D0094100

THE 214 HISTORICAL RADICALS

THE 214 HISTORICAL RADICALS			**1**	一 1	一 (1)	丨 2	丶 (2)	丿 3	´ 4	´ (4)	一 (4)	
乙 5	ㄴ (5)	ㄴ (5)	亅 6	**2**	二 7	二 (7)	亠 8	亠 (8)				
人 9	亻 (9)	ハ (9)	儿 10	入 11	入 (11)	八 12	八 (12)	ソ (12)	冂 13	冂 (13)	刂 (13)	刀 (13)
宀 14	冫 15	几 16	几 (16)	凵 17	刀 18	刂 (18)	力 19	勹 20	匕 21	七 (21)	匸 22	匚 (22)
匚 23	十 24	卉 (24)	廾 (24)	卜 25	卜 (25)	ㅏ (25)	卩 26	㔾 (26)	厂 27	厶 28	又 29	又 (29)
辶 [162]	阝 [163]	阝 [170]	**3**	口 30	囗 31	土 32	士 (32)	圡 (32)	士 33	夂 34	夂 (34)	夊 (34)
夊 35	夕 36	大 37	夻 (37)	女 38	子 39	宀 40	寸 41	小 42	⺌ (42)	尢 43	尸 44	屮 45
屯 (45)	屮 (45)	山 46	川 47	巛 (47)	工 48	工 (48)	己 49	已 (49)	巳 (49)	巾 50	干 51	幺 52
广 53	廴 54	廾 55	廾 (55)	弋 56	弓 57	彐 58	彑 (58)	彐 (58)	彑 (58)	彡 59	彳 60	忄 [61]
扌 [64]	氵 [85]	丬 [90]	犭 [94]	艹 [140]	辶 [162]	**4**	心 61	小 (61)	忄 [61]	戈 62	戈 (62)	戶 63
戶 (63)	手 64	手 (64)	扌 (64)	支 65	攴 (65)	支 66	攵 (66)	文 67	斗 68	斤 69	方 70	无 71
旡 (71)	旡 [71]	尢 [71]	日 72	曰 (72)	曰 73	月 74	木 75	欠 76	止 77	⺊ (77)	歹 78	歺 (78)
殳 79	冊 80	母 [80]	比 81	毛 82	毛 (82)	氏 83	气 84	水 85	氵 [85]	米 [85]	火 86	灬 (86)
爪 87	爪 (87)	⺥ (87)	⺥ (87)	父 88	爻 89	爻 (89)	爿 90	丬 [90]	片 91	牙 92	牙 (92)	牛 93
牛 (93)	犬 94	犭 [94]	王 96	王 (96)	壬 (96)	正 [103]	礻 [113]	内 [114]	岁 [125]	月 [130]	月 [130]	艹 [140]
5	旡 [71]	尢 [71]	母 [80]	比 [81]	米 [85]	牙 [92]	玄 95	玉 96	王 [96]	王 [96]	壬 [96]	瓜 97
瓦 98	瓦 (98)	甘 99	生 100	用 101	田 102	疋 103	正 (103)	广 104	癶 105	白 106	皮 107	皿 108

5 cont.	目 109	矛 110	矢 111	石 112	示 113	礻 (113)	礻 [113]	内 114	禾 115	穴 116	穴 (116)	宂 (116)
立 117	立 (117)	立 (117)	罒 [122]	貝 [138]	衤 [145]	**6**	竹 118	⺮ (118)	米 119	糸 120	缶 121	网 122
罒 [122]	羊 123	羊 (123)	羊 (123)	羽 124	羽 (124)	老 125	耂 [125]	而 126	耒 127	耒 (127)	耳 128	耴 (128)
聿 129	聿 (129)	肉 130	肉 (130)	月 [130]	月 [130]	臣 131	自 132	至 133	臼 134	舌 135	舛 136	舟 137
舟 (137)	艮 138	艮 [138]	色 139	艸 140	⺿ [140]	⺾ [140]	虍 141	虫 142	血 143	血 (143)	行 144	衣 145
衤 [145]	西 146	覀 (146)	覀 (146)	豕 [152]	𧾷 [157]	**7**	臣 [131]	舛 [136]	見 147	角 148	言 149	谷 150
豆 151	豆 (151)	豕 152	豕 [152]	豸 153	貝 154	赤 155	走 156	走 (156)	足 157	𧾷 (157)	身 158	車 159
辛 160	辛 (160)	辛 (160)	辰 161	辰 (161)	辵 162	辶 [162]	辶 [162]	邑 163	阝 [163]	酉 164	釆 165	里 166
镸 [168]	麦 [199]	**8**	金 167	金 (167)	長 168	镸 [168]	門 169	阜 170	阝 [170]	隶 171	隹 172	雨 173
覀 (173)	青 174	青 (174)	非 175	食 [184]	齐 [210]	**9**	面 176	革 177	韋 178	韭 179		
音 180	音 (180)	頁 181	風 182	風 (182)	飛 183	食 184	食 (184)	倉 (184)	食 (184)	首 185		
香 186	**10**	韋 [178]	馬 187	骨 188	高 189	高 [189]	髟 190	鬥 191	鬯 192	鬲 193		
鬼 194	鬼 (194)	竜 [212]	竜 [212]	**11**	高 [189]	魚 195	鳥 196	鹵 197	鹿 198	麂 (198)		
麥 199	麥 (199)	麦 [199]	麻 200	麻 (200)	麻 [200]	黃 (200)	黄 201	黑 [203]	亀 [213]	**12**	黃 201	
黃 [201]	黍 202	黑 203	黑 [203]	黹 204	黽 205	鼎 206	齒 [211]	**13**	黽 205	鼎 206		
鼓 207	皷 [207]	鼠 208	鼠 (208)	**14**	皷 [207]	鼻 209	鼻 (209)	齊 210	齐 [210]			
15	齒 211	齒 [211]	**16/17**	龍 212	竜 212	竜 [212]	龜 213	亀 [213]	龜 [213]	龠 214		

THE 12 STEPS

1. All
2. Lone
3. Enclosure
4. Left
5. Right
6. Top
7. Bottom
8. NW
9. NE
10. SE
11. SW
12. High

THE COMPACT NELSON
JAPANESE-ENGLISH
CHARACTER DICTIONARY

NOTE CONCERNING CHART INSIDE FRONT COVER   The use of the Radical Chart is explained in the first five appendices. The tables in Appendix 5, in particular, indicate whether a given element of a character is likely to be a radical in the position in which it occurs. If the reader is unable to locate the radical or cannot find the character under the radical selected, Appendix 11 crosslists characters under every radical or radical-like element appearing in the character.

The chart shows all 214 historic radicals arranged by stroke count, together with their numbers and variants. The *large numeral* indicates the stroke count of the radicals that follow it. An unadorned *small numeral* shows the number of the radical. *Small numbers in parentheses* show a variant form of the radical with the same stroke count as its parent. A *small number in brackets* designates a variant form having a different stroke count than its parent or a second entry of a radical that may appear to have more strokes than traditionally counted.

新版ネルソン漢英中辞典

The Compact Nelson

JAPANESE-ENGLISH

CHARACTER

DICTIONARY

Based on the Revised Version
of the Classic Edition
by Andrew N. Nelson

ABRIDGED
by JOHN H. HAIG
and the Department of East Asian
Languages and Literatures
University of Hawai'i at Mânoa

CHARLES E. TUTTLE COMPANY: PUBLISHERS
Rutland, Vermont
Tokyo, Japan

Published by the Charles E. Tuttle Company, Inc.
of Rutland, Vermont & Tokyo, Japan
with editorial offices at
Suido 1-chome, 2-6, Bunkyo-ku, Tokyo 112

LCC Card No. 98-89058
ISBN 0-8048-2037-6
ISBN 4-8053-0574-6 (Japan)

First edition, 1999

Printed in Singapore

Distributed by:

USA   Charles E. Tuttle Company, Inc.
Airport Industrial Park
RRI Box 231-5
North Clarendon, VT 05759
Tel: (802) 773-8930
Fax: (802) 773-6993

Japan   Tuttle Shokai Ltd.
1-21-13 Seki
Tama-ku, Kawasaki-shi
Kanagawa-ken 214-0022, Japan
Tel: (81) (44) 833-0225
Fax: (81) (44) 822-0413

Southeast Asia
Berkeley Books Pte Ltd.
5 Little Road #08-01
Singapore 536983
Tel: (65) 280 3220
Fax: (65) 280 6290

Boston Editorial Office:
153 Milk Street, 5th Floor
Boston, MA 02109, USA

Tokyo Editorial Office:
1-21-13 Seki
Tama-ku, Kawasaki-shi
Kanagawa-ken 214-0022, Japan

Singapore Editorial Office:
5 Little Road #08-01
Singapore 536983

TABLE OF CONTENTS

FOREWORD

This dictionary is based on The New Nelson Japanese-English Character Dictionary. It contains 3,068 characters, including all of the Joyo Kanji and the Additional Kanji for Proper Names. These characters are essential for everyday use. It also includes The New Nelson's innovative features, including the **Universal Radical Index,** which cross-indexes each entry by every one of its radicals or radical-like elements. *The Compact Nelson's* unprecedented level of cross-referencing and the URI's ease of use, as well as its compatibility with traditional dictionaries thanks to the reversion to the traditional radical system, offer numerous advantages over the former radical priority system. In addition, the URI has eliminated cross-listing of the same character. For greater portability, we have incorporated all of the JIS level 1 and related characters.

The support and advice of general editor Tamura Tatsuya and DTP operator Dong Guangliang at Charles E. Tuttle Co., have been invaluable.

TYPOGRAPHICAL EXPLANATIONS

THE PAGE IN GENERAL

N.B. The first five items below pertain to the first main-character entry on a left-hand page and to the last on a right-hand page.

1. The topmost boldface numeral in the upper, outer corner shows the traditional number of the radical under which the main character entries on the page are classified.

2. The vertical string of radicals in the outer margin shows all the radicals containing the relevant number of strokes, plus their more important variants.

3. The heavy brackets enclose the radical (and important variants) under which the main character entries on the page are classified. As the reader spins the pages, the brackets will seem to run up and down the string of radicals, providing a rapid visual aid to locating the relevant radical.

4. The boldface number at the head of a radical string shows the number of strokes in the radicals in the string.

5. The tiny numeral outside the radical (and variants) enclosed by the brackets show the number of strokes in the non-radical part of the main character entries on the page.

6. Boldface numbers in the lower, outer corner show the inclusive numbers of the character entries on the page.

7. Numerals centered at the bottom of each page are page numbers.

8. A column-wide divider consisting of a boldface numeral flanked by horizontal lines shows the beginning of a group of characters each having the indicated number of strokes in its non-radical part.

9. A page-wide divider consisting of a radical and its traditional number flanked by heavy horizontal lines shows the beginning of a new radical section. Shown immediately below the divider are the variants of the radical, its names in Japanese and English, and other pertinent information. Each radical is also given an English "nickname" in an effort to standardize the English nomenclature of the radicals.

THE ENTRIES

10. The large boldface character at the left of a column indicates a main entry character.

11. Three numbers separated by horizontal lines immediately follow each main entry. The top number is the character's Nelson number and is assigned sequentially through the dictionary to every main entry. This number is used in all cross-refer-

Typographical Explanations

ences. The middle number, preceded by a J, is the character's Japan Industrial Standard code number. "J-X" indicates that the character is not found in the JIS character set. The bottom number, preceded by an M, is the number assigned to the character in Morohashi's *Dai Kanwa Jiten*. "M-X" means that the character is not found in Morohashi.

12. A capital A immediately to the left of a main character entry indicates that the character is one of the 1006 characters designated by the Ministry of Education to be learned in the six years of elementary school (See Appendix 13). A capital B indicates that the character is one of the other 939 characters in the Jōyō Kanji List. If no small capital letter precedes a main entry character, it is to be understood that the character, while outside the 1,945 list, is still sufficiently common in modern literature to be important in a wide mastery of Japanese.

13. Other large boldface characters to the right of a main entry show alternative forms of the character. The Nelson, JIS, and Morohashi numbers of these variants are also given.

14. Reading of a character in small capital letters show the *on* or Sino-Japanese readings. These are defined only if they have distinctive meanings; otherwise they partake of the English meanings which follow other readings of the character. (Note that many *on* readings have gone out of use. As a rule, only those *on* that have independent use or appear in compounds in this dictionary are listed. For a complete listing of all the *on* readings of a character, see the Morohashi dictionary. See our character 6997 for an example of the great number of *on* readings that a character may have.)

15. Readings of a character in italics show the *kun* or native Japanese readings. The Hepburn system of romanization is employed in this dictionary. In general, the order of listing of the *kun* readings is, first, verbs, then other parts of speech, and finally prefixes and suffixes. The punctuation of the *on* and *kun* readings provides information about their uses and meanings as shown in the following examples: (a) "ON meaning. *kun* meaning." or "ON meaning. ON meaning. *kun* meaning. *kun* meaning." shows *on* and *kun* readings with separate meanings. (b) "ON. *kun* meaning." shows that the *on* reading is not used alone, but partakes of the *kun* meaning in compounds. (c) "ON. ON meaning. *kun* meaning." shows that the first *on* is not used alone, but partakes of the meanings of the other readings in compounds. (d) "ON *kun* meaning." or "ON, ON *kun* meaning." shows that the *on* may be used alone and share the meaning of the *kun* readings.

16. Syllables of a reading enclosed in parentheses show syllables comprising the *okurigana*, i.e., the inflected part of the word written in the kana syllabary. We follow recent Ministry of Education recommendations, but there is considerable variation in actual use. The auxiliary verbs *suru*, *nasu*, and *naru* and particles (*na, no, ni, de*, etc.) are not parts of the preceding words and are therefore not enclosed in parentheses; they should, of course, be written in the kana syllabary in a text.

17. The characters 国字 (*kokuji*) following a main entry indicate that the character is made in Japan and not inherited from China.

18. A radical enclosed in heavy brackets at the end of a main entry shows the character's traditional radical, which may differ from the radical under which we

have classified it in several cases. These cases are described in the material described in Paragraph 9 above.

THE COMPOUNDS

19. Small characters at the left of a column following a main entry are the compound entries and are followed by their readings in italics. No distinction is made between *on* and *kun* readings in compound entries. Parentheses are used to indicate *okurigana* as described in Paragraph 16 above. Note that in listing compounds the main-entry character is not repeated since it is the first member of every compound.

20. Superscript numerals immediately to the left of a list of compounds show the full stroke count of the second character of the compound (the main-character entry being counted as the first character). A new numeral appears whenever the stroke count changes.

THE CROSS-REFERENCES

The two types of cross-references used in the text are illustrated below.

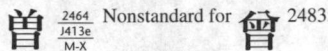

曾 is not one of the traditional variants listed in standard character dictionaries, but is quite widely used for 曾 2483.

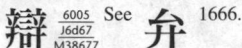

The information concerning the character 辯 is to be found under its Jōyō equivalent 弁 1666.

THE COMPACT NELSON
JAPANESE-ENGLISH
CHARACTER DICTIONARY

1-STROKE RADICALS

RAD. ━▲━ 1

A ━▶ $\frac{1}{\text{J306c}}$ ICHI one; a. ITSU one. *hi*
M1 one. *hito(tsu)* one, a unit;
the same; just; once. *itsu wa, hito(tsu) wa*
for one thing, partly. *itsu ni* solely,
entirely, only; or. *hitotsu ni* as one.
hitotsu ni wa for one thing, partly. *ichi-*
one, a certain; the whole; the same (time);
petty, worthless. *-ichi* the best, the first.
hito- one; a.

[1] 一 *ichi-ichi, hito(tsu)-hito(tsu)* one by
one, separately; everything; in detail

[2] 八 *ichi(ka)bachi(ka)* sink or swim
二無 *ichi(mo)ni(mo)na(ku)*
unhesitatingly
刀両断 *ittō-ryōdan* cutting in two with
one stroke; a swift and decisive action
or measure
人 *hitori, ichinin* one person. *hitori de*
alone; by oneself, voluntarily,
spontaneously, automatically
人一人 *hitoribitori* one by one
人子 *hitorigo, hitorikko* an only child
人当 *hitoria(tari), hitoria(te)* per person
人前 *hitorimae, ichinimmae* full
manhood, adult; a plate, one helping
人娘 *hitori musume* an only daughter
人称 *ichininshō* first person (in
grammar)
人息子 *hitori musuko* an only son
人舞台 *hitori butai* one's unrivaled field

[3] 山 *hitoyama* a mountain; the whole
mountain; a pile (of something)
丸 *ichigan* a lump, (into) one
才 *issai* one year old
ケ月 *ikkagetsu* one month
大事 *ichidaiji* a serious matter
寸 *issun* one inch. *chotto* just a minute;
a short time; just a little, somewhat;
easily, readily, rather
口 *hitokuchi* a mouthful, a bite, a sip, a
draft

[4] 月 *Ichigatsu* January. *hitotsuki,
ichigetsu* one month

片 *ippen* a piece, a bit
円 *ichien* the whole area; one yen
介 *ikkai no* mere, only a...
辺倒 *ippentō* complete devotion to one
side
夫一婦 *ippuippu* monogamy
夫多妻 *ipputasai* polygamy
心 *isshin, hito(tsu)kokoro* one mind, the
whole heart, wholeheartedness
心不乱 *isshin-furan ni* wholeheartedly,
intently
心同体 *isshin-dōtai* one flesh, union
方 *ippō* a quarter, a side; one direction;
one hand; the other hand; one party;
the other party; on the other hand;
meanwhile; only, simply; in turn.
hitokata(naranu) extraordinary;
special. *hitokata(narazu)* unusually,
greatly
方的 *ippōteki* one-sided, unilateral,
arbitrary
切 *issai* all, everything, the whole;
entirely, absolutely. *hitoki(re)* a slice,
a small piece. *hitoki(ri)* a pause, a
period, a step; once, some years ago
切合財 *issai-gassai* any and every
thing; altogether, without reserve
元 *ichigen no* unitary
元的 *ichigenteki* monistic, unitary,
unified, centralized
分 *ippun* a minute. *ichibu* one tenth;
one hundredth, one percent; one tenth
of a *sun*; one quarter *ryō* (an old coin).
ichibun duty, honor
business on a small scale
日 *ichinichi, ichijitsu, hitohi* one day, a
day. *tsuitachi* the first day (of the
month)
日一日 *ichinichi-ichinichi* gradually,
day by day
日中 *ichinichijū* all day long
[5] 礼 *ichirei* a bow, a salute, a greeting
旦 *ittan* once; one morning; temporarily

冊 *issatsu* one copy (of a book)

石二鳥 *isseki-nichō* killing two birds with one stone

代 *ichidai* one generation; a lifetime; an age

生 *isshō* a lifetime, one's (whole) life; all through life

生涯 *isshōgai* a lifetime, one's (whole) life; all through life

生懸命 *isshōkemmei ni* with all one's might

目 *hitome* glimpse, a glance. *ichimoku* a glance, a look. *hito(tsu)me* a one-eyed monster

目散 *ichimokusan ni* at full speed

目瞭然 *ichimoku-ryōzen* very clear

世 *issei* a first generation immigrant. *isse, issei* one existence, a lifetime, a generation, an age; the era

世紀 *isseiki* a century

本 *ippon* one (long object); one version; a certain book; a blow; a full-fledged geisha

本立 *ipponda(chi)* independence

本気 *ippongi* a one-track mind, single-minded

⁶色 *isshoku, hitoiro* one color; one kind. *isshiki* one color; pure; one article

行 *ichigyō, ikkō* a line, a row. *ikkō* a party; a troupe; an act

同 *ichidō* all present, all concerned, all of us

因 *ichiin* a cause

式 *isshiki* a complete set, all, the whole, everything

任 *ichinin suru* entrust (to someone)

件 *ikken* a matter, an item

考 *ikkō* consideration, a thought

名 *ichimei* one person; another name

存 *ichizon* one's own discretion; one's own idea; one's own responsibility

安心 *hitoanshin* a feeling of relief

気 *ikki ni* at a breath, at a stroke, at a sitting

字 *ichiji* a character, a letter

次 *ichiji* the first; a linear (equation)

両日 *ichiryōjitsu* a day or two

年 *ichinen* one year. *hitotose* one year; some time ago

年中 *ichinenjū* through the year

年生 *ichinensei* first-year student; annual (plant)

回 *ikkai* once, a time, one time, a round, a game, a bout, a heat, an inning.
hitomawa(ri) a turn, a round

巡 *hitomegu(ri)* a turn, a round; one full year. *ichijun* a beat, a round

⁷応 *ichiō* once; tentatively; in outline

位 *ichii* first place, first rank; unit's place (in figures)

対 *ittsui* a pair (of screens, vases, etc.)

決 *ikketsu suru* be agreed, be settled

別 *ichibetsu* parting

助 *ichijo* a help

束 *issoku, hitotaba* a bundle, a hundred

見 *ikken* a look, a glimpse; first meeting; apparently. *ichigen* first meeting; first-time (customer)

角 *ikkaku* corner, section; point; a narwhal. *hitokado, ikkado* superiority, something uncommon. *hitokado no* respectable; full-fledged

身 *isshin* throughout the body; oneself, one's own interests. *hito(tsu)mi* baby clothes

身上 *isshinjō no* personal (affairs)

里 *ichiri* 2.44 miles

利 *ichiri* one advantage

体 *ittai* one body, one flesh; what on earth, really, in fact, properly speaking; originally. *ittai ni* generally

体化 *ittaika* unification, integration

体全体 *ittai-zentai* Whatever (is the matter)?; What on earth (is going on)?

言 *hitokoto, ichigen, ichigon* a word, a single word

言半句 *ichigen-hanku, ichigon-hanku* a word, a few words

⁸門 *ichimon* the family, dependents, the household

例 *ichirei* one example, an instance

味 *ichimi* one flavor; an ingredient (of medicine); a touch, a tinge; conspirators; a gang

往 *ichiō* once, tentatively, in outline; go once

抹 *ichimatsu* a touch of, a tinge of, a wreath (of smoke)

服 *ippuku* a dose; a puff, a smoke; lull, dull market; short rest

念 *ichinen* a determined purpose

直線 *itchokusen* a straight line

長一短 *itchō-ittan* good points and

shortcomings

知半解 *itchi-hankai* superficial knowledge

泊 *ippaku* stopping one night

所 *ik(ka)sho, hitotokoro, issho* one place; the same place

所懸命 *isshokemmei ni* with all one's might

杯 *ippai* a cup of; a drink; full; to the utmost; up to (one's income)

定 *ittei suru* fix, settle, regularize, define; unify; standardize. *ichijō* something definitely settled. *ittei no* certain, uniform, prescribed, standard, regular, fixed, definite

刻 *ikkoku* a moment, an instant. *ikkoku na* stubborn, hotheaded

周 *hitomegu(ri)* a turn, a round; one full year. *isshū* once around, a revolution, a tour, a lap

周年 *isshūnen* one full year

周忌 *isshūki* first death anniversary

枚 *ichimai* one sheet

斉 *issei ni* simultaneously, all at once

歩 *ippo* a step

歩一歩 *ippo-ippo* step by step, by degrees

夜 *ichiya, hitoyo* one night, all night, one evening, overnight

夜漬 *ichiyazuke* salted just overnight; cramming

9度 *ichido, hitotabi* once, one time, on one occasion

通 *ittsū* one copy (of a document). *hitotō(ri)* in general, briefly. *hitotō(ri) no* ordinary, usual

連 *ichiren* a series, a chain; 1,000 sheets (of paper)

途 *itto* a way, a course; the only way. *ichizu ni* wholeheartedly

律 *ichiritsu* evenness, uniformity, equality, monotony. *ichiritsu ni* in the same way

指 *isshi* a finger

括 *ikkatsu* one lump, one bundle; summing up. *hitokuku(ri)* a bundle. *hitokuru(me)* a bunch, a bundle, a lot

派 *ippa* a school, a sect, a party

級 *ikkyū* one grade; first class

陣 *ichijin* vanguard; a gust of wind

変 *ippen* complete change

発 *ippatsu* a shot, a round, a charge

巻 *ikkan* one volume. *hitomaki* one roll

昼夜 *itchūya* a whole day and night, 24 hours

段 *ichidan* more, still more, much more, all the more; a part (of a talk). *ittan* 反 hectare

段落 *ichidanraku* a pause

品料理 *ippin-ryōri* service à la carte

点 *itten* a speck, dot, point, particle; a very little; one item

面 *ichimen* one side, one phase; the whole surface; first page (of a newspaper); (on) the other hand; all over

面識 *ichimenshiki* a passing acquaintance

重 *hitoe* one layer; single. *hitokasa(ne)* a suit; a set of boxes

昨日 *issakujitsu, ototoi, ototsui* day before yesterday

昨年 *issakunen, ototoshi* year before last

昨夜 *issakuya* night before last

昨晩 *issakuban* night before last

10座 *ichiza* the party; those present; a troupe; the first seat

席 *isseki* a sitting; a speech; a feast

流 *ichiryū* a school (of art); foremost, first-class, top-notch; unique

員 *ichiin* a member

案 *ichian* an idea, a plan

帯 *ittai* a region, a zone; the whole place

個人 *ikkojin, ichikojin* a private person, an individual

進一退 *isshin-ittai* advance and retreat, ebb and flow, seesawing, fluctuating

笑付 *isshō ni fu(su)* laugh (someone) down

致 *itchi* agreement, conformity, consistency; union, cooperation

週 *isshū* a week

週間 *isshūkan* a week

部 *ichibu* a part; a copy (of a publication)

部分 *ichibubun* a part

部始終 *ichibu-shijū* full particulars

家 *ikka, ikke* a house, a home, a family, a household, one's family, one's folks; a style

軒 *ikken* a house

挙 *ikkyo* one effort, one action

挙一動 *ikkyo-ichidō* one's every action

挙両得 *ikkyo-ryōtoku* killing two birds with one stone

時 *ichiji* one o'clock; a time; temporarily; at one time. *hitotoki* a little while, at one time. *ittoki* 12th part of a day; a short period. *ichidoki ni* at a time, at one time

時払 *ichijibarai* lump sum payment

時金 *ichijikin* lump sum

時的 *ichijiteki* temporary

時預 *ichijiazu(kari)* (baggage) checking, temporary custody. *ichijiazu(ke)* (baggage) checking, temporary depositing

般 *ippan no* general, universal, ordinary, average

般化 *ippanka* generalization, popularization

般性 *ippansei* generality

般的 *ippanteki* general

般論 *ippanron* general consideration

11 掃 *issō* a clean sweep

族 *ichizoku* a family, dependents, relatives, a household

理 *ichiri* a principle, a reason

組 *hitokumi, ichikumi* one class. *hitokumi* one set

階 *ikkai* ground floor, first floor

票 *ippyō* a vote, a ballot

問一答 *ichimon-itō* answering each question one by one

転 *itten* a turn, complete change

貫 *ikkan* consistency, coherence, integration; 8⅓ pounds

望 *ichibō* one sweep, an unbroken view

12 間 *ikken* one *ken*, six feet. *hitoma* one room, one *ken*

喝 *ikkatsu* a roar, a thundering cry

場 *ichijō* one time, one place. *ichiba* one scene (of a play)

晩 *hitoban* one evening; a night; all night; overnight

晩中 *hitobanjū* all night long

割 *ichiwari* ten percent

散 *issan ni* at top speed

期 *ikki* a term, the first term

畳 *ichijō* one mat

着 *itchaku* first arrival; first (in the race); a suit (of clothes); wear clothes

報 *ippō* information; a report

喜一憂 *ikki-ichiyū* alternation of hope and fear, alternation of joys and sorrows

朝一夕 *itchō-isseki ni* in a day, in a brief interval

番 *ichiban* number one, the first; most, best; a game, a round, a bout, an event (in a meet). *hitotsugai* a pair, a couple, a brace

番乗 *ichibannori* leader of a charge; first to arrive

等 *ittō* first class, first rank, A-1; the most, the best

13 睡 *issui, hitonemuri* a nap, a short sleep

路 *ichiro* one road, one way; straight; earnestly

群 *ichigun, hitomu(re)* a group; a flock, a crowd, a herd, a cluster (of flowers)

歳 *issai* one year old

触即発 *isshoku-sokuhatsu* delicate situation, explosive situation

新 *isshin* complete change, reform, remodeling, renewal

節 *issetsu* a verse (in the Bible), a stanza, a paragraph, a passage. *hito fushi* a joint, section; a tune, note, strain, measure

義的 *ichigiteki* having a single meaning; being the first principle

14 層 *issō* more, still more, much more, all the more

概 *ichigai ni* unconditionally, sweepingly

様 *ichiyō* uniformity, evenness, similarity, equality, impartiality

滴 *itteki* a drop

種 *isshu* a kind, a species, a variety

端 *ittan* one end; a part

緒 *issho* the same; company. *issho ni* together (with); at the same time; in a lump. *issho ni suru* unite; confuse with. *issho(kuta)* mix up; heterogeneous mixture

読 *ichidoku* a perusal; one reading

説 *issetsu* an opinion; a report; another opinion

酸化炭素 *issanka tanso* carbon monoxide

語 *ichigo* one word

箇 *ikko* one; a piece

15 億 *ichioku* one hundred million

線 *issen* a line; line of demarcation

審 *isshin* first instance; first trial

撃 *ichigeki* a blow, a hit, a poke

徹 *ittetsu na* obstinate, stubborn, inflexible

輪車 *ichirinsha* unicycle, wheelbarrow
16 興 *ikkyō* amusement, fun
覧 *ichiran* a look, a glance; a summary
覧表 *ichiranhyō* list, table, schedule, catalog
頭 *ittō* a head (of cattle)
17 瞥 *ichibetsu* a glance, a look
瞬 *isshun* a blink; a moment, an instant
18 難 *ichinan* one difficulty, one danger
類 *ichirui* same kind; accomplices, companions; same clan
騎 *ikki* one horseman
19 蹴 *isshū, hitoke(ri)* a kick; a rejection; easy victory
21 躍 *ichiyaku* one bound; at one bound
23 攫千金 *ikkaku-senkin* getting rich quick

──────────── 1 ────────────

A 丁 $\frac{2}{\text{J437a}}$ M2 TEI D, fourth; adult male; servant. CHŌ counter for guns, tools, orders of food, leaves, blocks, or cakes of something; even number. TŌ. *hinoto* fourth calendar sign. *-chō*. leaf (of paper), block, cake (of something).
5 目 *chōme* city block (of irregular size)
6 字形 *teijikei* T-shaped
9 度 *chōdo* exactly, just right
重 *teichō* courtesy; politeness
14 寧 *teinei* politeness, courtesy, care, conscientiousness

A 七 $\frac{3}{\text{J3c37}}$ M6 SHICHI *nana(tsu), na, nana* seven.
3 夕 *Tanabata, shichiseki* July 7 Festival of the Weaver; prayer ceremony for children's artistic development
4 日 *nanoka, nanuka* seven days; the seventh day (of the month)
月 *Shichigatsu* July
不思議 *nanafushigi* the seven wonders
五三 *shichi-go-san* the lucky numbers seven, five, and three; shrine visit by children aged seven, five, and three
五調 *shichigochō* seven-and-five-syllable meter
分三分 *shichibu-sambu* seven to three (chances)
分袖 *shichibusode* three-quarter sleeves
6 色 *nanairo, shichishoku* the seven prismatic colors
8 宝焼 *shippōyaki* cloisonné

9 草 *nanakusa* the seven spring flowers; the seven fall flowers
面鳥 *shichimenchō* turkey
11 転八起 *nanakoro(bi)-yao(ki)* the vicissitudes of life; always rising after a fall
転八倒 *shittembattō* writhing in agony
13 福神 *Shichifukujin* Seven Gods of Luck
18 曜 *shichiyō* the seven luminaries (sun, moon, and five planets); the seven days of the week

──────────── 2 ────────────

B 丈 $\frac{5}{\text{J3e66}}$ M11 JŌ 10 feet; length, measure; Mr. or Mrs. (re: artists). *dake* only; alone; no more; merely.

B 与 $\frac{6}{\text{J4d3f}}$ M20 YO. *ata(eru)* give, award, impart, provide, allot, cause (pain or damage). *azuka(ru)* participate in. *kumi(suru)* take part in; be implicated in; side with; support.
4 太者 *yotamono, yotamon* good-for-nothing fellow, hoodlum
10 党 *yotō* party in power
11 野党 *yoyatō* majority and minority parties

A 万 $\frac{7}{\text{J4b7c}}$ M10 MAN ten thousand; myriad. BAN ten thousand, myriad; fully; if by any chance. *yorozu* ten thousand, myriads, all, everything.
1 一 *man'ichi, man(ga)ichi* if by any chance, 10,000 to 1
2 人 *bannin, banjin* all people, everybody
4 引 *mambiki* shoplifting; shoplifter
5 世 *bansei* all ages, eternity. *yorozuyo* thousands of years, all generations, eternity
6 全 *banzen* perfection
有引力 *ban'yū inryoku* universal gravitation
年 *mannen* 10,000 years; eternity
年床 *mannendoko* always leaving bedquilts unfolded
年雪 *mannen'yuki* perpetual snow
年筆 *mannenhitsu* fountain pen
7 里 *banri* 10,000 miles; great distance
里長城 *Banri (no) Chōjō* Great Wall of China

8 物 *bambutsu* all things, all creation
物霊長 *bambutsu (no) reichō* mankind
事 *banji* all, everything
国 *bankoku* all nations
国旗 *bankokki, bankokuki* flags of all nations
9 点 *manten* perfect, perfect score
10 病 *mambyō* all kinds of sickness
般 *bampan* all things
能 *bannō, mannō* all-purpose; all-around. *bannō* omnipotence
12 策 *bansaku* all means
場一致 *manjō-itchi de* unanimously
葉仮名 *man'yōgana* an early Japanese syllabary composed of Chinese characters used phonetically
葉集 *Man'yōshū* Japan's oldest anthology of poems
13 歳 *banzai* hurrah; long life; congratulations. *manzai* strolling dancer for New Year's celebration; a pair of comic dialogists
18 難 *bannan* innumerable difficulties, all obstacles

三 $\frac{8}{\substack{J3b30\\M12}}$ SAN three. *mi(tsu), mi(ttsu), mi* three.
A
2 人称 *sanninshō* third person (in grammar)
3 三五五 *sansan-gogo* by twos and threes
千 *sanzen* 3,000; many
4 方 *sambō* three sides; small offering stand. *sampō* three sides
分 *sambun suru* trisect; divide by three. *sambu* ⌐ō (of various units). *sampun* three minutes
巴 *mi(tsu)domoe* three fat comma shapes arranged to form a circle; three parties in mutual conflict
月 *Sangatsu* March. *mitsuki* three months
文 *sammon* three coppers; farthing; cheapness
文判 *sammomban* ready-made seal
尺 *sanjaku* three Japanese feet; waistband, belt
日 *mikka* three days; the third day (of the month)
日月 *mikkazuki* crescent moon, new moon
6 次元 *sanjigen* three dimensions

百 *sambyaku* 300; petty sum; cheap
色 *sanshoku* three colors. *sanshiki* three colors; three kinds
7 役 *san'yaku* the three highest sumo ranks below the grand champion; the three highest officials (in companies, etc.)
男 *sannan* third son
角 *mi(tsu)kado* three corders; three-forked intersection. *sankaku* triangle
角形 *sankakukei* triangle
角函数 *sankaku kansū* trigonometrical function
角洲 *sankakusu* delta
角測量 *sankaku sokuryō* triangulation
角関係 *sankaku kankei* love triangle
8 拍子 *sambyōshi* triple time (in music); three important requisites ⌐lute
味線 *samisen, shamisen* three-stringed
拝九拝 *sampai-kyūhai* kowtowing, bowing repeatedly
9 食 *sanshoku* three meals (a day)
乗 *sanjō* cube (in math); three vehicles to truth (in Buddhism)
乗根 *sanjōkon* cube root
面 *sammen* three sides, three faces; page three (of a newspaper)
面記事 *sammenkiji* page-three news, police news, human-interest stories
段論法 *sandanrompō* syllogism
重 *mie* three-fold, triple, three-ply. *sanjū* triple, treble, three-fold, three-ply, triplicate
重奏 *sanjūsō* instrumental trio
10 倍 *sambai* threefold, three times
時 *sanji* three o'clock; afternoon snack; three seasons important in agriculture (spring, summer, fall); three ages of Buddhist law after Buddha's entering nirvana. *(o)sanji* three-o'clock snack
流 *sanryū* third rate
原色 *sangenshoku* three primary colors
11 脚 *sankyaku* tripod; three legs
12 等 *santō* third class; third rate; third place
等分 *santōbun suru* trisect
14 箇日 *sanganichi* January first through third
15 権分立 *sanken bunritsu* separation of powers (executive, legislative, and judicial)
輪車 *sanrinsha* tricycle, three-wheeled truck

A 下 ‹9 J323c M14› KA, GE low class; inferiority; second, or last volume. *kuda(ru)* come down, go down; get down, descend; be given; be less than; have diarrhea; retire; leave the capital. *kuda(saru)* give, confer; oblige, favor with. *kuda(sai)* please give me. *kuda(su)* let down, lower; give, confer; issue (orders); hand down (decisions); have diarrhea; lay (hands) on. *o(riru)* come down, go down, step down, descend; get off; swoop down; land. *o(rosu)* take down, lower, pull down, lift down, let down, drop; launch; let off (passengers); wear (for the first time); cause (abortion); grate; invoke; exercise; borrow (in subtraction); lock. *sa(garu)* vi hang down, dangle; fall, go down, come down; abate; wane; retire; stand back; go behind; be granted. *sa(geru)* vt hang; wear (a decoration); reduce (rank); move back; let go, dismiss; remove; grant; draw (money), withdraw. *shita* lower part, bottom, base, foot; downstairs; subordinate place; below average; part payment; under, lower; sub-, subordinate; preliminary. *kuda(ranai)* trivial, worthless; absurd, silly; nasty. *kuda(ri)* descent; leaving the capital; diarrhea. *kuda(shi)* purgation, evacuation. *o(roshi)* grating; grater; grated radish. *(o)sa(gari)* former offering to deities; used clothes; leavings (of food). *sa(gari)* decline. *shimo* bottom, lower part, the foot; lower stream; latter; lower part of the body; the masses, the servants; the governed. *shimo ni* below, down, downward. *moto* vicinity. *moto de, moto ni* under (a tree); under (the jurisdiction of).

³ 山 *gezan, gesan* descent from the mountain; leaving a temple

士官 *kashikan* noncommissioned officer

⁴ 心 *shitagokoro* secret intention, motive

水 *gesui* sewer, drain, ditch, gutter; sewerage

水道 *gesuidō* drainage system; drain; sewer

手 *heta* unskillful, awkward. *shimote* lower part; stage right. *shitade, shitate* lower part; humble position; underhand grip (in sumo)

⁵ 句 *shimo (no) ku* the second half (of a *tanka*)

付 *kafu suru* grant, issue

半 *kahan* lower half

半身 *shimo hanshin, kahanshin* lower half of the body

半期 *shimo hanki* the second half of the year; the second half of a term

⁶ 旬 *gejun* last ten days (of a month)

回 *shitamawa(ri)* subordinate part; menial service; subordinate; utility man (in theater). *shitamawa(ru)* be less than, be lower than

向 *shitamu(ki)* downward look; beginning of decline; downturn. *shitamu(ku)* look down; decline. *gekō suru* leave the capital; move from high to low

地 *shitaji* groundwork, foundation; inclination, makings; elementary knowledge of, grounding in; prearrangement, spadework; first coat of plastering; soy

列車 *kuda(ri) ressha* trains going away from the capital

⁷ 車 *gesha* alighting

位 *kai* low rank, subordinate position

坂 *kuda(ri)zaka* downhill; decline; waning

克上 *gekokujō* a retainer supplanting his lord; juniors dominating seniors

見 *shitami* preliminary inspection, preview; siding (on a house)

町 *shitamachi* downtown section

足 *gesoku* footgear checked at public places

⁸ 弦 *kagen* last quarter (of the moon)

⁹ 降 *kakō* descent, fall; drop, subsidence

降線 *kakōsen* downward curve

院 *kain* the lower (legislative) body

段 *gedan* lower (horizontal) column (of print); lowest step, lowest tier, lower berth; low positioning (of sword, spear)

品 *gehin* vulgarity, coarseness; indecency; inferior article. *kahin* inferior article; person of low birth

界 *gekai* this world; the lower world; the earth

草 *shitakusa* weeds beneath a tree

巻 *gekan* last volume (in a set of 2 or 3)

剋上 *gekokujō* a retainer supplanting his lord; juniors dominating seniors

級 *kakyū* lower grade, low class; junior officer

¹⁰記 *kaki no* the following

剤 *gezai* laxative

書 *shitaga(ki), gesho* rough copy, draft

流 *karyū* downstream, lower reaches of a river; lower classes

部 *kabu* lower part, lower order; subordinate (offices)

馬評 *gebahyō* outsider's irresponsible talk, hearsay, rumor

¹¹達 *katatsu suru* command a subordinate

船 *gesen* going ashore

野 *geya* retirement from public office

宿 *geshuku* room and board, lodging; boarding house

¹²痢 *geri* diarrhea

絵 *shitae* rough sketch, design

着 *shitagi* underwear

落 *geraku* depreciation, decline, fall, slump

等 *katō* low grade, lower class. *katō na* inferior, base, vulgar

¹³働 *shitabatara(ki)* subordinate work; assistant, servant

塗 *shitanu(ri)* first coat; undercoating

準備 *shita jumbi* preliminary arrangements, spade work

腹 *shitahara, shita(p)para, shitabara, kafuku* abdomen. *kudaribara* diarrhea

腹部 *kafukubu* abdominal region

¹⁴僕 *geboku, kaboku* servant; your humble servant

端 *katan* lower end. *shita(p)pa* underling

層 *kasō* lower strata; lower classes

層階級 *kasō kaikyū* lower classes

駄 *geta* wooden clogs, geta

駄箱 *getabako* cupboard (for shoes and clogs)

¹⁵履 *shitabaki* footgear for outdoors

潮 *sa(ge)shio* ebb tide

調 *shitashira(be)* preliminary investigation; preparation

敷 *shitaji(ki)* desk pad; something lying underneath; model; pattern; a thin plastic board (laid under writing

paper); pinned under, crushed beneath

請 *shitauke* subcontractor

¹⁶積 *shitazu(mi)* goods piled beneath; being in a subservient position

A 上 [10 J3e65 M13] Jō top; best; first volume. SHŌ upper part; government. *ue* up, upper part, top, summit; surface; far better; higher; (in) authority; as far as... is concerned; besides; after; emperor, sovereign; upon (examination); influence of (liquor); lord, shogun; superior. *a(garu)* rise, go up; climb up; advance, appreciate; be promoted; improve; enter, call on; be offered; accrue; be finished; (expenses) come to; go bankrupt; begin spinning (cocoons); be caught; get ruffled; eat, drink; die; weaken (as a battery); let up (rain). *a(geru)* raise, elevate; fly (kites); praise; increase, advance; promote, elevate; vomit; usher in, admit; send (to school); offer; present, leave with; finish; arrange (expenses); observe, perform; quote, mention, give (examples); bear (a child); improve (talents); do up (the hair); arrest; engage; fry; (rains) stop. *a(gattari)* poor business. *a(gari)* ascent, rise, advance; yield; death; spinning; completion; stop; finish. *nobo(ru)* rise, ascend, go up, climb; go to (the capital); add up to; be promoted; advance (in price); sail up; come up (on the agenda). *nobo(su), nobo(seru)* raise; record; bring up (a matter); serve (food); send some one out (from Kyoto). *nobo(ri)* ascent; up train (toward the capital). *kami* top; head; upper part; upper stream; emperor; a superior; upper part of the body; the above. *-ue* my dear (father). *-jō* aboard a ship or vehicle; from the standpoint of; as a matter of (fact). *jō-* governmental; imperial; best; high class; going up; presenting; showing. *uwa-* upper, upward, outer, surface, top. *-a(gezu)* every (two days, etc.). *-a(gari)* after (rain); ex- (official, etc.).

² 人 *shōnin* Buddhist saint, priest

³ 口 *nobo(ri)guchi* starting point for a mountain ascent. *a(gari)guchi, a(gari)kuchi* entrance

上 *jōjō* the best

下 *shōka, jōge* high and low; the government and the people; going up and down. *a(ge)oro(shi)* raising and lowering; loading and unloading. *a(ge)sa(ge)* raising and lowering; praising and blaming; modulation. *nobo(ri)kuda(ri)* going up and down. *a(gari)sa(gari)* rise and fall, fluctuation. *kamishimo* samurai garb; old ceremonial garb; the government and the people; the upper and lower parts of the body

下水道 *jōgesuidō* water and sewer services

下動 *jōgedō* vertical motion (in earthquakes)

⁴中下 *jō-chū-ge* excellent-good-poor; first-second-third (class)

手 *uwate, kamite* upper part; upper stream; overhand grip (in sumo); left side (of a stage). *jōzu na* skillful, dexterous

方 *jōhō* upper part. *kamigata* Kyoto and vicinity. *ue(tsu)gata* nobles, the upper class.

水 *jōsui* water supply

水道 *jōsuidō* waterworks

天気 *jōtenki* fair weather

⁵目 *uwame* upward glance, upturned eyes. *a(gari)me* eyes slanting upward; rising tendency

句 *kami (no) ku, jōku* the first part of a poem or verse

代 *jōdai* ancient times

司 *jōshi* superior authorities

出来 *jōdeki* good performance

申 *jōshin* report to a superior

古 *jōko* ancient times

半身 *jōhanshin* bust, upper half of the body

半期 *kamihanki* first half of a year

⁶衣 *uwagi, jōi* coat, tunic, jacket, outer garment

旬 *jōjun* first ten days of a month

回 *uwamawa(ru)* exceed

気 *jōki* dizziness; rush of blood to the head

列車 *nobo(ri) ressha* trains going toward the capital

向 *uwamu(ku), uemu(ku)* look upward, turn upward, rise. *uwamu(ki), uemu(ki)* upturn; tendency; looking upward

⁷述 *jōjutsu* the above-mentioned

位 *jōi* high rank, precedence

体 *jōtai* upper part of the body

役 *uwayaku* senior official, one's superior

告 *jōkoku* appeal (of a case)

⁸弦 *jōgen* first quarter (of a moon); a crescent moon

限 *jōgen* maximum (in math)

官 *jōkan* superior officer

空 *uwa(no)sora* inattention, absentmindedness. *jōkū* high-altitude sky, upper air

京 *jōkyō* proceeding to the capital

昇 *jōshō suru* rise, ascend, climb

昇気流 *jōshō kiryū* ascending air current

⁹面 *jōmen* surface, top, exterior. *uwatsura, uwa(t)tsura* surface, appearances

映 *jōei* screen projection

段 *jōdan* dais, raised part of the floor; seats of honor, upper row of seats; upper berth; upper (horizontal) column (of print). *a(gari)dan* staircase, doorsteps

品 *jōhin* refinement, decency; first-class article. *jōbon* Buddhism's highest paradise

巻 *jōkan* volume one

級 *jōkyū* higher grade, advanced class, high class

級生 *jōkyūsei* upperclassman

院 *jōin* Upper House, Senate, Lords

奏 *jōsō* report to the throne

¹⁰座 *jōza, kamiza* chief seat, seat of honor

記 *jōki no* the above-mentioned

陸 *jōriku* landing, disembarkation

書 *uwaga(ki)* address; superscription. *jōsho* memorial to the throne

流 *jōryū* upper stream; upper classes

流社会 *jōryū shakai* upper classes

部 *jōbu* upper part, top, upper side, surface

¹¹達 *jōtatsu* progress, proficiency

¹²程 *jōtei* introducing (a bill)

策 *jōsaku* excellent plan; best policy

着 *uwagi* coat, tunic, jacket, outer garment

棟式 *jōtōshiki* ridgepole-raising ceremony

等 *jōtō* superiority, first class, very good
¹³ 塗 *uwanu(ri)* last plaster coat, last painting, finish
¹⁴ 演 *jōen* stage performance
端 *jōtan* top, tip, upper end
製 *jōsei* superior make; superior binding
層 *jōsō* upper layer; upper air; upper story; higher class
層気流 *jōsō kiryū* upper air currents
層階級 *jōsō kaikyū* upper classes, high society
¹⁵ 履 *uwabaki* hallway slippers, inside shoes
潮 *a(ge)shio* incoming tide
質 *jōshitsu* fine quality
¹⁶ 機嫌 *jōkigen* good humor
¹⁸ 瞼 *uwamabuta* upper eyelid
²⁰ 欄 *jōran* top or preceding horizontal column

———— 3 ————

丑 $\frac{12}{\text{J312f}}$ $\frac{}{\text{M23}}$ CHŪ . *ushi* 1–3 a.m.; second zodiac sign; cow.

不 $\frac{13}{\text{J4954}}$ $\frac{}{\text{M19}}$ FU negation; bad; clumsy;
A ugly. BU bad; clumsy; ugly.
-*zu* negation.
¹ 一致 *fuitchi* discord, disagreement, dissonance
² 十分 *fujūbun* insufficiency, imperfection
人気 *funinki* unpopularity
人情 *funinjō* unkindness, inhumanity, heartlessness
³ 干渉 *fukanshō* nonintervention, noninterference
⁴ 分明 *fubummei* indistinct, obscure
介入 *fukainyū* noninvolvement, nonintervention, neutrality
心得 *fukokoroe* indiscretion, imprudence
手際 *futegiwa* clumsiness, ineptitude
毛 *fumō* barren, sour, unproductive (land)
公平 *fukōhei* unfairness, injustice, partiality
公正 *fukōsei* injustice, unfairness
文律 *fubunritsu* unwritten law, unwritten rule, common law
⁵ 払 *fubara(i)* nonpayment, default
世出 *fuseishutsu* rare, extraordinary, unparalleled

出来 *fudeki* poor workmanship, bad job, bungle
必要 *fuhitsuyō* unnecessary
本意 *fuhon'i* reluctance, unwillingness
甲斐無 *fugaina(i)* spiritless, cowardly, worthless
仕合 *fushia(wase)* unhappiness, misfortune, ill luck
平 *fuhei* discontent, dissatisfaction, complaint
平不満 *fuhei-fuman* discontent and grumbling
平等 *fubyōdō* inequality; unequal (treaties)
用心 *buyōjin, fuyōjin* insecurity; carelessness
用品 *fuyōhin* disused article
用意 *fuyōi* unpreparedness, carelessness
正 *fusei* injustice, iniquity, impropriety, irregularity, dishonesty, illegality
正行為 *fusei kōi* unfair practices, wrongdoing, malpractice, cheating, foul play
正確 *fuseikaku* inaccuracy, uncertainty
可 *fuka* wrong, bad, improper, unjustifiable, inadvisable
可欠 *fukaketsu na* indispensable
可分 *fukabun* indivisibility
可抗力 *fukakōryoku* act of God; irresistible force; inevitability
可知 *fukachi na* unknowable, mysterious
可侵 *fukashin* inviolability, nonaggression
可思議 *fukashigi* mystery, wonder, miracle
可能 *fukanō* impossibility
可解 *fukakai* mystery, incomprehensibility
可避 *fukahi* inescapable, inevitable, unavoidable
⁶ 向 *fumu(ki) na* unfit, unsuitable, unmarketable
仲 *funaka* discord
朽 *fukyū* immortality
吉 *fukitsu* bad luck, ill omen, inauspiciousness
充分 *fujūbun* insufficiency, shortage, imperfection, inadequacy
似合 *funia(i)* unbecoming, improper, unsuitable, ill-matched, unworthy of
気味 *bukimi* ill feeling. *bukimi na*

uncanny, weird, ghastly, ominous

如意 *funyoi* contrary to one's wishes; short of money

自由 *fujiyū* inconvenience, discomfort; destitution; disability

自然 *fushizen* unnatural, artificial, affected, strained

合格 *fugōkaku* failure (in an examination), rejection, disqualification

合理 *fugōri na* unreasonable, irrational, absurd, inconsistent

名誉 *fumeiyo* dishonor, disgrace, shame

同意 *fudōi* disagreement, objection

成立 *fuseiritsu* failure, rupture, rejection

成功 *fuseikō* failure

成績 *fuseiseki* poor result, bad record, failure

死 *fushi* immortality, eternal life

死鳥 *fushichō* phoenix bird

死身 *fujimi* invulnerability, immortality, insensibility to pain

行届 *fuyu(ki)todo(ki)* negligence, carelessness, incompetence, mismanagement

安 *fuan* anxiety, uneasiness; insecurity; suspense

安定 *fuantei* instability; insecurity; crankiness

当 *fua(tari)* failure, unpopularity. *futō na* unjust, unreasonable, undeserved. *futō* injustice, impropriety, unreasonableness

在 *fuzai* absence

[7] 快 *fukai* displeasure, discomfort; indisposition, malaise

完全 *fukanzen na* imperfect, incomplete, faulty, defective

沙汰 *busata* silence, neglect to write, neglect to call

条理 *fujōri* irrationality, absurdity, inconsistency

即不離 *fusoku-furi* neutral, noncommittal

作 *fusaku* poor crop, crop failure

作法 *busahō* bad manners, discourtesy

妊 *funin* sterility, barrenness

利 *furi* disadvantage, drawback, handicap

見識 *fukenshiki na* undignified, unprincipled, disgraceful

足 *fusoku* shortage, lack, deficiency,

dearth

均等 *fukintō* imbalance, inequality, unevenness

均衡 *fukinkō* out of balance, imbalance, disparity, inequality

承認 *fushōnin* disapproval, dissent, veto

良 *furyō* bad, poor, inferior; wicked, delinquent

[8] 屈 *fukutsu* fortitude, indomitability

況 *fukyō* depression, slump, recession

治 *fuchi, fuji* incurability

服 *fufuku* dissatisfaction, discontent; disagreement, disapproval; objection, protest, complaint

服従 *fufukujū* insubordination, disobedience

幸 *fukō* unhappiness, misfortune; death (of family or relative)

実 *fujitsu* faithlessness, inconstancy, insincerity; falsehood

始末 *fushimatsu* mismanagement, wastefulness, carelessness, misconduct

退転 *futaiten* firm determination, indomitableness

注意 *fuchūi* carelessness, negligence

和 *fuwa* discord, trouble, dissension, disagreement

参加 *fusanka* nonparticipation

具 *fugu* deformity; distortion; disability; cripple; Sincerely yours (letter ending)

明 *fumei* obscurity, indistinctness, uncertainty, ambiguity; ignorance, lack of wisdom

明朗 *fumeirō* gloomy; dubious; underhand

明瞭 *fumeiryō* indistinctness, dimness, obscurity

法 *fuhō* lawlessness, injustice, illegality, unlawfulness

定 *futei* uncertainty, indefiniteness, indeterminateness, mutability. *fujō* uncertainty, mutability

[9] 通 *futsū* suspension, stoppage, tie-up, cessation, impassability

便 *fuben* inconvenience, inexpediency. *fubin* inconvenience; caring; pity, compassion

変 *fuhen* unchangeability, immutability, constancy, permanence, indestructibility

要 *fuyō* unnecessary; waste (products)

面目 *fumemmoku, fumemboku* shame, disgrace

品行 *fuhinkō* unchastity, misconduct, dissipation, loose conduct

格好 *bukakkō* unshapeliness; clumsiness

相応 *fusōō, busōō* unsuited, inappropriate, improper, undeserved

首尾 *fushubi* failure, fizzle; disgrace, disfavor. *bushubi* inconsistency

透明 *futōmei* opacity

連続 *furenzoku* discontinuity

祝儀 *bushūgi* an occasion for mourning; a funeral

浄 *fujō* uncleanliness, impurity, filthiness, defilement; menses; toilet, latrine

思議 *fushigi* wonder, mystery, marvel, miracle; curiosity

発 *fuhatsu* misfire

貞 *futei* unchastity, unfaithfulness, (conjugal) infidelity

信 *fushin* unfaithfulness, insincerity; perfidy; mistrust, distrust, discredit

信任 *fushinnin* nonconfidence

10 倫 *furin* impropriety, immorality; infidelity, unfaithfulness

振 *fushin* dullness, depression, slump, stagnation

粋 *busui na* inelegant, lacking in polish

能 *funō* incompetency, lack of ability; impossibility; weak point; impotence

案内 *fuannai, buannai* ignorance, inexperience, unfamiliarity

都合 *futsugō* inconvenience, inexpedience; trouble, harm; impropriety, wrongdoing

真面目 *fumajime* unsteadiness; lack of sincerity

倶戴天 *fugutaiten* irreconcilable (enemy)

起訴 *fukiso* nonprosecution, nonindictment

純 *fujun* impurity, adulteration; dishonesty; irregularity

純物 *fujumbutsu* foreign matter, impurities

時着 *fujichaku* emergency landing

眠 *fumin* wakefulness, sleeplessness

眠不休 *fumin-fukyū* without sleep or rest, day and night

眠症 *fuminshō* insomnia, sleepless- ness

随 *fuzui* paralysis, palsy

11 運 *fuun* misfortune, bad luck, fate

遇 *fugū* misfortune, bad luck, obscurity

敗 *fuhai* invincibility

細工 *busaiku* clumsy work; poor shape; awkward, clumsy; homely, plain

経済 *fukeizai* poor economy, waste

道徳 *fudōtoku* immorality, iniquity

健全 *fukenzen* unhealthful

健康 *fukenkō* poor health; unhealthi ness

偏不党 *fuhen-futō* neutrality

断 *fudan* usually, habitually, continually; constantly; indecision, irresolution

動 *fudō* immobility, firmness, steadfastness; fixed, motionless, idle

動産 *fudōsan* real estate

規則 *fukisoku* irregularity, unsteadi- ness

得意 *futokui* one's weak point

12 備 *fubi* deficiency, imperfection , defect, inadequacy; Yours in haste

順 *fujun* irregularity, unseasonableness

渡 *fuwata(ri)* nonpayment, dishonoring (a bill); bouncing (check)

測 *fusoku* unexpectedness

統一 *futōitsu* disunity, disharmony

景気 *fukeiki* hard times, depression; gloom, sullenness, cheerlessness

愉快 *fuyukai* unpleasantness, disagreeableness, unhappiness

満 *fuman* dissatisfaction, displeasure, discontent

評 *fuhyō* bad reputation, disgrace, unpopularity

等辺 *futōhen* unequal sides

買 *fubai* not buying

覚 *fukaku* fault, failure, negligence, indiscretion

13 滅 *fumetsu* immortality, indestructibility

詳 *fushō* unknown, unidentified

馴 *funare* inexperience, unfamiliarity

摂生 *fusessei* neglect of health, intemperance

寛容 *fukan'yō* intolerance

寝番 *fushimban* night watch; sleepless vigil, vigilance. *nezuban, nezu(no)ban* sleepless vigil

誠実 *fuseijitsu* insincerity, dishonesty, untruthfulness, bad faith

義 *fugi* immorality; injustice;

impropriety; misconduct; adultery; perfidy

義理 *fugiri* dishonesty, injustice; dishonor; ingratitude

適 *futeki* unfitness, inappropriateness, inadequacy, impropriety

適切 *futekisetsu na* unsuitable, inappropriate

適格 *futekikaku, futekkaku* disqualification, unfitness

意 *fui* suddenness, unexpectedness

14 慣 *funa(re)* inexperience, unfamiliarity

様 *buzama na* unshapely, unsightly, unpresentable, uncouth, clumsy

徳 *futoku* depravity, immorality, unworthiness

認可 *funinka* disapproval, rejection

精 *bushō* laziness, indolence

15 慮 *furyo no* unforeseen, accidental

憫 *fubin* pity, compassion

撓不屈 *futō-fukutsu* inflexibility, tenacity, indomitableness

潔 *fuketsu* uncleanliness, dirtiness, impurity

遇 *fugū* misfortune; obscurity

敵 *futeki na* bold, fearless, daring, tough

衛生 *fueisei* unsanitary condition

履行 *furikō* nonperformance, default

徹底 *futettei* not thoroughgoing, unconvincing, inconclusive, inconsistent, illogical, indefinite, half-way

確実 *fukakujitsu na* uncertain, unreliable, inauthentic

審 *fushin* incomplete understanding; doubt, question; distrust, suspicion; strangeness; infidelity

調 *fuchō* disagreement, break-off, disorder; slump; out of form

器用 *bukiyō* clumsiness, unskillfulness

器量 *bukiryō, fukiryō* ugliness, homeliness; lack of ability, incompetence

16 興 *fukyō* displeasure, ill-humor

親切 *fushinsetsu* unkindliness, unfriendliness

機嫌 *fukigen* displeasure, ill humor, sullenness

燃性 *funensei* incombustibility

穏 *fuon* unrest, turbulence; impropriety unreasonableness

17 鮮明 *fusemmei* blurring

謹慎 *fukinshin* indiscretion, imprudence

———— **4** ————

B 丙 $\frac{16}{\underset{M35}{J4a3a}}$ HEI C, third. *hinoe* third calendar sign.

B 且 $\frac{17}{\underset{M29}{J336e}}$ SHO. *katsu* also, furthermore.

B 丘 $\frac{19}{\underset{M33}{J3556}}$ KYŪ. KU. *oka* hill, knoll, rising ground.

10 陵 *kyūryō* hill, hillock

A 世 $\frac{20}{\underset{M31}{J4024}}$ SE generation; world. SEI generation; age, world, counter for kings of the same name. *yo* world, society, public; life, existence, career, life-time; age, era, generation, times; reign.

2 人 *sejin* people, the public, the world

3 上 *sejō* the world

4 中 *yo (no) naka* society, the world, the times

5 代 *sedai, seidai* generation; the world; the age

8 事 *seji* worldly affairs

知辛 *sechigara(i)* a hard (life); a tough (world)

9 相 *sesō* phase of life; sign of the times; world conditions

紀 *seiki* century; era

俗 *sezoku* common customs; worldliness; the world, the common people. *sezoku no* common, worldly, vulgar, popular

俗的 *sezokuteki* worldly

界 *sekai* the world; society; the universe

界一 *sekaiichi* best in the world

界一周 *sekaiisshū* round-the-world trip, circumnavigation, globe-trotting

界大戦 *Sekai Taisen* World War

界的 *sekaiteki* world, world-wide, international, universal

界記録 *sekai kiroku* world record

界選手権 *sekai senshuken* world championship

界銀行 *Sekai Ginkō* the World Bank

10 帯 *setai* household, home

帯主 *setainushi* householder

11 情 *sejō* world conditions; worldly affairs; human nature

1

4 [二]
一、ノ乙亅

¹² 渡 *yowata(ri)* living, subsistence, getting along in the world

評 *sehyō* popular opinion; popularity; rumor

間 *seken* world, society, life, people, the public; rumor, gossip

間体 *sekentei* decency, reputation, appearance

間的 *sekenteki* worldly, earthly

間知 *sekenshi(razu)* ignorance of the world; a person ignorant of the world

間話 *sekembanashi* gossip, chitchat

¹³ 辞 *seji* flattery, compliment

話 *sewa* help, aid; good offices, service, recommendation; care, trouble; everyday life

¹⁴ 慣 *yona(reru)* get used to the world; grow worldly

¹⁵ 論 *seron, seiron, yoron* public opinion

論調査 *seron chōsa* public-opinion research

²² 襲 *seshū* heredity; heritage

性 *ryōsei* both sexes

⁹ 院 *ryōin* both houses (of a legislative assembly)

陛下 *Ryōheika* Their Majesties

面 *ryōmen* both faces, both sides

¹⁰ 脇 *ryōwaki* both sides

¹¹ 側 *ryōgawa, ryōsoku* both sides

眼 *ryōgan* both eyes

¹² 腕 *ryōude* both arms

棲動物 *ryōsei dōbutsu* amphibious animal

極 *ryōkyoku* both extremities; north and south poles, positive and negative poles

替 *ryōgae* money exchange

¹⁴ 様 *ryōyō* two ways, both ways, two kinds

種 *ryōshu* both kinds

端 *ryōtan, ryōhashi* both ends, either end; both edges; sitting on the fence

¹⁶ 親 *ryōshin, futaoya* parents, both parents

5

丞 $\frac{22}{\text{J3e67}}$ M40 Jō, SHŌ help.

両 $\frac{23}{\text{J4e3e}}$ M46 A RYŌ old Japanese coin; both; two; vehicle counter. *tēru* tael.

² 刀遣 *ryōtōtsuka(i)* two-sword fencer; expert in two lines; man of broad tastes; bisexual man

⁴ 方 *ryōhō* both

日 *ryōjitsu* both days; two days

手 *ryōte* both hands

⁵ 立 *ryōritsu* coexistence, standing together, compatibility

生動物 *ryōsei dōbutsu* amphibious animal

用 *ryōyō* dual use

⁷ 足 *ryōashi, ryōsoku* both feet; both legs

⁸ 岸 *ryōgan, ryōgishi* both banks (of a river)

者 *ryōsha* both persons; both things

国 *ryōkoku* both countries

7

並 $\frac{24}{\text{J4a42}}$ M54 A HEI. *nara(bu)* line up, bez in a row; rank with, rival, equal. *nara(beru)* arrange, place in order, marshal, put side by side, display, serve (food); enumerate; compare with. *nara(mi)* common, ordinary, average. *nara(bi) ni* and, besides, as well as. *nara(bi)* row, line, side. *na(bete)* all.

³ 大抵 *na(mi)-taitei no* ordinary

⁴ 木 *namiki* roadside tree; row of trees

⁵ 外 *na(mi)hazu(re)* above the average, extraordinary; abnormal; unreasonable

⁶ 列 *heiretsu* arrangement; row, parallel

存 *heizon* coexistence

行 *heikō* parallel

⁸ 居 *na(mi)-i(ru)* sit in a row

¹³ 置 *heichi* juxtaposition, placing side by side

¹⁴ 製 *namisei* ordinary make

丨

RAD. 2

Bō rod, stick, line. Variant: a shorter vertical. Nickname: Rod.

─────── 3 ───────

A 中 $\frac{28}{\text{J4366}}$ CHŪ center, middle; middle
M73 (course); (golden) mean;
medium, mediocrity, average; second
volume (of three). *naka* inside, interior,
midst, middle, mean, midway. *uchi*
inside, interior; house, home; within;
between, among, out of; mind; myself.
chū(suru) reach the middle; reach the
height (of prosperity). *-chū, -jū* through,
throughout, during; all over (town);
within, among, in.

² 二階 *chūnikai* mezzanine floor
³ 小 *chūshō* medium and small
　小企業 *chūshō kigyō* medium and small
　　enterprises
⁴ 止 *chūshi* suspension, stoppage,
　　interruption
　天 *chūten* mid-air; mid-heaven, zenith
　元 *chūgen* 15th day of the seventh lunar
　　month; last day of Bon Lantern
　　Festival; Bon gifts
　心 *chūshin* center, heart; pivot,
　　emphasis; balance
　心地 *chūshinchi* center, metropolis
⁵ 世 *chūsei* medieval times; Middle
　　Ages
　立 *chūritsu* neutrality
　古 *chūko, chūburu* secondhand, *chūko*
　　medieval times
　央 *chūō* center, middle
　央集権 *chūō shūken* centralized
　　authoritarian rule
⁶ 米 *Chūbei* Central America
　旬 *chūjun* middle ten days of a month
　近東 *Chūkintō* Near and Middle East
　耳炎 *chūjien* tympanitis
　肉中背 *chūniku-chūzei* medium build
　年 *chūnen* middle age
⁷ 形 *chūgata* medium size
⁸ 退 *chūtai* leaving school during a
　　term
　味 *nakami* interior, contents, substance,
　　filling; (sword) blade
　和 *chūwa suru* neutralize, counteract
　空 *chūkū* mid-air, the air; emptiness.
　　nakazora mid-air
　毒 *chūdoku* poisoning; addiction
　東 *Chūtō* Middle East
　波 *chūha* medium wave (in
　　broadcasting)

国 *Chūgoku* China; middle of a country;
　　the Hiroshima area
性 *chūsei* neutral gender; (chemical)
　　neutrality; sterility; indifference
性子 *chūseishi* neutron
性洗剤 *chūseisenzai* a detergent
枢 *chūsū* center, pivot, nucleus,
　　backbone, central figure, mainstay,
　　pillar, key man
枢神経系 *chūsū shinkei kei* central
　　nervous system
学 *chūgaku* middle school; junior high
　　school
学生 *chūgakusei* middle school pupil;
　　junior high school pupil
学校 *chūgakkō* middle school; junior
　　high school
⁹ 風 *chūbu, chūbū, chūfū* palsy,
　　paralysis
　段 *chūdan* half way up a slope or
　　stairway, the landing; center of three
　　(horizontal) columns (of print)
　巻 *chūkan* middle volume (of three)
　南米 *Chūnambei* Central and South
　　America
　級品 *chūkyūhin* fair average quality
　途 *chūto* midway, half way
　途半端 *chūto-hampa* half finished,
　　incomplete
¹⁰ 座 *chūza suru* leave before an affair is
　　over
　庭 *nakaniwa* courtyard, quadrangle,
　　middle court
　核 *chūkaku* kernel, core, nucleus
　流 *chūryū* mid-stream; middle course;
　　middle class
　部 *chūbu* central part, center, middle,
　　heart
　華 *Chūka* Middle Kingdom, China
　華人民共和国 *Chūka Jimmin
　　Kyōwakoku* the People's Republic of
　　China
　華民国 *Chūka Minkoku* Republic of
　　China (Taiwan)
¹¹ 庸 *chūyō* mean, golden mean,
　　moderation, middle path; Doctrine of
　　the Mean
　頃 *nakagoro* about the middle
　略 *chūryaku* omission of a part (of an
　　article)
　断 *chūdan* break, interruption,
　　suspension

1

一
[｜]
丶
ノ
乙
｜

距離 *chūkyori* middle distance (race)
産階級 *chūsan kaikyū* middle class, bourgeoisie
道 *chūdō* the middle road, middle of the road, mean, moderation
堅 *chūken* main body (of troops); center field, center fielder; nucleus, backbone, mainstay
¹² 程 *nakahodo* middle, midway
絶 *chūzetsu* interruption, discontinuance, suspension, abeyance, abortion
軸 *chūjiku* axis, pivot, central figure, key man
期 *chūki* middle period
葉 *chūyō* about the middle of (an era)
等 *chūtō* second grade, medium quality, average; middle class; secondary grade
等教育 *chūtō kyōiku* secondary education
間 *chūkan* middle, midway; interim
間子 *chūkanshi* meson, mesotron

間層 *chūkansō* the middle class
¹³ 傷 *chūshō* slander, libel, defamation
腰 *chūgoshi* half-sitting or half-standing posture
腹 *chūfuku* mountain side, halfway up
継 *chūkei* (radio) relay, hookup
継放送 *chūkei hōsō* relay broadcasting
¹⁵ 盤戦 *chūbansen* the midst of a campaign

───── 6 ─────

串 $\frac{30}{\frac{J367a}{M80}}$ KAN. KEN. SEN. *kushi* spit, skewer.
⁸ 刺 *kushiza(shi)* skewering
¹² 焼 *kushiya(ki)* food cooked on skewers

───── 8 ─────

衷 $\frac{31}{\frac{J436f}{M-X}}$ CHŪ heart, mind; inside.
B *uchi* the inside.

━━━━━━━━━━━ RAD. 丶 3 ━━━━━━━━━━━

Ten dot, point (the Japanese comma, like the grave accent). Nickname: Dot.

───── 1 ─────

乄 $\frac{33}{\frac{J213a}{M116}}$ (国字) *shime* adding up; bundle; ream; seal.
kan 8⅓ pounds. *shime(te)* totalling. *shi(meru)* sum up.
⁴ 切 *shimeki(ri)* closing; closing up
切日 *shimekiribi* deadline

───── 2 ─────

丸 $\frac{34}{\frac{J345d}{M94}}$ GAN. *maru* full (month);
A perfection; purity; the ship-name suffix anciently used after the name of a sword or a child. *maru(meru)* make round, round off, roll up, curl up; seduce; cajole; explain away. *tama* pills. *maru de* quite, completely, absolutely; just like; as it were. *maru(i), maru(kkoi)* round, circular, spherical.
³ 丸 *marumaru* completely. *marumaru to* plump

⁴ 込 *maru(me)-ko(mu)* coax, seduce
刈 *maruga(ri)* close clipping
太 *maruta* log
太小屋 *marutagoya* log cabin, blockhouse
木 *maruki* log
木舟 *marukibune* dugout canoe
木橋 *marukibashi* log bridge
⁵ 出 *maruda(shi)* bare, exposed, undisguised; broad (provincial accent)
⁷ 見 *marumi(e)* completely visible
坊主 *marubōzu* close-cropped head; bald hill
⁸ 味 *marumi* roundness, rotundity
⁹ 括弧 *marugakko* parentheses
¹² 焼 *maruya(ke)* total fire loss; completely burned. *maruya(ki)* barbecue
¹³ 損 *maruzon* total loss
暗記 *maru anki* indiscriminate memorizing
腰 *marugoshi* unarmed
裸 *maruhadaka* nude

¹⁵ 潰 *marutsubu(re)* complete ruin, collapse

¹⁶ 薬 *gan'yaku* pill

―――――――― **3** ――――――――

丹 $\frac{36}{\frac{J4330}{M99}}$ TAN red; red lead; pills. *ni* red; red earth.

B

⁸ 青 *tansei* red and blue; painting

念 *tannen* application, diligence

⁹ 前 *tanzen* large padded kimono

¹³ 誠 *tansei* sincerity; efforts, diligence

塗 *ninu(ri) no* red painted, vermilion lacquered

¹⁴ 精 *tansei suru* work earnestly

―――――――― **4** ――――――――

主 $\frac{38}{\frac{J3c67}{M100}}$ SU. SHŪ. SHU Lord; lord,

A master, employer; aim; main thing. *aruji* head of the house, master, mistress, husband. *nushi* owner; master, husband; lover; a god; you. *omo(na), omo(naru)* main, principal, important. *omo(ni)* chiefly, principally, mostly. *shu(taru)* main, principal, major. *shu toshite* mainly, chiefly. *omo-* main.

² 人 *shujin, aruji* master, head (of a household), landlord; one's husband; employer; host

人公 *shujinkō* master, head (of a household); hero or heroine (of a story)

力 *shuryoku* main force, main strength

⁴ 文 *shubun* the text; the main clause (in grammar); the main part of a document

⁵ 犯 *shuhan* principal offense; principal offender

⁶ 因 *shuin* primary cause, prime factor

旨 *shushi* opinion, idea; meaning, gist, tenor; aim, motive, purpose

成分 *shuseibun* main ingredient

任 *shunin* person in charge

⁷ 位 *shui* first place, leading position

役 *shuyaku* a major role; a big part; a star

君 *shukun* lord, master

体的 *shutaiteki* subjective

体性 *shutaisei* independence, autonomy

⁸ 事 *shuji* manager, director, secretary

治医 *shujii* attending physician

⁹ 査 *shusa* chief investigator

食 *shushoku* staple food; main article of diet

計 *shukei* paymaster, accountant

客 *shukaku, shukyaku* host and guest; principal and auxiliary

客転倒 *shukaku tentō* opposites; reverse order

要 *shuyō na* main, principal, chief, essential, staple

要人物 *shuyō jimbutsu* key people

¹⁰ 従 *shujū, shūjū* master and servant, lord and retainer, employer and employee

格 *shukaku* nominative case

流 *shuryū* main current

宰 *shusai* supervision; chairmanship

席 *shuseki* head seat, head, chief, president, governor, chairman

¹¹ 婦 *shufu* housewife, mistress

張 *shuchō* assertion, claim, advocacy; emphasis, contention, insistence; opinion, tenet

眼 *shugan* chief aim; main point

産地 *shusanchi* chief producing center

産物 *shusambutsu* main product

¹² 軸 *shujiku* main shaft

筆 *shuhitsu* editor in chief

¹³ 意 *shui* main meaning; opinion, idea; aim, motive

幹 *shukan* chief editor, managing editor; manager

義 *shugi* principle, policy, basis; -ism

催 *shusai* sponsorship, promotion

¹⁴ 語 *shugo* subject (of a sentence)

演 *shuen* starring, playing the leading part

導 *shudō* main leadership

導権 *shudōken* leadership, initiative

¹⁵ 賓 *shuhin* main guest, guest of honor

権 *shuken* sovereignty, dominion

¹⁶ 謀者 *shubōsha* leader

¹⁷ 翼 *shuyoku* main wings (of an airplane)

¹⁸ 題 *shudai* subject, theme, motif

観 *shukan* subjectivity; subject, ego

⁴ 心 *chūshin* innermost feelings, true heart

4

1

No (the katakana). At top: ⌐ *no kammuri*. Variants of varying lengths.
Nickname: *Kana No.*

──────── **1** ────────

乃 ── 42 / J4735 / M113 ── DAI. NAI. *sunawa(chi)*
no whereupon, accordingly.
no possessive particle. *soko de* then,
thereupon, accordingly.
⁶ 至 *naishi* from… to…; or

──────── **2** ────────

々 ── 45 / J2139 / M97 ── Character repetition.

B 乏 ── 46 / J4b33 / M133 ── BŌ. *tobo(shii), tomo(shii)*
meager, scarce, limited;
destitute, hard up.

A 久 ── 47 / J3557 / M118 ── KYŪ. KU. *hisa(shii)* long,
long-continued, an old
(story). *hisa(shiku)* for a long time.
³ 久 *hisabisa* a long time, many days
¹⁰ 振 *hisa(shi)buri* a long time, many days
¹⁶ 懐 *kyūkai* a long-cherished hope

──────── **3** ────────

之 ── 48 / J4737 / M125 ── SHI. *kore* this. *ko(no)* this.

──────── **4** ────────

乎 ── 49 / J3843 / M131 ── KO. *ya, ka* question mark.

乍 ── 50 / J4663 / M130 ── SA. *-naga(ra)* though,
notwithstanding; while,
during; both, all. *tachima(chi)* in a
moment, instantly, immediately, all of a
sudden.

──────── **8** ────────

A 乗 ── 54 / J3e68 / M153 ── JŌ power (in math):
multiplication; record;
vehicle; vehicle counter. *no(ru),*
no(kkaru) ride, board, mount; get up on;

spread (paints); be taken in; share in, join;
be found in (a dictionary); feel like doing;
be mentioned in; be in harmony with.
no(seru) place, put, lay, set; let (one) take
part; impose on; record, mention. *no(ri-*
konasu) manage (a horse). *jō(jiru),*
jō(zuru) take advantage of; multiply
(in math); follow blindly. *no(ri)* riding,
ride; (two)-seater; spread (of paints).
² 入 *no(ri)-i(reru)* vi ride or drive
into (a place); extend (a line into a
city). *no(ri)-i(ru)* ride or drive into
(a place). *no(ri)-i(re)* driving into
⁴ 込 *no(ri)-ko(mu)* vt and vi board, embark
on, get into (a car); ship (passengers);
man (a ship); help (someone) into;
march into, enter
心地 *no(ri)gokochi* one's feeling while
riding
⁵ 出 *no(ri)-da(su)* set out, set sail; embark
on; lean forward; begin to ride
用車 *jōyōsha* passenger auto
⁶ 回 *no(ri)-ma(waru)* ride around.
no(ri)-ma(wasu) vt drive (a car)
around, ride (a bicycle) around.
気 *no(ri)ki* interest, eagerness
合 *no(ri)-a(wasu), no(ri)-a(waseru)*
happen to ride together, share a
vehicle. *noriai* bus, stagecoach;
riding together; fellow passenger; joint
partnership
⁷ 車 *jōsha* entraining
車券 *jōshaken* passenger ticket
⁸ 物 *no(ri)mono* vehicle
取 *no(t)to(ru), no(ri)-to(ru)* capture,
occupy, usurp
⁹ 除 *jōjo* multiplication and
division
客 *jōkyaku, jōkaku* passenger
降 *jōkō, no(ri)o(ri)* getting on and off
¹⁰ 員 *jōin* crew
馬 *jōba, no(ri)uma* riding horse; saddle
horse
¹¹ 遅 *no(ri)-oku(reru)* miss (a train)
過 *no(ri)-su(gosu)* ride past
捨 *no(ri)-su(teru)* get off, abandon (a
ship)

移 *no(ri)-utsu(su)* transfer (a stowaway). *no(ri)-utsu(ru)* change (cars or horses), transfer; possess; inspire

船 *jōsen* embark; be on board

務員 *jōmuin* trainman, train crew

組 *no(ri)-ku(mu)* get on aboard; join a ship. *noriku(mi)* crew

組員 *norikumiin* crew

¹²越 *no(ri)-ko(eru)* climb over; ride across; surmount. *no(ri)-ko(su)* ride past; pass; outdistance. *noriko(shi)* riding past (one's station)

場 *no(ri)ba* car stop, platform

換 *no(ri)-ka(eru)* transfer. *norika(e)* transfer

—————— **9** ——————

乗 $\frac{55}{\substack{J502b \\ M154}}$ See 乗 54.

━━━━━━━ **RAD. 乙 5** ━━━━━━━

Otsu second (in order). Variants: 乚, ⼄ *tsuribari* fishhook. Nickname: Fishhook.

乙 $\frac{56}{\substack{J3235 \\ M161}}$ ITSU. OTSU B, second; the
B latter; duplicate. *otsu na* strange, queer, quaint; witty; stylish,

spicy, chic; tasty; romantic. *kinoto* second calendar sign.

³女 *otome* virgin, maiden

—————— **1** ——————

九 $\frac{57}{\substack{J3665 \\ M167}}$ KYŪ, KU *kokono(tsu), ko*
A nine.

²九表 *kuku (no) hyō* multiplication table

⁴日 *kokonoka* nine days; the ninth day (of the month)

月 *Kugatsu* September

⁶死一生 *kyūshi (ni) isshō* narrow escape from death

—————— **2** ——————

也 $\frac{58}{\substack{J4c69 \\ M171}}$ YA. *nari = desu* to be (classical).

乞 $\frac{59}{\substack{J3870 \\ M170}}$ KITSU. KOTSU. *ko(u)* ask, request; invite; pray for; beg, solicit.

⁹食 *kojiki* beggar; begging

—————— **6** ——————

乱 $\frac{60}{\substack{J4d70 \\ M187}}$ RAN, RON riot, rebellion,
A war, disorder. *mida(re)* disorder, disturbance, agitation. *mida(su), mida(ru)* put in disorder; disturb, agitate; corrupt; derange (the mind). *mida(reru)* be out of order, be confused; be disturbed, be disorganized; be demoralized, be lax; be disheveled. *mida(ri) ni* without authority, without reason, arbitrarily, unnecessarily, indiscriminately, recklessly. *mida(rigamashii)* morally corrupt.

²入 *rannyū* intrusion, raid. *rannyū suru* intrude, break into

⁴文 *rambun* careless writing (in composition)

反射 *ranhansha* diffused reflection

⁵用 *ran'yō* misuse, abuse, misappropriation

立 *ranritsu* flood (of candidates)

打 *randa* pummeling, random blows

世 *ransei* troubled times

⁶行 *rangyō* profligacy, debauchery, misconduct

⁹造 *ranzō* overproduction; careless manufacture

発 *rampatsu* random or reckless firing

¹⁰脈 *rammyaku* confusion, disorder, chaos

射 *ransha* random firing, wild shot

¹¹視 *ranshi* astigmatism, distorted vision

¹²筆 *rampitsu* bad writing, scribbling

¹⁴雑 *ranzatsu* disorder, confusion

舞 *rambu* boisterous dance

1

一 丨 丶 丿

⁶ 乙 亅

読 *randoku* indiscriminate reading
¹⁵ 暴 *rambō* violence, rudeness, rowdiness, carelessness, lawlessness, recklessness
¹⁶ 獲 *rankaku* indiscriminate fishing or hunting
¹⁸ 闘 *rantō* free-for-all fight, melee

─────── **7** ───────

乳 [61 / J467d / M190] NYŪ. *chi, chichi* milk; the breasts; loop.
⁴ 牛 *chichiushi, nyūgyū* milk cow, dairy cattle
⁵ 幼児 *nyūyōji* infant
母 *uba, nyūbo, omba* wet nurse, nursing mother
母車 *ubaguruma* baby buggy
白色 *nyūhakushoku* milk white
⁷ 状 *nyūjō* milky
児 *nyūji* suckling, infant, baby
⁸ 房 *chibusa, nyūbō* breast, nipple, udder
⁹ 首 *chikubi, chichi kubi* teat, nipple
¹⁰ 剤 *nyūzai* emulsion
¹¹ 液 *nyūeki* latex
¹² 歯 *nyūshi* first set of teeth
飲子 *chino(mi)go* baby, suckling child
¹³ 業 *nyūgyō* the dairy business
¹⁴ 製品 *nyūseihin* dairy products
酸菌 *nyūsankin* lactic acid bacilli
¹⁷ 癌 *nyūgan* breast cancer

─────── **10** ───────

亀 [62 / J3535 / M210] KI, KIN. *kame* turtle, tortoise.
⁵ 甲 *kikō, kikkō, kame(no)kō* tortoise shell
¹² 裂 *kiretsu* crack, crevice, fissure, chap

乾 [63 / J3425 / M204] KAN. KEN heaven; emperor. B *ho(su)* vt dry; desiccate; drain (off); drink up; dry up. *ka(seru)* dry up, scab, slough; be poisoned (with lacquer). *kawa(ku)* dry, dry up; be dry. *kawa(kasu)* vt dry, desiccate. *kara(biru)* dry up, shrivel. *kawa(ki)* drying; dryness. *hoshi-* dried, cured.
⁶ 肉 *hoshiniku* dried meat, pemmican
⁸ 杯 *kampai* a toast
季 *kanki* dry season
坤一擲 *kenkon'itteki* throwing all into a task; staking all on
物 *kambutsu* groceries. *hoshimono* laundry on the line. *karamono* dried fish
⁹ 草 *kansō, magusa, hoshi kusa* hay, dry grass ⌈fish
¹¹ 魚 *hoshiuo, hizakana, hiuo, kangyo* dried
菓子 *higashi* candy; cookies
¹² 湿計 *kanshitsukei* humidity meter
¹³ 電池 *kandenchi* dry cell
¹⁶ 瓢 *kampyō* dried gourd strings
¹⁷ 燥 *kansō* drying; dryness, aridity; insipid; dehydrated
燥地 *kansōchi* dry land
燥室 *kansōshitsu* drying room
燥剤 *kansōzai* a drying agent
燥機 *kansōki* dryer

───────────── **RAD.** ⌋ **6** ─────────────

Hane bō feathered stick or *kagi* hook, barb. Nickname: Barb.

─────── **1** ───────

了 [67 / J4e3b / M226] RYŌ. *ryō(suru)* finish, B complete; understand. *ryō to suru* acknowledge. *shima(u)* get through with.
⁷ 見 *ryōken* idea, thought, intention, inclination, motive, decision; discretion; forgiveness; toleration
承 *ryōshō* acknowledgment

¹³ 解 *ryōkai* understanding, comprehension
¹⁸ 簡 *ryōken* idea, thought, intention, inclination, motive, decision; discretion; forgiveness; toleration

─────── **3** ───────

予 [68 / J4d3d / M231] YO I, myself, the writer. A *arakaji(me)* previously. *kane(te)* previously, already, lately.

61–68

⁶ 行 *yokō* rehearsal
行演習 *yokō enshū* rehearsal
防 *yobō* prevention, protection against
防注射 *yobō chūsha* immunization, shots
防策 *yobōsaku* precautionary measures
⁷ 見 *yoken suru* foresee, foreknow. *yoken* divination
告 *yokoku* previous notice, preliminary announcement
言 *yogen* prediction, prognostication. *kanegoto* prediction; promise
⁸ 知 *yochi* intimation, premonition, foreknowledge, prediction
定 *yotei* prearrangement; program, plan; expectation; estimate
定日 *yoteibi* scheduled date, expected date
⁹ 後 *yogo* prognosis, aftereffects, recuperation, convalescence
科 *yoka* preparatory course; preparatory department
約 *yoyaku* contract, subscription, booking, reservation, pledge, advance order
約済 *yoyakuzu(mi)* reserved, engaged
¹¹ 習 *yoshū* lesson preparation; rehearsal
断 *yodan suru* guess, predict, conclude
¹² 測 *yosoku* forecast, estimate
期 *yoki* expectation, anticipation, hope, foresight, forecast
報 *yohō* forecasting, prediction, previous notification
備 *yobi* preparation; preliminaries; reserve; spare
備知識 *yobi chishiki* background knowledge
備校 *yobikō* preparatory school
備運動 *yobi undō* limbering up
備費 *yobihi* reserve fund, emergency fund, preliminary expenses
¹³ 感 *yokan* premonition, hunch
想 *yosō* anticipation, forecast, conjecture, imagination; estimate
想外 *yosōgai* unexpected, unforeseen, strange
¹⁴ 選 *yosen* nomination, primary election, elimination match
算 *yosan* estimate, appropriation, budget
算案 *yosan'an* budget proposal

──────── **5** ────────

争 ⁶⁹ / J4168 / M236 A Sō. *araso(u)* dispute, argue; be at variance; compete
araso(i) dispute, strife, quarrel, dissension, conflict; rivalry, contest. *araso(warenai)* indisputable, undeniable, unmistakable. *ika(de)* how.
⁷ 乱 *sōran* rioting, disturbances
⁸ 事 *araso(i)goto* dispute
⁹ 点 *sōten* point at issue
¹⁴ 奪 *sōdatsu* contest, competition, struggle, challenge
¹⁵ 論 *sōron* argument, dispute, controversy
²⁰ 議 *sōgi* dispute, conflict

──────── **7** ────────

事 ⁷¹ / J3b76 / M241 A JI thing, matter. *koto* thing, matter, fact, circumstances, business, reason, experience. *tsuka(eru)* serve, work for. *koto (ni yoru to)* possibly, probably. *koto to suru* deal in; take pleasure in; make it your business. *-ji* fact, matter. *-koto* alias.
³ 大主義 *jidai shugi* worship of the powerful
⁵ 由 *jiyū* reason, cause
犯 *jihan* crime
⁶ 毎 *kotogoto ni* in everything; always
件 *jiken* event, incident, affair, case, plot, trouble, scandal
⁷ 局 *jikyoku* circumstances
⁸ 例 *jirei* example; precedent
物 *jibutsu* things, affairs
宜 *jigi* a fitting thing
典 *jiten* encyclopedia
実 *jijitsu* fact; reality; as a matter of fact
実上 *jijitsujō* actually, in fact
実無根 *jijitsu-mukon* contrary to fact
⁹ 柄 *kotogara* matter, affair, circumstance
故 *jiko* accident, incident, trouble; circumstances, reasons
変 *jihen* accident, disaster; incident, uprising, emergency 「approval
後承諾 *jigo shōdaku* ex-post-facto
前 *jizen no* prior, before the fact
¹¹ 情 *jijō* circumstances, reasons
務 *jimu* business, clerical work
務当局 *jimu tōkyoku* officials in charge
務次官 *jimu jikan* permanent vice-minister, undersecretary
務局 *jimukyoku* secretariat, executive office

務所 *jimusho* office
務的 *jimuteki* businesslike, practical
務長 *jimuchō* manager; purser
務室 *jimushitsu* office
務員 *jimuin* clerk
務総長 *jimu sōchō* secretary-general, director
¹²項 *jikō* matters, facts, items

象 *jishō* phenomenon, a matter
¹³跡 *jiseki* evidence, trace, vestige
業 *jigyō* enterprise, business, industry; operation
業家 *jigyōka* enterprising man; businessman; industrialist
¹⁴態 *jitai* situation, state of affairs
¹⁸蹟 *jiseki* evidence, trace, vestige

2-STROKE RADICALS

―

RAD. ➤ 7

Ni two. Variant: shorter horizontals. Nickname: Two.

一 | 72 / J4673 / M247 | NI two; second. JI.
A ― *futa(tsu), fu, fū, futa* two.

² 人 *futari, ninin* two persons, pair, couple
人三脚 *nininsankyaku* three-legged race
人連 *futarizu(re)* a party of two
人称 *nininshō* second person (in grammar)
十日 *hatsuka* 20 days; 20th day (of the month)
十代 *nijūdai* one's twenties
十世紀 *nijisseiki* 20th century
十歳 *hatachi* age 20
⁴ 心 *futagokoro, nishin* duplicity, treachery
手 *futate* two groups, two bands
月 *Nigatsu* February. *futatsuki* two months
毛作 *nimōsaku* two crops a year
日 *futsuka* two days; the second day (of the month)
日酔 *futsukayoi* a hangover
分 *nibun suru* halve, bisect
元的 *nigenteki* dual
⁵ 目 *futame to* for a second time
号 *nigō* number two; concubine
句 *ni (no) ku* another word, answer
世 *nise* two existences, the present and the future. *nisei* junior; the second (king of the same name); two generations; the second generation (of immigrants)
⁶ 列 *niretsu* two rows; double file
返事 *futa(tsu) henji* an immediate (happy) reply
次 *niji* second, secondary. *ni (no) tsugi* secondary, subordinate

次元 *nijigen* two dimensions
次方程式 *niji hōteishiki* quadratic equation ⌈night
次会 *nijikai* a second party the same
⁷ 位 *nii* second place
束三文 *nisokusammon* cheap
足動物 *nisokudōbutsu* bipeds
⁸ 拍子 *nibyōshi* double time
股 *futamata* bifurcation, fork, parting of the way
者択一 *nisha takuitsu* an alternative
枚舌 *nimaijita* double tongue, double dealing
枚貝 *nimaigai* bivalve
⁹ 院制 *niinsei* bicameral system
連式 *nirenshiki* duplex
度 *nido* two times
度三度 *nido sando* again and again
度手間 *nido tema nidodema* double effort
重 *futae, nijū* double, twofold
重人格 *nijū jinkaku* double personality
重否定 *nijū hitei* double negative
重国籍 *nijū kokuseki* dual nationality
重奏 *nijūsō* instrumental duet
重唱 *nijūshō* vocal duet
重露出 *nijū roshutsu* double exposure
¹⁰ 倍 *nibai* double, twice, twofold
桁 *futaketa* tens (in figures)
流 *niryū* second-rate, inferior ⌈part
部 *nibu* two parts, two copies; the second
¹¹ 階 *nikai* second floor, upstairs
階建 *nikaidate* two-storied building
¹² 着 *nichaku* runner-up, second (in a race)

等 *nitō* second class; second
等辺三角形 *nitōhen sankakukei* isosceles triangle
等分 *nitōbun* bisection
番 *niban* second, number two, runner-up
番煎 *nibansen(ji)* a rehash
[13] 義的 *nigiteki ni* secondarily
[15] 輪 *nirin* two wheels, two flowers
輪車 *nirinsha* child's bicycle; two-wheeled vehicle

———— 2 ————

云 [74] [J313e] [M254] UN. *yu(u), i(u)* say, tell, talk, speak, declare; call, term, name.
[4] 云 *shikajika, unnun* and so forth, and so on, and the like

互 B [75] [J385f] [M255] GO. *tagai ni, katami ni* mutually, reciprocally, reciprocally, together.
[7] 角 *gokaku* equality, evenness, par; good match
助 *gojo* mutual aid, co-operation
[10] 恵 *gokei* reciprocity, mutual benefits
[12] 違 *taga(i)chiga(i) ni* alternately
換性 *gokansei* compatibility
[14] 選 *gosen* co-optation; mutual election

井 B [76] [J3066] [M258] SHŌ. SEI *i* well.
[4] 戸 *ido* well
戸水 *ido mizu* well water
戸掘 *idoho(ri)* well digging; well digger
戸端 *idobata* well side
戸端会議 *idobata kaigi* well-side gossip
[10] 桁 *igeta* well crib; parallel crosses

五 A [77] [J385e] [M257] GO five. *itsu(tsu), itsu* five; *itsu(tsu)* five years old.
[2] 十三次 *gojūsan tsugi* the 53 Tōkaidō stages
十歩百歩 *gojippo-hyappo, gojuppo-hyappo* six of one and a half dozen of the other
十音 *gojūon* the Japanese syllabary
十音順 *gojūonjun* the syllabary order
[4] 日 *itsuka* five days; the fifth day (of the month)

辺形 *gohenkei* pentagon
分 *gobu* five-tenths of a *wari* (ten percent); five-tenths of a *sun* 寸 (3 cm); 50%, half; a tie; evenness. *gofun* five minutes
分五分 *gobugobu* evenly matched; tie
月 *Gogatsu* May. *satsuki* lunar fifth month
月雨 *samidare, satsuki ame* early summer rain
月晴 *satsukibare(re)* fine weather during the rainy season; fine weather in May
[5] 目 *gomoku* a mixture; simplified game of go; *gomokumeshi* (飯) and *gomokuzushi* (鮨)
目飯 *gomokumeshi* boiled rice mixed with vegetables and fish
目鮨 *gomokuzushi* rice mixed with various delicacies and seasoned with vinegar
[6] 色 *goshiki, goshoku* five colors; variegated colors; the five cardinal colors; various kinds
行 *gogyō* the five elements (wood, fire, earth, metal, and water)
[7] 体 *gotai* five component parts of the body; the whole body; five styles of calligraphy
角形 *gokakukei, gokakkei* pentagon
[8] 官 *gokan* the five sensory organs
[9] 重塔 *gojū no tō* five-storied pagoda
[10] 桁 *go keta* ten thousands (in figures)
[11] 彩 *gosai* the five colors (blue, yellow, red, white, and black); five-colored porcelain
[13] 感 *gokan* the five senses
[14] 穀 *gokoku* the five grains (rice, *mugi* [wheat and barley], beans, and millet [*awa* and *kibi*])
種競技 *goshu kyōgi* pentathlon
[15] 線紙 *gosenshi* music paper
輪大会 *Gorin Taikai* Olympic Games
輪聖火 *Gorin Seika* Olympic Torch
[18] 臓六腑 *gozō-roppu* the internal organs; inside one's mind

———— 4 ————

亙 [79] [J414b] [M262] SEN, KAN, KŌ request. *wata(ru)* range, reach, extend, last, cover, be spread over.

二上人イ入儿入八 ゝ冂冖冫几凵刀刂力勹匕匚匸十卜卩厂厶又

互 $\frac{80}{\text{J4f4a}}$ M265 Kō . wata(ru)range, reach, extend, last, cover, be spread over.

5

B 亜 $\frac{81}{\text{J3021}}$ M272 A. tsu(gu) rank, next, come, after. -A- Asia. a- sub-, -ous (in acids).
⁶ 米利加 Amerika America
米利加合衆国 Amerika Gasshūkoku
   The United States of America
¹⁰ 流 aryū adherent, follower, imitator
¹¹ 麻 ama flax, hemp, linen

麻仁油 amaniyu linseed oil
¹² 属 azoku subgroup
温帯 aontai subtemperate zone
寒帯 akantai subarctic zone
¹³ 鉛 aen zinc
¹⁴ 種 ashu subspecies
¹⁵ 熱帯 anettai subtropics

6

此 $\frac{84}{\text{J3a33}}$ M268 SA. chi(to), chit(to), isasaka a little, a bit, sometimes.
⁴ 少 sashō no trifling, little, few, slight
⁸ 事 saji something small or petty
¹¹ 細 sasai na trivial, small, petty

████ **RAD.** 亠 **8** ████ • ████

Nabebuta kettle lid, *ten'ichi* (Rad. 3 *ten* plus Rad. 1 *ichi*), or *keisan kammuri* (crown shaped like a Japanese paperweight). Variant: 亠. Nickname: Lid.

1

A 亡 $\frac{86}{\text{J4b34}}$ M287 BU. MU. MŌ. BŌ . my late, the late; dying; being destroyed. *na(ku)naru* be lost; run short, be used up; disappear; die. *na(ku)suru* lose. *horo(biru)* perish, be ruined. *horo(bosu)* ruin, destroy, overthrow. *na(ki)* the late, the deceased. *na(shi) ni, na(shi) de* without.
² 人 na(ki)hito the deceased
⁴ 父 bōfu one's late father
夫 bōfu one's late husband
⁵ 母 bōbo one's late mother
失 bōshitsu loss
⁸ 国 bōkoku ruined country
妻 bōsai one's late wife   ⌈kill
者 mōja the dead. na(ki)mono ni suru
命 bōmei exile   ⌈apparition, ghost
¹⁵ 霊 bōrei the dead, departed spirits,

4

亦 $\frac{88}{\text{J4b72}}$ M293 EKI. YAKU. mata also, again.

亥 $\frac{89}{\text{J3067}}$ M292 GAI. inoshishi, i 9–11 p.m.; 12th zodiac sign; wild boar.

A 交 $\frac{90}{\text{J3872}}$ M291 Kō coming and going; association; change of seasons. *maji(waru), maji(ru)* associate with, mingle with; interest; join. *maji(eru)* mix; converse with, cross (swords). *ma(zeru)* mix, blend, mingle; include, let in on. *ma(jiru)* vi be mixed, be blended; mingle with. *kawa(su)* exchange (messages); dodge, parry, avoid, turn aside.
³ 叉 kōsa crossing, intersection
⁴ 互 kōgo no mutual, reciprocal, alternate
友 kōyū friend, companion
⁵ 付 kōfu suru deliver, furnish with
   (copies)
付金 kōfukin grant, subsidy, bounty
代 kōtai alternation, change, relief, relay,
   shift
代制 kōtaisei shift system
⁷ 尾 kōbi copulation (in animals)
⁸ 易 kōeki trade, commerce
⁹ 信 kōshin correspondence,
   communication
点 kōten point of intersection
通 kōtsū traffic; communication;
   transport; navigation
通公社 kōtsū kōsha travel bureau
通巡査 kōtsū junsa traffic officer

通安全 *kōtsū anzen* traffic safety
通妨害 *kōtsū bōgai* traffic obstruction
通事故 *kōtsū jiko* traffic accident
通信号 *kōtsū shingō* traffic signal
通違反 *kōtsū ihan* traffic violation
通規則 *kōtsū kisoku* traffic rules
通道徳 *kōtsū dōtoku* traffic ethics
通費 *kōtsūhi* traveling expenses, carfare
通網 *kōtsūmō* traffic network
通整理 *kōtsū seiri* traffic control
通機関 *kōtsū kikan* transportation facilities
¹⁰ 配 *kōhai* mating, crossbreeding, cross-fertilization
流 *kōryū* alternating current; (cultural) exchange; intermingling
差 *kōsa suru* to cross
差点 *kōsaten* crossing, intersection
¹¹ 渉 *kōshō* negotiation, discussion; connection
¹² 番 *kōban* police box
替 *kōtai* deliver, furnish, with (copies)
換 *kōkan* exchange, reciprocity, barter; substitution; clearing (of checks)
換手 *kōkanshu* switchboard operator
¹³ 感神経 *kōkan shinkei* sympathetic nerves
戦 *kōsen* war, battle, hostilities
際 *kōsai* association, intercourse, comradeship, acquaintance
際費 *kōsaihi* entertainment expenses
際範囲 *kōsai han'i* circle of acquaintance
¹⁵ 誼 *kōgi* friendship
歓 *kōkan* exchange of courtesies, fraternization
¹⁶ 錯 *kōsaku* mixture, blending, complication
¹⁹ 響曲 *kōkyōkyoku* symphony
響楽団 *kōkyōgakudan* symphony (orchestra)

--------- 5 ---------

亨 — 91 / J357c / M295 — Kō. Kyō. *tō(ru)* pass through.

--------- 6 ---------

享 — 92 / J357d / M298 — B — Kyō. *u(keru)* receive, take, get, obtain; accept, take, get, obtain; catch (a ball); stop (a blow), parry; answer (the phone); undergo (an operation); take (an exam); sustain (a loss); be exposed to (ridicule); face, front on; inherit; catch the public fancy.
⁶ 年 *kyōnen* age at death
⁸ 受 *kyōju suru* receive, accept, enjoy, be given
¹³ 楽 *kyōraku* enjoyment, pleasure
楽主義 *kyōraku shugi* epicureanism
楽的 *kyōrakuteki* pleasure-seeking

京 — 93 / J357e / M299 — A — KEI ten quadrillion. Kyō capital, metropolis; ten quadrillion; Kyoto. *miyako* capital, metropolis.
² 人形 *kyōningyō* Kyoto doll
³ 女 *kyōonna* Kyoto woman
⁶ 阪 *Keihan* Kyoto and Osaka
阪神 *Keihanshin* Kyoto-Osaka-Kobe
⁹ 風 *kyōfū* Kyoto style; urbanity, refinement
洛 *keiraku, kyōraku* capital; Kyoto
¹⁰ 師 *keishi* capital, metropolis; old Kyoto
浜 *Keihin* Tokyo and Yokohama
¹² 葉 *Keiyō* Tokyo and Chiba

--------- 7 ---------

亮 — 95 / J4e3c / M304 — Ryō clear; help.

亭 — 96 / J4462 / M303 — B — TEI restaurant; mansion; arbor; cottage; vaudeville, music hall, stage name. CHIN arbor, pavilion, summer house.
⁵ 主 *teishu* master, host; landlord, innkeeper; husband
土関白 *teishu kampaku* autocratic husband
⁹ 亭 *teitei(taru)* lofty, towering

2

Hito man. At left: イ *nimben*. At top: 𠆢 *yane* roof, *hito-yane* or *hitogashira*.

二十 【人イ𠆢】 儿 入 八 丷 冂 宀 冫 几 凵 刀 刂 力 勹 匕 匚 匸 十 卜 卩 厂 厶 又

A 人 $\frac{99}{\substack{J3f4d \\ M344}}$ JIN man, person, people. NIN man, person. *hito* man, human being, mankind, person, people; character, personality; true man; man of talent; adult; other people; messenger; visitor. *hito(rashii)* like a decent person, human. *hito(tonari)* hereditary disposition. *-jin* man; expert. *-nin* man, person. *-to* person.

1 一倍 *hito-ichibai* unusual; more than all others

2 人 *hitobito* men, people everybody. *ninnin* each person

力 *jinriki* human power. *jinryoku* human strength, human effort, human agency

3 士 *jinshi* well-bred man; people

口 *jinkō* population; common talk

口密度 *jinkō mitsudo* population density

口調査 *jinkō chōsa* census

工 *jinkō* human work, human skill; artificial; artificiality

工的 *jinkōteki* artificial, unnatural

工呼吸 *jinkō kokyū* artificial respiration

工受精 *jinkō jusei* artificial insemination

工流産 *jinkō ryūzan* abortion

工衛星 *jinkō eisei* manmade satellite

4 手 *hitode* a worker, a hand

込 *hitogo(mi)* a crowd of people

夫 *nimpu, nimbu* coolie, laborer, carrier

心 *jinshin, hitogokoro* human nature; sentiment

文 *jimmon, jimbun* humanity; civilization

文地理 *jimbun chiri* descriptive geography

文科学 *jimbun kagaku* human and cultural sciences; social sciences

5 出 *hitode* crowd, turnout

付合 *hitozu(ki)a(i)* social disposition

民 *jimmin* people, subjects, the public

生 *jinsei* human life

生哲学 *jinsei tetsugaku* philosophy of life

生観 *jinseikan* view of life

6 件費 *jinkenhi* personnel expenses

名 *jimmei* a person's given name

名辞典 *jimmei jiten* biographical dictionary

名録 *jimmeiroku* directory, name list

名簿 *jimmeibo* directory, name list

気 *ninki* popularity; business conditions; popular feeling. *hitoke* signs of life (in a place)

気役者 *ninki yakusha* stage favorite, star

気投票 *ninki tōhyō* popularity contest

気者 *ninkimono* popular person, favorite

7 足 *ninsoku* coolie, laborer, carrier. *hitoashi* pedestrian traffic

材 *jinzai* man of talent

形 *ningyō* doll, puppet, figure

形芝居 *ningyō shibai* puppet show

見知 *hitomishi(ri)* shyness

里 *hitozato* human habitation

体 *jintai* human body. *nintei* personal appearance

体実験 *jintai jikken* testing on a living person

身 *jinshin, hitomi* the human body, one's person

身攻撃 *jinshin kōgeki* personal attack

身保護 *jinshin hogo* habeas corpus

8 知 *jinchi* human intellect, knowledge. *hitoshi(renu), hitoshi(rezu)* secret, hidden, unseen, inward

並 *hitona(mi) no* ordinary

参 *ninjin* carrot; ginseng

妻 *hitozuma* a married woman

非人 *nimpinin* a brute of a man

的資源 *jinteki shigen* man-power resources

命 *jimmei* (human) life

命救助 *jimmei kyūjo* lifesaving

物 *jimbutsu* person, man; character, personage; talented man

物画 *jimbutsuga* portrait painting

物評 *jimbutsuhyō* personal criticism; character sketch

物像 *jimbutsuzō* statue; picture; a

picture revealing character

事 *hitogoto* others' affairs. *jinji*
　personal affairs; personnel affairs
事不省 *jinji-fusei* unconsciousness
事院 *Jinjiin* National Personnel
　Authority
事異動 *jinji idō* personnel changes
9 通 *hitodō(ri)*, *hitotō(ri)* pedestrian
　traffic
垣 *hitogaki* a crowd of people
柄 *hitogara* character; personality;
　personal appearance; gentility
前 *hitomae* the public, company.
　hitomae de in public, in
　company
品 *jimpin* personal appearance;
　character, personality
待顔 *hitoma(chi)gao* a look of
　expectation
海戦術 *jinkai senjutsu* infiltration
　tactics, human-wave tactics
為的 *jin'iteki* artificial, unnatural
為淘汰 *jin'i tōta* artificial selection (in
　biology)
相 *ninsō* physiognomy, looks,
　countenance
相占 *ninsō urana(i)* divination by facial
　features
相見 *ninsōmi* physiognomist
相書 *ninsōga(ki)* personal description
造 *jinzō* artificial, synthetic; imitation
造人間 *jinzō ningen* robot
造石油 *jinzō sekiyu* synthetic oil
造真珠 *jinzō shinju* artificial pearls
10 馬 *jimba* men and horses
骨 *jinkotsu* human bones
称 *ninshō* person; personal
　(in grammar)
殺 *hitogoro(shi)* murder; murderer
家 *jinka* house, human habitation
畜 *jinchiku* men and animal
真似 *hitomane* mimicry, imitation
差指 *hitosa(shi) yubi* index finger
格 *jinkaku* character, personality,
　individuality
格者 *Jinkakusha* man of character;
　person
員 *jin'in* staff, personnel, crew; the
　number of persons
員整理 *jin'in seiri* personnel cut
員縮少 *jin'in shukushō* personnel
　reduction

11 魚 *ningyo* mermaid, merman
達 *hitotachi* people
望 *jimbō* popularity
望家 *jimbōka* popular character
道 *jindō* humanity; sidewalk
道主義 *jindō shugi* humanism;
　humanitarianism
道的 *jindōteki* humane
情 *ninjō* humanity, sympathy, kindness;
　human nature; common sense;
　customs and manners
情味 *ninjōmi* human interest,
　kindness
12 間 *ningen* man, person, human being
間工学 *ningen kōgaku* ergonomics
間味 *ningemmi* human kindness; human
　weakness
間性 *ningensei* human nature,
　humanity
間的 *ningenteki* human
間並 *ningenna(mi)* the common run of
　people
間嫌 *ningengira(i)* misanthropy;
　misanthropist
間離 *ningembana(re)* unworldly;
　superhuman
13 数 *ninzu*, *ninzū*, *hitokazu* the number of
　people
意 *jin'i* public sentiment
猿同祖説 *jin'en dōsosetsu* monkey-
　ancestry theory
跡 *jinseki*, *hitoato* signs of human
　habitation
跡未踏 *jinseki-mitō* unexplored
14 選 *jinsen* personnel selection
徳 *jintoku*, *nintoku* personal virtue;
　natural virtue
様 *hitosama* (polite) other people,
　another
種 *jinshu* race of people
種的 *jinshuteki* racial
種学 *jinshugaku* ethnology
15 影 *hitokage*, *jin'ei* a person's shadow;
　a form
質 *hitojichi* hostage, prisoner
権 *jinken* human rights
権蹂躙 *jinken-jūrin* trampling on
　human rights
18 類 *jinrui* man, mankind, humanity
類学 *jinruigaku* anthropology,
　ethnology
類愛 *jinruiai* love for humanity

2 ——————— 2 ———————

什 [105 J3d3a M348] JŪ ten; utensil, thing.

15 器 *jūki* utensil, appliance, furniture

仇 [106 J3558 M355] KYŪ. *ada, ata, kataki* foe, enemy; revenge; enmity, grudge, feud; harm, evil; ruin; invasion.
10 討 *adauchi* vengeance, retaliation
15 敵 *kyūteki* bitter enemy

介 B [108 J3270 M359] KAI shell, shellfish. *kai(suru)* be in between; mediate; concern oneself with. *kai(shite)* through the medium of.
2 入 *kainyū* intervention
6 在 *kaizai* intervention
8 抱 *kaihō suru* nurse; look after
11 添 *kaizo(e)* helper, assistant, second

以 A [109 J304a M388] I. *mot(te)* with, by, by means of; because; in view of.
3 下 *ika* less than, under, below; and downward; not exceeding; the following; the rest
上 *ijō* more than, over, above; and up; beyond; the above-mentioned; since, as long as; the end
4 内 *inai* within, less than
心伝心 *ishin-denshin* telepathy; sympathy, quiet understanding
5 外 *igai ni* with the exception of; excepting. *mot(te) (no) hoka* absurd, unreasonable
北 *ihoku* north of; and northward
6 西 *isei* west of; and westward
7 来 *irai* since
8 東 *itō* east of; and eastward
9 後 *igo* hereafter; thereafter
降 *ikō* on and after; hereafter; thereafter
前 *izen ni* ago, since, before, previously
南 *inan* south of; and south
12 遠 *ien* and beyond

仁 A [110 J3f4e M349] JIN virtue, benevolence, humanity, charity; man. NIN kernel.
4 王 *Niō* Guardian Deva Kings
王門 *niōmon* temple gate guarded by fierce Deva Kings
9 侠 *ninkyō, jinkyō* chivalrous spirit

13 義 *jingi* humanity and justice; duty; moral code (of a gang)
14 徳 *jintoku* benevolence, goodness

仏 A [111 J4a29 M364] BUTSU Buddha, Buddhism. FUTSU French. *hotoke* Buddha; merciful person; Buddhist image; the dead.
4 心 *busshin, hotokegokoro* the Buddha heart, the Buddha mind
文 *Futsubun* French, French writing, French literature
6 式 *busshiki* Buddhist ritual
寺 *butsuji* Buddhist temple
7 陀 *Budda, Butsuda* Buddha
8 門 *Butsumon* Buddhism; priesthood
国 *Fukkoku* France
具 *butsugu* Buddhist altar equipment
典 *butten* Buddhist scriptures, sutras
事 *butsuji* Buddhist memorial service
舎利 *busshari* Buddha's ashes
9 前 *butsuzen* before the Buddha or a mortuary tablet
10 師 *busshi* Buddhist image maker
11 道 *butsudō* Buddhism, Buddhist teachings
教 *Bukkyō* Buddhism
頂面 *butchōzura* sour look
12 間 *butsuma* Buddhist family chapel
13 滅 *butsumetsu* Buddha's death; unlucky day
14 閣 *bukkaku* Buddhist temple
像 *butsuzō* Buddhist image
様 *hotokesama* a Buddha; a deceased person
語 *Futsugo* French language. *butsugo* Buddhist term
領 *Futsuryō* French possession, French territory
16 壇 *butsudan* Buddhist household altar
20 蘭西 *Furansu* France

今 A [112 J3a23 M358] KIN. KON now, the present; the coming; this. *ima* now, present time; just now, soon, immediately; (one) more. *ima demo* even now, still, as yet. *ima dewa* now, nowadays. *ima ni* before long; even now, still. *ima nimo* at any time, soon. *ima ya* now. *ima(mekashii)* fashionable. *ima(mekasu)* modernize. *ima(motte)* until now. *ima-modern.*

¹一度 *ima ichido* once more
³夕 *konseki, kon'yū* this evening, tonight
⁴方 *ima(shi)gata, imagata* a moment ago
以 *ima mot(te)* still, yet, (not) yet
月 *kongetsu* this month
日 *kyō, konnichi* today, this day. *Konnichi wa* Good afternoon
日的 *konnichiteki* modern, up-to-date
日明日 *kyō-asu* today and tomorrow; today or tomorrow; in a day or two
⁵生 *konjō* this life, this world
世紀 *konseiki* this century
⁶回 *konkai* lately; this time
年 *konnen, kotoshi* this year
⁷更 *imasara* now, at this late hour
⁸夜 *kon'ya* tonight, this evening
昔 *konjaku, konseki* past and present
明日 *kommyōnichi* today and (or) tomorrow
⁹風 *imafū* modern style
度 *kondo* this time, now; next time; another time
後 *kongo* after this, hereafter
¹⁰週 *konshū* this week
般 *kompan* now, recently; this time
宵 *koyoi* this evening, tonight
時 *imadoki* recently, these days; at this ⌐hour
¹¹頃 *imagoro* about this time
¹²晩 *komban* tonight, this evening. *Komban wa* Good evening.
期 *konki* the present term
朝 *kesa, konchō* this morning

───── 3 ─────

全 $\frac{114}{J2138}$ See 同 ⁷¹⁷ and 全 ¹⁴⁵.
   $\overline{M378}$

仔 $\frac{119}{J3b46}$ SHI *ko-* (animal) offspring.
   $\overline{M367}$
¹¹細 *shisai* reasons, circumstances; significance; particulars; hindrance, obstruction, interference

仙 $\frac{120}{I4067}$ SEN hermit; wizard. *sento* cent.
B $\overline{M374}$
²人 *sennin* hermit; wizard; fairy; otherworldly person
³女 *sennyo, senjo* fairy, nymph

令 $\frac{121}{J4e61}$ RYŌ ancient laws. REI order, command; ordinance,
A $\overline{M387}$

law, decree. *rei(suru)* command, order, dictate. *-shi(mu)* old causative verbal ending.
⁴夫人 *reifujin* Mrs., Lady, Madam; your wife
⁶名 *reimei* good reputation, fame
⁷状 *reijō* warrant, summons; written order
¹⁰息 *reisoku* your son
¹⁶嬢 *reijō* your daughter, your lady

他 $\frac{122}{J423e}$ TA. another, the other, others, another thing; the
A $\overline{M370}$ rest; another place. *ta-* another, other. *hoka* some other place; outside; the rest.
²力 *tariki* outside help; salvation by faith
力本願 *tariki-hongan* salvation by faith in Amida Buddha; reliance upon others
人 *tanin, adabito* another person, unrelated person, outsider, stranger
人行儀 *tanin gyōgi* reserved manners
人空似 *tanin (no) sorani* accidental resemblance
³山石 *tazan (no) ishi* object lesson, food for thought
⁴方 *tahō* another side; different direction; (on) the other hand
日 *tajitsu* some day; hereafter, at some future time
⁷言 *tagen, tagon* telling others; revealing to others
⁸所 *yoso, tasho* another place
国 *takoku* foreign country; another province
国民 *takokumin* other nations, other peoples
⁹面 *tamen* the other side; another direction; (on) the other hand
界 *takai suru* die. *takai* the next world; death
¹⁰殺 *tasatsu* murder
家 *take* another family
流 *taryū* another style; another school (of thought); different blood
¹¹動詞 *tadōshi* transitive verb
¹³意 *tai* other intention, secret purpose, ulterior motive, ill will, fickleness, doublemindedness
¹⁴聞 *tabun* publicity, reaching other ears

二 亠 【 人 亻 人 儿 入 八 丷 冂 冖 冫 几 凵 刀 刂 力 勹 匕 匚 匸 十 卜 卩 厂 厶 又

2

A 仕 123 J3b45 M368 SHI official; civil service. *tsuka(eru)* serve, work for. *tsukamatsu(ru)* serve; do (polite).

² 入 *shi-i(reru)* laying in stock, purchase

³ 上 *shi-a(garu) vi* be finished. *shi-a(geru) vt* finish

⁴ 手 *shite* protagonist; hero; leading part

切 *shi-ki(ru)* partition, divide; mark off; settle accounts; toe the mark. *shiki(ri)* partition, division, boundary; compartment; settlement of accounts; toeing the mark. *shi-ki(renai)* impossible to do

分 *shi-wa(keru)* assort, classify; journalize (in accounting)

込 *shi-ko(mu)* train, bring up, educate; fit into, stock up on. *shiko(mi)* training; stocking up; preparation

方 *shikata* way, method, resource, course, means

方無 *shikata (no) na(i), shikata (ga) na(i), shikatana(i)* it can't be helped, it's inevitable; it's no use; can't stand it; be impatient; be annoyed. *shikatana(ku), shikatana(shi) ni* helplessly, reluctantly

⁵ 打 *shiu(chi)* treatment; behavior, conduct

払 *shi-hara(u)* pay

出 *shida(shi)* catering; shipment. *shida(su)* begin to do; cater

立 *shi-ta(teru)* tailor; make; prepare; train; send (a messenger). *shita(te)* tailoring, dressmaking, sewing; making; preparation

立物 *shitatemono* sewing, tailoring; newly-tailored clothes

立屋 *shita(te)ya* tailor; dressmaker

⁶ 返 *shikae(shi)* doing over; tit for tat; retaliation, revenge

向 *shi-mu(keru)* treat, act toward, handle (men); send, forward to

合 *shiai* contest, match, game, bout, tournament, joust. *shia(wase)* fortune, luck; happiness, blessing

⁷ 来 *shikita(ri)* custom, conventional practice

⁸ 送 *shioku(ri)* allowance, remittance

官 *shikan* government service; samurai's service

放題 *shihōdai* having one's own way

事 *shigoto* work, employment, occupation

事場 *shigotoba* place where one works; construction site

⁹ 度 *shitaku* preparation, arrangements; costume, dress; trousseau

草 *shigusa* treatment; behavior, action; gestures

¹¹ 遂 *shi-to(geru)* accomplish, finish, fulfill

組 *shi-ku(mu)* devise, arrange, plan, plot. *shiku(mi)* construction; contrivance, arrangement; plan, plot

訳 *shi-wa(keru)* assort, classify; journalize (in accounting)

掛 *shi-ka(keru)* commence; lay (mines); set (traps); wage (war); challenge. *shikaka(ri)* commencement. *shika(ke)* mechanism, gadget; (small) scale; half-finished

¹³ 業 *shiwaza* act, action, deed

置 *shio(ki)* execution; punishment

¹⁴ 種 *shigusa* method; attitude; actor's expressions; actions.

様 *shiyō* way, method, resource; remedy, help

様書 *shiyōga(ki), shiyōsho* specifications

様無 *shiyō (ga) na(i)* It can't be helped. *shiyō (no) na(i)* hopeless, good-for-nothing, incorrigible

舞 *shima(u)* finish, conclude; put away; save; close, wind up. *shimai* end, termination; informal noh play

A 付 124 J4955 M373 FU. *fu(suru)* give to, submit to, refer to; affix, attach, append. *tsu(keru) vt* attach, join, stick, glue, fasten; sew on; furnish (a house with); wear, put on; make an entry; appraise, set (a price); apply (ointment); bring alongside; place (under guard or a doctor); follow, shadow; add, append, affix; load; give (courage to); keep (an eye on); establish (relations or understanding). *tsu(ku) vi* be connected with; be dyed; be stained; be scarred; be recorded; be attached to; (fires) start; follow; become allied to; accompany; study with; increase, be added to. *(o)tsu(ki)* attendant, escort. *tsu(ke)* bill, bill of sale. *(ni) tsu(ki)* per, apiece; because of; regarding. *tsu(ki)* (printing) impression; sociability; appearance. *tsu(ketari)* addition, accessory, appendage, supplement,

appendix; complement; an excuse. *(ni)*
tsu(ite) concerning; along; under; per. -
zu(ke) dated. *-zu(ki)* attached to,
furnished with. *tsu(ke)-* fixed, external. -
tsu(ke) date. *-tsuki)* attached to, under,
to.

² 人 *tsu(ke)bito* assistant, attendant;
chaperon; suite

入 *tsu(ke)-i(ru)* take advantage of,
impose on

³ 上 *tsu(ke)-a(garu)* be elated; be spoiled;
take advantage of

与 *fuyo* grant, allowance, endowment

⁴ 込 *tsu(ke)-ko(mu)* take advantage of,
impose on; make an entry.
tsu(ke)ko(mi) entry, booking

切 *tsu(ki)ki(ri), tsu(k)ki(ri)* constant
attendance (by a doctor)

⁵ 目 *tsu(ke)me* aim; (to aim at) a weak
point

加 *tsu(ke)-kuwa(eru)* add to. *fuka*
addition, annexation, supplement,
appendage

⁶ 回 *tsu(ke)-mawa(su), tsu(ke)-mawa(ru)*
follow, shadow, hanker after, hover
around

近 *fukin* neighborhood, environs, vicinity

合 *tsu(ke)-a(waseru)* add to. *tsu(ki)-a(u)*
keep company with, associate with,
get along with. *tsu(ki)a(i)*
association, fellowship, acquaintance,
friendship. *tsu(ki)a(wase)* perfect
occlusion; vegetable relish with meat

⁷ 言 *fugen* postscript, additional remarks

足 *tsu(ke)-ta(su)* add to. *tsu(ke)ta(shi)*
addition, appendix, supplement,
postscript

⁸ 届 *tsu(ke)todo(ke)* tip, present

狙 *tsu(ke)-nera(u)* prowl after, shadow,
keep watch on

和雷同 *fuwa-raidō* following blindly

⁹ 則 *fusoku* additional rules, by-laws,
supplementary provisions

¹⁰ 記 *fuki* appendix, addition, note

託 *futaku suru* commit to, refer to,
submit to

随 *tsu(ki)-shitaga(u)* follow, accompany,
cleave to. *fuzui* incidental, attendant,
annexed; accompanying

帯 *futai* incidental, accessory, secondary,
collateral

帯事項 *futai jikō* supplementary item

¹¹ 添 *tsu(ki)-so(u)* escort and wait on,
accompany, chaperon. *tsukiso(i)*
attendance on; attendant, escort,
chaperon, retinue

¹² 着 *fuchaku* adhesion, cohesion,
agglutination

焼刃 *tsu(ke)yakiba* pretension,
affectation

属 *fuzoku* attached, annexed; affiliated;
associated; subordinate, incidental,
dependent, auxiliary

属品 *fuzokuhin* accessory, fittings,
appurtenances

¹⁴ 箋 *fusen* tag, slip, label

¹⁶ 録 *furoku* supplement, appendix

代 125 J4265 M386
A DAI period, age, generation;
charge, rate, fee, cost, price.
yo world, society, public; life, existence,
career, lifetime; age, era, generation,
times; reign. *ka(eru)* change, turn,
convert, exchange, renew, substitute,
replace. *ka(waru)* replace, relieve.
kawa(ri) substitute, deputy, proxy,
alternate, relief; compensation; second
helping. *shiro* price; substitution;
materials. *kawa(ri) ni* instead of. *(sono)*
kawa(ri) ni on the other hand.

⁵ 代 *daidai, yoyo* for generations;
hereditary. *kawa(ru)gawa(ru),*
kawa(ri)gawa(ri) alternately

弁 *daiben suru* pay by proxy; act for
another; speak for another

用 *daiyō* substitution

用品 *daiyōhin* a substitute

⁶ 名詞 *daimeishi* pronoun

行 *daikō* acting as an agent

⁷ 役 *daiyaku, kawa(ri)yaku* substitute
actor, a stand-in, a double

⁸ 価 *daika* price, cost, charge

金 *daikin* price, cost, charge, the money,
the bill

表 *daihyō* representation, type, example,
model; delegate

表団 *daihyōdan* delegation

表作 *daihyōsaku* masterpiece, a
representative work

表者 *daihyōsha* representative, delegate

表的 *daihyōteki* representative,
exemplary, model

¹⁰ 案 *daian* alternate plan

書 *daisho* scribe, amanuensis

2
二丁
人
イ
𠆢
儿
入
八
丷
冂
冖
冫
几
凵
刀
刂
力
勹
匕
匚
匸
十
卜
卩
厂
厶
又
3

9

2

二十【人 イ 个 儿 入 八 ソ 冂 冖 冫 几 凵 刀 刂 力 勹 匕 匚 匸 十 卜 卩 厂 厶 又

¹¹理 *dairi* representation, agency, proxy, deputy, agent, attorney; substitute, alternate; acting (principal, etc.)

理人 *dairinin* proxy, agent, substitute, deputy, alternate, representative, attorney

理店 *dairiten* agency

¹²診 *daishin* doctor's assistance; doctor's assistant; locum tenens

筆 *daihitsu* amanuensis

¹³数 *daisū* algebra

¹⁷償 *daishō* compensation, indemnification, reparation; consideration

²⁰議士 *daigishi* member of a congress

議制度 *daigi seido* parliamentary system

議政治 *daigi seiji* representative government

議員 *daigiin* representative, delegate

——————— 4 ———————

件 A 130 J376f M410 KEN matter, case, item. *kudan* example, precedent. *kudan no* the usual; the said; the above-mentioned. *kudari* the above-mentioned.
¹³数 *kensū* number of cases or items

伍 131 J3860 M435 GO five; five-man squad; file, line. *go(suru)* rank with, associate with. *itsu(tsu)* five.

伐 B 132 J4832 M439 BATSU. *u(tsu)* strike, attack; punish. *ki(ru)* cut, chop, hash; carve; saw; clip, shear; slice, strip; fell, cut down; punch; sever (connections); pause, break off; disconnect, turn off; hang up; cross (a street); discount, sell below cost; shake (water) off.
¹¹採 *bassai* felling, deforestation, lumbering

伎 133 J346c M436 GI, KI deed; skill.
⁷芸 *gigei* accomplishments
¹⁰倆 *giryō* ability, talent, skill, capacity

伊 134 J304b M432 I that one. *I-, -I* Italy.
⁴太利 *Itaria, Itarī* Italy

⁷呂波 *i-ro-ha* the first three *kana* of the syllabary
¹¹達 *date na* vainglorious, showy

企 B 135 J346b M422 KI. *kuwada(teru)* plan, plot, propose, design, intend, contemplate; attempt, undertake. *taku(ramu)* scheme, plan, play a trick, invent, conspire, frame up. *takura(mi)* plan, design, artifice; trick, intrigue. *kuwada(te)* plan, attempt, undertaking.
⁷図 *kito* plan, project, scheme
⁸画 *kikaku* plan; planning
¹³業 *kigyō* an enterprise
業化 *kigyōka* commercialization
業家 *kigyōka* industrialist

任 A 136 J4724 M416 JIN, NIN duty, responsibility; office; mission; term. *maka(su), maka(seru)* entrust to, leave to. *nin(jiru), nin(zuru)* appoint, nominate; assume (responsibility); pose as. *mama* as it is; as one likes; because.
⁵用 *nin'yō* appointment, employment
^地 *ninchi* one's post, appointment
⁸官 *ninkan* appointment, investiture
免 *nimmen* appointments and dismissals
命 *nimmei* appointment, nomination, ordination, commission, designation
⁹侠 *ninkyō* chivalry, generosity, heroism, chivalrous spirit
¹¹務 *nimmu* duty, function, office, mission
¹²期 *ninki* term of office
¹³意 *nin'i* option, pleasure, discretion, free will
意出頭 *nin'i shuttō* voluntarily appearing for police questioning

仰 B 137 J3644 M400 GYŌ. KŌ. *ao(gu)* look up, look up to; ask for, depend on; seek; respect, revere; drink, take. *ao(muku), ao(noku)* look up. *ao(nokeru)* turn up (one's face or a card). *os(sharu)* say, speak, tell, talk (polite). *ō(serareru)* say, state (polite). *ō(se)* statement, command, wishes (of a superior).
³天 *gyōten suru* be amazed, be horrified
⁶仰 *gyōgyō(shii)* exaggerated, bombastic, highly colored
向 *aomu(keru)* turn up (one's face or a card). *aomu(ku)* look up, lie face up
⁷見 *ao(gi)-mi(ru)* look up to, look up at;

130–137

32

revere
角 *gyōkaku* angle of elevation
8 臥 *gyōga* sleeping face up

A 似 $\frac{138}{\substack{J3b77 \\ M485}}$ JI. *ni(ru)* resemble. *nise(ru)* copy, imitate; counterfeit, forge. *ni(tsukawashii)* suitable, appropriate, becoming. *-ni* takes after (a parent).
6 合 *ni-a(u)* become, suit, be like, match well. *nia(i)* well matched; suitable, becoming. *nia(washii)* well matched, suitable, becoming
而非 *ese-* false, would-be, sham, pretended, mock, spurious, pseudo-, quasi-
9 通 *ni-kayo(u)* resemble closely
18 顔 *nigao* likeness, portrait
顔絵 *nigaoe* likeness, portrait

B 伏 $\frac{139}{\substack{J497a \\ M438}}$ FUKU. *fu(su)* vi bend down, bow down, lie prostrate. *fu(seru)* vt turn over, lay face down; cover; lay (pipes), lay (an ambush); hide. *fuku(suru)* stoop, bend down, crouch; lie down, prostrate oneself, fall prostrate; hide; yield to, submit to. *fu(shite)* bowing down; humbly, respectfully.
5 目 *fu(shi)me* downcast look
6 在 *fukuzai suru* lie concealed, be hidden
7 兵 *fukuhei* ambush, troops in ambush
15 線 *fukusen* underplot (in a novel); precautionary measures

A 仲 $\frac{140}{\substack{J4367 \\ M403}}$ CHŪ. *naka* relation; relationship.
2 人 *nakōdo, chūnin* go-between; matchmaking
4 介 *chūkai* agency, intermediation
介者 *chūkaisha* mediator, go-between, middleman
5 立 *nakada(chi)* mediation, agency; agent, mediator, middleman, go-between
6 好 *nakayoshi* intimacy; chum
7 良 *nakayo(ku)* on cordial terms. *nakayo(shi)* intimacy; chum
8 直 *nakanao(ri)* reconciliation.
12 違 *nakataga(i)* discord, estrangement
買人 *nakagainin* broker, jobber
裁 *chūsai* arbitration, mediation,

peacemaking, intercession
間 *nakama* company, circle, party; associate, confederate, accomplice. *chūgen* samurai's attendant, footman
間入 *nakamai(ri)* joining a group
間外 *nakamahazu(re)* being left out
間同士 *nakamadōshi* comrades

A 伝 $\frac{141}{\substack{J4541 \\ M462'}}$ TEN. DEN. legend, tradition; life, biography; commentary; communicating. *tsuta(u)* go along, walk along, follow. *tsuta(waru)* be transmitted, be circulated, be introduced into; go along, walk along. *tsuta(eru)* report, tell, impart, transmit, propagate, teach, bequeath. *tsuta(e)* legend, tradition. *tsute* intermediary, good offices, connections; someone to trust. *-zuta(i) ni* along (the wall).
5 令 *denrei* messenger, orderly, runner
7 来 *denrai suru* be transmitted, be handed down; be imported. *denrai no* ancestral, hereditary; imported
言 *dengon* verbal message, word. *tsutegoto* verbal message; rumor
言板 *dengomban* message board
承 *denshō* transmission, legend, tradition, folklore
承文学 *denshō bungaku* oral literature
8 奇 *denki* romance (fiction)
奇的 *denkiteki* legendary
9 染 *densen* contagion
染病 *densembyō* contagious disease, infectious disease, epidemic
10 書鳩 *denshobato* carrier pigeon, homing pigeon
馬船 *temmasen* large sculling boat
記 *denki* biography
記文学 *denki bungaku* biographical literature
11 達 *dentatsu* transmission, communication, delivery
授 *denju* initiation, instruction
票 *dempyō* chit, sales slip, voucher
道 *dendō suru* evangelize. *dendō* evangelism, missionary work
12 統 *dentō* tradition, convention
統的 *dentōteki* traditional, conventional
14 聞 *dembun suru, tsuta(e)-ki(ku)* learn by hearsay. *dembun* hearsay, rumor, report

2

二十一【人イ𠆢儿入八丷冂冖冫几凵刀刂力ケ匕匚匸十卜卩厂厶又】

説 *densetsu* legend, tradition
導 *dendō* conduction, transmission
¹⁵ 播 *dempa* propagation, circulation, diffusion, dissemination

休 ¹⁴²/J3559/M440 **A** KYŪ. *yasu(mu), kyū(suru)* *vi* rest; take a day off; be absent; retire, sleep. *yasu(meru)* *vt* rest (oneself); let idle; suspend; have (someone) rest; set at ease, give relief to; fallow (land). *yasu(maru)* be rested, feel at ease, repose, be relieved. *yasu(maseru)* excuse (someone); give a holiday to; make (someone) rest. *yasura(u)* rest, relax. *yasu(mi)* rest, recess, respite, suspension; vacation, holiday; absence; molting.
⁴ 火山 *kyūkazan* dormant volcano
日 *kyūjitsu* holiday, rest day
日明 *kyūjitsua(ke)* the day after a holiday
止 *kyūshi* pause, cessation, rest
止符 *kyūshifu* rest (in music); period, full stop
⁵ 刊 *kyūkan* suspension of publication
⁶ 会 *kyūkai* adjournment, recess
⁸ 学 *kyūgaku* temporary absence from school; suspension
¹⁰ 校 *kyūkō* closing school (temporarily); dropping one's studies
眠 *kyūmin* idle (facility); dormant
息 *kyūsoku* rest, relief, relaxation
¹² 閑地 *kyūkanchi* fallow land
診 *kyūshin* no medical examinations (today)
¹³ 暇 *kyūka* holiday, vacation, furlough
業 *kyūgyō* shop closed, business suspended, shutdown, holiday
業日 *kyūgyōbi* business holiday
戦 *kyūsen* truce, armistice
戦協定 *kyūsen kyōtei* cease-fire agreement
¹⁴ 演 *kyūen suru* suspend performance
¹⁵ 養 *kyūyō* rest, recreation
¹⁶ 憩 *kyūkei* rest, recess, intermission
憩所 *kyūkeijo* restroom, lounge
¹⁷ 講 *kyūkō* lecture cancelled
¹⁸ 職 *kyūshoku* temporary retirement; suspension from office

会 ¹⁴³/J3271/M460 **A** E Buddhist ceremony; understanding.
KAI meeting, assembly; party; association, club. *a(u)* meet, interview. *a(waseru)* expose to, subject to. *kai(suru)* meet, assemble; join. *e(suru)* understand. *tamatama* casually, unexpectedly; few.
⁴ 心 *kaishin* congeniality, satisfaction
⁶ 同 *kaidō* an assembly, a meeting
合 *kaigō* meeting, assembly
⁷ 社 *kaisha* company, corporation
社員 *kaishain* company employee
見 *kaiken* interview, audience
⁸ 長 *kaichō* chairman, president (of a society)
⁹ 食 *kaishoku* dining together; mess
則 *kaisoku* society regulations, constitution
計 *kaikei* account; finance; accountant; treasurer; paymaster; a reckoning; bill
計士 *kaikeishi* certified public accountant
計年度 *kaikei nendo* fiscal year
計検査 *kaikei kensa* audit, auditing
¹⁰ 員 *kaiin* member; the membership
員証 *kaiinshō* membership certificate
席料理 *kaiseki ryōri* set menu of select food served on an individual tray in the banquet
¹¹ 得 *etoku* understanding, comprehension, grasp, perception, appreciation
釈 *eshaku* salutation, greeting, recognition, bow
¹² 場 *kaijō* meeting place, the grounds
費 *kaihi* membership fee
報 *kaihō* bulletin, report
期 *kaiki* session (of a legislature)
葬 *kaisō* attendance at a funeral
¹³ 話 *kaiwa* conversation
¹⁵ 談 *kaidan* conversation, discussion, interview
¹⁶ 頭 *kaitō* society president
館 *kaikan* assembly hall
²⁰ 議 *kaigi* conference, assembly, council, convention, congress, meeting
議事項 *kaigi jikō* agenda
議室 *kaigishitsu* council room
議録 *kaigiroku* minutes, proceedings

仮 ¹⁴⁴/J323e/M398 **A** KA. KE (Buddhist) vanity. *kari no* temporary, provisional; informal, unauthorized; fleeting; assumed (name); interim; acting. *kari ni* temporarily, provisionally; for example; for argument's sake. *kari nimo*

even for an instant, even as a joke.
⁵ 令 *tatoe, tatoi* if, even if, though, although
処分 *kari shobun* temporary measures
払 *karibara(i)* temporary advance (of money)
⁶ 死 *kashi* apparent death; asphyxiation
名 *kana* Japanese syllabaries. *kamei, kemyō, karina* pseudonym, alias, pen name
名交文 *kanama(jiri)bun* mixed writing (characters and *kana*)
名遣 *kanazuka(i)* syllabary spelling
⁷ 初 *karisome* temporariness, transience; trifle; negligence. *karisome nimo* for a moment; even as a joke; even in the slightest degree
住 *karizuma(i)* temporary residence
⁸ 免状 *kari menjō* temporary certificate
定 *katei* assumption, supposition, hypothesis
定法 *kateihō* subjunctive mood
⁹ 面 *kamen* mask, disguise
¹⁰ 病 *kebyō* feigned illness
眠 *kamin* nap
称 *kashō* temporary name
託 *kataku* pretense, pretext
¹¹ 設 *kasetsu* temporary, provisional; hypothesis, supposition; fiction
釈放 *kari shakuhō* release on parole
¹² 装 *kasō* masquerade, disguise, fancy dress
¹⁴ 説 *kasetsu* hypothesis, supposition
綴 *karitoji* temporary binding; paper binding
¹⁵ 縫 *karinu(i)* temporary sewing, basting
調印 *kari chōin* initialing (a pact)

A **全** $\frac{145}{\text{J4134}}$ **全** $\frac{114}{\text{J2138}}$ ZEN all.
M1424 M378 *mattō(suru)* accomplish, fulfill, complete, preserve (life). *matta(ki)* perfect, complete, whole, sound, intact. *matta(ku)* entirely, completely, wholly, perfectly; truly, indeed. *zen-* all, whole, entire, complete, overall; pan-. 〔入〕
² 力 *zenryoku* all one's energy, full capacity
人格 *zenjinkaku* one's whole personality
³ 土 *zendo* the whole land, the whole country
⁴ 文 *zembun* whole sentence; full paragraph; full text
日制 *zennichisei* the full-day (school system)
⁵ 世界 *zensekai* the whole world
市 *zenshi* the whole city
⁶ 米 *zen-Bei* all America, pan-American
会一致 *zenkai-itchi* unanimous
⁷ 角 *zenkaku* em, em quad (in printing)
図 *zenzu* complete map, whole view
局 *zenkyoku* general situation, whole aspect
快 *zenkai* complete recovery of health
形 *zenkei* the whole form; a perfect form
体 *zentai* the whole; whatever (is the matter). *zentai de* in all
体主義 *zentai shugi* totalitarianism
身 *zenshin* the whole body; full-length (portrait)
身麻酔 *zenshin masui* general anesthesia
身像 *zenshinzō* full-length portrait or statue
⁸ 長 *zenchō* over-all length, span
治 *zenchi, zenji* complete recovery
店 *zenten* the whole store
知全能 *zenchi-zennō* omniscience and omnipotence
国 *zenkoku, zengoku* the whole country; nationwide, national
国大会 *zenkoku taikai* national convention; national athletic meet
国区 *zenkokuku* national constituency
国中継 *zenkoku chūkei* nationwide hookup
国民 *zenkokumin* the whole nation
国的 *zenkokuteki* nationwide
国放送 *zenkoku hōsō* national network broadcast
⁹ 通 *zentsū* opening of the whole (railway line)
速 *zensoku* full speed
速力 *zensokuryoku* full speed
面 *zemmen* the whole surface
面的 *zemmenteki* all-out, general, over-all, complete, extensive, full-scale
面戦争 *zemmen sensō* total war, all-out war
¹⁰ 校 *zenkō* the whole school
員 *zen'in* all members; all hands, the whole crew
容 *zen'yō* full portrait; whole aspect; full story

2

二十一〔人〕
⁴〔イ〕⼋
儿 入 八 ⼅ 冂 冖 ⼎ 几 凵 刀 刂 力 勹 匕 匚 匸 十 卜 卩 厂 厶 又

般的 *zempanteki ni* generally, universally, wholly
部 *zembu* all, the whole; entirely, altogether
能 *zennō* omnipotence
能力 *zennōryoku* full capacity, all one's ability
¹¹ 道 *zendō* all Hokkaido
域 *zen'iki* the whole area
訳 *zen'yaku* complete translation
敗 *zempai* complete defeat
責任 *zensekinin* full responsibility
盛 *zensei* height of prosperity
盛期 *zenseiki* golden age
¹² 開 *zenkai suru* open fully. *zenkai* full throttle
焼 *zenshō* total destruction by fire
集 *zenshū* complete works
然 *zenzen* wholly, entirely, completely, absolutely
幅 *zempuku* overall width; wing span. *zempuku no* all, every, utmost
勝 *zenshō* complete victory
景 *zenkei* panoramic view, bird's-eye view
廃 *zempai* total abolition
¹³ 滅 *zemmetsu* annihilation, complete destruction
勢力 *zenseiryoku* full force
裸 *zenra* nude
¹⁴ 貌 *zembō* full portrait; whole aspect; full story
¹⁵ 編 *zempen* whole book, whole volume
篇 *zempen* whole book, whole volume
霊 *zenrei* one's whole soul
権 *zenken* plenipotentiary powers; full authority
¹⁶ 壊 *zenkai* complete destruction
¹⁸ 額 *zengaku* total, full amount

───── 5 ─────

伶 $\frac{149}{\substack{J4e62 \\ M478}}$ REI actor.

佑 $\frac{150}{\substack{J4d24 \\ M507}}$ U, YŪ help.

佃 $\frac{151}{\substack{J4451 \\ M492}}$ TEN. *tsukuda* cultivated rice field.
¹² 煮 *tsukudani* food preserved by boiling down in soy

但 $\frac{154}{\substack{J4322 \\ M495}}$ TAN. DAN. *tadashi* but, however, excepting that.
B
¹⁰ 書 *tadashiga(ki)* proviso

佐 $\frac{155}{\substack{J3a34 \\ M506}}$ SA help.
B

伺 $\frac{156}{\substack{J3b47 \\ M483}}$ SHI. *ukaga(u)* vt and vi visit; ask, inquire, question; hear, be told; implore (a god for an oracle).
B
¹⁰ 候 *shikō suru* wait upon (someone)

伴 $\frac{157}{\substack{J483c \\ M475}}$ HAN. BAN. *tomona(u)* accompany, bring with; be accompanied by; be involved in. *tomo* companion, follower.
B
⁴ 天連 *Bateren* Portuguese missionaries; Christianity
⁹ 侶 *hanryo* companion
奏 *bansō* accompaniment

伯 $\frac{158}{\substack{J476c \\ M466}}$ HAKU count; earl; eldest brother; uncle; chief official.
B
⁴ 父 *oji, hakufu* uncle
⁵ 母 *oba, hakubo* aunt
⁶ 仲 *hakuchū suru* be evenly matched
¹⁷ 爵 *hakushaku* count; earl

伽 $\frac{159}{\substack{J3240 \\ M486}}$ GA. KA. KYA. *togi* nursing; nurse; attending; attendant; entertainer.
B
⁹ 草子 *(o)togizōshi* fairy-tale book
¹⁵ 噺 *(o)togibanashi* fairy tale, nursery tale
¹⁷ 藍 *garan* temple, monastery

位 $\frac{162}{\substack{J304c \\ M503}}$ I rank, place, grade. *kurai* grade, rank; court order, dignity, nobility; situation; throne, crown. *kurai suru* occupy a position. *-kurai, -gurai* about, almost, as; rather; at least; enough to. *-i* rank, place.
A
¹¹ 階 *ikai* court rank
¹² 牌 *ihai* Buddhist mortuary tablet
¹³ 置 *ichi* situation, position, location, place

伸 $\frac{163}{\substack{J3f2d \\ M481}}$ SHIN stretching. *no(biru)* extend, lengthen, stretch, spread; be postponed; increase; grow; progress, develop; be straightened, be flattened, be smoothed; be exhausted. *no(basu)* lengthen, stretch, extend; let
B

(nails) grow; straighten; uncoil; spread out; reach out; postpone; dilute; smooth out; develop (talents); amass (riches). *no(beru)* make (a bed); stretch, widen, lengthen. *no(su)* stretch, spread, smooth out; roll out; iron; stretch, extend; gain influence; knock out. *no(bi)* stretching (the body); excess, surplus; postponement; growth; spread. *no(biyakana)* comfortable, carefree. *noshi* an iron.

¹⁰ 展 *shinten* expansion, extension

悩 *no(bi)-naya(mu)* be sluggish (business)

¹¹ 張 *shinchō* expansion, extension, elongation

¹⁷ 縮 *shinshuku, no(bi)chiji(mi)* expansion and contraction; elasticity, flexibility

縮自在 *shinshuku jizai na* elastic, flexible, telescoping, expandable

縮性 *shinshukusei* elasticity

Λ **住** <u>164 J3d3b M505</u> JŪ dwelling, living. *su(mu), su(mau), jū(suru)* live, reside, inhabit. *su(mai)* residence.

² 人 *jūnin* resident, inhabitant

⁵ 処 *su(mi)ka* dwelling; den (of robbers); nest

民 *jūmin* inhabitants, residents, population

民税 *jūminzei* municipal tax

民登録 *jūmin tōroku* resident registration

⁶ 宅 *jūtaku* residence, house

宅地 *jūtakuchi* residential district

宅難 *jūtakunan* housing shortage

⁸ 居 *jūkyo, sumai* dwelling, residence, address

居手当 *jūkyo teate* rent allowance

所 *jūsho, su(mi)dokoro* residence, address, domicile

所録 *jūshoroku* address book

¹⁸ 職 *jūshoku* chief priest (of a Buddhist temple)

Λ **体** <u>165 J424e M509</u> TAI the body; substance, object; reality, style, form; image counter. TEI appearance, air; condition, state, form. *tai(suru)* obey, comply with; keep in mind. *karada* body; health.

² 力 *tairyoku* physical strength

⁴ 内 *tainai* interior of the body

⁶ 当 *taiata(ri)* body blow, ramming attack, sacrifice attack

⁷ 言 *taigen* uninflected word

形 *taikei* form, figure

系 *taikei* system, organization

系化 *taikeika* organization, systematization

系的 *taikeiteki* systematic

⁸ 長 *taichō* length of an animal

制 *taisei* structure, system, setup, organization

育 *taiiku* physical education, gymnastics, athletics

育館 *taiikukan* gymnasium

⁹ 面 *taimen* honor, reputation; dignity; prestige; appearances

重 *taijū* body weight

臭 *taishū* body odor; a characteristic (of someone)

¹⁰ 格 *taikaku* physique, constitution

¹¹ 得 *taitoku* realization, experience; comprehension; mastery

現 *taigen suru* personify, impersonate, embody

¹² 温 *taion* body temperature

温計 *taionkei* clinical thermometer

裁 *teisai* form, style; appearance, show; get-up, format; decency

¹³ 感 *taikan* bodily sensation

¹⁴ 罰 *taibatsu* corporal punishment

¹⁵ 熱 *tainetsu* body heat

質 *taishitsu* physical constitution

¹⁶ 積 *taiseki* volume, capacity

操 *taisō* gymnastics, calisthenics

¹⁸ ɣ *taiku* the body, stature, physique, constitution

験 *taiken* experience

Λ **低** <u>166 J4463 M504</u> TEI low. *hiku(i)* low, short; humble; low (voice)

³ 下 *teika* fall, decline, lowering, deterioration

⁵ 圧 *teiatsu* low pressure; low voltage

⁶ 地 *teichi* low ground, bottom land, plain

劣 *teiretsu* low grade, inferiority; coarseness, vulgarity

気圧 *teikiatsu* low atmospheric pressure, cyclone; bad temper, tense situation

⁸ 迷 *teimei* low-hanging (clouds)

学年 *teigakunen* lower grades in school

2

二十【人 イ 个 儿 入 八 丷 冂 冖 冫 几 凵 刀 刂 力 勹 匕 匚 匸 十 卜 卩 厂 厶 又

金利 *teikinri* low interest
周波 *teishūha* low frequency
性能 *teiseinō* low efficiency
空 *teikū* low ceiling; low altitude
空飛行 *teikū hikō* low-altitude flying
⁹速 *teisoku* low (gear), slow speed
俗 *teizoku* vulgar
徊 *teikai* loitering, lingering, reluctance to leave
級 *teikyū* low grade; vulgar
音 *teion* bass (in music); low voice
¹⁰能 *teinō* low intelligence, feeblemindedness, imbecility
¹¹率 *teiritsu* low rate
¹²温 *teion* low temperature
減 *teigen* decrease, reduction, fall, depreciation, mitigation
¹³廉 *teiren* cheap, inexpensive
賃金 *teichingin* low wages
¹⁵調 *teichō* low tone, undertone, dullness, (market) weakness

A 作 ¹⁶⁷ J3a6e M518 SA. SAKU a work, a production; tillage; harvest; ridge (in a field). *tsuku(ru)* make, create, manufacture, prepare, draw up, write, compose; build; coin; cultivate; organize, establish; make up (a face), trim (a tree); fabricate; prepare food; commit (sin). *(o)tsuku(ri)* makeup; sliced raw fish. *tsuku(ri)* make, structure, construction; physique, build; workmanship; (a woman's) makeup; cultivation; a mounting.
⁴手 *tsuku(ri)te* maker, builder, creator; tenant farmer
文 *sakubun* composition, writing
方 *tsuku(ri)kata* way of making; recipe, how to grow (something); style of building; construction; workmanship
⁵用 *sayō* action, operation, function, effect
付 *tsuku(ri)tsu(ke)* fixed. *sakuzuke* planting
出 *tsuku(ri)-da(su)* manufacture, raise (crops), turn out, create, make; invent; dream up
⁶成 *sakusei* framing, drawing up, making; writing
曲 *sakkyoku* musical composition
曲家 *sakkyokuka* composer

(professional)
⁷図 *sakuzu suru* draw figures; construct (in geometry). *sakuzu* drawing
声 *tsuku(ri)goe* feigned voice; unnatural voice
⁸例 *sakurei* model of writing
法 *sahō* manners, etiquette, propriety
物 *sakumotsu* crops. *tsuku(ri)mono* artificial product; decoration; fake; crop. *sakubutsu* literary work
事 *tsuku(ri)goto* fabrication, lie, fiction
者 *sakusha* author
者未詳 *sakusha mishō* anonymous, author unknown
⁹風 *sakufū* literary style
品 *sakuhin* work, performance, production, opus
為 *sakui* artificiality; act; commission (of a crime)
¹⁰家 *sakka* writer, novelist; artist
¹³話 *tsuku(ri)banashi* fable, fabrication, fiction, myth
意 *sakui* design, motif, idea, conception, intention
詩 *sakushi* writing poetry; poem
戦 *sakusen* military or naval operations
戦計画 *sakusen keikaku* campaign plan
業 *sagyō* work, operations, manufacturing; fatigue duty
業用 *sagyōyō* for work, for manufacturing
業衣 *sagyōi* work clothes
業服 *sagyōfuku* work clothes
業場 *sagyōba, sagyōjō* works; workshop
¹⁴製 *sakusei* manufacture

A 余 ¹⁶⁸ J4d3e M515 YO I, myself, the writer; surplus, other; remainder. *ama(ri)* rest, remainder, remnant; surplus, balance; excess; remains, scraps, residue; fullness. *ama(ru)* remain, be in excess, be too many. *ama(su)* leave, spare, save. *-yo* over, more than. *ama(ri) ni* too much, excessively, too. *yo no* other, the rest. *-ama(ri)* upward of, over, more than.
²人 *yonin, yojin* others, other people
力 *yoryoku* remaining strength; reserve power; money to spare
⁴分 *yobun* extra, excess, surplus
⁵生 *yosei* one's remaining years
白 *yohaku* blank space, margin

⁶地 *yochi* place, room, margin; scope

⁷技 *yogi* avocation, hobby

⁸波 *yoha* secondary effect, aftermath; trail (of a storm), sequel, consequence. *nagori* farewell; keepsake, remembrance; remains, relics

物 *ama(ri)mono* remains, leavings, remnant; surplus. *ama(shi)mono* something not needed; a person who is in the way

命 *yomei* one's remaining days

念 *yonen* another idea

念無 *yonenna(ku)* earnestly, intently

所 *yoso* another place

所目 *yosome* another's eyes, casual observer

所行 *yosoyu(ki), yosoi(ki)* going out; company manners, one's best (clothes)

所見 *yosomi suru* look away

所者 *yosomono* stranger

⁹音 *yoin* reverberation; swelling (of a hymn); trailing note; lingering memory

計 *yokei* abundance, surplus, excess, superfluity

¹⁰病 *yobyō* secondary disease, complications

¹¹得 *yotoku* emoluments, additional ⌐profits

情 *yojō* suggestiveness (of a poem), lingering charm, lasting impression

剰 *yojō* surplus, balance, residue

¹²禄 *yoroku* additional gain

程 *yohodo, yo(p)podo* very, greatly, much, to a large extent

裕 *yoyū* surplus, margin, room, time, allowance, scope, rope

¹³暇 *yoka* spare time, leisure

罪 *yozai* other crimes, further offenses

勢 *yosei* surplus power, force, momentum, impetus, inertia

¹⁵談 *yodan* sequel (of a story); digression

震 *yoshin* aftershock

熱 *yonetsu* waste heat; remaining heat

¹⁶興 *yokyō* side show, entertainment

¹⁹韻 *yoin* reverberation; swelling (of a hymn); trailing note; lingering memory

---

何 ⸤169 J323f M511⸥ KA. *nan, nani* what. *dore* which; who. *nan da* What! Why! Well! What do you mean! *nan da ka* some way or other. *nan dattara* if you

like. *nan de* why, what for. *nan demo* anything; by all means; probably. *nani* Oh! What! why, well. *nani ka* something, anything. *nanikashira* something or other; I don't know what it is but… *nani kato* one way or another. *nanni(mo), nani(mo)* nothing, no (with neg.). *nan ni seyo, nani(shiro), nani(se)* at any rate, anyhow. *nani yori no* most, best. *nani yori mo* first of all. *nan nara* if you wish, if you can, if desirable. *nan no* what, what kind of. *nani, nan to, nan te* what, whatever; What! How! Look here! *nan toka* some way or other; so and so. *nan tomo* nothing; quite. *nan to nareba* for, because. *izu(re)* where, which, who. *izu(re) mo* both; (neg.) neither. *izu(re) ni seyo, izu(re) ni shitemo* either way, in any case. *nan da ga, nan da kedo* to speak frankly. *nani(ka), nani(yara)* some, any, something anything. *nan(narito)* anything, whatever. *nan(taru)* How! What! (beautiful, etc.). *dō(shite)* how; why; absurd, on the contrary. *dō(shitemo)* by all means, surely; no matter what you do; by no means; willy-nilly; after all; all things considered. *dō(se)* anyway, in any case, after all, at all (neg. implication). *nani(kanitsuke)* concerning many things. *nani(kuso)* an interjection of determination. *nani(watomoare)* nevertheless, anyway. *nan-* some (thousands).

²人 *nannin* how many (people). *nampito mo, nambito mo* everyone, all

³千 *nanzen* many thousands. *nanzen… ka* how many thousands

⁴方 *donata* who. *dotchi, dochira* where, what place; which; who. *dochira demo, dochira ka* either

日 *nannichi* how many days, what day

月 *nangatsu* what month

分 *nanibun* anyway, please. *nanibun no* some, something or other, as much as possible

⁵奴 *doitsu, doyatsu* who

代目 *nandaime* what ordinal number (of a president, daimyo, etc.)

処 *doko, dokoira, izuko, izuku* where. *doko ka* somewhere, anywhere, in some respects

2

二 亻〔人〕
イ 亻〔人〕
5 仌 亼
儿 入
八 ソ
冂 宀
冫 几
凵 刀
刂 力
勹 匕
匚 匸
十 卜
卩 厂
厶 又

処其処 *dokosoko* such and such a place

6 回 *nankai* how many times. *nankai mo* time and time again

年 *nannen* how many years; what year

気無 *nanigena(i)* casual, unconcerned. *nanigena(ku)* unintentionally, calmly, innocently, inadvertently

8 物 *nanimono* something; nothing (neg.)

者 *nanimono* who, what kind of a person. *nanimono ka* someone

事 *nanigoto* what; something, everything, nothing (neg.)

9 度 *nando* how many times, how often. *nando mo* many times, often. *nando demo* any number of times. *nando ka* many times

故 *naze, naniyue* why, how

10 個 *nanko* how many pieces

時 *itsu* when, how soon. *nanji, nandoki* what time. *itsu demo* any time; always; never (with neg.). *itsu ka* some time, some day; at one time, one day, the other day, before we know it. *itsu kara* since when, how long. *itsu mo* always, usually; never (with neg.); every time. *itsumo no* usual, habitual. *itsu demo, nandoki demo* whenever, at any time. *itsu shika* unawares, before you know it. *itsu zoya* once, some time ago

時頃 *nanjigoro, itsugoro* about when, how soon

時間 *nan jikan* how many hours. *itsu(no)ma(nika), itsu(no)ma(niyara)* unawares, unnoticed; before you know it

11 遍 *namben* how many times, how often. *namben mo* repeatedly

12 程 *dorehodo* how much, how long, how far. *nanihodo* how much, how many

等 *nanra, nanira* what, whatever, what sort of, any kind of, nothing whatever (with neg.). *nanra(ka) no* some… or other

番 *namban* what number

13 歳 *nansai* how old (are you, is she)

14 様 *nanisama* what kind; how; indeed, truly; extremely; to be sure

箇 *nanko* how many pieces

箇月 *nankagetsu* how many months

18 曜日 *naniyōbi, nan'yōbi* what day of the week

───── **6** ─────

侭 | 170 J4b79 M-X | Nonstandard for | 儘 327.

侠 | 171 J3622 M625 | Nonstandard for | 俠 213.

佼 | 175 J3873 M570 | Kō, Kyō attractive; clever; deceive; line up. *utsuku(shii)* beautiful, attractive.

侃 | 182 J3426 M577 | Kan strong; just; right; love of peace.
8 侃諤諤 *kankan-gakugaku no* outspoken

侮 | 187 J496e M629' | B Bu. *anado(ru), anazu(ru)* despise, make light of. *anado(ri)* contempt, scorn.
10 辱 *bujoku* insult, contempt; slight; humiliation
14 蔑 *bubetsu* contempt, scorn, slight

価 | 188 J3241 M628' | A Ka. *atai* price, cost, value, worth. *atai suru* be worth, merit; cost, be valued at.
10 値 *kachi* value, merit
格 *kakaku* price, cost, value

舍 | 189 J3c4b M30278' | A Seki. Sha inn; hut, house, mansion

併 | 190 J4a3b M561 | B Hei. *awa(saru)* vi get together, unite. *awa(seru)* vt put together, unite. *awa(sete)* collectively, altogether; in addition, besides; at the same time. *shika(shi)* however, but. *shika(mo)* moreover, furthermore, nevertheless, and yet.
5 用 *heiyō suru, awa(se)-mochi(iru)* use jointly, use at the same time
6 合 *heigō* annexation, merger, absorption
考 *awa(se)-kanga(eru)* consider together
7 呑 *heidon* annexation, merger, swallowing up

^{9} 発 *heihatsu* complications (in illness)

^{10} 記 *heiki suru* line up together (in writing)

依 $\frac{191}{\substack{J304d \\ M607}}$ B I. E. *yo(ru)* depend on. *yo(tte)* therefore, consequently. *(ni) yo(ri)* due to, depending on.

^{6} 存 *izon, ison* dependence, reliance

^{8} 怙地 *ikoji* obstinacy, stubbornness

怙贔屓 *ekohiiki* favoritism, partiality, prejudice, bias

拠 *ikyo* dependence

^{10} 託 *itaku* dependence (on someone)

^{12} 然 *izen toshite* still, as yet, as of old

^{15} 嘱 *ishoku suru* entrust with

^{16} 頼 *irai* request; trust; dependence

頼心 *iraishin* spirit of dependence

頼状 *iraijō* written request

^{19} 願免官 *igan menkan* retirement at one's own request

侍 $\frac{192}{\substack{J3b78 \\ M589}}$ B Jı. *habe(ru), ji(suru)* wait upon, serve. *samurai* warrior, samurai.

^{3} 女 *jijo* lady attendant, a lady in waiting

^{7} 医 *jii* court physician

^{10} 従 *jijū* chamberlain

従長 *jijucho* grand chamberlain

^{15} 衛 *jiei* bodyguard

例 $\frac{193}{\substack{J4e63 \\ M587}}$ A REI custom, usage, precedent; case, example, parallel, illustration. *tato(eru)* compare to, speak figuratively, illustrate. *tatoe* parable, illustration, figure of speech. *tato(eba)* for example. *tameshi* instance, example, case, precedent, an experience.

^{4} 文 *reibun* model sentence

^{5} 示 *reiji* illustration

外 *reigai* exception. *reigai na* exceptional

外無 *reigai na(ku)* without exception

^{6} 会 *reikai* regular meeting

年 *reinen* normal year, average year; every year, annually

^{12} 証 *reishō* illustration, example

^{18} 題 *reidai* example, exercises (in a textbook)

佳 $\frac{194}{\substack{J3242 \\ M557}}$ B KA beautiful; good; excellent. *i(i), yo(i), yo(shi)*

good, good-natured; pleasing; precious; noble; lovely, beautiful, fine; lucky; efficacious; right; suitable; justifiable; appropriate, satisfactory; better; all right; unnecessary; no objection; intimate, friendly; easy; well; desirous.

^{2} 人 *kajin* a beautiful woman

^{7} 作 *kasaku* a good piece of work 「fish

^{8} 肴 *kakō* delicacy, rare treat; good-eating

^{14} 境 *kakyō* climax (of a story)

供 $\frac{195}{\substack{J3621 \\ M605}}$ A KYŌ. KU. GU. *kyō(suru)* offer, present, submit; serve (a meal); supply. *sona(eru)* offer, sacrifice, dedicate. *(o)tomo suru* accompany. *(o)sona(e)* offering. *tomo* attendant, companion, retinue.

^{3} 与 *kyōyo suru* give, furnish, provide

^{5} 出 *kyōshutsu* delivery

出米 *kyōshutsumai* (farmers') rice deliveries

^{7} 応 *kyōō* treat, feast, banquet

述 *kyōjutsu* affidavit, deposition, testimony

述者 *kyōjutsusha* deponent, testifier

述書 *kyōjutsusho* affidavit, deposition, testimony

^{8} 物 *kumotsu, sona(e)mono* an offering

^{10} 託 *kyōtaku* deposit

託金 *kyōtakukin* deposit of money

^{12} 給 *kyōkyū* supply

給地 *kyōkyūchi* supply center

給者 *kyōkyūsha* supplier

給源 *kyōkyūgen* source of supply

給路 *kyōkyūro* supply route

^{15} 養 *kuyō* memorial service

使 $\frac{196}{\substack{J3b48 \\ M573}}$ A SHI use; messenger. *tsuka(u)* use; handle, manipulate; employ; need, want; spend, consume; speak (English); practice (fencing); take (one's lunch); circulate (bad money). *tsuka(i) suru* go as an envoy. *tsuka(eru)* useful, serviceable. *tsuka(wasu)* send, dispatch; give, donate, bestow on; do for (someone). *tsuka(i-konasu)* handle (men); master (a tool); acquire a command of (a language). *-shi(mu)* old causative verbal ending. *tsuka(i)* mission, errand, message; messenger, bearer; trainer, tamer; familiar spirit.

6

二 亠 人 イ 𠆢 儿 入 八 丷 冂 冖 冫 几 凵 刀 刂 力 勹 匕 匚 匸 十 卜 卩 厂 厶 又

2

二 十 〔人 亻 人 儿 入 八 ソ 冂 宀 冫 几 凵 刀 刂 力 勹 匕 匚 匸 十 卜 卩 厂 厶 又

⁴手 *tsuka(i)te* user, consumer; employer; prodigal, spendthrift; fencing master

方 *tsuka(i)kata* how to use, treatment, management (of help)

込 *tsuka(i)-ko(mu)* embezzle; accustom oneself to using

切 *tsuka(i)-ki(ru)* use up, exhaust, wear out

分 *tsuka(i)wa(ke)* proper use. *tsuka(i)-wa(keru)* use properly

⁵用 *shiyō suru* employ, use, utilize

用人 *shiyōnin* employee, servant

用例 *shiyōrei* examples showing the use (of a word)

用法 *shiyōhō* use, directions

用者 *shiyōsha* user, consumer

用料 *shiyōryō* rent, hire

用量 *shiyōryō* amount used

用権 *shiyōken* use, right to use

⁷役 *shieki suru* employ, use, set to word; enslave

役動詞 *shieki dōshi* causative verb

⁸果 *tsuka(i)-hata(su)* use up, squander

者 *shisha* messenger; envoy

命 *shimei* mission, errand; message

⁹途 *shito* purpose for which money is spent; the way money is spent

¹⁰残 *tsuka(i)noko(ri), tsuka(i)noko(shi)* remnant, remainder, odds and ends, leavings

¹¹過 *tsuka(i)-su(giru)* use excessively, use too much; spend too much; overwork someone

¹³節 *shisetsu* envoy; embassy; mission; delegate

節団 *shisetsudan* mission, delegation

¹⁴慣 *tsuka(i)-na(rasu)* accustom oneself to using; train; break in (horses). *tsuka(i)-na(reru)* get accustomed to using

───── **7** ─────

俣 | 202 J4b73 M718 | (国字) *mata* crotch, thigh, groin.

侶 | 205 J3e37 M647 | RYO. RO. *tomo* companion, follower.

侯 B | 211 J3874 M633 | KŌ marquis; lord, daimyo.

¹⁷爵 *kōshaku* marquis, marquess

促 B | 212 J4225 M664 | SOKU. SAKU. *unaga(su)* urge, press, demand; stimulate; quicken; incite; invite (attention to).

⁶成 *sokusei* growth promotion

成栽培 *sokusei saibai* raising out-of-season crops with artificial heat

⁹音 *sokuon* assimilated obstruent sound (represented by つ [*tsu*] in Japanese)

¹⁰進 *sokushin suru* promote, encourage, facilitate, accelerate, spur on

俠 | 213 J-X M706 | KYŌ chivalry. *kyan* tomboy, bobby soxer, flapper.

⁶気 *kyōki, otokogi*, chivalrous spirit

⁹客 *kyōkaku, otokodate* one who champions the underdog

俄 | 215 J3264 M665 | GA. *niwaka* sudden, abrupt, unexpected; improvised, offhand.

⁵仕込 *niwakajiko(mi)* hasty preparation

仕立 *niwakajita(te)* extemporary, improvised

⁶成金 *niwaka narikin* overnight millionaire

⁸雨 *niwaka ame* shower

¹²然 *gazen* suddenly, abruptly

俊 B | 216 J3d53 M674 | SHUN excellence, genius.

³才 *shunsai* genius; talented person, prodigy

⁷足 *shunsoku* swift of foot, talented person

秀 *shunshū* genius; talented man, prodigy

¹⁰敏 *shumbin na* keen, quick-witted

係 A | 217 J3738 M663 | KEI. *kakari, -gakari* duty; person in charge. *kaka(ru)* concern oneself in, have to do with; affect, influence; stick to (opinions). *kaka(ru)* is the work of. *kaka(wari)* relation, connection. *ka(karu)* *vi* hang on, be suspended from, be caught, be trapped; be built; begin; arrive at; require, cost; play against, oppose; be splashed; weigh (a pound); be levied; (the instrument or tool) works; attack, fall on;

is now showing at; consult; depend (on a son); concern, affect, involve.

⁶ 合 *kaka(ri)a(i)* unfortunate relationship

争 *keisō* dispute, contention

⁸ 長 *kakarichō* chief clerk

官 *kaka(ri)kan* official in charge

¹⁰ 員 *kaka(ri)in* clerk in charge

留 *keiryū* mooring, anchorage

¹¹ 船 *keisen* mooring a ship

累 *keirui* encumbrances, dependents; implication, complicity

¹² 属 *keizoku* relationship

¹³ 数 *keisū* coefficient (in math)

侵 $\frac{218}{\frac{J3f2f}{M646}}$ B SHIN. *oka(su)* invade, raid; violate, trespass, intrude on.

² 入 *shinnyū* invasion, raid, aggression, trespass

入者 *shinnyūsha* invader, trespasser, raider

⁴ 水 *shinsui* inundation, flood, submersion; leaking

⁵ 犯 *shimpan* invasion, violation, infringement

⁹ 食 *shinshoku* erosion; corrosion

¹⁰ 害 *shingai* infringement, violation, trespass, impairment

¹¹ 略 *shinryaku* aggression, invasion, raid

略的 *shinryakuteki* aggressive

略者 *shinryakusha* aggressor, invader

¹⁵ 蝕 *shinshoku* erosion; corrosion

便 $\frac{219}{\frac{J4a58}{M659}}$ A BEN convenience, facility; excreta, stools; evacuation. BIN chance; mail, letter. *ben(jiru)*, *ben(zuru)* will do, answer the purpose, make convenient. *tayo(ru)* rely on, have recourse to. *tayo(ri)* news, tidings; connection. *yosuga* way, means.

⁷ 利 *benri na* convenient, handy, useful

⁸ 所 *benjo* lavatory, latrine, comfort station, toilet

法 *bempō* handy method, shortcut, expedient

宜 *bengi* convenience, accommodation, advantage, expedience

宜上 *bengijō* for convenience sake

⁹ 通 *bentsū* bowel movement

乗 *binjō* taking advantage of a ride or an opportunity, taking a ship

乗者 *binjōsha* hitchhiker; one who catches a ride (with a friend)

¹⁰ 益 *ben'eki* convenience; benefit, profit

秘 *bempi* constipation

¹³ 意 *ben'i* call of nature, bowel-movement inclination

¹⁴ 箋 *binsen* stationery, writing paper

¹⁵ 器 *benki* toilet; bedpan, chamber pot, urinal

¹⁶ 覧 *benran* manual, handbook, compendium

俗 $\frac{220}{\frac{J422f}{M695}}$ B ZOKU customs, manners; the world; worldliness; vulgarity; mundane things; the laity. *zoku(ppoi)* cheap (reading); vulgar, worldly-minded.

² 人 *zokujin* layman; worldling

⁴ 化 *zokka suru* vulgarize, secularize, popularize

文学 *zokubungaku* popular literature

⁵ 世間 *zokuseken* everyday world

⁶ 耳 *zokuji* vulgar ears, attention of the masses

気 *zokki, zokke* vulgarity, worldliness, worldly ambition

字 *zokuji* popular characters; nonstandard characters

名 *zokumei* popular name; common name; secular name; bad reputation. *zokumyō* secular name

⁸ 物 *zokubutsu* worldly-minded person, vulgar person

念 *zokunen* worldliness, worldly ambition, unholy desires

事 *zokuji* worldly affairs; daily

⁹ 界 *zokkai* secular life, workaday world

¹⁰ 称 *zokushō* popular name, common name

¹¹ 情 *zokujō* worldly-mindedness; worldly affairs

悪 *zokuaku* worldliness, vulgarity, coarseness

¹² 間 *zokkan* the world; the public

¹⁴ 語 *zokugo* colloquial language; colloquialism

説 *zokusetsu* common saying, popular version; folklore, tradition

¹⁵ 論 *zokuron* popular opinion

趣味 *zokushumi* vulgar taste

¹⁶ 謡 *zokuyō* popular song, folk song, ballad, ditty

諺 *zokugen* proverb, popular saying

2

二十一【人イ⼈】
7 人イ⼈儿入八丷冂宀冫几凵刀刂力勹匕匚匸十卜卩厂厶又

A 信 221 J3f2e M707

SHIN truth; faith, fidelity, sincerity; trust, confidence, reliance. *shin(jiru), shin(zuru)* believe; believe in; place trust in, confide in, have faith in. *makoto* sincerity, fidelity, devotion.

⁴ 天翁 *shinten'ō, ahōdori* albatross
心 *shinjin* faith, belief, devotion, godliness
心深 *shinjimbuka(i)* deeply religious, devout, godly, faithful
⁵ 号 *shingō* signal, semaphore; signaling
用 *shin'yō* confidence, trust, faith; dependence, reliance; belief, credence; credit
用協同組合 *shin'yō kyōdō kumiai* cooperative credit association
用組合 *shin'yō kumiai* credit association
⁶ 任 *shinnin* trust, confidence, credence
任状 *shinninjō* credentials
任投票 *shinnin tōhyō* vote of confidence
仰 *shinkō* belief, creed; religious faith
⁷ 条 *shinjō* article of faith, creed, belief
⁸ 服 *shimpuku suru* be convinced
念 *shinnen* belief, faith, conviction
者 *shinja* believer, devotee, adherent; Christian
奉 *shimpō* belief, faith
奉者 *shimpōsha* adherent, devotee, believer
¹⁰ 徒 *shinto* layman, believer, adherent, follower, laity
託 *shintaku* trust; entrusting
託投資 *shintaku tōshi* trust investment
託統治 *shintaku tōchi* trusteeship
¹¹ 教 *shinkyō* religion, faith, belief
¹² 義 *shingi* faith, fidelity, loyalty
¹⁵ 賞必罰 *shinshō-hitsubatsu* sure penalty and certain rewards
¹⁶ 憑性 *shimpyōsei* authenticity, credibility
頼 *shinrai* reliance, trust, confidence
頼性 *shinraisei* credibility, authenticity
頼感 *shinraikan* feeling of trust

A 保 222 J4a5d M702

Ho. Hō. *ho(suru)* guarantee. *tamo(tsu)* keep, preserve, hold, retain, maintain; support, sustain; last, endure, keep well (food), wear well, be durable.

⁵ 母 *hobo* kindergarten teacher
⁶ 存 *hozon* preservation, conservation, storage, maintenance
全 *hozen* integrity; preservation, conservation
安 *hoan* peace preservation, security
安林 *hoanrin* forest reserve
有 *hoyū* possession, retention, maintenance
守 *hoshu* conservatism
守的 *hoshuteki* conservative
⁷ 身 *hoshin* self-protection
⁸ 育 *hoiku suru* nurse, nurture, rear
育園 *hoikuen* nursery school, day nursery
⁹ 持 *hoji* maintenance, preservation
持者 *hojisha* holder (of a record)
¹⁰ 留 *horyū suru* reserve, defer
険 *hoken* insurance, guarantee
険会社 *hokengaisha* insurance company
険金 *hokenkin* insurance money
険料 *hokenryō* insurance premium
¹¹ 菌者 *hokinsha* germ carrier
釈 *hoshaku* bail
釈金 *hoshakukin* bail
健 *hoken* health preservation, hygiene, sanitation
健所 *hokenjo* health center
健婦 *hokenfu* public-health nurse
¹² 温 *hoon* keeping warm; heat insulation
税 *hozei* customs bond
証 *hoshō* guarantee, security, pledge
証人 *hoshōnin* guarantor, bondsman
証金 *hoshōkin* security money, bond, deposit
¹³ 障 *hoshō* guarantee, security
¹⁴ 管 *hokan* custody, deposit, storage
管物 *hokambutsu* goods in custody, property in trust
管料 *hokanryō* custody fee, storage charge
¹⁵ 線 *hosen* track maintenance
養 *hoyō* health preservation; recuperation; recreation
養地 *hoyōchi* health resort
養所 *hoyōjo* sanatorium
²⁰ 護 *hogo* care, shelter, protection; favor, patronage
護色 *hogoshoku* protective coloration
護者 *hogosha* protector, guardian, patron
護観察 *hogo kansatsu* probation

倖 228 J3876 M771 Kō happiness, luck.

B 倣 235 J4a6f M785 Hō. *nara(u)* imitate, follow, emulate.

俺 240 J3236 M736 En. *ore* I.
¹² 等 *oira* I; we. *orera* we

倭 242 J4f41 M796 Wa *Yamato* ancient Japan.
² 人 *wajin* (an old word for) a Japanese
¹¹ 冠 *wakō* Japanese pirates

A 俵 243 J4936 M730 Hyō bag, bale, sack; bag counter. *tawara* straw bag.

倶 245 J3666 M724 Gu. Ku. *tomo ni* both; alike; together, along with, including.
¹³ 楽部 *kurabu* club, fraternity, sorority; clubhouse

B 倫 246 J4e51 M793 Rin companion.
¹¹ 理 *rinri* ethics, morals
理的 *rinriteki* ethical
理学 *rinrigaku* ethics, moral philosophy

B 倹 248 J3770 M823 Ken economy. *tsuma(shii)* thrifty, economical.
⁹ 約 *ken'yaku* economy, frugality

B 俸 249 J4a70 M734 Hō salary.
¹² 給 *hōkyū* salary, pay
給日 *hōkyūbi* pay day
給生活者 *hōkyū-seikatsusha* salaried man

A 候 250 J3875 M775 Kō season, weather. *sōrō* classical verbal ending equivalent to colloquial -*masu*.
¹² 補 *kōho* candidacy
補生 *kōhosei* cadet
補者 *kōhosha* candidate, applicant

倦 251 J3771 M788 Ken. *u(mu), aki(ru), agu(mu)* get tired of, lose interest in.
⁹ 怠 *kentai* fatigue, weariness, boredom

怠期 *kentaiki* the stage of fatigue
怠感 *kentaikan* a washed-out feeling

A 倍 252 J475c M760 Bai double, twice; times, -fold. *bai(suru)* vi and vt double; be doubled; increase.
⁵ 旧 *baikyū no* redoubled, increased
加 *baika* doubling
¹¹ 率 *bairitsu* magnification, magnifying power
¹³ 数 *baisū* multiple
¹⁴ 増 *baima(shi), baizō* doubling
¹⁸ 額 *baigaku* double amount

A 俳 254 J4750 M726 Hai actor.
² 人 *haijin* a haiku poet
⁴ 文 *haibun* prose with a poetic haiku flavor
⁵ 句 *haiku* 17-syllable poem in three lines of five, seven, and five syllables; *hokku*
⁸ 画 *haiga* briefly drawn picture, haiku picture
¹⁶ 壇 *haidan* the world of the haiku
諧 *haikai* 17- syllable poem, haiku; humorous haiku
¹⁷ 優 *haiyū* actor, actress, player

A 倉 255 J4152 M756 Sō storehouse. *kura* warehouse, godown; cellar; depository, treasury; granary, elevator.
¹⁰ 庫 *sōko* storehouse, godown; magazine

B 倒 256 J455d M767 Tō. *tao(reru), ko(keru)* fall, collapse, drop; break down, die, succumb to; fall senseless; be ruined; have a bad debt. *tao(su)* bring down, throw down, blow down, fell, knock down, trip up; defeat; ruin, overthrow; kill; leave unpaid; cheat. *tao(re)* bad debt. *saka(sa), saka(sama), saka(shima)* reverse, inversion, upside down.
¹¹ 産 *tōsan* insolvency, bankruptcy
¹³ 幕 *tōbaku suru* overthrow the shogunate
置 *tōchi* turning things upside down; placing nonessentials before essentials
¹⁴ 閣 *tōkaku suru* overthrow the cabinet
¹⁵ 影 *tōei* reflection
¹⁶ 壊 *tōkai suru* collapse, be destroyed
錯 *tōsaku* perversion

二 十 人 イ 八 丷 冂 冖 冫 几 凵 刀 刂 力 勹 匕 匚 匸 十 卜 卩 厂 厶 又 ⁸

2

二十
【人
⁸亻
⼂
儿
入
八
丷
冂
宀
冫
几
凵
刀
刂
力
勹
匕
匚
匸
十
卜
卩
厂
厶
又】

値 ²⁵⁷ J434d M786 CHI *atai, ne* price, cost,
A value. *atai suru* value.

³ 下 *nesa(gari)* price decline. *nesa(ge)*
price reduction

上 *nea(gari)* price advance, increase in
value. *nea(ge)* price hike, markup

⁴ 引 *nebiki* price reduction, discount

切 *negi(ru)* haggle, bargain

⁵ 打 *neuchi* value, worth, price; dignity

⁹ 段 *nedan* price, cost

¹⁵ 踏 *nebu(mi)* appraisal, estimation,
evaluation

個 ²⁵⁸ J3844 M758 KA article counter.
A Ko individual; article
counter.

² 人 *kojin* private person, individual. *kojin
no* personal, private, individual

人主義 *kojin shugi* individualism

人的 *kojinteki* individual, personal, self-
centered

人差 *kojinsa* individual differences;
personal equation

⁷ 体 *kotai* an individual

別 *kobetsu* a particular case

別的 *kobetsuteki ni* individually

条 *kajō* article, clause, item

条書 *kajōgaki* itemization

⁸ 性 *kosei* personality; individuality,
idiosyncrasy

性的 *koseiteki* personal, individual

¹⁰ 展 *koten* personal exhibition

個 *koko* one by one; individuals. *koko ni*
individually, separately

借 ²⁵⁹ J3c5a M781 SHA, SHAKU borrowing.
A *ka(riru), ka(ru)* borrow;
have a loan; hire, rent. *ka(ri)* borrowing;
debt; loan.

² 入 *ka(ri)-i(reru)* borrow, rent, lease,
charter. *karii(re)* debt

入金 *kariirekin* loan, debt

³ 上 *ka(ri)-a(geru)* hire, lease, requisition,
charter

⁴ 手 *ka(ri)te* borrower, debtor; tenant

切 *ka(ri)-ki(ru)* reserve. *ka(ri)ki(ri)*
reserved (car)

⁵ 出 *ka(ri)-da(su)* borrow, check out

用 *shakuyō* borrowing, loan

用証書 *shakuyō shōsho* promissory note

⁶ 地 *shakuchi, ka(ri)chi* leased land

地権 *shakuchiken* lease, leasehold

⁸ 放 *ka(rip)pana(shi)* borrowing without
returning

物 *ka(ri)mono* something borrowed

金 *shakkin* loan, debt, liabilities

金取 *shakkinto(ri)* bill collection; bill
collector

¹⁰ 倒 *ka(ri)-tao(su)* evade payment

財 *shakuzai* loan, debt, liability

家 *shakuya, shakka, ka(ri)ie, ka(ri)ya*
house for rent, rented house, renting a
house

家人 *shakkanin, shakuyanin* tenant,
renter

¹² 換 *ka(ri)-ka(eru)* convert (a loan).
ka(ri)ka(e) conversion, refunding,
renewal

款 *shakkan* loan

集 *ka(ri)-atsu(meru)* borrow money, call
for loans

越 *ka(ri)-ko(su)* overdraw. *ka(ri)ko(shi)*
outstanding debt; overdraft

¹³ 賃 *ka(ri)chin* rent, hire

修 ²⁶⁰ J3d24 M721 SHŪ. SHU. *osa(maru)*
A govern oneself, conduct
oneself well. *osa(meru)* study, complete
(a course); cultivate; master; order (one's
life); repair.

² 了 *shūryō* completion (of a course)

³ 士 *Shūshi* Master of Arts

⁵ 正 *shūsei* amendment, revision,
modification, alteration, correction,
retouching

正案 *shūseian* proposed amendment

⁶ 好 *shūkō* amity, friendship

行 *shugyō* training, practice, ascetic
practices, discipline; pursuit of
knowledge

行者 *shugyōsha* practitioner of
(Buddhist) austerities

⁸ 学 *shūgaku* learning

学旅行 *shūgaku ryokō* school
excursion, study tour

⁹ 訂 *shūtei* correction, revision

¹¹ 得 *shūtoku* learning, acquirement

理 *shūri, shuri* repair, mending

理工 *shūrikō* repair man

道士 *shūdōshi* (Catholic) monk, friar

道女 *shūdōjo* (Catholic) nun

道院 *shūdōin* monastery, convent,
cloister

¹² 復 *shūfuku* repair, mending

¹³ 飾 *shūshoku suru* decorate, adorn; polish up (writing); modify (in grammar)
飾語 *shūshokugo* modifier
業 *shūgyō, shugyō* pursuit of knowledge
辞 *shūji* figure of speech; rhetorical flourish
辞学 *shūjigaku* rhetoric
¹⁴ 練 *shūren* drill, practice, training, culture
¹⁵ 養 *shūyō* culture, (mental) training, self-discipline
¹⁶ 築 *shūchiku* repair, renovation, restoration
整 *shūsei* adjustment; retouching (in photography)
¹⁸ 験者 *shugenja* mountaineering ascetic
繕 *shūzen* repairs, mending
¹⁹ 羅場 *shuraba* fighting scene *shurajō* scene of carnage

――――― 9 ―――――

偲 $\frac{266}{J3c45}$ M895 SHI. SAI. *shino(bu)* recollect, remember.

B 偵 $\frac{270}{J4465}$ M898 TEI spy.
¹⁴ 察 *teisatsu* scouting, reconnaissance

A 停 $\frac{273}{J4464}$ M864 TEI stopping. *todo(maru)* stop, halt, stay, remain, stay behind; be limited to. *todo(meru)* stop, cease, detain, put an end to; leave; fix; remain in (a certain condition); content oneself with. *to(maru)* stop, halt, stand still, pull up; cease, be interrupted, be discontinued; be choked; alight on, perch, roost; be held in position.
⁴ 止 *teishi* suspension, ban; stop, standstill; deadlock, stalemate; interruption; abeyance
止線 *teishisen* stop line
⁶ 年 *teinen* mandatory retirement age
⁷ 車 *teisha* stopping a vehicle
⁸ 泊 *teihaku* anchorage moorings
学 *teigaku* suspension from school
¹⁰ 留 *teiryū suru* stop, halt
留所 *teiryūjo* bus or streetcar stop
¹¹ 船 *teisen* stopping a ship, detention, quarantine
¹³ 滞 *teitai* stagnation, tie-up; retention, accumulation, congestion; failing into arrears
戦 *teisen* armistice, cease fire
頓 *teiton* standstill, stalemate, setback, abeyance
電 *teiden* electricity failure; interruption of electrical service
¹⁸ 職 *teishoku* suspension from office

B 偶 $\frac{274}{J3676}$ M899 GŪ even number; couple; man and wife; friend; same kind; doll. *tama no* occasional, rare. *tamasaka* occasionally. *tamatama* casually, unexpectedly; accidentally.
⁹ 発 *gūhatsu* sudden outbreak; accidental, incidental
発的 *gūhatsuteki* accidental, incidental, occasional, casual
¹¹ 偶 *tamatama* casually, unexpectedly, accidentally
¹² 然 *gūzen* chance, accident, fortuity
¹³ 数 *gūsū* even number
¹⁴ 像 *gūzō* image, idol, statue
像視 *gūzōshi* idolization
像崇拝 *gūzō sūhai* idol worship, idolatry

A 側 $\frac{275}{J4226}$ M897 SOKU. *soba(mu) vi* lean to one side, oppose, look aside, regret. *soba(meru)* shove to one side, look at out of the corner of one's eyes. *gawa* a side; surroundings; (watch) case. *hata* side, edge; a third person. *kawa* side; row. *soba* side, vicinity. *katawara* side; besides; while. *hono(kana)* faint, indistinct; stupid; few.
⁶ 近 *sobachika(ku)*, nearby. *sokkin* close associate, braintruster
⁹ 室 *sokushitsu* a noble's concubine
背 *sokuhai* flank
面 *sokumen* side, flank; sidelight; lateral
面図 *sokumenzu* side view
¹⁰ 部 *sokubu* the side
¹⁴ 聞 *sokubun suru* hear casually
¹⁶ 壁 *sokuheki* side wall

B 偽 $\frac{276}{J3536}$ M927' GI. *itsuwa(ru)* lie, falsify; deceive; pretend; deceive, cheat. *nise* sham, counterfeit, forgery, imitation, false (prophet).
⁵ 札 *nise satsu, gisatsu* forged document, counterfeit money
⁶ 名 *gimei* false name, assumed name

2

二十〔人イ⼈〕儿入八丷冂冖冫几凵刀刂力勹匕匚匸十卜卩厂厶又

⁷ 作 *gisaku* apocryphal work, forgery, spurious article
⁸ 物 *nisemono, gibutsu* spurious article, a forgery, counterfeit
⁹ 造 *gizō* forgery, falsification, fabrication, counterfeiting
¹⁰ 称 *gishō suru* assume a false name
¹¹ 悪 *giaku* pretense of evil
¹² 装 *gisō* camouflage
善 *gizen* hypocrisy
善者 *gizensha* hypocrite
証 *gishō* perjury, false testimony
証罪 *gishōzai* crime of perjury

B 偏 | 277 / J4a50 / M848 | HEN side; left radical of a character; inclining.
hen(suru) incline toward, be biased.
katayo(ru) lean, incline; be biased.
katayo(ri) inclination; offset; polarization.
hitoe ni earnestly; humbly; solely.
⁶ 向 *henkō* propensity, inclination; deflection
在 *henzai* maldistribution
⁷ 見 *katayo(ri)-mi(ru)* show partiality.
henken prejudice, narrow view
⁸ 屈 *henkutsu* eccentricity, bigotry, obstinacy
⁹ 食 *henshoku* unbalanced diet
狭 *henkyō* narrow-mindedness; narrowness
重 *henchō suru* make too much of.
henchō, henjū preponderance
¹⁰ 差 *hensa* declination, deflection, variation, deviation, drift
¹¹ 執 *henshū* bias, eccentricity, obstinacy
¹³ 愛 *hen'ai* partiality, favoritism
¹⁶ 頭痛 *henzutsū, hentōtsū* headache on one side; migraine

A 健 | 278 / J3772 / M875 | KEN health, strength; stick-to-itiveness. *suko(yakana)* vigorous, healthy, sound. *shitataka ni* heartily; severely.
⁶ 気 *kenage* courage. *kenage na* manly, heroic, brave; praiseworthy; industrious
全 *kenzen* health, soundness. *kenzen na* healthy, sound, wholesome
在 *kenzai* good health
⁷ 児 *kenji* stalwart youth
忘症 *kembōshō* amnesia, loss of memory
⁹ 胃剤 *ken'izai* stomach medicine
¹¹ 啖家 *kentanka* glutton, gormand-izer
脚 *kenkyaku* good walker
康 *kenkō* health. *kenkō na* sound; wholesome
康体 *kenkōtai* healthy body
康児 *kenkōji* healthy child
康法 *kenkōhō* hygiene
康的 *kenkōteki* hygienic, healthful, sanitary
康美 *kenkōbi* physical beauty
康保険 *kenkō hoken* health insurance
康診断 *kenkō shindan* physical examination
¹² 勝 *kenshō* good health
筆 *kempitsu* powerful pen
¹⁸ 闘 *kentō* good fight, strenuous efforts

─── **10** ───

僅 | 279 / J364f / M-X | Nonstandard for 僅 292.

B 傘 | 283 / J3b31 / M966 | SAN. *kasa* umbrella, parasol. *karakasa* paper umbrella.
³ 下 *sanka* affiliated with; under the jurisdiction of
⁵ 立 *kasata(te)* umbrella stand
¹² 歯車 *kasaguruma* bevel gear

A 備 | 284 / J4877 / M967 | BI. *sona(waru)* be furnished with, be endowed with, possess; be among, be one of. *sona(eru)* furnish, provide, equip, install; have ready; prepare; possess, have; be endowed with; be armed with. *sona(e)* preparation, provision, guarding. *tsubu(sa) ni* in detail, with great care; completely; again and again.
⁵ 付 *sona(e)tsu(ke)* equipment, provision *sona(e)-tsu(keru)* provide, furnish, equip, install
⁶ 考 *bikō* note, remarks, N. B.
⁷ 忘録 *bibōroku* memorandum, notebook
⁹ 品 *bihin* fixtures, furnishings, equipment
¹³ 蓄 *bichiku* stored, reserved

B 偉 | 285 / J304e / M837 | I greatness. *era(garu)* be conceited. *era(i)* great,

famous, remarkable, excellent.
²人 *ijin* great man
力 *iryoku* power, might, authority, influence
³大 *idai* greatness, grandeur
才 *isai* remarkable man
丈夫 *ijōfu* a hero, a great man, a big man
¹⁰容 *iyō* majestic appearance, dignity
¹³業 *igyō* great enterprise, exploits
¹⁸観 *ikan* grand sight

傍 [286] [J4b35] [M948] B Hō . Bō *katawa(ra), waki, soba* side; besides; while. *katawa(ra) no* nearby. *katawa(ra) ni* beside, nearby. *hata* side; edge; a third person.
⁷系 *bōkei* collateral family; subsidiary; affiliated
⁸受 *bōju* interception, tapping
迷惑 *hata meiwaku* inconvenience to those nearby
若無人 *bōjaku-bujin* arrogance, audacity, insolence, defiance
⁹点 *bōten* marks to facilitate reading of Chinese
¹⁵線 *bōsen* side line, underline
¹⁷聴 *bōchō* hearing, attendance, auditing
聴人 *bōchōnin* hearer, auditor, audience
聴席 *bōchōseki* visitor's gallery, seats for the public
¹⁸観 *bōkan suru* look on, remain a spectator
観者 *bōkansha* bystander, onlooker
観的 *bōkanteki ni* as a spectator

─────── **11** ───────

僅 [292] [J-X] [M1048] 僅 [279] [J364f] [M-X] KIN. *wazu(ka)* a little, a small quantity.
⁴少 *kinshō* few, little, insignificant
¹⁰差 *kinsa* narrow majority; a shade of difference
¹³僅 *kinkin* merely, no more than

傑 [293] [J3766] [M955] B KETSU excellence. *sugu(reru)* excel.
⁵出 *kesshutsu suru* excel, be foremost
⁷作 *kessaku* masterpiece; gross mistake, blunder
⁸物 *ketsubutsu* remarkable character, great man

傭 [295] [J4d43] [M1007] YŌ . *yato(u)* employ, hire.
⁷兵 *yōhei, yato(i)hei* mercenary soldier

債 [296] [J3a44] [M1022] B SAI debt; loan.
⁸券 *saiken* bond, debenture
¹¹務 *saimu* debt; liabilities
務者 *saimusha* debtor
¹⁵権 *saiken* credit; claim
権者 *saikensha* creditor

働 [297] [J462f] [M1079] (国字) DŌ . *hatara(ku)* A work, labor; do, act, commit, practice; work on; come into play; be conjugated; reduce the price. *hatara(ki)* work, labor; action, function, operation; movement, motion; conjugation, inflection; talent; achievement.
³口 *hatara(ki)guchi* position, opening
⁴手 *hatara(ki)te, hatara(ki)de* a worker; a good worker, a breadwinner, an able worker
⁸者 *hatara(ki)mono* hard worker
¹⁰振 *hatara(ki)bu(ri)* way of working, discharge of duty
¹¹掛 *hatara(ki)-ka(keru)* work on someone, influence, appeal to; begin to work
盛 *hatara(ki)zaka(ri)* prime of life
¹³蜂 *hatara(ki)bachi* worker bee

催 [298] [J3a45] [M1005] B SAI. *moyō(su)* hold (a meeting); give (a dinner); feel; show signs of, develop symptoms of, feel (sick). *moyō(shi)* meeting, gathering; (bodily) urge.
⁷告 *saikoku* notification
⁸物 *moyō(shi)mono* points of interest; tourist attraction; an exhibit; events
⁹促 *saisoku suru* demand, request, urge (action), press for
促状 *saisokujō* dun, letter requesting money, etc.
¹⁰涙瓦斯 *sairui gasu* tear gas
涙弾 *sairuidan* tear-gas bomb
眠術 *saiminjutsu* hypnotism

傾 [299] [J3739] [M1038] B KEI. *kashi(gu)* vi lean, incline, tilt, list, tip, careen, lurch. *kashi(geru)* vt lean, incline, tilt.

katamu(ku), katabu(ku), kata(gu) incline
toward, tilt, slant, slope, lurch, heel over;
be disposed to; trend toward, be prone to;
go down (sun); wane, sink, decline.
katamu(keru) vt incline, list, bend, lean,
tip, tilt, slant; concentrate on; devote to;
ruin; squander; empty. *kata(geru)* vt
incline, tilt, slant. *nada(reru)* slope,
descend, slide (snow, etc.). *katamu(ki)*
slope, inclination, list; tendency, trend;
bent; disposition, bias. *nada(re)*
avalanche; snowslide; slope, sloping;
surging (crowd).

6 向 *keikō* tendency, trend; disposition
8 国 *keikoku* a matchless beauty, a siren
注 *keichū* devotion, concentration
9 城 *keisei* a matchless beauty, a siren
10 倒 *katamu(ke)-tao(su)* cast down, lay
low. *keitō suru* devote oneself to,
concentrate on; admire, idolize
11 斜 *keisha* inclination, level, slope, list,
dip
17 聴 *keichō* listening closely

僧 300
J414e
M1076
B Sō monk,
priest.
5 尼 *sōni* monks and nuns
正 *sōjō* high priest of a Buddhist sect
7 坊 *sōbō* priests' quarters
8 房 *sōbō* priests' temple quarters
服 *sōfuku* priest's garb
9 俗 *sōzoku* priests and laymen
侶 *sōryo* (Buddhist) priest, monk
院 *sōin* monastery, temple
18 職 *sōshoku* (Buddhist) priesthood
20 籍 *sōseki* (Buddhist) priesthood

傷 301
J3d7d
M1029
A SHŌ wound, injury. *ita(mu)*
feel a pain, hurt; be hurt,
be damaged, be spoiled, be bruised, wear
out, be worn out. *ita(meru)* hurt, injure,
impair, spoil, worry, bother, afflict, cause
pain. *kizu* wound, injury, hurt; cut, gash,
bruise, scratch; scar; weak point. *ita(mi)*
pain, ache.
3 口 *kizuguchi* wound
4 心 *shōshin* heartbreak, grief
5 付 *kizutsu(keru)* wound, injure; damage,
mar; disgrace. *kizutsu(ku)* get injured,
be wounded
8 物 *kizumono* defective article, damaged
goods

10 害 *shōgai* wound, injury, accident,
casualty
害保険 *shōgai hoken* accident
insurance
病 *shōbyō* injuries and sickness
11 痕 *kizuato, shōkon* scar
13 跡 *kizuato* scar
16 薬 *kizugusuri* salve, ointment

———— **12** ————

僑 307
J3623
M1088
Kyō temporary home.

像 308
J417c
M1084
A Zō image, statue, figure,
picture, portrait.

僕 313
J4b4d
M1094
B BOKU manservant, I (used
by male speakers.
shimobe manservant; servant (of God).

僚 314
J4e3d
M1100
B RYŌ official; companion.

———— **13** ————

億 321
J322f
M1178
A OKU 100,000,000.
3 万長者 *okumanchōja* billionaire
6 兆 *okuchō* people, multitude, masses
7 劫 *okkū na* troublesome, annoying

舗 322
J4a5e
M30323'
鋪 6269
J4a5f
M40491
B Ho shop,
store; pave
11 道 *hodō* pavement; paved street
12 装 *hosō* paving

僻 323
J4a48
M1166
HEKI prejudice, bias; rural
area. *heki(suru)* be biased,
be warped. *higa(mu)* be prejudiced, be
soured. *higami* prejudice, bias; inferiority
complex. *higa-* evil, untrue, erroneous.
6 地 *hekichi* remote place
7 村 *hekison* remote village
12 遠 *hekien no* remote, outlying

儀 324
J3537
M1172
B GI rule; ceremony; affair,
case, a matter.
5 仗 *gijō* cortege, guard
仗兵 *gijōhei* guard of honor
礼 *girei* courtesy, etiquette
礼的 *gireiteki* formal

⁶式 *gishiki* ceremony, rite, ritual, service
⁸典 *giten* ceremony, rite, ritual, service

―――――― 14 ――――――

儘 327 J5056 M1234　侭 170 J4b79 M-X JIN. *mama* as it is; as one likes; because.

B 儒 330 J3c74 M1220 JU Confucianism; Confucianist; Chinese scholar.

⁸者 *Jusha* a Confucianist
学 *Jugaku* Confucianism
¹¹教 *Jukyō* Confucianism

―――――― 15 ――――――

儲 331 J4c59 M-X See 儲 335.

B 償 333 J3d7e M1245 SHŌ. *tsuguna(u)* make up for, recompense, redeem (one's faults), compensate for, indemnify, atone for.

⁷却 *shōkyaku* repayment, redemption, amortization
⁸金 *shōkin* reparation, redemption
¹⁵還 *shōkan* repayment, redemption, amortization

A 優 334 J4d25 M1261 YŪ actor; superiority; gentleness. *sugu(reru)* excel, surpass; have advantages over; be excellent. *masa(ru)* excel, surpass, outrival. *yasa(shii)* gentle, tender, graceful, affectionate, kind, amiable, suave. *yasa-* gentle, affectionate. *yasa(shige) na* gentle, kind, sweet-looking. *yū ni* easily, amply, sufficiently, well, skillfully.

⁵生学 *yūseigaku* eugenics
⁶劣 *yūretsu* superiority or inferiority, quality
先 *yūsen* preference, priority
先的 *yūsenteki* preferential
先権 *yūsenken* priority, preference, preferential right
⁷位 *yūi* predominance, ascendancy, superiority
秀 *yūshū* excellence, superiority
良 *yūryō* excellence, superiority
⁹美 *yūbi* grace, refinement, elegance
待 *yūtai suru* treat kindly, receive hospitably, welcome
待券 *yūtaiken* complimentary ticket
柔不断 *yūjū-fudan* indecisiveness
¹¹遇 *yūgū* hearty welcome, hospitality, good treatment
¹²越 *yūetsu* supremacy, predominance
越感 *yūetsukan* superiority complex
越権 *yūetsuken* special rights, predominant rights
等 *yūtō* excellency, superiority
等生 *yūtōsei* honor student
等賞 *yūtōshō* honor prize
勝 *yūshō* victory, championship
勝杯 *yūshōhai* championship cup
勝旗 *yūshōki* championship pennant
¹³雅 *yūga* elegance, refinement
勢 *yūsei* superiority, superior power, preponderance, predominance

―――――― 16 ――――――

儲 335 J-X M1284　儲 331 J4c59 M-X CHO. *mō(karu)* be profitable, yield a profit. *mō(keru)* get, earn, gain. *mōke* profits, earnings.

³口 *mōkeguchi* profitable job
⁸物 *mōkemono* good bargain; a find

■■■■■ RAD. 儿 10 ■■■■■

Hito-ashi human legs. Nickname: Legs.

―――――― 2 ――――――

允 342 J3074 M1338 IN sincerity; permit.

¹¹許 *inkyo* permission, license

A 元 343 J3835 M1340 GAN, GEN yuan; origin; New Year's Day; first year

2

二 亠 人 イ 八 〔儿〕 入 八 丷 冂 冖 冫 几 凵 刀 刂 力 勹 匕 匚 匸 十 卜 卩 厂 厶 又

of an era. GEN Mongol (dynasty). *moto* beginning, origin; foundation, basis, source; cause; root (of a tree); (raw) material, base; capital; principal; cost; forebears; formerly. *moto(yori)* originally; of course.

⁴手 *motode* funds, capital, stock
　日 *Ganjitsu* New Year's Day
　凶 *genkyō* ringleader
　元 *motomoto* from the first, originally; by nature, naturally
⁵払 *motobara(i)* prepayment
　旦 *Gantan* New Year's morning; New Year's Day
　本 *gampon* principal, capital
　号 *gengō* era name
⁶兇 *genkyō* ringleader
　年 *gannen* first year (of a reign)
　老 *genrō* elder statesman, veteran, authority
　気 *genki* vigor, energy, vitality, vim, stamina, spirit, courage, pep
　気付 *genkizu(keru)* vt pep up, cheer up
　気者 *genkimono* a live wire (a person)
⁷利 *ganri* principal and interest
　来 *ganrai* originally, primarily, logically, naturally, essentially
⁸金 *motokin, gankin* capital, principal
　価 *genka* cost price
　始 *genshi* origin
⁹首 *genshu* ruler, sovereign
　通 *motodō(ri)* as ever, as before
　祖 *ganso* originator, founder, pioneer, inventor
¹⁰値 *motone* cost
　素 *genso* element
¹¹寇 *Genkō* the Mongol Invasion
¹⁵締 *motoji(me)* manager, boss, promoter
　勲 *genkun* elder statesman

————— **3** —————

A 兄 $\frac{344}{\text{J373b} \atop \text{M1343}}$ KEI brother; you. KYŌ . *ani*, *nii(san)* elder brother. *se* a women's familiar call for her husband or elder brother.

⁷弟 *kyōdai, keitei, anioto, aniotōto* brother, brethren
　弟子 *anideshi* senior schoolmate, senior apprentice
　弟分 *kyōdaibun* buddy, pal, sworn brother
　弟姉妹 *keitei-shimai* brothers and sisters, brethren
¹²貴 *aniki* elder brother, one's senior

————— **4** —————

A 兆 $\frac{346}{\text{J437b} \atop \text{M1347}}$ CHŌ sign, omen, indication, portent; trillion. *kiza(su)* show signs or symptoms of. *kizashi* signs, omen, symptoms.

¹⁰候 *chōkō* sign, indication, omen, symptom

兇 $\frac{347}{\text{J3624} \atop \text{M1348}}$ KYŌ wickedness.

³刃 *kyōjin* assassin's dagger
⁶行 *kyōkō* violence, murder, crime
⁷状 *kyōjō* crime, offense
　状持 *kyōjōmo(chi)* a criminal
⁹変 *kyōhen* catastrophe; assassination
¹¹悪 *kyōaku na* atrocious, fiendish, brutal
¹³漢 *kyōkan* villain, outlaw, assassin
¹⁵暴 *kyōbō* brutality, ferocity, atrocity
　器 *kyōki* dangerous weapon

B 充 $\frac{348}{\text{J3d3c} \atop \text{M1345}}$ JŪ fill. *ate(ru)* apply, place, put; hit (the mark); guess; succeed; expose to; sit (on a cushion); assign, allocate; call on (a pupil). *mi(chiru)* be full; mature, expire. *mi(tasu)* fill; supply, make good; satisfy, appease, answer (the need), meet (the demand).

⁴分 *jūbun* enough; satisfactory, adequate; perfect; thorough
⁶血 *jūketsu* congestion (medical); engorgement
　当 *jūtō suru* allot, appropriate
⁷足 *jūsoku* sufficiency
⁸実 *jūjitsu* substantiality; fullness, completion, perfection. *jūjitsu shita* full, complete; replete with; substantial (meal), solid (reading)
¹²満 *jūman suru, michimichi(te) iru* be filled with, be pregnant with, teem with
¹³電 *jūden* charging (batteries)
　電器 *jūdenki* charger

A 光 ³⁴⁹ J3877 M1350 **Kō** light. *hika(ru)* shine, glitter, sparkle, twinkle, flash. *hika(rakasu), hika(rasu)* show one's authority, strut around; shine (a light) on. *hikari* light, beam, flash, glare, gleam, twinkle, sparkle, glimmer, glow, brightness, radiance, glitter, luster; influence (of parents).

⁴化学 *kōkagaku* photochemistry
⁶芒 *kōbō* shaft of light, flash of lightning
 年 *kōnen* light year
 合成 *kōgōsei* photosynthesis
⁷束 *kōsoku* a beam of light
 沢 *kōtaku* brilliance, polish, luster
⁸波 *kōha* light wave
 明 *kōmyō* light, hope, bright future; glory; halo
 学 *kōgaku* optics
⁹速 *kōsoku* speed of light
 栄 *kōei* honor, glory; privilege
 度 *kōdo* brightness, luminosity
¹⁰陰 *kōin* time
¹¹彩 *kōsai* brilliance, splendor
¹²景 *kōkei* scene, spectacle; aspect
¹³源 *kōgen* light source
¹⁵線 *kōsen* light; light ray, beam
 輝 *hika(ri)-kagaya(ku)* shine, glitter. *kōki* brightness, splendor
 熱 *kōnetsu* light and heat
 熱費 *kōnetsuhi* fuel-and-light expense, utilities
¹⁷臨 *kōrin* our visit, your company

A 先 ³⁵⁰ J4068 M1349 **Sen** the future; priority, precedence. *saki(njiru), saki(nzuru)* precede; forestall, anticipate. *saki* point, tip, end; nozzle; head (of a line); the first priority; the future; objective, destination; sequel, remainder; the other party; future. *saki no* previous, prior. *saki ni* before, earlier than; ahead, beyond, away; previously; recently. *ma(zu)* first (of all); about, almost, hardly (with neg.); anyway; well, now. *sen ni* formerly. *sen no* former, previous, old, late.

²人 *senjin* predecessor, pioneer, ancestor
 入 *sennyū* preconception, prejudice
 入主 *sennyūshu* preconception, prejudice
 入観 *sennyūkan* preconception, prejudice, preoccupation

³口 *senkuchi* previous application; previous engagement
⁴手 *sente* the first move; initiative, forestalling. *sakite* front lines, vanguard
 方 *sempō* the other party, he, they; destination. *sakikata* the person in front; companion
 日 *senjitsu, saki(no)hi* the other day, a few days ago
 月 *sengetsu* last month
 天性 *sentensei* hereditary
 天的 *sententeki* inborn, innate, inherent, congenital, hereditary
⁵生 *sensei* teacher, master, doctor
 立 *sakida(tsu)* go before, precede; die before; take precedence *sakida(teru)* have (someone) go ahead
 付 *sakizu(ke)* dating forward
 代 *sendai* family predecessor; previous age; previous generation
 払 *sakibara(i)* advance payment; payment on delivery; forerunner
 史学 *senshigaku* prehistory
⁶行 *sakiyu(ki), sakii(ki)* the future. *senkō* preceding, going first
 回 *sakimawa(ri)* going on ahead; forestalling; anticipating; arrival before another
 年 *sennen* former years, formerly, a few years ago
 先 *ma(zu)ma(zu)* tolerable. *sakizaki* the distant future; places one visits. *mama* well, well
先月 *sensengetsu* month before last
 任 *sennin* seniority, predecessor
⁷走 *sakibashi(ru)* be forward, be impertinent
 攻 *senkō* batting first
 見明 *senken (no) mei* foresight, anticipation
 住民族 *senjū minzoku* aborigines
 住者 *senjūsha* former occupant
 決 *senketsu* previous decision, prior settlement
 決問題 *senketsu mondai* question to be settled first
⁸例 *senrei* precedent
 制 *sensei* headstart (of several runs)
 刻 *senkoku* already, a while ago
 夜 *sen'ya* a few nights ago
 妻 *sensai* former wife; late wife

2

二
十
人
イ
入
【儿】⁴
入
八
ハ
冂
宀
冫
几
凵
刀
刂
力
勹
匕
匚
匸
十
卜
卩
厂
厶
又

取 *senshu suru* earn the first (runs); preoccupy. *sakido(ri)* taking before others

⁹ 約 *sen'yaku* previous engagement; prior contract

陣 *senjin* vanguard, advance guard

客 *senkyaku* the preceding visitor

祖 *saki(no)oya, saki(tsu)oya, senzo* ancestor

祖伝来 *senzo-denrai no* inherited

発 *sempatsu* forerunner, advance party. *sempatsu suru* go on ahead

¹⁰ 週 *senshū* last week

進 *senshin* seniority; advance; leadership

進国 *senshinkoku* advanced nations

般 *sempan* the other day, some time ago

¹¹ 達 *sendatsu* guide, leader, pioneer. *senda(tte)* recently, the other day

頃 *sakigoro, senkoro* recently, the other day

¹² 程 *sakihodo* some time ago

着 *senchaku* first arrival

遣 *senken suru* send ahead

覚者 *senkakusha* seer, pioneer, leading spirit, enlightened person

¹³ 触 *sakibu(re)* previous or preliminary announcement

¹⁴ 端 *sentan* pointed end, tip; fine point; cusp; spearhead, vanguard

導 *sendō* guidance, leadership

駆 *sakiga(keru)* be the first. *sakiga(ke)* charging ahead of others; the first to charge; the initiative, the lead; pioneer, forerunner, harbinger. *senku* outrider, forerunner; pilot car; pioneer, herald, precursor

駆者 *senkusha* pioneer, forerunner

¹⁵ 鋭 *sen'ei* radical; acute

輩 *sempai* senior, superior, elder, older graduate; progenitor; old-timer

¹⁶ 頭 *sentō* the head, the lead, the van, the first; advance guard

¹⁸ 鞭 *semben* initiative; pioneering

––––––– 5 –––––––

克 $\frac{354}{\text{J396e} \\ \text{M1355}}$ Koku. *ka(tsu)* win; prevail,
B predominate, surpass. *yo(ku)* kindly; skillfully.

³ 己 *kokki* self-denial, self-control

己心 *kokkishin* spirit of self-denial

⁸ 明 *kokumei* faithfulness, diligence, conscientiousness

服 *kokufuku* subjugation, conquest

児 $\frac{355}{\text{J3b79} \\ \text{M1364}}$ JI, NI child. *ko* child;
A the young of animals.
chigo baby, child; page; festive children.

³ 女 *jijo* boys and girls; children

¹² 童 *jidō* child, juvenile

童文学 *jidō bungaku* juvenile literature

童心理学 *jidō shinrigaku* child psychology

童福祉 *jidō fukushi* child welfare

¹⁵ 戯 *jigi* mere child's play

兎 $\frac{358}{\text{J4546} \\ \text{M-X}}$ To. *usagi* rabbit, hare,
cony.

––––––– 6 –––––––

免 $\frac{361}{\text{J4c48} \\ \text{M-X}}$ MEN dismissal.
B *manuga(reru), manuka(reru)*
escape from, be rescued from, avoid, evade, avert, elude, be exempted, be relieved from pain, get rid of. *men(jiru), men(zuru)* dismiss; exempt. *(ni) men(jite)* in deference to.

⁷ 状 *menjō* diploma; license

⁸ 官 *menkan* dismissal, discharge

⁹ 除 *menjo* exemption, discharge, exoneration

疫 *men'eki* immunity; immunization

¹¹ 責 *menseki* exemption from responsibility

許 *menkyo* license, certificate, permit

許状 *menkyojō* license, certificate, permit

許証 *menkyoshō* license, permit

¹² 税 *menzei* tax exemption; duty exemption

税店 *menzeiten* duty-free shop

税品 *menzeihin* duty-free articles

¹³ 罪 *menzai* acquittal, pardon; papal indulgence

罪符 *menzaifu* an indulgence

¹⁸ 職 *menshoku* dismissal, discharge

––––––– 8 –––––––

党 $\frac{363}{\text{J455e} \\ \text{M1381}}$ Tō party, faction, clique;
A companions.

tō(suru) side with, make common cause with.
⁷利 tōri party interests
利党略 tōri-tōryaku (thinking of) party interests and policies
⁹首 tōshu party leader
則 tōsoku party rules
是 tōze party platform
派 tōha party, faction, clique
¹⁰員 tōin party member, partisan
¹¹略 tōryaku party policy, party platform

規 tōki party regulations
¹²費 tōhi party expenses; party dues
²⁰籍 tōseki party registration, membership (in a party)

— 9 —

兜 [364 J3375 M1386] Tō. To. kabuto helmet, headpiece.
⁶虫 kabuto mushi beetle

━━━━ RAD. 入 11 ━━━━

Iru enter. At top: 𠆢 *iri-yane* "entering" roof or *iri-gashira*
"entering" top. Nickname: Entering.
Note that it is often very difficult to distinguish between Rads. 9 and 11
when these occur at the top as *hito-yane* and *iri-yane*; therefore,
we have treated all such cases as Rad. 9.

A 入 [366 J467e M1415] Nyū. Ju. i(ru) go in, come in; flow into; set; set in. hai(ru) enter; break into; join; enroll; contain, hold; accommodate; have (an income of). i(reru) put in, take in, bring in, let in, admit, introduce, commit (to prison), usher in; insert; set (jewels); employ; listen to; tolerate, comprehend; include; pay (interest); cast (votes). i(ri) entering, setting (of the sun); audience; capacity; income; beginning. -i(re) container, receptacle.
³口 irikuchi, iriguchi, hai(ri)guchi entrance, gate, approach, mouth
⁴日 i(ri)hi setting sun
水 jusui, nyūsui suicide by drowning, drowning oneself
手 nyūshu receipt, procurement
⁵用 i(ri)yō, nyūyō need, demand, necessity
札 nyūsatsu bid, bidding
⁶舟 i(ri)bune, i(ri)fune incoming ship; ship's arrival
江 i(ri)e inlet, cove, creek, bay
交 i(ri)-ma(jiru) mix with, be mixed. i(re)-ma(zeru) vt mix
会 nyūkai admission, joining, enrollment
会金 nyūkaikin admission fee, initiation fee
会者 nyūkaisha entrant, new member

⁷廷 nyūtei admission to the courtroom
乱 i(ri)-mida(reru) be jumbled together
社 nyūsha joining a company
⁸金 nyūkin payment, money received; money due
門 nyūmon entering an institute; primer; manual; introduction to
門者 nyūmonsha beginner
所 nyūsho entrance, admission; imprisonment, internment
念 nyūnen ni with scrupulous care
知恵 i(re)jie suggestion, hint
国 nyūkoku, nyūgoku entering a country
学 nyūgaku matriculation
学生 nyūgakusei new student
学式 nyūgakushiki entrance ceremony
学金 nyūgakukin matriculation fee
学試験 nyūgaku shiken entrance examinations
学願書 nyūgaku gansho application for admittance to a school
⁹信 nyūshin entering the faith
城 nyūjō triumphant entry into a castle
室 nyūshitsu entering a room
院 nyūin hospitalization
院患者 nyūin kanja in-patients
¹⁰庫 nyūko warehousing, storing; entering the car barn
梅 nyūbai entering the rainy season
浴 nyūyoku bath, bathing

2

党 *nyūtō* joining a political party

荷 *nyūka, i(ri)ni* arrival of goods; goods received

[11] 組 *i(ri)-ku(mu)* be or become complicated

隊 *nyūtai* enlistment

道雲 *nyūdōgumo* great columns of clouds; cumulo-nimbus

[12] 歯 *i(re)ba* artificial tooth, denture

超 *nyūchō* excess of imports

違 *i(re)-chiga(eru)* misplace. *i(re)chiga(i)* passing each other

植 *nyūshoku* settlement, immigration

港 *nyūkō* entering a port

湯客 *nyūtōkyaku* a bathing guest at a hot spring

場 *nyūjō* admission; entrance, entering

場券 *nyūjōken* admission ticket; platform ticket

場者 *nyūjōsha* visitors, attendance

場料 *nyūjōryō* admission fee, gate receipts

[13] 試 *nyūshi* entrance examinations

電 *nyūden* telegram received

[14] 閣 *nyūkaku* joining the cabinet

獄 *nyūgoku* imprisonment

墨 *i(re)zumi* tattooing

選 *nyūsen* chosen (in a competition)

選者 *nyūsensha* winner, winning candidate

漁料 *nyūgyoryō* fishing-lot charge

[15] 賞 *nyūshō* winning a prize

[20] 籍 *nyūseki* entrance in the family register

RAD. 八 12

Hachi eight. At top: 八 or *hachigashira*. Variants: 八 and 丷. Nickname: Eight.

A 八 369 J482c M1450 HATSU, HACHI *ya(tsu), ya(ttsu), ya* eight. *(o)ya(tsu)* between-meal snack.

[2] 九分 *hakkubu* nearly, almost

[4] 日 *yōka* eight days; the eighth (day of the month)

月 *Hachigatsu* August

分目 *hachibumme, hachibume* eight-tenths; moderation

方 *happō* all sides, directions, quarters, or corners

方美人 *happō-bijin* a person beautiful from all angles; everybody's friend

方塞 *happō fusaga(ri)* all doors closed, blocked in every direction

[6] 当 *ya(tsu)ata(ri)* outburst of anger. *ya(tsu)ata(ri) ni* indiscriminately, recklessly

百長 *yaochō* put-up job, prearranged affair, logrolling

百屋 *yaoya* vegetable store; Jack-of-all-trades; dabbling in all lines of knowledge

[7] 角形 *hakkakkei* octagon

[8] 卦 *hakke* eight divination signs; divination

[9] 面 *hachimen* eight faces; all sides

面六臂 *hachimen-roppi* eight faces and six arms; versatile, all-round, many-sided

重咲 *yaeza(ki)* double blossom

重桜 *yaezakura* double cherry blossoms

重歯 *yaeba* double tooth; oblique tooth

[15] 幡 *Hachiman* God of War; shrine of the God of War

幡宮 *Hachimangū* Shrine of the God of War

--- 2 ---

A 六 371 J4f3b M1453 RIKU, ROKU *mu(tsu), mu(ttsu), mu* six. *mu(zukashii)* hard, difficult; delicate; troublesome; doubtful; hopeless; stern; sullen; hard to please; serious; technical.

[3] 三制 *roku-sansei* 6-3 system of education

[4] 日 *muika* six days; the sixth (day of the month)

月 *Rokugatsu* June

分儀 *rokubungi* sextant

[7] 角形 *rokkakukei* hexagon

[8] 法全書 *Roppō Zensho* the Statute Books

A 公 372 J3878 M1452 KŌ prince, duke, lord; public. KU. *ōyake* public,

open; official, governmental; formal. *kimi*
prince, lord. -*kō* lord, daimyo;
companion; a subordinate.

² 人 *kōjin* public character
⁴ 文書 *kōbunsho* official document;
archives
⁵ 示 *kōji* public announcement
布 *kōfu* proclamation, announcement
立 *kōritsu* public (institution)
立学校 *koritsu gakkō* public school
正 *kōsei* justice, fairness, impartiality
正証書 *kōsei shōsho* notarized
document
用 *kōyō* government business; public
use; public expense
用文 *kōyōbun* official terminology
用車 *kōyōsha* official vehicle
平 *kōhei* justice, fairness
平無私 *kōhei-mushi* impartiality, fair
play
民 *kōmin* citizens, freemen
民権 *kōminken* civil rights, citizenship,
franchise
民館 *kōminkan* public hall, community
center
⁶ 団 *kōdan* public corporation
休日 *kōkyūbi* national holiday
安 *kōan* public welfare, public safety
式 *koshiki* formula; formality
会堂 *kōkaidō* public hall; town hall
有 *kōyū* public ownership
有地 *kōyūchi* public land
共 *kōkyō* society, the community. *kōkyō
no* public, communal
共団体 *kōkyō dantai* public
organization
共物 *kōkyōbutsu* public property
共事業 *kōkyō jigyō* public utilities
⁷ 言 *kōgen* declaration, profession
私 *kōshi* government and people; public
and personal affairs. *kōshi no* public
and private
邸 *kōtei* official residence
告 *kōkoku* public notice
社 *kōsha* public corporation
判 *kōhan* public hearing, trial
⁸ 金 *kōkin* public funds
的 *kōteki* public, official
表 *kōhyō* official proclamation
使 *kōshi* minister (of a legation)
使館 *kōshikan* legation
明 *kōmei* fairness, justice

明正大 *kōmei-seidai* fairness, justice
定価格 *kōtei kakaku* ceiling or fixed
price
定相場 *kōtei sōba* ceiling price, official
quotation
⁹ 約 *kōyaku* public commitment or
promise
海 *kōkai* high seas
¹⁰ 庫 *kōko* finance corporation
租 *kōso* public tax
家 *kuge* Imperial Court; court noble
害 *kōgai* pollution
差 *kōsa* common difference (in math);
allowance, margin, tolerance
孫樹 *ichō* gingko or maidenhair tree
称 *kōshō* public name, announcing
publicly
益 *kōeki* public good
益法人 *kōeki hōjin* legal person
working for the public weal
¹¹ 道 *kōdō* public highway; justice
転 *kōten* revolution (around the sun)
務 *kōmu* public service, official business
務員 *kōmuin* government worker
¹² 評 *kōhyō* popular opinion
訴 *kōso* accusation, prosecution
募 *kōbo* public appeal, public
contribution
営 *kōei* public management
費 *kōhi* public expenditure
報 *kōhō* official bulletin, communiqué
然 *kōzen no* open, avowed, public,
official
証人 *kōshōnin* notary public
開 *kōkai suru* present to the public
開講座 *kōkai kōza* extension lectures
衆 *kōshū* the public
衆便所 *kōshū benjo* public lavatory
衆浴場 *kōshū yokujō* public bathhouse
衆道徳 *kōshū dōtoku* public morals
衆電話 *kōshū denwa* public telephone
衆衛生 *kōshū eisei* public health and
sanitation
¹³ 園 *kōen* park
債 *kōsai* public debt, public bond or
securities
電 *kōden* official telegram
¹⁴ 選 *kōsen* public election
僕 *kōboku* public servant
演 *kōen* public performance
算 *kōsan* probability
徳心 *kōtokushin* public spirit

2

二
十
人
イ
八
儿
入
【八〃】
冂
〇
冫
几
凵
刀
刂
力
勹
匕
匚
匸
十
卜
卩
厂
厶
又

認 *kōnin* official authorization, recognition, license, accreditation

認会計士 *kōnin kaikeishi* certified public accountant

認候補 *kōnin kōho* official candidate

15 儀 *kōgi* imperial court; shogunate government; authorities; public affairs. *kōgi no* official, government

論 *kōron* public opinion, unbiased criticism

課 *kōka* public imposts, taxes

16 館 *kōkan* official residence

17 聴会 *kōchōkai* public hearing

爵 *kōshaku* prince, duke

18 職 *kōshoku* public office

————— 4 —————

共 373 J3626 M1458 A KYŌ. *tomo* both; neither (with neg.); all; and, as well as; including; with, together with; plural ending. *tomo ni suru* share with, participate in. *tomo ni* both; alike; together, along with, with; including. *(to) tomo ni* together with.

5 用 *kyōyō* common use

犯 *kyōhan* complicity

犯者 *kyōhansha* accomplice

6 共 *tomodomo ni* together, in company

存 *kyōson, kyōzon* coexistence

存共栄 *kyōson-kyōei* coexistence and coprosperity

有 *kyōyū* joint ownership

有地 *kyōyūchi* public land; a common

有物 *kyōyūbutsu* common property

有者 *kyōyūsha* joint owners, part owners

有財産 *kyōyū zaisan* community property

同 *kyōdō* cooperation, collaboration, association; joint (defense)

同生活 *kyōdō seikatsu* community life; cohabitation

同会見 *kyōdō kaiken* news conference

同体 *kyōdōtai* cooperative body; cooperative system

同住宅 *kyōdō jūtaku* a settlement; an apartment house

同声明 *kyōdō seimei* joint declaration

同責任 *kyōdō sekinin* joint responsibility; solidarity

同組合 *kyōdō kumiai* a cooperative; a partnership

同募金 *kyōdō bokin* community chest

同墓地 *kyōdō bochi* public cemetery

同戦線 *kyōdō sensen* united front

7 助 *kyōjo* cooperation

8 学 *kyōgaku* coeducation

和国 *kyōwakoku* republic

和制 *kyōwasei* republicanism

和党 *Kyōwatō* Republican Party

9 食 *tomogu(i)* cannibalism (in animals), mutual destruction, internecine struggle, eating each other; damaging each other

栄 *kyōei* mutual prosperity

通 *kyōtsū no* common

通点 *kyōtsūten* common feature

通語 *kyōtsūgo* common term, common language

10 倒 *tomodao(re)* falling together, mutual destruction, joint bankruptcy

11 訳 *kyōyaku* joint translation

著 *kyōcho* coauthorship

済組合 *kyōsai kumiai* a cooperative society, a mutual-benefit association

産主義 *kyōsan shugi* communism, collectivism

産主義者 *kyōsan shugisha* a communist

産党 *Kyōsantō* Communist Party

12 営 *kyōei* joint management

13 催 *kyōsai* two or more organizations sponsoring a meeting together

感 *kyōkan* sympathy, response

14 鳴 *kyōmei, tomona(ri)* resonance, sympathy

演 *kyōen* coacting, costarring

15 稼 *tomokase(gi)* (husband and wife) earning a living together

編 *kyōhen* joint editorship

16 謀 *kyōbō* conspiracy, complicity

————— 5 —————

兵 374 J4a3c M1462 A HEI, HYŌ soldier, private; troops, army; warfare; arms; strategy, tactics. *tsuwamono* soldier, warrior.

2 力 *heiryoku* military force; force of arms; strength of an army

3 士 *heishi* soldier

4 火 *heika* fire caused by war

6 団 *heidan* army corps

7 役 *heieki* military service

⁸卒 *heisotsu* soldier, private
舎 *heisha* barracks
法 *heihō* art of war, strategy, tactics
学 *heigaku* military science, strategy, tactics
⁹変 *heihen* military disturbance
¹⁰馬 *heiba* arms and cavalry; troops; war; military affairs
員 *heiin* military strength, military personnel
站 *heitan* supply train, communications
¹¹隊 *heitai* soldier; sailor
¹²備 *heibi* war preparations
営 *heiei* barracks
¹⁴端 *heitan* hostilities; beginning of hostilities
¹⁵器 *heiki* arms, ordnance
¹⁸糧 *hyōrō* (army) provisions; food
糧攻 *hyōrōze(me)* starvation tactics

————— **6** —————

典 _{375 J4535 M1474} TEN ceremony, celebration; law code. *nori* rule, law.
A
⁵礼 *tenrei* ceremony; etiquette, courtesy; (Catholic) liturgy
⁸拠 *tenkyo* authority
⁹故 *tenko* authentic precedent
型 *tenkei* type, pattern
型的 *tenkeiteki* typical, model, ideal
¹³雅 *tenga na* refined, graceful, elegant, classic

具 _{376 J3671 M1473} GU tool; vessel; means; ingredients (in a dish);
A
counter for armor, suits, sets of furniture. *gu(suru)* possess, have; be accompanied by. *sona(waru)* be furnished with, be endowed with, possess; be among, be one of. *sona(eru)* furnish, provide, equip, install; have ready; prepare; possess, have; be endowed with; be armed with. *tsubusa ni* minutely, fully.
⁵申 *gushin* reporting (to a superior)
⁶合 *guai* fitness, order, condition; way, style; convenience; decency; propriety; state of health; situation; arrangements
⁷体 *gutai* concreteness
体化 *gutaika* embodiment, materialization
体的 *gutaiteki* concrete, tangible,

definite
体策 *gutaisaku* concrete plan
¹¹現 *gugen* incarnation, embodiment
¹²備 *gubi suru* have, possess, be endowed with
象 *gushō suru* embody, express concretely
象的 *gushōteki* concrete, material

其 _{378 J4236 M1472} KI. *so(no)* that (adj.). *sore* that, it. *sore da kara* therefore. *sore datte* but. *sore de* thereupon, therefore. *sore de koso* all the more. *sore da noni, sore na noni* nevertheless. *sore wa sō toshite* be that as it may. *sore tomo* or. *sore ja, sore dewa* then, in that case; well. *sore demo* nevertheless. *sore kara* after that; since; and then, and; from then on. *sore koso* the very thing. *sore nara* if so. *sore ni* besides, moreover, what is more. *sore ni shite mo* even so, nevertheless. *sore ni shite wa* considering that. *sore wa sō to* but now, to change the subject.
³上 *so(no)ue* on top of that, over and above, in addition, besides
丈 *sore dake* that much; only that; only that much. *soredake ni* all the more because
⁴辺 *so(no) hen* thereabouts, in the neighborhood
手 *so(no) te* that trick, that move, that ⌐way
内 *so(no) uchi* soon, before long; some day; meanwhile; among the number
日暮 *so(no)higura(shi)* hand-to-mouth existence
方 *sochira, sonata, sochi, so(no)hō* over there, your place; you, your family; the other one. *sotchi, so(no)hō, sonata* that direction, that way, that one, that
⁵他 *so(no)ta* the others, the rest
外 *so(no) hoka* the rest, the others
迄 *sore made* till then; so long, so far, so much, to that extent; the end
処 *soko* that place, there; to that extent; when, at this juncture. *soredokoro ka* on the contrary, out of the question (too busy). *soko(ra), soko(ira)* about there, around there. *soko de* then, thereupon, accordingly
処此処 *soko-koko ni* here and there, in places; sporadically

[8] 実 *so(no)jitsu* really, in reality
[9] 通 *so(no) tō(ri)* That's right; exactly, just like that
後 *so(no)go* thereafter, later, since then
故 *soreyue* therefore
相応 *sore sōō ni* in a corresponding degree
[11] 道 *so(no) michi* line of business, profession, trade, art
頃 *so(no) koro* about that time
許 *sore bakari* only that, about that much
[12] 程 *sore hodo* so, so far, to that extent; (not) very
筋 *so(no) suji* the authorities concerned
筈 *so(no) hazu* proper, just, reasonable
場 *so(no)ba* the place, the spot, the occasion, the situation
場逃 *so(no)banoga(re)* temporizing, stopgap
場限 *so(no)bakagi(ri)* on the spur of the moment. *so(no)bakagi(ri) no* temporary, makeshift

[13] 節 *so(no) setsu* at that time
[16] 儘 *so(no)mama* as it is, in that condition
積 *so(no) tsumo(ri) de* with that in mind

—————— 8 ——————

兼 B $\frac{381}{\text{J3773}}$ M1483 KEN and, in addition, concurrently. *ka(neru)* combine with, serve as both; hold an additional post; use with. *ka(nete)* simultaneously. *-ka(neru)* cannot; hesitate to; be impatient.
[5] 用 *ken'yō* combined use, combination, serving two purposes
[6] 任 *kennin* concurrent post
[11] 務 *kemmu* additional post
[12] 備 *kembi suru* be proficient in both, combining both. *ka(ne)-sona(eru)* have both, combine with
[13] 業 *kengyō* side line
[18] 職 *kenshoku* concurrent post

━━━━━ RAD. 冂 13 ━━━━━

Dōgamae (enclosure like that of *dō* "same"), *makigamae*, or *keigamae*.
Variants: 冂, 冂, 冂. Nickname: Upside-down Box.

—————— 2 ——————

円 A $\frac{385}{\text{J315f}}$ M1513 EN circle; yen. *mado (ka)* *mado(ka) na* round; tranquil. *maru(i), maro(yaka) na* round, circular, spherical. *tsubura na* round, rotund. *maru* circle; money.
[4] 内 *ennai* within the circle
[6] 安 *en'yasu* cheap yen
[8] 形 *enkei, marugata* circle, round shape
価 *enka* value of the yen
弧 *enko* arc
周 *enshū* circumference
周率 *enshūritsu* circular constant, pi
卓 *entaku* round table
[9] 建 *enda(te)* yen base
柱 *enchū* column, shaft, cylinder. *marubashira* cylindrical column
陣 *enjin* circle, ring
屋根 *maru yane* dome, cupola
[10] 高 *endaka* exchange in favor of the yen, strong yen
[11] 窓 *marumado* round window

貨 *enka* yen currency
運動 *en'undō* circular motion
[12] 満 *emman* perfection, harmony, peace, satisfaction, smoothness, integrity, completeness
筒 *entō* cylinder
[13] 滑 *enkatsu, enkotsu* smoothness, harmony
[14] 舞 *embu* waltz
[15] 熟 *enjuku* ripeness, mellowness, maturity, perfection
盤 *emban* disk; discus
[16] 錐 *ensui* cone. *marugiri* round gimlet
錐形 *ensuikei* cone

内 A $\frac{386}{\text{J4662}}$ M1512 DAI. NAI inside, interior, within, between, among. *uchi* inside, interior; house, home; within; between, among, out of; mind; myself. *uchi-* inner. *-nai* within, within the scope of.
[4] 心 *naishin* inmost heart, one's mind, in the heart

内 *uchiuchi* family circle, the inside.
uchiuchi no, nainai private, informal;
secret, confidential

分 *naibun* secret, confidential

分泌 *naibumpi, naibumpitsu* internal
secretion

⁵示 *naiji, naishi* unofficial announcement

圧 *naiatsu* internal pressure

包 *naihō* connotation, comprehension

出血 *naishukketsu* internal hemorrhage

弁慶 *uchibenkei* braggart

用薬 *naiyōyaku* medicine taken
internally

申 *naishin* unofficial report

外 *naigai* inside and outside; domestic
and foreign; approximately. *uchi-soto*
inside and out

外人 *naigaijin* nationals and foreigners

⁶因 *naiin* the actual reason

気 *uchiki* timidity, shyness, bashfulness

向性 *naikōsei* introversion

耳 *naiji* inner ear

地 *naichi* homeland; mainland; inland

在 *naizai* immanence, inherence,
indwelling

在的 *naizaiteki* immanent, internal,
intrinsic

⁷局 *naikyoku* a bureau in a ministry

応 *naiō* secret understanding, collusion;
betrayal

状 *naijō* internal conditions; true state of
affairs

乱 *nairan* civil war, rebellion

助 *naijo* a wife's help

弟子 *uchi deshi* live-in apprentice

⁸金 *uchikin* bargain money, money paid
on account

径 *naikei* bore, inside diameter

命 *naimei* private or secret orders

実 *naijitsu* the facts

定 *naitei* tentative decision

妻 *naisai* common-law wife

事 *naiji* personal affairs; internal affairs

国 *naikoku* home country

的 *naiteki* inner, intrinsic, mental,
inherited

服 *naifuku* internal use

⁹海 *uchi umi, naikai* inlet, bay, inland sea

約 *naiyaku* (marriage) engagement;
secret treaty; tacit understanding;
private contract

政 *naisei* internal administration;
domestic affairs

奏 *naisō* secret report to the emperor

省 *naisei* introspection, reflection

祝 *uchi iwai* family celebration; small
present on such an occasion

面 *naimen* inside, interior

面的 *naimenteki* inner, internal, inside

通 *naitsū* secret understanding, collusion

科 *naika* internal medicine

科医 *naikai* physician, internist

¹⁰紛 *naifun* domestic or internal discord

陸 *nairiku* inland

陸国 *nairikukoku* landlocked country

部 *naibu* interior, inside. *naibu no*
internal

容 *naiyō* contents, detail, import

容証明 *naiyō shōmei* certification of
contents

¹¹偵 *naitei* scouting

側 *uchigawa* inside, interior, inner part

情 *naijō* internal conditions; true state of
affairs

張 *uchiba(ri)* lining, ceiling, wainscoting

訳 *uchiwake* items, breakdown;
classification

規 *naiki* private regulations, bylaws,
tradition

密 *naimitsu* privacy, secrecy. *naimitsu
ni* confidentially, privately, off the
record

¹²湯 *uchiyu* hotsprings water in the home,
indoor bathplace

診 *naishin* pelvic examination

勤 *naikin* office or indoor work

報 *naihō* secret information

¹³戦 *naisen* civil war

意 *naii* intention, personal opinion

裏 *dairi* imperial palace

蒙古 *Uchi Mōko* Inner Mongolia

幕 *uchimaku* inside curtain; inside
information. *uchimaku, naimaku* the
inside; hidden circumstances

¹⁴聞 *naibun no* secret, private
(information)

需 *naiju* domestic demand

閣 *naikaku* cabinet, ministry

閣総理大臣 *Naikaku Sōri Daijin*
Premier

緒 *naisho* secret, privacy; internal
evidence; one's circumstances

緒話 *naishobanashi* secret talk

¹⁵線 *naisen* indoor wiring; inner line

2
二 亠 人 イ ハ 几 入 八 ソ ⼌ ⼀ ⼂ ⼃ 几 凵 刀 刂 力 勹 匕 匚 匸 十 卜 卩 厂 ム 又

縁 *naien* common-law marriage
諾 *naidaku* informal consent
憂 *naiyū* internal or domestic troubles
輪 *uchiwa* family circle, the inside.
　uchiwa no moderate, conservative; pigeon-toed
輪揉 *uchiwamome* internal dissension; family trouble
¹⁶ 壁 *naiheki* inner wall
親王 *naishinnō* imperial or royal princess
燃機関 *nainen kikan* internal-combustion engine
¹⁷ 濠 *uchibori* inner moat
¹⁸ 職 *naishoku* home industry; side line
臓 *naizō* internal organs, intestines, viscera

——————— **3** ———————

A 冊 $\frac{389}{\text{J3a7d}}$ M1515 Saku. Satsu book counter; volume, book, letter.
³ 子 *sasshi* book, booklet, pamphlet; notebook. *sōshi* copy-book; storybook
¹³ 数 *sassū* number of books

——————— **4** ———————

A 再 $\frac{391}{\text{J3a46}}$ M1524 Sai. *futata(bi)* again, twice. *sai-* re-; second time, again.
² 入学 *sainyūgaku* readmission to a school
入国 *sainyūkoku* re-entry into a country
³ 上映 *saijōei* rerun (of a film)
三 *saisan* again and again, repeatedly
三再四 *saisan-saishi* repeatedly
⁴ 分配 *saibumpai* redistribution
⁵ 刊 *saikan* reprint, republication
犯 *saihan* second offense
出発 *saishuppatu* restart, fresh start
生 *saisei* regeneration, resuscitation; return to life; rebirth, reincarnation; narrow escape; reclamation; recycling; reproduction
生品 *saiseihin* recycled goods
⁶ 任 *sainin* reappointment
会 *saikai* another meeting; meeting again, reunion
交付 *saikōfu* reissue, regrant
考 *saikō* reconsideration

⁷ 来 *sairai* return; second coming; Second Advent; reincarnation
来月 *saraigetsu* month after next
来年 *sarainen* year after next
来週 *saraishū* week after next
⁸ 征 *saisei* second punitive expedition
拝 *saihai* worshipping again; bowing twice; epistolary closing
⁸ 版 *saihan* reprinting; reprint; second edition
放送 *saihōsō* rebroadcasting
武装 *saibusō* rearmament
注文 *saichūmon* repeat order
⁹ 度 *saido* twice, again, second time
軍備 *saigumbi* rearmament
降臨 *Saikōrin* Second Advent
封鎖 *saifūsa suru* reblock, refreeze
訂 *saitei* second revision
訂版 *saiteihan* second revised edition
建 *saikon* (temple or shrine) rebuilding.
　saiken reconstruction, rebuilding
建築 *saikenchiku* reconstruction, rebuilding
発 *saihatsu* relapse; recurrence
発足 *saihossoku* restart, fresh start
¹⁰ 起 *saiki* a comeback, recovery, restoration, rally; reflexive (in grammar)
校 *saikō* second proof; reinvestigation
挙 *saikyo* another attempt
配置 *saihaichi* reallocation, realignment
¹¹ 遊 *saiyū* revisit
¹¹ 婚 *saikon* second marriage
現 *saigen* reappearance, return; revival
教育 *saikyōiku* retraining, re-education
¹² 開 *saikai* reopening, resumption
評価 *saihyōka* reassessment, reappraisal
検査 *saikensa* re-examination
検討 *saikentō* re-examination, review, reappraisal
¹³ 試合 *saishiai* resumption of a game
試験 *saishiken* re-examination
¹⁴ 選 *saisen* re-election
選挙 *saisenkyo* re-election
製 *saisei* remanufacture, reconditioning
¹⁵ 調査 *saichōsa* re-examination, reinvestigation
確認 *saikakunin* reaffirmation, reconfirmation
編 *saihen* reorganization, reshuffle
編成 *saihensei* reorganization, reshuffle

審 *saishin* re-examination, retrial, review
審査 *saishinsa* re-examination
¹⁶燃 *sainen* recurrence, revival,
resuscitation, rekindling
興 *saikō* revival, restoration,
resuscitation, rehabilitation

RAD. **14**

Wa kammuri (crown shaped like the katakana *wa*) or *beki kammuri* "covering" crown. Nickname: *Kana Wa*.

2

冗 $\frac{399}{\text{J3e69}}$ Jō uselessness.
B M1566

⁵句 *jōku* redundant phrase
⁸長 *jōchō* verbosity, tediousness
¹⁰員 *jōin* supernumerary
¹²費 *jōhi* unnecessary expenses
¹⁴漫 *jōman* verbosity
¹⁵談 *jōdan* joke

3

写 $\frac{400}{\text{J4c4c}}$ SHA. *utsu(ru)* be
A M1570 photographed; be projected
(on a screen); (light or shadows) fall on.
utsu(su) copy, transcribe, duplicate,
reproduce, trace; describe, picture,
photograph. *utsu(shi)* copy, duplicate,
facsimile, transcript.

⁵出 *utsu(shi)-da(su)* reveal, show
本 *shahon* manuscript, written copy,
codex
生 *shasei* sketching; drawing from
nature; portrayal, description
生帖 *shaseichō* sketchbook
⁸実 *shajitsu* a real picture; realism
実主義 *shajitsu shugi* realism, literalism
実的 *shajitsuteki* realistic, graphic, true
to life
¹⁰真 *shashin* photograph
真判定 *shashin hantei* deciding the
winner from a photo
真屋 *shashin'ya* photographer, photo
studio
真植字 *shashinshokuji* photosetting (in
printing)
真館 *shashinkan* photo studio
真機 *shashinki* camera

¹¹経 *shakyō* copying Buddhist scriptures or
sutras; a copied Buddhist scripture
¹²植 *shashoku* photosetting (in printing)

7

冠 $\frac{401}{\text{J3427}}$ KAN crown, diadem; first,
B M1580 best, peerless. *kamu(ru)* vt
and vi wear, put on; take (the blame);
pour on; be covered with; ship (a wave);
have (labor pains); be accidentally
exposed (a film). *kan(suru)* crown, cap;
name, designate; entitle; initiate on
coming of age. *kammuri* crown, diadem;
a top character radical.

⁴水 *kansui* flooding, submergence
¹¹婚葬祭 *kankonsōsai* ceremonial
occasion
¹²詞 *kanshi* article (in grammar)

8

冥 $\frac{405}{\text{J4c3d}}$ MEI, MYŌ dark.
M1588

³土 *meido* hades, realm of the dead
⁴王星 *Meiōsei* (planet) Pluto
⁷利 *myōri* providence, luck, favor,
advantage
⁸府 *meifu* hades, realm of the dead, sheol
⁹界 *meikai* hades, realm of the dead

¹³福 *meifuku* happiness in the next world
想 *meisō* meditation, contemplation

9

冨 $\frac{406}{\text{J495a}}$ See 富 1349.
M1592

Ni-sui (two-stroke "water," as distinguished from Rad. 85). Also known as the "ice" radical because of its use in the early form of the character for *kōri* "ice." Nickname: Ice.

2

二 亠 人 亻 ハ 儿 入 八 丷 冂 冖 冫 几 凵 刀 刂 力 勹 匕 匚 匸 十 卜 卩 厂 厶 又

3

冬 ⟨410 / J455f / M1610⟩ **Tō** *fuyu* winter. *fuyu(meku)* become wintry.

- ⁶休 *fuyu yasu(mi)* winter vacation, winter holidays
- 至 *tōji* winter solstice
- ⁸物 *fuyumono* winter clothing
- 服 *fuyufuku* winter clothing
- 季 *tōki* winter season
- 空 *fuyuzora* winter sky
- ⁹枯 *fuyuga(re)* winter decay, winter withering, winter business slump
- ¹⁰眠 *tōmin* hibernation
- 将軍 *Fuyu Shōgun* Jack Frost
- ¹²場 *fuyuba* winter season
- 着 *fuyugi* winter clothing
- ²²籠 *fuyugomori* hibernation, wintering

4

冴 ⟨417 / J3a63 / M-X⟩ **Go.** *sa(eru)* be clear; be serene; be cold, be skillful.

- ⁷冴 *sa(e)za(e) shita* cold and clear
- ¹²渡 *sa(e)-wata(ru)* get cold; freeze over

5

冶 ⟨418 / J4c6a / M1621⟩ **Ya** melting.

- ⁸金 *yakin* metallurgy

冷 ⟨419 / J4e64 / M1622⟩ **Rei** cold, cool. *hi(eru)* cool down, grow cold; feel chilly. *hiya(su)* cool, refrigerate. *hi(yakasu)* cool (in water or ice); banter, make fun, speak playfully, tease; window-shop, look in at a shop. *same(ru)* vi cool, get cold; abate, subside; dampen, cool down (interest); come down (interest, enthusiasm, etc.). *sama(su)* vt cool, let cool; dampen, throw a damper on, spoil. *hi(e)* chilling, exposure. *hiya* cold drinking water. *hi(yayakana)* cold; chilly; indifferent, coldhearted; surly, curt,

cool, composed. *(o)hi(ya)* cold water; cold boiled rice. *tsume(tai)* cold, chilly, icy, freezing; coldhearted. *hi(yari)* cool, chilly, *toshita* cold.

- ⁴込 *hi(e)-ko(mu)* get colder; get chilled
- 水 *hi(ya)mizu, reisui* cold water
- ⁶気 *reiki* cold, chill; cold weather; cold wave; cold air
- 汗 *hi(ya)ase, reikan* cold sweat
- 血 *reiketsu* coldbloodedness; coldheartedness
- 血動物 *reiketsu dōbutsu* coldblooded animal
- 血漢 *reiketsukan* coldblooded person
- ⁷冷 *hi(ya)hi(ya) suru, hi(e)bi(e) suru* feel chilly; be fearful
- 却 *reikyaku* cooling, refrigeration
- 却期間 *reikyaku kikan* cooling-off period
- 却器 *reikyakuki* refrigerator, cooler, freezer; radiator (of a car)
- ⁸雨 *reiu* chilly rain
- 性 *hi(e)shō* sensitivity to cold
- 房 *reibō* air conditioning, air-cooling
- 房車 *reibōsha* air-conditioned car
- 房装置 *reibō sōchi* air-conditioning; air-cooling apparatus
- ¹⁰酒 *hi(ya)zake, reishu* cold saké
- 害 *reigai* cold-weather damage
- 笑 *reishō* derisive smile, scornful laugh, sneer, cynicism
- 凍 *reitō* refrigeration, freezing, cold storage
- 凍車 *reitōsha* refrigerator car
- 凍食品 *reitō shokuhin* frozen food
- 凍庫 *reitōko* freezer, freezer compartment
- 凍器 *reitōki* deep freeze; freezer; refrigerating machine
- ¹¹遇 *reigū* frigid reception, cold treatment
- 淡 *reitan* indifference, coolness, lukewarmness; coldheartedness
- ¹²然 *reizen* indifference, coolness, lukewarmness; coldheartedness
- ¹³戦 *reisen* cold war
- ¹⁴酷 *reikoku* cruelty; heartlessness;

bitterness

静 *reisei* calmness, coolness, composure, serenity

蔵 *reizō* cold storage, refrigeration

蔵庫 *reizōko* refrigerator

17 厳 *reigen na* grim, stern, stark, heartless

———————— 8 ————————

凋 ⁴²³/J437c/M1668 CHŌ. *shibo(mu)* droop, wither, wilt, fade; be downcast.

12 落 *chōraku* decline, decay, fall, withering

凌 ⁴²⁴/J4e3f/M1669 RYŌ. *shino(gu)* endure; keep out (rain); stave off; tide over, pull through; defy; slight; surpass, excel, eclipse. *shinogi* tiding over.

8 波性 *ryōhasei* seaworthiness

10 辱 *ryōjoku* insult; outrage, rape

15 駕 *ryōga suru* excel, surpass, outdo

凄 ⁴²⁵/J4028/M1657 SEI. *sugo(mu)* threaten. *sugo(i)* uncanny, weird; ghastly, horrible; intimidating; enormous; amazing. *susama(jii)* terrible; amazing; absurd.

8 味 *sugomi* weirdness, ghastliness, dreadfulness

11 惨 *seisan* ghastliness, gruesomeness

12 絶 *seizetsu na* weird, gruesome, lurid

准 B ⁴²⁶/J3d5a/M1661 ³²⁷⁸/J3d60/M17934 JUN quasi-, semi-, associate. *jun(jiru), jun(zuru)* apply correspondingly, correspond to, be proportionate to, conform to. *nazora(eru)* pattern after, liken to, imitate. *(ni) jun(jite)* in proportion (to).

凍 B ⁴²⁷/J4560/M1670 TŌ. *kō(ru), shi(miru), i(teru)* freeze; be frozen

over; congeal. *kō(rasu)* vt freeze, refrigerate. *kogo(ru)* vi congeal, freeze. *kogo(eru)* freeze, be chilled, be frozen. *kogo(raseru)* vt freeze, congeal, condense.

3 土 *tōdo* frozen soil

土帯 *tōdotai* tundra

6 死 *kogo(e)ji(nu), kogo(e)-shi(nu), tōshi suru* freeze to death, die of cold

10 害 *tōgai* frost damage

12 結 *tōketsu* freezing

13 傷 *shimoyake, tōshō* frostbite, chilblains

———————— 14 ————————

凝 B ⁴³¹/J3645/M1720 GYŌ. *kogo(rasu), kogo(raseru)* vt freeze, congeal. *ko(ru)* feel stiff, get stiff; be absorbed in, be devoted to, be a fanatic; elaborate. *kogo(ru)* congeal, freeze. *ko(rasu)* concentrate, devote, apply, strain, rack. *shiko(ru)* stiffen, harden. *kori* stiffness, swelling, hardening. *ko(tta)* elaborate, exquisite, tasty, refined, artistic. *shiko(ri)* muscle stiffness.

6 血 *gyōketsu suru* curdle. *gyōketsu* blood clot

8 性 *ko(ri)shō* enthusiasm for one thing; fastidiousness

固 *ko(ri)-kata(maru)* coagulate, curdle, clot; be fanatical. *korikata(mari)* coagulation, clot; enthusiast, fanatic. *gyōko* solidification, congealing, coagulation, condensation

固点 *gyōkoten* freezing point

11 視 *gyōshi* stare, steady gaze, fixation. *mitsu(meru)* stare at, gaze at, fix the eyes on

12 結 *gyōketsu* coagulation, curdling, setting, congealing, freezing, refrigeration, condensation, solidification

集 *gyōshū* cohesion; condensation

17 縮 *gyōshuku* condensation

2

二
十
人
イ
八
儿
入
八
ハ
冂
冖
冫
几
凵
刀
刂
力
勹
匕
匸
匚
十
卜
卩
厂
厶
又

━━━━━━━ RAD. 几 16 ━━━━━━━

Tsukue table or *ki-nyō* "table" enclosure. Variant: 几 *kazegamae* (enclosure like that of *kaze* "wind"). Nickname: Windy (cf. Rad. 182).

─────── **1** ───────

B 凡 [433 / J4b5e / M1739] HAN. Bon mediocrity. *oyo(so)*, *ōyo(so)* as a rule; approximately. *sube(te)* all, the whole; entirely; in general. *a(rayuru)* all, every.

² 人 *bonjin, bonnin* ordinary person, mediocre

³ 才 *bonsai* mediocrity, ordinary ability

⁴ 夫 *bompu, bombu* ordinary man

⁶ 百 *bompyaku* many, many kinds

⁷ 作 *bonsaku* poor piece of writing

⁸ 退 *bontai* put in 1-2-3 order

⁸ 例 *hanrei* introductory remarks, explanatory notes

⁹ 俗 *bonzoku* mediocrity; the masses, ordinary person

¹¹ 庸 *bon'yō* mediocrity; commonplace

¹³ 愚 *bongu* common person; foolish commoner

─────── **3** ───────

凧 [434 / J427c / M1749] (国字) *ikanobori, tako* kite.

¹² 揚 *takoa(ge)* kite flying

A 処 [435 / J3d68 / M1745] SHO. *sho(suru)* manage, deal with; sentence, condemn; act, behave; conduct oneself (well). *tokoro* place, spot, scene, site, seat; locality, district; room; distance; address; point, feature; passage (in a book), part; thing; time, moment; extent; matter of course. *-ka* place.

³ 女 *shojo, otome* virgin, maiden

女地 *shojochi* virgin soil ⌈work

女作 *shojosaku* one's first published

女峰 *shojohō* an unclimbed mountain

女航海 *shojo kōkai* maiden voyage

⁴ 分 *shobun* disposition of, disposal, management; measure, action; punishment

方 *shohō* prescription, formula

方箋 *shohōsen* (doctor's) prescription

⁵ 世 *shosei* conduct of life, getting on

世術 *shoseijutsu* secret of success

⁶ 刑 *shokei* (infliction of) punishment, ⌊execution

¹¹ 遇 *shogū* treatment

理 *shori* procedure, management, treatment. *shori suru* manage, dispose of, settle, adjust

断 *shodan* judgment, decision

¹³ 置 *shochi* disposal, management; action, measure; treatment

¹⁴ 罰 *shobatsu* penalty, punishment

─────── **4** ───────

凪 [437 / J4664 / M1758] (国字) *nagi* lull, calm. *na(gu)* become calm, die down.

─────── **10** ───────

凱 [440 / J332e / M1790] GAI. victory song.

¹¹ 旋 *gaisen* triumphal return

旋門 *gaisemmon* arch of triumph

旋軍 *gaisengun* returning victorious army

¹⁴ 歌 *gaika* victory song; victory

━━━━━━━ RAD. 凵 17 ━━━━━━━

Ukebako open box or *kangamae* "open box" enclosure. Nickname: Open Box.

─────── **2** ───────

B 凶 [442 / J3627 / M1803] KYŌ. evil; bad luck; disaster; bad harvest.

³ 刃 *kyōjin* assassin's dagger

⁶ 行 *kyōkō* violence, murder, crime

年 *kyōnen* bad year, bad harvest

⁷ 作 *kyōsaku* bad harvest, poor crop

状 *kyōjō* crime, offense
状持 *kyōjōmo(chi)* a criminal
⁸事 *kyōji* calamity, misfortune
⁹変 *kyōhen* catastrophe; assassination
¹¹猛 *kyōmō* fierce
悪 *kyōaku na* atrocious, fiendish, brutal
¹²報 *kyōhō* bad news
¹³漢 *kyōkan* villain, outlaw, assassin
¹⁵暴 *kyōbō* brutality, ferocity, atrocity
器 *kyōki* dangerous weapon

─────── **3** ───────

B 凸 <u>443</u> J464c M1809 TOTSU *deko* projecting, beetle brow.
⁵凹 *dekoboko, totsuō* unevenness, ruggedness, roughness
⁸版 *toppan* relief printing
⁹面 *totsumen* convex surface
面鏡 *totsumenkyō* convex lens

B 凹 <u>444</u> J317a M1810 Ō hollow, sunken.
heko(mu) be dented, be indented, yield to, give, sink, collapse, cave in; be snubbed; be defeated. *heko(maseru), heko(masu)* vt dent, indent, depress; humiliate. *kubo(maru)* be low (as a hollow). *kubo(meru)* hollow out. *kubo, boko* hollow, depression. *heko(mi)* dent, hollow, depression. ⌐ruggedness
⁵凸 *ōtotsu* unevenness, roughness,
⁸版 *ōhan, ōban* intaglio (printing)
⁹面 *ōmen* concavity
面鏡 *ōmenkyō* concave lens or mirror

A 出 <u>445</u> J3d50 M1811 SUI. SHUTSU born of; appearing from; going out; sending out. *da(su), ida(su)* put out, take out, pull out, stick out; draw (a gun); stretch out, extend; save (from a fire); expose, bare; exhibit; send, forward, post; publish; hoist (a flag); hang out; present, send in, tender, submit; serve; run (extra trains); produce; pay, contribute; invest; advance (money). *de(ru)* appear, come out, emerge; haunt, infest; be found, get back; be served (meals); lead to, enter; find (oneself) at; come out (as a result); leave, go out, get out; attend, appear; work (at); participate; launch (into); run (for an office); be published; sell; depart; graduate; break out, originate; be raised, be produced; issue from, be traced to, derive from, stem from; protrude, stick out; exceed; interfere; intrude. *-de, de-* turnout, attendance, appearance, flow, outflow; pouring; outlay, expenditure, crop, yield, supply; sale, demand; start, outset, origin, birth, stock; one's turn; drawing (of tea). *de(shaburu)* intrude, butt in. *(o)i(de)* being; coming; going; come, come on. *(o)i(deninaru)* be; come; go. *da(shi)* broth, soup stock; pretext, excuse; cat's-paw, a dupe, a tool. *-da(su)* begin to.

²力 *shutsuryoku* output (of a dynamo)
入 *de-i(ru)* go in and out; quarrel; have the freedom of the home. *de(zu)-i(razu)* moderation; neither gain nor loss. *da(shi)i(re)* taking in and out, depositing and withdrawing; receipts and expenditures. *shutsunyū* going in and out; entrance and exit; receipts and expenditures. *dei(ri), dehai(ri)* free association, going in and out, entrance and exit; receipts and payments, surplus and deficit; indentation (of a coast)
入口 *deiriguchi* entrance and exit, a doorway, a gateway
入国 *shutsunyūkoku* emigration and immigration ⌐vent
³口 *deguchi* exit, way out; outlet, leak,
土 *shutsudo* appearance of an archeological find
土品 *shutsudohin* artifacts
刃 *deba* knife, pointed carver
⁴方 *dekata* attitude; a move; theater usher
欠 *shukketsu* presence or absence
水 *shussui, demizu* flood, freshlet, inundation
火 *shukka* fire, outbreak of fire
不精 *debushō* a stay-at-home; homekeeping
⁵立 *i(de)-ta(tsu)* start, leave. *idetachi* start, departure; dress, attire, outfit. *shuttatsu* departure
払 *dehara(u)* be all out, have none left
処 *shussho, dedokoro* birthplace; origin; source, authority; exit
処進退 *shussho-shintai* advancing and retreating; appearance and disappearance; one's daily activities; one's course of action; one's attitude

2

二
十
人 イ へ 几 入 八 ｀丷 冂 冖 冫 几 〔匚〕

³凵 刀 刂 力 勹 匕 匸 匚 十 卜 卩 厂 厶 又

札 *shussatsu* issuing tickets
札口 *shussatsuguchi* ticket window
札所 *shussatsujo* ticket office
生 *shusshō* birth
生地 *shusshōchi* birthplace 「birth
生年月日 *shusshō nengappi* date of
生率 *shusshōritsu* birth rate
世 *shusse* successful career, eminence
世作 *shussesaku* a work of art or
　literature that brings fame
世頭 *shussegashira* most successful man
⁶色 *shusshoku* prominence; excellence
回 *de-mawa(ru)* arrive on the market, be
　moving
迎 *de-muka(eru)* (go to) meet, (come to)
　meet, greet, receive. *demuka(e)*
　meeting, reception
向 *de-mu(ku), shukkō suru* go to,
　proceed to, leave for
任 *demaka(se)* random speech
帆 *shuppan* sailing, departure
会 *de-a(u)* meet, encounter, run across.
　shukkai an encounter
先 *desaki* destination
先機関 *desaki kikan* branch office
血 *shukketsu* hemorrhage, bleeding
⁷足 *deashi* start; turnout
戻 *demodo(ri)* divorced woman
抜 *da(shi)-nu(ku)* forestall, anticipate,
　jump the gun on, outwit, circumvent,
　steal a march on. *da(shi)nu(ke) ni*
　suddenly, without notice,
　unexpectedly
没 *shutsubotsu* appearance and
　disappearance
社 *shussha* going to the office
兵 *shuppei* dispatch of troops; expedition
廷 *shuttei* appearance in court
初式 *dezome shiki* firemen's New
　Year's demonstrations
身 *shusshin* graduate from; hailing from
身地 *shusshinchi* birthplace, native
　place
身者 *shusshinsha* alumnus
身校 *shusshinkō* alma mater
来 *deki(ru)* can, be able to; be possible;
　be done, be finished, be ready; be
　made of; be established, be set up; be
　formed; come into being; grow, be
　produced; break out; be good at; be
　versed in; become intimate with.
　deki(su) complete, accomplish

praiseworthily. *deka(shita)* well
done, bravo. *deki(ta)* fully developed,
mature, cultured, well-balanced. *deki*
make, workmanship; result; crop,
harvest. *shuttai, shutsurai*
occurrence; completion; fulfillment
来上 *dekia(garu)* be finished, be ready,
　be made for, be cut out
来心 *dekigokoro* sudden impulse,
　passing fancy
来立 *dekita(te)* new, newly made, fresh,
　brand-new
来合 *deki-a(u)* be ready-made; become
　intimate with. *dekia(i)* ready-made;
　common-law (wife)
来事 *dekigoto* incident, affair
来映 *dekibae* result, effect, performance,
　success; excellently made; shape and
　quality of (an article)
来高 *dekidaka* yield, crop, production
⁸国 *shukkoku* departure from a country
店 *demise* branch store
物 *demono* rash, boil; secondhand
　article. *da(shi)mono* performance,
　program
歩 *de-aru(ku)* go out, take a stroll, go
　about
典 *shutten* source, authority
放 *da(ship)panasu, da(shi)-hana(su)*
　leave on, leave running, leave lying
　around, leave (a faucet) open
奔 *shuppon* abscondence; flight
金 *shukkin* payment, contribution,
　investment, financing
所 *shussho, dedoko, dedokoro* origin,
　source; authority; exit; point of
　departure; release from prison
征 *shussei* departure for the front
版 *shuppan* publication
版元 *shuppammoto* publisher
版社 *shuppansha* publishing house
版物 *shuppambutsu* publications
版界 *shuppankai* the publishing world
版業 *shuppangyō* publishing business
⁹陣 *shutsujin* departure for the front
前 *demae* restaurant delivery service.
　da(shi)mae one's share (in the
　expenses)
前持 *demaemo(chi)* boy who delivers
　take-out food
発 *shuppatsu* departure
発点 *shuppatsuten* starting point; point

of departure

品 *shuppin* exhibit, display

10 馬 *shutsuba suru* go on horseback; go in person; run for election

庫 *shukko* delivery from a storehouse

航 *shukkō* departure, sailing

荷 *shukka* forwarding, shipping; outgoing freight

家 *shukke* entering the priesthood; priest, monk

納 *suitō* receipts and disbursements

納係 *suitōgakari* cashier, treasurer; teller

席 *shusseki* attendance

11 過 *de-su(giru)* project or protrude too much; be too forward, obtrude

惜 *da(shi)-oshi(mu)* grudge, be stingy, be unwilling to pay

掛 *de-ka(keru)* depart, go out, set out, start, be going out. *degake* about to start out

現 *shutsugen* appearance, arrival

船 *debune, defune, idebune* weighing anchor, setting sail; outgoing ship

窓 *demado* bay window

動 *shutsudō* sailing, marching, going out

産 *shussan* childbirth; production (of goods)

張 *de-ba(ru), de(p)pa(ru)* project, stand out, jut out, protrude. *deba(ri)* projection, ledge. *shutchō* business trip, official trip

張所 *shutchōjo* branch office

12 超 *shutchō* excess of exports, favorable balance of trade

揃 *de-soro(u)* appear all together, be all present

棺 *shukkan* carrying out a coffin

湯 *i(de)yu* hot springs

番 *deban* one's turn

費 *shuppi* expenses, disbursements

場 *shutsujō* stage appearance, performance; participation. *deba* one's turn; place of projection; production center

場者 *shutsujōsha* participants, participating athletes

港 *shukkō* departure; clearance (of a ship)

勤 *shukkin* at work; going to work

13 資 *shusshi* investment, financing, contribution

資金 *shusshikin* capital

14 鼻 *debana, dehana* projecting part (of a headland, etc.); outset, starting out

獄 *shutsugoku* release from prison

端 *deha* chance of going out, opportunity (to succeed). *debana, hehana* moment of departure, beginning of work

演 *shutsuen* stage appearance, performance

演者 *shutsuensha* performer, entertainer, actor

漁 *shutsugyo, shutsuryō* going fishing

15 稼 *dekasegi* working away from home

撃 *shutsugeki* sortie, sally

稽古 *degeiko* giving lessons at pupils' homes

16 頭 *shuttō* appearance, presence

18 題 *shutsudai* proposing a question

19 願 *shutsugan* application

22 鱈目 *detarame* irresponsible utterance, nonsense

----------- 6 -----------

函 446 / J4821 / M1826 KAN. *hako* box. *i(reru)* put into.

13 数 *kansū* function (in math)

================ RAD. 18 ================

Katana sword. At right: 刂 *rittō* standing "sword." Nickname: Sword.

A 刀 448 / J4561 / M1845 TŌ sword, saber, knife, engraving tool, *katana* sword, blade.

3 工 *tōkō* swordsmith

7 身 *tōshin* sword blade

10 剣 *tōken* sword

11 疵 *katana kizu* sword wound

17 鍛治 *katana kaji* swordsmith

二十
人
イ
亻
几
入
八
丷
冂
冫
几
凵
〔刀
刂〕
力
勹
匕
匸
匚
十
卜
卩
厂
厶
又

刃 ⁴⁴⁹ J3f4f M1850 **B** JIN blade, sword, cutting tool. NIN. *ha* blade, edge. *yaiba* blade, sword.
⁶ 向 *hamu(kau)* strike at; bite back; turn on, rise against, oppose, defy
⁸ 物 *hamono* edged tool, cutlery
¹² 渡 *hawata(ri)* sword length, walking on a sword
¹³ 傷 *ninjō* bloodshed
傷沙汰 *ninjōzata* bloodshed

— 2 —

刈 ⁴⁵² J3422 M1859 **B** KAI. *ka(ru)* cut, clip; shear; reap; trim, prune.
² 入 *ka(ri)-i(reru)* harvest, reap
⁴ 込 *ka(ri)-ko(mu)* cut, trim, clip; dress, prune. *kariko(mi)* haircut, pruning
⁸ 取 *ka(ri)-to(ru)* mow, reap, harvest

切 ⁴⁵³ J405a M1858 **A** SETSU. SAI. *ki(ru)* cut, chop, hash; carve; saw; clip; shear; slice, strip; fell, cut down; punch; sever (connections); pause, break off; disconnect, turn off; hang up; cross a street); discount, sell below cost; shake (water) off. *ki(reru)* cut well, be sharp; break, snap; wear out; be injured; burst, collapse; break off, be disconnected; be out of; expire; sever (connections) with; sharp, shrewd; less than. *ki(rasu)* vt be out of, be short of. *ki(re)* cloth; piece, cut, chop, strip, slice, scrap; counter for such. *ki(ri)* limits, end, bounds; period, place to leave off, closing sentence. *setsu na* earnest, eager; kind; keen, acute. *setsu(nai)* oppressive, suffocating; painful, trying. *-kitte no* the most… of all. *-ki(ru)* finish, be through, complete; be able to. *-ki(ri)* all there is; only; since.
³ 下 *ki(ri)-o(rosu)* slash downward. *ki(ri)-sa(geru)* cut down, prune; cut and hang down; reduce, cut shorter
上 *ki(ri)-a(geru)* close, finish. *kiria(ge)* end, conclusion
口 *ki(ri)kuchi* cut end, section; opening, slit
口上 *ki(ri)kōjō* stiff formality, set terms
⁴ 方 *ki(ri)kata* how to cut, how to slice
切 *ki(re)gi(re)* pieces, scraps. *setsusetsu*

politeness; feeling of loneliness
支丹 *Kirishitan* (early) Japanese Christianity
手 *kitte* postage stamp; merchandise certificate.
手蒐集 *kitte shūshū* philately
込 *ki(ri)-ko(mu)* cut into; raid, attack; cut up. *ki(re)-ko(mu)* cut into. *ki(re)ko(mi)* cut, notch, incision
⁵ 目 *ki(re)me* rift, gap, break; pause, interruption. *ki(ri)me* cut, section, notch, incision; end (of a task)
立 *ki(ri)-ta(teru)* cut, slash, slay all. *ki(ri)-ta(tsu)* rise perpendicularly. *ki(ri)ta(te)* freshly cut. *ki(ri)ta(tta)* steep, precipitous
付 *ki(ri)-tsu(keru)* slash at a person
払 *ki(ri)-hara(u)* clear away; clear land; prune, lop off
札 *ki(ri)fuda* trump card
出 *ki(ri)-da(su), ki(ri)-ida(su)* quarry; cut (timber); cut and carry off; begin to talk, break the ice. *ki(ri)da(shi)* pointed knife; logging; (beef) scraps; starting to speak
⁶ 回 *ki(ri)-mawa(su)* run around killing; manage everything, control; cut carelessly (a cook or a surgeon)
先 *ki(s)saki* point of a sword; spearhead
羽詰 *seppatsu(maru)* be at one's wit's end, be cornered
⁷ 身 *ki(ri)mi* slice, chop
迫 *seppaku* pressure, urgency; imminence; acuteness, tenseness
花 *ki(ri)bana* cut flowers
抜 *ki(ri)-nu(keru)* cut one's way through, tide over, struggle through. *ki(ri)-nu(ku)* cut out, clip from, extract. *kirinu(ki)* scraps
売 *kiriu(ri)* selling by the piece
⁸ 味 *ki(re)aji* sharpness (of the sword), the feel of a cutting edge
放 *ki(ri)-hana(su), ki(ri)-hana(tsu)* cut loose, let loose, cut off, detach, dismember, cut in two
者 *ki(re)mono* able man, shrewd businessman
刻 *ki(ri)-kiza(mu)* hew, chop up, mangle, mince
実 *setsujitsu ni* strongly, keenly, vividly, sincerely, urgently
取 *ki(ri)-to(ru)* cut off, cut out; whittle

down; tear out; cut down, amputate. *kirito(ri)* cutting; tearing off, cutting off; robbery with assault, burglary; robber, burglar

取線 *kirito(ri) sen* perforated line

9 通 *ki(ri)-tō(su)* cut through (with a road, tunnel, or canal). *kiridō(shi)* (railway or road) cut

10 屑 *ki(ri)kuzu* scraps, chips. *ki(re)kuzu* cloth scraps

倒 *ki(ri)-tao(su)* cut down, chop down, fell

株 *ki(ri)kabu* stump, stubble

11 捨 *ki(ri)-su(teru)* cut down, slay; omit, discard

崩 *ki(ri)-kuzu(su)* level (a hill); cut through (a mountain); break (a strike); split (the opposition)

望 *setsubō* earnest desire, longing

符 *kippu* ticket

断 *setsudan* section; cutting, severance, amputation

断図 *setsudanzu* sectional drawing

断面 *setsudammen* section (in drawing)

12 開 *sekkai suru, ki(ri)-hira(ku)* clear (land), open up; cut through. *sekkai* incision, operation, section. *ki(ri)hira(ki)* clearing (land); excavating

間 *ki(re)ma* interval, break, rift (in clouds)

揃 *ki(ri)-soro(eru)* cut and even up, cut several pieces to the same size

落 *ki(ri)-oto(su)* cut down, lop off, prune

裂 *ki(ri)-sa(ku)* cut off, cut up; cut to pieces

歯扼腕 *sesshi-yakuwan suru* be enraged, be indignant, be impatient, gnashing the teeth and clenching the arms on the breast (in anger or regret)

換 *ki(ri)-ka(eru)* change, exchange, convert, renew; throw a switch; replace; switch over

替 *ki(ri)-kawa(ru)* change completely. *ki(ri)-ka(eru)* change, exchange, convert, renew, throw a switch, replace; switch over

13 傷 *ki(ri)kizu* cut, gash

腹 *seppuku* disembowelment, harakiri

詰 *ki(ri)-tsu(meru)* shorten, reduce, economize. *ki(ri)tsu(me)* retrenchment, curtailment

15 磋琢磨 *sessa-takuma* apply oneself closely to (one's study), study hard, diligent application

A 分 454 J4a2c M1853 BUN dividing; part, segment; share; ration; rate; degree; one's lot, one's status; relation; duty; kind, lot. FUN a minute of time; one-sixtieth of a degree; one-tenth of a *momme* (see Weights and Measures). BU rate, part, percentage; one percent; thickness; odds; chance of winning; one-tenth of a *shaku* (see Weights and Measures); one quarter of a *ryō*. *wa(karu)* understand, comprehend; know, be known, be identified; be open to reason, be sensible; can tell (what will happen); appreciate; be announced; be discovered, recognize. *wa(keru)* divide, split, separate; isolate; distribute, share; distinguish; spare. *wa(katsu)* divide, separate; share with; distinguish between. *wa(kazu)* without differentiation. *wa(kare)* branch, fork; division, section; farewell. *wa(kareru)* branch off, diverge from, fork; split; be divided; part with; be divorced; bid farewell; break up, disperse, scatter. *wa(kari)* understanding, comprehension. *wa(ke)* sharing, division; draw, tie. *wa(kachi)* distinction, differentiation, discrimination. *bun-* branch, detached.

2 入 *wa(ke)-i(ru)* force one's way, push through

3 子 *bunshi* numerator; molecule; (bad) elements

与 *wa(ke)-ata(eru), waka(chi)-ata(eru)* apportion to, share. *bun'yo suru* distribute. *bun'yo* distribution, allocation; dispensation; impartation

4 化 *bunka* specialization, differentiation

水嶺 *bunsuirei* watershed, divide

5 母 *bumbo* denominator

目 *wa(ke)me* dividing line; parting (of the hair); partition; crisis

布 *bumpu* distribution

冊 *bunsatsu* separate volume, installment

7 身 *bunshin* parturition, delivery; one's child; branch, offshoot; one's other self

別 *fumbetsu* discernment, judgment, wisdom. *bumbetsu* discrimination;

2

二十人イ八几入

separation, division; classification; distinction

岐 *bunki* divergence, ramification, forking

岐点 *bunkiten* diverging point; turning point; fork, crossroads; junction; parting of the ways

⁸明 *bummei, bummyō* clearness; clear understanding

泌 *bumpitsu, bumpi* secretion

限者 *bungenja* a rich man

担 *buntan* apportionment

担金 *buntankin* share of expenses; contribution

析 *bunseki* analysis, assaying

⁹厚 *buatsu na, buatsu(i)* thick, bulky, massive

院 *bun'in* branch (of an institution); branch temple; detached building

乗 *bunjō* riding separately

前 *wa(ke)mae* share, quota

室 *bunshitsu* isolated room, detached office, annex

度器 *bundoki* protractor

派 *bumpa* denomination, sect, branch, faction. *bumpa suru* separate from

科会 *bunkakai* subcommittee meeting

界線 *bunkaisen* line of demarcation

¹⁰骨 *bunkotsu* part of a person's ashes

校 *bunkō* branch school

納 *bunnō* installment payment or delivery

針 *funshin* minute hand

家 *bunke* branch family

配 *bumpai* division, sharing; distribution, allotment

捕 *bundo(ru)* capture, seize, plunder

¹¹野 *bun'ya* field, sphere, division, branch

隊 *buntai* squad; division (in the navy); small unit

娩 *bumben* delivery, confinement, childbirth

¹²遣 *bunken* detachment, detail

散 *bunsan* breakup, dispersion, decentralization, divergence; bankruptcy

掌 *bunshō* division of duties

量 *bunryō* quantity, amount, dose

極化 *bunkyokuka* polarization; lining up with

割 *bunkatsu* partition, division, dismemberment

割払 *bunkatsubara(i)* installment paying

裂 *bunretsu* dissolution, dismemberment, breakup, disintegration, segmentation, fission, split, schism, separation

¹³際 *bunzai* social standing

数 *bunsū* fraction

業 *bungyō* division of labor, specialization, assembly-line production

解 *bunkai* analysis; parsing; decomposition; dismantling; disintegration; dissolution; reduction (in chemistry)

¹⁴銅 *fundō* weight, counterweight

¹⁵権 *bunken* decentralization of authority

¹⁸類 *bunrui* classification, group

¹⁹離 *bunri* division, separation. *wa(ke)-hana(su)* separate from, detach

²⁰譲 *bunjō* selling (real-estate) lots

3

A 刊 | 456 / J3429 / M1865 | KAN publishing; carve, engrave.

⁵本 *kampon* printed book

⁶行 *kankō* publication

行物 *kankōbutsu* a publication

4

A 列 | 460 / J4e73 / M1901 | RETSU row, rank, tier, file, column, line; procession; queue. *res(suru)* vi attend, rank with. *vt* line up. *tsura(naru)* range, be connected with, join; stand in a row; attend; join one's people (in death). *tsura(neru)* put in a row, join.

⁶伝 *retsuden* series of biographies

⁷車 *ressha* train

¹⁰記 *rekki* enumeration, listing

島 *rettō* archipelago, chain of islands

挙 *rekkyo* enumeration

席 *resseki* attendance, presence

¹¹強 *rekkyō* the great powers

B 刑 | 461 / J373a / M1886 | KEI penalty, sentence, punishment. *kei(suru)* sentence.

⁶死 *keishi* execution

⁸法 *keihō* criminal law

事 *keiji* criminal case; criminal

事犯 *kaijihan* criminal offense
事処分 *keiji shobun* punishment of a criminal
事事件 *keiji jiken* criminal case
事被告人 *keiji hikokunin* the accused
事裁判 *keiji saiban* criminal trial
事訴訟 *keiji soshō* criminal action
¹¹ 務官 *keimukan* prison guard
務所 *keimusho* prison, penitentiary
¹² 場 *keijō* place of execution
期 *keiki* prison term
¹⁴ 罰 *keibatsu* judgment, penalty, punishment

———— 5 ————

判 ⁴⁶⁵ J483d M1923 HAN stamp, seal; a
A monogram signature; judgment. *han(jiru)* judge, decide; guess; solve, decipher, interpret; divine. *waka(ru)* understand, comprehend; know, be known, be identified; be open to reason, be sensible; can tell (what will happen); appreciate; be announced; be discovered; recognize. *-ban* size (of paper or books).
³ 子 *hanko* personal seal
⁷ 決 *hanketsu* judgment, decision, decree, sentence
別 *hambetsu* distinction, discrimination
⁸ 例 *hanrei* judicial precedent
明 *hammei suru* become clear, be confirmed
事 *hanji* judge
定 *hantei* judgment, decision, award, verdict
¹¹ 断 *handan* judgment, decision, adjudication, conclusion; decipherment; divination
¹² 然 *hanzen(taru)* clear, distinct, evident, definite
¹⁴ 読 *handoku* decipherment, interpretation, making out

利 ⁴⁶⁶ J4d78 M1932 RI advantage, benefit, gain;
A interest; victory. *ri(suru)* benefit, do good, profit, gain. *ki(ku)* take effect, do (a person) good; work, operate; tell (on one's strength); be available (bus or phone). *ki(kasu)* use (one's head); exert (influence). *ki(keru)* be influential. *kiki* efficacy.
³ 子 *rishi* interest

口 *rikō* cleverness, wisdom, intelligence
己 *riko* selfishness
己主義 *riko shugi* egoism, selfishness
⁵ 目 *kikime* effect, efficacy, impression
用 *riyō* use, utilization; improvement (of opportunities); making a tool of
⁶ 回 *rimawa(ri)* interest, yield, profit
⁹ 便 *riben* convenience
点 *riten* advantage, point in favor
発 *rihatsu* cleverness, wisdom, intelligence
¹⁰ 害 *rigai* advantages and disadvantages, interests
息 *risoku* interest
益 *rieki* profit, gain; benefit, advantage.
  riyaku the favor of a Buddha; answer to prayer, help
¹¹ 率 *riritsu* rate of interest
得 *ritoku* profit, benefit
¹² 殖 *rishoku* moneymaking
¹⁵ 潤 *rijun* profit
¹⁵ 権 *riken* rights, concessions

別 ⁴⁶⁷ J4a4c M1924 BETSU. *wa(keru)* divide,
A split, separate; isolate; distribute, share; distinguish; spare. *waka(tsu)* divide, separate; share with; distinguish between. *waka(reru)* branch off, diverge from, fork; split; be divided; part with; be divorced; bid farewell; break up, disperse, scatter. *betsu no* another, different, particular, separate; extra; exception; difference, distinction. *betsu ni* (with neg.) not especially, not particularly. *bes(shite)* especially, particularly. *waka(chi)* distinction, discrimination; differentiation. *waka(re)* branch, fork; division, section; farewell. *wake(te)* above all, especially, all the more. *-betsu* classified by.
² 人 *betsujin, betsunin* different person, changed man
³ 口 *betsukuchi* different item, different lot, different kind
⁴ 天地 *bettenchi* another world
⁵ 冊 *bessatsu* separate volume, extra issue, supplement
世界 *bessekai* another world
⁶ 宅 *bettaku* secondary residence
名 *betsumei, betsumyō* another name, alias, pseudonym
⁷ 状 *betsujō* a different situation

2

二 十 人 イ 八 几 入 八 ソ 冂 ハ ; 几 凵 【刀 刂】 力 ク ヒ 匚 匸 十 卜 卩 厂 ム 又

別 *betsubetsu ni, waka(re)-waka(re) ni* separately, apart, severally, individually

邸 *bettei* villa, detached residence

⁸居 *bekkyo* separation, limited divorce

送 *bessō* separate mail, separate shipment

物 *betsumono* another thing, exception, special case

⁹途 *betto* special, special reserve (account)

便 *betsubin de* by separate post

段 *betsudan* (with neg.) not in particular, not especially

室 *besshitsu* separate room, special room

荘 *bessō* villa, second house

¹⁰席 *besseki* different seat, special seat, separate room

個 *bekko no* several, separate, different, another

格 *bekkaku* special, extraordinary

称 *besshō* another name, alias, pseudonym

紙 *besshi* enclosed paper, attached paper

¹¹道 *waka(re)michi* forked road, crossroads, branch road, parting of the ways

勘定 *betsu kanjō* separate account

問題 *betsu mondai* a different thing, another question, a different case

¹²項 *bekkō* separate paragraph; special heading

棟 *betsumune* outbuilding, detached building

¹³誂 *betsu atsura(e)* special order

働隊 *betsu dōtai* flying column, detached force

¹⁴種 *besshu* another kind, distinct species, variety

¹⁶館 *bekkan* annex

¹⁷嬪 *beppin* beauty, beautiful woman, pretty girl

¹⁹離 *betsuri* parting, separation

初 ₄₆₉ _{J3d69} _{M1911} SHO beginning; first.
A *haji(meru)* vt begin, open, start, originate, inaugurate, initiate. *haji(maru)* vi begin, start, open; date from; (season) sets in; arise, break out; originate in. *haji(mete)* (for) the first time; not until. *hatsu* beginning, first, new. *haji(me)* beginning, origin. *-haji(me)*

including, and, as well as. *-so(meru)* begin to. *ui-* first(time), beginning. *hatsu-* new, the first (snow), maiden (voyage). *-some* begin to.

⁴手 *shote* beginning, start

心 *shoshin* original aim, original intention; inexperience

心者 *shoshinsha* beginner

日 *hatsuhi* New Year's Day sunrise. *shonichi* first day, opening day, first performance. *shojitsu* first day; dawn

⁵犯 *shohan* first offense; first offender

冬 *shotō* beginning of winter; tenth lunar month

出 *shoshutsu* first appearance

代 *shodai* the first generation; the founder

⁶老 *shorō* middle-aged

耳 *hatsumimi* something heard for the first time

旬 *shojun* first ten days of the month

回 *shokai* first time; first inning

任給 *shoninkyū* initial salary

年 *shonen* first year, early years

⁷初 *uiui(shii)* innocent, artless, unsophisticated

志 *shoshi* original aim, original intention

対面 *shotaimen* first meeting, first interview

見 *shoken* seeing for the first time

⁸版 *shohan* first edition

物 *hatsumono* season's first product

夜 *shoya* first watch of the night; bridal night

歩 *shoho* first steps, elements, primer

学 *shogaku* beginning to study; a person beginning a course of study

⁹秋 *hatsuaki, shoshū* early fall

級 *shokyū* beginners' class

段 *shodan* lowest grade; first-degree black belt (martial arts)

春 *hatsuharu, shoshun* early spring

¹⁰校 *shokō* first proof

夏 *shoka, hatsunatsu* early summer

恋 *hatsukoi* first love; puppy love

¹¹雪 *hatsuyuki* the first snow

産 *hatsusan, uizan, shozan* first childbirth

¹²期 *shoki* early days, early years, early stage, beginning

診 *shoshin* first medical examination

等 *shotō* elementary

¹³詣 *hatsumōde* first shrine or temple visit

469

in the new year
¹⁴演 *shoen* first performance
¹⁵審 *shoshin* first trial
¹⁶頭 *shotō* early, elementary; at first
¹⁸顔合 *hatsukaoa(wase)* first meeting

———— **6** ————

券 A ⁴⁷³ J3774 M1966 KEN ticket, coupon, bond, certificate.

到 B ⁴⁷⁷ J457e M1950 TŌ. *ita(ru)* go, proceed, come; arrive, reach, attain; result in, lead to.
⁷来 *tōrai* arrival, advent, visitation
⁸底 *tōtei* after all, in the long run; (with neg.) (cannot) possibly, (none) at all, impossible; absolutely
¹¹達 *tōtatsu* arrival
¹²着 *tōchaku* arrival
¹⁶頭 *tōtō* at last, finally, after all

刻 A ⁴⁷⁸ J396f M1970 KOKU time; carving, engraving, cutting. *kiza(mu)* cut fine, chop up; mince, hash; carve (images); engrave (seals); chisel, cut, notch. *ho(ru)* carve, engrave, chisel, sculpture, inscribe. *kiza(mi)* shredded tobacco; notch, nick. *kiza* scratch.
¹一刻 *koku-ikkoku* moment by moment; hour by hour ⌐ruler
⁵目 *kiza(mi)me* notch, nick, marks on a
⁶印 *kokuin* carved seal
⁸限 *kokugen* time, appointed time
刻 *kokukoku, kokkoku to* moment by moment; hour by hour
苦 *kokku* hard work

刷 A ⁴⁷⁹ J3a7e M1964 SATSU. *su(ru)* print.
⁴毛 *hake* paint brush
⁸物 *su(ri)mono* printed matter
¹³損 *su(ri)-soko(nau)* misprint, spoil in printing
新 *sasshin* reform, renovation, innovation

刺 B ⁴⁸⁰ J3b49 M1969 SHI calling card. *sa(su)* pierce, thrust, stab, prick; bite, sting; pin down; sew, stitch; put (a runner) out; pole (a boat); stick. *sa(saru)* stick, be stuck. *ira, toge* thorn, splinter;

spine; biting words. *sashi* sharpened tube for testing rice in bags.
⁷身 *sashimi* sliced raw fish
⁸青 *irezumi, shisei* tattooing
刺 *togetoge(shii)* sharp, harsh, stinging
⁹客 *shikaku, sekkaku, shikyaku* assassin
¹⁰殺 *sa(shi)-koro(su)* stab to death. *shisatsu suru* put out (in baseball); stab to death
¹⁶激 *shigeki* stimulus, impetus, incentive, excitement, irritation, encouragement
激的 *shigekiteki* stimulating
¹⁷繍 *shishū* embroidery.

制 A ⁴⁸¹ J4029 M1961 SEI system, organization; imperial command; laws, regulation. *sei(suru)* control, govern, suppress, restrain, hold back; establish.
⁴止 *seishi* control, check, restraint, inhibition
⁵圧 *seiatsu* oppression, control, mastery, ascendancy, supremacy
⁷肘 *seichū* restraint, check, restriction, control, interference
作 *seisaku* production (of a painting, book, etc.)
⁸定 *seitei* enactment, establishment, ⌐creation
服 *seifuku* uniform
空権 *seikūken* mastery of the air
限 *seigen* limit, limitation, restriction
⁹度 *seido* system, organization, institution
約 *seiyaku* condition, limitation, restriction
海権 *seikaiken* control of the seas
¹¹動 *seidō* braking (mechanism)
動機 *seidōki* brake
¹²帽 *seibō* regulation cap; school cap
裁 *seisai* restraint, punishment, sanctions
御 *seigyo* control, governing; checking; suppression; repression; restraint; mastery; management
¹⁹覇 *seiha* conquest, domination, supremacy, mastery; championship

———— **7** ————

則 A ⁴⁸⁷ J4227 M1994 SOKU. *norito(ru), notto(ru)* follow (precedent), be based on, go by; live up to; model after; be in accordance with. *nori* law, rule; model, doctrine. *sunawa(chi)* whereupon, accordingly.

2

B 削 488 J3a6f M2000 SAKU. *kezu(ru)* plane, sharpen, whittle, pare, shave (leather); scrape off; cross out; reduce, curtail. *so(gu)* vt chip, slice off, cut aslant, split off; diminish, reduce; dampen, spoil, mar. *so(geru)* vi split, splinter; be sunken; be sharpened; miss the mark. *hatsu(ru)* cutting down little by little; taking a percentage.

⁹除 *sakujo* elimination, cancellation, deletion, erasure
¹²減 *sakugen* reduction, curtailment

剃 489 J4466 M1989 TEI. *so(ru), su(ru)* shave.

²刀 *kamisori* razor
¹⁴髪 *teihatsu* tonsure, cutting off the hair

A 前 490 J4130 M2011 SEN. ZEN before. *mae* front, fore part; head (of a line); presence; ago, before; previously; (five minutes) to. *mae ni* ahead, before. *(o)mae(san)* you; my dear; hey. *-mae* a helping, portion; lady (So-and-so). *-zen* ago, before. *zen-* former, previous, one-time; the above. *saki ni* before, earlier that; ahead, beyond, away; previously; recently.

²人未到 *zenjin-mitō* unexplored
³口上 *mae kōjō* introductory remarks
⁴文 *zembun* the above statement; preamble
方 *zempō* front
日 *zenjitsu, maebi* the day before
⁵号 *zengō* preceding issue
払 *maebara(i)* advance payment
立腺 *zenritsusen* prostate gland
史 *zenshi* prehistory
代 *zendai* previous generation; former ages
代未聞 *zendaimimon* unparalleled, unheard of, record-breaking
半 *zempan, zenhan* first half
世 *zense, mae (no) yo, saki (no) yo* previous existence. *zensei* antiquity; the previous era
世紀 *zenseiki* last century; ancient times
⁶回 *zenkai* last time; last session
向 *maemu(ki)* facing forward
兆 *zenchō* omen, portent, sign, premonition, harbinger
列 *zenretsu* front row

年 *zennen* the preceding year, last year
年度 *zennendo* preceding fiscal year
任地 *zenninchi* former post
任者 *zenninsha* predecessor
⁷言 *zengen* previous remarks
足 *mae ashi* forefeet
身 *zenshin* antecedents, ancestor; previous position; previous existence; predecessor organization
述 *zenjutsu no* the above-mentioned
条 *zenjō* preceding article, preceding entry
売 *maeu(ri)* advance sale, booking
売券 *maeu(ri) ken,* ticket sold in advance
⁸門 *zemmon* front gate
非 *zempi* past folly, past sin
屈 *zenkutsu suru* bend forward. *maekaga(mi)* slouch
例 *zenrei* precedent
者 *zensha* the former
金 *maekin, zenkin* advance payment
金払 *maekinbara(i)* payment in advance
夜 *zen'ya* last night, the previous night
夜祭 *zen'yasai* eve
⁹面 *zemmen* front part, frontage, façade
祝 *mae iwa(i)* celebration in anticipation
段 *zendan* preceding paragraph; first part
途 *zento* one's future prospects; outlook; the journey ahead
途有望 *zento yūbō* promising future
途多難 *zento tanan* a future fraught with difficulty
科 *zenka* criminal record, previous offense
奏曲 *zensōkyoku* prelude, overture
後 *zengo, mae-ushi(ro)* front and back, before and behind, before and after. *zengo* about that (time); longitudinal; context, order, sequence. *-zengo* nearly, approximately
後不覚 *zengo-fukaku* unconsciousness
後左右 *zengo-sayū* in all directions
¹⁰庭 *zentei* front yard
座 *zenza* opening performance; minor performer
納 *zennō* prepayment, advance payment
記 *zenki no* the above-mentioned
部 *zembu* front part, fore, front
書 *maega(ki)* preface, preamble

借 *maega(ri), zenshaku* getting an advance; a loan
借金 *zenshakukin* loan, advance
進 *zenshin* advance, drive, progress
哨 *zenshō* outpost
哨戦 *zenshōsen* skirmish; prefinals (in games)
¹¹ 掛 *maeka(ke)* apron
略 *zenryaku* first part omitted; salutation of a brief letter
脚 *mae ashi, zenkyaku* forelegs
菜 *zensai* appetizers, hors d'œuvres
揭 *zenkei no* the above-named
¹² 歯 *maeba, zenshi* front tooth
開 *maebira(ki)* open in front
項 *zenkō* the preceding clause
提 *zentei* preamble, premise, reason, prerequisite
渡 *maewata(shi)* advance payment; advance delivery
腕 *maeude, zenwan* forearm
期 *zenki* first term, first half year, preceding period, early period
景 *zenkei* foreground, front view
景気 *maegeiki* prospect, promise, outlook
¹³ 触 *maebu(re)* previous notice; herald; harbinger, portent
節 *zensetsu* preceding paragraph, section, or verse
照灯 *zenshōtō* headlights
置詞 *zenchishi* preposition
¹⁴ 歴 *zenreki* personal history
髪 *maegami* forelock
駆 *zenku* vanguard, precursor, forerunner, leader
¹⁵ 線 *zensen* front line; (weather) front
輪 *zenrin, maewa* front wheel
衛 *zen'ei* advance guard, vanguard
¹⁶ 頭部 *zentōbu* the front, the forehead
¹⁸ 額部 *zengakubu* forehead. *zengakubu no* frontal

──────── 8 ────────

剖 $\frac{492}{\text{J4b36}}$ Hō. Bō divide.
B M2034

剤 $\frac{493}{\text{J3a5e}}$ Zai medicine, drug, dose.
B M2076′

剥 $\frac{496}{\text{J476d}}$ Haku. *ha(geru)* come off,
M48939 peel off, be worn off; fade, discolor. *ha(gu), ha(gasu), he(gu)* tear off, peel off, rip off, strip off; skin, flay; disrobe; deprive of. *mu(keru)* peel off, come off, be taken off. *mu(ku)* peel, pare, hull. *hezu(ru)* pilfer, steal a portion. *muku(reru)* be tangled up with, be connected with.
⁵ 出 *mu(ki)-da(su)* show, bare (the teeth). *mu(ki)da(shi)* nakedness; frankness
⁷ 身 *sukimi* a meat or fish slicer. *mukimi* shellfish removed from the shell
⁸ 取 *ha(gi)-to(ru)* tear off; strip; rob. *ha(gi)to(ri)* pad of paper
¹² 落 *hakuraku suru, ha(ge)-o(chiru)* peel off
¹⁴ 奪 *hakudatsu suru* deprive of, divest of
製 *hakusei* stuffing
¹⁹ 離 *hakuri suru vt* and *vi* peel off

剛 $\frac{497}{\text{J3964}}$ Gō strength.
B M2042
⁴ 毛 *gōmō* bristle
⁶ 気 *gōki* bravery, stoutheartedness
⁷ 体 *gōtai* a rigid body
⁸ 性 *gōsei* hardness, rigidity
直 *gōchoku* integrity, moral courage
者 *gō(no)mono* very strong person, brave warrior, veteran
⁹ 胆 *gōtan* boldness, hardihood, courage
勇 *gōyū* bravery, prowess
¹¹ 健 *gōken* vigor, virility, sturdiness, health
¹⁵ 毅 *gōki* fortitude, firmness of character, hardihood, manliness

剣 $\frac{498}{\text{J3775}}$ Ken sword, saber, blade,
B M2076 bayonet; sting; clock hand. *tsurugi* sword.
³ 士 *kenshi* fencer
⁶ 先 *kensaki* point of a sword
⁷ 呑 *kennon na* risky, dangerous, insecure
⁸ 法 *kempō* fencing
突 *kentsuku* rough scolding
⁹ 客 *kenkaku* fencer, swordsman
¹¹ 道 *kendō* fencing, swordsmanship
術 *kenjutsu* fencing
¹² 戟 *kengeki* weapons, arms
¹³ 幕 *kemmaku* threatening attitude
¹⁴ 豪 *kengō* master fencer
舞 *kembu* sword dance

2

二 亠 人 イ 入 八 ソ 冂 冖 冫 几 凵 【刀 刂 】⁸ 力 勹 匕 匚 匸 十 卜 卩 厂 厶 又

2

――――― **9** ―――――

剩 [501 | J3e6a | M2107] B Jō . *amatsusa(e)* besides.

⁷余 *jōyo* surplus, balance

副 [503 | J497b | M2097] A FUKU duplicate, copy; assistant, associate. *so(u)* *vi* suit, meet, satisfy; marry; accompany; be added to; be adjusted to. *so(eru) vt* add to, attach, append; accompany; garnish; imitate. *fuku-* vice-, sub-, deputy, assistant, substitute; auxiliary, supplementary, additional; collateral.

³大統領 *fukudaitōryō* vice-president
⁵本 *fukuhon* duplicate, copy
収入 *fukushūnyū* additional income
⁶次的 *fukujiteki* secondary
会長 *fukukaichō* vice-president (of a society)
⁷見出 *fukumida(shi)* subtitle
作用 *fukusayō* reaction, secondary effect
社長 *fukushachō* vice-president of a firm
⁸官 *fukukan, fukkan* adjutant, aide, aide-de-camp
⁹食 *fukushoku* side dish; supplementary food
食物 *fukushokubutsu* side dish; supplementary food
¹¹産物 *fukusambutsu* by-product, side line
¹²詞 *fukushi* adverb
葬品 *fukusōhin* articles buried with the dead
¹³業 *fukugyō* subsidiary business, side line
¹⁴読本 *fukutokuhon* supplementary reader
¹⁵審 *fukushin* sub-umpire, sub-referee
賞 *fukushō* extra prize
¹⁸題 *fukudai* subtitle, subheading
²⁰議長 *fukugichō* vice-chairman

――――― **10** ―――――

創 [506 | J414f | M2127] A SŌ . *kizu* wound, injury, hurt; cut, gash, bruise; scratch; scar; weak point. *haji(meru)* start, originate.

⁵立 *sōritsu* establishment, founding, organization
立者 *sōritsusha* founder, organizer
刊 *sōkan* launching a magazine; first issue
世 *sōsei* creation of the world

世記 *Sōseiki* Genesis
⁷見 *sōken* originality, creation, invention
作 *sōsaku* production, literary creation; work
⁸始 *sōshi* creation, founding, initiating
始者 *sōshisha* originator
⁹建 *sōken* establishment, foundation
建者 *sōkensha* founder
造 *sōzō* creation
造的 *sōzōteki* creative
¹⁰案 *sōan* original idea
案者 *sōansha* originator, inventor
設 *sōsetsu* establishment, founding, organization
設者 *sōsetsusha* founder
¹³意 *sōi* original idea; originality
業 *sōgyō* establishment
業者 *sōgyōsha* founder, promoter

割 [507 | J3364 | M2112] A KATSU. *wa(ru)* divide, cut, break; separate; split, rip; break, crack, smash; dilute. *wa(reru)* break, split, cleave, fissure, be smashed. *sa(ku)* cut up, cleave; sever, separate, divide; spare (time); cede, alienate. *wa(re)* broken piece. *wa(ri)* rate, ratio, proportion, percentage, profit, assignment. *wa(ri) ni* comparatively. *-wari* ten percent.

⁴込 *wa(ri)-ko(mu)* wedge oneself in, cut in, muscle in on. *wa(ri)ko(mi)* sharing a theater box; muscling in on; wedging oneself in
切 *wa(ri)-ki(reru)* be divisible by. *wa(ri)-ki(ru)* divide; give a clear explanation. *wa(ri)-ki(renai)* indivisible; unconvincing; incomprehensible; unaccounted for
引 *wa(ri)-bi(ku)* discount. *waribiki* discount, reduction, rebate
引券 *waribikiken* a discount coupon
⁵目 *wa(re)me* crevice, crack, split, rift, chasm, fissure
付 *wa(ri)-tsu(keru)* allot, assign, distribute, percentage, divide among. *waritsu(ke)* allotment, assignment, distribution; layout, editing
出 *wa(ri)-da(su)* calculate, compute; infer
礼 *katsurei* circumcision
⁶印 *wa(ri)in* a seal over the edges of adjacent sheets

二十人イ八儿入八丷冂冖冫几凵【刀刂】⁹力勹匕匚匸十卜卩厂厶又

合 *wariai* rate, ratio, proportion, percentage. *wariai ni* comparatively; contrary to expectations

安 *wariyasu na* comparatively cheap

当 *wa(ri)-a(teru)* assign, allot, divide among, distribute, prorate, assess. *waria(te)* assignment, allotment, quota, rationing

⁷判 *wa(ri)ban* a seal over the edges of adjacent sheets

戻金 *wa(ri)modo(shi)kin* rebate money

⁸拠 *kakkyo suru* hold one's ground; defend local authority

物 *wa(re)mono* broken article; fragile article

¹⁰高 *waridaka na* comparatively high

振 *wa(ri)-fu(ru)* assign, allot, divide among, distribute, prorate, assess. *wa(ri)fu(ri)* assignment, allotment, quota, rationing

烹 *kappō* cooking, cuisine

¹¹勘 *wa(ri)kan* divide the bill equally, each person pays his or her own share

¹³腹 *kappuku* disembowelment, harakiri

愛 *katsuai suru* share, spare, part with reluctantly

¹⁴算 *wa(ri)zan* division (in math)

増 *warima(shi)* extra wages, premium, bonus

¹⁵賦 *kappu, wappu* allotment, quota

箸 *wa(ri)bashi* split chopsticks, disposable chopsticks

²⁰譲 *katsujō* cession of territory

──────── **12** ────────

劃 〔513〕 〔J3344〕 〔M2193〕 KAKU divide.

¹一 *kakuitsu* uniformity, standardization

¹²然 *kakuzen(taru)* distinct, clear-cut

期的 *kakkiteki* epoch-making

──────── **13** ────────

劉 〔515〕 〔J4e2d〕 〔M2224〕 RYŪ axe; kill.

劇 〔517〕 〔J3760〕 〔M2218〕 GEKI drama, play.
A *hage(shii)* violent, vehement, furious, severe, acute, intense, extreme, passionate, heated, stormy (applause); tempestuous (temperament); mighty.

⁴文学 *geki bungaku* dramatic literature

⁶団 *gekidan* troupe, theatrical company

⁷作家 *gekisakuka* playwright, dramatist

⁸的 *gekiteki* dramatic

毒 *gekidoku* deadly poison

⁹変 *gekihen* sudden change, upheaval, convulsion, cataclysm

甚 *gekijin* intenseness, violence, severity, vehemence, keenness

映画 *geki eiga* film drama

¹⁰烈 *gekiretsu* violence, severity, intenseness, fierceness

¹¹務 *gekimu* exhausting work

¹²痛 *gekitsū* intense pain, sharp pain

評 *gekihyō* drama criticism

場 *gekijō* theater

¹⁵論 *gekiron* heated discussion

震 *gekishin* severe earthquake

¹⁶壇 *gekidan* the stage, the theatrical world

薬 *gekiyaku* powerful medicine; violent poison

¹⁸職 *gekishoku* exhausting work

═════════ **RAD. 力 19** ═════════

Chikara strength. Nickname: Strong.

力 〔521〕 〔J4e4f〕 〔M2288〕 RIKI. RYOKU. *riki(mu)*
A strain, bear up, exert one's strength; swagger, bluff, boast. *tsuto (meru)* serve, fill a post, serve under; exert oneself, endeavor, work. be diligent; play (the part of). *chikara* strength, energy, force, might, power; agency; authority, influence; vigor; stress, emphasis; exertions, endeavors; efficacy; help, support, good offices; ability, faculty, capability, attainment; means, resources. -*riki* strength. -*ryoku* strength, power.

2

二十人イヘ儿入八丷冂冖冫儿凵刀刂【力】クヒ匚匸十卜卩厂厶又

¹一杯 *chikaraippai ni* with all one's strength

³士 *rikishi* Japanese sumo wrestler; a strong man

⁵付 *chikarazu(ku) vi* be strengthened, revive, be invigorated, be encouraged. *chikarazu(keru) vt* strengthen (someone)

仕事 *chikara shigoto* physical work

⁶尽 *chikarazu(ku) de* by sheer strength

任 *chikaramaka(se) ni* with all one's might

⁷走 *rikisō* hard running

作 *rikisaku* literary masterpiece

⁸泳 *rikiei* powerful swimming

学 *rikigaku* dynamics, mechanics

⁹持 *chikaramo(chi)* strong man

点 *rikiten* leverage; emphasis, importance

¹¹強 *chikarazuyo(i)* reassuring, emboldened

¹²量 *rikiryō* physical strength; capacity, ability; tact

¹³戦 *rikisen* hard fighting

¹⁴説 *rikisetsu* emphasis, stress

¹⁵瘤 *chikarakobu* large biceps

--- **3** ---

A 功 $\frac{522}{\substack{J3879 \\ M2295}}$ Kō merits, meritorious deeds; success; credit, honor; effect; class (in court orders). KU merits. *isao, isaoshi* merit; meritorious deed.

⁶名 *kōmyō* great achievement

名心 *kōmyōshin* ambition, love of fame

⁷利 *kōri* utility; utilitarian

利主義 *kōri shugi* utilitarianism

利的 *kōriteki* utilitarian, businesslike

労 *kōrō* meritorious deed; services

労者 *kōrōsha* man of distinguished service

¹⁰能 *kōnō* work; efficiency

¹³罪 *kōzai* merits and demerits

業 *kōgyō* exploit, achievement

¹⁴徳 *kōtoku, kudoku* charity, virtue, merit

¹⁷績 *kōseki* meritorious service, merit

A 加 $\frac{523}{\substack{J3243 \\ M2297}}$ KA addition, increase. *kuwa(waru)* join in; accede to; gain in (influence); increase.

kuwa(eru) add, sum up; append; include; increase; inflict. *kuwa(uru) ni* besides, furthermore. *kuwa(ete)* and, in addition, furthermore.

²入 *kanyū* joining, entry, admission, affiliation, adherence, signing, subscription

入金 *kanyūkin* admission fee

入者 *kanyūsha* member, entrant, participant; (telephone) subscriber

³工 *kakō* processing, manufacturing, treatment

工品 *kakōhin* processed goods, finished goods

⁵圧 *kaatsu* increasing pressure

⁸味 *kami* seasoning, flavoring

担 *katan* support; conspiracy, complicity

⁹重 *kajū, kachō* weighting (in averaging); aggravation

速度 *kasokudo* acceleration

除 *kajo* insertion and deletion

¹⁰害 *kagai* assault, violence, damaging (someone)

害者 *kagaisha* assailant

¹²湿 *kashitsu* humidification

筆 *kahitsu* correction, revision

減 *kagen* addition and subtraction; allowance for; degree; condition; seasoning, flavor; moderation; adjustment; influence (of the weather); state of health; chance

減乗除 *kagenjōjo* the four arithmetical operations (addition, subtraction, mulitplication, and division)

¹³勢 *kasei* assistance, backing, reinforcements; assistant

盟 *kamei* participation, affiliation

¹⁴算 *kasan, kuwa(e)zan* addition

¹⁵熱 *kanetsu* heating

¹⁷療 *karyō* medical treatment

²⁰護 *kago* divine protection

--- **4** ---

B 劣 $\frac{524}{\substack{J4e74 \\ M2302}}$ RETSU. *oto(ru)* be inferior to, be worse than.

¹⁰弱 *retsujaku* inferiority

¹¹情 *retsujō* animal passions, carnal desire, lust

悪 *retsuaku na* inferior, coarse

¹²等 *rettō* inferiority, low grade
等感 *rettōkan* inferiority complex
¹³勢 *ressei* numerical inferiority; weakness

───── 5 ─────

努 $\frac{527}{\text{J4558}}$ M2314 Do *tsuto(meru)* serve, fill a post, serve under; exert oneself, endeavor, work, be diligent; play (the part of). *tsuto(mete)* as much as possible; diligently.

²力 *doryoku* endeavor, exertion, effort, labor, strain, industry
力家 *doryokuka* hard worker

励 $\frac{528}{\text{J4e65}}$ M2326 REI *hage(mu)* be diligent. *hage(masu)* encourage, inspire; raise (the voice). *hage(mi)* encouragement, stimulation; incentive.

⁶行 *reikō suru* enforce strictly, carry out (regulations)

劫 $\frac{529}{\text{J3965}}$ M2316 Kō, Gō, Kyō threat; long ages. *obiya(kasu)* threaten.

⁴火 *gōka* world-destroying conflagration
¹¹掠 *kyōryaku, gōryaku* pillage, plunder
略 *kyōryaku, gōryaku* pillage, plunder

助 $\frac{530}{\text{J3d75}}$ M2313 Jo help, rescue. *tasu(karu)* be saved, be rescued, survive; be helpful. *tasu(keru)* help; save, rescue; give relief to; spare (life); reinforce; promote; abet. *su(keru)* help. *tasu(ke), suke* assistance. *jo-* assistant.

²力 *joryoku* assistance, support
³上 *tasu(ke)-a(geru)* help up; pick up, bring safely to land
⁴手 *tasu(ke)te, su(ke)te* helper, helpmeet. *joshu* helper, assistant, tutor; intern
太刀 *sukedachi* help, assistance, helper, supporter, backer
⁵出 *tasu(ke)-da(su)* help out of (trouble), extricate
⁶合 *tasu(ke)-a(u)* help each other, cooperate
成 *josei* fostering, aiding
成金 *joseikin* subsidy, grant-in-aid
⁷役 *joyaku* deputy mayor, deputy

stationmaster
言 *jogon, jogen* advice, suggestion
言者 *jogonsha, jogensha* adviser, counsellor
⁸長 *jochō* promotion, fostering
命 *jomei* sparing a life, clemency, reconsidering a dismissal
¹¹船 *tasu(ke)bune* lifeboat; a friend in need, help
動詞 *jodoshi* auxiliary verb
教授 *jokyōju* assistant or associate professor
産婦 *josampu* midwife
¹²詞 *joshi* a particle (in grammar)
¹³数詞 *josūshi* counters for various categories of objects
¹⁴監督 *jokantoku* assistant director (in taking professional movies)

労 $\frac{531}{\text{J4f2b}}$ M2329 Rō labor, toil, trouble. *rō(suru)* labor, toil, strive; put (someone) to work; thank (someone) for their efforts; comfort. *itawa(ru)* pity, sympathize with, console, care for, be kind to. *negira(u)* thank for, reward for. *itawa(ri)* trouble, service, labor; sympathy; illness; carefulness, attention. *itazuki* pain, trouble.

²力 *rōryoku* labor; toil, trouble
⁷災保険 *rōsai hoken* worker's accident insurance
作 *rōsaku* toil, labor; laborious task
役 *rōeki* work, labor, toil
⁸使 *rōshi* laborers and employers
苦 *rōku* labor, toil, hardship
¹¹務 *rōmu* labor, work, service
¹³賃 *rōchin* wages
働 *rōdō* manual labor, work, toil
働力 *rōdōryoku* labor, manpower, working force
働大臣 *Rōdō Daijin* Minister of Labor
働争議 *rōdō sōgi* labor trouble, strike
働条件 *rōdō jōken* working conditions
働者 *rōdōsha* laborer, worker
働省 *Rōdōshō* Ministry of Labor
働時間 *rōdō jikan* working hours; man hours
働組合 *rōdō kumiai* labor union

2

二
亠
人
イ
ハ
几
入
八
ソ
冂
冖
冫
几
凵
刀
刂
[力]
勹
匕
匚
匸
十
卜
卩
厂
ム
又

6⁶

—————— 6 ——————

劢 B 534 J332f M2342 GAI criminal investigation.

効 A 535 J387a M2334 Kō efficacy, benefit; efficiency; effect, result; success. *ki(ku)* be effective.

² 力 *kōryoku* effect, efficacy; validity
⁵ 用 *kōyō* use, utility, effect, benefit
　目 *kikime* effect, efficacy, impression
⁸ 果 *kōka* effect, efficacy, result
　果的 *kōkateki* effective, successful
¹⁰ 能 *kōnō* effect, efficacy, virtue, benefit
　能書 *kōnōga(ki)* statement of the efficacy of a medicine
¹¹ 率 *kōritsu* efficiency
¹⁸ 験 *kōken* efficacy, effect

—————— 7 ——————

勃 539 J4b56 M2351 BOTSU suddenness; rise.

⁹ 勃 *botsubotsu(taru)* spirited, rising energetic
　発 *boppatsu* outbreak, outburst, sudden occurrence
¹⁰ 起 *bokki suru* stand erect, stiffen
¹² 然 *botsuzen to* suddenly; in fit of anger
¹⁶ 興 *bokkō* sudden rise to power

勅 B 540 J443c M2354 CHOKU *mikotonori* imperial decree.

⁵ 令 *chokurei* imperial edict
⁶ 旨 *chokushi* imperial order, imperial will
　任 *chokunin* imperial appointment
⁸ 使 *chokushi* imperial messenger
　命 *chokumei* imperial command
¹¹ 許 *chokkyo* imperial sanction
¹⁴ 語 *chokugo* imperial rescript
¹⁵ 撰 *chokusen* compilation for the emperor; emperor's literary production
¹⁶ 諭 *chokuyu* imperial instructions

勇 A 541 J4d26 M2360 YŪ bravery, courage, heroism. *isa(mu)* cheer up, be in high spirits. *isa(mashii)* courageous, valiant.

³ 士 *yūshi* brave man, hero
⁵ 立 *isa(mi)-ta(tsu)* cheer up, be encouraged (by)

⁶ 壮 *yūsō* bravery, heroism
　肌 *isa(mi)hada* gallantry
　名 *yūmei* fame, great renown
　気 *yūki* courage, bravery, valor, nerve, boldness.
　気付 *yūkizu(ke)* have a burst of courage
⁸ 退 *yūtai suru* retire voluntarily, bow out
　者 *yūsha* hero, man of valor
　往 *yūō* spirited advance, energetically going forward
⁹ 姿 *yūshi* gallant figure
¹¹ 断 *yūdan* resolute decision
　猛 *yūmō* daring, bravery, valor
¹² 敢 *yūkan* heroism, gallantry, bravery
¹³ 戦 *yūsen* brave fight, desperate fight
²¹ 躍 *yūyaku suru* take heart, be in high spirits

—————— 8 ——————

勉 A 543 J4a59 M2384' BEN. *tsuto(meru)* serve, fill a post, serve under; exert oneself, endeavor, work, be diligent; play (the part of). *tsuto(mete)* as much as possible; diligently.

⁷ 励 *benrei* diligence
⁸ 学 *bengaku* study
¹¹ 強 *benkyō* study; diligence; discount, reduction
　強家 *benkyōka* scholar, diligent student

—————— 9 ——————

務 A 546 J4c33 M2394 MU. *tsuto(meru)* serve, fill a post, serve under; exert oneself, endeavor, work, be diligent; play (the part of). *tsuto(me)* service, duty, business; Buddhist religious services.

勘 B 548 J342a M2393 KAN perception, intuition; the sixth sense.

⁵ 弁 *kamben* pardon, forgiveness, forbearance
⁶ 気 *kanki* disfavor, disinheritance
　当 *kandō* disinheritance
⁷ 忍 *kannin* patient endurance
⁸ 所 *kandokoro* finger board (of an instrument); vital point
　定 *kanjō* calculation; account; settlement of an account; consideration, allowance
　定取 *kanjōto(ri)* bill collector

定係 *kanjōgakari* cashier, accountant, treasurer

定書 *kanjōga(ki)* bill, one's account

定高 *kanjōdaka(i)* calculating, mercenary, closefisted

¹⁰校 *kankō suru* examine and correct

案 *kan'an suru* think

¹²違 *kanchiga(i)* misunderstanding, wrong guess

¹⁹繰 *kangu(ru)* be suspicious of

動 A | 549 J4630 M2390 | Dō motion; change; confusion. *dō(jiru), dō(zuru)* be perturbed, be agitated. *ugo(ku) vi* move, stir, shift, shake, swing; operate, run, go, work; be touched, be influenced, waver, fluctuate, vary, change, be transferred. *ugo(kasu) vt* move, shift; set in motion, operate; inspire, rouse, influence; mobilize; deny; change. *ugo(ki)* movement, activity, trend, development, change. *yaya(mosureba), yaya(tomosureba)* be apt to, be liable to, be inclined to.

²力 *dōryoku* power, motive power, dynamic force

力学 *dōryokugaku* kinetics, dynamics

力源 *dōryokugen* source of power

⁶向 *dōkō* trend, tendency, movement, attitude

名詞 *dōmeishi* gerund

⁷作 *dōsa* action, movements, motions; bearing, behavior, manners

乱 *dōran* agitation, commotion, riot

⁸的 *dōteki* dynamic, kinetic

物 *dōbutsu* animal

物学 *dōbutsugaku* zoology

物園 *dōbutsuen* zoo

物誌 *dōbutsushi* fauna

¹⁰員 *dōin* mobilization

脈 *dōmyaku* artery

脈硬化 *dōmyaku kōka* arteriosclerosis

¹¹悸 *dōki* palpitation, pulsation, throbbing

転 *dōten* being surprised and stunned; transition, change

産 *dōsan* personal property, personal effects

¹²揺 *dōyō* shaking, trembling, pitching, rolling, oscillation; agitation, excitement; unrest, commotion

---

植物 *dōshokubutsu* plants and animals, flora and fauna

詞 *dōshi* verb

¹⁴静 *dōsei* state, condition, movements

態 *dōtai* movement; vital (statistics)

¹⁶機 *dōki* motive, incentive

²⁰議 *dōgi* a motion

--- **10** ---

募 B | 551 J4a67 M2416 | Bo. *tsuno(ru)* gather (contributions); campaign (for students); float (a loan); enlist (troops); grow violent.

⁸金 *bokin* fund raising

¹²集 *boshū* recruiting; invitation, collection; enrollment; solicitation; flotation

勤 A | 552 J3650 M2415' | KIN. GON. *tsuto(maru)* be fit for, be equal to, function properly. *tsuto(meru)* serve, fill a post, serve under; exert oneself, endeavor, work, be diligent; play (the part of). *tsuto(me)* service, duty, business; Buddhist religious services.

²人 *tsuto(me)nin* office worker, salaried man, white-collar worker

³口 *tsuto(me)guchi* position, place of employment

⁶行 *tsuto(me)-okona(u)* carry on (work). *gongyō* Buddhist religious service

先 *tsuto(me)saki* place of work

⁷求 *gongu* inquiring about the Buddha way

⁷労 *kinrō* labor, exertion

労者 *kinrōsha* working man

労奉仕 *kinrō hōshi* labor service

労所得 *kinrō shotoku* earned income

労感謝日 *Kinrō Kansha no Hi* (Labor) Thanksgiving Day, November 23

⁹怠 *kintai* diligence and indolence; diligence; attendance

皇 *kinnō* imperialism

¹⁰倹 *kinken* industry, diligence, frugality

勉 *kimben* industry, diligence

¹¹務 *kimmu* service, duty, work

務先 *kimmusaki* place of employment

務評定 *kimmu hyōtei* evaluation of workers

¹³続 *kinzoku* continuous service

2

二
十
人
イ
ヘ
儿
入
八
丷
冂
冖
冫
几
凵
刀
刂
【力】¹⁰
勹
匕
匚
匸
十
卜
卩
厂
厶
又

2

二亠人イ八丷冂冖冫几凵刀刂【力】勹匕匸匚十卜卩厂厶又

A 勝 ₅₅₃ J3e21 M2409 SHŌ victory; beauty spot. *ka(tsu)* win; prevail, predominate, surpass. *masa(ru)* excel, surpass, outrival. *sugu(reru)* excel, surpass; have advantages over; be excellent. *ka(chi)* victory, success. *-ga(chi)* be apt to, be prone to, be liable to, tend to; predominating.

⁴手 *katte* kitchen; condition, circumstances; one's own convenience; wilfulness, selfishness. *katte(gamashii)* selfish

手口 *katteguchi* back door, service door

手気盡 *kattekimama* selfishness

⁵目 *ka(chi)me* chances of winning

⁶因 *shōin* cause of victory

地 *shōchi* scenic spot

⁷抜 *ka(chi)-nu(ku)* win one game after another

抜戦 *ka(chi)nu(ki)sen* tournament

利 *shōri* victory

⁸者 *shōsha* winner, victor, conqueror

⁹負 *shōbu* victory or defeat; game, bout. *ka(chi)ma(ke)* victory or defeat

負事 *shōbugoto* game of skill; gambling

負師 *shōbushi* gambler; chess or go player

¹¹敗 *shōhai* victory or defeat; the issue (of a battle)

¹²訴 *shōso* winning a lawsuit

景 *shōkei* beautiful view, scenic spot

¹³誇 *ka(chi)-hoko(ru)* triumph, be elated with success

¹⁴算 *shōsan* chances of victory

¹⁶鬨 *ka(chi)doki* shout of victory; victory song

───────── 11 ─────────

A 勢 ₅₅₈ J402a M2422 SE. SEI. energy; military strength. *ikio(izuku)* gather strength. *ikio(i)* force, vigor, energy, spirit, life; authority, influence, power, might; impetus; course (of events), tendency; necessarily. *hazumi* spring, bound, rebound; inertia, momentum; impetus, stimulus, impulse; instant; chance.

²力 *seiryoku* influence, power, might, strength; force, energy

力下 *seiryokuka ni* under the influence or power of

力家 *seiryokuka, seiryokka* man of influence

力圏 *seiryokuken* sphere of influence

力範囲 *seiryoku han'i* sphere of influence

⁴込 *ikio(i)-ko(mu)* brace oneself

⁹威 *seii* power, might, authority, influence; high spirits

¹²揃 *seizoro(i)* array, muster, lineup; full force

B 勧 ₅₅₉ J342b M2433 KAN. *susu(meru)* recommend, advise, encourage; offer (wine). *susu(me)* recommendation, advice, encouragement.

⁷告 *kankoku* advice, counsel, recommendation

¹⁰進 *kanjin* temple solicitation

進元 *kanjimmoto* backer, promoter

¹²善懲悪 *kanzen-chōaku* rewarding good and punishing evil; political justice; moral purpose

¹³奨 *kanshō* encouragement, stimulation

業 *kangyō* encouragement of industry; industry

¹⁴誘 *kan'yū* invitation, inducement, solicitation, canvassing; persuasion, encouragement

誘員 *kan'yūin* canvasser, traveling salesman

───────── 13 ─────────

B 勲 ₅₆₀ J372e M2463 KUN merit, order of merit. *isao, isaoshi* meritorious deed; merit.

⁵功 *kunkō* merits, distinguished services

⁷位 *kun'i* order of merit

¹⁰記 *kunki* decoration diploma

¹¹章 *kunshō* decoration, order, medal

¹²等 *kuntō* order of merit

¹⁷爵 *kunshaku* peerage and order of merit

勹 RAD. 勹 20

Tsutsumigamae "wrapping" enclosure. Nickname: Wrapping.

1

勺 $\frac{565}{\text{J3c5b}}$ SHAKU one-tenth of a *gō*
B M2495 (see Weights and
Measures); dip, ladle.

2

匆 $\frac{566}{\text{J4c68}}$ （国字）*momme, me* $\frac{1}{100}$
B M2502 *hyakume* (See Weights and
Measures)

匂 $\frac{567}{\text{J4677}}$ （国字）*nio(u)* be fragant,
M2503 smell; stink; glow, be bright.
nio(wasu), nio(waseru) vt give out an
odor, scent, or perfume; suggest,
insinuate. *nioi* smell, odor, scent; stench;
fragrance, aroma, perfume.

勾 $\frac{568}{\text{J387b}}$ KŌ be bent.
M2500
⁴引 *kōin suru* arrest, seduce, abduct. *kōin*
arrest, custody.
⁵玉 *magatama* comma-shaped jewels
¹⁰配 *kōbai* slope, incline, gradient, grade,
pitch
留 *kōryū* detention, confinement

勿 $\frac{569}{\text{J4c5e}}$ MOCHI. BUTSU. *naka(re)*
M2501 must not, do not, be not.
⁷忘草 *wasurenagusa* forget-me-not
体 *mottai* overemphasis. *mottai(buru)*
assume airs. *mottai(rashiku)*
exaggeratedly, importantly

体無 *mottaina(i)* sacrilegious; unworthy
of; wasteful
⁸怪幸 *mokke (no) saiwa(i)* stroke of luck,
godsend, windfall
¹⁵論 *mochiron* naturally, of course

3

包 $\frac{572}{\text{J4a71}}$ HŌ. *tsutsu(mu)* wrap,
A M2506' pack up; cover with; dress
in; conceal. *kuru(mu)* wrap up, tuck in.
kuru(meru) lump together, include, sum
up; quibble. *tsutsu(mi)* bundle, package,
parcel, bale. *tsutsu(minaku)* without
concealment, without reserve, frankly.
²丁 *hōchō* kitchen knife; cooking
⁴込 *tsutsu(mi)-ko(mu)* wrap up
⁷囲 *hōi* siege, encirclement
含 *hōgan suru* include, comprise,
comprehend, cover, imply
⁹括 *hōkatsu* include, comprise,
comprehend, cover, imply
括的 *hōkatsuteki* inclusive,
comprehensive
¹⁰紙 *tsutsu(mi)gami* wrapping
paper
容 *hōyō suru* comprehend, embrace,
imply, tolerate
帯 *hōtai* bandage, dressing
¹²装 *hōsō* packing, wrapping
¹³摂 *hōsetsu* connotation
隠 *tsutsu(mi)-kaku(su)* conceal, keep
secret, cover up. *tsutsu(mi)kaku(shi)*
concealment

ヒ RAD. ヒ 21

Saji spoon or *hi* (the katakana). Variant: ヒ. Nickname: *Kana Hi*.

2

化 $\frac{580}{\text{J323d}}$ KA influence. KE.
A M2572 *ba(kasu)* bewitch, enchant,
confuse, delude. *ba(keru)* appear in
disguise. *ka(suru), ka(su), ke(suru)*

change into, convert into, transform, be
reduced; influence, improve (someone).
fu(keru) steam (rice); change with age,
spoil from weathering. *(o)ba(ke)* goblin,
apparition. *-ka* -ize (a verbal ending
meaning "to change").

2

二十人イ几入八丷冂冖冫几凵刀刂力勹【匕】匚匸匚十卜卩厂厶又

⁵ 石 *kaseki* petrifaction, fossilization; fossil

石学 *kasekigaku* paleontology

⁶ 合 *kagō* compounding (in chemistry)

合物 *kagōbutsu* chemical compound

成 *kasei* change, transformation

⁷ 身 *keshin* (Buddhist) incarnation; personification; impersonation

⁸ 物 *ba(ke)mono* goblin, apparition

学 *kagaku* chemistry

学工業 *kagaku kōgyō* chemical industry

学反応 *kagaku hannō* chemical reaction

学式 *kagaku shiki* chemical formula

学兵器 *kagaku heiki* chemical weapons

学者 *kagakusha* chemist

学肥料 *kagaku hiryō* chemical fertilizer

学変化 *kagaku henka* chemical change

学記号 *kagaku kigō* chemical symbols (for the elements)

学療法 *kagaku ryōhō* chemotherapy

学繊維 *kagaku sen'i* synthetic fibers

¹² 粧 *keshō* makeup

粧台 *keshōdai* dressing table, dresser

粧石鹸 *keshō sekken* toilet soap

粧品 *keshōhin* toilet articles

粧室 *keshōshitsu* powder room, lavatory

粧箱 *keshōbako* vanity case; fancy box

¹⁷ 繊 *kasen* synthetic fibers

膿 *kanō suru* suppurate, fester, come to a head

--- **3** ---

北 ⁵⁸¹ J4b4c M2574 A Hoku. *kita* north.

³ 上 *hokujō* going north

⁴ 方 *hoppō* north, northward; northern

斗七星 *Hokuto Shichisei* Big Dipper

⁵ 半球 *Kita Hankyū* Northern Hemisphere

氷洋 *Hokuhyōyō, Hoppyōyō* Arctic Ocean

北西 *hokuhokusei* north-northwest

北東 *hokuhokutō* north-northeast

⁶ 行 *hokkō* northbound; sailing north

向 *kitamu(ki)* facing north, northern exposure

米 *Hokubei* North America

回帰線 *Kita Kaikisen* Tropic of Cancer

西 *hokusei, kitanishi* northwest

⁸ 枕 *kitamakura* turning the head to the north in sleeping

東 *hokutō, kitahigashi* northeast

国 *hokkoku, kitaguni* northern provinces, northern countries

欧 *Hokuō* Northern Europe; land of the Norsemen, Scandinavia

岸 *hokugan* north coast; north bank

⁹ 面 *hokumen* north face, north side; the north; facing north

風 *hokufū, kitakaze* north wind

海 *hokkai* northern sea, the North Sea

洋 *hokuyō* northern waters

¹⁰ 進 *hokushin suru* proceed north

部 *hokubu* north, northern part

¹¹ 側 *kitagawa* north side, north bank. *hokusoku* north side

寄 *kitayo(ri)* northerly (wind)

¹² 極 *Hokkyoku* North Pole

極光 *hokkyokukō* northern lights, aurora borealis

極海 *Hokkyokukai* Arctic Ocean

極星 *Hokkyokusei* North Star

極圏 *Hokkyokuken* Arctic Circle

極熊 *hokkyokuguma* polar bear

¹⁴ 端 *hokutan* northern extremity

¹⁶ 緯 *hokui* north latitude

--- **9** ---

匙 ⁵⁸² J3a7c M2590 Shi. Ji. *saji* spoon.

⁵ 加減 *saji kagen* about a spoonful; dosage, prescription; discretion, consideration, allowance

⁷ 投 *saji (o) na(geru)* withdraw, give up as hopeless

━━━━━━━━━ **RAD.** 匚 **22** ━━━━━━━━━

Hakogamae (box-on-side enclosure). Variant: 匚. This variant is actually
Rad. 23 but is treated herein as Rad. 22. Nickname: Box on Side.

─────────── **2** ───────────

B 匹 584 / J4924 / M2673 HITSU. HIKI head, counter
(small animals); roll of cloth.
⁴夫 *hippu* a man; a coarse man; a rustic
夫勇 *hippu (no) yū* rash courage
¹¹婦 *hippu* coarse woman; country woman
¹⁵敵 *hitteki suru* compare with, match,
rival, be equal to

A 区 585 / J3668 / M2674 KU ward, district,
section
⁴区 *kuku(taru), machimachi no* several,
various, divergent, conflicting
切 *kugi(ru)* punctuate; cut off; mark off.
kugi(ri) punctuation
分 *kuwa(ke), kubun* division, section,
demarcation; (traffic) lane;
compartment; classification, sorting
⁵民 *kumin* ward residents
⁷別 *kubetsu* distinction, difference;
classification
役所 *kuyakusho* ward office
⁸画 *kukaku* division, section;
compartment; boundary; area;
block
画整理 *kukaku seiri* land readjustment,
town planning
¹¹域 *kuiki* limits, boundary; domain, zone,
sphere, territory
¹²間 *kukan* section (of track, etc.)
²⁰議 *kugi* ward assemblyman

─────────── **3** ───────────

匝 586 / J4159 / M2599 SŌ go around.

─────────── **4** ───────────

匡 587 / J3629 / M2606 KYŌ correct; save; assist.

B 匠 588 / J3e22 / M2605 SHŌ workman, artisan;
means; idea. *takumi*
artisan, mechanic; carpenter.

─────────── **5** ───────────

A 医 590 / J3065 / M2680 I medicine, the
healing art; doctor.
i(suru), iya(su) cure, heal; quench (thirst).
³大 *idai* medical university
⁷局 *ikyoku* medical office, dispensary
⁸長 *ichō* head doctor
者 *isha* doctor
学 *igaku* medical science, medicine
学界 *igakukai* medical world
学博士 *Igaku Hakushi, Igaku Hakase*
M.D., Doctor of Medicine
⁹界 *ikai* medical world
⁹科 *ika* medical department
院 *iin* doctor's office, dispensary
¹⁰書 *isho* medical book
師 *ishi* doctor
師会 *ishikai* medical association
¹¹術 *ijutsu* medicine, healing art
務 *imu* medical affairs
務室 *imushitsu* medical office
¹⁶薬 *iyaku* medicine
薬品 *iyakuhin* medical supplies
¹⁷療 *iryō* medical care; medical
療保険 *iryō hoken* medical-care
insurance
療施設 *iryō shisetsu* medical facilities
療機関 *iryō kikan* medical institution

─────────── **8** ───────────

B 匿 591 / J463f / M2690 TOKU. *kakuma(u)* shelter,
shield, hide.
⁶名 *tokumei* anonymity; pseudonym

匪 592 / J485b / M2629 HI negation; wicked person.
¹³賊 *hizoku* bandit, rebel

2

二 亠 人 亻 入 八 丷 冂 冖 冫 几 凵 刀 刂 力 勹 匕 匚 匸 十 卜 卩 厂 厶 又

RAD. ⼕ 23

Kakushi-gamae "hiding" enclosure. This radical is treated herein as a
variant of Rad. 22. Nickname: Hiding.

RAD. 十 24

Jū ten. Variants: 十, ナ. The enclosure ナ is sometimes included as a
variant of this, but not herein. Nickname: Cross.

A **十** | 598 / J3d3d / M2695 | JŪ *tō, to* ten.

¹ 一月 *Jūichigatsu* November
² 八番 *jūhachiban* No. 18; one's favorite
stunt; one's hobby. *ohako* one's
favorite stunt, one's hobby
人力 *jūninriki* the strength of ten
人十色 *jūnin-toiro* Everyone has his
own interests and ideas.
人並 *jūninna(mi)* average, mediocrity
二支 *jūnishi* the 12 signs of the
zodiac
二月 *Jūnigatsu* December
二分 *jūnibun* more than enough
二単衣 *jūnihitoe* lady's ceremonial
court dress
二指腸 *jūnishichō* duodenum
二時 *jūniji* 12 o'clock; noon; midnight
³ 干 *jikkan* the ten calendar signs
三夜 *jūsan'ya* the 13th day (of the
moon); the night of the 13th day of the
ninth lunar moon
万 *jūman* 100,000
⁴ 手 *jitte* short metal truncheon
五夜 *jūgoya* night of the full moon; the
night of the 15th day of the eighth
lunar month
文字 *jūmonji* cross. *jūmonji no*
cruciform. *jūmonji ni* crosswise.
中八九 *jitchū-hakku* eight or nine cases
out of ten
日 *tōka* ten days; the tenth (day of the
month)
月 *Jūgatsu* October
分 *jūbun* enough, satisfactory; perfect;
thorough. *juppun* ten minutes.
⁵ 代 *jūdai* the teens; the tenth generation
⁶ 全 *jūzen* perfection, consummation;
absolute safety
字 *jūji* cross. *jūji ni* crosswise. *jūji no*

crossed, cruciform
字架 *jūjika* cross; the Cross (of Christ)
字軍 *Jūjigun* Crusades; Crusaders
字路 *jūjiro* crossroads
⁹ 指 *jisshi, jusshi* the ten fingers
重 *toe* tenfold
¹⁰ 倍 *jūbai* ten times, tenfold
進法 *jisshinhō* decimal system
¹⁴ 種競技 *jisshu kyōgi* decathlon
¹⁵ 億 *jūoku* a billion

1

A **千** | 599 / J4069 / M2697 | SEN *chi*
thousand; many.

¹ 一夜 *Sen'ichiya* Thousand and One
Nights
² 人力 *senninriki* strength of a thousand
men
³ 千 *chiji* thousands. *chiji* a great number
of; variety
万 *chiyorozu* a great many. *semman*
10,000,000; myriad. *semban*
exceedingly, very many, very much,
indeed
⁴ 切 *chigi(ru)* cut up fine; pick (fruit).
sengiri short small pieces of
vegetables
⁵ 古 *senko* all ages; great antiquity;
eternity
代 *chiyo, sendai* 1,000 years; a very long
period
代紙 *chiyogami* gaily colored paper
⁶ 両 *senryō* 1,000 *ryō* (an old Japanese
coin)
両役者 *senryō yakusha* star (actor),
prima donna; leading figure
年 *sennen* millennium, 1,000 years
⁷ 里 *senri* 1,000 *ri*; a long distance
里眼 *senrigan* clairvoyance; clairvoyant

⁸金 *senkin* 1,000 yen; 1,000 pieces of gold; pricelessness

枚通 *semmaidō(shi)* an awl

⁹草 *chigusa* great variety of flowering plants

変万化 *sempembanka* innumerable changes, infinite variety

客万来 *senkaku-banrai, senkyaku-banrai* flood of customers

軍万馬 *sengumbamba* series of battles

秋 *senshū* 1,000 years; many years

秋楽 *senshūraku* the last day of a sumo tournament; the concluding program

¹⁰倍 *sembai* 1,000-fold

島 *Chishima* the Kurile Islands

差万別 *sensa-bambetsu* infinite variety

¹¹鳥 *chidori* plover

鳥足 *chidori ashi* tottering steps

¹²鈞 *senkin* 1,000 pounds; 1,000 *kan*; great weight

¹³歳 *chitose* 1,000 years

載 *senzai* 1,000 years; a long time; a millennium; perpetuity

載一遇 *senzai-ichigū* experienced once in 1,000 times; once in a lifetime opportunity

¹⁵慮一失 *senryo (no) isshitsu* the mistake of a wise man

篇一律 *sempen-ichiritsu* monotony, lack of variety

--- 2 ---

升 $\frac{603}{\text{J3e23}}$ SHō 1.8 liter. *masu* a
B $\overline{\text{M2702}}$ measuring box.

午 $\frac{604}{\text{J3861}}$ Go *uma* 11 a.m. – 1 p.m.;
A $\overline{\text{M2703}}$ seventh zodiac sign. *uma* horse; south.

⁹後 *gogo* afternoon, p.m.

前 *gozen* forenoon, a.m.

¹³睡 *gosui* nap, siesta

--- 3 ---

半 $\frac{608}{\text{J483e}}$ HAN half; odd number;
A $\overline{\text{M2707}}$ semi-, hemi-, demi-.
naka(ba) half, semi-, middle, halfway; partly.

²人前 *hannimmae* half share; half a person

⁴日 *hunnichi, hanjitsu* a half day

分 *hambun* half. *hampun* half minute

円 *han'en* semicircle

円形 *han'enkei* semicircle

月 *hantsuki, hangetsu* half moon; half month; semicircle

⁵生 *hansei* half a lifetime. *hanshō* half death

半 *hanhan* half and half, fifty-fifty

母音 *hamboin* semivowel

世紀 *hanseiki* a half century

永久的 *han'eikyūteki* semipermanent

可通 *hankatsū* superficial knowledge; smatterer

⁶休 *hankyū* half holiday

死半生 *hanshi-hanshō* half dead

年 *hantoshi, hannen* a half year

⁷里 *hanri* half a *ri* (see Weights and Measures)

狂乱 *hankyōran* half-crazed

身不随 *hunshin fuzui* paralyzed on one side

身像 *hanshinzō* half-length statue or portrait, bust

⁸金 *hankin* half the amount

周 *hanshū* semicircle

径 *hankei* radius

夜 *han'ya* midnight

官半民 *hankan-hammin* semi-governmental

⁹音 *han'on* half tone (in music)

透明 *hantōmei* semi-transparency

信半疑 *hanshin-hangi* dubious, incredulous

面 *hammen* half the face; one side, half; the other side the reverse; the contrary

¹⁰値 *hanne* half price

時 *hantoki* about an hour; a short time

紙 *hanshi* rice paper, thin Japanese writing paper

袖 *hansode* short sleeves

島 *hantō* peninsula

¹²期 *hanki* half term, half year, half period

畳 *hanjō* half mat; hissing, heckling

開 *hankai* semicivilized. *hambira(ki)* partly open, in half bloom

減 *hangen* reduction by half

¹³数 *hansū* half the number

農 *hannō* part-time farming

¹⁴旗 *hanki* flag at half-mast

端 *hampa* fragment; incomplete set; fraction, odd sum; remnant; incompleteness

2

二 亠 人 イ ハ 入 八 ソ 冂 宀 冫 几 凵 刀 刂 力 勹 匕 匚 匸 十 ³ 卜 卩 厂 厶 又

2

導体 *handōtai* semiconductor
製品 *hanseihin* semiprocessed goods
¹⁶ 壊 *hankai* partial destruction
濁点 *handakuten* circle used in *kana* to indicate p-sound
濁音 *handakuon* p-sound
¹⁸ 額 *hangaku* half price, half amount, half fare
²⁰ 鐘 *hanshō* fire alarm
²¹ 纏 *hanten* short coat; workman's livery coat

──────── 6 ────────

尭 ⁶¹⁴ J3646 M-X Gyō high; valuable; rich; abundant.

A 卒 ⁶¹⁵ J4234 M2740 Sotsu soldier, private; graduate. *sos(suru)* die, pass away.
⁴ 中 *sotchū* apoplexy, cerebral stroke
¹⁰ 倒 *sottō* fainting, swooning
¹² 塔婆 *sotoba* wooden grave tablet; stupa
¹³ 業 *sotsugyō* graduation
業生 *sotsugyōsei* graduate, alumnus
業式 *sotsugyōshiki* graduation exercises
業証書 *sotsugyō shōsho* graduation certificate

B 卓 ⁶¹⁶ J426e M2741 Taku table, desk; high.
³ 子 *takushi, tēburu* table
上 *takujō* after-dinner (speech); on the table, on the desk
⁷ 見 *takken* clearsightedness, penetration, farsightedness; excellent idea
抜 *takubatsu* excellence, superiority, preeminence; prevalence
⁸ 効 *takkō* great efficiency
¹¹ 球 *takkyū* pingpong, table tennis
袱台 *chabudai* tea table
¹² 絶 *takuzetsu* excellence, superiority, preeminence; prevalence
越 *takuetsu* excellence, superiority, preeminence; prevalence
¹⁴ 説 *takusetsu* excellent opinion
¹⁵ 論 *takuron* sound argument, clever presentation
¹⁹ 識 *takushiki* clearsightedness, penetration, farsightedness; excellent idea

A 協 ⁶¹⁷ J3628 M2742 Kyō cooperation.
² 力 *kyōryoku* cooperation
力者 *kyōryokusha* co-worker; cooperator
⁶ 会 *kyōkai* association, society
同 *kyōdō* cooperation, collaboration, association
同組合 *kyōdō kumiai* a cooperative; a partnership
⁸ 和 *kyōwa* concord, harmony, concert
定 *kyōtei* pact, agreement
⁹ 奏曲 *kyōsōkyoku* concerto
約 *kyōyaku* pact, convention, agreement
¹⁵ 賛 *kyōsan* mutual aid, cooperation; approval, authorization
調 *kyōchō* cooperation, conciliation, harmony; firm (market) tone
²⁰ 議 *kyōgi* conference, deliberation
議会 *kyōgikai* council, conference, convention
議事項 *kyōgi jikō* agenda

──────── 7 ────────

B 卑 ⁶¹⁸ J485c M2751 Hi. *iya(shii)* humble; base, mean, vile, vulgar; greedy. *iya(shimu), iyashi(meru)* despise.
³ 小 *hishō* petty, trifling
下 *hige* humility, self-deprecation
⁶ 近 *hikin* common, simple
劣 *hiretsu* meanness, foul play
⁷ 見 *hiken* my humble opinion
⁸ 屈 *hikutsu* meanness servility
怯 *hikyō* cowardice; meanness; unfairness
金属 *hikinzoku* base metals
⁹ 俗 *hizoku na* vulgar, coarse
¹² 猥 *hiwai* indecency, obscenity
¹⁵ 賤 *hisen* low class

A 南 ⁶¹⁹ J466e M2750 Nan. *minami, minnami* south.
² 十字星 *Minami Jūjisei* Southern Cross
³ 下 *nanka suru* go south
⁴ 中 *nanchū suru* crossing the meridian
太平洋 *Minami Taiheiyō* South Pacific
支那海 *Minami Shinakai* South China Sea
方 *nampō* south; southern, southward
⁵ 瓜 *kabocha, nanka, tōnasu* squash,

pumpkin

氷洋 *Nanhyōyō, Nampyōyō* Antarctic Ocean

半球 *Minami Hankyū* Southern Hemisphere

北 *namboku* north and south

⁶米 *Nambei* South America

向 *minamimu(ki)* southern exposure, facing south

回帰線 *Minami Kaikisen* Tropic of Capricorn

西 *nansei, minaminishi* southwest

⁸国 *nangoku* southern countries

欧 *Nan'ō* Southern Europe

東 *nantō, minamihigashi* southeast

岸 *nangan* south coast; south bank

京豆 *nankimmame* peanut

⁹面 *nammen* south face, south side; the south. *nammen suru* face the south; ascend the throne; rule

風 *nampū, minami kaze* south wind

海 *nankai* southern sea

洋 *Nan'yō* South Seas

南西 *nannansei* south-southwest

南東 *nannantō* south-southeast

¹⁰進 *nanshin suru* proceed south

部 *nambu* southern part

¹¹側 *minamigawa, nansoku* south side

寄 *minamiyo(ri)* southerly (wind)

¹²蛮 *namban* southern barbarians; red pepper

蛮人 *nambanjin* the southern barbarians, the early Europeans

極 *Nankyoku* South Pole

極大陸 *Nankyoku Tairiku* Antarctica

極星 *nankyokusei* the southern polar stars

極海 *Nankyokukai* Antarctic Ocean

¹⁴端 *nantan* southern tip

¹⁶緯 *nan'i* south latitude

A 単 620 / J4331 / M2752 TAN one, single, simple, singular, individual. *tan(naru)* mere, simple, sheer. *tan ni* simply, merely, only, solely. *hitoe* one layer, single.

¹一 *tan'itsu na* single, simple, sole, individual

一化 *tan'itsuka* simplification

²刀直入 *tantō-chokunyū* getting right into the subject, frankness

⁴文 *tambun* simple sentence

元 *tangen* a teaching unit

⁶行本 *tankōbon* separate volume

式 *tanshiki* simple system; single-entry (bookkeeping)

⁷作 *tansaku* single crop

身 *tanshin* alone; unaided; away from home

身赴任 *tanshin funin* working separated from home and family

利 *tanri* simple interest

位 *tan'i* unit, denomination; credit (in school)

⁸価 *tanka* unit cost, unit price

⁹音 *tan'on* monosyllable; monotony

音節 *tan'onsetsu no* monosyllabic

発 *tampatsu* single-engined, single-shot

独 *tandoku* solo (flight); independence; singleness. *tandoku no* single, sole, lone. *tandoku de* independently, individually, separately, alone, single-handed, unassisted

¹⁰純 *tanjun* simplicity

純化 *tanjunka* simplification

¹¹細胞 *tansaibō* single cell

¹²葉機 *tan'yōki* monoplane

¹³数 *tansū* singular number

¹⁴複 *tanpuku* simplicity and complexity; singular and plural; single and double; single and doubles (in tennis)

語 *tango* word; vocabulary; single-character word ⌐track

¹⁵線 *tansen* single line; solid wire; single

調 *tanchō* monotone, monotony, dullness

—— 10 ——

A 博 621 / J476e / M2761′ HAKU. BAKU. *haku(suru)* command esteem, win acclaim; gain, receive. *-haku* doctor, PhD; exposition, fair, exhibition.

³士 *Hakase, Hakushi* PhD

⁵打 *bakuchi* gambling

⁷労 *bakurō* horse trader

⁸学 *hakugaku* erudition

物 *hakubutsu* wide learning; natural history

物学 *hakubutsugaku* natural history

物館 *hakubutsukan* museum

⁹奕 *bakuchi, bakueki* gambling

¹⁰徒 *bakuto* gambler

¹³愛 *hakuai* charity, benevolence, philanthropy, humanity

二 亠 人 イ 入 八 ソ 冂 冖 冫 几 凵 刀 刂 力 勹 匕 匚 匸 十 卜 卩 厂 厶 又

2

二十人イ入几入八丷冂冖冫几凵刀刂力勹匕匚匸十卜卩厂厶又

¹⁴ 聞 *hakubun no* well-informed, erudite
¹⁶ 覧 *hakuran* extensive reading, wide knowledge
覧会 *hakurankai* fair, exhibition, exposition
覧強記 *hakuran-kyōki* wide reading and recording
¹⁹ 識 *hakushiki* extensive knowledge

RAD. 卜 25

Uranai divination or *to* (the katakana). Variants: ⼘ , ⼘. Nickname: *Kana To.*

卜 _{622 J4b4e M2774} BOKU divining. *boku suru, urana(u)* tell a fortune, predict; choose, settle, fix. *uranai, ura* divination.

--- **3** ---

B 占 _{624 J406a M2780} SEN. *shi(meru)* occupy, hold, have, get, take (a seat). *urana(u)* divine, forecast, augur. *uranai* divination, fortunetelling, soothsaying. *shi(meta)* I've got it; all right, fine.
⁵ 用 *sen'yō* exclusive use
⁶ 有 *sen'yū* exclusive possession, occupancy
⁷ 住 *senjū suru* occupy

⁸ 拠 *senkyo* occupation
取 *senshu* preoccupation
⁹ 星術 *senseijutsu* astrology
¹⁰ 師 *uranaishi* diviner, fortuneteller, soothsayer, palmist
¹⁴ 領 *senryō* capture, possession, occupation. *senryō suru* have a room to oneself
領下 *senryōka no* occupied (by an army)
領地 *senryōchi* occupied territory
領軍 *senryōgun* army of occupation

--- **6** ---

卦 _{625 J3735 M2798} KA. KE a divination sign.

RAD. 卩 26

Warifu seal or *fushizukuri* right-side "joint." Variant: 巳 *mage warifu* crooked seal. Nickname: Seal.

--- **3** ---

卯 _{628 J312c M2847} Bō. *u* 5–7 am; fourth zodiac sign; rabbit; east.
⁴ 月 *uzuki* fourth lunar month

--- **4** ---

A 危 _{629 J346d M2849} KI. *abu(nagaru)* be afraid of, feel uneasy about, shrink from. *aya(bumu)* fear, have misgivings, be doubtful, mistrust. *aya(meru)* wound; murder. *abu(nai), abu(nakkashii), ayau(i)* dangerous; critical, grave; uncertain, unreliable; limping; narrow, close; watch out.

⁶ 気 *abu(na)ge* possibility of danger
⁹ 殆 *kitai* danger, jeopardy, distress
急 *kikyū* emergency, crisis
急存亡 *kikyū-sombō* a life-and-death matter
¹⁰ 害 *kigai* injury, harm; danger
険 *kiken* danger, risk
険性 *kikensei* riskiness, danger
険物 *kikembutsu* dangerous goods, explosives, combustibles
険視 *kikinshi suru* regard as dangerous
¹¹ 惧 *kigu* fear, misgivings
¹⁶ 篤 *kitoku* on the verge of death
機 *kiki* crisis, emergency
機一髪 *kiki-ippatsu* critical moment
¹⁸ 難 *kinan* danger, hazard, distress

印 $\frac{630}{\text{J3075}}$ M2848 IN seal, stamp, mark. *in(suru)* print, imprint, impress. *shirushi* sign, mark; symbol, emblem; badge; evidence; souvenir; token; brand, trademark; signs, indications; omen; seal. *-In-* Indian.

⁶ 肉 *inniku* a seal stamp pad
字 *inji* copying
⁷ 材 *inzai* seal stock
⁸ 刻 *inkoku* seal engraving
画 *inga* (photographic) print
画紙 *ingashi* (photographic) printing paper
刷 *insatsu* printing
刷所 *insatsujo* press, print shop
刷物 *insatsubutsu* printed matter
刷者 *insatsusha* printer
刷機 *insatsuki* printing press
⁸ 度 *Indo* India, Hindustan. *Indo no* Indian, Hindu
度洋 *Indoyō* Indian Ocean
¹⁰ 紙 *inshi* revenue stamp
¹¹ 章 *inshō* seal, signet
¹² 税 *inzei* royalty (on a book)
象 *inshō* impression
象的 *inshōteki* graphic, impressive
象派 *inshōha* impressionist school
²² 鑑 *inkan* seal impression
籠 *inrō* seal case; pill box, medicine case

───── 5 ─────

却 $\frac{631}{\text{J3551}}$ M2856 KYAKU. *kae(tte)* instead, on the contrary; rather, all the more.

³ 下 *kyakka suru* reject, dismiss, ignore

卵 $\frac{632}{\text{J4d71}}$ M2857 RAN ovum. *tamago* egg; spawn, roe; (an expert) in the making.

³ 子 *ranshi* ovum, ovule, egg cell
⁵ 白 *rampaku* white of an egg, albumin
⁶ 色 *tamago iro* yellowish color
⁷ 形 *tamagogata, rankei* egg-shaped, oval
¹¹ 黄 *ran'ō* yolk of an egg
殻 *rankaku* eggshell
巣 *ransō* ovary
¹² 焼 *tamagoyaki* fried eggs; omelet
¹⁴ 管 *rankan* fallopian tube, oviduct

即 $\frac{633}{\text{J4228}}$ M2855 SOKU namely; as is. *soku (suru)* conform to, agree

with; be adapted to; be based on. *sunawa(chi)* namely, viz. *tsu(ku)* ascend (a throne); take root; begin work; be settled (questions).

⁴ 日 *sokujitsu* the same day
⁶ 死 *sokushi* instant death
⁷ 応 *sokuō* adaptation, compliance, conformity
応性 *sokuōsei* relevance
妙 *sokumyō* tact
売 *sokubai* sale on the spot
位 *sokui* enthronement, coronation, accession. *sokui suru* ascend the throne
決 *sokketsu* prompt decision, snap judgment
⁸ 金 *sokkin, sokukin* spot cash, down payment
刻 *sokkoku* instantly, immediately
効 *sokkō* immediate effect
¹⁰ 座 *sokuza* prompt; impromptu
席 *sokuseki* extemporaneous, offhand, ad lib
時 *sokuji* promptly, immediately
¹¹ 達 *sokutatsu* special delivery
断 *sokudan* prompt decision, snap judgment
¹² 答 *sokutō* prompt answer
¹⁴ 製 *sokusei* making on the spot
¹⁶ 興 *sokkyō* improvisation, impromptu

───── 7 ─────

卸 $\frac{641}{\text{J3237}}$ M2861 SHA. *oro(su)* sell at wholesale; grated (vegetables). *oroshi* wholesale.

⁷ 売 *oroshiuri* wholesale
¹⁰ 値 *oroshine* wholesale price
¹¹ 商 *oro(shi)shō* wholesaler
問屋 *oro(shi) don'ya* wholesaler

───── 8 ─────

卿 $\frac{642}{\text{J362a}}$ M2878 See 643.

───── 10 ─────

卿 $\frac{643}{\text{J-X}}$ M2880   **卿** $\frac{642}{\text{J362a}}$ M2878

KEI, KYŌ you; lord; secretary; state minister.

2

二
亠
人
亻
八
儿
入
八
丷
冂
冖
冫
几
凵
刀
刂
力
勹
匕
匚
匸
十
卜
卩
²厂
厶
又

RAD. 厂 27

Gandare trailing "cliff" or *ichidare* (a trailing *ichi* "one"). Also known as the "trailing goose" radical because it is the enclosure in the character for *gan* "wild goose." Nickname: Cliff.

2

厄 $\frac{646}{\text{J4c71}}$ $\frac{}{\text{M2893}}$ **B** YAKU misfortune, bad luck, evil, disaster.

⁴日 *yakubi* critical day, unlucky day
介 *yakkai* trouble, bother, worry; dependence, support; kindness; obligation
　介払 *yakkaibara(i)* good riddance
　介者 *yakkaimono* dependent, hanger-on
　介事 *yakkaigoto* trouble, difficulty, burden
⁵払 *yakubara(i)* good riddance; exorcism. *yakuhara(i)* exorcism.
⁶年 *yakudoshi* critical age, unlucky year
⁹除 *yakuyo(ke)* warding off evil

7

厘 $\frac{650}{\text{J4e52}}$ $\frac{}{\text{M2946}}$ **B** RIN one-tenth of a *sen;* one-tenth of a *bu* (See Weights and Measures).

厚 $\frac{651}{\text{J387c}}$ $\frac{}{\text{M2949}}$ **A** KŌ . *atsu(bottai)* very thick; heavy. *atsu(i)* thick; kind, cordial. *atsu(kamashii)* impudent, shameless, brazen. *atsu(sa)* thickness.

⁴手 *atsude no* thick (paper, etc.)
切 *atsugi(ri)* thick slice
化粧 *atsugeshō* heavy makeup
⁵生 *kōsei* public welfare, health promotion
生大臣 *Kōsei Daijin* Minister of Health and Welfare
生年金 *kōsei nenkin* welfare pension
生省 *Kōseishō* Ministry of Health and Welfare
⁶地 *atsuji* thick cloth
⁷志 *kōshi* kindness, kind intention
⁸味 *atsumi* thickness
⁹相 *Kōshō* Minister of Health and Welfare
¹⁰紙 *atsugami* thick paper, cardboard
¹¹遇 *kōgū* cordial welcome, kind treatment
情 *kōjō* kindness, favor, hospitality

¹²着 *atsugi* wearing thick clothes
¹⁸顔 *kōgan* impudence, audacity

8

原 $\frac{652}{\text{J3836}}$ $\frac{}{\text{M2973}}$ **A** GEN original, primitive. *hara* field, plain, prairie, tundra, moor, wilderness. *hara(ppa)* plain. gen- original, primitive, primary, fundamental; raw.

²人 *genjin* primitive man
³寸 *gensun* actual size, full size
寸大 *gensundai* actual size, full size
子 *genshi* atom
子力 *genshiryoku* atomic energy
子物理学 *genshi butsurigaku* atomic physics
子核 *genshikaku* atomic nucleus
子爆弾 *genshi bakudan* atomic bomb
⁴文 *gembun* the text, the original
木 *gemboku* pulpwood
水爆 *gensuibaku* atom and hydrogen bombs
⁵本 *gempon* the original, original copy, script primitive
生林 *genseirin* primeval forest, virgin forest
生動物 *gensei dōbutsu* protozoa
⁶色 *genshoku* primary color
因 *gen'in* root cause, factor, occasion, origin, source
因不明 *gen'in fumei* cause unknown
⁷図 *genzu* original drawing
状 *genjō* original state
告 *genkoku* plaintiff, accuser, prosecutor
住民 *genjūmin* natives, aborigines
材料 *genzairyō* raw material
作 *gensaku* original work
作者 *gensakusha* the original author (of a translated work)
形 *genkei* original form
⁸油 *gen'yu* crude oil
画 *genga* original picture
典 *genten* original document
価 *genka* original price
価計算 *genka seisan* cost accounting

646–652

始 *genshi* origin; primitive, primeval
始人 *genshijin* primitive man
始林 *genshirin* primeval forest, primeval virgin forest
始的 *genshiteki* primitive, original, primeval
始時代 *genshi jidai* primitive times
⁹点 *genten* starting point
型 *genkei* prototype; model, pattern
則 *gensoku* principle, general rule
則的 *gensokuteki* general
¹⁰料 *genryō* raw materials
紙 *genshi* stencil; silkworm eggsheet
案 *gen'an* original bill, motion, draft, or plan
書 *gensho* the original document
素 *genso* chemical element
¹¹理 *genri* principle, theory, basic truth
野 *gen'ya* waste land, wilderness, moor, field, plain. *harano* plain, field, wilderness, moor, prairie
動力 *gendōryoku* motive power
産地 *gensanchi* place of origin; home, habitat
産物 *gensambutsu* primary product
¹³罪 *genzai* original sin
義 *gengi* original meaning
¹⁴種 *genshu* pure breed
語 *gengo* original word or language
¹⁵稿 *genkō* manuscript
稿料 *genkōryō* payment for a manuscript
¹⁹簿 *gembo* ledger, original record
爆 *gembaku* atom bomb
²⁰籍 *genseki* original domicile, permanent address

─────── 10 ───────

厩 $\frac{654}{\text{J3139}}$ See 厩 660
M-X

厨 $\frac{657}{\text{J3f5f}}$ CHŪ. ZU. *kuriya* kitchen.
M3005
³子 *zushi* miniature shrine in a temple
⁸房 *chūbō* kitchen, galley

─────── 12 ───────

厩 $\frac{660}{\text{J-X}}$ 厩 $\frac{654}{\text{J3139}}$ KYŪ. *umaya* barn, stable.
M3006   M-X

⁸肥 *kyūhi* manure, compost
舍 *kyūsha* barn

厭 $\frac{662}{\text{J315e}}$ EN. YŌ. YŪ. *a(kiru)* get tired of, lose interest in, have enough. *a(kasu)* satiate, surfeit; bore, tire, weary. *ito(u)* dislike, hate; grudge (doing), spare (oneself); be weary of; take (good) care of, *agu(mu)* be weary of doing. *i(yarashii), ito(washii), i(yana)* detestable, diagreeable.
⁵世 *ensei* pessimism, weariness with life
世的 *enseiteki* pessimistic
世家 *enseika* pessimist
世観 *enseikan* pessimistic view of life, pessimism
¹³戦 *ensen* war weariness

─────── 15 ───────

厳 $\frac{663}{\text{J3837}}$ GON. GEN strictness, severity. *gen ni* strictly, severely, rigidly. *gen (ni) suru* fortify, strengthen, secure. *gen(taru)* strict, severe, stern. *ikame(shii)* solemn, majestic; dreadful, stern, ostentatious. *kibi(shii)* severe, strict, stern; intense (cold). *ogoso(kana)* austere, majestic, dignified, stately, awful, impressive. *ikatsu(i)* grim, stern.
⁵冬 *gentō* severe winter
正 *gensei* strictness, impartiality, exactness, rigidness
正中立 *gensei chūritsu* strict neutrality
⁶守 *genshu* strict observance
⁷戒 *genkai* strict guard
⁸命 *gemmei* strict order, peremptory command
⁹封 *gempū suru* seal hermetically
重 *genjū* strictness, rigor, severity. *genjū na* firm, strong, secure
¹⁰格 *genkaku* strictness, rigor, austerity, severity
¹¹密 *gemmitsu* strictness
粛 *genshuku* gravity, solemnity, seriousness, dignity, rigor, austerity
¹²寒 *genkan* intense cold
然 *genzen to* solemnly, gravely, majestically, authoritatively

2

二十人イ八ソ几凵刀刂力勹匕匚匸十卜卩厂【厶】又

¹³ 禁 *genkin* ban, interdict, strict prohibition

¹⁴ 選 *gensen* careful selection

罰 *gembatsu* severe punishment, rigorous measures

RAD. 厶 28

Mu (the katakana). Nickname: *Kana Mu.*

3

去 ⁶⁶⁵ J356e M3070 A KYO. KO. *sa(ru)* *vi* leave, move away, quit; pass, elapse, be gone, be over; be distant from., *vt* remove, eliminate, get rid of; divorce. *sa(ru)-* used in specifying a certain day in the past, last (June).

⁶ 行 *sa(ri)-yu(ku)* go away

年 *kyonen, kozo* last year

⁷ 来 *kyorai* coming and going; past and future

¹² 就 *kyoshū* course of action; attitude

¹³ 勢 *kyosei* castration; enervation; emasculation

6

参 ⁶⁶⁶ J3b32 M3090 A SHIN. SAN three; going; coming; visiting. *mai(ru)* go; come; call, visit; visit a shrine; be defeated; be nonplussed; be madly in love; die. *mai(raseru)* beat, floor (someone), bring (someone) to his knees. *san(jiru), san(zuru)* go; visit; come. *(o)mai(ri)* visits to shrines or temples.

³ 上 *sanjō suru* call on, visit

与 *san'yo* participation (in public affairs); counselor, consultant

⁴ 内 *sandai* palace visit

⁵ 加 *sanka* participation, joining, intervention

加者 *sankasha* participant, entrant

⁶ 列 *sanretsu* attendance, presence, participation

会 *sankai* attendance (at a meeting)

考 *sankō* reference, consultation

考人 *sankōnin* a person given as a reference

考品 *sankōhin* reference materials

考書 *sankōsho* reference book

考書目 *sankō shomoku* bibliography

⁸ 拝 *sampai* worship, visits to shrines or tombs

画 *sankaku suru* take part in planning

事 *sanji* secretary, councilor

事会 *sanjikai* a council

事官 *sanjikan* counselor

⁹ 院 *San'in* House of Councilors

政権 *sanseiken* suffrage, franchise

¹⁰ 酌 *sanshaku suru* compare and choose the good; consult, refer to

宮 *sangū* visit to the Ise Shrine

¹¹ 道 *sandō* approaching a shrine

¹² 集 *sanshū* assembling (of people)

賀 *sanga* congratulatory palace visit

¹³ 禅 *sanzen* Zen meditation

詣 *sankei* temple or shrine visit, pilgrimage, homage

戦 *sansen* participation in a war

照 *sanshō* reference, comparison

¹⁶ 謀 *sambō* staff officer; participation in planning

¹⁸ 観 *sankan* visit, inspection

²⁰ 議院 *Sangiin* House of Councilors, Upper House

議院議員 *Sangiin giin* member of the House of Councilors

RAD. 又 29

Mata again. Variant: . Nickname: Again.

B 又 668 J4b74 M3115 Yū. *mata* again, and, furthermore; on the other hand. *mata (moya)* again. *mata (shitemo)* again. *mata (wa)* or.

───── 1 ─────

叉 669 J3a35 M3116 Sa. Sha. *mata* fork (of a road); crotch (of a tree).

───── 2 ─────

B 及 670 J355a M3118' Kyū. *oyo(bosu)* exert, exercise, cause. *oyo(bu)* reach, come up to, amount to; befall, happen to; extend; match, equal. *oyo(banai)* unnecessary; unattainable. *oyo(bi)* and, as well as.

¹¹ 第 *kyūdai* passing an examination
¹² 落 *kyūraku* success or failure (in exams)
¹³ 腰 *oyo(bi)goshi* a bent back

A 友 672 J4d27 M3119 Yū. *tomo* friend, companion, pal.

² 人 *yūjin* friend
⁶ 邦 *yūhō* friendly nation, ally
好 *yūkō* friendship, amity, companionship
好国 *yūkōkoku* friendly nation
好的 *yūkōteki* friendly, amicable
¹¹ 情 *yūjō* friendship, fellowship
達 *tomodachi* friend, companion
¹³ 愛 *yūai* friendship
¹⁵ 誼 *yūgi* friendship, friendly relations

B 双 673 J4150 M3125 Sō. a pair; a set; comparison; counter for pairs.

³ 子 *futago* twins, twin
⁴ 方 *sōhō* both sides, both parties. *sōhō no* mutual, both
六 *sugoroku* a child's dice game
⁵ 生児 *sōseiji* twins
⁶ 曲線 *sōkyokusen* hyperbola
⁸ 肩 *sōken* shoulders
⁹ 発 *sōhatsu* two-motored
¹⁰ 胴船 *sōdōsen* catamaran
¹¹ 眸 *sōbō* the pupils of both eyes; both eyes
眼鏡 *sōgankyō* field glasses, binoculars
¹⁶ 頭 *sōtō no* double-headed

¹⁸ 璧 *sōheki* pair of bright jewels; matchless things; matchless people

A 反 674 J483f M3127 Hon. Tan roll of cloth (c. 10 yds.); .245 acres, 300 *tsubo*. Han antithesis, opposite, antagonism; anti-. *so(ru)* vi warp; curve; lean backward. *so(rasu), so(raseru)* vt bend, warp. *han(suru)* be inconsistent with, oppose; contradict; transgress; rebel. *kae(ru)* vi change, turn over, turn upside down. *kae(su)* vt change, turn over, turn upside down. *sori* warp, curvature, curve, arch. *kae(tte)* instead, on the contrary; rather, all the more.

⁴ 日 *hannichi* anti-Japanese
比例 *hampirei* inverse proportion
⁵ 目 *hommoku* antagonism, hostility
古 *hogu, hogo* wastepaper
⁶ 米 *hambei* anti-American
共 *hankyō* anticommunist
⁷ 応 *hannō* reaction, response
攻 *hankō* counteroffensive
抗 *hankō* resistance, insubordination, defiance, opposition, hostility, rebellion
作用 *hansayō* reaction
社会的 *hanshakaiteki* antisocial
乱 *hanran* rebellion
対 *hantai* opposition, resistance, antagonism, hostility, contrast, objection, dissension; reverse, opposite, vice versa
対色 *hantaishoku* clashing colors
対訊問 *hantai jimmon* cross-examination
対側 *hantaigawa* the opposite side
⁸ 逆 *hangyaku* treason, treachery, rebellion, insurrection, mutiny
物 *tammono* cloth; textiles, drapery; dry goods, piece goods
⁹ 面 *hammen ni* on the other hand
映 *han'ei* reflection, influence
則 *hansoku* transgression; default; foul; balk, irregularity
故 *hogu, hogo* wastepaper
省 *hansei* reflection, introspection; reconsideration; meditation, contemplation
発 *hampatsu suru* repel, repulse; rebound; recover; resist
¹⁰ 徒 *hanto* rebels, insurgents

2

二十人イ八几入八ソ冂冖冫几凵刀刂力勹匕匚匸十卜卩厂厶又

²

芻 *hansū* chewing the cud, rumination
射 *hansha* reflection, reverberation
射的 *hanshateki* reflective; reflecting; reflexive. *hanshateki ni* reminiscingly
¹¹問 *hammon suru* cross-examine; retort; ask in return
転 *hanten suru* turn around, roll over, turn from side to side
動 *handō* reaction; recoil, kick
動的 *handōteki* reactionary
¹²復 *hampuku* repetition
証 *hanshō* counterevidence
¹³戦 *hansen* antiwar
感 *hankan* antipathy, animosity
意語 *han'igo* antonym
¹⁴旗 *hanki* standard of revolt
語 *hango* irony; rhetorical question; antonym; word in reverse
駁 *hambaku, hampaku* refutation, rebuttal
¹⁵撥 *hampatsu* repel, repulse; rebound; recover; resist
論 *hanron* refutation; rebuttal
撃 *hangeki* counterattack
¹⁹響 *hankyō* echo, reverberation; repercussion, reaction, influence

———————— 3 ————————

A 収 ⁶⁷⁵ _{J3c7d} _{M3128} SHŪ income. *osa(meru)* obtain, reap; dedicate, consecrate; pay; supply; store; finish; collect; restore, replace; accept (a present); bury, gather; rally (troops); sheathe (the sword). *osa(maru)* be paid; be restored; stay (in the stomach); look composed; be contented; be satisfied; be settled.
²入 *shūnyū* receipts, income, revenue, proceeds, earnings
入印紙 *shūnyū inshi* revenue stamp
入役 *shūnyūyaku* government treasurer
入源 *shūnyūgen* source of income
⁴支 *shūshi* income and expenditure
⁵用 *shūyō* expropriation
⁷束 *shūsoku suru* tie up
⁸受 *shūju suru* receive
⁹拾 *shūshū suru* get under control, save (the situation)
¹⁰益 *shūeki* earnings, proceeds, returns
納 *shūnō* crop, harvest; receipts
容 *shūyō* accommodation, seating, housing custody, admission; entering (in a dictionary)
容力 *shūyōryoku* capacity, accommodation
容所 *shūyōjo* home, asylum, camp
容者 *shūyōsha* inmates
容能力 *shūyō nōryoku* capacity, accommodation
¹¹得 *shūtoku suru* receive
¹²集 *shūshū* gathering up; collection; accumulation
税 *shūzei* tax collection, taxation
¹³賄 *shūwai* accepting bribes, corruption, graft
¹⁴奪 *shūdatsu suru* rob
蔵 *shūzō* garnering, collection
監 *shūkan* imprisonment
¹⁶録 *shūroku suru* collect, record
¹⁷斂 *shūren* exaction (of taxes); convergence, contraction, astriction
縮 *shūshuku* contraction, shrinking, constriction
¹⁸穫 *shūkaku* harvest, harvesting, ingathering, crop
穫物 *shūkakubutsu* the harvest, the yield
穫高 *shūkakudaka* the income, the crop, the yield
穫期 *shūkakuki* harvest time
²⁴攬 *shūran* grasping, winning over

———————— 6 ————————

B 叔 ⁶⁷⁷ _{J3d47} _{M3154} SHUKU uncle; youth.
⁴父 *oji* uncle (parent's younger brother)
⁵母 *oba* aunt (parent's younger sister)

A 受 ⁶⁷⁸ _{J3c75} _{M3159} JU receive. *u(keru)* receive, accept, take, get, obtain; catch (a ball); stop (a blow), parry; answer (the phone); undergo (an operation); take (an exam); sustain (a loss); be exposed to (ridicule); face, front on; inherit; catch the public fancy. *uka(ru)* pass (an examination). *u(ke)* receiving; receptacle; support, prop; (pot) holder; popularity; agreement.
²入 *u(ke)-i(reru)* accept, receive; assent to, grant
入態勢 *u(ke)i(re) taisei* preparedness (for new personnel), reception set-up (for immigrants)
⁴止 *u(ke)-to(meru)* stop, catch; parry,

ward off
5 皿 *u(ke)zara* saucer
付 *u(ke)-tsu(keru)* receive, accept (an application). *uketsuke* receipt, acceptance; receptionist; information desk
付係 *uketsukegakari* receptionist, usher
6 刑者 *jukeisha* convict, convicted person
7 身 *ukemi* being acted upon, passivity, defensive position; passive voice; safe ways to fall
売 *ukeu(ri)* retailing; second hand (knowledge)
8 注 *juchū suru* accept an order
取 *u(ke)-to(ru)* receive, take delivery, accept; believe; understand, interpret. *uketori* receipt, acknowledgment
取人 *uketorinin* recipient, payee
取証 *uketorishō* receipt, voucher
9 胎 *jutai* conception, fertilization
持 *u(ke)-mo(tsu)* take charge of, be in charge of. *ukemo(chi)* charge (of something); matter in one's charge
信 *jushin* receipt of a message; radio reception
信機 *jushinki* receiver
負 *u(ke)-o(u)* contract for, undertake. *ukeoi* a contract
負人 *ukeoinin* contractor
10 容 *u(ke)-i(reru), juyō suru* accept
益者 *juekisha* beneficiary
11 授 *juju* receiving and giving
理 *juri suru* entertain (an action against), accept, take up (a report)
動的 *judōteki* passive
動態 *judōtai* passive voice
12 診 *jushin* getting a physical examination
給者 *jukyūsha* pensioner
渡 *ukewata(shi)* delivery, transfer, payment; give-and-take
13 継 *u(ke)-tsu(gu)* inherit, succeed to, take over
話器 *juwaki* receiver, headphones
14 精 *jusei* fertilization, pollination
像 *juzō suru* receive TV broadcasts
像機 *juzōki* TV set
領 *juryō* receipt, acceptance
領証 *juryōshō* receipt
15 諾 *judaku* acceptance
賞 *jushō* receiving a prize
賞者 *jushōsha* prize winner
17 講 *jukō* taking lectures

講生 *jukōsei* trainee; a person present at a lecture class; a participant
18 難 *junan* ordeal, trouble, sufferings; the crucifixion
験 *juken suru* take an examination

A 取 679 J3c68 M3158 SHU. *to(ru)* take, hold, seize, catch, capture; fetch; receive, procure, obtain; adopt (a measure); engage (graduates); choose; order (foodstuffs); pick, pluck; make, produce; eat; set up (camp); charge; administer; transact; take (pains); make out (the meaning); remove; take off (one's hat); take out (spots); strike out (words); weed, catch (fish); deprive of; steal; capture (territory), annex; need, require; reserve (rooms); subscribe to; press (a point home); take (a picture); possess. *to(reru)* can be held, can take; come off, come apart, be off, be removed; be relieved (of pain); be obtained, be produced; be caught; be earned; come out (well) (a photo); require (time); be interpreted as; can get; let (light) in; take (one's measure); can feel (the pulse); take (a pen and write). *to(tchimeru)* drive into a corner, take to task, take it out on. *to(ttoku), to(tte)o(ku)* keep, hold, save, reserve, set aside. *to(tte)* to, for, in the case of; including.
2 入 *to(ri)-i(reru)* take in, gather in, harvest; accept, adopt, introduce (customs). *to(ri)-i(ru)* get into (someone's favor), win (another's heart), ingratiate oneself with. *to(ri)i(re)* ingathering, taking in, harvest
入口 *toriireguchi* intake
3 下 *to(ri)-sa(geru)* withdraw, dismiss. *to(ri)-o(rosu)* take down, lower, pull down, lift down, let down, drop
上 *to(ri)-a(geru)* take up, pick up; deal with; adopt, accept, listen to; dispossess, expropriate, confiscate, revoke; deliver (a baby)
4 手 *to(ri)te* receiver, recipient, taker. *to(t)te* handle, knob, grip
止 *to(ri)-ya(meru)* stop, withdraw. *to(ri)-to(meru)* ascertain, make sure, save (a life). *to(ri)ya(me)* cancellation
分 *to(ri)-wa(keru)* divide, separate;

2
二
人
イ
人
儿
入
八
冂
冖
冫
几
凵
刀
刂
力
勹
匕
匚
匸
十
卜
卩
厂
厶
又 6

2

二
十
人
イ
へ
儿
入
八
ハ
冂
冖
冫
几
凵
刀
刂
力
勹
匕
匚
匸
十
卜
卩
厂
厶
[又]

---

distribute; assort. *to(ri)wa(ke),*
to(ri)wa(kete) especially, particularly.
toribun share, portion

引 *torihiki* transactions, deal, business

引先 *torihikisaki* customer, client,
business connection

引所 *torihikijo, torihikisho* stock
exchange

引高 *torihikidaka* turnover, volume of
business

⁵外 *to(ri)-hazu(su)* remove, take away;
dismantle; demount

去 *to(ri)-sa(ru)* take away, remove, leave
out

出 *to(ri)-da(su)* take out; produce; pick
out

立 *to(ri)-ta(teru)* collect; employ,
appoint; promote; patronize; exact
(taxes). *torita(te)* collection, levy;
appointment, employment; promotion;
patronage. *torita(te) no* fresh, freshly
picked. *torita(tete)* particularly

付 *to(ri)-tsu(keru)* draw, cash; patronize;
furnish, install; establish (regulations).
to(ri)-tsu(ku) hold fast to, catch hold
of; possess, obsess, haunt. *toritsu(ke)*
run on a bank; drawing, cashing;
installation, furnishing. *toritsu(ke) no*
regular (tradesman). *toritsu(ki)*
beginning; rudiments; foot (of a hill
road); edge (of town). *to(t)tsu(ki)* the
beginning; the first you come to; first
impression

⁶返 *tori-kae(su)* get back, regain, retrieve,
recover; recuperate; recall; undo;
make good, make up for, redeem;
withdraw. *to(tte) kae(su)* turn back,
hurry back. *to(ri)kae(shi)* recovery,
making up for, catching up

次 *to(ri)-tsu(gu)* act as agent;
intermediate; transmit, convey.
toritsu(gi) agency; agent;
intermediation; relaying (a telegram)

次店 *toritsugiten* agency

扱 *to(ri)-atsuka(u)* treat; manage;
handle, manipulate; conduct, transact;
take charge of; accept (telegrams).
toriatsuka(i) treatment, dealing,
service; handling, manipulation;
transaction, management

⁷囲 *to(ri)-kako(mu)* surround, crowd
against

戻 *to(ri)-modo(su)* take back, regain,
resume, recover, redeem, recapture

抑 *to(ri)-osa(eru)* catch, seize, capture;
quiet (a horse)

材 *shuzai* choice of subject. *shuzai suru*
gather material for a report

決 *to(ri)-ki(meru)* arrange, agree upon,
settle, make an appointment.
toriki(me) arrangement, agreement,
settlement

乱 *to(ri)-mida(su)* mess up, disturb; be
agitated

⁹柄 *to(ri)e* worth, merit, redeeming
feature

除 *to(ri)-no(keru)* remove, clear away,
get rid of; make an exception of; lay
aside, reserve. *to(ri)-nozo(ku)*
remove, take away; set apart

急 *to(ri)-iso(gu)* hurry. *to(ri)iso(gi)* in
haste

¹⁰残 *to(ri)-noko(su)* leave behind

消 *to(ri)-ke(su)* cancel, nullify, revoke,
rescind, withdraw, retract, take back,
repeal, quash, abrogate, annul,
countermand, recall

¹¹掛 *to(ri)-kaka(ru), to(k)kaka(ru)* begin,
set to work, proceed to business.
to(ri)-ka(keru) begin to take

捨 *shusha* adoption or rejection, choice,
option

舵 *to(ri)kaji* port; turning (a ship) to port

寄 *to(ri)-yo(seru)* send for, write for,
procure, order, obtain

崩 *to(ri)kuzu(su)* break down, dismantle;
tear down, demolish

得 *to(ri)doku* gain, profit. *shutoku*
acquisition, possession.

組 *to(ri)-ku(mu)* wrestle; be matched
against, tackle. *torikumi* match, bout

¹²違 *to(ri)-chiga(eru)* mistake, take the
wrong one; misunderstand

揃 *to(ri)-soro(eru)* arrange; make even;
complete, get ready

結 *to(ri)-musu(bu)* conclude; act as go-
between; curry favor

敢 *to(ri)a(ezu)* immediately; for the
present; first of all

越苦労 *torikoshigurō, torikoshi kurō*
unnecessary worry

替 *to(ri)-ka(eru)* exchange; barter;
change, renew. *torika(e), torika(ekko)*
a swap, an exchange

---

¹³ 置 *to(tte) o(ku)* keep, hold, save, reserve, set aside

¹⁵ 澄 *to(ri)-su(masu)* put on airs, put on company manners ⌈examine

調 *to(ri)-shira(beru)* investigate,

締 *to(ri)-shi(maru)* manage, control, oversee. *torishima(ri)* control, management, regulation, discipline, supervision; good order; supervisor, superintendent, director, foreman

締役 *torishimariyaku* director

¹⁶ 壊 *to(ri)-kowa(su)* break down, dismantle; tear down, demolish

²² 纏 *to(ri)-mato(meru)* settle, complete, agree upon, arrange; collect; put in order; unify; coordinate

──────── 7 ────────

叛 680 J4840 M3166 Hon. Han rebellion. *somu(ku)* act contrary to, go back on, disobey, defy, rebel against, turn one's back on.

⁷ 乱 *hanran* rebellion

⁸ 逆 *hangyaku* treason, treachery, rebellion, insurrection, mutiny

¹⁰ 徒 *hanto* rebels, insurgents

¹³ 意 *han'i* spirit of rebellion

¹⁴ 旗 *hanki* standard of revolt

叙 681 J3d76 M3163 Jo. *jo(suru)* relate, narrate, write; confer (a rank);
B
write a preface.

⁶ 任 *jonin* investiture

⁷ 述 *jojutsu* description, narration

⁸ 事 *joji* narration, description

事詩 *jojishi* descriptive poetry, epic poem

¹¹ 情 *jojō* description of feelings; lyricism

¹² 景 *jokei* scenery description

¹⁵ 勲 *jokun* conferring of decorations

──────── 14 ────────

叡 683 J3143 M3214 Ei intelligence; imperial

⁸ 知 *eichi* wisdom, intelligence, intellect

¹² 智 *eichi* wisdom, intelligence; intellect

──────── 16 ────────

叢 684 J4151 M3220 Sō plexus. *kusamura* clump of bushes, grassy place, thicket, the bush. *mura-, mura(garu)* crowd, flock, swarm.

⁵ 生 *sōsei* dense growth; healthy growth

⁸ 雨 *murasame* passing shower

¹⁰ 書 *sōsho* series (of publications); a library (of literature)

¹² 雲 *murakumo* cloud masses

¹⁵ 談 *sōdan* collection of stories

3-STROKE RADICALS

━━━━━ RAD. 口 30 ━━━━━

Kuchi mouth. At left: *kuchi hen*. Nickname: Mouth.

口 685 J387d M3227 Ku. Kō mouth. *kuchi*
A
mouth, lips; speech, words; one's taste, stopper, plug; nozzle, orifice, slit, aperture; door, gate, entrance; route, ascent; employment, job; call (for a doctor); share; kind, lot, brand; beginning; rumor, opening (of a boil).

² 八丁 *kuchihatchō* voluble, eloquent

³ 口 *kuchiguchi* each entrance, every mouth. *kuchiguchi ni* severally, unanimously

下手 *kuchibeta* defective speech, slowness of speech; poor talker

上 *kōjō* verbal message, statement; introduction

上書 *kōjōga(ki)* verbal statement

⁴ 元 *kuchimoto* the mouth; the shape of the mouth; near an entrance

2

⁰口

土
士
夂
夊
夕
大
女
子
宀
寸
小
尢
尸
屮
山
川
巛
工
己
巾
干
幺
广
廴
廾
弋
弓
ヨ
彑
彡
彳

止 *kuchido(me) suru* forbid to speak, muzzle (a person)

火 *kuchibi* fuse; spark plug; cause (of war); origin (of a quarrel)

内炎 *kōnaien* stomatitis

⁵外 *kōgai suru* tell, divulge

出 *kuchida(shi)* interference. *kuchi (o) da(su)* interrupt a conversation

付 *kuchizu(ke) suru* kiss. *kuchitsu(ki)* the mouth; manner of speaking; mouthpiece (of a cigarette)

⁶舌 *kōzetsu* words, tongue. *kōzetsu, kuzetsu* talking recklessly; quarreling; curtain lecture

伝 *kuden, kuchizuta(e), kuchizute* oral tradition; tradition

汚 *kuchigitana(i)* foul-mouthed, abusive. *kuchiyogo(shi)* tantalizing sample (of food)

当 *kuchia(tari)* taste; reception, hospitality

先 *kuchisaki* lips, mouth; snout; proboscis; professions, lip service, mere words

争 *kuchiaraso(i)* quarreling

⁷走 *kuchibashi(ru)* speak carelessly, tell, blurt out

車 *kuchiguruma* cajolery

吻 *kōfun* way of speaking; intimation

利 *kuchikiki* eloquent person; mouthpiece; man of influence; mediator, middleman

承 *kōshō* passing on by word of mouth, oral tradition

述 *kōjutsu* oral statement, dictation, lecture

⁸金 *kuchigane* bottle cap; clasp, base (of a light bulb)

径 *kōkei* aperture, bore, caliber

直 *kuchinao(shi)* removing a bad taste by eating something else

実 *kōjitsu* excuse, pretext

⁹拭 *kuchifu(ki)* napkin

紅 *kuchibeni* lipstick; red-rimmed

重 *kuchiomo na, kuchiomo(i)* slow of speech

臭 *kōshū* bad breath, halitosis

約束 *kuchi yakusoku* verbal promise

¹⁰座 *kōza* account

振 *kuchiburi* way of speaking; intimation

真似 *kuchimane* mimicry

¹¹惜 *kuya(shii)* vexing, regrettable, mortifying. *kuya(shigaru)* be chagrined (at one's failure); regret (a circumstance); resent (an insult). *kuchio(shii)* regrettable, mortifying

添 *kuchizo(e)* advice, support, good offices

移 *kuchiutsu(shi)* mouth-to-mouth feeding; oral transmission, tradition

許 *kuchimoto* the mouth; shape of the mouth; near an entrance

笛 *kuchibue* whistling

堅 *kuchigata(i)* closed mouthed, discreet

達 *kōtatsu, kōdatsu* verbal message, oral instructions

達者 *kuchidassha na* talkative

¹²開 *kuchia(ke)* beginning

絵 *kuchie* frontispiece

軽 *kuchi (ga) karu(i)* careless (talker). *kuchigaru* glibness, volubility

飲 *kuchino(mi)* drinking from the bottle

割 *kuchi (o) wa(ru)* confess to a crime

喧 *kuchiyakama(shii)* nagging, faultfinding, scolding; talkative, gossipy

喧嘩 *kuchigenka* quarreling

腔 *kōkō, kōkū* oral cavity

答 *kuchigota(e)* talking back, retort, oral answer. *kōtō* oral answer

¹³煩 *kuchiurusa(i)* nagging

数 *kuchikazu* number of dependents; words, speech; number of shares. *kōsū* number of accounts; number of times

¹⁴誦 *kōshō* humming; reading aloud

酸 *kuchi (ga) suppa(ku) naru, kuchi (o) suppa(ku) suru* repeat tediously

銭 *kōsen* commission, brokerage; net profit

説 *kudo(ku)* persuade, entreat, woo, seduce. *kuzetsu* quarrel; curtain lecture; jabbering

説落 *kudo(ki)-o(tosu)* persuade, talk (someone) into (something), seduce

語 *kōgo* colloquial language

語文 *kōgobun* colloquial language

語体 *kōgotai* colloquial style; colloquialism

¹⁵論 *kōron* dispute, argument

調 *kuchō* tone, expression

¹⁶髭 *kuchi hige* moustache

頭 *kōtō* oral

頭弁論 *kōtō benron* oral argument

頭試問 *kōtō shimon* oral examination
18 癖 *kuchiguse* way of saying, favorite phrase
糧 *kōryō* rations

2

叶 689 J3370 M3255 Kyō. *kana(eru)* grant, answer, hear (a prayer). *kana(u)* suit, be capable of; measure up to expectations; match, rival, keep up with; stand (the work); bear (the heat).

叱 691 J3c38 M3247 Shitsu. *shika(ru)* scold, reprove.
5 付 *shika(ri)-tsu(keru)* scold severely
正 *shissei* correction, improvement
7 声 *shissei* hiss
9 咤 *shitta* scolding
11 責 *shisseki* rebuke, reprimand

号 692 J3966 M3256 A Gō. number; item, title, pseudonym; Buddhist name. *gō(suru)* assume the name of; name, call, style; declare, announce. *-gō* suffix after a foreign ship name.
5 外 *gōgai* newspaper extra
令 *gōrei* order, command
8 泣 *gōkyū* lamentation, wailing
9 音 *gōon* reverberating sound; audible signal, a call
10 砲 *gōhō* signal gun
11 笛 *gōteki* whistle
20 鐘 *gōshō* signal bell

句 693 J3667 M3234 A Kō. Ku phrase, clause, sentence, passage, paragraph; expression; line, verse, stanza; 17-syllable poem.
4 切 *kugi(ru)* punctuate; cut off; mark off, stop *kugi(ri)* stopping place, punctuation, pause
6 会 *kukai* a gathering of haiku poets
7 作 *kusaku* composing haiku poems
9 点 *kuten* period (in punctuation)
12 集 *kushū* collection of haiku poems
14 読点 *kutōten* punctuation marks

只 694 J427e M3239 Shi *tada* free; only, just. *tada sae* in addition to, to add to.

4 中 *tadanaka ni* in the midst of
今 *tadaima* now, at present; right now; soon; Here I am. I just got back. I'm home
9 乗 *tadano(ri)* stolen ride, free ride
13 働 *tadabatara(ki)* working for nothing
14 管 *hitasura* earnestly

召 695 J3e24 M3241 B Shō. *me(su)* call, send for; wear, put on; take (a bath); ride in; buy; eat, drink; catch (a cold). *me(shi)* summons, a call. *(o)me (shi)* summons, a call; dressing; clothing; striped crepe.
3 上 *me(shi)-a(garu)* eat (honorific). *me(shi)-a(geru)* forfeit, confiscate; call out
上物 *me(shi)a(gari)mono* food
5 出 *me(shi)-da(su)* call out, summon
8 使 *me(shi)tsuka(i)* servant. *me(shi)-tsuka(u)* employ
抱 *me(shi)-kaka(eru)* employ, engage, take into one's service. *me(shi)kaka(e)* mercenary troops
物 *(o)me(shi)mono* clothing (polite)
10 捕 *me(shi)-to(ru)* arrest, apprehend
致 *shōchi suru* call together
12 募 *shōbo* levy, enlistment
喚 *shōkan* summons
集 *shōshū suru, me(shi)-atsu(meru)* call 「together
15 還 *shōkan* recall
請 *shōsei suru* call together

叩 696 J4321 M3238 Kō. *tata(ku)* strike, beat, hit, knock, knock, thrash, slap, rap, pat, pound, maul, clap (the hands); sound out (views); criticize. *tata(ki-nomesu)* knock down, beat up. *tata(ki)* dusting; duster.
3 上 *tata(ki)-a(geru)* work up; improve by training
4 込 *tata(ki)-ko(mu)* drive into; throw (into prison); hammer in, inculcate
切 *tata(ki)-ki(ru)* hack down, chop down, mangle
5 出 *tata(ki)-da(su)* begin to beat (a drum); beat and drive out; dismiss, send away
8 直 *tata(ki)-nao(su)* beat back into shape; correct by discipline
10 起 *tata(ki)-oko(su)* rouse, shake, awake
倒 *tata(ki)-tao(su)* knock down, beat down

2

²[口]

口 土 士 夂 夕 大 女 子 宀 寸 小 尢 尸 屮 山 川 巛 工 己 巾 干 幺 广 廴 廾 弋 弓 ヨ 彑 彡 彳

¹²割 *tata(ki)-wa(ru)* break to pieces, smash
落 *tata(ki)-oto(su)* knock down, knock off
¹⁵潰 *tata(ki)-tsubu(su)* smash up, crushing defeat
¹⁶壊 *tata(ki)-kowa(su)* knock to pieces, smash up, wreck
頭 *nukazu(ku)* bow, kowtow, prostrate oneself. *kōtō* kowtow, bow

A **史** 697 J3b4b M3249 SHI history, chronicles; historian; book.
³上 *shijō no* historical. *shijō ni* in history
⁸実 *shijitsu* historical fact
的 *shiteki* historic, historical
学 *shigaku* (study of) history
¹⁰料 *shiryō* historical records
家 *shika* historian
書 *shisho* history book
¹³跡 *shiseki* historical landmark
¹⁸蹟 *shiseki* historical landmark
観 *shikan* historical view

A **司** 698 J3b4a M3257 SHI official; government office. *tsukasado(ru)* rule, administer, conduct. *tsukasa* office, government office; director, head official.
⁵令 *shirei* command, control; commander
令官 *shireikan* commanding officer
令長官 *shirei chōkan* commander-in-chief
令部 *shireibu* headquarters, the command
令塔 *shireitō* conning tower
⁶会 *shikai* chairmanship; chairman
会者 *shikaisha* chairman, toastmaster, moderator
⁸直 *shichoku* judicial authorities, the court, the bench, a judge
法 *shihō* administration of justice
法官 *shihōkan* judicial official
⁹政官 *shiseikan* civil administrator
¹⁰書 *shisho* librarian
¹¹教 *shikyō* (Catholic) bishop
祭 *shisai* (Catholic) priest

A **台** 699 J4266 M3246 TAI. DAI stand, pedestal, rack, table, dais, bench, block; holder, support; mounting, setting. *utena* calyx; tower; platform. *tsukasa* office, government office; director, head official. *-dai* level, mark; the decade of

one's age; plateau, height, eminence; counter for vehicles, machines, tables, benches, etc.
⁶地 *daichi* plateau, tableland, eminence
⁷車 *daisha* push car; flatcar
形 *daikei* echelon formation; trapezoid
⁸所 *daidokoro* kitchen
⁹風 *taifū* typhoon
¹⁰座 *daiza* pedestal
紙 *daishi* cardboard; mat, mount
¹¹帳 *daichō* ledger, register
¹²場 *daiba* fort, battery
無 *daina(shi) ni suru* spoil, mar, ruin, destroy, make a mess of
湾 *Taiwan* Taiwan
詞 *serifu* speech, words, lines, remarks
¹⁶頭 *taitō* raise one's head, come to the fore, become influential, gain power, become famous

A **右** 700 J3126 M3250 YŪ. U. *migi, migiri* right, right hand. *migi suru* turn to the right.
⁴手 *migite, mete* right hand
⁵左 *migi-hidari* right and left
⁶回 *migimawa(ri)* right-handed rotation, clockwise
⁷折 *usetsu suru* turn to the right
利 *migiki(ki)* right-handedness; right-hander
⁸岸 *ugan, migi kishi* right bank, right shore (as you go down a river)
往左往 *uōsaō suru* go right and left, go this way and that
⁹派 *uha* rightists, the Right
¹¹舷 *ugen* starboard
側 *usoku, migigawa* right hand, right side
¹²腕 *migi ude, uwan* right arm, one's right-hand man
¹³傾 *ukei* leaning to the right, rightist
¹⁴端 *utan* right edge; right end; right lane
¹⁷翼 *uyoku* right wing, rightists; right field; right flank
²¹顧左眄 *uko-saben suru* look right and left; vacillate, waver

A **可** 701 J3244 M3245 KOKU. KA good, passable; approval; safe to say, ability to do. *-be(karazu)* must not, should not; do not. *i(i), yo(i), yo(shi)* good, good

natured; pleasing; precious; lovely, beautiful, fine; lucky; efficacious; right; suitable; justifiable; appropriate; satisfactory; better; all right; unneccessary; unobjectionable; intimate, friendly; easy, well; desirous. *-be(shi)*, *-be(ki)* shall, should, must, ought to, be expected to; seem to, look like; can; will.

3 也 *kanari* considerably, fairly, quite

及的 *kakyūteki* as ... as possible

7 決 *kaketsu* approval, adoption

否 *kahi* right or wrong, propriety, advisability, pro and con

9 哀想 *kawaisō na* poor, pitiable, pathetic; pitiless; unjust

変 *kahen* variable, changeable, convertible,controllable

10 笑 *oka(shii)* funny amusing, ridiculous

能 *kanō* possible

能性 *kanōsei* possibility

11 動 *kadō* movable, mobile

動性 *kadōsei* mobility

13 塑性 *kasosei* plasticity

溶性 *kayōsei* solubility

愛 *kawai(garu)* love, hold dear; *kawai(rashii)* lovely, sweet. *kawai(i)* dear, darling, charming, lovely, sweet

愛気 *kawaige* loveliness

15 憐 *karen na* poor, pitiful; cute, sweet, lovely

撓性 *katōsei* flexibility

16 燃性 *kanensei* combustibility, inflammability

燃物 *kanembutsu* a combustible, inflammables

A 古 702 / J3845 / M3233 **Ko** old. *furu(i)* old, aged, ancient, antiquated; stale, threadbare; outmoded, obsolete article. *furu(biru)* look old, get old. *furu(bokeru)* look old; become musty; wear out. *furu, furu-* used, secondhand. *furu(ku)* anciently, formerly. *inishie* antiquity, ancient times. *(o)furu* used article. *furu(mekashii)* old and familiar.

2 人 *kojin* ancient people

4 手 *furute* disused article, secondhand article; ex-soldier; retired official

木 *koboku* an old tree

井戸 *furuido* an old unused well

文 *kobun, komon* ancient writing

文書 *kobunsho, komonjo* ancient documents

今 *kokon* ancient and modern times, all ages, past and present

今東西 *kokon-tōzai* all times and places

5 史 *koshi* ancient history

写本 *koshahon* an old manuscript; a codex

生物 *koseibutsu* extinct plants and animals

生物学 *koseibutsugaku* paleontology

本 *furuhon, furubon* old book, secondhand book

本屋 *furuhon'ya* secondhand book store

代 *kodai* ancient times

代人 *kodaijin* the ancients

代史 *kodaishi* ancient history

代語 *kodaigo* ancient language

6 米 *komai* old rice

老 *korō* old people, seniors, elders

式 *koshiki* old style; ancient rites

寺 *furudera, koji* an old temple

色 *koshoku* faded color, antique look

色蒼然 *koshoku-sōzen(taru)* antique-looking

7 来 *korai* from time immemorial. *korai no* ancient, time-honored

8 刹 *kosatsu* ancient temple

武士 *kobushi* feudal warrior, samurai. *furutsuwamono* an old veteran, an old hand

物 *furumono, kobutsu* antique, old article, secondhand goods

物商 *kobutsushō* curio or secondhand dealer

参 *kosan* seniority, long service

事 *koji* ancient events

事記 *Kojiki* Japan's Ancient Chronicle

典 *koten* old book; classics; classic

典文学 *koten bungaku* classical literature

典主義 *koten shugi* classicism

典的 *kotenteki* classical

9 風 *kofū* old customs, old style

城 *kojō* old castle

臭 *furukusa(i)* stale, old fashioned; hackneyed, trite

美術品 *kobijutsuhin* old art object

10 株 *furukabu* old-timer, veteran, senior

狸 *furudanuki* old badger, veteran, old-timer, schemer, old fox

3 〔口〕
口
土
士
夂
夊
夕
大
女
子
宀
寸
小
⺌
尢
尸
屮
山
川
巛
工
己
巾
干
幺
广
廴
廾
弋
弓
彐
彑
彡
彳

都 *koto* ancient city; former capital
書 *kosho* old book, rare book
11 巣 *furusu* old home, former haunt
道 *kodō* old road; ancient methods; ancient moral teachings; the way of learning
道具 *furudōgu, kodōgu* old furniture; curious; secondhand goods
12 稀 *koki* seventy years of age
着 *furugi* old clothes, secondhand clothing
13 傷 *furukizu* scar, old wound; old unpleasant incident
雅 *koga* classical elegance, antiquity
跡 *koseki, furuato* historic spot, ruins
戦場 *kosenjō* ancient battlefield
14 語 *kogo* obsolete word; old proverb
豪 *kogō* veteran, old-timer, a person of experience
銭 *kosen* old coin
15 墳 *kofun* old mound, old grave, ancient tomb
18 蹟 *koseki* historic spot, ruins
顔 *furugao* familiar face, old-timer

───── 3 ─────

吋 703 J3125 M3292 Tō. *inchi* inch.

后 704 J3921 M3298 **A** Kō. Go after; behind; back; later. *kisaki* empress, queen.
6 妃 *kōhi* queen

吏 706 J4d79 M3299 **B** Ri an official.
10 員 *riin* officials

吃 707 J3549 M3280 Kitsu. *domo(ru)* stammer, stutter.
4 水 *kissui* draft (of a ship)
水線 *kissuisen* (loaded) water line
9 音 *kitsuon* stammering, stuttering
22 驚 *bikkuri suru* be surprised. *kikkyō* being surprised
驚仰天 *bikkuri-gyōten suru* be startled, be shocked, be stunned

叫 708 J362b M3240 **B** Kyō. *sake(bu)* shout, exclaim, cry, yell, roar,

howl; cry for, clamor for, advocate. *wame(ku)* shout, cry, yell, clamor.
7 声 *sake(bi)goe* shout, cry, yell, scream, wail, roar, howl

吐 709 J4547 M3300 **B** To. *ha(ku)* disgorge, vomit; belch, emit; give vent to; confess; tell (lies), speak. *tsu(ku)* breathe; disgorge; tell (lies).
3 口 *ha(ke)guchi* outlet, vent; *ha(ki)guchi* spillway; marketing.
5 出 *ha(ki)-da(su)* vomit, disgorge, spit out; breathe out; send out (smoke); belch (fire and smoke); say (angrily)
6 血 *toketsu* vomiting blood
気 *ha(ki)ke* nausea
10 息 *toiki* sigh, a long breath
18 瀉 *tosha* vomiting and diarrhea
21 露 *toro suru* express one's mind, give vent to, open (one's heart)

吊 710 J445f M3291 Chō. *tsuru(su), tsu(ru)* hang, suspend; wear (a sword).
3 下 *tsu(ri)-sa(garu)* dangle, be suspended, be hung down from. *tsu(ri)-sa(geru)* dangle, suspend, hang down
上 *tsu(ri)-a(geru)* hang up, haul up, suspend, raise, hoist, weigh (an anchor). *tsuru(shi)a(ge)* kangaroo court; impeachment
9 革 *tsurikawa* (hanging) strap.
12 棚 *tsuridana* hanging shelf
16 橋 *tsuribashi* suspension bridge
17 環 *tsuriwa* flying ring (in a gym); watch fob
22 籠 *tsurikago* hanging basket; nacelle, gondola

吉 711 J3548 M3289 **B** Kichi, Kitsu *yoshi* good luck; joy, congratulations.
4 日 *kichinichi , kitsujitsu* lucky day
凶 *kikkyō* fortune, sunshine and shadow
6 兆 *kitchō* lucky omen
事 *kichiji, kitsuji* auspicious event
10 祥 *kisshō* lucky omen
12 報 *kippō* good news

向 712 J387e M3301 **A** Kō. Kyō. *mu(kau)* face, confront; oppose, defy; proceed to; get, tend toward; approach. *mu(keru)* turn, face; point (a gun); send (a

messenger or letter). *mu(ku)* turn towards, (a needle) points to; lean towards; face, front on; suit. *mu(kai)* opposite. *mu(ke), mu(kete)* bound for. *mu(ki)* direction; exposure; aspect; suitability; position (on a proposition). *mu(kō)* the other side; opposite direction; the other party; destination; the next (few years); opposition to.

3 二軒 *mukō sangen* one's three neighbors across the way

上 *kōjō* advancement, progress, improvement, elevation, rise

上心 *kōjōshin* ambition, aspiration

4 日性 *kōjitsusei, kōnichisei* disposition (in flowers) to turn toward the sun

日葵 *himawari* sunflower

7 見 *mu(kō)-mi(zu)* recklessness

8 岸 *mu(kō)gishi* the opposite bank

学心 *kōgakushin* love of learning

9 風 *mu(kai)kaze* headwind

後 *kōgo* hereafter

背 *kōhai* one's attitude; state of affairs

11 側 *mu(kō)gawa* the opposite side; the other party

脛 *mu(kō)zune* shin, front of lower leg

13 鉢巻 *mu(kō)hachimaki* folded or rolled head towel

吸 [713] [J355b] [M3372] KYŪ. *su(u)* inhale; imbibe, A sip; suck, suck out.

2 入 *kyūnyū* inhalation. *su(i)-i(reru)* suck in

3 口 *su(i)kuchi* cigarette holder, mouthpiece (on a pipe)

上 *su(i)-a(geru)* suck in, pump up. *suia(ge)* suction; sucking

4 込 *su(i)-ko(mu)* inhale, imbibe; suck in; absorb, engulf, swallow up; suck down

引 *kyūin* absorption, suction, attraction

5 出 *su(i)-da(su)* suck out, draw out, pump out

収 *kyūshū* absorption; suction; attraction; extinction (of light)

収力 *kyūshūryoku* absorptive power

6 気 *kyūki* breathing in

血鬼 *kyūketsuki* a vampire, an extortioner

8 物 *su(i)mono* soup

取 *su(i)-to(ru)* suck up, soak up, suck out; extort, squeeze out (money)

取紙 *suitorigami* blotting paper, blotter

12 殻 *su(i)gara* tobacco ashes

殻皿 *suigarai(re)* ash tray

飲 *kyūin* (opium) smoking. *suino(mi)* feeding cup (for a patient)

着 *kyūchaku suru* adhere, stick fast

15 盤 *kyūban* sucker (on an octopus)

各 [714] [J3346] [M3281] KAKU each. *ono-ono* each, A every, either, respectively. *kaku-* each.

2 人 *kakujin* each individual

4 方面 *kakuhōmen* every direction; all quarters

6 自 *kakuji* each individual

地 *kakuchi* each place; various areas

各 *onoono* each, every, either, respectively

7 位 *kakui* gentlemen, sirs

8 国 *kakkoku* all countries, various nations, each nation.

所 *kakusho* each place, various places

宗 *kakushū* all sects ⌈faction

9 派 *kakuha* each party, all sects, each

界 *kakkai* each field, various circles

10 部 *kakubu* every part; various parts; every department

員 *kakuin* each one

個 *kakko* every one, each. *kakko ni* individually, respectively, each

11 階 *kakkai* each floor

12 項 *kakkō, kakukō* each item, each clause

14 層 *kakusō* each stratum; each class

種 *kakushu* each kind, all kinds

種学校 *kakushu gakkō* miscellaneous schools

駅停車 *kakueki teisha* local train

15 論 *kakuron* detailed exposition

合 [715] [J3967] [M3287] GŌ one-tenth *shō* (see A Weights and Measures); one of ten stations up a mountain. *a(u)* fit, suit; agree with, match, be correct; pay, be profitable. *a(wasu), a(waseru)* join together; be opposite, face; unite, combine, connect; add up; mix; match; overlap; compare; check with. *a(wasaru)* get together, unite. *gas(suru) vi* and *vt* join together; sum up; combine, unite, mix; agree with. *a(i)-* joint; associate, accomplice. *a(wase)-* joined together; opposite, facing.

口 土 士 夂 夕 大 女 子 宀 寸 小 尢 尸 屮 山 川 巛 工 己 巾 干 幺 广 廴 廾 弋 弓 彐 彡 彳

3

口
土
士
夂
夊
夕
大
女
子
宀
寸
小
⺌
尢
尸
屮
山
川
巛
工
己
巾
干
幺
广
廴
廾
弋
弓
彐
彑
彡
彳

¹ 一 *gōitsu* unification, union, oneness
² 力 *gōryoku* resultant force; cooperation.
    gōriki alms, assistance, contribution;
    Buddhist almsgiving
⁴ 手 *a(ino)te* interlude; accompaniment;
    sideshow; strain of music
⁵ 札 *a(i)fuda* check
  弁 *gōben* joint management; pool
  本 *gappon* a collection in one volume
  冊 *gassatsu, gōsatsu* a collection in one
    volume
⁶ 羽 *kappa* raincoat, foul-weather gear; an
    oil-skin
  同 *gōdō* union, combination,
    amalgamation, fusion; congruence
  同会議 *gōdō kaigi* joint session
  成 *gōsei* synthesis, composition;
    synthetic; composite, mixed,
    combined, compound
  成力 *gōseiryoku* resultant force
  成物 *gōseibutsu* a compound
  成樹脂 *gōsei jushi* plastics, synthetic
    resins
  成繊維 *gōsei sen'i* synthetic fiber
⁷ 図 *aizu* sign, signal
  体 *gattai* union, combination, alliance,
    annexation
  作 *gassaku* joint work, collaboration
  言葉 *a(i)kotoba* password, watchword
⁸ 金 *gōkin* alloy
  板 *gōhan, gōban, a(wase)ita* veneer
    board, plywood
  併 *gappei, gōhei* combination, union,
    amalgamation, consolidation, merger,
    coalition, fusion, annexation,
    affiliation, incorporation
  併症 *gappeishō* complications (in an
    illness)
  法 *gōhō* legality, legitimacy, lawfulness
  法的 *gōhōteki* legal, lawful, legitimate,
    law-abiding, in order
  法性 *gōhōsei* lawfulness, validity
⁹ 計 *gōkei* total
  乗 *a(i)no(ri)* riding together
  点 *gaten, gatten* understanding,
    comprehension, grasp; consent
  奏 *gassō* concert, ensemble
¹⁰ 流 *gōryū* confluence; union,
    linking up
  致 *gatchi* agreement, concurrence,
    conforming to
  格 *gōkaku* passing an examination;
eligibility
  格者 *gōkakusha* successful applicant
¹¹ 宿 *gasshuku* lodging together
  唱 *gasshō* chorus
  唱団 *gasshōdan* chorus, choir
  理 *gōri* rationality
  理化 *gōrika* rationalization
  理主義 *gōri shugi* rationalism
  理性 *gōrisei* rationality, reasonableness
  理的 *gōriteki* reasonable, rational,
    logical
¹² 間 *aima* interval
  掌 *gasshō* pressing palms together (in
    prayer)
  衆国 *Gasshūkoku* The United States of
    America; a federal state
¹³ 戦 *kassen* battle, engagement
  意 *gōi* agreement, consent, mutual
    understanding
¹⁴ 算 *gassan* totaling
¹⁶ 憲性 *gōkensei* constitutionality
¹⁷ 鍵 *aikagi* pass key, duplicate key, master
    key
²⁰ 議 *gōgi* consultation, conference
  議制 *gōgisei* parliamentary system

名 716 J4c3e M3297 MYŌ. MEI distinguished,
A noted; wise; name. *na*
name; fame, reputation; pretext.
na(zukeru) name, call. *na(ute) no*
notorious, famous. *-mei* counter for
persons.
² 人 *meijin* master, expert
  人芸 *meijingei* expert skill
³ 士 *meishi* a celebrity
⁴ 手 *meishu* expert
  月 *meigetsu* moon of the 15th day of the
    eighth lunar month and the 13th day of
    the ninth month
  分 *meibun* moral duty; justice
  文 *meibun* fine prose; beautiful passage
  文句 *meimonku* a fine expression;
    famous words
  文家 *meibunka* fine writer
⁵ 立 *nada(taru)* famous, notorious
  句 *meiku* happy expression; famous
    phrase; wise saying; excellent haiku
    poem
  代 *myōdai* proxy, deputy, representative.
    nadai star (actor), famous, notorious
  札 *nafuda* name plate; name card; place
    card; identification tag

付 *nazu(keru)* name, call, entitle, christen

目 *meimoku, myōmoku* title, name; pretext; nominal

目的 *meimokuteki ni* nominally

⁶曲 *meikyoku* famous music

字 *myōji* surname

⁷医 *meii* famous doctor

折 *nao(re)* disgrace

状 *meijō suru* describe

君 *meikun* wise ruler

言 *meigen* beautiful words, famous words

作 *meisaku* literary masterpiece

利 *meiri, myōri* wealth and honor

声 *meisei* fame, reputation

⁸門 *meimon* noble or illustrious family

取 *natori* a professional name (in the arts) received from one's teacher

刹 *meisatsu* famous temple

所 *meisho* place of interest, beauty spot. *nadokoro* name and address; beauty spot

所旧跡 *meisho-kyūseki* scenic and historical places

物 *meibutsu* specialty, noted product

画 *meiga* famous picture, masterpiece

宛人 *naatenin* addressee

実 *meijitsu* name and reality

刺 *meishi* (calling) card

⁹前 *namae* name; given name

負 *na(ni)o(u), na(nishi)o(u)* (reputation) agrees with facts; be famous

指 *naza(shi)* naming, designation. *naza(su)* name, mention by name

乗 *nano(ru)* profess to be, introduce oneself as. *nano(ri)* announcing one's candidacy; self-introduction

¹⁰馬 *meiba* fine horse

高 *nadaka(i)* famous, notorious

流 *meiryū* famous people. *na (o) naga(su)* become famous

将 *meishō* famous commander

称 *meishō* name, title, term

家 *meika* good family; a celebrity, an authority

案 *meian* splendid idea, good plan

残 *nagori* farewell; keepsake, remembrance; remains, relics

残惜 *nagorio(shii)* reluctant to part

¹¹惜 *na (o) osh(mu)* be careful to preserve one's reputation

訳 *meiyaku* excellent translation

産 *meisan* noted product, specialty

著 *meicho* famous work, masterpiece

望 *meibō* reputation, popularity

¹²揚 *na (o) a(geru)* become famous

勝 *meishō* scenic spot

詞 *meishi* noun

答 *meitō* right answer, excellent answer

無 *nana(shi)* nameless, anonymous, unknown

¹³園 *meien* famous garden

義 *meigi* name; justice, moral duty

義人 *meiginin* nominal person

誉 *meiyo* honor, credit, glory; dignity; prestige; honorary

誉心 *meiyoshin* desire for fame

誉欲 *meiyoyoku* desire for fame

誉職 *meiyoshoku* honorary position

¹⁴聞 *meibun, myōbun* fame, honor

説 *meisetsu* excellent idea

歌 *meika* famous poem

¹⁵器 *meiki* rare utensil, curio

調子 *meichōshi* eloquence

¹⁷優 *meiyū* great actor, star

¹⁹簿 *meibo* register of names

²²鑑 *meikan* directory

A 同 ⁷¹⁷ J4631 M3294　全 ¹¹⁴ J2138 M378 **Dō** the same, the same, the said, ibid. *dō(jiru), dō(zuru)* agree. *ona(ji), onna(ji)* same, identical, equal; uniform; equivalent; similar; common (origin); changeless. *ona(jiku) suru* make similar; have the same (idea). *ona(jiku)* the same (name).

¹一 *dōitsu* sameness, similarity, identity, equality; fairness

一人 *dōitsunin* the same person

一視 *dōitsushi suru* class with, put on a par with, regard in the same light

²人 *dōjin, dōnin* same person, said person; clique; fraternity; kindred spirits; comrade, colleague

人雑誌 *dojin zasshi* a magazine of a society

³上 *dōjō* same as above, ditto, ibid.

士 *dōshi* fellow, companion

士討 *dōshiu(chi)* killing each other by mistake

工異曲 *dōkō-ikyoku* practically the same

3 〔口〕

口
土
士
夂
夊
夕
大
女
子
宀
寸
小
⺌
尢
尸
屮
山
川
巛
工
己
巾
干
幺
广
廴
廾
弋
弓
ヨ
彑
彡
彳

⁴日 *dōjitsu* the same day
月 *dōgetsu* the same month
氏 *dōshi* the same person, the said person
文 *dōbun* same script; same language
心円 *dōshin'en* concentric circles
化 *dōka* assimilation, adaptation, absorption
化作用 *dōka sayō* assimilation, metabolism, anabolism
⁶色 *dōshoku* the same color
地 *dōchi* the same place; that place
列 *dōretsu* same rank, same file; company; attendance
行 *dōkō* travelling together. *dōgyō* fellow pilgrim, fellow practicer of austerities
行者 *dōkōsha* fellow travellers
年 *ona(ji)doshi, ona(i)doshi* same age. *dōnen* that year, same year; same age
年輩 *dōnempai* persons of the same age
名 *dōmei, dōmyō* the same name
名異人 *dōmei-ijin* namesake; person with the same name
好 *dōkō* similar tastes
好会 *dōkōkai* association of like-minded people
好者 *dōkōsha* people of similar tastes
⁷体 *dōtai ni* as one, together
役 *dōyaku* colleague
形 *dōkei* the same shape
伴 *dōhan suru* accompany, go with
伴者 *dōhansha* companion
位元素 *dōi genso* isotope
志 *dōshi* same mind; kindred soul, comrade
⁸門 *dōmon* fellow student
姓 *dōsei* the same surname
所 *dōsho* the same place, the same address, the said place
国 *dōkoku* the same country, the same province, the said country
居 *dōkyo* living with (someone)
居人 *dōkyonin* a person living with the family
性 *dōsei* the same sex; homosexuality; homogeneity; congeniality
性愛 *dōseiai* homosexual love
⁹封 *dōfū* enclosure. *dōfū suru* enclose
乗 *dōjō* riding together
前 *dōzen* same as above, ditto, ibid.
点 *dōten* tie, draw

室 *dōshitsu* the same room
型 *dōkei* the same type, the same pattern
音語 *dōongo* homonym
級 *dōkyū* the same grade, same class
級生 *dōkyūsei* classmates
胞 *dōhō, harakara, dōbō* brothers, brethren, fellow countrymen, fellowmen
¹⁰席 *dōseki* sitting together, being present together
病 *dōbyō* the same sickness
格 *dōkaku* the same rank, equality; apposition
郷 *dōkyō* same village, town, or province
衾 *dōkin* sharing the bed
時 *dōji* the same time. *dōji no* synchronous, simultaneous. *dōji ni* coincident with; on the other hand; while
時代 *dōjidai* the same age, same period
¹¹道 *dōdō suru* go with, accompany
断 *dōdan* the same, ditto
宿 *dōshuku* lodging in the same hotel
情 *dōjō* sympathy
族 *dōzoku* the same family, same tribe, same race
窓 *dōsō* the same school
窓生 *dōsōsei* schoolmate, fellow student, alumnus
窓会 *dōsōkai* alumni meeting
¹²棲 *dōsei suru* cohabit with, live together
等 *dōtō* equality, same rights; same rank
然 *dōzen* the same
期 *dōki* the same period; same class; synchronism
期生 *dōkisei* classmate
¹³数 *dōsū* same number
罪 *dōzai* the same offense
感 *dōkan* the same feeling, sympathy; concurrence
義 *dōgi* the same meaning
義語 *dōgigo* synonym
業 *dōgyō* the same trade, same business
意 *dōi* the same meaning; same opinion; agreement, consent, approval
意語 *dōigo* synonym
盟 *dōmei* alliance, league, union
盟条約 *dōmei jōyaku* treaty of alliance
盟国 *dōmeikoku* ally (of another nation)
盟罷業 *dōmei higyō* strike
¹⁴僚 *dōryō* associate, colleague
様 *dōyō* same, same kind, identical, like,

equal. *ona(ji) yō ni* similarly

説 *dōsetsu* the same opinion

種 *dōshu* the same kind; homogeneousness; the same race

15 慶 *dōkei* a matter for mutual congratulation

権 *dōken* the same rights, equal rights

輩 *dōhai* comrade, colleague, one's equal

調 *dōcho* alignment; tuning

質 *dōshitsu* the same quality, same nature, homogeneity

18 類 *dōrui* the same kind; accomplice

額 *dōgaku* the same amount

--- **4** ---

呂 728 / J4t24 / M3386 RYO, RO backbone.

9 律 *roretsu* articulation, pronunciation

吻 729 / J4a2d / M3375 FUN proboscis. *kuchiwaki* sides of the mouth

6 合 *fungō* coincidence, conformity, concurrence; union; junction

吾 733 / J3863 / M3379 GO. *waga* my, our, one's own. *ware* I, oneself, self, ego.

15 輩 *wagahai* I

呈 B 734 / J4468 / M3401 TEI *tei(suru)* offer, present; send (a letter); exhibit; develop (symptoms); assume (airs).

5 出 *teishutsu* presentation

示 *teishi, teiji* presentation

呑 737 / J465d / M3329 DON. *no(mu)* drink, taste, take; swallow, devour; smoke; conceal (a weapon); accept (an idea); despise.

4 込 *no(mi)-ko(mu)* swallow, gulp down; understand

6 気 *nonki* optimistic, carefree, careless, heedless

7 兵衛 *nombē* heavy drinker

呆 738 / J4a72 / M3395 HŌ. BŌ. *aki(reru)* be amazed, be aghast, be disgusted, be shocked. *boke* dullheadedness.

6 返 *aki(re)-kae(ru)* be amazed at, be disgusted with

気 *akke* blank amazement. *utsuke* stupid fellow

気無 *akkena(i)* disappointing

8 果 *aki(re)-ha(teru)* be amazed at, be disgusted with

12 然 *bōzen to* in blank amazement

18 顔 *aki(re)gao* amazed look

吠 739 / J4b4a / M3331 HAI. BEI. *ho(eru)* bark, bay, howl, bellow, roar, cry.

吟 B 740 / J3663 / M3330 GIN singing; recital; song; poem. *gin(jiru), gin(zuru)* sing, chant, recite.

8 味 *gimmi* testing, scrutinizing, careful inquiry

11 遊詩人 *gin'yū shijin* troubadour, minnesinger, minstrel

12 詠 *gin'ei* singing, recital; song, poem

14 誦 *ginshō suru* recite, chant

呉 B 741 / J3862 / M3365 GO. *ku(reru)* give; do (something) for.

7 呉 *kuregure mo* repeatedly, sincerely, earnestly

8 服 *gofuku* piece goods, dry-goods, draperies

服店 *gofukuten* dry-goods store

服屋 *gofukuya* dry-goods store

12 越同舟 *goetsu-dōshū* enemies in the same boat

否 A 742 / J485d / M3340 HI no, noes. *ina(mu)* refuse, decline; deny. *iya(mu)* detest, dislike. *ina* no, nay. *ina(ya)* as soon as, no sooner than, the moment; yes or no; objection; if, whether. *ie, iie* no. *iya, iiya* no, nay; yes, well.

7 決 *hiketsu* rejection, voting down

応無 *iyaōna(shi) no* compulsory

8 定 *hitei* denial

定文 *hiteibun* negative sentence

定的 *hiteiteki* negative, contradictory

14 認 *hinin* denial, disapproval, repudiation, veto, nonrecognition

含 B 743 / J345e / M3330 GAN. *fuku(mu)* hold in the mouth; bear in mind; understand; cherish, harbor; contain, comprise, have, hold, include, embrace, be

3

［口］

口
土
士
夂
夕
大
女
子
宀
寸
小
⺌
尢
尸
屮
山
川
巛
工
己
巾
干
幺
广
廴
廾
弋
弓
彐
彑
彡
彳

charged or loaded with, be dripping with, be full of, be suffused with. *fuku(maseru)*, *fuku(masu)* soak, saturate; suckle, make one hold something in the mouth; include; instruct, make one understand.

fuku(meru) include, instruct, make one understand. *fuku(mi)* implication, hidden meaning; latitude; atmosphere, tone, sentiment; inclusion.

6 有 *gan'yū suru* contain, have, hold, include

有量 *gan'yūryō* content (of a mineral, etc.)

8 味 *gammi suru* taste; think over carefully

10 笑 *fuku(mi)wara(i)* suppressed laugh, smile, giggle, chuckle

13 蓄 *ganchiku* implication, significance

A 告 $\frac{744}{J3970}$ M3381' KOKU. *tsu(geru)* tell, inform, announce, proclaim; bid, order. *tsu(ge)* oracle, revelation, inspiration.

3 口 *tsu(ge)guchi* talebearing

5 白 *kokuhaku* confession, acknowledgment

示 *tsu(ge)-shime(su)* tell, proclaim. *kokuji* notification, bulletin

7 別 *kokubetsu* leave-taking, farewell

別式 *kokubetsushiki* funeral service

8 知 *tsu(ge)-shi(raseru)*, *tsu(ge)-shi(rasu)*, *kokuchi suru* tell, notify, reveal. *kokuchi* notice, announcement

9 発 *kokuhatsu* prosecution; indictment; accusation, complaint, denunciation

発者 *kokuhatsusha* prosecutor, accuser, informant

12 訴 *kokuso* accusation, complaint

訴人 *kokusonin* one who brings suit

A 君 $\frac{746}{J372f}$ M3323 KUN mister (familiar). *kimi* you (familiar); ruler.

3 子 *kunshi* true gentleman, wise man; an official

5 代 *Kimi(ga)yo* Japan's national anthem

主 *kunshu* ruler

主国 *kunshukoku* monarchy

主専制 *kunshu sensei* autocratic monarchy

主制 *kunshusei* monarchy

6 臣 *kunshin* ruler and ruled; master and servant

17 臨 *kunrin suru* reign; control, dictate

B 吹 $\frac{747}{J3161}$ M3373 SUI. *fu(ku)* vi and vt breathe, blow; play (a wind instrument); emit; smelt; mint; brag. *fu(kasu)* vt smoke, puff.

3 下 *fu(ki)-o(rosu)* blow down (from a mountain)

上 *fu(ki)-a(garu)* be blown up high (as dust, or water in geysers). *fu(ki)-a(geru)* spout (water), blow up; wash ashore. *fu(ki)a(ge)* fountain, spouting, spray

4 込 *fu(ki)-ko(mu)* blow into, breathe into; record; inspire, instill. *fukiko(mi)* recording

5 矢 *fu(ki)ya* blowgun

付 *fu(ki)-tsu(keru)* blow against (a house), blow (sparks) upon; blow ashore. *fu(ki)-tsu(ku)* (winds) blow against (something), blow (something) along; blow up (a fire in a brazier). *fu(ki)tsu(ke)* spraying; air blast

払 *fu(ki)-hara(u)* drive away (clouds)

出 *fu(ki)-da(su)* begin to blow; breathe out; burst out laughing. *fu(ki)-de(ru)* begin to blow; break out (in sores)

出物 *fu(ki)demono* skin eruption, rash, pimple, eczema, boil, ulcer

7 抜 *fu(ki)-nu(ku)* blow through, blow over, blow itself out. *fu(ki)nu(ki)* ventilation, draft; streamer, pennant

9 飛 *fu(t)to(bu)* vi be blown off, blow off. *fu(ki)-to(basu)* vt blow away, blow off

降 *fu(ki)bu(ri)* driving rain

荒 *fu(ki)-susa(mu)*, *fu(ki)-susa(bu)*, *fu(ki)-a(reru)*, *fu(ki)-a(rasu)* blow violently, sweep over, devastate

奏 *suisō* playing wind instruments

奏楽 *suisōgaku* wind-instrument music

奏楽器 *suisō gakki* wind instruments

10 倒 *fu(ki)-tao(su)* blow down

消 *fu(ki)-ke(su)* blow out (a fire)

流 *fu(ki)-naga(su)* blow away, drive out of course. *fukinaga(shi)* streamer, pennant

破 *fu(ki)-yabu(ru)* blow to pieces

11 過 *fu(ki)-su(giru)* blow past, sweep past

寄 *fu(ki)-yo(seru)* drift, blow together. *fu(ki)yo(se)* collection; drift (of sand or snow)

雪 *fubuki* snowstorm, blizzard. *fubu(ku)* (winds) blow hard; (snow) is driven

¹² 募 *fu(ki)-tsuno(ru)* blow with growing intensity

替 *fu(ki)ka(e)* substitute actor; dummy; stand-in; recasting, reminting

¹³ 溜 *fu(ki)damari* snowdrift

¹⁴ 鳴 *suimei suru* blow (a whistle) *fu(ki)-na(rasu)* blow a blast

¹⁷ 聴 *fuichō* announcement, publicity, advertisement, notification, recommendation

¹⁹ 曝 *fu(ki)-sara(su)* blow with unhindered sweep. *fu(ki)sara(shi) no, fu(ki)zara(shi) no* exposed to the wind, weather-beaten, wind-blown, wind-swept, bleak, bare

---

5

呪 ⁷⁶⁴ J3c76 M3443 JU spell, curse, incantation. *majina(u)* charm, cast a spell over. *noro(u)* curse. *noroi* curse, anathema, malediction. *majinai* spell, charm, enchantment

⁴ 文 *jumon* magic formula, incantation, curse, spell, charm

¹¹ 術 *jujutsu* magic, incantation, sorcery

¹² 詛 *juso* curse, anathema

¹⁶ 縛 *jubaku* a spell

味 ⁷⁶⁶ J4c23 M3456 A MI taste, flavor, dash; touch, tinge; counter for foods and drinks. *aji(wau)* taste; appreciate, experience. *aji, aji(wai)* taste, flavor, aroma; zest; experience; tinge. *aji na* clever, witty, smart.

⁴ 方 *mikata* friend, ally, supporter. *ajiwa(i)kata* way to taste

⁵ 付 *ajitsu(ke)* seasoning

加減 *aji kagen* seasoning

⁶ 気無 *ajikena(i)* irksome, insipid, wretched, vain

⁷ 見 *ajimi* sampling, foretaste

¹¹ 得 *mitoku suru* taste thoroughly

¹² 覚 *mikaku* sense of taste

¹⁴ 読 *midoku suru* appreciate a book

¹⁵ 醂 *mirin* sweet saké

噌 *miso* fermented bean paste; flattery

噌汁 *misoshiru, misojiru* bean-paste soup

噌漬 *misozuke* pickled in bean paste

命 ⁷⁶⁷ J4c3f M3473 A MYŌ. MEI command, decree; life; destiny. *mei(jiru), mei(zuru)* command; appoint. *inochi* life. *mikoto* words of a ruler; lord, prince.

³ 乞 *inochigoi* pleading for one's life

⁴ 日 *meinichi* death anniversary

中 *meichū* a hit

⁵ 令 *meirei* command, decree, directive, order

令形 *meireikei* imperative form

⁶ 名 *meimei* naming, christening

⁸ 取 *inochito(ri) no* fatal

知 *inochishi(razu)* recklessness; daredevil. *inochishi(razu) no* long-lasting

⁹ 拾 *inochibiro(i)* narrow escape from death

¹¹ 運 *meiun* fate, doom

¹³ 数 *meisū* span of life; destiny

¹⁸ 題 *meidai* thesis, proposition

²⁰ 懸 *inochigake no* risky, desperate. *inochigake de* at the risk of life

周 ⁷⁶⁸ J3c7e M3441' A SHŪ circuit, lap, circumference, vicinity; Chou (dynasty). *mawa(ri)* rotation; circumference, girth; surroundings, border; detour; tour; efficacy or effect (of something taken); spread (of flames). *gururi* surroundings.

⁴ 辺 *shūhen* circumference, perimeter; environs, outskirts

⁶ 回 *shūkai* circumference, girth, surroundings

年 *shūnen* whole year; anniversary (used after number)

⁷ 囲 *shūi* circumference, girth; surroundings

忌 *shūki* anniversary of a person's death (used after number)

⁸ 到 *shūtō na* scrupulous, careful, meticulous, complete

知 *shūchi* common knowledge

知徹底 *shūchi-tettei* (something) known to all

波数 *shūhasū* frequency (in electricity)

¹⁰ 航 *shūkō* circumnavigation; a circle tour by ship

¹¹ 遊 *shūyū* tour, round trip

章 *awa(teru)* be confused, lose one's head, be hurried, be hasty. *shūshō*

3

agitation, frustration

旋 *shūsen* good offices, recommendation, mediation; (Tokugawa-era) employment office

旋人 *shūsennin* agent, middleman

¹² 期 *shūki* period, cycle

期性 *shūkisei* cyclic, periodic

呼 $\frac{769}{J3846}$ $\overline{\text{M3471}}$ Ko. *yo(bu)* call, call out to; invoke; summon; invite; attract; send for; name, designate; bring about. *yo(bawaru)* shout, exclaim, cry, yell, roar, howl; cry for, clamor for, advocate. *-yo(bawari) suru* treat as, denounce as, call (someone something).

² 入 *yo(bi)-i(reru)* call in, restore (a disowned son)

³ 子 *yo(bu)ko, yo(bi)ko* police whistle

⁴ 止 *yo(bi)-to(meru)* call (to someone) to stop, challenge; call back

水 *yo(bi)mizu* priming water

込 *yo(bi)-ko(mu)* call in; restore a disowned son

⁵ 立 *yo(bi)-ta(teru)* call out, call (someone to) come, summon

付 *yo(bi)-tsu(keru)* call (to someone), send for, summon

号 *kogō suru* cry out, proclaim; appeal to; exaggerate

出 *yo(bi)-da(su)* call out, call before, call up; summon, subpoena; decoy; conjure up, involve

⁶ 気 *koki* exhalation

合 *yo(bi)-a(u)* call each other (brethren); call to each other

名 *yo(bi)na* given name, popular name, alias

吸 *kokyū* breath, respiration; knack, secret; tone, time. *kokyū suru* breathe

吸器 *kokyūki* respiratory organs

⁷ 応 *koō suru* hail each other; act in concert; respond to

戻 *yo(bi)-modo(su)* call back, call home; resuscitate, recall

声 *yo(bi)goe* call, yell, hail; street huckster's call; rumor

売 *yo(bi)u(ri)* hawking, peddling

求 *yo(bi)-moto(meru)* call upon, call for (help)

⁸ 物 *yo(bi)mono* attraction, feature, main event

¹⁰ 起 *yo(bi)-oko(su)* *vt* wake, rouse, call; call up; recall

称 *koshō suru* call out, call (someone by name or title)

¹¹ 掛 *yo(bi)-ka(keru)* call out to, accost; address (a crowd). *yo(bi)ka(ke)* a call (to prayer)

捨 *yobisu(te)* calling to someone disrespectfully

寄 *yo(bi)-yo(seru)* send for, summon, call together

¹² 集 *yo(bi)-atsu(meru)* assemble. *yo(bawari)-atsu(meru)* call together. *yo(bawari)-atsu(maru)* be called together

覚 *yo(bi)-sa(masu)* *vt* wake up

¹³ 鈴 *yo(bi)rin* buzzer, door bell, call bell

¹⁴ 慣 *yo(bi)-na(reru)* be used to calling (someone by a certain name)

和 $\frac{770}{J4142}$ $\overline{\text{M3490}}$ KA. WA sum; peace, harmony, reconciliation, unity. *wa(suru)* harmonize, be in harmony with; make peace, be reconciled; respond, echo. *yawa(ragu)* *vi* soften, be reconciled; lessen; calm down. *yawa(rageru)* *vt* soften, moderate, ease, alleviate, mitigate, relax; appease; dilute (wine); tone down (colors); comfort; pacify, quiet. *nago(mu)* *vi* be softened; get quiet. *nago(meru)* *vt* soften, quiet down. *na(gu)* get calm, die down. *nago(yakana)* mellow, matured, refined, genial. *nagi* lull, calm.

² 人 *Wajin* (an old word for) a Japanese

⁴ 文 *wabun* Japanese, Japanese writing

文英訳 *wabun'eiyaku* Japanese-English translation

⁵ 平 *wahei* peace

⁶ 合 *wagō* harmony, unity, union

名 *wamyō, wamei* Japanese name

気 *waki* harmony, peacefulness

気藹藹 *wakiaiai* maturity; refinement; harmony

⁸ 服 *wafuku* Japanese clothes, kimono

尚 *oshō* chief priest of a temple

英 *Wa-Ei* Japanese-English

⁹ 風 *wafū* light breeze; Japanese style

食 *washoku* Japanese food

約 *wayaku* treaty of peace

室 *washitsu* Japanese-style room

洋 *wayō* Japanese and Western

洋折衷 *wayō setchū* semi-European

style
10 紙 *washi* Japanese paper
書 *washo* Japanese book, book bound in Japanese style
11 船 *wasen* Japanese-style ship
訳 *wayaku* Japanese translation
菓子 *wagashi* Japanese confectionery
12 装 *wasō* Japanese dress; Japanese binding
裁 *wasai* Japanese sewing
13 睦 *waboku* reconciliation, conclusion of a peace treaty
解 *wakai* reconciliation; atonement; compromise. *wakai, wage* translation; rewriting Chinese *(kambun)* in mixed script
戦 *wasen* peace and war
漢 *Wa-Kan* Japan and China; Japanese and Chinese
14 語 *wago* pure Japanese words
歌 *waka* thirty-one-syllable poem, tanka
算 *wasan* Japanese mathematics; abacus calculation
製 *wasei* Japanese manufacture
16 親 *washin* harmony, amity, friendship
親条約 *washin jōyaku* treaty of friendship
19 蘭 *Oranda* Holland, Netherlands
20 議 *wagi* peace negotiations, reconciliation

──── 6 ────

哉 779 J3a48 M3596 SAI. *Kana* How! What! Alas! *ya* question mark.

咽 788 J3076 M3577 IN. EN. ETSU. *muse(ru), muse(bu)* be choked, be smothered. *muse(ppoi)* stuffy, suffocating. *nodo* throat, gullet, windpipe; voice.
6 返 *mu(se)-kae(ru)* be severely choked
8 泣 *muse(bi)-na(ku)* sob
12 喉 *inkō* throat
頭 *intō* pharynx
頭炎 *intōen* pharyngitis

咳 789 J3331 M3555 GAI cough. *se(ku)* cough. *shiwabu(ku)* cough, clear one's throat. *seki* cough. *shiwabuki* cough, clearing one's throat.
4 止 *sekido(me)* cough medicine, throat

tablet
込 *se(ki)-ko(mu)* have a fit of coughing
5 払 *sekibara(i)* clearing the throat; coughing

咲 790 J3a69 M3554 SHŌ. *sa(ku)* bloom, blossom. *-sa(ki)* blooming.
4 匂 *sa(ki)-nio(u)* bloom beautifully and fragrantly
5 出 *sa(ki)-de(ru), sa(ki)-da(su)* begin to bloom, come out
7 乱 *sa(ki)-mida(reru)* bloom in profusion
初 *sa(ki)-so(meru)* begin to bloom
12 揃 *sa(ki)-soro(u)* be in full bloom
13 誇 *sa(ki)-hoko(ru)* bloom in glory

哀 791 J3025 M3580 AI. *awa(remu)* pity, have mercy on, sympathize with. *awa(re)* grief, sorrow; misery; compassion, pathos. *awa(reppoi)* plaintive, piteous, doleful.
4 切 *aisetsu na* pathetic
5 史 *aishi* sad story, tragic history
6 気 *awa(re)ge na* sad, sorrowful, pensive
11 悼 *aitō* condolence, regret, sympathy, sorrow, lament
惜 *aiseki* grief, sorrow
12 痛 *aitsū* sorrowing with the bereaved
13 傷 *aishō* sorrow, grief
話 *aiwa* sad tale
愁 *aishū* sorrow, grief
感 *aikan* pathos
14 歌 *aika* elegy, dirge, sad song, lamentation
15 調 *aichō* mournful melody; minor key
19 願 *aigan* appeal, entreaty, petition

品 792 J494a M3581 HIN refinement, dignity; article. HON item, course (in a meal). *shina* article, goods, thing; quality; brand; kind, type; ways, conditions; character.
4 切 *shinagi(re)* out of stock, sold out
5 目 *himmoku* list of articles
6 行 *hinkō* conduct, behavior; moral character, respectability
行方正 *hinkō-hōsei* respectability
7 位 *hin'i* dignity, nobility; grade, quality, fineness; character
8 物 *shinamono* goods, stock, articles
定 *shinasada(me)* estimation, judgment, criticism (of goods)

性 *hinsei* character

9 品 *shinajina* various articles

10 格 *hinkaku* grace, dignity

12 詞 *hinshi* part of speech

評会 *himpyōkai* competitive exhibition, a fair

13 数 *shinakazu, hinsū* number of articles, amount of stock

14 種 *hinshu* kind, description, grade, variety, breed

15 調 *shinashira(be)* stock taking

質 *hinshitsu* quality

16 薄 *shinausu* shortage of goods

------ 7 ------

啄 793 J426f M-X Nonstandard for 啄 821.

唖 795 J3022 M3743 Nonstandard for 啞 827.

唄 802 J3134 M3694 BAI. *uta* songs accompanied by the samisen.

B 唆 803 J3a36 M3696 SA. *sosonoka(su)* tempt, seduce; instigate; promote.

哩 805 J4b69 M3649 RI. *mairu* mile.

B 唇 807 J3f30 M3697 SHIN. *kuchibiru* lip.

9 音 *shin'on* labial sound

12 歯輔車 *shinshi-hosha* interdependence

A 員 808 J3077 M3633 EN. IN -*in* member; number; the one in charge.

5 外 *ingai* nonmembership

13 数 *inzū, inzu, insū* number of members, things, or people

哨 809 J3e25 M3646 SHŌ scout, sentinel

7 戒 *shōkai* patrol, patrolling

兵 *shōhei* sentry, sentinel

8 舎 *shōsha* sentry box

9 海艇 *shōkaitei* patrol vessel

B 哲 811 J452f M3667 TETSU clear.

2 人 *tetsujin* wise man, sage, philosopher

8 学 *tetsugaku* philosophy

学的 *tetsugakuteki* philosophical

学者 *tetsugakusha* philosopher

11 理 *tetsuri* the philosophy (of something)

B 唐 812 J4562 M3709 TŌ Tang (dynasty); China; foreign countries. *Kara* China; Cathay; Korea; foreign countries. *Kara-, Tō-* Chinese; Korean; foreign. *kara(meku)* look like something Chinese.

2 人 *Tōjin, karabito* a Chinese; a foreigner

3 土 *Tōdo, Morokoshi* China, Cathay

4 手 *karate* a weaponless defense system

5 本 *tōhon* books from China

7 辛子 *tōgarashi* red pepper

8 突 *tōtotsu* suddenly, unexpectedly

物 *karamono* goods from China or Korea. *tōbutsu, tōmotsu* imported goods

物屋 *tōbutsuya* foreign-goods store

9 風 *karafū* Chinese style

変木 *tōhemboku* a blockhead

草模様 *karakusa moyō* arabesque design

10 紙 *karakami* thick door paper; opaque sliding paper door

11 船 *karafune, tōsen* Chinese ship; foreign ship

12 朝 *Tōchō* the Tang dynasty

傘 *karakasa* paper umbrella

13 詩 *tōshi* Tang-dynasty poem

獅子 *kara shishi* lion

14 様 *karayō* Chinese style

16 錦 *karanishiki* Chinese brocade

17 薯 *karaimo* sweet potato

------ 8 ------

啄 821 J-X M3801 TAKU. *tsuiba(mu)* peck, pick up.

4 木鳥 *kitsutsuki* woodpecker

B 喝 824 J3365 M-X KATSU scold; get hoarse

8 采 *kassai* applause, cheers

10 破 *kappa suru* declare, proclaim

唾 826 J4243 M3785 DA. *tsuba, tsubaki* sputum; saliva.

¹¹ 液 *daeki* saliva

¹³ 棄 *daki subeki* detestable, disgusting, revolting. *daki suru* spit; detest, hate, abhor, reject

啞 ⁸²⁷ / J-X / M3835 — A. *oshi* deaf-mute.

⁸ 者 *asha* deaf-mute

¹² 然 *azen to* in mute amazement

¹³ 鈴 *arei* dumbbell

啓 ⁸²⁸ / J373c / M3820 — B KEI open; say.

³ 上 *keijō* speak respectfully

⁵ 白 *keihaku* informing

示 *keiji* revelation

⁹ 発 *keihatsu* enlightenment, development, improvement, education, edification

¹³ 蒙 *keimō* enlightenment, instruction

唱 ⁸²⁹ / J3e27 / M3765 — A SHŌ. *tona(eru)* recite, chant; call upon; cry, yell (*banzai*); advocate, preach; quote (prices).

⁸ 和 *shōwa* cheering in chorus

¹¹ 道 *shōdō* advocacy

道者 *shōdōsha* proponent

¹⁴ 導 *shōdō* advocacy

歌 *shōka* song; singing

問 ⁸³⁰ / J4c64 / M3814 — A MON question, problem, subject, discussion. *to(u)* ask, question, inquire; accuse. *to(i)* question, inquiry. *-to(wazu)* without distinction, regardless of, irrespective.

⁶ 合 *to(i)-a(waseru), to(i)-a(wasu)* inquire of

⁹ 屋 *ton'ya, toiya* wholesaler, forwarding agent

¹¹ 掛 *to(i)-ka(keru)* inquire of; begin to ask

責 *monseki* reproof, censure

¹² 答 *mondō* questions and answers; catechism; discussion; dispute

¹³ 詰 *to(i)-tsu(meru)* press for an answer, cross-examine

罪 *monzai* accusation, indictment

¹⁵ 質 *to(i)-tada(su)* inquire of, question

¹⁸ 題 *mondai* problem, question, issue, case, matter; discussion; trouble

題点 *mondaiten* the point at issue

唯 ⁸³¹ / J4d23 / M3761 — B YUI. I. *tatta* only, merely, solely, simply. *tada* only,

merely, solely, simply; earnestly; perfectly, generally.

¹ 一 *yuiitsu, yuitsu* sole, unique, the one and only. *tada hitotsu* sole, only one

⁴ 今 *tadaima* now, at present; right now; soon; Here I am. I just got back. I'm home.

⁷ 我独尊 *yuigadokuson* self-conceit, self-righteousness

⁸ 物主義 *yuibutsu shugi* materialism

物史観 *yuibutsu shikan* materialistic conception of history

物論 *yuibutsuron* materialism

⁹ 美主義 *yuibi shugi* estheticism

美的 *yuibiteki* esthetic

¹¹ 唯 *ii toshite* willingly, meekly

唯諾諾 *iidakudaku toshite* quite willing; readily; submissively; meekly; at one's beck

商 ⁸³² / J3e26 / M3803 — A SHŌ trade; merchant; quotient. *akina(u)* sell, handle, trade in. *akina(i)* trade, business.

² 人 *shōnin, akindo, akyūdo, akiudo* trader, shopkeeper, merchant

³ 才 *shōsai* business ability

工会議所 *Shōkō Kaigisho* Chamber of Commerce and Industry

工業 *shōkōgyō* commerce and industry

⁵ 号 *shōgō* firm name, trade name

用 *shōyō* business

用文 *shōyōbun* business correspondence

⁶ 会 *shōkai* company, firm

⁷ 社 *shōsha* company, firm

売 *shōbai* trade, business, commerce; transaction, occupation, trade

売人 *shōbainin* merchant; professional, expert

売柄 *shūbaigara* nature of one's business; business instinct

売道具 *shōbai dōgu* stock-in-trade

売敵 *shōbaigataki* professional jealousy; business rivalry

⁸ 法 *shōhō* trade, business, commerce; commercial law

取引 *shōtorihiki* business transaction

店 *shōten* shop, store

店街 *shōtengai* shopping district; shopping street

事会社 *shōjigaisha* commercial 「company

⁹ 科大学 *shōka daigaku* commercial college

3

品 *shōhin* goods, stock, merchandise

品目録 *shōhin mokuroku* inventory, catalog

品券 *shōhinken* merchandise certificate

¹⁰ 家 *shōka* mercantile house, store; merchant

¹¹ 務官 *shōmukan* commercial attaché

船 *shōsen* merchant ship

船大学 *shōsen daigaku* merchantile-marine college

¹³ 業 *shōgyō* commerce, trade, business

業化 *shōgyōka* commercialization

業主義 *shōgyō shugi* commercialism

¹⁴ 魂 *shōkon* commercial spirit

慣習 *shōkanshū* commercial practice

¹⁵ 談 *shōdan* business transaction

標 *shōhyō* trademark

───── 9 ─────

喬 ⁸⁴¹ J362c M3990 Kyō high; boasting.

⁴ 木 *kyōboku* tall tree, forest tree, arbor

喰 ⁸⁴⁹ J3674 M4015 （国字） *kura(u), ku(u)* eat, drink; receive (a blow).

ku(u) eat; subsist on; support oneself; consume; get (a scolding); encroach; bite at, gnaw at; (shoes) pinch; be cheated.

⁴ 込 *kura(i)-ko(mu)* go to jail; shoulder a debt or other load; be deceived; abandon oneself to vice; fall heir (to trouble)

⁵ 付 *kura(i)-tsu(ku)* bite

喋 ⁸⁵⁰ J437d M3917 Chō. *shabe(ru), shabe(kuru)* talk, chat, chatter.

喚 ⁸⁵² J342d M3953 Kan. *ome(ku), wame(ku)* cry, scream, yell, shout, clamor. *yo(bu)* call, call out to; invoke; summon; invite; attract; send for; name, designate; bring about.

⁷ 声 *kansei, wame(ki)goe* shout, yell, scream, clamor

¹⁰ 起 *kanki suru* arouse, evoke

¹¹ 問 *kammon* summons

喪 ⁸⁵³ J4153 M3985 Sō. *mo* mourning.

⁴ 心 *sōshin* absentmindedness; stupor, dejection

中 *mochū* mourning

⁵ 主 *moshu* chief mourner

失 *sōshitsu* loss, forfeit, forfeiture

⁸ 服 *mofuku* mourning dress

喉 ⁸⁵⁴ J3922 M3913 Kō. *nodo* throat, voice.

⁴ 仏 *nodobotoke* Adam's apple

元 *nodomoto* throat

⁶ 自慢 *nodojiman* pride of voice

¹⁶ 頭 *kōtō* larynx

喫 ⁸⁵⁵ J354a M3987 Kitsu. Keki. *kis(suru)* eat, drink, smoke; receive (a blow, etc.).

⁴ 水 *kissui* draft (of a ship)

水線 *kissuisen* water line (of loaded ship)

⁹ 茶 *kissa, kitcha* tea drinking, tea house

茶店 *kissaten* tea house, coffee shop

¹³ 煙 *kitsuen* smoking (tobacco)

煙車 *kitsuensha* smoking car

煙者 *kitsuensha* smoker

煙室 *kitsuenshitsu* smoking room

¹⁴ 緊 *kikkin* very urgent

緊事 *kikkinji* a very urgent matter

²² 驚 *bikkuri suru* be surprised. *kikkyō* surprise, astonishment

喧 ⁸⁵⁶ J3776 M3976 Ken. *kamabisu(shii)* noisy, boisterous. *yakama(shii)* noisy, boisterous; critical; troublesome; much-discussed; fastidious.

⁶ 伝 *kenden suru* noise abroad, circulate

¹² 喧囂囂 *kenken-gōgō* pandemonium

¹³ 嘩 *kenka* quarrel, dispute

嘩腰 *kenkagoshi* defiant attitude

¹⁶ 噪 *kensō* noisy, uproarious; nuisance

¹⁸ 騒 *kensō* noisy, uproar, a nuisance

営 ⁸⁵⁷ J3144 M4025 Ei camp; performing. *itona(mu)* perform (ceremonies); build; conduct (business); follow (a profession), operate (a store); build. *itona(mi)* business, occupation, operation.

⁶ 団 *eidan* corporation, foundation

⁷ 利 *eiri* gain, money-making

利事業 *eiri jigyō* business enterprise

⁸ 門 *eimon* barracks gate

林 *eirin* forestry
⁹造 *eizō* building, construction
¹⁰庭 *eitei* barracks' parade ground
倉 *eisō* guardhouse, detention barracks
¹¹巣 *eisō* building a nest
¹²営 *eiei to* strenuously, eagerly, diligently
¹³業 *eigyō* business, trade
業所 *eigyōsho* place of business
¹⁸繕 *eizen* upkeep (of equipment)

A 喜 ⸤858 J346e M3957⸥ KI. *yoroko(bu)* rejoice, be glad, be pleased.
yoroko(basu) gladden, please, make happy. *yoroko(bi)* joy, delight, pleasure.
yoroko(bashii) joyful, glad, pleasant.
⁶色 *kishoku* joyful countenance
⁷寿 *kiju* 77th birthday
⁹怒哀楽 *kido-airaku* joy and anger, feelings
¹⁰悦 *kietsu* gladness, delight
¹¹捨 *kisha* charity, donation
¹⁵劇 *kigeki* comedy

A 善 ⸤859 J4131 M3904⸥ ZEN good, goodness, right, virtue. *i(i), yo(i)* good, good-natured; pleasing; precious; noble; lovely, beautiful, fine; lucky; efficacious; right; suitable; justifiable; appropriate, satisfactory; better; all right; unnecessary; no objection; intimate, friendly; easy; well; desirous. *yo(ku) suru* be skilled in. *yo(shi)* good, all right, well, so. *yō(koso)* Well, good for you. Well, that's a rude thing to do.
²人 *zennin* good people
⁴心 *zenshin* virtue, moral sense, conscience
⁵玉 *zendama* good person, goodie
用 *zen'yō* good use
処 *zensho suru* tide over, make the best of, use discretion
⁶行 *zenkō* good deed, good conduct; benevolence
⁷良 *zenryō* goodness, virtue, excellence
男善女 *zennan-zennyo* pious men and women
⁹政 *zensei* good government
後 *zengo* giving careful thought to the future; finishing up carefully
後策 *zengosaku* relief measure, remedy, countermeasure, means of settling a problem

¹¹悪 *zen'aku, zennaku* good and evil.
yo(shi)-waru(shi), yo(shi)-a(shi), yo(i)-waru(i) good or bad; merits or demerits; quality; suitability.
yo(kare)-a(shikare) good or bad, right or wrong
¹³戦 *zensen suru* fight a good fight
意 *zen'i* good faith; good will, good intentions; favorable sense
¹⁴隣 *zenrin* good neighbor
導 *zendō* proper guidance

───── **10** ─────

嘩 ⸤861 J325e M-X⸥ KA noisy.

B 嗣 ⸤868 J3b4c M4109⸥ SHI heir. *tsu(gu)* succeed to, inherit; follow; patch.
³子 *shishi* heir, successor

B 嘆 ⸤872 J4332 M4138⸥ TAN sigh. *nage(ku)* sigh, lament, moan, grieve; regret, deplore, sorrow. *tan(jiru), tan(zuru)* deplore, mourn, regret, be indignant. *nage(kawashii)* sad, wretched, deplorable.
⁶叫 *nage(ki)-sake(bu)* wail
⁷声 *tansei* sigh, lamentation; sigh of admiration
⁹美 *tambi* admiration, adoration
¹⁰息 *tansoku* sigh, grief, deploring
¹²訴 *nage(ki)-utta(eru)* complain
悲 *nage(ki)-kana(shimu)* lament, mourn
¹⁵賞 *tanshō* praise, admiration, applause
¹⁹願 *tangan* entreaty, appeal, petition, suit

───── **11** ─────

噌 ⸤873 J4139 M-X⸥ See 噲 889.

嘗 ⸤878 J3e28 M4205⸥ SHŌ. *na(meru)* lick; lap up; burn up; taste; undergo; underrate, despise. *katsu(te)* once, before, formerly; ever, never (neg.); former, ex-.

嘘 ⸤885 J-X M4206⸥ 嘘 ⸤886 J3133 M-X⸥ KYO. *uso* lie, falsehood, fib, fabrication
²八百 *usohappyaku* full of lies

3

[口]

口
土
士
夂
夕
大
女
子
宀
寸
小
ⴑ
尢
尸
屮
山
川
巛
工
己
巾
干
幺
广
廴
廾
弋
弓
彐
彑
彡
彳

嘉 887 J3245 M4176 **KA.** *yomi(suru)* applaud, praise, esteem, appreciate, approve of.
⁴ 日 *kajitsu* auspicious day, good day
月 *kagetsu* auspicious month; beautiful moonlight; lunar third month
⁷ 言 *kagen* wise saying
¹³ 節 *kasetsu* auspicious occasion
¹⁵ 賞 *kashō* approval

──── 12 ────

嚙 888 J337a M-X See 嚙 921.

噌 889 J-X M4303 噌 873 J4139 M-X **Sō, Zō, Shō** throat.

嘱 B 894 J3e7c M4249 **Shoku** requesting. *shoku suru* request; send a message.
⁵ 目 *shokumoku suru* pay attention to, notice, observe, watch
¹⁰ 託 *shokutaku suru* commission, charge (a person) with, give (a person) charge of. *shokutaku* part-time employment
¹¹ 望 *shokubō* expectation

噂 896 J313d M4286 **Son.** *uwasa* rumor, gossip, hearsay.
⁵ 主 *uwasa (no) nushi* the person talked about
¹³ 話 *uwasabanashi* rumor, gossip, hearsay
¹⁴ 種 *uwasa (no) tane* source of rumor, subject of gossip

器 A 898 J346f M4349 **Ki** container; utensil; instrument, tool apparatus; set; ability. *utsuwa* vessel, receptacle, utensil, implement, instrument; capacity, ability.
⁵ 用 *kiyō* cleverness, ingenuity; shrewdness; versatility
用貧乏 *kiyō-bimbō* Jack-of-all-trades and master of none
⁷ 材 *kizai* machine parts
⁸ 物 *utsuwamono, kibutsu* container, receptacle, utensil, tool, furnishings
官 *kikan* organ (of the body)
具 *kigu* utensil, appliance; apparatus; tool; fixtures
¹⁰ 財 *kizai* tools

¹¹ 械 *kikai* appliance; apparatus; instrument
¹² 量 *kiryō* looks, features, personal beauty; ability; dignity
¹³ 楽 *kigaku* instrumental music

噴 B 900 J4a2e M4345 **Fun.** *fu(ku)* spout, emit, flush out.
⁴ 水 *funsui* jet of water, squirt, fountain
火 *funka* eruption, volcanic activity
火口 *funkakō* crater
⁵ 出 *fu(ki)-da(su)* spout out, gush out, spurt out, shoot out, send out, discharge, exude. *funshutsu* gushing, spouting, eruption
⁶ 気 *funki suru* flutter, puff (as a locomotive)
⁹ 泉 *funsen* fountain, spring, geyser
¹⁰ 射 *funsha* jet, jet propulsion
¹² 飯 *fumpan suru* burst out laughing
¹³ 煙 *fun'en* smoke (out of a chimney)
¹⁹ 霧 *fummu* spray

──── 13 ────

噺 903 J4838 M4433 （国字） *hanashi* talk, chat, conversation; story; rumor; news; consultation, negotiations; facts, reasons.

噸 910 J4655 M4429 （国字） **Ton** ton.
¹³ 数 *tonsū* tonnage

──── 14 ────

嚇 B 915 J3345 M4459 **Kaku.** *odo(su), odo(kasu)* threaten; frighten; intimidate.
¹⁷ 嚇 *kakukaku(taru)* brilliant, glorious

──── 15 ────

嚙 921 J-X M4516 嚙 888 J337a M-X **Gō.** *ka(mu)* bite, gnaw, chew; gear with; (waves) dash against.
⁴ 切 *ka(mi)-ki(ru)* bite off, gnaw off
⁵ 付 *ka(mi)-tsu(ku)* bite at
⁶ 合 *ka(mi)-a(u) vi* fight or bite each other; engage (gears); occlude (teeth). *ka(mi)-a(waseru) vt* clench (teeth); engage (gears); set (animals fighting)
⁹ 砕 *ka(mi)-kuda(ku)* crunch, crush with

the teeth
10 殺 *ka(mi)-koro(su)* bite to death; keep
back, suppress
13 締 *ka(mi)-shi(meru)* chew well; meditate
on; digest (ideas); appreciate
(kindness)

─── **19** ───

囊 | 933 / J-X / M4633 | Nō pouch, purse. *fukuro* bag, sack, pouch.

■■■ RAD. 口 31 ■■■

Kunigamae (enclosure as in *kuni* "country"). Nickname: Box.

─── **2** ───

囚 | 937 / J3c7c / M4680 | SHŪ criminal, arrest.
B *tora(eru)* catch, arrest,
capture. *torawa(reru)* be caught, be
captured, be arrested; be a slave to; be
seized with.
2 人 *meshiudo, shūjin, torawa(re)bito*
prisoner, convict

四 | 938 / J3b4d / M4682 | SHI four. *yo(tsu), yo(ttsu),*
A *yo, yon* four.
2 十 *yonjū, shijū* 40
人 *yonin, yottari* four people
4 日 *yokka* four days; the fourth day (of
the month)
切 *yo(tsu)gi(ri)* quartering; quarter
月 *Shigatsu* April. *yotsuki* four months
月馬鹿 *shigatsu baka* April fool
辺形 *shihenkei* quadrilateral, quadrangle
六時中 *shirokujichū* 24 hours, day and
night; constantly, always
方 *shihō, yomo* four directions; all
directions
方八方 *shihō-happō* far and wide, in all
directions
方山 *yomoyama no* various, sundry
分六 *shiburoku* six-to-four ratio
分五裂 *shibun-goretsu* disruption
5 辻 *yo(tsu)tsuji* street crossing, four
corners
半分 *shihambun* quarter, fourth
半世紀 *shihanseiki* a quarter of a
century
半期 *shihanki* quarter (of a year)
6 次元 *yojigen, yonjigen* fourth
dimension
7 囲 *shii* circumference, girth;
surroundings

阿 *azumaya* arbor, summer house
足 *yo(tsu) ashi* four legs. *yo(tsu)ashi*
beast, animal
角 *yosumi* all the corners, four corners.
yotsukado four corners; intersection,
street crossing. *shikaku* square;
quadrilateral
角四面 *shikaku-shimen na* methodical,
prim
角形 *shikakkei* quadrilateral, square
角張 *shikakuba(ru)* be formal
8 周 *shishū* surroundings
肢 *shishi* the limbs, the extremities, the
arms and legs
苦八苦 *shiku-hakku* much agony
季 *shiki* the four seasons
9 則 *shisoku* the four arithmetical
operations
通八達 *shitsū-hattatsu* accessible from
all directions
面 *shimen* four sides, all sides
面楚歌 *shimensoka* completely
surrounded (by the enemy)
10 這 *yo(tsu)bai* crawling. *yo(tsum)bai* on
all fours, falling flat, sprawling
書五経 *Shisho-Gokyō* the Nine Chinese
Classics
11 隅 *yosumi* four corners
捨五入 *shisha-gonyū* counting .5 and
over as 1 and discarding .4 and less;
rounding
12 散 *shisan suru* disperse, scatter
15 輪車 *yonrinsha, shirinsha, yorinsha*
four-wheeled vehicle

─── **3** ───

因 | 939 / J3078 / M4693 | IN cause, factor.
A *china(mu)* be associated
with. *yo(ru)* depend on, be limited to.

3

口
�口
土
士
夊
夂
夕
大
女
子
宀
寸
小
⺌
尢
尸
屮
山
川
巛
工
己
巾
干
幺
广
廴
廾
弋
弓
ヨ
彑
彡
彳

yo(tte) therefore, consequently. *chinami ni* by the way, in this connection.
³ 子 *inshi* factor, element (in math)
⁸ 果 *inga* cause and effect; retribution, karma; fate, destiny; misfortune
果応報 *inga-ōhō* reward according to deeds, retribution
¹¹ 習 *inshū* custom, convention, tradition
¹² 循 *injun* indecision, vacillation
循姑息 *injunkosoku na* temporizing, tardy, time-serving
¹³ 業 *ingō* causes and actions, results of one's actions in a former existence
数 *insū* factor (in math)
¹⁵ 縁 *innen* cause and effect; karma; fate; affinity, connection; origin, history; pretext

---

団 ⁹⁴⁰ / J4344 / M4703' TON. DON. DAN body, group, corps, gang, party, company, troupe; circle.
A

³ 子 *dango* dumpling
⁶ 交 *dankō* collective bargaining
⁷ 体 *dantai* corporation, party, body, organization, group, association, entity
⁸ 長 *danchō* leader of a group
¹⁰ 員 *dan'in* member of a group
扇 *uchiwa* round fan; referee's fan
栗 *donguri* acorn
¹² 結 *danketsu* unity, union, combination
²³ 欒 *danran* family circle; harmony

回 ⁹⁴¹ / J3273 / M4690 E. KAI time; round, game, bout, heat, inning, innings; go around. *megu(ru), mawa(ru)* vi and vt turn, go around; revolve, rotate, spin, gyrate; patrol, tour; take effect (medicine); be distributed; be past (time); be transferred. *mawa(rasu), mawa(su)* turn, revolve, rotate; circularize; pass around; forward, transmit; refer to; transfer; lend money. *motō(ru)* wander around. *mawa(ri)* rotation; circumference, girth, surroundings, border; detour; tour; efficacy or effect (of something taken); spread (of flames). *mawa(shi)* loin cloth; cape, mantle. *megu(rasu)* enclose, surround; turn, turn around; ponder; devise. *mawa(rikudoi)* circuitous. *-mawa(ri)* via; a round, a turn; a size; a cycle (12 years). (See also 廻 1659 for related compounds)
A

⁵ 付 *kaifu suru* transmit, refer to, send to, pass on to
収 *kaishū* collection (of materials); recovery (of something)
⁶ 米 *kaimai* rice transportation; rice deliveries
虫 *kaichū* roundworm, ascarid
向 *ekō* Buddhist memorial service
合 *mawa(ri)a(wase), megu(ri)awase)* turn of fortune, chance, fate. *kaigō* chance meeting
⁸ 者 *mawa(shi)mono* spy, secret agent
送 *kaisō* forwarding, transportation
送車 *kaisōsha* out-of-service bus, train, or streetcar
⁹ 持 *mawa(ri)mo(chi)* doing by turns
春 *kaishun* return of spring; recovery (from an illness); rejuvenation
¹⁰ 航 *kaikō* navigation, cruise
帰 *kaiki* revolution, recurrence. *kaiki suru* revolve, return, recur
帰線 *kaikisen* the tropics (of Cancer and Capricorn)
¹¹ 廊 *kairō* corridor
道 *mawa(ri)michi* detour, roundabout way
遊 *kaiyū* excursion, circular tour
船 *kaisen* barge; cargo vessel
教 *Kaikyō* Muhammedanism; Islam
教徒 *Kaikyōto* a Mohammedan, a Moslem
転 *kaiten* revolution, rotation; revolving, swivel; turnover
転椅子 *kaiten isu* swivel chair
転資金 *kaiten shikin* revolving fund
転翼 *kaiten'yoku* rotor
¹² 遊 *kaiyū* a run of fish; traveling around for pleasure
診 *kaishin* doctor's hospital rounds
飲 *mawa(shi)no(mi)* drink in turn from one cup
答 *kaitō* reply
復 *kaifuku* recovery, restoration, rehabilitation
¹³ 路 *kairo* (electric) circuit
想 *kaisō* reflection, reminiscence
想録 *kaisōroku* memoirs
数 *kaisū* frequency, number of times
¹⁴ 舞台 *mawa(ri)butai* revolving stage
漕 *kaisō* marine transportation
¹⁵ 線 *kaisen* (electric) circuit
避 *kaihi* evasion, shirking, dodging,

circumvention, avoiding
¹⁶ 燈籠 *mawa(ri)dōrō* revolving lantern
覧 *kairan* circulation
²¹ 顧 *kaiko* recollection, retrospect
顧的 *kaikoteki* retrospective
顧録 *kaikoroku* memoirs, reminiscences

———————— 4 ————————

A 囲 $\frac{945}{\substack{J304f\\M4722}}$ I enclosure. *kako(mu),*
kako(u) enclose, surround,
encircle; besiege; preserve, store; keep.
kako(mi), kako(i) enclosure, paling; tea
arbor; storage.
⁸ 炉裏 *irori* sunken hearth
¹³ 碁 *igo* (the game of) *go*
¹⁸ 繞 *inyō suru, ijō suru* surround

A 困 $\frac{946}{\substack{J3a24\\M4717}}$ KON. *koma(ru)* be
distressed be in trouble,
be destitute, be embarrassed, be perplexed,
be annoyed. *koma(raseru), koma(rasu)*
embarrass, annoy.
⁷ 抜 *koma(ri)-nu(ku)* be greatly perplexed;
be greatly embarrassed
⁸ 果 *koma(ri)-ha(teru)* be greatly
perplexed; be greatly embarrassed
者 *koma(ri)mono* good-for-nothing
person; source of trouble
苦 *konku* hardships, privation
¹² 惑 *konwaku* perplexity, embarrassment;
doubt; confusion
¹⁵ 窮 *konkyū* poverty, distress
¹⁶ 憊 *kompai* exhaustion, fatigue
¹⁸ 難 *konnan* trouble, distress, perplexity

A 図 $\frac{947}{\substack{J3f5e\\M4734}}$ To plan. ZU drawing,
plan, figure, cut, chart,
diagram, illustration, graph. *haka(ru)*
measure, gauge, weigh; fathom, sound;
compute, estimate; plan, devise, scheme;
counsel with; have in mind; aim at;
deceive, impose on. *haka(razaru)*
unexpected. *haka(razu) mo*
unexpectedly, unintentionally,
accidentally.
² 入 *zui(ri)* illustrated (book)
³ 工 *zukō* drawing and manual arts (the
study)
⁴ 太 *zubuto(i)* bold, audacious, impudent
⁵ 示 *zushi* explanatory diagram,
illustration

⁶ 式 *zushiki* diagram, graph
⁷ 図 *zūzū(shii)* impudent, audacious, bold,
brazenfaced
体 *zūtai* body
抜 *zunu(keru)* tower above, be
outstanding
形 *zukei* figure, diagram
⁸ 版 *zuhan* plate, figure, illustration
画 *zuga* drawing (the study); a drawing,
a picture
表 *zuhyō* chart, diagram, graph
⁹ 面 *zumen* drawing, plan, map, sketch
柄 *zugara* a design
星 *zuboshi* the bull's-eye, the mark
¹⁰ 案 *zuan* design, plan, sketch, drawing
書 *tosho* books
書目録 *tosho mokuroku* catalog of
publications
¹³ 解 *zukai* illustration, explanatory
diagram
¹⁴ 説 *zusetsu* explanatory diagram;
illustrated book
像学 *zuzōgaku* iconology, iconography
¹⁹ 譜 *zufu* chart, picture, figure
²² 鑑 *zukan* picture book, illustrated
reference book

———————— 5 ————————

A 固 $\frac{949}{\substack{J3847\\M4745}}$ KO. *kata(maru) vi* harden,
stiffen, solidify, set, settle,
congeal, clot, curdle, conglomerate; get
together; be devoted to; settle down
(weather). *kata(meru) vt* harden;
tighten; freeze; curdle; strengthen;
stabilize; defend, fortify; collect, amass;
settle down, locate. *kata(me)* defense,
fortification; guard; pledge, engagement.
katama(ri) lump, chunk, cold, mass;
clump, cluster, group; flock; bigotry;
personification (of). *kata(i)* hard, solid;
tough, rigid; tight; steady, firm; strict;
safe, reliable, upright; chaste, constant;
stiff; bookish; classical; stubborn.
moto(yori) from the beginning; of course.
⁶ 守 *koshu* persistence, tenacity, adhering
有 *koyū no* personal, characteristic,
peculiar to, inherent
有名詞 *koyū meishi* proper noun
⁷ 体 *kotai* a solid (body)
形 *kokei* a solid (body)
形物 *kokeibutsu* a solid ; solid food

3

口【口】₅
土
士
夂
夊
夕
大
女
子
宀
寸
小
尤
尸
屮
山
川
巛
工
己
巾
干
幺
广
廴
廾
弋
弓
彐
彑
彡
彳

3

口【口】

土 士 久 夂 夕 大 女 子 宀 寸 小 尢 尸 屮 山 川 巛 工 己 巾 干 幺 广 廴 廾 弋 弓 ヨ 彑 彡 彳

⁸陋 *korō* perversity, bigotry, conservatism
苦 *katakuru(shii)* formal, ceremonious; awkward; punctilious; strict
定 *kotei* fixing, fixation, fixed; identification (of biological specimens)
定化 *koteika* fixation, freezing (credits)
⁹持 *koji suru* persist in (a belief), adhere to (a cause)
¹¹執 *koshū, koshitsu* adherence; persistence
唾飲 *katazu (o) no(mu)* be intensely anxious
¹²着 *kochaku suru* adhere to
¹³辞 *koji suru* positively decline

A 国 $\frac{950}{\text{J3971}}$ Koku country. *kuni* M4752 country, land, realm; province; native land. *(o)kuni* your country; hometown, province.
²力 *kokuryoku* national strength, national resources
³土 *kokudo* country, territory, domain
土防衛 *kokudo bōei* national defense
土計画 *kokudo keikaku* land planning
⁴王 *kokuō* king, monarch
内 *kokunai* domestic; the interior of a country
文 *kokubun* national literature; national language
文法 *kokubumpō* Japanese grammar
文学 *kokubungaku* Japanese literature
文科 *kokubunka* Japanese literature course
⁵号 *kokugō* name of a country
史 *kokushi* national history
外 *kokugai* overseas, outside the country
外追放 *kokugai tsuihō* deportation
立 *kokuritsu* national (institution)
立公園 *kokuritsu kōen* national park
民 *kokumin, kunitami* the people, a national; national
民文学 *kokumin bungaku* national literature
民投票 *kokumin tōhyō* plebiscite
民性 *kokuminsei* national character
民的 *kokuminteki* national
民所得 *kokumin shotoku* national income
民感情 *kokumin kanjō* national sentiment

⁶交 *kokkō* diplomatic relations
名 *kokumei* name of a country
自慢 *kuni jiman* provincial pride
字 *kokuji* native script; the *kana* syllabary; characters made in Japan
防 *kokubō* national defense
防軍 *kokubōgun* national defense force
会 *kokkai* national assembly, diet, congress, parliament
会図書館 *Kokkai Toshokan* Library of Congress, National Diet Library
会議事堂 *Kokkai Gijidō* Diet Building; House of Parliament; U.S. Capitol, National Assembly Building
会議員 *kokkai giin* national assemblyman
有 *kokuyū* national ownership
有化 *kokuyūka* nationalization
有地 *kokuyūchi* national land
有林 *kokuyūrin* national forest
有財産 *kokuyū zaisan* national resources
⁷体 *kokutai* national structure, national polity; national athletic meet
技 *kokugi* national skills; national sport
状 *kokujō* condition of the country
別 *kunibetsu* classification by nations
花 *kokka* national flower
言葉 *kuni kotoba* local dialect
⁸国 *kuniguni* nations
使 *kokushi* envoy
法 *kokuhō* national law, public law
宝 *kokuhō* national treasure; national hero
定 *kokutei* stipulated by law, compiled by the state
定公園 *kokutei kōen* semi-national park
学 *kokugaku* study of Japanese literature
事 *kokuji* national affairs
事行為 *kokuji kōi* matters of state
事犯 *kokujihan* political offense, treason
⁹風 *kokufū, kuniburi* national customs; popular songs, folk songs
威 *kokui* national prestige
政 *kokusei* government, national administration
軍 *kokugun* national armed forces
是 *kokuze* national policy
連 *Kokuren* United Nations
連安全保障理事会 *Kokuren Anzen Hoshō Rijikai* UN Security Council

連事務総長 *Kokuren Jimu Sōchō* UN Secretary General

連軍 *Kokuren Gun* UN Forces

連教育科学文化機構 *Kokuren Kyōiku Kagaku Bunka Kikō* UNESCO

連旗 *Kokurenki* UN flag

連総会 *Kokuren Sōkai* UN General Assembly

¹⁰ 庫 *kokko* national treasury

辱 *kokujoku* national dishonor

都 *kokuto* national capital

益 *kokueki* national prosperity

書 *kokusho* credentials (to a ruler); a ruler's message; national record; national literature

粋主義 *kokusui shugi* nationalism, ultranationalism

家 *kokka* nation, country

家公務員 *kokka kōmuin* government officials

家主義 *kokka shugi* nationalism

家的 *kokkateki* national, state

家試験 *kokka shiken* government examinations

¹¹ 道 *kokudō* national highway

運 *kokuun* national destiny, national fortunes

情 *kokujō* condition of the country

設 *kokusetsu* provided by the government

許 *kunimoto* birthplace, one's country, one's home province

章 *kokushō* national emblem

務 *kokumu* state affairs

務大臣 *kokumu daijin* minister of state; minister without portfolio

務長官 *Kokumu Chōkan* The Secretary of State (USA)

産 *kokusan* domestic products

産品 *kokusanhin* domestic products

祭日 *kokusaibi* national holiday

¹² 税 *kokuzei* national tax

朝 *kokuchō* imperial court

富 *kokufu* national wealth

策 *kokusaku* national policy

葬 *kokusō* state funeral

営 *kokuei* government-operated

¹³ 債 *kokusai* national debt; national bonds, national securities

賊 *kokuzoku* traitor, rebel

禁 *kokkin* a national prohibition

勢 *kunizei* local armed forces. *kokusei*

national strength; condition of the country

勢調査 *kokusei chōsa* national census

際 *kokusai* international (intercourse)

際化 *kokusaika* internationalization

際的 *kokusaiteki* international

際司法裁判所 *Kokusai Shihō Saibansho* International Court of Justice

際主義 *kokusai shugi* internationalism

際赤十字 *Kokusai Sekijūji* International Red Cross

際社会 *kokusai shakai* community of nations

際法 *kokusaihō* international law

際連合 *Kokusai Rengō* United Nations

際連盟 *Kokusai Remmei* League of Nations

際通貨基金 *Kokusai Tsūka Kikin* International Monetary Fund

際間 *kokusaikan no* international

際結婚 *kokusai kekkon* international marriage

¹⁴ 旗 *kokki* national flag

歌 *kokka* national anthem

選弁護人 *kokusen bengonin* counsel assigned by the court

語 *kokugo* national language; Japanese

境 *kokkyō, kunizakai* frontier, national boundary

境線 *kokkyōsen* boundary line

境警備 *kokkyō keibi* border guards

¹⁵ 権 *kokken* sovereign rights; national prestige

論 *kokuron* public opinion, public discussion

賓 *kokuhin* national guest

¹⁸ 難 *kokunan* national crisis, national disaster

²⁰ 籍 *kokuseki* nationality, citizenship

--------------------- 7 ---------------------

圃 $\frac{954}{\text{J4a60}}$ Ho field (for crops); garden.
    M4774

--------------------- 9 ---------------------

圏 $\frac{960}{\text{J3777}}$ KEN sphere, circle, range, radius.
B   M4815'

⁴ 内 *kennai* within the range or orbit

⁵ 外 *kengai* outside the range or orbit

3
口口【土土】夂夂夕大女子宀寸小ⱱ尢尸中山川巛工己巾干幺广廴廾弋弓ヨ且彡彳

— 10 —

A 園 $\frac{962}{J3160}$ M4818 **En** garden, yard, plantation, farm. *sono* garden, park.

2 丁 *entei* gardener

6 地 *enchi* park
7 児 *enji* kindergarten pupil
芸 *engei* horticulture, floriculture, gardening
8 長 *enchō* kindergarten principal
11 遊会 *en'yūkai* garden party

▇ RAD. 土 32 ▇

Tsuchi earth. At left: 土 *tsuchi-hen*. Variant: 士. This variant is actually Rad. 33 but, except for the radical character itself, is herein treated as a variant of Rad. 32. Nickname: Earth.

A 土 $\frac{966}{J455a}$ M4867 **To**. Do earth, ground; Saturday; Turkey.
tsuchi earth, soil, ground.

3 工 *dokō* earthwork; coolie, laborer
下座 *dogeza suru* prostrate oneself
4 手 *dote* bank, dike, embankment
方 *dokata* laborer, coolie
木 *doboku* engineering, public works
木工学 *doboku kōgaku* civil engineering
5 台 *dodai* foundation, groundwork, base; fundamentally, entirely
民 *domin* natives, aborigines
左衛門 *dozaemon* drowned person
用 *doyō* dog days, midsummer
用波 *doyō nami* high waves in the dog days
6 色 *tsuchi iro* earth color
気色 *tsuchike iro* earth color
地 *tochi* land, tract, lot; estate; soil; locality; territory; the neighborhood
地付 *tochitsu(ki)* land attached, with land
地収用 *tochi shūyō* expropriation of land
地台帳 *tochi daichō* land register
地改良 *tochi kairyō* land improvement
地言葉 *tochi kotoba* dialect
地柄 *tochigara* nature of the locality
地訛 *tochi namari* colloquial expression
7 足 *dosoku de* with footgear on
8 性骨 *doshōbone* (derisive for) disposition, nature
9 星 *Dosei* Saturn
俗 *dozoku* local customs
建 *doken* civil engineering and construction

建屋 *doken'ya* contractor
建業 *dokengyō* civil engineering and construction
砂 *dosha* earth and sand
砂降 *doshabu(ri)* downpour
砂崩 *doshakuzu(re)* landslide
10 埃 *tsuchibokori, tsuchihokori* dust
俵 *dohyō* sandbag; ring, wrestling arena
俵際 *dohyōgiwa* scaffold, place of execution
11 偶 *dogū* earthen figure, wooden image, dummy, puppet
瓶 *dobin* earthen teapot
崩瓦解 *dohō-gakai* collapse, downfall
産 *miyage* souvenir, present
産物 *miyagemono* souvenir, present
産話 *miyagebanashi* story of one's travels
12 間 *doma* unfloored room; dirt floor
塀 *dobei* mud wall
塁 *dorui* earthwork, breastwork
葬 *dosō* burial, interment
着 *dochaku no* aboriginal, indigenous, native
着民 *dochakumin* natives, aborigines
13 煙 *tsuchikemuri* cloud of dust
14 語 *dogo* native tongue, dialect
管 *dokan* earthen pipe, drainpipe
蔵 *dozō* warehouse, storehouse, godown
豪 *dogō* (ancient) powerful provincial family
15 踏 *tsuchifu(mazu)* arch of the foot
質 *doshitsu* nature of the soil
器 *doki, kawarake* unglazed earthenware, earthenware, crockery,

pottery

16 壌 *dojō* soil, earth
橋 *dobashi* earthen bridge
壇場 *dotamba* place of execution, scaffold

17 鍋 *donabe, tsuchi nabe* earthen pot

18 曜 *Doyō* Saturday
曜日 *Doyōbi* Saturday
嚢 *donō* sandbag

20 饅頭 *domanjū, tsuchi manjū* grave mound

1

壬 ⟨968 / J3f51 / M5639⟩ NIN. JIN I, ninth. *mizunoe* ninth calendar sign. [土]

2

圧 ⟨970 / J3035 / M4879⟩ EN. ATSU. *as(suru)*
A press, oppress, dominate, overwhelm. *he(su)* push, press. *o(su)* push, shove; press, squash, compress; stamp, seal; do in spite of. *o(shi)-* emphatic verbal prefix.

2 力 *atsuryoku* pressure, stress
力計 *atsuryokukei* pressure gauge

6 死 *asshi* crushing to death

7 迫 *appaku* pressure, coercion, oppression
迫感 *appakukan* feeling of oppression

8 制 *assei* oppression, tyranny, despotism
延 *atsuen* rolling
延鋼 *atsuenkō* rolled steel

8 巻 *akkan* best part (of a book); masterpiece; highlight; best in the lot

10 殺 *o(shi)-koro(su)* crush, stifle, or squeeze to death. *assatsu* crushing to death
倒 *attō suru* overwhelm, overpower, crush; outdo, surpass
倒的 *attōteki* overwhelming

12 勝 *asshō* complete victory

13 搾 *assaku* pressure, compressing
搾空気 *assaku kūki* compressed air
搾機 *ussukuki* press, compressor

17 縮 *asshuku* compression, pressing, constriction, condensation

---
3

圭 ⟨973 / J373d / M4887⟩ KEI corner, angle, edge; jewel.

壮 ⟨974 / J4154 / M5642⟩ Sō manhood;
B prosperity. saka(n) prosperous. [士]

2 丁 *sōtei* a young man, an able-bodied youth

3 士 *sōshi* henchman, political bully
大 *sōdai* grandeur, splendor

6 年 *sōnen* the prime of life
行会 *sōkōkai* farewell party

7 図 *sōto* great undertaking; heroic attempt
快 *sōkai na* stirring, thrilling, exciting

8 者 *sōsha* man in his prime

9 途 *sōto* ambitious course
重 *sōchō* solemnity, gravity, impressiveness

10 挙 *sōkyo* great undertaking; heroic attempt
烈 *sōretsu na* heroic, brave

11 健 *sōken na* healthy, robust

12 絶 *sōzetsu na* sublime, heroic, magnificent

17 厳 *sōgon* solemnity, sublimity, impressiveness, magnificence, majesty

18 観 *sōkan* grandeur, grand spectacle

19 麗 *sōrei* splendor, grandeur

在 ⟨975 / J3a5f / M4881⟩ ZAI outskirts, suburbs,
A country. *a(ru)* there is, have, exist; occur; be located, be contained in; (it) measures; happen; be found; be held; consist of. *owa(su)* to be (polite). *a(ri) to arayuru* all, every. *zai-* located in.

4 方 *a(ri)kata* way something should be; the way something is
中 *zaichū* within
日 *zai-Nichi* resident in Japan. *ari(shi)hi* bygone days; during one's lifetime

5 処 *arika* one's whereabouts, retreat, refuge, hiding place; location (of something)
世 *zaisei* on the earth. *ari(shi)yo* on the earth; past days
外 *zaigai* abroad
外邦人 *zaigai hōjin* Japanese residents abroad

6 宅 *zaitaku suru* be in, be at home
米 *zai-Bei* resident in America
任 *zainin suru* hold office
任中 *zaininchū* while in office

7 来 *zairai, a(ri)ki(tari)* usage, tradition
位 *zaii* reigning

口口【土士】夂夂夕大女子宀寸小⺌尢尸屮山川巛工己巾干幺广廴廾弋弓彐彑彡彳 3 ³

3

口口口【土‐土】
夂夂夕大女子宀寸小尢尸屮山川巛工己巾干幺广廴廾弋弓ヨ彑彡彳

住 *zaijū suru* live, reside, dwell
住者 *zaijūsha* resident
[8] 所 *zaisho* the country; one's residence; one's home town. *a(ri)dokoro* one's whereabouts, retreat, refuge, hiding place; location (of something)
京 *zaikyō* resident in the capital
学 *zaigaku* enrolled in school
学生 *zaigakusei* student; undergraduate
[9] 室 *zaishitsu suru* be in the room
[10] 家 *zaike* layman (Buddhist)
庫 *zaiko* stock, stockpile
庫品 *zaikohin* goods on hand, inventory
校 *zaikō suru* be in school
校生 *zaikōsei* present students
留 *zairyū suru* reside temporarily
留民 *zairyūmin* residents
[11] 野 *zaiya* out of office; the party out of power
[12] 勤 *zaikin suru* serve, hold office
[18] 職 *zaishoku suru* hold office, remain in office
[20] 籍 *zaiseki* be enrolled

地 976 / J434f / M4890 A Cʜɪ earth, land, ground, the surface of the earth; soil; place, region; territory; room, space; position; site; foundation. *ji* ground, land, earth; the surface of the earth; foundation, soil; texture, weave, fabric; field (of a flag); region; disposition; respectability; accompaniment; narrative part; fact. *ji(beta)* the ground, the earth. *tsuchi* earth, soil, ground.
[2] 力 *chiryoku* fertility
[3] 上 *chijō no* terrestrial, earthly, mundane, temporal. *chijō ni* on the ground, on earth, in this world
上軍 *chijō gun* ground forces
下 *chika* underground, subterranean; basement
下水 *chikasui* subterranean water
下牢 *chikarō* underground dungeon
下足袋 *jika tabi* heavy-soled work tabi
下茎 *chikakei* rhizome
下室 *chikashitsu* basement, cellar
下道 *chikadō* underground passage
下街 *chikagai* underground market
下鉄 *chikatetsu* subway
下資源 *chika shigen* underground resources
[4] 区 *chiku* area, region, lot

中 *chichū* underground, subterranean
中海 *Chichūkai* Mediterranean Sea
元 *jimoto no* local. *jimoto* that country
引網 *jibikiami* dragnet, seine (for inshore fishing)
方 *chihō* locality, region, area, section; the country; vicinity, neighborhood. *jigata* rural locality; coastal waters
方色 *chihōshoku* local color
方的 *chihōteki* local
方訛 *chihō namari* provincialism, local dialect, local accent
方税 *chihōzei* local taxes
[5] 目 *chimoku* land category
代 *jidai, chidai* land rent
主 *jinushi* landlord
平 *chihei* ground level
平線 *chiheisen* horizon, skyline
[6] 肌 *jihada* texture, grain
名 *chimei* place name
団駄 *jidanda* stamping with vexation
回 *jimawa(ri)* neighborhood, neighboring districts; provincial, local; a street tough
曳網 *jibiki ami* dragnet, seine (for inshore fishing)
[7] 図 *chizu* map, chart, plan
位 *chii* position, status, place, office, post
利 *chi(no)ri* geographical advantage
声 *jigoe* natural voice
卵 *jitamago* home-grown eggs; local eggs
吹雪 *jifubuki* drifting snow
均 *jinarashi* ground leveling
形 *chikei* topography.
形図 *chikeizu* topographical map
[8] 金 *jigane* metal, ore, ground metal; true character
固 *jigata(me)* ground leveling; ground tamping
底 *chitei* the bowels of the earth; underground
価 *chika* land value
味 *chimi* nature of the soil. *jimi na* plain, simple, quiet, sober, modest, conservative
物 *chibutsu* natural objects, landmarks, places to hide. *jimono* local product
歩 *chiho* one's ground, one's stand, standing, position, footing
学 *chigaku* physiography
表 *chihyō* surface of the earth

所 *jisho* land, ground, tract, plot
⁹ 廻 *jimawa(ri)* neighborhood, neighboring districts; provincial, local; a street tough
峡 *chikyō* isthmus
点 *chiten* spot, point, place, position
政学 *chiseigaku* geopolitics
面 *jimen* surface (of land), ground, land, lot
¹⁰ 核 *chikaku* earth's nucleus
酒 *jizake* locally brewed saké
紋 *jimon* pattern
帯 *chitai* zone, belt, region, area
¹¹ 道 *jimichi na* fair, honest
階 *chikai* basement
殻 *chikaku* the earth's crust
異 *chii* physiographical changes
動説 *chidōsetsu* heliocentric or Copernican theory
域 *chiiki* region area zone
域的 *chiikiteki* local, regional
域差 *chiikisa* regional differences
理 *chiri* geography, topography
理学 *chirigaku* geography
球 *chikyū* earth, globe
球人 *chikyūjin* earthdwellers
球物理学 *chikyū butsurigaku* geophysics
球儀 *chikyūgi* terrestial globe
¹² 軸 *chijiku* earth's axis
割 *jiwa(re)* earth fissure or crack. *jiwa(ri)* land allotment
¹³ 続 *jitsuzu(ki)* land contiguity
勢 *chisei* topography
滑 *jisube(ri)* landslide
雷 *jirai* land mine
¹⁴ 鳴 *jina(ri), chimei* earth tremor
誌 *chishi* topography, geographical description
磁気 *chijiki* terrestial magnetism
模様 *jimoyō* background pattern (woven into cloth)
層 *chisō* stratum, layer
獄 *jigoku* hell
獄耳 *jigoku mimi* sharp ears
蔵 *Jizō* a Buddhist guardian deity of children
¹⁵ 熱 *chinetsu, jinetsu* subterranean heat
盤 *jiban* base, foundation, the ground; footing, foothold; sphere of influence; constituency
質 *chishitsu* geology, geological features; nature of the soil. *jishitsu* texture
質学 *chishitsugaku* geology
震 *jishin* earthquake
震計 *jishinkei* seismograph
¹⁸ 鎮祭 *jichinsai* ground-breaking ceremony
¹⁹ 響 *jihibi(ki)* earth tremor

─────── 4 ───────

坐 | 978 J3a41 M4931 | See 座 1619.

壱 | 983 J306d M5647 | B | ICHI, ITSU one. [士]

坂 | 985 J3a64 M4910 | A | HAN. *saka* incline, slope, hill.
¹¹ 道 *sakamichi* hill road

坊 | 986 J4b37 M4924 | B | BŌ priest's residence; (Buddhist) priest; boy. *bō(ya)* boy. *bo(tchan)* your, his, or her boy. *tsukasa* office, government office; director, head official.
⁵ 主 *bōzu* Buddhist priest, monk; shaven head; boy; rascal
主頭 *bōzu atama* tonsure, shaven head

坑 | 987 J3923 M4932 | B | KŌ pit, hole.
³ 口 *kōkō* mine entrance
⁴ 区 *kōku* mine area
木 *kōboku* mine pillars
夫 *kōfu* miner
内 *kōnai* mine pit, shaft
⁵ 外 *kōgai* surface, out of the pit
¹¹ 道 *kōdō* (mine) level; tunnel

均 | 988 J3651 M4916 | A | KIN. *nara(su)* to level, to average. *hito(shii)* equal, similar, alike, equivalent.
¹ 一 *kin'itsu* uniformity, equality
⁴ 分 *kimbun* equal division
⁸ 斉 *kinsei* symmetry, balance
¹² 等 *kintō* equality, uniformity, evenness, identity
¹⁵ 質 *kinshitsu* homogeneity
¹⁶ 衡 *kinkō* equilibrium, balance
整 *kinsei* symmetry, balance

口 口【土 士】 攵 攵 夕 大 女 子 宀 寸 小 ⺌ 尢 屮 山 川 巛 工 己 巾 干 幺 广 廴 廾 弋 弓 彐 彑 彡 彳

⁴

3

口口【土士】夊夊夕大女子宀寸小⺌尢尸屮山川巛工己巾干幺广廴廾弋弓ヨ彑彡彳

声 ⁹⁸⁹ J403c M5645 SHŌ. SEI koe voice;
tone; alarm, cry; (bird) song, chirp. [士]

⁵立 koe (o) ta(teru) speak
⁶名 seimei fame, popularity
色 seishoku voice and countenance; songs and women. kowairo tone of voice
⁷呑 koe (o) no(mu) keep quiet, say nothing
⁸価 seika good reputation, fame, popularity
明 seimei declaration, statement, proclamation
⁹音 kowane tone of voice, timber of the voice. seion voice quality, vocal sound
変 koegawa(ri) change of voice.
¹⁰高 kowadaka ni, koetaka(rakani), koedaka(ku), koetaka(ku) with a loud voice
涙 seirui tears in the voice
帯 seitai vocal chords
帯模写 seitai mosha vocal mimicry
¹¹掛 koe (o) ka(keru) call to (someone). koegaka(ri) influence, recommendation
望 seibō popularity, fame
¹²援 seien encouragement, support, rooting, cheering
量 seiryō voice volume
¹³楽 seigaku vocal music
楽家 seigakuka vocalist
¹⁵調 seichō tone of voice
¹⁷優 seiyū radio actor

売 ⁹⁹⁰ J4764 M5647 MAI. BAI selling. u(ru)
A sell, deal in, betray, deceive, impose on, tell on, pick (a quarrel). u(reru) sell, be in demand, enjoy a large sale; be well known. u(ri) sale, selling. u(re) sale, demand. [士]

³口 u(re)kuchi, u(ri)guchi outlet, market, demand
子 u(rek)ko popular person. u(ri)ko sales clerk
上 u(ri)-a(geru) sell out. uria(ge) sales, proceeds; sale, closing sale
上金 uriagekin amount sold, sales
上高 uria(ge)daka amount sold, sales
⁴切 u(ri)-ki(reru) be sold out. u(ri)-ki(ru) sell out, clear out. uriki(re) sold out,

a sellout
文業 baibungyō hack writing
込 u(ri)-ko(mu) sell, find a market for
⁵付 u(ri)-tsu(keru) palm off, force a sale
払 u(ri)-hara(u) sell off, close out
主 urinushi seller, vendor
出 u(ri)-da(su), u(ri)-ida(su) offer for sale; gain a reputation. urida(shi) sale
⁶行 ureyu(ki), urei(ki) sale, demand, a run
尽 u(ri)-tsuku(su) sell off, clear out
先 u(ri)saki, u(re)saki market, outlet, demand, buyer
名 baimei self-advertisement
⁷足 u(re)ashi selling; a sale
戻 u(ri)modo(shi) resale (on the stock market)
却 baikyaku sale
声 u(ri)goe peddler's cry
言葉 u(ri)kotoba tit-for-tat; exchange of complements
⁸店 baiten booth, stand, store
価 baika selling price
物 urimono article for sale, offerings, for sale
歩 u(ri)-aru(ku) peddle
国奴 baikokudo traitor
⁹飛 u(ri)-toba(su) sell off
食 urigu(i) live by selling one's property
約 baiyaku sales contract
春 baishun prostitution
春婦 baishunfu prostitute
¹⁰高 u(re)daka, u(ri)daka amount of sales
値 urine selling price
残 u(re)-noko(ru) remain unsold, remain unmarried. u(re)noko(ri) goods left unsold; unmarried woman
家 u(ri)ya, u(ri)ie house for sale
捌 u(ri)sabaki sale; selling. u(ri)-saba(ku) sell, deal in, dispose of; sell widely
¹¹惜 u(ri)-oshi(mu) be indisposed to sell, hoard, restrict sales
¹²渡 u(ri)-wata(su) sell, negotiate, sign away. uriwata(shi) sale and delivery
買 baibai, u(ri)ka(i) trading, buying and selling; sale
場 uriba counter, salesroom, shop, store
場係 uribagakari sales clerk
¹³損 u(ri)-sokona(u) lose a sale, fail to find a market ⌐drugs
¹⁶薬 baiyaku, u(ri)gusuri patent medicine,

───── 5 ─────

坤 996 / J3a25 / M4969　KON divination sign; land, earth.

坦 997 / J4333 / M4971　TAN level; wide.

8 坦 *tantan(taru)* level, even; peaceful

B **坪** 998 / J445a / M4976　HEI. HYŌ. *tsubo* area about 36 square feet.

6 当 *tsuboa(tari)* per *tsubo*
10 庭 *tsuboniwa* a small court garden
13 数 *tsubosū* area in *tsubo*, floor space

A **垂** 999 / J3l62 / M5012　SUI *ta(rasu)* suspend, hang down; slouch. *ta(reru)*, *shida(reru)* vt and vi hang, droop, drop, lower, pull down; dangle; sag; drip, ooze, trickle; leave behind (at death); give, confer. *tare* hanging; straw curtain; lapel; pocket flap; skirts of a coat; gravy; soy sauce. *nannan to suru* be on the verge of (doing), be close to.

3 下 *suika suru* be pendent, hang down. *ta(re)-sa(garu)* vi hang, dangle. *ta(re)-sa(geru)* vt hang (a curtain); droop (a tail); lower (a blind)
4 込 *ta(rashi)-ko(mu)* vt drop into drop by drop
木 *taruki* rafter
8 直 *suichoku* vertical, perpendicular
直線 *suichokusen* perpendicular line
10 涎 *suizen* watering at the mouth
13 幕 *taremaku* hanging screen, curtain
15 範 *suihan suru* set an example

───── 6 ─────

垢 1008 / J3924 / M5058　KŌ. KU. *aka* dirt, grime, scale.

1 抜 *akanu(ke)* refined, elegant, urbane
9 染 *akaji(miru)* become grimy

B **垣** 1009 / J3340 / M5060　EN. *kaki* fence, hedge, wall.

10 根 *kakine* fence, hedge
12 間見 *kaimami(ru)* peep at, glimpse

A **型** 1010 / J373f / M5030　KEI *kata* model, mold, matrix, impression; style, type, pattern, make; set form; usage.

10 破 *katayabu(ri) no* unusual, queer, novel
紙 *katagami* sewing pattern
16 録 *katarogu* catalog

A **城** 1011 / J3e6b / M5086′　JŌ castle. SEI. *shiro* castle, citadel.

3 下町 *jōkamachi* castle town, the town around a castle
4 内 *jōnai* inside the castle
5 外 *jōgai* outside the castle
市 *jōshi* castle town, fortified town
主 *jōshu* lord of a castle
7 址 *jōshi* castle ruins
8 門 *jōmon* castle gate
10 郭 *jōkaku* castle, citadel
11 砦 *jōsai* fort, stronghold, citadel
13 楼 *jōrō* castle tower, watchtower
跡 *shiro ato* castle ruins, castle site
16 壁 *jōheki* castle wall, rampart

───── 7 ─────

B **埋** 1020 / J4b64 / M5116　MAI. *uzu(maru)*, *u(maru)* be filled up, be buried, be imbedded in. *uzu(meru)*, *u(meru)* bury, inter, fill up, pour in, plug up, inlay; make up for. *i(keru)* bury (in the ound); band (a fire). *uzu(moreru)*, *u(moreru)* be buried, be covered; live in obscurity.

4 込 *u(me)-ko(mu)* bury in the ground
5 立 *u(me)-ta(teru)* reclaim, fill in, fill up. *umeta(te)* reclamation, filling in
立地 *umetatechi* reclaimed land
6 合 *u(me)-a(waseru)* make amends, compensate for
7 没 *maibotsu suru* be buried, be entombed; remain obscure
9 草 *u(me)kusa* padding, stuffing, filler
11 設 *maisetsu suru* vt lay underground
12 葬 *maisō* burial, interment
14 蔵 *maizō suru* burying or hiding underground
蔵物 *maizōbutsu* buried treasure
蔵量 *maizōryō* amount of underground deposits

3

口 口 【土 士】

7

夂 夊 夕 大 女 子 宀 寸 小 ⺌ 尢 尸 屮 山 川 巛 工 己 巾 干 幺 广 廴 廾 弋 弓 彐 彑 彡 彳

3

口口
[土土]
夂夂夕大女子宀寸小⺌尢尸屮山川巛工己巾干幺广廴廾弋弓彐彑彡彳

─────── 8 ───────

堵 ₁₀₂₁ J4548 M-X　See 堵 1053.

埜 ₁₀₂₂ J4738 M5154　See 野 6208.

埼 ₁₀₂₈ J3a6b M5201　KI. *saki* cape, spit, promontory.

埠 ₁₀₂₉ J4956 M5161　FU wharf.
¹⁶頭 *futō* wharf, pier, quay

A 域 ₁₀₃₀ J3068 M5158　IKI region; limits; stage, level.
⁴内 *ikinai* inside the area
⁵外 *ikigai* outside the area

埴 ₁₀₃₁ J3e7d M5188　SHOKU. *hani, hena* clay.
¹⁵輪 *haniwa* ancient clay images buried with the dead

B 培 ₁₀₃₂ J475d M5195　BAI. HŌ. *tsuchika(u)* cultivate, foster.
¹⁵養 *baiyō* cultivation, nurture, culture

B 堕 ₁₀₃₃ J4244 M-X　DA. *da(suru)* descend to, lapse into, degenerate.
⁹胎 *datai* miscarriage, abortion
¹²落 *daraku* depravity, corruption, degradation, delinquency, apostasy, degeneration

壷 ₁₀₃₄ J445b M5657　KO. *tsubo* jar, pot; hinge knuckle; one's aim. [士]

堆 ₁₀₃₅ J424f M5211　TAI. *uzutaka(i)* piled high.
⁵石 *taiseki* moraine
⁸肥 *taihi, tsumigoe* compost, barnyard manure
¹⁶積 *taiseki* accumulation, pile, heap

B 堀 ₁₀₃₆ J4b59 M5205　KUTSU. *hori* moat, canal, ditch.
¹²割 *horiwa(ri)* canal, dock, ditch
¹⁴端 *horibata* edge of a moat

A 堂 ₁₀₃₇ J4632 M5207　DŌ temple; shrine; hall; reception room; firm; state chamber. *-dō* temple, shrine; shop, store.
⁴内 *dōnai* in the temple
¹¹堂 *dōdō(taru)* imposing, majestic, grand, magnificent, stately; fair, square
堂巡 *dōdōmegu(ri)* roll-call vote; vicious circle; going round and round (in an argument); circling a shrine or temple in worship

B 堅 ₁₀₃₈ J3778 M5210　KEN. *kata(i)* hard, solid; tough, rigid; tight; steady, firm; strict; safe, reliable, upright; chaste, constant; stiff; bookish; classical; stubborn.
⁶気 *katagi na* honest, upright, steady
⁷牢 *kenrō* solidity, stability, durability
忍不抜 *kennin fubatsu* perseverance, fortitude
⁸固 *kengo na* strong, solid, secure, firm
実 *kenjitsu na* steady, sound, reliable
苦 *katakuru(shii)* formal; punctilious; awkward
⁹持 *kenji suru* hold on to, stick to
陣 *kenjin* stronghold
¹²棧 *tatesan* vertical framework
¹²塁 *kenrui* stronghold

B 執 ₁₀₃₉ J3c39 M5193　SHITSU. SHŪ. *to(ru)* take, hold, seize, catch, capture; fetch; receive, procure, obtain; adopt (a measure); engage (graduates); choose; order (foodstuffs); pick, pluck; make, produce; eat; set up (camp); charge; administer; transact; take (pains); make out (the meaning); remove; take off (one's hat); take out (spots); strike out (words); weed, catch (fish); deprive of; steal; capture (territory), annex; need, require; reserve (rooms); subscribe to; press (a point home); take (a picture); possess. *shi(ssuru)* take, hold, grasp; take to heart; form an attachment; persist in.
²刀 *shittō* operating (in a hospital)
⁴心 *shūshin* devotion, attachment, infatuation
⁶成 *to(ri)-na(su)* mediate, intervene, intercede for, recommend. *to(ri)-na(shi)* arrangement; influence; mediation, intercession; good offices

行 *to(ri)-okona(u)* do, act, conduct oneself; carry out; perform, conduct (school); exercise (control); hold (a ceremony). *shikkō* performance

行委員 *shikkō iin* executive committee; executive officer

行猶予 *shikkō yūyo* stay of execution, suspended sentence

8 拗 *shitsuyō* obstinacy, persistence

念 *shūnen* tenacity; implacability

念深 *shūnembuka(i)* unforgiving, revengeful, vindictive; tenacious

事 *shitsuji* steward, deacon

11 務 *shitsumu* discharging one's office duties

12 着 *shūchaku, shūjaku* attachment, adhesion, tenacity

筆 *shippitsu* writing

基 | 1040 / J3470 / M5197 | A

KI radical (in chemistry); counter for lanterns, wreaths, motors, silos, and heavy machines; foundation; fundamentals; basis. *motoi, moto* basis, foundation, origin. *motozu(ku)* be based on, be founded on.

5 本 *kihon* basis, standard

本的 *kihonteki* basic, fundamental, standard

本的人権 *kihonteki jinken* basic human rights

本原理 *kihon genri* basic principles

本給 *kihonkyū* basic salary or wages

6 地 *kichi* base

8 金 *kikin* fund, endowment, foundation

底 *kitei* base, basis, foundation

9 点 *kiten* cardinal point

10 部 *kibu* base, pedestal, foundation

13 数 *kisū* cardinal number

幹 *kikan* mainstay, nucleus

準 *kijun* standard, basis, norm, criterion

督教 *Kirisutokyō* Christianity

15 線 *kisen* base line; base of a triangle

盤 *kiban* base, foundation, basis

調 *kichō* keynote, basis

18 礎 *kiso* foundation

礎的 *kisoteki* fundamental, basic

堺 | 1045 / J3a66 / M5289 | See 界 3739.

塚 | 1048 / J444d / M-X | B

CHŌ. *tsuka* mound, hillock, tumulus.

塀 | 1051 / J4a3d / M5316 | B

(国字) HEI wall, fence.

塔 | 1052 / J4563 / M5332 | B

TŌ tower, pagoda, steeple, obelisk, monument.

9 型 *tōgata* tower or steeple type

11 婆 *tōba* wooden grave tablet; stupa; pagoda

堵 | 1053 / J-X / M5279 |

To fence, railing, enclosure; dwelling.

6 列 *toretsu* line (of men)

堤 | 1054 / J4469 / M5259 | B

TEI *tsutsumi* dike, bank, embankment.

6 防 *teibō* bank, dike, levee

堰 | 1055 / J3161 / M5274 | B

EN. *se(ku)* dam up; check, stop, prevent. *seki* dam, embankment.

4 止 *se(ki)-to(meru)* intercept, check; dam up

12 堤 *entei* dike, weir

塁 | 1056 / J4e5d / M5316′ | B

RUI fort, rampart, walls; base (in baseball).

堪 | 1057 / J342e / M5266 | B

KAN. *ta(eru)* endure; support; withstand, resist, brave, weather; be fit for, be equal to. *ko(raeru)* endure; tolerate; control, stifle; pardon. *kota(eru)* endure. *tama(ranai)* be unbearable; be "dying" to (do something).

4 切 *ta(e)-ki(reru), kora(e)-ki(reru)* endure to the end, bear up. *kora(e)-ki(renai), ta(e)-ki(renai)* be unable to stand it any longer

7 忍 *kannin* pardon; patience, patient endurance. *ta(e)-shino(bu)* endure, bear patiently

忍袋 *kannimbukuro* patience

8 性 *kora(e)shō* patience

10 能 *tannō, kannō* skill, mastery; sufficiency

3

口 口【土 土】夊 夊 夕 大 女 子 宀 寸 小 ⺌ 尢 尸 屮 山 川 巛 工 己 巾 干 幺 广 廴 廾 弋 弓 ヨ 彑 彡 彳

9

3

口 口 【土 士】
夂 夊 夕 大 女 子 宀 寸 小 ⺌ 尢 尸 屮 山 川 巛 工 己 巾 干 幺 广 廴 廾 弋 弓 彐 彑 彡 彳

A 場 $\frac{1058}{\text{J3e6c}}$ Jō place, grounds, links,
M5278 range, course, track, ring.
ba place, site; space; seat; scene;
occasion, situation.
⁴ 内 *jōnai* within the grounds or hall
⁵ 末 *basue* outskirts, suburbs
外 *jōgai* outside the premises; outside
the market, on the curb; over the
fence
⁶ 合 *baai* occasion, circumstances, case
当 *baa(tari)* applause-seeking, claptrap,
sensational (speech)
⁸ 所 *basho* place, area, locality, quarter;
position, location; seat, site; scene;
room, space; experiences; sumo
tournament
⁹ 面 *bamen* place, scene, spectacle
¹² 違 *bachiga(i)* wrong place, different
place
¹³ 馴 *banare* experience
数 *bakazu* experience; many places

A 報 $\frac{1059}{\text{J4a73}}$ Hō news, report; reward,
M5275 retribution. *hō(jiru)*,
hō(zuru) repay, requite; report, inform,
disseminate. *muku(iru)* reward,
compensate; repay; revenge. *muku(i)*
reward; retribution. *shirase* information,
report, news; omen.
⁷ 告 *hōkoku* report, information, returns,
statement
告書 *hōkokusho* written statement,
written report
⁸ 知 *hōchi* news, report, intelligence,
information
知器 *hōchiki* alarm, communicator
¹¹ 道 *hōdō* news, report, intelligence,
information
道陣 *hōdōjin* a camp of reporters
waiting for news; the news front
¹² 復 *hōfuku* retaliation, revenge
¹³ 酬 *hōshū* remuneration, reward,
honorarium, fee, pay, salary
奨 *hōshō* compensation
奨金 *hōshōkin* cash bonus, reward,
bounty

--- **10** ---

塙 $\frac{1063}{\text{J4839}}$ KAKU. Kō . *hanawa*
M5341 projecting tableland,
projecting mountain.

塘 $\frac{1066}{\text{J4564}}$ Tō dike, embankment.
M5340

B 塑 $\frac{1068}{\text{J413a}}$ So modeling, molding.
M5328
⁹ 造 *sozō* modeling, molding
¹⁴ 像 *sozō* plaster image, clay figure, plastic
image

塞 $\frac{1069}{\text{J3a49}}$ SOKU. SAI. *fusa(gu)*,
M5349 *fusa(geru)* vt close, shut,
cover, block, wall up obstruct, fill; occupy.
fusa(garu) be closed, be blocked, be
obstructed, be clogged, be shut; be
occupied. *se(ku)* dam up; check, stop,
prevent.

B 塊 $\frac{1070}{\text{J3274}}$ KAI lump, chunk, clod,
M5319 mass, clot, ingot. *katamari*
lump, chunk, clod, mass; clump, cluster,
group; flock; bigotry; personification (of).
-*kure* lump, clod.

填 $\frac{1072}{\text{J4536}}$ TEN. *ha(maru)* go into, fit
M-X into; fall into, plunge into;
be deceived. *ha(meru)* put on, pull on;
inlay, set in; fit in; fill in; throw into;
ensnare, cheat.
⁴ 込 *ha(me)-ko(mu)* go into, fit into; fall
into, plunge into; be deceived.
hama(ri)-ko(mu) telescope, fall into,
get into (trouble), be infatuated with;
be addicted to

A 墓 $\frac{1073}{\text{J4a68}}$ Bo. *haka* grave, tomb.
M5431
⁵ 石 *boseki, hakaishi* tombstone
穴 *boketsu* grave hole
⁶ 地 *bochi* cemetery
守 *hakamori* grave keeper
⁸ 所 *bosho, hakadokoro, hakasho*
cemetery
参 *bosan, hakamai(ri)* visit to a grave
⁹ 前 *bozen* before the grave
¹² 場 *hakaba* cemetery
¹⁴ 碑 *bohi* tombstone
碑銘 *bohimei* epitaph
誌 *boshi* epitaph
¹⁵ 標 *bohyō* grave marker, tombstone

B 塗 $\frac{1074}{\text{J4549}}$ To. *nu(ru)* paint; plaster;
M5338 daub, lacquer. *mabu(su)*

smear, sprinkle or cover with.
mabu(reru), mami(reru) be covered or
smeared with. *nu(ri)* coating, lacquering,
varnishing, painting; lacquered.

³ 上 *nu(ri)-a(geru)* finish painting or
lacquering
⁵ 立 *nu(ri)-ta(teru)* put on thick makeup.
nu(ri)ta(te) no newly painted or
plastered
付 *nu(ri)-tsu(keru)* daub, smear
布 *tofu suru* apply (ointment)
⁸ 物 *nurimono* lacquerware
⁹ 炭苦 *totan (no) kuru(shimi)* very sad
situation
¹⁰ 師 *nu(ri)shi* lacquerer
料 *toryō* paints
¹² 椀 *nu(ri)wan* lacquered bowl
絵 *nu(ri)e* picture card for coloring
装 *tosō* painting, coating
装屋 *tosōya* painter
¹⁵ 潰 *nu(ri)-tsubu(su)* paint out
¹⁶ 薬 *nu(ri)gusuri* liniment, ointment
壁 *nu(ri)kabe* plastered wall

塩 A ⸺ 1075. J3176 M5382 ⸺ EN salt. *shio* salt;
seasoning.

⁴ 分 *embun* salt, salinity
水 *ensui, shiomizu* brine, salt water
⁵ 田 *enden* salt field, salt farm
出 *shioda(shi) suru* steep out the salt
加減 *shiokagen* seasoning
⁶ 気 *shioke* saltiness
⁷ 辛 *shiokara* salted fish; salted fish
entrails. *shiokara(i)* salty,
brackish
⁸ 味 *shioaji* seasoning
¹⁰ 梅 *ambai* seasoning; condition; manner;
state of health
浜 *shiohama* salt farm
害 *engai* salt-air damage
素 *enso* chlorine
¹¹ 魚 *shiozakana* salted fish
基 *enki* base (in chemistry)
¹² 焼 *shioyaki* fish broiled with salt; boiling
off sea water to make salt
¹⁴ 漬 *shiozuke* pickling in salt
酸 *ensan* hydrochloric acid
¹⁷ 鮭 *shiozake, shiojake* salted salmon

⸺ **11** ⸺

墜 B ⸺ 1082. J4446 M5451 ⸺ TSUI fall.

⁶ 死 *tsuishi suru* fall to one's death
¹² 落 *tsuiraku suru* fall, crash

塾 B ⸺ 1083. J3d4e M5402 ⸺ JUKU private school;
boarding school; gate house.

⁵ 生 *jukusei* private-school student
⁸ 長 *jukuchō* private-school
principal

境 A ⸺ 1085. J362d M5409 ⸺ KYŌ, KEI boundary;
region; condition; stage.
sakai boundary, border, frontier; place.

⁴ 内 *keidai* compound, grounds, precincts
⁵ 目 *sakaime* border, boundary line; crisis
⁹ 界 *kyōkai* boundary, limits, frontier;
environment determined by karma;
environment; rank. *keikai* border
界線 *kyōkaisen* boundary line
¹¹ 遇 *kyōgū* environment,
circumstances
域 *kyōiki* boundary; precincts
涯 *kyōgai* environment, circumstances,
one's lot, in life

墨 B ⸺ 1086. J4b4f M-X ⸺ BOKU. *sumi* India ink;
Chinese ink; ink stick;
inked marking string; ink (of a squid).

⁵ 汁 *bokujū* India ink
⁶ 守 *bokushu* strict adherence
⁹ 客 *bokkaku, bokkyaku* artist; writer
染 *sumizo(me)* dying black; dyed black;
dark
¹¹ 書 *bokusho* writing in India ink
¹¹ 痕 *bokkon* ink marks; handwriting
壷 *sumitsubo* ink bottle; carpenter's
inking device
¹² 堤 *bokutei* banks of the Sumida river
絵 *sumie* India-ink drawing, black-and-
white drawing

塵 ⸺ 1087. J3f50 M5388 ⸺ CHIN. JIN dust. *chiri, gomi*
dust, trash, rubbish.
chiri(bamu) be covered with dust.

⁵ 外 *jingai ni* aloof from the world
⁷ 芥 *chiriakuta, jinkai* rubbish,
garbage
⁸ 取 *chirito(ri)* dustpan
¹⁰ 埃 *jin'ai, chirihokori* dust, dirt; this drab
world
紙 *chirigami* coarse toilet paper

3

口 口 【土 ⌐
11 土】
夂 夂 夕 大 女 子
宀 寸 小 ⺌ 尢 尸
屮 山 川 巛 工 己
巾 干 幺 广 廴 廾
弋 弓 ヨ 彑 彡 彳

A 増 1088 / J417d / M5448′ Zō increase. *masa(ru)*, *ma(su)* vt increase, add to, augment, gain; promote (health); enlarge, extend; vi increase. *fu(yasu)* vt increase. *fu(eru)* vi increase. *ma(shi)* increase, extra; every (day). *ma(shi) na* better.

³大 *zōdai suru* increase, enlarge, enhance

⁴水 *zōsui suru* rise, swell, flood

⁵加 *zōka suru, ma(shi)-kuwa(waru)* vi increase, add, multiply. *ma(shi)-kuwa(eru)* vt increase, add, multiply. *zōka* increase, addition

収 *zōshū* increased yield, increased income

刊号 *zōkangō* special number (of a magazine)

⁸長 *zōchō suru* grow presumptuous, get puffed up

刷 *zōsatsu* additional printing

⁹派 *zōha* reinforcements

発 *zōhatsu suru* increase (a bond) issue; put on an extra train

¹⁰進 *zōshin suru* promote, increase, advance

員 *zōin* personnel increase

¹¹強 *zōkyō suru* augment, reinforce, increase

設 *zōsetsu* building enlargement, additional installations

産 *zōsan* production increase

¹²減 *zōgen* increase and decrease, rise and fall

税 *zōzei* tax increase

補 *zōho* enlargement, supplement

量 *zōryō* quantity increase

援 *zōen* reinforcement

幅 *zōfuku* amplification (in electricity)

幅器 *zōfukuki* amplifier

¹³資 *zōshi* capital increase

¹⁶築 *zōchiku suru* extend (a building)

¹⁸額 *zōgaku* increased amount

12

B 墳 1095 / J4a2f / M5488 FUN mound; tomb.

¹³墓 *fumbo* grave, tomb

墓地 *fumbo (no) chi* native country

13

B 墾 1097 / J3a26 / M5509 KON *ha(ru)* open up farmland.

B 壤 1098 / J3e6d / M-X JŌ earth, soil.

B 壇 1101 / J4345 / M5528 DAN stage, rostrum, dais; terrace; altar; world (of literature, etc.).

³上 *danjō* on the platform; on the stage; on the altar

¹⁰家 *danka* families which are temple supporters

B 壊 E. 1102 / J3275 / M5541′ KAI break. *kowa(su)* break; destroy; tear up; crack; smack; mar. *kowa(reru)* be broken; be demolished; fall into ruin.

⁶血病 *kaiketsubyō* scurvy

⁷乱 *kairan* corruption, demoralization, subversion, disturbance, destruction

¹⁰疽 *eso* gangrene

¹³滅 *kaimetsu* destruction, annihilation

B 壁 1103 / J4a49 / M5516 HEKI wall; lining (of the stomach); fence; partition. *kabe* wall.

³土 *kabetsuchi* wall mud, plaster, stucco

⁸板 *kabeita* wainscoting

画 *hekiga* fresco, wall painting; picture hanging on a wall

¹⁰紙 *kabegami* wallpaper

¹¹掛 *kabeka(ke)* tapestry

¹³際 *kabegiwa ni* near the wall

新聞 *kabe shimbun* wall newssheet (often handwritten)

14

B 壕 1108 / J3968 / M5559 KŌ. GŌ trench, dugout, air-raid shelter. *hori* moat; ditch; canal.

3

====== RAD. 土 33 ======

Samurai warrior. Except for the radical character itself, entered below, this radical is treated herein as a variant of Rad. 32. Nickname: Samurai.

A 土 $\frac{1117}{J3b4e}$ M5638 SHI samurai; man, gentleman; scholar. *samurai*, knight. *-shi* suffix for academic degrees.
⁶ 気 *shiki* morale; martial spirit
⁸ 官 *shikan* (military or naval) officer

官学校 *shikan gakkō* military academy
¹¹ 族 *shizoku* descendants of samurai
¹³ 農工商 *shi-nō-kō-shō* warriors-farmers-artisans-tradesmen; class distinction

====== RAD. 夂 34 ======

At top: *fuyugashira* (like crown of *fuyu* "winter"). At bottom: *natsuashi* (like legs of *natsu* "summer"). As enclosure: 夂 *suinyō*. This variant and some of the foregoing terms are actually Rad. 35 but are treated herein as Rad. 34. Nickname: Winter.

──────── 3 ────────

A 変 $\frac{1119}{J4a51}$ M5703 HEN cjange; accident, calamity; uprising; something strange. *hen(jiru), hen(zuru)* vi change into, be transformed, be transfigured. vt transform, alter, convert. *ka(waru)* change, vary; be revised; be different; be queer; move; be transferred. *ka(eru)* change, vary convert; revise, amend. *kawa(ri)* change, alteration; difference. *kawa(tta)* another, different; various; particular; unusual; novel; peculiar. *kawa(ranu)* constant, unchangeable. *kawa(rinaku)* unchangeably, constantly; eternally; uneventfully. *hen na* strange, suspicious-looking; queer, eccentric, funny. *hen ni* curiously, strangely.
² 人 *henjin* eccentric person ⌈apostasy
⁴ 心 *henshin* change of mind, inconstancy,
化 *henka* change, variation, alteration, mutation, transition; transformation, transfiguration, metamorphosis; variety, diversity; infection, declension, conjugation. *henge* goblin, ghost, apparition, bugbear
幻自在 *hengenjizai* ever-changing
⁵ 目 *kawa(ri)me* change, turning point, transition, new program

圧 *hen'atsu* transformation (of a current)
圧器 *hen'atsuki* transformer
⁶ 色 *henshoku* change of color; fading, discoloration
名 *hemmei* assumed name, alias
死 *henshi* accidental death
⁷ 身 *henshin* disguise
位 *hen'i* change of position
体 *hentai* anomaly, anomalous state
形 *henkei* transformation, metamorphosis, modification, variation, deformation; variety, deformity, monster
更 *henkō* change, modification, alteration
⁸ 果 *kawa(ri)-ha(teru)* be completely changed
者 *kawa(ri)mono* an eccentric
事 *henji* accident, emergency, calamity
⁹ 革 *henkaku* change, reform
造 *henzō* alteration, defacement, debasement, falsification, forgery
則 *hensoku* irregularity
奏曲 *hensōkyoku* variation (in music)
速 *hensoku* shifting gears
速機 *hensokuki* transmission
¹⁰ 容 *hen'yō* changed appearance
¹¹ 移 *hen'i* change, alteration, transmutation, mutation
転 *henten* mutation, change, vicissitude

3
口
口
口
土
士
夂
夊
【夕】
0
大
女
子
宀
寸
小
尚
尢
尸
屮
山
川
巛
工
己
巾
干
幺
广
廴
廾
弋
弓
彐
互
彡
彳

動 *hendō* change, fluctuation
異 *hen'i* accident; variation, mutation
12 換 *henkan* change, conversion, diversion, transformation
装 *hensō* disguise, masquerade
13 数 *hensū* variable (in math)
節 *hensetsu* apostasy, betrayal
電所 *hendensho* transformer substation
14 遷 *hensen* transition, vicissitudes, change
種 *henshu, kawa(ri)dane* novelty, exception; hybrid, mutation, variety, freak; eccentric personality
貌 *hembō* transfiguration
態 *hentai* transformation, metamorphosis; abnormality
15 調 *henchō* change of tone, variation (in music); irregularity, anomaly, abnormality; modulation (in radio)
質 *henshitsu* deterioration, degeneration

──────── **7** ────────

A 夏 1120 J3246 M5720 GE. KA *natsu* summer.
3 山 *natsuyama* mountains in summer

4 日 *kajitsu, natsubi* summer day
木立 *natsukodachi* a grove in summer
6 衣 *natsugoromo* summer clothes
向 *natsumu(ki)* suitable for summer
休 *natsuyasu(mi)* summer vacation
至 *geshi* summer solstice
8 物 *natsumono* summer goods
服 *natsufuku* summer clothes
季 *kaki* summer season
炉冬扇 *karo-tōsen* summer fires and winter fans; useless things
9 枯 *natsuga(re)* summer slump
草 *natsukusa* summer grass
負 *natsuma(ke)* suffering from summer heat
10 時間 *natsu jikan* daylight-saving time
11 祭 *natsumatsu(ri)* summer festival
12 場 *natsuba* summertime
期 *kaki* summer season
期講座 *kaki kōza* summer school, summer course of study
14 蜜柑 *natsu mikan* bitter summer orange, Chinese citron
15 痩 *natsuyase* summer loss of weight
18 蝉 *natsuzemi* summer cicadas

━━━━━━ RAD. 夂 35 ━━━━━━

Sui or *yuku* to go. This radical is treated herein as a variant of Rad. 34.
Nickname: Winter Variant.

━━━━━━ RAD. 夕 36 ━━━━━━

Yūbe evening or *ta* (the katakana). Nickname: *Kana Ta.*

A 夕 1123 J4d3c M5749 SEKI. *yū, yū(be)* evening.
4 方 *yūgata* evening
日 *yūhi* setting sun
月 *yūzuki* evening moon
5 立 *yūdachi* sudden shower, evening shower
刊 *yūkan* evening paper
6 凪 *yūnagi* evening calm
8 刻 *yūkoku* evening
空 *yūzora* evening sky
9 映 *yūbae* sunset glow
食 *yūge, yūshoku* supper, evening meal
11 涼 *yūsuzu(mi)* enjoying the evening cool

12 焼 *yūya(ke)* sunset colors
雲 *yūgumo* evening clouds
景色 *yūgeshiki* evening scene
飯 *yūhan, yūmeshi* evening meal
14 暮 *yūgu(re)* evening
15 餉 *yūge* evening meal
17 闇 *yūyami* dusk, twilight
19 霧 *yūgiri* evening mist

──────── **2** ────────

A 外 1125 J3330 M5750 GE. GAI outside, without, beside, beyond the scope of.
hazu(su) take off, remove, unfasten, undo,

detach, disconnect, put out off gear; miss, fail; avoid, evade, dodge. *hazu(reru)* be off, come off, be or get out of place, be out of gear, run off the track, slip out or off, be dislocated, be disconnected, be off the hook (a phone), be unbuttoned, be unzipped. *soto* outside, exterior, open air. *hazu(re)* end, verge, extremity, tip; outskirts; miss, failure. *hoka* some other place; outside; the rest. *hoka no* other, another, different. *no hoka ni* with the exception of. *hoka naranu* none other than, nothing but.

2 力 *gairyoku* external force
人 *gaijin* foreigner, alien
4 方 *gaihō* outward. *soppo, soppō* the other way, outside, another direction, off to the side
5 皮 *gaihi* outer cover, crust, shell, husk, shuck, hull, cuticle, skin
圧 *gaiatsu* external pressure, outside pressure
出 *gaishutsu, sotode* going out, outting, airing
6 米 *gaimai* foreign rice
因 *gaiin* the surface reason
回 *sotomawa(ri)* circumference, perimeter; outside work; circumferential line
気 *gaiki* the air, the open air
地 *gaichi* overseas territory, outlying territory
向性 *gaikōsei* extroversion
耳 *gaiji* external ear
字 *gaiji* characters not among the JIS Kanji; foreign letters, foreign language
交 *gaikō* diplomacy, foreign relations
交白書 *gaikō hakusho* diplomatic white paper
交官 *gaikōkan* diplomat, diplomatic official
交員 *gaikōin* canvasser, traveling salesman
交辞令 *gaikō jirei* diplomacy; flattery
7 見 *gaiken, sotomi* external appearance
車 *gaisha* foreign automobile
局 *gaikyoku* external bureau
形 *gaikei* external form, externals, appearance
来 *gairai no* foreign, imported
来患者 *gairai kanja* outpatient
来語 *gairaigo* word of foreign origin
8 征 *gaisei* foreign campaigns

径 *gaikei* outside diameter
泊 *gaihaku* overnight stay
的 *gaiteki* external, exterior, outside
歩 *sotoaru(ki)* going out for a walk
事 *gaiji* foreign affairs
国 *gaikoku, totsukuni* foreign country
国人 *gaikokujin* foreigner, alien
国風 *gaikokufū* foreign style
国為替 *gaikoku kawase* foreign exchange
国語 *gaikokugo* foreign language
9 面 *gaimen* exterior, surface, outside, outward appearance. *tonomo* outside the house
相 *Gaishō* the Minister of Foreign Affairs
海 *gaikai, sotoumi* open sea, the high seas
洋 *gaiyō* ocean, open sea
界 *gaikai* outside world; physical world; the externals
食 *gaishoku* eating out
祖父 *gaisofu* maternal grandfather
祖母 *gaisobo* maternal grandmother
科 *geka* surgery
科医 *gekai* surgeon
10 孫 *gaison, sotomago* child of a daughter who enters another home
部 *gaibu* exterior, outside world
套 *gaitō* overcoat, cloak
郭 *gaikaku* outer wall; outline; contour
郭団体 *gaikaku dantai* auxiliary organization
11 戚 *gaiseki* maternal relative
側 *gaisoku, sotogawa* exterior outside
商 *gaishō* going round for orders, large customer department, foreign merchant
患 *gaikan* foreign troubles, outside troubles
遊 *gaiyū* foreign travel
貨 *gaika* imported goods; foreign money
務 *gaimu* foreign affairs
務大臣 *Gaimu Daijin* the Minister of Foreign Affairs
務省 *Gaimushō* Ministry of Foreign Affairs
12 港 *gaikō* outer port
勤 *gaikin* outside duty, canvassing
13 債 *gaisai* foreign loan, foreign bond, foreign debt

3
口
口
土
夂
夊【夕】2
大
女
子
宀
寸
小
⺌
尢
尸
屮
山
川
巛
工
己
巾
干
幺
广
廴
廾
弋
弓
彐
彑
彡
彳

口 口 土 士 夂 夊 【夕】 大 女 子 宀 寸 小 ⺌ 尢 尸 屮 山 巛 工 己 巾 干 幺 广 廴 廾 弋 弓 ヨ 彑 彡 彳

傷 *gaishō* external wound
電 *gaiden* foreign cable
資 *gaishi* foreign capital, foreign money
14 聞 *gaibun* reputation, honor; respectability
語 *gaigo* foreign language
貌 *gaibō* one's looks, external appearance, externals, exterior
様 *tozama* outside the group; non-Tokugawa daimyo
15 線 *gaisen* outside telephone line; outer circle; outside wire
敵 *gaiteki* foreign enemy
賓 *gaihin* foreign visitor
輪山 *gairinzan* the outer crater
輪船 *gairinsen* paddle-wheel steamer
16 壁 *gaiheki* outer wall
17 濠 *sotobori* outer moat
18 観 *gaikan* external appearance, outside view
題 *gedai* title (of a play or book); a play, a piece

————— 3 —————

夙 1126 J3d48 M5755 SHUKU. *tsuto ni* bright and early; early in life; long ago; for a long time. *madoki ni* earlier, already, beforehand.

多 1127 J423f M5756 TA much. *ō(i)* many; copious, abundant; much; frequent. *ta-* many- (sided); multi-; poly-. *ta to suru* appreciate, thank.
2 人数 *taninzu* multitude
3 大 *tadai* great quantity, great number
才 *tasai na* talented
士済済 *tashiseisei* galaxy of able men
4 分 *tabun* probably, maybe; very likely, presumably; a great deal, a great many
方面 *tahōmen no* various, different, manysided, versatile
辺形 *tahenkei* polygon
少 *tashō* a little, somewhat, any, some, slightly, more or less
元 *tagen* pluralism
5 用 *tayō* pressure of business
弁 *taben* talkativeness, verbosity
6 忙 *tabō* pressure of work
多 *tata* very many, very much; more and more
年 *tanen* many years

7 言 *tagen, tagon* loquacity, verbosity; many words
岐 *taki* digression; many branches (of a road); many divergences
芸 *tagei* versatility
作 *tasaku* being prolific in writing
角的 *takakuteki* many-sided, versatile, diversified, multilateral
角経営 *takaku keiei* many-sided enterprise
8 雨 *tau* a heavy rain
幸 *takō* great happiness, good fortune
事 *taji* eventfulness; storm and stress; press of business
9 段式 *tadanshiki* multistage (rocket)
面 *tamen* many sides, many phases
面体 *tamentai* polyhedron
重 *tajū* multiplex, multiple
重処理 *tajū shori* multiprocessing
発 *tahatsu suru* happen frequently, occur in many places, occur in many cases
神教 *tashinkyō* polytheism
10 病 *tabyō* frail health
11 彩 *tasai na* colorful, varicolored
産 *tasan* fecundity, bearing more than one offspring at a time; productivity
情 *tajō* inconstancy, licentiousness; sentimentalism
12 量 *taryō* large quantity, a great deal
13 勢 *tazei* a crowd of people, numerical superiority
感 *takan* sensibility, susceptibility, sentimentality
数 *tasū* large number, multitude; majority
数決 *tasūketsu* decision by the majority
14 端 *tatan* many items; pressure of business
寡 *taka* quantity, number, amount
様 *tayō* diversity, variety
様性 *tayōsei* diversity, variety
種 *tashu* various kinds, many kinds
種多様 *tashu-tayō na* various, multifarious, diversified
読 *tadoku* extensive reading
15 趣味 *tashumi* many-sided interests
18 難 *tanan na* full of difficulties, thorny, tumultuous
額 *tagaku* large sum

————— 5 —————

夜 ¹¹²⁹ J4c6b M5763 YA night. *yo* evening, night. *yoru* night, nighttime, evening; at night. *yo(nabe)* night work. *yo(mosugara)* all night.

A

3 叉 *yasha* female demon

4 中 *yachū, yojū* all night, the whole night. *yonaka* midnight, dead of night

分 *yabun* evening, night, nighttime

5 半 *yowa, yahan* midnight, dead of night

6 色 *yashoku* shades of night; night scene

行 *yakō* night travel, night train. *yagyō* walking around at night

回 *yomawa(ri)* night watch; night watchman

気 *yaki* night air, stillness of night, cool evening

曲 *yakyoku* a nocturne

毎 *yogoto* every night

会 *yakai* evening party

光 *yakō* nocturnal luminescence

光虫 *yakōchū* phosphorescent animalcule

光塗料 *yakō toryō* luminous paint

7 更 *yofuka(shi)* staying up late, nightowl. *yofuke ni, yofuke(te)* late at night

来 *yorai* overnight; since last night

汽車 *yogisha* night train

尿症 *yanyōshō* bed-wetting

見世 *yomise* night shop, night fair

8 長 *yonaga* long night

雨 *yau* night rain

店 *yomise* night stall, night booth; night fair

逃 *yoni(ge)* night flight

歩 *yoaru(ki)* walking around at night

具 *yagu* bedding

空 *yozora* night sky

明 *yoa(kashi)* staying up all night, all-night vigil. *yoa(ke)* dawn, daybreak

学 *yagaku* night class, night school

9 風 *yokaze* night wind

食 *yashoku* supper, night meal

通 *yodō(shi)* all night

10 桜 *yozakura* cherry trees at evening

討 *you(chi)* night attack

陰 *yain* shades of evening, dead of night

11 道 *yomichi* going out at night, night trip, road at night

遊 *yoaso(bi)* night amusements

船 *yofune* night boat

釣 *yozu(ri)* night angling

12 勤 *yakin* night duty, night shift

寒 *yosamu, yozamu* night cold; cold night

景 *yakei* night view

着 *yogi* nightclothes; heavy kimono-like quilt

間 *yakan* night, nighttime

13 話 *yawa, yobanashi* night talks; evening tea parties

戦 *yasen* night warfare

想曲 *yasōkyoku* a nocturne

14 鳴 *yona(ki)* crying at night

19 霧 *yogiri* night fog

警 *yakei* night watchman

21 露 *yotsuyu* evening dew, night dew

22 襲 *yashū* night attack

24 鷹 *yotaka* nighthawk, prostitute

───── **10** ─────

夢 ¹¹³¹ J4c34 M5801 MU. *yume* dream; vision; illusion, delusion; reverie.

A

4 幻 *mugen* dreams, visions. *yume-maboroshi* dreams and visions; something visionary

心地 *yumegokochi* trance, ecstasy

中 *muchū* unconscious; ecstasy; absorption; abstraction

7 見 *yumemi(ru)* dream, fancy. *yumemi* a dream

8 枕 *yume makura ni* in a dream

物語 *yume monogatari* story of a dream; fantastic story

11 現 *yumeutsutsu* trance, ecstasy; dream and reality

遊病 *muyūbyō* sleepwalking

13 路 *yumeji* traveling in a dream; Land of Nod

想 *musō* dream, vision, reverie

21 魔 *muma* a fearful disturbing dream

3

口
口
土
士
夂
夕
【大】
女
子
宀
寸
小
尢
尸
屮
山
川
巛
工
己
巾
干
幺
广
廴
廾
弋
弓
彐
彑
彡
彳

━━━━━━ RAD. 大 37 ━━━━━━

Dai large. At top: *dai kashira*. Variant: 𡗜. Nickname: Big.

大 A
¹¹³³ ^{J4267} ^{M5831}
TAI, DAI large, huge, grand; the greater; size; very; inveterate (smoker); severe (damage); success. *ō(kii)* large, great, grand, mighty, immense; severe; heavy. *ō(inaru)* big, large, great. *ō(i) ni* very, much, greatly, exceedingly. *ō(zappana)* rough (estimate); loose (talk); generous. *ō(makana)* rough (estimate); general, generous. *tai-* big, huge, grand, major. *·tai(shita)* many, much, enormous; great, grand; important; serious; severe, intense; very; what a lot of. *ō(ki)ni* greatly, very much. *ō(isa), ō(kisa)* size, dimensions, volume. *tai(shite)* very, much, greatly, seriously. *ō(bira) ni* openly, publicly. *dai(soreta)* ambitious; daring; outrageous, atrocious. *-dai* the size of.... *dai-* great, prominent, large-scale, serious, severe, gross. *ō-* large, great; heavy (rain); loud (voice); full-size, life-size.

²刀 *daitō, tachi* long sword

八車 *daihachiguruma* large wagon, dray

八洲 *Ōyashima* the Eight Great Islands (of Japan)

入 *ōi(ri)* full house

人 *otona* adult. *otona(buru)* act like an adult. *otona(biru)* look grown up; become precocious. *taijin* giant; adult; man of virtue. *taijin, ushi* polite term used in addressing an important person. *otona(shii)* gentle, quiet, good-tempered.

人気無 *otonagena(i)* childish; mean

人物 *daijimbutsu* great person, person of great character

³丈夫 *daijōbu* safe, secure, all right; sure; infallible. *daijōfu* a man, a great man, a brave man

大的 *daidaiteki* great, grand, immense; sweeping (victory); wholesale, large-scale

上段 *daijōdan* holding a sword over one's head; taking a highhanded attitude

川 *ōkawa, taisen* large river

川端 *ōkawabata* Sumida riverside

工 *daiku* carpenter

口 *ōguchi* large mouth; bragging; exaggeration; large amount. *ōkuchi* large mouth; large amount, large opening

小 *daishō* great and small (people); size; large and small sizes; long and short sword. *dai(nari)-shō(nari)* whether large or small

⁴方 *ōkata* probably; almost, mostly; the public. *taihō* in general; broad-mindedness; the public

水 *ōmizu* flood, inundation

王 *daiō* the great king

切 *taisetsu* important, momentous, significant. *ōgi(ri)* large cut; last scene of a drama; catastrophe; end

分 *daibu, daibun* greatly, considerably

文字 *daimonji* large characters; the character 大; *ōmoji* capital letters

反対 *daihantai* intense opposition

木 *taiboku, ōki* large tree

火 *taika* big fire, conflagration, holocaust

内裏 *daidairi* (ancient) imperial palace

仏 *daibutsu* large image of a Buddha

手 *ōte* front castle gate; unit attacking front castle gate. *ōde* both arms; arms spread out

手柄 *ōtegara* great exploit

公使 *taikōshi* ambassadors and ministers

⁵皿 *ōzara* large plate, platter, charger

穴 *ōana* big hole; huge deficit; (make) a killing; a big upset (at the races)

外 *ōhazu(re)* utter failure; big mistake; wild guess

正 *Taishō* Taisho era (1912-1925)

兄 *ōani* eldest brother. *taikei* polite word for elder brother or someone a little older

半 *taihan* majority, greater part; mostly, nearly all, generally

冊 *taisatsu* bulky volume

主教 *daishukyō* archbishop (Protestant)

司教 *daishikyō* archbishop (Catholic)

広間 *ōhiroma* grand hall; rotunda

立回 *ōta(chi)mawa(ri)* serious quarrel

立物 *ōda(te)mono* principal actor; prominent figure

仕事 *ōshigoto* big business

仕掛 *ōshika(ke)* large scale

礼服 *taireifuku* court dress, full-dress uniform

目玉 *ōmedama* big eyes; scolding

目見 *ōme(ni)mi(ru)* overlook, let go, connive at

本 *ōmoto* foundation, base, source, fountainhead; fundamentals. *taihon* cardinal principles, great foundation

本山 *daihonzan* important sectarian-headquarters temple

本営 *Daihon'ei* Imperial Headquarters

⁶臣 *daijin* cabinet minister; high government official

成 *taisei* completion, accomplishment; compilation; attainment of greatness, success

向 *ōmuko(u)* standing section, the gallery, the masses

任 *tainin* great task, important position, important mission

仰 *ōgyō* exaggeration

全 *taizen* encyclopedia, complete works

旨 *ōmune, taishi* the main idea

吉 *daikichi* excellent luck

字 *ōaza* major section of a village. *taiji* large characters. *dai (no) ji* spread-eagle form like the character 大

当 *ōata(ri)* good luck; great success; a killing; bumper crop

休止 *daikyūshi* (soldier's) long rest period

団円 *daidan'en* end, grand finale; catastrophe

西洋 *Taiseiyō* Atlantic Ocean

自然 *daishizen* Mother Nature

多数 *daitasū* the great majority

地 *daichi* ground, earth, the solid earth

好 *daisu(ki)* very fond of

好物 *daikōbutsu* favorite dish

会 *taikai* large meeting, mass meeting, rally, general meeting, conference, convention; tournament, meet

同 *daidō* general resemblance; combination, union

同小異 *daidō-shōi* substantial identity

同団結 *daidō-danketsu* merger, combination

気 *taiki* atmosphere, the air

安 *taian* lucky day

安売 *ōyasuu(ri)* big bargain sale

名 *daimyō* feudal lord, daimyo. *taimei* great honor

名旅行 *daimyō ryokō* junket, spendthrift tour

⁷豆 *daizu, ōmame* soy bean

佐 *taisa* colonel; (navy) captain

作 *taisaku* masterpiece, monumental work

体 *daitai* outline, summary; generally, on the whole; in substance; originally

役 *taiyaku* important task, important role

別 *taibetsu* general classification

判 *ōban* large old Japanese gold coin; large size (paper of book), folio

助 *ōtasu(kari), ōdasu(kari)* a big help

形 *ōgata* large size, large pattern. *ōgyō* exaggeration, bombast

系 *taikei* outline (of a subject)

兵 *taihei* large army. *taihyō* great stature, large body

志 *taishi* great ambition, aspiration

男 *ōotoko* giant. *dai (no) otoko* a real man, a big man

君 *ōkimi, ōgimi* sovereign. *taikun* tycoon

売出 *ōu(ri)da(shi)* large sale

見出 *ōmida(shi)* big headline

見得 *ōmie* magnificent gesture

言壮語 *taigen-sōgo* bragging; exaggeration

身 *taishin* man of rank; man of wealth

車輪 *daisharin* large wheel; giant swing; feverishly at work

声 *ōgoe* loud voice. *taisei* stentorian voice, sonorous tone

麦 *ōmugi* barley

局 *taikyoku* the general situation; the issue

⁸門 *daimon* large outer gate of a Buddhist temple. *ōmon* front gate

雨 *ōame, taiu* heavy rainfall, downpour

国 *taikoku* large country; major power

店 *ōmise, ōdana* large store

味 *ōaji na* tasteless, insipid

所 *ōdokoro, ōdoko* powerful family, great house. *taisho* wide viewpoint

所高所 *taisho kōsho* taking a wide view (of the situation)

抵 *taitei* generally, usually, probably; nearly, almost

枚 *taimai* large sum

河 *taiga, ōkawa* large river

3

口 口 土 士 夂 夂 夕 【大】。 女 子 宀 寸 小 ⺌ 尢 尸 屮 山 川 巛 工 己 巾 干 幺 广 廾 弋 弓 ヨ 彑 彡 彳

3

口口土士夂夊夕【大】女子宀寸小⺌尢尸屮山川巛工己巾干幺广廴廾弋弓彐彑彡彳

股 *ōmata* straddle; long stride
命 *taimei* a ruler's command
官 *taikan* high official, dignitary
受 *ōu(ke)* great popularity, a hit
空 *ōzora, taikū* sky, firmament, space
典 *taiten* state ceremony; important law; excellent publication
昔 *ōmukashi* great antiquity
往生 *daiōjō* peaceful death; the death of a priest; euthanasia
使 *taishi* ambassador
使館 *taishikan* embassy
物 *ōmono* big thing; big shot; big game
事 *daiji, taiji* great thing, great undertaking; serious affair, emergency; importance, significance. *daiji ni suru* value, prize, esteem, be careful of. *Daiji(nai)* It matters little. *ōgoto* serious matter
金 *taikin, ōgane* enormous sum, great cost
金持 *ōganemochi* very rich man
逆 *taigyaku* hideous wickedness; treason; patricide
英帝国 *Daei Teikoku* British Empire
東亜 *Daitōa* Greater East Asia
学 *daigaku* college, university
学生 *daigakusei* university or college student
学出 *daigakude* college graduate
学院 *daigakuin* graduate school
和 *Yamato* ancient Japan
和言葉 *Yamato kotoba* classical Japanese, native Japanese vocabulary
和魂 *Yamatodamashii* Japanese spirit
和撫子 *Yamato nadeshiko* women of Japan
9 食 *taishoku, ōgu(i)* gluttony, voracity; glutton
通 *ōdō(ri)* main street, highway, thoroughfare.
便 *daiben* feces, excrement
柄 *ōgara* large build; large pattern (in kimonos)
約 *taiyaku* summary, outline; great plan; approximately
計 *taikei* far-reaching policy, long-range plan, great plan
軍 *taigun* large army, large force, mighty host. *ōikusa* a big battle; a great war
荒 *ōa(re)* severe storm; great violence
要 *taiyō* summary, outline

型 *ōgata* large size, large pattern
急 *ōiso(gi)* great haste
負 *ōma(ke)* crushing defeat; great bargain
威張 *ōiba(ri)* great bragging; great braggart
活躍 *daikatsuyaku* vigorous personal activity
屋 *ōya* landlord
屋根 *ōyane* main roof
相撲 *ōzumō* annual sumo matches; exciting sumo match
海 *taikai, daikai, ōumi* the ocean, the open sea ⌐deep
海原 *ōunabara* the ocean, the mighty
胆 *daitan* boldness, intrepidity, hardihood; audacity
胆不敵 *daitan-futeki na* bold and willful; daredevil; audacious; undaunted
降 *ōbu(ri)* heavy precipitation
乗的 *daijōteki* broad-minded
乗仏教 *Daijō Bukkyō* Mahayana Buddhism, Greater-Vehicle Buddhism
変 *taihen* serious, terrible; innumerable; immense; What!; a great change
前提 *daizentei* the major premise
音声 *daionjō* stentorian voice
音響 *daionkyō* a great noise
風 *ōkaze, taifū* strong wind, storm, hurricane, typhoon. *ōfū* arrogance
風呂敷 *ōburoshiki* big cloth wrapper; bragging
神宮 *Daijingū* the Ise Shrine
洋 *taiyō* ocean
洋州 *Taiyōshū* Oceania
10 病 *taibyō* serious illness
振 *ōbu(ri)* big things; large size
砲 *taihō* gun, cannon, artillery
破 *taiha* dilapidation, run, havoc, serious damage
笑 *ōwara(i), taishō* loud laughter
差 *taisa* wide difference, great discrepancy, striking contrast
書 *taisho suru* write in large letters
恩 *daion, taion* great kindness; great obligation
挙 *taikyo* great enterprise; united effort
時代 *ōjidai* great antiquity. *ōjidai na* old-fashioned
株主 *ōkabunushi* large stockholder

流行 *dairyūkō, ōhayari* the fashion, the rage

馬鹿 *ōbaka* big fool

恐慌 *daikyōkō* great panic

真面目 *ōmajime* great earnestness

原則 *daigensoku* broad principle

酒 *ōzake, taishu* heavy drinking

将 *taishō* general; admiral; head, leader, boss

都会 *daitokai* big city

家 *taika* mansion, large building; rich or illustrious family; great master, authority. *taike* wealthy family, aristocratic family; an authority, a scholar. *ōya* main building, main house; landlord

部 *daibu, taibu* the larger part; a many-volume set. *taibu no, daibu no* voluminous, copious, bulky

部分 *daibubun* greater part, majority; mostly, largely

部屋 *ōbeya* large room; actors' room; utility man; lesser stars

根 *daikon* the huge white radish, daikon

陸 *tairiku* continent; the Continent (of Asia)

陸棚 *tairikubō, tairikuhō, tairikudana* continental shelf

11 喝 *daikatsu suru, taikatsu suru* thunder, roar, yell at

麻 *ōasa, taima* hemp; marijuana

尉 *taii* captain; lieutenant junior grade

婚 *taikon* imperial wedding

掛 *ōgaka(ri)* large-scale

略 *tairyaku* summary, outline; great plan; approximately

脳 *dainō* brain, cerebrum

蛇 *daija, orochi* monster serpent, boa; large snake

敗 *taihai* crushing defeat, complete rout

赦 *taisha* amnesty; plenary indulgence

隊 *daitai* battalion

著 *taicho* great work, voluminous work

雪 *ōyuki, taisetsu* heavy snow; heavy snow season

患 *taikan, ōwazura(i)* serious illness; disaster; great trial

望 *taibō, taimō* aspiration, ambition

盛 *ōmo(ri)* heaping measure, large serving

匙 *osaji* tablespoon

晦日 *Ōmisoka* December 31; New Year's Eve

理石 *dairiseki* marble

掃除 *ōsōji* semiannual house cleaning

動脈 *daidōmyaku* aorta, main artery

袈裟 *ōgesa* exaggeration; grandiosity; large-scale

規模 *daikibo no* large-scale

過 *taika* serious error, grave fault

黒柱 *daikokubashira* central pillar, king post; pillar, mainstay; family head

祭 *taisai, ōmatsu(ri)* grand festival

道 *daidō, taidō* highway, street; great moral principle. *ōdō(ri)* main street

道具 *ōdōgu* stage setting, scene; large stage equipment

道商人 *daidō shōnin* street vendor

12 慌 *ōawate* great excitement

寒 *daikan, taikan* midwinter, coldest period

嵐 *ōarashi* severe storm

暑 *taisho* midsummer day (about July 23)

童 *ōwarawa ni* with all one's might

筋 *ōsuji* outline, summary

評判 *daihyōban, ōhyōban* sensation

勝利 *daishōri* great victory

圏航路 *taiken kōro* great-circle route

幅 *ōhaba* full width; big scale

奥 *ōoku* inner palace; harem

量 *tairyō, dairyō* large quantity

量生産 *tairyō seisan* mass production

統領 *daitōryō* president

御心 *ōmikokoro* imperial heart or will

御所 *ōgosho* retired shogun; boss

衆 *taishū* a crowd, the masses; general public

衆化 *taishūka* popularization

衆向 *taishūmu(ki)* for everybody, popular

13 路 *ōji* highway, main street, thoroughfare

鉈 *ōnata* large hatchet

蒜 *ninniku* garlic

意 *taii* gist, outline, summary

勢 *taizei, ōzei* crowd, multitude. *taisei* general trend, current thought

僧正 *daisōjō* high priest of a Buddhist sect

福 *daifuku* great fortune, good luck

福帳 *daifukuchō* old-fashioned account book

腿部 *daitaibu* thigh

3

腸 *daichō* colon, large intestine
群 *taigun* large crowd, large herd, large flock, large school (of fish)
聖堂 *daiseidō* cathedral
業 *taigyō* great undertaking, noble work, great achievement
戦 *taisen* great war, world war
義 *taigi* law of justice; moral obligation; righteousness; loyalty and patriotism; a great cause
義名分 *taigi-meibun* true sovereign-subject relations; justice
¹⁴層 *taisō* very, very much. *taisō na* a great deal, plenty; exaggerated, extravagant
関 *ōzeki* champion sumo wrestler
掴 *ōzukami* big handful; the whole (of a problem), outline; summary
概 *taigai* in general; mostly, principally, almost; probably; about, roughly. *taigai ni* moderately, reasonably
様 *ōyō na* easygoing, generous; haughty
綱 *ōzuna* hawser, cable. *taikō* general rules, fundamental principles; outline, general features
雑把 *ōzappa* rough (estimate); loose (talk); generous
漁 *tairyō* large catch
蔵大臣 *Ōkura Daijin* Minister of Finance
蔵省 *Ōkurashō* Ministry of Finance
蔵経 *Daizōkyō* complete Buddhist scriptures
¹⁵慶 *taikei* great happiness
儀 *taigi* national ceremony. *taigi na* laborious; troublesome; wearisome; languid
権 *taiken* supreme power, sovereignty
潮 *ōshio* spring tide, flood tide
震災 *daishinsai* a great earthquake; the 1923 Tokyo earthquake
器 *taiki* large receptacle; great genius
器晩成 *taikibansei* Great talents mature late.
¹⁶樹 *taiju* large tree
憲章 *Daikenshō* Magna Carta, Great Charter
鋸屑 *ogakuzu* sawdust
¹⁷鼾 *ōibiki* loud snoring
¹⁸儲 *ōmōke* large profit
韓民国 *Daikamminkoku* Republic of Korea

騒 *ōsawa(gi)* clamor, uproar, tumult
観 *taikan* general view, general survey; philosophical view
¹⁹願 *daigan, taigan* ambition, aspiration; earnest prayer; the heart's desire

──────── **1** ────────

夫 | 1136 J4957 M5835 | FŪ, FU husband; man. *otto, tsuma* husband, spouse. *se* a woman's familiar call for her husband or elder brother. *so(re)* that.
²人 *fujin* wife, married lady, Mrs.
⁷君 *fukun, se(no)kimi* one's husband (honorific)
⁸妻 *fusai* husband and wife; Mr. and Mrs.
¹¹婦 *fūfu, meoto, myōto* husband and wife; couple; pair
婦仲 *fūfunaka* conjugal relations, conjugal affection
婦共稼 *fūfu-tomokase(gi)* dual income, husband and wife both working
婦喧嘩 *fūfugenka* matrimonial quarrel
¹⁵権 *fuken* husband's marital rights

太 | 1137 J4240 M5834 | TAI, TA. *futo(ru)* get fat, gain, fill out. *futo(rasu), futo(raseru)* fatten, feed up; enrich. *futo(i)* big, thick, burly, fat; deep, sonorous (voice); shameless, audacious, insolent. *futo-* big, fat, noble. *hanaha(da)* extreme, excessive, intense severe, serious, terrible, tremendous, heavy (damage).
²刀 *tachi* long sword
刀持 *tachimo(chi)* swordbearer
³子 *taishi* crown prince; prince
⁴夫 *tayū, taifu* chief actor in a Noh play; entertainer; courtesan; kabuki female-role actor; main actor
公望 *taikōbō* angler
⁵古 *taiko* ancient times
白星 *yūzutsu, taihakusei* evening star; Venus
平 *taihei* peace, tranquility
平洋 *Taiheiyō* Pacific Ocean
平楽 *taiheiraku* irresponsible talk
⁶后 *taikō* empress dowager, queen dowager
字 *futoji* bold-faced type
⁷初 *taisho* the beginning of the world

3

⁸ 股 *futomomo* thigh
⁹ 祖 *taiso* founder, progenitor, first emperor (of a dynasty)
皇太后 *taikōtaigō* the empress dowager
¹⁰ 宰府 *Dazaifu* (ancient) Kyūshū government headquarters
陰 *taiin* moon
陰暦 *taiinreki* lunar calendar
¹¹ 陽 *taiyō* sun
陽系 *taiyōkei* solar system
陽暦 *taiyōreki* solar calendar, Julian calendar
陽熱 *taiyōnetsu* solar heat
¹³ 腹 *futo(p)para no* generous, magnanimous
鼓 *taiko* a big drum; professional jester; flatterer; big obi bow
鼓判 *taikoban* seal of approval; vouching
¹⁴ 閣 *taikō* the father of an imperial adviser; Toyotomi Hideyoshi

天 $\frac{1138}{J4537}$ TEN sky, air, heavens,
A celestial sphere, firmament; M5833
heaven, Providence, God, Nature; weather; top; beginning. *ame* sky, heaven. *ama-* heavenly. *amatsu-* heavenly, imperial.

² 人 *tenjin* nature and man; God and man; celestial being.
³ 女 *tennyo* heavenly maiden; goddess
子 *tenshi* son of Heaven; the emperor
与 *ten'yo* heaven's gift, a godsend
才 *tensai* genius, prodigy; natural gift
上 *tenjō* the heavens
下 *amakuda(ri)* descent from heaven; appointment through influence; top-down decision making. *amakuda(ru)* descend from heaven. *tenka, tenga, ame(ga)shita, ame(no)shita* the whole country; the public, the world; the ruling power; having one's own way; the shogun
下一 *tenkaichi* matchless; best on earth
下一品 *tenka ippin* best article under heaven
下分目 *tenkawa(ke)me* fateful, decisive (war)
下晴 *tenka ha(rete)* right and proper, legal
⁴ 火 *tempi* oven
辺 *teppen* top, summit, apex, pate.

tempen ni high up in the sky
引 *tembi(ki)* lending money and taking out the interest in advance; payroll deduction
分 *tembun* one's nature, talents, sphere of activity, mission, destiny
手古舞 *tentekomai* whirl of business; have an extremely busy time
水 *tensui* rain water
王山 *Tennōzan* Tennozan Hill; strategic point
王星 *Tennōsei, Ten'ōsei* Uranus
文 *temmon* astronomy
文台 *temmondai* astronomical observatory
文学 *temmongaku* astronomy
日 *tenjitsu* the sun. *tempi* sun, sunlight
井 *tenjō* ceiling
井川 *tenjogawa* a river raised above the surrounding land
井桟敷 *tenjō sajiki* gallery
井裏 *tenjō ura* above the ceiling
⁵ 平 *Tempyō* era name during Emperor Shōmu's reign (8th c.)
台 *Tendai* Buddhist sect introduced into Japan in the eighth century
丼 *tendon* bowl of rice topped with tempura
主教 *Tenshukyō* Roman Catholicism
⁶ 衣無縫 *ten'i-muhō* perfect beauty with no trace of artifice; artless and endearing (person)
守閣 *tenshukaku* castle tower
地 *tenchi, amatsuchi* heaven and earth, the universe, nature; top and bottom; world, realm, sphere
地人 *tenchijin* heaven, earth, and man; all things in the universe; three-part hierarchical categorization
地無用 *tenchimuyō* this side up; Do not turn over.
地創造 *Tenchi Sōzō* the Creation
気 *tenki* weather; the elements; fine weather. *(o)tenki* weather; the elements; fine weather; temper, mood
気予報 *tenki yohō* weather forecast
気図 *tenkizu* weather map
気屋 *tenkiya* moody person
⁷ 佑 *ten'yū* divine aid
災 *tensai* natural calamity
寿 *tenju* natural life span
邪鬼 *amanojaku* a perverse person; a

3

口 口 土 士 夂 夂 夕 【大】 女 子 宀 寸 小 尷 尢 尸 屮 山 川 巛 工 己 巾 干 幺 广 廴 廾 弋 弓 ヨ 彑 彡 彳

devil in folklore; the devil beneath temple guardian deities' statues

体 *tentai* celestial bodies

体図 *tentaizu* star map

体物理学 *tentai butsurigaku* astrophysics

[8] 金 *tenkin* gilt-top (book)

国 *tengoku* Kingdom of Heaven, paradise, heaven

府 *tempu* nature's storehouse; fertile land; deep scholarship; imperial storehouse; a part of timepiece mechanism

使 *tenshi, ten (no) tsuka(i)* angel; imperial messenger

性 *tensei* nature; innate disposition. *tensei no* natural, born (musician)

明 *temmei* dawn, daybreak

河 *Ama(no)gawa, Tenga* the Milky Way

命 *temmei* God's will, Heaven's decree; destiny, karma; one's life

空 *tenkū* sky, air, firmament, space

狗 *tengu* long-nosed goblin, boaster

竺 *Tenjiku* (old term for) India

[9] 降 *amakuda(ru)* descend from heaven. *amakuda(ri)* descend from heaven; top-down decision making; appointment through influence

帝 *Tentei* Lord, God, Creator, Heavenly King

変地異 *tempen-chii* striking phenomena in heaven and earth; natural disaster

神 *tenjin* heavenly gods; Michizane's deified spirit

祐 *ten'yū* divine grace, providential help

皇 *Tennō, Sumeragi, Sumerogi, Sumeramikoto* Emperor of Japan

皇杯 *Tennōhai* Emperor's Trophy

皇制 *Tennōsei* Emperor system

皇陛下 *Tennō Heika* His Majesty the Emperor

[10] 候 *tenkō* weather

孫 *tenson* descendant of the heavenly gods; grandson of the Sun Goddess

険 *tenken* natural stronghold; rugged place

恵 *tenkei* heaven's blessings

宮図 *tenkyūzu* horoscope

馬 *temba* flying horse, Pegasus; a fine steed

秤 *tembin* (balance) scales, steelyard; shoulder carrying pole

秤棒 *tembimbō* shoulder carrying pole

真爛漫 *tenshin-ramman* naivete, guilelessness, innocence

[11] 運 *ten'un* destiny, will of Heaven, luck; movement of celestial bodies

涯 *tengai* horizon, skyline; remote region; the whole wide world

理 *tenri* rule of heaven, natural laws

堂 *tendō* heaven, paradise, palace of heaven ⌈head

窓 *temmado* skylight. *tensō* skylight;

動説 *tendōsetsu* Ptolemaic theory

球 *tenkyū* celestial sphere

球儀 *tenkyūgi* celestial globe

眼鏡 *tengankyō* physiognomist's magnifying glass; old term for telescope

頂 *tenchō* zenith

道 *tentō* Providence, heaven; the sun. *tendō* the way of heaven; Providence; orbits of celestial bodies

道様 *tentōsama* the sun

[12] 晴 *appa(re)* splendid, praiseworthy; well done

測 *tensoku* astronomical observation; observing heavenly bodies in celestial navigation

朝 *tenchō* imperial court (polite); emperor

象 *tenshō* astronomical phenomenon; weather

然 *tennen* nature; spontaneity. *tennen ni* naturally, spontaneously

然色 *tennenshoku* natural color; technicolor

然記念物 *tennen kinembutsu* natural monument

然痘 *tennentō* smallpox

然資源 *tennen shigen* natural resources

[13] 誅 *tenchū* Heaven's punishment; punishing (someone) in Heaven's name

蓋 *tengai* canopy; dome; priestly minstrel's reed hood

意 *ten'i* divine will, providence; natural laws; emperor's will

照大神 *Amaterasu Ōmikami* the Sun Goddess

幕 *temmaku* curtain hung from the ceiling; tent, pavilion; (ship's) awning

[14] 聞 *tembun* emperor's knowledge

網 *temmō* heaven's net, heaven's justice

領 *tenryō* imperial fief; shogunate control

罰 *tembatsu* divine wrath, divine punishment

罰覿面 *tembatsu-tekimen* the swiftness of divine punishment

¹⁵敵 *tenteki* natural enemy

麩羅 *tempura* (Japanese) deep-fat fried food; plating; sham

賦 *tempu* innate quality, endowment

¹⁶覧 *tenran* imperial inspection

¹⁸職 *tenshoku* one's divinely appointed work in life; emperor's work of ruling; vocation, calling

─────── 2 ───────

央 _{1140
J317b
M5840} Ō middle.
A

失 _{1141
J3c3a
M5844} SHITSU error; fault;
A disadvantage; loss; demerit. *na(kunaru)* be lost; run short, be used up; disappear; die. *na(ku) nasu, na(ku) suru, na(kusu)* vt lose; run out of; remove; absorb. *shis(suru)* lose, miss; forget; be excessive. *u(seru)* disappear, vanish. *ushina(u)* lose, miss (a chance).

⁴心 *shisshin* trance, stupefaction, faint

火 *shikka* accidental fire

⁵礼 *shitsurei* discourtesy, impoliteness, rudeness

⁶血 *shikketsu* loss of blood

地 *shitchi* lost territory

当 *shittō* injustice; impropriety; unreasonableness

名 *shitsumei* name unknown

⁷言 *shitsugen* improper language, a slip

体 *shittai* mismanagement, fault, error, failure; disgrace, discredit

⁸物 *u(se)mono* lost article

効 *shikkō* lapse, abatement, invalidation

念 *shitsunen* lapse of memory, forgetting; oblivion

明 *shitsumei* loss of eyesight

⁹速 *shissoku* a stall (in flying)

神 *shisshin* trance, stupefaction, faint

陥 *shikkan* surrender, fall

政 *shissei* misgovernment

点 *shitten* a run charged to the pitcher

¹⁰恋 *shitsuren* unrequited love

笑 *shisshō* spontaneous laughter

格 *shikkaku* disqualification, elimination; incapacity (legal)

¹¹脚 *shikkyaku suru* lose one's standing, fall, be overthrown, stumble

敗 *shippai* failure, mistake, blunder

望 *shitsubō* disappointment, despair

¹²敬 *shikkei* rudeness, impoliteness, disrespect. *shikkei suru* say goodbye; act impolitely; steal

策 *shissaku* blunder, slip, error

¹³跡 *shisseki* abscondence, disappearance

意 *shitsui* despair, disappointment; adversity

禁 *shikkin* incontinence (of urine or feces)

業 *shitsugyō* unemployment

¹⁴墜 *shittsui suru* lose, forfeit, fall, sink (in a person's estimation)

態 *shittai* mismanagement, fault, error, failure; disgrace, discredit

語症 *shitsugoshō* loss of speech; agnosia

¹⁵調 *shitchō* lack of harmony

踪 *shissō* abscondence, disappearance

¹⁸職 *shisshoku* unemployment

─────── 3 ───────

夷 _{1143
J3050
M5852} I barbarian. *ebisu* barbarian, savage; Ainu.

⁷狄 *iteki* barbarians, aliens

─────── 5 ───────

奄 _{1146
J3162
M5881} EN cover

奈 _{1147
J4660
M5893} NA What?

⁷何 *ikan* what, how

良朝 *Narachō* Nara period (710–794)

¹²落 *naraku* hell, hades; eternity; theater basement

奔 _{1148
J4b5b
M-X} HON *hashi(ru)*
B run.

⁷走 *honsō* bustle; activity, good offices

⁸放 *hompō na* wild, incorrigible, extravagant

命 *hommei* bustle; activity, good offices

¹⁰馬 *homba* galloping horse; runaway horse

口 口 土 士 夂 夕 【大】 5 女 子 宀 寸 小 尢 尸 屮 山 川 巛 工 己 巾 干 幺 广 廴 廾 弋 弓 ヨ 互 彡 彳

3

口 口 土 士 夂 夊 夕 【大】 女 子 宀 寸 小 ⺌ 尢 尸 屮 山 巛 工 己 巾 幺 广 廴 廾 弋 弓 ヨ 彑 彡 彳

流 *honryū* torrent, rapids
20 騰 *hontō* price jump, boom

B **奉** $\frac{1149}{\substack{J4a74 \\ M5894}}$ Hō . Bu. *hō(zuru)* present, dedicate; obey, follow, believe in, serve. *matsu(ru), tatematsu(ru)* offer, present; revere; do respectfully.
4 公 *hōkō* public service; apprenticeship
公人 *hōkōnin* servant, employee
公先 *hōkōsaki* place of employment
5 加帳 *hōgachō* subscription list
仕 *hōshi* service, serving
6 行 *bugyō* shogunate administrator
迎 *hōgei* welcome
7 呈 *hōtei* dedication, presentation
9 祝 *hōshuku* celebration
10 書 *hōsho* high-quality paper
納 *hōnō* dedication, offering, oblation
13 献 *hōken suru* offer (to a shrine)
18 職 *hōshoku suru* be in the service of

B **奇** $\frac{1150}{\substack{J3471 \\ M5892}}$ KI strangeness, curiosity, eccentricity. *kusu(shiki), ku(shiki)* strange, mysterious. *kusu(shiku) mo, ku(shiku) mo* strangely, mysteriously, ironically. *ki (to) suru* regard as wonderful.
2 人 *kijin* eccentric person
3 才 *kisai* genius, wizard, prodigy
6 行 *kikō* eccentric conduct
7 妙 *kimyō na* strange, queer, wonderful
抜 *kibatsu na* novel, original, striking, extraordinary, strange
形 *kikei* deformity, abnormality
声 *kisei* strange voice, squeaky voice
8 知 *kichi* genius
岩 *kigan* fantastic crag
怪 *kikai na, ki(k)kai na* strange, wonderful; weird; outrageous, scandalous, insolent
奇怪怪 *kiki-kaikai* something very strange
9 計 *kikei* ingenuity, clever plan
10 病 *kibyō* strange disease
特 *kitoku* miracle. *kitoku na, kidoku na* commendable; charitable
書 *kisho* strange book
11 遇 *kigū* chance meeting
異 *kii na* odd, strange, wonderful
習 *kishū* strange custom
貨 *kika* curiosity; good opportunity (to make a profit)

術 *kijutsu* jugglery; magic
12 勝 *kishō* surprise victory; successful execution; beauty spot
策 *kisaku* clever plan
13 跡 *kiseki* miracle, wonder, mystery
跡的 *kisekiteki* miraculous
数 *kisū* odd number; masculine number
想 *kisō* original idea, strange notion
想天外 *kisō-tengai* original idea
17 矯 *kikyō* eccentric conduct
18 観 *kikan* strange sight
蹟 *kiseki* miracle, wonder, mystery
19 麗 *kirei na* beautiful, lively; clean, neat. *kirei ni* completely, beautifully
22 襲 *kishū* surprise attack

━━━━━━ **6** ━━━━━━

B **契** $\frac{1155}{\substack{J3740 \\ M5917}}$ KEI *chigi(ru)* pledge, vow, swear, promise.
9 約 *keiyaku* contract, agreement, covenant, testament
約書 *keiyakusho* contract
16 機 *keiki* opportunity, chance

A **奏** $\frac{1156}{\substack{J4155 \\ M5915}}$ Sō . *kanade(ru)* play (an instrument). *sō(suru)* play on; speak to a ruler; report to (the emperor); complete.
3 上 *sōjō* report to the emperor
5 功 *sōkō* fruition, success, efficacy
8 法 *sōhō* playing (an instrument); touch
13 楽 *sōgaku* instrumental music
14 鳴曲 *sōmeikyoku* sonata (in music)
15 請 *sōsei* petitioning the emperor

━━━━━━ **7** ━━━━━━

套 $\frac{1161}{\substack{J4565 \\ M5926}}$ Tō hackneyed.

━━━━━━ **9** ━━━━━━

B **奥** $\frac{1165}{\substack{J317c \\ M5981}}$ Ō. OKU heart, interior. *oku(maru)* lie deep in, extend far back. *oku(matte)* secluded, innermost.
3 山 *okuyama* remote mountain, mountain recesses
4 手 *okute* late crops. *oku(no)te* left hand; upper hand; secret skills; secret, mystery; last resort, trump card

方 *okugata* lady, nobleman's wife
⁵付 *okuzuke* colophon, (publisher's) imprint
⁶行 *okuyuki* depth, length, in depth
地 *okuchi, ōchi* interior, backwoods, hinterland
州 *ōshū* northern part of Japan
⁷床 *okuyuka(shii)* refined, graceful, modest
⁸底 *okusoko, okuzoko* depth, bottom (of one's heart)
⁹院 *oku(no)in* inner sanctuary
¹⁰庭 *oku niwa* inner garden, back yard
書 *okugaki* postscript (to a book); verification; publication data (in a book)
座敷 *oku zashiki* inner parlor
¹¹深 *okubuka(i)* deep, profound
¹²歯 *okuba* molars, back teeth
間 *oku(no)ma* inner room
御殿 *okugoten* noble's private quarters
¹³義 *okugi, ōgi* mystery, secret, hidden, purpose
¹⁴様 *okusama, okusan* your or his wife; married lady; madam

───── 10 ─────

奨 1167 J3e29 M5990' Sнō *susu(meru)* urge, encourage.
B
⁷励 *shōrei* encouragement, promotion, exhortation; message, address
励金 *shōreikin* incentive pay, subsidy

⁸学 *shōgaku* encouragement of learning
学金 *shōgakukin* scholarship (grant)

───── 11 ─────

奪 1171 J4325 M5994 DATSU. *uba(u)* take by force, snatch away, oust, dispossess, deprive of, plunder, usurp; absorb (attention); fascinate.
B
⁶回 *dakkai* recovery, recapture, rescue
返 *uba(i)-kae(su)* take back, recapture
合 *uba(i)-a(u)* scramble for, struggle for
⁸取 *uba(i)-to(ru), dasshu suru* plunder. *dasshu* capture, seizure, occupation
¹⁵還 *dakkan* recovery, recapture, rescue

───── 13 ─────

奮 1172 J4a33 M6012 FUN. *furu(u)* be invigorated, be spirited, flourish. *furu(tte)* energetically, heartily.
A
⁵立 *furu(i)-ta(tsu)* rouse oneself, be inspired. *furu(i)-ta(taseru)* stir up, arouse
迅 *funjin* dashing forward impetuously
⁷励 *funrei* strenuous efforts, push, hustle
⁹発 *fumpatsu* strenuous, effort, spurt
¹⁰起 *furu(i)-oki(ru), funki suru* rouse oneself
¹³戦 *funsen* hard fighting
¹⁵撃 *fungeki* fierce attack
¹⁸闘 *funtō* hard struggle, desperate fight, strenuous effort

■■■■■■■■■■ **RAD.** 女 **38** ■■■■■■■■■■
Onna woman. At left: *onna hen.* Nickname: Woman.

女 1173 J3d77 M6036 Jō, Nyō, Nyō woman, girl, daughter. *onna, omina* woman, female, sweetheart, girl. *onna(rashii)* womanly, ladylike; effeminate. *onna(datera) ni* unladylike. *me-* female.
A
²人 *nyonin, jonin* woman
人禁制 *nyonin kinsei* no admittance to women
³女 *meme(shii)* effeminate, unmanly
工 *jokō* woman factory worker

丈夫 *jojōfu* heroine; outstanding woman
子 *joshi, nyoshi* woman, female, girl. *onna (no) ko* girl; daughter; baby girl. *onago* girl, woman, maid.
子供 *onna kodomo* a woman and her child; a nonentity; a man of straw; an encumbrance
⁴心 *onnagokoro* a woman's heart
手 *onnade* the cursive (*hiragana*) syllabary; a woman's handwriting; the work of women

女 0

子宀寸小⺌尢尸屮山川巛工己巾干幺广廴廾弋弓ヨ彑彡彳

3

口 口 土 士 夂 夊 夕 大 **【女】** 子 宀 寸 小 尢 尸 屮 山 川 巛 工 己 巾 干 幺 广 廴 廾 弋 弓 彐 彑 彡 彳

文字 *onna moji* the cursive (*hiragana*) syllabary; a woman's handwriting
王 *joō, nyoō* queen; belle; princess
中 *jochū* servant, maid; waitress, barmaid
⁵ 史 *joshi* Mrs., Miss
犯 *nyobon* (priest's) clandestine romance
生徒 *joseito* schoolgirl; coed
⁶ 色 *joshoku* feminine charms; sensuality
⁷ 医 *joi* woman doctor
体 *jotai, nyotai* a woman's body
形 *onnagata, oyama* female impersonator
系 *jokei* female line
児 *joji* baby girl, primary schoolgirl
⁸ 官 *jokan, nyokan* court lady, maid of honor
店員 *joten'in* saleswoman
郎 *jorō* prostitute, geisha
房 *nyōbō, nyōbo* court lady; wife
学生 *jogakusei* girl student
学院 *jogakuin* girls' school
性 *josei* woman; womanhood; feminine gender
性的 *joseiteki* feminine, effeminate
⁹ 神 *megami, joshin* goddess
帝 *jotei* empress
姿 *onna sugata* the guise of a woman; a womanish pose
¹⁰ 振 *onnabu(ri)* a woman's charms, a woman's looks
将 *okami, joshō* landlady, hostess (of a restaurant)
流 *joryū* accomplished woman; fair sex; female
流作家 *joryū sakka* women novelist
¹¹ 盛 *onnazaka(ri)* the prime of womanhood
教師 *jokyōshi* woman teacher
¹² 傑 *joketsu* heroine; outstanding woman
婿 *josei* son-in-law
湯 *onnayu* ladies' bath
装 *josō* female attire; dressing in female attire
給 *jokyū* waitress
¹³ 嫌 *onnagira(i)* woman-hater
¹⁵ 権 *joken* women's rights; woman suffrage
¹⁶ 親 *onna oya* mother
¹⁷ 優 *joyū* actress
¹⁸ 難 *jonan* trouble with women

―――――――― **2** ――――――――

奴 〔1174 J455b M6039〕 B Do manservant, slave; fellow. Nu manservant. *yakko* servant, valet, footman; clown; the fellow, the guy. *yatsu* fellow, guy. *-me* suffix indicating ridicule or despite.
⁵ 凧 *yakkodako* kites shaped like ancient footmen
⁷ 豆腐 *yakkodōfu* tofu cut in cubes
¹¹ 婢 *dohi, nuhi* servant; male or female slaves
¹² 等 *yatsura* fellows, guys
¹⁴ 僕 *nuboku* manservant; slave
¹⁶ 隷 *dorei* slave, servant
隷制 *doreisei* slavery

―――――――― **3** ――――――――

妃 〔1176 J485e M6061〕 B Hi queen; princess. *kisaki* queen.
¹³ 殿下 *Hidenka* Her Imperial Highness (a princess or consort)

妄 〔1177 J4c51 M6063〕 B Bō. Mō. *mida(ri) ni* without authority, without reason, arbitrarily, unnecessarily, indiscriminately, recklessly. *mida(rigamashii)* morally corrupt.
⁷ 言 *bōgen, mōgen* reckless remark, abusive language
⁸ 念 *mōnen* distracting ideas, irrelevant thoughts
⁹ 信 *mōshin, bōshin* blind belief, credulity
¹¹ 動 *mōdō suru, bōdō suru* act blindly
執 *mōshū* deep-rooted delusion
¹³ 想 *mōsō, bōsō* wild idea, delusion

如 〔1178 J4721 M6060〕 B Jo. Nyo. *-goto(ki)* like, such as, as if. *shi(kazu)* be better, be best. *shi(ku)* be equal to, be like. *-goto(ku)* like, as, as if. *-goto(shi)* seem to be, be like.
³ 才無 *josaina(i), josai (no) na(i)* clever, shrewd, smart, adroit, tactful; sociable
⁴ 月 *Kisaragi* second lunar month
⁷ 来 *Nyorai* Buddha
何 *ikaga* How (about it)? How (are you)? What (do you think)? *ikan* what, how. *ikaga(washi)* unreliable; questionable. *ika(na), ika(naru)* what (kind), anybody, everybody; nobody (with neg.). *ika ni* how. *ika ni mo* indeed, really, certainly; apparently, as

if. *ikan nimo shite* by all means
何様 *ikayō* how; what kind. *ikasama*
how; what kind; fraud, swindle; I see;
to be sure
[8] 実 *nyojitsu ni* truly, realistically
雨露 *jōro* watering can
[13] 意 *nyoi* priest's staff; ease, comfort

好 $\frac{1180}{J3925}$ Kō. *kono(mu)* like, be
A M6053 fond of. *su(ku)* like, love,
be fond of. *kono(mi)* taste, fondness,
bent, choice, wish; fashion, mode.
kono(mashii) desirable, pleasant,
enviable. *kono(nde)* by choice,
willingly; often. *suki* liking, love, taste,
bent. *yo(shi)* good, all right, well, so.
yo(shimi) friendship, intimacy, good will.
su(kanai) odious, disagreeable. *i(i), yo(i)*
good, good-natured; pleasing; precious;
noble; lovely, beautiful, fine; lucky;
efficacious; right; suitable; justifiable;
appropriate, satisfactory; better; all right;
unnecessary; no objection; intimate,
friendly; easy; well; desirous.
su(itarashii) lovable, charming, nice.
-zu(ki) lover of, fan, enthusiast, maniac.
[1] 一対 *kōittsui* well-matched couple
[2] 人物 *kōjimbutsu* good-natured man
[5] 加減 *i(i) kagen no, yo(i) kagen no*
moderate, temperate, proper;
haphazard; unconvincing, halfhearted.
i(i) kagen quite, rather (old)
古 *kōko* love of antiquities
[6] 印象 *kōinshō* good impression
成績 *kōseiseki* good results
好爺 *kōkōya* a good-natured old man
色 *kōshoku* sensuality, lewdness, lust
色漢 *kōshokukan* sensual person
[7] 男子 *kōdanshi* handsome man
[8] 例 *kōrei* good illustration
況 *kōkyō* prosperity, boom
物 *i(i) mono, yo(i) mono* a good thing.
kōbutsu something good; a favorite
dish
尚 *kōshō* taste, fashion
取組 *kōtorikumi* good game, good match
放題 *su(ki)hōdai* doing just as one
pleases
奇 *kōki* curiosity, inquisitiveness
奇心 *kōkishin* curiosity, inquisitiveness
事 *kōji* happy event; good act; curiosity.
kōzu curiosity, amateurism,

dilettantism
事家 *kōzuka* dilettante, amateur
[10] 個 *kōko* propriety. *kōko no* ideal,
excellent
都合 *kōtsugō na* favorable, fortunate
[11] 運 *kōun* good fortune, lucky break
転 *kōten* favorable turn, improvement
悪 *kōo* likes and dislikes; fancy;
partiality
[12] 景気 *kōkeiki* boom, good times
結果 *kōkekka* good results, success
評 *kōhyō* public favor, favorable
criticism
[13] 適 *kōteki* very suitable, ideal
嫌 *su(ki)-kira(i)* likes and dislikes, taste
漢 *kōkan* fine fellow
感 *kōkan* good feeling, good impression
意 *kōi* good will, friendliness, favor,
kindness, courtesy, good offices
戦的 *kōsenteki* warlike
[15] 誼 *kōgi* friendship, intimacy, your
kindness
調 *kōchō no* favorable, promising,
satisfactory
餌 *kōji* bait, decoy; lure, temptation
敵手 *kōtekishu* worthy opponent
[16] 機 *kōki* good chance, psychological
moment

———— 4 ————

妓 $\frac{1185}{J3538}$ Gi singing girl, geisha,
M6083 courtesan, prostitute.
[13] 楼 *girō* brothel
[16] 館 *gikan* brothel

妨 $\frac{1187}{J4b38}$ Bō. Hō. *samata(geru)*
B M6111 disturb, prevent, hamper,
hinder, obstruct. *samata(ge)* hindrance,
obstacle, barrier, disturbance,
inconvenience, encumbrance, interference.
[10] 害 *bōgai* interference, obstruction,
disturbance
害物 *bōgaibutsu* obstacle, impediment

妥 $\frac{1188}{J4245}$ Da peace; depravity.
B M6107
[6] 当 *datō* appropriateness, propriety
当性 *datōsei* propriety, adequacy,
pertinence, soundness
[8] 協 *dakyō* compromise, understanding,
agreement

口 口 土 士 夂 夊 夕 大 **[女]** 子 宀 寸 小 ⺌ 尢 尸 屮 山 川 巛 工 己 巾 干 幺 广 廴 廾 弋 弓 彐 彑 彡 彳

協的 *dakyōteki* compromising
12 結 *daketsu* an agreement

妊 ⎡1189 J4725 M6072⎤ B NIN. *hara(mu)*, *migomo(ru)* become
pregnant; be pregnant; be filled with.
10 娠 *ninshin* pregnancy, conception
娠中絶 *ninshin chūzetsu* artificial abortion
11 産婦 *ninsampu* expectant and nursing mothers
婦 *nimpu* pregnant woman

妖 ⎡1190 J4d45 M6086⎤ Yō attractive, bewitching; calamity.
3 女 *yōjo* fairy, witch, enchantress, vampire
6 気 *yōki* ghostly, spooky
8 怪 *yōkai* ghost, apparition
11 婦 *yōfu* enchantress, a Jezebel
術 *yōjutsu* magic, sorcery, witchcraft
婆 *yōba* witch, hag
14 精 *yōsei* elf, sprite, fairy
19 艶 *yōen* voluptuous charm
21 魔 *yōma* ghost, apparition

妙 ⎡1191 J4c2f M6090⎤ B MYŌ strange, queer; mystery, miracle; cleverness. *tae(naru)* exquisite, excellent; melodious; delicate; charming; marvelous. *myō(chikirin)* strange, queer.
4 手 *myōshu* excellent skill; expert; good move
5 句 *myōku* clever expression; fine verse
7 技 *myōgi* outstanding skill, splendid feat, stunt
8 味 *myōmi* charms, exquisite beauty
法 *myōhō* clever method; marvelous law of Buddha; mystery
9 計 *myōkei* wise plan, clever trick
10 案 *myōan* bright idea, excellent plan
12 策 *myōsaku* clever plan
16 薬 *myōyaku* miracle drug
17 齢 *myōrei* youth

————— 5 —————

姑 ⎡1194 J3848 M6174⎤ Ko. *shūtome, shūto* mother-in-law.
10 息 *kosoku* makeshift

姐 ⎡1195 J3039 M6172⎤ B So girl; elder sister; maidservant.
12 御 *anego* elder sister (polite)

姓 ⎡1196 J402b M6178⎤ B SHŌ. SEI surname, family name. *kabane* new name conferred by the emperor.
4 氏 *seishi* surname
6 名 *seimei* name

妬 ⎡1197 J454a M6121⎤ To. *neta(mu)* be jealous of, be envious of. *neta(mi)* jealousy. *neta(mashii)* jealous of, envious of; enviable.

妾 ⎡1198 J3e2a M6147⎤ SHŌ *mekake, sobame* concubine. *warawa* I.
6 宅 *shōtaku* concubine's house
13 腹 *shōfuku* illegitimate birth. *mekakebara* illegitimate child

妹 ⎡1199 J4b65 M6138⎤ A MAI. *imōto, imoto, imo* younger sister.

妻 ⎡1200 J3a4a M6140⎤ A SAI (my) wife. *tsuma* wife, spouse.
3 女 *saijo* wife; wife and daughters
子 *saishi, tsumako* wife and children, one's family
7 君 *saikun* wife
8 妾 *saishō* wife and concubines
10 帯 *saitai* marriage, matrimony
帯者 *saitaisha* married man

姉 ⎡1201 J3b50 M6165⎤ A SHI. *ane* elder sister. *ne(san)* elder sister; waitress; girl. *nē(ya)* maid. -*shi* Miss, Mrs.
8 妹 *shimai, ane-imōto* sisters

始 ⎡1203 J3b4f M6166⎤ A SHI beginning. *haji(maru) vi* begin, start, open; date from; (season) sets in; arise, break out; originate in. *haji(maranai)* be of no avail, accomplish nothing. *haji(meru) vt* begin, open, start, originate, inaugurate, initiate. *haji(mari)* beginning, inception, opening, start, origin. *haji(me)* beginning, origin. *haji(mete)* (for) the first time; not until. *haji(memashite)* for the first time (I greet you).
5 末 *shimatsu* circumstances;

management; disposal, settlement; control

末書 *shimatsusho* written explanation, written apology

5 祖 *shiso* founder, originator, pioneer, progenitor ⌈(station)

発 *shihatsu* first train, first bus; starting

11 終 *shijū, shotchū* all the time, always, constantly. *shijū no* the whole, all

動 *shidō* starting (in machines)

13 業 *shigyō* commencement of work; beginning of a class

業式 *shigyōshiki* opening ceremony

A 委 $\frac{1204}{\text{J3051}}$ M6181 I. *i(suru)* entrust to, discard. *yuda(neru)* entrust to, devote (oneself) to. *maka(su), maka(seru)* entrust to, leave to. *kuwa(shii)* full, detailed, minute, accurate; versed in, well-informed on.

6 任 *inin* trust, delegation, authorization, charge, commission, mandate

任状 *ininjō* power of attorney

10 託 *itaku* trust, consignment, commission

員 *iin* committeeman, committee, commission ⌈board

員会 *iinkai* committee (meeting),

員長 *iinchō* chairman

11 細 *isai* details, particulars

15 嘱 *ishoku suru* entrust with

20 譲 *ijō suru* transfer to

6

姶 $\frac{1208}{\text{J3028}}$ M6242 Ō attractive; quiet.

姪 $\frac{1209}{\text{J4c45}}$ M6226 TETSU. *mei* niece.

姥 $\frac{1212}{\text{J3138}}$ M6216 BO. MO. *uba* aged woman.

10 桜 *ubazakura* a faded beauty

娃 $\frac{1213}{\text{J3023}}$ M6262 AI, A beautiful, attractive, beautiful woman. *utsuku(shii)* beautiful, attractive.

B 姻 $\frac{1215}{\text{J3079}}$ M6250 IN marry.

---

11 戚 *inseki* in-laws

A 姿 $\frac{1216}{\text{J3b51}}$ M6257 SHI. *sugata* figure, form, shape; appearance, attire; posture; oneself; portrait; aspect.

7 見 *sugatami* dresser, full-length mirror

12 絵 *sugatae* portrait

13 勢 *shisei* posture, pose

14 態 *shitai* figure, form, style

B 姫 $\frac{1217}{\text{J4931}}$ M6229 KI. *hime* princess; young lady of birth. *hime-* little, pretty.

7 君 *himegimi* princess, young lady of birth

14 様 *hiisama* daughter of a noble

姦 $\frac{1218}{\text{J342f}}$ M6217 KAN wickedness, mischief. *kan(suru)* seduce, assault, rape. *kashima(shii)* noisy, boisterous.

4 夫 *kampu* adulterer, paramour

9 計 *kankei* trick, evil design, sharp practice

通 *kantsū* adultery

11 婦 *kampu* adulteress

淫 *kan'in* adultery

悪 *kan'aku* wickedness, treachery

B 威 $\frac{1219}{\text{J3052}}$ M6259 I dignity, majesty, authority. *odo(su)* threaten; frighten; intimidate. *odoshi* menace, threat; scarecrow.

2 力 *iryoku* power, might, authority, influence

3 丈高 *itakedaka ni* angrily

4 文句 *odoshi monku* bluff, threatening language

5 令 *irei* authority

圧 *iatsu* coercion

圧的 *iatsuteki* domineering, coercive

6 光 *ikō* power, authority, influence

9 風 *ifū* majesty, dignity

信 *ishin* prestige, authority, honor

10 容 *iyō* dignity, majestic appearance

11 張 *iba(ru), eba(ru)* be proud, swagger

13 勢 *isei* power, might, authority, influence; high spirits

15 儀 *igi* dignity, majesty; dignified manner

17 厳 *igen* dignity, majesty

嚇 *ikaku* menace, threat

3

口 口 土 士 夂 夊 夕 大 **[女]** 子 宀 寸 小 尢 尢 尸 屮 山 川 巛 工 己 巾 干 幺 广 廴 廾 弋 弓 彐 彑 彡 彳

───── 7 ─────

娠 B | 1224 / J3f31 / M6322 | SHIN pregnancy.

娘 B | 1230 / J4c3c / M6304 | JŌ . *musume* daughter, girl, young woman.
³ 子軍 *jōshigun* Amazonian troops
⁴ 心 *musumegokoro* girlish innocence
¹¹ 盛 *musumezaka(ri)* the prime of young womanhood
¹² 婿 *musumemuko* adopted son-in-law

娯 B | 1231 / J3864 / M6307' | GO pleasure.
¹³ 楽 *goraku* pleasure, amusement, recreation, entertainment

───── 8 ─────

娩 | 1233 / J4a5a / M6337 | BEN bear (children).

婁 | 1235 / J4f2c / M6383 | RU, RŌ frequently; tie.

婆 B | 1240 / J474c / M6390 | BA. *baba* old woman; grandmother. *baba, babā* old woman; wet nurse. *bā(ya)* wet nurse; old maid; old housekeeper.

娼 | 1241 / J3e2b / M6376 | SHŌ prostitute.
⁷ 妓 *shōgi* prostitute, harlot
¹⁰ 家 *shōka* brothel
¹¹ 婦 *shōfu* prostitute, harlot

婚 B | 1242 / J3a27 / M6418 | KON marriage.
⁵ 礼 *konrei* wedding ceremony
⁹ 姻 *kon'in* marriage
姻届 *kon'in todoke* marriage registration
約 *kon'yaku* engagement, betrothal
約者 *kon'yakusha* fiancé, fiancée
¹⁰ 家 *konka* one's husband's family
¹² 期 *konki* marriageable age
¹⁵ 儀 *kongi* wedding ceremony

婦 A | 1243 / J4958 / M6432' | FU woman; wife; bride.
² 人 *fujin* lady, woman, female
人科 *fujinka* gynecology

人病 *fujinbyō* women's diseases
³ 女 *fujo* woman, womankind
女子 *fujoshi* woman and child
¹⁹ 警 *fukei* policewoman

───── 9 ─────

媛 | 1244 / J4932 / M6516 | EN. *hime* princess; young lady of noble birth.

婿 B | 1246 / J4c3b / M6470 | SEI. *muko* son-in-law.
² 入 *mukoi(ri) suru* become the heir of one's wife's family
⁸ 取 *mukoto(ri)* adopting a son-in-law
¹⁵ 養子 *mukoyōshi* son-in-law adopted as an heir

媒 B | 1247 / J475e / M6498 | BAI. *nakadachi* go-between.
⁴ 介 *baikai* mediation, intervention, agency
介物 *baikaibutsu* medium, agency; carrier (of germs), vehicle
⁷ 体 *baitai* medium (in biology)
¹⁰ 酌 *baishaku* matchmaking
酌人 *baishakunin* matchmaker, go-between

───── 10 ─────

嫉 B | 1255 / J3c3b / M6611 | SHITSU. *sone(mu)* be jealous, envy. *neta(mu)* be jealous of, be envious of. *sone(mi), neta(mi)* jealousy, envy.
⁸ 妬 *shitto* jealousy, envy
妬心 *shittoshin* jealousy, envy

嫁 B | 1256 / J3247 / M6602 | KA. *ka(suru), ka(su)* marry (a man); be married to; blame. *totsu(gu)* marry off; get married. *yome* bride, young wife, daughter-in-law.
² 入 *yomei(ri)* marriage, wedding
入支度 *yomei(ri)jitaku* trousseau
入衣裳 *yomei(ri) ishō* trousseau
⁸ 取 *yometo(ri)* taking a wife

嫌 B | 1257 / J3779 / M6618 | KEN. *iya(garu)* dislike, hate; be unwilling (to do something). *kira(u)* hate, detest, dislike. *kira(i)* dislike, disinclination, abhorrence,

prejudice; tinge, touch, suspicion. *kira(i) na* distasteful, disagreeable, repugnant. *iya na* disagreeable. *iya(garase)* a disagreeable thing *iya(rashii)* unpleasant, offensive *iya ni* disagreeably, offensively.

⁶ 気 *iyaki, iyake* aversion, repugnance
⁸ 味 *iyami* disagreeableness; gaudiness; mannerism; sarcasm
¹¹ 悪 *ken'o* dislike, hatred, abhorrence
悪感 *ken'okan* dislike, hatred
¹³ 嫌 *iyaiya* reluctantly
¹⁴ 疑 *kengi* suspicion; accusation

━━━━━ 11 ━━━━━

嫡 $\frac{1263}{M6656}$ J4364 CHAKU, TEKI legitimacy; legitimate child; legitimate wife; direct descent.
B
³ 子 *chakushi* legitimate child
⁵ 出 *chakushutsu* legitimacy (of birth)
出子 *chakushutsushi* legitimate child
⁷ 男 *chakunan* heir, eldest son
⁹ 室 *chakushitsu* legitimate wife
¹⁰ 流 *chakuryū* lineage of the eldest son

━━━━━ 12 ━━━━━

嬉 $\frac{1267}{M6736}$ J3472 KI. *ure(shigaru)* be glad, be pleased, rejoice. *ure(shigaraseru)* please, delight, flatter. *ure(shisōna), ure(shigena)* delightful, joyful, happy. *ure(shii)* glad, happy, delightful, pleasant.
⁸ 泣 *ure(shi)na(ki)* crying for joy
¹⁰ 涙 *ure(shi)namida* tears of joy
¹⁵ 嬉 *kiki(taru)* gleeful, joyful

━━━━━ 13 ━━━━━

嬢 $\frac{1270}{M6807}$ J3e6e JŌ girl, daughter, young lady; Miss.
B

━━━━━ 14 ━━━━━

嬬 $\frac{1271}{M6821}$ J445c JU. NYU wife; mistress; weak.

嬰 $\frac{1273}{M6828}$ J3145 EI sharp (in music); baby.
⁷ 児 *eiji, midorigo* infant, baby

━━━━━━━━━ RAD. 子 39 ━━━━━━━━━

Ko child. At left: *ko hen*. Nickname: Child.

子 $\frac{1281}{M6930}$ J3b52 SHI viscount, master; child; male; fruit; seed. SU. *ko* child, offspring; the young (of animals). *ne* 11 p.m. to 1 a.m.; first zodiac sign, rat; north. *ko-* small.
A
³ 女 *shijo* children
子孫孫 *shishi-sonson* descendants, posterity
⁴ 分 *kobun* follower, protégé, apprentice; adopted son; bad elements
午線 *shigosen* the meridian
⁶ 会社 *kogaisha* subsidiary company
守 *komori* amah; baby tending; baby sitter
守歌 *komori uta* lullaby, nursery rhyme
⁷ 役 *koyaku* child actor, child actress; child's role
弟 *shitei* children
沢山 *kodakusan* many children (in the family)
⁸ 宝 *kodakara* treasure of children
供 *kodomo* child *kodomo(rashii)* childlike
供扱 *kodomoatsuka(i)* treating like a child
供染 *kodomoji(mita)* childish
供騙 *kodomodama(shi)* fooling a child; childish trick
⁹ 音 *shiin, shion* consonant
持 *komo(chi)* a mother; maternity; pregnancy
¹⁰ 孫 *shison* posterity, descendants
息 *shisoku* son
宮 *shikyū* womb
¹¹ 細 *shisai* reasons, circumstances; significance; particulars; hindrance, obstruction, interference
¹³ 煩悩 *kobonnō* fondness for children

口 口 土 士 夂 夂 夕 大 女 [子]⁰ 宀 寸 小 小 尢 尸 屮 山 川 巛 工 己 巾 干 幺 广 廴 廾 弋 弓 ヨ 彑 彡 彳

3

口 口 口 土 士 夂 夕 大 女 [子] 宀 寸 小 ⺌ 尢 尸 屮 山 川 巛 工 己 巾 干 幺 广 廴 廾 弋 弓 彐 彑 彡 彳

福者 *kobukusha, kofukusha* a person blessed with a large family

飼 *koga(i)* raising from infancy; raising animals from birth

¹⁷ 爵 *shishaku* viscount

———— **1** ————

孔 | 1282 J3926 M6933 | Kō. Ku. *ana* hole,
B aperture, slit; gap, stop (of musical instrument); eyelet; cavity; socket; cave; den; hiding place; pit; fault, defect; deficit; grave; dark horse. *hanaha(da)* very, greatly, exceedingly.

³ 子 *Kōshi* Confucius
⁷ 廟 *Kōshibyō* Confucian shrine
⁸ 孟 *Kō-Mō* Confucius and Mencius
¹¹ 雀 *kujaku* peacock

———— **3** ————

存 | 1284 J4238 M6943 | Son. Zon. *zon(jiru),*
A *zon(zuru)* know, be aware of, be acquainted with; think, believe, feel. *son(suru)* exist, be extant, remain, live; retain, maintain, preserve; consist of; depend on. *nagara(eru)* live on, live long.

³ 亡 *sombō* life or death, existence, fate
⁴ 分 *zombun ni* to one's heart's content, freely, without reserve
⁵ 立 *sonritsu* existence, subsistence
外 *zongai* contrary to expectations; beyond expectations
⁶ 在 *sonzai* existence, subsistence, being
⁷ 否 *sompi* existence, life or death
⁸ 念 *zonnen* thought, idea, concept
命 *zommei* alive, living; existence
¹² 廃 *sompai* continuance or abolition; existence
¹³ 置 *sonchi suru* maintain, retain, continue
続 *sonzoku* continuance, continued existence, duration

字 | 1285 J3b7a M6942 | Ji character, letter, word,
A handwriting. *aza* section of a village. *azana* nickname, alias, pseudonym.

⁴ 引 *jibiki* dictionary
⁵ 母 *jibo* letter, alphabet, syllabic character; matrix; type
句 *jiku* terms, wording

⁷ 体 *jitai* form or style of a character
⁸ 画 *jikaku* character strokes
典 *jiten* character dictionary
⁹ 面 *jimen, jizura* the appearance of the writing
音 *jion* Chinese (on) pronunciation of a character
¹⁰ 消 *jike(shi)* eraser
訓 *jikun* the Japanese (kun) reading of a character
書 *jisho* character dictionary
¹³ 源 *jigen* construction of a character
数 *jisū* number of characters
彙 *jii* glossary, dictionary
幕 *jimaku* title, caption
義 *jigi* meaning of a word

———— **4** ————

孜 | 1287 J3b5a M6951 | Shi industriousness.

⁷ 孜 *shishi to shite* untiringly, diligently

孝 | 1289 J3927 M6952 | Kō filial piety.
A

³ 子 *kōshi* filial child
⁴ 心 *kōshin* filial devotion
⁶ 行 *kōkō* filial piety
¹⁵ 養 *kōyō* discharge of filial duties

———— **5** ————

孟 | 1291 J4c52 M6960 | Mō chief; beginning.

³ 子 *Mōshi* Mencius
¹⁰ 夏 *mōka* early summer

季 | 1292 J3528 M6965 | Ki season. *sue* end.
A

⁵ 刊 *kikan* quarterly publication
刊誌 *kikanshi* quarterly magazine
¹³ 節 *kisetsu* the seasons, the time of year
節的 *kisetsuteki* seasonal
節風 *kisetsufū* seasonal wind, monsoon
¹⁴ 語 *kigo* word referring to seasons (in poetry)

孤 | 1293 J3849 M6966 | Ko orphan. *minashigo*
B orphan. *hitori de* alone.
⁵ 立 *koritsu* isolation; helplessness
⁷ 児 *koji, minashigo* orphan

⁹ 独 *kodoku* solitude, isolation, loneliness
軍 *kogun* isolated force
¹⁰ 高 *kokō* splendid isolation, proud loneliness; nobility of character
島 *kotō* a solitary island
¹³ 愁 *koshū* lonely contemplation
¹⁵ 影 *koei* a lone figure; lonesome person
影悄然 *koei shōzen toshite* forlorn and crestfallen

学 A | 1294 J3358 M6974 | GAKU learning, study, science, scholarship, erudition. *mana(bu)* learn, study. *mana(bi)* learning, knowledge; study.

² 力 *gakuryoku* scholarship, knowledge, literary ability
力考査 *gakuryoku kōsa* achievement test
³ 才 *gakusai* scholastic ability
士 *Gakushi* Bachelor of Arts; college graduate
士院 *Gakushi'in* the Academy
⁴ 区 *gakku* school district
内 *gakunai* within the campus
友 *gakuyū* schoolmate, classmate, alumnus
⁵ 外 *gakugai* off-campus, outside the school
用品 *gakuyōhin* school supplies
生 *gakusei* student
⁶ 会 *gakkai* institute, academy, learned society, literary society
年 *gakunen* school year
名 *gakumei* technical name
⁷ 位 *gakui* academic degree
究 *gakkyū* scholar, student
芸 *gakugei* art and science, literary attainments, culture
⁸ 長 *gakuchō* college president, rector
府 *gakufu* educational institution, seat of learning
制 *gakusei* educational system
舎 *gakusha* school building
事 *gakuji* educational affairs; learning, studies
者 *gakusha* scholar, learned man, scribe
⁹ 風 *gakufū* academic traditions, school character, method of study, a school (of thought)
派 *gakuha* school, sect
級 *gakkyū* school class, grade, form, standard

則 *gakusoku* school regulations
院 *gakuin* school, academy, seminary
界 *gakkai* academic or scientific world
科 *gakka* curriculum, course
科目 *gakkamoku* school subjects
¹⁰ 徒 *gakuto* scholar, student, disciple, follower
部 *gakubu* faculty, department, college, school
校 *gakkō* school, educational institution
校長 *gakkōchō* school principal
¹¹ 務 *gakumu* educational affairs
堂 *gakudō* educational institution, academy
窓 *gakusō* school
問 *gakumon* learning, studies, scholarship, knowledge, education, culture, science
問的 *gakumonteki* scholarly
理 *gakuri* scientific principle, a theory
習 *gakushū* learning, study
術 *gakujutsu* science, learning, scholarship, art and science
術用語 *gakujutsu yōgo* technical term
術的 *gakujutsuteki* scientific
¹² 帽 *gakubō* school cap
童 *gakudō* school child, pupil
費 *gakuhi* school expenses
期 *gakki* school term
期末 *gakkimatsu* end of a school term
期試験 *gakki shiken* term examinations
¹³ 園 *gakuen* school, educational institution; campus
僧 *gakusō* a learned priest pursuing his studies
業 *gakugyō* studies, schoolwork, classwork, scholarship
際的 *gakusaiteki* interdisciplinary
¹⁴ 歴 *gakureki* school career, academic record
閥 *gakubatsu* academic clique, school fraternity
説 *gakusetsu* theory
¹⁵ 課 *gakka* lesson, schoolwork, classwork, subject
寮 *gakuryō* school dormitory
¹⁷ 齢 *gakurei* school age
¹⁹ 識 *gakushiki* scholarship, learning, scientific attainments
²⁰ 籍簿 *gakusekibo* school register

口 口 土 士 夂 夊 夕 大 女 子 [宀] 寸 小 尢 尣 尸 屮 山 川 巛 工 己 巾 干 幺 广 廴 廾 弋 弓 彐 彑 彡 彳

——— 7 ———

A **孫** $\frac{1296}{\text{J4239}}$ Son descendants. *mago,*
$\overline{\text{M6987}}$ *hiko* grandchild.
³ 子 *magoko* children and grandchildren, descendants

⁴ 手 *mago(no)te* back scratcher
引 *magobi(ki)* reference to secondary sources
⁷ 弟子 *mago deshi* disciples of one's disciples
¹⁰ 娘 *mago musume* granddaughter

━━━━━━━━━━ 宀 **RAD.** 40 ━━━━━━━━━━

U kammuri (crown like the katakana *u*). Note that the crown 穴 is Rad. 116.
Nickname: *Kana U.*

——— 3 ———

A **宅** $\frac{1308}{\text{J4270}}$ Taku home, house,
$\overline{\text{M7064}}$ residence; our home;
my husband.
⁶ 地 *takuchi* building lot, residential land; homestead
⁹ 急便 *takkyūbin* parcel delivery service
¹⁰ 配便 *takuhaibin* parcel delivery service
¹² 診 *takushin* home consultation

A **宇** $\frac{1309}{\text{J3127}}$ U eaves; roof; house;
$\overline{\text{M7067}}$ heaven.
⁸ 宙 *uchū* universe, cosmos
宙人 *uchūjin* alien
宙的 *uchūteki* universal
宙船 *uchūsen* space ship
宙線 *uchūsen* cosmic rays
宙論 *uchūron* cosmology

A **守** $\frac{1310}{\text{J3c69}}$ Shu. Su. *mamo(ru)* defend,
$\overline{\text{M7071}}$ protect; keep, observe,
obey; abide by; stick to; be true to. *mo(ru)*
observe. *mamo(ri)* defense; guarding.
mori nursemaid, baby sitter; baby sitting;
(lighthouse) keeper. *(o)mamo(ri)* charm,
amulet. *kami* feudal lord.
² 刀 *mamo(ri)gatana* self-defense sword
⁵ 旧 *shukyū* conservatism
札 *mamo(ri)fuda* paper charm
⁶ 成 *shusei* preservation, maintenance
⁷ 抜 *mamo(ri)-nu(ku)* hold fast, protect to the end
兵 *shuhei* guards
⁹ 神 *mamo(ri)gami, shushin* guardian deity
¹⁰ 宮 *yamori* gecko, wall lizard
¹² 備 *shubi* garrison, defense; fielding

(baseball)
¹³ 勢 *shusei* the defensive; defensive attitude; passive attitude
¹⁴ 歌 *moriuta* lullaby, nursery rhyme
銭奴 *shusendo* a miser, a niggard
¹⁵ 衛 *shuei* a guard; a watchman, a doorkeeper
²⁰ 護 *shugo* protection; guard; safeguard
護神 *shugoshin* guardian deity

A **安** $\frac{1311}{\text{J3042}}$ An. *yasu(maru)* be rested,
$\overline{\text{M7072}}$ feel at ease, be relieved,
repose. *yasu(njiru), yasu(nzuru)* be
contented, be at ease. *yasura(u)* rest,
relax. *yasu(i)* cheap, inexpensive;
peaceful, quiet; gossipy, thoughtless. *yasu*
cheap, low; drop (in prices). *yasu(ppoi)*
cheap-looking, tawdry, insignificant.
yasu(rakana) peaceful, tranquil, calm,
restful. *yasu(pika)* knickknack, cheap
finery.
³ 上 *yasua(gari)* economy. *yasua(gari) no*
cheap, economical
⁴ 手 *yasude* cheap kind
心 *anshin* peace of mind, freedom from
care; (sense of) relief or security;
reassurance
心感 *anshinkan* sense of security
⁶ 気 *anki* ease, comfort, feeling at home
全 *anzen* safety, security
全弁 *anzemben* safety valve
全地帯 *anzen chitai* safety zone, safety
island
全保障 *anzen hoshō* security
全第一 *Anzen Daiichi* Safety First
全装置 *anzen sōchi* safety device
⁷ 住 *anjū suru* live peaceably
否 *ampi* safety, welfare, well-being

売 *yasuu(ri)* selling cheap
8 居 *ankyo* an easy life
価 *anka* low price
物 *yasumono* cheap article, bargain
直 *anchoku* cheapness, low price
易 *an'i* ease
定 *antei* stability, equilibrium, stabilization, composure. *an(no)jō* as expected
定性 *anteisei* inclined to be stable or composed
定感 *anteikan* sense of security
10 逸 *an'itsu* ease, idleness
値 *yasune* low price
眠 *ammin* quiet sleep
泰 *antai* peace, security, tranquility
息 *ansoku* rest, repose
息日 *ansokubi, ansokunichi, ansokujitsu* the Sabbath; a sabbath; a day of rest
11 産 *anzan* easy delivery
12 閑 *ankan to* idly, indolently
堵 *ando* relief, reassurance
着 *anchaku* safe arrival
普請 *yasubushin* cheap structure
13 置 *anchi* enshrinement, installation (of an image)
楽 *anraku* ease, comfort
楽死 *anrakushi* euthanasia, mercy killing
14 静 *ansei* rest, quiet, tranquility
寧 *annei* public peace, tranquility
15 請合 *yasuu(ke)a(i)* rash promise, lightly undertaking (something)
16 穏 *annon, an'on* peace, quiet, tranquility

———— 4 ————

宋 $\frac{1312}{\text{J3c35}}$ $\frac{}{\text{M7084}}$ See 肉 4753.

宋 $\frac{1313}{\text{J4157}}$ $\frac{}{\text{M7078}}$ Sō Sung (dynasty); dwell.
12 朝 *Sōchō* Sung dynasty

宏 $\frac{1314}{\text{J3928}}$ $\frac{}{\text{M7086}}$ Kō wide, large.
3 大 *kōdai na* vast, extensive, magnificent
6 壮 *kōsō na* grand, imposing
7 図 *kōto* large plans
12 遠 *kōen na* vast and far-reaching

13 業 *kōgyō* large extensive enterprise

A 完 $\frac{1315}{\text{13430}}$ $\frac{}{\text{M7079}}$ Kan completion, end. *mattō(suru)* accomplish, fulfill, complete, preserve (life). *matta(ku)* entirely, completely, wholly, perfectly; truly, indeed.
2 了 *kanryō* completion, conclusion
了形 *kanryōkei* perfect tense
3 止 *kankō* completion
6 成 *kansei suru* finish; be finished
成品 *kanseihin* finished goods
全 *kanzen* perfection, completeness
全主義 *kanzen shugi* perfectionism
全性 *kanzensei* state of perfection
全無欠 *kanzen-muketsu* absolute perfection
10 納 *kannō* full payment; full delivery
11 遂 *kansui* completion
済 *kansai* full payment, liquidation
訳 *kan'yaku* complete translation
敗 *kampai* complete defeat
12 備 *kambi* perfection, completion
結 *kanketsu* conclusion, completion
勝 *kanshō* complete victory
膚無迄 *kampuna(ki) made* thoroughly, completely; scathingly
18 璧 *kampeki* perfect gem, flawlessness; perfection, completeness

———— 5 ————

宕 $\frac{1316}{\text{J4566}}$ $\frac{}{\text{M7103}}$ Tō cave.

B 宜 $\frac{1317}{\text{J3539}}$ $\frac{}{\text{M7111}}$ Gi. *yo(i), i(i)* good, good-natured; pleasing; precious; noble; lovely, beautiful, fine; lucky; efficacious; right; suitable, justifiable; appropriate, satisfactory; better; all right; unnecessary; no objection; intimate, friendly; easy; well; desirous. *yoro(shiku)* regards, greetings; well, properly, at your own discretion. *yo(shi)* good, all right, well, so. *mube, ube* truly ⌈ship).
10 候 *yōsōrō, yōsoro* Hold her steady (a

A 宙 $\frac{1318}{\text{J4368}}$ $\frac{}{\text{M7108}}$ Chū air, space, mid-air, sky, heaven; memorization; interval of time.
6 返 *chūgae(ri)* somersault; looping the loop

3

口 口 口 土 士 夂 夂 夕 大 女 子 〔宀〕 寸 小 尐 尢 尸 屮 山 川 巛 工 己 巾 干 幺 广 廴 廾 弋 弓 彐 彑 彡 彳

宛 $\frac{1319}{\substack{J3038\\M7110}}$ EN. *a(teru)* address (a letter). *sanaga(ra)* just like. *-zutsu* apiece; each. *ataka(mo)* just as; as it were; fortunately. *-ate* addressed to.

⁶先 *atesaki* address
名 *atena* address
⁷扶持 *a(tegai)buchi* discretionary allowance
¹¹転 *enten(taru)* smoothly rolling
¹²然 *enzen* just as, as though; fortunately.

宝 $\frac{1320}{\substack{J4a7.5\\M7122}}$ A Ho treasure. *takara* treasure, valuables; wealth; jewels; mammon.

²刀 *hōtō* sacred sword; treasured sword
⁵玉 *hōgyoku* gem, jewel, precious stone
石 *hōseki* gem, jewel
⁷貝 *takaragai* cowrie, porcelain shell
⁸典 *hōten* thesaurus, treasury of words; manual; precious book
物 *hōmotsu, takaramono* a treasure
⁹冠 *hōkan* crown, diadem
¹⁰庫 *hōko* treasure house, treasury
剣 *hōken* sacred sword
島 *takarajima* treasure island
¹¹探 *takarasaga(shi)* treasure hunt
船 *takarabune* treasure-ship picture
¹⁴蔵 *hōzō* the treasury; treasure house
¹⁵器 *hōki* treasured article
²¹籤 *takarakuji* raffle, lottery
²²鑑 *hōkan* handbook, thesaurus, dictionary

宗 $\frac{1321}{\substack{J3d2.1\\M7106}}$ A Sō. Shū religion, sect, denomination. *mune* main point, essence; origin.

⁵主 *sōshu* suzerain
⁶匠 *sōshō* master (in an art), teacher
旨 *shūshi* doctrine, creed; sect, religion, a faith; one's line, one's taste
⁷社 *sōsha* the state; the world
⁸門 *shūmon* doctrine, creed; sect, religion, a faith; one's line, one's taste
⁹派 *shūha* sect, denomination
派的 *shūhateki* sectarian, denominational
¹⁰徒 *shūto* believer, devotee, follower. *muneto* principal vassal; important people
家 *sōka, sōke* head family, main stock; originator
¹¹族 *sōzoku* relative; one's whole family

務 *shūmu* (Buddhist) sectarian affairs
教 *shūkyō* religion, a faith, creed, cult
教心 *shūkyōshin* religious sentiment, piety
教団体 *shūkyō dantai* religious organization
教的 *shūkyōteki* religious
教法人 *shūkyō hōjin* registered religious organization
教界 *shūkyōkai* the religious world
教観 *shūkyōkan* religious view
¹⁵廟 *sōbyō* ancestral mausoleum

官 $\frac{1322}{\substack{J3431\\M7107}}$ A KAN the Government, the authorities; the Court. *tsukasa* office, government office; director, head official.

³女 *kanjo* court lady. *kannyo* women workers in the palace of the shogun or emperor
⁴辺筋 *kampen suji* government circles, officialdom
公庁 *kankōchō* government and public agencies
公吏 *kankōri* public officials
公署 *kankōsho* public offices
⁵用 *kan'yō* government business; official use
立 *kanritsu* government-operated
民 *kammin* government and people
庁 *kanchō* government office; authorities
⁶印 *kan'in* government seal
名 *kammei, kammyō* official title
吏 *kanri* government official or clerk
有 *kan'yū* government ownership
⁷位 *kan'i* office and rank; official rank
邸 *kantei* official residence
兵 *kampei* government forces
⁸姓名 *kanseimei* official title and name
制 *kansei* government organization
命 *kammei* official orders, official business
舎 *kansha* official residence
房 *kambō* secretariat
房長官 *Kambō Chōkan* Chief Secretary of the Cabinet
⁹途 *kanto* government service
軍 *kangun* government forces, imperial army
界 *kankai* officialdom
¹⁰員 *kan'in* officials

能 *kannō* body functions; carnal desire

能的 *kannōteki* sensual

¹¹ 許 *kankyo* government license

設 *kansetsu* established by the government

¹² 営 *kan'ei* government operation

報 *kampō* official telegram; official gazette

給 *kankyū* government supply

給品 *kankyūhin* government issues

費 *kampi* government expense

費生 *kampisei* government student

¹³ 衙 *kanga* government office

業 *kangyō* government enterprise

¹⁴ 選 *kansen* government-appointed (official)

製 *kansei* government manufacture

僚 *kanryō* bureaucracy, officialdom

僚主義 *kanryō shugi* bureaucracy

僚的 *kanryōteki* bureaucratic

僚制 *kanryōsei* bureaucracy

¹⁵ 撰 *kansen* government compilation

¹⁶ 憲 *kanken* officials, authorities

¹⁸ 職 *kanshoku* government service

定 ^1323 ^J446a ^M7109 TEI deciding. JŌ.
sada(maru) be decided, be settled, quiet down. *sada(meru)* establish, lay down, stipulate; decide, determine; appoint, set (a date); pacify. *kima(ru)* be decided, be settled, be arranged; be certain to, be doomed to. *sada(me)* law, rule, regulation, provision; decision; appointment, arrangements; destiny, fate, karma. *sada(mari)* usage, custom, routine, rule; tranquility. *sada(kana)* sure, positive; accurate; reliable; sound, firm; clear, evident; genuine; able, competent; sober, sane; I think; if I remember right. *sada(mete), sada(meshi)* presumably, surely. *ki(matte)* usually, always, invariably. *jō-* regular, permanent.

⁵ 石 *jōseki* formula, rules

本 *teihon* authentic book or manuscript

収入 *teishūnyū* fixed income

⁶ 式 *jōshiki, teishiki* prescribed form; formula, formality. *teishiki no* regular, formal

年 *teinen* age limit, retirement age

休 *teikyū* regular holiday

休日 *teikyūbi* regular holiday

⁷ 見 *teiken* definite opinion

形 *teikei* fixed form, regular shape

足数 *teisokusū* quorum

住 *teijū suru* settle down

住地 *teijūchi* permanent abode

住者 *teijūsha* permanent resident

⁸ 例 *jōrei, teirei* usage, precedent; standing orders; regular (meeting)

刻 *teikoku* regular time, appointed time

価 *teika* fixed price

⁹ 食 *teishoku* regular meal; table d'hôte

律 *teiritsu* fixed law, fixed rhythm

則 *teisoku* established rule, law

点 *teiten* fixed point

冠詞 *teikanshi* definite article

型 *teikei* definite form, type

型化 *teikeika* standardization

型詩 *teikeishi* rhymed verse or poems with fixed forms (such as tanka, haiku, sonnets, etc.)

¹⁰ 紋 *jōmon* family crest

案 *teian* fixed plan, definite plan

員 *teiin* regular staff, full number; seating capacity; quorum; full complement

時 *teiji* regular time, stated period. *jōtoki* ancient gun or drum time signal; the signaler

時制 *teijisei* part-time (school system)

¹¹ 理 *teiri* theorem, proposition. *jōri* accepted truth

規 *teiki* prescribed, regular. *jōgi* a ruler; a (carpenter's) square; a standard

率 *teiritsu* fixed rate

宿 *jōyado* regular hotel

常 *teijō no* regular; stationary

¹² 評 *teihyō* public acknowledgment, general opinion

款 *teikan* articles of incorporation

温 *teion* fixed temperature

量 *teiryō* fixed quantity; calculation; dose

着 *teichaku* fixing, fastening, fixation; stationed (at)

期 *teiki* stated period; season (train) ticket; rice sold on time; time transaction; time deposit; regular

期刊行物 *teiki kankōbutsu* periodicals

期的 *teikiteki* periodic

期券 *teikiken* season (train) ticket, commuter pass

3
口
口
土
士
夂
夂
夕
大
女
子
宀 ⁵
寸
小
⺌
尢
尸
屮
山
川
巛
工
己
巾
干
幺
广
廴
廾
弋
弓
⺕
⺜
彡
彳

3

口 口 土 士 夂 夕 大 女 子 【宀】 寸 小 丷 尢 尸 屮 山 川 巛 工 己 巾 干 幺 广 廴 廾 弋 弓 彐 彑 彡 彳

期預金 *teiki yokin* time deposit
¹³ 数 *teisū* fixed number, full number, quorum; constant; destiny
置 *teichi* stationary, fixed
義 *teigi* definition
¹⁴ 説 *teisetsu* definite opinion, established theory
¹⁵ 論 *teiron* fixed opinion, established theory
¹⁸ 礎式 *teisoshiki* cornerstone ceremony
職 *teishoku* regular occupation, steady job
額 *teigaku* fixed amount, flat sum
額預金 *teigaku yokin* fixed deposit
¹⁹ 繋場 *teikeijō* anchorage area

⁵ A **実** ¹³²⁴ J3c42 M7124 JITSU truth, reality; sincerity, fidelity; kindness; faith; substance, essence. *mino(ru)* ripen; bear fruit. *jitsu ni, ge ni* truly, really, in truth, surely, in fact. *jitsu wa* really, in fact. *mi* seed, berry, nut, fruit; substance, contents; ingredients; (soup) stock. *makoto* sincerity, honesty, fidelity; truth. *sane* fruit stone, kernel; nucleus.
² 入 *mii(ri)* crop; earnings, gains
力 *jitsuryoku* real ability, merit, efficiency; arms, force
力行使 *jitsuryoku kōshi* use of force, wildcat strike
力者 *jitsuryokusha* powerful person
³ 子 *jisshi* one's own child
⁴ 父 *jippu* one's real father
⁵ 母 *jitsubo* one's real mother
写 *jissha* on-the-spot photograph
兄 *jikkei* one's own elder brother
包 *jippō* real cartridge
生活 *jisseikatsu* real life
収入 *jisshūnyū* actual income, take-home pay
世間 *jisseken* the everyday world
用 *jitsuyō* utility; practical use
用主義 *jitsuyō shugi* pragmatism
用的 *jitsuyōteki* practical
用品 *jitsuyōhin* utility article
用新案 *jitsuyō shin'an* utility model; practical design
⁶ 印 *jitsuin* registered seal
刑 *jikkei* prompt corporal punishment
名 *jitsumei, jitsumyō* real name
存 *jitsuzon* existence
存主義 *jitsuzon shugi* existentialism

在 *jitsuzai* real existence, reality
地 *jitchi* practice; the actual site
地試験 *jitchi shiken* practical examination, driving test
行 *jikkō* practice, performance, action, execution, realization
行力 *jikkōryoku* executive ability
行委員 *jikkōiin* executive committee; action committee
⁷ 見 *jikken* actual observation
状 *jitsujō* actual state of affairs
弟 *jittei* one's real younger brother
社会 *jisshakai* the real world, actual society
利 *jitsuri* utility, benefit, profit
利主義 *jitsuri shugi* materialism, utilitarianism
体 *jittai* substance, entity; antitype
体論 *jittairon* substantialism, ontology, noumenalism
⁸ 例 *jitsurei* example, illustration
妹 *jitsumai* one's real younger sister
姉 *jisshi* one's real elder sister
効 *jikkō* efficacy, efficiency
直 *jitchoku* steadfastness; seriousness
学 *jitsugaku* practical learning, realism
況 *jikkyō* real condition
況放送 *jikkyō hōsō* on-the-spot broadcast
物 *jitsubutsu* substance; the real thing, genuine article, the original
物大 *jitsubutsudai* life-size
⁹ 施 *jisshi* execution, enforcement
相 *jissō* actual facts; reality
¹⁰ 益 *jitsueki* net profit
家 *jikka* one's original family
¹¹ 現 *jitsugen* realization, fruition, materialization
理 *jitsuri* principles actually practiced
情 *jitsujō* actual state of affairs
習 *jisshū* practice
習生 *jisshūsei* student apprentice, student assistant
務 *jitsumu* business affairs, business practice
¹² 費 *jippi* actual expense; cost price
弾 *jitsudan* real cartridge, live shell; solid shot; money
測 *jissoku* actual survey
測図 *jissokuzu* accurate ordnance map

証 *jisshō* actual proof
証主義 *jisshō shugi* positivism
¹³話 *jitsuwa* true story
戦 *jissen* actual fighting
数 *jissū* actual number
感 *jikkan* actual sensation, realization, low passions
働 *jitsudō* actual work
践 *jissen* practice
践的 *jissenteki* practical
業 *jitsugyō* industry, business
業界 *jitsugyōkai* industrial circles, business world
業家 *jitsugyōka* industrialist, businessman
際 *jissai* truth, fact, practice, reality, actual situation; actually; indeed. *jissai no* real, actual
際上 *jissaijō no* effective, real, actual, substantial. *jissaijō* as a matter of fact
際的 *jissaiteki* practical
¹⁴像 *jitsuzō* real image
演 *jitsuen* stage show; exhibition, demonstration
態 *jittai* actual condition, realities
¹⁵権 *jikken* real power
線 *jissen* solid line
質 *jisshitsu* substance, essence, quality; material, contents
質上 *jisshitsujō* in substance, substantially
質的 *jisshitsuteki* substantial, essential, material, real
¹⁶録 *jitsuroku* authentic account
¹⁷績 *jisseki* actual results
¹⁸験 *jikken* experimentation; experience
験的 *jikkenteki* experimental, empirical
験室 *jikkenshitsu* laboratory

───── 6 ─────

宥 1326 J4d28 M7137 YŪ. *nada(meru)* soothe, calm, pacify. *nada(me)* expiation, atonement, reconciliation.
⁸和 *yūwa* appeasement

室 1327 J3c3c M7136 A SHITSU room, apartment, compartment, chamber. *muro* greenhouse; (ice) house; cellar.
⁴内 *shitsunai* indoor, indoors, interior of a room

内装飾 *shitsunai sōshoku* interior decorating; upholstering
内楽 *shitsunaigaku* chamber music
⁵外 *shitsugai* outdoors
⁷町 *Muromachi* Muromachi era (1392–1573)
¹²温 *shitsuon* room temperature

宣 1328 J406b M7132 A SEN. *notama(u)* be pleased to say, say. *sen(suru), no(ru)* proclaim, announce. *nobe(ru)* state, speak, recite, relate, mention.
⁵布 *sempu* proclamation, promulgation
⁶伝 *no(be)-tsuta(eru)* proclaim, preach. *senden* propaganda, publicity
伝業者 *senden gyōsha* publicity agent
伝機関 *senden kikan* propaganda machinery
⁷告 *senkoku* sentence, verdict, pronouncement
言 *sengen* declaration, proclamation, profession, statement
⁸明 *semmei* enunciation
¹¹教 *senkyō* missionary work; preaching; evangelism
教師 *senkyōshi* missionary
¹²揚 *sen'yō suru* enhance, increase, exalt
¹³戦 *sensen* declaration of war
戦布告 *sensen-fukoku* declaration of war
¹⁴誓 *sensei* vowing, swearing
¹⁵撫 *sembu* placation, pacification

客 1329 J3552 M7128 A KAKU, KYAKU visitor; guest, customer, client; passenger. *kaku-* last (month).
²人 *kyakujin, marōdo* visitor, guest
⁴引 *kyakuhi(ki)* soliciting patronage; barker; hotel runner; procurer
分 *kyakubun* guest, honorary member
⁵用 *kyakuyō* for guests
⁶死 *kakushi, kyakushi* dying abroad
気 *kakki* youthful ardor; rashness
扱 *kyakuatsuka(i)* entertainment of guests
⁷足 *kyakuashi* customers, clientele
車 *kyakusha, kakusha* railway passenger coach
体 *kakutai, kyakutai* object (in law and philosophy)
⁸舎 *kakusha* hotel, inn
⁹待 *kyakuma(chi)* waiting for passengers

3

口 口 土 士 夂 夊 夕 大 女 子 [宀] 寸 小 ⺌ 尢 尸 屮 山 川 巛 工 己 巾 干 幺 广 廴 廾 弋 弓 ヨ 彑 彡 彳

室 *kyakushitsu, kakushitsu* stateroom; guest room; parlor

10 席 *kyakuseki* seats for guests

員 *kakuin, kyakuin* associate or honorary member; guest (editor)

員教授 *kyakuin kyōju* visiting professor

11 船 *kyakusen, kakusen* passenger boat

商売 *kyaku shōbai* hotel, restaurant, or entertainment business

12 間 *kyakuma* parlor, guest room

筋 *kyaku suji* character of a customer

14 語 *kakugo, kyakugo* object (in grammar)

18 観 *kyakkan, kakkan* the object; the material world

観性 *kyakkansei, kakkansei* objectivity

観的 *kyakkanteki, kakkanteki* objective

観視 *kyakkanshi suru* look at objectively

─── **7** ───

宰 $\frac{1330}{\text{J3a4b}}$ $\overline{\text{M7160}}$ S**AI** manager; rule.

B

9 相 *saishō* prime minister; councilor

14 領 *sairyō* management, supervision; manager, supervisor

宴 $\frac{1332}{\text{J3163}}$ $\overline{\text{M7166}}$ E**N** feast, banquet, party, entertainment. *utage* party, banquet.

B

6 会 *enkai* feast, banquet, party, entertainment

会場 *enkaijō* banquet hall

10 席 *enseki* banquet, dinner party; banquet

11 遊 *en'yū* drinking party hall; banquet seat

害 $\frac{1333}{\text{J3332}}$ $\overline{\text{M7165}}$ G**AI** injury, harm, damage, mischief, interference.

A

gai(suru), sokona(u) injure, harm, mar, spoil, damage, impair.

6 虫 *gaichū* harmful insect, blight, vermin

8 毒 *gaidoku* evil, harm; mischief; virus; poison; evil influence; blight

11 鳥 *gaichō* injurious bird

悪 *gaiaku* harm, injury, evil, mischief, evil influence

13 意 *gaii* malice, ill will, murderous intent

宵 $\frac{1334}{\text{J3e2c}}$ $\overline{\text{M7168}}$ S**HŌ** . *yoi* evening, early night hours.

B

3 口 *yoi (no) kuchi* nightfall, early evening

4 月 *yoizuki* evening moon

月夜 *yoizukiyo* moonlit evening

8 明星 *yoi (no) myōjō* evening star, Venus

11 張 *yoi(p)pa(ri)* sitting up late; nighthawk

祭 *yoimatsu(ri)* eve of a festival, vigil

12 越 *yoigo(shi)* (kept) overnight

17 闇 *yoiyami* moonless night, dark evening

容 $\frac{1335}{\text{J4d46}}$ $\overline{\text{M7172}}$ Y**Ō** form; looks. *i(reru)* put into; permit; accept (advice). *katachi* form, shape; personal appearance.

A

6 色 *yōshoku* looks, personal appearance

共 *yōkyō* pro-Communist

7 体 *yōtai, yōdai* state of health, condition (of a patient)

8 易 *tayasu(i)* easy, simple, light. *yōi na* easy, simple. *yōi(narazu),* *yōi(naranu)* serious, dangerous, important

9 姿 *yōshi* form, figure, appearance

11 赦 *yōsha* pardon, forgiveness, mercy

赦無 *yōshana(ku)* mercilessly

12 喙 *yōkai* meddling, interference, interrupting a conversation

量 *yōryō* capacity, content, volume

14 認 *yōnin suru* tolerate, approve of, admit

貌 *yōbō* looks, personal appearance

疑 *yōgi* suspicion

疑者 *yōgisha* suspected person

15 器 *yōki* container, receptacle, capsule

16 積 *yōseki* capacity, volume, bulk, measurement, content

宮 $\frac{1336}{\text{J355c}}$ $\overline{\text{M7156}}$ K**U**. K**YŪ** , G**Ū** constellations (of the zodiac); palace. *miya* Shinto shrine; Imperial Palace; prince, princess.

A

3 女 *kyūjo* court lady

4 内庁 *Kunaichō* Imperial Household Agency

中 *kyūchū, kujū* imperial court

5 仕 *miyazuka(e)* court or government service

司 *gūji* chief priest of a Shinto shrine

7 作 *miyazuku(ri)* palace construction; shrine construction

7 廷 *kyūtei* the Court, the Palace

8 門 *kyūmon* palace gate

参 *miyamai(ri)* shrine visit

9 室 *kyūshitsu* palace

城 *Kyūjō* the Imperial Palace

10 家 *miyake* imperial prince's home or

family
¹³ 殿 *kyūden* palace
¹⁴ 様 *miyasama* prince; princess
¹⁸ 闕 *kyūketsu* imperial palace

家 ¹³³⁷ / ^{J3248} / ^{M7169} KA, KE house. *ie, uchi*
A house, home, residence; housing; family, household; family name; fortune. -*ya* house, shop, store, seller; dealer. *ke* family. -*ka* person, profession.

² 人 *iebito* people living in the house. *kajin* the family, one's folks. *kenin* retainer, follower
³ 子郎党 *ie(no)ko rōtō* family followers, clansmen, adherents
⁴ 中 *uchijū, kachū, iejū* the whole family; all over the house. *kachū* retainer
元 *iemoto* the head family of a school
内 *kanai* family, household; one's wife
内工業 *kanai kōgyō* home industry
⁵ 主 *yanushi, ienushi, iearuji* head of the house, houseowner, landlord
出 *iede* leaving home; abscondence
⁶ 老 *karō* chief retainer, daimyo's minister
臣 *kashin* vassal, retainer
名 *iena, kamei* the name of the house, the family name. *kamei, kamyō, kemyō* family name, family honor
伝 *kaden* family history; family (secret) formula; family tradition
宅 *kataku* domicile; premises
⁷ 作 *kasaku* house for rent; building. *ietsuku(ri)* style of house. *iezuku(ri)* house building
来 *kerai* retainer, retinue, servant
系 *kakei* family lineage
系図 *kakeizu* family tree
⁸ 長 *kachō* family head, patriarch
門 *kamon* one's family or clan
並 *iena(mi), yana(mi)* row of houses, every door
宝 *kahō* heirloom
具 *kagu* furniture, fixtures
事 *kaji* household affairs; housework; household economy
⁹ 風 *kafū* family tradition
相 *kasō* the construction of a house (of importance in divination)
柄 *iegara* parentage, pedigree; a good family
計 *kakei* household economy, family

finances; livelihood
計費 *kakeihi* household expenses
計簿 *kakeibo* household account book
屋 *kaoku* house; building
屋敷 *ieyashiki* houses and lands, estate, homestead
政 *kasei* household economy
政学 *kaseigaku* domestic science
政婦 *kaseifu* housekeeper
¹⁰ 紋 *kamon* family crest
訓 *kakun* family precepts
畜 *kachiku* domestic animals
財 *kazai* household goods; family wealth
財道具 *kazai dōgu* household goods
庭 *katei* home; family
庭的 *kateiteki* domestic or family (affairs)
庭教師 *katei kyōshi* private tutor; governess
庭裁判所 *katei saibansho* domestic-affairs court
¹¹ 運 *kaun* family fortunes
探 *iesaga(shi), yasaga(shi)* searching a house (for something); domiciliary search; house hunting
産 *kasan* family property
族 *kazoku* family, household
族的 *kazokuteki ni* like a member of the family
¹² 筋 *iesuji* lineage, pedigree, family line
¹³ 路 *ieji* the road home
賃 *yachin* house rent
業 *kagyō* one's occupation or business
禽 *kakin* poultry, fowls
督 *katoku* family headship; inheritance; family estate
¹⁴ 僕 *kaboku* house boy, manservant
構 *iegama(e)* house structure, style, or appearance
塾 *kajuku* private school

———— **8** ————

寅 ¹³⁴¹ / ^{J4652} / ^{M7204} IN. *tora* 3–5 a.m.; third zodiac sign; tiger.

寂 ¹³⁴² / ^{J3c64} / ^{M7200} JAKU death of a priest;
B quietly. SEKI quietly. *sa(biru)* mellow, mature. *sabi(shigaru)* feel lonely, miss someone. *sabi* patina, antique look; elegant simplicity; trained

口 口 土 夂 夕 大 女 子 【宀】⁸ 寸 小 尢 尸 屮 山 川 巛 工 己 巾 干 幺 广 廴 廾 弋 弓 彐 彑 彡 彳

3

口 口 土 士 夂 夂 夕 大 女 子 【宀】 寸 小 尢 尢 尸 屮 山 川 巛 工 己 巾 干 幺 广 廴 廾 弋 弓 彐 彑 彡 彳

reciter's voice. *sami(shii), sabi(shii)* lonely, lonesome; solitary, deserted, desolate. *seki to shita* hushed, still, silent.

¹² 然 *sekizen(taru)* lonely, lonesome, desolate

¹³ 寞 *sekibaku(taru)* lonely, lonesome, desolate

　 滅 *jakumetsu* Nirvana, death, annihilation

¹⁴ 寥 *sekiryō* loneliness, desolateness

A 密 $\frac{1343}{\text{J4c29}}$ M7205 Mɪᴛꜱᴜ secrecy; denseness (of population); minuteness; carefulness; fineness. *hiso(kana), hiso(yakana)* secret, private, stealthy, hushed, still. *misoka* secret.

² 入国 *mitsunyūgoku* smuggling oneself into a country

⁵ 生 *missei suru* grow luxuriantly

⁶ 会 *mikkai* clandestine meeting

　 行 *mikkō suru* prowl about

⁷ 告 *mikkoku* secret information

　 売 *mitsubai* smuggling, bootlegging, illicit sale

⁸ 送 *missō suru* send secretly

　 使 *misshi* secret messenger, secret agent

　 林 *mitsurin* thicket, jungle, dense forest

⁹ 度 *mitsudo* density

　 造 *mitsuzō* illicit manufacture, moonshining

　 約 *mitsuyaku* secret agreement

　 計 *mikkei* secret plan

　 封 *mippū suru* seal tight

　 室 *misshitsu* secret room

　 通 *mittsū* misconduct, adultery; intrigue; criminal connection

¹⁰ 書 *missho* secret message

　 航 *mikkō* stowing away (on a ship)

¹¹ 閉 *mippei suru* seal tight

　 偵 *mittei* spy

　 接 *missetsu na* close, intimate. *missetsu suru* stand close together; stick together

　 猟 *mitsuryō* poaching (in hunting)

　 教 *mikkyō* esoteric Buddhism; mysterious religion; the mysteries

¹² 着 *mitchaku suru* adhere to, be glued to

　 葬 *missō* private funeral

　 雲 *mitsuun* thick clouds

　 集 *misshū suru* swarm, crowd together

　 貿易 *mitsubōeki* smuggling, contraband trade

¹⁴ 漁 *mitsuryō, mitsugyo* secret unlicensed fishing

¹⁵ 談 *mitsudan* secret or confidential talk

¹⁶ 謀 *mitsubō* plot, intrigue, conspiracy

　 輸 *mitsuyu* smuggling; contraband

²⁰ 議 *mitsugi* secret conference; private consultation

A 宿 $\frac{1344}{\text{J3d49}}$ M7195 Sʜᴜᴋᴜ lodging; inn; post town, relay station, stage. *yado(ru)* lodge, dwell, live in; roost, be pregnant. *yado(su)* keep (a guest); carry (a virus); conceive (a child). *yado* house, home, dwelling; address; inn, lodgings, shelter. *yado(ri)* shelter, taking shelter, lodging.

⁴ 六 *yadoroku* my hubby, my old man (the husband)

⁵ 外 *shukuhazu(re)* edge of a stage town

　 主 *yadonushi* landlord, host

　 世 *sukuse, shukuse* previous existence; karma; fate

⁷ 坊 *shukubō* temple lodgings

⁸ 舎 *shukusha* lodging, quarters, billet

　 直 *shukuchoku, tonoi* night duty, night watch

　 所 *shukusho* address, quarters, lodgings

　 泊 *shukuhaku* lodging

　 命 *shukumei* fate, destiny, predestination

　 命的 *shukumeiteki* fatal

⁹ 屋 *yadoya* inn, hotel, lodginghouse

¹⁰ 病 *shukubyō* chronic illness

¹¹ 帳 *yadochō* hotel register

　 酔 *shukusui, futsukayo(i)* a hangover

　 望 *shukubō* a long-cherished desire

¹² 痾 *shukua* chronic disease

　 営 *shukuei* billeting; camp

　 場 *shukuba* post town, relay station, stage

¹³ 業 *shukugyō* karma's reward

¹⁴ 駅 *shukueki* post town, relay station; stage

¹⁵ 縁 *shukuen* karma; destiny, fate

　 敵 *shukuteki* old enemy

¹⁶ 謀 *shukubō* premeditated plan

¹⁸ 題 *shukudai* homework, lessons; pending questions

¹⁹ 願 *shukugan* long-cherished desire

A 寄 $\frac{1345}{\text{J3473}}$ M7203 Kɪ. *yo(seru)* let approach, bring near; gather, collect, summon, muster; add up; push aside;

——— **9** ———

attack; send a letter; contribute to; become dependent on, take refuge with. *yo(kosu)* send, forward, deliver. *yori* attendance, gathering; collection (of money). *yo(ru)* approach; assemble; call at; come; lean toward; obey; lean on, depend on; conclude; be possessed (by devils); present (offerings). *yo(tte-takatte)* in a crowd. *-yori* from (the north).

³ 与 *kiyo* contribution; service
⁴ 辺 *yo(ru)be* friend; protector, helper
　手 *yo(se)te* enemy, attacking force, onset
⁵ 付 *yo(se)-tsu(keru)* let come near. *yo(ri)-tsu(ku)* approach; open (the stock market). *kifu* donation, endowment
　付金 *kifukin* donation, endowment
　生 *kisei* parasitism
　生虫 *kiseichū* parasite, parasitic insects
⁶ 年波 *yo(ru) toshinami* oncoming age, old age
　合 *yo(ri)-a(u)* vi assemble, meet, grow together. *yo(ri)-a(waseru)* vt intertwine. *yoriai* meeting, assembly, party. *yo(se)-a(waseru)* get (people or things) together
　合所帯 *yoria(i)jotai* heterogeneous group (of people)
⁹ 食 *kishoku* parasitism, dependency, sponging
¹⁰ 席 *yose* variety hall, storytellers' hall, music hall, vaudeville
　進 *kishin* contribution, donation
　航 *kikō suru* call at a port, anchor
　託 *kitaku* deposition
　留 *kiryū* temporary residence, sojourn
¹¹ 道 *yo(ri)michi suru* call on the way; detour; stop over
　添 *yo(ri)-so(u)* draw near; snuggle against
　宿 *kishuku* lodging, board
　宿舎 *kishukusha* boarding house; school dormitory
¹² 港 *kikō suru* call at a port
　寓 *kigū* lodger, paying guest
　棟造 *yo(se)munezuku(ri)* hip roof
¹⁴ 算 *yo(se)zan* addition (in math)
¹⁵ 稿 *kikō suru* contribute (to a newspaper)
¹⁸ 贈 *kizō, kisō* donation, presentation
　贈品 *kizōhin, kisōhin* present, donation

寓 [1348] [J3677] [M7243] Gū temporary abode. *gū(suru)* reside temporarily; keep; imply, suggest.
⁷ 言 *gūgen* allegory, parable
⁸ 居 *gūkyo* temporary residence
¹³ 話 *gūwa* allegory, fable, parable
　意 *gūi* hidden meaning; symbolism; implication; moral

富 A [1349] [J4959] [M7230] 冨 [406] [J495a] [M1592] Fu. Fū. *to(masu)* enrich. *to(meru)* wealthy; abundant. *to(mu)* be rich, become wealthy; teem with, abound in; be fruitful; be rife; be replete. *tomi* wealth, mammon, fortune; resources; lottery.
⁸ 岳 *Fugaku* Mt. Fuji
　者 *fūsha, fusha* rich person, millionaire
　国 *fukoku* rich country, national resources, national enrichment
　国強兵 *fukoku-kyōhei* national wealth and military strength
⁹ 栄 *to(mi)-saka(eru)* prosper
¹¹ 強 *fukyō* wealth and power
¹² 裕 *fuyū* wealth, affluence
　貴 *fuki, fūki, fukki* wealth and honor
¹³ 農 *funō* rich farmer
¹⁴ 豪 *fugō* wealthy man, millionaire
²³ 籤 *tomikuji* lottery, lottery ticket

寒 A [1350] [J3428] [M7239] KAN midwinter, coldest season. *samu(garu)* be sensitive to cold. *samu(gari)* a person sensitive to cold. *samu(i)* cold, chilly.
⁴ 心 *kanshin suru* shudder at, be alarmed
　月 *kangetsu* wintry moon
　中 *kanchū* midwinter, cold season
　天 *kanten* freezing weather; wintry sky; agar-agar, vegetable gelatin
⁶ 色 *kanshoku* cold color
　地 *kanchi* cold region
　気 *kanki, samuke* cold, cold weather; chill
⁷ 村 *kanson* deserted village, poor village, out-of-the-way village
　冷 *kanrei* cold, chilliness
　冷地 *kanreichi* cold district
　冷前線 *kanrei zensen* cold front
⁸ 波 *kampa* cold wave
　夜 *kan'ya* cold night, winter night

3

口
口
土
士
夂
夊
夕
大
女
子
[宀]
⁹
寸
小
⺌
尢
尸
⼬
山
川
巛
工
己
巾
干
幺
广
廴
廾
弋
弓
彐
彑
彡
彳

空 *samuzora* wintry sky, cold weather

苦 *kanku* suffering from the cold

⁹風 *kampū, samukaze* cold wind, winter wind

¹⁰梅 *kambai* early plum blossoms

流 *kanryū* cold current

帯 *kantai* frigid zone

烈 *kanretsu* severe cold weather

¹²暑 *kansho* hot and cold; temperature; summer and winter

¹³暖 *kandan* heat and cold, temperature

暖計 *kandankei* thermometer

¹⁵熱 *kannetsu* heat and cold; chills and fever

稽古 *kangeiko* winter exercise

━━━━━ 10 ━━━━━

寛 1352 J3432 M7276 KAN leniency, generosity. **B** *kutsuro(gu)* relax, feel at home. *kutsuro(geru)* loosen, ease, relax. *yutta(ri) suru* make oneself at home. *yutta(ri) toshite* at ease, composed. *yutta(ri) shita* quiet, calm, leisurely, composed. *kutsuro(gi)* ease; room, space. *hiro(i)* broad-minded. *yuru(yakana)* loose; easy (slope); gentle, lenient, generous; slow (stream).

³大 *kandai* magnanimity, liberality; tolerance, leniency

⁴仁 *kanjin* magnanimity, generosity

¹⁰恕 *kanjo* generosity; forgiveness; mercy, leniency

容 *kan'yō* forbearance, tolerance, generosity. *kan'yō no* generous, lenient, long-suffering, broad-minded, tolerant, liberal

寝 1353 J3J32 M7278 SHIN sleeping; resting; bed. **B** *ne(ru)* sleep; retire; be bedridden; lie down; lie idle; remain unsold. *ne(kasu), ne(kaseru), ne(seru)* put to sleep; send to bed; lay down, let lie idle. *ne(soberu)* sprawl, lie sprawled. *ne(sobireru)* be wakeful, fail to sleep. *i(nu)* sleep. *ne* sleep. *ne(shina) ni* on retiring *ne(zu) ni* sleeplessly.

²入 *ne-i(ru)* fall asleep; be dull (the stock market)

入端 *nei(ri)bana* first part of a night's sleep

⁴込 *neko(mi), nego(mi)* asleep; in bed. *neko(mu)* fall asleep; oversleep; be sick in bed

不足 *nebusoku* lack of sleep

心地 *negokochi* sleeping comfort

⁵圧 *neo(shi)* pressing clothes under bedding

付 *shin (ni) tsu(ku)* retire, go to bed. *ne-tsu(ku)* fall asleep, be confined to bed. *ne-tsu(kaseru)* put to sleep. *ne(kashi)-tsu(keru)* put to sleep, send to bed

台 *shindai, nedai* bed, bedstead, bunk, berth, couch, crib, cot

⁶返 *negaeri* tossing or turning in bed; changing sides; betrayal. *negae(ru)* change sides; betray

汗 *nease* night sweat

耳水 *nemimi (ni) mizu* great surprise, thunderbolt

⁷言 *negoto* talking in sleep, nonsense

床 *nedoko* bed, cot, berth

冷 *nebi(e)* catching cold while sleeping

坊 *nebō* oversleeping, late rising

⁸泊 *netoma(ri) suru* stay with, lodge

取 *ne-to(ru)* steal another's lover

具 *shingu* bedding

物語 *nemonogatari* bedtime story

⁹首 *nekubi* head of a sleeping person

食 *shinshoku* food and sleep. *negu(i)* living in idleness

相 *nezō* sleeping posture

室 *shinshitsu* bedroom

姿 *nesugata* sleeping form

巻 *nemaki* night clothes

¹⁰起 *neoki* lying down and arising; waking; daily living

息 *neiki* a sleeper's breathing

¹¹惚 *ne-bo(keru), ne-tobo(keru)* be half asleep

転 *ne-koro(bu)* lie down, throw oneself down

¹²違 *ne-chiga(eru)* strain (the back) in sleep

椅子 *neisu* couch, lounge

間 *nema* bedroom

間着 *nemaki* night clothes

¹³殿造 *shindenzuku(ri)* Heian residential architecture

¹⁸顔 *negao* sleeping face

━━━━━ 11 ━━━━━

口
口
土
夂
夊
夕
大
女
宀
[寸]⁰
小
⺌
尢
尸
屮
山
川
巛
工
己
巾
干
幺
广
廴
廾
弋
弓
ヨ
彑
彡
彳

A 察 _{1360 J3b21 M7283} Satsu. *sas(suru), sas(shiru)* presume, surmise; judge; realize, understand; imagine, suppose; sympathize with. *sas(shi)* conjecture; judgment; understanding, consideration, sympathy.
⁸ 知 *satchi* inference

B 寧 _{1361 J472b M7296′} Nei. *mushi(ro)* rather, preferably.
⁴ 日 *neijitsu* peaceful day, quiet day

B 寡 _{1363 J3249 M7286} Ka minority, few, minimum; widow. *yamome* widow. *sukuna(i)* few, a little, scarce, insufficient, seldom.
⁴ 少 *kashō no* little, few, scanty
⁷ 言 *kagen* taciturnity, reticence
作 *kasaku* low production
兵 *kahei* small army force
男 *yamome, yamome otoko, yamoo* widower
¹¹ 婦 *kafu, yamome* widow
欲 *kayoku* unselfishness
¹⁴ 聞 *kabun* limited information
¹⁵ 黙 *kamoku* taciturnity, reticence
¹⁶ 頭政治 *katō seiji* oligarchy

──── 12 ────

B 賓 _{1365 J4950 M-X} Hin guest. [貝]
⁹ 客 *hinkyaku* guest, guest of honor

B 寮 _{1366 J4e40 M7325} Ryō hostel, dormitory; villa; tea pavilion.

tsukasa office, government office; director, head official.
⁵ 母 *ryōbo* matron (of a dormitory)
生 *ryōsei* boarding student
⁸ 長 *ryōchō* one in charge of a dormitory
¹⁴ 歌 *ryōka* dormitory song

B 審 _{1367 J3f33 M7316} Shin hearing, trial, investigation.
saba(ku) judge. *saba(ki)* judgment.
tsumabira(ka) full, detailed, minute, accurate; versed in, well-informed on.
⁷ 判 *shimpan, shimban* refereeing, umpireship; trial, judgment
⁹ 査 *shinsa* judgment, examination, inspection, investigation, screening, auditing (of salaries)
査員 *shinsain* judges, examiners
美 *shimbi* appreciation of the beautiful
美学 *shimbigaku* aesthetics
美眼 *shimbigan* aesthetic sense
¹¹ 問 *shimmon* interrogation, hearing, trial
理 *shinri* trial, hearing, examination
²⁰ 議 *shingi* deliberation, discussion, review

──── 16 ────

寵 _{1370 J437e M7368} Chō favor, affection, love, patronage.
⁵ 用 *chōyō suru* show favor to
⁶ 臣 *chōshin* favorite retainer; court favorite
⁷ 児 *chōji* favorite child, pet
⁹ 姫 *chōki* favorite imperial concubine
¹³ 愛 *chōai* favor, affection, love, patronage

■■■■ RAD. 41 ■■■■
Sun (the Japanese inch). At right: *sunzukuri*. Nickname: Inch.

A 寸 _{1372 J4023 M7411} Sun one-tenth of a foot; measure.
³ 土 *sundo* an inch of land
⁴ 分 *sumbun* a bit, a little
⁷ 言 *sungen* short but significant words
余 *sun'yo* a small amount remaining, a small remnant
志 *sunshi* small token of appreciation
⁸ 法 *sumpō* measure, dimension; plan,
program, arrangement
法通 *sumpōdō(ri)* to measure; as specified
⁹ 前 *sunzen* just before
¹⁰ 時 *sunji* a moment, a minute
書 *sunsho* note, short letter
¹¹ 描 *sumbyō* thumbnail sketch
断 *sundan suru* cut to pieces, tear to pieces

3

口
口
土
士
久
夊
夕
大
女
子
宀
【寸】
小
ゖ
尢
尸
屮
山
川
巛
工
己
巾
干
幺
广
廴
廾
弋
弓
ヨ
彑
彡
彳

毫 *sungō* (not) a bit
12 評 *sumpyō* brief review, thumbnail sketch
13 暇 *sunka* a moment's leisure
鉄 *suntetsu* small weapon; pithy saying
隙 *sungeki* moment of leisure
15 劇 *sungeki* short play, skit

———————— 3 ————————

寺 $\frac{1373}{\text{J3b7b}}$ JI *-ji*, *tera* temple.
A   M7414

3 子屋 *terakoya* temple primary school
小屋 *terakoya* temple primary school
5 巡 *teramegu(ri)* temple-pilgrimage journey
号 *jigō* Buddhist temple name
7 社 *jisha* temples and shrines
8 参 *teramai(ri)* temple visit
9 院 *jiin* temple
11 務所 *jimusho* temple office
13 詣 *teramō(de)*, *teramai(ri)* visiting a temple
14 銭 *terasen* charge for the temporary use of land or buildings
領 *jiryō* temple estate, glebe

———————— 4 ————————

寿 $\frac{1374}{\text{J3c77}}$ SU. JU age; one's natural
B   M7419 life; longevity; congratulations. *kotobu(ku)* congratulate; wish one well. *kotoho(gu)* congratulate. *kotobuki* long life; congratulations.

5 司 *sushi* sushi, rice mixed with other foods
6 老人 *Jurōjin* a god of longevity
8 命 *jumyō* life, life span

対 $\frac{1375}{\text{J4250}}$ TAI the opposite; antonym;
A   M7419 even, equal; versus; (score of three) to (one); counter-, anti-, versus. *tai(suru)* face, confront, be opposite; receive (visitors); subtend. *(ni) tai(suru)* toward, to, in, by, against, in answer to; in contrast to; compared with. *tai(shi)*, *tai(shite)* against, opposite, face to face; before; at; contrary to; in preparation for; toward; in return for; as compared with, in contrast to. *tsui* pair, couple, set.

2 人 *taijin* personal, personnel (affairs)
4 比 *taihi* contrast, comparison,

opposition, dissimilitude, analogy
手 *aite, taishu* opponent, adversary; the other party
内 *tainai* internal or domestic (affairs)
内的 *tainaiteki* internal, domestic
中 *tai-Chū* toward China, with China
日 *tai-Nichi* toward Japan, with Japan
5 句 *tsuiku* couplet, distich; antithesis
処 *taisho suru* deal with, cope with
立 *tairitsu* opposition, antagonism; correlation, coordination
外 *taigai* international (problems), foreign (relations), overseas
外的 *taigaiteki* external (affairs)
6 米 *tai-Bei* with America, toward America
7 局 *taikyoku* facing a situation
決 *taiketsu* showdown, confrontation
坐 *taiza suru* sit facing each other, sit opposite to
角線 *taikakusen* diagonal line
応 *taiō* correspondence, equivalence, opposition
応策 *taiōsaku* countermeasure
抗 *taikō* opposition, antagonism, rivalry; counteraction
抗馬 *taikōba* rival horse; rival candidate
抗策 *taikōsaku* countermeasure
8 価 *taika* compensation; equivalent; consideration; prices
岸 *taigan* opposite shore
物鏡 *taibutsukyō* objective lens
空 *taikū* antiaircraft
9 峙 *taiji suru* confront each other, keep up rivalry, hold one's own against
陣 *taijin suru* encamp opposite the enemy, confront each other
面 *taimen* interview, meeting, facing (someone)
10 席 *taiseki suru* sit facing each other, attend together
座 *taiza suru* sit facing each other, sit opposite to
流 *tairyū* convection current
案 *taian* counterproposal
称 *taishō* symmetry (in math); second person
称的 *taishōteki* symmetrical
症 *taishō* specific (treatment)
校 *taikō* interschool, intercollegiate
11 訳 *taiyaku* parallel versions

策 *taisaku* countermeasure
等 *taitō* equality, par, parity, equivalent
象 *taishō* object (of worship); subject (of taxation); concern
13 置 *taichi suru* set opposite or against
戦 *taisen* waging war, competition
数 *taisū* logarithms
照 *taishō* contrast, antithesis, comparison
照的 *taishōteki* diametrically opposite
話 *taiwa* conversation, dialogue
15 論 *tairon* arguing face to face; arguing against a proposition
敵 *taiteki* hostile; (trade) with the enemy
談 *taidan* conversation, interview, dialogue
17 聯 *tairen, tsuiren* couplet
18 蹠 *taiseki, taisho* diametrical opposition
蹠的 *taisekiteki, taishoteki* diametrically opposite

──────── 6 ────────

封 $\frac{1376}{J4975}$ Fū seal; sealing; closing.
B $\overline{M7426}$ Hō fief. *fū(jiru), fū(zuru)* seal, close up, confine, blockade.
hō(zuru) appoint; invest with a fief; erect a mound.
2 入 *fūnyū* enclosure (in a letter)
4 込 *fū(ji)-ko(meru), fū(ji)-ko(mu)* enclose, confine, contain, seal up
切 *fūkiri* release of the first run (of a film); beginning
5 冊 *hōsaku* imperial order to invest with a fief
6 印 *fūin* seal
9 建 *hōken* feudalism
建的 *hōkenteki* feudal
建制度 *hōken seido* feudalism
10 書 *fūsho* sealed letter, sealed document
12 筒 *fūtō* envelope
15 緘 *fūkan* seal
18 鎖 *fūsa* blockade; freezing (funds)

専 $\frac{1377}{J406c}$ Sen. *moppa(ra)* mainly,
A $\overline{M-X}$ solely.
1 一 *sen'itsu, sen'ichi* concentration; best care; primary importance. *sen'itsu no* special, exclusive, principal
4 心 *senshin* undivided attention, concentration; singleness of purpose
5 用 *sen'yō* private use, personal use, exclusive use
6 任 *sennin* full-time service
有 *sen'yū* exclusive possession
7 攻 *senkō* special research
決 *senketsu* arbitrariness
売 *sembai* monopoly
売特許 *sembai tokkyo* patent
8 念 *sennen* close attention
制 *sensei* despotism, autocracy
制君主 *sensei kunshu* autocrat, tyrant
制的 *senseiteki* despotic, autocratic, arbitrary
門 *semmon* specialty, line, profession
門用語 *semmon yōgo* technical term
門的 *semmonteki* professional, technical
門学校 *semmon gakkō* professional school
門家 *semmonka* specialist, professional, expert
門書 *semmonsho* books in special fields
9 科 *senka* special course
10 修科 *senshūka* special course
従 *senjū suru* specialize
従者 *senjūsha* full-time worker
11 断 *sendan* arbitrary action
務 *semmu* special duty; main business; (train) conductor; managing director
12 属 *senzoku* attached to; exclusive; specialization; specialist
13 業 *sengyō* specialty, monopoly, main occupation
15 権 *senken* exclusive right; despotism, arbitrary power
横 *sen'ō* arbitrariness; despotism, tyranny
横的 *sen'ōteki* arbitrary

──────── 7 ────────

将 $\frac{1379}{J3e2d}$ Shō commander, general,
A $\overline{M7437}$ admiral. *hata* or, and again. *masa ni* soon, from now on; just about.
7 兵 *shōhei* officers and men
来 *shōrai* future, prospects
来性 *shōraisei* future, possibilities, prospects
8 官 *shōkan* general, admiral
9 星 *shōsei* a general
軍 *shōgun* general, commander, shogun
10 校 *shōkō* commissioned officer
12 棋 *shōgi* Japanese chess game
棋倒 *shōgidao(shi)* falling one after another in a row

3

口
口
土
士
夂
夕
大
女
子
宀
[寸]
小
⺌
尢
尸
屮
山
川
巛
工
己
巾
干
幺
广
廴
廾
弋
弓
彐
彑
彡
彳

射 $\frac{1380}{\underset{M7434}{J3c4d}}$ SHA archery; shooting.
A i(ru) shoot. sa(su) shine into, shine upon.

⁴ 止 i-to(meru) shoot (an animal) to death; win (a girl)
込 sa(shi)-ko(mu) shine into. i-ko(mu) hit the mark
手 ite, shashu archer, bowman, shooter
⁵ 出 i-da(su) shoot. shashutsu suru emit, project, shoot out, catapult, radiate, be radiant
⁷ 角 shakaku angle of fire
抜 i-nu(ku) shoot through
⁸ 的 shateki target practice
幸 shakō speculative spirit
幸心 shakōshin speculative spirit
⁹ 界 shakai field of fire
¹⁰ 殺 i-koro(su), shasatsu suru shoot to death
倖 shakō speculative spirit
倖心 shakōshin speculative spirit
¹¹ 距離 shakyori rifle range
¹² 落 i-oto(su) shoot down
程 shatei rifle range
程距離 shatei kyori range of fire, sphere of interest
¹⁴ 精 shasei ejaculation, emission
¹⁵ 撃 shageki shooting; gunshot; marksmanship
撃場 shagekijō target range, rifle range

———————— **8** ————————

尉 $\frac{1383}{\underset{M7440}{J3053}}$ I. jō jailer; old man; rank;
B company officer.
⁸ 官 ikan company officer

———————— **9** ————————

尋 $\frac{1385}{\underset{M7447}{J3f52}}$ JIN fathom. tazu(neru)
B look for, inquire for, ask (someone) a question. hiro fathom. tsu(ide) next, secondly, subsequently.

² 人 tazu(ne)bito missing person, wanted person
⁷ 求 tazu(ne)-moto(meru) inquire of ; seek for
⁸ 者 (o)tazu(ne)mono fugitive from justice, man wanted by the police
¹¹ 問 jimmon questioning
常 jinjō no common, usual

尊 $\frac{1386}{\underset{M7445}{J423a}}$ SON. tatto(bu), tōto(bu),
A tatto(mu), tōto(mu) value, prize, esteem; respect, honor, revere. tatto(i), tōto(i) precious, valuable, priceless; noble, exalted, sacred. mikoto lord, prince.

³ 大 sondai haughtiness, pomposity, self-sufficiency
⁴ 父 sompu your father
王 sonnō reverence for the emperor, advocate of imperial rule
⁵ 号 songō honorary title
⁶ 宅 sontaku your house
名 sommei your name
⁸ 者 sonja Buddhist saint; man of high repute; guest of honor
⁹ 重 sonchō respect, esteem, regard
皇 sonnō reverence for the emperor, advocate of imperial rule
皇攘夷 sonnō-jōi reverence for the emperor and expulsion of the barbarians
¹⁰ 称 sonshō honorary title
¹¹ 族 sonzoku direct ancestors
崇 sonsū reverence, veneration
¹² 属 sonzoku direct ancestors; noble ancestors
敬 sonkei respect, esteem, honor, reverence
貴 sonki noble (person)
¹⁴ 像 sonzō statue of a noble character; your picture
¹⁷ 厳 songen dignity, majesty, sanctity
¹⁸ 顔 songan your countenance

———————— **11** ————————

導 $\frac{1388}{\underset{M7463}{J4633}}$ DŌ leading. michibi(ku)
A guide, lead, conduct, usher. michibi(ki) guidance. shirube guide; guiding; road sign.

² 入 michibi(ki)-i(reru), dōnyū suru lead into, bring into; induce; invite; import; introduce
⁴ 水 dōsui conducting water; hydraulic
水路 dōsuiro raceway, canal
火線 dōkasen fuse; cause, agency, incentive, impetus, occasion
⁵ 出 michibi(ki)-da(su) bring out, bring forth, lead out
⁷ 体 dōtai conductor; medium

¹⁰ 師 *dōshi* officiating (Buddhist) priest

¹³ 電体 *dōdentai* conductor of electricity

電性 *dōdensei* conductivity

¹⁴ 管 *dōkan* conduit, pipe, aqueduct; standpipe; duct

¹⁵ 線 *dōsen* leading wire

RAD. 小 42

Shō small. Variant: ⺌. Nickname: Little.

A 小 1389 / J3e2e / M7473 SHŌ smallness; minor; small. *chii(sai), chii(sana), chi(sai)* small, little, diminutive, minute, fine, trivial. *isasa* small. *ko-* small; short; pretty; petty; nearly. *o-* little; nice, pretty. *shō-* humility prefix; small. *sa-* honorary prefix.

² 刀 *shōtō* the shorter sword. *kogatana* knife, pocket knife

人 *shōjin* small person, dwarf; child; mean person; person of small caliber. *shōnin* child. *kobito* dwarf, Lilliputian, pygmy, manikin

人物 *shōjimbutsu* ungenerous person; low-charactered person

人数 *koninzū* small number of people

³ 川 *ogawa, kogawa* brook, creek

口 *koguchi* end, edge; clue; beginning, small lots; small sum

山 *koyama* hill, mound

⁴ 水 *shōsui* urine, urination

片 *shōhen* piece, fragment

文字 *komoji* small letters, lower-case letters

火器 *shōkaki* light weapons

天地 *shōtenchi* a small world

心 *shōshin* timidity, cowardice; prudence

心翼翼 *shōshin-yokuyoku* infinite care; trembling

手先 *kotesaki* (a good) hand (at)

手調 *koteshira(be)* tryout, rehearsal, workout, preliminary examination

切手 *kogitte* check

⁵ 用 *shōyō, koyō* small matter; urination

皿 *kozara* saucer, small plate

出 *koda(shi)* passing out a small quantity; frugal use; choosing some out of many; articles so chosen

市民 *shōshimin* lower middle class

母様 *obusan, obasama* aunt; lady

生 *shōsei* I

生意気 *konamaiki* impertinence, conceit, impudence

包 *kozutsumi* parcel, package

冊子 *shōsasshi* booklet, pamphlet, tract, brochure

半時 *kohantoki* quarter hour; nearly half an hour

田原評定 *odawara hyōjō* endless talk, fruitless debate

⁶ 耳 *komimi* little ears (that happen to overhear)

回 *komawa(ri)* sharp turn

字 *shōji* small characters, small type; one's baby name. *koaza* small village subsection

気味 *kokimi, kokibi* sentiment, feeling

休止 *shōkyūshi* short rest

⁷ 言 *kogoto* scolding, faultfinding

豆 *azuki* red bean

走 *kobashi(ri)* hurrying along with small steps

兵 *kohyō* small stature

弟 *shōtei* the younger of two younger brothers; (humble) my younger brother

声 *kogoe* low voice, whisper

男 *kootoko* young man; short man

見出 *komida(shi)* subtitle, subheading

亜細亜 *Shōajiya* Asia Minor

身 *shōshin* humble position; persons of low rank

町 *komachi* beauty, belle, queen

判 *koban* small size (in printing); small Edo gold coin

利 *shōri* small profit

利口 *korikō* somewhat talented, cleverness

売 *kouri* retail sale

売店 *kouriten* retail store

麦 *komugi* wheat

麦色 *komugi iro* cocoa brown

3

口 口 土 士 夂 夕 大 女 子 宀 寸 【小 ⺌】 尢 尸 屮 山 川 巛 工 己 巾 干 幺 广 廴 廾 弋 弓 ヨ 彑 彡 彳

麦粉 *komugiko* wheat flour
児 *shōni* little child, infant
児科 *shōnika* pediatrics
作 *kosaku* (firm) tenancy. *kozuku(ri)* small size; small stature; small physique
作人 *kosakunin* tenant farmer
⁸金 *kogane* small fortune; small sum
雨 *kosame, koame* light rain, drizzle
使 *kozukai* janitor; errand boy, servant; spending money
咄 *kobanashi* short story
姓 *koshō* child, youth; page to a noble
姑 *kojūto, kojūtome* sister-in-law
径 *shōkei* lane, path
枝 *koeda* twig; spray
波 *sazanami, sasanami, konami* ripples
股 *komata* short steps; crotch, thigh, groin
肥 *kobuto(ri)* somewhat fat
刻 *kokiza(mi)* mincing, chopping fine
者 *komono* menial, servant; small fry
事 *shōji* small matter
奇麗 *kogirei na* trim, neat, snug
国 *shōkoku* small country, weak nation
物 *komono* small articles, a little thing
突 *kozu(ku)* prod, poke, thrust, push, shake; swing; irritate; thrash
突回 *kozu(ki)-mawa(su)* manhandle, shake; tease; find fault with
学生 *shōgakusei* elementary pupil
学校 *shōgakkō* elementary school
夜嵐 *sayo arashi* night wind, night storm
⁹食 *shōshoku, kogu(i)* light eating, spare diet
柄 *kogara* short stature. *kozuka* knife attached to a sword sheath
計 *shōkei* subtotal
降 *koburi* light snow, light rain, drizzle
首 *kokubi* neck; head
便 *shōben, shomben* urine, urination
指 *koyubi, shōshi* little finger
乗仏教 *Shōjō Bukkyō* Hinayana or Lesser-Vehicle Buddhism
乗的 *shōjōteki* narrow-minded
品 *shōhin* something very small; an essay, a literary sketch
型 *kogata* small size, small design
春日和 *koharubiyori* Indian-summer day, balmy autumn day
屋 *shōoku, koya* cottage, hut, booth,

cabin, shed. *koya* theater
¹⁰高 *kodaka(i)* slightly elevated
倅 *kosegare* one's little son, little fellow, kid
唄 *kouta* ditty, ballad
娘 *komusume* girl in her early teens; young woman before reaching maturity
振 *kobu(ri)* small size
破 *shōha* slight damage
恥 *kohazu(kashii)* ashamed, embarrassed, shy
脇 *kowaki* side (of the body)
袖 *kosode* padded silk garment
差 *shōsa* small difference, narrow margin
馬鹿 *kobaka* somewhat of a fool. *kobaka ni suru* treat with contempt
骨 *kobone* small bones
料理屋 *koryōriya* small restaurant
荷物 *konimotsu* parcel, package
¹¹魚 *kozakana, kouo* small fish, fingerling
康 *shōkō* lull, respite, some improvement (in a patient)
脳 *shōnō* cerebellum
隊 *shōtai* platoon, troop
瓶 *kobin* small bottle
異 *shōi* minor differences
規模 *shōkibo* small scale
鳥 *kotori* small bird
道 *komichi* path, lane, alley, byway
道具 *kodōgu* small pieces of equipment; small tools; small stage properties
細工 *kozaiku* handiwork; tricks; tinkering
粒 *kotsubu, shōryū* grain, fine particle
¹²惑星 *shōwakusei* asteroid
幅 *kohaba* single or narrow width
遣 *kozukai* spending money, incidental expenses
遣銭 *kozukaisen, kozukai zeni* spending money, incidental expenses
間切 *komagi(re)* small pieces of cloth; chopped meat
間使 *komazukai* maid
間物 *komamono* notions, knickknacks, sundry wares
¹³鼓 *kotsuzumi* hand drum
僧 *kozō* young Buddhist priest; errand boy, shop boy; youngster
暗 *kogura(i), ogura(i)* dusky; shady
槌 *kozuchi* small mallet; gavel; wand

腸 *shōchō* small intestines

路 *komichi, kōji* path, lane, alley, byway, narrow street

節 *shōsetsu* a small knot (in wood); bar (in music); faithfulness in small matters

舅 *kojūto* brother-in-law

意気 *koiki na* stylish, chic, neat, tasteful

数 *shōsū* a fraction; a comparatively small number

数点 *shōsūten* decimal point

¹⁴ 鼻 *kobana* wings of the nose

銭 *kozeni* small change, loose coins

綺麗 *kogirei na* trim, neat, snug

説 *shōsetsu* novel, romance, story, fiction

説家 *shōsetsuka* novelist, fiction writer

銃 *shōjū* rifle, small arms

¹⁵ 皺 *kojiwa* little wrinkles, crow's feet

賢 *kozaka(shii), kogashiko(i)* smart, conceited; tricky, shrewd

¹⁶ 憩 *shōkei* short rest, recess

¹⁷ 糠雨 *konuka ame* drizzling rain

¹⁸ 難 *komuzuka(shii)* bothersome, troublesome, finicky, peevish. *shōnan* small misfortune; minor fault

額 *shōgaku* small amount

²⁰ 競合 *kozeria(i)* skirmish, bickering; wrangle

²¹ 癪 *koshaku na* impertinent, impudent

躍 *koodo(ri)* dancing or jumping for joy

——— **1** ———

少 1390 J3e2f M7475 SHŌ small; few; young. *suko(shi)* a small quantity, a little; a few; something; a little while; a short distance. *suko(shimo)* (not) at all. *suku(nai), suke(nai)* few, a little, scarce, insufficient, seldom. *suku(nakarazu)* not a little, in no small numbers. *suku(nage)* scarcity. *suku(nakutomo), suku(nakumo)* at least.

³ 女 *shōjo, otome* daughter, young lady, virgin

⁴ 少 *shōshō* a little, a few, slightly

⁶ 壮 *shōsō* youth

年 *shōnen* boy, juvenile

年法 *shōnenhō* juvenile law

年院 *shōnen'in* reform school

⁷ 佐 *shōsa* major; lieutenant commander; wing commander

⁹ 食 *shōshoku* light eating, spare diet

¹⁰ 将 *shōshō* major general, rear admiral; air commodore

¹¹ 康 *shōkō* small improvement (in a patient)

¹¹ 尉 *shōi* second lieutenant; ensign

¹² 量 *shōryō* small quantity, small dose

¹³ 数 *shōsū* few; minority

数民族 *shōsū minzoku* minority peoples

——— **3** ———

尖 1393 J406d M7480 SEN. *toga(ru), tonga(ru)* be pointed, be sharp, taper off; be displeased, get angry. *toga(rasu), tonga(rasu), toga(rakasu)* sharpen, point; raise (one's voice); put (one's nerves) on edge. *tonga(ru), tonga(rakaru)* get cross. *toga(ri), tongar(i)* point, tip, peak.

⁷ 兵 *sempei* advance guard

¹² 塔 *sentō* pinnacle, spire, steeple

¹⁴ 端 *sentan* pointed end, tip; fine point; cusp; spearhead, vanguard

¹⁵ 鋒 *sempō* point

鋭 *sen'ei* radical; acute

鋭化 *sen'eika suru* become acute, be aggravated

¹⁶ 頭 *sentō* pinnacle, spire, steeple

——— **5** ———

尚 1395 J3e30 M7493 SHŌ. *nao* further, furthermore, still, still more, yet; just like. *tatto(bu)* value, prize, esteem; respect, honor, revere. *hisa(shii)* long, long-continued, an old (story).

² 又 *naomata* further, besides

⁵ 且 *naokatsu* and yet

古 *shōko* worship of ancient civilizations

⁶ 早 *shōsō* prematurity

⁷ 更 *naosara* still, still more, all the more

⁸ 武 *shōbu* militarism, warlike spirit

3

口 口 土 士 夂 夕 大 女 子 宀 寸 【小 ⺍】⁵ 尢 尸 屮 山 川 巛 工 己 巾 干 幺 广 廴 廾 弋 弓 ヨ 彑 彡 彳

3

口 口 土 士 夂 夊 夕 大 女 子 宀 寸 小 ⺌ [尢] 尸 屮 山 川 巛 工 己 巾 干 幺 广 廴 廾 弋 弓 彐 互 彡 彳

RAD. 尢 43

Dai no mageashi crooked-leg *dai* (large). *Mottomo* just, right, reasonable, natural.
Nickname: Crooked Big (cf. 37).

1

尢 $\frac{1399}{\frac{J4c60}{M7543}}$ YŪ superb, outstanding. *motto(morashii)* plausible. *yū(naru)* superb, outstanding. *motto(mo)* reasonable, right, just, natural; of course; although.

9

就 $\frac{1401}{\frac{J3d22}{M7599}}$ SHŪ . JU. *tsu(ku)* settle in (place); take (a seat); take (a position); depart; study (under a teacher). *(ni) tsu(ite)* concerning; along; under; per. *tsu(ite) wa, tsu(kimashite) wa* concerning. *-zu(ku)* to become.
A
⁴ 中 *nakanzuku* especially, above all, among other things

⁶ 任 *shūnin* assumption of office, inauguration
⁷ 役 *shūeki suru* be placed in commission; enter servitude
労 *shūrō* actual work
⁸ 学 *shūgaku* entering school; school attendance
¹⁰ 眠 *shūmin* retiring, going to sleep
航 *shūkō* commissioning a ship
¹³ 寝 *shūshin suru* go to bed, retire
業 *shūgyō* employment, starting work
¹⁸ 職 *shūshoku* finding employment
職口 *shūshokuguchi* position, opening, employment
職先 *shūshokusaki* place of employment
職難 *shūshokunan* scarcity of employment

RAD. 尸 44

Shikabane or *kabane* corpse. Nickname: Flag.

1

尺 $\frac{1404}{\frac{J3c5c}{M7632}}$ SEKI. SHAKU Japanese foot (1 *shaku* = .994 foot); rule; measure, scale; length. *sashi* measure, rule.
A
² 八 *shakuhachi* bamboo flute
³ 寸 *shakusun, sekisun* a bit, a little; a strip (of land); short length
⁸ 取虫 *shakuto(ri)mushi* measuring worm
⁹ 度 *shakudo* linear measure, scale, gauge, standard
¹¹ 貫法 *shakkanhō* Japanese system of weights and measures

2

尼 $\frac{1405}{\frac{J4674}{M7635}}$ JI. NI *ama* nun.
B
⁶ 寺 *amadera* convent
¹³ 僧 *nisō* (Buddhist) priestess

尻 $\frac{1407}{\frac{J3f2c}{M7634}}$ KŌ . *shiri* buttocks, hips; rear or back of a person; bottom (of a kettle); tail end, tag end.
³ 下 *shirisa(gari)* a drop in the back part of anything; lowering the voice at the end of a sentence
上 *shiria(gari)* rising intonation; head over heels; rising market
⁴ 込 *shirigo(mu)* flinch, shrink back, hesitate
切 *shiriki(re)* half-finished
⁵ 目 *shirime ni* looking askance
⁶ 当 *shiria(te)* trouser-seat lining
⁷ 尾 *shirio, shippo* tail; end
抜 *shirinu(ke)* forgetfulness
⁸ 長 *shiri (ga) naga(i)* overstaying (guest)
⁹ 拭 *shirinugu(i)* taking the blame or loss for another
¹⁰ 馬 *shiriuma* blindly following, indiscriminate imitation
¹² 軽 *shirigaru ni* lightly. *shirigaru na* wanton, loose

割 *shiri (ga) wa(reru)* (a secret) is exposed
¹⁴ 端折 *shiri(p)pasho(ri), shirihasho(ri)* tucking up the kimono behind
¹⁵ 餅 *shirimochi* falling on one's buttocks

——————— 3 ———————

尽 <u>1408 J3f54 M7642</u> **B** JIN. *tsu(kusu)* use up, run out of, exhaust; serve, befriend, work for, endeavor, do (one's duty). *tsu(kiru)* become exhausted, be consumed, spend, end. *kotogoto(ku)* all, entirely, completely. *-zu(ku) de* for the sake of, by means of, by force of. *-zu(kushi)* a full enumeration of. *-jin* last day of the month.
² 力 *jinryoku* efforts; assistance
⁸ 果 *tsu(ki)-ha(teru)* be exhausted
忠 *jinchū* loyalty

——————— 4 ———————

尿 <u>1410 J4722 M7651</u> **B** NYŌ *shito, yubari, ibari* urine.
¹⁰ 素 *nyōso* urea
¹¹ 道 *nyōdō* urethra
¹³ 意 *nyōi* the urge to urinate

尾 <u>1411 J4878 M7650</u> **B** BI tail; end; counter for fish. *o* tail; trail (of a meteor); lower slope (of a mountain).
⁶ 羽 *oha* wing and tail feather
行 *bikō* following, trailing, shadowing
灯 *bitō* taillight; stop light
⁷ 花 *obana* Japanese pampas grass
¹⁰ 根 *one* a mountain ridge
部 *bibu* tail
¹⁴ 端 *bitan* tail tip
¹⁵ 骶骨 *biteikotsu* coccyx
¹⁶ 橇 *bisori* tail skid
錠 *bijō* buckle, clasp
¹⁷ 翼 *biyoku* tail, tail plane
²¹ 鰭 *obire* caudal fin. *ohire* tail and fin; exaggeration
²² 籠 *birō* indelicate, indecent, vulgar language

局 <u>1412 J3649 M7653</u> **A** KYOKU bureau, board, office; central; post office; affair; duty; situation; conclusion. *tsubone* court lady; her apartment; lady-in-waiting.
⁵ 外 *kyokugai* the outside; an independent position; irrelevance
⁶ 名 *kyokumei* call sign, station name
地 *kyokuchi* locality, the site (of the occurrence)
⁸ 長 *kyokuchō* bureau chief, director, postmaster
限 *kyokugen suru* limit, localize
所 *kyokusho* part, section; local
⁹ 面 *kyokumen* checkerboard; aspect, situation
¹⁰ 留 *kyokudo(me)* general delivery
部 *kyokubu* part, section; affected region; privates ⌈number
¹² 番 *kyokuban* telephone-exchange

——————— 5 ———————

届 <u>1413 J464f M7667</u> **A** KAI. *todo(ku)* reach, arrive, be received; be attentive, be realized. *todo(keru)* report, notify; forward. *todoke* report, notice; forwarding, delivery.
⁵ 出 *todo(ke)-de(ru)* report. *todokeide, todokede* report, notice; forwarding, delivery
⁶ 先 *todo(ke)saki* destination, address, consignee
¹⁰ 書 *todo(ke)sho, todo(ke)ga(ki)* notice, written report
¹¹ 済 *todo(ke)zu(mi)* filed

屈 <u>1415 J367e M7669</u> **B** KUTSU. *kus(suru)* bend, bend over; give in, submit to, yield to; flinch. *kaga(mu), kaga(maru), kogo(meru)* stop, lean over, crouch. *kago(mu)* bow, stoop, bend over. *kaga(meru)* bow (the knee); bend (the legs).
⁴ 込 *kaga(mi)-ko(mu)* bend over
⁶ 曲 *kukkyoku suru* be crooked, bend, wind; be indented; be refracted
伏 *kuppuku* surrender, submission
⁷ 伸 *kusshin* extension and contraction; bending and stretching; flexibility
折 *kussetsu* bending; indentation; refraction
⁸ 服 *kuppuku* surrender, submission
⁹ 指 *kusshi* counting on the fingers; prominence
¹⁰ 託 *kuttaku* worry, trouble; preoccupation; boredom, ennui

3
口
口
土
士
夂
夊
夕
大
女
子
宀
寸
小
尢
〔尸〕 5
屮
山
川
巛
工
己
巾
干
幺
广
廾
弋
弓
彐
彑
彡
彳

辱 *kutsujoku* humiliation, insult; defeat
¹¹ 強 *kukkyō* robust health; obstinacy

A 居 1416 J356f M7663 KO. KYO residence.
i(ru), o(ru) be, exist; be found in, stay in; inhabit; live with, reside; be present; remain (sitting).
³ 士 *koji* active (Buddhist) layman
丈高 *itakedaka ni, idakedaka ni* domineeringly
⁴ 心地 *igokochi* relaxation (at home)
⁵ 民 *kyomin* residents, inhabitants
⁶ 宅 *kyotaku* a residence
合 *i-a(wasu), i-a(waseru)* happen to be present
合抜 *ia(i)nu(ki)* swordplay, swordplayer
⁷ 抜 *inu(ki)* a going concern
坐 *i-suwa(ru)* stay on, settle down, remain (in office). *isuwa(ri) no* stationary, permanent
住 *kyojū suru* reside. *izuma(i)* sitting position. *kyojū* residence; address
住地 *kyojūchi* residence; address
住者 *kyojūsha* resident, inhabitant
⁸ 所 *idokoro, kyosho* residence, whereabouts, address. *o(ri)dokoro* the place where one is
並 *i-nara(bu)* sit in a row, be arrayed
直 *i-nao(ru)* sit straight; change one's attitude; come out strong; turn into a robber; resort to threat
⁹ 城 *kyojō* daimyo's residential castle
室 *kyoshitsu* living room; private room, den
¹⁰ 候 *isōrō* hanger-on, dependent, parasite
残 *i-noko(ru)* work overtime; remain behind
眠 *inemu(ri)* doze, nap
酒屋 *izakaya* saloon, pub
留民 *kyoryūmin* residents
留地 *kyoryūchi* settlement, concession
留守 *irusu* "not at home" (said when someone does not want to see the callers)
¹¹ 据 *i-su(waru)* stay on, settle down, remain (in office)
¹² 間 *ima* living room, private room
場所 *ibasho* residence; whereabouts

— 6 —

屍 1420 J3b53 M7688 SHI corpse. *shikabane* corpse, remains.
⁷ 体 *shitai* corpse
⁹ 姦 *shikan* violating a corpse; necrophelia
臭 *shishū* smell of death, putrid smell
¹⁶ 諫 *shikan* admonishing a ruler by one's death

A 屋 1421 J3230 M7684 OKU roof; house. *-ya* shop, store; seller, dealer; business.
³ 上 *okujō* housetop, roof
⁴ 内 *okunai* indoors
⁵ 外 *okugai* open air, outdoors
号 *yagō* store name, house name, hereditary family name, a stage-family name
台 *yatai* a float; a stall
台骨 *yataibone* framework, foundation; means, property
⁷ 体 *yatai* a float; a stall
形 *yakata* house, mansion, boat cabin
形船 *yakatabune* houseboat, barge, pleasure boat
⁸ 舎 *okusha* house, building
並 *yana(mi)* row of houses
¹⁰ 根 *yane* roof, roofing, housetop
根裏 *yaneura* attic; loft
¹⁵ 敷 *yashiki* mansion, residence, premises; residential site

— 7 —

屑 1424 J367d M7709 SETSU. *kuzu* rubbish, junk, trash, waste, scraps, rags, crumbs, waste paper; the scum of society.
² 入 *kuzui(re)* garbage can
⁸ 物 *kuzumono* trash, junk
⁹ 屋 *kuzuya* junk man
拾 *kuzuhiro(i)* ragpicking; ragpicker
¹³ 鉄 *kuzu tetsu* scrap iron
²² 籠 *kuzu kago* wastebasket

A 展 1425 J4538 M7715 TEN expand.
⁵ 示 *tenji* exhibition, display
示会 *tenjikai* exhibition
示場 *tenjijō* (place of) an exhibition
⁸ 性 *tensei* malleability
¹¹ 転 *tenten* rolling
望 *tembō* view, outlook, prospect

望台 *tembōdai* observatory; observation platform
望車 *tembōsha* observation car
12 開 *tenkai suru* unfold, develop, evolve; deploy
16 覧 *tenran* exhibition
覧会 *tenrankai* exhibition, exhibit
18 観 *tenkan* exhibition

8

屠 1426 / J454b / M-X Nonstandard for **屠** 1429.

9

屢 1428 / J3c48 / M7770 Nonstandard for **屢** 1431.

屠 1429 / J-X / M7761 To. *hofu(ru)* slaughter, butcher, massacre, slay.
8 所 *tosho* slaughterhouse
10 畜 *tochiku* butchering, slaughtering
殺 *tosatsu* slaughter, butchering; massacre
殺場 *tosatsujō* slaughterhouse
12 場 *tojō* slaughterhouse
19 蘇 *toso* spiced saké

A **属** 1430 / J4230 / M7754 Zoku genus; subordinate official. Shoku. *zoku(suru), zoku(su)* belong to, be among; fall under; be affiliated with; be subject to; be vested in, be inherent in.
6 地 *zokuchi* dependency, territory
名 *zokumei* generic name
吏 *zokuri* subordinate official
8 国 *zokkoku* vassal state, dependency
性 *zokusei* attribute
11 望 *shokubo* expectation
14 領 *zokuryō* possession, dependency, dominion

11

屢 1431 / J-X / M7787 Ru. *shibashiba* often, frequently.
14 屢 *shibashiba* often, frequently

A **層** 1432 / J4158 / M-X Sō (social) class; stratum, layer, seam, bed, formation; story, floor; course (of stones).
7 位 *sōi* layer, stratum (of soil)
状 *sōjō* stratified
12 雲 *sōun* stratus clouds
16 積雲 *sōsekiun* strato-cumulus clouds

12

B **履** 1434 / J4d7a / M7799 Ri. *fu(mu)* step on, trample on, stamp on; carry through, practice; appraise; set foot on; evade payment. *ha(ku)* put on (the feet). *kutsu* shoes, boots.
6 行 *rikō* performance, fulfillment, execution, observance
8 物 *hakimono* footwear
10 修 *rishū suru* study, complete (a course)
12 違 *ha(ki)-chiga(eru)* to put on someone else's footwear; be mistaken
14 歴 *rireki* personal history, career
歴書 *rirekisho* personal history, vita, resumé

RAD. 屮 45

Furukusa old "grass" (i.e., the less complicated "grass," as distinguished from Rad. 140). Variants: 屮, 屮. Nickname: Old Grass.

1

B **屯** 1438 / J4656 / M7828 Ton ton. Chun. *tamuro* police station; camp, barracks.
5 田 *tonden* colonization
田兵 *tondenhei* agricultural soldiers, colonizers
8 所 *tonsho* post, quarters, military station; police station
12 営 *ton'ei* military camp, barracks, camping

3

口
口
土
士
夂
夂
夕
大
女
子
宀
寸
小
⺌
尢
尸
屮
[山]
川
巛
工
己
巾
干
幺
广
廴
廾
弋
弓
彐
彑
彡
彳

Yama mountain. At left: *yamahen*. Nickname: Mountain.

A 山 $\frac{1439}{\text{J3b33}}$ M7869 SAN mount, mountain.
yama mountain, hill, height, knoll; heap, pile; crown (of a hat); seam (of an obi); speculation, adventure; climax, acme, crisis; forest; mine.

² 刀 *yamagatana* woodman's hatchet

³ 女 *yamame* trout, young salmon

山 *yamayama* mountains; very much

川 *yamagawa* mountain stream. *sansen, yama-kawa* mountains and rivers

小屋 *yamagoya* mountain hut

上 *sanjō* mountain top

⁴ 手 *yamate, yama(no)te* hilly section of Tokyo; bluff; uptown

月 *sangetsu* the moon above a mountain

犬 *yama inu* wild dog, wolf, coyote, jackal

中 *yamanaka, sanchū* in the mountains

内 *sannai* in the mountains; in a temple compound

火事 *yama kaji* forest fire

水 *yama mizu* mountain spring water. *sansui* hills and water; landscape, scenery; landscape painting; landscape garden

水画 *sansuiga* landscape painting; a landscape

⁵ 号 *sangō* temple name

出 *yamada(shi)* a rustic

⁶ 色 *sanshoku* mountain scenery; color of the mountains

行 *sankō, yamayu(ki), yamai(ki)* trip into the mountains

向 *yamamu(kō)* across the mountain

伏 *yamabushi* mountain priest, itinerant priest, hermit

地 *yamachi, sanchi* hilly country, mountain area

肌 *yamahada* mountain surface

寺 *yamadera* mountain temple

羊 *yagi* goat

⁷ 里 *yamazato* mountain village, hilly district

村 *sanson* mountain village

系 *sankei* mountain system

男 *yama otoko* wild man; woodsman; hillbilly; mountaineer

吹 *yamabuki* yellow rose

吹色 *yamabuki iro* bright yellow, golden; gold

形 *yamagata* chevron

⁸ 門 *sammon* main (two-story) temple gate

国 *yamaguni* mountainous province

房 *sambō* a mountain villa; a home in the mountains

河 *sanga, sanka* mountains and rivers; stronghold

幸 *yama (no) sachi, yama sachi* mountain food products

沿 *yamazo(i)* along the foot of a mountain

岳 *sangaku* mountains

林 *sanrin* mountains and forests; mountain forest

⁹ 峡 *yamagai, yamakai, sankyō* gorge, ravine, gap, vale

相 *sansō* the form of a mountain

海 *sankai* mountains and seas; land and sea

狩 *yamaga(ri)* hunting in the mountains

神 *yama (no) kami* god of the mountain; a wife

彦 *yamabiko* mountain echo; mountain god

荘 *sansō* mountain villa, mountain retreat

津浪 *yama tsunami* landslide

¹⁰ 師 *yamashi* speculator; adventurer; impostor, swindler; miner; lumber dealer

桜 *yamazakura* a wild cherry tree, prunus serrulata

脈 *sammyaku* mountain range

陰 *yama kage, san'in* shelter of the mountains; northern slopes

陵 *sanryō* mountains and hills; imperial tomb

容 *san'yō* the form of a mountain

高帽 *yamatakabō* derby hat

家 *sanka, yamaga* mountain home, chalet. *yama (no) ie* mountaineers' hut

¹¹ 道 *sandō* mountain pass, mountain path. *yama michi* mountain path

1439

野 *san'ya* fields and mountains
陽 *san'yō* the southern face of a mountain; the sunny slopes
勘 *yamakan* speculation in business
頂 *sanchō* mountain top
崩 *yamakuzure* landslide
盛 *yamamo(ri)* heap, pile; full measure
砦 *sansai* mountain fortifications; bandit den
猫 *yamaneko* wildcat, lynx
¹²越 *yamago(e), yamago(shi)* crossing a mountain
開 *yamabira(ki)* opening of the mountain-climbing season
焼 *yamaya(ki)* burning of dead grass
奥 *yamaoku* mountain recesses
嵐 *yama arashi* mountain storm
登 *yamanobo(ri)* mountain climbing
紫水明 *sanshi-suimei* scenic beauty
間 *sankan* in the mountains. *yamaai* glen, ravine, gorge
間僻地 *sankan-hekichi* deep mountain recesses
椒魚 *sanshō uo* salamander
¹³塊 *sankai* isolated mountains; mountain range
猿 *yamazaru* wild monkey; a rustic
稜 *sanryō* mountain ridge
続 *yamatsuzu(ki)* mountain chain
腹 *sampuku* hillside, mountainside
裾 *yama suso, yamazuso* foot of a mountain
賊 *sanzoku* mountain bandit
路 *yamaji, sanro* mountain road
際 *yamagiwa* mountain ridge, skyline, base of a mountain
群 *sangun* mountain range
塞 *sansai* mountain fortress; den of bandits
勢 *sansei* condition in the mountains; shape of the mountains
¹⁴鳴 *yamana(ri)* rumbling in the mountains. *yamana(rashi)* poplar
寨 *sansai* mountain fortification; bandit den
窩 *sanka* roving mountainous tribes; nomads; outcast tribe; ancient hermit people
¹⁵稼 *yamakasegi* work in the mountains
¹⁶懐 *yamabutokoro* mountain valley, heart of the mountains
積 *yamazu(mi), sanseki* mountainous

pile, big pile
¹⁹鯨 *yama kujira* wild-boar meat
霧 *yamagiri* fog in the mountains
麓 *sanroku* the foot of a mountain
²²嶺 *santen* mountain top
籠 *yamagomo(ri)* retiring in the mountains; retiring to a mountain temple

─────── 4 ───────

岐 $\frac{1447}{\text{J3474}}$ M7936 KI. *chimata* forking road; street; scene; quarters; arena, theater.
¹³路 *kiro* forked road, branch road, crossroad

─────── 5 ───────

岱 $\frac{1452}{\text{J4252}}$ M7997 TAI. DAI. name of mountain in China.

岨 $\frac{1456}{\text{J413b}}$ M7984 SO a rocky mountain.

岳 $\frac{1457}{\text{J3359}}$ M8001 GAKU. *take* peak, mountain.
⁴父 *gakufu* father-in-law

岬 $\frac{1458}{\text{J4c28}}$ M7992 KŌ. *misaki, saki* cape, spit, promontory.

岸 $\frac{1459}{\text{J3455f}}$ M8009 GAN. *kishi* bank, shore, coast, brink.
⁴辺 *kishibe* shore
⁶向 *kishimu(kō)* opposite bank
¹⁶頭 *gantō* top of a riverbank
壁 *gampeki* wharf, breakwater; steep coastal cliff

岡 $\frac{1460}{\text{J322c}}$ M7962 KŌ. *oka* hill, knoll, rising ground.
⁴辺 *okabe* vicinity of a hill
⁵目八目 *okamehachimoku* The onlooker sees better than the players.
⁹持 *okamo(chi)* wooden carrying box
¹¹惚 *okabore* unrequited love, secret affections
¹²場所 *okabasho* red-light district

岩 $\frac{1461}{\text{J3464}}$ M7985 GAN. *iwa* rock, crag; reef.

3
口
口
土
士
夂
夕
大
女
子
宀
寸
小
尢
尸
屮
【山】⁵
川
巛
工
己
巾
幺
广
廴
廾
弋
弓
ヨ
彑
彡
彳

3

口 口 土 士 夂 夂 夕 大 女 子 宀 寸 小 ⺌ 尢 尸 屮 [山] 川 巛 工 己 巾 干 幺 广 廴 廾 弋 弓 彐 彑 彡 彳

³ 山 *iwayama* rocky mountain (large or small)

⁵ 石 *ganseki* rock, crag

穴 *iwa ana* rocky cave

⁸ 苔 *iwagoke* rock moss

⁹ 屋 *iwaya* cavern, grotto, rocky cave

乗 *ganjō na* solid, firm, stout. *ganjō* excellent horse; 5-to-15-year-old horse

室 *iwamuro* stone hut

¹¹ 魚 *iwana* bull trout

清水 *iwa shimizu* spring water among rocks

¹² 棚 *iwatana* ledge

¹³ 塩 *gan'en, iwashio* rock salt

窟 *gankutsu* rocky cave

¹⁴ 層 *gansō* rock formation

¹⁷ 礁 *ganshō* reef

───── 6 ─────

B 峠 [1464 / J463d / M8068] （国字）*tōge* mountain pass; crisis, crest, climax.

¹¹ 道 *tōge michi* a road over a mountain pass

B 峡 [1465 / J362e / M8068'] Kyō gorge, ravine. *hazama* interval, interstice; ravine, glen; loophole (in a castle).

⁷ 谷 *kyōkoku* glen, ravine, gorge, canyon

¹² 湾 *kyōwan* fjord

───── 7 ─────

B 峨 [1471 / J3265 / M8071] Ga high mountain.

¹⁰ 峨 *gaga(taru)* rugged, craggy

B 峰 [1473 / J4a76 / M8094] 峯 [1474 / J4a77 / M8093] Hō. *mine, ne* peak, summit, top; back (of a sword).

⁵ 打 *mineu(chi)* striking with the back of a sword

¹⁰ 峰 *minemine* peaks

¹³ 続 *minetsuzu(ki)* succession of peaks

B 峻 [1475 / J3d54 / M8116] Shun high; steep.

⁷ 拒 *shunkyo* positive refusal

別 *shumbetsu* sharp distinction

¹⁰ 烈 *shunretsu na* unrelenting, severity, sternness

¹⁷ 厳 *shungen na* strict, harsh, severe

A 島 [1476 / J4567 / M8108] 嶋 [1503 / J4568 / M8434] Tō *shima* island.

⁴ 内 *tōnai* on the island

⁵ 民 *tōmin* islanders

⁶ 伝 *shimazuta(i)* island-hopping

⁸ 育 *shimasoda(chi)* brought up on an island

国 *shimaguni, tōgoku* island country

¹⁰ 流 *shimanaga(shi)* exile, banishment

破 *shimayabu(ri)* escaping from an island exile

陰 *shimakage* the other side of the island

島 *shimajima* islands

¹⁶ 嶼 *tōsho* islands

───── 8 ─────

B 崎 [1485 / J3a6a / M8169] Ki steep. *misaki, saki* cape, spit, promontory.

B 崖 [1488 / J3333 / M8180] Gai. *gake* cliff, bluff, precipice.

¹¹ 崩 *gakekuzu(re)* landslide

B 崇 [1490 / J3f72 / M8152] Sū, Shū high. *aga(meru)* respect, revere, adore, worship.

⁴ 仏 *sūbutsu* revering the Buddhas

⁸ 拝 *sūhai* worship; admiration, adoration; cult

拝者 *sūhaisha* worshiper, admirer, idolater, devotee

¹⁰ 高 *sūkō na* lofty, noble, sublime

¹² 敬 *sūkei* reverence, adoration, veneration

B 崩 [1491 / J4a78 / M8212] Hō. *hō(jiru), hō(zuru)* die. *kuzu(su)* demolish, destroy; level (a hill); crumble (bread); change (money); simplify; put in disorder; cut (prices). *kuzu(reru)* crumble, collapse, cave in, be destroyed, get out of shape; be routed; worsen (weather). *kuzu(shi)* simplified form. -*kuzu(re)* delinquent, degenerate.

⁵ 去 *kuzu(re)-sa(ru)* collapse, crumble away

⁶ 字 *kuzu(shi)ji* abbreviated character

¹⁰ 書 *kuzu(shi)ga(ki)* grass-hand penmanship

¹² 御 *hōgyo* demise, death of an emperor

落 *kuzu(re)-o(chiru)* fall down flat; dissolve. *hōraku* collapse, cave-in; slump, crash, heavy decline
15 潰 *hōkai* collapse, cave-in
16 壊 *hōkai* collapse, cave-in

─────── 9 ───────

嵐 1496 | J4d72 | M8289 RAN. *arashi* storm, tempest.

─────── 10 ───────

嵯 1500 | J3a37 | M8363 SA. SHI craggy; steeply towering mountain; boulders scattered on mountain.

嵩 1502 | J3f73 | M8348 SŪ. *kō(zuru), kō(jiru)* be aggravated, grow worse. *kasa(mu)* grow bulky, rise, swell, increase in volume; mount up. *kasa* bulk, volume, quantity, size.
10 高 *kasadaka na* bulky, voluminous; high-handed
11 張 *kasaba(ru)* be bulky

─────── 11 ───────

嶋 1503 | J4568 | M8434 See 島 1476.

─────── 14 ───────

嶺 1517 | J4e66 | M8553 REI. RYŌ. *mine, ne* peak, summit, top; back (of a sword).

─────── 17 ───────

巌 1521 | J3460 | M8624' GAN. *iwa* rock, crag, reef. *iwao* (massive) rock.

═══════ RAD. 川 47 ═══════

Kawa river or *sambon kawa* 3-stroke "river" (to distinguish it from the 8-stroke river 河). Variant: 巛 *magari kawa* curving "river." Nickname: River.

A 川 1526 | J406e | M8673 SEN. *kawa* river, stream, brook.
3 口 *kawaguchi* mouth of a river
下 *kawashimo* downstream. *kawakuda(ri)* going down a river
上 *kawakami* upper stream; upstream. *kawanobo(ri)* going up a river
4 止 *kawado(me)* no ferry service
辺 *kawabe* riverside
5 尻 *kawajiri* river mouth; lower stream
6 向 *kawamuka(i), kawamu(kō)* the opposite side of the river
伝 *kawazuta(i) ni* along the river
7 床 *kawadoko, kawatoko* riverbed
8 沿 *kawazo(i) ni* along the river
岸 *kawagishi* riverbank
9 面 *kawazura, kawamo, kawa(no)omo* river surface
風 *kawa kaze* river breeze
柳 *kawa yanagi* purple willow, river willow. *senryū* comic haiku poem
10 原 *kawara, kawahara* dry riverbed; river beach
11 魚 *kawauo, kawazakana* river fish
遊 *kawaaso(bi)* boating, rowing
船 *kawabune, kawa fune* river boat, barge, ferry
12 開 *kawabira(ki)* river festival
幅 *kawa haba* river width
渡 *kawawata(shi)* crossing a river
筋 *kawa suji* river course
越 *kawago(e), kawago(shi)* crossing a river
14 端 *kawabata* riverside
15 縁 *kawabuchi, kawaberi* riverside

─────── 2 ───────

B 巡 1528 | J3d64 | M8680 JUN going around; circumference. *megu(ru)* go around; in connection with,

口 口 土 士 夂 夊 夕 大 女 子 宀 寸 小 丬 尢 尸 屮 山【川】巛 工 己 巾 干 幺 广 廴 廾 弋 弓 ヨ 彑 彡 彳

3

口 口 土 士 夂 夕 大 女 子 宀 寸 小 ⺌ 尢 尸 屮 山 【川】 巛 工 己 巾 干 幺 广 廴 廾 弋 弓 ヨ 彑 彡 彳

concering. *megu(ri)* girth, circumference; tour, round, pilgrimage; flow, circulation; menstruation. *megu(rasu)* surround, make (someone) go around. *(o)mawa(ri)san* policeman.

⁵礼 *junrei* pilgrimage; pilgrim
礼者 *junreisha* pilgrim
⁶合 *megu(ri)-a(u)* meet by chance, come across
回 *junkai* tour, round, patrol
⁸拝 *jumpai* circuit pilgrimage
幸 *junkō* imperial tour
歩 *megu(ri)-aru(ku)* walk around, travel around
⁹洋艦 *jun'yōkan* (navy) cruiser
査 *junsa* police, patrolman
¹⁰航 *junkō* cruise; cruising
航船 *junkōsen* cruiser
¹¹遊 *jun'yū* tour
視 *junshi* inspection tour

¹³業 *jungyō* provincial tour
¹⁴歴 *junreki* tour, trip
察 *junsatsu* patrol, inspection round; visitation
¹⁵閲 *jun'etsu* tour of inspection
¹⁶覧 *junran* tour, sightseeing
²²邏 *junra* patrol, round, beat

─────────── **3** ───────────

A 州 $\frac{1529}{\text{J3d23}}$ SHŪ province, state; continent. Su sandbar, shallows.

⁵立 *shūritsu* state-owned, state-operated
⁸知事 *shūchiji* state or provincial governor
¹⁴境 *shūkyō* state boundary, provincial boundary

████ RAD. 工 48 ████

E (the katakana). At left: 工 *takumi hen* (left-side "carpenter's square").
Nickname: *Kana E.*

A 工 $\frac{1532}{\text{J3929}}$ KU. Kō artisan, mechanic; manufacture; work.
takumi artisan, mechanic; carpenter.
taku(mu) plan; scheme.

⁴夫 *kufū* device, invention, scheme, means. *kōfu* coolie, workman, laborer
⁶匠 *kōshō* mechanic, artisan, craftsman
合 *guai, guwai* fitness, order, condition; way, style; convenience; decency, propriety; state of health; situation; arrangements
⁷兵 *kōhei* army engineers
作 *kōsaku* building, engineering; handicraft; maneuvering (in politics)
作物 *kōsakubutsu* building; manufactured articles
作機械 *kōsaku kikai* machine tools
芸 *kōgei* industrial arts, artistic handicraft
芸品 *kōgeihin* craft object, art work, craft products
芸美術 *kōgei bijutsu* applied fine art
⁸房 *kōbō* (artisan's) studio
具 *kōgu* tool, implement

学 *kōgaku* engineering
事 *kōji* construction
事中 *kōjichū* under construction
事場 *kōjiba* construction site
⁹面 *kumen* contriving, managing, raising (funds); circumstances, pecuniary status
科 *kōka* engineering course
¹⁰員 *kōin* factory worker, artisan
¹¹商 *kōshō* industry and commerce; workmen and businessmen
務店 *kōmuten* engineering firm
¹²程 *kōtei* process; work progress
費 *kōhi* construction costs
場 *kōjō, kōba* factory, workshop, mill
¹³賃 *kōchin* wages, pay, labor cost
業 *kōgyō* industry
業大学 *kōgyō daigaku* technical college
業化 *kōgyōka* industrialization
業地帯 *kōgyō chitai* industrial area
業国 *kōgyōkoku* industrial nation
¹⁵廠 *kōshō* arsenal

─────────── **2** ───────────

巧 ⸺ 1533 / J392a / M8721 ⸺ Kō. *taku(mi) na* skilled. *taku(manai)*, *taku(manu)* artless, natural, unintentional. *taku(mi)* skill, ingenuity.

⁷ 妙 *kōmyō* skill, cleverness, ingenuity

言令色 *kōgen-reishoku* ingratiating geniality

⁸ 拙 *kōsetsu* tact, skill, performance, workmanship

知 *kōchi* cleverness, tact

者 *kōsha* cleverness, skill, tact

¹² 智 *kōchi* cleverness, tact

¹⁶ 緻 *kōchi na* elaborate, finely wrought

巨 ⸺ 1534 / J3570 / M8722 ⸺ KYO. KO. *ōki(i)*, *ōi(naru)* big, large, great.

² 人 *kyojin* giant; great person

³ 万 *kyoman* huge fortune, millions

大 *kyodai na* huge, enormous

⁵ 石 *kyoseki* megalith

⁶ 匠 *kyoshō* master, masterhand, maestro

⁷ 体 *kyotai* large build

利 *kyori* huge profit

⁸ 刹 *kyosatsu* large temple

岩 *kyogan* huge rock, crag

歩 *kyoho* long strides

⁹ 星 *kyosei* giant sun; great man, big shot

¹¹ 細 *kyosai* large and small matters; particulars, details. *kosai* greatness and smallness; details, particulars, circumstances

視的 *kyoshiteki* macroscopic

¹² 富 *kyofu* great riches

費 *kyohi* great cost

¹³ 漢 *kyokan* giant

¹⁴ 魁 *kyokai* ringleader, chief

像 *kyozō* huge image

¹⁶ 頭 *kyotō* leader, magnate, big name

¹⁸ 額 *kyogaku* enormous sum

左 ⸺ 1535 / J3a38 / M8720 ⸺ SA left; the following. *hidari* left; the left; leftist. *hidari suru* turn to the left.

⁴ 手 *hidarite* left hand; the left

方 *sahō* the left

辺 *sahen* left side

⁵ 右 *sayū suru* command, dominate, control, sway. *sayū* left and right; one's side; one's attendants. *tokō* this or that. *sau* left and right; news; condition; criticism; command. *to(ni)kaku(ni)* anyway. *to(mo)kaku*

(mo), *to(mo)kaku* anyhow, in any case. *hidari-migi* left and right

⁶ 回 *hidarimawa(ri)* counterclockwise

向 *hidarimu(ki)* turning to the left

団扇 *hidari uchiwa* living in comfort

⁷ 折 *sasetsu suru* turn to the left

利 *hidarikiki* left-handedness; left-hander; saké drinker. *hidarigitcho* left-handedness; left-hander

⁸ 岸 *sagan* left bank (of a river)

官 *sakan, shakan* plasterer

⁹ 派 *saha* left wing; left faction; leftist

前 *hidarimae* the wrong way, folding left side of a kimono under the right; adversity. *sazen* front of left field

巻 *hidarima(ki)* counterclockwise; perverse; mentally off

¹⁰ 記 *saki* the following

書 *hidariga(ki)* writing from the left

¹¹ 眼 *sagan* left eye

舷 *sagen* port, port side

寄 *hidariyo(ri)* leaning toward the left; leftist

側 *hidarigawa, sasoku* left side; the left

側通行 *hidarigawa tsūkō* Keep to the Left

¹² 程 *sahodo* so much, much, very

¹³ 傾 *sakei* leftist, radical, inclination to the left

¹⁴ 遷 *sasen* demotion, degradation

様 *sayō* such, like that; yes, indeed; well, let me see. *sayo(nara), sayō(nara)* goodbye. *sonna* that kind of. *hidarizama* wicked way

端 *satan* left edge; left end; left lane

¹⁷ 翼 *sayoku* left flank; left wing, leftist, radical movement; left field

⸺ **7** ⸺

差 ⸺ 1537 / J3a39 / M8732 ⸺ SHI, SA difference, variation; discrepancy; margin; balance; remainder (in subtraction). *sa(su)* vt raise (the hands); stretch out (the hands in dancing); put up (an umbrella); carry (on the shoulder); build (a hut); stretch (a rope); graft (trees); carry (in the belt); lift up; offer. *vi* (the sun) shines; appear on the surface. *su(shi)* sharpened tube for testing rice in bags; ruler (for measuring); face to face;

3

口
口
土
士
夂
夂
夕
大
女
子
宀
寸
小
⺌
尢
尸
屮
川
巛
7 [工]
已
巾
干
幺
广
廴
廾
弋
弓
彐
彑
彡
彳

hindrance; sharing a load. *sa(shi)de* between two persons. *sa(shi)-* emphatic verbal prefix.

² 入 *sa(shi)-i(reru)* insert; send to a prisoner. *sa(shi)i(re)* insertion; something sent to a prisoner

³ 上 *sa(shi)-a(geru)* lift up, raise; give, present, offer; let (a person) have

⁴ 止 *sa(shi)-to(meru)* prohibit, forbid, ban

込 *sa(shi)-ko(mu)* insert, thrust in; flow into; plug in; have a sharp pain. *sashiko(mi)* thrusting; insertion; socket; plug; cap; sharp pain

支 *sa(shi)-tsuka(eru)* be hindered, be interrupted, be prevented; be engaged; suffer inconvenience, have difficulty (in doing); be unable to; be hard up. *sa(shi)tsuka(e)* hindrance, impediment, interference, interruption; previous engagement

引 *sa(shi)-hi(ku), sa(p)pi(ku)* deduct. *sashihi(ki)* deduction, subtraction; balance; ebb and flow, rise and fall; intermittence

⁵ 出 *sa(shi)-da(su), sa(shi)-ida(su)* present, tender; send in (a card); produce (evidence); file (a petition); send; forward; reach out; extend; mail (a letter). *sa(shi)de(gamashii)* forward, intrusive, impertinent. *sa(shi)-de(ru)* push oneself forward. *sa(shi)ide, sa(shi)de* impertinence

出人 *sashidashinin* sender; addresser

⁶ 回 *sa(shi)-mawa(su)* send (a car) around

向 *sa(shi)-mu(keru)* send around; direct; turn (the light) toward; cover (with a gun). *sashimu(ki)* for the time being. *sashimuka(i)* face to face

当 *sa(shi)ata(ri)* for the time being. *sa(shi)-ata(ru)* happen to meet; (the sun) shines in

⁷ 戻 *sa(shi)-modo(su)* send back, refer back

迫 *sa(shi)-sema(ru)* be imminent, be impending

別 *sabetsu* discrimination, distinction, differentiation

別的 *sabetsuteki* discriminatory

⁸ 金 *sakin, sa(shi)kin* difference; margin; balance. *sa(shi)gane* carpenter's square; metal foot rule; tip; suggestion; inspiration; instigation

押 *sa(shi)-osa(eru)* seize, attach, garnishee, impound

¹⁰ 益 *saeki* marginal profit

配 *sahai* conduct of business; management; agency, agent

¹¹ 控 *sa(shi)-hika(eru)* be temperate, use moderation; withhold, refrain from

許 *sa(shi)-yuru(su)* permit, approve; authorize; acknowledge; confide in; forgive, pardon; release; acquit; overlook

異 *sai* difference, disparity

掛 *sa(shi)-ka(keru)* hold (an umbrella) over (someone). *sa(shi)-ka(karu)* approach, come near, arrive, hang over, overhang; be urgent, be imminent; be on the point of; be covered; pass by. *sa(shi)ka(ke)* penthouse, lean-to

¹² 遣 *saken suru* dispatch

渡 *sa(shi)-wata(ru)* cross in a boat. *sa(shi)wata(shi)* diameter, caliber, distance across

替 *sa(shi)-ka(eru)* replace, substitute, change

¹³ 詰 *sa(shi)zu(me)* for the time being

障 *sa(shi)-sawa(ru)* be obstructed, be hindered. *sa(shi)sawa(ri)* obstacle, hindrance; offense

置 *sa(shi)-o(ku)* leave, let alone; ignore, neglect, slight

¹⁵ 潮 *sa(shi)shio, sa(shi)jio* rising tide

¹⁸ 額 *sagaku* balance, difference, margin

RAD. 己 49

Onore self. Variants: 已 *sude ni* already, 巳 *mi* snake. Nickname: Snake.

己 $\frac{1538}{\substack{J4c26 \\ M8744}}$ SHI. *mi* 9–11 a.m.; sixth zodiac sign; serpent.

A 己 $\frac{1540}{\substack{J384a \\ M8742}}$ KO. KI F, sixth. *onore*, *ono* oneself, myself,

yourself. *ono(gajishi)* as one pleases.
tsuchinoto sixth calendar sign.

————— **1** —————

巴 _{1541 J4743 M8745} HA. *tomoe* huge comma design.

————— **6** —————

巷 _{1543 J392b M-X} Kō. *chimata* forking road; stree; scene; quarters; arena, theater.
¹² 間 *kōkan* the world
¹⁴ 説 *kōsetsu* rumor, talk of the town

巻 _{1545 J342c M8759ʹ} A KEN, KAN volume, book, part; reel. *ma(ku)* roll up; wind, coil; tie around; wind up. *maki* roll (of silk); volume, book; winding (of a clock).
³ 上 *ma(ki)-a(geru) vt* roll up; hoist, hoist, heave up; take away, rob; blow up (dust). *ma(ki)-a(garu) vi* curl up into the air (smoke); roll up. *ma(ki)a(ge)* lifting, hoisting
⁴ 尺 *makijaku* measuring tape
込 *ma(ki)-ko(mu) vt* roll up, enfold; engulf, swallow up, drag into, involve in
⁵ 付 *ma(ki)-tsu(keru)* wind or tie around, coil. *ma(ki)-tsu(ku)* coil or wind

around; twist about
末 *kammatsu* end of a book
⁶ 舌 *ma(ki)jita* trill, rolling the tongue
返 *makikae(shi)* bickering; give and take; fighting back and forth
⁸ 物 *makimono* a (horizontal) scroll
直 *ma(ki)nao(shi)* rebinding (a scroll); rewinding
⁹ 狩 *ma(ki)ga(ri)* grand hunt
¹⁰ 起 *ma(ki)-o(kosu)* stir up
紙 *makigami* rolled paper
¹¹ 添 *ma(ki)zo(e)* involvement, entanglement
¹² 雲 *ma(ki)gumo, ken'un* cirrus clouds
軸 *ma(ki)jiku* scroll
揚 *ma(ki)-a(geru) vt* roll up; hoist, heave up; take away, rob; blow up (dust). *ma(ki)-a(garu) vi* curl up into the air (smoke); roll up. *ma(ki)a(ge)* lifting, hoisting
揚機 *ma(ki)a(ge)ki* hoist, winch, windlass
¹³ 煙草 *ma(ki)tabako* cigarette
¹⁴ 層雲 *kensōun* cirro-stratus clouds
¹⁶ 頭 *kantō* beginning of a book
積雲 *kensekiun* cirro-cumulus clouds
¹⁷ 鮨 *ma(ki)zushi* sushi rolled in seaweed or egg-omelet strips

————— **9** —————

巽 _{1546 J4327 M8765} Son. *tatsumi* southeast.

—————— **RAD.** 巾 **50** ——————

Haba width or *kin, kire* cloth. At left: *haba hen* or *kimben*. Nickname: Cloth.

巾 _{1547 J3652 M8771} KIN towel. *haba* width, breadth, range; difference (in price); power, influence.
⁴ 木 *habaki* baseboard
⁵ 広 *hababiro no* wider than usual
¹² 着 *kinchaku* purse, money bag

————— **2** —————

布 _{1548 J495b M8778} A Ho. FU. *nuno* cloth.
³ 巾 *fukin* dish cloth; napkin
⁴ 切 *nunogi(re)* piece of cloth

⁵ 目 *nunome* texture
石 *fuseki* arrange stones (in a *go* game); place party members in strategic government positions
令 *furei* official notice, proclamation, announcement
⁶ 団 *futon* bedding, mattress
地 *nunoji* cloth
⁷ 局 *fukyoku* arrangement, composition
告 *fukoku* proclamation, declaration, notification, decree, edict
⁹ 施 *fuse* alms, charity; temple offering

口
口
土
士
夂
夊
夕
大
女
子
宀
寸
小
⺌
尢
尸
屮
山
川
巛
工
己
[²巾]
干
幺
广
廴
廾
弋
弓
彐
彑
彡
彳

3

陣 *fujin* lineup. *fujin suru* take up a position

¹¹ 袋 *Hotei* a god of fortune
教 *fukyō* missionary work, propaganda, proselytism
¹³ 置 *fuchi* arrangement, composition, design

市 $\frac{1549}{\substack{J3b54 \\ M8775}}$ A SHI city, town; market. *ichi* market; fair.

⁴ 日 *ichibi* market day
区 *shiku* municipal district; streets
中 *shichū* in the city
内 *shinai* the city, within the city limits
井 *shisei* the street; the town
⁵ 庁 *shichō* municipal office
立 *shiritsu* municipal, city
外 *shigai* outside the city limits; suburbs
民 *shimin* citizen, townspeople
民権 *shiminken* citizenship
⁶ 会 *shikai* city council
会議員 *shikai giin* city councilman
有 *shiyū* owned by the city
⁷ 役所 *shiyakusho* city hall
町村 *shichōson* cities, towns, and villages; municipalities
⁸ 長 *shichō* mayor
価 *shika* market price, current price
松 *ichimatsu* checked (pattern)
況 *shikyō* market conditions
制 *shisei* municipal organization, municipality
⁹ 政 *shisei* municipal government
¹¹ 販 *shihan* marketing
¹² 場 *ichiba, shijō* market
費 *shihi* municipal expenditure
営 *shiei* municipal operation
街地 *shigaichi* town areas
¹³ 電 *shiden* municipal railway; city streetcar
²⁰ 議 *shigi* city assemblyman

——— **3** ———

帆 $\frac{1551}{\substack{J4841 \\ M8787}}$ B HAN. *ho* sail.

⁵ 布 *honuno, hampu* sailcloth, canvas
立貝 *hotategai* scallop (shell)
⁷ 走 *hobashi(ru)* sail, be under sail. *hansō* sailing; gliding
⁹ 柱 *hobashira* mast
前船 *homaesen* sailing vessel

¹⁰ 桁 *hogeta* (sail) boom, yard
¹¹ 船 *hansen, hobune* sailing vessel
掛船 *hoka(ke)bune* sailboat

——— **4** ———

希 $\frac{1553}{\substack{J3475 \\ M8813}}$ A KI. KE. -*Gi*- Greece. *koinega(u)* beg, request, pray, beseech; hope, desire. *mare na* rare, few, phenomenal. *ki*- dilute (acid).

⁴ 少 *kishō* scarcity
⁵ 代 *kidai, kitai* uncommon, remarkable, matchless
⁶ 有 *keu* rare, extraordinary
⁷ 求 *kikyū suru* aspire to, seek, demand, ask for
¹¹ 釈 *kishaku* dilution
望 *kibō* hope, desire, aspiration, anticipation; request
望者 *kibōsha* candidate, applicant, aspirant, one who desires
望的観測 *kibōteki kansoku* wishful thinking
¹⁶ 薄 *kihaku na* thin, dilute, sparse, weak

——— **5** ———

帖 $\frac{1558}{\substack{J4421 \\ M8849}}$ CHŌ. JŌ quire (of paper); bundle of seaweed; screen counter; notebook. Also used for 畳 3763.

⁹ 面 *chōmen* notebook
面面 *chōmenzura* accounts; appearance
¹⁹ 簿 *chōbo* account book

——— **6** ———

帥 $\frac{1559}{\substack{J3f63 \\ M8886}}$ B SOCHI, SOTSU, SHUTSU, SUI leading (troops). *sotsu, sochi* (ancient) governor.

帝 $\frac{1560}{\substack{J446b \\ M8865}}$ B TEI emperor; the god of heaven; the creator. *mikado* emperor (of Japan).

⁴ 王 *teiō* sovereign, emperor
王切開術 *teiō sekkaijutsu* Caesarian section
⁷ 位 *teii* the throne, the crown
⁸ 制 *teisei* imperial government, imperialism
京 *teikyō* the capital
国 *teikoku* empire; imperial
国主義 *teikoku shugi* imperialism

⁹ 冠 *teikan* imperial crown, diadem
室 *teishitsu* Imperial Family; Imperial Household
¹⁰ 都 *teito* imperial capital
¹³ 業 *teigyō* imperial task

───────── 7 ─────────

席 ‹1561 / J404a / M8926› SEKI seat; mat; a place, room, occasion. *mushiro* straw mat, matting.

³ 上 *sekijō* in the seat, in the assembly. *sekijō de* at the meeting, on the occasion
⁵ 代 *sekidai* room charge; cover charge; admission fee, price of a seat
⁶ 次 *sekiji* seating order, precedence
⁹ 亭 *sekitei* variety hall, storytellers' hall, music hall, vaudeville
巻 *sekken suru* conquer everything
¹⁰ 料 *sekiryō* room charge; cover charge; admission fee, price of a seat
¹¹ 捲 *sekken suru* sweep over and completely subdue
¹² 順 *sekijun* seating order, precedence
貸 *sekiga(shi)* renting seats

師 ‹1562 / J3b55 / M8916› SHI teacher, master; exemplary person; army; war.

⁴ 父 *shifu* fatherly master
⁶ 匠 *shishō* master, teacher
団 *shidan* army division
⁷ 走 *shiwasu, shihasu* 12th lunar month, December
弟 *shitei* teacher and student
⁸ 事 *shiji suru* study under; look up to; apprentice oneself to
¹⁵ 範 *shihan* model; teacher; fencing teacher
範学校 *shihan gakkō* normal school

帯 ‹1563 / J4253 / M8929› TAI belt; zone. *obi* obi, belt, sash, girdle, band; belting. *obi(ru), tai(suru)* wear (at the belt), carry, be armed with; be entrusted with; assume, take on (the character of), be tinged with; gird up (one's loins). *-tai* zone, region.

² 刀 *taitō* the sword at one's side
⁴ 止 *obidome* obi clip, obi band

⁵ 皮 *obikawa* leather belt
⁶ 同 *taidō suru* be accompanied by
地 *obiji* sash material, obi cloth
⁷ 状 *obijō* long narrow strip
⁸ 金 *obigane* banding iron
⁹ 革 *obikawa* leather belt
¹⁰ 剣 *taiken* sword at one's side
¹³ 鉄 *obitetsu* band iron
電 *taiden* electric charge
¹⁶ 鋼 *obikō* band steel, hoop
鋸 *obi nokogiri, obi noko* band saw

帰 ‹1564 / J3522 / M8930› KI. *kae(ru)* return; take one's leave; come again; come around (time). *kae(su)* send (someone) back. *ki(suru)* come to, arrive at, result in, end in, lead to; belong to, ascribe to; put down to; impute; be due to; fall into (one's power); (his blood) be upon (him). *kae(ri)* return; return trip. *kae(rigake) ni, kae(rishina) ni, kae(rusa) ni* on returning. *(o)kae(ri)nasai* welcome home, welcome back.

¹ 一 *kiitsu* unity, unification. *kiitsu suru* be united into one, be reduced to one
⁴ 心 *kishin* longing for home
支度 *kae(ri)jitaku* preparations to return
化 *kika* naturalization
⁶ 任 *kinin* returning to one's post
帆 *kihan* returning sailing ship
宅 *kitaku* homecoming, returning home
⁷ 来 *kirai* coming back
⁸ 国 *kikoku* returning to one's country
依 *kie* conversion. *kie suru* believe (in Buddhism)
服 *kifuku* surrender, submission
京 *kikyō, kikei* returning to the capital
参 *kisan* returning to a former service
⁹ 途 *kito* homeward journey
省 *kisei* homecoming
¹⁰ 校 *kikō suru* return to school
航 *kikō* homeward passage
郷 *kikyō* returning home
納 *kinō* induction (in argumentation)
納的 *kinōteki* inductive
納法 *kinōhō* inductive method
¹¹ 道 *kae(ri)michi* the way back, return trip
隊 *kitai* returning to one's unit
巣本能 *kisō honnō* homing instinct
¹² 属 *kizoku suru* revert to, be returned to, be restored to
順 *kijun* submission, return to allegiance

口口土士夂夊夕大女子宀寸小⺌尢尸屮山川巛工己【巾】⁷干幺广廴廾弋弓彐彑彡彳

50

口口土夂夊夕大女子宀寸小⺌尢尸⺍山川巛工己[巾]干幺广廴廾弋弓彐彡彳

3

港 *kikō suru* return to port

結 *kiketsu* conclusion, end, result

着 *kichaku* return, conclusion

朝 *kichō* returning from abroad

¹³路 *kiro* homeward journey, return circuit. *kae(ri)michi* the way back, return trip

農 *kinō* going back to the soil

¹⁵還 *kikan* return, repatriation; feedback

¹⁷趨 *kishu* conclusion. *kisū* trend, tendency; direction

──────────── **8** ────────────

帳 1568 / J4422 / M8939 CHŌ notebook; account book; register; album; curtain dividing a room. *tobari* curtain.

A

⁴元 *chōmoto* manager, promoter, bookmaker

⁵尻 *chōjiri* footings, account balance

⁶合 *chōa(i)* balance of accounts; keeping accounts; comparison

⁹面 *chōmen* notebook, account book, register

¹⁰消 *chōke(shi)* cancellation, writing off

¹²場 *chōba* counter, desk; office; jinricksha pool

¹⁹簿 *chōbo* account book, register

常 1569 / J3e6f / M8955 JŌ. SHŌ. *tsune* normal conditions, regular course of events; one's habit. *tsune no* ordinary, normal, continual. *tsune ni* always, continually. *towa* eternity. *tada* ordinarily. *tsune(naranu)* in vain. *toko-* ever-, endless.

A

⁴日頃 *tsunehigoro* always, usually

⁵世国 *tokoyo (no) kuni* distant country; heaven; hades

用 *jōyō* common use; addition

⁶会 *jōkai* regular meeting

任委員 *jōnin iin* standing committee

⁷住 *jōjū* constancy, continuity; always; usually

住坐臥 *jōjūzaga ni* always

⁸例 *jōrei* custom, usual practice

法 *jōhō* usual method

夜灯 *jōyatō* light kept lit through the night

⁹食 *jōshoku* daily diet, staple food

連 *jōren* regular companions, regular customers, frequenters, patrons

軌 *jōki* proper course; beaten track

客 *jōkyaku* regular customer; frequent visitor

春 *tokoharu* eternal spring

¹⁰時 *jōji* usually, habitually, ordinarily

夏 *tokonatsu* perennial summer; a wild pink (flower)

套手段 *jōtō shudan* old trick, usual practice, regular means

套句 *jōtōku* stock phrase

¹¹道 *jōdō* ordinary way, universal practice

宿 *jōyado* regular hotel

常 *tsunezune* always, usually

務委員会 *jōmu iinkai* executive committee

務取締役 *jōmu torishimariyaku* executive director

設 *jōsetsu* permanent; standing (committee)

習 *jōshū* usage, custom, common practice

習犯 *jōshūhan* habitual crime; habitual criminal

¹²雇 *jōyatoi* regular employee

温 *jōon* normal temperature

勤 *jōkin no* full-time (official)

備 *jōbi no* standing, permanent, regular

備薬 *jōbiyaku* household remedy

¹⁴態 *jōtai* normalcy

緑樹 *jōryokuju* evergreen tree

¹⁵駐 *jōchū* staying permanently

¹⁹識 *jōshiki* common sense

識的 *jōshikiteki* sensible, practical

──────────── **9** ────────────

帽 1573 / J4b39 / M8971 BŌ cap, headgear.

B

³子 *bōshi* cap, hat, headgear

幅 1574 / J497d / M8995 FUKU hanging scroll, picture; width; counter for scrolls. *haba* width, breadth, range; difference (in price); power, influence.

B

⁵広 *hababiro* wide width; wide obi

¹⁰員 *fukuin* width, beam, breadth, extend

¹³跳 *habato(bi)* broad jump

──────────── **10** ────────────

幌 1577 / J4b5a / M9022 KŌ. *horo* awning, hood, (folding) top. *tobari* curtain.

¹⁰ 馬車 *horo basha* covered wagon, covered carriage

A 幕 | 1578 / J4b6b / M9051 | BAKU, MAKU curtain; bunting; an act (in a play); end; first rank (in sumo); a matter, a case. *tobari* curtain.

³ 下 *bakka* shogun; shogun's staff; vassal, feudatory, follower. *makushita* second-class Japanese wrestler
⁴ 切 *makugi(re)* fall of the curtain
内 *makuuchi* first-class wrestler. *maku(no)uchi* first-class wrestler. *maku(no)uchi* a Japanese lunch
⁵ 末 *bakumatsu* latter days of the Tokugawas
⁶ 臣 *bakushin* shogun's vassal
⁸ 府 *bakufu* shogunate

舎 *bakusha* barracks; camp
¹² 間 *makuai* interval between acts
開 *makuaki* opening of a play; beginning
¹⁰ 僚 *bakuryō* staff; staff officer; brain trust; brain truster; adviser

——— 12 ———

幡 | 1584 / J4828 / M9086 | HAN. HON. *hata* flag.

B 幣 | 1585 / J4a3e / M9088 | HEI Shinto zigzag paper offerings; bad habit; humble prefix; gift. *nusa* Shinto offerings of cloth, rope, or cut paper.

⁸ 制 *heisei* monetary system
帛 *heihaku* Shinto offerings of cloth or cut paper

■■■■■■■ RAD. 干 51 ■■■■■■■

Kan dry or *ichi-jū* (*ichi* "one" plus *jū* "ten"). Nickname: One Ten.

A 干 | 1589 / J3433 / M9165 | KAN. *hi(ru)* parch, get dry; ebb, recede. *ho(su)* vt dry; desiccate; drain (off); drink up; dry up. *tate* shield. *hidaru(i)* hungry.

³ 上 *hiaga(ru)* dry up, parch; ebb away
⁴ 戈 *kanka* shield and spear; weapons; war
支 *kanshi* sexagenary cycle
天 *kanten* drought, dry weather
⁵ 犯 *kampan* infringement, violation
⁶ 肉 *ho(shi)niku* dried meat, pemmican
⁸ 固 *ho(shi)-kata(meru)* vt *ho(shi)-kata(maru)* vi dry up, harden by drying. *hi-kata(maru)* vi dry and harden
物 *himono, karamono* dried fish. *ho(shi)mono* laundry on the line
拓 *kantaku suru* reclaim by drainage
拓地 *kantakuchi* reclaimed land
⁹ 柿 *ho(shi)gaki* dried persimmons
草 *ho(shi)gusa, hoshikusa, kansō* hay, dry grass
¹⁰ 害 *kangai* drought damage
¹¹ 魚 *hiuo, kangyo, hizakana, ho(shi)uo, ho(shi)zakana* dried fish
涸 *hi-kara(biru)* vi completely dry up. *ho(shi)-ka(rasu)* vt dry up (a river)

渉 *kanshō* interference, intervention
乾 *hiboshi ni suru* vt starve to death. *hiboshi ni na(ru)* vi starve to death
菓子 *higashi* candy; cookies
¹² 場 *ho(shi)ba* drying ground
満 *kamman* ebb and flow, tide
飯 *hoshii* cooked and dried (for preservation) rice
¹⁵ 魃 *kambatsu* drought
潮 *kanchō, hikishio, hishio* ebb tide
潟 *higata, hikata* tideland; dry beach

——— 2 ———

A 平 | 1590 / J4a3f / M9167 | HYŌ. BYŌ. HEI level, peaceful. *taira(geru)* subjugate; put down (trouble); consume (food), eat up. *taira(gu)* be suppressed. *hei(tsukubaru)* make a deep bow. *hira ni* earnestly, humbly *hira(tai)* flat, even, level; simple, plain. *tai(ra) na* flat, smooth; calm; a plain; sitting tailor fashion. *tai(rakana)* level; just; peaceful. *hira-* common, ordinary.

³ 凡 *heibon na* common, commonplace, ordinary, mediocre
⁴ 日 *heijitsu* weekday, ordinary days

口 口 土 士 夂 夊 夕 大 女 子 宀 寸 小 ⺌ 尢 尸 屮 山 川 巛 工 己 巾 干 幺 广 廴 廾 弋 弓 彐 彑 彡 彳

3

口 口 土 士 夂 夕 大 女 子 宀 寸 小 ⺌ 尢 尸 屮 山 川 巛 工 己 巾 [干] 幺 广 廴 廾 弋 弓 彐 彑 彡 彳

氏 *Heishi* the Tairas
水 *heisui* the usual amount of water; calm water
仄 *hyōsoku* meter (in Chinese poetry); consistency
手 *hirate* palm; equality
手打 *hirateu(chi)* a slap, spanking
方 *heihō* square (of a number); square
方形 *heihōkei* square
方根 *heihōkon* square root
⁵生 *heizei no* usual, ordinary
平凡凡 *heihei-bombon(taru)* ordinary, mediocre
民 *heimin* commoner, plebeian
⁶気 *heiki* composure; unconcern
伏 *hirefu(su)* prostrate oneself before. *heifuku suru* fall prostrate
地 *heichi, hirachi* level ground, plain
仮名 *hiragana* the cursive syllabary
年 *heinen* normal year, civil year
年作 *heinensaku* normal crop
年並 *heinennami* the same (harvest, rain fall, etc.) as in an average year
安 *heian* peace, tranquility; Heian era (794-1185)
安京 *Heiankyō* ancient Kyoto
行 *heikō* parallelism, parallel
行四辺形 *heikōshihenkei* parallelogram
行棒 *heikōbō* parallel bars
行線 *heikōsen* parallel line
⁷身低頭 *heishin teitō suru* prostrate oneself
均 *heikin, narashi* equilibrium, balance, average, mean
均点 *heikinten* average mark, mean point
均値 *heikinchi* average value, mean value
⁸坦 *heitan na* even, flat, level
明 *heimei na* clear, simple
泳 *hiraoyo(gi)* breast stroke
版 *heihan* lithography
服 *heifuku* civilian clothes, plain clothes, ordinary clothes
定 *heitei* suppression, repression, subjugation
底 *hirazoko* flat bottom
価 *heika* normal prices; par; parity
板 *heiban* slab, flat board; monotony; lithography
易 *heii* easiness; simplicity
和 *heiwa* peace, harmony

和主義 *heiwa shugi* pacifism
和共存 *heiwa kyōzon* peaceful coexistence
和条約 *heiwa jōyaku* peace treaty
⁹城京 *Heijōkyō* ancient Nara
屋 *hiraya* bungalow, one-story house
面 *heimen* level surface, plane
面図 *heimenzu* ground plan; plane figure
面形 *heimenkei* plane figure
¹⁰原 *heigen* plain, moor, prairie
時 *heiji* normal times, peace time
家 *hiraya* one-story house. *Heike* the Taira family
素 *heiso* ordinarily, in the past
¹¹野 *heiya* a plain, open field
常 *heijō* normal; normally, usually
常通 *heijōdō(ri)* as usual
¹²温 *heion* the usual temperature
然 *heizen(taru)* calm, composed
等 *byōdō* equality, impartiality
¹³滑 *heikatsu na* smooth, even, level, flat
¹⁴静 *heisei* tranquility, calm, equanimity
¹⁵熱 *heinetsu* normal (body) temperature
¹⁶穏 *heion* tranquility, calmness, rest
衡 *heikō* equilibrium, balance; equalization
¹⁸癒 *heiyu* convalescence

———— **3** ————

A 年 $\frac{1593}{J472f}$ NEN year; term of service. $\overline{M9168}$ *toshi* year; age, time of life.
³子 *toshigo* second child born within a year
下 *toshishita* younger, junior
上 *toshiue* older, senior
⁴内 *nennai* within the year
月 *nengetsu, toshitsuki* months and years, time
月日 *nengappi* date
中 *nenjū* throughout the year
中行事 *nenjū gyōji, nenchū gyōji* annual functions or events
少 *nenshō* youth
少者 *nenshōsha* youth, minor, young people
⁵玉 *(o)toshidama* New Year's gift
収 *nenshū* annual income
号 *nengō* era name
末 *nemmatsu* year end
甲斐無 *toshigai (mo) na(i)* unbecoming, unsuitable; disgraceful

功 *nenkō* long service, long experience
功序列 *nenkō joretsu* seniority system
代 *nendai* age, era, period; date
代記 *nendaiki* chronicle, chronology
代順 *nendaijun* chronological order
⁶回 *toshimawa(ri)* age relationship, luck concerning age. *nenkai* anniversary service (in Buddhism)
次 *nenji* annual; dates
毎 *toshigoto (ni)* annually, yearly
百年中 *nembyaku-nenjū* all year round; year after year
会 *nenkai* conference; annual convention
年 *toshidoshi, nennen* years, year by year, annually. *toshi (ga) toshi* considering his age
年歳歳 *nennen-saisai* annually, every year
⁷利 *nenri* annual interest rate
初 *nensho* beginning of the year; New Year's greetings
別 *nembetsu* by years
来 *nenrai* for some years
⁸金 *nenkin* annuity, pension
取 *toshito(ru), toshi (o) to(ru)* grow old, age
限 *nengen* length of time, term
若 *toshiwaka(i), toshiwaka no* young, youthful
表 *nempyō* chronological tables, chronology
長 *nenchō* seniority
長者 *nenchōsha* a senior, elderly people
始 *nenshi* beginning of the year; New Year's greetings, New Year's calls
季 *nenki* one's term of service; apprenticeship
⁹度 *nendo* year; fiscal year; school year; term
格好 *toshi kakkō, toshigakkō* approximate age
¹⁰俸 *nempō* annual salary
配 *nempai* age
配者 *nempaisha* elderly person
貢 *nengu* land tax (in kind); tribute; ground rent
¹¹頃 *toshigoro* age; marriageable age; age of puberty; adolescence; for some years
産 *nensan* annual production
寄 *toshiyo(ru), toshi (ga) yoru* grow old. *toshiyo(ri)* old person, an elder; older

councillor
¹²越 *toshiko(shi)* year end, New Year's Eve. *toshi (o) ko(su)* the year ends
間 *nenkan* era, period of a year; for the year
報 *nempō* annual report
賀 *nenga* New Year's greetings; New Year's call
賀状 *nengajō* New Year's card
¹³数 *nensu* number of years
嵩 *toshikasa* senior, older, elderly
¹⁴増 *toshima* mature woman, middle-aged woman
暮 *toshi (no) kure* year end. *toshiku(reru)* the year ends
¹⁵賦 *nempu* annual installment
輪 *nenrin* annual tree ring
輩 *nempai* age, age of experience
輩者 *nempaisha* elderly person
¹⁶頭 *nentō* beginning of the year
¹⁷齢 *nenrei* age
¹⁸額 *nengaku* yearly amount
¹⁹瀬 *toshi (no) se* New Year's Eve, the year end
²²鑑 *nenkan* yearbook

———— 5 ————

幸 $\frac{1595}{\substack{J392c \\ M9176}}$ Kō happiness, fortune.
A *sachi, saiwa(i)* happiness; blessing; good fortune. *shiawase* good fortune, happiness, blessing, mercy. *kō(su)* (the emperor) travels.
⁴不幸 *kōfukō* weal or woe, good or evil, sunshine and shadow
⁶先 *saisaki* good omen; good beginning
⁹甚 *kōjin* a favor; supreme happiness
¹¹運 *kōun* good fortune
¹³福 *kōfuku* happiness, welfare

———— 10 ————

幹 $\frac{1596}{\substack{J3434 \\ M9183}}$ KAN. *miki* (tree) trunk.
A
⁸事 *kanji* manager, secretary
事長 *kanjichō* chief secretary (of a party)
¹⁰部 *kambu* management, the executives, the leaders
¹⁵線 *kansen* main line, trunk line

3
口
口
土
士
夂
夊
夕
大
女
子
宀
寸
小
⺌
尢
尸
屮
山
川
巛
工
己
巾
干 ¹⁰
幺
广
廴
廾
弋
弓
彐
彑
彡
彳

3

口
口
土
士
夂
夕
大
女
子
宀
寸
小
小
尢
尸
屮
山
川
巛
工
己
巾
干
[幺]
广
廴
廾
弋
弓
彐
彑
彡
彳

At top: *itogashira* "thread" top. At left: *yō hen* left-side "young."
Nickname: Short Thread (cf. Rad. 120).

---- **1** ----

幻 | 1598 J3838 M9190 | Gen. *maboroshi* vision,
B dream; illusion, apparition.
⁶ 灯 *gentō* stereopticon, magic lantern
¹¹ 術 *genjutsu* magic, witchcraft, sorcery
視 *genshi* visual hallucination
¹² 惑 *genwaku* fascination, bewitching
覚 *genkaku* illusion, hallucination
¹³ 滅 *gemmetsu* disillusionment
夢 *gemmu* dreams, visions
想 *gensō* illusions
想曲 *gensōkyoku* fantasy
¹⁴ 像 *genzō* phantom, vision, illusion
¹⁵ 影 *gen'ei* phantom, vision, illusion
¹⁷ 聴 *genchō* auditory hallucination

---- **2** ----

幼 | 1599 J4d44 M9193 | Yō infancy, childhood;
A infants, children. *osana(i)*,
itokena(i) infant. *ito* very young.
³ 女 *yōjo* baby girl, little girl
子 *osanago* baby, infant, child
⁴ 心 *osanagokoro* child's mind; innocent heart
友達 *osanatomodachi* childhood friend
少 *yōshō* infancy, childhood
⁶ 虫 *yōchū* larva
名 *yōmei, yōmyō* one's infant name
年 *yōnen* infancy, childhood
⁷ 児 *yōji* infant, baby, little child
¹⁰ 時 *yōji* infancy, childhood
弱 *yōjaku* young and weak
¹³ 馴染 *osananajimi* childhood playmate
稚 *yōchi* infancy, babyhood; crudeness
稚園 *yōchien* kindergarten, preschool
¹⁷ 齢 *yōrei* tender age

---- **6** ----

幽 | 1600 J4d29 M9205 | Yū . *yū(suru)* confine to a
B room. *kasu(kana)* faint,
dim, weak, indistinct, hazy; poor, wretched.
⁵ 玄 *yūgen* mystery, the occult
囚 *yūshū* imprisonment
⁷ 谷 *yūkoku* ravine, glen
⁸ 明 *yūmei* the present and the other world; dark and light
⁹ 界 *yūkai* Hades, realm of the dead
¹⁰ 冥 *yūmei* semidarkness; deep and strange; Hades
冥界 *yūmeikai* Hades, realm of the dead
¹¹ 寂 *yūjaku* quiet, sequestered
¹³ 暗 *yūan na* dark and secluded
雅 *yūga* refinement
愁 *yūshū* deep contemplation
¹⁴ 境 *yūkyō* solitude; secluded place
魂 *yūkon* spirits of the dead
¹⁵ 趣 *yūshu* a quiet, natural setting
霊 *yūrei* ghost, apparition, spirit
¹⁷ 邃 *yūsui na* retired and quiet
邃境 *yūsuikyō* secluded place

---- **9** ----

幾 | 1601 J3476 M9208 | Ki. *iku(ra)* how many, how
B much; how far, how long;
so much per; however (difficult).
iku(raka) some, something, anything; somewhat, a little, to some extent, partly; in a way. *iku(ra)mo* any amount, any number; (neg.) not many, not much. *iku(tsu)* how many; how old. *hotohoto* almost, quite, really. *iku-* some, several, many; how many, how much.
² 人 *ikunin, ikutari* how many people. *ikunin ka* several people. *ikunin demo* any number of people
³ 久 *ikuhisa(shiku)* eternally, forever
万 *ikuman* many tens of thousands
千 *ikusen* thousands (of people)
⁴ 月 *ikutsuki* how many months
分 *ikubun* some, something, a part. *ikubun ka* somewhat, partly
日 *ikunichi, ikka* how many days; what day (of the month). *ikunichi ni* what

day. *ikunichi demo* for any number of days

⁶年 *ikutose, ikunen* how many years. *ikunen mo* for many years

多 *ikuta no* many

⁷何 *ikubaku* how much, how many. *kika* geometry

何学 *kikagaku* geometry

何的 *kikagakuteki* geometric

何級数 *kika kyūsū* geometrical series, geometrical progression

⁸夜 *ikuyo* how many nights; night after night

⁹度 *ikudo, ikutabi* how often, how many times. *ikudo mo* frequently, many times

通 *ikutō(ri)* how many kinds. *ikutsū* how many copies; how many letters

重 *ikue nimo* again and again; earnestly

RAD. 广 53

Madare trailing *ma* (i.e., the enclosure of Rad. 200 *ma* "hemp").
Also called *ten'ichi-dare* (i.e., a trailing Rad.8). Nickname: Dotted Cliff (cf. Rad. 27).

2

庁 A $\frac{1603}{\substack{J4423 \\ M9223}}$ Chō government office.

⁸舎 *chōsha* government office building

広 A $\frac{1604}{\substack{J392d \\ M9224'}}$ Kō. *hiro(garu) vi* sprrad out, extend, reach to. *hiro(geru) vt* expand, enlarge, widen; unfurl; open (arms or a package), stretch, spread.
hiro(maru) spread, be diffused, prevail, be propagated, pervade, be circulated, become popular. *hiro(meru)* extend, widen, enlarge; spread, disseminate; popularize; advertise, introduce, announce. *hiro(me)* announcement, advertisement. *hiro(i), hiro(yakana)* wide, broad, extensive, spacious.

³口 *hirokuchi* broad mouth; large-mouthed bottle

小路 *hirokōji* thoroughfare

大 *kōdai na* vast, extensive, magnificent

⁵広 *hirobiro toshita* extensive, spacious, roomy

⁶汎 *kōhan na* wide, extensive, widespread, comprehensive

壮 *kōsō na* grand, imposing

⁷角 *kōkaku* wide angle

言 *kōgen* boastful speech

告 *kōkoku* advertisement; public notice; poster, handbill; publicity

告社 *kōkokusha* advertising agency; publicity bureau

⁹軌 *kōki* wide gauge

¹¹野 *kōya, hirono* open field, open country, wilderness, moorland, plain, prairie

域 *kōiki* wide area

¹²遠 *kōen na* vast and far-reaching

間 *hiroma* hall, saloon (on a ship)

場 *hiroba* open field, public square

報 *kōhō* publicity

¹³漠 *kōbaku(taru)* vast, wide, boundless

義 *kōgi* broad sense, broad application

¹⁵縁 *hiroen* broad veranda; eaves

範 *kōhan* wide, extensive, widespread, comprehensive

範囲 *kōhan'i* wide scope, vast range

¹⁷闊 *kōkatsu na* spacious, wide, extensive

3

庄 $\frac{1605}{\substack{J3e31 \\ M9234}}$ Shō level.

⁹屋 *shōya* village headman

¹³園 *shōen* manor

4

庇 $\frac{1606}{\substack{J485f \\ M9239}}$ Hi. *kaba(u)* protect, shield; defend, plead for; harbor (criminals). *hisashi* waves; canopy; penthouse; visor.

⁵立 *kaba(i)-ta(te) suru* protect, shield; defend, plead for; harbor (criminals)

3

口
口
土
士
夂
夂
夕
大
女
子
宀
寸
小
⺌
尢
尸
屮
山
川
巛
工
己
巾
干
幺
[广]⁴
廴
廾
弋
弓
彐
彑
彡
彳

[20] 護 *higo* protection, patronage
護者 *higosha* patron, guardian

序 | 1607 J3d78 M9253 | Jo beginning; preface;
A order, precedence; farewell address; curtain raiser. *tsuide* order; occasion, chance. *tsuide ni* while, on the way, incidentally, while you're about it.

[4] 文 *jobun* preface, foreword, introduction
[6] 曲 *jokyoku* prelude, overture
列 *joretsu* rank, grade, order
[7] 言 *jogen* preface, foreword
[9] 奏 *josō* introduction (in music)
[13] 数 *josū* ordinal number; numbering
幕 *jomaku* curtain raiser
[14] 説 *josetsu* introduction
[15] 論 *joron* introduction, preface
盤戦 *jobansen* the beginning of a campaign

床 | 1608 J3e32 M9242 | SHŌ floor; bed. *toko* bed;
B sickbed; floor; alcove; padding. *yuka* floor. *yuka(shii)* admirable, respectable; sweet, charming; interesting; tasteful, mysterious. *-shō* counter for beds.

[2] 几 *shōgi* camp stool, folding stool
[3] 山 *tokoyama* wrestler's hairdresser; wig maker; a theatrical coiffeur
下 *yukashita* under the floor
上 *tokoa(ge)* recovery from a long illness. *shōjō* on the bed. *yukaue* on the floor, above the floor, floor (lamp).
[8] 板 *tokoita* alcove floor board. *yukaita* floor boards
[9] 屋 *tokoya* barber; barber shop
柱 *tokobashira* ornamental alcove post
[11] 張 *yukaba(ri)* flooring
[12] 間 *toko(no)ma* large ornamental livingroom alcove
就 *toko(ni) tsu(ku)* go to bed
[17] 擦 *tokozure* bedsore

─────── **5** ───────

庚 | 1609 J392e M9278 | KŌ G, seventh. *kanoe* seventh calendar sign.
[5] 申塚 *kōshinzuka* stone image of travelers' guardian deity

庖 | 1610 J4a79 M9266 | HŌ kitchen.
[2] 丁 *hōchō* kitchen knife; cooking; cook

府 | 1611 J495c M9283 | FU urban prefecture;
A government office; representative body; storehouse. *tsukasa* office, government office; director, head official.

[3] 下 *fuka* metropolitan suburban districts
[5] 立 *furitsu* managed by an urban prefecture
庁 *fuchō* urban prefectural office
[8] 知事 *fu chiji* urban prefectural governor
[12] 営 *fuei* urban prefectural enterprise
[20] 議会 *fugikai* urban prefectural assembly

底 | 1612 J446c M9262 | TEI bottom, base; kind,
A sort. *soko* bottom; sole; depth, bowels (of the earth); bottom price.

[2] 入 *sokoi(re)* touching bottom (stock market)
力 *sokojikara* latent energy, reserve strength
[3] 土 *sokotsuchi* subsoil
[4] 辺 *teihen* base (in geometry)
引網 *sokobi(ki)ami* dragnet; dragnet fishing
[5] 石 *soko ishi* hard core
払 *soko (o) hara(u)* empty completely
本 *teihon* original text
[6] 光 *sokobika(ri)* lurking luster, latent light
冷 *sokobi(e)* chilling to the bone
抜 *sokonu(ke)* bottomless; unbounded; extreme; self-indulgent; indiscreet
[8] 波 *sokonami* ground swell (the wave)
知 *sokoshi(ranu)*, *sokoshi(renu)* bottomless
[10] 値 *sokone* bottom price
流 *teiryū* bottom current, undercurrent
荷 *sokoni* ballast
[12] 無 *sokona(shi)* bottomless
[13] 意 *sokoi* innermost thoughts; secret intention; ulterior motive; undertone (in stock market)
意地 *sokoiji* bottom of one's heart

店 | 1613 J4539 M9267 | TEN shop, store. *mise, tana*
A shop, store, booth. *tana* house (for rent).

[3] 子 *tanako* tenant
[5] 主 *tenshu* storekeeper, shopkeeper

仕舞 *misejimai* closing a business
⁶先 *misesaki* shop front
⁷売 *miseu(ri)* sale at a store
⁹屋物 *ten'yamono* caterer's dishes
¹⁰晒 *tanazara(shi)* shopworn goods
浚 *tanazarae* clearance (sale)
員 *ten'in* clerk
¹²開 *misebira(ki)* opening a store
番 *miseban* tending a shop, salesperson
¹⁵舗 *tempo* shop, store
¹⁶頭 *tentō* shop front, shop window; counter; store

───── 6 ─────

度 [1616] [J4559] [M9313] **Do** degree; extent, measure, limit; a time; graduation, scale; composure. **Taku. To.** *do(suru)* save, redeem, reclaim. *wata(su)* carry across, ferry over, bring over; hand over, deliver; deal (cards); transfer (a business); pay (wages); bridge; stretch (something) across, lay across. *tabi* time, occasion; repetition. *-tai* desiderative verbal suffix.
⁵失 *do (o) ushina(u)* wander aimlessly
外 *dohazu(re), dogai* out of one's consideration, extraordinary, excessive
外視 *dogaishi suru* disregard, neglect, overlook
⁶合 *doa(i)* degree, extent, rate
⁷忘 *dowasu(re)* memory slip, forgetting for the moment
⁹度 *tabitabi, dodo* often, frequently
重 *tabikasa(naru)* occur repeatedly; repeated
胆抜 *dogimo (o) nu(ku)* startle (someone)
¹⁰胸 *dokyō* courage, pluck, nerve, bravery
¹²量 *doryō* magnanimity, generosity
量衡 *doryōkō* weights and measures
¹³数 *dosū* frequency, number of times
¹⁸難 *do(shi)gata(i)* incorrigible, inveterate, hopeless, beyond saving

───── 7 ─────

庫 [1617] [J384b] [M9330] **Ku. Ko** storehouse. *kura* warehouse, godown; cellar; depository; treasury; granary; elevator.
⁵出 *kurada(shi)* releasing stored goods

¹³裏 *kuri* priests' quarters; monastery kitchen

庭 [1618] [J446d] [M9337] **Tei.** *niwa* yard, courtyard, garden.
⁴内 *teinai* in the garden
木 *niwaki* garden tree, shrub, shrubbery
木戸 *niwa kido* garden gate
⁵石 *niwa ishi* decorative garden stones; steppingstones; flagstones
⁶先 *niwasaki de* in the garden
⁷作 *niwatsuku(ri)* gardening
¹⁰師 *niwashi* landscape gardener
¹¹球 *teikyū* tennis
¹²番 *niwaban* guard of the inner garden
¹³園 *teien* garden, park
園師 *teienshi* gardener, landscape architect

座 [1619] [J3a42] [M9319] 坐 [978] [J3a41] [M4931] **Za** seat, throne; a gathering; stand, pedestal, platform; (metal) washer; theater; troupe; constellation. *suwa(ru)* squat down, sit down, (eyes) are fixed on. *za(suru)* be involved in; squat; sit down. *i(masu)* be, go, come (polite). *suwa(ri)* stability. *-za* (ancient) guild.
⁴中 *zachū* in the room; member of the troupe
込 *suwa(ri)-ko(mu)* sit down, plant oneself down
⁵白 *za (ga) shira(keru)* a chill falls over the gathering
付 *zatsu(ki)* regular actor attached to a theater
主 *zasu, zashu* head priest of a temple. *zashu* theater owner
右 *zayū ni* at one's right; at one's side
右銘 *zayū (no) mei* desk motto
⁷位 *zai* seating order, precedence
⁸金 *zagane* metal washer
長 *zachō* chairman, president, moderator; troupe owner-leader
所 *zasho* one's seat; one's location; emperor's residence
臥 *zaga* sitting and lying down
⁹持 *za (o) mo(tsu)* act as hostess or master of ceremonies
洲 *zasu suru* run aground
乗 *zajō suru* be on board
¹⁰高 *zakō* sitting height

3

口 口 土 士 夂 夊 夕 大 女 子 宀 寸 小 小 尢 尸 屮 山 川 巛 工 己 巾 干 幺 [广] 廴 廾 弋 弓 彐 互 彡 彳

員 *zain* troupe personnel
席 *zaseki* seat, pew; cockpit
骨 *zakotsu* hip bone
[11] 視 *zashi suru* look on indifferently, be a mere spectator
[13] 禅 *zazen* meditation (in Zen Buddhism)
蒲団 *zabuton* cushion
業 *zagyō* sedentary work
[14] 像 *zazō* seated image
[15] 標 *zahyō* coordinates (in math)
談 *zadan* discussion, talking things over
談会 *zadankai* round-table talk, discussion group
敷 *zashiki* room, apartment, drawing room; giving a banquet; entertainer's evening engagement
[16] 薬 *zayaku* suppository
興 *zakyō* amusement, entertainment, fun, party games
頭 *zagashira* theater-troupe leader; leading man. *zatō* ancient blind official; blind masseur; blind man; blind musician
[17] 礁 *zashō* running aground

---------- **8** ----------

A 康 $\frac{1621}{\frac{J392f}{M9376}}$ Kō peace.

B 廊 $\frac{1622}{\frac{J4f2d}{M-X}}$ Rō corridor, hall, lobby; tower; watchtower.
[3] 下 *rōka* corridor, hall, lobby, vestibule

庵 $\frac{1623}{\frac{J3043}{M9369}}$ An hermitage, retreat. *io, iori* hermitage; living in a hermitage.
[5] 主 *anshu* owner of a hermitage

B 庸 $\frac{1624}{\frac{J4d47}{M9378}}$ Yō tax paid in labor; ordinary; employment.
[2] 人 *yōjin* ordinary people. *yōnin* employee

B 庶 $\frac{1625}{\frac{J3d6e}{M9373}}$ Sho all; illegitimate child.
[2] 人 *shonin, shojin* masses, (common) people
[3] 子 *shoshi* illegitimate child
[5] 出 *shoshutsu* illegitimate birth
民 *shomin* masses, the common people
[8] 事 *shoji* various matters, everything

[11] 務 *shomu* general affairs, miscellaneous affairs

---------- **9** ----------

B 廃 $\frac{1630}{\frac{J4751}{M9425}}$ Hai obsolescence; cessation; discarding.
hai(suru) abolish, abandon; repeal, annul; depose; discontinue. *suta(reru), suta(ru)* become useless, get out of date, die out; be abolished; decline(in prosperity).
ya(meru) vt end, discontinue; give up, abandon; abolish; resign, retire. *suta(ri)* waste. *ya(me)* end, discontinuance, stop.
[2] 人 *haijin* invalid, cripple; useless person; abandoned person
[4] 止 *haishi* abolition, discontinuance, abrogation
[5] 刊 *haikan* discontinuance of publication
[6] 気 *haiki* exhaust, ventilation
寺 *haiji* ruined temple
[7] 位 *haii* dethronement
坑 *haikō* abandoned mine
材 *haizai* scrap wood
[8] 物 *haibutsu* scrap, waste, refuse. *suta(ri)mono* useless thing, obsolete thing
[9] 屋 *haioku* deserted house
除 *haijo suru* remove, take away
品 *haihin* scrap, waste
[10] 残 *haizan* survival after defeat; decline; ruin ⌈draft
案 *haian* rejected measure, discarded
[11] 船 *haisen* scrapped vessel; superannuated ship
[12] 絶 *haizetsu* extinction
[13] 滅 *haimetsu* ruin, decay
鉱 *haikō* abandoned mine
棄 *haiki* abandonment, repeal, annulment, abrogation
業 *haigyō* closing up shop, quitting the business
[15] 墟 *haikyo* ruins
[18] 藩置県 *haihan-chiken* the abolition of the clans and the setting up of prefectures

---------- **10** ----------

廓 $\frac{1633}{\frac{J3347}{M9461}}$ Kaku enclosure; quarter. *kuruwa* enclosure, quarter; red-light district.

廉 B $\frac{1634}{\text{J4e77}}$ $\frac{}{\text{M9436}}$ REN purity; honesty; low price; corner. *yasu(i)* cheap, inexpensive; peaceful; quiet; gossipy, thoughtless. *kado* reason, charge, suspicion; point, account.
⁷ 売 *rembai* bargain sale, dumping
⁸ 直 *renchoku* integrity, honor, uprightness
　価 *renka* low price
¹⁰ 恥 *renchi* honor, integrity
　恥心 *renchishin* sense of shame; sense of honor
¹⁵ 潔 *renketsu* honesty, integrity, uprightness

———————— 12 ————————

廠 $\frac{1643}{\text{J3e33}}$ $\frac{}{\text{M9490}}$ SHŌ workshop.

廟 $\frac{1645}{\text{J4940}}$ $\frac{}{\text{M9489}}$ BYŌ mausoleum; shrine; palace.
⁶ 宇 *byōu* mausoleum, shrine
¹¹ 堂 *byōdō* the court, cabinet, ministry
²⁰ 議 *byōgi* cabinet council; cabinet decision

■■■■■■■■■■■■ RAD. 廴 54 ■■■■■■■■■■■■

Ennyō (Enclosure for 延 *en*, *nobiru* "stretch, lengthen"). Also *innyō* or *innyū*, the "long stride" radical. Nickname: Stretching.

———————— 4 ————————

廷 B $\frac{1654}{\text{J446e}}$ $\frac{}{\text{M9571}}$ TEI imperial court; government office.
² 丁 *teitei* court attendant
⁴ 内 *teinai* in the court
⁶ 臣 *teishin* courtier, court official
　史 *teiri* lesser court official

———————— 5 ————————

延 A $\frac{1657}{\text{J3164}}$ $\frac{}{\text{M-X}}$ EN stretching. *no(biru)* extend, lengthen, stretch, spread; be postponed; increase; grow; progress, develop; be straightened, be flattened, be smoothed; be exhausted. *no(bi)* stretching (the body); excess, surplus; postponement; growth; spread. *no(basu)* lengthen, stretch, extend; let (nails) grow; straighten; uncoil; spread out; reach out; postpone; dilute; smooth out; develop (talents); amass (riches). *no(beru)* make (a bed); stretch, widen, lengthen. *no(be)* futures, credit (buying); stretching; total.
² 人員 *no(be) jin'in* total personnel
⁴ 引 *en'in, ennin* delay, postponement, procrastination
　日数 *no(be) nissū* total days
⁵ 払 *no(be)bara(i)* deferred payment

⁸ 金 *no(be)gane* sheet metal; hammered-out sheets; sword, dagger
　延 *no(bi)no(bi)* stretching. *no(bi)no(bi) ni naru* be delayed. *en'en(taru)* meandering, serpentine
　命 *emmei* prolongation of life; long life, longevity
　取引 *no(be) torihiki* dealing in futures
　長 *enchō* extension, elongation, prolongation; continuation; extent, length
　長戦 *enchōsen* extra-inning game
¹⁰ 納 *ennō* deferred payment
　時間 *no(be) jikan* total hours
¹² 棒 *no(be) bō* (metal) bar
　渡 *no(be)wata(shi)* forward delivery
　焼 *enshō* spread of a fire
　期 *enki* postponement, adjournment, deferment, respite
　着 *enchaku* delayed arrival
¹³ 滞 *entai* delay, procrastination, arrearage

———————— 6 ————————

廼 $\frac{1658}{\text{J4736}}$ $\frac{}{\text{M9576}}$ DAI. NAI namely; you; go; arrive; far, this. *sunawa(chi)* namely. *nanji* you. *no* used phonetically.

3
口
口
土
士
夂
夂
夕
大
女
子
宀
寸
小
⺌
尢
尸
屮
山
川
巛
工
己
巾
干
幺
广
廴
[廾]
弋
弓
彐
彑
彡
彳

廻 ₁₆₅₉ J3276 M9575 KAI. *mawa(su)* turn, revolve, rotate; circularize; pass around; forward, transmit; refer to; transfer; lend money. *mawa(ru)* turn, go around; revolve, rotate, spin, gyrate; patrol, tour; take effect (medicine); be distributed; be past (time); be transferred. *megu(ru)* go around. *megu(ri)* girth, circumference; tour, round, pilgrimage; flow, circulation; menstruation. (See 回 941 for other related compounds.)

⁶米 *kaimai* rice arrivals
合 *megu(ri)-a(u)* meet by chance
⁸国 *kaikoku* pilgrimage, tour
送 *kaisō* forwarding, transportation
¹⁰航 *kaikō* navigation, cruise
¹¹船 *kaisen* barge; cargo vessel
転 *kaiten* revolution, rotation
¹⁴漕 *kaisō* marine transportation
¹⁶覧 *kairan* circulation of letter or document

建 ₁₆₆₀ J377a M9574 KON, KEN build, raise. A *ta(tsu)* stand, rise; rouse oneself; be built, be established; go up (smoke); burn out; depart; take flight; run high (waves); stick into; be worked out; be maintained; save (face); establish oneself; begin life; spread (rumors); shut (doors); be active; open (markets); be excited; come (seasons); makes (a total of thirty). *ta(teru)* stand something up, set up, raise; put up; set on edge; prick up (one's ears); build, erect; close (a door); establish; institute, enact; lay (plans); map out; set forth, lay down (a proposition); formulate; render (services), perform; look up to, respect; be loyal to; do justice to; circulate (rumors); have (an aim); establish

(oneself), make (a success); support (oneself), make (an oath); sharpen, set (a saw); put up (a candidate); make (tea); save (face).

⁴方 *ta(te)kata* architectural style; how to build
込 *ta(te)-ko(mu)* be closely built up
⁵立 *konryū* building, erection
白 *kempaku* memorial, petition
⁶回 *ta(te)-megu(rasu)* build around
⁷言 *kengen* memorial, petition, proposal
材 *kenzai* building materials
売 *ta(te)u(ri)* ready-built (house)
⁸国 *kenkoku, kengoku* establishing a nation
坪 *tatetsubo* floor space
物 *tatemono* building; architecture
直 *ta(te)-nao(ru)* be rebuilt. *ta(te)-nao(su)* rebuild
具 *tategu* house fittings (doors and windows)
⁹前 *tatemae* framework-erection ceremony; framing a house; fundamental principles
造 *kenzō* building, construction
造物 *kenzōbutsu* building, edifice
¹¹設 *kensetsu* building, establishment
設的 *kensetsuteki* constructive
設省 *Kensetsushō* Ministry of Construction
¹²策 *kensaku* recommendation, suggestion
¹⁴増 *ta(te)-ma(su)* build on. *tatema(shi)* extension, annex
¹⁶築 *kenchiku* building, architecture
築物 *kenchikubutsu* building, edifice
築学 *kenchikugaku* architecture
築家 *kenchikuka* architect
築業 *kenchikugyō* building industry
²⁰議 *kengi* proposal, petition, recommendation

■ RAD. 廾 55 ■

Nijū-ashi "twenty" legs (i.e. legs resembling *nijū* "twenty").
Variant: 艹. Nickname: Letter H.

--- **1** ---

廿 ₁₆₆₂ J467b M9586 JŪ. *nijū* twenty.

--- **2** ---

弁 ₁₆₆₄ J4a5b M9588 瓣 ₃₆₈₉ J6122 M21425 A BEN petal, valve.

¹⁴膜 *bemmaku* valve (in internal organs)

A 弁 | 1665 J4a5b M9588 | 辨 | 6002 J517e M38657 | 辧 | 6003 J5221 M38656

BEN discrimination. *ben(jiru), ben(zuru)* manage, dispose of, carry through; distinguish, discriminate. *wakima(eru)* discern, discriminate, know, understand, bear in mind.

⁴天 *Benten* god of wealth, music, eloquence, and water

⁶当 *bentō* lunch, box lunch, lunch box
当屋 *bentōya* lunch vendor
当箱 *bentōbako* lunch box

⁷別 *bembetsu* discrimination

¹⁰財天 *Benzaiten* god of wealth, music, eloquence, and water

¹¹済 *bensai* settlement, payment
理 *benri* management
理士 *benrishi* patent attorney
務官 *bemmukan* commissioner

¹²証 *benshō* demonstration, proof
証法 *benshōhō* dialectic, dialectics

¹⁷償 *benshō* reparation, indemnity, compensation, reimbursement

A 弁 | 1666 J4a5b M9588 | 辯 | 6005 J6d67 M38677

BEN speech, oratory. *ben(jiru), ben(zuru)* speak, talk, argue. (See also 1663, 1664, 1665)

³士 *benshi* speaker, orator
才 *bensai* eloquence, oratorical talent
舌 *benzetsu* speech

⁸明 *bemmei* explanation, defense, justification

¹³解 *benkai* explanation, justification, defense, excuse, apology

¹⁴駁 *bembaku, bempaku* refutation, contradiction, rebuttal, disproof, disputation

¹⁵論 *benron* discussion, argument, debate; oral proceedings, pleading

²⁰護 *bengo* defense, vindication, explanation, pleading
護人 *bengonin* counsel, defender, advocate
護士 *bengoshi* lawyer, attorney

——————— 4 ———————

弄 | 1668 J4f2e M9596

RŌ . *ijiku(ru), rō(suru)* play with, trifle with. *iji(ru)* touch, tamper with, play with. *moteaso(bu)* play; take pleasure in; play (on an instrument); play with; make sport of; trifle with (affections).

——————— 12 ———————

B 弊 | 1670 J4a40 M9644

HEI evil, abuse, vice, bad custom; breakage; our (humble); Shinto zigzag paper offering; tribute. *tsuie* expenses. *hei-* our (humble).

⁶衣 *heii* shabby clothes
衣破帽 *heii habō* shabby clothes and an old hat

⁷社 *heisha* our firm

⁸店 *heiten* our shop

⁹風 *heifū* evil habit, bad custom, abuse

¹⁰害 *heigai* evil, vice, abuse; harmful influence; bad effect

¹¹習 *heishū* corrupt custom, bad habit

¹⁵履 *heiri* worn-out sandals or shoes

RAD. 弋 **56**

Shikigamae (enclosure for 式 *shiki* "ceremony"). Nickname: Ceremony.

——————— 3 ———————

B 弐 | 1675 J4675 M-X

JI, NI two; second. *futa(tsu)* two.

A 式 | 1676 J3c30 M9663

SHIKI ceremony, rite, function; method, system; style, form, type, plan; formula, expression (in math); model; law; standard. *-shiki* style, type.

⁵台 *shikidai* step or platform in an entranceway; slatted removable floor in an entrance hall

⁶次 *shikiji* the order of a ceremony

3

口
口
土
士
夂
夊
夕
大
女
子
宀
寸
小
⺌
尢
尸
屮
山
巛
巜
工
己
巾
干
幺
广
廴
廾
弋
【弓】
ヨ
彑
彡
彳

⁸服 *shikifuku* ceremonial dress
典 *shikiten* ceremony, celebration, rites
¹⁰部官 *shikibukan* master of court

ceremonies
¹²場 *shikijō* place of the ceremony; ceremonial hall
¹³辞 *shikiji* address, speech

RAD. 弓 57

Yumi bow (for arrows). At left: *yumi hen*. Nickname: Bow.

弓 A
₁₆₇₈
_{J355d}
_{M9692}
KYŪ bow; violin bow.
yumi bow; archery; violin
violin bow; bow shape.
⁴手 *yunde* archer's hand; the left hand
引 *yumi (o) hi(ku)* draw the bow; rebel
⁵矢 *yumiya* bow and arrow
⁷形 *kyūkei* crescent form, circle segment. *yuminari, yumigata* arch, arc, curve
⁸弦 *yumizuru, yuzuru* bowstring
取 *yumito(ri)* archer, warrior, samurai; famous archer; archery
¹⁰馬 *kyūba* bow and horse; archery and horsemanship
¹¹道 *kyūdō* archery
術 *kyūjutsu* archery
張月 *yumiha(ri)zuki* crescent moon; waxing moon; waning moon
¹⁵箭 *kyūsen* bows and arrows; arms; war

1

弔 B
₁₆₈₀
_{J4424}
_{M9698}
CHŌ mourning. *chō(suru)* mourn, condole with.
tomura(u), tobura(u) mourn for; hold a memorial service for; condole. *tomura(i), tobura(i)* funeral, burial, condolence.
⁴文 *chōbun* funeral address
⁶合戦 *tomura(i) gassen* battle of revenge
¹¹問 *chōmon* condolence call
¹³辞 *chōji* message of condolence, memorial address
電 *chōden* telegram of condolence
意 *chōi* condolence, sympathy, mourning
¹⁴旗 *chōki* flag at half-mast
歌 *chōka* elegy, dirge
¹⁵慰 *chōi* condolence, sympathy

引 A
₁₆₈₁
_{J307a}
_{M9699}
IN. *hi(ku) vt* draw, pull, haul, tug, jerk, drag, trail, bend, attract; lead (horses or captives); draw (lines); admit; install (utilities);

quote, refer to; look up (words); subtract, reduce; apply, daub on; blunt (a sword); patronize; choose; draw (a line); catch (a cold). *vi* retreat, withdraw, retire; subside. *hi(kaseru)* redeem, ransom. *hi(keru)* close, be over; can discount; slink away. *hi(ke)* closing (of office, school, etc.); leaving (work); retiring; defeat, reverse; loss. *hi(ki)* flattery, patronage, pull, backing; discount. *-bi(ki)* coated with, plated with. *hi(ki)-* emphatic verbal prefix.
²入 *hi(ki)-i(reru)* drag in, bring into; win over, interest, entice; pull in, pull back
力 *inryoku* gravitation, attraction
³下 *hi(ki)-sa(garu) vi* retire, withdraw. *hi(ki)-sa(geru)* pull down, lower, reduce. *hi(ki)-oro(su)* pull down; drag off (the rocks), refloat
上 *hi(ki)-a(geru) vi* withdraw, retire, leave; be repatriated. *vt* pull up; increase (fares); evacuate; refloat, salvage; recover (a body); promote
⁴戸 *hi(ki)do* sliding door
比 *hi(ki)-kura(beru)* compare
分 *hi(ki)-wa(keru)* pull apart, separate. *hikiwake* a drawn game
手 *hi(ki)te* knob, handle, catch; patron, admirer. *hi(ku)te* admirer; inducer
手繰 *hi(t)taku(ru)* snatch away, wrest from
止 *hi(ki)-to(meru)* restrain, check; detain, keep back, hold, stop
切 *hi(ki)-ki(ru)* pull and cut; saw off. *hi(kimo)-ki(ranu), hi(kimo)-ki(razu)* uninterrupted. *hi(kimo)-ki(razu) ni* uninterruptedly
切無 *hi(k)ki(ri)na(shi) ni* incessantly, continuously, in rapid succession
火 *inka suru* ignite, catch fire

込 *hi(ki)-ko(mu)* drag in, bring into; win over, interest, entice; pull in, pull back. *hi(k)ko(mu)* draw back, retire; sink, cave in; keep behind; disappear. *hi(k)ko(masu), hi(k)ko(meru), hi(k)ko(mu)* vt draw in, take in; withdraw, retract, pull inside. *hikko(mi), hikiko(mi)* retreat, withdrawal; retirement; depression (a hole)

込思案 *hikko(mi)jian* conservatism

⁵目 *hi(ke)me* weakness; drawing back

付 *hi(t)tsu(keru), hi(ki)-tsu(keru)* fascinate; pull up (at a gate); have a convulsion. *hi(t)tsu(ku)* stick to, cling to. *hi(ki)tsu(ke)* fit, convulsion

叩 *hi(p)pata(ku)* thrash, box, slap, strike

外 *hi(ki)-hazu(su), hi(p)pazu(su)* pull down, take off, unfasten. *hi(p)pazu(su)* dodge, parry off

払 *hi(ki)-hara(u)* evacuate, vacate

写 *hi(ki)utsu(shi)* copy, tracing

立 *hi(t)ta(teru), hi(ki)-ta(teru)* favor; patronize; support; promote; rouse; enhance; emphasize; shut; escort (a prisoner), march (a person) off. *hi(ki)-ta(tsu)* become active; be inspired; become brisk; set off (to advantage), look better

出 *hi(ki)-da(su)* take out, extract; drag out; draw out, lead out, entice out, bring out. *hikida(shi)* (desk) drawer; withdrawal

出物 *hi(ki)demono* gift, souvenir

用 *in'yō* a quotation

用文 *in'yōbun* a quotation

用句 *in'yōku* a quotation

用符 *in'yōfu* quotation marks

⁶回 *hi(ki)-mawa(su)* draw (a curtain); parade about; guide

返 *hi(ki)-kae(su)* repeat; send back; reverse; bring back; turn back, retrace (steps)

合 *hi(ki)-a(u)* be profitable, pay; pull against each other. *hi(ki)-a(waseru)* introduce; compare, collate, check. *hi(ki)a(i)* reference, comparison; witness; a deal

当 *hi(ki)-a(teru)* apply, compare. *hi(ki)a(te)* mortgage, security

⁷見 *inken* audience, interview

戻 *hi(ki)-modo(su)* bring back, restore;

improve (business); turn back, retrace (steps)

伸 *hi(ki)-noba(su), hi(ki)-no(beru)* stretch out, prolong; elongate; extend; beat out; spin out; enlarge; postpone; filibuster. *hikinoba(shi)* photographic enlargement

抜 *hi(ki)-nu(ku), hi(kko)nu(ku)* extract; uproot; select, pull out

⁸金 *hi(ki)gane* trigger

延 *hi(ki)-no(beru), hi(ki)-noba(su)* stretch out, prolong; elongate; extend; beat out; spin out; enlarge; postpone; filibuster

退 *intai suru, hi(ki)-shirizo(ku)* draw back, retreat. *hi(ki)-no(keru)* drag out of the way. *intai* retirement

例 *inrei* quotation, referring to precedent

放 *hi(ki)-hana(tsu), hi(ki)-hana(su)* pull apart

波 *hi(ki)nami* backwash

直 *hi(ki)-nao(su)* restore, bring back, redraw (lines, etc.)

取 *hi(ki)-to(ru)* take charge of, respond to; take delivery of; claim (a body); retire; die

受 *hi(ki)-u(keru)* be responsible for; take charge of, undertake; consent to; accept, guarantee; contract (a disease). *hikiu(ke)* undertaking; acceptance, underwriting; guarantee, guarantor

受人 *hikiukenin* guarantor; acceptor (of a draft); underwriter

⁹連 *hi(ki)-tsu(reru)* bring along

括 *hi(k)kuru(meru), hi(ki)-kuru(meru)* bring to a conclusion

降 *hi(ki)-o(rosu)* pull down, bring down

¹⁰起 *hi(ki)-oko(su)* raise up, pull up; cause, bring about; raise (questions); create (trouble), provoke, stir up

倒 *hi(ki)-tao(su)* pull down, drag down

捕 *hi(ki)-tora(eru), hi(t)tora(eru)* capture, seize, arrest

時 *hi(ke)doki* closing time

破 *hi(ki)-yabu(ru)* tear, tear up, tear away

被 *hi(k)kabu(ru)* pull (bedclothes) over the head

剥 *hi(ki)-ha(gu), hi(ki)-ha(gasu)* tear off, peel off, rip off, strip off; skin, flay; disrobe; deprive of. *hi(ki)-mu(ku)*

3

口
口
土
士
夂
夂
夕
大
女
子
宀
寸
小
⺌
尢
尸
屮
山
川
巛
工
己
巾
干
幺
广
廴
廾
弋
[弓]
彐
彑
彡
彳

peel, pare, hull

留 *hi(ki)-to(meru)* restrain, check; detain, keep back, hold, stop

[11] 掛 *hi(k)ka(karu)* be caught in, get stuck; be involved; be cheated. *hi(k)ka(keru)* hang on, hook, throw on; ensnare; defraud, evade (payment); drink (saké). *hi(ki)-ka(keru)* hang up (something); pull (something) over one; request; make connections with. *hi(k)ka(kari)* a hold; connection, complicity, involvement; affair; unsettled account. *hi(k)ka(ke)* hook

据 *hi(ki)-su(eru)* set (a table); lay (a foundation); place (a gun); install, equip; appoint (to a position)

移 *hi(ki)-utsu(ru)* move to. *hi(ki)-utsu(su)* move, transfer; pour into, divert (attention), give (a disease to someone)

船 *hi(ki)fune* tugboat

寄 *hi(ki)-yo(seru)* draw nearer, drag in; attract

責 *inseki suru* take the responsibility

率 *insotsu suru* lead, command

張 *hi(p)pa(ru)* pull, draw, jerk, drag, tug at; stretch over; take (someone) to; entice, invite; delay (payment)

張出 *hi(p)pa(ri)-da(su)* take out, drag out, bring out, lead out, pull out

[12] 喩 *in'yu* allusion

換 *hi(ki)-ka(eru)* exchange, change, convert. *hikika(ete)*, *hikika(e)* on the contrary, on the other hand; while, when

渡 *hi(ki)-wata(su)* deliver, transfer, hand over; extradite; stretch across. *hikiwata(shi)* delivery, turning over to, extradition

絞 *hi(ki)-shibo(ru)* wring, squeeze, press, extract; milk; close tight; extort; scold; draw a bow to the limit; draw aside (curtains); tuck up; strain (the voice)

着 *hi(ki)-tsu(keru)*, *hi(t)tsu(keru)* fascinate; pull up (at a gate); have a convulsion

裂 *hi(s)sa(ku)*, *hi(ki)-sa(ku)* tear off, tear up, rip open; split; separate

越 *hi(k)ko(su)*, *hi(ki)-ko(su)* move, change quarters

揚 *hi(ki)-a(geru)* *vi* withdraw, retire, leave; be repatriated. *vt* pull up;

increase (fares); evacuate; refloat, salvage; recover (a body); promote

替 *hi(ki)-kae(ru)*, *hi(k)kae(ru)* exchange (things); change from; reverse

[13] 継 *hi(ki)-tsu(gu)* take over or hand over (duties); inherit

続 *hi(ki)-tsuzu(ku)* continue, occur in succession. *hi(ki)tsuzu(ki)* continually

掻 *hi(k)ka(ku)* scratch, claw, maul

掻回 *hi(k)ka(ki)-mawa(su)* ransack, mess up, carry on high-handedly

[14] 綱 *hi(ki)zuna* tow rope; bell rope

算 *hi(ki)zan* subtraction

導 *indō* guidance; address to the departed soul

摺 *hi(ki)-zu(ru)* drag along; seduce; prolong. *hi(ki)zuri* train (of a dress); a low woman

摺込 *hi(ki)-zu(ri)-ko(mu)* drag in

摺出 *hi(ki)-zu(ri)-da(su)* drag out

摺回 *hi(ki)-zu(ri)-mawa(su)* drag around

[15] 潮 *hi(ki)shio* ebb tide

締 *hi(ki)-shi(maru)* become tense; be tightened. *hi(ki)-shi(meru)* tighten; stiffen; strain, brace

[19] 離 *hi(ki)-hana(su)*, *hi(p)pana(su)* pull apart, separate; outdistance

繰返 *hi(k)ku(ri)-kae(ru)* capsize; collapse; lie on one's back; be reversed; betray. *hi(k)ku(ri)-kae(su)* capsize; knock down; turn over; turn inside out; turn up (a card). *hi(k)ku(ri)kae(shi)* topsy-turvy, upside down, inside out

[20] 懸 *hi(k)ka(karu)* be caught in, get stuck; be involved; be cheated. *hi(k)ka(keru)* hang on, hook, throw on; ensnare; defraud, evade (payment); drink (saké). *hi(k)ka(kari)* a hold; connection, complicity, involvement; affair; unsettled account. *hi(k)ka(ke)* hook

[22] 籠 *hi(ki)-komo(ru)*, *hi(k)komo(ru)* stay indoors; be confined indoors

[23] 攣 *hi(ki)-tsu(ru)* have a cramp or spasm; twitch; strain (a ligament); have a convulsion. *hikitsuri* scar; spasm, cramp, twitch, convulsion

———— **2** ————

弘 1682 J3930 M9709 Ku. Kō. *hiro(i)* broad, wide.

11 済会 *kōsaikai* benefit association
12 報 *kōhō* publicity

弗 1683 J4a26 M9708 Futsu. *doru* dollar.

9 相場 *doru sōba* dollar exchange
10 素 *fusso* fluorine
12 箱 *dorubako* cashbox; backer, patron

--- 3 ---

弛 1684 J4350 M9724 Chi. Shi. *taru(mu) vi* slacken, loosen, relax. *tayu(mu)* slacken one's efforts. *taru(meru) vt* loosen slack up on. *tayu(i)* tired and weak, listless; without any ambition. *yuru(mu) vi* loosen, lessen; relax; be unguarded; be moderate. *yuru(meru) vt* loosen, unbend, unfasten; relax, ease, slacken; mitigate. *yuru(i)* loose, slack; lenient, generous, slow.

15 緩 *chikan, shikan* relaxation; getting careless

弟 1685 J446f M9737 Dai. Tei younger brother,

A faithful service to those older; brotherly affection. *otōto, ototo, oto* younger brother.
3 子 *deshi, teishi* pupil, disciple, adherent, follower; apprentice. *teishi* young person; teacher's student-helper
子入 *deshii(ri)* apprenticeship; enrolling
4 分 *otōtobun* a friend treated as a younger brother
8 妹 *teimai* younger brothers and sisters

--- 5 ---

弧 1687 J384c M9757 Ko arc; arch; bow.

B
6 光 *kokō* arc light
7 状 *kojō no* arc-shaped
形 *kokei* an arc
15 線 *kosen* an arc

弦 1688 J3639 M9754 Gen bowstring; chord (in

B geometry); hypotenuse; crescent (moon); bowstring; string (of an instrument). *tsuru* bowstring; teakettle handle made of bamboo or vines.

4 月 *gengetsu* crescent moon
7 声 *gensei* sound of the strings
13 楽 *gengaku* singing accompanied by stringed instruments
楽器 *gengakki* stringed instruments
14 歌 *genka* singing

弥 1689 J4c6f M9753 Bi. Mi. *iya* all the more, increasingly.

5 生 *yayoi* spring; third lunar month
6 次 *yaji(ru)* cheer, support, root for; hoot at, obstruct; jeer at. *yaji* cheering, rooting; heckling, jeering; rooters, hecklers, mob; spectators; busybody; intruder
次馬 *yajiuma* rabble, mob; spectators; busybody; intruder
9 栄 *iyasaka(eru)* prosper more and more. *iyasaka* increasing prosperity
15 縫策 *bihōsaku* makeshift, stopgap policy

--- 7 ---

弱 1692 J3c65 M-X Jaku weakness; the weak.

A *yowa(maru), yowa(ru) vi* weaken, be emaciated; be dejected; be perplexed. *yowa(meru) vt* weaken. *yowa(ru) vt* impair, weaken, enfeeble. *yowa(i)* weak, feeble, frail, tender; unskilled; weak (alcoholic beverage). *(ka)yowa(i)* frail, feeble. *(hi)yowa(i)* weak, sickly. *-jaku* a little less than.

3 小 *jakushō* puniness; youth
4 込 *yowa(ri)-ko(mu)* weaken, be at wits' end
切 *yowa(ri)-ki(ru)* faint, be exhausted
5 目 *yowa(ri)me* a time of weakness
目祟目 *yowa(ri)me (ni) tata(ri)me* misfortunes never come singly
6 虫 *yowamushi* weakling, coward
気 *yowaki* faintheartedness; bearish sentiment
肉強食 *jakuniku-kyōshoku* survival of the fittest
年 *jakunen* youth
7 体 *jakutai* weak (organization)
体化 *jakutaika* weakening
8 卒 *jakusotsu* cowardly soldier
者 *yowa(i)mono, yowa(ki)mono* weak person, the weak *jakusha* the weak, the underdog

3

口 口 土 士 夂 夊 夕 大 女 子 宀 寸 小 ⺌ 尢 尸 屮 山 川 巛 工 己 巾 干 幺 广 廾 弋 【弓】 ヨ 彑 彡 彳

3

口
口
土
士
夊
夕
大
女
子
宀
寸
小
⺌
尢
尸
屮
山
川
巛
工
己
巾
干
幺
广
廴
廾
弋
【弓】
ヨ
⺕
彡
彳

昩 *yowami* weakness
⁹冠 *jakkan* age 20; youth
点 *jakuten* weak point
音 *yowane* complaints. *jakuon* soft
　　sound
¹⁰弱 *yowayowa(shii)* frail, slender,
　　feminine
¹¹視 *jakushi* weak sight
¹³腰 *yowagoshi* weak attitude
¹⁵震 *jakushin* weak earthquake shock, a
　　minor tremor
輩 *jakuhai* young person; inexperienced
　　person, a novice

──────── **8** ────────

A 張 ⟨1694 / J4425 / M9812⟩ CHŌ counter for bows and
　　stringed instruments.
ha(ru) vt put up (a tent); stretch, spread,
string, tighten; cover, line; strain; square
(elbows); give (a banquet); run (a store);
stake (money); display; slap, box, spank;
lay (flooring); insist on (one's own way);
guard; run after (a girl); fill (with water).
vi swell, be full; form (ice); be expensive;
increase; be heavy; grow stiff; brace up.
ha(ri) tension; will power, pluck, pride;
expansion steadiness. *-ba(ri)* fashion.
²力 *chōryoku* tension, tensile strength
³子 *ha(ri)ko* papier-mâché
⁴手 *ha(ri)te* slapping (someone)
込 *ha(ri)-ko(mu)* keep watch; be eager
　　for; invest in
切 *ha(ri)-ki(reru)* burst out. *ha(ri)-ki(ru)*
　　string up, stretch tight; be tense, be
　　enthusiastic
⁵巡 *ha(ri)-megu(rasu)* ramify
付 *ha(ri)-tsu(keru)* stick on, paste up (a
　　notice), affix (stamps)
札 *ha(ri)fuda* placard, bill, poster; tag
出 *ha(ri)-da(su)* put up a notice, project,
　　jut out. *harida(shi)* bill, poster,
　　notice; overhang
出窓 *harida(shi) mado* bay window
本人 *chōhonnin, chōbonnin* originator,
　　ringleader, perpetrator
⁶合 *ha(ri)-a(u)* vie with, emulate,
　　compete with. *haria(i)* rivalry,
　　competition; responsiveness;
　　inducement
¹⁰倒 *ha(ri)-tao(su)* knock down, floor (a

man)
紙 *ha(ri)gami* sticker, bills, label, tag
¹²番 *ha(ri)ban* watch, guard; watchman,
　　sentinel
替 *ha(ri)-ka(eru)* repaper, replaster, re-
　　upholster, recover
裂 *ha(ri)-sa(keru)* burst open; split,
　　break, splinter
¹³詰 *ha(ri)-tsu(meru)* strain, stretch, string
　　up, make tense, cover over, freeze
　　over
¹⁴綱 *ha(ri)zuna* guy rope

A 強 ⟨1695 / J362f / M9815⟩ KYŌ, GŌ strength; might;
　　strong person.
tsuyo(i) strong, powerful, mighty, robust,
vigorous, healthy; brave, courageous;
severe, intense; durable, solid.
tsuyo(maru) get strong. *tsuyo(meru)* vt
strengthen, intensify, invigorate; confirm;
emphasize, increase, redouble.
tsuyo(garu) show one's toughness.
tsuyo(gari) bluff, show of strength.
shi(iru) force, coerce, constrain, compel.
shi(ite) forcibly, against one's will.
anaga(chi) necessarily, wholly. *kowa(i)*
tough, hard, stiff. *-kyō* a little over, and a
fraction.
-zuyo(i) very.
²力 *kyōryoku* power, might. *gōriki*
　　Herculean strength; mountain carrier-
　　guide
³大 *kyōdai na* mighty, powerful
弓 *gōkyū* strong bow
⁴火 *tsuyobi* a good (cooking) fire
化 *kyōka suru* strengthen, reinforce,
　　intensity, step up, build up
引 *gōin ni* by main force, forcibly
心剤 *kyōshinzai* heart stimulant
⁵圧 *kyōatsu* pressure, oppression,
　　coercion
弁 *kyōben suru* quibble, sophisticate
打 *kyōda* hard blow; heavy hit (in
　　baseball); drive (in tennis)
⁶気 *tsuyoki* strong spirit. *gōgi na* great,
　　powerful, grand
壮 *kyōsō na* robust, sturdy, strong,
　　vigorous
壮剤 *kyōsōzai* tonic
行 *kyōkō* forcing; enforcement
行軍 *kyōkōgun* forced march
⁷迫 *kyōhaku suru* compel, use duress

⁸ 固 *kyōko* firmness, stability, security, strength

国 *kyōkoku* strong nation, powerful country

肩 *kyōken* strong-armed (player)

味 *tsuyomi* strength, strong point

者 *kyōsha* strong person. *gō(no)mono* very strong person; brave warrior

突張 *gōtsu(ku)ha(ri)* hardheartedness; headstrong person

制 *kyōsei* coercion, compulsion, enforcement

制力 *kyōseiryoku* authority, legal power

制的 *kyōseiteki* compulsory, forced

⁹ 風 *kyōfū* moderate gale, strong wind

度 *kyōdo* intensity, strength

姦 *gōkan* rape, violation, assault

要 *kyōyō* coercion, enforcement, extortion, persistent demand. *shi(i)-sema(ru)* coerce

¹⁰ 剛 *kyōgō* strong man

烈 *kyōretsu na* strong, intense; gaudy

弱 *kyōjaku* strength, power

¹¹ 健 *kyōken* robust health

情 *gōjō* obstinacy, stubbornness

盗 *gōtō* burglar, robber; burglary, robbery

欲 *gōyoku* greed, avarice

¹² 訴 *gōso* direct petition

靭 *kyōjin na* tough, tenacious, stiff

硬 *kyōkō na* firm, vigorous, unbending

¹³ 腰 *tsuyogoshi* firm attitude

¹⁴ 豪 *kyōgō* strong man; champion

奪 *gōdatsu* pillage, plunder, extortion; violence

¹⁵ 調 *kyōchō* emphasis

敵 *gōteki, kyōteki* formidable enemy

震 *kyōshin* severe earthquake

権 *kyōken* the power of the state

²² 襲 *kyōshū* assault, storming; terrific hitting

弾 $\frac{1699}{\text{J4346}}$ $\frac{}{\text{M9836}}$ Dan bullet. *dan(jiru)*,
B *dan(zuru), tan(zuru)* play or twang on a stringed instrument. *hi(ku)* play on. *haji(ku)* fillip, flip, snap; repel, shed (water); use (an abacus). *haji(keru)* split open; spring off. *hazu(mu)* spring, bound, rebound; be inspired, be spurred on; invest in; be generous (in tipping); breathe with difficulty. *hajiki* (metal) spring; marbles. *tama* bullet, shot, shell.

² 力 *danryoku* elasticity, flexibility

力性 *danryokusei* elasticity, resilience, flexibility; adaptability

³ 丸 *dangan, tama* bullet, shot, shell, cannon ball, projectile

丸列車 *dangan ressha* super-express, flier

⁴ 手 *hi(ki)te* player, performer

片 *dampen* shell splinter

⁵ 圧 *dan'atsu* pressure, oppression, suppression

出 *haji(ki)-da(su)* snap out; expel; calculate; squeeze out (the money needed)

⁶ 返 *haji(ki)-kae(ru)* spring back, rebound, boomerang

⁸ 雨 *dan'u* hail of bullets

性 *dansei* elasticity

劾 *dangai* impeachment, accusation, censure, criticism

⁹ 除 *tamayoke* protection against bullets, bulletproof

奏 *dansō* playing on stringed instruments

¹¹ 痕 *dankon* bullet hole, bullet mark

道 *dandō* trajectory, line of fire

¹² 着 *danchaku* hit, impact

¹³ 幕 *dammaku* barrage

¹⁴ 語 *hi(ki)gata(ri)* reciting with one's own stringed accompaniment

¹⁶ 頭 *dantō* warhead

薬 *dan'yaku* ammunition

9

彌 $\frac{1697}{\text{J492b}}$ $\frac{}{\text{M9826}}$ Hitsu help.

13

彊 $\frac{1702}{\text{J3630}}$ $\frac{}{\text{M9872}}$ Kyō, Gō strong.

3

口 口 土 士 夂 夊 夕 大 女 子 宀 寸 小 ⺌ 尢 尸 屮 山 川 巛 工 己 巾 干 幺 广 廴 廾 弋 【弓】¹³ ヨ 彑 彡 彳

口
口
土
士
夂
夕
大
女
子
宀
寸
小
⺌
尢
尸
屮
山
川
巛
工
己
巾
干
幺
广
廴
廾
弋
弓
【ヨ
彑】
彡
彳

Kei-gashira or *ino-kashira* pig's head. Also called *yo* (the katakana).
Variants: ⺕, ⺔, 彑. Nickname: Pig's Head.

----- 3 -----

当 $\frac{1706}{\substack{J4576 \\ M9913}}$ Tō right; appropriateness,
A fairness; himself; itself;
at the time. *a(taru)* vi and vt hit, strike,
dash into; touch; shine on; guess right, be
fulfilled; succeed; confront; lie (to the
south); treat; feel out; undertake; be worth;
correspond to; be related to; apply to;
draw (a prize); be assigned to; be affected
by; be spoiling; be exposed to; warm
oneself; shave; grind; this coming (15th);
turn out well; take well; be punished (by
heaven); stand to reason; deal with;
engage (the enemy); need not to (with
negative); have (one's turn); be charged
with. *a(teru)* apply, place, put; hit (the
mark); guess; succeed; expose to; sit (on a
cushion); assign, allocate; call on (a
pupil). *a(terareru)* be affected (by),
suffer (from); be bored, be annoyed. *masa
ni* properly, naturally. *a(taranai)* do not
deserve, be not justifiable, be not proper.
a(tari) bruise; bite; exposure (to wind);
success, hit; clue, trail, scent; batting
average; on this (occasion); in the
direction (of). *a(te)* aim; hopes,
reckoning; dependence, confidence; clue;
pad; blow, stroke. *a(tezuppō)* guesswork,
haphazard work. *a(tekko)* guesswork,
guessing game. *tō no* the said (person or
thing). *-a(tari)* per. *tō-* this (city, etc.).

² 人 *tōnin* the one concerned, the said
person, the man himself
⁴ 日 *tōjitsu* the appointed day, the
occasion
月 *tōgetsu* this month
木 *a(te)gi* batten, scantling
込 *a(te)-ko(mu)* count on, anticipate,
expect
今 *tōkon* the present, these days
分 *tōbun* for the present, temporarily
方 *tōhō* I; our part
⁵ 付 *a(te)-tsu(keru)* insinuate
代 *tōdai* the present generation; those
days; the present family head
外 *a(tari)hazu(re)* success or failure,

risk. *a(te)hazu(re)* disappointment
主 *tōshu* the present head of the family
用漢字 *Tōyō Kanji* the official 1850
"Current Characters" used till 1981
世 *tōsei* the present time
世風 *tōseifū* the latest fashion, the
fashionable style
⁶ 地 *tōchi* this locality
字 *a(te)ji* a phonetic-equivalent
character; a substitute character
年 *tōnen* the current year; that year.
a(tari)doshi bumper year
⁷ 身 *a(te)mi* body blow, knockout punch
役 *a(tari)yaku* successful role. *tōyaku*
this role; this officer
社 *tōsha* this shrine, this firm
初 *tōsho* original; at the beginning
否 *tōhi* right or wrong; justice; propriety,
suitability
局 *tōkyoku* the authorities concerned, the
powers that be, the one in authority;
an insider
⁸ 店 *tōten* this shop, this store, we
所 *tōsho* this place. *a(te)do* aim
夜 *tōya* that night
直 *tōchoku* on duty
事者 *tōjisha* the person concerned
⁹ 面 *tōmen suru* face, confront. *tōmen no*
immediate, urgent.
前 *a(tari)mae* proper, just, fair,
reasonable, natural, ordinary, normal,
usual
為 *tōi* what should be
¹⁰ 馬 *a(te)uma* confronting a mare with a
stallion to test readiness to mate;
preparatory move
時 *tōji* in these days; in those days; time
家 *tōke* this house, this family
座 *tōza* the present; for some time;
current; temporary; immediate; current
checking account
座預金 *tōza yokin* current checking
account
¹¹ 得 *tō (o) e(ta)* accurate, correct
¹² 散 *a(tari)-chi(rasu)* find fault with
everybody
期 *tōki* the present period, this term

嵌 *a(te)-ha(meru) vt* apply to; assign to.
a(te)-ha(maru) vi apply to; be true of; conform to
落 *tōraku* election result
然 *tōzen* justly, properly, naturally, necessarily, of course
番 *tōban* being on duty or on guard; man on duty
惑 *tōwaku* perplexity, embarrassment; doubt; confusion

¹³ 該 *tōgai* the appropriate (authorities)
節 *tōsetsu* these times
障無 *a(tari)sawa(ri) ga na(i)* be harmless; be noncommittal, be neutral
意即妙 *tōi-sokumyō* ready wit
歳 *tōsai* this year; a yearling
¹⁴ 選 *tōsen* election to office; winning (a lottery)

RAD. 彡 59

Kami kazari hair ornament. On right: *sanzukuri* right-hand "hair ornament" or right-hand "three." Nickname: Short Hair (cf. Rad. 190)

──────── **4** ────────

形 [1713 / J3741 / M9969] Gyō. Kei shape. *kata*
A shape, form, make, size, format, mark; pattern, design. *katachi* form, shape; personal appearance. *nari* form, figure, appearance; dress.
⁶ 成 *keisei* formation
而下 *keijika no* physical, material
而上 *keijijō no* metaphysical
式 *keishiki* form; formality
式化 *keishikika* formalization
式主義 *keishiki shugi* formalism, red-tapism
式的 *keishikiteki* formal
式論 *keishikiron* formalism
⁷ 体 *keitai* shape, form. *narikatachi* appearance
作 *katachizuku(ru)* form, shape, make, mold; buildup
状 *keijō* shape, form
見 *katami* memento, souvenir
⁹ 相 *gyōsō* features, expression; aspect. *keisō* phase, form
¹⁰ 容 *keiyō* form, figure, appearance; qualification, description; modifying; figure of speech
容詞 *keiyōshi* adjective
¹⁷ 無 *katana(shi)* all knocked out of shape, worthless
象 *keishō* shape, figure; appearance; phenomenon
¹³ 跡 *keiseki* traces, evidences, indications
勢 *keisei* condition, situation, prospects
¹⁴ 態 *keitai* shape, form, structure
¹⁶ 骸 *keigai* framework; wreck

──────── **6** ────────

彦 [1714 / J4927 / M9981] Gen. *hiko* (ancient) boy.

──────── **8** ────────

彪 [1716 / J4937 / M9993] Hyō. Hyū spots; a tiger's spots; small tiger; *aya* figure, design.

彬 [1717 / J493b / M9996] Hin harmony; pleasing balance between figure and background.

彩 [1718 / J3a4c / M9992] Sai. *irodo(ru)* color, paint,
B makeup.
⁶ 色 *saishiki, saishoku* coloring, painting
色画 *saishikiga* colored painting
⁸ 画 *saiga* painting, colored picture
¹² 雲 *saiun* cloudscape; glowing clouds

彫 [1719 / J4426 / M9995] Chō carving. *ho(ru)*
B carve, engrave, chisel, sculpture, inscribe.
⁸ 金 *chōkin* metal carving
物 *ho(ri)mono* carving; engraving; sculpture; tattooing
刻 *ho(ri)kıza(mu)* engrave, carve. *chōkoku* carving, engraving, sculpture
刻刀 *chōkokutō* graver, chisel
刻家 *chōkokuka* engraver; carver
¹² 琢 *chōtaku* carving and polishing
¹³ 塑 *choso* carving and modeling
¹⁴ 像 *chōzō* sculpture; carved statue, graven image

3
ロ
ロ
土
士
夂
夊
夕
大
女
子
宀
寸
小
尢
尸
屮
山
川
巛
工
已
巾
干
幺
广
廴
廾
弋
弓
彐
彑
彡
[彳]
4

---------- 11 ----------

B 彰 $\frac{1721}{\text{J3e34}}$ SHŌ. *aki(rakana)* clear.
M10015

---------- 12 ----------

B 影 $\frac{1722}{\text{J3146}}$ EI shadow. *kage* light;
M10019 shadow; silhouette; phantom; reflection; figure; trace.

[8] 武者 *kagemusha* general's double; wirepuller; man behind the scenes

法師 *kagebōshi* shadow, shadowy figure, silhouette

[12] 絵 *kagee* silhouette
[14] 像 *eizō* shadow, image, phantom
[16] 薄 *kage (ga) usu(i)* emaciated
[19] 響 *eikyō* influence, effect, consequences

████████████ RAD. 彳 60 ████████████

Gyōnimben (a left-hand element like the first part of Rad. 144 *gyō,* the "going" radical, but used only at the left like Rad. 9 *nimben* left-hand "man"; hence, the "going man" radical). All characters historically treated under Rad. 144 行 are, with the exception of the radical character itself, treated herein as Rad. 60. Nickname: Going Man.

---------- 4 ----------

A 役 $\frac{1726}{\text{J4c72}}$ EKI war, campaign, battle,
M10057 expedition; exacted unpaid labor. YAKU office, post, position, appointment, duty; role; use, service, help. *eki(suru)* employ, enlist the services of, press into service.

[2] 人 *yakunin* official, officer, office holder
[4] 不足 *yakubusoku* dissatisfaction with one's lot
[5] 立 *yakuda(teru), yakuda(tsu), yaku (ni) ta(tsu)* be useful, be helpful, serve the purpose
付 *yakuzu(ke)* allotment of duties; role. *yakuzu(ki)* responsible person; assuming office
目 *yakume* duty, office, business, role
目柄 *yakumegara de* by virtue of office
[6] 回 *yakumawa(ri)* part, burden, responsibility
向 *yakumu(ki)* nature of one's office, one's position
[8] 者 *yakusha* actor, actress, performer, ⌈official
所 *yakusho* government office
[9] 柄 *yakugara* nature of one's office, one's position
[10] 員 *yakuin* officer, official, person in charge; board; staff
[11] 得 *yakutoku* the extra emoluments of office

務 *ekimu* labor, service
[12] 場 *yakuba* city hall, a public office
割 *yakuwa(ri)* allotment of duties; role

---------- 5 ----------

A 径 $\frac{1730}{\text{J3742}}$ KEI path; diameter;
M10080' method. *michi* road, path, lane, way, street, highway, route; journey; distance; course, way, means; duty, morality, moral doctrine; teachings; specialty; an art; reason, justice.

[13] 路 *keiro* course, route, channel

B 征 $\frac{1731}{\text{J402c}}$ SEI. *sei(suru)* attack the
M10077 rebellious; collect taxes.

[5] 圧 *seiatsu* control, conquest
[6] 伐 *seibatsu* subjection, conquest; chastisement, punishment, extermination

夷大将軍 *Seii Taishōgun* Commander-in-Chief of the Expeditionary Force Against the Barbarians

[8] 服 *seifuku* conquest, subjugation; mastery, overcoming

服者 *seifukusha* conqueror, overcomer
[9] 途 *seito* military expedition; journey, travel
[10] 討 *seitō* subjection, conquest; chastisement, punishment, extermination

彼 ₁₇₃₂ J4860 M10066 HI he; that. *kare* he.
B *ka(no), a(no)* that, the. *are* that, that time. *are(demo)* in a way, in spite of appearances, as it is.

³ 女 *kanojo* she; girl friend
⁴ 氏 *kareshi* he; beau, lover
方 *anata, kanata, achi, atchi, achira* that; the other; the other side; there, yonder; foreign country. *atchi* Get out of here.
方任 *anatamaka(se)* letting things slide
方此方 *anata-konata, achikochi, achira-kochira* here and there, to and fro, fore and aft
⁵ 処 *asuko, asoko, kashiko* yonder, over there, that place
奴 *aitsu, ayatsu, kyatsu, kayatsu* that fellow, that guy
世 *a(no)yo* the next world
⁶ 此 *are kore, kare kore, are(ya)-kore(ya)* this and that, one thing or another
⁷ 我 *higa* oneself and others, each other
⁸ 岸 *higan* equinoctial week; Buddhist services during equinoctial week; the other shore; goal
¹² 等 *karera* they

往 ₁₇₃₃ J317d M10073 Ō. *ina(su)* let go; chase
A away. *yuki* going; travel. *yu(ku)* go; run (water).

⁴ 日 *ōjitsu* ancient times
⁵ 古 *ōko* ancient times
生 *ōjō* death, submission. *ōjō suru* be at one's wit's end
生際 *ōjōgiwa* the point of death
⁶ 年 *ōnen* years ago, formerly, the years past
⁷ 来 *yukiki, ōrai* coming and going; street traffic; road, street, highway, boulevard; fluctuations; correspondence, association; occurring to the mind
⁸ 往 *ōō* sometimes, occasionally, often
昔 *ōjaku, ōseki* ancient times
事 *ōji* the past, past events
⁹ 信 *ōshin* first half of a reply card
¹⁰ 時 *ōji* ancient times
帰 *yu(ki)kae(ri)* round trip
¹² 診 *ōshin* doctor's visit, house call
復 *ōfuku* round trip; correspondence; association
復切符 *ōfuku kippu* return ticket

復葉書 *ōfuku hagaki* return postcard
¹³ 路 *ōro* outward journey
¹⁵ 還 *yu(ki)kae(ri), ōkan* traffic, coming and going, round trip; highway

──────── 6 ────────

律 ₁₇₄₀ J4e27 M10097 RICHI, RITSU law,
A regulation; rhythm. *ris(suru)* judge, settle, gauge, control. *Ritsu* Buddhist sect originating in the eighth century.

⁵ 令 *ritsuryō* ancient laws. *ritsurei* national laws
⁸ 例 *ritsurei* ordinance, criminal law
法 *rippō* law, rule, legislation; Law of God
¹¹ 動 *ritsudō* rhythm, rhythmic movement, periodic motion
¹³ 義 *richigi* honesty, integrity, simplicity, sincerity, loyalty
¹⁵ 儀 *richigi* honesty, integrity, simplicity, sincerity, loyalty

待 ₁₇₄₁ J4254 M10085 TAI waiting. *ma(tsu)* vi
A and *vt* wait, wait for; expect, watch for; depend on; treat, deal with. *ma(chiagumu)* be tired of waiting. *ma(tta)* hold on, not ready. *ma(taseru)* detain, keep waiting.

² 人 *ma(chi)bito* expected visitor
⁴ 伏 *ma(chi)bu(seru)* lie in wait for
合 *ma(chi)-a(u)* wait for each other. *ma(chi)-a(waseru)* waiting at a set time. *machiai* tea-ceremony waiting room; geisha entertainment place
合室 *machiaishitsu* waiting room
⁸ 侘 *ma(chi)-wa(biru)* be tired of waiting
明 *ma(chi)-a(kasu)* wait all night
命 *taimei* awaiting orders; being put on the waiting list
受 *ma(chi)-u(keru)* await, expect
¹⁰ 針 *ma(chi)bari* marking pin
兼 *ma(chi)-ka(neru)* wait impatiently for
時間 *ma(chi)jikan* waiting time
¹¹ 遇 *taigū* treatment, reception, entertainment, (hotel) service; salary, remuneration; rank
惚 *ma(chi)-bo(ke), ma(chi)-bō(ke)* wait in vain

3

口
口
土
士
夂
夊
夕
大
女
子
宀
寸
小
⺌
尢
尸
屮
山
川
巛
工
已
巾
干
幺
广
廾
弋
弓
彐
彡
[彳]⁶

3

口 口 土 士 夂 夕 大 女 子 宀 寸 小 ⺌ 尢 尸 屮 山 川 巛 工 己 巾 干 幺 广 廴 廾 弋 弓 彐 彑 彡 [彳]

望 ma(chi)-nozo(mu) look for, wait eagerly for. *taibō* expectant waiting

12 遠 ma(chi)dō(shii), machidō(i) being long in coming; waiting anxiously for

焦 ma(chi)-ko(gareru) wait eagerly for

無 ma(tta)na(shi)de without waiting

14 構 ma(chi)-kama(eru) watch for, wait eagerly for, be prepared for

暮 ma(chi)-ku(rasu) wait all day for

15 避 *taihi* shunting (in railroading); taking shelter; escaping

機 *taiki suru* watch and wait, stand by, wait for a chance

A 後 1742 J3865 M10098 Go, Kō back, rear, behind. *ato* back, rear; results; remainder, sequel; posterity; successor; survivor; effect, influence; estate. *ato no* back, rear, posterior; previous, last; later, subsequent; next, following; future. *ato ni* after, behind, back, backward; ago; next. *oku(rasu), oku(raseru)* retard, delay, defer. *oku(re)* failure, defeat; backwardness, shyness, fear. *oku(reru)* be late, be delayed, be overdue; lag behind; (clocks) lose. *ushi(ro)* back, rear, behind. *ushiro(metai)* underhanded, suspicious. *nochi* after, since then; future; after one's death. *-go* after, afterwards, later on, since, hence.

2 人 *kōjin* posterity, future generations

4 手 ushi(ro)de (tied with) hands behind the back. *gote* passivity

片付 atokatazu(ke) clearing up, putting things in order

日 *gojitsu, gonichi* later on, some other day later on

日談 *gojitsudan* reminiscences, recollections

方 *kōhō, shirie, atokata* rear, back. *nochikata* later

天性 *kōtensei* characteristics acquired from one's environment

天的 *kōtenteki* acquired, cultivated

5 代 *kōdai* future generations, posterity

払 atobara(i) deferred payment

半 *kōhan* latter half

世 *kōsei, nochi (no) yo* coming age; last days, posterity. *gose, nochi (no) yo* the next world, the future life

生 *kōsei* being born later; younger

people. *goshō* the future life

生大事 *goshō daiji ni* religiously, earnestly, carefully

半生 *kōhansei* latter half of life

半期 *kōhanki* latter half of a year

半戦 *kōhansen* latter half of a game

6 回 atomawa(shi) postponement

向 ushi(ro)mu(ki) looking backward

列 *kōretsu* rear, back row

光 *gokō* halo, corona

先 atosaki front and rear; first and last; both ends; context; circumstances, consequences. *atosaki ni suru* reverse, invert

年 *kōnen* in later years, afterward

任 *kōnin* successor

7 足 atoashi, ushi(ro) ashi hind leg

身 *kōshin* one's future rebirth; a successor organization

図 *kōto* plans for the future

戻 atomodo(ri) going backward, retrogression

述 *kōjutsu suru* state hereafter

見 *kōken, ushi(ro)mi* guardianship; assistance

見人 *kōkennin* guardian, tutor, assistant

尾 *kōbi* rear, tail

8 金 atokin, atogane balance of payment

門 *kōmon* back gate; back door

送 *kōsō suru* send to the rear; send later

退 atozusa(ri), atoshiza(ri), atojisa(ri) falling back, drawing back. *kōtai* retreat

味 atoaji aftertaste

押 atoo(shi) pushing, backing, boosting

刻 *gokoku* later on, afterward

命 *kōmei* further instructions

妻 *gosai* second wife

学 *kōgaku* younger scholars; younger generation; knowledge to be available in the future

者 *kōsha* the latter

始末 atoshimatsu settlement, liquidation, clearing up

知恵 atojie hindsight

事 *kōji* future affairs; affairs after one's death

9 後 atoato distant future. *nochinochi* distant future; future life

悔 *kōkai* repentance, remorse

段 *kōdan* latter part (of a story)

前 *ushi(ro)-mae* with front side back

姿 *ushi(ro) sugata* retreating figure, appearance from the back

¹⁰記 *kōki* postscript

宮 *kōkyū* imperial consort; harem; palace

家 *goke* the bereaved family, widow, widowhood

釜 *atogama* successor

書 *atoga(ki)* postscript. *kōsho* sequel to a book

部 *kōbu* rear, stern, back part

進 *kōshin* retreat, moving backward; younger generation

¹¹添 *nochizo(i)* second wife

略 *kōryaku* omitting the last part of an article

祭 *ato (no) matsu(ri)* too late for the fair, too late for the doctor

¹²程 *nochihodo* later on

期 *kōki* latter period; late (Nara); latter half year; second semester

援 *kōen* assistance, support, backing

¹³暗 *ushi(ro)gura(i)* shady, underhanded, suspicious, secretive

楯 *ushi(ro)date* backing, support, protection; backer, supporter

詰 *gozu(me)* rear guard

裔 *kōei* descendants

続 *kōzoku no* succeeding, following

継 *kōkei* succession; successor, heir

¹⁴腐 *atokusa(re)* trouble afterward

塵 *kōjin* second best; subordination; second best; second fiddle; dust raised after vehicles

¹⁵衛 *kōei* rear guard

篇 *kōhen* last volume, later volumes, last part of the book; sequel

輩 *kōhai* younger men; younger generation; one's juniors

¹⁶頭部 *kōtōbu* back of the head

¹⁸難 *gonan, kōnan* future trouble, consequences

²¹顧 *kōko* looking back; anxiety

---------------- 7 ----------------

B 徐 1744 J3d79 M10110 Jo. *omomu(ro) ni* slowly, deliberately, gently.

³行 *jokō suru* go slowly

¹⁰徐 *jojo ni, sorosoro* gradually, steadily, slowly; quietly

A 從 1745 J3d3e M10133 SHŌ. JU. JŪ secondary, incidental, subordinate, accessory, junior; retainer; follow.

shitaga(u) obey, submit to, comply with, observe (a law); follow; accompany.

shitaga(eru) be accompanied by, take (someone) with you; subjugate, subdue.

shitaga(tte) consequently, therefore; in accordance with, in proportion to, as. *ju-* junior or second (in court ranks).

⁵犯 *jūhan* accomplice; complicity

兄 *jūkei, itoko* elder male cousin

兄弟 *jūkeitei, itoko* male cousin

⁷弟 *jūtei, itoko* younger male cousin

来 *jūrai* heretofore; existing

⁸妹 *jūmai, itoko* younger female cousin

卒 *jūsotsu* a soldier servant, an officer's servant

者 *jūsha* follower, attendant, valet, retinue, servant

事 *jūji suru* engage in, carry on, practice medicine

姉 *jūshi, itoko* elder female cousin

姉妹 *jūshimai, itoko* female cousin

⁹前 *jūzen ni* heretofore. *jūzen no* previous, former

軍 *jūgun suru* follow the army; join the colors

¹⁰容 *shōyō(taru)* composed, calm, tranquil

¹²順 *jūjun na* submissive, obedient, docile, gentle, meek, tame, pliant, amenable

属 *jūzoku* subordination; dependency

⁷業員 *jūgyōin* employee, working force

¹⁴僕 *jūboku* attendant male servant

¹⁵横 *jūō* length and breadth; every direction; right and left; warp and woof

---

A 徒 1746 J454c M10121 To. party, set, gang, companions; people. *ada* emptiness, vanity, futility, uselessness, faithlessness, ephemeral thing. *itazura* vanity; uselessness. *itazu(ra)ni* in vain, uselessly, aimlessly. *tada, tadano* free, gratis. *tada(narunu)* unusual, extraordinary, serious. *tada* ordinarily. *ada(shi)* fickle, vain; another. *kachi* walking. *muda* futility, uselessness, waste. *kachi de* on foot.

³士 *kachi* foot soldier

⁴手 *toshu* empty-handed, penniless

手体操 *toshu taisō* calisthenics

3

口口土士夂夂夕大女子宀寸小小尤尸屮山川巛工己巾干幺广廴廾弋弓ヨ彑彡〔彳〕

3

口
口
土
士
夂
夂
夕
大
女
子
宀
寸
小
小
尢
尸
屮
山
川
巛
工
己
巾
干
幺
广
廴
廾
弋
弓
ヨ
彑
彡

[彳]

手空拳 *toshukūken de* empty-handed; without capital

⁶死 *toshi suru* die in vain. *toshi* a dog's death

刑 *tokei* penal servitude, prison term

⁷花 *adabana* an abortive flower

労 *torō* wasted effort, lost labor

弟 *totei* apprenticeship; apprentice; errand boy

⁸歩 *toho, kachi* walking

⁹食 *toshoku* life of idleness

¹⁰党 *totō* conspirators; conspiracy; faction, junta

¹¹渉 *kachiwata(ri), toshō* fording

¹²然 *tsurezure, tozen* tedium, leisure hours

²⁰競走 *tokyōsō* footrace, race on foot

---------- 8 ----------

術 ₁₇₅₄ J3d51 M34046 A JUTSU art, technique, skill; means; artifice, trick, stratagem; resources; magic, conjury. *sube* way, means, resource. [行]

⁴中 *jutchū* trick, trap

¹²策 *jussaku* artifice, stratagem, trick, intrigue, policy

¹³数 *jussū* artifice, stratagem, trick, intrigue, policy

¹⁴語 *jutsugo* technical term, terminology

得 ₁₇₅₅ J4640 M10137 A TOKU profit, advantage, benefit. *e(ru), u(ru)* get, acquire, find, earn, win, gain, receive; can, be able to, may; commit (sin). *e(tagaru)* covet, have a desire for. *toku(suru)* gain, save; benefit. *e(tari)* fine, excellent. *e(te)* being apt to.

⁴心 *tokushin* consent; conviction; satisfaction

手 *ete* strong point, specialty, forte

手勝手 *etegatte, etekatte* selfishness, wilfulness

⁵失 *tokushitsu* pros and cons, gains and losses, desirability

⁷体 *etai* nature, character

⁸物 *emono* weapon

⁹度 *tokudo suru* enter the (Buddhist) priesthood

点 *tokuten* marks, score, runs

¹¹得 *tokutoku(toshite)* proudly, triumphantly

票 *tokuhyō* votes obtained

¹²策 *tokusaku* profitable plan, good plan. *tokusaku na* advisable, wise, expedient

¹³意 *tokui(garu)* be elated. *tokui* prosperity; triumph, elation; strong point; customer, client

意回 *tokuimawa(ri)* calling on customers; traveling salesman

意気 *tokuige na* proud, elated

意先 *tokuisaki* customer, client; credit customer

¹⁸難 *egata(i)* rare, hard to get

---------- 9 ----------

循 ₁₇₅₈ J3d5b M10187 B JUN follow.

¹⁵環 *junkan* circulation, rotation, cycle

街 ₁₇₅₉ J3339 M34051 A KAI, GAI street, avenue; town. *machi* town; quarters; street. [行]

⁶灯 *gaitō* street light, road lamp

⁷角 *machi kado* street corner

¹¹道 *kaidō, gaidō* highway

¹³路 *gairo* road, street, avenue, arcade

路樹 *gairoju* shade tree, roadside tree

¹⁶頭 *gaitō* street

復 ₁₇₆₀ J497c M10183 A FUKU. *fuku(suru)* return to, revert to, be restored to, resume (one's duties); revenge; reward. *mata, mata to* again.

⁴仇 *fukkyū, fukukyū* revenge, reprisal

元 *fukugen* restoration to original state

⁵旧 *fukkyū, fukukyū* recovery, restoration, restitution, rehabilitation

刊 *fukkan* reissue, revived publication

古 *fukko* restoration, revival (of a former regime), reaction

古調 *fukkochō* trend toward old styles

⁸刻 *fukkoku* reproducing a book from identical plates

命 *fukumei* report

⁹活 *fukkatsu* revival, rebirth, resuscitation, regeneration, resurrection

活祭 *Fukkatsusai* Easter

¹⁰原 *fukugen* restoration (to original state)

帰 *fukki* return, comeback, reinstatement, reversion

員 *fukuin* demobilization

11 唱 *fukushō suru* recite, rehearse; repeat (a command)

習 *fukushū* review. *sarai* review; rehearsal

13 辟 *fukuheki* restoration of a ruler

路 *fukuro* return trip

業 *fukugyō suru* return to work

14 誦 *fukushō suru* recite, rehearse; repeat (a command)

15 権 *fukken, fukuken* reinstatement, rehabilitation, restoration of rights

縁 *fukuen* restoring marital or other relations

調 *fukuchō* a comeback

16 興 *fukkō* revival, resuscitation, resurgence, restoration, rehabilitation, a comeback, renaissance

18 職 *fukushoku* reinstatement, resumption of office, reappointment

20 籍 *fukuseki* reinstating as a member; returning to original domicile

23 讐 *fukushū* revenge, reprisal, retaliation

御 ──1761── Go honorific prefix. Gyo
B ──J3866── imperial honorary prefix.
──M10157── prefix. *gyo(suru)* control, manage, manipulate, govern; handle; drive (a cart). *o-, on-, mi-* honorific prefixes.

3 大 *ontai* boss, governor, general

下 *osa(ge)* hair hanging down the back

上 *okami* emperor, government, authorities; a noble; hostess at a restaurant

上様 *okamisan* wife, madame. *onobo(ri)san* visitor from the country

4 方 *onkata* person (polite)

中 *onchū* and Company; Messrs.

尤 *gomotto(mo)* quite right, reasonable

日様 *ohisama* the sun

月様 *otsukisama* the moon

父様 *otōsama, otōsan* father

手玉 *otedama* jackstones; bean bags

手洗 *mitarashi* holy water at a shrine. *oteara(i)* toilet, lavatory, washstand

代 *miyo* reign, period

5 札 *ofuda* Shinto talisman

礼 *orei* salutation, salute, bow, courtesy, propriety, ceremony, thanks, appreciation, remuneration, return present

世 *miyo* reign, period

出 *oide* (polite) coming; going; being

召 *ome(shi) ni naru* ride; call (someone); wear

召物 *ome(shi)mono* clothes

目玉 *omedama* scolding, reprimand

目出度 *omedeta(i)* happy, auspicious. *omedetō* congratulations

目通 *omedō(ri)* an audience (with), interview; presence

目掛 *ome(ni)ka(karu)* meet (someone). *ome(ni)ka(keru)* show someone (something)

用 *goyō* your order; your business; official business; king's business

用地 *goyōchi* imperial estate

用邸 *goyōtei* detached palace, imperial villa

用始 *goyō haji(me)* reopening of offices after New Year's

用納 *goyō osa(me)* year-end office closing

用達 *goyōtashi* purveyors to the government

6 好 *okono(mi) no* favorite, requested

字 *on(no)ji* enough

守 *omamori* a charm

先 *osaki* the future. *osaki e, osaki ni* (go) ahead of me; first. *onsaki* one who walked before a noble

存 *gozon(ji)* your acknowledgment; your knowledge; your acquaintance, your awareness

自身 *gojishin* himself, herself

朱印 *goshuin* shogun's sealed letter

名 *mina* God's name. *gyomei* emperor's name, imperial signature

名御爾 *gyomeigyoji* imperial seal, privy seal

7 身 *omi, ommi* you (familiar)

来光 *goraikō* mountain-top sunrise viewing; mountain-top sunrise

沙汰 *gosata* words of a ruler

見外 *omiso(re)* failure to recognize

見知置 *omishi(ri)o(ki)* meeting you

伽 *otogi* keeping (a person) company; nursing (a patient)

伽国 *otogi(no)kuni* fairyland

3
口
口
士
士
夂
夊
夕
大
女
子
宀
寸
小
⺌
尢
尸
屮
山
川
巛
工
己
巾
干
幺
广
廴
廾
弋
弓
彐
彑
彡
彳 9

口 口 土 士 夂 夊 夕 大 女 子 宀 寸 小 尤 尸 屮 山 川 巛 工 己 巾 干 幺 广 廴 廾 弋 弓 彐 彑 彡 〔彳〕

3

⁸ 金 *okane* money

物 *gyobutsu* imperial property

参 *omai(ri)* visiting a shrine or temple

苑 *gyoen* imperial garden

免 *gomen* your pardon; declining (something); dismissal; permission; licensed, chartered. *gomen nasai* Pardon me.

者 *gyosha* driver, coachman, bus driver

法度 *gohatto* law, ordinance; prohibition

供 *otomo suru* accompany. *osona(e) goku*, *gokū* an offering

所 *gosho* an old imperial palace

⁹ 通夜 *otsuya*, *otsūya* a wake

星様 *ohoshisama* the stars

神酒 *omiki* sacred wine, wine offering

前 *omae* you; Hey there you. *gozen* before a noble; you (polite); (an ancient) term of address for a titled lady

前会議 *gozen kaigi* imperial conference

¹⁰ 株 *okabu* one's position; favorite trick; forte; characteristic

酒 *miki* sacred wine, wine offering. *goshu, osake* saké

破算 *gohasan* recalculation; fresh start

託 *gotaku* tedious talk; impertinent talk; oracle; stating something trivial as if important

都合 *gotsugō* your convenience

都合主義 *gotsugō shugi* opportunism, time-serving

料地 *goryōchi* imperial estate

家人 *gokenin* a lower-grade retainer

家芸 *oiegei* specialty, monopoly

家騒動 *oie sōdō* family quarrel

¹¹ 経 *okyō* sutras

堂 *midō* main temple of a monastery

袋 *ofukuro* mama

曹子 *onzōshi* son of noble

転婆 *otemba* tomboy, flapper

遍路 *ohenro* pilgrimage

¹² 裁可 *gosaika* imperial sanction

無沙汰 *gobusata* neglect to get in touch with

偉方 *oeragata* dignitary

開 *ohira(ki)* adjournment, close

飯 *gohan, omamma* boiled rice; a meal

¹³ 預 *oazu(ke)* wait (command to a dog); postponement

裾分 *osusowa(ke)* sharing a gift

馳走 *gochisō* entertainment, treat, feast, dinner, banquet, hospitality

愛想 *oaisō* hospitality; cuteness; (restaurant) bill; attachment

殿 *goten* palace; court; mansion, home of a noble

辞儀 *ojigi* bow, greeting; refusal, hesitation

陰 *okage* indebtedness, favor, help, support

陰様 *okagesama de* thanks to you

意 *gyoi* your will, your pleasure

¹⁴ 製 *gyosei* an emperor's poem or song

¹⁵ 影石 *mikage ishi* granite

幣担 *gohei-katsugi* superstitious person

霊 *mitama* departed spirit; Holy Spirit

¹⁶ 膳 *gozen* meal, rice, tray, low table

覧 *goran ni naru* see, look, inspect; try (to do). *gorō(jiru)* see (polite)

嬢様 *ojōsama, ojōsan* young lady, (your) daughter

¹⁷ 輿 *mikoshi* palanquin of a Shinto god

¹⁸ 雛様 *ohinasama* festival dolls

題 *gyodai* theme of Imperial Poetry Contest

¹⁹ 簾 *misu* bamboo screen

──────── **10** ────────

微 | 1765 / J4879 / M10203 | BI, MI minuteness; insignificance; vagueness; fewness. *kasu(kana)* faint, dim, weak, indistinct, hazy; poor, wretched.

² 力 *biryoku* poor ability; the little one can do; slender means; little influence

³ 才 *bisai* minor talent; my talents (humble)

小 *bishō* minuteness

⁴ 少 *bishō* minute quantity

分 *bibun* differential calculus

分子 *bibunshi* atom; molecule; tiny particle

分積分学 *bibun-sekibungaku* differential and integral calculus

⁵ 生物 *biseibutsu* microscopic organism, microbe, germ

生物学 *biseibutsugaku* microbiology

⁶ 行 *bikō* traveling incognito

⁷ 妙 *bimyō* delicacy, subtlety, nicety

⁸ 雨 *biu* light rain

⁹ 風 *bifū* breeze, zephyr

¹⁰笑 *bishō, hohoe(mi)* smile. *hohoe(mu)* smile; begin to bloom

弱 *bijaku* feebleness

¹¹細 *bisai* minuteness, fineness; details

粒子 *biryūshi* a very tiny particle

視的 *bishiteki* microscopic

動 *bidō* tremor, quiver

¹²量 *biryō* very small amount

温 *bion* lukewarmness, low temperature

温的 *bionteki* indifferent, lukewarm

¹³微 *bibi(taru)* slight, small, tiny, petty, feeble, insignificant

禄 *biroku* small stipend, pittance

罪 *bizai* minor offense

意 *bii* small token (of gratitude), my (humble) feelings

¹⁴塵 *mijin* particle, bit, atom

¹⁵熱 *binetsu* slight fever

震 *bishin* slight earthquake

¹⁶積分 *bisekibun* differential and integral calculus

───────── **11** ─────────

德 A | 1767 J4641 M10237' | TOKU virtue, goodness; good; gain; power to command respect.

⁵目 *tokumoku* virtues

用 *tokuyō na* economical

用品 *tokuyōhin* bargain goods

⁶行 *tokkō* virtuous deeds, goodness

⁷利 *tokkuri, tokuri* bottle

⁸育 *tokuiku* spiritual education, moral training

⁹政 *tokusei* benevolent government; moratorium

¹¹望 *tokubō* moral influence

¹³義 *tokugi* morality, integrity, sincerity

徴 B | 1768 J4427 M10238' | CHŌ sign, symptom, omen. *chō(suru)* collect, solicit, seek; judge by; question; refer to; call for (someone); demand. *shirushi* sign, indication, omen.

⁵用 *chōyō* commandeering, drafting, requisitioning, expropriating

収 *chōshū* collection, levy, assessment

⁷兵 *chōhei* conscription, recruitment, enlistment

兵制 *chōheisei* conscription system

⁹発 *chōhatsu* levy, forage, requisition, commandeering

¹⁰候 *chōkō* sign, indication, omen, symptom

¹²税 *chōzei* tax collection, taxation

募 *chōbo* enlistment, recruitment

集 *chōshū* levy, enlistment, recruiting

───────── **12** ─────────

徹 B | 1771 J4530 M10245 | TETSU clear. *tes(suru)* pierce, penetrate, strike home; go through, sit up (all night). *tō(ru)* penetrate, permeate. *tō(su)* walk along, pass by; pass through; pass (exams); be known as; be admissible; come in; be understood; reach; draw (on a pipe); drain (as a sink); be consistent.

⁸夜 *tetsuya* all night; all-night vigil; sleepless night

底 *tettei* thoroughness, completion

底的 *tetteiteki* thorough, exhaustive, complete

¹⁰宵 *tesshō* all night, without sleep

¹⁶頭徹尾 *tettō-tetsubi* thoroughly, through and through, completely, from start to finish

衝 B | 1772 J3e57 M34069 | SHŌ brunt; opposition (in astronomy); highway; collision; important point. *tsu(ku)* thrust, pierce, spear, stab, prick; gore; lunge at; push, poke; strike (a bell); attack, strike (at the heart); brave (a storm); be pungent; strike against; (words) rush (to one's lips). [行]

⁵立 *tsuita(te)* single-leaf screen

⁸突 *shōtotsu* collision, bump, impact; conflict, discord, quarrel; encounter, clash

¹¹動 *shōdō* shock; impulse, impetus

動的 *shōdōteki* impulsive

¹⁵撃 *shōgeki* shock, crash, impact; bombardment (in physics); (emotional) shock; trauma

───────── **13** ─────────

徽 | 1773 J352b M-X | Nonstandard for 徽 1778.

衡 B | 1775 J3955 M34078 | KŌ measuring rod; scales. *kubiki* yoke. [行]

3

口 口 土 士 夂 夊 夕 大 女 子 宀 寸 小 ⺌ 尢 尸 屮 山 川 巛 工 己 巾 干 幺 广 廾 弋 弓 彐 彑 彡 [彳]₁₃

4
【心忄⺗】

戈戸手扌支攴攵文斗斤方无日曰月木欠止歹殳毋比毛氏气水氵氺火灬爪爫父爻爿丬片牙牛犬犭

衛 $\frac{1776}{J3152}$ $\frac{}{M34073}$ Eɪ protection.
A [行]
³士 *eji, eishi* ancient imperial guard; soldiers on guard
⁵生 *eisei* health, hygiene, sanitation
生的 *eiseiteki* hygienic, sanitary
生学 *eiseigaku* hygiene, hygienics
⁷兵 *eihei* palace guards; guard, sentinel; garrison

⁹星 *eisei* satellite
¹¹視 *eishi* guards at a parliament

---- **14** ----

徽 $\frac{1778}{J\text{-}X}$ $\frac{}{M10267}$ 徽 $\frac{1773}{J352b}$ $\frac{}{M\text{-}X}$ Kɪ good; beautiful; badge.
¹⁵章 *kishō* badge, emblem, ensign

4-STROKE RADICALS

RAD. 心 61

Kokoro heart. At left: 忄 (3 strokes) *risshimben* left-side standing "heart." At bottom: 心 or ⺗ *shitagokoro* bottom "heart." Nickname: Heart.

心 $\frac{1780}{J3f34}$ $\frac{}{M10295}$ SHIN heart, mind, spirit;
A motive, sense (of duty); padding; wick; core; marrow; vitality. *kokoro* mind, spirit; mentality; idea, thought; heart, feeling; wholeheartedness,

sincerity, sympathy; attention; interest, care; will; intention; taste, mood; true meaning (of a poem). *kokoro kara, shin kara* wholeheartedly, sincerely, cordially. *kokoro(narazumo)* unwillingly, reluctantly. *kokoro suru* attend to, care for, mind, notice, pay attention to; take heed.
³丈夫 *kokorojōbu na* courageous, secure
⁴中 *shinjū* double suicide, lover's suicide. *shinchū* heart, mind, inmost thoughts, true motive; at heart
⁵付 *kokorozu(ku)* notice, realize, sense; exercise care. *kokorozu(ke)* tip, gratuity; suggestion
外 *shingai* unexpected, regrettable, mortifying
⁶血 *shinketsu* sincerity
尽 *kokorozu(kushi)* earnest work, kindness, solicitude, efforts
任 *kokoromaka(se)* one's own way, as one desires
忙 *kokorozewa(shii)* rushed (feeling)
当 *kokoroa(tari)* knowledge, idea, clue;

guess. *kokoroa(te)* hope, expectation, reliance; guess
次第 *kokoro shidai* depending on how one feels
気 *shinki* mind
安 *kokoroyasu(i)* intimate, friendly, feeling at ease
行迄 *kokoroyu(ku) made* to one's heart's content
地 *kokochi, shinchi* feeling, sensation, mood; idea; mental attitude, mental state
地好 *kokochiyo(ku)* pleasantly; willingly
⁷床 *kokoroyuka(shii)* refined
乱 *kokoromida(re)* lack of prudence
忘 *kokorowasu(re)* sudden failure of memory
労 *shinrō* anxiety, worry, fear, suspense; trouble, care; good offices
身 *shinshin* mind and body
⁸底 *kokoro (no) soko, shinsoko, shintei* bottom of one's heart, real intention, motive
房 *shimbō* auricle, atrium
易 *kokoroyasu(i)* intimate, friendly, feeling at ease
的 *shinteki* mental, psychological, psychical
服 *shimpuku* admiration and devotion, hearty submission
苦 *kokoroguru(shii)* regrettable, sorry,

conscience-stricken, unfortunate

事 *shinji* one's thoughts

9 音 *shin'on* heart tone

待 *kokoroma(chi)* anticipation, expectation

持 *kokoromo(chi)* feeling, sensation, mood; somewhat, a little

砕 *kokoro (o) kuda(ku)* worry

胆 *shintan* one's heart

変 *kokorogawa(ri)* change of mind; inconstancy

室 *shinshitsu* ventricle of the heart

神 *shinshin* mind

神喪失 *shinshin sōshitsu* mental derangement

10 根 *kokorone* inner feelings; motive; disposition; character

残 *kokoronoko(ri)* regret, reluctance

浮 *kokoro (ni) uka(bu)* think about

恥 *kokoroha(zukashii)* shameful

留 *kokoro (ni) to(meru)* pay attention to

弱 *kokoroyowa(i)* weak-willed, fickle

配 *shimpai, kokorokuba(ri)* anxiety, worry, fear, suspense; trouble, care; good offices

配性 *shimpaishō* worry habit

配事 *shimpaigoto* cares, worries, troubles

11 強 *kokorozuyo(i)* feeling reassured, confident; heartening (news). *kokorogowa(i)* stout-hearted; headstrong

情 *shinjō* one's heart, feelings. *kokoronasake* kind heart

惜 *kokoroo(shii)* regrettable

掛 *kokoroga(keru), kokoro (ni) ka(keru)* intend, lean, aim; look forward to; bear in mind; be careful to provide for. *kokoroga(kari)* worry, anxiety. *kokoroga(ke)* readiness, intention, aim; study, effort; attention, care

淋 *kokorosabi(shii)* somewhat lonely. *urasabi(shii)* lonely, lonesome

眼 *shingan* mind's eye, mental vision

移 *kokoroutsu(ri)* inconstancy, change of heart

細 *kokoroboso(i)* lonely, depressed, disheartening, helpless, forlorn

動 *kokoro (o) ugo(kasu)* be stirred up; apply one's mind to. *kokoro (ga) ugo(ku)* worry

密 *kokorohiso(kani)* inwardly, secretly

寂 *kokorosabi(shii)* somewhat lonely

悸 *shinki* palpitation of the heart

許 *kokorobaka(ri)* just a little, mere token

許無 *kokoromotona(i)* uneasy, apprehensive; insecure; unreliable

酔 *shinsui* fascination, admiration, devotion

酔者 *shinsuisha* enthusiast, admirer, fan

得 *kokoroe(ru)* know, understand, be aware of; regard as; give consent. *kokoroe* rules, instructions, information; acting (principal); understanding

得違 *kokoroechiga(i)* mistake, misunderstanding; indiscretion

得顔 *kokoroegao* proud face

理 *shinri* mentality, psychology

埋的 *shinriteki* mental, psychological, psychical

理学 *shinrigaku* psychology, mental philosophy

12 痛 *shintsū* anxiety, worry, fear, suspense; trouble, care; good offices

遣 *kokoroya(ri)* relaxation, recreation; sympathy; comfort. *kokorozuka(i)* solicitude, anxiety, regard for ⌐rod

棒 *shimbō* axle, shaft, mandrel, piston

証 *shinshō* a judge's conviction of a prisoner's guilt or innocence; one's impression of a person

寒 *kokorosamu(i)* deeply impressed

悲 *uragana(shii), kokorogana(shii)* sad, sorrowful

覚 *kokoroobo(e)* remembrance; memo

象 *shinshō* mental image

筋 *shinkin* heart muscle

無 *kokoro (nimo) na(i)* insincere; unintentional. *kokorona(i)* without ideas, unsympathetic; unrefined; heartless, thoughtless, indiscreet; cruel

13 豊 *kokoroyuta(kani)* without fear

置無 *kokoroo(ki)na(ku)* frankly; confidentially; without anxiety; heartily; without hesitation

電図 *shindenzu* electrocardiogram

電計 *shindenkei* electrocardiograph

意 *shin'i, kokorobae* mind, heart. *kokorobase* mind, heart; thoughtfulness

意気 *kokoroiki* disposition, spirit, feeling

4

心 忄 小

戈 戸 手 扌 支 攴 文 斗 斤 方 无 日 曰 月 木 欠 止 歹 殳 毋 比 毛 氏 气 水 氵 氺 火 灬 爪 爫 父 爻 爿 片 牙 牛 犬 犭

¹⁴ 境 *shinkyō* mental state; mental attitude
憎 *kokoroniku(i)* detestable; refined, graceful, excellent; reticent
構 *kokorogama(e)* mental attitude, preparation
静 *kokoroshizu(kani)* calmly, serenely. *kokoroshizu(ka)* at peace
算 *shinsan, tsumori* intention, purpose; belief; motive; expectation; idea; estimate
¹⁵ 霊 *shinrei* the spirit, soul
霊学 *shinreigaku* occultism, spiritism
¹⁶ 積 *kokorozumo(ri)* expectation
頭 *shintō* mind, heart
頼 *kokorodano(mi)* dependence, hope, expectation
機 *shinki* mind, mental attitude
機一転 *shinki itten* changing one's mind
¹⁷ 優 *kokoroyasa(shii)* kindhearted
¹⁸ 臓 *shinzō* heart; nerve, cheek
臓麻痺 *shinzō mahi* heart failure, heart attack
¹⁹ 願 *shingan* heart's desire; prayer

—————— **1** ——————

A 必 1781 / J492c / M10299 HITSU certainly. *kanara(zu)* certainly, positively, invariably. *kanara(zushimo)* (not) always, (not) necessarily, (not) all, (not) entirely.
⁴ 中 *hitchū* hitting the target
⁶ 至 *hisshi no* inevitable, necessary
死 *hisshi* inevitable death; desperation. *hisshi no* frantic, desperate
⁸ 定 *hitsujō* certainly, inevitably
⁹ 要 *hitsuyō* need, necessity
¹⁰ 衰 *hissui* bound to decline, decay, or collapse
修 *hisshū* required (subject)
¹² 勝 *hisshō* certain victory
須 *hissu* indispensable, necessary, mandatory
然 *hitsuzen* necessity
然的 *hitsuzenteki ni* inevitably, necessarily
¹³ 携 *hikkei* indispensability; manual, handbook
滅 *hitsumetsu* annihilation; death; doomed to perish
¹⁴ 読 *hitsudoku* required reading

罰 *hitsubatsu* inevitability of punishment
需 *hitsuju* necessary
需品 *hitsujuhin* necessities, essentials

—————— **3** ——————

B 忙 1783 / J4b3b / M10334 BŌ . *isoga(shii), sewa(shii)* busy, occupied. *sewa(shinai)* restless, fidgety, in a hurry.
⁴ 中 *bōchū* during pressure of business
¹⁰ 殺 *bōsatsu* being worked to death, being pressed with work

A 忘 1784 / J4b3a / M10333 BŌ . *wasu(reru)* forget; be forgetful of; forget about; forget (an article). *wasu(reppoi)* forgetful.
⁶ 年会 *bōnenkai* year-end party
⁷ 却 *bōkyaku* memory lapse, forgetfulness
我 *bōga* selflessness, trance, ecstasy; enthusiasm
形身 *wasu(re)gatami* memento, souvenir, keepsake; posthumous child
⁸ 物 *wasu(re)mono* something forgotten
¹⁰ 恩 *bōon* ingratitude

A 志 1785 / J3b56 / M10331 SHI record; shilling; will, intention, aim; ambition, hopes; gift; kindness; offering (Buddhist). *kokoroza(su)* plan, intend, aim at, aspire to, resolve, determine. *kokorozashi* will, intention, motive; determination; aim; ambition, hopes; gift; kindness; offering (Buddhist). *shiringu* shilling.
³ 士 *shishi* patriot, public-spirited man
⁶ 向 *shikō* intention, aim
¹¹ 望 *shibō* desire, ambition, choice
望者 *shibōsha* aspirant; applicant
¹⁶ 操 *shisō* constancy, purpose, integrity
¹⁹ 願 *shigan* desire, aspiration; application, volunteering
願者 *shigansha* applicant, volunteer, aspirant, candidate

B 忌 1786 / J3477 / M10310 KI mourning; death anniversary; something detestable. *i(mu)* abhor, have an aversion for, avoid, shun; taboo; abstain from.

ima(washii) objectionable, abominable, offensive; ominous, unlucky. *i(mi)* mourning; taboo.

[superscript 4] 日 *i(mi)bi* unlucky day; death anniversary; purification and fast day. *kijitsu, kinichi* death anniversary

中 *kichū* in mourning

引 *kibi(ki)* absence from work due to mourning

[superscript 7] 忌 *i(ma)i(mashii)* annoying, provoking

[superscript 8] 明 *kimei, i(mi)a(ke), i(mi)a(ki), kia(ke)* end of mourning ; end of childbirth-purification period

[superscript 13] 嫌 *i(mi)-kira(u)* detest, hate

[superscript 15] 避 *kihi* evasion, shirking; challenge (in law)

憚無 *kitanna(ku)* frankly, without reserve

[superscript 17] 諱 *kii, kiki* offense displeasure

B 忍 [1787 / J4726 / M10312] NIN. *shino(bu)* bear, endure, put up with; hide (oneself). *shino(baseru), shino(basu)* conceal, secrete. *shino(bi)* stealing (into); spy; sneak thief; surreptitious visit to a house of ill fame. *shino(biyakani)* stealthily, secretly.

[superscript 2] 入 *shino(bi)-i(ru)* slip in, sneak in, steal into

[superscript 4] 込 *shino(bi)-ko(mu)* slip in, sneak in, steal into

[superscript 5] 出 *shino(bi)-de(ru)* slip out, sneak out

[superscript 6] 返 *shino(bi)gae(shi)* sharp-pointed wooden or metal prongs atop fences or walls

[superscript 7] 足 *shino(bi) ashi* tiptoeing, stealthy steps

声 *shino(bi)goe* whisper, suppressed voice

[superscript 8] 泣 *shino(bi)na(ki)* subdued sobbing

歩 *shino(bi)-aru(ku)* sneak around. *shino(bi)aru(ki)* traveling incognito

者 *ninja* (ancient) spy, a ninja. *shino(bi) mono* spy, scout

[superscript 9] 音 *shino(bi) ne* weak voice; tearful voice

耐 *nintai* patience, perseverance, fortitude

[superscript 10] 逢 *shino(bi)ai* secret meeting. *shino(bi)-a(u)* meet clandestinely

従 *ninjū* submission, resignation, meekness

笑 *shinobiwara(i)* stifled laugh, giggle, chuckle

[superscript 11] 術 *ninjutsu* occult art; art of the *ninja*

寄 *shino(bi)-yo(ru)* steal up to, steal upon

A 応 [1789 / J317e / M10347'] Ō yes, all right. *ō(jiru), ō(zuru)* answer, reply to; respond to, accept, obey, comply with, accede to, agree to; subscribe for; apply for (admission); meet, supply; fulfill, satisfy. *kota(eru)* respond, answer; be affected by (pain or stimulation); be effective. *(ni) ō(jite)* in proportion to, in answer to, in obedience to. *irae* answer. *masa(ni)* in the act of, on the point of.

[superscript 2] 力 *ōryoku* stress

[superscript 4] 分 *ōbun* appropriate, reasonable

[superscript 5] 召 *ōshō suru* be drafted

用 *ōyō* practical application; practice; adaptation; improvement; applied (physics)

[superscript 7] 対 *ōtai suru* receive, deal with, grant an interview

[superscript 9] 信 *ōshin* answer signal

変 *ōhen* expediency

急 *ōkyū* temporary, emergency

急手当 *ōkyū teate* first aid

急策 *ōkyūsaku* emergency measures

[superscript 11] 接 *ōsetsu* reception

接室 *ōsetsushitsu* drawing room, reception room

接間 *ōsetsuma* drawing room, parlor

[superscript 12] 訴 *ōso* countersuit

答 *ōtō* answer, reply, response

報 *ōhō* retribution

募 *ōbo* subscription; application; enlistment, enrollment, entry; response

募者 *ōbosha* subscriber, applicant, entrant, volunteer; buyer (of bonds)

援 *ōen* aid; reinforcement; rescue; backing; cheering

[superscript 13] 酬 *ōshū* reply

戦 *ōsen suru* accept a challenge, return the fire

[superscript 15] 諾 *ōdaku* consent; compliance

——————— **4** ———————

忽 [1799 / J397a / M10405] KOTSU. *tachima(chi)* in a moment, instantly, immediately, all of a sudden. *yuruga(se)* neglect, disregard.

4

〔心忄⺗〕

⼽戸扌支攴文斗斤方无日月木欠止歹殳毋比毛氏气水氵氺火灬爪爫父爻爿丬片牙牛犭

---

¹² 然 *kotsuzen, kotsunen* suddenly

念 `1800 J4730 M10390` A **NEN** sense, idea, thought; feeling; desire; concern, attention, care. *nen(jiru), nen(zuru)* pray silently; have in mind, be anxious about. *omo(u)* think, believe, judge, esteem; consider, realize; feel like; regard as; anticipate; imagine, suppose, guess; mistake for; recall; intend; desire; love, care for, yearn after; wonder; suspect.

² 力 *nenriki, nenryoku* will power; faith
入 *nen'i(ri), nen'i(re)* care, scrupulousness, conscientiousness
⁴ 仏 *Nembutsu* the Buddhist prayer formula; Hail Amida
⁹ 為 *nen (no) tame* just to be sure
¹⁰ 珠 *nenju* rosary
書 *nensho* memorandum
¹⁶ 頭 *nentō* mind
¹⁹ 願 *nengan* one's heart's desire; an earnest petition

忠 `1801 J4369 M10353` A **CHŪ** loyalty, devotion, fidelity, faithfulness.

⁴ 犬 *chūken* faithful dog
⁶ 臣 *chūshin* loyal subject, faithful retainer
⁷ 言 *chūgen* good advice
告 *chūkoku* advice, warning
良 *chūryō* loyalty
孝 *chūkō* loyalty and filial piety
君 *chūkun* loyalty to the ruler
⁸ 実 *chūjitsu, mame, mame(yaka)* faithfulness, devotion, honesty, fidelity
⁹ 勇 *chūyū* loyalty and bravery
¹⁰ 純 *chūjun* loyalty, obedience
烈 *chūretsu* unswerving loyalty
¹² 順 *chūjun* allegiance, loyalty, obedience
勤 *chūkin* faithful service, devotion
¹³ 愛 *chūai* loyalty, devotion
節 *chūsetsu* loyalty, devotion
誠 *chūsei* loyalty, sincerity, integrity
義 *chūgi* loyalty, devotion
¹⁴ 僕 *chūboku* faithful manservant
魂 *chūkon* the loyal dead, faithful spirit

快 `1802 J3277 M10369` A **KAI** pleasure, enjoyment. *kokoroyo(i)* pleasant, agreeable, comfortable, refreshing, delightful; well (from illness).

kokoroyo(ku) cheerfully, comfortably, gladly. *kokoroyo(shi)* willing, happy. *kokoroyo(ge) na* cheerful, pleasant, comfortable.

² 刀 *kaitō* sharp sword
⁴ 心 *kaishin no* agreeable, congenial
方 *kaihō* convalescence
⁷ 足 *kaisoku* quick of foot
男子 *kaidanshi* an agreeable man
男児 *kaidanji* a fine fellow
走 *kaisō* fast sailing, fast running
⁹ 活 *kaikatsu na* cheery, jovial
哉 *kaisai* shout of joy
美 *kaibi* good feeling
速 *kaisoku* high speed; celerity; mobility
¹⁰ 眠 *kaimin* pleasant sleep
挙 *kaikyo* brilliant achievement
記録 *kaikiroku* fine record
¹² 傑 *kaiketsu* a handsome man
晴 *kaisei* fine weather
勝 *kaishō* easy victory
腕 *kaiwan* shrewdness, remarkable ability
報 *kaihō* good news
¹³ 適 *kaiteki na* comfortable, pleasant, agreeable
漢 *kaikan* jolly fellow
感 *kaikan* agreeable sensation, comfort
楽 *kairaku, keraku* pleasure, enjoyment
楽主義 *Kairaku Shugi* Epicureanism
¹⁵ 諾 *kaidaku* ready consent
調 *kaichō* harmony; excellent condition
¹⁸ 癒 *kaiyu* recovery from illness

5

怜 `1812 J4e67 M10461` **REI** wise.

¹⁰ 悧 *reiri* cleverness, sagacity

怯 `1816 J3631 M10491` **KYŌ** cowardice. *hiru(mu)* wince, flinch, hesitate, waver, fear. *obi(eru)* get frightened; be intimidated; feel shy; have a nightmare.

怖 `1817 J495d M10450` B **FU** *o(jiru), oji(keru)* fear, be frightened; be timid; get nervous. *oso(reru)* fear, be overawed, be apprehensive. *kowa(garu)* fear, be afraid of. *kowa(i)* fearful, frightful,

terrible, weird. *kowa(garaseru)* frighten, terrorize. *kowa(gari)* timidity, cowardice.
⁶ 気 *ojike, ozoke* fear; awe; timidity; nervousness

怠 ₁₈₁₈ _{J4255} _{M10469} TAI laziness, neglect.
B *okota(ru)* neglect; be off guard; be feeling better. *nama(keru)* be lazy, be idle; neglect. *okota(rinaku)* diligently. *okota(razu) ni* carefully.
⁸ 者 *nama(ke)mono* sloth; a lazy person
¹² 惰 *taida* laziness, idleness
¹³ 業 *taigyō* slowdown tactics, sabotage
¹⁴ 慢 *taiman* negligence; procrastination; carelessness

怨 ₁₈₁₉ _{J3165} _{M10479} EN. ON. *ura(mu), en(zuru)* bear a grudge, show resentment; be jealous. *ura(meshii), ura(migamashii)* hateful, bitter. *urami* grudge, hatred, malice, bitterness.
⁷ 言 *engen, uramigoto* grudge, complaint, murmuring
⁸ 念 *onnen* grudge, malice, hatred
⁹ 恨 *enkon* enmity, grudge
¹³ 嗟 *ensa* grudge, resentment
¹⁵ 霊 *onryō* revengeful ghost; apparition

怒 ₁₈₂₀ _{J455c} _{M10439} DO. NU. *ika(ru), oko(ru)*
B become angry, be offended, become excited. *ika(ri)* anger, indignation, rage, wrath. *ika(raseru), oko(raseru)* offend, anger, irritate. *oko(rippoi)* touchy, excitable, hot-tempered.
⁵ 出 *oko(ri)-da(su)* fly into a rage
号 *dogō* roar, outcry, howl
⁶ 気 *doki* anger; indignation, resentment
⁷ 坊 *oko(rim)bō* hotheaded person
狂 *ika(ri)-kuru(u)* be terribly angry
声 *dosei* harsh words; angry voice; excited voice
⁸ 肩 *ika(ri)kata* square shoulders
¹⁴ 鳴 *dona(ru)* shout at
髪 *dohatsu* anger; hair standing on end
¹⁷ 濤 *dotō* raging billows, high waves

怪 ₁₈₂₁ _{J3278} _{M10483} KE, KAI mystery;
B apparition. *aya(shimu)* doubt; be suspicious of; wonder at. *aya(shigena), aya(shii)* undependable,

strange, mysterious. *ke(shikaran), ke(shikaranu)* rude, disgraceful, indecent, unpardonable, outrageous, absurd.
² 力 *kairiki* superhuman strength
人物 *kaijimbutsu* mystery man
⁴ 火 *kaika* mysterious fire, will-o'-the-wisp
文書 *kaibunsho* objectionable literature
⁶ 死 *kaishi* mysterious death
気 *aya(shi)ge na* questionable, shady, suspicious; unsteady; threatening (rain); broken (English)
⁷ 我 *kega* wound, injury; accident, error; casualty
我人 *keganin* injured or wounded person
⁸ 物 *kaibutsu* monster, apparition
奇 *kaiki na* strange, wonderful; weird; outrageous, scandalous, insolent
事件 *kaijiken* mystery case
¹¹ 異 *kaii* monster. *kaii na* mysterious; marvelous; grotesque
盗 *kaitō* mysterious thief
¹² 傑 *kaiketsu* prodigy, extraordinary man
訝 *kegen na, kaiga na* suspicious, puzzled, dubious
¹⁵ 談 *kaidan* ghost story
¹⁶ 獣 *kaijū* monster

性 ₁₈₂₂ _{J402d} _{M10478} SEI sex, gender; nature,
A attribute. SHŌ nature, disposition; quality; purity. *saga* one's nature; custom.
⁴ 分 *shōbun* nature, disposition
⁵ 生活 *sei seikatsu* sex life
犯罪 *sei hanzai* sex crime
⁶ 向 *seikō* inclination, disposition
行為 *sei kōi* sexual act
交 *seikō* sexual intercourse
⁷ 状 *seijō* characteristics
別 *seibetsu* distinction by sex, sex (male or female)
⁸ 的 *seiteki* sexual
⁹ 急 *seikyū* quick temper, impatience
¹⁰ 病 *seibyō* sexually transmitted disease
根 *shōne* nature, disposition, spirit, mind
能 *seinō* performance, efficiency
格 *seikaku* character, personality
¹¹ 情 *seijō* character, disposition, nature
悪 *seiaku, shōwaru* evil disposition

4

5 戈 戸 手 扌 支 攴 文 斗 斤 方 无 日 曰 月 木 欠 止 歹 殳 毋 比 毛 氏 气 水 氵 氺 火 灬 爪 爫 父 爻 爿 丬 片 牙 牛 犬 犭

悪説　*seiakusetsu* doctrine of original sin
欲　*seiyoku* sexual desire
12 善説　*seizensetsu* doctrine of man's innate goodness
13 愛　*seiai* sexual love
感　*seikan* sexual emotion, sexual sensibility
15 質　*seishitsu* nature, disposition, temperament; qualities, properties; nature (of an undertaking)
器　*seiki* reproductive organs
18 癖　*seiheki* disposition, inclination, characteristic, idiosyncrasy

急 ‹1823 / J355e / M10475› A KYŪ emergency; suddenness; danger; haste; steep. *iso(gu)* hurry, hasten. *se(kasu)* rush, hurry, expedite. *se(ku)* vi and vt hurry, make haste; be impatient; press, urge, hurry up. *a(seru)* be hasty, be in a hurry, be impatient. *kyū na* urgent, sudden; precipitous; sharp (turn); swift. *kyū ni* in a hurry, promptly; suddenly; at a moment's notice.
4 込　*se(ki)-ko(mu), se(k)ko(mu)* become excited, be agitated, be in a hurry, become impatient
勾配　*kyūkōbai* steep slope
5 用　*kyūyō* urgent business
立　*se(ki)-ta(teru)* hurry, urge, speed up, urge on
6 死　*kyūshi* sudden death
先峰　*kyūsempō* leader, champion, forerunner, vanguard
行　*kyūkō* express train; going in a hurry
7 足　*iso(gi)ashi* fast pace. *iso(gi)ashi de* at a quick pace
迫　*kyūhaku* urgency; imminence
告　*kyūkoku* urgent notice
坂　*kyūhan* steep hill
8 送　*kyūsō suru* rush (something), dispatch
追　*kyūtsui* hot pursuit
所　*kyūsho* vital point, vitals, tender spot, vulnerable spot; secret, key (to)
性　*kyūsei* acute (illness)
9 派　*kyūha suru* dispatch, expedite
変　*kyūhen* sudden turn; emergency, accident
逝　*kyūsei* sudden death
造　*kyūzō* hurried construction
降下　*kyūkōka* swoop, nose dive
速　*kyūsoku na* swift, prompt

速度　*kyūsokudo* high speed
10 峻　*kyūshun na* steep
流　*kyūryū* swift current; rapids
病　*kyūbyō* sudden illness
病人　*kyūbyōnin* emergency case
進主義　*kyūshin shugi* radicalism
進的　*kyūshinteki* radical, extreme
進派　*kyūshinha* radicals
11 務　*kyūmu* urgent business, pressing need
患　*kyūkan* emergency patient
停車　*kyūteisha* sudden stop
斜面　*kyūshamen* steep slope
転　*kyūten* sudden change
転直下　*kyūtenchokka suru* fall headlong; take a sudden turn
12 場　*kyūba* emergency, crisis
須　*kyūsu, kibisho* teapot
募　*kyūbo* recruiting (workers) in a hurry
落　*kyūraku* slump (in prices)
報　*kyūhō* urgent message, alarm
13 傾斜　*kyūkeisha* steep slope; heavy list
14 増　*kyūzō* surge, sudden increase
16 遽　*kyūkyo* hastily, hurriedly
激　*kyūgeki na* sudden, precipitous; radical
20 騰　*kyūtō* sudden jump in prices
22 襲　*kyūshū* surprise attack; raid

思 ‹1824 / J3b57 / M10462› A SHI. *omo(u)* think, believe, judge, esteem; realize; feel like; regard as; anticipate; imagine, suppose, guess; mistake for; recall; intend; desire; love, care for, yearn after; wonder; suspect. *omo(wareru)* seem, appear. *omo(waseru)* give the impression that. *omo(eba)* come to think about it. *omo(eraku)* it seems to me. *omo(i)* thought, idea, mind, heart, sense; feeling, emotion; affection; desire, wish; expectation; intention, will; pleasure, care, worry; experience. *omo(inashi)* fancy, imagination. *omo(wanu)* unexpected, inconceivable. *omo(washii)* satisfactory, desirable. *omo(wazu)* unintentionally, spontaneously, unconsciously.
2 入　*omo(i)-i(ru)* consider, ponder
　omo(i)i(re) one's pleasure, heart's desire; meditation, reverie. *omoi(re)* one's pleasure, heart's desire; meditation, reverie; supposition
3 及　*omo(i)-oyo(bu)* think up, remember, hit upon, think of

4

上 *omo(i)-a(garu)* be conceited
⁴止 *omo(i)-to(maru), omo(i)-todo(maru)* drop (the idea)
込 *omo(i)-ko(mu)* be impressed with (an idea); set one's heart on; imagine (something)
切 *omo(i)-ki(ru)* resign to fate; get over (a loss); give up, despair of; resolve. *omo(i)ki(ri)* resignation, determination, decision; vehemently, vigorously; terribly; to heart's content; with all one's might; thoroughly, completely. *omo(i)ki(tta)* drastic, radical
⁵立 *omo(i)-ta(tsu)* plan, resolve. *omo(i)ta(chi)* resolve, intention, idea, plan, whim, impulse
巡 *omo(i)-megu(rasu), omo(i)-mawa(su)* recall, ponder over
付 *omo(i)-tsu(kaseru)* remind of, suggest. *omo(i)-tsu(ku)* hit upon, think up (ideas). *omo(i)tsu(ki)* plan, suggestion, casual idea
外 *omo(i) (no) hoka* unexpectedly, beyond expectations
召 *obo(shi)-me(su)* think, believe, judge, esteem; consider, realize; feel like; regard as; anticipate; imagine, suppose, guess; mistake for; recall; intend; desire; love, care for, yearn after; wonder; suspect. *obo(shi)me(shi)* your opinion; your desire; token of gratitude; liking, fancy
弁 *shiben* discrimination, speculation
出 *omo(i)-da(su)* recall, remember. *omo(i)de* memories, recollections
⁶交 *omo(i)-ka(wasu)* love each other
合 *omo(i)-a(u)* love each other. *omo(i)-a(waseru)* consider together. *omo(i)a(i)* mutual love
当 *omo(i)-a(taru), omo(i)-a(teru)* occur to one, think of; suspect
存分 *omo(u)zombun* as one pleases
考 *shikō* thought, consideration, contemplation
考力 *shikōryoku* mental faculties
⁷沈 *omo(i)-shizu(mu)* worry
乱 *omo(i)-mida(reru)* be distracted with the thought of
余 *omo(i)-ama(ru)* be overcome with emotion

⁸迷 *omo(i)-mayo(u)* be unable to decide
知 *omo(i)-shi(ru)* perceive, realize; repent of. *omo(i)-shi(raseru)* teach (someone a lesson). *omo(wazu)-shi(razu)* unintentionally, unconsciously
念 *shinen* thought
直 *omo(i)-nao(su)* reconsider, change one's mind
定 *omo(i)-sada(meru)* resolve
⁹通 *omo(i)dō(ri) ni* to one's satisfaction, as much as one likes
思 *omo(i)omo(i) ni* as one pleases
春期 *shishunki* puberty
¹⁰起 *omo(i)-oko(su)* remember, recall
悩 *omo(i)-naya(mu)* be depressed, be dejected, worry
残 *omo(i)-noko(su)* leave with regret
浮 *omo(i)-u(kaberu)* recall, remember, hit upon, think up. *omo(i)-u(kabu)* occur to, remind of
料 *shiryō* consideration
索 *shisaku* speculation, thinking, meditation
索的 *shisakuteki* meditative, speculative
案 *shian* thought, consideration, meditation; plan, resources
¹¹過 *omo(i)-su(gosu)* worry too much, be over-anxious
惟 *shii* speculation, thinking
掛無 *omo(i)ga(ke)na(i)* unexpected
¹²遣 *omo(i)-ya(ru)* sympathize with, have consideration for. *omo(i)ya(ri)* sympathy, consideration, compassion
違 *omo(i)chiga(i)* misunderstanding
壷 *omo(u) tsubo* one's wishes or expectations
量 *shiryō* consideration
募 *omo(i)-tsuno(ru)* think more and more of
焦 *omo(i)-koga(reru)* pine for, be deeply in love
惑 *omo(i)-mado(u)* be unable to decide. *omowaku* thought, opinion; intention; expectation; ulterior aim; rumor
¹³煩 *omo(i)-wazura(u)* worry about, be concerned about
詰 *omo(i)-tsu(meru)* think hard, brood over
想 *shisō* thought, idea

4

【心忄小】

5 小

戈戸手扌支攴攵文斗斤方无日曰月木欠止歹殳毋比毛氏气水氵氺火灬爪爫父爻爿片牙牛犬犭

14 様 *omo(u)sama, omo(u) yō ni* as one pleases

慕 *shibo* yearning, deep affection

15 潮 *shichō* trend of thought

慮 *shiryo* discretion, thought, consideration

慮深 *shiryobuka(ku)* discreetly, prudently, judiciously, sensibly

16 儘 *omo(u)mama, omo(i) (no) mama* as one pleases

———— 6 ————

恕 $\frac{1834}{\text{J3d7a}}$ Jo. *jo(suru)* excuse, M10560 tolerate, forgive.

恰 $\frac{1838}{\text{J3366}}$ Kō . *ataka(mo), adaka(mo)* M10603 just as, as though; fortunately.

6 好 *kakkō* shape, form, appearance; pose, posture; manner; approximately. *kakkō na* suitable, reasonable

12 幅 *kappuku* build, physique

恨 $\frac{1842}{\text{J3a28}}$ Kon. *ura(mu)* bear a M10588 grudge, show resentment. B
ura(mi) grudge, hatred, malice. *ura(meshii)* hateful, bitter.

7 言 *ura(mi)goto* grudge, grievance, complaint

恢 $\frac{1843}{\text{J327a}}$ Kai wide; large; enlarge. M10577

12 復 *kaifuku* recovery, restoration, rehabilitation

恭 $\frac{1845}{\text{J3633}}$ Kyō . *uyauya(shii)* M10596 respectful, reverent. B

10 倹 *kyōken* modesty, humility; courtesy, respect

12 順 *kyōjun* allegiance

賀 *kyōga* respectful congratulations

17 謙 *kyōken* modesty, humility

恥 $\frac{1846}{\text{J4351}}$ Chi. *haji* shame, dishonor, M10585 disgrace, humiliation, B
insult. *ha(jiru), ha(zuru)* feel ashamed. *ha(zubeki)* disgraceful, unbecoming. *ha(jirau)* feel shy, be coy, be bashful, blush. *ha(zukashigaru)* be shy, be bashful, be ashamed. *ha(zukashii)* bashful, ashamed, coy; disgraceful,

shameful. *ha(zukashikaranu)* worthy, decent, honorable.

2 入 *ha(ji)-i(ru)* feel ashamed

8 知 *hajishi(razu)* shameless. *haji (o) shi(ru)* refrain from shameful acts

10 辱 *chijoku* disgrace, shame, insult

18 曝 *hajisara(shi)* shame, disgrace

恵 $\frac{1847}{\text{J3743}}$ Kei. E. *megu(mi)* M10618' blessing, grace, favor; B
kindness, mercy, benevolence, charity. *megu(mu)* bless; show mercy to, render benevolence to.

3 与 *keiyo suru* present, give, bestow

4 比須 *Ebisu* a god of wealth
比須顔 *ebisugao* smiling face

7 沢 *keitaku* blessing; pity; favor; benefit

18 贈 *keizō* presentation

悔 $\frac{1848}{\text{J3279}}$ Kai. Ge. *ku(iru)* repent, M10617' regret. *ku(yamu)* regret, B
repent of; mourn for, condole with. *ku(i)* regret, repentance. *ku(yami)* condolence visit; regret, repentance. *ku(yashigaru)* be chagrined (at one's failure); regret (a circumstance); resent (an insult). *kuya(shii)* vexing, regrettable, mortifying.

7 言 *kuya(mi)goto* words of condolence

改 *ku(i)-arata(meru)* repent of. *ku(i)arata(me)* repentance, penitence

8 泣 *ku(yashi)naki* cry of remorse

9 恨 *kaikon* remorse; regret; contrition, repentance

10 悛 *kaishun* penitence, repentance (Catholic)

涙 *ku(yashi) namida* tears of regret or remorse

紛 *ku(yashi)magi(re) ni* out of spite

悟 *kaigo* repentance, penitence, contrition, remorse

恒 $\frac{1849}{\text{J3931}}$ Kō always. *tsune ni* M10527 always. B

3 久 *kōkyū* perpetuity, permanency
久的 *kōkyūteki* permanent

心 *kōshin* steadiness, constancy

6 存 *kōzon* conservation (of energy)

8 例 *kōrei* regular ceremony; established custom, common usage

9 風 *kōfū* constant wind, trade wind

星 *kōsei* fixed star
11 産 *kōsan* fixed property
常 *kōjō* constancy
常的 *kōjōteki* constant
12 温線 *kōonsen* isotherm
13 数 *kōsū* constant (in science)

A 息 1850 J4229 M1060T SOKU son; interest (on money). *iki* breath, respiration. *iki(mu)* strain, bear up, exert one's strength; swagger, bluff, boast. *iki(ru)* be hot with anger. *iko(u)* rest, relax, repose.
3 女 *sokujo* daughter
子 *musuko* son, boy, young man
切 *iki-gi(re)* breathlessness
5 付 *ikitsu(ku)* have a respite. *iki (mo) tsu(kasezu)* without giving any respite. *iki (mo) tsu(kazu) ni* holding one's breath
7 吹 *ibu(ki)* breath
抜 *ikinu(ki)* ventilator; breathing space; diversion. *iki-nu(ku)* live through, survive
災 *sokusai* safety, security; peace, tranquility; good health; boredom
男 *sokunan* son
8 苦 *ikiguru(shii)* stuffy, suffocating
9 巻 *iki-ma(ku)* fume, be enraged
急 *iki-se(ku)* breathe hard
急切 *iki-se(ki)-ki(ru)* gasp, pant
12 遣 *ikizu(kai)* breathing
絶 *iki-ta(eru)* die
13 継 *ikitsu(gi)* breathing spell
詰 *ikizu(maru)* be choked, be stifled

A 恩 1851 J3238 M1059T ON kindness, goodness, favor, mercy, blessing, benefit.
2 人 *onjin* benefactor, patron
6 返 *ongae(shi)* requital of a favor
7 沢 *ontaku* favor, benefit
8 知 *onshi(razu)* ingratitude; ungrateful person
典 *onten* favor, act of grace, special privilege
10 師 *onshi* one's honored teacher
恵 *onkei* grace, favor, benefit, blessings
11 情 *onjō* compassion; affection
赦 *onsha* amnesty, general pardon
12 給 *onkyū* pension

13 愛 *on'ai, onnai* kindness and affection, love
義 *ongi* favor, obligation, debt of gratitude
14 徳 *ontoku* sympathy, mercy, grace
15 賜 *onshi* imperial gift; gracious gift
賞 *onshō* reward
19 寵 *onchō* grace, favor
21 顧 *onko* favor, patronage
23 讐 *onshū* love and hate

B 恋 1852 J4e78 M10537 REN. *ko(u)* be in love. *koi(suru)* love, fall in love with. *koi(shigaru)* yearn for, miss. *koi* love, tender sentiment. *koi(shii)* dear, beloved, darling.
2 人 *koibito* lover, sweetheart
4 心 *koigokoro* love, love's awakening
文 *koibumi* love letter
仇 *koigataki* one's rival in love
6 仲 *koinaka* love, love relationship
10 恋 *renren toshite* fondly, longingly
11 情 *renjō* love, attachment. *koinsake* lovesickness
12 着 *renchaku* attachment, love
焦 *ko(i)-ko(gareru)* yearn for, be deeply in love with
13 煩 *koiwazura(i)* lovesickness
路 *koiji* romance, love's pathway
愛 *ren'ai* love, lovemaking, passion, emotion, affections
14 歌 *koiuta, koika, renka* love song, love poem
慕 *ko(i)-shita(u)* miss, yearn for. *rembo suru* love, fall in love with

B 恐 1853 J3632 M10552 KYŌ. *oso(reru)*, *oso(roshigaru)* fear, dread, be afraid; be overawed; be apprehensive. *oso(raku)* perhaps, possibly. *oso(re)* fear, dread; consternation; anxiety; reverence, awe; danger, risk; chance, signs. *oso(renagara)* most respectfully. *oso(roshii)* terrible, awful, fierce; tremendous, marvelous. *kowa(l)* fearful, dreadful.
2 入 *oso(re)-i(ru)* be awestruck; be overwhelmed; be humiliated; be astonished, be sorry to trouble, beg pardon; be disconcerted; plead guilty, stand corrected
6 気 *osoro(shi)ge na* frightening, awful

4 【心 忄 小】 戈 戸 手 扌 支 攴 父 文 斗 斤 方 旡 日 曰 月 木 欠 止 歹 殳 毋 比 毛 氏 气 水 氵 氺 火 灬 爪 爫 父 爻 爿 丬 片 牙 牛 犬 犭

4

【心 忄 㣺】

6 戈 戸 手 扌 支 攴 攵 文 斗 斤 方 无 日 曰 月 木 欠 止 歹 殳 毋 比 毛 氏 气 水 氵 氺 火 灬 爪 爫 父 爻 爿 丬 片 牙 牛 犬 犭

多 oso(re)-ō(i) august, gracious, awe-inspiring, awful

8 妻病 kyōsaibyō fear of one's wife
怖 kyōfu fear, terror, panic
怖心 kyōfushin feeling of terror
怖感 kyōfukan sense of fear

10 悦 kyōetsu delight, pleasure
恐 oso(ru)-oso(ru) nervously, timidly, cautiously, reverently. kowagowa fearfully. kyōkyō respect (in letters)
竜 kyōryū dinosaur

11 喝 kyōkatsu threat, blackmail

12 慌 kyōkō panic, scare, consternation
惶 kyōkō fear and trembling; your humble servant

13 戦 oso(re)-onono(ku) tremble, shudder

16 龍 kyōryū dinosaur

17 縮 kyōshuku obligation, appreciation; regret; shame

21 懼 kyōku fear, awe, dread

────────── 7 ──────────

悌 $\frac{1861}{J4470 \mid M10642}$ TEI serving our elders.

悉 $\frac{1864}{J3c3d \mid M10635}$ SHITSU. tsu(kusu) use up, run out of, exhaust; serve, befriend, work for, endeavor, do (one's duty). kotogoto(ku) all, entirely, altogether, completely. tsubusa ni minutely, fully.

9 皆 shikkai entirely, without exception

悩 B $\frac{1867}{J473a \mid M10716'}$ NŌ distress, illness. naya(mu) worry, be troubled, be afflicted, be in pain. naya(masu) annoy, embarrass, afflict, worry, oppress, torment. naya(mi) anguish, worry, distress, pain. naya(mashii) painful, distressing; melancholy; teasing.

8 苦 naya(mi)-kuru(shimu) be sorely troubled

10 殺 nōsatsu suru captivate, charm, fascinate

悦 B $\frac{1868}{J3159 \mid M10629'}$ ETSU joy, rapture, ecstasy, amusement. yoroko(bashii) joyful, glad, pleasant. yoroko(bi) joy, delight, pleasure. yoroko(bu) rejoice, be glad, be pleased.

13 楽 etsuraku enjoyment, pleasure

悟 B $\frac{1870}{J3867 \mid M10680}$ GO. sato(ru) perceive, discern, realize, understand, comprehend; attain enlightenment, find one's philosophy. sato(ri) understanding, comprehension; Buddhist enlightenment; philosophy.

患 B $\frac{1871}{J3435 \mid M10691}$ GEN. KAN disease. wazura(u) be ill, suffer from; be afflicted. ure(e), ure(i) distress, sorrow, trouble, anxiety, grief.

8 者 kanja patient, victim (of a disease)

10 部 kambu diseased part, the affected area
家 kanka (doctor's) patient

悠 B $\frac{1872}{J4d2a \mid M10681}$ YU. YŪ distant, longtime; leisure.

3 久 yūkyū eternity, permanence

8 長 yūchō na slow, tedious, deliberate, leisurely

11 悠 yūyū(taru) quiet, calm, composed, leisurely, deliberate; eternal, boundless, vast
悠自適 yūyūjiteki easy comfortable retirement

12 遠 yūen remoteness; eternity; repose
揚 yūyō repose, composure, serenity; easy climbing (in a plane)
然 yūzen(taru) quiet, calm, composed, leisurely, deliberate; eternal, boundless, vast

悪 A $\frac{1873}{J302d \mid M10717}$ O. AKU evil, wrong, vice, wickedness, lawlessness. a(shikarazu) do not take offense. waru(i), a(shii) bad, evil, wrong; immoral; malicious; blamable; injurious; detrimental, malignant; be indisposed; inferior; homely; poor (memory); inclement; unlucky; out of order; unsavory. niku(mu) hate, detest. niku(i) hateful, abominable, poor-looking. waru(bireru) be timid, be ashamed. aku(tareru) be mischievous. aku(tare) rowdiness; a rowdy. waru rascal, ruffian; wickedness. niku(shimi) hatred, enmity. aku- bad, wrong, evil, vicious, wicked; unfavorable, false; perverted; treacherous. -niku(i) difficult, awkward.

² 人 *akunin* bad man, villain

³ 女 *akujo* wicked woman, ugly woman

口 *akkō, warukuchi, waruguchi, aku(tare)guchi* verbal abuse, insult, slander, evil speaking

口雑言 *akkō-zōgon* all kinds of malicious gossip

⁴ 心 *akushin* evil thought, malicious motive. *oshin* nausea, urge to vomit

文 *akubun* poor writing, bad style, bad sentence

化 *akka* worsening, deterioration, aggravation, degeneration, corruption

友 *akuyū* bad companion

⁵ 玉 *akudama* bad character, bad person; the villain

用 *akuyō* misuse, abuse, perversion

巧 *warudaku(mi)* wiles, sinister design, trick, conspiracy, intrigue

⁶ 行 *akugyō, akkō* misdeed, wrongdoing, wickedness

気 *warugi* ill will, evil intent, ill feeling, distrust

名 *akumei, akumyō* bad reputation, notoriety, bad name

⁷ 役 *akuyaku* the villain, the villain's part

投 *akutō* wild pitch

阻 *tsuwari, oso* morning sickness

足掻 *waruagaki* wicked mischief, wicked play

⁸ 例 *akurei* bad example

性 *akusei* virulence; malignant (cancer); pernicious (anemia). *akushō* evil nature; licentiousness, lewdness

所 *akusho* dangerous place; house of ill-fame, bad place

法 *akuhō* a bad law

妻 *akusai* a bad wife

果 *akka* bad results

者 *warumono* rascal, ruffian, scoundrel

事 *akuji* evil deed, crime, wickedness

知恵 *warujie* cunning, guile

逆 *akugyaku* treason, treachery, atrocity

⁹ 風 *akufū* vice, evil manners, bad custom

食 *akujiki suru* eat repulsive things, eat poor food, eat meat. *akushoku suru* eat poor food

疫 *akueki* a plague, pestilence, epidemic

政 *akusei* misgovernment

臭 *akushū* bad odor, stench

¹⁰ 鬼 *akki* evil spirit, demon, devil

党 *akutō* rascal, scoundrel, villain

¹¹ 運 *akuun* bad luck

酔 *waruyo(i)* drunken sickness, drunken frenzy

習 *akushū* bad habit, vice

¹² 評 *akuhyō* ill repute, bad reputation, unfavorable criticism

寒 *okan* chill

童 *akudō* bad boy, naughty boy

筆 *akuhitsu* poor handwriting

循環 *akujunkan* vicious circle

¹³ 漢 *akkan* rascal, villain, scoundrel, ruffian, crook

路 *akuro* bad road

夢 *akumu* nightmare, bad dream

意 *akui* ill will, malice

業 *akugyō* evil, sinful deeds. *akugō* evil karma

戦苦闘 *akusen-kutō* hard fighting

感情 *akkanjō* ill feeling, ill will, animosity, bad impression

¹⁴ 様 *a(shi)zama ni* unfavorably, slanderously

辣 *akuratsu* craftiness

銭 *akusen* ill-gotten money; bad coin

態 *akutai* abusive language

徳 *akutoku* vices, corruption, immorality

¹⁵ 罵 *akuba* cursing, vilification

霊 *akurei, akuryō, akurō* evil spirit

弊 *akuhei* vice, abuse, evil

賢 *warugashiko(i)* cunning, crafty, wily, sly

質 *akushitsu* poor quality, malignancy; viciousness

戯 *itazura, warusa, waruitazura* mean mischief. *akugi* practical joke

戯子 *itazurakko* mischievous boy

戯小僧 *itazura kozō* mischievous boy

戯坊主 *itazura bōzu* mischievous boy

戯書 *itazuraga(ki)* scribbling, doodling

¹⁸ 癖 *akuheki, waruguse* bad habit, vice

²¹ 魔 *akuma* Satan; devil, demon, evil spirit; fiend

───── 8 ─────

惹 ⟨1886 / J3c66 / M10866⟩ JAKU attract, captivate.

¹⁰ 起 *jakki suru* bring about, cause, provoke (discussion)

4

【心忄㣺】

8 戈戸手扌支攴文斗斤方无日曰月木欠止歹殳毋比毛氏气水氵氺火灬爪爫父爻爿片牙牛犬犭

惇 1887 J4657 M10759 TON. JUN *atsu(i)* thick; warm hearted; sincere.

惣 1889 J415a M10829 SŌ all.
11 菜 *sōzai* side dish

惟 1890 J3054 M10820 I. *omom(miru)* consider, reflect. *omo(u)* think, believe, judge, esteem; consider, realize; feel like; regard as; anticipate; imagine, suppose, guess; mistake for; recall; intend; desire; love, care for, yearn after; wonder; suspect.

B 悼 1891 J4569 M10738 TŌ . *ita(mu)* grieve over.
13 辞 *tōji* message of condolence, funeral oration

B 惑 1892 J4f47 M10789 WAKU. *mado(u)* be perplexed, be in doubt, hesitate, vacillate, go astray, err; be tempted; be infatuated; be misguided. *mado(wasu), mado(wakasu)* perplex; mislead, deceive; tempt; seduce; charm, infatuate. *mado(i)* delusion; perplexity.
7 乱 *wakuran* bewilderment, confusion
9 星 *wakusei* planet
13 溺 *wakudeki* indulgence, addiction; infatuation

惚 1893 J397b M10811 KOTSU. *ho(reru)* fall in love with, admire, be entranced with. *boke(ru)* grow senile; become mentally weak; fade, discolor. *hoke(ru)* grow senile; become mentally weak; become enthusiastic; be beside oneself. *hoke, boke* dull; dull-headedness.
4 込 *ho(re)-ko(mu)* fall deeply in love
6 気 *noroke(ru)* boast of love conquests. *noroke* love affair
11 惚 *horebore to* fondly. *horebore suru* be charmed

B 惜 1894 J404b M10814 SEKI. SHAKU. *o(shimu), o(shigaru)* be sparing of; be frugal with; be stingy with; regret; value, prize; be reluctant. *o(shii)* regrettable, pitiful, disappointing; precious; wasteful. *o(shimazu)* without regret, ungrudgingly; generously. *o(shiminaku)* freely, regardless of expenses. *o(shisō) ni* grudgingly, reluctantly.
6 気無 *o(shi)ge(mo)na(ku)* without regret, ungrudgingly; generously
7 別 *sekibetsu* parting regrets
11 敗 *sekihai* regrettable defeat; defeat by a narrow margin

悶 1895 J4c65 M10729 MON. *moda(eru)* be in agony, be worried.
6 死 *monshi* agonizing death
8 苦 *moda(e)-kuru(shimu)* writhe in pain
12 悶 *mommon(taru)* discontented
絶 *monzetsu suru* faint; fall in convulsions
着 *monchaku* trouble; dispute

B 惨 1896 J3b34 M10850 SAN. ZAN disaster; cruelty; wretchedness. *mugo(i)* cruel, merciless, harsh. *mugo(tarashii)* cruel; horrible; tragic. *san(taru)* disastrous, appalling. *mijime na* sad, pitiful, wretched.
6 死 *zanshi, sanshi* tragic death, violent death
7 状 *sanjō* pitiful situation
8 事 *sanji* disaster, tragedy, terrible accident
10 害 *sangai* ravages, havoc, heavy damage
10 殺 *zansatsu* slaughter, massacre, murder
11 敗 *zampai, sampai* overwhelming defeat, crushing defeat
13 禍 *sanka* terrible disaster, calamity, horrors (of war)
15 劇 *sangeki* tragedy, tragic event
16 憺 *santan(taru)* pitiable, wretched, tragic
澹 *santan(taru)* pitiable, wretched, tragic

A 悲 1897 J4861 M10720 HI. *kana(shimu), kana(shigaru)* grieve, be sad, deplore, mourn for, regret. *kana(shimi)* sorrow, grief. *kana(shige) na* sad, sorrowful, plaintive. *kana(shii)* sad, pathetic, plaintive.
6 壮 *hisō na* pathetic, tragic
8 況 *hikyō* distress, adversity
9 哀 *hiai* sorrow, grief, misery, pathos
10 恋 *hiren* disappointed love

¹¹ 運 *hiun* bad luck, misfortune, sad fate

惨 *hisan* misery, wretchedness

¹² 痛 *hitsū* bitterness, pathos

報 *hihō* sad news, news of a death

喜 *hiki* joy and sorrow

喜劇 *hikigeki* tragicomedy

¹³ 嘆 *kana(shimi)-nage(ku)* weep and wail. *hitan* grief, sorrow

愴 *hisō* pathetic, sad

話 *hiwa* sad story

愁 *hishū* pathos, sorrow

¹⁴ 鳴 *himei* shriek, scream

境 *hikyō* adversity, distress

歌 *hika* elegy, dirge

¹⁵ 憤 *hifun* indignation, resentment

憤慷慨 *hifun-kōgai* give vent to a jeremiad

歎 *hitan* grief, sorrow

劇 *higeki* tragedy, tragic drama

劇的 *higekiteki* tragic

¹⁸ 観 *hikan* pessimism, disappointment

観主義 *hikan shugi* pessimism

観的 *hikanteki* pessimistic

¹⁹ 願 *higan* Buddhist prayer for mankind

情 ¹⁸⁹⁸ J3e70 M10756 SEI. JŌ feeling, emotion; passion; affection; heart; human nature; sympathy; sincerity; circumstances, facts; obstinacy. *nasake* sympathy, compassion.

² 人 *jōnin, jōjin* sweetheart, lover

⁴ 心 *nasakegokoro* sympathy, compassion

夫 *jōfu* adulterer, paramour

⁶ 死 *jōshi* double love suicide

交 *jōkō* intimacy; illicit relations. *nasake (o) kawa(su)* have illicit relations with

⁷ 状 *jōjō* circumstances, conditions

状酌量 *jōjō shakuryō* sentence reduction due to commiserative circumstances

⁸ 念 *jōnen* sentiment

実 *jōjitsu* personal considerations; favoritism; actual circumstances

事 *jōji* love affair, liaison

況 *jōkyō* circumstances

¹¹ 婦 *jōfu* adulteress

深 *nasakebuka(i)* tenderhearted, compassionate

理 *jōri* heart and mind; reason and sentiment

欲 *jōyoku* passions, carnal desire

¹² 景 *jōkei* scene; nature and sentiment

無 *nasakena(i)* heartless, cruel; pitiful, shameful, regrettable

報 *jōhō* information, news, intelligence report

¹³ 話 *jōwa* lover's talk; love story

愛 *jōai* affection, love

義 *jōgi* friendship

勢 *jōsei* state of affairs, condition, indication, appearance

感 *jōkan* emotion, feeling

¹⁴ 緒 *jōcho, jōsho* emotion, feeling

¹⁵ 趣 *jōshu* mood, sentiment; artistic effect

誼 *jōgi* friendship

熱 *jōnetsu* passion; enthusiasm

¹⁶ 操 *jōso* sentiment

--- 9 ---

愈 ¹⁹¹⁰ J4c7c M-X YU. *iyoiyo* more and more, increasingly; at last; beyond doubt.

慌 ¹⁹¹⁷ J3932 M11057 KŌ. *awa(teru)* be confused, lose one's head, be hurried, be hasty. *awa(tefutameku)* be confused, be disconcerted, be panicked. *awatada(shii)* busy, bustling, hurried, confused.

愉 ¹⁹²⁰ J4c7b M10905 YU rejoice. *tano(shimu)* enjoy, amuse oneself; anticipate. *tano(shii)* merry, pleasant, cheerful, joyful.

⁷ 快 *yukai na* happy, pleasant, delightful; cheerful

¹⁰ 悦 *yuetsu* joy

¹³ 楽 *yuraku* pleasure, joy

惰 ¹⁹²¹ J4246 M10855 DA laziness. *okota(ru)* neglect; be off guard; be feeling better.

² 力 *daryoku* inertia, momentum, force of habit

⁸ 性 *dasei* inertia, momentum, force of habit

¹⁰ 眠 *damin* indolence, inactivity, idle slumber

弱 *dajaku* effeminacy, emasculation, laziness

心 忄 ⺗ 9

戈 戶 手 扌 支 攴 文 斗 斤 方 无 日 曰 月 木 欠 歹 殳 毋 比 毛 氏 气 水 氵 氺 火 灬 爪 爫 父 爻 爿 片 牙 牛 犬 犭

4

想 ₁₉₂₂ J415b M10858 Sō idea, conception, A thought. *omo(u)* think, believe, judge, esteem; consider, realize; feel like; regard as; anticipate; imagine, suppose, guess; mistake for; recall; intend; desire; love, care for, yearn after; wonder; suspect.

8 念 *sōnen* idea, conception
定 *sōtei* hypothesis, assumption
9 思 *sōshi* mutual love
10 起 *sōki* recollection, remembrances
14 像 *sōzō* imagination, supposition, conjecture
像力 *sōzōryoku* imagination, imaginative power

愁 ₁₉₂₃ J3d25 M10885 Shū. *ure(u), ure(eru)* B grieve, lament, be anxious. *ure(i), ure(e)* sad, unhappy, gloomy.

6 色 *shūshoku* melancholy air, anxious look, traces of sorrow, gloom
9 眉 *shūbi* worried look, knitted brows, anxiety
眉開 *shūbi (o) hira(ku)* be relieved of worry
12 訴 *shūso* appeal, petition, supplication
13 嘆 *shūtan* lamentation, sorrow
傷 *shūshō* grief, lamentation; condolence
15 歎 *shūtan* grief, lamentation
歎場 *shūtamba* tragic scene

慈 ₁₉₂₄ J3b7c M10980 Ji. *itsuku(shimu)* love, B be affectionate to; pity. *itsuku(shimi)* affection, love.

4 父 *jifu* affectionate father
5 母 *jibo* affectionate mother
8 雨 *jiu* beneficial or welcome rain
11 眼 *jigen* merciful eye
12 悲 *jihi* compassion, benevolence, charity, mercy
悲心 *jihishin* benevolence
善 *jizen* charity, philanthropy
13 愛 *jiai* affection, kindness, love, benevolence

愚 ₁₉₂₅ J3672 M10946 Gu folly, foolishness, B absurdity; fool. *oro(kana), oro(kashii)* foolish, stupid, dull. *gu-* my humble (opinion).

2 人 *gujin* fool, dunce
3 女 *gujo* my (foolish) daughter (humble)
才 *gusai* poor ability, my poor intelligence
5 生 *gusei* I (humble)
民 *gumin* ignorant people
6 行 *gukō* folly, foolish move
劣 *guretsu* foolishness, stupidity, absurdity
考 *gukō* my humble opinion
7 作 *gusaku* poor piece of writing
弄 *gurō* mockery, ridicule
図 *guzu(ru)* grumble, criticize; tease; charge falsely; be cloudy. *guzu* dullard
8 物 *gubutsu* fool, bonehead
直 *guchoku* simple honesty; tactless frankness
妻 *gusai* my (foolish) wife (humble)
忠 *guchū* my loyalty
者 *gusha, oro(ka)mono* fool, dunce
9 昧 *gumai* stupidity, ignorance
計 *gukei* a foolish plan; my (foolish) plan (humble)
衷 *guchū* my feelings
連隊 *gurentai* gang of young toughs
10 息 *gusoku* my (foolish) son (humble)
挙 *gukyo* foolish undertaking
11 問 *gumon* foolish question
鈍 *gudon* stupidity, silliness
策 *gusaku* my (foolish) plan (humble); foolish plan, poor policy
13 僧 *gusō* foolish priest; I (humble, used by a priest)
痴 *guchi* grumbling; folly, foolishness *guchi(ru)* complain
15 論 *guron* foolish argument, absurd opinion; my humble opinion

意 ₁₉₂₆ J3055 M10921 I mind, heart; care; liking, A taste; inclination, will, intention; thought, idea; desire.

4 中 *ichū* intention
中人 *ichū (no) hito* lovers
5 外 *igai na* unexpected, surprising
6 向 *ikō* intention, idea, inclination
匠 *ishō* design, idea
地 *iji* temper; disposition; will power; obstinacy
地汚 *ijikitana(i)* greedy, gluttonous
地張 *ijiba(ru)* persist in, be obstinate. *iji(p)pa(ri)* obstinacy; obstinate person
地悪 *ijiwaru(i)* ill-tempered, unfortunate
気 *iki* spirit, heart; disposition
気込 *ikigo(mu)* be enthusiastic about

気地 *ikuji, ikiji* self-respect, honor, pride
気投合 *ikitōgō* sympathy, mutual understanding
気阻喪 *ikisosō* depression, dejection
気消沈 *ikishōchin* depression, dejection
気軒昂 *ikikenkō* high spirits, high morale
気盛 *ikisaka(n)* high spirits
気揚揚 *iki-yōyō(taru)* triumphant, exultant
⁷図 *ito* intention, aim
見 *iken* opinion, idea, suggestion; remonstrance, admonition
志 *ishi* will, mind, volition
⁸表 *ihyō* surprise, something unexpected
味 *imi* meaning, significance
味合 *imia(i)* meaning, reason
味深長 *imishinchō na* significant
⁹思 *ishi* intention, purpose, mind
¹¹訳 *iyaku* free translation, broad translation
欲 *iyoku* volition, will
¹³想 *isō* thoughts
想外 *isōgai no* unexpected, unsuspected
義 *igi* meaning, significance
義深 *igibuka(i)* full of meaning; of great value
¹⁵趣 *ishu* grudge, malice, spite; thoughts, intention
趣返 *ishugae(shi)* revenge
¹⁹識 *ishiki* consciousness
識不明 *ishiki fumei* unconsciousness
識的 *ishikiteki ni* consciously

愛 $\frac{1927}{\text{J3026}}$ Aı love, affection, favorite.
A M10947 *ai(suru), me(zuru), me(deru)* love; admire, appreciate. *ai(rashii)* lovely, pretty, sweet. *ito(shii)* beloved, dear, loving, pitiable. *mana-* love.
²人 *aijin* lover; lover of mankind
⁵用 *aiyō* habitual use; favorite
⁶好 *aikō* love for, liking for
好者 *aikōsha* lover of
好家 *aikōka* lover of
⁷児 *aiji* beloved child
弟子 *manadeshi* favorite pupil
⁸育 *aiiku* tender nurture
妾 *aishō* prostitute
妻 *aisai* beloved wife
妻家 *aisaika* devoted husband
国 *aikoku* patriotism

国心 *aikokushin* patriotism
国者 *aikokusha* patriot
玩 *aigan suru* be fond of
玩物 *aigambutsu* prized article; pet
¹⁰娘 *manamusume* favorite daughter
称 *aishō* pet name, term of endearment
息 *aisoku* cute boy, beloved son; your son
郷心 *aikyōshin* local patriotism
¹¹唱 *aishō suru* love to read
情 *aijō* love, affection
惜 *aiseki suru* miss (someone); be loathe to part
欲 *aiyoku* passion, love and lust
¹²着 *aichaku, aijaku* attachment, covetous affection
飲家 *aiinka* habitual drinker
敬 *aikei, aikyō* love and respect; charm, winsomenes, attractiveness, courtesy
¹³煙家 *aienka* habitual smoker
想 *aiso, aisō* civility, amiability, courtesy, compliments, entertainment, hospitality, sociability
想尽 *aisozu(kashi), aisōzu(kashi)* alienating (someone)
¹⁴憎 *aizō* likes and dislikes, love and hatred, partiality
慕 *aibo* love, attachment, adoration
読 *aidoku* reading with pleasure
読者 *aidokusha* reader, subscriber, admirer (of a writer)
読書 *aidokusho* favorite book
¹⁵撫 *aibu suru* love dearly. *aibu* caress
嬌 *aikyō* charm, winsomeness, attractiveness, courtesy
²⁰護 *aigo* protection, tender care
²¹顧 *aiko* patronage, favor

感 $\frac{1928}{\text{J3436}}$ Kan feeling, sensation,
A M10953 sentiment; sense; emotion; impression; intuition. *kan(jiru), kan(zuru)* feel, experience, be conscious of; be impressed by; respond to. *kan(ji)* feeling, sense, sensation; perception; sensibility; impression; sentiment, effect, influence; touch, the feel.
²入 *kan(ji)-i(ru)* be deeply impressed
⁴心 *kanshin* admiration, wonder
化 *kanka* influence, inspiration; reform, correction
⁵付 *kanzu(ku)* suspect, sense, scent
⁶光 *kankō* exposure to light; sensitization

4

光紙 *kankōshi* photographic printing paper

7 応 *kannō* inspiration; divine response; sympathy; effect, efficacy; influence; induction (in electricity)

状 *kanjō* letter of commendation; letter of approval

8 性 *kansei* sensitivity, sensitiveness, sense

泣 *kankyū suru* be deeply affected, be touched. *kankyū* crying for joy

知 *kanchi* perception

取 *kan(ji)-to(ru)* take in; appreciate (a poem)

服 *kampuku* admiration, wonder

易 *kan(ji)yasu(i)* sensitive to, excitable, nervous, emotional; impressionable

受性 *kanjusei* receptivity, sensitivity, susceptibility; irritability

9 度 *kando* sensitivity; severity (of a quake)

冒 *kambō, kaze* a cold, influenza

染 *kansen* infection

10 涙 *kanrui* tears of gratitude

11 得 *kantoku suru* get wind of, become aware of, realize

動 *kandō* impression, inspiration, emotion, excitement

情 *kanjō* feelings; emotion; sentiment; impulse; passion

情的 *kanjōteki* emotional, impulsive

12 喜 *kanki* joy, delight, ecstasy

覚 *kankaku* feeling, sensation; senses

13 嘆 *kantan* admiration, wonder

嘆詞 *kantanshi* interjection

触 *kanshoku* sense of touch, feeling, sensation

電 *kanden* electric shock

傷 *kanshō* sentimentality

傷的 *kanshōteki* sentimental

慨 *kangai* deep emotion

慨無量 *kangai-muryō* full of deep emotion

想 *kansō* thoughts, impressions, sentiments, feelings

想文 *kansōbun* description of impressions

14 銘 *kammei* deep impression

銘深 *kammeifuka(i)* impressive

15 歎 *kantan* admiration; wonder

歎符 *kantanfu* exclamation point

歎詞 *kantanshi* interjection

---

16 懐 *kankai* deep impression

激 *kangeki* deep emotion, inspiration, impression

興 *kankyō* interest; fun

奮 *kampun* deep emotion, impression, inspiration

17 謝 *kansha* thanks; appreciation; thanksgiving; grace

謝状 *kanshajō* letter of thanks, testimonial, citation

謝祭 *kanshasai* Thanksgiving Day; thanks offering

────── **10** ──────

慨
B 慨 | 1944 J3334 M-X | GAI be sad. *nage(ku)* sigh, lament.

13 嘆 *gaitan* deploring, regret

慎
B 慎 | 1945 J3f35 M11024′ | SHIN *tsutsu(shimu)* be discreet, be careful, be prudent, be cautious; restrain oneself, be moderate. *tsutsu(mashige) ni* reverently, respectfully, humbly, modestly. *tsutsu(mashii), tsutsu(mashiyaka) na* modest, reserved, humble, bashful. *tsutsu(shimi)* prudence, modesty, discretion, self-control.

9 重 *shinchō* caution, prudence, discretion

11 深 *tsutsu(shimi)buka(i)* discreet, prudent, cautious, modest, self-denying

態
A 態 | 1947 J4256 M11052 | TAI condition, figure, appearance; voice (of verbs). *waza to* intentionally, deliberately, knowingly. *zama* plight, state, appearance, spectacle.

9 度 *taido* attitude; posture, bearing, manner

13 勢 *taisei* attitude; arrangements

14 様 *taiyō* situation, terms

慕
B 慕 | 1948 J4a69 M11088 | BO. *shita(u)* yearn for, love dearly, adore, follow. *shita(washii)* dear, beloved, fond of.

11 情 *bojō* longing, affection

────── **11** ──────

慾
慾 | 1951 J4d5d M11163 | See 欲 2936.

慮 1962 J4e38 M11132 B RYO thought, concern, agreement. *omombaka(ru)*, *omompaka(ru)* consider, deliberate, fear. *omombaka(ri)*, *omompaka(ri)* thought, consideration, prudence; fears, apprehension, strategy.
5 外 *ryogai* emergency; unexpectedness; impoliteness

慧 1964 J3745 M11116 KEI wise.
11 眼 *keigan* keen eye

慶 1967 J3744 M11145 B KYŌ. KEI. *kei(suru)* congratulate. *yoroko(bu)* rejoice, be happy over.
4 弔 *keichō* congratulations and condolences
8 事 *keiji* auspicious event
9 祝 *keishuku* congratulation, celebration
12 賀 *keiga* congratulation

慢 1968 J4b7d M11110 B MAN laziness; ridicule.
4 心 *manshin* self-conceit, pride
8 性 *mansei* chronic

憎 1969 I417e M11188′ B ZŌ. *niku(mu)* hate, detest. *niku(garu)* hate. *niku(i)* hateful, abominable; poor-looking. *niku(rashii)* hateful, horrible, provoking. *niku(shimi)* hatred, enmity. *niku(rashige) ni* hatefully, maliciously.
3 口 *niku(mare)guchi* abusive language
子 *niku(mare)ko, niku(marek)ko* bad boy
6 合 *niku(mi)-a(u)* hate one another
7 役 *niku(mare)yaku* unpopular role
11 悪 *zōo* malice, hatred, abhorrence
13 嫌 *niku(mi)-kira(u)* detest ⌈loathsome
14 憎 *nikuniku(shii)* hateful, detestable,

慣 1970 J3437 M11111 A KAN. *nara(u)* experience; become a habit. *na(rasu)* tame, charm (animals); train, exercise, drill; habituate, accustom to. *na(reru)* get used to, become experienced; be tamed; get too familiar, mature. *na(re)* practice, habit, skill, experience.
5 用 *kan'yō no* common, customary, conventional; colloquial
用句 *kan'yōku* an idiom; a common expression

用的 *kan'yōteki* common, colloquial, customary
用語 *kan'yōgo* idiom; colloquial expression
6 行 *kankō* usual practice, routine
8 性 *kansei* inertia
例 *kanrei* custom, usage, precedent
11 習 *kanshū* custom, common practice
16 親 *na(re)-shita(shimu)* get used to

憂 1971 J4d2b M11170 B YŪ. *ure(u), ure(eru)* grieve, lament, be anxious. *u(ki), u(i)* sad, unhappy, gloomy. *ure(e), ure(i)* distress, sorrow, trouble, anxiety, grief. *usa* gloom, sorrow, melancholy.
4 心 *yūshin* grieving heart
5 目 *u(ki)me* bitter experience, misery, distress, grief, sad thoughts
6 色 *yūshoku* melancholy air, anxious look, traces of sorrow, gloom
8 国 *yūkoku* patriotism
苦 *yūku* trouble, distress, sorrow
11 患 *yūkan* sorrow, worry, distress
12 悶 *yūmon* anguish, mortification
晴 *usabara(shi)* diversion, distraction
13 愁 *yūshū* grief, melancholy, gloom
15 慮 *yūryo* anxiety, dread, cares, solicitude
18 顔 *ure(i)gao* anxious look, sad countenance
26 欝 *yūutsu* melancholy, dejection, gloom

慰 1972 J3056 M11135 B I. *nagusa(mu) vt and vi* amuse oneself; make sport of; seduce. *nagusa(meru), i(suru)* comfort, console, cheer. *nagusa(me)* comfort, consolation, diversion. *nagusa(mi)* amusement, pleasure.
6 合 *nagusa(me)-a(u)* comfort one another
安 *ian* solace, comfort; relaxation, recreation
安婦 *ianfu* army prostitute, comfort woman
7 労 *irō suru* recognize (a person's) services
8 物 *nagusa(mi)mono* object of pleasure; plaything, laughingstock
10 留 *iryū suru* dissuade from resigning
11 問 *imon* condolences; a sympathy call
15 撫 *ibu* pacification, soothing
霊祭 *ireisai* memorial service for the dead

戈戸手扌支攴文斗斤方无日曰月木欠止歹殳毋比毛氏气水氵氺火灬爪爫父爻爿丬片牙牛犬犭

4
【心忄小】

11 忄小 戈戸手扌支攴文斗斤方无日曰月木欠止歹殳毋比毛氏气水氵氺火灬爪爫父爻爿丬片牙牛犬犭

17 謝 *isha* consolation
謝料 *isharyō* consolation money
藉 *isha* consolation
藉料 *isharyō* consolation money

———— **12** ————

B 憩 $\frac{1980}{\text{J3746}}$ M11246 KEI. KATSU. *iko(u)* rest, relax, repose.
12 場 *iko(i) (no) ba* place for relaxation

憧 $\frac{1982}{\text{J4634}}$ M11242 SHŌ. TŌ. DŌ. *akoga(reru)* yearn after, long for; thirst for; aspire to; admire, adore.
15 憬 *dōkei, shōkei, akoga(re)* longing, aspiration

憐 $\frac{1987}{\text{J4e79}}$ M11206 REN. *awa(remu)* pity, have mercy on, sympathize with. *awa(remi)* pity, compassion.
13 愍 *rembin* compassion, pity, mercy
15 憫 *rembin* compassion, pity, mercy

A 憲 $\frac{1988}{\text{J377b}}$ M11269' KEN law.
7 兵 *kempei* military police
8 法 *kempō* constitution; constitutional law
9 政 *kensei* constitutional government

B 憤 $\frac{1990}{\text{J4a30}}$ M11239 FUN. *ikidō(ru)* resent, be indignant, become angry. *mutsuka(ru)* be angry (because of being unhappy); be always crying. *ikidōri* resentment, indignation.
6 死 *funshi suru* die in a fit of anger; be unfortunately put out (in baseball)
9 怒 *fundo, funnu* anger, rage, resentment, indignation, exasperation
10 起 *funki suru* rouse oneself, be stirred up
12 然 *funzen to* indignantly, in a rage
13 慨 *fungai* resentment, indignation
16 激 *fungeki* resentment; indignation
18 懣 *fumman* anger, resentment, indignation, chagrin, irritation

———— **13** ————

B 憾 $\frac{1999}{\text{J3438}}$ M11312 KAN. *ura(mu)* regret, be sorry for. *ura(mi)* regret. *ura(murakuwa)* regrettably.

B 憶 $\frac{2001}{\text{J3231}}$ M11295 OKU think, remember. *omo(u)* think.
11 断 *okudan* deciding without the facts
12 測 *okusoku* guess, speculation, supposition
14 説 *okusetsu* hypothesis, speculation, surmise

B 懇 $\frac{2002}{\text{J3a29}}$ M11326 KON. *nengo(ro) na* kind, courteous, hospitable, cordial.
4 切 *konsetsu* kindness, cordiality, exhaustiveness
7 求 *konkyū* earnest desire
11 望 *kombō, kommō* entreaty
13 意 *kon'i* kindness, intimacy, friendship
話 *konwa* friendly chat
15 請 *konsei* entreaty, request
談 *kondan* chat; consultation
談会 *kondankai* social gathering; roundtable discussion
16 篤 *kontoku* kindness, cordiality
親 *konshin* friendship, intimacy
親会 *konshinkai* social gathering
17 懇 *konkon to* earnestly, repeatedly
19 願 *kongan* entreaty, supplication, petition

B 懐 $\frac{2003}{\text{J327b}}$ M11351 KAI heart, feeling. *natsu(kashima), natsu(kashigaru)* yearn for, miss someone. *natsu(keru)* win over, win another's heart. *natsu(ku)* become attached to. *omo(u)* think, believe, judge, esteem; consider, realize; feel like; regard as; anticipate; imagine, suppose, guess; mistake for; recall; intend; desire; love, care for, yearn after; wonder; suspect. *futokoro* bosom, breast, heart; pocket, purse. *natsu(kkoi)* affectionate, affable, tame. *natsu(kashii)* dear, longed-for; yearning for. *natsu(kashimi)* yearning, nostalgia, kindly feeling.
2 刀 *futokorogatana* dagger; confidant
4 手 *futokorode* hands in pockets, folded arms
中 *kaichū* one's pocket
5 旧 *kaikyū* longing for the old days
古 *kaiko* recalling the old days
古談 *kaikodan* reminiscences
7 妊 *kainin* conception, pregnancy
8 抱 *kaihō suru* entertain, harbor. *da(ki)-*

kaka(eru) embrace; hold in the arms

具合 *futokoro-guai* one's financial situation

炉 *kairo* pocket heater

⁹胎 *kaitai* conception, becoming pregnant

柔 *kaijū* conciliation, pacification, appeasement

¹⁰紙 *futokorogami, kaishi* handkerchief paper; paper used in lieu of plate in tea ceremony; paper to be used for writing poetry

剣 *kaiken* dagger (for self-defense)

郷 *kaikyō* nostalgic reminiscence

¹⁴疑 *kaigi* disbelief, skepticism, doubt

------ 14 ------

懲 B $\frac{2006}{J4428}$ M11399⁰ CHŌ. *ko(rasu), ko(rashimeru), chō(zuru)* chastise, punish, discipline. *ko(riru)* learn by experience; be disgusted with.

⁷役 *chōeki* penal servitude

戒 *chōkai* disciplinary punishment, official reprimand

¹¹悪 *chōaku* chastisement, punishment

罰 *chōbatsu* discipline, punishment

¹⁸懲 *korigori suru, korikori suru* learn from experience; have had enough

------ 16 ------

懸 B $\frac{2011}{J377c}$ M11462 KEN. KE. *ka(keru)* vt hang; set up (a ladder); cover; construct, install; sit down; sprinkle, pour on; put on; ring up; weigh; multiply; levy; pay (in installments); anchor; start (a machine); wind; turn on (radio); spend on; offer (prizes); put (under treatment); set (on fire). *ka(karu)* vi hang on, be suspended from, be caught, be trapped; be built; begin; arrive at; require, cost; play against, oppose; be splashed; weigh (a pound); be levied; (the instrument or tool) works; attack, fall on; is now showing at; consult; depend (on a son).

⁸念 *kenen* fear, anxiety, concern

命 *kemmei* eagerness, earnestness; risking one's life

垂 *kensui* chinning

¹⁰釘 *kakekugi* peg

案 *ken'an* pending question or problem

¹¹崖 *kengai* overhanging cliff, precipice

¹²絶 *kenzetsu* great difference

隔 *kenkaku* difference, discrepancy, gap

¹³想 *kesō* falling in love, attachment

¹⁵賞 *kenshō* offering prizes; prize winning; prize, reward

¹⁶橋 *kakehashi* viaduct; suspension bridge; intermediary

¹⁹離 *ka(ke)-hana(reru)* be far from; be different from

━━━━━ RAD. 戈 62 ━━━━━

Hoko tasseled spear. At right: *hokozukuri* or *hokogamae*.
Variant, at right: 戈. Nickname: Tasseled Spear (cf. Rads. 56 and 110).

------ 1 ------

戊 $\frac{2020}{J4a6a}$ M11532 Bo E, fifth. *tsuchinoe* fifth calendar sign.

------ 2 ------

戎 $\frac{2024}{J3d3f}$ M11539 JŪ warrior; arms. *ebisu* barbarian, savage; Ainu.

⁶衣 *jūi* armor; military uniform

成 A $\frac{2025}{J402e}$ M11542⁰ SEI. JŌ. *na(ru)* become, get or grow (old), form

(a part of); set in, come (time or seasons); turn into; be reduced to; consist of; be accomplished; result in; prove (fatal); amount to; play the part of; elapse; reach (a certain age); bear, stand; be promoted; be pleased to. *na(su)* do, perform, accomplish; form, make, accomplish. *(o)na(ri)* departure of a high personage; visit of a high personage.

²人 *seijin* adult. *seijin suru* come of age

³下 *na(ri)-sa(garu)* stoop to, be reduced to

心 忄 小
【戈】²
戸 手 扌 支 攴 攵 文 斗 斤 方 无 日 曰 月 木 欠 歹 殳 毋 比 毛 氏 气 水 氵 氺 火 灬 爪 爫 父 爻 爿 片 牙 牛 犬 犭

4

心 忄 小 【戈】 戸 手 扌 支 攴 文 斗 斤 方 无 日 曰 月 木 欠 止 歹 殳 毋 比 毛 氏 气 水 氵 灬 火 爪 爻 父 爿 片 牛 犬 犭

上 *na(ri)-a(garu)* rise from the ranks, rise suddenly. *na(ri)a(gari)* upstart

⁴仏 *jōbutsu* attaining Buddhahood, entering Nirvana; death

分 *seibun* ingredient; component; contents

文 *seibun* writing a document; a document

⁵立 *na(ri)-ta(tsu)* consist of; materialize; be concluded, be valid. *seiritsu* materialization, realization, formation, organization, completion. *na(ri)ta(chi)* origin, history

句 *seiku* set phrase, idiomatic phrase

功 *seikō* success, achievement, prosperity

⁶虫 *seichū* adult insect; adult invertebrate animal

行 *na(ri)-yu(ku)* turn out, become of (a person). *nariyu(ki)* developments, course of events; outcome, consequences, destiny

因 *seiin* origin, cause

年 *seinen* majority, adult age, legal age, man's estate

⁷否 *seihi* success or failure

⁸金 *narikin* the newly rich

長 *seichō* growth

育 *seiiku* growth, development; birth and breeding

果 *na(ri)-ha(teru)* be reduced to, become. *seika* results, outcome. *na(re) (no) ha(te)* shadow of one's former self

⁹約 *seiyaku* promise

型 *seikei* plastic surgery

¹⁰員 *seiin* charter members

案 *seian* definite plan

¹¹婚 *seikon* marriage

敗 *seibai suru* punish, judge, bring to justice, deal with (a culprit). *seihai* success or failure

規 *seiki no* regular, formal, official, prescribed

¹²程 *na(ru)hodo* I see, well, really, to be sure

就 *jōju* fulfillment; completion, realization, consummation

¹³損 *na(ri)-sokona(u)* fail to become, be unsuccessful in

¹⁴語 *seigo* a set phrase, an idiom

算 *seisan* prospects of success

層圏 *seisōken* stratosphere

¹⁵熟 *seijuku* ripeness; maturity, maturation, attainment of skill

¹⁷績 *seiseki* results, marks, rating, score

——————— **3** ———————

戒 2027 J327c M11548 B KAI commandment; admonition. *imashi(meru)* admonish, warn, prohibit. *imashi(me)* precept, exhortation, instruction, commandment.

⁴心 *kaishin* caution, vigilance, discretion

⁶名 *kaimyō* Buddhist initiation name; posthumous name

⁷告 *kaikoku* warning, caution

⁹律 *kairitsu* precepts, commandments

¹⁶壇 *kaidan* temple ordination platform

¹⁷厳 *kaigen* guarding against danger

厳令 *kaigenrei* martial law

我 2028 J3266 M11545 A GA ego, self, selfishness, egotism. *waga* my, our, one's own. *ware* I, oneself, self, ego.

⁴方 *wa(ga)hō* our side, we

⁵田引水 *gaden insui* drawing water for one's own field, promoting one's own interests

⁶先 *waresaki ni* self first

⁷身 *wa(ga)mi* myself, oneself

我 *wareware* we. *ware(mo)ware(mo)* vying with one another

⁸国 *wa(ga) kuni* our country

武者羅 *gamushara na* reckless, daredevil

物顔 *wagamonogao* like one's own. *waga monogao ni* in a lordly manner

⁹通 *ga (o) tō(su)* insist on one's own ideas

¹⁰流 *garyū* self-taught; one's own way

家 *wa(ga)ya* our home, our house

¹¹欲 *gayoku* selfishness

執 *gashū* egotism; obstinacy

¹²勝 *warega(chi)* everybody for himself

等 *warera* we

¹³意 *gai* self-will, obstinacy

¹⁴慢 *gaman* patience, perseverance, endurance, tolerance, self-control, self-denial

¹⁵輩 *wagahai* I

¹⁶儘 *wagamama* selfishness, egoism; willfulness, disobedience; whim

—— 4 ——

或 _{2030 / J303f / M11563} WAKU. KOKU. *a(ru)* some, one, a certain, a. *arui(wa)* or; possibly.

—— 7 ——

戚 _{2032 / J404r / M11594} SOKU. SEKI relative; sadness.

—— 8 ——

戟 _{2035 / J3761 / M11606} GEKI. *hoko* halberd; arms.

—— 9 ——

A 戦 _{2037 / J406f / M11631'} SEN war; battle; game, match. *tataka(u)* wage war; fight; engage in a contest; struggle against. *onono(ku)* tremble, shudder. *wanana(ku)* tremble. *tataka(wasu)* cause a quarrel; bring about a war between other nations; argue hotly; compete. *soyo(gu)* rustle, tremble, quiver, sway, stir. *tataka(i)* war, fight; battle, encounter, strife, conflict; contest (in athletics). *ikusa* war, fight, battle, encounter.

² 力 *senryoku* war potential
³ 士 *senshi* soldier, combatant, warrior
⁴ 火 *senka* war conflagration; war disasters; sword and fire
　 中 *senchū* during the war
　 友 *sen'yū* comrade-in-arms
⁵ 史 *senshi* military history; history of the war
　 功 *senkō* distinguished war service, military merit
　 犯 *sempan* war crime; war criminal
⁶ 地 *senchi* battlefield, war front
　 列 *senretsu* line of battle; line (of ships)
　 死 *senshi* death in action
　 争 *sensō* war, warfare, campaign; battle
⁷ 局 *senkyoku* war situation
　 役 *sen'eki* war, battle, campaign
　 抜 *tataka(i)-nu(ku)* fight to a finish
　 乱 *senran* wars, disturbances
　 利品 *senrihin* war spoils, trophies
　 没 *sembotsu* death in battle, killed in action
　 車 *sensha* tank; chariot

　 災 *sensai* war damage
⁸ 法 *sempō* strategy, tactics, campaign plan
　 況 *senkyō* war situation
　 果 *senka* war results
⁹ 陣 *senjin* war preparations; battlefield
　 後 *sengo* after the war
　 前 *senzen* prewar days, before the war
¹⁰ 記 *senki* military history
　 時 *senji* wartime, war period
　 時中 *senjichū* during the war, in wartime
¹¹ 域 *sen'iki* war area, theater of war
　 敗 *sempai* defeat in war
　 術 *senjutsu* tactics, strategy, art of war, campaign plan
　 略 *senryaku* strategy, tactics
¹² 備 *sembi* war preparations; war preparedness
　 場 *senjō* battlefield, the front, war theater
　 渦 *senka* the confusion of war
　 雲 *sen'un* war clouds
　 費 *sempi* war expenditures
　 勝 *senshō* victory, triumph
¹³ 慄 *senritsu* shuddering; frightfulness; shivering
　 跡 *senseki* old battlefield; aftermath of war
　 意 *sen'i* fighting spirit, hostile intention
　 戦恐恐 *sensen-kyōkyō toshite* nervously, gingerly
　 傷 *senshō* war wound
　 傷病 *senshōbyō* war injury or illness
¹⁴ 歴 *senreki* war experience, war service
　 塵 *senjin* dust of battle
　 端 *sentan* hostilities
¹⁵ 線 *sensen* battle line, front
¹⁶ 機 *senki* time to strike; military secret
¹⁷ 績 *senseki* war record; score
¹⁸ 闘 *sentō* battle, action, combat
²⁰ 艦 *senkan* battleship

—— 14 ——

B 戯 _{2041 / J353a / M11665} GI. GE. *tawamu(reru)* play, sport, frolic, joke; flirt with. *tawa(keru)* fool, play the fool, act indecently; be silly over; talk foolishly. *ja(reru), za(reru)* be playful, gambol. *jara(kasu)* calling for jokes. *odo(keru)* joke. *soba(eru)* play pranks, be spoiled.

4

心 忄 小 戈 【戸】 手 扌 支 攵 文 斗 斤 方 无 日 曰 月 木 欠 止 歹 殳 毋 比 毛 氏 气 水 氵 氺 火 灬 爪 爫 父 爻 爿 丬 片 牙 牛 犬 犭

6 曲 *gikyoku* drama, play
7 言 *zaregoto, gigen* joke
作 *gesaku, gisaku* cheap literature, fiction; writing for amusement
作者 *gesakusha* fiction writer, dime novelist
8 画 *giga* cartoon, comics

───── 13 ─────

戴 $\frac{2045}{\text{J4257} \atop \text{M11685}}$ TAI. *itada(ku)* *vi* and *vt* be crowned with, wear; live under (a ruler); install (a president); receive, accept; buy; take, eat, drink (humble).
9 冠式 *taikanshiki* coronation

━━━━━ RAD. 戸 63 ━━━━━

To door. Also called *togashira*, *to kammuri*, or *todare*. Variant: 戸. Nickname: Door.

A 戸 $\frac{2048}{\text{J384d} \atop \text{M11696}}$ Ko house; door; family; counter for houses.
to door.
3 口 *toguchi* door, doorway. *kokō* number of houses; population
4 戸 *koko* houses; *koko ni* at each door, from door to door
5 外 *kogai* open-air, outdoors
主 *koshu* head of a family
6 毎 *kogoto ni* at every door; from door to door
7 別 *kobetsu* each house, house to house
8 板 *toita* rain shutter (when used for carrying)
11 袋 *tobukuro* built-in box for shutters
12 棚 *todana* locker, cabinet, closet, sideboard, cupboard
惑 *tomado(u)* be at sea, lose one's bearings
13 数 *kosū* number of houses
15 締 *tojima(ri)* fastening the doors, closing up. *tojime* shutting a door
20 籍 *koseki* census; family register
籍抄本 *koseki shōhon* abstract of a family register
籍謄本 *koseki tōhon* copy of a family register

───── 3 ─────

B 戻 $\frac{2051}{\text{J4c61} \atop \text{M11707}}$ REI. *modo(ru)* return, turn back; revert to, resume; return to; be returned; go backward. *modo(su)* return, restore; turn back (a clock); reject; vomit. *moto(ru)* be contrary (to), go against, deviate from.
2 入 *modo(shi)-i(re)* reimbursement
11 道 *modo(ri)michi* the way back, return journey

───── 4 ─────

B 房 $\frac{2053}{\text{J4b3c} \atop \text{M11714}}$ Bō house, room; tassel. *fusa* tuft, tassel, fringe; lock (of hair); cluster, bunch, segment (of an orange).
4 中 *bōchū* in the room; in the bedroom
8 房 *fusafusa* tufty, fringy, bushy (tail), fleecy
事 *bōji* sexual intercourse

A 所 $\frac{2054}{\text{J3d6a} \atop \text{M11715}}$ So. SHO place. *tokoro* place, spot, scene, site, seat; locality, district; room; distance; address; point, feature; passage (in a book), part; thing; time, moment; extent; matter of course. *tokoro ga* but, however, on the contrary. *toko* place. *tokoro de* well, by the way. *-sho, -jo* place, office, bureau.
4 以 *yuen* reason, the reason why
5 用 *shoyō* errand, business, appointment
6 行 *shogyō* acts, works
存 *shozon* thought, opinion
在 *shozai* whereabouts, site, position, location, place where something is kept
有 *shoyū* possession, ownership; property
7 見 *shoken* view, opinion, impressions, findings
作 *shosa* conduct; gesture

⁸長 *shochō* office head, factory head, institute head

定 *shotei no* fixed, prescribed

所 *shosho, tokorodokoro* here and there, several places

⁹信 *shoshin* belief, conviction, opinion

要 *shoyō* need

為 *shoi* results; influence, effect; fault. *sei, shoi* act, action, deed, results, results of one's actions

持 *shoji suru* possess, have, own; carry

持品 *shojihin* one's personal effects

¹⁰員 *shoin* staff, personnel; staff member

帯 *shotai* household, home

帯道具 *shotai dōgu* household goods

¹¹産 *shosan* result, outcome

¹¹望 *shomō* desire, request, wish

得 *shotoku* income, earnings; possessions. *tokoro (o) e(ru)* secure a position exactly to one's liking

¹²属 *shozoku* attached to; one's post

期 *shoki* anticipation, expectation

番地 *tokorobanchi* address

¹³嫌 *tokorokira(wazu)* anywhere, everywhere; indiscriminately

詮 *shosen* after all

感 *shokan* impressions

業 *shogyō* acts, works

載 *shosai no* printed, published, reported

¹⁴領 *shoryō* territory, dominion, possession; fief

蔵 *shozō* possession

管 *shokan* jurisdiction

¹⁶謂 *iwayuru* the so-called

¹⁷轄 *shokatsu* jurisdiction

───── 6 ─────

扇 $\frac{2056}{\begin{smallmatrix}J4070\\M11743\end{smallmatrix}}$ B SEN. *ao(gu)* fan. *ōgi* folding fan.

³子 *sensu* folding fan

⁷形 *senkei, ōgigata* fan shape

状地 *senjōchi* alluvial delta

⁹風機 *sempūki* electric fan

¹¹情的 *senjōteki* lascivious, sensational, suggestive

動 *sendō* instigation, agitation

───── 8 ─────

扉 $\frac{2058}{\begin{smallmatrix}J4862\\M11750\end{smallmatrix}}$ B HI. *tobira* door; title page; front page.

═════ RAD. 手 64 ═════

Te hand. At left: 手, 扌, and 扌 (3 strokes) *tehen*. Nickname: Hand.

才 $\frac{2059}{\begin{smallmatrix}J3a4d\\M11769\end{smallmatrix}}$ A SAI ability, talent, aptitude, genius, acumen, intelligence, wit; cubic foot; year, age; time; occasion; opportunity; limit; vicinity. *-sai* years old, age, year. *zae* intelligence, ability, talent.

²人 *saijin* talented person, clever person

³女 *saijo* talented woman

子 *saishi* talented man, clever man

⁶色 *saishoku* wit and beauty

気 *saiki* wisdom

気煥発 *saiki kampatsu* great wisdom

気縦横 *saiki jūō* great wisdom

⁷走 *saibashi(ru)* be clever, be quick-witted, be precocious

⁸知 *saichi* wit and intelligence

¹⁰能 *saino* talent, ability

¹²媛 *saien* literary woman; talented woman

腕 *saiwan* skill, ability

筆 *saihitsu* literary talent, clever style

覚 *saikaku* ready wit; raising (money); plan, device

¹³幹 *saikan* ability

槌 *saizuchi* small wooden mallet

¹⁴徳 *saitoku* intelligence and virtue

手 $\frac{2060}{\begin{smallmatrix}J3c6a\\M11768\end{smallmatrix}}$ A SHU. *te* hand, arm; help; handwriting; handle, means; trick, snare; skill; kind; direction, side; trouble, care; control, management; possession; connection; injury. *te ni suru* carry. *te(bura) de* empty-handed. *te(zukara)* personally, with one's own hands. *te(gusune)* prepared and waiting. *-te* person; kind; direction; money.

4

心 忄 小 戈 戸 【手 扌】

支 攴 文 斗 斤 方 无 日 曰 月 木 欠 止 歹 殳 毋 比 毛 氏 气 水 氵 氺 火 灬 爪 爫 父 爻 爿 片 牙 牛 犬 犭

[1] 一杯 *te-ippai* hands full; barely making ends meet; full operation

[2] 入 *te (o) i(reru)* reach into; correct, retouch, repair; raid; interfere. *tei(razu)* requiring little trouble; untouched, virgin (forest). *tei(re)* repair, remodeling; care, trimming; raid, round-up

八丁口八丁 *tehatchō-kuchihatchō no* very skilled (person)

[3] 口 *teguchi* style of work; method employed

下 *te (o) kuda(su)* set to work; do in person; participate; murder. *teshita* subordinate, follower

土産 *temiyage* visitor's present

工芸 *shukōgei* handicraft

工業 *shukōgyō* manual labor, handicrafts

[4] 心 *tegokoro* discretion, consideration, allowance

手 *tete* hands (child's word). *te(ni)te(ni)* in everyone's hands

込 *tego(me)* rape, violation, outrage. *te (no) ko(nda)* complicated, laborious, elaborate

中 *shuchū ni* in the hand

元 *temoto* money on hand, one's purse; usual skill

分 *tewa(ke)* division of work. *te (o) wa(katsu)* break off relations with

内 *te(no)uchi* palm; skill, capacity; gift, alms; scope of one's ability

内職 *tenaishoku* piecework at home

引 *te (o) hi(ku)* lead by the hand; sever connections with. *tebi(ki)* guidance; introduction, primer; good offices, pull; introducer, backer; guide; spinning (silk) by hand

引書 *tebi(ki)sho* guidebook

不足 *tebusoku* shorthanded

水 *temizu, chōzu* water for washing the hands

切 *te (o) ki(ru)* cut the hand; sever connections with. *tegi(re)* severance of connections

切金 *tegirekin* alimony, heart balm

[5] 玉 *tedama* jackstones; bean bags. *tedama ni* (leading) by the nose

立 *teda(te)* method, means

広 *te (o) hiro(geru)* extend operations. *tebiro(i)* roomy, spacious; large

(practice); extensive (trade)

甲 *te(no)kō, tekkō* covering for the back of the hand. *tekkō* old-style Japanese glove

打 *te (o) u(tsu)* clap hands; adopt (a measure); strike a bargain. *teu(chi)* striking a bargain; reconciliation, handmade; killing by one's own hands

出 *teda(shi)* interference; striking the first blow

本 *tehon* model, pattern, copy, standard

加減 *tekagen* allowance, discretion; tact; skill; measuring in the hand

古摺 *tekozu(ru)* be at wit's end, have a hard time with

付 *te (o) tsu(keru)* touch, lay hands on; attempt, have carnal connections with. *te (ni) tsu(kanai)* unable to settle down (to anything). *tetsu(ke)* way of doing; earnest money, deposit. *tetsu(ki)* way of using the hand

付金 *tezukekin, tetsukekin* earnest money, deposit

弁当 *tebentō de* furnishing one's own lunch

仕事 *teshigoto* manual labor, hand work

札 *tefuda* name card; a hand (in card playing)

[6] 尽 *te (o) tsu(kusu)* take pains, do everything possible

近 *tejika (na), tejika (i)* near, handy, familiar

休 *teyasu(mi), teyasu(me)* rest, pause

交 *shukō (suru)* hand over, deliver

合 *tea(i)* fellow, chap; party, company, set (of people). *tea(wase)* game, contest, sale, transaction

早 *tebaya(i)* quick, nimble, agile

先 *tesaki* fingers; cat's-paw, tool, agent

向 *tamu(keru)* offer, pay tribute (to the dead). *temu(kau)* resist, oppose, lift one's hand against. *tamu(ke)* offering, parting gift, tribute (to the dead)

伝 *tetsuda(u)* help, take part in. *tetsuda(i)* help; helper, assistant

当 *tea(tari)* the feel; within reach. *tea(tari-battari)* hit-and-miss manner. *teate* allowance, compensation, tip, bonus. *tea(te)* (police) search; treatment, dressing, medical care

当次第 *tea(tari) shidai ni* at random, haphazardly

回 *temawa(shi)* preparation. *te (o) mawa(su)* send out agents, use spies. *temawa(ri)* personal effects; personal surroundings; bodyguard. *te (ga) mawa(ru)* be attentive to, attend to everything

回品 *temawa(ri)hin* personal effects

7 応 *tegota(e)* resistance, response; effect, result

作 *tezuku(ri) no* handmade, homemade, homegrown.

折 *tao(ru)* break off, pluck; deflower

技 *shugi* technique, procedure

抜 *te (o) nu(ku)* eliminate steps, save labor; drop out (of a project); do slipshod work. *tenu(kari)* omission, oversight, error, slip. *tenu(ki)* omission; intentional negligence

助 *tedasu(ke)* help, assistance

兵 *shuhei* soldiers under direct command

足 *teashi* hands and feet, limbs. *shusoku* hands and feet; subordinates

足纏 *teashimato(i)* encumbrance

余 *teama(su), te (ni) ama(ru)* be beyond one's power; incorrigible

芸 *shugei* handicrafts, manual arts, useful arts

形 *tegata* draft, promissory note

8 金 *tekin* key money, earnest money, deposit. *tegane* ready money

届 *te (ga) todo(ku)* reach (a goal)

刷 *tezu(ri)* hand printing

始 *tehajime* beginning, outset

招 *temane(ku)* beckon

放 *tebana(su)* let go, release; part with, dispose of, send away; leave uncared for; leave off work. *tebana(shi)* hands off (in driving); leaving alone. *tebana(shi) de* freely, uncritically

明 *tea(ki)* leisure, spare time

枕 *temakura suru* use the arm for a pillow

法 *shuhō* technique, technical skill; execution

並 *tena(mi)* skill, performance

直 *tenao(shi)* later adjustment

者 *te(no)mono* one's men.

押車 *teo(shi)guruma* handcart; wheelbarrow

長猿 *tenagazaru* gibbon

拍子 *tebyōshi* beating time; careless move

取 *tedo(ri)* net profit; net income; take-home pay

取早 *te(t)to(ri)bayai* quick; rough and ready

取足取 *teto(ri)-ashito(ri), te(o)to(ri)-ashi(o)to(ri)* by main force, by the hands and feet, bodily

9 首 *tekubi* wrist

厚 *teatsu(i)* cordial, courteous, hospitable; liberal (gift)

垢 *teaka* soil from handling

拱 *te (o) komanu(ku)* fold the arms; do nothing to help; meditate

拭 *tenugui, tefuki* towel

狭 *tezema na, tezema(i)* narrow, cramped, small

段 *shudan, tedate* resources, way, means, device, expedient, measures

柔 *teyawa(rakani)* gently, kindly, leniently

荒 *teara(i), teara na* rough, rude, harsh; violent; outrageous. *teara(ku), teara ni* roughly, violently, rudely

巻 *tema(ki)* hand-rolled; hand-wound

風琴 *tefūkin* accordion, hand organ

品 *tejina* sleight of hand, tricks, juggling

洗 *teara(i)* washing the hands; washbasin; washstand; lavatory, toilet

前 *temae* I; you; this side of; this way, toward you; living, livelihood; due to; for the sake of, tea-ceremony procedures; self, ones' own. *(o)temae* tea-serving skill

前味噌 *temae miso* self-praise; bean paste of one's own making

前勝手 *temaegatte* selfishness

負 *te (o) o(u)* hurt yourself. *te(ni)o(enai)* unmanageable, incorrigible. *teo(i)* wound; wounded person

持 *temo(chi)* holdings, goods on hand

持無沙汰 *temo(chi)busata* idleness, suspense; ennui

柄 *tegara* merit, feat, exploit

相 *tesō* lines of the palm

相見 *tesōmi* palmist, palm reader

10 振 *te (o) fu(ru)* shake one's hand. *tebu(ri)* gesture

捕 *tedo(ri)* capturing

捌 *tesaba(ki)* processing, maneuvering

4

心 忄 小 戈 戸 【手 扌】 ⁰ 支 攴 攵 文 斗 斤 方 无 日 曰 月 木 欠 止 歹 殳 毋 比 毛 氏 气 水 氵 氺 火 灬 爪 宀 父 爻 爿 丬 片 牙 牛 犬 犭

紙	*tegami* letter, note, epistle
記	*shuki* taking notes; memo
討	*teu(chi)* killing with one's own sword
配	*tekuba(ri), tehai* arrangements; disposition (of men); preparations
酌	*tejaku* drinking alone
書	*tega(ki)* hand-written
挙	*te (o) a(geru)* raise a hand; show one's hand; give up
真似	*temane* gesture, signs; dumb show, pantomime
荷物	*tenimotsu* luggage, baggage, personal effects
料理	*teryōri* home cooking
¹¹ 疵	*tekizu* wound (on the battlefield)
遊	*teaso(bi)* playing; plaything; gambling. *tesusabi* patting to comfort; play with
遅	*teoku(re)* too late, belated treatment
彫	*tebo(ri)* hand carving
頃	*tegoro na* handy, suitable, moderate
帳	*techō* notebook
強	*tezuyo(i)* strong, firm; severe. *tegowa(i)* stiff, unyielding, stubborn
掛	*tega(keru)* handle, manage, work with; rear, look after; have experience with. *te (o) ka(keru)* touch, handle. *te (ni) ka(karu)* fall into another's hand. *te (ga) ka(karu)* require a lot of care. *te (ni) ka(keru)* kill by one's hand; take care of, bring up. *tega(kari)* contact, trail, scent; on hand; hand hold; clue, key
控	*tebika(eru)* hold back, hold off, refrain from. *tebika(e)* note, memorandum; holding back
探	*tesagu(ri)* fumbling, groping
桶	*teoke* wooden bucket
淫	*shuin* masturbation
堅	*tegata(i)* steady, firm; solid, secure
袋	*tebukuro* gloves, mittens; gauntlet; mitt
許	*temoto* money on hand, one's purse; usual skill. *temoto ni* at hand, under one's care
毬	*temari* handball
習	*tenara(i)* penmanship; practice; learning
動	*shudō* hand-operated
術	*shujutsu* surgical operation
¹² 痛	*teita(i)* severe, serious, hard (blow)
違	*techiga(i)* hitch, something wrong

順	*tejun* process, routine, procedure
渡	*tewata(shi)* personal delivery
焼	*te (o) ya(ku)* burn one's fingers, have a bitter experience with. *teya(ki) no* home-baked
短	*temiji(kana)* short, brief
掌	*shushō, te(no)hira* the palm of the hand
筋	*tesuji, te (no) suji* palm lines; skill (in writing, painting, etc.); means; method; connections. *te (no) suji* veins on the hand
筈	*tehazu* program, plan
着	*te (o) tsu(keru)* begin, start work on
落	*teo(chi)* omission, slip, oversight, neglect
軽	*tegaru na* easy, ready; simple, informal, offhand; cheap. *tegaru(i)* easy (to do)
腕	*shuwan* ability, skill
提	*tesage* handbag
間	*tema* time; labor; trouble; wages
間仕事	*tema shigoto* piecework, odd jobs
間取	*temado(ru)* take time, be delayed
間賃	*temachin* wages
¹³ 傷	*tekizu* wound (on the battlefield)
煩	*te (o) wazura(wasu)* trouble someone
解	*tehodo(ki)* introduction, primer, rudiments
話	*shuwa* sign language
詰	*tezu(maru)* be hard up, be driven to the wall. *tezu(me)* forced liquidation. *tezu(mari)* hard up; stalemate
跡	*shuseki* handwriting (specimen)
馴	*tena(rasu)* tame; train (a person). *tena(reru)* get used to; become skilled in
勢	*tezei* troops under one's command
業	*tewaza* manual work; skill; art
続	*tetsuzu(ki)* procedure, process (of laws), formalities
際	*tegiwa* performance, execution; skill; tact
数	*tekazu* trouble; number of moves (in a game). *tesū* trouble, pains, care
数料	*tesūryō* handling charge, commission
塩掛	*teshio (ni) ka(keru)* rear, raise, tame; train (flower)
¹⁴ 慣	*tena(reru)* get used to; become skilled in

掴	*tezukami* taking with the fingers
摺	*tesuri* railing, balustrade
綱	*tazuna* bridle, reins
酷	*tehido(i)* severe, cruel, merciless
管	*tekuda* art, technique; guile, wiles, coquetry; deceit
蔓	*tezuru* interest, influence, connections, good offices, medium
製	*tesei* handmade, homespun
榴弾	*shuryūdan, teryūdan* hand grenade
旗	*tebata* hand flag
漉	*tesuki* handmade paper
練	*shuren* manual skill. *teren* methods of deception
練手管	*teren-tekuda* method of deception
15 編	*tea(mi)* hand knitting
縫	*tenu(i) no* hand-sewn, hand-tailored
緩	*tenuru(i)* mild, lenient; relaxed, lukewarm; slow, dilatory
縄	*tenawa* curtain rope; rope binding a criminal; halter rope
慰	*tenagusa(mi)* fingering; gambling
16 懐	*tenazu(keru)* tame, domesticate; win over; win one's heart
積	*tezumo(ri)* rough measurement
錠	*tejō* handcuffs, manacles
薄	*teusu* weakness, shortage; inadequate preparations. *teusu(i)* scarce, short of; slender (means)
17 厳	*tekibi(shii)* severe, scathing, cruel
濡	*te (o) nu(rasazu) ni* without getting wet; without lifting a finger
鞠	*temari* handball
鞠唄	*temari uta* handball song
18 癖	*tekuse* kleptomania; hand mannerisms
織	*teo(ri)* hand weaving
蹟	*shuseki* handwriting (specimen)
19 鏡	*tekagami* hand mirror; copybook; model
離	*tebana(reru)* to not need constant care; be finished and ready to deliver
繰	*tagu(ru)* haul in, reel in; trace; unravel. *teguri* spinning by hand; dragnet; arrangement; management
繰上	*taku(shi)-a(geru)* tuck up. *tagu(shi)-a(geru)* haul in
繰込	*tagu(ri)-ko(mu)* haul in
繰揚	*tagu(ri)-a(geru)* haul in
20 懸	*tekake* handling something; concubine. *tega(kari)* contact, trail,

scent; on hand; hand hold; clue, key

――――――― 2 ―――――――

B 払 $\frac{2062}{\text{J4a27}}$ FUTSU *hara(u)* clear out, M11784 sweep away, wipe off, brush off, drive away, banish; prune; parry; pay; dispose of; wield (a sword) sideways; show interest in. *(o)hara(i)* payment; unneeded things for sale.

3 下	*hara(i)-sa(geru)* sell, dispose of
4 手	*hara(i)te* payer
込	*hara(i)-ko(mu)* pay in, pay up, pay an installment. *haraiko(mi)* payment, installment, subscription
5 出	*hara(i)-da(su)* disburse, pay out; drive away
7 戻	*hara(i)-modo(su)* refund, reimburse
8 底	*futtei* shortage, scarcity, famine
退	*hara(i)-no(keru)* brush aside, ward off, drive away
9 拭	*fusshoku suru* wipe out, sweep away
除	*hara(i)-nozo(ku)* remove, sweep away
12 暁	*futsugyō* dawn
落	*hara(i)-oto(su)* shake off, brush off
15 箱	*(o)hara(i)bako* dismissal

A 打 $\frac{2063}{\text{J4247}}$ CHŌ, DA striking. *u(tsu)* M11781 strike, hit, beat, knock, slap, punch, thrash, smite; clap (one's hands); beat (a drum); ring (a bell); (clocks) strike; impress, touch; shoot; pound in (a nail); water, sprinkle; braid; play (checkers); till (the soil); temper (a sword); prepare (buckwheat noodles); present (a play); cast (a net); pay (earnest money). *bu(tsu)* strike, beat; tell, speak; address (an audience). *dāsu* dozen. *u(chi-nomesu)* knock down, beat up. *u(chi)-* emphatic verbal prefix.

3 下	*u(chi)-o(rosu)* strike on the head, strike down on, bring an ax down on
上	*u(chi)-a(geru)* shoot up, send up, set off (fireworks); dash against; cast up on shore, wash ashore; finish, end (a performance)
4 手	*dashu* (cricket) bowler. *u(chi)te, u(t)te* attacking party, punitive force, pursuers; shooter, murderer
方	*u(chi)kata* how to shoot; batting, stroking (in tennis); how to punctuate

4

心 忄 小 戈 戸 【手 扌】

2

支 攴 攵 文 斗 斤 方 无 日 曰 月 木 欠 止 歹 殳 毋 比 毛 氏 气 水 氵 氺 火 灬 爪 爫 父 爻 爿 丬 片 牙 牛 犬 犭

止 u(chi)-ya(mu) vi end, stop, cease; subside, calm down, pass; die out, be extinguished; leave, go off; be abandoned. u(chi)-to(meru) kill, bring down (a bird). u(chi)do(me) end of an entertainment or match

水 u(chi)mizu watering, sprinkling

込 u(chi)-ko(mu) drive in, pound in, shoot into, fall deeply in love, be thrown into, be absorbed in

切 bu(t)tagi(ru) cut off, chop off. u(chi)-ki(ru) vt end, close, discontinue. bu(k)ki(ru) chop, mangle

5 立 u(chi)-ta(teru) establish

付 u(chi)-tsu(keru) strike, knock; pound in (a nail); throw at. u(tte)-tsu(ke) appropriateness of work

叩 u(chi)-tata(ku), bu(t)tata(ku) bruise, pound, strike

払 u(chi)-hara(u) beat off, shake off, sweep off, brush off, drive off, repel, rout

出 u(chi)-da(su) begin to beat; open fire; emboss; end, be over. u(chi)-de(ru), u(tte)-de(ru) sally out, come forward, be a candidate; fire. u(chi)da(shi) close of a performance; embossing; delivery (of a ball)

6 尽 u(chi)-tsu(kusu) shoot up all (ammunition)

返 u(chi)-kae(su) strike back; return (the ball); rally; repeat; plow up; renovate (old cotton). u(chi)kae(shi) striking back; change of scene

向 u(chi)-mu(kau) face, be opposite, meet, confront; oppose, defy; proceed to; get, tend toward; approach

伏 u(chi)-fu(seru) overpower, have power over. u(chi)-fu(su) humble oneself

当 u(chi)-a(teru) dash against

合 u(chi)-a(u) fight, exchange blows. u(chi)-a(waseru) strike (a thing) against (another). uchia(wase) previous arrangement; preliminaries, appointment

7 身 u(chi)mi bruise, contusion

抜 u(chi)-nu(ku) punch, perforate; stamp out (coins); penetrate, pierce; shoot through

沈 u(chi)-shizu(mu) be completely discouraged

8 固 u(chi)-kata(meru) harden by tamping

延 u(chi)-no(basu), u(chi)-no(beru) hammer out

取 u(chi)-to(ru) catch, arrest; take possession of; kill

者 dasha batter, hitter

明 u(chi)-a(keru), u(chi)-a(kasu) reveal, confide in

9 飛 bu(t)to(basu) (emphatic), beat, strike, knock; let go off. bu(t)to(bu) (emphatic) jump

首 u(chi)kubi decapitation

連 u(chi)-tsu(reru) take (someone) along

砕 u(chi)-kuda(ku), bu(chi)-kuda(ku) smash, crush

負 u(chi)-ma(kasu) overcome, outrival, defeat

10 倒 bu(t)tao(su) knock down. bu(t)tao(reru) fall down, be knocked down. u(chi)-tao(reru) fall, collapse, drop; break down, die, succumb to; fall senseless; be ruined; have a bad debt. u(chi)-tao(su) knock down; overthrow. datō knockout; overthrowing

振 u(chi)-fu(ru) wave, wag, swing, shake; sprinkle; brandish; jilt, reject; attach, allot

消 u(chi)-ke(su) deny, contradict. uchike(shi) denial, negation; negative (in grammar)

破 u(chi)-yabu(ru) vt tear, rip, rend; break, crush, destroy; violate, transgress; defeat; baffle, frustrate. daha breaking, destruction, defeat, conquest, overthrow

留 u(chi)-to(meru) kill, bring down (a bird). u(chi)do(me) end of a match or an entertainment

11 掛 u(tte)-kaka(ru) attack a person. u(chi)-ka(karu), bu(chi)-ka(karu) strike at (someone). u(chi)ka(ke) long outer robe

捨 u(chi)-su(teru) throw away, discard, abandon, desert; discard, give up, abandon; renounce, relinquish; resign; lay down (one's life); part with; sacrifice; reject, condemn

寄 u(chi)-yo(seru) break upon (the shore), beat upon

貫 u(chi)-nu(ku), u(chi)-tsuranu(ku) pierce

¹² 開 *u(chi)hira(ku)* open, unfold, unroll, uncover, unpack, unite, unseal; establish; clear (land); pioneer; clear the way; convene; enlighten (a country); bloom; differ, have a margin; widen (the space between). *dakai* break, development, new turn, solution

勝 *u(chi)-ka(tsu)* defeat, conquer, overcome, surmount, recover from (illnesses)

診 *dashin* percussion, tapping (in medicine)

割 *u(chi)-wa(ru)* divide, cut, halve; separate; split, rip; break, crack, smash; dilute

落 *u(chi)-o(tosu)* knock down; shoot down; knock out (a tooth); thresh out; lop off (branches)

集 *u(chi)-tsudo(u)* meet, assemble, congregate; swarm, flock or gather together; be collected, be gathered together; converge

¹³ 傷 *u(chi)kizu* bruise, contusion

損 *u(chi)-sokona(u)* miss, fail to hit

続 *u(chi)-tsuzu(keru)* give repeated blows; fire in succession; batter; continue. *u(chi)-tsuzu(ku)* long, long-continued

電 *daden suru* send a telegram

楽器 *dagakki* percussion instrument

解 *u(chi)-to(keru)* open one's heart, be frank, throw aside reserve

¹⁴ 鳴 *u(chi)-na(rasu)* vt ring, sound, blow (a whistle), beat (drums), clank, clink, clap, crack (a whip), smack (lips), cluck (one's tongue), honk; air (grievances); attain (celebrity)

算 *dasan* calculation, self-interest, selfishness

算的 *dasanteki* calculating, mercenary, self-centered

¹⁵ 撲 *daboku* contusion, blow

撲傷 *dabokushō* bruise, contusion

撃 *dageki* blow, hit, shock; batting, hitting

¹⁶ 壊 *u(chi)-kowa(su), bu(chi)-kowa(su)* break, shatter, smash; upset (a plan), ruin, spoil, frustrate; bungle

¹⁸ 懲 *u(chi)-ko(rasu)* discipline, chasten, punish by whipping

───── 3 ─────

托 2069 J4271 M11793 TAKU. *taku(suru)* entrust with, charge with; pretend; hint.

¹³ 鉢 *takuhatsu* religious mendicancy; begging priest

扱 2070 J3037 M-X Sō. KYŪ. *atsuka(u)* B treat; entertain; manage, deal with, conduct, work on; handle; manipulate. *shigo(ku)* squeeze through the hand, strip off. *ko(ku)* thresh, strip. *shigoki* woman's undergirdle, waistband; squeezing through.

³ 下 *ko(ki)-oro(su)* thresh; strip off; criticize meanly

⁸ 使 *ko(ki)-tsuka(u)* work (a person) hard

───── 4 ─────

扮 2080 J4a31 M11830 FUN. *fun(suru), yatsu(su)* impersonate, dress up (as), disguise oneself (as).

¹² 装 *funsō suru* impersonate. *funsō* garb, style of dress

択 2082 J4272 M11902 TAKU. *yo(ru), era(bu),* B *e(ru)* choose, select; cull out; elect; prefer; decide on.

¹ 一 *takuitsu* choosing an alternative

把 2083 J4744 M11874 HA bundle, bunch, sheaf, B coil. *to(ru)* take, hold, seize, catch, capture; fetch; receive, procure, obtain; adopt (a measure); engage (graduates); choose; order (foodstuffs); pick, pluck; make, produce; eat; set up (camp); charge; administer; transact; take (pains); make out (the meaning); remove; take off (one's hat); take out (spots); strike out (words); weed, catch (fish); deprive of ; steal; capture (territory), annex; need, require; reserve (rooms); subscribe to; press (a point home); take (a picture); possess. *wa* bundle, faggot, sheaf.

⁴ 手 *totte, torite, hashu* handle, knob, grip. *hashu* grasping the hand

¹² 握 *haaku* grasp, hold, grip

4

心 忄 小 戈 戸 【手 扌】 支 攴 攵 文 斗 斤 方 无 日 曰 月 木 欠 止 歹 殳 毋 比 毛 氏 气 水 氵 氺 火 灬 爪 爫 父 爻 爿 丬 片 牙 牛 犬 犭

B 拒 2084 J3571 M-X KYO *koba(mu)* refuse, reject, decline; repudiate; resist, oppose, prevent; deny. *fuse(gu)* defend, protect; resist; keep away, shut out, ward off; prevent.

7 否 *kyohi* denial, veto, rejection
食症 *kyoyokushō* anorexia
12 絶 *kyozetsu* refusal, rejection, rebuff

A 批 2086 J4863 M11845 HI strike.

7 判 *hihan* criticism, comment
判的 *hihanteki* critical
10 准 *hijun* ratification
12 評 *hihyō* criticism, comment
18 難 *hinan* criticism, denunciation

B 抄 2087 J3e36 M11863 SHŌ selection, summary; one tenth of a *shaku* (勺). *shō(suru)* copy; copy out. *su(ku)* spread out thin; manufacture (paper).

5 本 *shōhon* excerpt, abridgment, book of selections
11 訳 *shōyaku* abridged translation
16 録 *shōroku* quotation, selection; summary

A 承 2088 J3e35 M11852 JŌ. SHŌ. *u(keru)* receive, accept, take, get, obtain; catch (a ball); stop (a blow), parry; answer (the phone); undergo (an operation); take (an exam); sustain (a loss); be exposed to (ridicule); face, front on; inherit; catch the public fancy. *uketamawa(ru)* hear, listen to, be informed.

8 服 *shōfuku* compliance, consent, submission
知 *shōchi* consent, assent, admitting, acknowledgment, compliance, agreement
9 前 *shōzen* continued (from)
13 継 *shōkei* succession, accession, inheritance
14 認 *shōnin* approval, consent, agreement, recognition, acknowledgment
15 諾 *shōdaku* acquiescence, consent, agreement

B 扶 2089 J495e M11840 FU. *tasu(keru)* help; save, rescue; give relief to; spare (life); reinforce; promote; abet.

7 助 *fujo* aid, help, support, relief
8 育 *fuiku* bringing up (children)
9 持 *fuchi* stipend, allowance, sustenance
10 桑 *Fusō* Japan
12 植 *fushoku* implantation; establishment; extension
15 養 *fuyō* support, maintenance

B 抑 2090 J4d5e M11883 YOKU *osa(eru)* stop, check, restrain, pin down; suppress, subdue, control; catch, arrest; govern; stop (the ears); withhold; attach, seize; secure (evidence), estimate conservatively. *osa(e)* weight, paperweight; rear guard; defense; pressure, suppression; control. *somosomo* well, now; in the first place.

4 止 *yokushi suru* check, checkmate, stave off
5 圧 *yokuatsu* oppression, repression, pressure, suppression, restraint
付 *osa(e)-tsu(keru)* hold down, curb, control
8 制 *yokusei suru* control, restrain, suppress
10 留 *yokuryū* internment
12 揚 *yokuyō* modulation, intonation, accent, rhythm, cadence
26 欝 *yokuutsu* depression (in psychiatry)

B 抗 2091 J3933 M11889 KŌ. *kō(suru)* resist, defy, oppose, antagonize.

4 日 *kō-Nichi* anti-Japanese
5 弁 *kōben* plea, defense, protest, refutation, contradiction, answer
生物質 *kōsei busshitsu* an antibiotic
6 争 *kōsō* dispute; resistance
7 告 *kōkoku* protest, appeal
8 命 *kōmei* disobedience
13 戦 *kōsen* resistance
20 議 *kōgi* protest, objection

A 技 2092 J353b M11855 GI art, craft; ability, skill, feat, performance. *waza* deed, act, work, art, performance, trick.

3 工 *gikō* artisan, craftsman
4 手 *gishu, gite* assistant engineer; (telegraph) operator
5 巧 *gikō* art, craftmanship, skill, technique; trick
巧的 *gikōteki* skillful, clever; ornate
7 芸 *gigei* arts, crafts, accomplishments

⁸ 法 *gihō* technique
官 *gikan* technical official
¹⁰ 師 *gishi* engineer, technician
倆 *giryō* skill
能 *ginō* ability, capacity, skill, talent
¹¹ 術 *gijutsu* art, technique, skill
術者 *gijutsusha* technician, engineer
¹² 量 *giryō* skill

抜 B $\frac{2093}{\substack{J4834\\M11901}}$ BATSU. *nu(ku)* extract, uncork, pull out; root up; unsheathe; pilfer; quote; remove; omit; capture; outrun; shoot through. *nu(keru)* come off, fall out, slip out; be omitted; be missing; be rid of; pass through; escape; be captured; withdraw; be less than. *nu(kasu)* omit, skip over. *nuki(nderu)* excel in, surpass. *nu(karu)* be careless; slip, make a mistake. *nu(kari)* negligence; carelessness. *nu(ki)* omission, removal; defeating. *nu(karanu)* shrewd, on one's guard.

² 刀 *battō* drawing a sword; drawn sword
³ 小路 *nu(ke) kōji* a through passage
⁴ 手 *nu(ki)te, nu(ki)de* overhand stroke
毛 *nu(ke)ge* falling hair, combings, molt
⁵ 目 *nu(ke)me* imprudence. *nu(ke)me(nai)* shrewd, alert, careful, tactful, clever
穴 *nu(ke)ana* secret passage, ⌈escape underground exit; loophole; way of去 *nu(ke)-sa(ru)* lose all (strength). *nu(ki)-sa(ru)* pull out. *bakkyo* extraction (of teeth)
出 *nu(ki)-da(su), nu(ki)-ida(su)* select, extract, pull out. *nu(ke)-da(su), nu(ke)-de(ru)* slip out, sneak away, break out, get loose; excel, surpass, choose the best. *nu(ki)-de(ru)* be outstanding
本的 *bapponteki* radical, drastic
打 *nukiu(chi)* sudden attack
打的 *nukiu(chi)teki ni* without notice
⁶ 糸 *basshi* removal of stitches. *nu(ki)ito* drawn thread
⁷ 身 *nu(ki)mi* drawn sword
作 *nu(ke)saku* dunce, simpleton
足差足 *nu(ki)ashi-sa(shi)ashi de* stealthily, gingerly
⁸ 刷 *nu(ki)zu(ri)* a publication of the important parts of a book
放 *nu(ki)-hana(su), nu(ki)-hana(tsu)* unsheathe, draw out, take out

取 *nu(ki)-to(ru)* pilfer, steal; pull out, extract, take out, tear off
取検査 *nukito(ri) kensa* sampling inspection
¹⁰ 粋 *bassui* quotation, selection, excerpt; abstract, summary
剣 *bakken* drawing a sword
差 *nu(ki)sa(shi)* slipping off and on; taking on and off. *nu(ki)sa(shinaranu)* impossible; being in a dilemma
書 *nukiga(ki)* selection, excerpt
荷 *nu(ki)ni* pilfered goods. *nukeni* smuggled goods
¹¹ 道 *nu(ke)michi* bypass; secret path; way of escape, loophole; last resources; excuse
殻 *nu(ke)gara* the shed skin (of a snake or cicada); a person whose mind is elsewhere
¹² 歯 *basshi* extraction of teeth
落 *nu(ke)-o(chiru)* fall out
¹³ 群 *batsugun* pre-eminence
¹⁴ 読 *nukiyo(mi) suru* read or tell part of a story
駆 *nu(ke)ga(ke)* stealing a march on; forestalling; scoop
¹⁶ 錨 *batsubyō* weighing anchor
¹⁷ 擢 *batteki* selection, choice

折 A $\frac{2094}{\substack{J405e\\M11890}}$ SETSU. *o(ru) vt* break, snap, fracture, knock out (teeth); fold, turn down; bend; make (a paper toy); yield (oneself), give in. *o(reru)* snap, break; be folded; give in, submit; turn (to the left or right). *o(re)* fragment, broken piece. *o(ri)* breaking; small food box; time, occasion, juncture; opportunity. *ori(shimo)* just then. *o(ri) kara* just at that time. *-ori-* folding; signature (of a book).

² 入 *o(ri)-i(reru)* fold and insert; tuck in; turn in; read into. *o(ri)-i(tte)* earnestly
³ 口 *o(re)kuchi* a split, a break
山 *o(ri)yama* the outside edge of a fold
⁴ 戸 *o(ri)do* folding doors
方 *o(ri)kata* how to fold
尺 *o(ri)jaku* folded ruler
込 *o(ri)-ko(mu)* tuck, turn in; insert. *o(re)-ko(mu)* fold and insert. *o(ri)ko(mi)* insert

4

心 忄 小 戈 戸 【手 扌】 支 攴 攵 文 斗 斤 方 无 日 曰 月 木 欠 止 歹 殳 毋 比 毛 氏 气 水 氵 氺 火 灬 爪 爫 父 爻 爿 丬 片 牙 牛 犭

⁵ 半 *seppan* halving

本 *o(ri)bon, o(ri)hon* a folding book, a folder

目 *o(re)me, o(ri)me* fold, crease, dog-ear

目正 *o(ri)metada(shii)* well-mannered; ceremonious

⁶ 曲 *o(ri)-ma(geru)* bend, turn up, turn down

合 *o(ri)-a(u), o(re)-a(u)* come to an agreement. *o(ri)a(i), o(re)a(i)* mutual relations; compromise, agreement, understanding

返 *o(re)-kae(ru)* tell again and again. *o(ri)-kae(su)* turn up, turn down, fold back; repeat. *o(ri)kae(shi)* lapel, cuffs, flap; chorus, refrain; repetition

返点 *o(ri)kae(shi)ten* turn-back point

返運転 *o(ri)kae(shi) unten* shuttle service

⁷ 角 *sekkaku* at great pains; on purpose, expressly; kindly. *sekkaku no* valuable, long-awaited

折 *o(ri)o(ri)* occasionally

⁸ 屈 *o(re)-kaga(mu)* bend. *o(ri)kaga(mi)* bend, curtsy

取 *o(ri)-to(ru)* break off a branch, pick (flowers)

⁹ 柄 *o(ri)kara* just then, at that time

重 *o(ri)-kasa(naru)* vi overlap; telescope. *o(ri)-kasa(neru)* vt fold back, turn down

衷 *setchū* compromise; cross, blending, eclecticism

¹⁰ 紙 *o(ri)gami* folded paper; colored folding paper, origami; affidavit, testimonial

紙付 *o(ri)gamizu(ki)* certified; guaranteed; notorious

釘 *o(re)kugi, o(ri)kugi* hooked nail; broken nail

¹¹ 悪 *o(ri)a(shiku)* inopportunely, unfortunately

崩 *o(ri)-kuzu(reru)* collapse

¹² 畳 *o(ri)-tata(mu)* fold up

畳式 *o(ri)tatamishiki* folding, collapsible

¹³ 詰 *orizume* food packed in a small box

節 *o(ri)fushi* chance, occasion; just then; occasionally; opportunity, time

¹⁴ 鞄 *o(ri)kaban* folding brief case

¹⁵ 衝 *sesshō* negotiation

¹⁸ 檻 *sekkan* chastisement, correction; whipping, spanking

襟 *o(ri)eri* turned-down collar; sack coat

投 [2095 / J456a / M11887] Tō throw. *tō(jiru)*, *tō(zuru)* throw, throw away, throw into; abandon; launch into, embark on; join (a party); invest in; seize (an opportunity); agree with; catch (the public eye). *na(geru)* throw, hurl; give up; sell at a loss. *na(ge)* a throw, a spill, a fall. A

² 入 *na(ge)-i(reru)* throw into; dump in together. *tōnyū suru* throw into; invest. *na(ge)-i(re)* free-style flower arrangement

³ 下 *tōka suru* throw down, drop; invest

上 *na(ge)-a(geru)* throw up (in the air)

与 *tōyo suru, na(ge)-ata(eru)* throw to (the dogs)

⁴ 込 *na(ge)-ko(mu)* throw into, dump into. *na(ge)ko(mi)* free-style flower arrangement

手 *tōshu* pitcher, bowler (in cricket)

⁵ 付 *na(ge)-tsu(keru)* throw at; throw (someone) down

出 *na(ge)-da(su)* throw out, throw down; stretch out (legs); give up, renounce

石 *tōseki* throwing stones

⁶ 返 *na(ge)-kae(su)* throw back

光器 *tōkōki* floodlight projector

⁷ 足 *na(ge)ashi* sitting with legs stretched out

身 *tōshin* suicide by drowning

売 *nageu(ri)* bargain sale

⁸ 函 *tōkan suru* mail (a letter). *tōkan* throwing into a box

⁹ 飛 *na(ge)-to(basu)* throw away

首 *na(ge)kubi* dropping the head (in thought)

降 *tōkō* surrender

¹⁰ 倒 *na(ge)-tao(su)* throw (someone) down

射 *tōsha* projection (in math); incidence (in physics); throwing (spears)

書 *tōsho* correspondence, contribution

¹¹ 捨 *na(ge)-su(teru)* throw away

球 *tōkyū* throwing a ball, pitching, bowling (in cricket); a pitched ball

宿 *tōshuku suru* put up at a hotel

票 *tōhyō* vote, voting; ballot; suffrage

¹² 遣 *na(ge)-ya(ru)* throw away, leave to

chance. *na(ge)ya(ri)* negligence, irresponsibility

弾 *tōdan* dropping a bomb

落 *na(ge)-oto(su)* throw down, drop

¹³棄 *na(ge)-su(teru)* throw away. *tōki suru* abandon, give up

資 *tōshi* investment

¹⁴槍 *na(ge)yari* dart, javelin, lance; javelin throw

網 *na(ge)ami, toami* casting net

獄 *tōgoku* imprisonment

¹⁵縄 *na(ge)nawa* a lasso

影 *tōei suru* reflect, project (an image)

稿 *tōkō* contribution (to a magazine)

¹⁶錨 *tōbyō* anchoring, anchorage

薬 *tōyaku* medication, prescription, dosage

機 *tōki* speculation

¹⁷環 *na(ge)wa* quoits

擲 *tōteki suru* throw

5

拐 ₂₁₀₇ / J327d / M11955 KAI falsify; kidnap. B

抹 ₂₁₁₂ / J4b75 / M11926 MATSU paint, erase, rub. B

⁹茶 *matcha* powdered green tea

香 *makkō* incense; incense powder

香鯨 *makkō kujira* sperm whale

¹⁰消 *masshō* erasure, obliteration; denial; ignoring (an opinion); execution, liquidation

殺 *massatsu* erasure, obliteration; denial; ignoring (an opinion); execution, liquidation

拠 ₂₁₁₃ / J3572 / M11985 KYO. KO. *yo(ru)* be based on, follow. *yo(tte)* therefore, consequently. B

⁵出 *kyoshutsu* contribution, donation

⁸所 *yo(ri)dokoro* source, authority

⁹点 *kyoten* position, point, base

拍 ₂₁₁₄ / J476f / M11952 HYŌ. HAKU. beat (in music). *u(tsu)* strike, hit, beat, knock, slap, punch, thrash, smite; clap (one's hands); beat (a drum); ring (a bell); (clocks) strike; impress, touch; shoot; pound in (a nail); water, sprinkle; B

braid; play (checkers); till (the soil); temper (a sword); prepare (buckwheat noodles); present (a play); cast (a net); pay (earnest money).

³子 *hyōshi* time, rhythm, beat, measure, number; tact; chance, the moment

子木 *hyōshigi* wooden clappers, bones

子抜 *hyōshinu(ke)* disappointment

⁴手 *hakushu* applause, handclapping. *kashiwade* handclapping (at a shrine)

⁷車 *hakusha* spur (on boots)

拓 ₂₁₁₅ / J4273 / M11958 TAKU *hira(ku)* open, clear, break up (land). B

⁵本 *takuhon* rubbed copy; folio of rubbings

¹²殖 *takushoku* colonization, exploitation

披 ₂₁₁₆ / J4864 / M11909 HI open. B

⁷見 *hiken suru* peruse (a letter)

¹⁹瀝 *hireki suru* express (opinions)

²¹露 *hirō* announcement

露目 *hirome* announcement, advertisement

露宴 *hirōen* reception (wedding, etc.)

拡 ₂₁₁₈ / J3348 / M11985′ KAKU. *hiro(geru)* vt expand, enlarge, widen; unfurl; open (arms or a package), stretch, spread. *hiro(garu)* vi spread out, extend, reach to. A

³大 *kakudai* magnification, enlargement

⁶充 *kakujū* expansion; amplification; generalization

⁷声器 *kakuseiki* loudspeaker

¹¹張 *kakuchō* extension, expansion, increase, enlargement, aggrandizement, increase, dilation

¹²散 *kakusan* scattering, diffusion

抽 ₂₁₁₉ / J436a / M11930 CHŪ pull; extract; excel. *nuki(nderu)* excel in, surpass; choose the best. *nu(ku)* extract, uncork, pull out; root up; unsheathe; pilfer; quote; remove; omit; capture; outrun; shoot through. *hi(ku)* pull. A

⁴斗 *hikidashi* (desk) drawer

⁵出 *chūshutsu suru* educe, abstract, extract. *hikidashi* (desk) drawer; withdrawal

¹²象 *chūshō* abstraction

4

心 忄 小 戈 戸 【手 扌】 支 攴 攵 文 斗 斤 方 无 日 曰 月 木 欠 止 歹 殳 母 比 毛 氏 气 水 氵 氺 火 灬 爪 爫 父 爻 爿 爿 片 牙 牛 犬 犭

象的 *chūshōteki* abstract

¹⁴選 *chūsen* lottery, raffle, drawing

²¹籤 *chūsen* lottery, raffle, drawing

抵 2120 J4471 M11921 **B** TEI touch, reach, resist.

⁶当 *teitō* mortgage, hypothec, security

当流 *teitōnaga(re)* foreclosure

当権 *teitōken* mortgage

⁷抗 *teikō* resistance, opposition, defiance; (electrical) resistance

¹³触 *teishoku* conflict, contradiction, infringement

担 2121 J4334 M11941 **A** TAN carry; raise. *katsu(gu)* shoulder (a load). *kata(geru)* shoulder, carry on the shoulder. *nina(u)* carry on the shoulder; bear a burden. *katsugi* carrier, coolie.

²入 *katsu(gi)-i(reru)* carry in

³上 *katsu(gi)-a(geru), katsu(gi)-nobo(ru)* carry up

⁴手 *ninaite* bearer, carrier

⁶任 *tannin* charge (of something)

当 *tantō* charge (of something)

当者 *tantōsha* the one in charge

⁹保 *tampo* mortgage, security, guarantee

架 *tanka* stretcher, litter

拙 2122 J405b M11965 **B** SETSU clumsy, unskillful. *tsutana(i), mazu(i)* clumsy, bungling, unskillful.

⁴文 *setsubun* poor writing, my writing

⁶宅 *settaku* my humble home

劣 *setsuretsu na* clumsy, unskillful

⁸者 *sessha* I (humble); an untalented person; an ignorant person

⁹速 *sessoku* rough-and-ready, hasty

¹¹訳 *setsuyaku* (my) poor translation

著 *setcho* my (humble) production

¹²策 *sessaku* poor policy, poor plan

¹³僧 *sessō* your humble priest; a foolish priest

拘 2123 J3934 M11963 **B** KŌ seize, arrest. *kakawa(ru)* be concerned with; adhere to; be wedded to one's opinion. *kakawa(razu)* in spite of, regardless of.

⁴引 *kōin* arrest, custody

⁷束 *kōsoku* restriction, binding, duress

⁸泥 *kōdei suru* adhere to, be a stickler for

¹⁰留 *kōryū* detention, arrest, custody

¹³禁 *kōkin* confinement, detention, imprisonment

置 *kōchi* detention, confinement, arrest

置所 *kōchisho* detention house, prison

招 2124 J3e37 M11968 **A** SHŌ . *mane(ku)* beckon to, invite, summon; engage (someone), call (a doctor); incur, cause. *mane(ki)* invitation.

⁷来 *shōrai suru* lead to, invite, incur, cause

⁹待 *shōtai, shōdai* invitation

待券 *shōtaiken* complimentary ticket

待客 *shōtaikyaku* invited guest

¹⁰致 *shōchi* summons, invitation

宴 *shōen* giving an invitation to a banquet

¹¹寄 *mane(ki)-yo(seru)* call from, bring from

¹³聘 *shōhei* engagement, employment

¹⁴魂 *shōkon* invocation of spirits of the dead

¹⁵請 *shōsei* invitation, call

抱 2125 J4a7a M11917 **B** HŌ . *da(ku)* hug, embrace, hold in the arms; sit (on eggs). *ida(ku)* hug, embrace, hold in the arms; entertain (hope); cherish (a desire); harbor (malice); hold, have. *da(kasu)* set a hen. *da(kko) suru* hug, embrace, hold in the arms. *kaka(eru)* hold or carry under or in the arms. *kaka(e)* armful; employee.

³上 *da(ki)-a(geru)* take up in one's arms

⁴止 *da(ki)-to(meru)* hold (a person) back, restrain, catch

込 *da(ki)-ko(mu)* win over, carry in the arms. *kaka(e)-ko(mu)* hold or carry under or in the arms

⁵付 *da(ki)-tsu(ku)* embrace; hold forcibly

主 *kaka(e)nushi* employer

⁶合 *da(ki)-a(u)* hug, embrace. *da(ki)-a(waseru)* cause to embrace; pawn off poor articles. *hōgō* combination; embrace

⁷卵 *hōran* incubation

⁹負 *hōfu* aspiration, ambition, pretension

¹⁰起 *da(ki)-oko(su)* lift (a person) up, help (a person) to his feet or to sit up (in bed)

¹¹ 寄 *da(ki)-yo(seru)* embrace

¹² 竦 *da(ki)-suku(meru)* hug tight

着 *da(ki)-tsu(ku)* embrace; hold forcibly

¹³ 腹絶倒 *hōfuku-zettō* convulsed with laughter

¹⁵ 締 *da(ki)-shi(meru), ida(ki)-shi(meru)* embrace closely, cuddle, hug

¹⁶ 懐 *hōkai* harboring, cherishing, entertaining

擁 *hōyō* a hug, an embrace

A 拝 _{2126 J4752 M11969} HAI worship. *hai(suru)* worship, bow in veneration, pay respects to; receive (an imperial command); see (the emperor). *oga(mu), oroga(mu)* worship, pray to, adore, reverence; look at (with reverence).

⁴ 火教 *Haikakyō* Zoroastrianism

⁵ 礼 *hairei* worship

⁷ 見 *haiken suru* see, look at, inspect

⁸ 命 *haimei* receiving an official appointment

受 *haiju suru* receive, accept

金主義 *haikin shugi* mammonism

⁹ 眉 *haibi* personal meeting

¹⁰ 借 *haishaku* loan, borrowing

倒 *oga(mi)-tao(su)* entreat into consenting

¹¹ 啓 *huikei* Dear Sir, Dear Madam

¹² 復 *haifuku* in reply to your esteemed letter; Dear Sir, Dear Madam

診 *haishin* medical examination (polite)

¹³ 殿 *haiden* outer shrine, hall of worship; holy place; nave

辞 *haiji suru* resign, decline

跪 *haiki suru* kneel reverently

¹⁴ 読 *haidoku suru* read, note. *haidoku* reverent reading

察 *haisatsu* guess

領 *hairyō suru* receive (from a superior)

¹⁵ 謁 *haietsu* an audience (with the emperor)

¹⁷ 聴 *haichō suru* listen attentively

¹⁸ 観 *haikan* inspection, visit

観料 *haikanryō* (museum) admission charge

B 押 _{2128 J3221 M11929} Ō. *o(su)* push, shove; press, squash, compress; stamp, seal; do in spite of. *osa(eru)* stop, check, restrain, pin down; suppress, subdue, control; catch, arrest; govern; stop

---

(the ears); withhold; attach, seize; secure (evidence), estimate conservatively. *oshi* weight; authority, influence; self-confidence; a fall (in the stock market). *osa(e)* weight, paperweight; rear guard; defense; pressure, suppression; control. *o(shite)* forcibly; importunately; in spite of. *o(shi)-* emphatic verbal prefix.

² 入 *o(shi)-i(reru)* push in, force in, squeeze in. *oshi-i(ru)* break in *oshii(re)* clothes closet. *o(shi)i(ri)* burglar, robber

³ 下 *o(shi)-sa(geru)* depress, force down. *o(shi)-o(rosu)* take down, lower, pull down, lift down, let down, drop; launch; let off (passengers); wear (for the first time); cause (abortion); grate; invoke; exercise; borrow (in subtraction); lock

上 *o(shi)-a(geru)* force up, push up, boost

⁴ 止 *o(shi)-to(meru), o(shi)-todo(meru)* stop, prevent, restrain

切 *o(shi)-ki(ru)* have one's own way, push through, push and cut. *osa(e)-ki(ru)* shutout (in baseball). *o(shi)ki(tte)* boldly, daringly. *o(shi)ki(ri)* straw cutter; short mane

分 *o(shi)-wa(keru)* push apart, elbow through

込 *o(shi)-ko(mu)* vi push in, crowd into, herd into. *o(shi)-ko(meru)* vt shut up, imprison. *o(shi)ko(mi)* clothes closet; burglar

⁵ 立 *o(shi)-ta(teru), o(t)ta(teru)* raise, set up, erect; hoist

広 *o(shi)-hiro(geru), o(p)piro(geru)* vt expand, enlarge, widen; unfurl; open (arms or a package), stretch, spread

付 *o(shi)-tsu(keru), o(t)tsu(keru)* push against, press down, thrust on; compel, urge; force on, intrude on, impose on. *o(shi)tsu(kegamashii)* unreasonable

収 *ōshū* seizure, confiscation

出 *oshida(shi)* presence, appearance; forced (run); pushing out of. *o(shi)-da(su), o(shi)-ida(su)* push out; squeeze out; crowd out; set out all together. *o(shi)-de(ru)* force one's way out

⁶ 返 *o(shi)-kae(su)* force back, jostle

支 支 攵 文 斗 斤 方 无 日 日 月 木 欠 止 歹 父 毋 比 毛 氏 气 水 氵 氺 火 灬 爪 爫 父 爻 爿 丬 片 牙 牛 犬 犭

心 忄 小 戈 戸【手扌】
⁵
支 攴 攵 文 斗 斤 方 无 日 曰 月 木 欠 止 歹 殳 毋 比 毛 氏 气 水 氵 氺 火 灬 爪 爫 父 爻 爿 丬 片 牙 牛 犬 犭

印 *ōin* affixing one's seal
当 *o(shi)-a(teru)* push (something) against
合 *o(shi)-a(u), o(shi)a(i) suru* jostle, crowd; haggle
⁷戻 *o(shi)-modo(su)* force back; reject, turn down
売 *o(shi)u(ri)* high-pressure salesmanship
花 *o(shi)bana* pressed flowers
⁸固 *o(shi)-kata(meru)* press together
退 *o(shi)-no(keru)* push away, brush aside, elbow through, crowd out
送 *ōsō* escort
拡 *o(shi)-hiro(geru), o(p)piro(geru) vt* expand, enlarge, widen; unfurl; open (arms or a package), stretch, spread
並 *o(shi)na(bete)* generally
⁹通 *o(shi)-tō(ru)* force one's way through. *o(shi)-tō(su)* carry through, accomplish, persevere; insist on
型 *o(shi)gata* impression taken by pressing
¹⁰進 *o(shi)-susu(meru)* push, push through, expedite. *o(shi)-susu(mu)* push on, press onward
倒 *o(shi)-tao(su)* push down; overwhelm
流 *o(shi)-naga(su)* wash away, sweep away; (waves) drive on
破 *o(shi)-yabu(ru)* break through
¹¹捺 *ōnatsu* sealing (a document)
寄 *o(shi)-yo(seru)* push aside; advance on; besiege (an office); bear down upon; make for the door. *o(shi)-yo(ru)* press together, come close
問答 *o(shi)mondō* heated questioning and answering, dispute
掛 *o(shi)-ka(karu)* lean on, rely on. *o(shi)-ka(keru)* intrude on, throng into
¹²遣 *o(shi)-ya(ru)* push away
開 *o(shi)-hira(ku), o(shi)-a(keru)* force open, push open
渡 *o(shi)-wata(su)* cross over; force one's way across
葉 *o(shi)ba* pressed leaves
¹³詰 *o(shi)-tsu(maru)* approach the year end; be jammed, be tight. *o(shi)-tsu(meru)* pack (in a box); drive to the wall
¹⁵潰 *o(shi)-tsubu(su)* smash, crush
黙 *o(shi)-dama(ru)* keep silent
¹⁹韻 *ōin* rhyme, rhyming

─────── **6** ───────

拶 $\frac{2134}{\text{J3b22}}$ $\frac{}{\text{M12004}}$ Satsu be imminent.

拷 B $\frac{2142}{\text{J3969}}$ $\frac{}{\text{M12006}}$ Kō, Gō beat, torture.
¹¹問 *gōmon* torture, the rack, third degree

括 B $\frac{2143}{\text{J3367}}$ $\frac{}{\text{M11988}}$ Katsu. *kuku(ru)* tie up, hang (someone); arrest; fasten. *kuru(mu)* wrap up, tuck in. *kuru(meru)* lump together, include, sum up; quibble. *kubi(ru)* constrict. *kubi(reru)* be constricted, contracted, or compressed. *ko(ru)* pack, tie up. *kuku(ri)* tying; bundle; knot; management; conclusion; trap. *kubi(re)* constriction, compression.
⁵付 *kuku(ri)-tsu(keru)* tie up, hang (someone); arrest; fasten
⁸弧 *kakko* parentheses; brackets

拭 $\frac{2144}{\text{J3f21}}$ $\frac{}{\text{M11989}}$ Shoku. *fu(ku)* wipe, mop, swab. *nugu(u)* wipe, mop.
⁵去 *nugu(i)-sa(ru)* put off, wipe off, wipe away
⁸取 *fu(ki)-to(ru)* wipe off, wipe out, mop up. *nugu(i)-to(ru)* wipe away
¹⁰消 *fu(ki)-ke(su)* wipe out, wipe off, erase
¹¹掃除 *fuki sōji* wiping; scrubbing
¹²落 *nugu(i)-oto(su)* wipe off, wipe away. *fu(ki)-oto(su)* rub out (a stain)

挑 B $\frac{2145}{\text{J4429}}$ $\frac{}{\text{M12055}}$ Chō. *ido(mu)* challenge; contend for; make love to.
⁹発 *chōhatsu* provocation, excitement, encouragement, suggestion
発的 *chōhatsuteki* provocative, suggestive, lascivious, seditious
¹³戦 *chōsen* challenge, defiance
戦的 *chōsenteki* defiant, aggressive, provocative, challenging

挟 B $\frac{2146}{\text{J3634}}$ $\frac{}{\text{M-X}}$ Kyō. *hasa(mu), sashihasa(mu)*, put put between, hold between; insert, jam into; nip; interpose. *hasa(maru)* get between, be caught in, be jammed in, be hemmed in, be sandwiched between, be pinned under, lie between.

⁴込 *hasa(mi)-ko(mu)* insert
¹⁵撃 *kyōgeki* pincer operation. *hasamiuchi* pincer attack

按 <u>2147</u> AN. *an(zuru)* hold; J3044 M12038 consider, investigate.
⁴分 *ambun* proportional division
¹⁰配 *ambai* arrangement, assignment; adjustment, modification, tempering
¹¹排 *ambai* arrangement, assignment; adjustment, modification, tempering
¹⁵摩 *amma* massage; masseur

拳 <u>2148</u> GEN. KEN *kobushi* fist. J377d M11996
⁸固 *genko* fists and knuckles
¹⁰骨 *genkotsu* fists and knuckles
¹⁴銃 *kenjū* pistol, revolver
¹⁸闘 *kentō* boxing, prizefighting

拾 <u>2149</u> SHŪ. JŪ ten. *hiro(u)* A J3d26 M12014 pick up, gather; find; set (type); go on foot.
³上 *hiro(i)-a(geru)* pick up, pick out
¹¹得 *shūtoku suru* pick up, find
得物 *shūtokubutsu* found article
¹⁴遺 *shūi* gleanings

挙 <u>2150</u> KYO plan, project; A J3573 M12081 behavior; actions; step. *a(geru)* celebrate (a ceremony); join (hands in an effort); have (a child); arrest. *a(garu)* become prosperous; be captured. *kozo(ru)* meet all together. *a(gete)* all, whole, in a body. *kozo(tte)* all, all together.
⁴手 *kyoshu* show of hands, raising the hand; salute, touching the cap
止 *kyoshi* bearing, deportment
⁵句 *ageku* in the end, finally
世 *kyosei* all the people of the world
⁶行 *kyokō* performance, celebration, solemnization
式 *kyoshiki* holding a ceremony
⁷足 *ageashi* faultfinding
兵 *kyohei* raising an army
⁸国 *kyokoku* the whole nation
¹¹動 *kyodō* deportment, conduct
措 *kyoso* deportment, conduct
¹²証 *kyoshō* presentation of proof

持 <u>2151</u> JI. *ji(suru)* hold, entertain, A J3b7d M12019 maintain; observe (principles). *mo(tsu)* vi and vt hold, take, have, possess; carry; maintain; have charge of; wear, last long; pay; bear (a grudge). *mo(teru)* be warmly welcomed; can hold, can carry; propertied, wealthy. *mo(taseru)* let (a person) have, give; get (a wife) for; give to carry; send by; keep, preserve; lean or set against; make (someone) pay. *mo(tanu), mo(tanai)* propertyless, have-not. *mo(chi)* wear, durability; (my) charge; (ladies') wear.
³上 *mo(chi)-a(geru)* raise, lift, jack up; flatter, praise. *mo(chi)-a(garu)* be raised, be lifted; happen; be promoted with one's class, teaching the same group through the years
久 *jikyū* endurance, persistence
久力 *jikyūryoku* endurance, persistence
久戦 *jikyūsen* delaying action, holding action
⁴込 *mo(chi)-ko(mu)* bring in; lodge (a protest); bring to (a decision)
切 *mo(chi)-ki(ru)* keep, continue to hold; hold all; maintain; talk of nothing else. *mo(chi)ki(ri)* sole topic (of conversation)
分 *mo(chi)bun* share (of costs); interest in (a business)
⁵主 *mo(chi)nushi* proprietor, owner, possessor
去 *mo(chi)-sa(ru)* carry away; make off with
出 *mo(chi)-da(su)* take out; rescue; embezzle; offer (a plan)
⁶行 *mo(tte)-yu(ku), mo(tte)-i(ku)* take along
回 *mo(tte)-mawa(ru), mo(chi)-mawa(ru), mo(chi)-mawa(su)* carry around. *mo(tte)-mawa(tta)* circuitous. *mochimawa(ri)* securing decisions by circularizing members
成 *mo(te)na(shi)* treatment, service, reception, hospitality, entertainment. *mo(te)-na(su)* welcome, entertain, treat
合 *mo(chi)-a(waseru)* have on hand. *mo(chi)-a(u)* maintain equilibrium; share expenses. *mo(chi)a(wase)* things on hand; money on hand. *mo(chi)a(i)* interdependence; steadiness (of the market)

4

心 忄 小 戈 戸 【手 扌】 ⁶ 扌 支 攴 攵 文 斗 斤 方 无 日 曰 月 木 欠 止 歹 殳 毋 比 毛 氏 气 水 氵 氺 火 灬 爪 爫 父 爻 爿 丬 片 牙 牛 犬 犭

⁷来 *mo(tte)-ku(ru)* bring, fetch. *mo(chi)-ki(tasu)* take, bring; bring about. *mo(tte)ko(i)* ideal, excellent, just right

余 *mo(te)ama(su)* be embarrassed with; find unmanageable; have too much of

⁸送 *mo(chi)oku(ri)* bracket, truss

逃 *mochini(ge) suru* make off with, abscond with

味 *mo(chi)aji* natural flavor, characteristic quality

物 *mochimono* property, belongings

直 *mo(chi)-nao(su) vi* and *vt* change one's hold; improve, rally, recover

歩 *mo(chi)-aru(ku)* carry about

参 *jisan suru* bring, take along. *jisan* (by the) kindness of

参金 *jisankin* dowry

⁹持 *mo(chitsu)-mo(taretsu)* helping one another

前 *mo(chi)mae* nature, property; share

¹⁰病 *jibyō* chronic illness

家 *mo(chi)ie* one's own house

帰 *mo(chi)-kae(ru)*, *mo(tte)-kae(ru)* carry back

株 *mo(chi)kabu* one's stock holdings

¹¹運 *mo(chi)-hako(bu)* carry, transport. *mo(chi)-hako(bi)* portable, carrying

掛 *mo(chi)-ka(keru)* offer, propose. *mo(tase)-ka(keru)* lean against

寄 *mo(chi)-yo(ru)* (each) contributes

崩 *mo(chi)-kuzu(su)* ruin oneself by dissipation ⌐hold over

¹²越 *mo(chi)-ko(su)* defer; carry forward;

場 *mo(chi)ba* place of duty, one's post, one's beat; jurisdiction

堪 *mo(chi)-kota(eru)* maintain, keep; hold out (longer)

¹³続 *mo(chi)-tsuzu(keru)* persist in. *jizoku* continuation

続的 *jizokuteki* continuous, lasting

¹⁴腐 *mo(chi)gusa(re)* useless possession

説 *jisetsu* pet theory

¹⁵論 *jiron* pet theory

指 2152 J3b58 M12034
A SHI finger. *sa(su)* point to, indicate; name, designate; insert, put into; fill, pour into, drop into (eyes); hold up (an umbrella); wear (a sword); offer (a cup); play; move (in games); rise, flow; be tinged with; point to; proceed to; fix (a day); measure (with a ruler); measure and make (a box); play

(chess or checkers). *yubi* finger. *sa(shite)* for, to, toward.

⁴手 *sashite* a move; a hand (in playing)

切 *yubiki(ri)* a pledge by hooking each other's little fingers

⁵令 *shirei* order, notice, instructions, directive ⌐treatment

圧療法 *shiatsu ryōhō* finger-pressure

示 *sa(shi)-shime(su)*, *shishi suru* indicate, point out. *shiji, shishi* indication, instructions, directions. *shiji* a type of character depicting numerals or directions (e.g. 三 and 上)

⁶先 *yubisaki* fingertip

名 *shimei suru* name, mention, designate, nominate

向 *shikō* directional (antenna)

⁷折数 *yubio(ri)-kazo(eru)* count on one's fingers

図 *sashizu* instructions, orders

⁸定 *shitei* appointment, designation, authorization

定席 *shiteiseki* reserved seat

呼間 *shiko (no) aida, shiko (no) kan* hailing distance

物 *sashimono* cabinet work, joinery; armor ornament

物師 *sashimonoshi* cabinet maker

⁹南 *shinan* instruction, guidance

南番 *shinamban* instructor, teacher, master

¹⁰値 *sashine* buying-price limits

紋 *shimon* fingerprint, thumb print

差 *yubisa(shi)* pointing with the finger; index tabs. *yubisa(su)* point to

針 *shishin* compass needle; guide, manual

¹¹貫 *yubinuki* thimble

弾 *yubihaji(ki)* flip, fillip. *shidan, shitan* flip, fillip; rejection; disdain

揮 *shiki* command, supervision, instructions, direction, leading

揮者 *shikisha* commander, director; conductor (of a band), leader

¹³数 *shisū* index, index number; exponent

¹⁴摘 *shiteki* pointing out, indication

導 *shidō* guidance, leadership, coaching

導者 *shidōsha* leader

導権 *shidōken* leadership

¹⁵標 *shihyō* indication, index

輪 *yubiwa* finger ring

捉 2159 J422a M12136 SOKU. SAKU. *tora(eru)* catch, arrest, capture. *tsukama(eru), tsura(maeru), torama(eru)* catch, seize, arrest, capture. *tsuka(maru), tsura(maru)* be caught, be arrested; cling to.
- 8 所 *tora(e)dokoro* the point, meaning. *tsuka(mae)dokoro* grip, hold
- 所無 *tsuka(mae)dokoro (no) na(i)* slippery; sly; vague

挨 2160 J3027 M12082 AI push open.
- 9 拶 *aisatsu* greeting, salutation; address, reply, response; notice

捗 2161 J-X M12160 捗 2173 J443d M-X CHOKU. HO. *hakado(ru)* make progress.
- 8 取 *hakado(ru)* advance, make headway
- 10 捗 *hakabaka(shii)* rapid, expeditious, active; favorable

捌 2162 J3b2b M12141 HACHI, HATSU. *saba(ku)* sell; dispose of, deal with; handle, manipulate; loosen (the hair). *saba(keru)* sell, be in demand; be worldly wise; be disentangled; tear, break. *ha(keru)* drain, flow off, run out; sell, be in demand. *ha(ke)* drainage; draining; sale, demand. *saba(keta)* sociable, frank.

挫 2163 J3a43 M12087 ZA. *kuji(ku)* crush, break, sprain, dislocate; frustrate; unnerve; dampen (spirits). *kuji(keru)* be broken, crushed, or sprained; be discouraged.
- 7 折 *zasetsu* frustration, collapse, setback, reverses, discouragement
- 13 傷 *zashō* bruise, sprain, strain, contusion

挺 2164 J4472 M12106 TEI. CHŌ counter for guns, tools, inksticks, oars, candles, palanquins, and jinrickshas. *tei(suru)* bravely volunteer.
- 3 子 *teko* lever
- 7 身 *teishin* volunteer
- 10 進 *teishin suru* go ahead of, dash ⌈forward

挿 2167 J415e M12119 SŌ. *sa(su)* insert, put in; graft (a branch); wear (a sword); carry (in the belt). *hasa(mu),*

sashihasa(mu) put between, hold between; insert, jam into; nip; interpose. *hasa(maru)* get between, be caught in, be jammed in, be hemmed in, be sandwiched between, be pinned under, lie between.
- 2 入 *sōnyū* insertion, incorporation, interpolation
- 4 木 *sashiki* a cutting; planting
- 5 句 *sōku* parenthetical expression
- 7 図 *sōzu* illustration (in a book)
- 8 画 *sashie, sōga* illustration (in a book)
- 12 絵 *sashie* illustration (in a book)
- 13 話 *sōwa* episode

搜 2168 J415c M12179 SŌ. *saga(su)* search, look for, locate; glean.
- 5 出 *saga(shi)-da(su)* find out, discover, detect, locate, search out, hunt up
- 6 回 *saga(shi)-mawa(ru)* hunt around
- 当 *saga(shi)-a(teru)* find out, discover, detect, locate, search out, hunt up
- 7 求 *saga(shi)-moto(meru)* seek for
- 8 物 *saga(shi)mono* something one is looking for
- 9 査 *sōsa* investigation, search
- 10 索 *sōsaku* search, investigation; dragging (a river)

挽 2169 J-X M12111 BAN. *hi(ku)* saw; turn (on a lathe); pull (a cart); grind (in a mill).
- 6 肉 *hikiniku* ground meat, minced meat
- 回 *bankai* recovery, restoration, retrieval⌉
- 8 物 *hikimono* lathe work
- 10 馬 *bamba* work horse
- 12 割 *hi(ki)-wa(ru)* saw. *hikiwa(ri)* lumber
- 14 歌 *banka* elegy, dirge

捕 2170 J4a61 M12157 BU. HO. *tora(eru), torama(eru), tsukama(eru), to(ru)* catch, arrest, capture. *tsukama(ru)* be caught, be captured. *to(reru)* can be held, can take; come off, come apart, be off, be removed; be relieved (of pain); be obtained, be produced; be caught; be earned; come out (well) (a photo); require (time); be interpreted as; can get; let (light) in; take (one's measure); can feel (the pulse); take (a pen and write). *tora(wareru)* be caught, be captured, be arrested; be a slave to; be seized with.

心 忄 小 戈 戸 【手 扌】 支 攴 攵 文 斗 斤 方 无 日 曰 月 木 欠 止 歹 殳 毋 比 毛 氏 气 水 氵 氺 火 灬 爪 爫 父 爻 爿 丬 片 牙 牛 犬 犭

4

心 忄 小 戈 戸 【手 扌】

⁷ 手 扌

支 支 攵 文 斗 斤 方 无 日 曰 月 木 欠 止 歹 殳 毋 比 毛 氏 气 水 氵 氺 火 灬 爪 爫 父 爻 爿 丬 片 牛 犬 犭

---

⁴ 手 *hoshu* catcher. *torite* (ancient) policeman

⁵ 囚 *hoshū* prisoner, captive, captivity

⁷ 身 *torawa(re) (no) mi* a captive

⁸ 物 *torimono* a capture, an arrest

⁹ 食 *hoshoku suru* prey upon

¹⁰ 捉 *hosoku* capture, seizure

殺 *hosatsu suru* catch and kill; assist (in baseball)

¹³ 虜 *horyo* prisoner, captive; captivity

¹⁶ 獲 *hokaku* capture, seizure

縛 *hobaku* arrest, seizure

鯨 *hogei* whaling

B 振 $\frac{2171}{\substack{J3f36 \\ M12093}}$ SHIN *fu(ru)* wave, wag, swing, shake; sprinkle; brandish; jilt, reject; attach, allot. *fu(reru)* lean toward, deflect, tend; shake, swing, oscillate. *furu(u)* shake, wield, brandish; be invigorated, be spirited, flourish. *fu(rareru)* be jilted, be rejected. *fu(ri)* appearance, manners, air, dress, form, posture; pretense, affectation; discipline; custom; swing, shaking; (dance) postures; slant, inclination, deviation, deflection; casual customer; sword counter. *fu(re)* deflection, deviation. *fu(rutta)* splendid, extraordinary, striking, original. *-bu(ri)* lapse of -, after (two years, etc.); for (three days, etc.); manner, style.

³ 子 *fu(ri)ko, shinshi* pendulum, bob

上 *fu(ri)-a(geru)* fling up, swing up, whip out, brandish; toss (the head)

⁴ 込 *fu(ri)-ko(mu)* pay in, pay up, pay an installment

切 *fu(ri)-ki(ru)* sever, shake off, free oneself

分 *fu(ri)-wa(keru)* divide in half, distribute. *furiwa(ke)* hair parted and hanging down; carrying packages on a strap over the shoulders

⁵ 付 *furitsu(ke)* Japanese dance composition; dance coaching

払 *fu(ri)-hara(u)* shake off, whisk off

出 *fu(ri)-da(su)* shake out; infuse, decoct; write (a check). *furida(shi)* start; drawing or issuing (a draft)

⁶ 回 *fu(ri)-mawa(su)* brandish, wave, flourish, wave about, swing; display, show off

返 *fu(ri)-kae(ru)* turn the head, look over one's shoulder, turn around, look back

---

向 *fu(ri)-mu(keru)* turn toward; apply toward, appropriate to. *fu(ri)-mu(ku)* turn toward, look back

当 *fu(ri)-a(teru)* assign (work)

仮名 *fu(ri)gana* side *kana* (to show the pronunciation of characters)

⁷ 作 *shinsaku* prosperity

乱 *fu(ri)-mida(su)* shake (one's hair) loose, dishevel

⁸ 放 *fu(ri)-hana(su), fu(ri)-hana(tsu)* shake oneself loose, tear away from

⁹ 飛 *fu(ri)-to(basu)* swing and throw

¹⁰ 袖 *fu(ri) sode* long sleeves, long-sleeved kimono

起 *furu(i)-oko(su)* arouse, awaken, promote. *shinki* encouragement, stimulation

¹¹ 捨 *fu(ri)-su(teru)* shake off; discard, forsake, abandon, desert, leave off

掛 *fu(ri)-ka(keru)* sprinkle over, splash on. *fu(ri)-ka(karu)* be splashed. *furika(ke)* flakes of fish, seaweed, or other seasonings sprinkled over rice

動 *fu(ri)-ugo(kasu)* vt swing, shake, wag. *fu(ri)-ugo(ku)* vi swing, shake, oscillate. *shindō* oscillation, swing, vibration

¹² 幅 *shimpuku* amplitude (of vibrations); the swing of a pendulum

落 *fu(ri)-oto(su), furu(i)-oto(su)* shake off, throw off, spill, sift out, eliminate

替 *fu(ri)-ka(eru)* transfer (funds). *furikae* change, transfer, postal-transfer account

¹³ 解 *fu(ri)-hodo(ku)* shake and untangle

鈴 *shinrei* ringing a bell; hand bell

¹⁴ 撒 *fu(ri)-ma(ku)* sprinkle, scatter, diffuse, disperse; lavish

舞 *furuma(u)* behave oneself, entertain, treat. *furumai* behavior, deportment, demeanor, conduct, manners; entertainment, feast

¹⁶ 興 *shinkō* promotion, encouragement, arousing

— 8 —

挽 $\frac{2172}{\substack{J4854 \\ M-X}}$ Nonstandard for **挽** 2169.

捗 $\frac{2173}{\substack{J443d \\ M-X}}$ Nonstandard for **捗** 2161.

捆 ⎯2174⎯ J44f M-X Nonstandard for **掆** 2263.

掻 ⎯2175⎯ J415f M-X See **掻** 2256.

捺 ⎯2189⎯ J4668 M12221 NATSU press, print. *o(su)*, *sa(su)* affix a seal, stamp.
⁶印 *natsuin* sealing (a document)
⁹染 *nassen, oshizome, nasen* (textile) printing

措 B ⎯2190⎯ J413c M12286 SO. *o(ku)* give up, suspend, discontinue, lay aside, set apart; except.
¹³置 *sochi* measure, step, move, action
辞 *soji* phraseology, wording, diction

掠 ⎯2191⎯ J4e2b M12273 RYAKU. *kasu(meru)* rob, pillage; graze (in passing), skim, sweep over; cheat; hint, suggest. *kasu(ru)* graze (one's leg); squeeze, exploit. *kasu(reru)* be grazed, touch, chip; become hoarse. *kasuri* grazing (something); squeeze, percentage, kickback.
⁸取 *kasu(me)-to(ru), ryakushu suru* rob, cheat, despoil; seize, capture
¹³傷 *kasu(ri) kizu* scratch, bruise; slight damage; slight (business) failure
¹⁴奪 *kasu(me)-uba(u)* plunder. *ryakudatsu* pillage, plunder, looting

掩 ⎯2192⎯ J3166 M12285 EN *ō(u)* cover, shade, conceal, shelter
¹³蓋 *engai* cover, covering 「blanketing
¹⁵蔽 *empei* cover, obscuration, occultation
²⁰護 *engo* covering, protection, aegis, backing, relief

捲 ⎯2193⎯ J377e M12208 KEN. *ma(ku)* roll, wind, coil; tie around, wind up. *maku(ru), meku(ru)* turn over (pages); turn up (a card); tear off, take up, rip off; tuck up, bare (one's arm), roll up (one's sleeves). *maku(reru) vi* turn over, turn up; tear off, rip; be rolled up. *makure* burr, snag, catch.
³上 *maku(ri)-a(geru), maku(shi)-a(geru), ma(ki)-a(geru) vt* roll up; hoist, heave up; take away, rob; blow up (dust)

土重来 *kendochōrai, kendojūrai* making a success after failure 「on
⁵立 *maku(shi)-ta(teru)* talk volubly, rattle

掲 B ⎯2194⎯ J3747 M12311ʼ KEI. KETSU. *kaka(geru)* put up, hang out, hoist, display; publish, insert; describe; mention.
⁵示 *keiji* bulletin, notice
示板 *keijiban* bulletin board
¹²揚 *keiyō suru* hoist, fly, display
¹³載 *keisai* publication, insertion

据 B ⎯2195⎯ J3178 M12204 KYO. *su(eru)* set (a table); lay (a foundation); place (a gun); install, equip; appoint (to a position). *su(waru)* squat down, sit down, (eyes) are fixed on.
⁵付 *su(e)-tsu(keru)* install, equip; set up; mount, place in position; set (a charge)
¹³置 *su(e)-o(ku)* leave as it is, defer; leave (a loan) unredeemed; establish
¹⁶膳 *suezen* an individually served meal

描 B ⎯2196⎯ J4941 M12339 BYŌ. *ka(ku)* write, compose; draw, paint. *ega(ku)* paint, sketch, draw, describe.
⁴切 *ega(ki)-ki(ru)* draw exactly
⁵写 *byōsha* description; portrayal; drawing, painting, picture
出 *ega(ki)-da(su)* portray, delineate, depict. *byōshutsu* description; portrayal; drawing, painting, picture
⁸画 *byōga* drawing, painting
¹⁵線 *byōsen* a drawn line.

掬 ⎯2197⎯ J3545 M12204 KIKU. *kiku(su), musu(bu)* scoop up water with the hand. *suku(u)* scoop, dip, ladle.
³上 *suku(i)-a(geru)* dip up, scoop up
⁵出 *suku(i)-da(su)* bail out
⁷投 *suku(i)na(ge)* tripping up (someone)
¹⁴網 *suku(i)ami* scoop net, dip net

捷 ⎯2198⎯ J3e39 M12216 SHŌ victory; fast.
⁸径 *shōkei* short cut; expedient
¹²報 *shōhō* news of victory

捧 ⎯2199⎯ J4a7b M12189 HŌ *sasa(geru)* lift up; give; offer, consecrate, devote, sacrifice, dedicate.

心 忄 小 戈 戸 【手 扌】 支 攴 攵 文 斗 斤 方 无 日 曰 月 木 欠 止 歹 殳 毋 比 毛 氏 气 水 氵 氺 火 灬 爪 爫 父 爻 爿 丬 片 牙 牛 犬 犭

4

心 忄 小 戈 戸 【手 扌】 支 攴 攵 文 斗 斤 方 旡 日 曰 月 木 欠 止 歹 殳 毋 比 毛 氏 气 水 氵 氺 火 灬 爪 爫 父 爻 爿 片 牙 牛 犬 犭

---

⁷ 呈 *hōtei* dedication, presentation; gift
⁸ 物 *sasa(ge)mono* offering, sacrifice
⁹ 持 *hōji suru* bear, present, hold up (the emperor's picture)
¹⁴ 読 *hōdoku suru* read reverently
　銃 *sasa(ge)tsutsu* presenting arms.

掌 〔2200 J3e38 M12248〕 B SHŌ. *tsukasado(ru)* rule, administer, conduct.
tanagokoro palm, hollow of the hand.
⁴ 中 *shōchū* in the hand; (something) very small; (something) easily manipulated
¹² 握 *shōaku suru* grasp, seize, hold, command

捻 〔2201 J4731 M12222〕 NEN. *hine(ri)* pinch (of salt); small gift of money; a twist. *hine(ru)* twirl, twist, twiddle; wring, wrench; bend (the body); incline (the head); pinch; defeat. *ne(jiru)* screw, twist, wrench, distort, wring, turn (a faucet); make capital out of someone's slip of the tongue. *neji(reru)* be twisted, be distorted, kink, twist, be awry; be perverse. *hineku(ru)* twirl, twist, play with; twist (the truth in reasoning).
³ 子 *neji* screw, faucet, watch spring
⁵ 出 *hine(ri)-da(su)* squeeze out; work out a plan. *nenshutsu suru* contrive, devise (means), raise (money)
⁶ 回 *hineku(ri)-mawa(su)*, *hine(ri)-mawa(su)* tinker with, twist up, twirl
⁸ 取 *hine(ri)-to(ru)* pinch (something) from
¹⁰ 挫 *nenza* sprain
¹¹ 転 *nenten* twisting, torsion
¹⁵ 潰 *hine(ri)-tsubu(su)* crush between fingers

控 〔2202 J3935 M12283〕 B KŌ. *hika(eru)* draw in; hold back, suspend (judgment); refrain from; be moderate; write, make notes; wait; have; moderate (a report). *hika(e)* memo; duplicate; waiting; prop; reserve.
⁵ 目 *hika(e)me no* moderate, temperate, reserved, conservative
⁸ 制 *kōsei* checking, controlling
⁹ 除 *kōjo* subtraction, deduction
　室 *hika(e)shitsu* waiting room
¹⁰ 書 *hika(e)ga(ki)* notes, memo
¹¹ 帳 *hika(e)chō* notebook
¹² 訴 *kōso* (legal) appeal
　訴審 *kōsoshin* appeal trial

掘 〔2204 J3721 M12264〕 B KUTSU. *ho(ru)* dig, delve; core; excavate; sink (wells); dig up; scoop out; pick (the ear); probe.
³ 下 *ho(ri)-sa(geru)* dig down; delve, investigate
⁴ 込 *ho(ri)-ko(mu)* dig in, dig into
⁵ 出 *ho(ri)-da(su)* dig out, unearth, exhume, extricate, excavate; pick up (a rare book)
　出物 *horida(shi)mono* treasure trove; lucky find; bargain
⁶ 返 *ho(ri)-kae(su)* turn up (the soil); tear up (a road)
　池 *ho(ri)ike* an artificial pool
　当 *ho(ri)-a(teru)* find, dig up, strike (oil)
⁷ 抜 *ho(ri)-nu(ku)* bore through, bore into
　抜井戸 *horinuki ido* bored well
⁹ 削 *kussaku* excavation
　建小屋 *ho(t)ta(te)goya* hut, shack, cabin
¹⁰ 起 *ho(ri)-o(kosu)* dig up; plow up
　進 *kusshin suru* excavate, tunnel
¹¹ 崩 *ho(ri)-kuzu(su)* demolish
¹² 開 *ho(ri)-hira(ku)* excavate

捨 〔2205 J3c4e M12191〕 A SHA. *su(teru)* throw away, discard, abandon, desert, give up; renounce, relinquish; resign; lay down (one's life); part with; sacrifice; reject, condemn.
³ 子 *su(te)go* foundling
⁵ 石 *su(te)ishi* ornamental garden rocks; road ballast; preparatory work
　去 *su(te)-sa(ru)* forsake; send away; throw away
　台詞 *su(te)zerifu* sharp parting remark
⁷ 身 *su(te)mi* self-abandonment. *shashin* becoming a priest
　売 *su(te)u(ri)* sacrifice sale
¹⁰ 値 *su(te)ne* sacrifice price
¹² 場 *su(te)ba* dumping ground, dump
¹³ 鉢 *su(te)bachi* despair, desperation
　置 *su(te)-o(ku)* let alone, let pass, overlook

掃 〔2207 J415d M12237'〕 B SŌ. *ha(ku)* sweep; brush; gather up.
⁵ 出 *ha(ki)-da(su)* sweep out
⁹ 海 *sōkai* mine sweeping
　海艇 *sōkaitei* mine sweeper
　除 *sōji* cleaning, sweeping; cleanup, purge

除機 *sōjiki* vacuum cleaner
¹⁰討 *sōtō* cleaning up, sweeping, mopping up
射 *sōsha* sweeping fire
¹¹捨 *ha(ki)-su(teru)* sweep away, sweep out
寄 *ha(ki)-yo(seru)* sweep up
¹²集 *ha(ki)-atsu(meru)* sweep up
¹³滅 *sōmetsu* clean sweep, annihilation
溜 *hu(ki)da(me)* sweepings, rubbish heap, dump
¹⁵蕩 *sōtō* clearing up, sweeping, mopping up

授 ₂₂₀₈ _{J3c78} _{M12242} Ju give, grant. *sazu(keru)*
A grant, confer, award, invest (with authority); impart, teach.
sazu(karu), *sazu(keraru)* be gifted with, be granted, be awarded, be accorded, be blessed with; be taught.
³与 *juyo* awarding, conferring
⁸物 *sazu(kari)mono* godsend, windfall, gift, boon, blessing
受 *juju suru* give and receive, deliver and receive
乳 *junyū* lactation, suckling
⁹洗 *jusen suru* baptize (by sprinkling)
¹¹産 *jusan* placement, employment
産所 *jusanjo* vocational institute (to help the unemployed)
¹³業 *jugyō* teaching, instruction, classwork
¹⁴精 *jusei* fertilization, pollination
¹⁵賞 *jushō* awarding a prize

採 ₂₂₀₉ _{J3a4e} _{M12274} SAI. *to(ru)* take, hold,
A seize, catch, capture; fetch; receive, procure, obtain; adopt (a measure); engage (graduates); choose; order (foodstuffs); pick, pluck; make, produce; eat; set up (camp); charge; administer; transact; take (pains); make out (the meaning); remove; take off (one's hat); take out (spots); strike out (words); weed, catch (fish); deprive of; steal; capture (territory), annex; need, require; reserve (rooms); subscribe to; press (a point home); take (a picture); possess.
to(reru) can be held, can take; come off, come apart, be off, be removed; be relieved (of pain); be obtained, be produced; be caught; be earned; come out (well) (a photo); require (time); be

interpreted as; can get; let (light) in; take (one's measure); can feel (the pulse); take (a pen and write).
²入 *to(ri)-i(reru)* take in, gather in, harvest; accept, adopt, introduce (customs)
³上 *to(ri)-a(geru)* take up, pick up; deal with; adopt, accept, listen to; dispossess, expropriate, confiscate, revoke; deliver (a baby)
⁵用 *saiyō suru* use, adopt, employ. *saiyō* introduction, adoption, acceptance; appointment, employment
石 *saiseki* quarrying
⁶血 *saiketsu suru* take a blood sample
光 *saikō* lighting
⁷択 *saitaku suru* adopt, select
決 *saiketsu* vote, roll call, ballot taking
否 *saihi* adoption or rejection; employment or rejection
⁸取 *saishu* picking, gathering, collecting, harvesting; extracting (alcohol)
⁹点 *saiten* marking, grading
炭 *saitan* coal mining
¹¹掘 *saikutsu* mining
¹²集 *saishū* collecting, gathering
¹³鉱 *saikō* mining
¹⁴算 *saisan* profit
¹⁶録 *sairoku suru* transcribe, record

排 ₂₂₁₀ _{J4753} _{M12256} HAI *hai(suru)* exclude,
B expel, reject; push aside, push open; defy; disregard; anti-(Japanese, etc.).
⁴水 *haisui* drainage; draining; bailing; displacement
⁵斥 *haiseki* rejection, exclusion, ostracism, expulsion
外 *haigai* antiforeign
他 *haita* exclusion
他的 *haitateki* exclusive
出 *haishutsu* discharge, exhaust, evacuation
⁶列 *hairetsu* arrangement, grouping, disposition
気 *haiki* exhaust, ventilation
⁷尿 *hainyō* urination
卵 *hairan* ovulation
⁸泄 *haisetsu* evacuation, discharge, exhaust
泄物 *haisetsubutsu* excrement, excretion
⁹便 *haiben* evacuation, bowel movement

4

心 忄 小 戈 戸【手 扌】
8
支 攴 攵 文 斗 斤 方 无 日 日 月 木 欠 止 歹 殳 毋 比 毛 氏 气 水 氵 氺 火 灬 爪 爫 父 爻 爿 丬 片 牙 牛 犬 犭

除 *haijo* exclusion, removal
11 球 *haikyū* volleyball
15 撃 *haigeki* denouncement, rejection

探 _A 2211 J4335 M12276 TAN. *sagu(ru)* search, look for; explore; spy upon, sound out; probe (a wound). *saga(su)* search. *sagu(ri)* sounding out; spy; probe.
5 出 *sagu(ri)-da(su)* spy out, worm out, smell out, search out
6 回 *sagu(ri)-mawa(su), sagu(ri)-mawa(ru)* grope for, fumble for
合 *sagu(ri)a(i)* testing each other's feelings
当 *sagu(ri)-a(teru)* grope and find, discover, locate
7 求 *saga(shi)-moto(meru)* search for. *tankyū* quest, pursuit, research
究 *tankyū* search, research, inquiry
8 知 *tanchi* detection
9 査 *tansa* inquiry, investigation
10 険 *tanken* exploration, expedition
索 *tansaku* search; inquiry, investigation
11 訪 *tambō* searching; hunting a news story; journalist
偵 *tantei* detective work; espionage; detective; spy, investigator, agent
12 測 *tansoku* search, observation
勝 *tanshō* sightseeing
検 *tanken* exploration, expedition
13 照灯 *tanshōtō* searchlight

推 _A 2212 J3f64 M12284 SUI conjecture. *o(su)* infer, conclude; guess, suppose; recommend, support. *o(shite)* by conjecture, by deduction.
2 力 *suiryoku* thrust, driving power
6 考 *suikō* inference, deduction, deliberation
8 知 *suichi* inference, deduction, conjecture
参 *suisan* visiting; discourtesy
定 *suitei* presumption, conclusion, estimation
9 計 *suikei* estimate
10 称 *suishō* praise; admiration
挙 *suikyo suru* propose (for office)
進 *suishin* propulsion, drive, promotion
進力 *suishinryoku* impulse, propulsion
進機 *suishinki* propeller
11 移 *suii* transition, change. *o(shi)-utsu(ru)*

(times) change, (months) pass
断 *suidan* inference, deduction, conclusion
理 *suiri* reasoning, inference, presumption
理小説 *suiri shōsetsu* detective story
12 測 *suisoku* conjecture, supposition. *o(shi)-haka(ru)* enter into another's feelings
量 *suiryō* guess, inference, imagination; consideration, sympathy
14 選 *suisen* recommendation
輓 *suiban* recommendation
敲 *suikō* polish, elaboration, choice of diction
察 *suisatsu* guess, inference, imagination; consideration, sympathy
算 *suisan* calculation, reckoning
15 賞 *suishō* recommendation, commendation
論 *suiron* reasoning, inference, deduction
16 薦 *suisen* recommendation, nomination

接 _A 2213 J405c M12280 SETSU. *ses(suru)* touch, contact; adjoin; receive (visitors); be in receipt of; encounter, experience; draw near. *tsu(gu)* join, piece together, splice, cement, set (broken bones); graft (trees). *ha(gu)* patch. *ha(gi)* patch, patches; patching; seam, joint.
4 手 *tsugite* joint, pipe coupling
木 *tsugiki* grafting; grafted tree
5 目 *tsugime, hagime* joint, seam, suture
収 *sesshū* seizure, requisition
6 近 *sekkin* proximity, approach; intimate relations
地 *setchi* ground (connection)
合 *ha(gi)-a(waseru)* sew together; join. *setsugō* union, joining
7 伴 *seppan* reception, welcome; serving (food)
吻 *seppun* kiss, kissing
見 *sekken* interview, reception
尾辞 *setsubiji* suffix
8 受 *setsuju suru* receive, intercept
9 待 *settai* reception, welcome; serving (food)
客 *sekkyaku* receiving visitors
客業 *sekkyakugyō* hotel and restaurant business
10 骨 *sekkotsu* bonesetting
11 眼鏡 *setsugankyō* eyepiece

¹² 着 *setchaku* adhesion, glueing

¹³ 戦 *sessen* hand-to-hand fighting; close game

続 *setsuzoku* connection, junction, joining

続詞 *setsuzokushi* conjunction

触 *sesshoku* contact, touch, tangency

¹⁴ 種 *sesshu* inoculation, vaccination

¹⁶ 頭辞 *settōji* prefix

掛 B $\frac{2214}{\substack{J335d \\ M12267}}$ KAI. KEI. *ka(karu) vi* hang on, be suspended from; be caught, be trapped; be built; begin; arrive at; require, cost; play against, oppose; be splashed; weigh (a pound); be levied; (the instrument or tool) works; attack, fall on; is now showing at; consult; depend (on a son). *ka(keru) vt* hang, set up (a ladder); cover; construct, install; sit down; sprinkle, pour on; put on; ring up; weigh; multiply; levy; pay (in installments); anchor; start (a machine); wind; turn on (radio); spend on; offer (prizes); put (under treatment); set (on fire). *kakari* duty; person in charge; expenses, charges; tax; dependence (on someone); scale; outward appearance; construction; beginning; bite (of a tool). *ka(ke)* buckwheat noodles in soup; credit; overcharge; installment. *-ka(keru)* begin, start to. *-ka(ketewa)* (in) the matter of, in. *-ga(ke)* wearing; on (the way); ten percent; times (as large). *-ka(ke)* half finished; (clothes) hook; (table) cover.

³ 小屋 *ka(ke)goya* lean-to, temporary hut

⁵ 付 *ka(kari)tsu(ke)no* one's regular (physician)

札 *ka(ke)fuda* small hanging plaque for notices; nameplate

払 *ka(ke)bara(i)* settlement of accounts

布団 *ka(ke)buton* covering quilt

⁶ 合 *ka(ke)-a(u)* negotiate with, bargain with. *ka(ke)-a(wasu) vt* multiply; cross, interbreed. *ka(kari)-a(u)* have dealings with; be involved in. *ka(kari)a(i)* implication, involvement. *kakea(i)* negotiations; dialogue

⁷ 図 *kakezu* wall map, wall picture

声 *ka(ke)goe* shouting encouragement; shouting in unison to aid effort

売 *kakeu(ri)* selling on credit

⁸ 金 *kakekin* installment payments; credit

sales. *ka(ke)gane* hatch, hasp, latch

⁹ 持 *ka(ke)mo(chi)* holding positions concurrently

竿 *ka(ke)zao* clothes-drying pole

¹⁰ 値 *ka(ke)ne* overcharge; exaggeration

時計 *ka(ke)dokei* wall clock

¹¹ 捨 *kakezu(te)* abandoning an installment contract

¹² 詞 *ka(ke)kotoba* play on words

軸 *kakejiku* hanging scroll

違 *ka(ke)-chiga(u)* cross (on the way)

替 *ka(ke)-ka(eru)* replace, rebuild, substitute. *kakeka(e)* rebuilding (a bridge); rehanging (a scroll). *kakega(e)* substitute

¹³ 蒲団 *ka(ke)buton* covering quilt

¹⁴ 暦 *ka(ke)goyomi* wall calendar

樋 *ka(ke)hi*, *ka(ke)doi* water pipe, conduit, flume

算 *ka(ke)zan* multiplication

¹⁵ 蕎麦 *ka(ke)soba* buckwheat noodles in seasoned broth

¹⁶ 橋 *ka(ke)hashi* viaduct, suspension bridge

--- **9** ---

揖 $\frac{2222}{\substack{J4d2c \\ M12351}}$ YŪ bow with hands clasped at breast; give way; advance; scoop up. SHŪ gather, assemble.

揃 $\frac{2226}{\substack{J4237 \\ M12319}}$ SEN. *soro(u)* be complete; be equal; be even, be uniform; be all present. *soro(eru)* arrange; make even; complete, get ready. *soroi* all, both, together; uniform; uniformity; attendance. *soro(tte)* in a body, en masse; all alike. *-soroi* set; suit.

搭 B $\frac{2228}{\substack{J456b \\ M12508}}$ TŌ load (a vehicle); ride.

⁹ 乗 *tōjō suru* board, get on

乗者 *tōjōsha* passenger, occupant

¹³ 載 *tōsai suru* load; entrain; embark

揮 A $\frac{2229}{\substack{J3478 \\ M12394}}$ KI. *furu(u)* shake, wield, brandish; be invigorated, be spirited, flourish.

⁹ 発 *kihatsu* volatilization

発油 *kihatsuyu* gasoline

¹¹ 毫 *kigō* writing, painting, drawing

4

心 忄 小 戈 戸 【手扌】支 攴 攵 文 斗 斤 方 无 日 曰 月 木 欠 止 歹 殳 毋 比 毛 氏 气 水 氵 氺 火 灬 爪 爫 父 爻 爿 丬 片 牙 牛 犬 犭

援 B 2230 J3167 M12407 EN *tasu(keru)* help, save.

4 引 *en'in* reference
5 用 *en'yō suru* claim, quote, invoke
8 助 *enjo* assistance, help, pay, support
9 軍 *engun* relief, reinforcements
20 護 *engo* covering, protection, aegis, backing, relief

握 B 2232 J302e M12366 AKU. *nigi(ru)* grasp, hold; make (sushi balls); assume (power); make (money); get (proof). *nigi(rasu)* let (someone) take hold of your hand; slip money to, bribe. *nigi(ri)* grasp, grip, handful; handle; rice ball, sushi ball.

2 力 *akuryoku* grasping power
4 手 *akushu* handshaking; reconciliation; harmony
10 拳 *nigi(ri)kobushi* clenched fist
12 飯 *nigi(ri)meshi, musubi* rice ball
15 潰 *nigi(ri)-tsubu(su)* crush, crumple; shelve, table
締 *nigi(ri)-shi(meru)* squeeze, wring, clasp, hold tightly
17 鮨 *nigi(ri)zushi* sushi ball

換 B 2233 J3439 M12358 KAN. *ka(eru)* change, turn, convert, exchange, renew, substitute, replace. *ka(waru)* replace, relieve.

6 気 *kanki* ventilation
7 言 *kangen (sureba)* in other words
8 金 *kankin suru* realize, turn into money
10 骨奪胎 *kankotsu-dattai* adaptation, modification; plagiarism
14 算 *kansan* conversion, change, exchange

揺 B 2235 J4d49 M12445 YŌ. *yu(reru), yu(rameku), yu(ratsuku), yu(ragu), vi* shake, sway, rock, roll, pitch, tremble, quake, flicker, vibrate, jolt. *yu(suru), yu(suburu), yu(saburu) vt* swing, shake, rock. *yu(rugasu)* shake, wave, swing, sway. *yu(re)* vibration; shock; variety.

3 上 *yu(ri)-a(geru)* swing up, jiggle (a baby on one's back)
6 返 *yu(ri)kae(shi)* an aftershock
曳 *yōei suru* flutter, tremble; trail, linger
10 起 *yu(ri)-oko(su), yu(suri)-oko(su)* wake (someone) up
11 動 *yu(ri)-ugo(ku) vi* quake; swing. *yu(ri)-ugo(kasu) vt* shake, wave,

---

swing, sway. *yu(re)-ugo(ku)* tremble
12 無 *yu(rugi)na(i)* firm, steady, secure
椅子 *yu(ri)isu* rocking chair
20 籃 *yōran, yu(ri)kago* cradle
籃地 *yōran (no) chi* the home of, the cradle of, birthplace
籃期 *yōranki* infancy, babyhood
22 籠 *yu(ri)kago* cradle

揚 B 2236 J4d48 M12355 YŌ praise. *a(garu)* rise, go up; climb up; advance, appreciate; be promoted; improve; enter, call on; be offered; accrue; be finished; (expenses) come to; go bankrupt; begin spinning (cocoons); be caught; get ruffled; eat, drink; die; weaken (as a battery); let up (rain). *a(geru)* raise, elevate; fly (kites); praise; increase, advance; promote, elevate; vomit; usher in, admit; send (to school); offer; present, leave with; finish; arrange (expenses); observe, perform; quote, mention, give (examples); bear (a child); improve (talents); do up (the hair); arrest; engage; fry; (rains) stop; fry in deep fat. *a(ge)* tuck; fried tofu; fried food.

2 力 *yōryoku* lifting power
3 子江 *Yōsukō* Yangtze River
4 水 *yōsui* pumping water
5 句 *a(ge)ku* in the end, finally
7 言 *yōgen* declare, assert, profess
足 *a(ge)ashi* faultfinding
8 板 *a(ge)ita* removable floor boards, trap door
物 *a(ge)mono* fried food
油 *a(ge)abura* frying oil
10 荷 *a(ge)ni* cargo being unloaded
陸 *yōriku* disembarkation; unloading
12 場 *a(ge)ba* wharf, landing (place)
揚 *yōyō(taru)* triumphant, exultant
13 幕 *a(ge)maku* noh theater-entrance curtain
16 錨機 *yōbyōki* anchor windlass

提 B 2237 J4473 M12344 TEI. CHŌ. *sa(geru)* take along, carry in the hand. *hissa(geru)* carry.

5 示 *teiji suru, teishi suru* present; exhibit; suggest
出 *teishutsu suru* present, introduce (a bill), tender (a resignation), lodge (a petition)

---

⁶灯 *chōchin* paper lantern

灯持 *chōchimmo(chi)* lantern carrier; exaggerated propaganda

⁷言 *teigen* proposal, motion

⁸供 *teikyō* offer, tender

⁹要 *teiyō* summary

¹⁰起 *teiki suru* bring suit; raise a question; file a claim

案 *teian* proposition, suggestion, overture, proposal

¹¹唱 *teishō* (Buddhist) lecture; advocacy

¹²訴 *teiso suru* sue

琴 *teikin* violin

¹³携 *teikei* concert, cooperation

督 *teitoku* admiral, commodore

²⁰議 *teigi* proposal, motion

─────── **10** ───────

搬 ²²⁴⁹ J4842 M12507 HAN carry, transport.
B

²入 *hannyū suru* carry in

⁵出 *hanshutsu suru* carry out

⁸送 *hansō suru* convey

摸 ²²⁵⁰ J4c4e M12644 MO. search. *mo(suru)* imitate; copy.

⁵写 *mosha* copying; copy, replica

¹⁰倣 *mohō* copy, imitation

索 *mosaku* groping

¹⁷擬 *mogi* imitation

擬戦 *mogisen* sham fight

擬試験 *mogi shiken* trial examination

搾 ²²⁵¹ J3a71 M12553 SAKU. *shibo(ru)* wring, squeeze, press, extract; milk; close tight; extort; scold. *shi(meru)* strangle, constrict, wring.
B

⁵汁 *shibo(ri)jiru* juices

出 *shiborida(shi)* (toothpaste) tube

⁸油 *sakuyu* expressing oil (from seeds or nuts)

取 *shibo(ri)-to(ru)* wring, squeeze, press, extract; milk; close tight; extort; scold. *sakushu* exploitation; squeezing; sweating

乳 *sakunyū* milking

¹³滓 *shibo(ri)kasu, shimekasu* strained lees

摂 ²²⁵² J405d M12557 SETSU. *ses(suru)* act in place of; carry on in addition to. *to(ru)* take, hold, seize,
B

catch, capture; fetch; receive, procure, obtain; adopt (a measure); engage (graduates); choose; order (foodstuffs); pick, pluck; make, produce; eat; set up (camp); charge, administer; transact; take (pains); make out (the meaning); remove; take off (one's hat); take out (spots); strike out (words); weed, catch (fish); deprive of; steal; capture (territory), annex; need, require, reserve (rooms); subscribe to; press (a point home); take (a picture); possess.

⁴氏 *sesshi* centigrade

⁵生 *sessei* health preservation, hygiene

⁸取 *sesshu* intake, absorption; adoption

⁹政 *sesshō, sessei* regency; regent

¹¹理 *setsuri* providence

携 ²²⁵³ J3748 M12529 KEI. *tazusa(eru)* carry (in the hand); be armed with; carry along, bring (someone) along. *tazusa(waru)* participate in, be concerned in.
B

⁶行 *keikō suru* carry along, bring. *tazusa(e)-yu(ku)* carry to, bring to, carry away

¹⁰帰 *tazusa(e)-kae(ru)* bring back

¹⁰帯 *keitai* portable. *keitai suru* carry along

帯品 *keitaihin* personal effects, luggage

損 ²²⁵⁵ J423b M12459 SON loss; disadvantage, handicap. *son(suru)* lose, suffer loss. *sokona(u), sokone(ru), son(zuru), son(jiru)* harm, hurt, injure, damage, mar; lose, oppress. *-son(jiru), -sokona(u)* fail in (doing), fail to (do), miss, err in. *-son(ji), -sokona(i)* slip, error, failure.
A

³亡 *sommō* loss

⁵失 *sonshitsu* loss

⁸金 *sonkin* money loss

¹⁰耗 *sommō* loss

益 *son'eki* loss and gain; advantage and disadvantage

料 *sonryō* charge for the use of certain articles

害 *songai* damage, injury, loss; casualties; prejudice

害保険 *songai hoken* insurance against loss

4

心 忄 小 戈 戸【手扌】支 支 攵 文 斗 斤 方 无 日 曰 月 木 欠 止 歹 殳 毋 比 毛 氏 气 水 氵 氺 火 灬 爪 爫 父 爻 爿 片 牙 牛 犬 犭

害賠償 *songai baishō* restitution, compensation for damages or injuries

¹¹ 得 *sontoku* loss and gain; advantages and disadvantages

¹³ 傷 *sonshō* damage, injury, casualty

掻 _{2256 J-X M12477} 搔 _{2175 J415f M-X} Sō . *ka(ku)* scratch; clear away; rake; comb; paddle; cut off (a head). *ka(ki)-* emphatic prefix.

³ 口説 *ka(ki)-kudo(ku)* complain of

⁴ 込 *ka(ki)-ko(mu)* carry under the arm, rake in. *kakko(mu)* eat fast

切 *ka(ki)-ki(ru)* cut; cut off; cut and take

分 *ka(ki)-wa(keru)* push or shove aside

立 *ka(ki)-ta(teru)* stir; rake (the fire); beat, whip; turn up (a wick); arouse (interest), stir up (trouble)

払 *kappara(u)* pilfer, filch. *kappara(i)* sneak thief; shoplifter

出 *ka(i)-da(su)* bail out (a boat); drain out. *ka(ki)-da(su)* scrape out, rake out

⁶ 回 *ka(ki)-mawa(su)* stir, churn, beat, whip; ransack; have one's own way

合 *ka(ki)-a(waseru)* adjust, arrange

⁷ 乱 *ka(ki)-mida(su)* disturb, ruffle, disarrange

⁸ 爬 *sōha* curetting, scraping, scooping out

抱 *ka(ki)-ida(ku)* emphatic for *idaku*: hug, embrace, hold in the arms; entertain (hope); cherish (a desire); harbor (malice); hold, have

取 *ka(i)-do(ru)* take; tuck up. *ka(ki)-to(ru)* scrape off, scrape out

¹⁰ 消 *ka(ki)-ke(su)* wipe out, efface

¹¹ 疵 *kakikizu* scratch

痒 *sōyō* scratching an itchy place

寄 *ka(ki)-yo(seru)* rake up, gather up

混 *ka(ki)-ma(zeru)* mix, mix up

¹² 揚 *kakia(ge)* fritters; combing upward

落 *ka(ki)-oto(su)* scrape off (mud); cut off (a head)

集 *ka(ki)-atsu(meru)* rake up, gather up

¹⁴ 鳴 *ka(ki)-na(rasu)* thrum, strum

摘 *ka(i)-tsuma(mu)* summarize ⌐under

¹⁵ 潜 *ka(i)-kugu(ru)* pass through, pass

----------- **11** -----------

摺 _{2262 J4022 M12647} SHŌ , SHŪ fold; rub. *su(ru)* rub; print (on cloth).

⁵ 本 *surihon* printed book

---

⁷ 足 *suriashi* shuffling feet, dragging feet

摑 _{2263 J-X M12572} KAKU. *tsuka(mu)* catch, seize, grasp, hold, lay hands on. *tsuka(maru)* hang onto, grab onto. *tsuka(maeru)* catch, seize, arrest, capture. *tsuka(maseru)* make (a person) catch hold of, let (a person) grasp; bribe; palm off; impose upon. *tsuka(mi)* handful, grip.

摩 B _{2264 J4b60 M12613} MA. *ma(suru)* rub; rub off; polish; grind; graze; scrape; be equal to; be about to reach. *sa(suru)* pat, stroke. *su(ru)* rub, chafe; strike (a match); frost (glass). *su(reru)* rub, chafe, wear; become sophisticated.

⁴ 天楼 *matenrō* skyscraper ⌐abrade

¹³ 滅 *mametsu* wear away, rub down,

¹⁷ 擦 *masatsu* rubbing, chafing; friction; discord

撃 B _{2265 J3762 M12674} GEKI. *u(tsu)* attack, defeat, destroy, conquer. *uchi-, u(tsu)* strike, hit, beat, knock, slap, punch, thrash, smite; clap (one's hands); beat (a drum); ring (a bell); (clocks) strike; impress, touch; shoot; pound in (a nail); water, sprinkle; braid; play (checkers); till (the soil); temper (a sword); prepare (buckwheat noodles); present (a play); cast (a net); pay (earnest money). *bu(tsu)* strike, beat; tell, speak; address (an audience).

⁷ 沈 *gekichin suru* sink a ship

⁸ 退 *gekitai suru* repulse, dislodge, reject, refuse, rebuff

¹⁰ 破 *gekiha suru, u(chi)-yabu(ru)* defeat, crush, rout, overthrow; refute

剣 *gekken* fencing ⌐shooting

殺 *gekisatsu suru* kill (a person) by

¹³ 滅 *gekimetsu* destruction, annihilation, extermination

鉄 *gekitetsu, u(chi)gane* gun hammer

¹⁴ 墜 *gekitsui suru* shoot down

²⁰ 攘 *gekijō suru*, repulse, dislodge, reject, refuse, rebuff. *u(chi)-hara(u)* beat off, shake off, sweep off, brush off, drive off, repel, rout

摘 B _{2266 J4526 M12582} TEKI. *tsuma(mu)* pick, pinch; hold in the fingers; summarize. *tsu(mu)* pick, pluck, pull out;

trim, clip, nip; gather.
⁴切 *tsu(mi)-ki(ru)* pick off; pick all, strip
⁵示 *tekishi suru, tekiji suru* point out, give the gist
　出 *tekishutsu suru* pick out, take out, extract; expose, point out
⁸果 *tekika* thinning fruit
　取 *tsu(mi)-to(ru)* pick, pluck. *tsu(mi)to(ri)* picking
⁹食 *tsuma(mi)gu(i)* picking and eating; eating stealthily
　草 *tsu(mi)kusa* gathering wild greens
　要 *tekiyō* summary, outline
　発 *tekihatsu suru* expose, unmask, lay bare, point out
¹⁰記 *tekki suru* sum up, summarize
¹⁶録 *tekiroku* summary

───── **12** ─────

撹 2267 J3349 M-X　See 攬 2322.

播 2273 J4745 M12747　HA. BAN. HAN. *ma(ku)* plant, sow.
¹⁴種 *hashu* sowing, planting

撲 2274 J4b50 M12755　B BOKU. *u(tsu)* strike, hit, beat, knock, slap, punch, thrash, smite; clap (one's hands); beat (a drum); ring (a bell); (clocks) strike; impress, touch; shoot; pound in (a nail); water, sprinkle; braid; play (checkers); till (the soil); temper (a sword); prepare (buckwheat noodles); present (a play); cast (a net); pay (earnest money). *bu(tsu)* strike, beat; tell, speak; address (an audience). *ha(ru)* slap, strike.
¹⁰殺 *bokusatsu* clubbing to death
¹³滅 *bokumetsu* eradication, destruction, extermination

撞 2276 J4635 M12717　DŌ. TŌ. *tsu(ku)* thrust, pierce, spear, stab, prick; gore; lunge at; push, poke; strike (a bell); attack; strike (at the heart); brave (a storm); be pungent; strike against; (words) rush (to one's lips).
⁴木 *shumoku* wooden bell hammer
¹¹球 *tamatsuki, dōkyū* billiards
¹²着 *dōchaku* conflict, inconsistency, contradiction

撰 2277 J4071 M12753　SAN. SEN composing, editing, compiling, selecting. *sen(suru)* write, compose. *era(bu), era(mu)* choose, select; cull out; elect; prefer; decide on.
⁷述 *senjutsu* editing, compilation
⁸定 *sentei* choice
⁹食 *e(ri)gu(i)* being choosy in eating
¹⁰修 *senshū* writing, editing
¹²集 *senshū* compiling writings; compilation

撚 2278 J4732 M12713　NEN. *yo(ru)* vt twist, twine. *yo(reru)* get twisted, be kinky. *yori* twist, strand. *hine(ru)* twirl, twist, twiddle; wring, wrench; bend (the body); incline (the head); pinch; defeat.
⁶糸 *yoriito* twisted thread, twine, yarn
¹⁰索 *yorisaku* stranded cable
¹⁵線 *yorisen* stranded wire

撒 2279 J3b35 M12697　SATSU. *ma(ku)* scatter; sprinkle; give (someone) the slip.
⁴水 *ma(ki)mizu, sassui, sansui* watering, sprinkling
　水車 *sansuisha* water cart, street sprinkler
⁵布 *sappu suru* spread, scatter, sprinkle. *sampu* scattering; sprinkling; dispersion
¹⁵餌 *makie* scattered food; ground bait

撤 2280 J4531 M12726　B TETSU. *tes(suru)* withdraw; disarm (a ship); dismantle (a fort); remove, reject, exclude.
⁵収 *tesshū* withdrawal
　去 *tekkyo* withdrawal, evacuation, removal
⁶回 *tekkai suru* withdraw, revoke, retract, relinquish, forgo, repeal
⁷兵 *teppei suru* evacuate troops
⁸退 *tettai* withdrawal, evacuation
¹²廃 *teppai* abolition, removal

撫 2281 J496f M12743　BU. *na(deru)* stroke, pat, smooth down.
³子 *nadeshiko* a pink
　下 *na(de)-o(rosu)* stroke down
　上 *na(de)-a(geru)* comb back
⁴切 *nadegi(ri)* killing several with one sweep of the sword; a clean sweep

4

心 忄 小 戈 戸 【手 扌】 支 支 攵 文 斗 斤 方 无 日 曰 月 木 欠 止 歹 殳 毋 比 毛 氏 气 水 氵 氺 火 灬 爪 爫 父 爻 爿 丬 片 牙 牛 犬 犭

²扌

⁵付 *na(de)-tsu(keru)* comb down, smooth down. *nadetsu(ke)* smooth hair, flowing hair

⁸肩 *nadegata* sloping shoulders

育 *buiku* care, tending

¹¹斬 *nadegi(ri)* killing several with one sweep of the sword; a clean sweep

B 撮 2282 J3b23 M12748 SATSU. *tsuma(mu)* pick, pinch; hold in the fingers; summarize. *to(ru)* take (pictures). *tsuma(mi)* knob, (bell) button; pinch (of salt).

⁵出 *tsuma(mi)-da(su)* pick out, drag out, throw out

⁹要 *satsuyō* summary, outline, compendium

¹⁵影 *satsuei* photographing

影所 *satsueijo* studio; movie lot

─────── 13 ───────

B 擁 2294 J4d4a M12781 YŌ. *yō(suru)* embrace, hug; possess; protect; lead.

⁵立 *yōritsu suru* back, support

²⁰護 *yōgo* protection, defense, assistance; indication

A 操 2296 J4160 M12806 SŌ. *ayatsu(ru)* manipulate, operate, steer; pull strings. *ayado(ru)* tie across (the back). *misao* chastity, virginity, constancy, fidelity, honor. ⌐marionette

²人形 *ayatsu(ri) ningyō* puppet;

⁶行 *sōkō* conduct, deportment

⁷作 *sōsa* operation, handling, managing

車 *sōsha* operation (of trains)

車場 *sōshajō* switchyard

⁸典 *sōten* drill manual

¹¹船 *sōsen* controlling a ship

舵 *sōda* steering (of a ship)

¹²短 *sōtan* curtailed operation

¹³業 *sōgyō* operation, work

¹⁴練 *sōren* military exercises, drill

¹⁶縦 *sōjū* management, manipulation, piloting, operation, control, maneuvering, driving, steering

縦士 *sōjūshi* pilot; manipulator; wirepuller; manager

─────── 14 ───────

擢 2303 J4527 M12852 TEKI. TAKU. *nuki(nderu)* excel in, surpass. *nu(ku)* pull out, select.

B 擦 2306 J3b24 M12862 SATSU. *kosu(ru)* rub, scour, scrub, scratch, scrape, brush. *kosu(reru)* be rubbed. *su(ru)* rub, chafe; strike (a match); frost (glass). *su(reru)* rub, chafe, wear; become sophisticated. *nasu(ru)* rub on, smear; blame another. *kasu(reru), kasu(ru)* graze; squeeze; exploit. *suri* frosted, ground. *-zure* bedsores; sophistication.

⁴込 *su(ri)-ko(mu)* rub in, grind and mix

切 *su(ri)-ki(reru)* wear out; *su(ri)-ki(ru)* cut by rubbing; spend all

⁵付 *kosu(ri)-tsu(keru), su(ri)-tsu(keru)* rub on, rub against; strike (a match), rub hard. *nasu(ri)-tsu(keru)* blame another; rub on, smear

⁶合 *su(re)-a(u)* rub against, chafe, jostle with, be at variance with, quarrel

⁹枯 *sure(k)ka(rashi), sureka(rashi)* sophisticated person

¹⁰剥 *su(ri)-mu(keru)* vi be grazed, be abraded; be chafed. *su(ri)-mu(ku)* vt graze, abrade, chafe

¹¹過傷 *sakkashō* abrasion, scratch

¹²違 *su(ri)-chiga(u), su(re)-chiga(u)* pass each other

¹³傷 *surikizu* scratch, graze, abrasion. *surekizu* marring caused by rubbing

¹⁷擦 *suresure ni* close by; by a shave; barely. *suresure* unfriendly

B 擬 2307 J353c M12870 GI. *gi(suru)* aim (a gun) at; nominate for office; imitate, mimic; compare. *nazora(eru)* pattern after, imitate, liken to. *ni(seru), nise* sham, counterfeit, forgery, imitation. *magai* imitation, sham.

²人化 *gijinka* personification

人法 *gijinhō* personification

⁵古文 *gikobun* classical style

古的 *gikoteki* classical

⁶似 *giji-* suspected, quasi-, pseudo-, sham

⁷声 *gisei* onomotopoeia (for sounds)

⁸宝珠 *giboshi, gibōshu* stone-leek flower, bridge railing-post knob

制 *gisei* legal fiction ⌐background

⁹音 *gion* sound effects, imitation sound,

¹²装 *gisō* camouflage, disguise

[14]態 *gitai* onomotopoeia (for actions).
gitai suru simulate, imitate

──────── 15 ────────

擾 2314 J3e71 M12920 *Jō* disturb, throw into confusion.
[7]乱 *jōran* riot, commotion

──────── 20 ────────

攪 2322 J5978 M13041 KAKU, Kō disturb, throw into confusion.
[7]乱 *kōran, kakuran* disturbance, agitation
[8]拌 *kōhan suru, kakuhan suru* agitate, stir, whip, beat, churn, mix

━━━━ RAD. 支 65 ━━━━

Shi or *eda* branch. Also called *jū-mata* (*jū* "ten" plus *mata* "also").
As enclosure: 支 *shinyō* or *edanyō*. Nickname: Branch.

A 支 2324 J3b59 M13061 SHI branch. *sasa(eru)* support, maintain, sustain, hold; prop, bolster, check, stem. *tsuka(eru)* be obstructed, be blocked, be stopped up, break down, be choked. *ka(u)* prop up. *sasae* prop, fulcrum. -*Shi-* China.
[5]庁 *shichō* government branch office
弁 *shiben* payment, disbursement
出 *shishutsu* expenditure, disbursement
払 *shihara(u)* pay. *shiharai* payment
[6]那 *Shina* China
[7]社 *shisha* branch office
局 *shikyoku* branch office
[8]店 *shiten* branch store, branch office
所 *shisho* branch office, substation
[9]度 *shitaku* preparation, arrangements; costume, dress; trousseau
途 *shito* account for the money spent
柱 *shichū* prop, brace, support, fulcrum, underpinning
点 *shiten* fulcrum, bearing
持 *shiji* support, maintenance
[10]流 *shiryū* tributary, branch
脈 *shimyaku* spur, branch, feeder
部 *shibu* branch office
配 *shihai* management, control, rule, guidance
配人 *shihainin* manager
配層 *shihaisō* the ruling class
[12]援 *shien* aid, support
給 *shikyū* supply, allowance, payment
[13]障 *shishō* obstacle, hindrance; trouble
[15]線 *shisen* branch line, spur
[19]離滅裂 *shirimetsuretsu* incoherence, inconsistency, disruption

━━━━ RAD. 攴 66 ━━━━

Boku strike. Generally called *to-mata* (the katakana *to* plus *mata* "again").
At right: 攵 *bokunyō, bokuzukuri*, or *no-bun* (like Rad. 67 *bun* but with first stroke changed to katakana *no*). Nickname: Folding Chair.

──────── 3 ────────

B 攻 2331 J3936 M13120 Kō . *se(meru)* attack, assault. *se(me)* attack, offensive.
[2]入 *se(me)-i(ru)* invade, raid, rush in to attack, penetrate into
[3]下 *se(me)-kuda(ru)* go down and attack
上 *se(me)-nobo(ru)* go up against, attack
[4]手 *se(me)te* assailant, assaulter; attacking force; offensive
込 *se(me)-ko(mu)* attack and invade
[5]立 *se(me)-ta(teru)* attack incessantly
[6]防 *kōbō* offense and defense
守 *kōshu* offense and defense; batting and fielding
[7]囲 *se(me)-kako(mu)* besiege. *kōi* siege
抜 *se(me)-nu(ku)* successfully storm a castle; attack fiercely
究 *kōkyū* investigation, research

4

心 忄 小 戈 戸 手 扌 支 【支 攵】

³

文 斗 斤 方 无 日 曰 月 木 欠 止 歹 殳 毋 比 毛 氏 气 水 氵 氺 火 灬 爪 爫 父 爻 爿 爿 片 牙 牛 犬 犭

⁸ 取 *se(me)-to(ru)*, *kōshu suru* take by storm, capture
⁹ 城 *kōjō* siege
¹¹ 略 *kōryaku* capture, occupation, invasion
寄 *se(me)-yo(ru)*, *se(me)-yo(seru)* overtake and attack
¹² 落 *se(me)-o(tosu)* take by storm. *kōraku* capturing (a castle)
¹³ 滅 *se(me)-horo(bosu)* attack and overthrow; utterly destroy; subdue
勢 *kōsei* offensive, aggression
¹⁵ 撃 *kōgeki suru*, *se(me)-u(tsu)* attack and crush, cut down. *kōgeki* attack, assault, raid; criticism, denunciation
撃的 *kōgekiteki* aggressive, offensive

改 $\frac{2332}{\text{J327e}}$ KAI. *arata(meru)* change, M13114 modify, convert; renew, renovate; reform, mend, rectify; amend, revise, improve; examine, inspect, search. *arata(maru)* be renewed, be renovated; change, be modified, be revised; be improved, be reformed; be ceremonious. *arata(mete)* again, anew, formally.
A
⁴ 元 *kaigen* change of the era
心 *kaishin* conversion; reform
⁵ 札 *kaisatsu* ticket examination
札口 *kaisatsuguchi* ticket gate
正 *arata(me)-tada(su)* revise. *kaisei* revision, amendment; improvement, amelioration
⁶ 行 *kaigyō suru* begin new line
名 *kaimei* changing a name
⁷ 良 *kairyō* improvement, reform
⁸ 姓 *kaisei* changing a family name
版 *kaihan* revised edition
定 *kaitei* reform
宗 *kaishū* conversion (to another faith); proselytism
⁹ 変 *kaihen* change, innovation, reformation, transformation
革 *kaikaku* reform, reformation
造 *kaizō* remodeling, reconstruction
訂 *kaitei* revision ⌜works
¹⁰ 修 *kaishū* repair, improvement, (riparian)
悛 *kaishun* penitence, repentance
悟 *kaigo* repentance
称 *kaishō suru* rename, retitle
進 *kaishin* reform; progress
¹¹ 組 *kaiso* reorganization
悪 *kaiaku* change for the worse, deterioration

訳 *kaiyaku* retranslation, revision
¹² 廃 *kaihai* reorganization, change
善 *kaizen* reform, improvement, amelioration
装 *kaisō* remodeling, modernization
¹³ 新 *kaishin* renovation, innovation, reformation
¹⁴ 選 *kaisen* re-election
¹⁵ 編 *kaihen* reorganization
¹⁶ 築 *kaichiku* rebuilding, remodeling
¹⁸ 竄 *kaizan* falsification, mutilation, alteration; correction, amendment, revision
題 *kaidai* retitling

5

放 $\frac{2333}{\text{J4a7c}}$ HŌ . *hana(tsu)* set free, M13133 release, fire, shoot; circulate (rumors); emit, give out; set fire to; banish. *hana(su)* let go, release, disengage; liberate. *hana(reru)* free oneself from. *hō(ru)* throw, hurl, toss; give up; neglect; let alone. *ho(ttarakasu)* neglect, leave undone, lay aside.
A
³ 上 *hō(ri)-a(geru)* hurl up ⌜mind
⁴ 心 *hōshin* absentmindedness; peace of
水 *hōsui* drainage, discharge
水路 *hōsuiro* drainage canal
火 *hōka* arson, incendiarism
⁵ 生 *hōjō* setting (birds) free
出 *hō(ri)-da(su)* throw out; dismiss, fire; throw up (a job). *hōshutsu* release, discharge, exhaust
⁶ 任 *hōnin* nonintervention
⁷ 言 *hōgen* irresponsible talk
尿 *hōnyō* urination
屁 *hōhi* breaking wind, passing gas
技 *hana(re)waza* a grand work
⁸ 念 *hōnen* relaxation, ease
免 *hōmen* release, acquittal
物線 *hōbutsusen* parabola
牧 *hōboku* grazing, pasturage
送 *hōsō* broadcasting
送局 *hōsōkyoku* broadcasting station
⁹ 逐 *hōchiku suru* expel, banish, deport; dismiss
神 *hōshin* freedom from care. *hōshin suru* be dumbfounded
胆 *hōtan* fearlessness
¹⁰ 逸 *hōitsu* self-indulgence, debauchery

埒 *hōratsu* dissipation, debauchery

校 *hōkō* expulsion from school

恣 *hōshi* self-indulgence

流 *hōryū suru* stock (with fish), let loose

浪 *hōrō* wandering

射 *hōsha* emanation, radiation, emission, discharge

射性 *hōshasei* radioactive

射性同位元素 *hōshasei dōi genso* radioisotope

射能 *hōshanō* radioactivity, radiation

射線 *hōshasen* radiation

¹² 散 *hōsan* radiation; emanation; diffusion; evaporation

¹³ 飼 *hana(chi)ga(i), hana(shi)ga(i)* grazing, pasturage

棄 *hōki* abandonment, resignation, renunciation, waiving

置 *hōchi suru* leave alone, neglect, let lie

電 *hōden* electric discharge

¹⁴ 漫 *hōman* recklessness, laxity, indiscretion

歌 *hōka* loud singing

歌高吟 *hōka kōgin* loud singing

¹⁵ 談 *hōdan* irresponsible talk; chat

課後 *hōkago* after school

熱 *hōnetsu* radiation; radiant heat

熱器 *hōnetsuki* radiator

蕩 *hōtō* dissipation, prodigality

¹⁶ 縦 *hōjū, hōshō* self-indulgence, debauchery

¹⁷ 擲 *hōteki suru* abandon, give up, neglect

¹⁸ 題 *-hōdai* at will, to one's heart's content

故 A ²³³⁴ J384e M13161 **Ko.** *yue* reason, cause; circumstances. *yue ni* therefore, consequently. *kotosara ni* especially, intentionally. *furu(i)* old, aged, ancient, antiquated; stale, threadbare; outmoded, obsolete article. *ko-* the late.

² 人 *kojin* the deceased; an old friend. *furubito* the ancients; elderly persons; longtime residents

⁵ 旧 *kokyū* old acquaintance

⁶ 老 *korō* old people, seniors

宅 *kotaku* old home, former home

⁷ 里 *furusato, kori* hometown, birthplace ⌜country

⁸ 国 *kokoku* one's native land; an old

知 *kochi* an old acquaintance; an old intimacy

制 *kosei* former laws; the old system

京 *kokyō* old capital

実 *kojitsu* ancient customs

事 *koji* origin; historical fact; tradition

事来歴 *koji-raireki* origin and history; particulars

¹⁰ 郷 *kokyō* birthplace, homeland, hometown

¹¹ 道 *kodō* the old morality; an old road

¹³ 意 *koi* intention, purpose; bad faith

障 *koshō* hindrance, obstacle; difficulty; breakdown; accident; objection

---

政 A ²³³⁵ J402f M13135 **SHŌ . SEI.** *matsurigoto* government, rule.

⁵ 庁 *seichō* government office

令 *seirei* government ordinance, cabinet order

⁶ 争 *seisō* political controversy

⁷ 見 *seiken* political views

局 *seikyoku* political situation

体 *seitai* form of government, polity

⁸ 況 *seikyō* political situation

事 *seiji* political affairs; administrative business

府 *seifu* the government, the administration

治 *seiji* government, administration, politics

治的 *seijiteki* political

治家 *seijika* politician, statesman

治運動 *seiji undō* political campaign, political agitation

治結社 *seiji kessha* political organization

⁹ 変 *seihen* political change, change of government

界 *seikai* political world, political circles

¹⁰ 党 *seitō* political party

党政治 *seitō seiji* party government

¹¹ 情 *seijō* political conditions

商 *seishō* businessman with political ties

経学 *seikeigaku* politics and economics

務 *seimu* political affairs, affairs of state

務次官 *seimu-jikan* parliamentary vice-minister

教分離 *seikyō bunri* separation of Church and State, disestablishment of a church

略 *seiryaku* statecraft, political strategy; expedient

¹² 策 *seisaku* policy; political measures

4

心 忄 小 戈 戸 手 扌 支

【支攵】

5

文 斗 斤 方 无 日 曰 月 木 欠 止 歹 殳 毋 比 毛 氏 气 水 氵 氺 火 灬 爪 爫 父 爻 爿 丬 片 牙 牛 犬 犭

---

¹⁴ 綱 *seikō* political creed; political platform
¹⁵ 論 *seiron* politics, political discussion
敵 *seiteki* political opponent
権 *seiken* political power; reins of government, administration
談 *seidan* a talk on politics or a law case
談演説 *seidan enzetsu* political speech, campaign speech

――――― 6 ―――――

敏 $\frac{2337}{\text{J4952}}$ Bin agility; alertness. *hashiko(i)*, *hashi(k)ko(i)*
B M13202 clever; agile.

⁹ 速 *binsoku* quickness, agility, activity
活 *binkatsu* quickness, agility, activity
¹¹ 捷 *binshō* agility, promptness, shrewdness
¹² 腕 *binwan* ability, capacity
¹³ 感 *binkan* sensitivity, susceptibility

――――― 7 ―――――

敗 $\frac{2343}{\text{J4754}}$ Hai defeat, reversal. *yabu(ru)* vt defeat.
A M13227 *yabu(reru)* vi be defeated.

⁵ 北 *haiboku* defeat, reversal, rout
⁶ 色 *haishoku* omens of defeat
因 *haiin* cause of defeat
死 *haishi suru* be defeated and killed
血症 *haiketsushō* blood poisoning
⁷ 走 *haisō* rout, flight
兵 *haihei* routed troops
⁸ 退 *haitai* defeat, retreat
者 *haisha* the defeated
⁹ 軍 *haigun* defeated army
¹⁰ 将 *haishō* defeated general
残 *haizan* survival after defeat; decline; ruin. *haizan no* defeated, vanquished
¹² 訴 *haiso* lost case; losing a case
報 *haihō* news of defeat
¹³ 戦 *haisen* defeat, a lost battle

救 $\frac{2344}{\text{J355f}}$ Kyū. *suku(u)* save, help,
A M13221 rescue, relieve (suffering); redeem, reclaim. *suku(i)* salvation, help, rescue, relief.

³ 上 *suku(i)-a(geru)* pick up and rescue, save from
⁴ 手 *suku(i) (no) te* helping hand
⁵ 民 *kyūmin* helping and saving the people

出 *suku(i)-da(su)* help out of (trouble), extricate, rescue from, reclaim (from a life of sin). *kyūshutsu* deliverance, rescue
世主 *Kyūseishu* the Saviour, the Messiah
世軍 *Kyūseigun* Salvation Army
⁶ 米 *kyūmai, suku(i)mai* relief rice
⁷ 助 *kyūjo* rescue, relief, aid
助信号 *kyūjo shingō* SOS, distress signal
⁸ 国 *kyūkoku* national salvation
命 *kyūmei* lifesaving
命具 *kyūmeigu* life preserver
⁹ 神 *suku(i) (no) kami* a special providence
恤 *kyūjutsu* relief, aid
急 *kyūkyū* deliverance in an emergency
急処置 *kyūkyū shochi* applying first aid
急車 *kyūkyūsha* ambulance
急箱 *kyūkyūbako* first-aid kit
¹¹ 貧 *kyūhin* poor relief
済 *kyūsai* relief, aid; emancipation; salvation; rescue
¹² 援 *kyūen* relief, rescue, reinforcement
¹⁸ 難 *kyūnan* rescue, salvage
²⁰ 護 *kyūgo* relief, rescue

教 $\frac{2345}{\text{J3635}}$ Kyō faith. *oshi(eru)*
A M13213 teach, give lessons; inform; coach. *oso(waru)* learn, be taught, take lessons in. *oshi(e)* teaching; lesson; precept; doctrine, tenet; creed, faith; religion; philosophy.

³ 子 *oshi(e)go* pupil, disciple
⁴ 込 *oshi(e)-ko(mu)* inculcate, implant
化 *kyōka* culture, education; civilization; evangelization
⁵ 示 *kyōji* instruction, teaching
本 *kyōhon* textbook
⁶ 団 *kyōdan* religious body, a religious order
会 *kyōkai* church; church building
会堂 *kyōkaidō* church, chapel, cathedral, tabernacle
⁷ 材 *kyōzai* teaching materials
戒 *kyōkai* exhortation, preaching
⁸ 知 *oshi(e)-shi(raseru)* inform, teach
官 *kyōkan* educational official; public school teacher; national university professor
具 *kyōgu* teaching tools, teaching aids

典 *kyōten* canon, sacred scriptures of a religion; teaching guide

学 *kyōgaku* education, educational affairs

育 *kyōiku* education

育界 *kyōikukai* educational circles

育勅語 *Kyōiku Chokugo* Imperial Rescript on Education

育費 *kyōikuhi* school expenses; educational fund

育課程 *kyōiku katei* course, curriculum

育機関 *kyōiku kikan* educational institutions

9 祖 *kyōso* founder or head of a sect

室 *kyōshitsu* classroom

派 *kyōha* sect, denomination

則 *kyōsoku* teaching rules; school rules

科 *kyōka* lesson; course, curriculum

科書 *kyōkasho* textbook

皇 *kyōō, kyōkō* pope

10 徒 *kyōto* believer, adherent ⌈plan

案 *kyōan* teaching program, teaching

師 *kyōshi* teacher, minister, rabbi, missionary

唆 *kyōsa* instigation

訓 *kyōkun* lesson, precept, moral, instruction

員 *kyōin* teacher; faculty

11 務 *kyōmu* school affairs; religious affairs

習 *kyōshū* training, instruction

授 *kyōju* teaching; professor

理 *kyōri* doctrine, tenet, creed, dogma

12 程 *kyōtei* teaching method

13 義 *kyōgi* doctrine, tenet, creed, dogma

14 練 *kyōren* military drill

導 *oshi(e)-michibi(ku)* instruct and guide

誨 *kyōdō* instruction, training

誨 *kyōkai* exhortation, preaching

誨師 *kyōkaishi* prison chaplain, prison missionary

15 課 *kyōka* a course; a textbook

範 *kyōhan* teaching methods; model teaching; textbooks

養 *kyōyō* culture, education, refinement

養学科 *kyōyō gakka* liberal arts

16 壇 *kyōdan* rostrum, platform

頭 *kyōtō* head teacher; vice principal

18 鞭 *kyōben* a teacher's whip; teaching school

職 *kyōshoku* teaching; ministry, priesthood, clergy

————— 8 —————

敦 ²³⁴⁹ J4658 M13276 TON industry; kindliness.

敢 ²³⁵⁰ J343a M13260 KAN. *ae(nai)* sad, tragic, pitiful; frail, feeble; fleeting; unkind. *ae(te)* positively, daringly.

B

6 行 *kankō* execution, decisive action

12 然 *kanzen to* boldly, fearlessly, bravely

18 闘 *kantō suru* fight bravely. *kantō* determined fighting

敬 ²³⁵¹ J3749 M13285 KEI. KYŌ. *kei(suru)* respect, honor, revere. *uyama(u)* respect, honor, revere, venerate.

A

5 白 *Keihaku* Sincerely yours

礼 *keirei* bow, salutation, salute

6 仰 *keigyō suru* respect, revere

老 *keirō* respect for the aged

服 *keifuku suru* admire and respect

具 *keigu* Sincerely yours

10 称 *keishō* title of honor

虔 *keiken* piety, devotion, reverence

12 遠 *keien suru* keep (a person) at a distance; give (a batter) a walk; kick (a person) upstairs

13 愛 *keiai* respect and affection

意 *keii* respect, honor

14 語 *keigo* honorific word

慕 *keibo* love and respect

20 譲 *keijō suru* respect; take a humble attitude

散 ²³⁵² J3b36 M13265 SAN. *san(jiru), san(zuru)* scatter, disperse; spend; squander; dispel, dissipate, chase away. *bara(su)* pull down; take apart; sell (to get rid of); liquidate; defeat; expose. *chi(ru)* fall, scatter, be scattered, be shed; disperse; (rumor) spreads; run, spread, blur. *chi(rasu)* scatter; disperse; dissipate (fog); dispel; take down or loosen (the hair); rout; distribute (handbills); distract (attention); splash on (a pattern). *chi(rakasu)* scatter (around), disarrange, leave untidy. *chi(rakaru)* lie scattered around, be in disorder. *chi(rabaru)* scatter, be scattered (about), lie around. *chi(rashi)* handbill, leaflet. *bara* bulk. *-san* (medicinal) powder.

A

4 水 *sansui* water sprinkling

4

心 忄 小 戈 戸 手 扌 支 【攴 攵】 文 斗 斤 方 无 日 曰 月 木 欠 止 歹 殳 毋 比 毛 氏 气 水 氵 氺 火 灬 爪 爫 父 爻 爿 丬 片 牙 牛 犬 犭

文 *sambun* prose
文的 *sambunteki* prosaic
文詩 *sambunshi* poetry in prose
布 *sampu* scattering; sprinkling; dispersion
⁶ 会 *sankai* adjournment
在 *sanzai suru* be scattered, straggle, be dotted with
⁷ 見 *sanken suru* be seen here and there
佚 *san'itsu suru* get scattered and lost
乱 *chi(ri)-mida(reru)* disperse in all directions, be scattered around. *sanran* dispersion, scattering
⁸ 歩 *sampo* walk, stroll
⁹ 発 *sampatsu* scattered shots; scattered hits
¹⁰ 逸 *san'itsu suru* get scattered and lost
財 *sanzai* expense, wasted of money, extravagance, spree
書 *chi(rashi)ga(ki)* irregular writing; writing on alternate lines; writing on odds and ends of paper
華 *sange* Buddhist flower-scattering ceremony. *sange suru* die a heroic death
¹¹ 掛 *chi(ri)-ka(karu)* begin to fall; fall on (something)
¹² 開 *sankai* deployment (of skirmishers)
弾 *sandan, baradama* shot, case shot
散 *sanzan, sanza(ppara)* severely, harshly, terribly; thoroughly, utterly. *chi(ri)chi(ri), chi(ri)ji(ri)* sporadically, separately
策 *sansaku* walk, stroll
¹³ 蓮華 *chi(ri)renge* porcelain spoon
¹⁴ 漫 *samman na* vague, desultory, distracted
模様 *chi(rashi) moyō* scattered pattern
髪屋 *sampatsuya* barber
¹⁵ 敷 *chi(ri)-shi(ku)* lie scattered
¹⁶ 積 *barazu(mi)* bulk shipment
薬 *san'yaku* powdered medicine. *chi(rashi)gusuri* a cure-all medicine

━━━━━━ 9 ━━━━━━

A 数 ²³⁵³ J3174 M13319 SAKU. SOKU. SU. SŪ strenght; fate; law; numbers, figures; numerical. *kazo(eru)* count, calculate, enumerate. *kazu* number, figure. *kazu(naranu)* insignificant, humble. *shibashiba* often,

frequently. *sū-* several.
² 人 *sūnin* several people
十 *sūjū* scores (of people)
³ 子 *kazu(no)ko* herring roe
万 *sūman* tens of thousands
千 *sūsen* thousands
上 *kazo(e)-a(geru)* count up, enumerate
ヶ所 *sūkasho* several places
⁴ 切 *kazo(e)-ki(renai), kazo(e)-ki(renu)* countless, incalculable
分間 *sūfunkan* a few minutes
日 *sūjitsu* a few days, several days
⁵ 立 *kazo(e)-ta(teru)* count up, enumerate
台 *sūdai* several vehicles
⁶ 行 *sūgyō, sūkō* several lines
回 *sūkai* several times
百 *sūhyaku* several hundred
年 *sūnen* several years. *kazo(e)doshi* Japanese age
名 *sūmei* several people
多 *amata, sūta* many, multitude. *kazu ō(ku)* in great numbers
字 *sūji* figure, numeral; tabular matter
⁸ 限無 *kazukagi(ri)na(ku)* numberless
奇 *suki* fancy, artistic taste; refined arts. colorfulness; varied fortunes. *sūki na* unlucky
学 *sūgaku* mathematics
⁹ 度 *sūdo* several times
秒 *sūbyō* several seconds
¹⁰ 個 *sūko* several (objects)
倍 *sūbai* several times as (large)
値 *sūchi* numerical value
珠 *juzu, zuzu* a string of beads; a (Buddhist) rosary
¹¹ 寄 *suki* fancy, artistic taste; refined arts.
寄屋 *sukiya* tea-ceremony parlor; detached tea-ceremony house
理 *sūri* mathematical principle; mathematics
¹² 渡 *kazo(e)-wata(su)* count out (things)
詞 *sūshi* numeral
量 *sūryō* quantity, volume
¹³ 数 *kazukazu* many
¹⁴ 種 *sūshu* several kinds
種類 *sūshurui* several kinds
¹⁵ 億 *sūoku* hundreds of millions

━━━━━━ 11 ━━━━━━

B 敷 ²³⁵⁷ J495f M13359 FU. *shi(ku)* spread; pave; sit (on a cushion); lay

(a railway); gravel (a road); promulgate; draw up. *shi(ki)* (flower) stand; deposit money.

⁵ 瓦 *shi(ki)gawara* floor tile
皮 *shi(ki)gawa* fur cushion, bearskin, etc.
石 *shi(ki)ishi* paving stone, flagstone, pavement
台 *shi(ki)dai* step or platform in an entranceway; slatted removable floor in an entrance hall
布 *shikifu* (bed) sheet, sheeting
布団 *shikibuton* the lower futon
⁶ 地 *shikichi* site
⁸ 金 *shikikin* deposit money
居 *shikii* threshold, doorsill
物 *shikimono* carpet, rug, matting, cushion
¹⁰ 島 *Shikishima* (ancient) Japan
¹¹ 設 *fusetsu* construction, laying (a railroad, mine, etc.)
¹³ 詰 *shi(ki)-tsu(meru)* cover over, spread all over
蒲団 *shi(ki)buton* the lower futon

敵 ²³⁵⁹ / J4528 / M13354 TEKI enemy, foe, opponent. *teki(suru)* turn against, fight against, antagonize, be a match for. *kataki* enemy; competitor; revenge.

⁴ 中 *tekichū* midst of the enemy
⁶ 地 *tekichi* enemy territory
同士 *katakidōshi* mutual enemies
⁷ 役 *katakiyaku, tekiyaku* villain's role
兵 *tekihei* enemy troops
対 *tekitai* hostility, antagonism, contention
対心 *tekitaishin* hostility, enmity, animosity
⁸ 味方 *teki-mikata* friend or foe; opposing forces
国 *tekikoku, tekkoku* enemy's country
性 *tekisei* enemy character
⁹ 陣 *tekijin* enemy camp, enemy position
軍 *tekigun* enemy army

前 *tekizen* before the enemy
¹⁰ 討 *katakiu(chi)* vengeance, revenge
¹¹ 情 *tekijō* enemy movements the condition of the enemy
視 *tekishi suru* regard with hostility; show enmity toward. *tekishi* hostility, enmity
¹³ 意 *tekii* hostility, animosity
勢 *tekizei* enemy strength
愾心 *tekigaishin* hostility, enmity, animosity
¹⁵ 影 *tekiei* signs of the enemy
²² 襲 *tekishū* enemy attack

--- **12** ---

整 ²³⁶⁰ / J4030 / M13394 SEI arranging. *totono(eru)* prepare, arrange; fill (orders); supply; raise (money); put in order, tidy up, adjust (clothes); regulate; settle; purchase. *totono(u)* be prepared, be arranged, be in order, be adjusted, be well regulated; be settled.

⁶ 地 *seichi* land readjustment; soil preparation
列 *seiretsu* array, lineup, parade
合 *seigō* adjustment, coordination; integration; consolidation; conformity (in geology)
⁷ 形 *seikei* plastic surgery
¹⁰ 骨 *seikotsu* osteopathy, bone-setting
¹¹ 理 *seiri* arrangement, adjustment, regulation, consolidation; liquidation, reorganization; retrenchment, curtailment, shake-up, abridgement
¹² 備 *seibi* complete equipment; consolidation
然 *seizen(taru)* orderly, regular, systematic, trim, accurate, well-organized
¹³ 数 *seisū* integer, whole number
頓 *seiton* (good) order, arrangement, regulation

━━━ RAD. **文** 67 ━━━

Bun literature. Nickname: Literary.

文 ²³⁶⁴ / J4a38 / M13450 MON ¹⁄₁₀₀ of a *hyakume*; crest; figures; = BUN. BUN

literary text, production, composition; sentence; style; literature, art; the pen;

4
心 忄 小 戈 戸 手 扌 支 攵 【文】° 斗 斤 方 无 日 曰 月 木 欠 止 歹 毋 比 毛 氏 气 水 氵 氺 火 灬 爪 爫 父 爻 爿 丬 片 牙 牛 犬 犭

4

心 忄 小 ⺍ 戈 戶 手 扌 支 攴 【文】 ⁰【文】 斗 斤 方 无 日 曰 月 木 欠 止 歹 殳 毋 比 毛 氏 气 水 氵 氺 火 灬 爪 爫 父 爻 爿 丬 片 牙 牛 犬 犭

civil affairs; decoration; characters; elegance. *aya* design; figure of speech; plan, plot. *fumi* letter, note. *-mon* size (of tabi).

² 人 *bunjin* a writer, the literati
³ 才 *bunsai* literary talent
　士 *bunshi* a writer, the literati
⁴ 月 *fuzuki, fumizuki* seventh lunar month
　中 *bunchū* in the document
　化 *bunka* culture, civilization
　化的 *bunkateki* cultural
　化財 *bunkazai* cultural assets
⁵ 民 *bummin* civilian
　句 *monku* phrase, expression; complaint; objection; excuse
　句無 *monkuna(shi)* perfect, satisfactory
⁶ 臣 *bunshin* civil official
　名 *bummei* literary fame
　字 *moji, monji* letter, character; writings
　字盤 *mojiban* dial, clock face
⁷ 言 *bungen, mongon* phrase, expression
　体 *buntai* literary style
　芸 *bungei* liberal arts, literary arts, learning
　芸批評 *bungei hihyō* literary criticism
　芸復興 *bungei fukkō* renaissance, revival of learning
⁸ 例 *bunrei* model sentence; model for writing
　物 *bumbutsu* civilization
　盲 *mommō* ignorance, illiteracy
　具 *bungu* writing materials, stationery
　典 *bunten* grammar book
　房具 *bumbōgu* writing materials, stationery
　治 *bunchi, bunji* civilian administration
　官 *bunkan* civil official
　武 *bumbu* literary and military arts, the sword and the pen
　法 *bumpō* grammar
　明 *bummei* civilization, culture
　明開化 *bummei-kaika* civilization and enlightenment
　学 *bungaku* literature
　学的 *bungakuteki* literary
　学界 *bungakukai* literary world
　学博士 *Bungaku Hakushi* Doctor of Literature, PhD
⁹ 面 *bummen* contents of a letter
　通 *buntsū* correspondence, communication
　科 *bunka* department of literature;

literary course
¹⁰ 庫 *bunko* hand box, bookcase; library, archives
　脈 *bummyaku* context
　案 *bun'an* draft
　弱 *bunjaku* frivolity, effeminacy
　書 *bunsho, monjo* document, writing, letter, note, archives, literature, correspondence, records
　部大臣 *Mombu Daijin* Education Minister
　部省 *Mombushō* Ministry of Education
¹¹ 鳥 *bunchō* Java sparrow, paddy bird
　運 *bun'un* cultural progress, enlightenment
　責 *bunseki* responsibility for the wording of an article
　理 *bunri* context, line of thought; science and literature
　教 *bunkyō* education, culture
　章 *bunshō* sentence; article, composition; style
¹² 集 *bunshū* anthology, prose collection
　無 *monna(shi) no* penniless
　筆 *bumpitsu* writing, literary art
¹³ 雅 *bunga* elegance, grace (in literature)
　辞 *bunji* the words of a sentence
　飾 *bunshoku* rhetorical flourishes
　意 *bun'i* meaning (of a passage)
　楽 *bunraku* puppet theatre, *Bunraku*
　献 *bunken* literature; records, documents; bibliography
¹⁴ 様 *mon'yō* design; figure of speech; plan, plot
　豪 *bungō* literary master
　選 *bunsen* anthology; typesetting
　語 *bungo* literary language
　語文 *bungobun* literary language
¹⁶ 壇 *bundan* literary circles; literary column
¹⁸ 鎮 *bunchin* paperweight
¹⁹ 藻 *bunsō* rhetorical flourishes; literary talent

——————— 4 ———————

斉 B 斉 ²³⁶⁶ J4046 M13454 SEI. *hito(shii)* equal, similar. *totono(eru)* prepare, arrange, fill (orders); supply; raise (money); put in order, tidy up, adjust (clothes); regulate; settle; purchase.
¹ 一 *seiitsu* equality; good order

¹¹ 唱 *seishō suru* sing in unison

---— 6 —---

斎 <u>2368</u> J3a58 / M13467 **SAI**, **SET** Buddhist food; B room. *imi* religious purification. *itsu(ku)* worship, enshrine. *i(mu)* abhor, avoid, taboo, shun. *toki* meals exchanged by parishioners and priests. *hito(shii)* equal, similar, like, equivalent.

⁴ 日 *saijitsu* fast day. *i(mi)bi* unlucky day; death anniversary; purification and fast day

⁷ 戒 *saikai* purification

¹² 場 *saijō* place of ceremony, place of a funeral service

斌 <u>2369</u> J494c / M13468 **HIN** pleasing balance between figure and background. *uruwa(shii)* beautiful, lively, fine.

斐 <u>2370</u> J4865 / M13469 **HI** beautiful; patterned.

斑 <u>2371</u> J4843 / M13470 **HAN** spot. *buchi, madara, hadare* spots, specks, patches. *fu* spot, speck, speckle, stripe, streak. *mura* unevenness, inequality; blemishes; capriciousness.

⁹ 点 *hanten* spot, speck

¹⁰ 紋 *hammon* spot, speck

▬▬▬▬▬ **RAD.** 斗 **68** ▬▬▬▬▬

To or *to masu* (a unit of measure). Also, at right, *tozukuri*. Nickname: Dots and Cross.

斗 <u>2373</u> J454d / M13489 **TO** ten *shō* (1 *to* = 4.8 B gallons (U.S.) = 18 liters); a one-*to* measure; saké ladle; the Big Dipper. *-bakari* approximately; only, merely, alone; degree; almost, practically; absorbed in; continue doing; just now; be about to do; be ready for; have no alternative; now or never. (Also non-standard for 闘 6418 and pronounced Tō.)

⁹ 南 *tonan* south of the Big Dipper; the whole world

¹⁰ 酒 *toshu* a *to* of saké; a big supply of saké

---— 6 —---

料 <u>2374</u> J4e41 / M13501 **Ryō** charge, rate, fee; A allowance; materials; measuring.

⁸ 金 *ryōkin* charge, rate, fee, fare

⁹ 亭 *ryotei* restaurant

¹¹ 理 *ryōri* cooking, cuisine; dish; food; fare; management; administration

理屋 *ryōriya* restaurant

¹⁸ 簡 *ryōken* idea, thought, intention, inclination, motive, decision; discretion; forgiveness; toleration

---— 7 —---

斜 <u>2376</u> J3c50 / M13509 **SHA** slanting, oblique. B *hasu, hasukai* slanting, diagonal, oblique. *nana(me)* slanting, diagonal, oblique, askew; unpleasant, disagreeable. *nana(menarazu)* exceedingly.

⁶ 向 *nana(me)-mu(kō) ni* diagonally across

⁹ 面 *shamen* slope, inclined plane

前 *nana(me)mae* advancing obliquely

巷 *shakō* red-light district

¹¹ 視 *shashi, yabunira(mi)* strabismus, squint (cross-eye or walleye)

陽 *shayō* setting sun

¹⁵ 線 *shasen* oblique line

影 *shaei* slanting shadow

---— 10 —---

斡 <u>2378</u> J3036 / M13522 **ATSU** go around; rule, administer.

¹¹ 旋 *assen* kind offices, mediation

旋人 *assennin* mediator, agent, go-between

旋業 *assengyō* agency; intermediary

Kin (a Japanese pound) or *ono* axe. On right: *onozukuri*. Nickname: Axe.

B 斤 2379 / J3654 / M13534 KIN *kin* 1⅓ pounds, catty; axe.

1

B 斥 2380 / J404d / M13535 SEKI. *shirizo(ku) vi* retreat, recede, withdraw. *shirizo(keru) vt* repel, repulse, reject.
10 候 *sekkō* scout, patrol, spy

4

斧 2382 / J4960 / M13539 FU. *ono* axe, hatchet.

7

斬 2384 / J3b42 / M13555 ZAN beheading. *ki(ru)* kill; cut. *-kiri* murder.
9 首 *zanshu* decapitation. *ki(ri)kubi* decapitation; a severed head
10 殺 *zansatsu suru* slay, kill
13 新 *zanshin* novelty, originality, newness

A 断 2385 / J4347 / M13557 DAN decision, judgment; cutting. *dan(jiru)*, *dan(zuru)* conclude, judge. *ta(tsu)* sever, cut off; shut off, interrupt; abstain from; eradicate; suppress. *kotowa(ru)* decline, refuse; apologize; give notice; warn; dismiss; prohibit. *dan(jite)* positively, decidedly; by no means. *kotowa(ri)* refusal; excuse, apology; notice, warning; permission; prohibition. *(o)kotowa(ri)* not allowed.
4 水 *dansui* suspension of water supply, no water
切 *ta(chi)-ki(ru)* cut off; disconnect; block
片 *dampen* fragment, piece, bit, crumb, odds and ends, shred, scrap
片的 *dampenteki* fragmentary, piecemeal
5 乎 *danko* firm, decisive, resolute, determined, drastic, conclusive
去 *ta(chi)-sa(ru)* cut off, do away with
末魔 *dammatsuma* the hour of death

6 行 *dankō* decisive action, resolute enforcement
交 *dankō* rupture of relations
7 言 *dangen* (positive) assertion, declaration, affirmation
8 固 *danko* firm, decisive, resolute, determined, drastic, conclusive
念 *dannen* abandonment, relinquishment, despairing of
定 *dantei* decision, conclusion
郊競走 *dankōkyōsō* cross-country race
9 食 *danjiki* fast, fasting
面 *dammen* section; cross section
面図 *dammenzu* cross-section drawing
10 案 *dan'an* decision, conclusion
書 *kotowa(ri)ga(ki)* proviso, explanatory note
酒 *danshu* giving up alcohol
11 崖 *dangai* precipice, cliff
章 *danshō* literary fragment
12 絶 *danzetsu* extinction, rupture, severance
割 *ta(chi)-wa(ru)* cut open, cut apart
雲 *dan'un* scattered clouds
然 *danzen* resolutely, decisively, positively, absolutely
裁 *dansai* cutting (paper, etc.)
腸 *danchō* heartbreak
罪 *danzai* conviction, condemnation; decapitation
想 *dansō* random thoughts
続 *danzoku* stopping and starting
続的 *danzokuteki* intermittent, fitful, off and on
14 層 *dansō* (geological) fault, shift, slip
種 *danshu* castration, sterilization
髪 *dampatsu* haircutting; bobbed hair
15 線 *dansen* disconnection, broken wire
16 頭台 *dantōdai* guillotine
18 簡 *dankan* fragmentary documents

8

斯 2386 / J3b5b / M13563 SHI this. *ka(karu)* such. *ka(ku)*, *ka(kute)*, *ka(kushite)* thus, in this way. *kō* thus, so, like this, in

this way. *kō to* a word filling in awkward spaces in conversation. *ka(no)* that.

⁶ 如 *ka(ku) no goto(ku)* thus. *ka(ku) no goto(ki)* such (a)

⁷ 言 *kō i(u)* this kind of, such

⁹ 界 *shikai* this field (of medicine), this circle (of experts), this society

¹¹ 道 *shidō* profession, line, craft; field

¹⁴ 様 *kayō na* such

───────── 9 ─────────

新 $\frac{2387}{\text{J3f37}}$ SHIN newness, novelty.
A   M13572 *atara(shii)* new, novel, fresh, recent, modern. *atara(shigaru)* be fond of. *ara(ta) ni suru* make new. *ara-, ara(tana)* new, fresh, novel. *ara, sara* newness; something new. *nii-* new, *shin-* new, modern, novel, fresh, neo-.

² 人 *shinjin* new face; new star; man of advanced ideas

人類 *shinjinrui* new breed (of young person)

入 *shinnyū* new, incoming, entering

³ 大陸 *shintairiku* new continent; New World

⁴ 手 *arate* new move, new form, new trick; reinforcements

月 *shingetsu* new moon, crescent moon

天地 *shintenchi* the new world

⁵ 田 *arata, shinden* new rice field

古 *shinko* new and old

出 *shinshutsu* new appearance

旧 *shinkyū* new and old; incoming and outgoing

刊 *shinkan* new publication

世代 *shinsedai* new era

世界 *shinsekai* new world; the New World

生 *shinsei* new life; new birth, rebirth, regeneration; reincarnation

生児 *shinseiji* newborn baby

⁶ 米 *shimmai* new rice; novice, beginner, newcomer

式 *shinshiki* a new form; a new formula

曲 *shinkyoku* new tune, new musical composition

任 *shinnin* new appointment

年 *Shinnen* New Year

⁷ 車 *shinsha* new car   ⌈book

作 *shinsaku* a new production, a new

形 *shingata* new style

来 *shinrai* newcomer

局面 *shinkyokumen* new aspect

体 *shintai* new style

体制 *shintaisei* new system, new structure

⁸ 居 *shinkyo* new residence, new home

味 *shimmi* fresh taste, freshness; novelty

宗教 *shinshūkyō* new religion

所帯 *shinjotai, arajotai* a new home

法 *shimpō* new method; new law

奇 *shinki* novelty, originality

芽 *shimme* sprout, bud, shoot

妻 *niizuma* bride, young wife

学期 *shingakki* new school term

版 *shimpan* new publication

郎 *shinrō* bridegroom

郎新婦 *shinrō shimpu* the bride and bridegroom

参者 *shinzanmono* newcomer, novice

事実 *shinjijitsu* new facts

事業 *shinjigyō* new enterprise

⁹ 風 *shimpū* new style

香 *shinko, shinkō* pickled vegetables, (Japanese) pickles

柄 *shingara* new pattern

派 *shimpa* new school (of thought); new-style kabuki

秋 *shinshū* early autumn

盆 *niibon* first *Bon* festival after death

前 *shimmae, shimmai* novice, beginner, newcomer

星 *shinsei* a nova; a new star; a new movie star

茶 *shincha* first tea of the season

型 *shingata* new style

造 *shinzō* new construction; new wife; single young lady

約聖書 *Shin'yaku Seisho* the New Testament

訂 *shintei* new revision

春 *Shinshun* the New Year

品 *shimpin* new article

発見 *shinhakken* new discovery

発足 *shinhossoku* new start

発明 *shinhatsumei* recent invention

¹⁰ 進 *shinshin no* rising (scholar), up-and-coming (leader)

造 *shinzō, shinzo* new construction; new wife; single young lady

案 *shin'an* new idea, new design, novelty, new departure

4

心 忄 小 戈 戸 手 扌 支 攴 文 斗 斤 〔方〕 无 日 曰 月 木 欠 止 歹 殳 毋 比 毛 氏 气 水 氵 氺 火 灬 爪 爫 父 爻 爿 丬 片 牙 牛 犬 犭

党 *shintō* new political party
書 *shinsho* new book
記録 *shinkiroku* new record
陳代謝 *shinchintaisha* renewal, replacement, regeneration; metabolism
11 婦 *shimpu* bride
設 *shinsetsu* new organization
規 *shinki* novelty, originality, new, newly created
教 *Shinkyō* Protestantism
婚 *shinkon* new marriage; newly married
12 装 *shinsō* new garb; new equipment; new binding; new finish
開地 *shinkaichi* reclaimed land, newly opened land
着 *shinchaku* new arrivals
13 傾向 *shinkeikō* new trend
14 暦 *shinreki* new calendar; solar calendar
選 *shinsen* newly elected; newly compiled
種 *shinshu* new species
緑 *shinryoku* fresh verdure
説 *shinsetsu* new theory
語 *shingo* new word
境地 *shinkyōchi* a new area; a new field of endeavor
製品 *shinseihin* new products

聞 *shimbun* newspaper
聞広告 *shimbun kōkoku* newspaper advertising
聞社 *shimbunsha* newspaper company
聞紙 *shimbunshi* newspapers
聞記者 *shimbun kisha* journalist, reporter
15 劇 *shingeki* new drama; new school of acting
編 *shimpen* new edition
鋭 *shin'ei* freshly picked, newly produced; newly built
趣向 *shinshukō* new idea; novel device; novelty; originality
16 館 *shinkan* new building, annex
機軸 *shinkijiku* new device; new departure; new idea
築 *shinchiku* new building, new construction
興 *shinkō* new, rising, newly established, newly awakened
興勢力 *shinkō seiryoku* resurgence of power
17 鮮 *shinsen* freshness
18 顔 *shingao* newcomer, new face
19 羅 *Shiragi* the ancient Korean kingdom of Silla

RAD. 方 70

Hō direction or *kata* side, person. On left: *hōhen* or *kata hen*. Nickname: Direction.

A 方 2389 J4a7d M13620 *Hō* direction, way; side; part; square; way, method, means, scheme, process. *kata* direction; settlement; person. *masa(ni)* right now. *-gata* type, style. *-kata* manner, method, fashion; side, party; toward (evening); person in charge; care of. *-e* direction; location; time. *(ni) ata(ri)* at the time of.

3 丈 *hōjō* ten feet square; superior priest's quarters; chief priest of a temple
寸 *hōsun* square *sun*; one's ideas; one's object
4 方 *katagata* people, persons; everywhere; this and that; any way. *hōbō* every direction, everywhere
今 *hōkon* the present time
5 正 *hōsei* contract, behavior, moral character

6 舟 *hakobune* an ark; (Noah's) ark; the ark (of the covenant)
式 *hōshiki* formula; form; method, system; formalities, usage
向 *hōkō* direction, bearings, course, line, destination, aim
向板 *hōkōban* destination sign
向舵 *hōkōda* rudder
向探知機 *hōkō tanchiki* radar
7 角 *hōgaku* direction, quarter
言 *hōgen* dialect; provincialism
形 *hōkei* square
位 *hōi* direction, course
8 法 *hōhō* way, method, means, scheme, process
9 面 *hōmen* direction, way; side; district; sphere; line; phase
途 *hōto* means, way

便 *hōben* expedient, means, instrument

10 針 *hōshin* magnetic needle; course, policy, plan, principle, purpose

案 *hōan* plan, program

11 術 *hōjutsu* art, method, magic

略 *hōryaku* plan, scheme, program

眼紙 *hōganshi* graph paper

12 策 *hōsaku* plan, policy

程式 *hōteishiki* equation

------- 4 -------

於 2390 J3177 M13628 O. *(ni) oi(te)* at, in, on, as for, as to. *(ni) o(keru)* at, in.

------- 5 -------

施 B 2391 J3b5c M13629 SHI. SE. *hodoko(su)* give alms; conduct (educational work); carry out; administer (first aid); apply (bandages); perform (an operation). *hodoko(shi)* alms, almsgiving.

3 工 *shikō suru, sekō suru* carry out, execute, operate

与 *hodoko(shi)-ata(eru)* give alms. *seyo* charity

5 主 *seshu* chief mourner; donor, benefactor

6 行 *shikō suru* execute, carry out. *segyō suru* give alms

8 物 *hodoko(shi)mono* alms, almsgiving

肥 *sehi* fertilization, manuring

9 政 *shisei* government, administration, statesmanship

政方針 *shisei hōshin* party line; the administration program

11 設 *shisetsu* institution, establishment; equipment, facilities

12 策 *shisaku* a policy, a measure

17 療 *seryō* free medical tratment

旅 A 2396 J4e39 M-X RYO journey; go around. *tabi* journey. *tabi suru* make a trip.

2 人 *tabibito, ryojin* traveler, wayfarer

4 中 *ryochū* on a journey

支度 *tabijitaku* journey preparation; traveling outfit

5 用 *ryoyō* traveling expenses

立 *tabida(tsu)* set out on a trip.

tabida(chi) departure

6 回 *tabimawa(ri)* touring

団 *ryodan* brigade

先 *tabisaki* destination; place of sojourn. *tabisaki de* while traveling

行 *ryokō* travel, trip, journey

行先 *ryokōsaki* destination

行者 *ryokōsha* traveler, tourist

行案内 *ryokō annai* guidebook; itinerary

7 住 *tabizuma(i)* one's stopping place on a trip

芸人 *tabi geinin* itinerant player

8 枕 *tabimakura* sleeping away from home; journey

舎 *ryosha* hotel, inn

空 *tabi (no) sora* strange land

券 *ryoken* passport

9 姿 *tabi sugata* traveling outfit

客 *ryokaku, ryokyaku* traveler, passenger, tourist

客機 *ryokakki* passenger plane

10 烏 *tabigarasu* one who is always traveling

11 情 *ryojō* travel weariness

宿 *tabiyado, ryoshuku* hotel

商人 *tabi shōnin* peddler, commercial traveler

12 程 *ryotei* distance, journey

費 *ryohi* traveling expenses

装 *ryosō* traveling outfit

13 路 *tabiji* journey

愁 *ryoshū* lonesomeness on a journey

16 館 *ryokan* hotel

22 籠 *hatago* inn

族 A 2399 J4232 M13661 ZOKU family, relatives, clan, tribe, race. *yakara* family, relatives; party, colleagues, gang.

8 長 *zokuchō* patriarch, chief, family head

制 *zokusei* patriarchal family system

10 称 *zokushō* family-rank designation

党 *zokutō* companions

旋 B 2400 J407b M13656 SEN go around.

4 毛 *tsumuji, semmō* a whirl of hair on the head; a cowlick

6 回 *senkai* revolution, rotation, turning, circling

4

心 忄 小 戈 戸 手 扌 支 攴 攵 文 斗 斤 方 【旡】 日 日 月 木 欠 止 歹 殳 毋 比 毛 氏 气 水 氵 氺 火 灬 爪 爫 父 爻 爿 丬 片 牙 牛 犭

⁹風 *sempū, tsumujikaze* whirlwind
律 *senritsu* melody
¹⁵盤 *semban* lathe

—————— **10** ——————

旗 A 2402 J347a M13687 KI. *hata* flag, banner, standard, ensign, pennant, streamer.
³下 *kika, hatashita* beneath the banner.
⁴手 *kishu* standard bearer
日 *hatabi* national holiday
⁵本 *hatamoto* a vassal directly under the shogun
⁶色 *hatairo* tide of war; outlook. *kishoku* flag, banner; one's attitude, one's stand

印 *hatajirushi* flag, banner; one's attitude, one's stand
⁹持 *hatamo(chi)* standard bearer
亭 *kitei* inn, restaurant
竿 *hatazao* flagstaff, flagpole
巻 *hata (o) ma(ku)* surrender, give up
¹⁰振 *hatafu(ri)* flagman; starter; flag wagging
¹¹章 *hatajirushi, kishō* flag mark, ensign; slogan
¹²揚 *hataa(ge)* raising an army; launching a business
¹⁵幟 *kishi* flag, banner; one's attitude, one's stand
¹⁶頭 *hatagashira* top of the flagpole; chief
²⁰艦 *kikan* flagship

■■■■■■ **RAD. 无 71** ■■■■■■
Mu or *nashi* nothing. Also *munyō*. Variants: 无 and 旡 or 无 (5 strokes). Do not confuse with Rad. 92. Nickname: Crooked Heaven (cf. 天 *ten* heaven).

—————— **5** ——————

既 B 2407 J347b M13721 KI. *sude ni, sunde ni* previously; already, long ago; on the point of; actually. *sude ni shite* meanwhile.
⁵刊 *kikan* already published
⁶存 *kizon* existing
成 *kisei* existing, accomplished, completed, established
成事実 *kisei jijitsu* accomplished fact
⁷決因 *kiketsushū* convict, convicted person

⁸定 *kitei* fixed, prearranged already, long ago; on the point of; actually
知 *kichi* (already) known, well-known
往 *kiō* the past
往症 *kiōshō* patient's history
¹¹習 *kishū* already learned
婚 *kikon* already married
得権 *kitokuken* vested interests
設 *kisetsu* already constructed, established, existing
¹⁴製 *kisei* ready-made
製品 *kiseihin* manufactured goods, ready-made goods

■■■■■■ **RAD. 日 72** ■■■■■■
Hi or *nichi* day. At left: *hi hen* or *nichi hen*. Variant: 日. This variant is actually Rad. 73 but, with the exception of the radical character itself, is treated herein as a variant of Rad. 72. Nickname: Sun.

日 A 2410 J467c M13733 JITSU, NICHI, NITSU day; Sunday. *hi* sun; time; day, date. *hi(narazu)* before long, in a few days. *hi niwa* if, in case. *hi(mosugara)* all day long. -*ka* day. -*Nichi*- Japanese.
¹一日 *hihitohi, hiichinichi,* 「day *hi(gana)ichinichi* all day long, day by day

4

² 入 *hi(no)i(ri)* sunset
³ 夕 *nisseki* day and night
干 *hibo(shi)* sun-dried, sun-baked
下 *hi (no) shita ni* under the sun, in the whole world
丸 *Hi(no)maru* the Japanese flag, the ball of the sun, sun flag
⁴ 日 *hi(ni)hi(ni)* daily. *hibi* daily; days. *nichinichi* daily, every day
中 *nitchū* during the day. *hinaka* broad daylight, daytime. *Nitchū* Japan and China
仏 *Nichi-Futsu* Japan and France
月 *jitsugetsu* sun and moon; time, days, years
加 *Nikka* Japan and Canada; Japan and California
収 *nisshū* one day's income
用 *nichiyō* daily use, of daily necessity
用品 *nichiyōhin* daily necessities
付 *hizuke* date, dating
付変更線 *hizuke henkōsen* the international date line
刊 *nikkan* daily publication, a daily
出 *hi(no)de, nisshutsu* sunrise
本 *Nihon, Nippon* Japan. *Hi(no)moto* Land of the Rising Sun
本一 *Nihon'ichi, Nippon'ichi* Japan's best
本刀 *Nihontō* Japanese sword
本風 *Nihonfū* Japanese style
本海 *Nihonkai* the Japan Sea
本酒 *Nihonshu* saké
本間 *Nihomma* Japanese-style room
本晴 *Nihomba(re)* ideal weather, clear sky, glorious weather
本語 *Nihongo, Nippongo* Japanese language
本髪 *Nihongami* Japanese hairdo
本製 *Nihonsei* Japanese make
⁶ 米 *Nichi-Bei* Japan and America
印 *Nichi-In* Japan and India
伊 *Nichi-I* Japan and Italy
次 *nichiji* the date
当 *hiata(ri)* sunny place; exposure to the sun. *nittō* daily allowance, a day's pay
毎 *higoto ni* daily
向 *hinata* sunny place, sunshine. *hinata(bokko)* basking in the sun
光 *nikkō* sunshine, sunlight, sun
光浴 *nikkōyoku* sun-bath
⁷ 足 *hiashi* daytime; sun's position

系 *Nikkei* Japanese descent
没 *nichibotsu* sunset
⁸ 延 *hino(be)* postponement
送 *hioku(ri)* passing the time (days)
限 *nichigen* time limit, date, term
取 *hido(ri)* setting a date; the date
夜 *nichiya* day and night; always
直 *nitchoku* a day shift; the day's work
参 *nissan* daily visits (to a shrine, etc.)
歩 *hibu* daily interest
英 *Nichi-Ei* Japan and England
長 *hinaga* a long day
和 *hiyori* weather conditions; fair weather; situation
和見 *hiyorimi* weather forecasting; weather vane; opportunism; marking time; wait-and-see (policy)
周運動 *nisshū undō* diurnal motion
⁹ 食 *nisshoku* solar eclipse
遂 *hi (o) o(tte)* day by day
柄 *higara* kind of day (lucky or unlucky)
計 *nikkei* daily account, daily expenses; the day's total
除 *hiyoke* sunshade, awning, blind
独 *Nichi-Doku* Japan and Germany
¹⁰ 差 *hiza(shi)* sunlight; sun's height
帰 *higae(ri)* a one-day (trip)
進月歩 *nisshin geppo* steady advance
時 *nichiji* date; time; date and hour
記 *nikki* diary, journal
陰 *hikage* shade
陰者 *hikagemono* one who stays out of the public eye, an obscure person; a concubine
¹¹ 頃 *higoro* normally, habitually, always; for a long time
捲 *himeku(ri)* calendar pad
掛 *higake* daily installment
脚 *hiashi* daytime; sun's position
産 *nissan* daily output
盛 *hizakari* high noon
章旗 *Nisshōki* Rising Sun Flag
清 *Nisshin* Sino (Manchu)-Japanese
常 *nichijō* everyday, usually, always; daily; ordinary
常用品 *nichijō yōhin* daily necessities
常茶飯事 *nichijō sahanji* an everyday occurrence
¹² 雇 *hiyatoi* day-to-day employment
焼 *hiya(ke)* sunburn
短 *himijika* shortening of the days
程 *nittei* day's schedule

心 忄 小 戸 手 扌 支 攴 攵 文 斗 斤 方 无 【日曰】 月 木 欠 止 歹 殳 毋 比 毛 氏 气 水 氵 氺 火 灬 爪 爫 父 爻 爿 丬 片 牙 牛 犬 犭

4

心 忄 小 戈 戸 手 扌 支 攴 攵 文 斗 斤 方 无 【日曰】月 木 欠 止 歹 殳 毋 比 毛 氏 气 水 氵 氺 火 灬 爪 爫 父 爻 爿 片 牙 牛 犬 犭

給 *nikkyū* day wages, daily wages

割 *hiwa(ri)* daily rate, daily quota. *hiwari de* by the day

勤 *nikkin* daily work

傘 *higasa* parasol

報 *nippō* daily news, daily report

¹³ 蓮宗 *Nichirenshū* Buddhist sect originating in the thirteenth century

溜 *hidama(ri)* sunny place; exposure to the sun

数 *nissū* number of days, time. *hikazu* number of days; the kind of day (lucky or unlucky)

新 *nisshin* starting each day anew

蔭 *hikage* shade

照 *hide(ri), nisshō* sunshine, drought, dry weather

傭 *hiyō, hiyatoi* day-to-day employment

¹⁴ 誌 *nisshi* diary, journal

語 *Nichigo* Japanese language

銀 *Nichigin* Bank of Japan

銭 *hizeni* daily receipts; a loan to be repaid in daily installments

増 *hima(shi) ni* daily, day by day, gradually

暮 *higu(re), hi (no) ku(re)* twilight; sunset, dusk, evening. *higu(rashi)* a day's living

暮方 *higu(re)gata* sunset, twilight, dusk, evening

¹⁵ 課 *nikka* daily lesson; one's regular work

賦 *hibu* daily installments

輪 *nichirin* sun, orb of day

蝕 *nisshoku* solar eclipse

影 *hikage* sunlight; sun's shadow

¹⁶ 録 *nichiroku* journal

¹⁷ 濠 *Nichi-Gō* Japan and Australia

鮮 *Nissen* Japan and Korea

¹⁸ 韓 *Nikkan* Japan and Korea

覆 *hiōi, hioi* sunshade, awning, curtain, blind

曜 *Nichiyō* Sunday

曜日 *Nichiyōbi* Sunday

²¹ 露 *Nichi-Ro* Japan and Russia

───── **1** ─────

旦 2411 / J4336 / M13734 TAN dawn, early morning.

³ 夕 *tanseki* morning and evening, day and night

⁶ 那 *danna* master; husband; gentleman

A 旧 2412 / J356c / M13737 KYŪ old things; old times; old friend; old calendar; former, ex-. *furu-* used article, secondhand. *furu(i)* old, aged, ancient, antiquated; stale, threadbare; outmoded, obsolete article.

大陸 *Kyūtairiku* the Old World

⁴ 友 *kyūyū* an old friend

⁵ 刊 *kyūkan* back number; old edition

正月 *Kyūshōgatsu* New Year's Day in the lunar calendar

世界 *Kyūsekai* the Old World

市街 *kyūshigai* old town

⁶ 式 *kyūshiki* old type, old style

交 *kyūkō* an old friendship

宅 *kyūtaku* former residence

年 *kyūnen* the old year, last year

⁷ 来 *kyūrai* from ancient times, formerly. *kyūrai no* traditional

体制 *kyūtaisei* old regime

⁸ 居 *kyūkyo* former residence

例 *kyūrei* old custom, tradition

姓 *kyūsei* former name, maiden name

知 *kyūchi* an old friend; an old friendship

事 *kyūji, kuji* past events, bygones

制 *kyūsei* old system, old order

制度 *kyūseido* old system, old order

⁹ 風 *kyūfū* old customs

型 *kyūgata, kyūkei* old style, old type

約聖書 *Kyūyaku Seisho* Old Testament

¹⁰ 師 *kyūshi* one's old teacher; one's old master

記 *kyūki* an old chronicle, an old record

都 *kyūto* the old capital

家 *kyūka* an old family

教 *Kyūkyō* Roman Catholicism

¹³ 跡 *kyūseki* historic ruins

¹⁴ 暦 *kyūreki* the old lunar calendar

聞 *kyūbun* old news

態 *kyūtai* old state of affairs

¹⁵ 墟 *kyūkyo* ruins, remains

敵 *kyūteki* old enemy

弊 *kyūhei* standing evil; conservatism; the old school. *kyūhei na* old-fashioned, antiquated, conservative

¹⁸ 蹟 *kyūseki* historic ruins

観 *kyūkan* former state, former appearance

───── **2** ─────

旨 B $\frac{2414}{\underset{M13738}{J3b5d}}$ SHI. *uma(garu)* relish, show a liking for. *mune* purport; principle; instructions; will, thinking. *uma(i)* delicious, appetizing; skillful, clever, expert; wise; successful; fortunate; splendid; promising.

旬 B $\frac{2415}{\underset{M13746}{J3d5c}}$ JUN ten-day period. SHUN season (for specific products).

4 日 *junjitsu* ten-day period
刊 *junkan* published every ten days
12 報 *jumpō* ten-day report

旭 $\frac{2416}{\underset{M13747}{J3030}}$ KYOKU. *asahi* the morning sun, the rising sun.

4 日 *kyokujitsu* the rising sun
日旗 *Kyokujitsuki* Rising Sun Flag
6 光 *kyokkō* rays of the rising sun

曳 $\frac{2417}{\underset{M14282}{J3148}}$ EI. *hi(ku)* draw, pull, haul, tug, jerk, drag, trail, bend, attract; lead (horses or captives); draw (lines); admit; install (utilities); quote, refer to; look up (words); subtract, reduce; apply, daub on; blunt (a sword); patronize; choose; catch (a cold). [日]
光弾 *eikōdan* tracer bullet, star shell, flare bomb
11 船 *hikifune, hikibune, eisen* tug boat
14 網 *hikiami* seine, dragnet

曲 A $\frac{2418}{\underset{M14280}{J364a}}$ KYOKU music, tone, melody, composition; fault. *ma(garu)* vi bend, curve, swerve; be crooked; turn; be awry; be perverse; lean; decline. *ma(geru)* vt bend, curve; lean, bow; distort; depart from (principles); pawn. *ma(gari-kuneru)* curve, meander, wind. *kuma* corner, nook, recess; indentation, bend, turn; shade, shading; make-up. *ma(gatta)* leaning, bent, curved, crooked; winding, meandering, zigzag; perverse, wicked; distorted. *kune(ri)* bend, twist. *ma(garinari) ni* some way or other. [日]
尺 *kanejaku, kyokushaku, maga(ri)jaku, kanezashi* common Japanese foot; carpenter's square
5 玉 *magatama* (ancient) comma-shaped jewels
目 *maga(ri)me* turn, bend, curve.

kyokumoku musical selection, program; tunes
7 角 *maga(ri)kado* street corner, road turn
技 *kyokugi* acrobatic feats
折 *kyokusetsu* winding, meandering; indentations; vicissitudes, complications
芸 *kyokugei* tricks, acrobatic stunts
芸師 *kyokugeishi* acrobat, tumbler
8 直 *kyokuchoku* merits (of a case); right or wrong
者 *kusemono* ruffian, villain, knave; thief; suspicious fellow
10 馬団 *kyokubadan* circus troupe
11 道 *maga(ri)michi* roundabout road; curving road
解 *kyokkai* misconstruction, distortion
15 調 *kyokuchō* melody, tune
線 *kyokusen* curve, curved line
線美 *kyokusembi* linear beauty
19 譜 *kyokufu* musical composition; notes

早 A $\frac{2419}{\underset{M13742}{J4161}}$ SA. SŌ. SATSU. *haya(i)* quick, fast, speedy; brisk; prompt; early; premature. *haya(meru)* vt hasten, precipitate, accelerate, expedite; advance (the date). *haya(maru)* be hasty, be rash. *haya(ru)* be hasty, be rash. *(O)ha(yō)* Good Morning. *haya(sa)* swiftness; being early; speed. *ha(ya)* already, now, so soon.
3 口 *hayakuchi, hayaguchi* fast talking; tongue twister
口言葉 *hayakuchi kotoba* tongue twister
天 *sōten* dawn, early morning
分 *hayawa(kari)* quick understanding; easy guide
手回 *hayatemawa(shi)* early precipitation
5 目 *hayame ni* early, ahead of time
立 *hayada(chi)* early morning departure
世 *sōsei* early death
仕舞 *hayajimai* early closing
生 *hayauma(re)* born between January 1 and March 31. *hayana(ri)* early crop, early fruit. *wase* early ripening; a precocious child
生児 *sōseiji* premature baby
6 耳 *hayamimi* insider; keen of hearing
成 *sōsei* early maturity

4 心 忄 小 戈 戸 手 扌 支 攴 文 斗 斤 方 无 [日 曰]² 月 木 欠 止 歹 殳 毋 比 毛 氏 气 水 氵 氺 火 灬 爪 爫 父 爻 爿 片 牙 牛 犬 犭

4

死 *hayaji(ni), sōshi* premature death

早 *sōsō, hayahaya* Hurry up. *hayabaya* early; immediately. *sōsō* Hurriedly yours.

年 *sōnen* youth, early years

合点 *hayaga(t)ten, hayagaten* hasty conclusion, premature judgment

⁷足 *hayaashi* quick pace, quick march, trot, fast walking

技 *hayawaza* quick work; sleight of hand

見表 *hayamihyō* chart, table

⁸退 *sōtai, hayabiki* leaving early

者勝 *haya(i)monoga(chi)* first-come-first-served

苗 *sanae* rice seedlings

⁹速 *sassoku* immediately, speedily

咲 *hayaza(ki)* early blooming; precocious

秋 *sōshū* early fall

計 *sōkei na* rash, premature, hasty

変 *hayagawa(ri)* quick change of costume, sudden transformation

春 *sōshun* early spring

急 *sōkyū, sakkyū* urgent, pressing; great speed

¹⁰起 *hayao(ki)* early rising

¹¹道 *hayamichi* shortcut

婚 *sōkon* early marriage

¹²晚 *sōban* early and late; sometime or other; finally, after all

暁 *sōgyō* daybreak, dawn

朝 *sōchō* early morning

場米 *hayabamai* early rice

期 *sōki* early stage

期診断 *sōki shindan* early diagnosis

¹⁴稲 *wase* early rice. *wase no* early ripening; precocious

¹⁵熟 *sōjuku* precocity; premature development

¹⁹瀬 *hayase* swift current, rapids

---------- 3 ----------

更 2422 J3939 M14283 Kō a watch of the night. *fu(kasu)* sit up late. *fu(keru)* get late; grow old; reach the height of the season. *arata(maru)* be renewed, be renovated; change, be modified, be revised; be improved, be reformed; be ceremonious. *sara ni* again; after all; more and more. *sara(nari)* of course. [日]

⁵代 *kōtai suru* exchange (something)

正 *kōsei* correction, revision, rectification

生 *kōsei* rebirth; resuscitation; rehabilitation, reorganization, regeneration

⁶年期 *kōnenki* menopause, change of life

衣 *kōi* seasonal changing of clothes; lady court attendant; second lunar month. *koromogae* seasonal changing of clothes

衣室 *kōishitsu* dressing room

¹³新 *kōshin* renewal, innovation, renovation

---------- 4 ----------

昂 2424 J3937 M13783 See 昂 2447.

旺 2427 J3222 M13774 Ō. *sakan* flourishing, successful; beautiful; vigorous.

¹¹盛 *ōsei na* excellent, flourishing, prosperous

昌 2428 J3e3b M13803 SHŌ proseperous; bright, clear.

昆 2430 J3a2b M13792 KON descendants; elder brother.

⁵布 *kombu, kobu* kombu, tangle, kelp, sea tang, devil's apron

⁶虫 *konchū* insect, bug

昏 2431 J3a2a M13806 KON dark; evening, dusk.

⁸迷 *kommei* confusion, bewilderment, stupor, unconsciousness

昏 *konkon to* unconsciously

¹⁰倒 *kontō* swoon, faint

冥 *kommei* complete darkness

¹¹酔 *konsui* dead drunk

¹²惑 *konwaku* ignorance of the truth and lack of judgment

¹³睡 *konsui* coma, stupor, dead sleep

易 2432 J3057 M13814 EKI divination, augury, fortunetelling. I easiness.

yasu(i) easy, simple, light; habitual.

yasu(i) be liable to, be ready to, be easy to.

8 易 *ii(taru)* simple, easy. *yasuyasu* very easy

学 *ekigaku* study of divination

者 *ekisha* fortuneteller, diviner

11 道 *ekidō* divination, fortunetelling

断 *ekidan* divination, fortunetelling

昔 ⟨2433 J404e M13816⟩ SHAKU. SEKI. *mukashi*
A antiquity, old times.

4 日 *sekijitsu* old times

6 年 *sekinen* antiquity; formerly; years ago

気質 *mukashi-katagi* old-time spirit

8 昔 *mukashimukashi* long ago

9 風 *mukashifū no* old-fashioned

10 時 *sekiji* old times

13 話 *mukashibanashi* folklore, legend; reminiscences

馴染 *mukashinajimi* old friend, crony

14 語 *mukashigata(ri)* an ancient tale

昇 ⟨2434 J3e3a M13794⟩ SHŌ. *nobo(ru)* rise, ascend,
B go up, climb; go to (the capital); add up to; be promoted; advance (in price); sail up; come up (on the agenda). *nobo(ri)* ascent; up train (toward the capital).

3 口 *nobo(ri)kuchi, nobo(ri)guchi* way up (to trains)

4 天 *shōten* ascension; the Ascension (of Christ)

6 任 *shōnin* promotion

9 級 *shōkyū* promotion, advancement

降 *shōkō* rise and fall; ascent and descent; fluctuations

降口 *shōkōguchi* companionway, hatchway, (ship) entrance

降機 *shōkōki* elevator, hoist, dumb-waiter

10 進 *shōshin* promotion, advancement

格 *shōkaku* raising of status

12 給 *shōkyū* salary raise

明 ⟨2435 J4c40 M13805⟩ MEI clearness, shining;
A eyesight; discernment.
MYŌ next (week), tomorrow (morning).
MIN Ming (Dynasty). *a(keru)* open; empty, vacate; leave (a space); clear (the table); make (a hole), reserve (a seat), stay away from; dawn; end, expire, be over;

open, begin. *a(ku)* open, be opened; start, begin, commence; become vacant, become empty, be disengaged, be free; expire, be over. *a(kasu)* spend, pass the time; reveal, divulge. *a(ke)* expiration, end; dawn. akashi. proof. *aka(ri)* light, lamp; vindication. *aka(rui)* bright, light; cheerful, sunny; clear, clean; conversant with. *aki(raka)* bright; clear, plain, distinct, definite, obvious, indisputable, evident. *a(kuru)* next, following. *saya(keshi)* clear; refreshing; pure. *a(ki)*-empty, vacant, unoccupied, spare (time).

4 方 *a(ke)gata* dawn

月 *meigetsu* bright moon, bright moonlight

文 *meibun* express provision

日 *myōnichi, ashita, asu* tomorrow. *a(keno)hi* the next day; tomorrow

5 白 *meihaku na* clear, unmistakable

示 *meiji, meishi* clear statement

払 *a(ke)-hara(u)* leave open (a house or window); throw open

6 色 *meishoku* bright color

年 *myōnen* next year

7 言 *meigen* declaration, assertion

快 *meikai* clear, explicit

君 *meikun* wise ruler

8 放 *a(ke)-hana(su)* throw open, open wide; leave open. *a(ke)-hana(reru)* grow light, dawn. *a(kep)pana(shi)* leaving (a door) open; blunt, frank, openhearted

盲 *a(ki)mekura* illiterate

治維新 *Meiji Ishin* Meiji Restoration

明 *akaaka to* brightly. *meimei* very clear

明白白 *meimei-hakuhaku* very clear

明星 *a(ke) (no) myōjō* morning star, Venus

明後日 *myōmyōgonichi, shiasatte, yanoasatte, yanaasatte* two days after tomorrow

9 屋 *a(ki)ya* vacant house

度 *meido* brightness

星 *myōjō* morning star; Venus; Lucifer; (literary) star

春 *myōshun* next spring

後日 *myōgonichi, asatte* day after tomorrow

後年 *myōgonen* year after next

10 記 *meiki suru* specify

4

心 忄 小 戈 戸 手 扌 支 攴 攵 文 斗 斤 方 无 【日 日】 月 木 欠 止 歹 殳 母 比 毛 氏 气 水 氵 氺 火 灬 爪 爫 父 爻 爿 丬 片 牙 牛 犭

敏 *meibin* intelligence, discernment
家 *a(ki)ya, a(ki)ie* vacant house, empty house
哲 *meitetsu* wise man, sage
朗 *meirō na* clear, bright, cheerful
11 細 *meisai* details, particulars. *meisai na* obvious
細書 *meisaisho* detailed statement, specifications
12 媚 *meibi na* picturesque, beautiful
晩 *myōban* tomorrow night
晰 *meiseki na* clear, distinct
渡 *a(ke)-wata(ru)* dawn, become light. *a(ke)-wata(su)* vacate; evacuate; surrender
答 *meitō* definite answer
番 *a(ke)ban* off duty
朝 *myōchō, myōasa* tomorrow morning. *Minchō* Ming Dynasty; Ming style
朝活字 *Minchō katsuji* Ming-dynasty-style characters
13 解 *meikai* clear understanding
滅 *meimetsu suru* appear and disappear, flicker, glimmer
暗 *meian* light and darkness
14 徳 *meitoku* illustrious virtue
徴 *meichō* clarification
察 *meisatsu* discernment, insight
暮 *aka(shi)-ku(rasu), a(ke)-ku(rasu)* live. *a(ketemo)-ku(retemo)* always. *a(ke)-ku(re)* day and night, morning and evening; day in and day out, all the time, early and late
15 確 *meikaku na* clear, distinctive, definite
17 瞭 *meiryō* clearness
19 離 *a(ke)-hana(reru)* become light, dawn
鏡止水 *meikyō shisui* serene frame of mind

5

昧 $\frac{2444}{\text{J4b66}}$ MAI dark; foolish.
A M13846

昭 $\frac{2446}{\text{J3e3c}}$ SHŌ clear, bright.
A M13855
8 和 *Shōwa* the name of the era from 1926 to 1989

昂 $\frac{2447}{\text{J-X}}$ 昂 $\frac{2424}{\text{J3937}}$ KŌ rise.
M13885   M13783
10 進 *kōshin* rise; acceleration; exasperation

---

12 揚 *kōyō suru* exalt, promote, enhance
然 *kōzen(taru)* elated, triumphant
20 騰 *kōtō* sudden price jump

映 $\frac{2448}{\text{J3147}}$ EI reflecting; projection.
A M13838 *ei(jiru), ei(zuru)* be reflected in, shine on; impress, appear to. *ha(eru)* shine, be brilliant; look attractive. *utsu(ru)* be reflected; match, harmonize, be becoming; be taken (a photo). *utsu(su)* copy, transcribe, duplicate, reproduce, trace; describe, picture, photograph. *ha(yasu)* applaud, cheer. *utsu(ri)* reflection, print, impression; match, harmony, effect. *hae* glory.
5 写 *eisha* projection
写機 *eishaki* projector
8 画 *eiga* cinema, movie, moving picture, film
画化 *eigaka* filming, making a film version
画館 *eigakan* movie theater
12 渡 *ha(e)-wata(ru)* shine all over
14 像 *eizō* reflection, image, silhouette

昨 $\frac{2449}{\text{J3a72}}$ SAKU the past; yesterday,
A M13847 last (year). *saku-* last (year); yesterday.
3 夕 *sakuyū* last evening
4 今 *sakkon* nowadays, recently
日 *sakujitsu, kinō* yesterday
5 冬 *sakutō* last winter
6 年 *sakunen* last year
8 夜 *sakuya, yūbe* last night, last evening
9 秋 *sakushū* last fall
春 *sakushun* last spring
10 夏 *sakka* last summer
12 晩 *sakuban* last night, last evening

昼 $\frac{2450}{\text{J436b}}$ CHŪ daytime, midday.
A M13886 *hiru* midday, daytime, noon.
3 下 *hirusa(gari)* early afternoon
4 日中 *hiruhinaka* daytime; noon
6 休 *hiruyasu(mi)* noon recess, noon rest period
行灯 *hiruandon* (useless as) a lantern at noon day
8 夜 *chūya, hiru (mo) yoru (mo)* day and night
夜兼行 *chūya kenkō* working day and night

⁹食 *chūshoku, chūjiki, hiruge* lunch, midday meal

前 *hirumae* forenoon; just before noon

¹⁰時 *hirudoki* noon, lunch time

¹¹過 *hirusu(gi)* afternoon

¹²間 *hiruma, chūkan* daytime; during the day

飯 *hirumeshi, chūhan* lunch, midday meal

¹³寝 *hirune* siesta, nap

¹⁶興行 *hirukōgyō* matinee

B 是 2451 J4027 M13859 ZE right, justice. *kore* this. *kore de* with this. *kore demo* such as I am. *koko ni* here. *kore kara* now, from now on, from here.

⁵正 *zesei* correction, revision

⁸非 *zehi* right or wrong, pro and con; surely, by all means. *zehi suru* comment on, criticize

非共 *zehitomo* surely; please

非曲直 *zehi-kyokuchoku* good and bad; right and wrong

非無 *zehina(i)* inevitable; necessary, unavoidable

⁹是 *korekore* this and that; etc. *kore(wa)kore(wa)* an exclamation of surprise

是非非 *zeze hihi* fair and just, clear-cut (policy)

¹⁴認 *zenin* approval

A 星 2452 J4031 M13837 SEI, SHŌ star. *hoshi* star; spot, dot, mark; bull's eye; one's fortune; point, score.

⁴月夜 *hoshizukiyo* starlit night

⁵占 *hoshi urana(i), seisen* astrology,

⁶回 *hoshimawa(ri)* one's fortune horoscope

団 *seidan* star cluster

⁷図 *seizu* star map

形 *hoshigata* star shape

条旗 *Seijōki* the Stars and Stripes

辰 *seishin* stars, heavenly bodies

⁸明 *hoshi aka(ri)* starlight

夜 *setya* starry night

¹⁰座 *seiza* constellation

¹¹宿 *seishuku* constellation

章 *seishō* badge, star

¹²雲 *seiun* nebula

¹³群 *setgun* star cluster

¹⁵影 *hoshikage* starlight

¹⁷霜 *seisō* years, time

A 春 2453 J3d55 M13844 SHUN spring. *haru* spring, springtime. *haru(meku)* become springlike.

³山 *haruyama* mountains in the spring

⁴心 *shunshin* thoughts of spring; air of spring; sexual passion

日 *haruhi, shunjitsu* spring day

分 *shumbun* vernal equinox

分日 *Shumbun (no) Hi* the Vernal Equinox (holiday, March 21)

⁵立 *haruta(tsu)* Spring is coming on.

本 *shumpon* pornographic book

⁶色 *shunshoku* spring scenery

気 *shunki* atmosphere of spring, spring fever, spring landscape

帆 *shumpan* a boat floating on the water in spring; spring sailing

光 *shunkō* spring scenery

先 *harusaki* early spring

⁷売 *haru (o) u(ru)* sell one's virtue, prostitute oneself

⁸雨 *harusame, shun'u* spring rain; bean-jelly sticks

郊 *shunkō* spring countryside

画 *shunga* erotic *ukiyoe* print; pornography

季 *shunki* spring, springtime

⁹風 *harukaze, shumpū* spring breeze

秋 *haru-aki, shunjū* spring and fall; months and years

秋富 *shunjū (ni) to(mu)* be young

¹⁰時 *shunji* springtime

眠 *shummin* morning sleep in spring

宵 *shunshō* spring evening, spring night

夏秋冬 *shun-ka-shū-tō* the four seasons; the year round

¹¹情 *shunjō* sexual passion

陽 *shun'yō* springtime; spring sunshine

雪 *shunsetsu* spring snow

¹²景色 *harugeshiki* spring scenery

¹³暖 *shundan* warm spring weather

蒔 *harumaki* spring sowing

雷 *shunrai* spring thunder

¹⁷霞 *harugasumi* spring haze

───── **6** ─────

晦 2454 J3322 M-X Nonstandard for 晦 2478.

心忄小戈戸手扌支攴攵文斗斤方无【日曰】月木欠止歹殳毋比毛氏气水氵氺火灬爪爫父爻爿丬片牙牛犬犭

4

心 忄 小 戈 戸 手 扌 支 攴 文 斗 斤 方 无 【日日】 月 木 欠 止 歹 殳 毋 比 毛 氏 气 水 氵 氺 火 灬 爪 爫 父 爻 爿 丬 片 牙 牛 犬 犭

晋 2455 J3f38 M13899 SHIN advance.

晃 2458 J3938 M13891 KŌ clear.

晒 2461 J3b2f M13924 SAI. *sara(su)* bleach, refine; expose, air. *sarashi* bleaching; bleached cotton.
⁴ 木綿 *sarashimomen* bleached cotton cloth
⁸ 者 *sarashimono* exposed criminal
⁹ 首 *sarashikubi* unburied severed head
¹⁰ 粉 *sarashiko* bleaching powder, chloride of lime

A 時 2462 J3b7e M13890 JI hour, o'clock, time; Buddhist sect originating in the thirteenth century. *toki* time, hour, moment; occasion; season; opportunity; the times; tense. *toki(meku)* prosper, flourish, be influential; prosperous, influential. *toki ni* now, by the way, in passing. *toki(naranu)* unseasonable, untimely, inopportune; sudden, unexpected. *toki ni totte* on the occasion, for the occasion. *toki niwa, toki(tama), toki toshite* occasionally. *toki(shimo), toki(shimoare)* just then. *toki to shite* sometimes, in some cases. *-ji* time, period.
³ 下 *jika* at present
⁴ 化 *shike(ru)* be stormy; be gloomy. *shike* stormy weather, heavy sea; scarcity of fish; business depression
分 *jibun* time, hour, season, time of year; (proper) time, opportunity; those days
⁵ 世 *jisei* the times, the era. *tokiyo* era, age; current trends
代 *jidai* period, age, stage, antiquity
代遅 *jidaioku(re)* out-of-date
代劇 *jidaigeki* historic costume play; historical play
代錯誤 *jidai sakugo* anachronism; being behind the times
⁷ 局 *jikyoku* situation
折 *tokio(ri)* at times, occasionally
⁸ 雨 *shigu(reru)* the late rains fall; tears fall. *shigure, jiu* late fall or early winter rain; shedding tears
価 *jika* current price

制 *jisei* tense (in grammar)
効 *jikō* statute of limitations
宜 *jigi* the right time; season's greetings; bowing
刻 *jikoku* time, hour, the time
刻表 *jikokuhyō* time table, schedule
事 *jiji* current events
限 *jigen* time limit; period; limited
⁹ 速 *jisoku* speed per hour
点 *jiten* occasion
計 *tokei* clock, watch, timepiece
計回 *tokeimawa(ri)* clockwise
¹⁰ 流 *jiryū* trend of the times
時 *tokidoki* sometimes, occasionally, frequently; each time, each season. *tokidoki no* seasonal, occasional, recurrent. *jiji* from time to time
時刻刻 *jiji-kokkoku* hourly; momentarily
差 *jisa* time difference
差惚 *jisaboke* jetlag
差出勤 *jisa shukkin* staggered office hours, flexible worktime
候 *jikō* season, time of year; climate
¹¹ 運 *jiun* tide of fortune
移 *toki (o) utsu(sazu)* immediately
得 *toki (o) e(ru)* be prosperous
¹² 給 *jikyū* payment by the hour
評 *jihyō* editorial comment
期 *jiki* time, the times, season
報 *jihō* review; time siren
間 *jikan* an hour; time; period
間外 *jikangai* late; overtime; outside of hours
間割 *jikanwari* timetable, schedule
間給 *jikankyū* payment by the hour
¹³ 勢 *jisei* spirit of the age, trend of the times, conditions
節 *jisetsu* season; the times; opportunity
¹⁵ 論 *jiron* contemporary opinion, comment on current events
¹⁶ 機 *jiki* opportunity, time, occasion
²⁰ 鐘 *jishō* hour bells, (ship's) time bells

A 書 2463 J3d71 M14294 SHO handwriting; letter, note; book. *sho(suru)* write. *ka(ku)* write, compose; draw, paint. *fumi* letter, note. [日]
² 入 *ka(ki)-i(reru)* enter, write in, mortgage
入時 *kakii(re)doki* best season (for profits)

³下 *ka(ki)-kuda(su)* write down. *ka(ki)-oro(su)* write a new play

上 *ka(ki)-a(geru)* finish writing; write out

⁴手 *ka(ki)te* calligrapher, copyist; painter

方 *ka(ki)kata* manner of writing; penmanship, (prescribed) form

止 *ka(ki)-todo(meru)* record, chronicle. *ka(ki)-sa(su)* leave off writing, leave unfinished

込 *ka(ki)-ko(mu)* enter, write in; mortgage

中 *shochū* within the letter, the book, or the document

分 *ka(ki)-wa(keru)* classify and write up

⁵目 *shomoku* catalog of books

付 *ka(ki)-tsu(keru)* make a note of. *kakitsuke* note; bill

加 *ka(ki)-kuwa(eru)* add; add a postscript

写 *ka(ki)-utsu(su)* copy, transcribe. *shosha* copying

出 *ka(ki)-da(su)* begin to write; make an excerpt; make out a bill; present in writing. *ka(ki)da(shi)* opening paragraph; bill

生 *shosei* student; one studying while working in a teacher's home

生論 *shoseiron* impractical argument

⁶式 *shoshiki* blank form

名 *shomei* title of a book

⁷見 *shoken* reading

足 *ka(ki)-ta(su)* add, write a postscript

体 *shotai* penmanship style; style of one's characters

抜 *ka(ki)-nu(ku)* abstract, copy out, take an excerpt. *kakinu(ki)* quotation, excerpt

状 *shojō* letter

初 *ka(ki)zo(me)* first writing of the new year

言葉 *ka(ki)kotoba* written language

⁸店 *shoten* bookstore; publisher

房 *shobō* bookstore

送 *ka(ki)-oku(ru)* write a letter, send a letter

林 *shorin* bookstore

法 *shohō* calligraphy, penmanship

取 *ka(ki)-to(ru)* take down, write from dictation. *kakito(ri)* dictation

画 *shoga* pictures and writings

表 *ka(ki)-ara(wasu)* write out, express, publish

物 *shomotsu* books. *ka(ki)mono* something written, papers

⁹面 *shomen* letter, document, contents

信 *shoshin* letter, message, correspondence

架 *shoka* bookshelf, bookcase

院 *shoin* window writing alcove; drawing room; study; school; publishing house

¹⁰庫 *shoko* book room, library

残 *ka(ki)-noko(su)* omit (something) in writing; leave a will behind; leave a history behind

流 *ka(ki)-naga(su)* write with ease

家 *shoka* good penman, calligrapher

留 *ka(ki)-to(meru)* write down; make a note of; jot down. *kakitome* registered mail

留郵便 *kakitome yūbin* registered mail

記 *ka(ki)-shiru(su)* write down, record. *shoki* clerk, secretary, scribe

記長 *shokichō* chief clerk, chief secretary

記官 *shokikan* secretary

¹¹道 *shodō* calligraphy

添 *ka(ki)-so(eru)* add, write a postscript

著 *ka(ki)-arawa(su)* publish

斎 *shosai* study, library, den

¹²違 *ka(ki)-chiga(eru)* miswrite. *ka(ki)chiga(i)* clerical error, slip of the pen

棚 *shodana* bookshelf

散 *ka(ki)-chi(rasu)* scribble, scrawl

替 *ka(ki)-ka(eru)* rewrite; renew (a bond); transfer, convey

評 *shohyō* book review

評家 *shohyōka* book reviewer

¹³損 *ka(ki)-sokona(u)*, *ka(ki)-son(jiru)* miswrite

肆 *shoshi* bookstore

¹⁴誌学 *shoshigaku* bibliography

¹⁶翰 *shokan* letter, note, epistle

¹⁸類 *shorui* documents, papers

簡 *shokan* letter, note, epistle

²⁰籍 *shoseki*, *shojaku* books, publication

──────── **7** ────────

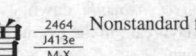

曽 — 2464 J413e M-X — Nonstandard for 會 2483.

4

心 忄 小 戈 戸 手 扌 支 攴 夂 文 斗 斤 方 尢 【日 曰】⁷ 月 木 欠 止 歹 殳 毋 比 毛 氏 气 水 氵 氺 火 灬 爪 爫 父 爻 爿 丬 片 牙 牛 犬 犭

心 忄 小 戈 戶 手 扌 支 攴 文 斗 斤 方 无 〔日 日〕 月 木 欠 止 歹 殳 母 比 毛 氏 气 水 氵 氺 火 灬 爪 爫 父 爻 爿 片 牙 牛 牜 犬 犭

曹 2477 J4162 M14297 Sō, Zō friend. [日]

⁸ 長 *sōchō* sergeant-major

¹¹ 達 *sōda* soda

晦 2478 J-X M13960 **晦** 2454 M-X Kai dark. *kura(masu)* give the slip to, disappear. *tsugomori* month end, last day of the month; the dark of the moon.

⁴ 日 *misoka* the last day of the month

¹⁰ 冥 *kaimei* darkness

¹¹ 渋 *kaijū* ambiguity, obscurity

────── 8 ──────

晶 2482 J3e3d M14000 Shō clear; crystal.

曾 2483 J413d M14299 Sō. So. *katsu(te), kat(te)* once, before, formerly; ever, never (neg.); former, ex-. [日]

⁹ 祖父 *sōsofu, hiijiji, hiōji* great-grandfather

祖母 *sōsobo, hiibaba, hiōba* great-grandmother

¹⁰ 孫 *hiimago, sōson, hiko, himago* great-grandchild

暑 2484 J3d6b M14031ˈ Sho summer heat. *atsu(ga ru)* feel the heat, swelter. *atsu(gari)* sensitivity to heat; a person sensitive to hot weather. *atsu(i)* hot, warm, sultry. *atsu(sa)* heat, hot weather.

⁴ 中 *shochū* midsummer, hot season. *atsusaata(ri)* heatstroke, sunstroke.

中見舞 *shochū mima(i)* summer health inquiry

中休暇 *shochū kyūka* summer vacation

⁶ 気 *atsuke, shoki* hot weather; heatstroke, sunstroke

気中 *shokiata(ri)* heatstroke, sunstroke

⁸ 苦 *atsuguru(shii), atsukuru(shii)* sultry, sweltering

⁹ 屋 *atsu(gari)ya* person sensitive to hot weather

¹⁵ 熱 *shonetsu* summer heat

暁 2485 J3647 M14031 Gyō. *akatsuki* dawn, daybreak; in the event (of).

⁴ 天 *gyōten* dawn

⁶ 光 *gyōkō* light at dawn

⁹ 星 *gyōsei* morning star, Venus; rarity

替 2486 J4258 M14300 Tai. Tei. *ka(eru)* change, renew, convert, exchange, substitute, replace. *kawa(ru)* replace, relieve. *kawa(ri)* substitute, deputy, proxy, alternate, relief; compensation; second helping. *ka(e)-* spare, substitute, exchange. *kae(de)* at, for, per. [日]

⁵ 玉 *ka(e)dama* substitute, a double

⁶ 地 *ka(e)chi* substitute land

¹² 着 *ka(e)gi* a change of clothing

¹⁴ 歌 *ka(e)uta* parody in song

景 2487 J374a M13983 Kei view, scene.

⁶ 色 *keshiki, keishoku* scenery, landscape

仰 *keikō* love of virtue. *keigyō* adoration, admiration; a love of virtue

気 *keiki* the times, business conditions; liveliness

気付 *keikizu(ku)* boom, become active. *keikizu(ke)* promotion stunt

⁸ 況 *keikyō* situation; outlook

物 *keibutsu* (seasonal) scenery; premium, present

⁹ 品 *keihin* premium, present, bonus

¹¹ 教 Keikyō Nestorianism

¹² 勝 *keishō* picturesque scenery; advantageous position

¹³ 福 *keifuku* great happiness

¹⁵ 趣 *keishu* scenery, landscape

¹⁸ 観 *keikan* spectacle, view

晴 2488 J4032 M13994ˈ Sei. *ha(reru)* clear up; (doubts) vanish; be refreshed. *ha(rasu)* dispel, clear away (gloom); refresh (oneself). *ha(re)* fine weather. *ha(reyakana)* clear, bright; radiant, cheerful. *ha(rete)* openly, publicly. *ha(regamashii)* openhearted, frank.

³ 上 *ha(re)-a(garu)* clear up

⁴ 天 *seiten* fine weather, clear sky

天白日 *seiten-hakujitsu* innocence; clear weather

⁶ 衣 *haregi, hareginu* one's best clothes

⁷ 雨 *seiu* rain or shine; weather conditions

雨計 *seiukei* barometer
9 姿 *ha(re)sugata* wearing one's best clothes
10 朗 *seirō* clear, fair, fine, bright
耕雨読 *seikō-udoku* working in fair weather and reading in wet
12 間 *ha(re)ma* clear interval
晴 *ha(re)ba(reshii), harebare(shita)* clear, cloudless; cheerful, refreshing; splendid
渡 *ha(re)-wata(ru)* clear up
着 *ha(re)gi* one's best clothes
14 模様 *ha(re) moyō* clearing weather

普 2489 J4961 M13982 **B** Fu. *amane(ku)* widely, generally.
3 及 *fukyū* diffusion, dissemination
及版 *fukyūban* cheap popular edition
9 段 *fudan* usually, habitually, continually; constantly; indecision, irresolution
段着 *fudangi* ordinary clothes
通 *futsū* ordinary, common, usual, mediocre
通科 *futsūka* regular or general course
11 遍 *fuhen* universality, ubiquity, omnipresence
遍性 *fuhensei* universality, ubiquity, omnipresence
遍的 *fuhenteki* universal, omnipresent
15 請 *fushin* building, construction
請場 *fushimba* building plot

智 2490 J4352 M14010 CHI wisdom, intellect; intelligence, reason; strategem.
2 力 *chiryoku* wisdom, intellectual power, mental capacity, intellect, mentality, brains
8 育 *chiiku* mental education
者 *chisha* wise person, sage
10 将 *chishō* resourceful general
能 *chinō* knowledge and ability
能指数 *chinō shisū* IQ, intelligence quotient
能検査 *chinō kensa* mental test
恵 *chie* wisdom, sense, sagacity, intelligence, resourcefulness
恵袋 *chiebukuro* one's close advisor; brain trust
11 略 *chiryaku* ingenuity, talents
12 歯 *chishi* wisdom tooth

13 愚 *chigu* wisdom and foolishness; wise men and fools
15 慮 *chiryo* wise idea; planning ability
慧 *chie* wisdom, sense, sagacity, intelligence, resourcefulness
16 謀 *chibō* ingenuity, resourcefulness
19 識 *chishiki* wisdom

晩 2491 J4855 M14030′ **A** BAN evening, night; the end of all things; late.
4 方 *bangata* toward evening
5 冬 *bantō* late winter
6 成 *bansei* late success; late development
年 *bannen* late in life
8 学 *bangaku* late education
9 秋 *banshū* late fall
春 *banshun* late spring
10 酌 *banshaku* an evening drink of saké
夏 *banka* late summer
婚 *bankon* late marriage
12 飯 *bammeshi* evening meal, supper
景 *bankei* evening; an evening scene
13 節 *bansetsu* life's closing years
16 餐 *bansan* supper, dinner
20 鐘 *banshō* curfew; evening bell

最 2492 J3a47 M14301 **A** SAI. *motto(mo)* most. *sai-* ultra, most, maximum, extreme. *ito-* extremely, greatly. [日]
3 小 *saishō* the smallest, the minimum
小限 *saishōgen* minimum
上 *saijō* the best; the highest
上級 *saijōkyū* superlative degree; highest class
大 *saidai* maximum, greatest, largest
大限 *saidaigen* maximum
大級 *saidaikyū* superlative degree; highest class
下位 *saikai* lowest position, lowest rank
下級 *saikakyū* lowest class, lowest grade
4 中 *saichū ni, sanaka ni* in the midst of, at the height of. *monaka* middle; bean-jam wafer
少 *saishō* the fewest, the least, the minimum; the youngest
5 古 *saiko* the oldest
6 早 *mohaya* now, soon, already, by now
多数 *saitasū* the largest number
近 *suikin* recently; latest, newest
初 *saisho* the first, the beginning
良 *sairyō* the best, the ideal

4

心 忄 小 戈 戸 手 扌 支 攴 文 斗 斤 方 无 【日曰】 月 木 欠 止 歹 殳 毋 比 毛 氏 气 水 氵 氺 火 灬 爪 爫 父 爻 爿 片 牙 牛 犭

低 *saitei* lowest, minimum

⁸長 *saichō no* longest

果 *saiha(te)* farthest limit; farthest land

⁹前 *saizen* foremost; short time ago; just now

前線 *saizensen* spearhead, front, first line

後 *saigo, iyahate* the last, the end. *saigo no* last, final. *saigo ni* in conclusion; in the long run

後通牒 *saigo tsūchō* ultimatum

¹⁰恵国 *saikeikoku* most-favored nation

恵国待遇 *saikeikoku taigū* most-favored-nation treatment

高 *saikō* maximum, supreme, highest, best

高司令官 *saikō shireikan* commander-in-chief

高司令部 *saikō shireibu* supreme command

高学府 *saikō gakufu* highest seat of learning

高峰 *saikōhō* highest peak; highest point reached

高裁 *Saikōsai* Supreme Court

高裁判所 *Saikō Saibansho* Supreme Court

高潮 *saikōchō* highwater mark; high tide; climax, peak, acme

¹¹深 *saishin* greatest depth

悪 *saiaku* the worst

寄 *moyo(ri) no* neighboring, nearest

盛期 *saiseiki* golden age, height of prosperity; the season, the best time (for)

強 *saikyō* strongest

終 *saishū* the last, the end; final

終的 *saishūteki* ultimate

¹²期 *saigo* one's last moments; death; fate

善 *saizen* the very best

敬礼 *saikeirei* profound obeisance, deep respect

短 *saitan* shortest

¹³愛 *saiai no* dearest, beloved

適 *saiteki* optimum

新 *saishin* newest, latest, up-to-date

———————— 9 ————————

暇 B ⟨2501 / J324b / M14036⟩ KA rest, leisure. *hima* time; leisure; poor business; leave of absence; dismissal; divorce.

itoma leisure, spare time; dismissal; divorce; leave; leave-taking.

³乞 *itomagoi* farewell visit

⁴日 *kajitsu* holiday, day off

⁸取 *himado(ru)* take time; be delayed

¹⁵潰 *himatsubu(shi)* waste of time, killing time

暖 A ⟨2502 / J4348 / M14064⟩ DAN warmth. *atata(meru), atata(meru)* vt warm, heat. *atata(maru), atta(maru)* warm oneself, sun oneself, get warm. *atataka(i), attaka(i)* warm, mild, genial, cordial.

⁵冬 *dantō* mild winter

⁶色 *danshoku* warm-looking (clothes)

気 *danki* heat, warmth, warm weather

地 *danchi* warm region

衣 *dan'i* warm clothes; dressing warmly

衣飽食 *dan'i hōshoku* warm clothing and plenty to eat, luxury

⁸房 *dambō* heating

炉 *danro* fireplace, hearth, stove

¹⁰流 *danryū* warm current

帯 *dantai* subtropics

¹⁹簾 *noren* shop curtain, sign curtain; reputation, goodwill

暗 A ⟨2503 / J3045 / M14065⟩ AN dark. *kura(mu)* grow dark; be dazzled; be blinded. *kura(masu)* disappear, give (a person) the slip. *kura(ku) suru* darken, shade, make dim. *kura(gari)* darkness, gloom. *kura(i)* dark, gloomy, somber; dim, faint; ignorant. *yami* darkness; grief, gloom; disorder; black market. *kura(me)* gathering darkness. *an(ni)* tacitly, implicity, informally, indirectly, obscurely.

⁴中 *anchū* in the dark

中模索 *anchū mosaku* groping in the dark

⁵示 *anji* hint, suggestion

号 *angō* code, password

⁶色 *anshoku* dark color

合 *angō* coincidence

灰色 *ankaishoku* dark gray, taupe

⁷車 *ansha* propeller, screw

君 *ankun* foolish ruler

赤色 *ansekishoku* dark red

⁸夜 *an'ya* dark night

⁹室 *anshitsu* dark room

¹⁰流 *anryū* undercurrent

涙 *anrui* silent tears

記 *anki* memorization

殺 *ansatsu* assassination
[11] 唱 *anshō* memorization, recitation
転 *anten* sudden darkening of the stage (to change scenery)
黒 *ankoku* darkness
黒街 *ankokugai* the underworld
[12] 喩 *an'yu* metaphor
雲 *an'un* dark clouds
渠 *ankyo* drain, culvert
然 *anzen* discouraged, disappointed, astonished
紫色 *anshishoku* dark purple
[13] 溝 *ankō* buried drain-tile sewer
愚 *angu* weak-mindedness, stupidity
褐色 *ankasshoku* dark brown
暗 *an'an* darkness; stillness in the depths
暗裏 *an'anri(ni)* tacitly, implicitly, obscurely, by implication, secretly
[14] 誦 *anshō* memorization, recitation
算 *anzan* mental arithmetic
緑色 *anryokushoku* dark green
[15] 影 *an'ei* shadow, gloom
黙 *ammoku* silence
黙了解 *ammoku (no) ryōkai* tacit understanding
[16] 澹 *antan* darkness, gloom
[17] 闇 *kurayami, kureyami* darkness; dark place; privacy; lawlessness
礁 *anshō* reef, sunken rock
[18] 闘 *antō* secret feud
[21] 躍 *an'yaku* secret maneuvers
[26] 欝 *an'utsu* gloom, melancholy

———— 10 ————

暢 ²⁵⁰⁶ J442a M14095 CHŌ stretch.
[6] 気 *nonki* optimistic; carefree; careless, reckless

B 暦 ²⁵⁰⁷ J4e71 M14111' RYAKU. REKI. *koyomi* calendar, almanac.
[4] 日 *rekijitsu* calendar day; time
[6] 年 *rekinen* calendar year, civil year; time
[8] 学 *rekigaku* the study of the calendar

A 暮 ²⁵⁰⁸ J4a6b M14128 BO. *kura(su)* live, make a living; spend (one's time). *ku(reru)* get dark; (the sun) sets; (the season) ends; (time) passes; be overwhelmed. *kura(shi)* living,

livelihood; circumstances. *ku(re)* sunset, nightfall; year-end; end.
[4] 方 *ku(rashi)kata* manner of living. *ku(re)gata, kure(tsu)kata* nightfall
[6] 色 *boshoku* twilight scene
行 *ku(re)-yu(ku)* get dark
向 *ku(rashi)mu(ki)* circumstances, livelihood
[8] 夜 *boya* evening, night
果 *ku(re)-ha(teru)* get completely dark
[9] 秋 *boshū* late fall
春 *boshun* late spring
[12] 渡 *ku(re)-wata(ru)* the whole landscape darkens
景 *bokei* twilight, evening scene
[13] 愁 *boshū* the loneliness of evening

———— 11 ————

B 暫 ²⁵¹⁰ J3b43 M14120 ZAN *shibara(ku)* for a while, a moment; for a long time.
[8] 定 *zantei* provisional, tentative
[10] 時 *zanji, shibashi* a short while, for some time. *zanji no* transient, momentary

A 暴 ²⁵¹¹ J4b3d M14137 BAKU, Bō violence, force, outrage, cruelty. *aba(reru)* rage, rave, fret; buck. *aba(ku)* unearth, disclose, rave, divulge, reveal; open (a grave).
[2] 力 *bōryoku* violence, force, terrorism
力団 *bōryokudan* terrorist organization, gangster group
[4] 込 *aba(re)-ko(mu)* storm into, burst into
[5] 令 *bōrei* wicked decree
出 *aba(re)-da(su)* grow restive, begin to act violently; begin to buck
民 *bōmin* mob, insurgents
[6] 行 *bōkō* act of violence, assault, outrage
回 *aba(re)-mawa(ru)* rampage, tear around, run riot
[7] 言 *bōgen* harsh or abusive language
走 *bōsō* running wildly
戻 *bōrei* tyranny, atrocity
状 *bōjō* atrocity, violence
狂 *aba(re)-kuru(u)* rage, run amuck, tear around
利 *bōri* excessive profits, usury
君 *bōkun* tyrant
坊 *aba(rem)bō* rascal
[8] 逆 *bōgyaku* violence, lawlessness

心 忄 小 戈 戸 手 扌 支 攴 攵 斗 方 无 【日 曰】 [11] 月 木 欠 止 歹 殳 毋 比 毛 氏 气 水 氵 氺 火 灬 爪 爫 父 爻 爿 丬 片 牛 犬 犭 [4]

者 *aba(re)mono* rowdy
9 威 *bōi* tyranny, great violence, havoc
虐 *bōgyaku* tyranny, atrocity
政 *bōsei* tyrannical government
発 *bōhatsu* accidental gun discharge
食 *bōshoku* gluttony, intemperance in eating
風 *bōfū* storm
風雨 *bōfūu* rainstorm
風雪 *bōfūsetsu* blizzard, snowstorm
10 徒 *bōto* mob, rioters, insurgents, mutineers
挙 *bōkyo* violence, outrage; riot
11 動 *bōdō* riot, uprising
12 落 *bōraku* slump, sharp break, crash, heavy decline (in prices)
飲 *bōin* heavy drinking, carousing
13 漢 *bōkan* ruffian, desperado
14 慢 *bōman* insolence, arrogance
説 *bōsetsu* preposterous theory
15 論 *bōron* irrational argument
20 騰 *bōtō* sudden (price) rise
21 露 *bakuro* exposure, disclosure

12

B **曇** 2518 / J465e / M14172 DON. *kumo(ru) vi* cloud up; fog up, become dim, be blurred; be gloomy. *kumo(rasu) vt* cloud up, dim, blur, fog, dull (the color); tarnish; shade (one's face); darken. *kumo(ri)* cloudiness, shadow, blur, dimness; gloom; suspicion; slur, stain; frosted (glass).
4 日 *kumo(ri)bi* cloudy day; the sun covered with clouds
天 *donten* cloudy weather, overcast sky
12 勝 *kumo(ri)ga(chi) na* cloudy

13

曙 2519 / J3d6c / M-X See **曙** 2523.

14

A **曜** 2522 / J4d4b / M14227' YŌ day of the week; light; shining.
4 日 *yōbi* weekday

曙 2523 / J-X / M14220 **曙** 2519 / J3d6c / M-X SHO. *akebono* dawn, daybreak.
6 光 *shokō* dawn; prospects

15

曝 2524 / J4778 / M14239 BAKU. *sara(su)* bleach; refine; expose, air.
10 書 *bakusho* airing of books

RAD. 日 73

Iwaku to speak or *hirabi* (a flattened Rad. 72 *hi*). With the exception of the radical itself, which follows, this radical is treated herein as a variant of Rad. 72.
Nickname: Flat Sun.

RAD. 月 74

Tsuki moon. At left: *tsuki hen*. With the exception of the radical character itself, which follows, this radical is herein treated as a variant of Rad. 130.
Nickname: Moon.

A **月** 2530 / J376e / M14330 GETSU moon; month; Monday. GATSU month (of the year). *tsuki* moon; month.
3 下 *gekka ni* on a moonlit night, in the moonlight
下氷人 *gekka hyōjin* go-between, matchmaker, Cupid
4 日 *gappi* date. *tsukihi* months and days,

time and tide; one's star

月 tsukizuki every month
5刊 gekkan monthly publication
払 tsukibarai monthly installments
収 gesshū monthly income
末 getsumatsu, tsukizue end of the month
次 getsuji monthly. tsukinami every month; common
光 gekkō moonlight, moonbeam
利 getsuri monthly interest
別 tsukibetsu by months
見 tsukimi viewing the moon; moonlight party
8例 getsurei monthly
始 tsukihaji(me) beginning of the month
明 getsumei, tsukiaka(ri) moonlight
並 tsukina(mi) every month; common
長石 getchōseki moonstone
夜 tsukiyo, getsuya moonlit night
9面 getsumen the moon's surface
食 gesshoku eclipse of the moon
後 tsukioku(re) back numbers (of a monthly)
10俸 geppō monthly salary

桂 gekkei laurel; moon; moonlight
11遅 tsukioku(re) a month or more older
掛 tsukigake monthly installments
産 gessan monthly output
経 gekkei menstruation
12越 tsukigo(shi) no (bill) hanging over from last month
極 tsukigime monthly contract. tsukigime no monthly
割 tsukiwari monthly allocation
報 geppō monthly report, monthly review
評 geppyō monthly review
給 gekkyū monthly salary
給取 gekkyūto(ri) white-collar worker
15蝕 gesshoku eclipse of the moon
影 tsukikage, getsuei moonlight, moonbeams
賦 geppu monthly installment
17謝 gessha monthly tuition
齢 getsurei age of the moon
18額 getsugaku monthly amount
曜 Getsuyō Monday
曜日 Getsuyōbi Monday

RAD. 木 75

Ki tree. At left: *ki hen*. Nickname: Tree.

木 A 2531 J4c5a M14415 BOKU tree. MOKU tree; Thursday. *ki, ko* tree; wood; timber; lumber; wooden clappers.

2刀 bokutō wooden sword
3口 koguchi cut end, butt end. kiguchi cross section of wood; lumber quality
工 mokkō woodworking; woodworker
4木 kigi every tree; many trees; all kinds of trees
片 mokuhen block; chip; splinter
戸 kido gate, wicket, wooden door, wooden gate; entrance; castle gate
戸銭 kidosen admission fee
5目 mokume wood grain. kime wood grain; texture
立 kodachi clump of trees, thicket, grove, standing trees
札 kifuda wooden tag or ticket
末 konure twig, tree top

石 bokuseki trees and stones, inanimate objects
6地 kiji grain of wood; plain wood
肌 kohada, kihada bark of a tree
7材 mokuzai wood, timber, lumber
8実 ko(no)mi, ki(no)mi fruit, nut, berry
芽 ko(no)me, ki(no)me leaf buds; roasted tea leaves
版 mokuhan wood-block printing; wood-block print
版画 mokuhanga wood-block print
9枯 koga(rashi) wintry wind
柵 mokusaku wooden barricade, fence
星 Mokusei Jupiter
造 mokuzō, kizuku(ri) sawmilling. mokuzō wooden
炭 mokutan, kizumi charcoal
10屑 kikuzu shavings, chips
陰 kokage tree shade, bower

心 忄 小 戈 戸 手 扌 支 攴 文 斗 斤 方 无 日 曰 月 【木】0 欠 止 歹 殳 毋 比 毛 氏 气 水 氵 氺 火 灬 爪 爫 父 爻 爿 丬 片 牙 牛 犬 犭

4

心 忄 小 戈 戸 手 扌 支 攴 攵 文 斗 斤 方 无 日 曰 月 〇【木】 欠 止 歹 殳 毋 比 毛 氏 气 水 氵 氺 火 灬 爪 爫 父 爻 爿 丬 片 牙 牛 犬 犭

剣 *bokken* wooden sword
馬 *mokuba* rocking horse
馬飛 *mokubato(bi)* horse vaulting (in a gym)
挽 *kobiki* sawyer
11 魚 *mokugyo* wooden temple drum
彫 *kibo(ri), mokuchō* wood carving
訥 *bokutotsu* rugged honesty
細工 *kizaiku* woodwork
偶 *deku, mokugū, bokugū* wooden figure, dummy, puppet
12 間 *ko(no)ma* through the trees; among the trees
場 *kiba* lumberyard
割 *kiwa(ri)* allotment of lumber
登 *kinobo(ri)* tree climbing
琴 *mokkin* marimba, xylophone
遣 *kiyari* workmen's chant; carrying a big load together
葉 *ko(no)ha, ki(no)ha* foliage of trees
13 蓮 *mokuren* magnolia
鉢 *kibachi* wooden bowl
賃宿 *kichin'yado* cheap lodging house
14 像 *mokuzō* wooden image; figurehead
精 *mokusei* wood alcohol, methyl alcohol; an echo
端 *ki(no)hashi, koppa, koba* block, chip (of wood); worthless thing; worthless person
端微塵 *koppa-mijin* smithereens
管 *mokkan* wooden pipe; bobbin
管楽器 *mokkan gakki* wind instruments of wood
製 *mokusei no* wooden, made of wood
綿 *momen* cotton, cotton cloth. *kiwata* cotton plant
15 箱 *kibako* wooden box
霊 *kodama* spirit of a tree; echo. *kodama suru* echo, resound
18 曜 *Mokuyō* Thursday
曜日 *Mokuyōbi* Thursday
21 鐸 *bokutaku* bell with a wooden clapper; a leader; a great teacher

———— **1** ————

札 2533 J3b25 M14422 SATSU paper money; counter for bonds, etc. *fuda* tag, placard; name plate; check; charm; (playing) card; tender, bid.
2 入 *satsui(re)* billfold, wallet
4 止 *fudado(me)* full house

5 付 *fudatsu(ki)* branded, marked (with prices); notorious; ex-convict
7 束 *satsu taba* bundle of paper money

末 2534 J4b76 M14420 BATSU. MATSU end; powder. *sue* end, close; tip, top; the future; posterity; youngest child. *sue ni* finally. *ura* top end, tip. *ure* new shoots, new growth (of a tree). *-matsu* the end of; powder.
3 子 *basshi, masshi, sueko, sue(k)ko* youngest child
4 日 *matsujitsu* last day (of the month)
5 広 *suehiro* folding fan. *suehiro(gari)* spreading out like an open fan
代 *matsudai* eternity
世 *sue(no)yo, masse* last days
6 寺 *matsuji* branch temple
7 尾 *matsubi* end, close
弟 *mattei, battei* youngest brother; last disciple
8 長 *suenaga(ku)* long, forever
法 *mappō* latter days (in Buddhism), age of decadence
法思想 *mappō-shisō* pessimism due to decadent-age theory
10 座 *matsuza* lowest seat
流 *matsuryū, batsuryū* descendants
恐 *sueoso(roshii)* ominous, uncertain of the future
席 *masseki, basseki* lowest seat
席汚 *masseki (o) kega(su)* attend a meeting (humble)
11 梢 *masshō* tree top, tip; periphery; minor details, nonessentials
梢的 *masshōteki* trivial, minor, insignificant
梢神経 *masshō shinkei* peripheral nerves
12 期 *makki* closing years, last stage. *matsugo* deathbed, hour of death
筆乍 *mappitsunaga(ra)* a letter-closing phrase expressing regret for a delay
13 路 *matsuro, batsuro* last days, end, fate
裔 *matsuei, batsuei* descendants
14 端 *mattan* end, tip, extremities
16 頼 *suetano(moshii)* promising (future)

未 2535 J4c24 M14419 MI not yet. *ima(da)* as yet, hitherto; not yet (with neg.). *ima(dani)* still, even now, until this very day. *mada* not yet; still; so far;

more, besides; only. *ima(dashi)* something to be desired. *hitsuji* 1–3 p.m.; eighth zodiac sign; sheep. *mi-* un-, not yet.

² 了 *miryō no* unfinished, unfilled (order), unexecuted

³ 亡人 *mibōjin* widow

⁴ 公表 *mikōhyō* not yet officially announced

⁵ 刊 *mikan no* unpublished

未 *madamada* still, still more, much more

処分 *mishobun* unsettled, unfinished, undivided (profits)

処置 *mishochi* untreated

払 *mihara(i)* unpaid

⁶ 成年 *miseinen* minority, not of age

成年者 *miseinensha* a minor

⁷ 完成 *mikunsei no* incomplete

来 *mirai* future; future life; future tense

来完了 *mirai kanryō* future perfect

決 *miketsu* pending, unsettled

決囚 *miketsushū* unconvicted prisoner

⁸ 届 *mitodo(ke)* failing to report

明 *mimei* early dawn

到 *mitō* untrodden, unexplored

知 *michi* unknown, strange

知数 *michisū* unknown number

定 *mitei* undecided, pending

⁹ 発見 *mihakken* undiscovered, unexplored

発表 *mihappyō* not yet announced

発達 *mihattatsu* undeveloped

¹¹ 組織 *misoshiki* unorganized

遂 *misui* attempted (crime)

婚 *mikon* unmarried

経験 *mikeiken no* inexperienced

¹² 満 *miman* less than, below

曾有 *mizou, misou* unprecedented, unheard of

登記 *mitōki* unregistered

着 *michaku* nonarrival

開 *mikai* uncivilized, barbarous; not blooming

開拓 *mikaitaku* undeveloped, wild (areas)

開発 *mikaihatsu* undeveloped (countries), backward, unentered

¹³ 詳 *mishō no* unknown, unidentified

解決 *mikaiketsu no* unsettled, pending

¹⁴ 練 *miren* unskilled; lingering affection

製品 *miseihin* unfinished article

¹⁵ 確定 *mikakutei* unsettled, pending

踏 *mitō* untrodden, unexplored

熟 *mijuku na* unripe, raw; unskilled; immature, inexperienced

A 本 $\frac{2536}{\text{J4b5c}}$ M14421 HON book; this, the same, the present, the current; main; true; real; regular, normal; counter for long things. *moto* beginning, origin; foundation, basis, source; cause; root (of a tree); (raw) material, base; capital; principal; cost; forebears; formerly.

² 人 *honnin* the person himself; the said person; the principal

³ 土 *hondo* mainland; Japan proper

山 *honzan* head temple; this temple

丸 *hommaru* inner citadel

⁴ 心 *honshin* one's right mind, real motive, true sentiment, real intention, conscience

日 *honjitsu* today

分 *hombun* one's duty; original position

文 *hombun, hommon* text (of a treaty); body (of a letter)

⁵ 立 *hontate* bookrack, book ends

庁 *honchō* head government office

代 *hondai* money for books

末 *hommatsu* cause and effect; the means and the end; root and branch; substance and shadow; beginning and end

末転倒 *hommatsu-tentō* overturning plans

⁶ 式 *honshiki* orthodox style. *honshiki no* formal, regular

件 *honken* this case

好 *honzu(ki)* a bookworm, bibliophile; fondness for books

州 *Honshū* Japan proper, Main Island

刑 *honkei* regular penalty

邦 *hompō* this country, our country

旨 *honshi* the main purpose; the true aim; the true reason

宅 *hontaku* principal residence

当 *hontō, hontō no* true, real, actual, proper, genuine; natural; veritable, substantial. *hontō ni* in earnest; very; really. *hontō(rashii)* probable, plausible, likely.

名 *hommyō, hommei* real name, family name

心 忄 小 戈 戸 手 扌 支 攴 攵 文 斗 斤 方 无 日 曰 月 【木】¹ 欠 止 歹 殳 毋 比 毛 氏 气 水 氵 氺 火 灬 爪 爫 父 爻 爿 片 牙 牛 犬 犭

4

心 忄 小 戈 戸 手 扌 支 攴 攵 文 斗 斤 方 无 日 曰 月 ⌊木⌋ 欠 止 歹 殳 毋 比 毛 氏 气 水 氵 氺 火 灬 爪 爫 父 爻 爿 片 牙 牛 犬 犭

気 *honki* earnestness, seriousness, soberness

会員 *honkaiin* regular member

会議 *honkaigi* plenary session, regular session

年 *honnen* this year

⁷局 *honkyoku* main office; telephone central

決 *hongima(ri)* final decision

社 *honsha* main shrine; this shrine; main office; our firm

来 *honrai* originally, primarily, essentially, naturally; properly speaking; just, proper

初子午線 *honsho shigosen* Greenwich Meridian

位 *hon'i* standard, basis, principle; system

位貨幣 *hon'i kahei* legal tender

体 *hontai* substance, entity, the thing itself; true form; antitype; object of worship; main part (of a book)

⁸店 *honten* head office; main store; this store

姓 *honsei* original surname

性 *honshō, honsei* original nature, real character, oneself

物 *hommono* real article, real thing; expert performance

命 *hommei* prospective winner, favorite in a contest

妻 *honsai* legal wife

国 *hongoku* one's own country

拠 *honkyo* stronghold, inner citadel; base, headquarters

拠地 *honkyochi* stronghold, inner citadel; base, headquarters

⁹音 *honne* real intention, motive

屋 *hon'ya* bookstore; publisher; main building. *hon'oku* principal residence

則 *honsoku* rules; original rules

省 *honshō* this ministry; the home office

契約 *honkeiyaku* formal contract

建築 *honkenchiku* permanent construction

草学 *honzōgaku* study of medicinal herbs

¹⁰棒 *hompō* regular salary; basic salary; full pay

校 *honkō* main school; this school

流 *honryū* main current; main current (of thought)

部 *hombu* headquarters

能 *honnō* instinct

家 *honke* main family; originator

格的 *honkakuteki* full-dress, regular; real, genuine, earnest; normal, typical; fundamental

¹¹隊 *hontai* main body (of an army)

望 *hommō* long-cherished ambition; satisfaction

¹²棚 *hondana* bookshelf

結 *hommusu(bi)* square knot

尊 *honzon* main image, the idol; the main image one worships; object of adoration; the man himself; the master of the house

筋 *honsuji* main thread (of a story)

葬 *honsō* formal funeral

番 *homban* the actual performance

営 *hon'ei* headquarters

塁打 *honruida* home run

場 *homba* home, habitat, center

¹³殿 *honden* main shrine; inner sanctuary

源 *hongen* origin, root, cause; principle

腰 *hongoshi* earnestness, seriousness

署 *honsho* police headquarters; main office; this office

義 *hongi* true meaning, underlying principle

意 *hon'i* motive, will, real intention, hopes

業 *hongyō* principal occupation

¹⁴誌 *honshi* this magazine

領 *honryō* characteristic; specialty; duty; proper function; original fief

¹⁵線 *honsen* main (railway) line

論 *honron* main discourse; this subject; body (of a speech)

箱 *hombako* bookcase

調子 *honchōshi* proper key; keynote; normal condition

質 *honshitsu* essence, reality

質的 *honshitsuteki ni* essentially, substantially

¹⁶懐 *honkai* long-cherished ambition; satisfaction

館 *honkan* main building; this building

¹⁸職 *honshoku* principal occupation; an expert; I

題 *hondai* the main question

¹⁹願 *hongan* Amida Buddha's original vow; long-cherished desire

²⁰籍 *honseki* permanent domicile

—— 2 ——

A 机 2543 J3479 M14435 KI. *tsukue* desk, table.

上 *kijō* top of a desk. *kijō no* academic, theoretical, impractical

B 朴 2544 J4b51 M14428 BOKU simple, plain; docile. *hō* tree used for the legs of geta, magnolia hypoleuca

8 直 *bokuchoku* simplicity, naïveté, honesty

念仁 *bokunenjin* a quiet unsociable person; blockhead

11 訥 *bokutotsu* rugged honesty

B 朽 2545 J3560 M14439 KYŪ. *ku(chiru)* decay, rot; remain in seclusion.

4 木 *kuchiki* decayed wood. *kyūboku* decayed wood; an old person

8 果 *ku(chi)-ha(teru)* rust away, rot away, completely decay

葉 *kuchiba* dead leaves

B 朱 2546 J3c6b M14424 SHU cinnabar; vermilion.

3 子学 *Shushigaku* Neo-Confucianism

6 肉 *shuniku* red ink pad

印 *shuin* red seal

13 塗 *shunu(ri)* red (lacquer)

—— 3 ——

垈 2548 J4c5d M14487 (国字) MOKU woodworker.

李 2549 J4d7b M14459 RI. *sumomo* plum.

杏 2554 J3049 M14461 KYŌ. *anzu* apricot.

3 子 *anzu* apricot

杖 2555 J3e73 M14469 JŌ. *tsue* staff, cane.

杓 2558 J4c5d M14466 SHAKU ladle, scoop.

3 子 *shakushi* dipper, ladle, scoop

子定規 *shakushi-jōgi* hard-and-fast rule, formalism, officialism

4 文字 *shamoji* dipper, ladle, scoop

A 束 2559 J422b M14480 SOKU bundle, sheaf, ream (of paper). *taba(neru)* bundle, tie in a bundle; govern, manage, control. *tsuka(neru)* tie in bundles; fold (one's arms); administer. *taba* bundle, bunch, sheaf, coil. *tabane* bundle; control, management. *tsuka* handbreadth; bundle.

12 間 *tsuka (no) ma* brief time, a moment

14 髪 *sokuhatsu* Western hairstyle

16 縛 *sokubaku* restraint, restriction, shackles

杜 2560 J454e M14477 TO. ZU. *mori* woods, grove.

4 氏 *tōji* saké brewer

12 絶 *tozetsu* suspension, interruption

15 撰 *zusan na* slovenly, careless, inaccurate

18 鵑 *token, hototogisu* cuckoo

鵑花 *tokenka, satsuki* an early small azalea

A 材 2561 J3a60 M14463 ZAI log; timber, lumber, wood; material; talent.

4 木 *zaimoku* logs, timber, lumber

木屋 *zaimokuya* lumberyard, lumber dealer

10 料 *zairyō* materials; factor; data

15 質 *zaishitsu* lumber quality

B 杉 2562 J3f79 M14452 SAN. *sugi* cryptomeria, sugi, Japan cedar.

A 条 2563 J3e72 M14486 JŌ article, clause, item; line, stripe, streak; column (of smoke); ray (of light). *kudari* article, clause, paragraph. *-jō* since, because, although, though; article (of a document).

4 文 *jōbun* text, provisions

5 令 *jōrei* law, ordinance, bylaw, rule, regulation

6 件 *jōken* proviso, stipulation, condition

8 例 *jōrei* law, ordinance, bylaw, rule

9 約 *jōyaku* treaty, pact

11 理 *jōri* logic, reason

12 項 *jōkō* clause, article, stipulations

款 *jōkan* stipulation, provision, article, clause

A 村 2564 J423c M14464 SON *mura* village, hamlet.

4

心 忄 小 戈 戸 手 扌 支 攴 攵 文 斗 斤 方 无 日 曰 月 【木】3 欠 止 歹 殳 毋 比 毛 氏 气 水 氵 氺 火 灬 爪 爫 父 爻 爿 片 牙 牛 犬 犭

4

² 人 *murabito* villager
八分 *murahachibu* ostracism
⁴ 内 *sonnai* within the village
⁵ 立 *sonritsu* established by the village
民 *sommin* villagers
⁶ 会 *sonkai* village assembly
名 *sommei* village name
⁷ 邑 *son'yū* village
里 *murazato* villages
村 *muramura* villages
役場 *mura yakuba* village office
⁸ 長 *sonchō* village mayor
雨 *murasame* passing shower
¹¹ 道 *sondō* village road
祭 *mura matsuri* village festival
¹² 落 *sonraku* village, hamlet
営 *son'ei* operated by the village
¹⁴ 境 *murazakai* edge of the village

A 来 2565 / J4d68 / M14489 RAI coming. *ki(taru)* come, arrive; be due to; next, forthcoming. *ki(tasu)* cause, bring about, produce. *ku(ru)* come, come to hand, arrive, approach; call on; come on (rain); set in, be due; become, grow, get; come from; be caused by; derive from. *-rai* since (last month); for (ten days). *rai-* next (year).

月 *raigetsu* next month
日 *rainichi* arrival in Japan; coming to Japan. *ku(ru)hi* the coming days
⁵ 世 *raisei* the future, posterity. *raise* next world
⁶ 宅 *raitaku* coming of a visitor to one's home
年 *rainen, ku(ru)toshi* the coming year
⁷ 攻 *raikō* invasion
社 *raisha* visit to a company
来週 *rairaishū* week after next
⁸ 店 *raiten* coming to the store
⁹ 院 *raiin* coming to the hospital
春 *raishun, raiharu* next spring
客 *raikyaku, raikaku* visitor, caller
¹⁰ 週 *raishū* next week
航 *raikō* arrival of ships; arrival by ship
¹¹ 遊 *raiyū* visit
訪 *raihō* visit, call
¹² 援 *raien* assistance, support
診 *raishin* doctor's visit
着 *raichaku* arrival
場 *raijō* attendance

¹³ 意 *raii* purpose of a visit
¹⁴ 歴 *raireki* history, career
¹⁵ 談 *raidan* interview
駕 *raiga* your coming, your presence
賓 *raihin* guest, visitor; visitor's arrival
賓席 *raihinseki* visitors' seats
¹⁷ 臨 *rairin* attendance, presence; visit, coming, advent

——————— 4 ———————

B 析 2574 / J404f / M14538 SEKI divide; tear; analyze.

杷 2575 / J4747 / M14505 HA a kind of rake.

枇 2580 / J487a / M14528 BI spoon.
⁸ 杷 *biwa* loquat

杵 2581 / J354f / M14503 SHO. SO. *kine* wooden pestle, pounder.
⁹ 柄 *kinezuka* long-handled pestle

A 枚 2582 / J4b67 / M14554 BAI. MAI counter for thin flat things. *-mai* page, leaf (of a book), sheet.
¹⁰ 挙 *maikyo suru* enumerate, mention
¹³ 数 *maisū* the number of flat things

杭 2583 / J393a / M14494 KŌ. GŌ. *kui* stake, post, picket, piling.
⁵ 打 *kuiu(chi)* driving a pile

B 枠 2585 / J4f48 / M14576 (国字) *waku* frame, framework; reel, spindle, spool; rim; box (in printing); limit.
⁴ 内 *wakunai* within the limits
⁵ 外 *wakugai* beyond the limits
¹¹ 組 *wakugu(mi)* frame, framework, framing

B 杯 2586 / J4755 / M14497 盃 3887 / J4756 / M22955 HAI cup, glass; toast, congratulatory cup; counter for cupfuls. *sakazuki* wine glass, saké cup; chalice, cup.
⁸ 事 *sakazukigoto* drinking feast; exchange of nuptial cups; pledging over winecups

⁹ 洗 *haisen* a sink
¹⁵ 盤 *haiban* glasses and plates
盤狼藉 *haiban-rōzeki* disorderly
  drinking party

枡 | 2587 / J5b46 / M14577 | 桝 | 2673 / J4b71 / M-X | (国字)
masu
measuring box.
⁵ 目 *masume* measure
⁷ 形 *masugata* square shape

枢 | 2588 / J3f75 / M14577 | B SŪ. *toboso*
pivot; door.
⁹ 要 *sūyō* importance
¹¹ 密院 *sūmitsuin* Privy Council
¹² 軸 *sūjiku* pivot; axle; center
¹⁶ 機 *sūki* important state affairs
機卿 *sūkikyō, sūkikei* (Catholic) cardinal

枕 | 2589 / J4b6d / M14546 | CHIN. *makura* pillow.
⁴ 木 *makuragi* railroad tie
辺 *makurabe, chimpen* bedside
元 *makuramoto* bedside
¹⁰ 紙 *makuragami* toilet paper
時計 *makuradokei* alarm clock
¹¹ 許 *makuramoto* bedside
¹² 詞 *makura kotoba* a 'pillow word'; a
  conventional epithet
¹⁶ 頭 *chintō* bedside

林 | 2590 / J4e51 / M14551 | A RIN. *hayashi* forest.
⁴ 木 *rimboku* forest tree
⁵ 立 *rinritsu* forest (of chimneys)
⁸ 学 *ringaku* forestry
⁹ 政 *rinsei* forestry management
泉 *rinsen* landscape garden
¹¹ 道 *rindō* forest road
産 *rinsan* forestry products
野 *rin'ya* woodland, forests
野庁 *rin'yachō* forestry agency
¹² 間 *rinkan* in the forest
間学校 *rinkan gakkō* outdoor school,
  camping school
¹³ 業 *ringyō* forestry
¹⁷ 檎 *ringo* apple

枝 | 2591 / J3b5e / M14557 | A SHI. KI. *eda, e* branch,
bow, twig, limb.
³ 川 *edagawa* branch of a river
⁴ 切 *edaki(ri)* pruning

⁷ 豆 *edamame* green soybeans
折 *edao(ri)* breaking branches (to mark a
  mountain trail). *shio(ri)* guide book
折戸 *shio(ri)do* garden gate, gate of
  branches
⁸ 垂柳 *shidare yanagi* weeping willow
垂桜 *shidarezakura* weeping cherry
⁹ 城 *edajiro* branch castle
¹⁰ 振 *edabu(ri)* ramifications; shape (of a
  tree)
¹¹ 道 *edamichi* branch road
接 *edatsugi* cleft grafting
¹² 葉 *edaha, shiyō* leaves and branches,
  foliage; ramifications; side issues;
  digression; minor details
葉末節 *shiyō-massetsu* branches and
  leaves; unimportant details

松 | 2592 / J3e3e / M14516 | A SHŌ. *matsu*
pine.
³ 山 *matsuyama* pine-covered hill
⁴ 内 *matsu(no)uchi* New Year's season
⁶ 虫 *matsumushi* a cricket
竹 *matsutake* New Year's pine-and-
  bamboo decorations
竹梅 *shō-chiku-bai* pine-bamboo-plum;
  congratulatory tree decorations
⁸ 明 *taimatsu* pine torch, torchlight,
  firebrand
林 *matsubayashi* pine forest
⁹ 風 *matsukaze, shōfū* wind through the
  pines
柏 *shōhaku* pines and oaks; faithfulness
茸 *matsutake, matsudake* a kind of
  edible mushroom
¹⁰ 原 *matsubara* pine grove
脂 *matsuyani, shōshi* rosin, pine resin
¹² 笹 *matsukasa* pine cone
葉 *matsuba* pine needles
葉杖 *matsubazue* crutches
¹³ 飾 *matsukaza(ri)* New Year's pine
  decorations
²¹ 露 *shōro* a kind of edible mushroom
²² 籟 *shōrai* sighing of the pine trees

果 | 2594 / J324c / M14556 | A KA fruit; reward. *ha(tasu)*
carry out, achieve,
complete; realize, perform, fulfill.
ha(teru) end, be finished, be exhausted;
die, perish *ōse(ru)* succeed in doing.
hatashite as was expected; really.
ha(teshi), ha(te) end, limit, bounds,

4
心 忄 小 戈 戸 手 扌 支 攴 攵 文 斗 斤 方 无 日 曰 月 【木】⁴ 欠 止 歹 殳 毋 比 毛 氏 气 水 氵 氺 火 灬 爪 爫 父 爻 爿 丬 片 牙 牛 犬 犭

4

心忄小戈戸手扌支攴攵文斗方无日曰月【木】欠止歹殳毋比毛氏气水氵永火灬爪爫父爻爿丬片牙牛犬犭

extremity, result; fate. *-ha(teru)* be tired out; be used up.

⁵ 汁 *kajū* fruit juice
⁶ 肉 *kaniku* the flesh of fruit
⁸ 物 *kudamono* fruit
実 *kajitsu* fruit; nut; berry
実酒 *kajitsushu* cider, wine, plum liquor
⁹ 食 *kashoku* living on fruit
¹¹ 断 *kadan na* decisive, resolute, drastic
¹² 敢 *hakana(i)* fleeting, momentary, ephemeral; vain, empty, hopeless; fickle, inconstant, unstable; fragile, frail; pitiful, poor, sad, miserable. *kakan na* resolute, determined, bold
然 *kazen* as was expected
無 *hakana(i)* fleeting, transitory, ephemeral. *ha(teshi)na(ku)* eternally, interminably. *ha(teshi) (ga) na(i)* endless, boundless, fathomless, eternal
報 *kahō* good fortune, luck; happiness
報者 *kahōmono* lucky fellow
¹⁶ 糖 *katō* fruit sugar
樹 *kaju* fruit tree
樹園 *kajuen* orchard

板 A 2595 J4844 M14518 HAN. BAN. *ita* board, plank; planking; plate, sheet; the stage.

³ 子 *itago* a board on which to practice swimming strokes (in water); floor planks in a small Japanese boat
⁴ 戸 *itado* wooden door
切 *itaki(re)* piece of wood, scrap lumber
仕切 *itajikiri* wooden partition
目 *itame* grain (in wood)
⁷ 囲 *itagako(i)* board fence, wooden fence
床 *itadoko* wooden-floored
材 *itazai* boards
⁸ 金 *itagane* metal plate, sheet metal; sheet gold or sheet silver. *bankin* sheet gold; sheet silver
⁹ 垣 *itagaki* wooden fence
前 *itamae* a cook
挟 *itabasami* dilemma, predicament
¹⁰ 挽 *itahiki* sawing lumber
¹¹ 張 *itaba(ri)* boarding; planking; boarded-up place
¹² 場 *itaba* a cook (in a restaurant)
塀 *itabei* wooden wall, board fence
葺 *itabuki* roofing of boards
硝子 *itagarasu* plate glass

間 *ita(no)ma* wooden floor
間稼 *ita(no)ma kase(gi)* bathhouse thief
¹⁵ 敷 *itaji(ki)* wooden floor; removable slatted floor
¹⁶ 橋 *itabashi* wooden bridge
壁 *itakabe* wooden wall

東 A 2596 J456c M14499 TŌ *higashi* east. *azuma* east; Eastern Japan.

⁴ 方 *tōhō, tōbō* east, eastward; eastern; the Orient
方教会 *Tōhō Kyōkai* The Eastern Church
天 *tōten* the eastern sky
⁵ 北 *tōhoku, higashikita* northeast. *Tōhoku* the Northeast
半球 *Higashi Hankyū* Eastern Hemisphere
⁶ 行 *tōkō* eastbound
向 *higashimu(ki)* facing east
夷 *tōi* eastern barbarians
印度 *Higashi Indo* East Indies
西 *tōzai* east and west; Orient and Occident; Your attention please.
西南北 *tōzainamboku* east, west, south, and north, all directions
⁷ 男 *azuma otoko* a man from East Japan
亜 *Tōa* East Asia, the Orient
⁸ 国 *tōgoku* eastern country; eastern provinces; Kanto Provinces
欧 *Tōō* Eastern Europe
郊 *tōkō* eastern suburbs
京都 *Tōkyōto* Tokyo Metropolis
奔西走 *tōhon-seisō suru* busy oneself, bestir oneself, be on the go, take an active interest
⁹ 面 *tōmen* facing the east; east face, east side; the east
風 *tōfū, kochi, kochi kaze* east wind; spring wind
南 *tōnan, higashiminami* southeast
南亜 *Tōnan'a* Southeast Asia
海地方 *Tōkai Chihō* Eastern-Sea Area
海道 *Tōkaidō* Eastern Sea Road
洋 *Tōyō* Orient
洋人 *Tōyōjin* Orientals
洋風 *tōyōfū no* Oriental
洋通 *Tōyōtsū* Orientalist
¹⁰ 進 *tōshin suru* proceed east
部 *tōbu* eastern part
都 *Tōto* the Eastern Capital, Yedo, Edo; Tokyo

宮 *tōgū, haru(no)miya* crown prince
11 側 *higashigawa* east side, east bank. *tōsoku* east side
経 *tōkei* east longitude
12 雲 *shinonome* daybreak, dawn
14 漸 *tōzen* eastward advance

────── 5 ──────

柁 2597 J4248 M14599 See 舵 4937.

栃 2613 J464a M14687 (国字) *tochi* horse chestnut.

柊 2614 J4922 M14610 SHU. SHŪ. *hiiragi* holly.

栂 2618 J444e M14686 (国字) *tsuga* hemlock, hemlock-spruce.

柾 2619 J4b6f M14675 (国字) *masa, masame* straight grain. *masaki* spindle tree.
5 目 *masame* straight grain

柵 2620 J3a74 M14665 SAKU stockade, fence, palisade. *shigara(mu)* entwine around; check (a current) with a weir. *shigarami* weir.
9 垣 *sakugaki* fence

柑 2621 J343b M14619 KON. KAN citrus fruit; orange.
16 橘類 *kankitsurui* citrus fruits

柚 2622 J4d2e M14629 YU. YŪ. JIKU. *yuzu* citron.

柏 2623 J4770 M14617 HAKU. HYAKU. *kashiwa* oak.
4 手 *kashiwade* handclapping in worship at a shrine ⌈oak leaf
15 餅 *kashiwa mochi* rice cake wrapped in

柿 2624 J3341 M14681 SHI. JI *kaki* persimmon. *kokera* shingle.
6 色 *kaki iro* yellowish brown
11 渋 *kakishibu* persimmon juice

柘 2626 J4453 M14626 SHA, SO wild mulberry.

榴 2633 *zakuro* pomegranate
榴石 *zakuroishi* garnet

柄 2627 J4a41 M14603 HEI. *e* handle, crank, grip; hilt, shaft, knob, spoke (of steering wheel on a ship). *gara* pattern, design; build; character, nature. *tsuka* hilt, grip, handle (of a knife).
7 杓 *hishaku* dipper, ladle, scoop
9 染 *garazo(me)* dyeing in designs

某 2628 J4b3f M14618 BŌ one, a certain; that person; that thing. *nanigashi* somebody, a certain person; a certain amount. *soregashi* somebody, a certain person; I.
4 月 *bōgetsu* a certain month
氏 *bōshi* a certain person
8 所 *bōsho* a certain place

柳 2629 J4c78 M14662 RYŪ. *yanagi* willow.
6 行李 *yanagigōri* wicker trunk
9 眉 *ryūbi* beautiful eyebrows
13 腰 *yanagigoshi* slender figure, slim waist; willowy

査 2630 J3a3a M14643 SA investigate.
5 収 *sashū suru* investigate and confiscate
8 定 *satei* assessment; revision; audit (of salaries); investigation and decision
11 問 *samon* inquiry, hearing
12 証 *sashō* visa; investigation and attestation
13 照 *sashō* a checkup
14 察 *sasatsu* inspection, investigation
15 閲 *saetsu* inspection, investigation

柱 2631 J436c M14660 CHŪ cylinder, supports for strings on a lute; pillar, post. *hashira* pillar, column, post, pole; support, prop, stay; sole support; counter for Shinto gods. *ji* bridge (of a stringed instrument).
5 石 *chūseki* pillar, mainstay, cornerstone
状 *chūjō* columnar, pillar-like
10 時計 *hashiradokei* wall clock
11 廊 *chūrō* colonnade, portico
14 暦 *hashiragoyomi* wall calendar
16 頭 *chūtō* capital of a column

心 忄 小 戈 戸 手 扌 支 攴 攵 文 斗 斤 方 无 日 曰 月 【木】5
欠 止 歹 殳 毋 比 毛 氏 气 水 氵 氺 火 灬 爪 爫 父 爻 爿 爿 片 牙 牛 犬 犭

4

心 忄 小 戈 戸 手 扌 支 攵 文 斗 斤 方 无 日 曰 月 【木】 欠 止 歹 殳 毋 比 毛 氏 气 水 氵 氺 火 灬 爪 爫 父 爻 爿 片 牙 牛 犬 犭

B 架 2632 J324d M14586 KA frame, mount, stand, support; hang up; shelf.
ka(suru) build (a bridge), construct.
ka(keru) vt hang.
⁵台 *kadai* abutment; stand, frame, holder
⁸空 *kakū* aerial, overhead, trolley; fiction.
kakū no fanciful, fictitious, Utopian
¹¹設 *kasetsu* construction, building
¹⁵線 *kasen* aerial wiring
¹⁶橋 *kakyō* bridge building

B 柔 2633 J3d40 M14622 JŪ, NYŪ weakness; gentleness; softness.
yawa(ragu) vi soften, be reconciled; lessen; calm down. *yawara(geru)* vt soften, moderate, ease, alleviate, mitigate, relax; appease; dilute (wine); tone down (colors); comfort; pacify, quiet.
yawa(rakai), yawa(rakana), yawa(i) soft, tender, plastic; limp; gentle; mellow.
yawa(ra) jujitsu.
⁶肌 *yawahada* soft skin
⁸和 *nyūwa* gentleness, meekness, mildness
¹⁰弱 *jūjaku, nyūjaku* weakness, effeminacy, enervation
¹¹術 *jūjutsu* jujitsu, jujutsu
道 *jūdō* jujitsu, jujutsu, judo
道家 *jūdōka* judo expert
軟 *jūnan na* soft, pliable, flexible, elastic
¹²順 *jūjun* obedience, meekness, docility

B 枯 2634 J384f M14579 KO. *ka(reru)* wither, die, be dead; age; be seasoned; fog up. *ka(rasu)* kill (vegetation); let dry; season (lumber). *ka(rebamu)* wither.
ka(re)-, ka(ra)- dead.
³山 *ka(re)yama* a hill covered with dead vegetation
⁴木 *ka(re)ki, ka(ra)ki, koboku* dead tree
⁶死 *koshi* withering, dying
⁷花 *ka(re)bana* faded flowers
枝 *ka(re)eda, ka(ra)eda, ka(re)e* dead branch
果 *ka(re)-ha(teru)* waste away
⁹草 *ka(re)gusa, ka(re)kusa* dry grass, hay
¹¹淡 *kotan* elegant simplicity
渇 *kokatsu suru* dry up; be exhausted; become poverty-stricken
野 *ka(re)no* desolate field
¹²葉 *ka(re)ha, ka(re)ba, koyō* dead leaf

A 栄 2635 J3149 M14687 EI prosperity, glory, splendor, honor. *saka(eru)* prosper, flourish, thrive. *ha(eru)* shine, be brilliant; look attractive. *saka(e)* glory, prosperity. *hae* glory. *hae(aru)* glorious.
光 *eikō* glory
⁷利 *eiri* wealth and fame
⁸典 *eiten* honors; ceremony, exercises
⁹冠 *eikan* laurels, garland
枯 *eiko* ups and downs, rise and fall, vicissitudes
枯盛衰 *eiko seisui* prosperity and decline, vicissitudes of fortune
¹⁰進 *eishin* promotion, advancement
華 *eiga* glory, splendor, prosperity; luxury; majesty
辱 *eijoku* honor and disgrace; prestige, dignity, honor, reputation
¹¹達 *eitatsu* fame, distinction, rise, advancement
転 *eiten* promotion
¹²落 *eiraku* flourishing and declining
¹³誉 *eiyo* honor, fame, glory
¹⁵養 *eiyō* nutrition, nourishment, sustenance
²⁰耀 *eyō, eiyō* luxury, splendor, prosperity

A 染 2636 J4077 M14621 SEN. *so(mu), so(maru)* be dyed, be imbued with, be tainted with. *so(meru)* dye, color, paint. *shi(miru)* soak in, permeate, infiltrate; pierce (as a wind); be imbued with, be influenced by; smart; be sensitive to pain. *shi(mi)* stain, blot, spot, smudge. *so(me)* dyeing, printing. *-zo(me)* dyed.
²入 *shi(mi)-i(ru)* soak into, permeate, infiltrate; be impressed with
³上 *so(me)-a(garu)* be completely dyed.
so(me)-a(geru) finish dyeing
⁴方 *so(me)kata* dyeing process
込 *so(me)-ko(mu)* dye in designs.
shi(mi)-ko(mu) soak into, permeate, infiltrate; be impressed with
分 *so(me)-wa(keru)* dye in different colors
毛 *semmō* dyeing the hair
⁵付 *shi(mi)-tsu(ku)* be dyed in deeply, be stained. *so(me)-tsu(keru)* dye in (patterns)
出 *so(me)-da(su)* dye (patterns)

⁶色 *senshoku* dyeing
色体 *senshokutai* chromosome
⁷抜 *so(me)-nu(ku)* dye in the grain.
shi(mi)-nu(ku) removal of stains
⁸直 *so(me)-nao(su)* redye
物 *somemono* dyeing; dyed goods
⁹透 *shi(mi)-tō(ru)* soak through, penetrate, permeate, infiltrate
柄 *so(me)gara* dyed designs
型 *so(me)gata* dyed pattern
¹⁰料 *senryō* dyes, dyestuffs
粉 *so(me)ko* dyestuff
¹²渡 *shi(mi)-wata(ru)* penetrate, spread, pervade
替 *so(me)ka(e)* redyeing
筆 *sempitsu* writing; painting
¹⁴髪剤 *sempatsuzai* hair dye
模様 *so(me)-moyō* printed pattern
¹⁸織 *senshoku* dyeing and weaving

————— 6 —————

桧 ₂₆₃₇ J4930 M-X Nonstandard for 檜 2894.

栢 ₂₆₃₈ J337c M14714 See 柏 2623.

栓 ₂₆₄₉ J4072 M14689 B SEN bolt, stopper, cork, plug, ear plug, bung, faucet, peg.
⁷抜 *sennu(ki)* corkscrew, bottle opener

栖 ₂₆₅₀ J4034 M14693 SEI. *su* nest, rookery, breeding place, beehive, cobweb; den, haunt.
¹⁰息 *seisoku suru* inhabit, live in, lodge in

栴 ₂₆₅₁ J4073 M14737 SEN Japanese bead tree.
¹⁷檀 *sendan* Japanese bead tree

桓 ₂₆₅₂ J343c M14774 KAN marking post.

桔 ₂₆₅₃ J354b M14777 KETSU, KITSU a sweep-well bucket; used in plant names.
¹¹梗 *kikyō* a root used in making cough medicine

栽 ₂₆₅₄ J3a4f M14750 B SAI planting.

¹¹培 *saibai* cultivation (of plants)

桐 ₂₆₅₅ J364d M14770 TŌ. *kiri* the paulownia tree.
³下駄 *kiri geta* geta made of paulownia wood
⁸油 *kiriyu, kiri abura, tōyu* wood oil, tung oil, nut oil, China wood oil
¹⁸箪笥 *kiri tansu* chest of drawers of paulownia wood

桁 ₂₆₅₆ J3765 M14754 KŌ. *keta* beam, girder, spar, yard; unit or column (in figures).
³下 *ketashita* clearance (under overpass)
⁵外 *ketahazu(re)* wide difference; extraordinary
¹²違 *ketachiga(i)* off on the decimal point; wide difference

柴 ₂₆₅₇ J3c46 M14664 SHI. SAI. *shiba* brushwood, firewood.
刈 *shibaka(ri)* gathering firewood; firewood gatherer 「cottage
⁸門 *saimon* brushwood gate, humble
¹¹笛 *shibabue* leaf flute

桟 ₂₆₅₈ J3b37 M14796 B SAN crosspiece, cleat, frame, door bolt; shelf; jetty; suspension bridge.
¹¹道 *sandō* plank road
¹⁵敷 *sajiki* reviewing stand, box, gallery
¹⁶橋 *sambashi* wharf, jetty. *sankyō* wharf; bridge

桂 ₂₆₅₉ J374b M14755 KEI. *katsura* Judas tree, katsura tree, cinnamon tree.
⁹冠 *keikan* crown of laurel
冠詩人 *keikan shijin* poet laureate

核 ₂₆₆₀ J334b M14743 B KAKU nucleus, core, seed, kernel. *kaku no* nuclear. *sane* fruit stone, kernel, nucleus.
⁴心 *kakushin* core, kernel
反応 *kaku hannō* nuclear reaction
分裂 *kaku bunretsu* nuclear fission
⁷兵器 *kaku heiki* nuclear weapons
⁸武装 *kaku busō* nuclear arms
実験 *kaku jikken* nuclear experiments
物理学 *kaku butsurigaku* nuclear physics

4

¹² 弾頭 *kaku dantō* nuclear warhead

B 桑 2661 J372c M14772 Sō. *kuwa* mulberry.

⁵ 田 *sōden* mulberry plantation
⁶ 色 *kuwa iro* light yellow
⁸ 門 *sōmon* priesthood; Buddhism
⁹ 海 *sōkai* this world's sudden changes
　畑 *kuwabatake* mulberry field
¹³ 園 *sōen* mulberry plantation

栗 2662 J372a M14695 Ritsu. *kuri* chestnut.

⁴ 毛 *kurige* chestnut color; bay horse, sorrel
⁶ 色 *kuri iro* chestnut color
¹³ 鼠 *risu* squirrel

B 桃 2663 J456d M14757 Tō. *momo* peach.

³ 山 *Momoyama* era (1576～1598)
⁶ 色 *momo iro* rose, pink
　色遊戯 *momo-iro yūgi* love affair
　色雑誌 *momo-iro zasshi* yellow journal
　花 *tōka* peach blossom
¹³ 園 *momozono* peach orchard
　節句 *Momo (no) Sekku* the Doll Festival
　源郷 *tōgenkyō* quiet country garden; heaven on earth; Shangri-La

A 桜 2664 J3a79 M14796 Ō. *sakura* flowering cherry; cherry blossoms; pink color; horse meat.

⁴ 月 *sakurazuki* third lunar month
　木 *sakuragi* cherry tree
⁶ 肉 *sakuraniku* horse meat
　色 *sakura iro* the color of cherry blossoms; pink, cerise
⁷ 坊 *sakurambō* edible cherry 「season
　花 *ōka, sakurabana* cherry-blossom
　貝 *sakuragai* a cherry shell
⁹ 狩 *sakuraga(ri)* looking for cherry blossoms
　草 *sakurasō* primrose
¹⁰ 桃 *sakurambō, ōtō* edible cherry
　紙 *sakuragami* handkerchief paper, toilet paper
¹⁵ 餅 *sakura mochi* a round glutenous-rice cake filled with sweet bean paste covered with a salted cherry leaf

A 株 2665 J3374 M14723 Shu. *kabu* stump; shares, stocks; connections; business; counter for small plants.

⁴ 分 *kabuwa(ke)* dividing roots
⁵ 主 *kabunushi* shareholder
　主総会 *kabunushi sōkai* stockholders' general meeting
⁶ 式 *kabushiki* shares, stocks
　式市場 *kabushiki shijō* stock market
　式会社 *kabushiki kaisha* joint-stock corporation
　式取引所 *kabushiki torihikijo* stock exchange
　式相場 *kabushiki sōba* stock quotations
⁸ 価 *kabuka* price of stocks
　券 *kabuken* stock certificate

A 梅 2666 J475f M14795' Bai. *ume* plum, plum tree.

³ 干 *umeboshi* pickled plums
⁷ 花 *baika* plum blossoms
⁸ 林 *bairin* plum orchard
　毒 *baidoku* syphilis
　雨 *baiu, tsuyu* rainy season
　雨明 *tsuyua(ke), baiua(ke)* end of the rainy season
　雨晴 *tsuyuba(re)* end of the rainy season
¹⁰ 酒 *umeshu, baishu* plum brandy
¹³ 園 *baien* plum orchard
¹⁴ 暦 *umegoyomi* harbingers of spring (plum blossoms)

A 案 2667 J3046 M14762 An proposition, suggestion, plan, idea; opinion; expectation; bill, draft, measure; table. *an(jiru), an(zuru)* worry, be anxious, be afraid, ponder, fear. *an(zuru) ni* it seems to me that.

³ 山子 *kakashi, kagashi* scarecrow; figurehead
⁴ 文 *ambun* draft
　内 *annai* guidance; guide; announcement, invitation, notice; familiarity (with)
　内者 *annaisha* guide
　内書 *annaisho* guidebook
⁵ 外 *angai* surprisingly; disappointingly; unexpectedly
　出 *anshutsu* contrivance, invention, studying out (something)
⁶ 件 *anken* item, case, matter
⁸ 定 *an(no)jō* as feared, as expected

A 格 2668 J334a M14749 Kō . KAKU status, rank; capacity, character; standard; a rule; a case (in law); case (in grammar).

³ 下 kakusa(ge) demotion, downgrading
上 kakua(ge) status elevation
子 kōshi lattice, coffer, grating, fretwork
子細工 kōshizaiku latticework
子縞 kōshijima checkered pattern
⁴ 天井 gōtenjo coffered ceiling
⁵ 付 kakuzu(ke), kakutsu(ke) rating, classification, allocation, conditioning
外 kakuhazu(re) inferior, ungraded (goods). kakugai special, exceptional
外品 kakugaihin inferior goods
⁶ 好 kakkō shape, form, appearance; pose, posture; manner; approximately. kakkō na suitable, reasonable
式 kakushiki status, rank, social standing; rules of etiquette
式張 kakushikiba(ru) be overly formal
安 kakuyasu na cheap, reasonable
⁷ 言 kakugen maxim, proverb
別 kakubetsu ni especially, exceptionally
⁸ 例 kakurei precedent; ruling
⁹ 段 kakudan no special, exceptional, remarkable, appreciable
¹⁰ 差 kakusa difference in quality
納 kakunō housing for equipment or machines
納庫 kakunōko hangar
¹⁵ 調 kakuchō the style and meter of a poem
¹⁸ 闘 kakutō fist fight; scuffle; wrestling

A 校 2669 J393b M14713 KYŌ . Kō school; (printing) proof; comparison; correction; investigation. kō(su) test, correct, proofread. -kō school; proof.

² 了 kōryō, kyōryō proofreading completed
⁴ 内 kōnai school grounds
友 kōyū schoolmate, alumnus
⁵ 本 kōhon perfected text
外 kōgai outside the school; extension
止 kōsei proofreading
正刷 kōseizu(ri) galley proofs
正済 kōseizu(mi) corrected proof, corrected
⁷ 医 kōi school doctor
⁸ 長 kōchō principal, schoolmaster, rector
門 kōmon school gate

舎 kōsha school building
定 kōtei revision
⁹ 風 kōfū school spirit; school customs
則 kōsoku school regulations
訂 kōtei revision
訂版 kōteiban revised edition
¹⁰ 庭 kōtei campus, school playground
訓 kōkun school rules; school mottos
倉 azekura a storehouse built of square logs; a log house
¹¹ 務 kōmu school affairs
勘 kōkan suru compare and consider; compare with the original and correct
¹⁴ 旗 kōki school flag
歌 kōka school song
¹⁵ 閲 kōetsu revision

A 根 2670 J3a2c M14745 KON root (of a plant); root, radical (in science and math.); stamina. ne root; base (of a hill); head (of a boil); origin; foundation; peak. ne(kosogi), ne(kosoge) all, completely, thoroughly. ne(kkara) (not) at all, (not) in the least.

⁴ 方 nekata the lower part; the root
比 konkura(be) endurance contest
元 kongen root, origin, cause, source. nemoto part near the root; base, bottom
⁵ 付 nezu(ku), netsu(ku) take root. netsu(ke) toggle for suspending a pouch from belt
本 kompon root, origin, cause; basis. nemoto part near the root; base, bottom
本法 komponhō fundamental law
本的 komponteki na fundamental, basic, drastic
⁶ 回 nemawa(ri) circumference of the root. nemawa(shi) digging around the root, negotiating with all concerned parties before making a formal decision
気 konki patience, perseverance, energy
⁸ 底 kontei root; basis, foundation
治 konchi, konji complete cure
限 konkagi(ri) with all one's might
茎 konkei root stalk, rhizome
性 konjō disposition, nature
拠 konkyo basis, foundation; authority
⁹ 城 nejiro stronghold, citadel; headquarters, base of operations

4

負 *komma(ke)* losing stamina; losing in a test of strength; losing patience

10 原 *kongen* root, origin, cause

差 *neza(su)* take root; originate in; show signs of. *neza(shi)* taking root; breeding, birth

11 強 *nezuyo(i)* firmly rooted; deep-seated. *nezuyo(ku)* firmly, steadfastly, tenaciously

張 *neba(ri)* deep spreading roots

深 *nebuka(i)* deep-rooted, ingrained

雪 *neyuki* lingering snow

菜類 *konsairui* root crops

掘葉掘 *neho(ri)-haho(ri)* inquisitively; completely

12 絶 *konzetsu, nedaya(shi)* eradication

葉無 *ne(mo) ha(mo) na(i)* without foundation

無草 *nena(shi)gusa* duckweed; something unsettled

13 源 *kongen* root, origin, cause, source

幹 *konkan* root and trunk; basis; nucleus; keynote

20 競 *konkura(be)* endurance contest

——————— **7** ———————

梼 ⌷2672 J456e M14911⌷ See 檮 2897.

檮 ⌷⌷

桝 ⌷2673 J4b71 M-X⌷ Nonstandard for 枡 2587.

枡 ⌷⌷

椛 ⌷2683 J3371 M15065⌷ (国字) *momiji* autumn foliage. Used also as a variant of 樺 2817.

A 械 ⌷2685 J3323 M14882⌷ KAI fetters; machine; instrument.

梓 ⌷2688 J3034 M14845⌷ SHI. *azusa* catalpa tree.

桶 ⌷2694 J3233 M14811⌷ YŌ. TŌ. *oke* tub, bucket.

9 屋 *okeya* cooper

梢 ⌷2695 J3e3f M14866⌷ SHŌ. *kozue* twig; treetop.

梱 ⌷2696 J3a2d M14883⌷ KON. *kō(ru)* pack, tie up. *kōri* bale (of silk or thread).

kori bale, pack, package.

5 包 *kompō* packing, crating; package

梨 ⌷2697 J4d7c M14873⌷ RI. *nashi* pear, Japanese pear; pear tree.

13 園 *rien* theatrical world; pear orchard

20 礫 *nashi (no) tsubute* no communication

梗 ⌷2698 J393c M14849⌷ KŌ, KYŌ for the most part; close up.

14 概 *kōgai* outline, summary

梶 ⌷2699 J3361 M14889⌷ BI. *kaji* oar, sculling oar, shaft.

12 棒 *kajibō* (wagon) shafts

梧 ⌷2700 J3868 M14872⌷ GO desk. *aogiri* Chinese parasol tree; phoenix tree. *sasa(eru)* support.

3 下 *goka* under a desk

10 桐 *godō* Chinese parasol tree; phoenix tree

梁 ⌷2702 J4e42 M14825⌷ RYŌ bridge beams. *hari, utsubari, uchibari* beam, girder. *yana* weir, fish trap, fish pond.

4 木 *ryōboku* beam

7 材 *harizai* beam, girder

12 間 *harima* span (in construction)

A 巣 ⌷2705 J4163 M8696⌷ SŌ. *su* nest, rookery, breeding place, beenhive, cobweb; den, haunt. *suku(u)* build (a nest).

5 立 *suda(chi)* leaving the nest; becoming independent; leaving one's confinement; graduation

13 窟 *sōkutsu* den, haunt, hangout, home

15 箱 *subako* nest box, hive

22 籠 *sugomo(ru)* to nest

梯 ⌷2706 J4474 M14881⌷ TEI. *hashigo* ladder, stairs; insatiable drinking.

3 子 *hashigo, teishi* ladder, stairs; insatiable drinking.

子段 *hashigodan* step, stair, stairway

子酒 *hashigozake* insatiable drinking; heaver drinker

7 状 *teijō* echelon formation; trapezoid

形 *hashigogata, teikei* echelon formation; trapezoid
[11] 隊 *teitai* echelon

――――――― **8** ―――――――

槌 | 2709 / J4448 / M-X | Nonstandard for 槌 2767.

椋 | 2725 / J4c3a / M15020 | RYŌ *muku* a kind of elm.

椙 | 2728 / J3f7a / M15063 | （国字） *sugi* Japanese cedar; cryptomeria.

椀 | 2732 / J4f50 / M15001 | WAN wooden bowl, lacquered bowl.

椅 | 2737 / J3058 / M15009 | I chair.
[3] 子 *isu* chair, seat, couch; office, position

棉 | 2741 / J4c49 / M14919 | MEN. *wata* cotton.
[7] 花 *menka* raw cotton

椎 | 2742 / J4447 / M15024 | TSUI. *tsuchi* hammer, mallet. *shii* an oak.
[9] 茸 *shiitake* a kind of edible mushroom
[10] 骨 *tsuikotsu* vertebra

棲 | 2743 / J4033 / M14980 | SEI. *su(mu)* live, dwell.
[5] 処 *sumika* dwelling; nest; den (of robbers)
[10] 息 *seisoku suru* inhabit, dwell in, lodge in

B 棋 | 2744 / J347d / M14922 | KI *go*; Japanese chess.
[3] 士 *kishi* a go player
[7] 局 *kikyoku* the game of go; the go board

B 棺 | 2746 / J343d / M14993 | KAN *hitsugi* casket, coffin.
[11] 桶 *kan'oke* casket, coffin

B 棟 | 2747 / J456f / M14949 | TŌ. *mune* ridge, ridgepole; counter for buildings.
[3] 上 *munea(ge)* ridgepole raising
[4] 木 *munagi* ridgepole

[5] 瓦 *munegawara* ridge tile
[11] 梁 *tōryō* chief support, pillar (in a nation); chief, leader, foreman

B 棚 | 2748 / J432a / M14941 | HŌ. BYŌ. *tana* shelf, ledge, rack, mount, mantelpiece; trellis, lattice.
[3] 上 *tanaa(ge) suru* shelve, pigeonhole, table (a motion), sidetrack
[4] 引 *tanabi(ku)* trail, hang over (fog or smoke)
[8] 承 *tanau(ke)* shelf bracket
[10] 晒 *tanazarashi* shopworn stock

A 森 | 2749 / J3f39 / M14974 | SHIN. *mori* woods, grove.
[8] 林 *shinrin* forest, wood
　　林学 *shinringaku* forestry
　　林限界 *shinrin genkai* timber line
　　林帯 *shinrintai* forest zone
[12] 閑 *shinkan to shita* silent, hushed, deserted
　　森 *shinshin* deeply forested; towering
[17] 厳 *shingen na* solemn, grave, awe-inspiring
　　羅万象 *shinra-banshō* all creation, the universe

A 棒 | 2750 / J4b40 / M14929 | BŌ. stick, cane, rod, pole, stake, pile, club, bar; line, dash.
[4] 引 *bōbi(ki)* cancellation, writing off
　　切 *bōki(re)* a piece of wood; a piece of a broken pole
[5] 立 *bōda(chi)* standing up straight (because of surprise)
[7] 状 *bōjō* cylindrical shape
[8] 杭 *bōgui* pile, stake
[10] 振 *bō (ni) fu(ru)* fail, come to naught
　　高跳 *bōtakato(bi)* pole vault
[11] 術 *bōjutsu* stick fighting
　　暗記 *bōanki* rote memorization
[14] 読 *bōyo(mi)* accentless reading; reading Chinese in the Chinese order

A 植 | 2751 / J3f22 / M15023 | SHOKU planting. *u(eru)* plant, set out, raise, sow; set type. *u(waru)* be planted.
[4] 込 *u(e)-ko(mu)* plant (trees). *u(e)ko(mi)* shrubbery, thick growth of plants
　　木 *ueki* garden plant, shrub, tree
　　木屋 *uekiya* gardener, nurseryman

4

心 忄 小 戈 戸 手 扌 支 攴 攵 文 斗 斤 方 无 日 曰 月 【木】 欠 止 歹 殳 毋 比 毛 氏 气 水 氵 氺 火 灬 爪 爫 父 爻 爿 片 牙 牛 犬 犭

木鉢 *uekibachi* flowerpot
5 付 *u(e)-tsu(keru)* plant, set out, transplant; implant
皮 *shokuhi* skin grafting
民 *shokumin* colonization, settlement; colonist, settler
民地 *shokuminchi* colony, settlement
民時代 *shokumin jidai* colonial period
6 字 *shokuji* typesetting, composition
8 林 *shokurin* afforestation
物 *shokubutsu* plant, vegetation, flora
物人間 *shokubutu ningen* human vegetable
物学 *shokubutsugaku* botany
物園 *shokubutsuen* botanical garden
12 替 *u(e)-ka(eru)* transplant, replant
16 樹 *shokuju* tree planting
樹祭 *Shokujusai* Arbor Day

検 A
2752
J3821
M15065
KEN investigation. *ken(suru)* investigate.
4 分 *kembun* inspection, examination
5 札 *kensatsu* examination of tickets
出 *kenshutsu* search; (chemical) detection
圧 *ken'atsu* measuring pressure
6 死 *kenshi* investigating a death; autopsy
印 *ken'in* stamp of approval
地 *kenchi* land survey
7 尿 *kennyō* urine examination
束 *kensoku* restraint, restriction; arrest, custody
8 事 *kenji* prosecuting attorney
事局 *kenjikyoku* prosecutor's office
定 *kentei* official certification, approval, authorization; examination, inspection; license
定済 *kenteizu(mi)* inspected (by the government)
定試験 *kentei shiken* licensing examination
9 便 *kemben* stool examination
屍 *kenshi* investigating a death; autopsy
屍官 *kenshikan* coroner
疫 *ken'eki* quarantine
疫所 *ken'ekisho* quarantine station
査 *kensa* inspection, examination
査役 *kensayaku* inspector, auditor
査官 *kensakan* inspector, auditor

10 梅 *kembai* syphilis test
討 *kentō* investigation, examination, study, test
針 *kenshin* inspection of a meter or a gauge
索 *kensaku suru* refer to, look up (a word); make a laboratory test
挙 *kenkyo* arrest, roundup
11 視 *kenshi* investigation of the facts
問 *kemmon* inspection, examination
眼 *kengan* optometry, eye examination
12 証 *kenshō* verification, inspection
温器 *ken'onki* clinical thermometer
診 *kenshin* medical examination
14 算 *kenzan* verification of accounts, checking figures
察 *kensatsu* investigation and prosecution
察庁 *kensatsuchō* prosecuting attorney's office
察官 *kensatsukan* prosecuting attorney
15 震器 *kenshinki* seismograph
閲 *ken'etsu* inspection, censorship
潮 *kenchō* tidal observation

極 A
2753
J364b
M15181
KYOKU end; highest rank; the poles; (electric) poles. GOKU very, extremely, highly, most, quite. *kiwa(maru)* terminate; reach an extreme; be in a dilemma. *kiwa(meru)* investigate thoroughly, master; carry to extremes. *ki(meru)* fix, decide, agree upon; appoint, choose; resolve. *ki(maru)* be decided, be settled, be arranged; be certain to, be doomed to. *kime* agreement, contract. *kima(ri)* settlement, conclusion, agreement; system, regularity; rule; habit. *kiwa(marinai)* endless, eternal. *kiwa(mete)* very, exceedingly. *kiwa(mi)* height, acme, extremity. *-gime* by (the month).
2 力 *kyokuryoku* with all one's might
3 大 *kyokudai* the greatest, maximum
上 *gokujō* first-rate, finest quality, the best
小 *kyokushō, gokushō* the smallest, minimum
4 手 *kimete* winning move, deciding factor

月 *gokugetsu* December; the last month of the year

⁵付 *ki(me)-tsu(keru)* scold, reprimand. *kiwa(me)tsu(ki)* guaranteed

北 *kyokuhoku* extreme north, North Pole

右 *kyokuu* extreme right

左 *kyokusa* extreme left

⁶尽 *kiwa(me)-tsuku(su)* know thoroughly; measure the full extent

印 *gokuin* seal, stamp die, hallmark, impression; proof of genuineness

地 *kyokuchi* the pole, polar regions

刑 *kyokkei* capital punishment; extreme penalty

光 *kyokkō* northern lights, aurora borealis; southern lights, aurora australis

⁷言 *kyokugen* extreme criticism

⁸所 *kyokusho* end, conclusion

限 *kyokugen* limit, extremity

東 *Kyokutō* Far East

⁹度 *kyokudo* highest degree, the extreme, maximum

点 *kyokuten* highest point, climax, summit, zenith; nadir, bottom

¹⁰秘 *gokuhi* top-secret, confidential

致 *kyokuchi* culmination, perfection

¹¹貧 *gokuhin* destitution

彩色 *gokusaishiki* brilliant coloring, full color (illustrations)

道 *gokudō na* wicked, villainous, brutal, dissipated

悪 *gokuaku* brutality, atrocity. *kima(ri) waru(i)* awkward, embarrassed

¹²極 *gokugoku* very, severely

寒 *gokkan* intense cold, midwinter

¹³微 *kyokubi, gokubi* infinitesimal, microscopic

意 *gokui* mystery; the secrets (of the art)

楽 *gokuraku* paradise

¹⁴端 *kyokutan* an extreme, extremity

¹⁵論 *kyokuron* extreme argument; extreme criticism

———— 9 ————

楳 2754 J4760 M15178 See 梅 2666.

榊 2756 J3a67 M-X Nonstandard for 榊 2808.

樋 2757 J4875 M-X Nonstandard for 樋 2816.

梛 2766 J4f31 M15226 Rō.

槌 2767 M15318 / 槌 2709 J4448 M-X Tsui. *tsuchi* hammer, mallet.

楢 2769 J466a M15154 Shū. Yū. *nara* oak.

楚 2771 J413f M15141 So whip; cane.

¹³楚 *soso(taru)* graceful, neat

椴 2772 J464e M15075 Tan fir.

⁸松 *todomatsu* fir, white fir

楯 2776 J3d5d M15173 Jun. *tate* shield, buckler, escutcheon; pretext.

⁸突 *tatetsu(ku)* oppose, defy

楓 2777 J4976 M15126 Fū. Fu. *kaede* maple tree.

楠 2779 J466f M15152 Nan. *kusu, kusunoki* camphor tree.

⁴木 *kusunoki* camphor tree

楕 2780 J424a M15133 Da ellipse.

⁴円 *daen* oval, ellipse

円形 *daenkei* oval ellipse

椿 2782 J4458 M15090 Chin. *tsubaki* camellia.

⁸油 *tsubaki yu; tsubaki abura* camellia oil

事 *chinji* accident; sudden occurrence

楊 2784 J4d4c M15112 Yō. *kawa yanagi* willow.

⁸枝 *yōji* toothpick; toothbrush

⁹柳 *yanagi, kawa yanagi, yōryū* riverside willows

楼 2785 J4f30 M15212 Rō tower, turret, lookout, high building. *takadono* stately mansion.

4
心 忄 小 戈 戸 手 扌 支 攴 攵 文 斗 斤 方 无 日 曰 月 【木】⁹ 欠 止 歹 殳 毋 比 毛 氏 气 水 氵 氺 火 灬 爪 爫 父 爻 爿 丬 片 牙 牛 犬 犭

4

心忄小戈戸手扌支攴文斗斤方无日曰月【木】欠止歹殳毋比毛氏气水氵氺火灬爪爫父爻爿片牙牛犬犭

³上 *rōjō* upper story; balcony; roof garden
⁸門 *rōmon* tower gate, two-story gate
¹⁴閣 *rōkaku* many-storied building

棄 B $\frac{2787}{\substack{J347e \\ M14913}}$ KI. *su(teru)* throw away, discard, abandon, desert, give up; renounce, relinquish; resign; lay down (one's life); part with; sacrifice; reject, condemn.
³子 *sutego* foundling
⁷却 *kikyaku suru* reject, dismiss; abandon, renounce waive
¹⁵権 *kiken suru* abstain from voting; renounce one's rights

業 A $\frac{2789}{\substack{J3648 \\ M15170}}$ GYŌ vocation, occupation, business, trade, profession; industry; undertaking; studies; arts; conduct, act; service; achievement. GŌ karma. *waza* deed, act, work, art, performance, trick.
⁴火 *gōka* hell fire
⁸物 *wazamono* sharp sword
者 *gyōsha* the trade, businessperson concerned
⁹界 *gyōkai* the business world, industry, the trade
¹⁰病 *gōbyō* incurable disease
¹¹務 *gyōmu* business, affairs, duties, work, service, operations
¹³腹 *gōhara* spite, resentment
¹⁴種 *gyōshu* business category
態 *gyōtai* business conditions
¹⁷績 *gyōseki* achievement, performance, results, work, contribution

楽 A $\frac{2790}{\substack{J335a \\ M15213}}$ RAKU comfort, ease, relief; pleasure; concluding program. GAKU music. *tano(shimu)*, *tano(shibu)* enjoy; amuse oneself; anticipate. *tano(shimi)*, *tano(shibi)* pleasure, enjoyment, happiness; amusement; anticipation. *tano(shii)* merry, pleasant, cheerful, joyful. *tano(shige) na* merry, pleasant, happy, gay. *raku na* easy.
²人 *gakujin* musician, minstrel. *rakujin* person living at ease
³土 *rakudo* paradise, a pleasant land

士 *gakushi* bandsman, musician
才 *gakusai* musical talent
⁴手 *gakushu* musician, bandsman
天 *rakuten* optimism
天地 *rakutenchi* paradise; amusement park
天的 *rakutenteki* optimistic, cheerful, happy-go-lucky
天家 *rakutenka* optimist, easygoing person
⁶団 *gakudan* band, orchestra
曲 *gakkyoku* musical composition, tune
⁸長 *gakuchō* bandmaster, conductor, musical director
典 *gakuten* musical grammar
⁹音 *gakuon* musical tone
屋 *gakuya* dressing room, greenroom; behind the scenes
屋落 *gakuyao(chi)* a matter not understand by the outside, inside information, shop talk
屋話 *gakuyabanashi* backstage talk
¹⁰員 *gakuin* bandsman
¹¹隊 *gakutai* band, orchestra
章 *gakushō* a movement (in music)
¹²焼 *rakuya(ki)* hand-molded pottery; *raku* ware
勝 *rakushō* easy victory
¹³園 *rakuen* pleasure garden, paradise
楽 *rakuraku to* comfortably; very easily. *rakuraku suru* feel relieved
聖 *gakusei* celebrated musician
隠居 *rakuinkyo* comfortable retirement
¹⁵劇 *gakugeki* opera, musical drama
調 *gakuchō* musical tone
器 *gakki* musical instrument
¹⁶壇 *gakudan* music circles
¹⁸観 *rakkan* optimism
観的 *rakkanteki* optimistic, hopeful
¹⁹譜 *gakufu* sheet music, music book, musical notation, the score

───── **10** ─────

榊 $\frac{2808}{\substack{J-X \\ M15352}}$ 榊 $\frac{2756}{\substack{J3a67 \\ M-X}}$ (国字) *sakaki* sacred Shinto tree, *cleyera ochnacea*.

榎 $\frac{2810}{\substack{J315d \\ M15219}}$ KA. *enoki* hackberry; nettle tree; lotus tree.

榛 2811 J3f3a M15240 SHIN. *hashibami* hazel, filbert. *han* black alder.
⁴木 *han(no)ki* black alder

樋 2816 J-X M15415 樋 2757 J4875 M-X TŌ. *hi, toi* water pipe, gutter, downspout; aqueduct, flume; conduit; trough.

樺 2817 J3372 M15497 KA. *kaba, kamba* birch.
⁴太 *Karafuto* Sakhalin

槇 2818 J7422 M15310 槙 2819 J4b6a M-X SHIN twig. *maki* an ornamental evergreen.

A 様 2821 J4d4d M15352ʹ YŌ. way, manner, method; kind, class; (to that) effect. *sama* situation, circumstances, condition. *sama* Mr., Mrs., Messrs., Mme., Miss, Master. *yō na* like, such as. *yō ni* in order to; in such a way, in such a manner. *zama* plight, state, appearance, spectacle.
³子 *yōsu* situation, aspect, circumstances, movements; appearance, behavior, signs
⁶式 *yōshiki* style, form, pattern
⁹相 *yōsō* aspect, phase, condition
¹⁴様 *samazama na* various, varied, sundry
態 *yōtai* form, situation; condition of the patient

槍 2822 J4164 M15319 SŌ. *yari* spear, lance, javelin.
⁵玉 *yaridama* victim, sacrifice
⁷投 *yarina(ge)* javelin throwing, javelin contest
¹¹術 *sōjutsu* drilling with spears
¹⁸騎兵 *sōkihei* lancer

A 構 2823 J393d M15317 KŌ. *kama(eru)* build; keep house; take a posture; assume an attitude; pose as; be ready for; feign, pretend; set up (camp). *kama(u)* mind, care about; pay attention to; interfere with; be hospitable; tease, molest; expel, banish. *ku(u)* build (a nest). *kama(e)* construction, architecture, style, appearance; posture; attitude; enclosure radical. *kama(i)* meddling, concern; entertainment, hospitality;

banishment. *(o)kama(i nashi ni)* regardless of.
⁴文 *kōbun* sentence construction, syntax
内 *kōnai, kama(e)uchi* compound, grounds, premises
⁵外 *kōgai* outside the premises
⁶成 *kōsei suru* comprise. *kōsei* composition, organization, construction, line-up
成員 *kōseiin* member
⁷図 *kōzu* plot (of a novel); plan (of a life); composition (of a painting); design; sketch
⁹造 *kōzō* construction, framework, structure; setup, organization
¹³想 *kōsō* plan, idea, conception, plot
¹⁶築 *kōchiku suru* build, construct

B 概 2824 J3335 M15217ʹ GAI condition, situation; approximation. *gai(shite)* generally, as a rule, on the whole. *ōmu(ne)* in general; mostly, principally, almost; probably; about, roughly.
⁸況 *gaikyō* outlook, over-all condition, general situation
念 *gainen* general idea, concept
念的 *gainenteki ni* roughly, generally
⁹括 *gaikatsu* summary, generalization
要 *gaiyō* summary, outline, synopsis, résumé
¹¹略 *gairyaku* outline, summary, gist, résumé; roughly, approximately, in brief
¹³数 *gaisū* round numbers
¹⁴説 *gaisetsu* general statement, outline
算 *gaisan* approximation, rough estimate
¹⁵論 *gairon* introduction, outline, general remarks
¹⁸観 *gaikan* general view, outline

A 模 2825 J4c4f M15453 MO. BO. *mo(suru)* copy, imitate, mock. *katado(ru)* pattern after, imitate, symbolize.
⁵写 *mosha* copying; copy, replica
⁹型 *mokei* model, pattern
造 *mozō* imitation, copy, reproduction; counterfeit
造紙 *mozōshi* vellum paper
¹⁰倣 *mohō* copy, imitation
索 *mosaku* groping
¹⁴様 *moyō* pattern, design; appearance; circumstances

4
心 忄 小 戈 戸 手 扌 支 攴 攵 文 斗 斤 方 无 日 曰 月 [10][木] 欠 止 歹 殳 毋 比 毛 氏 气 水 氵 氺 火 灬 爪 爫 父 爻 爿 片 牙 牛 犬 犭

---

¹⁵ 糊 *moko* dimness, vagueness, stupidity
範 *mohan* model, pattern, example
¹⁷ 擬 *mogi* imitation
擬店 *mogiten* buffet, refreshment booth (at a party)
擬試験 *mogi shiken* trial examination

───── **11** ─────

樗 [2841 J4374 M15438] CHO. *gonzui* a sumac. *ōchi* Japanese bead tree.

B 槽 [2844 J4165 M15393] SŌ tub, tank, vat.

槻 [2845 J4450 M15390] KI. *tsuki* a kind of Zelkova tree.

樫 [2849 J335f M15485] (国字) *kashi* evergreen oak.
¹² 棒 *kashibō* oak club, oak stick

樟 [2851 J3e40 M15451] SHŌ. *kusu* camphor tree; camphor.
⁴ 木 *kusu(no)ki* camphor tree
¹¹ 脳 *shōnō* camphor

A 標 [2852 J4938 M15442] HYŌ signpost; mark; target; designate. *shirushi* sign, mark; symbol, emblem; badge; evidence; souvenir; token; brand, trademark; signs, indications; omen; seal.
⁵ 示 *hyōji* indication, expression; marking
札 *hyōsatsu* nameplate, door plate
本 *hyōhon* specimen
⁸ 的 *hyōteki* mark, target
⁹ 柱 *hyōchū* pylon, guidepost
¹⁰ 高 *hyōkō* height above sea level
記 *hyōki* a mark; marking
¹³ 準 *hyōjun* standard, norm, level, criterion, canon, measure
準時 *hyōjunji* standard time, Greenwich time
準語 *hyōjungo* standard language
¹⁴ 榜 *hyōbō suru* profess, advocate. *hyōbō* sign, signboard, doorplate; poster, billboard; appearance; figurehead; policy; attraction; closing time
語 *hyōgo* slogan, motto
¹⁵ 縄 *shimenawa* sacred shrine rope
¹⁸ 題 *hyōdai* title (of a book)

¹⁹ 識 *hyōshiki* landmark; sign, signal, beacon; criterion

A 権 [2853 J3822 M15484] GON, KEN authority, power; rights, concession. *gon-* assistant (in the Shinto hierarchy).
² 力 *kenryoku* power, authority, influence
力争 *kenryoku araso(i)* struggle for supremacy
力者 *kenryokusha* man of power
⁴ 化 *gonge* (Buddhist) incarnation, avatar, embodiment, personification
⁵ 外 *kengai* outside the jurisdiction (of)
⁶ 臣 *kenshin* influential retainer
⁷ 利 *kenri* rights, claim, privilege, title; authority, powers; goodwill; franchise; agency
利金 *kenrikin* key money
⁸ 門 *kemmon* man of influence
限 *kengen* power, authority, jurisdiction
官 *kenkan* influential official
⁹ 柄尽 *kempeizu(ku)* authoritative, dictatorial
威 *ken'i* authority, power, dignity, prestige
威筋 *ken'i suji* authoritative sources
¹⁰ 益 *ken'eki* rights, interests
能 *kennō* authority, power; function, faculty
¹³ 勢 *kensei* power, influence
¹⁶ 謀 *kembō* scheme, stratagem, plot
謀術数 *kembō-jussū* trickery, diplomacy, Machiavellism

A 横 [2854 J3223 M15484'] Ō horizontal. *yoko* side, flank; horizontal direction; width, breadth, beam; woof. *yoko(taeru)* lay (oneself) down, lie down; place across. *yoko(tawaru)* lie down, stretch out on.
² 丁 *yokochō* lane, alley, side street
⁴ 辷 *yokosuberi* skid, slip, sideslip
切 *yokogi(ru)* intersect, cross
文字 *yokomoji* European writing, crosswise writing
⁵ 目 *yokome* side glance; amorous glance; crosscut saw
穴 *yokoana* cave, tunnel
⁶ 死 *ōshi* violent, tragic, accidental, or unnatural death; a dog's death

好 *yokozu(ki)* immoderately fond of

帆 *ōhan* square sail

合 *yokoa(i)* side, flank

行 *ōkō suru* walk sideways; swagger; stride

⁷見 *yokomi* side glance

町 *yokochō* lane, alley, side street

車 *yokoguruma* perverseness

車押 *yokoguruma (o) o(su)* be perverse

⁸長 *yokonaga* oblong

泳 *yokooyo(gi)* side stroke

波 *yokonami* side wave, broadside sea, transverse wave

取 *yokodo(ri)* usurpation; seizure; snatching; intercepting

臥 *ōga* lying on the side

歩 *yokoaru(ki) suru* walk sideways

⁹面 *yokotsura, yoko(t)tsura, yokozura* side of the face

風 *yokokaze, ōfū* crosswind

柄 *ōhei* arrogance

¹⁰流 *yokonaga(re)* flowing into blackmarket channels. *yokonaga(shi)* diversion into illegal channels

書 *yokoga(ki)* writing horizontally

紙破 *yokogamiyabu(ri)* perverseness, waywardness

恋慕 *yoko rembo* illicit love

¹¹道 *yokomichi* side street; crossroad; wrong way; side issue; evil course. *ōdō* wickedness, wrong, injustice; crossroad

転 *ōten* lateral turn; barrel roll (of a plane)

隊 *ōtai* rank, line

笛 *yokobue, ōteki* flute, fife

断 *ōdan* crossing, intersection

断歩道 *ōdan hodō* pedestrian crossing

¹²幅 *yokohaba* breadth, width

揺 *yokoyu(re)* rolling, a roll

棒 *yokobō* bar, horizontal bar; dash; horizontal line

軸 *yokojiku* horizontal shaft, cross axle

着 *ōchaku* dishonesty; cunning; impudence; laziness; selfishness

隔膜 *ōkakumaku* the diaphragm

¹³溢 *ōitsu* overflowing, inundation

睨 *yokonira(mi)* a sharp sidelong glance

腹 *yoko(p)para, yokohara, yokobara* side, flank

罫 *yokokei* horizontal lines

¹⁴槍 *yokoyari* interruption

綱 *yokozuna* champion sumo wrestler; top in the class

領 *ōryō* usurpation, seizure, dispossession; embezzlement, misappropriation

¹⁵暴 *ōbō* violence, oppression, high-handedness

¹⁶縞 *yokojima* lateral stripes

¹⁸顔 *yokogao* profile, side view, silhouette

──────── **12** ────────

橡 | 2863 / J464b / M15564 | SHŌ . *tochi* horse chestnut.

橘 | 2868 / J354c / M15551 | KITSU. *tachibana* mandarin orange; orange crest.

樵 | 2871 / J3e41 / M15489 | SHŌ . *kiko(ru), ko(ru)* cut wood. *kikori* woodcutting; woodcutter, lumberjack.

樽 | 2875 / J432e / M15500 | SON. *taru* barrel, cask, keg, tub.

⁹柿 *tarugaki* persimmons seasoned in saké barrels (to remove astringency)

¹³詰 *taruzume* barreled, casked

A 樹 | 2878 / J3c79 / M15496 | JU *ki* tree, wood. *ta(teru)* stand something up, set up, raise; put up; set on edge; prick up (one's ears); build, erect; close (a door); establish; institute, enact; lay (plans); map out; set forth, lay down (a proposition); formulate; render (services), perform; look up to, respect; be loyal to; do justice to; circulate (rumors); have (an aim); establish (oneself), make (a success); support (oneself); make (an oath); sharpen, set (a saw); put up (a candidate); make (tea); save (face).

³下 *juka ni* under a tree

上 *jujō no, jujō ni* on a tree

⁴木 *jumoku* trees and shrubs, ardor

⁵皮 *juhi* bark

立 *juritsu* establishment, setting (a record)

4

心 忄 小 戈 戸 手 扌 支 攴 攵 文 斗 斤 方 无 日 曰 月 【木】 ₁₂ 欠 止 歹 殳 毋 比 毛 氏 气 水 氵 氺 火 灬 爪 爫 父 爻 爿 丬 片 牙 牛 犬 犭

氷 *juhyō* silver frost (on trees)
⁸ 林 *jurin* forest
⁹ 海 *jukai* a sea of foliage, a sea of forests
¹⁰ 脂 *jushi* resin, rosin
¹¹ 液 *jueki* sap
¹² 葉 *juyō* leaves of a tree
¹³ 幹 *jukan* trunk of a tree
¹⁷ 齢 *jurei* a tree's age

A 橋 $\frac{2879}{\substack{J3636 \\ M15526}}$ Kyō. *hashi* bridge.

¹⁰ 桁 *hashigeta* bridge girder
¹¹ 脚 *kyōkyaku* bridge pier
梁 *kyōryō* bridge
¹² 渡 *hashiwata(shi)* building a bridge; mediation, good offices
¹³ 詰 *hashizume* bridge approach
¹⁶ 頭堡 *kyōtōhō* bridgehead, beachhead

A 機 $\frac{2880}{\substack{J3521 \\ M15561}}$ Kɪ opportunity; occasion, time; machine, airplane. *hata* loom.

上 *kijō* aboard a plane
⁴ 内 *kinai* within the plane
⁵ 甲 *kikō* armored
甲部隊 *kikō butai* armored corps
⁶ 先 *kisen* before the occurrence
帆船 *kihansen* steam-and-sail ships
会 *kikai* opportunity, chance
会均等 *kikai kintō* equal opportunity
⁷ 尾 *kibi* airplane tail
体 *kitai* fuselage
⁸ 知 *kichi* wit, resources, tact
⁹ 首 *kishu* nose of a plane
乗 *ki (ni) no(ru)* take advantage of an opportunity ⌐astuteness
¹⁰ 敏 *kibin* shrewdness, alertness
能 *kinō* faculty, function, process
能的 *kinōteki* functional
¹¹ 運 *kiun* luck; tendency; opportunity
略 *kiryaku* resources; expedient; tact
転 *kiten* tact, ready wit
密 *kimitsu* secrecy, secret
動 *kidō* mobile
動力 *kidōryoku* mobile power, motive force; maneuverability
械 *kikai* machine, mechanism, gear
械工学 *kikai kōgaku* mechanical engineering
械化 *kikaika* mechanization; mechanized

械体操 *kikai taisō* calisthenics using equipment
械的 *kikaiteki* mechanical
¹² 軸 *kijiku* axis; axle; plan; contrivance
智 *kichi* wit, resources, tact
¹³ 微 *kibi* secrets, inner workings, delicate turn
雷 *kirai* (sea) mine
業 *kigyō* the textile industry
嫌 *kigen* health; cheer; temper, mood
嫌良 *kigen'yo(ku)* cheerfully, with good grace
¹⁴ 構 *kikō* mechanism, structure, organization, setup
種 *kishu* the type of plane
銃 *kijū* machine gun
関 *kikan* engine, machine; means, instrument; agency, organization, facilities, institution; organ
関士 *kikanshi* engineer
関車 *kikansha* locomotive
関砲 *kikanhō* machine gun
関紙 *kikanshi* bulletin, organ
関誌 *kikanshi* bulletin, regular publication of a society
関銃 *kikanjū* machine gun
¹⁵ 器 *kiki* machinery and tools
¹⁸ 織 *hatao(ri)* weaving; weaver; grasshopper

──────── **13** ────────

櫛 $\frac{2884}{\substack{J367b \\ M-X}}$ Nonstandard for 櫛 2909.

檎 $\frac{2888}{\substack{J3869 \\ M15657}}$ Kɪɴ, Goɴ pear; apple; Pyrus.

橿 $\frac{2889}{\substack{J3360 \\ M15629}}$ Kyō a kind of oak.

檜 $\frac{2894}{\substack{J5b58 \\ M15676}}$ 桧 $\frac{2637}{\substack{J4930 \\ M-X}}$ Kaɪ. *hinoki*, *hi* Japanese cypress.

¹⁴ 舞台 *hinoki butai* cypress-floored stage, high-class stage

檀 $\frac{2895}{\substack{J4349 \\ M15632}}$ Daɴ, Taɴ a kind of cedar, sandalwood. *mayumi* spindletree.

⁶ 那 *danna* master; husband; gentleman
¹⁰ 家 *danka* families supporting a temple

---- 14 ----

檮 $\frac{2897}{\substack{J5b6d\\M15713}}$ Tō. Dō tree stump; foolish, ignorant.

櫓 $\frac{2908}{\substack{J4f26\\M15798}}$ Ro sculling oar; oar; tower. *yagura* tower, turret; scaffolding.

櫛 $\frac{2909}{\text{J-X}\\M15817}$ 櫛 $\frac{2884}{\substack{J367b\\M-X}}$ SHITSU. *kushi* comb.
⁴ 比 *shippi suru* stand in a long row
⁷ 形 *kushigata* comb-like; arch-shaped; arched window

---- 16 ----

櫨 $\frac{2910}{\substack{J4827\\M15844}}$ Ro (carpenter's) square. *haze* wax tree; sumac.

B 欄 $\frac{2914}{\substack{J4d73\\M15880'}}$ RAN column (in a newspaper); blank; space; railing. *obashima* handrail.
³ 干 *rankan* railing, balustrade
⁵ 外 *rangai* margin (of a page)

¹² 間 *ramma* transom; transom work

---- 21 ----

欝 $\frac{2924}{\substack{J3135\\M-X}}$ See 欝 2926.

---- 22 ----

欝 $\frac{2926}{\text{J-X}\\M15978}$ UTSU gloom, depression, melancholy. *us(suru)*, *fusa(gu)* be depressed, have the blues.
⁶ 血 *ukketsu* blood congestion
金色 *ukon iro* saffron color
金香 *ukkonkō* tulip
⁹ 勃 *utsubotsu(taru)* pent up, stored; energetic, irresistible
¹⁰ 陶 *uttō* sultriness, stuffiness; unpleasantness; bother. *uttō(shii)* gloomy, depressing; dull, cloudy
¹³ 蒼 *ussō(taru)* thick, dense, luxuriant
¹⁵ 憤 *uppun* resentment, grudge, anger
¹⁶ 積 *usseki* congestion, stagnation
²⁶ 欝 *utsuutsu to* gloomily, cheerlessly

========= RAD. 欠 76 =========

Akubi yawn; also *ken, ketsu,* or *kakeru* lacking. Nickname: Yawning.

A 欠 $\frac{2928}{\substack{J3767\\M15991}}$ KETSU lack, gap. *ka(ku)* lack; break, crack, chip; neglect; fail in; omit. *ka(keru)* be broken (off), be chipped; lack, be missing; wane; be vacant (a position). *ka(kasu)* miss (a meeting). *ka(ke)* broken piece (of glass, etc.). *akubi* yawn (欠 only).
³ 乏 *ketsubō* want; dearth, famine; scarcity, shortage
乏症 *ketsubōshō* deficiency disease
⁵ 礼 *ketsurei* neglect of courtesies
本 *keppon* missing volume
号 *ketsugō* missing number (of a magazine)
⁶ 如 *ketsujo* lack, privation, deficiency
⁷ 伸 *akubi* yawn
⁹ 除 *ketsujo* removal, omission
点 *ketten* faults, defect, weakness
食 *kesshoku* going without a meal
陥 *kekkan* defect, fault, deficiency

¹⁰ 航 *kekkō* steamship-service suspension
員 *ketsuin* vacant position
格 *kekkaku* lack of qualifications
席 *kesseki* absence; default
¹² 場 *ketsujō* not in the lineup
量 *ketsuryō* ullage
落 *ketsuraku* lack, absence
勤 *kekkin* absence
¹³ 損 *kesson* deficit, shortage, loss; damage

---- 2 ----

A 次 $\frac{2929}{\substack{J3c21\\M15992'}}$ SHI. JI order, sequence; times; next; below. *tsu(gu)* rank next to, come after. *tsugi* next; stage station, stage. *tsugi ni* then, subsequently. *tsu(ide)* next, secondly, subsequently. *-ji* order.
³ 女 *jijo* second daughter

4

心 忄 小 戈 戸 手 扌 支 攴 文 斗 斤 方 无 日 曰 月 木 ² [欠] 止 歹 殳 毋 比 毛 氏 气 水 氵 氺 火 灬 爪 爫 父 爻 爿 丬 片 牙 牛 犬 犭

⁴元 *jigen* dimension (in math)
⁵代 *jidai* the next era
号 *jigō* next issue
⁶回 *jikai* next time
次 *tsugitsugi ni* one by one, one after another, successively
会 *jikai* the next meeting
⁷序 *jijo* order, system
男 *jinan* second son
男坊 *jinambō* second son
⁸長 *jichō* vice- or assistant executive
官 *jikan* vice-minister, under-secretary, assistant secretary
⁹点 *jiten* runner-up
¹⁰席 *jiseki* associate, junior, assistant; runner-up
¹¹第 *shidai* order, precedence; circumstances, occasion; reason, cause; as soon as; at one's pleasure; according to. *shidai ni* gradually
¹²善 *jizen no* second best

――― **4** ―――

欣 [2930 / J3655 / M16008] KIN rejoice. *yoroko(bu)* rejoice, be glad, be pleased. *yoroko(bashii)* joyful, glad, pleasant.
⁷快 *kinkai na* pleasant, delightful
¹²喜 *kinki* joy, delight
然 *kinzen(taru)* joyful, cheerful

欧 B [2931 / J3224 / M16024'] Ō Europe.
⁴文 *ōbun* European language, foreign text
化 *ōka* Europeanization, Westernization
⁶米 *Ō-Bei* Europe and America
州 *Ōshū* Europe
州経済共同体 *Ōshū Keizai Kyōdōtai* European Economic Community
⁷亜 *Ō-A* Europe and Asia
⁹風 *Ōfū* European style, Occidental
¹⁹羅巴 *Yōroppa* Europe
²¹露 *Ō-Ro* European Russia

――― **7** ―――

欲 A [2936 / J4d5f / M16080] 慾 [1951 / J4d5d / M11163] YOKU covetousness; greed, passion, desire, craving, appetite. *hos(suru)* desire, want. *ho(shigaru)* desire, want, covet. *ho(shii)* desire, want.
⁴心 *yokushin* selfishness, acquisitiveness

⁵目 *yokume* partial view; partiality; sanguine hope
⁷求 *yokkyū* desire, craving, aspiration
¹¹張 *yokuba(ru)* be greedy, be covetous. *yokuba(ri)* greed, covetousness
得 *yokutoku* self-interest, selfishness. *yokutoku(zuku) no* selfish, mercenary
情 *yokujō* desire, craving, passion
深 *yokufuka* greed, covetousness. *yokufuka(i)* greedy; covetous
望 *yokubō* desire, craving; wants; ambition

――― **8** ―――

款 B [2938 / J343e / M16107] KAN article, section; goodwill, friendship; collusion.
⁹待 *kantai* entertainment, hospitality

欺 B [2939 / J353d / M16097] KI. GI *azamu(ku)*, *dama(su)* deceive, cheat, delude.
¹⁶瞞 *giman* deception, imposition

欽 [2940 / J3656 / M16104] KIN respect, revere; long for.
⁸定 *kintei* authorized, appointed
定詩人 *kintei shijin* poet laureate

――― **10** ―――

歌 A [2945 / J324e / M16167] KA. *uta(u)* sing, recite, chant, carol. *uta* poem, tanka, ballad, poetry; singing.
²人 *kajin, utabito* poet
⁴手 *kashu, uta(i)te* singer, vocal soloist
⁶曲 *kakyoku* melody, tune, song
会 *kakai, utakai* poetry party, poetry competition
会始 *utakaihaji(me)* Imperial Poetry Contest
⁷声 *utagoe* singing; singing voice. *uta(i)goe* singing voice. *kasei* singing
⁹風 *kafū* poetic style
姫 *utahime* songstress
¹²詞 *utakotoba* poetic diction. *kashi* the words of a song, lyrics
集 *kashū* anthology; a book of poetry
¹⁵劇 *kageki* opera

舞 *kabu* singing and dancing, entertainment

舞伎 *kabuki* popular drama, kabuki

舞妓 *kabuki* popular drama, kabuki

¹⁶壇 *kadan* poetry circles

謡 *kayō* song, ballad

謡曲 *kayōkyoku* popular song

───────── **11** ─────────

歎 ―――― 2947 / J4337 / M16182 ―――― TAN grief, lamentation. *nage(ku)* sigh, lament, moan, grieve; regret, deplore, sorrow. *nageka(shii), nagekawa(shii)* sad, wretched, deplorable.

⁷声 *tansei* sign, lamentation; sigh of admiration

⁹美 *tambi* admiration, adoration

¹⁰息 *tansoku* sigh, grief, deploring

¹⁹願 *tangan* entreaty, petition, appeal, suit

歡 ―――― 2948 / J343f / M16197 ―――― KAN joy, pleasure. B *yoroko(bi)* joy, delight, pleasure. *yoroko(bu)* rejoice, be glad, be pleased.

⁴心 *kanshin* favor

⁶迎 *kangei* welcome

迎会 *kangeikai* welcome meeting, reception

⁷声 *kansei* cheers, shout of joy

⁸送 *kansō* hearty send-off

送会 *kansōkai* farewell meeting

呼 *kanko* ovation, a cheer

呼声 *kanko (no) koe* shout of joy, a cheer

⁹待 *kantai* entertainment, hospitality, warm reception

¹²喜 *kanki, kangi* joy, gladness

¹³楽 *kanraku* pleasure, enjoyment

楽街 *kanrakugai* amusement center; red-light district

¹⁵談 *kandan* pleasant chat

────────── RAD. 止 77 ──────────

Tomeru to stop. At left: 止 *tome hen*. Nickname: Stopping.

止 ―――― 2954 / J3b5f / M16253 ―――― SHI. *to(maru)* stop, halt, stand still, pull up; cease, be interrupted, be discontinued; be choked; alight on, perch, roost; be held in position. *to(meru)* stop; check; allay (pain); fasten; turn off; detain; forbid to do; dissuade. *todo(maru)* stop, halt, stay, remain, stay behind; be limited to. *todo(meru)* stop, cease, detain, put an end to; leave; fix; remain in (a certain condition); content oneself with. *ya(mu)* vi end, stop, cease; subside, calm down, pass; die out, be extinguished; leave, go off; be abandoned. *ya(meru)* vt end, discontinue; give up, abandon; abolish; resign, retire. *yo(su)* stop, discontinue, give up. *sa(su)* stop; leave something unfinished. *to(me)* stopping; prohibition; end; a stop. *to(mare)* halt, stop. *ya(mi), ya(me)* end, discontinuance, stop. *yoshi* stop, discontinue. *todo(me)* finishing blow. *to(mari)* stop, stoppage; end, termination. *-sa(shi)* stopping.

⁶血 *shiketsu* stopping of bleeding, stanching

⁷役 *to(me)yaku* peacemaker (in a quarrel)

¹¹得 *ya(mu) (o) e(zu)* unavoidably, inevitably, necessarily. *ya(mu) (o) e(nai)* unavoidable, necessary, inevitable, obligatory

宿 *shishuku* lodging

────────── **1** ──────────

正 ―――― 2955 / J4035 / M16255 ―――― SEI right, righteousness, A justice; original; plus, positive; genuine. SHŌ just; punctual; senior; right, righteousness, justice. *tada(su)* correct; adjust; reform; redress, straighten; amend. *masa(ni)* correctly, surely. *masa(shiku)* surely, no doubt, evidently. *tada(shii)* right, righteous, just; honest, truthful, proper, correct; lawful; healthy; moral; straight; straightforward; perfect. *sei-* regular.

³大 *seidai* fairness, justice

心 忄 小 戈 戸 手 扌 支 攴 攵 文 斗 斤 方 无 日 曰 月 木 欠 〔止〕¹ 歹 殳 毋 比 毛 氏 气 水 氵 氺 火 灬 爪 爫 父 爻 爿 片 牙 牛 犬 犭

4

心 忄 小 戈 戸 手 扌 支 攴 攵 文 斗 斤 方 无 日 曰 月 木 欠 【止】 歹 殳 毋 比 毛 氏 气 水 氵 氺 火 灬 爪 爫 父 爻 爿 片 牙 牛 犬 犭

三角形 *seisankakukei* equilateral triangle

4 月 *Shōgatsu* the first month; January; the New Year

午 *shōgo* noon, midday

反対 *seihantai* exactly opposite

比例 *seihirei* direct proportion, direct ratio

中 *seichū* the exact middle

方形 *seihōkei* square

5 目 *masame* straight grain

史 *seishi* authentic history

正堂堂 *seisei-dōdō(taru)* fair and square, open and aboveboard

犯 *seihan* principal offense; principal offender

札 *shōfuda* correct-price tag

6 式 *seishiki* proper form, formality

気 *shōki* consciousness; sanity, reason; soberness. *seiki* true heart, true spirit, true character

会員 *seikaiin* regular member

当 *seitō na* just, justifiable, right, due, proper, equitable, reasonable, legitimate, lawful

当防衛 *seitō bōei* legitimate self-defense

7 体 *shōtai* natural shape; one's true colors, true character; consciousness; senses

邪 *seija* right and wrong

否 *seihi* right and wrong

坐 *seiza suru* sit (or squat) straight

攻法 *seikōhō* frontal attack

社員 *seishain* regular member, staff member

8 門 *seimon* main gate, main entrance

価 *seika* net price, regular price

宗 *masamune* sword blade by Masamune

妻 *seisai* legal wife

金 *shōkin* specie, bullion, cash

直 *shōjiki* honesty, integrity, frankness

味 *shōmi* net

9 則 *seisoku no* correct, proper, formal, regular, systematic, normal

負 *seifu* positive and negative, plus and minus

面 *matomo* the front; honesty. *shōmen* front, frontage, facade

面図 *shōmenzu* front elevation

面衝突 *shōmen shōtotsu* head-on collision

10 座 *seiza suru* sit (or squat) straight. *shōza* seat of honor

朔 *seisaku* beginning of the month or the year; New Year's Day; the calendar

員 *seiin* regular member

真正銘 *shōshin-shōmei* the genuine article

書 *seisho* square characters, printed style

書法 *seishohō* correct orthography

11 道 *seidō* righteousness; path of righteousness, path of duty, the right track

眼 *seigan* aiming at the eye (with a sword)

副 *seifuku* original and copy; chief and vice-chief

貨 *seika* specie, metallic currency

視 *seishi* looking straight ahead; viewing sincerely

視眼 *seishigan* correct vision

常 *seijō* normalcy, normality, normal

常化 *seijōka* normalization

教 *seikyō* orthodoxy; Greek Orthodox Church

教会 *Seikyōkai* Greek Orthodox Church

規 *seiki no* regular, legal, formal, established, legitimate

規曲線 *seiki kyokusen* probability curve, normal curve

規兵 *seikihei* regulars, regular soldiers

規軍 *seikigun* regular army

12 閏 *seijun* normal and leap (years); legitimate and illegitimate (dynasties)

12 装 *seisō* uniform, full dress

統 *seitō no* legitimate, orthodox, traditional

13 続 *seizoku* a book or document and its supplement

数 *seisū* positive number

夢 *masayume* a dream that comes true

業 *seigyō* legitimate occupation, honest business

義 *seigi* righteousness, justice, right, correct meaning

義感 *seigikan* sense of justice

14 誤 *seigo* correction

誤表 *seigohyō* errata

15 論 *seiron* sound argument

調 *seichō* traditional tune

確 *seikaku* exactness, authenticity, veracity

課 *seika* regular curriculum, required subject

18 鵠 *seikoku* the mark, the point, the bull's eye

――――――― **2** ―――――――

此 2956 J3a21 M16259 SHI. *ko(no)* this, current; next, coming; last, past. *kore* this. *koko ni* here.

4 辺 *ko(no) hen, ko(no) atari, kokora* in this area, around here

方 *ko(no)hō* this one; I, we. *kochira, konata, kotchi* here, this side. *ko(no) kata* since; this person

5 奴 *koitsu* this guy, this fellow

9 度 *ko(no) tabi* at this time

11 頃 *ko(no)goro, ko(no) koro* these days, recently, now

――――――― **4** ―――――――

歩 2958 J4a62 M16284 Ho. step, pace; foot soldier.
A Bu rate, six feel square, *tsubo*; chance of winning. *aru(ku)* walk, hike, step. *ayu(mu)* walk, step. *fu* pawn (in Japanese chess).

6 回 *aru(ki)-mawa(ru)* walk around, gad about

行 *hokō* walking

行者 *hokōsha* pedestrian

合 *ayu(mi)-a(u)* step up to, compromise. *buai* rate, ratio, percentage; commission

合高 *buaidaka* percentage

7 兵 *hohei* infantry, foot soldier

10 哨 *hoshō* sentinel, sentry

11 道 *hodō* footpath, sidewalk

寄 *ayu(mi)-yo(ru)* step up to, approach; compromise

12 測 *hosoku* pacing (a distance)

13 数 *hosū* number of steps

15 調 *hochō* pace, step, cadence, acting in unison

武 2959 J4970 M16273 Mu. Bu military affairs, military arts, chivalry,
A military glory, military power, arms. *take(shi)* brave.

2 人 *bujin* military man

力 *buryoku* armed might, the sword, force

3 士 *bushi, mononofu* samurai, warrior

士道 *bushidō* Bushido, samurai code of chivalry

7 芸 *bugei* martial arts

8 門 *bumon* military family, warrior class

官 *bukan* military or naval officer

具 *bugu* arms, armor

者 *musha* warrior

者振 *mushabu(ri)* prowess, gallantry. *mushaburu(i)* shaking with excitement

者修業 *musha shugyō* samurai drill, knight errantry

9 威 *bui* military power

勇 *buyū* bravery, valor, military prowess

勇伝 *buyūden* martial story; a heroic episode

10 将 *bushō* military commander

骨 *bukotsu* uncouth, clumsy, brusque

骨者 *bukotsumono* boor, rustic

家 *buke* samurai; warrior

11 道 *budō* military arts; Bushido

運 *buun* the fortunes of war

術 *bujutsu* military arts

断 *budan* militarism

12 備 *bubi* military preparation, armaments, defenses

装 *busō* arms, armament; armed. *busō suru* arm

装中立 *busō chūritsu* armed neutrality

装解除 *busō kaijo* disarmament

15 勲 *bukun* deeds of arms

器 *buki* weapon, arms, ordnance

――――――― **5** ―――――――

歪 2960 J4f44 M16286 WAI. E. *hizu(mu)* warp, be crooked, get bent, be strained. *yuga(mu), iga(mu)* warp, swerve, deflect, be crooked, be distorted, be bent, incline, slant; be perverted, be cross-grained. *iga(meru), yuga(meru)* vt bend, curve, warp, distort. *ibitsu no* oval, elliptical; distorted, crooked, irregular, warped. *iga(mi), yuga(mi)* strain, distortion, bend.

6 曲 *waikyoku* distortion, falsification, perversion

4
心 忄 小 戈 戸 手 扌 支 攴 攵 文 斗 方 无 日 曰 月 木 欠 止 【歹】 殳 毋 比 毛 氏 气 水 氵 氺 火 灬 爪 爫 父 爻 爿 片 牛 犬 犭

── 8 ──

歯 A
2961
J3b75
M16323
SHI tooth; age. *ha* tooth, cog, dent.

[4] 止 *hado(me)* brake

切 *hagi(ri)* gnashing the teeth; cutting cogs. *hagi(re)* the feel when biting; manner of enunciation

[5] 石 *shiseki* hard tooth tartar, calculus deposit

立 *ha (ga) ta(tanai)* hard to chew; unable to compete with

牙 *shiga* teeth; teeth and tusks

牙掛 *shiga (ni) ka(kenai)* no argument necessary

向 *hamu(kau)* strike at; bite back; turn on, rise against, oppose, defy

列 *shiretsu* row of teeth

[7] 車 *haguruma* cogwheel, gear

応 *hagota(e)* hard to chew; tough; crisp

医者 *haisha* dentist

[8] 並 *hanara(bi), hana(mi)* row of teeth; set of teeth; dentition

茎 *haguki* gum, tooth ridge

垢 *shikō* tooth tartar

科 *shika* dentistry

科大学 *shika daigaku* dental college

科医 *shikai* dentist

科医師 *shikaishi* dentist

[10] 根 *shikon, ha(no)ne* root of a tooth; fang

浮 *ha (ga) u(ku)* teeth get loose; to tire of someone's bragging

[11] 痒 *hagayu(i)* impatient, tantalized, chagrined, vexed

[12] 痛 *haita, shitsū* toothache

槽膿漏 *shisō nōrō* pyorrhea

[16] 磨 *hamiga(ki)* toothpaste; dentifrice

── 9 ──

歳 B
2962
J3a50
M16326'
SEI, SAI year, age; time; occasion; opportunity; limit; vicinity. *toshi* age. -*sai* years old, age, year.

[2] 入 *sainyū* annual revenue

[4] 月 *saigetsu* time

[5] 出 *saishutsu* annual expenditures

末 *saimatsu* year-end

[8] 事 *saiji* the year's events

[10] 時記 *saijiki* almanac

費 *saihi* annual expenditure

[13] 歳 *saisai* yearly, every year

[14] 暮 *seibo* year-end; year-end present

── 10 ──

歴 A
2964
J4e72
M16334'
REKI history; continuation; passing (of time). *rekki to shita* clear, plain, unmistakable.

[5] 代 *rekidai* successive generations, successive emperors

史 *rekishi* history

史的 *rekishiteki* historic, historical, traditional

史学 *rekishigaku* history

史家 *rekishika* historian

史観 *rekishikan* historical viewpoint

[6] 任 *rekinin suru* successively fill several posts

年 *rekinen* year after year

[11] 遊 *rekiyū suru* tour, itinerate

訪 *rekihō* round of calls; tour of visitation

[12] 然 *rekizen(taru)* plain, distinct, clear

[13] 戦 *rekisen* long military service

[14] 歴 *rekireki* notables, dignitaries; ⌈clear illustrious families. *rekireki(taru)*

━━━━━ RAD. 歹 78 ━━━━━

Ichi-ta (*ichi* "one" plus the katakana *ta*) or *gatsu* dried bones.
At left: *ichi-ta hen* or *gatsu hen*. As enclosure: 歹 *shinigamae* (enclosure like that of *shinu* "die") or *ichi-ta*. Nickname: Death.

── 2 ──

死 A
2968
J3b60
M16365
SHI death. *shi(nu)*, *shi(suru)* die. *shi(nareru)* be bereaved, have (someone) die.

[2] 人 *shinin, shibito, shi(ni)bito* dead person, the killed

力 *shiryoku* desperate effort

³亡 *shibō* death
亡率 *shibōritsu* mortality, death rate
⁴文 *shibun* a document no longer of any value
中 *shichū* fatal situation
火山 *shikazan* extinct volcano
⁵生 *shishō, shisei* life and death
目 *shi(ni)me* the moment of death
去 *shikyo* death
⁶灰 *shikai* cinders, ashes; lack of liveliness. *shi(no)kai* ashes of a nuclear bomb
地 *shichi* jaws of death, fatal situation; battlefield
守 *shishu* stubborn defense
因 *shiin* cause of death
刑 *shikei* capital punishment
刑囚 *shikeishū* criminals condemned to death
⁷角 *shikaku* dead space (in firing)
別 *shibetsu* bereavement
体 *shitai* corpse, remains
体解剖 *shitai kaibō* autopsy
⁸歿 *shibotsu* death
命 *shimei* life and death; fate
果 *shi(ni)-ha(teru)* die (out), become extinct
物狂 *shi(ni)monoguru(i)* death struggle; desperation, frantic efforts
者 *shisha* dead person
⁹相 *shisō* shadow of death
海 *Shikai* Dead Sea
活 *shikatsu* life and death
¹¹産 *shizan, shisan* stillbirth
¹²絶 *shi(ni)-ta(eru)* die out, become extinct. *shizetsu* extinction, destruction
期 *shiki, shigo* time of death, the last hour
¹³滅 *shimetsu* extinction, destruction
罪 *shizai* capital punishment
傷 *shishō* casualties, killed and wounded
¹⁴語 *shigo* dead language; obsolete word
蔵 *shizō* hoarding
¹⁵線 *shisen* the death line; dead wire (in electricity); crisis; the brink of death
¹⁶骸 *shigai* corpse, remains
¹⁸闘 *shitō* life-and-death struggle

──────── 5 ────────

殆 2972 J4b58 M16430 TAI. DAI. *hoton(do)*, *hotohoto* almost, quite, really.

──────── 6 ────────

殉 2974 J3d5e M16448 B JUN. *jun(jiru), jun(zuru)* die a martyr, follow (someone) by committing suicide; follow in resigning.
⁶死 *junshi suru* die a martyr, follow (someone) by committing suicide; follow in resigning
¹¹教 *junkyō* martyrdom
¹⁸職 *junshoku* dying at one's post
難 *junnan* martyrdom

殊 2975 J3c6c M16451 B SHU. *koto ni* especially, exceptionally, above all.
⁵外 *koto (no) hoka* exceedingly, unusually; unexpectedly
⁷更 *kotosara ni* especially, intentionally
¹²勝 *shushō na* laudable, admirable, commendable
¹⁵勲 *shukun* meritorious deeds

残 2976 J3b44 M16459 A ZAN remainder; balance. *noko(ru)* remain, be left over; stay, linger; survive. *noko(su)* leave behind; keep back; leave undone; reserve; save, amass; bequeath. *sokona(u)* harm, hurt, injure, damage, mar; lose, oppress. *noko(razu)* all, entirely, without exception. *noko(ri)* remainder, remnant, residue.
⁴月 *zangetsu* waning moon, morning moon
⁶存 *zanzon suru, zanson suru* survive, remain
⁷忍 *zannin* cruelty, atrocity, brutality
余 *zan'yo* remainder, residue, remnant, balance
⁸金 *zankin* balance, surplus
念 *zannen* regret, disappointment, chagrin
⁹虐 *zangyaku* cruelty, atrocity, brutality
品 *zampin* remnant sale
¹⁰高 *zandaka, noko(ri)daka* balance, remainder
殺 *zansatsu* slaughter, massacre, murder
留 *zanryū suru* remain behind
¹¹雪 *zansetsu* lingering snow

心 忄 小 戈 戸 手 扌 支 攴 攵 文 斗 斤 方 无 日 曰 月 木 欠 止 【歹】⁶ 殳 毋 比 毛 氏 气 水 氵 氺 火 灬 爪 爫 父 爻 爿 丬 片 牙 牛 犬 犭

4

心 忄 小 戈 戸 手 扌 支 攴 攵 文 斗 斤 方 无 日 曰 月 木 欠 止 歹 【殳】 毋 比 毛 氏 气 水 氵 氺 火 灬 爪 爫 父 爻 爿 片 牙 牛 犬 犭

務 *zammu* unfinished business
務整理 *zammu seiri* winding up business
[12] 飯 *zampan* left-over rice; leavings from a meal
期 *zanki* unexpired period
暑 *zansho* lingering summer heat
[13] 業 *zangyō* overtime
業手当 *zangyō teate* overtime pay
[14] 像 *zanzō* afterimage
酷 *zankoku* cruelty, atrocity, brutality
[15] 影 *zan'ei* traces, relics
[16] 骸 *zangai* corpse, carcass; ruins, debris, wreck, remains of
[18] 額 *zangaku* balance (of an account)

B 殖 $\frac{2981}{J3f23}$ M16502 SHOKU increasing. *fu(eru)* increase, multiply, accrue; (water) rises. *fu(yasu)* increase, add to, raise, multiply, augment.
民 *shokumin* colonization, settlement; colonist, settler
[10] 財 *shokuzai* saving money; money-making; increasing one's wealth
[11] 産 *shokusan* increase in production; industry; production

RAD. 殳 79

Ru-mata (the katakana *ru* plus *mata* "again").
Nickname: Windy Again (cf. Rads. 16 and 29).

4

B 殴 $\frac{2990}{J3225}$ M16618 Ō. *nagu(ru)* hit, beat, thrash.
[4] 込 *nagu(ri)-ko(mu)* attack, assault, break into
[5] 付 *nagu(ri)-tsu(keru)* strike, beat, thrash
打 *ōda* blow, assault (and battery)
[6] 合 *nagu(ri)-a(u)* fight, exchange blows
[10] 倒 *nagu(ri)-tao(su)* knock down
殺 *nagu(ri)-koro(su), ōsatsu suru* strike dead, beat to death

5

A 段 $\frac{2991}{J434a}$ M16619 DAN steps, stair, flight of stairs; column; paragraph; act, scene; case, question; grade, class, rank, level; degree, extent. TAN a measure of land. *kiza* scratches, mutilation (of furniture).
[5] 丘 *dankyū* terrace, bench
[8] 取 *dando(ri)* program, plan, arrangements
[9] 段 *dandan* steps, staircase, terrace; gradually, increasingly, one after another. *gizagiza* notches, indentation; ruggedness; fringes
段畑 *dandambatake* terraced fields
[11] 階 *dankai* grade, rank, step, phase, stage. *kizahashi* steps; arrangements
[12] 落 *danraku* period, stop, section, end of a paragraph; conclusion, settlement
違 *danchiga(i)* different class, different level

6

A 殺 $\frac{2994}{J3b26}$ M16629 SATSU. SAI. SETSU. *koro(su)* kill, murder, butcher; waste (money); suppress (anger); hold (breath); put out, strike out. *so(gu)* vt chip, slice off, cut aslant, split off; diminish, reduce; dampen, spoil, mar. *so(geru)* vi split, splinter; be sunken; be sharpened; miss the mark.
[2] 人 *satsujin* murder, homicide, manslaughter
人犯 *satsujinhan* the crime of murder
人光 *satsujinkō* death ray
人光線 *satsujin kōsen* death ray
人的 *satsujinteki* murderous; deadly (heat); hectic (situation); cutthroat (competition)
人鬼 *satsujinki* cutthroat, bloodthirsty felon
人罪 *satsujinzai* murder, competition
[4] 文句 *koro(shi) monku* a "killing" expression; cooing words
[5] 生 *sesshō suru* destroy life, kill animals. *sesshō na* cruel

生戒 *sesshōkai* Buddhist precept against killing

生禁断 *sesshō kindan* hunting and fishing prohibited

⁶竹 *so(gi)take* sharp bamboo sticks

伐 *satsubatsu na* bloodthirsty, brutal, savage, warlike, fierce

合 *koro(shi)-a(u)* kill one another

虫剤 *satchūzai* insecticide

気 *sakki* bloodthirstiness; fury; wild excitement

気立 *sakkida(tsu)* get excited; be bloodthirsty

⁸到 *sattō suru* rush in, pour in, throng to; descend on, storm, swoop down on

⁹屋 *koro(shi)ya* a hired assassin

風景 *sappūkei* inelegance, vulgarity, lack of taste; dreariness

¹⁰害 *satsugai, setsugai* murder, killing, manslaughter, assassination

害人 *satsugaijin* murderer, slayer

害者 *satsugaisha* murderer, slayer

¹¹掠 *satsuryaku* killing and robbing

略 *satsuryaku* killing and robbing

菌 *sakkin* sterilization, disinfection, pasteurization

菌力 *sakkinryoku* germicidal effect

菌剤 *sakkinzai* germicide, disinfectant

¹³傷 *sasshō* bloodshed; casualties

意 *satsui* murderous intent

鼠剤 *sassozai* rat poison

---

¹⁵戮 *satsuriku* massacre, slaughter

──────── 7 ────────

殻 | 2996 | J334c | M-X

B KAKU. *kara* husk, hull, nutshell; cast-off skin; tofu refuse; corpse; earth's crust.

──────── 9 ────────

殿 | 3001 | J4542 | M16651

B TEN. DEN hall, mansion, palace, temple, rear guard. *dono* mister. *shingari* rear. *tono* lord; mansion, place. *-dono* Mr.

³下 *Denka* Highness

上人 *tenjōbito, denjōbito* courtier, court official

⁴方 *tonogata* men, gentlemen

中 *denchū* in the palace

堂 *dendō* palatial building

¹⁴様 *tonosama* feudal lord

様芸 *tonosamagei* dilettantism; amateurism (in art)

様育 *tonosamasoda(chi)* brought up in luxury

様蛙 *tonosamagaeru* bullfrog

──────── 11 ────────

毅 | 3003 | J3523 | M16673

KI strong.

¹²然 *kizen(taru)* dauntless, firm, resolute

═══════ RAD. 母 80 ═══════

Haha mother, *kan no haha* (like the top element of *kan*, a unit of weight), or *nakare* not. Variant: 母 (5 strokes) *haha*. Nickname: Mother.

母 | 3005 | J4a6c | M16723

A BO. *haha* mother; cause; motive. *(o)kā(san)* mother, mama.

³子 *boshi, hahako* mother and child. *boshi* principal and interest

子家庭 *boshi katei* fatherless home

⁴方 *hahakata* the mother's side (of the family)

⁶后 *bokō* empress dowager

⁷体 *botai* mother's body; parent organization

系 *bokei* maternal line

⁸乳 *bonyū* mother's milk

国 *bokoku* mother country

国語 *bokokugo* mother tongue

性愛 *boseiai* a mother's love

⁹音 *boin, boon* vowel

4

心 忄 小 戈 戸 手 扌 支 攴 攵 文 斗 斤 方 无 日 曰 月 木 欠 止 歹 殳 毋 【比】 毛 氏 气 水 氵 氺 火 灬 爪 爫 父 爻 爿 丬 片 牙 牛 犬 犭

屋 *omoya, moya* main building (of a
noble's home)
指 *boshi* thumb
型 *bokei* matrix (in printing)
[10] 校 *bokō* one's alma mater
[11] 船 *bosen* mother ship
[12] 港 *bokō* home port
違 *hahachiga(i)* stepbrother,
stepsister
[16] 親 *hahaoya* mother
[20] 艦 *bokan* mother ship, tender,
carrier

——————— **2** ———————

毎 $\frac{3006}{\text{J4b68}}$ MAI. -*goto ni* each, every,
A 毎 $\overline{\text{M16724}^\text{i}}$ at an interval of, whenever.
mai- every, each, apiece.
[3] 夕 *maiyū* every evening
[4] 日 *mainichi* every day, daily
月 *maitsuki, maigetsu* monthly, every
month
[6] 回 *maikai* every time
年 *maitoshi, mainen* every year,
annually
[9] 度 *maido* each time, frequently;
always
[10] 週 *maishū* every week, weekly
[12] 晩 *maiban* every evening, every night
朝 *maiasa, maichō* every morning

——————— **4** ———————

毒 $\frac{3007}{\text{J4647}}$ DOKU poison; virus,
A 毒 $\overline{\text{M16730}}$ venom, germ, toxin; harm,
injury; malice, spite. *doku(suru)* poison,
harm, corrupt, spoil. *doku(zuku)* curse,
revile, abuse.
[4] 心 *dokushin* malice, spite
手 *dokushu* the clutches (of a usurer, a
villain, etc.)
[5] 牙 *dokuga* poison fang
[6] 舌 *dokuzetsu* wicked tongue; abusive
language
虫 *dokumushi, dokuchū* poisonous
insect
気 *dokuke, dokki, dokke* noxious air,
poisonous air, virulence, poisonous
breath; malice, spite
[7] 見 *dokumi* tasting for poison
[8] 物 *dokubutsu* poisonous substance,
toxicant
毒 *dokudoku(shii)* poisonous; venomous,
malicious, acrimonious; heavy, gross,
disagreeable
味 *dokumi* tasting for poison
草 *dokusō* poisonous plant
[10] 消 *dokuke(shi)* antidote
殺 *dokusatsu* poisoning
素 *dokuso* toxin, ptomaine, poison
[11] 蛇 *dokuja, dokuhebi* venomous
serpent
悪 *dokuaku* great wickedness
[16] 薬 *dokuyaku* poison, poisonous
drug

═══════════ **RAD. 比 81** ═══════════

Kuraberu to compare. Nickname: Comparing.

比 $\frac{3010}{\text{J4866}}$ HI ratio; comparison; an
A 比 $\overline{\text{M16743}}$ equal, a match. *hi(suru)*
compare. *kura(beru)* compare, balance,
contrast. *tagu(eru)* compare with.
kura(bekko) race. *tagui* kind, sort, class.
koro time; about, toward. -*Hi-*
Philippines. -*kura(be)* contest, trial (of
strength).
[8] 肩 *hiken suru* rank with
例 *hirei* proportion; ratio
例代表制 *hirei daihyōsei* proportional
representation
[9] 重 *hijū* specific gravity; density; priority,
relative importance
[11] 率 *hiritsu* ratio; percentage
[12] 喩 *hiyu* simile, metaphor; allegory,
parable, fable
喩的 *hiyuteki* figurative, allegorical
[13] 較 *hikaku* comparison; comparative
(anatomy)
較的 *hikakuteki* relative, comparative
[17] 翼塚 *hiyokuzuka* lover's double
grave
[18] 類 *hirui* a parallel, an equal

5

毘 $\frac{3011}{J487b}$ $\frac{}{M16753}$ Hɪ help, assist.

RAD. 毛 82

Ke hair (of animals). Nickname: Fur.

A 毛 $\frac{3013}{J4c53}$ $\frac{}{M16772}$ Mō hair, tenth of a *rin*. *ke* hair, fur, feather, down. *ke(darake)* hairy.

⁴孔 *keana* pores
⁵穴 *keana* pores
布 *mōfu* blanket, steamer rug
皮 *kegawa, mōhi* fur, skin, pelt
⁶糸 *keito* wool yarn, worsted
羽 *keba* nap, fuzz, pile
虫 *kemushi* caterpillar
⁸並 *kena(mi)* the lie of the hair; color of

the hair; disposition; lineage
¹⁰根 *mōkon* hair root
¹¹深 *kebuka(i)* hairy
脛 *kezune* hairy legs
細血管 *mōsai kekkan* capillaries
¹²筆 *mōhitsu* writing or painting brush
¹⁴髪 *mōhatsu* hair
¹⁶頭 *mōtō* (not) at all
¹⁷氈 *mōsen* rug, carpet
¹⁸織物 *keorimono* woolen goods

RAD. 氏 83

Uji surname, clan. Nickname: Clan.

A 氏 $\frac{3020}{J3b61}$ $\frac{}{M17026}$ Sнı Mr.; family, clan. *uji* clan; lineage, birth; surname.

⁶名 *shimei, ujina* surname
名点呼 *shimei tenko* roll call
⁹神 *ujigami* Shinto clan god, patron deity. *uji (no) kami* clan chieftain
¹¹族 *shizoku* family, clan

1

A 民 $\frac{3021}{J4c31}$ $\frac{}{M17028}$ Mɪɴ. *tami* people, nation, subjects.

²力 *minryoku* national manpower
⁴心 *minshin* popular sentiment
⁵生 *minsei* people's livelihood, people's welfare
生委員 *minsei iin* district welfare officer
主 *minshu* democracy
主化 *minshuka* democratization
主主義 *minshu shugi* democracy
主的 *minshuteki* democratic

有 *min'yū* private ownership
⁷兵 *mimpei* militia
芸 *mingei* folk craft, folk art
⁸国 *Minkoku* The Republic of China
法 *mimpō* civil law, civil code
事 *minji* civil affairs; civil case
事的 *minjiteki* civil
事裁判 *minji saiban* civil trial
事訴訟 *minji soshō* civil suit
⁹度 *mindo* cultural standard
俗 *minzoku* ethnic customs, folk customs
政 *minsei* civil government, democracy
¹⁰家 *minka* private house
¹¹宿 *minshuku* a private house providing lodging and meals to transient guests
情 *minjō* condition of the people; the sentiment of the people
族 *minzoku* race, people, ethnic group
族主義 *minzoku shugi* nationalism
族的 *minzokuteki* racial, ethnic

4

心 忄 小 戈 戸 手 扌 支 攴 文 斗 斤 方 无 日 曰 月 木 欠 止 歹 殳 毋 比 毛 氏 【气】 水 氵 氺 火 灬 爪 爫 父 爻 爿 丬 片 牙 牛 犬 犭

族学 *minzokugaku* ethnology
族学者 *minzokugakusha* ethnologist
族移動 *minzoku idō* racial migration
¹² 営 *min'ei* private management
間 *minkan no* private, civilian, civil, popular, folk, unofficial
衆 *minshū* people, populace,

masses
¹³ 話 *minwa* folklore
意 *min'i* popular will
¹⁴ 選 *minsen* popular election
需 *minju* civilian requirements
¹⁵ 権 *minken* civil rights
¹⁶ 謡 *min'yō* popular song, ballad, folk song

⽓ RAD. 84

Kigamae "vapor" enclosure. Nickname: Steam.

2

A 気 3025 / J3524 / M17046 KI, KE spirit, mind, soul, heart; intention; bent, interest; mood, feeling; temper, disposition, nature; care, attention; air, atmosphere; flavor; odor; energy, essence; air, indications, symptoms; taste; touch, dash, shade, trace; spark, flash; suspicion. *ki (ni) suru* mind, care, take to heart, be nervous about. *ki (ni) naru* weigh on the mind, get on one's nerves; take a fancy to; feel inclined to. *ki (ga) suru* think, feel. *ki (ga) aru* have the intention (of doing something). *-ke, -ge* feeling; taste.
² 入 *ki (ni) i(ru)* be pleased with, be satisfactory. *ki(ni)i(ri)* favorite, pet
力 *kiryoku* energy, vigor, vitality, mettle, push
³ 丈 *kijō na* stouthearted
⁴ 心 *kigokoro* temper, disposition
化 *kika* evaporation; vaporization
分 *kibun* feeling, mood, spirit

分転換 *kibun tenkan* mental diversion; change of environment
⁵ 立 *ki (ga) ta(tsu)* get excited, be aroused. *kida(te)* disposition, temperament
失 *ki (o) ushina(u)* faint
付 *ki (ga) tsu(ku)* be aware of, notice, realize. *ki (o) tsu(keru)* take care of, be careful, be attentive to, take note of; be on the lookout. *kizu(ku)* notice, perceive, find out, think of, get wind of. *kitsu(ke)* encouragement; restorative, stimulant, smelling salts; reviving. *ki (o) tsu(ke)* Attention!

-kitsuke, -kizuke in care of.
圧 *kiatsu* atmospheric pressure. *keo(sareru)* be overpowered, be overawed
圧計 *kiatsukei* barometer
⁶ 色 *keshiki(bamu)* look hurt; get excited; get angry. *kishoku* mood, feeling; expression; countenance; feelings. *kewai, kehai* sign, indication. *keshiki* signs, indications; feelings; popularity; your will, your pleasure; reason; getting excited, getting angry
回 *ki (o) ma(wasu), ki (ga) mawa(ru)* give play to imagination; make a suspicious conjecture
向 *ki (ga) mu(ku)* feel inclined
休 *kiyasu(me) ni* for peace of mind
忙 *kizewa(shii)* restless, bustling, fidgety
早 *kibaya na, ki (no) haya(i)* quick-tempered
合 *kia(i)* feeling, temper, disposition; a puff of breath; yell. *ki (ga) a(u)* congenial
⁷ 迫 *kihaku* soul; great energy, great mental power
抜 *ki (ga) nu(keru)* be discouraged. *ki (ga) nu(keta), ki (no) nu(keta)* insipid, stale. *kinu(ke)* absentmindedness, dejection
狂 *ki (ga) kuru(u)* go insane; lose one's head; run amuck, rave; be madly in love; go haywire. *kiguru(i)* out of one's senses, out of season (flowering)
利 *ki (ga) ki(ku)* have good judgment, be clever. *ki (o) ki(kasu)* use one's head, be sensible. *ki (no) ki(ita)* sensible, intelligent, clever, respectable, in good

3025

taste. *ki (no) ki(kanai)* dull, awkward, unrefined

位 *kigurai* feelings

体 *kitai* gas, vapor, gaseous body

⁸性 *kishō* disposition, temperament

易 *kiyasu(ku)* freely, with a light heart

苦労 *kigurō* worry, anxiety

所為 *ki (no) sei* fancy, imagination

泡 *kihō* air bubble

取 *kedo(ru)* suspect, sense. *kido(ru)* be affected, assume airs, pose as. *kido(ri)* affectation

炎 *kien* flame; bombast, tall talk

毒 *ki (no) doku* pitiable, miserable; regrettable; too bad

味 *kimi, kibi* feeling; touch, dash, shade, tinge; taste and savor; suspicion. *-kimi, -gimi* tendency

味悪 *kimiwaru(i), kibiwaru(i)* uncanny, weird, lurid, gruesome, ominous, repulsive, eerie, creepy

⁹風 *kippu, kifū* character, disposition, temper; morale, spirit

食 *ki (ni) ku(wanu)* go against the grain, be unsatisfactory, be disagreeable,

持 *kimochi* feeling, mood. *kimochi(yoku)* agreeably, cheerfully dislike

乗 *kino(ri) suru, ki (ga) no(ru)* be interested in

前 *kimae* temperament; generosity

品 *kihin* (moral) tone, dignity, grace, nobility, refinement

負 *kio(u)* brace oneself; stir up one's fighting spirit

¹⁰高 *kedaka(i)* noble, exalted, graceful

疲 *kizuka(re)* mental fatigue, worry, boredom

病 *ki (ni) ya(mu)* worry about, be sensitive about. *kiya(mi), kibyō* blues, depression. *ki (no) ya(mai)* anxiety, illness; nervous breakdown

進 *ki (ga) susu(mu)* feel inclined

振 *kebu(ri)* air, appearance; behavior; bearing; indications

根 *kikon* aerial root; energy, perseverance

流 *kiryū* air current

紛 *kimagure* caprice, whim, uneven temper

恥 *kihazu(kashii)* ashamed, bashful, shy, embarrassed

胸 *kikyō* pneumothorax

脈 *kimyaku* connection; collusion; communication

配 *kehai, kewai* sign, indication. *kikuba(ri)* vigilance; worry. *kihai* market trend

兼 *kiga(ne)* constraint, deference, scruple, hesitation

差 *ki (ga) sa(su)* be concerned

弱 *kiyowa(i)* timid, fainthearted

骨 *kikotsu* spirit, soul, mettle, backbone. *kibone* mental effort

随気儘 *kizui-kimama na* willful

息 *kisoku* breathing; breath

候 *kikō* climate; weather; season

¹¹運 *kiun* luck; tendency, opportunity

強 *kizuyo(i)* brave, resolute; reassuring; hardhearted. *kizuyo(ku)* resolutely, cheerfully, confidently

掛 *kiga(kari)* anxiety

済 *ki (ga) su(mu)* be satisfied, be appeased

転 *kiten* tact; ready wit

悪 *ki (o) waru(ku) suru* hurt one's feelings

動車 *kidōsha* diesel train

密 *kimitsu* airtight

密室 *kimitsushitsu* airtight chamber

球 *kikyū* balloon

¹²遣 *kizuka(u)* be anxious about, worry about. *kizuka(i)* fear, worry, solicitude. *kizuka(washii)* anxious

遠 *ki (ga) tō(ku) naru* feel dizzy

揉 *ki (o) mo(mu)* worry, be anxious

晴 *kiba(rashi)* diversion, recreation, relaxation, amusement. *ki(o)harasu* clear one's mind

温 *kion* air temperature

短 *kimijika na; ki (ga) mijika(i)* hot-tempered, impatient, touchy

絶 *kizetsu* fainting

筒 *kitō* steam cylinder

落 *kio(chi)* discouragement, despondency. *ki (o) oto(su)* be discouraged

軽 *kigaru na* cheerful; buoyant, lighthearted

違 *kichiga(i)* insanity; mania, fanaticism; lunatic; fanatic, enthusiast, fan

象 *kishō* climate, weather, weather conditions; meteorology (of a place);

4

心 忄 小 戈 戸 手 扌 支 攴 文 斗 斤 方 无 日 曰 月 木 欠 歹 殳 毋 比 毛 氏 【气】² 水 氵 氺 火 灬 爪 爫 父 爻 丬 片 牙 牛 犬 犭

4

心 忄 小 戈 戸 手 扌 支 攴 攵 文 斗 斤 方 无 日 曰 月 木 欠 止 歹 殳 毋 比 毛 氏 气 【水 氵 氺】 火 灬 爪 爫 父 爻 爿 片 牙 牛 犬 犭

disposition, temperament; characteristics

象庁 *Kishōchō* Weather Bureau

象台 *kishōdai* weather observatory

¹³ 障 *ki (ni) sawa(ru)* offend; get offended. *kiza* affectation. *kizawa(ri)* disagreeable feeling

節 *kisetsu* courage and integrity; weather

勢 *kisei* energy, enthusiasm, spirit

楽 *kiraku* feeling at home, ease, comfort

¹⁴ 概 *kigai* spirit, pep, pluck; backbone; self-respect; courage

---

管 *kikan* windpipe, trachea

管支 *kikanshi* bronchial tube

管支炎 *kikanshien* bronchitis

管支肺炎 *kikanshi haien* bronchial pneumonia

¹⁵ 魄 *kihaku* soul; great energy, great mental power

鋭 *kiei* spirit, impetuosity, energy

質 *kishitsu* temperament, disposition. *katagi* spirit, character, trait

¹⁶ 儘 *kimama, ki(no)mama* willfulness, selfishness, self-indulgence

¹⁸ 難 *kimuzuka(shii)* hard to please, moody

■ RAD. 水 85 ■

Sui or *mizu* water. At left: 氵 (3 strokes) *sanzui* (3-stroke "water," as distinguished from Rad. 15). At bottom: 氺 (5 strokes) *shita mizu*. Nickname: Water.

水 ³⁰³⁰ / J3165 / M17083 SUI water; ice water; Wednesday. *mizu* water. *mizu(ppoi)* watery.

² 入 *mizu-i(razu) de* privately, among ourselves. *mizui(re)* water jug, pitcher

力 *suiryoku* water power

力発電所 *suiryoku hatsudensho* hydroelectric plant

³ 上 *suijō* water (transportation); aquatic; floating. *minakami* headwater, source

上機 *suijōki* hydroplane, seaplane

上競技 *suijō kyōgi* water sports

⁴ 牛 *suigyū* water buffalo

辺 *suihen* water's edge, beach

引 *mizuhiki* two-color strings for tying gifts

分 *suibun* moisture, water, humidity; juice; water content

夫 *suifu, kako* sailor, mariner

中 *suichū* submarine, aquatic, underwater; in water. *mizuata(ri)* illness from water

⁵ 母 *kurage* jellyfish

玉 *mizutama* a drop of water; a drop of dew

仙 *suisen* daffodil; narcissus

仕事 *mizu shigoto* washing and scrubbing

田 *suiden, mizuta* paddy field

圧 *suiatsu* hydraulic pressure

平 *suihei* water level; horizontal

平線 *suiheisen* horizon

⁶ 色 *mizuiro* light blue, water green

虫 *mizumushi* water insect; athlete's foot

気 *mizuke* dampness, moisture, juice. *suiki* dropsy; moisture, humidity, vapor

汲 *mizuku(mi)* drawing water

防 *suibō* flood prevention

成岩 *suiseigan* sedimentary rock

死 *suishi* drowning

先案内 *mizusaki-annai* pilot; piloting

⁷ 車 *suisha, mizuguruma* water wheel

利 *suiri* water utilization; water supply; irrigation

系 *suikei* mountain drainage system, water system

冷式 *suireishiki* water-cooled

芭蕉 *mizubashō* a skunk cabbage

位 *suii* water level

兵 *suihei* (navy) sailor

⁸ 門 *suimon* floodgate, penstock, sluice

泡 *minawa* foam, bubbles. *mizu(no)awa* foam, bubbles; nothing; failure. *suihō* foam, bubbles; nothing; failure

底 *minasoko, suitei* sea bottom, river bottom

泳 *suiei, mizuoyo(gi)* swimming

⁹面 *suimen, minomo* surface of the water

屋 *mizuya* water carrier; water font at shrine or temple; dish cupboard, washing area in tea ceremony room

星 *Suisei* Mercury

臭 *mizukusa(i)* watery; reserved, formal, distant

洗 *mizuara(i), suisen* washing

洗式 *suisenshiki* flush type

洗式便所 *suisenshiki benjo* flush toilet

洗便所 *suisenbenjo* flush toilet

¹⁰流 *suiryū* current, stream, watercourse

浴 *suiyoku* bathing, cold bath. *mizua(bi)* bathing

脈 *suimyaku* water vein

陸 *suiriku* land and water

差 *mizusa(shi)* water jug, pitcher. *mizu (o) sa(su)* cause trouble between | people

疱 *suihō* blister

疱瘡 *mizubōsō* chicken pox

素 *suiso* hydrogen

害 *suigai* flood damage, inundation

¹¹鳥 *mizudori, mizutori, suichō* waterfowl

運 *suiun* water transportation

域 *suiiki* river basin; an area of the ocean

深 *suishin* water depth

球 *suikyū* water polo

瓶 *mizugame* water jar

密 *suimitsu* watertight

菓子 *mizugashi* fruit

商売 *mizu shōbai* the entertainment business

掛論 *mizuka(ke)ron* futile argument

眼鏡 *mizu megane* diver's goggles

魚交 *suigyo (no) majiwa(ri)* intimate friendship

彩画 *suisaiga* watercolor painting

道 *suidō* waterworks; water pipes; aqueduct; waterway, channel; city water

道局 *suidōkyoku* water bureau

産 *suisan* marine products

産物 *suisambutsu* marine products

産業 *suisangyō* fisheries, marine products industry

¹²温 *suion* water temperature

筒 *suitō* water bottle, canteen

着 *mizugi* swimming suit

葬 *suisō* burial at sea

無月 *minazuki* sixth lunar month

揚 *mizua(ge)* landing (goods); earnings; defloration; preservation (of cut flowers)

割 *mizuwa(ri)* diluting with water; packing inferior goods beneath a high-quality layer

晶 *suishō* quartz

量 *suiryō* water volume

¹³煙 *mizu kemuri, suien* spray, splashes

路 *suiro* waterway, channel; aqueduct

禽 *suikin* waterfowl

嵩 *mizu kasa* water volume

勢 *suisei* force of water

鉄砲 *mizudeppō* squirt gun

溶性 *suiyōsei* water-soluble

源 *suigen* river source, fountainhead

際 *mizugiwa, migiwa* water's edge, beach

準 *suijun* water level; standard

¹⁴増 *mizuma(shi)* dilution, watering

滴 *suiteki* drop of water

稲 *suitō* wet-land rice

練 *suiren* swimming practice; art of swimming

蜜 *suimitsu* (a quality) peach

墨画 *suibokuga* India-ink painting

銀 *suigin* mercury

¹⁵槽 *suisō* water tank, water trough, cistern

線 *suisen* water line

質 *suishitsu* water quality

¹⁶薬 *mizugusuri, suiyaku* liquid medicine

¹⁸曜 *Suiyō* Wednesday

¹⁹爆 *suibaku* hydrogen bomb

1

A 永 ³⁰³¹/_{J314a} M17088 Eɪ. *naga(i)* long, lengthy. *towa* eternity. *naga(raku)* a long time.

³久 *eikyū, tokoshie* eternity, perpetuity, immortality. *eikyū ni, tokoshie ni* everlastingly

⁵代 *eitai* permanence, eternity

代借地 *eitai shakuchi* perpetual lease

世 *eisei* eternity, perpetuity, immortality, permanence

世中立 *eisei chūritsu* permanent neutrality

⁶年 *einen* many years, a long time

⁷劫 *eigō* eternity, perpetuity

寿 *eiju* long life

住 *eijū* permanent residence

住権 *eijūken* denizenship; permanent residence

4

¹

¹⁰ 眠 *eimin* eternal sleep, death

¹¹ 訣 *eiketsu* last farewell

¹² 遠 *eien* eternity, immortality, perpetuity, permanence

¹³ 続 *eizoku, nagatsuzu(ki)* permanence, continuation

A 氷 ³⁰³²/J4939/M17087 Hyō. *kō(ru)* freeze; be frozen over; congeal. *kōri* ice; shaved ice. *hi* ice; hail.

³ 山 *hyōzan* iceberg

⁴ 水 *kōri mizu, kōrisui* shaved ice, ice water

⁸ 枕 *kōri makura* ice pillow

河 *hyōga* glacier

河時代 *hyōga jidai* glacial period

河期 *hyōgaki* glacial period

⁹ 柱 *hyōchū, tsurara* icicle, ice pillar

砂糖 *kōrizatō* rock candy, sugar candy

点 *hyōten* freezing point

点下 *hyōtenka* below freezing

¹⁰ 原 *hyōgen* ice field; ice floe; snow field

¹¹ 雪 *hyōsetsu* ice and snow

菓子 *kōrigashi* a frozen sweet; sherbert

¹² 結 *hyōketsu* freezing

¹³ 塊 *hyōkai* lump of ice, block of ice; ice floe

解 *hyōkai* melting, thawing

詰 *kōrizume* packing in ice

¹⁴ 漬 *kōrizuke* putting down in ice

¹⁸ 瀑 *hyōbaku* ice fall

嚢 *hyōnō* ice bag, ice pack

──────── **2** ────────

泛 ³⁰³³/J4845/M17101 Han spread out; wide.

¹⁷ 濫 *hanran* flooding

汀 ³⁰³⁴/J4475/M17103 Tei. *migiwa* water's edge, shore.

B 汁 ³⁰³⁵/J3d41/M17104 Jū, Shū juice. *shiru* juice; sap; soup, broth; gravy; pus. *tsuyu* juice; sap; soup, broth; gravy.

⁸ 物 *shirumono* soups

¹¹ 液 *jūeki* juice

A 求 ³⁰³⁶/J3561/M17105 Kyū. Gu. *moto(meru)* want, wish for, request, demand; seek, search for; pursue (pleasure); hunt (a job); buy.

² 人 *kyūjin* help wanted

人広告 *kyūjin kōkoku* help-wanted ad

⁴ 心力 *kyūshinryoku* centripetal force

⁶ 刑 *kyūkei suru* prosecute

¹¹ 道 *kyūdō, gudō* seeking for truth

婚 *kyūkon* proposal, courtship

婚者 *kyūkonsha* suitor

¹³ 愛 *kyūai* courtship

¹⁸ 職 *kyūshoku* job hunting, seeking employment

──────── **3** ────────

汝 ³⁰⁴⁰/J4672/M17138 Jo. *nanji, nare* you, thou.

汐 ³⁰⁴¹/J3c2e/M17122 Seki. Shaku. *shio* tide; salt water; opportunity.

³ 干狩 *shiohiga(ri)* low-tide shell gathering

¹² 焼 *shioya(ke)* tanned by salt air

A 池 ³⁰⁴²/J4353/M17141 Chi. *ike* pond, pool, cistern, basin, reservoir.

汎 ³⁰⁴³/J4846/M17120 Han pan-.

B 江 ³⁰⁴⁵/J393e/M17140 Kō. *e* inlet, bay.

戸 *Edo* Edo, Tokyo, Edo era (1603-1867)

戸子 *Edo(k)ko* true Tokyoite

戸前 *Edomae* Edo-style (cooking)

¹² 湖 *kōko* the public, the world; rivers and lakes

B 汗 ³⁰⁴⁶/J3440/M17130 Kan. *ase(bamu), ase suru* be sweaty. *ase* perspiration. *ase(daku)* dripping with sweat. *ase(mizuku)* dripping with sweat.

⁴ 水 *asemizu* copious sweating

⁸ 性 *aseshō* tendency to perspire

¹³ 搔 *ase(k)kaki, asekaki* heavy perspirer

腺 *kansen* sweat gland

¹⁵ 瘡 *asemo, asebo* prickly heat, heat rash

¹⁸ 顔 *kangan* sweating from shame

顔至 *kangan (no) ita(ri)* deeply ashamed, feeling awkward

B 汚 ³⁰⁴⁷/J3178/M17133 O. *kega(su)* make dirty, stain, pollute, defile,

contaminate; disgrace, dishonor; rape.
kega(reru) get dirty; be defiled; be
contaminated. *yogo(su)* vt stain, soil,
pollute; defile, debauch. *yogo(reru)* vi
get dirty, be stained, be contaminated,
tarnish. *yogo(reta)* loathsome; obscene.
kega(re) uncleanness, impurity, disgrace.
yogo(re) dirt, spot, stain, filth. *kitana(i)*
dirt, filthy, unclean, soiled; shabby;
indecent, obscene; base, sordid; stingy;
foul. *kega(rawashii)* filthy; unfair.

⁴ 水 *osui* filthy water, sewage
名 *omei* stigma, dishonor, disgrace, slur,
infamy
⁸ 物 *obutsu* dust, dirt, filth, garbage, ashes;
impurities; sewage. *yogo(re)mono*
the washing, laundry 「disgrace
⁹ 染 *osen* stain, blot, spot, smudge,
点 *oten* stain, blot, spot, smudge, blur;
flaw; disgrace
¹⁰ 辱 *ojoku* disgrace, humiliation, insult
¹³ 損 *oson* stain
¹⁶ 濁 *odaku* corruption, graft
¹⁸ 職 *oshoku* graft, bribery

——————— **4** ———————

沌 `3054 J4659 M17193` Ton primeval chaos.

汰 `3055 J4241 M17160` Da. Ta luxury; select.

沓 `3060 J3723 M17206` Tō. *kutsu* shoes, boots.

沃 `3061 J4d60 M17184` Yoku pour; fertility.

³ 土 *yokudo* fertile soil; mold
⁹ 度 *yōdo* iodine
¹⁰ 素 *yōso* iodine
¹¹ 野 *yokuya* fertile field

沢 `3062 J4274 M17234` Taku swamp; blessing.
B *sawa* swamp, marsh, dale,
valley.

³ 山 *takusan* a great many, a large
quantity, abundance, plenty
¹¹ 庵 *takuan* pickled daikon

沙 `3063 J3a3b M17212` Sa. Sha. *isago, suna* sand.

⁷ 汰 *sata* instructions, directions, orders;
notice, information message; report,
rumor; affair
¹³ 漠 *sabaku* desert

汲 `3064 J3562 M17163` Kyū. *ku(mu)* draw
(water), ladle, dip, scoop,
pump; consider; sympathize with; drink;
think.

² 入 *ku(mi)-i(reru)* draw in
⁴ 水 *ku(mi)mizu, kyūsui* pumping water
⁵ 出 *ku(mi)-da(su)* pump out, dip out, bail
out
⁸ 取 *ku(mi)-to(ru)* draw (water), dip, ladle,
drain, bail out; take into consideration,
make allowance for

沖 `3065 J322d M17209` Chū. *okitsu, oki* offing,
B open sea. *chū(suru)* rise
high in the sky.

⁶ 合 *okia(i)* offshore, offing
仲仕 *okinakashi* longshoreman
¹⁶ 積土 *chūsekido* alluvial soil

没 `3066 J4b57 M17233` Botsu. Motsu. *bos(suru)*
B sink, set, go down; hide,
be hidden, fall into; disappear; die. *botsu*
rejection of manuscript; deceased. (Some
scholars limit the meaning of 歿 to
dying).

² 入 *botsunyū suru, motsunyū suru* be
absorbed in
⁵ 収 *bosshū* confiscation
⁶ 年 *botsunen* year of death
交渉 *bokkōshō, botsukōshō* no
connection (with), no relation to
¹² 落 *botsuraku* ruin, downfall,
bankruptcy
落者 *botsurakusha* a bankrupt person; a
ruined people
¹⁶ 頭 *bottō suru* be absorbed in, be devoted
to

汽 `3068 J3525 M17177` Ki vapor; steam.
A

⁵ 圧 *kiatsu* steam pressure
⁶ 缶 *kikan* boiler, steam generator
缶室 *kikanshitsu* boiler room
⁷ 車 *kisha* train; steam train
車賃 *kishachin* railway fare
¹¹ 笛 *kiteki* steam whistle, siren
船 *kisen* steamship

4

沈 B　3069 / J4440 / M17189　CHIN. SHIN. JIN aloes. *shizu(mu)* vi sink, be submerged; subside, cave in; feel depressed, be overcome with. *shizu(meru)* vt sink, submerge, immerse. *shizu(me)* immersion.

³ 下 *chinka* sinking, subsidence, settlement, dip
⁷ 没 *chimbotsu* sinking, foundering, submersion
⁹ 降 *chinkō* sedimentation, settling, subsidence, sinking
¹¹ 船 *chinsen* sunken ship
¹² 痛 *chintsū* pathetic, sad
　着 *chinchaku* composure, calmness
¹³ 殿 *chinden* precipitation, sedimentation, subsidence
　滞 *chintai* stagnation, inactivity
¹⁴ 静 *chinsei* stillness, tranquility, placidity; slackness, dullness, stagnation, inactivity
¹⁵ 黙 *chimmoku* silence, reticence
¹⁶ 澱 *odo(mu)* precipitate, settle. *chinden* precipitation, sedimentation, subsidence
²⁵ 欝 *chin'utsu* melancholy, gloom

決 A　3070 / J3768 / M17174　KETSU decision, vote. *kes(suru)* vt settle, vote on, judge, decide. *vi* be settled, be decided; collapse, give way. *ki(maru)* be decided, be settled, be arranged; be certain to, be doomed to. *ki(meru)* fix, decide, agree upon; appoint, choose; resolve. *ki(me)* arrangement, contract. *(o)ki(mari)* usage, custom, routine; fixed charge. *kes(shite)* (with neg.) never, by no means.

⁴ 心 *kesshin* determination, resolution
　手 *ki(me)te* deciding factor, winning move
　文句 *ki(mari) monku* favorite phrase, ⌈cliché
⁶ 行 *kekkō* decisive action
　死 *kesshi* preparedness for death, do-or-die spirit
⁷ 別 *ketsubetsu* separation, farewell
　定 *kettei* decision, determination, conclusion, settlement
　定版 *ketteiban* final edition (of a book)
　定的 *ketteiteki* definite, final, decisive, conclusive, peremptory
¹⁰ 起 *kekki suru* rise, spring to one's feet

¹¹ 済 *kessai* settlement, liquidation
　断 *ketsudan* decision, determination
¹² 着 *ketchaku* conclusion, settlement
　然 *ketsuzen(taru)* firm, decisive, determined
　裂 *ketsuretsu* breakdown, rupture
　裁 *kessai* sanction, approval
　勝 *kesshō* decision (in a contest)
　勝戦 *kesshōsen* finals
¹³ 意 *ketsui* resolution, determination
　戦 *kessen* decisive battle; deciding match, finals
¹⁴ 算 *kessan* settlement, liquidation
¹⁵ 潰 *kekkai* rip, break
¹⁶ 壊 *kekkai* rip, break
¹⁸ 闘 *kettō* duel
²⁰ 議 *ketsugi* resolution, decision, vote

── **5** ──

沫 　3085 / J4b77 / M17235　MATSU. *awa* bubble, foam, froth, scum, suds. *shibuki* spray, splash.

況 B　3086 / J3637 / M17264　KYŌ. *ma(shite)* still more, still less (neg.) *iwa(n'ya)* still more; (neg.) much less.

泳 A　3090 / J314b / M17328　EI. *oyo(gu)* swim; totter; keep afloat, get along. *oyo(gi)* swim, swimming.
⁸ 法 *eihō* swimming style
　者 *eisha* swimmer

沼 B　3091 / J3e42 / M17257　SHŌ swamp, lake. *numa* swamp, bog, pond, lake.
⁶ 地 *numachi, shōchi* marsh land
⁷ 沢 *shōtaku* marsh, swamp

泌 B　3092 / J4867 / M17279　HITSU, HI flow; soak in; penetrate; secrete.
⁷ 尿 *hinyō, hitsunyō* urinary
　尿器 *hinyōki* urinary organs

泡 B　3093 / J4b22 / M17307　HŌ. *awa, abuku* bubble, foam, froth, scum, suds.
⁵ 立器 *awada(te)ki* eggbeater
⁸ 沫 *hōmatsu, utakata* bubble, foam, froth
¹¹ 雪 *awayuki* light snow

4

B 沸 3094 J4a28 M17251 FUTSU. *wa(ku) vi* boil, get hot; ferment; seethe; be in an uproar; gush out; grow, breed, be hatched. *wa(kasu) vt* boil; heat up (the bath); melt.

3 上 *wa(ki)-a(garu)* boil up; well up
5 立 *wa(ki)-ta(tsu)* boil up, seethe, ferment, stir
6 返 *wa(ki)-kae(ru)* seethe, boil up; be in an uproar
9 点 *futten* boiling point
20 騰 *futtō* boiling, seething, bubbling; agitation

A 泉 3095 J4074 M17274 SEN. *izumi* spring, fountain(head), source.

4 水 *sensui* fountain, miniature lake
13 源 *sengen* source of a stream

A 沿 3096 J3168 M17260 EN following along. *so(u)* run along; lie along; be situated on.

8 岸 *engan* coast, shore
9 革 *enkaku* history, development
海 *enkai* coast, shore, sea, inshore, coastal waters
11 道 *endō* route, course; roadside
13 路 *enro* route
15 線 *ensen no* along the railway line

B 泰 3098 J4259 M17325 TAI calm, peace; easy; large, wide. *Tai* Thai, Thailand, Siam.

4 斗 *taito* an authority
5 平 *taihei* peace, tranquility
6 西 *Taisei* the Occident
12 然 *taizen(taru)* calm, composed; firm
然自若 *taizen-jijaku* imperturbability, presence of mind

B 泊 3099 J4771 M17275 HAKU (three-day) stay. *to(maru)* stay at, put up at; ride at anchor. *to(meru)* lodge a person. *toma(ri)* anchorage; stopping (for the night); night duty.

6 地 *hakuchi* anchorage, berth
9 客 *toma(ri)kyaku* overnight guest

A 治 3100 J3c23 M17256 JI. CHI peace; government. *ji(suru)* cure, heal; rule; conserve (resources). *osa(meru)*, *chi(suru)* govern, manage, regulate; quell, subdue; patch up; heal. *osa(maru)* be at peace; calm down; be settled, be ruled. *nao(ru)* be mended; get well; be restored; return to normal; be installed (as a legal wife); change (from third to second class). *nao(su)* mend, repair, put in order, reform, correct; revise, amend; re-do, alter; cure; restore; adjust, regulate; convert (money).

3 山 *chisan* flood-control tree planting on a watershed
5 世 *chisei, jisei* reign, rule, regime, dynasty
外法権 *chigai-hōken* extraterritoriality
6 安 *chian* public peace and order
7 乱 *chiran* war and peace
17 績 *chiseki* administration's record
療 *chiryō* medical treatment
療法 *chiryōhō* therapeutics, cure, remedy
18 癒 *chiyu* healing, cure, recovery

A 波 3101 J4748 M17308 HA wave. *nami* wave, billows.

3 及 *hakyū suru* be propagated; extend, spread; affect, influence
4 止場 *hatoba* wharf, quay, jetty, pier
5 立 *namida(tsu)* be choppy, be wavy, be rolling (with billows); boil up; ripple
打 *namiu(tsu)* dash against; undulate
打際 *namiu(chi)giwa* beach
7 状 *hajō* wave, undulation
乱 *haran* waves, billows; commotion; wide fluctuations
8 長 *hachō* wave length
9 風 *namikaze* wind and waves; discord, trouble
乗 *namino(ri)* surf riding. *nami (ni) no(ru)* ride on a wave (of success)
10 高 *hakō* wave height
浪 *harō* waves, billows
紋 *hamon* ripple, wave ring
11 動 *hadō* wave motion, undulatory motion
16 頭 *hatō* on the waves; wave crest; on the sea; whitecaps. *namigashira* whitecaps
17 濤 *hatō* billows, rough seas, large waves

A 河 3102 J324f M17245 KA *kawa* river, stream.

3 口 *kakō* river mouth, estuary

心 忄 小 戈 戸 手 扌 支 攴 父 文 斗 方 无 日 曰 月 木 欠 止 歹 殳 毋 比 毛 氏 气 【水 氵 氺】5 火 灬 爪 爫 父 爻 爿 丬 片 牙 牛 犬 犭

心忄小戈戸手扌支攴攵文斗斤方无日曰月木欠止歹殳毋比毛氏气【水氵氺】火灬爪爫父爻爿丬片牙牛犬犭

4

川 *kasen* rivers
7 床 *kashō, kawadoko* river bed
系 *kakei* river system
8 岸 *kashi* riverside, waterfront; fish market; scene, place; one's trade or field. *kawagishi, kagan* riverside, river bank
10 馬 *kaba* hippopotamus
流 *karyū* stream
畔 *kahan* riverside
原 *kawara, kawahara* river beach, dry river bed
11 豚 *fugu, katon* puffer, globefish pufferfish, blowfish
12 港 *kakō* river port
童 *kappa, kawa(p)pa* a waterinp; a river monster; expert swimmer

注 3103 J436d M17316 CHŪ notes, comment; N.B. *chū(suru)* comment on; annotate. *soso(gu)* vt pour into, pour on, irrigate, sprinkle; shed (tears). *vi* (rain) falls; flow into; pay attention to, concentrate on. *tsu(gu)* pour in, fill, put in (more coal). *sa(su)* pour (a drink), serve (drinks); mix into.
A
2 入 *chūnyū suru* pour into, put into, inject, impregnate, infuse, instill, implant, imbue
4 水 *chūsui* flooding; douche
込 *soso(gi)-ko(mu)* pour into, flow into. *tsu(gi)-ko(mu)* pour into; invest, sink (money) into
文 *chūmon* an order
文先 *chūmonsaki* where you place your order
5 目 *chūmoku* attention, observation, notice
8 油 *chūyu* oiling, lubrication. *soso(gi) abura* anointing oil
10 記 *chūki suru* make entries, write down
射 *chūsha* injection, shot
11 釈 *chūshaku* notes, comment, exegesis
13 意 *chūi* attention, care, heed; warning, advice, hint; interest 「character
意人物 *chūi jimbutsu* suspicious
意事項 *chūi jikō* N.B.; suggestions; matters requiring attention
意報 *chūihō* storm warning

泣 3104 J3563 M17309 KYŪ. *na(ku)* cry, weep, wail, moan. *na(kasu)*,
A

na(kaseru) let cry, make cry; grieve, worry. *na(keru)* shed tears, be moved to tears.
5 出 *na(ki)-da(su)* burst into tears, begin to
6 虫 *na(ki)mushi* crybaby
伏 *na(ki)-fu(su)* throw oneself down crying; break down
叫 *na(ki)-sake(bu)* cry, yell, scream, wail
7 言 *na(ki)goto* complaint, grievance
別 *na(ki)waka(re)* tearful parting
声 *na(ki)goe* a cry, a crying voice
8 明 *na(ki)-a(kasu)* cry all night
泣 *na(ki)na(ki)* between sobs, with an aching heart; barely. *na(ku)na(ku)* tearfully, with an aching heart 「face
9 面 *na(ki)tsura, na(kit)tsura* tear-stained
10 涙 *na(ki) (no) namida (de)* in tears
笑 *na(ki)wara(i)* tearful smile, tragicomedy
11 崩 *na(ki)-kuzu(reru)* break down and cry
12 喚 *na(ki)-wame(ku)* cry, scream, wail
落 *na(ki)-o(tosu)* persuade in tears
13 腫 *na(ki)-ha(rasu)* cry one's eyes out
寝入 *na(ki)nei(ri)* crying oneself to sleep
14 暮 *na(ki)-ku(rasu)* live in sorrow
17 濡 *na(ki)-nu(reru)* be tearstained

泥 3105 J4525 M17311 DEI mud, mire. *nazu(mu)* adhere to, be attached to. *doro, hiji* mud, mire, dirt, slush; disgrace.
B
3 土 *deido* mud, mire
5 仕合 *dorojiai* corrupt campaign, mudslinging
6 地 *deichi* swamp, marsh, bog, morass
8 沼 *doronuma* bog, slough, quagmire
9 臭 *dorokusa(i)* smelling of mud
炭 *deitan, sukumo* peat
11 道 *doromichi* muddy road
酔 *deisui* dead drunk
12 棒 *dorobō* thief, burglar, robber
13 塗 *doromami(re)* covered with mud
15 縄 *doronawa* unpreparedness; last-minute preparations; locking the barn after the horse is gone
17 濘 *nuka(ru), nukaru(mu)* get muddy, be muddy, be slushy. *nukarumi, nukari, deinei* mud, slush, mire; muddy road

油 3106 J4c7d M17253 YU. YŪ. *abura* oil. *abura(giru)* be excessively fat.
A

⁴ 井 *yusei* oil well

⁵ 田 *yuden* oil field, oil well, oil land

圧 *yuatsu* oil pressure; hydraulic

⁶ 虫 *aburamushi* cockroach; plant louse; hanger-on

気 *aburake, abura(k)ke* greasiness, oiliness

汗 *aburaase* perspiration from pain

⁸ 性 *yusei no* oily

¹⁰ 脂 *yushi* fat, fats and oils

¹¹ 断 *yudan* negligence, unpreparedness, carelessness

¹² 揚 *aburaa(ge), aburage* fried tofu

絵 *aburae* oil painting

¹³ 煙 *yuen* lampblack, carbon black

¹⁴ 層 *yusō* oil strata

¹⁵ 槽 *yusō* oil tank

¹⁶ 濃 *abura(k)ko(i), aburako(i)* greasy, fatty, oily

¹⁸ 蝉 *aburazemi* common locust

法 ₃₁₀₇ _{J4b21} _{M17290} Hō law, rule, principle;
A legislation, regulation; code; method, way, model, manner, system, process, art, technique; rites, religion, doctrine; reason; mood (of verbs). *nori* law, rule; model; doctrine.

² 人 *hōjin* legal person, corporation

⁴ 文 *hōbun* the law; letter of the law, law and literature

王 *Hōō* Pope; Gautama; famous priest

⁵ 外 *hōgai* exorbitant, unreasonable; extraordinary

令 *hōrei* laws and ordinances

⁶ 会 *hōe* (Buddhist) memorial service

名 *hōmyō* (Buddhist) priest's name; posthumous name

⁷ 医学 *hōigaku* medical jurisprudence

廷 *hōtei* law court, courtroom

⁸ 例 *hōrei* regulations for carrying out laws

的 *hōteki* legal, legalistic

典 *hōten* code of laws, statute

事 *hōji* (Buddhist) memorial service

治 *hōchi* constitutional government

制 *hōsei* laws, legislation

学 *hōgaku* law, jurisprudence

定 *hōtei* legal, designated by law

⁹ 相 *Hōshō* Minister of Justice. *Hossō* Buddhist sect originating in the seventh century

科 *hōka* law course, law department

則 *hōsoku* law, rule

要 *hōyō* (Buddhist) memorial service

律 *hōritsu* law

¹⁰ 被 *happi* worker's livery coat

案 *hōan* bill, measure

華経 *Hokekyō* the Lotus Sutra

¹¹ 規 *hōki* regulations, laws; legislation

務大臣 *Hōmu Daijin* Minister of Justice

務省 *Hōmushō* Ministry of Justice

¹⁷ 螺 *hora* trumpet shell; boast

─── **6** ───

洩 ₃₁₁₈ _{J314c} _{M17401} EI. SETSU. *mo(ru)*,
mo(reru) leak, escape; shine through; find expression; be disclosed; be omitted, be excluded. *mo(rasu)* spill, let leak; omit, miss, leave out; divulge; betray; give vent to, express; let go. *mo(ri)* leak, leakage.

洛 ₃₁₁₉ _{J4d6c} _{M17383} RAKU Kyoto, the capital.

⁴ 中 *rakuchū* in Kyoto

⁵ 外 *rakugai* suburbs of Kyoto; metropolitan suburbs

洲 ₃₁₂₀ _{J3d27} _{M17413} SHŪ continent. SU sand
bar, shallows. *shima* island. *kuni* country.

¹¹ 崎 *susaki* sandspit

津 ₃₁₂₂ _{J4445} _{M17396} SHIN. *tsu* port, harbor;
B ferry. *tsuyu* juice; sap; soup, broth; gravy.

⁸ 波 *tsunami* tsunami, tidal wave

⁹ 津浦浦 *tsutsu-uraura ni* throughout the land, in every nook and corner

¹¹ 液 *shin'eki* sputum, saliva

洪 ₃₁₂₃ _{J393f} _{M17402} KŌ flood; vast.
B

⁴ 水 *kōzui, ōmizu* inundation, flood, deluge

⁷ 図 *kōto* ambitious scheme

洞 ₃₁₂₅ _{J4636} _{M17386} DŌ cavity. TŌ cave.
B *hora* cave, den, excavation.

⁵ 穴 *horaana dōketsu* cave, den, excavation

⁸ 門 *dōmon* tunnel

4

心 忄 小 戈 戸 手 扌 支 攴 攵 文 斗 斤 方 无 日 曰 月 木 欠 止 歹 殳 毋 比 毛 氏 气 〔水 氵 氺〕 火 灬 爪 爫 父 爻 爿 片 牛 犬 犭

4

心 忄 小 戈 戸 手 扌 支 攴 攵 文 斗 斤 方 无 日 曰 月 木 欠 止 歹 殳 毋 比 毛 氏 气 【水 氵 氺】 火 灬 爪 爫 父 爻 爿 片 牙 牛 犬 犭

¹³ 窟 *dōkutsu* cave

¹⁴ 察 *dōsatsu, tōsatsu* insight, discernment

派 $\frac{3126}{J4749}$ $\frac{}{M17428}$ HA group, party, clique;
A faction, sect; school
(of art, etc.). *ha(suru)* dispatch, send.

⁴ 手 *hade* flashiness, gaudiness, gaiety. *hade(yakana)* flashy, gaudy

⁵ 生 *hasei* derivation; dividing and growing

出 *hashutsu suru vi* and *vt* send out, dispatch; be derived from

出所 *hashutsujo* branch office; police box

兵 *hahei* dispatch of troops

¹² 遣 *haken suru* send, dispatch

¹⁴ 閥 *habatsu* clique, faction

浄 $\frac{3128}{J3e74}$ $\frac{}{M17451}$ JŌ. *kiyo(i)* clean, clear;
B pure, innocent, noble.
kiyo(meru) purify, cleanse; consecrate; exorcise. *kiyo(maru), kiyo(mawaru)* be purified, be cleansed.

³ 土 *jōdo* pure land, (Buddhist) paradise

土宗 *Jōdoshū* a Buddhist sect originating in the 12th century

土真宗 *Jōdo Shinshū* a Buddhist sect originating in *Jōdoshū*.

⁴ 水 *jōsui* clean water

¹⁰ 財 *jōzai* money offering, votive offering, collection

書 *jōsho* clean copy

¹⁴ 瑠璃 *jōruri* a ballad-drama

浅 $\frac{3129}{J4075}$ $\frac{}{M17452}$ SEN. *asa(i)* shallow;
A superficial; short (time);
slight (connection); pale, light (color). *asa(hakana)* frivolous, shallow, rash, foolish. *asa(mashii)* wretched, miserable, pitiable; despicable, base, shameful. *asa-* light (color); slight (wound).

⁸ 学 *sengaku* superficial knowledge, superficiality

⁹ 海 *senkai* shallow sea

¹¹ 黄 *asagi* light blue, pale blue

黒 *asaguro(i)* dark, dusky, swarthy, brunet, dark-complexioned, dark-skinned

¹² 葱 *asagi* light blue, pale blue

¹³ 蜊 *asari* short-necked clam

¹⁴ 緑 *asamidori* light green

¹⁵ 慮 *senryo* indiscretion, thoughtlessness

¹⁶ 薄 *sempaku* shallowness; superficiality, flimsiness, frivolity

¹⁹ 瀬 *asase* shoal, shallows, sand bar, ford

洋 $\frac{3130}{J4d4e}$ $\frac{}{M17363}$ YŌ ocean, sea, channel.
A *yō-* foreign, Western, European.

⁶ 行 *yōkō* foreign travel; company, firm

式 *yōshiki* Western style

⁸ 服 *yōfuku* Western clothes

学 *yōgaku* Western learning

画 *yōga* Western painting; Western film

⁹ 風 *yōfū* Western style

洋 *yōyō(taru)* vast, broad, wide

室 *yōshitsu* Western-style room

食 *yōshoku* Western food

品 *yōhin* haberdashery

¹⁰ 酒 *yōshu* Western liquor

書 *yōsho* Western book

¹¹ 梨 *yōnashi* Western pear

菓子 *yōgashi* Western confectionery

¹² 間 *yōma* Western-style room

傘 *yōgasa* Western umbrella

装 *yōsō* Western dress

裁 *yōsai* Western dressmaking

¹³ 楽 *yōgaku* Western music

¹⁶ 館 *yōkan* Western-style building

洗 $\frac{3131}{J4076}$ $\frac{}{M17379}$ SEN. *ara(u)* wash; inquire
A into, probe. *ara(i)* wash; washing.

⁵ 礼 *senrei* baptism by sprinkling

⁷ 車 *sensha* car wash

車場 *senshajō* car-washing place

⁸ 物 *ara(i)mono* the washing, laundry

⁹ 浄 *senjō* washing, cleaning, rinsing; ablution

面 *semmen* washing the face

面所 *semmenjo* washroom, lavatory

面器 *semmenki* washbasin, washbowl

剤 *senzai* cleansing agent, detergent

¹¹ 脳 *sennō* brainwashing

¹² 落 *ara(i)-oto(su)* wash off, wash out (stain), rinse out (soap)

¹⁴ 滌 *sendeki, senjō* washing, rinsing

練 *senren* refining; polishing

髪 *sempatsu* washing the hair, shampoo. *ara(i)gami* washed hair

¹⁷ 濯 *ara(i)susu(gi)* washing, laundry. *sentaku* laundering. *susugi* rinsing, washing; water for washing the feet

濯物 *sentakumono* the washing, laundry

濯挟 *sentakubasami* clothespins

濯機 *sentakuki* washing machine

活 $\frac{3132}{J3368}$ $\overline{M17423}$ KATSU resuscitation; living;
A being helped. *i(kiru)* live, subsist, exist; be enlivened; stet; be safe (on first). *i(kasu)* revive, resuscitate; restore to life; let live, spare a life; make the most of; give life to; stet. *hatara(ku)* work, labor; do, act, commit, practice, work on; come into play; be conjugated; reduce the price. *i(keru)* keep alive; arrange flowers (in a vase). *iki* freshness; stet.

² 力 *katsuryoku* vitality

⁴ 火山 *kakkazan* active volcano

⁵ 写 *kassha* candid photography

用 *katsuyō* practical use; declension, conjugation, inflection

用語 *katsuyōgo* inflected words

⁶ 気 *kakki* liveliness, vigor, activity

字 *katsuji* type

⁷ 作 *ikezuku(ri)* slicing live fish

⁸ 況 *kakkyō* vigor, activity, liveliness

性 *kassei* activated, active (oxygen)

性炭 *kasseitan* activated carbon

版 *kappan* type, printing

⁹ 発 *kappatsu* vigor, vivacity, activity

¹⁰ 断層 *katsudansō* active fault

動 *katsudō* activity, action, operations; energy; service; function; movies

¹³ 路 *katsuro* way of escape, last resort

²¹ 躍 *katsuyaku suru* be active in, jump into action

海 $\frac{3133}{J3324}$ $\overline{M17450}$ KAI *umi* sea, ocean.
A

³ 女 *ama* woman shell diver

千山千 *umisen-yamasen* an old codger

上 *kaijō* maritime, seafaring, seaborne, overseas

上自衛隊 *Kaijō Jieitai* Maritime Self-Defense Force

上保安庁 *Kaijō Hoanchō* Maritime Safety Agency

上保険 *kaijō hoken* maritime insurance

⁴ 辺 *kaihen, umibe, unabata, umibeta* seashore, beach, coast, seaside

中 *kaichū* in the sea; marine. *watanaka* in the ocean; on the ocean

王星 *Kaiōsei* Neptune

水 *kaisui* sea water

水浴 *kaisuiyoku* sea bathing

⁵ 外 *kaigai* overseas, foreign; abroad

⁶ 防 *kaibō* coast defense

老 *ebi* lobster; shrimp, prawn

老茶 *ebicha* maroon

⁷ 里 *kairi* knot, nautical mile

図 *kaizu* marine chart

抜 *kaibatsu* height above sea level

兵隊 *kaiheitai* (U.S.) marines

⁸ 苔 *nori* laver (an edible seaweed)

事 *kaiji* maritime affairs

事裁判所 *kaiji saibansho* maritime court

底 *kaitei* ocean floor; submarine

岸 *kaigan* seashore, coast, beach, waterfront. *umigishi* beach, seaside

⁹ 面 *kaimen* (surface of) the sea, sea level. *umizura* surface of the sea

峡 *kaikyō* straits, channel, sound

草 *kaisō, umikusa* seaweeds, marine plants

洋 *kaiyō* ocean

軍 *kaigun* navy

¹⁰ 原 *unabara, wata(no)hara* ocean, sea, the deep

浜 *kaihin* seashore, beach, coast

流 *kairyū* ocean current

¹¹ 魚 *kaigyo* sea fish

鳥 *kaichō, umidori* sea bird

亀 *umigame* sea turtle

域 *kaiiki* an area of the ocean

猫 *umi neko* sea gull

豚 *iruka* dolphin, porpoise

運 *kaiun* marine transportation, maritime

運業 *kaiungyō* shipping business; merchant marine

産物 *kaisambutsu* marine products

¹² 湾 *kaiwan* gulf, bay

¹³ 溝 *kaikō* an ocean deep

路 *kairo, umiji* ocean route, sea paths

戦 *kaisen* naval battle

賊 *kaizoku* pirate

賊版 *kaizokuban* pirated edition/version

心 忄 小 戈 戸 手 扌 支 攴 文 斗 斤 方 无 日 曰 月 木 欠 止 歹 殳 毋 比 毛 氏 气 【水 氵 氺】⁶ 火 灬 爪 爫 父 爻 爿 片 牙 牛 犬 犭

4

心 忄 小 戈 戸 手 扌 支 攴 攵 文 斗 斤 方 无 日 曰 月 木 欠 止 歹 殳 毋 比 毛 氏 气 【水 氵 氺】 火 灬 爪 爫 父 爻 爿 丬 片 牙 牛 犬 犭

¹⁴ 鳴 *umina(ri), kaimei* roar of the ocean
綿 *kaimen* sponge
¹⁸ 難 *kainan* sea disaster
¹⁹ 藻 *kaisō* sea weeds, marine plants

⁹ 室 *yokushitsu* bathroom
¹¹ 掛 *a(bise)-ka(keru)* pour on; subject to, impute to, deluge with
¹² 場 *yokujō* bathroom, bathhouse
¹⁵ 槽 *yokusō* bathtub

─────── 7 ───────

浣 | 3134 / J4642 / M-X | Nonstandard for 瀆 3373.

涛 | 3138 / J4573 / M-X | Nonstandard for 濤 3361.

浬 | 3142 / J333d / M17485 | RI nautical mile, knot. *kairi* knot, nautical mile.

浩 | 3147 / J3940 / M17479 | KŌ wide expanse; abundance; vigorous.
¹² 然 *kōzen taru* great and prosperous; broad-minded
然気 *kōzen (no) ki* energy, vigor
¹⁹ 瀚 *kōkan na* bulky, voluminous

涌 | 3150 / J4d30 / M17534 | 湧 | 3207 / J4d2f / M17862 | YŌ. YU. *wa(ku)* vi boil, get hot; ferment; seethe; be in an uproar; gush out; grow, breed, be hatched. *wa(kasu)* vt boil; heat up (the bath); melt.
⁵ 立 *wa(ki)-ta(tsu)* bubble up, well up
^出 *wa(ki)-de(ru), yōshutsu suru, yūshutsu suru* gush forth or out, spout, flow out, well up, bubble up. *wa(ki)-da(su)* cause to gush out
¹⁰ 起 *wa(ki)-oko(ru)* arise

浜 | 3152 / J494d / M17462 | HIN. *hama* beach, seashore; fishing village.
B
⁴ 辺 *hamabe* beach, seashore
⁹ 風 *hamakaze* beach wind

浴 | 3153 / J4d61 / M17496 | YOKU. *yoku(suru)* bathe, be favored with; bask in.
A
a(biru) bathe in, pour on oneself, bask in, be flooded with, be under (fire); be accused of, be charged with, expose oneself to, be subjected to, receive (applause). *a(biseru)* pour on; subject to, impute to, deluge with.
⁵ 用 *yokuyō* for the bath
⁶ 衣 *yokui, yukata* unlined cotton kimono, bathrobe, dressing gown

涙 | 3154 / J4e5e / M17577 | RUI. *namida* tear; sympathy. *namida(ppoi)* easily shedding tears.
B
¹³ 腺 *ruisen* tear gland
¹⁸ 顔 *namidagao* tearful face

浪 | 3155 / J4f32 / M17482 | RŌ. *nami* waves, billows.
B
² 人 *rōnin* lordless samurai, adventurer; unsuccessful examinee, jobless person
⁶ 曲 *rōkyoku* musical recital of ancient tales
⁷ 花節 *naniwabushi* minstrels; musical recital of ancient tales
¹² 費 *rōhi* waste, extravagance
¹⁴ 漫主義 *rōman shugi* romanticism
漫的 *rōmanteki* romantic (school)

浦 | 3156 / J313a / M17475 | HO. *ura* creek, inlet; bay, gulf; beach, seacoast.
B

浸 | 3157 / J3f3b / M17505 | SHIN. *hita(su)* soak, dip, steep, immerse, moisten, wet, dunk, drench. *hita(ru)* to soak in, be immersed in, be flooded, be submerged in; be bathed in; be addicted to. *tsuka(ru)* be soaked in; be submerged; be flooded; take a dip; be seasoned. *(o)hita(shi)* boiled greens with dressing.
B
² 入 *shinnyū suru* seep in, flow in
⁴ 水 *shinsui* inundation, flood, submersion; leaking
⁵ 出 *shinshutsu* exudation, percolation, effusion; extraction (in chemistry)
⁹ 食 *shinshoku* erosion; corrosion
^透 *shintō* permeation, infiltration, osmosis
¹⁵ 潤 *shinjun* permeation, infiltration, saturation
蝕 *shinshoku* erosion; corrosion

消 | 3158 / J3e43 / M17529 | SHŌ. *ke(su)* extinguish, blow out; turn off, erase, cross out; neutralize (odors or poisons); deaden (noise); cancel (in fractions).
A

ki(eru), ki(yuru) be extinguished; melt away; disappear, die out; wear away; burst (as a bubble).

² 入 *ki(e)-i(ru)* vanish

⁴ 火 *shōka* fire fighting

火栓 *shōkasen* fire hydrant

火器 *shōkaki* fire extinguisher

化 *shōka* digestion, assimilation

化器 *shōkaki* digestive organs

⁵ 去 *ke(shi)-sa(ru)* erase, blot out. *ki(e)-sa(ru)* disappear, die out, melt away. *shōkyo* elimination

失 *ki(e)-u(seru)* die out, disappear, fail. *shōshitsu* disappearance, vanishing

⁶ 印 *keshiin* postmark, cancellation stamp

灯 *shōtō* putting out the lights

防 *shōbō* fire fighting

防夫 *shōbōfu* fireman

防署 *shōbōsho* fire station

⁷ 却 *shōkyaku* erasure, effacement; expenditure; repayment, redemption, amortization

⁸ 長 *shōchō* ebb and flow, prosperity and decay

毒 *shōdoku* disinfection, sterilization, fumigation, pasteurization

⁹ 音器 *shōonki* silencer, muffler, mute, damper

¹⁰ 夏 *shōka* summering, going away for the summer

耗 *shōkō suru, shōmō suru* consume, exhaust, dissipate, use up

耗品 *shōmōhin* supplies, consumer goods

息 *shōsoku* news, letter, circumstances

息通 *shōsokutsū* informed person

息筋 *shōsoku suji* informed circles

¹² 極的 *shōkyokuteki* passive, negative, conservative, destructive

費 *shōhi* consumption; expenditure

費者 *shōhisha* consumer

費税 *shōhizei* excise tax, consumption tax

¹³ 滅 *ke(shi)-horo(bosu)* destroy, consume. *shōmetsu suru* be destroyed. *shōmetsu* extinction, disappearance, nullification

浮 ³¹⁵⁹ J4962 M17487 Fu. *u(ku)* float, be floated, rise to the surface; be
B cheered up; be set on edge, feel loose

(teeth); be left over, be saved. *u(kasu), u(kaberu)* vt float, launch, sail (a toy ship); refloat; waft; express (feelings in the face); recall. *u(kabu)* vi float, refloat, surface; flit across (the face), occur to; play (about the lips, as a smile); rise in the world; rest in peace. *u(kareru)* be in high spirits, go on a spree. *u(kasareru)* be carried off, be captivated, be exhilarated. *u(kanu)* gloomy. *u(ki)* cork, float, buoy, lifebuoy, life belt. *u(ita)* gay, cheerful, frivolous. *u(ki)-* floating.

² 力 *furyoku* buoyancy, lift

³ 上 *u(ki)-a(geru)* come to the surface, surface, float, refloat, be refloated; be lifted out of the water; come out in relief. *fujō suru, u(ki)-a(garu), u(kabi)-a(garu)* float, refloat, surface

⁵ 出 *u(ki)-de(ru)* come to the surface; loom. *u(ki)da(shi)* embossed

世 *ukiyo* this transitory world, the earth

世絵 *ukiyoe* genre picture, ukiyoe

⁶ 舟 *u(ki)bune* pontoon

名 *u(ki)na* romance, scandal, rumor, love affair

気 *u(wa)ki* inconstancy, faithless love, wantonness, affair

気者 *u(wa)kimono* inconstant lover, licentious person

⁷ 沈 *fuchin, u(ki)shizu(mi)* rise and fall, ebb and flow, ups and downs, vicissitudes

足立 *u(ki)ashida(tte)* ready to run away

⁹ 草 *u(ki) kusa* floating weed, duckweed; precarious business

¹⁰ 浮 *u(ki)u(ki) to* buoyantly, cheerfully, jauntily

流 *furyū* floating, drifting

浪者 *furōsha* hobo, tramp, vagabond

¹¹ 彫 *ukibori* relief, embossed carving

袋 *u(ki)bukuro* air bladder; water wings, life preserver, float, tire

遊 *fuyū* floating, suspension

動 *fudō suru* float; be wafted; fluctuate; be unsettled

動人口 *fudō jinkō* floating population

¹² 揚 *fuyō* floating, flotage, flotation

雲 *fuun, u(ki)gumo* floating cloud; something unsettled

桟橋 *u(ki)sambashi* floating pier

4

心 忄 小 戈 戸 手 扌 支 攴 文 斗 斤 方 无 日 曰 月 木 欠 止 歹 殳 毋 比 毛 氏 气 【水 氵 氺】火 灬 爪 爫 父 爻 爿 片 牙 牛 犬 犭

¹⁵ 標 *fuhyō* buoy

輪 *u(ki)wa* buoyant water ring

流 ³¹⁶⁰ / J4e2e / M17572 RU. RYŪ current; counter

A for flags. *naga(reru)* flow, trickle, ooze, drain, run down; be washed away; float, drift; wander; be forfeited, be foreclosed; lapse; incline to; be swayed by; (years) pass. *naga(su)* dash, pour, sluice, let run out, flush; float, set adrift; spill; shed (tears); wash away, wash off; forfeit, foreclose; exile; cruise (taxis). *naga(re)* flow, stream, waters, current; passage (of time), descent; school; abandonment; foreclosure; tendency. *naga(shi)* sink; bath-attendant service; cruising (taxi); strolling musician. *(o)naga(re)* suspension, adjournment, calling off. *-ryū* style, fashion, type, form, manner; school, system; class, order, rate, rank, grade.

² 入 *ryūnyū suru, naga(re)-i(ru)* flow into
³ 下 *naga(re)-kuda(ru)* flow down; drink down; descend
⁴ 木 *ryūboku, naga(re)gi* driftwood
込 *naga(re)-ko(mu)* flow into, run into, drift into. *naga(shi)-ko(mu)* wash down, pour into
⁵ 用 *ryūyō* diversion, misappropriation
氷 *ryūhyō* drift ice, ice drift
失 *ryūshitsu suru* be washed away
民 *ryūmin* drifting people, displaced persons
布 *rufu* circulation, diffusing, dissemination
⁶ 血 *ryūketsu* bloodshed
会 *ryūkai* adjournment for lack of a quorum
刑 *ryūkei, rukei* deportation, banishment, exile; transportation of a criminal
行 *naga(re)-yu(ku)* flow along. *haya(ru)* be fashionable, be popular, be prevalent; flourish, prosper, have a large practice. *ryūkō, hayari* fashion, popularity, prevalence
行言葉 *hayari kotoba* popular expression
行性感冒 *ryūkōsei kambō* flu, influenza
行語 *ryūkōgo* a word on everybody's lips
行歌 *hayari uta, ryūkōka* popular song
⁷ 作業 *naga(re) sagyō* assembly-line

operation
体 *ryūtai* fluid
体力学 *ryūtai rikigaku* hydrodynamics
言蜚語 *ryūgenhigo* rumor, gossip
⁹ 通 *ryūtsū* circulation of money; flow of water; ventilation
派 *ryūha* a school of thought; a system
砂 *ryūsa, ryūsha* river sand; sandy area, desert
星 *ryūsei, naga(re)boshi* falling star, meteor; skyrocket
星群 *ryūseigun* meteoric shower
¹⁰ 浪 *rurō* vagrancy, wandering, exile
¹¹ 域 *ryūiki* river basin
転 *ruten* perpetual motion; vicissitudes; wandering, vagrancy; transmigration
産 *ryūzan* abortion; miscarriage, failure
動 *ryūdō* flow, flowing, floating, circulation, fluidity, mobility; liquid (assets); current (liabilities)
¹² 弾 *ryūdan, naga(re)dama* stray bullet
量 *ryūryō* amount of flow
¹³ 感 *ryūkan* flu, influenza
¹⁴ 暢 *ryūchō* fluency, facility
¹⁵ 儀 *ryūgi* a school of thought; style; system; method, form, way
線型 *ryūsenkei* streamlined
¹⁸ 謫 *rutaku, ryūteki* exile, banishment
¹⁹ 麗 *ryūrei na* fluent, flowing, smooth
²¹ 露 *ryūro suru* disclose, reveal, express

──────── **8** ────────

渚 ³¹⁶⁴ / J3d6d / M-X See 渚 3228.

涯 ³¹⁸¹ / J3336 / M17582 GAI shore.

B

淀 ³¹⁸² / J4d64 / M17610 TEN. DEN. *yodo(mu)* stagnate, be stagnant; settle, deposit; be sluggish; hesitate; stammer. *yodo* pool (in a river), eddy.

淘 ³¹⁸⁷ / J4571 / M17642 TŌ select.
⁷ 汰 *tōta* selection; weeding out, reducing, retrenchment; dismissal, shake-up

淳 ³¹⁸⁹ / J3d5f / M17690 JUN pure.

⁶ 朴 *jumboku* simplicity and honesty

涉 B
3190
J3e44
M17749'
SHŌ. *wata(ru)* cross, ford, ferry; be imported; change hands; make one's way through life; sweep across; migrate; be provided.
⁵外 *shōgai* public relations, liaison
¹¹猟 *shōryō* extensive reading

淑 B
3191
J3d4a
M17634
SHUKU. *shito(yakana)* graceful, polite, gentle; pure.
³女 *shukujo* lady
¹⁴德 *shukutoku* womanly virtues

淋
3194
J4e54
M17626
RIN lonely. *sabi(reru)* become deserted, decline in prosperity. *sabi(shii), sami(shii), samu(shii)* lonely, lonesome, solitary, deserted, desolate.
⁴巴腺 *rimpasen* lymph gland

渇 B
3195
J3369
M17748
KATSU thirst. *kas(suru)* be thirsty; dry (up); long for. *kawa(ku)* be thirsty; feel dry; dry up, be parched. *kawa(ki)* thirst.
⁴水 *kassui* water shortage

渓 B
3196
J374c
M-X
KEI valley. *tani* valley.
⁷谷 *keikoku* valley, ravine, canyon
¹⁰流 *keiryū* mountain stream
¹²間 *keikan* ravine

済 A
3197
J3a51
M17749
SAI. SEI. *su(mu)* end; do without; avoid; be excusable; need not. *su(masu), su(maseru)* finish up; settle (one's account); make do. *na(su)* pay back. *suku(u)* save, help, rescue, relieve (suffering), redeem, reclaim. *su(manai)* inexcusable, unjustifiable, regrettable, repentant. *su(mimasen)* Excuse me; I'm sorry. *su(mi)* settled, O.K.. *-zu(mi)* finished.

涼 B
3198
J4e43
M17606
RYŌ cool. *suzu(mu)* cool oneself, enjoy the evening air. *suzu(shii), suzu(yaka) na* cool, refreshing.
⁶気 *ryōki* the cool air
⁹風 *suzukaze, ryōfū* cool breeze

液 A
3199
J3155
M17586
EKI liquid, fluid, juice, sap, secretion. *tsuyu* juice; sap; soup, broth; gravy.
⁴化 *ekika* liquefaction
⁷冷 *ekirei* liquid-cooling
⁷状 *ekijō* liquid state
体 *ekitai* liquid, fluid
¹²晶 *ekishō* liquid crystal

渋 B
3200
J3d42
M17750'
JŪ. SHŪ. *shibu(ru)* hesitate, be reluctant; have loose painful bowel movements. *shibu* puckery taste (of persimmons); sobriety, quietness. *shibu(i)* puckery, astringent; sullen; quiet, sober; tasteful (in dress).
⁵皮 *shibukawa* astringent skin (of a chestnut); discolored skin
⁸味 *shibumi* puckery taste, astringency; good taste, sobriety, refinement
⁹面 *jūmen, shibuzura, shibutsura* sullen face, grimace
柿 *shibugaki* puckery persimmon
茶 *shibucha* coarse tea
¹⁰紙 *shibukami, shibugami* paper treated with astringent persimmon juice
¹¹渋 *shibushibu, shibujibu, shibu(ri)-shibu(ri)* reluctantly, grudgingly
¹³滞 *jūtai* stagnation, retardation

添 B
3201
J453a
M17698
TEN. *so(u) vi* accompany; marry; be added to; suit, meet, satisfy, be adjusted to. *so(eru) vt* add to, attach, append; accompany; garnish; imitate.
⁵付 *tempu suru* append, accompany
加 *tenka suru* annex, append, add
⁸物 *so(e)mono* addition, supplement, premium
⁹削 *tensaku* correction
¹⁰書 *tensho, so(e)ga(ki)* postscript, additional writing, letter of introduction; accompanying letter
¹³寝 *so(i)ne* sleeping with one's child

淡 B
3202
J4338
M17660
TAN. *awa(i)* light, faint, pale, fleeting; a little.
⁴水 *tansui* fresh water
⁵白 *tampaku na* light; frank; indifferent to
⁹紅 *tankō* pink, rose pink
¹¹淡 *tantan(taru)* unconcerned, disinterested; plain, light
彩 *tansai* light coloring

4

雪 *awayuki* a light snowfall

淫 〔3203 J1307c M17678〕 IN lewdness, licentiousness. *in(suru)* indulge in, go to excess. *mida(rana), mida(rigawashii)* licentious, indecent, lewd.
6 行 *inkō* obscenity, harlotry
乱 *inran* debauchery, lewdness, lasciviousness
売 *imbai* prostitution
12 猥 *inwai* indecency, obscenity
15 蕩 *intō* dissipation, lewdness
19 靡 *imbi* impurity, obscenity

混 〔3204 J3a2e M17694〕 KON. *kon(jiru), kon(zuru)* A *vi* and *vt* mix; blend; adulterate; confound, confuse. *ma(zeru)* mix, blend, mingle; include, let in on. *ma(zaru), ma(jiru)* vi be mixed, be blended; mingle with.
2 入 *konnyū suru* vi and vt mingle, adulterate; get mixed
5 用 *kon'yō suru* vt mix, mingle
6 色 *konshoku* compound color, hue
同 *kondō* confusion; mixing; merger
気 *ma(jiri)ke* mixture, impurities
返 *ma(ze)-kae(su), ma(zek)kae(su)* stir up; interrupt, interfere with
交 *konkō* confusion, jumble, mixture
在 *konzai* mixture
血 *konketsu* racial mixture
成 *konsei* mixture, composition
合 *ma(ze)-a(waseru)* vt mix, blend, compound. *maji(ri)-a(u)* vi mix. *kongō* mixing; mixture
合物 *kongōbutsu* mixture, compound, amalgam
7 沌 *konton* chaos, nebulosity, confusion
乱 *konran* disorder, chaos, confusion
声合唱 *konsei gasshō* mixed chorus
8 迷 *kommei* confusion, bewilderment; stupor, unconsciousness
9 信 *konshin* jamming, interference
10 浴 *kon'yoku* mixed bathing (in a bath house)
紡 *kombō* mixed spinning; mixed yarn
11 淆 *konkō* mixture, confusion, jumble
12 然 *konzen(taru)* whole, entire, harmonious
13 戦 *konsen* free-for-all fight
載 *konsai* mixed loading; mixed freight
14 雑 *konzatsu* confusion, disorder,

congestion
15 線 *konsen* entanglement of wires; confusion
16 濁 *kondaku* turbidity, muddiness

清 〔3205 J4036 M17695〕 SHŌ. SEI. SHIN China, A Manchu (dynasty). *kiyo(meru)* purify, cleanse; consecrate; exorcise. *kiyo(maru), kiyo(mawaru)* be purified, be cleansed. *su(masu)* clear, clarify, settle; strain (one's ears); look grave. *kiyo(i)* clean, clear; pure, innocent; noble. *kiyo(me)* purification, sanctification; cleansing, purgation; exorcism; ablution. *kiyo(rakana)* clear.
4 水 *shimizu, seisui* clear water, pure water
8 冽 *seiretsu na* clear, limpid
明 *seimei* pure and clear
9 音 *seion* unvoiced sound
浄 *seijō, shōjō* purity, spotlessness
浄無垢 *shōjōmuku* perfect purity, innocence
10 流 *seiryū* clear stream
酒 *seishu, sumizake* refined saké
純 *seijun* purity
11 清 *seisei suru* feel refreshed, feel relieved. *sugasuga(shii)* refreshing, soothing
貧 *seihin* honorable poverty
掃 *seisō* cleaning
教 *Seikyō* Puritanism
涼 *seiryō na* cool, refreshing
涼飲料水 *seiryō inryōsui* cooling drink
12 朝 *Shinchō* Manchu dynasty. *seichō* square character with thin horizontal strokes
13 楚 *seiso* neatness
廉 *seiren* purity and unselfishness, honesty, integrity
廉潔白 *seiren-keppaku* uprightness
新 *seishin na* fresh, new
14 算 *seisan* liquidation, settlement
15 澄 *seichō na* clear; serene
潔 *seiketsu* cleanliness, neatness, purity
16 濁 *seidaku* purity and impurity; good and evil
17 聴 *seichō* your kind attention (to my talk)

深 〔3206 J3f3c M17687〕 SHIN deep. *fuka(meru)* vt, A *fuka(maru)* vi deepen, heighten, intensify, strengthen. *fuka(mi)*

a depth, deep place; profundity. *fuka(su)* sit up late. *fuke(ru)* get late; grow old; reach the height of the season. *fuka(i)* deep; thick, dense; profound, intense; intimate.

² 入 *fukai(ri) suru* be engrossed in, be taken up with, go too far into

³ 山 *miyama, shinzan* mountain recesses, remote mountains

山幽谷 *shinzan-yūkoku* distant mountains and solitary valleys

⁴ 手 *fukade* deep wound, severe injury, mortal wound

⁸ 呼吸 *shinkokyū* deep breathing, deep breath

夜 *shin'ya* dead of night, midnight

刻 *shinkoku na* serious, keen, acute, significant

⁹ 度 *shindo* depth

浅 *shinsen* depth

思 *shinshi* deep thinking

甚 *shinjin no* profound, deep

紅 *shinku* deep crimson

海 *shinkai* deep sea. *shinkai no* abysmal

¹⁰ 酒 *fukazake* heavy drinking

¹¹ 深 *fukabuka to* very deeply. *shinshin* getting later; getting quiet; deep interior; feeling (the cold)

酔 *fukayo(i)* deep drunkenness

窓 *shinsō* a secluded inner room. *shinsō ni* very carefully

¹² 遠 *shin'en na* profound, deep, unfathomable

閑 *shinkan toshita* silent, hushed, ⌈deserted

淵 *shin'en* abyss, ravine

¹³ 傷 *fukade* deep wound, severe injury

謀遠慮 *shimbōenryo* careful plans for the future

———————— 9 ————————

湧 3207 J4d2f M17862 See 涌 3150.

溌 3209 J482e M-X See 潑 3325.

漣 3210 J4e7a M-X See 漣 3259.

湘 3216 J3e45 M17842 SHŌ used in proper names; boil.

渥 3224 J302f M17770 AKU kindness.

湊 3226 J4c2b M17822 SŌ. *minato* harbor, port.

渚 3228 J-X M17758 渚 3164 J3d6d M-X SHO. *nagisa* beach, shore, strand.

渠 3230 J3574 M17764 KYO ditch, canal, dock.

湛 3234 J4339 M17846 TAN. *tata(eru)* fill; wear (a smile).

¹² 然 *tanzen(taru)* overflowing; deep, abysmal

淵 3237 J4a25 M17692 EN edge. *fuchi* deep pool, deep water, abyss, the depths.

¹³ 源 *engen* origin, source, fountainhead

¹⁸ 叢 *ensō* center, seat, home, cradle of

滋 3238 J3c22 M17919 JI more and more; be
B　luxuriant; planting; turbidity.

¹⁵ 養 *jiyō* nourishment

湾 3239 J4f51 M17920 WAN gulf,
B　bay, inlet.

² 入 *wannyū* inlet, gulf

³ 口 *wankō* bay entrance

⁴ 内 *wannai* inside the bay

⁶ 曲 *wankyoku* curve, crook, bend

⁸ 屈 *wankutsu* curve, crook, bend

岸 *wangan* gulf coast

¹⁶ 頭 *wantō* head of a bay

湖 3240 J3850 M17836 KO *mizuumi* lake.
A

³ 上 *kojō* on the lake

⁴ 心 *koshin* center of a lake

水 *kosui* lake

⁸ 底 *kotei* lake bottom

岸 *kogan* lake shore

沼 *koshō* lakes and marshes

¹⁰ 畔 *kohan* lake shore, lakeside

渦 3241 J3132 M17771 KA. *uzumaki, uzu* eddy,
B　whirlpool, vortex.

⁴ 中 *kachū* in the whirlpool

4

心 忄 小 戈 戸 手 扌 支 攵 文 斗 斤 方 无 日 曰 月 木 欠 止 歹 殳 毋 比 毛 氏 气 【水 氵 氺】 火 灬 爪 爫 父 爻 爿 片 牙 牛 犬 犭

⁹ 巻 *uzumaki* eddy, whirlpool, vortex; coil. *uzuma(ku)* eddy, whirl, swirl, curl (smoke)

¹⁰ 紋 *kamon* whirlpool design

¹⁵ 潮 *uzushio* whirling tides

港 [3242 / J3941 / M17783] **A** Kō *minato, -kō* port, harbor.

³ 口 *kōkō, minatoguchi* harbor entrance

⁷ 町 *minatomachi* harbor town

¹² 湾 *kōwan* harbors

湿 [3243 / J3c3e / M17920] **B** SHITSU dampness, moisture; itch. *shime(ru)* get damp, get moist, get wet. *shime(su), shime(rasu)* wet, moisten, dampen. *shito(ru)* get damp, become moist. *shime(ppoi)* damp, moist, humid, wet; gloomy, depressing. *shime(ri)* dampness, humidity, moisture; a sprinkle. *shime(yakana)* quiet, gentle; gloomy, dismal.

⁵ 布 *shippu* compress, fomentation

⁶ 気 *shike(ru), shikke(ru)* get damp, be moist, be wet. *shikke, shikki, shime(ri)ke* moisture, humidity, dampness. *shike* moisture

地 *shitchi* swampy land, damp ground

⁹ 度 *shitsudo* humidity

¹⁰ 疹 *shisshin* eczema, rash

¹⁵ 潤 *shitsujun* moisture, humidity, dampness

測 [3244 / J422c / M17780] **A** SOKU. *haka(ru)* measure, gauge, weigh; fathom, sound; compute, estimate.

⁶ 地 *sokuchi* land survey, geodetic survey

⁸ 知 *haka(ri)-shi(ru), sokuchi suru* infer, understand, fathom, determine

定 *sokutei* measurement, survey, sounding, calibration, determination, test

¹⁰ 候所 *sokkōjo* weather station

¹¹ 深 *sokushin* sounding

距儀 *sokkyogi* range finder

¹² 量 *sokuryō* survey; surveying; sounding; measurement

湯 [3245 / J4572 / M17874] **A** TŌ hot water. *yu* hot water, hot bath, hot spring.

³ 上 *yua(gari)* just after the bath; bathrobe

⁴ 水 *yumizu* hot and cold water; plenty of everything

元 *yumoto* the source of a hot spring

⁶ 気 *yuge* steam, vapor

⁷ 呑 *yunomi* teacup

豆腐 *yudōfu* boiled tofu

⁸ 沸 *yuwa(kashi)* teakettle

治場 *tōjiba* health resort

¹³ 殿 *yudono* bathroom

¹⁵ 槽 *yubune* bathtub

温 [3246 / J3239 / M17774] **A** ON. *atata(meru), atta(meru)* warm, heat. *atata(maru), atta(maru), nuku(maru)* warm oneself, sun oneself, get warm. *nukumo(ru)* warm oneself, get warm. *nuku(meru)* warm slightly. *nukumo(ri), nuku(mi)* (slight) warmth. *nukuto(i), nuku(i)* warm, mild, genial. *atataka(i), attaka(i)* warm, mild, genial, cordial.

⁶ 存 *onzon suru, onson suru* preserve, retain

⁷ 床 *onshō, ondoko* hotbed

⁸ 和 *onwa na* gentle, mild, temperate

⁹ 厚 *onkō na* gentle

室 *onshitsu* greenhouse

故知新 *onkochishin* learning from the past

度 *ondo* temperature

泉 *onsen, ideyu* hot spring

¹¹ 健 *onken na* quiet, dependable, uniform

情 *onjō* warm heart; kindliness

¹² 順 *onjun* gentleness, docility, obedience

暖 *ondan* warmth

¹⁸ 顔 *ongan* kindly face

渡 [3247 / J454f / M17765] **B** TO. *wata(ru)* cross, ford, ferry; be imported; change hands; make one's way through life; sweep across; migrate; be provided. *wata(su)* carry across, ferry over, bring over; hand over, deliver; deal (cards); transfer (a business); pay (wages); bridge; stretch (something) across; lay across. *wata(ri)* passage, transit; gangplank; length, diameter; negotiations; migration (of birds); payable at. *wata(shi)* ferry; delivery; transfer; ford. *watarai* one's occupation.

世 *tosei* living, livelihood, subsistence; business, trade, profession

⁶ 舟 *wata(shi)bune, wata(ri)bune* ferryboat

米 *to-Bei* going to the United States

来 *torai suru* visit; come across the sea. *torai* importation, influx, entrance (of a new religion)

⁸ 欧 *to-Ō* going to Europe

英 *to-Ei* going to England

河 *toka* river crossing

⁹ 海 *tokai* crossing the ocean; passage

¹⁰ 航 *tokō* voyage, tour; a sailing, a crossing

航地 *tokōchi* the land of one's sojourn

航者 *tokōsha* foreign traveler, passenger

¹¹ 鳥 *wata(ri)dori* migratory bird, bird of passage

廊下 *wata(ri) rōka* covered passageway

船 *wata(shi)bune, wata(ri)bune, tosen* ferry

満 3248 / J4b7e / M17921 MAN fullness, enough;
A pride. *mi(tsuru), mi(chiru)* be full; rise (tides); mature, expire. *mi(tasu)* fill; supply, make good; satisfy, appease, answer (the need), meet (the demand). *man-* full, fully, fulfillment; a full (year); a full (five years).

³ 干 *michihi, mankan* ebb and flow

⁴ 月 *mangetsu* full moon

水 *mansui* full to the brim

大 *manten* the whole sky

⁶ 州 *Manshū* Manchuria

⁷ 足 *manzoku* satisfaction, contentment. *manzoku na* satisfactory, complete, proper, sound (health). *mi(chi)-ta(riru)* fulfill, fill up

身 *manshin* the whole body

⁹ 面 *mammen* the whole face

洲 *Manshū* Manchuria

点 *manten* perfect, perfect score

¹⁰ 座 *manza* the whole assembly

悦 *man'etsu* great joy, rapture

員 *man'in* no vacancy, full house

¹² 開 *mankai* full bloom

幅 *mampuku* full width; full area

満 *mi(chi)-mi(chiru)* fill up. *mamman(taru)* full of (vigor, etc.)

期 *manki* expiration (of a period)

場 *manjō* the whole assembly

場一致 *manjō-itchi de* unanimously

¹³ 腹 *mampuku* satiety

載 *mansai* full load

¹⁵ 潮 *manchō, michishio* high tide

¹⁸ 額 *mangaku* full amount

減 3249 / J383a / M17759 GEN decrease, decline.
A *gen(jiru), gen(zuru)* decrease; mitigate, appease; dwindle; subtract, deduct. *he(ru), me(ru)* decrease, dwindle, subside; wear and tear; get hungry. *he(su), he(rasu)* reduce, decrease, shorten, curtail; be hungry. *me(ri), he(ri)* decrease, wear, loss, waste.

⁴ 水 *gensui* low water; subsiding water; reduced water supply

反 *gentan* acreage reduction

少 *genshō* decrease, reduction, decline

⁵ 収 *genshū* decrease in income or production

⁶ 刑 *genkei* reduction of penalty

⁸ 退 *gentai* decline, ebb, waning, subsiding; loss (of appetite); failing (eyesight)

免 *gemmen* reduction and exemption; mitigation and remission

⁹ 削 *gensaku* reduction

速 *gensoku* speed reduction

¹⁰ 俸 *gempō* salary reduction

殺 *gensatsu suru, gensai suru* diminish, reduce, attenuate, deaden, impair, detract from

¹¹ 産 *gensan* decreased production

¹² 税 *genzei* reduction of taxes

給 *genkyū* wage cut, salary reduction

軽 *genkei* reduction (of a penalty)

量 *genryō* loss in quantity

¹⁷ 縮 *genshuku* reduction, retrenchment

¹⁸ 額 *gengaku* reduction, cut

— 10 —

漣 3259 / J-X / M18155 REN. *sazanami* ripples.

漠 3268 / J4779 / M18149 BAKU vague, obscure;
B desert; wide.

¹² 然 *bakuzen* vague, obscure

¹³ 漠 *bakubaku* vague, obscure; vast, boundless

溢 3270 / J306e / M17951 ITSU. *afu(reru)* overflow,
flow over, inundate. *kobo(reru) vi* spill, overflow, be scattered. *kobo(su) vt* spill; grumble over.

⁵ 出 *isshutsu* overflowing, effusion, gushing out

4

心 忄 小 戈 戸 手 扌 支 攴 攵 文 斗 斤 方 无 日 曰 月 木 欠 止 歹 殳 毋 比 毛 氏 气 【水 氵 氺】火 灬 爪 爫 父 爻 爿 片 牙 牛 犬 犭

溺 `3271` `J452e` `M17990` DEKI *obo(reru)* drown, indulge in. *obo(rasu)*, *obo(rakasu)* drown (a person); cause to indulge in. ⌈drowning
6 死 *dekishi*, *obo(re)ji(ni)*, *obo(re)shi(ni)*
13 愛 *dekiai* dotage, infatuation

溯 `3272` `J5e6a` `M17975` 遡 `6094` `J414c` `M39048` SAKU. SO. *sakanobo(ru)* go upstream; retrace the past.
3 及 *sakkyū, sokyū* tracing back
6 行 *sokō* going upstream
10 航 *sokō* going up against a stream

B 滝 `3273` `J426c` `M18067` 瀧 `3376` `J426d` `M18671` RŌ. SŌ. *taki* waterfall; rapids, cascade.
12 壺 *takitsubo* pool below a waterfall
登 *takinobo(ri)* (fish) climbing a waterfall

A 源 `3274` `J383b` `M17926` GEN. *gen-, minamoto* source, origin. *Minamoto* Genji family, the Minamotos.
9 泉 *gensen* fountainhead, wellspring, source, origin
泉徴収 *gensen chōshū* collecting (taxes) at the source
10 流 *genryū* source, origin

B 溝 `3275` `J3942` `M17944` KŌ. *dobu* ditch, gutter, sewer, drain. *mizo* ditch, gutter, drain; groove, slot; gulf, gap.

溜 `3276` `J4e2f` `M17943` RYŪ. *tama(ru) vi* collect, gather, accumulate; be saved (money); be in arrears. *ta(meru) vt* accumulate, pile up, store, save, collect. *tama(ri)* waiting room, rendezvous, taxi stand, parking place; (stair) landing; (baseball) dugout; soy sauce. *tame* sink, sump, manure vat.
6 池 *tameike* reservoir, irrigation pond, tank, cistern
10 息 *tameiki* sigh, deep breath
12 飲下 *ryūin (ga) sa(garu)* feel at ease again

B 溶 `3277` `J4d4f` `M17983` YŌ. *to(keru) vi* melt, dissolve, thaw. *to(kasu)* melt, dissolve, liquefy. *to(ku) vt* dissolve, melt.

5 去 *to(ke)-sa(ru) vt* melt away. *to(kashi)-sa(ru) vt* melt (something) away
6 合 *to(ke)-a(u)* melt into, fade into
8 岩 *yōgan* lava
10 剤 *yōzai* solvent, solution; flux (in metallurgy)
11 接 *yōsetsu* welding
液 *yōeki* solution, solvent
13 鉱炉 *yōkōro* blast furnace
解 *yōkai* melting; solution; liquefaction

A 準 `3278` `J3d60` `M17934` JUN. *jun(jiru), jun(zuru)* apply correspondingly, correspond to, be proportionate to, conform to. *nazora(eru)* pattern after, liken to, imitate. *jun-* semi-, quasi-, associate; standard; rule; level; aim. *(ni) jun(jite)* in proportion to.
5 用 *jun'yō suru* apply
6 会員 *junkaiin* associate member
決勝 *junkesshō* semifinals
8 拠 *junkyo* conformity; authority (of); standard
9 則 *junsoku* regulations; standard
急 *junkyū* local express
12 備 *jumbi* preparation; provision, reserve
備中 *jumbichū* in preparation; not open for business
備金 *jumbikin* reserve fund

B 滅 `3279` `J4c47` `M18008` METSU. *horo(biru)* be ruined; perish. *horo(bosu)* ruin, destroy, overthrow. *mes(suru) vi* die, be destroyed, be extinguished. *mes(suru) vt* destroy, exterminate; extinguish. *meri* loss, waste, leakage.
3 亡 *metsubō* downfall, destruction
6 多 *metta na* reckless, careless. *metta ni* seldom, rarely
7 却 *mekkyaku* destruction, extinction
8 法 *meppō na* absurd, unreasonable, exorbitant; extraordinary; awful, horrible
9 相 *messō na* extraordinary, unreasonable
茶 *mecha na* absurd, unreasonable, unjust
茶苦茶 *mechakucha* confusion; absurdity, mess, wreck, ruin
茶滅茶 *mechamecha* mess, wreck, ruin, confusion

¹¹ 菌 *mekkin* sterilization, disinfection, pasteurization

滞 $\frac{3280}{\text{M18067'}}$ J425a TAI stopping. *todokō(ru)*
B stagnate; be delayed, be left undone; be overdue, fall into arrears. *nazu(mu)* lose heart; be in pain; be in earnest, adhere to, be attached to. *todokō(ri)* stagnation; hitch, hindrance, delay; arrearage, indebtedness. *tai-* staying in (a certain country).

⁶ 在 *taizai* stay, sojourn
⁸ 空 *taikū* staying in the air
⁹ 陣 *taijin* encampment
¹⁰ 留 *tairyū* stay, sojourn
納 *tainō* nonpayment, default, delinquency; back taxes
¹¹ 貨 *taika* freight congestion; accumulation of stocks

漢 $\frac{3281}{\text{M18068'}}$ J3441 KAN Han (Dynasty);
A (old name for) China; masculine suffix.

² 人 *Kanjin* a Chinese
⁴ 文 *kambun* Chinese writing, Chinese composition
方薬 *kampōyaku* Chinese medicine
⁵ 民族 *Kamminzoku* Chinese people
⁶ 字 *kanji* the Chinese characters
⁸ 学 *kangaku* Chinese literature
和 *Kan-Wa* China and Japan, Chinese and Japanese (languages)
¹¹ 族 *Kanzoku* Han (Chinese) race
¹² 朝 *kanchō* Han dynasty
¹³ 詩 *kanshi* Chinese poetry
¹⁴ 語 *kango* Chinese word
²⁰ 籍 *kanseki* Chinese book, Chinese classics

滑 $\frac{3282}{\text{M18032}}$ J336a KATSU. KOTSU. *sube(ru)*
B slide, glide, skate; be slippery; slip; fail in exams. *nume(rakasu), sube(rasu), sube(rakasu)* let slip, make slip. *nume(ru)* be lazy, play all the time. *sube(ri)* sliding, slipping; slippage; slide; slip; skid. *sube(rakana)* smooth. *name(rakana)* smooth. *nume(ri)* slime, slipperiness. *sube(kkoi)* smooth, slippery, velvety, slick.

⁴ 止 *suberido(me)* tire chains; nonskid heels

台 *suberidai* launching platform, ways; (children's) slide; sliding bed
⁷ 車 *kassha, sube(ri)guruma, semi* pulley, block, tackle
走 *kassō* gliding, planning, sliding, skating, coasting, taxiing
走路 *kassōro* runway
空 *kakkū suru* glide, volplane
⁹ 降 *kakkō* descent (by ski, glider, etc.)
¹⁵ 稽 *kokkei* joke, pleasantry, humor. *odoke* joke

——— 11 ———

潅 $\frac{3287}{\text{M18216}}$ J3443 See 灌 3390.

¹⁴ 滾 *konkon to* copiously (flowing)

滴 $\frac{3299}{\text{M18084}}$ J4529 TEKI *shizuku* drop.
B *shitata(ru)* drip, drop; trickle. *shitatari* drop; trickle.

¹⁶ 薬 *tekiyaku* (medicine) drops

漉 $\frac{3300}{\text{M18112}}$ J3977 ROKU. *su(ku)* manufacture
paper; spread out thin. *ko(su)* strain, filter, percolate.

¹⁰ 紙 *koshigami* filter paper
¹⁴ 網 *koshiami* strainer

漬 $\frac{3301}{\text{M18167}}$ J4452 SHI. *tsu(keru)* soak,
B moisten, steep; pickle, preserve, add (salt) to. *tsuka(ru)* be soaked in; be submerged; be flooded; take a dip; be seasoned. *hita(su)* soak, dip, steep, immerse, moisten, wet, dunk, drench. *hita(ru)* be soaked in, immersed in, be flooded, be submerged; be bathed in; be addicted to.

⁸ 物 *tsukemono* Japanese pickles

漂 $\frac{3303}{\text{M18102}}$ J493a HYŌ. *tadayo(u)* float (on
B the water).

⁵ 白 *hyōhaku* bleaching
⁸ 泊 *hyōhaku* wandering, vagabondage; drifting
¹⁰ 流 *hyōryū* drifting
流物 *hyōryūbutsu* flotsam
¹² 着 *hyōchaku* drifting ashore

漆 $\frac{3304}{\text{M18108}}$ J3c3f SHITSU. *urushi* lacquer,
B varnish.

心 忄 小 戈 手 扌 支 攴 攵 文 斗 斤 方 无 日 曰 月 木 欠 止 歹 殳 毋 比 毛 氏 气 【水 氵 氺】 火 灬 爪 父 爻 爿 片 牙 牛 犬 犭

4

¹¹ 黒 *shikkoku* jet black

¹² 喰 *shikkui* plaster, mortar, stucco, whitewash

¹³ 塗 *urushinu(ri)* lacquering; lacquer ware

¹⁵ 器 *shikki* lacquer ware

漸 | 3305 / J4132 / M18179 | ZEN gradually advancing.
B *yōya(ku), yōyō* gradually; finally; barely.

⁶ 次 *zenji* gradually

¹⁰ 進 *zenshin* gradual progress, steady advance

¹² 減 *zengen* gradual decrease

¹⁴ 増 *zenzō* gradual increase

漕 | 3306 / J4166 / M18131 | Sō. *ko(gu)* row, scull, paddle.

⁴ 手 *kogite, sōshu* rower, oarsman

⁵ 出 *ko(gi)-da(su), ko(gi)-ida(su)* begin to row

⁹ 通 *ko(gi)-kayo(u)* travel by rowboat

¹¹ 寄 *ko(gi)-yo(ru), ko(gi)-yo(seru)* row up to

¹² 着 *ko(gi)-tsu(keru), ko(gi)-tsu(ku)* row up to, reach

¹³ 艇 *sōtei* rowing, boating

漏 | 3307 / J4f33 / M18120 | Rō leaking; water clock;
B time. *mo(ru), mo(reru)* leak, escape; shine through; find expression; be disclosed; be omitted, be excluded. *mo(rasu)* spill, let leak; omit, miss, leave out; divulge; betray; give vent to, express; let go. *mo(ri)* leak, leakage.

⁴ 水 *rōsui* water leakage

斗 *jōgo, rōto* funnel

⁵ 出 *rōshutsu* leak, leakage, seepage

⁹ 洩 *rōei* leakage; disclosure

¹² 無 *mo(re)na(ku)* without exception

¹³ 電 *rōden* short circuit, leakage of electricity

漫 | 3308 / J4c21 / M18166 | MAN. *suzu(ro), sozo(ro)*
B involuntarily, in spite of oneself. *mida(ri) ni* without authority, without reason, arbitrarily, unnecessarily, indiscriminately, recklessly. *midari(gamashii)* morally corrupt.

³ 才 *manzai* comic dialogue

⁴ 文 *mambun* random notes

⁸ 歩 *mampo, sozo(ro)aru(ki)*, *suzu(ro)aru(ki)* a ramble, a stroll, a walk

画 *manga* comics, cartoon, caricature

¹¹ 遊 *man'yū* trip, tour, travel

¹⁵ 談 *mandan* idle talk, comic chat

漁 | 3309 / J3579 / M18101 | GYO, RYŌ fishing; fishery;
A catch, haul. *sunado(ru)*, *isa(ru)* to fish. *asa(ru)* fish, forage, browse, hunt for; gather (news).

⁴ 火 *gyoka, isaribi* fisher's fire lure

夫 *gyofu* fisherman

夫利 *gyofu(no)ri* running off with a prize while others are fighting for it

⁵ 民 *gyomin* fishers

⁶ 色 *gyoshoku* debauchery

⁷ 村 *gyoson* fishing village

労 *gyorō* fishing

⁸ 法 *gyohō* fishing method

具 *gyogu* fishing tackle

¹⁰ 師 *ryōshi* fisher

¹¹ 船 *gyosen, ryōsen* fishing boat

¹² 場 *gyojō, ryōba* fishing grounds

港 *gyokō* fishing port

¹³ 業 *gyogyō* fishing industry

¹⁴ 網 *gyomō* fishing net

¹⁶ 獲 *gyokaku* fishing; catch, haul

¹⁷ 礁 *gyoshō* artifically-made fishing grounds

演 | 3310 / J3169 / M18130 | EN. *en(jiru), en(zuru)*
A perform, play, act, enact, render, stage, put on.

⁵ 出 *enshutsu* production, performance, rendition, presentation; a play

出家 *enshutsuka* producer, director

⁷ 技 *engi* acting, performance

芸 *engei* entertainment, performance

⁸ 武 *embu* military exercises, fencing and judo

⁹ 奏 *ensō* (musical) performance, recital

奏会 *ensōkai* concert, recital

¹¹ 習 *enshū* practice, exercises; maneuvers, sham battle; seminar

¹⁴ 説 *enzetsu* speech, lecture, address, oration

¹⁵ 劇 *engeki* drama, play

¹⁶ 壇 *endan* rostrum, platform

¹⁸ 題 *endai* subject of an address

---

¹⁹ 繹 *en'eki* deductive reasoning

───────── **12** ─────────

潑 ³³²⁵ / J-X / M18225 — H<small>ATSU</small> leap; pour on.

⁹ 剌 *hatsuratsu(taru)* lively, animated

B 潟 ³³²⁸ / J3363 / M18247 — S<small>EKI</small>. *kata* lagoon.

澗 ³³²⁹ / J3442 / M-X — K<small>AN</small> valley river.

A 潔 ³³³² / J3769 / M18231 — K<small>ETSU</small>. *isagiyo(i)* pure, clean, righteous; manly, gallant, sportsmanlike.

⁵ 白 *keppaku* purity, innocence, integrity
¹⁸ 癖 *keppeki* fastidiousness

B 澄 ³³³³ / J4021 / M18315 — C<small>HŌ</small>. *su(mu)* be clear, become clear, clarify. *su(masu)* clear, clarify, settle; strain (one's ears); look grave.

⁵ 汁 *suma(shi)jiru* clear broth or stock (seasoned with shaved dried bonito, certain seaweeds, etc.)
⁸ 明 *chōmei* lucidity, serenity, clearness, clarity
¹² 渡 *su(mi)-wata(ru)* be perfectly clear

B 潤 ³³³⁴ / J3d61 / M18255 — J<small>UN</small>. *uruo(u)* vi be watered; profit by, receive benefits, become rich. *uruo(wasu), uruo(su)* vt moisten, water, irrigate, dip; enrich, profit. *uru(mu)* be dimmed, be clouded, get muddy; be wet. *fuya(kasu)* steep, soak. *fuya(keru)* swell up, become soaked. *uruo(i)* dampness, rain; gain; favor; charm. *uru(mi)* dimness, cloudiness, opacity, blur; moisture.

⁶ 色 *junshoku* rhetorical flourishes
⁷ 沢 *juntaku* gloss, luster; moisture, abundance; profit, favor
¹³ 滑 *junkatsu* lubrication
滑油 *junkatsuyu* lubricating oil

潰 ³³³⁵ / J4459 / M18281 — K<small>AI</small>. *tsubu(su)* crush, smash, break; dissipate; waste (time); kill, butcher; demolish; melt down. *tsubu(reru)* be smashed, break, be destroyed, collapse; be defaced (type); be ruined; be worn down. *tsui(eru)* be routed, collapse.

⁷ 走 *kaisō* rout, stampede
¹³ 滅 *kaimetsu* destruction, annihilation
¹⁴ 瘍 *kaiyō* ulcer

A 潮 ³³³⁶ / J442c / M18277 — C<small>HŌ</small>. *shio* tide; salt water; opportunity. *ushio* tide, sea water.

³ 干狩 *shiohiga(ri)* shell gathering at low tide
⁶ 気 *shioke* salt air
⁹ 風 *shio kaze* sea breeze, salt air
待 *shioma(chi)* waiting for the tide
¹⁰ 時 *shiodoki* tidal hour; favorable opportunity, psychological moment
流 *chōryū* tide, current; trend
¹² 焼 *shioya(ke)* tanned by salt air.
shioya(ki) broiling fish with salt
¹⁸ 騒 *shiosai* roar of the sea

B 潜 ³³³⁷ / J4078 / M18241 — S<small>EN</small>. *hiso(meru)* conceal, hide; lower (the voice). *hiso(maru)* be hushed. *hiso(mu)* lurk, lie dormant, be hidden. *kazu(ku)* dive, submerge. *kugu(ru)* pass through, pass under. *mogu(ru)* dive; get into, crawl into. *kugu(ri)* wicket gate, side gate. *hisoka ni* secretly.

² 入 *sennyū* infiltration, sneaking in
⁴ 込 *mogu(ri)-ko(mu)* get in, crawl in, slip in; hide
水 *sensui* diving
水艦 *sensuikan* submarine
⁶ 行 *senkō* traveling in disguise; submarine voyage
伏 *sempuku* concealment, hiding, ambush; incubation
在 *senzai* potentiality, latency, dormancy
在意識 *senzai ishiki* subconsciousness, subliminal self
¹⁰ 航 *senkō* submarine voyage
¹¹ 望鏡 *sembōkyō* periscope

───────── **13** ─────────

澱 ³³⁴⁷ / J4543 / M18410 — D<small>EN</small>. *ori* dregs, sediment, grounds. *yodo(mu)* stagnate, be stagnant; settle, deposit; be sluggish; hesitate; stammer. *yodo* pool (of a river).

¹⁰ 粉 *dempun* starch

4

心 忄 小 戈 戸 手 扌 支 攴 攵 文 斗 斤 方 无 日 曰 月 木 欠 止 歹 殳 毋 比 毛 氏 气 【水 氵 氺】 火 灬 爪 爫 父 爻 爿 片 牙 牛 犬 犭

B 濁 〔3348 J4279 M18440〕 JOKU, DAKU. *nigo(ri)* uncleanness; wrong; muddiness, impurity; voicing marks; voiced sound, voiced consonant; unrefined saké. *nigo(ru)* be muddy, be impure; be voiced; be vague. *nigo(su), nigo(rasu)* make muddy, make cloudy; quibble; prevaricate.

4 水 *dakusui* muddy water
9 音 *dakuon* voiced sound
　点 *dakuten, nigo(ri)ten* voiced consonant marks
10 流 *dakuryū* muddy stream
　酒 *dakushu, nigo(ri)zake, doburoku* unrefined saké, raw saké

B 濃 〔3349 J473b M18442〕 NŌ dark, thick, undiluted. *ko(i)* dark, deep; saturated; strong (drink); intimate; thick. *koma(yakana)* ardent.

9 厚 *nōkō* thickness, density, concentration; richness; elaborateness; ardency; tenseness
　度 *nōdo* density, thickness, consistency, concentration
11 淡 *nōtan* light and shade
　密 *nōmitsu na* thick; crowded
17 縮 *nōshuku* concentration
19 霧 *nōmu* dense fog

A 激 〔3350 J3763 M18438〕 GEKI. *geki(suru)* get excited, be agitated, be enraged, be exasperated, chafe; urge, encourage, incite. *hage(shii)* violent, vehement, furious, severe, acute, intense, extreme, passionate, heated, stormy (applause); tempestuous (temperament); mighty.

4 化 *gekka, gekika* intensification, aggravation
7 励 *gekirei* urging, encouragement, incitement
8 突 *gekitotsu* crash, collision
　昂 *gekkō, gekikō* excitement, exasperation, indignation, resentment
9 変 *gekihen* sudden change, upheaval, convulsion, cataclysm
　発 *gekihatsu* fit, spasm; outburst, explosion of anger
　怒 *gekido* rage, indignation, exasperation
　甚 *gekijin* violence, severity

10 浪 *gekirō* high waves, high seas; raging waves ⌐rapids
　流 *gekiryū* swift current, raging stream,
　烈 *gekiretsu* violence, severity, vehemence, fierceness
11 情 *gekijō* violent emotion, passion, fury, outburst
　務 *gekimu* exhausting work
　動 *gekidō* terrible shock, concussion, upheaval; agitation
12 痛 *gekitsū* sharp pain
　越 *gekietsu na* violent, vehement, fiery
13 戦 *gekisen* severe fight
15 論 *gekiron* heated argument
　賞 *gekishō* high praise
　震 *gekishin* severe earthquake

--- **14** ---

瀞 〔3356 J4654 M-X〕 See 瀞 3380.

B 濯 〔3360 J4275 M18532〕 TAKU. *soso(gu), susu(gu), yusu(gu), isu(gu)* wash, pour on, rinse.

濤 〔3361 J5e39 M18508〕 TŌ. *nami* waves, billows.

濠 〔3363 J396a M18502〕 GŌ. *hori* moat, ditch, canal. GŌ- Australia.

6 州 *Gōshū* Australia

濡 〔3365 J4728 M18504〕 JU. *nure(ru)* be wet, get wet, be damp, be soaked; make love. *nura(su)* wet, soak, dip, dampen.

4 文 *nurebumi* love letter
6 衣 *nureginu, nuregoromo* wet clothes; false charge
　衣着 *nureginu (o) ki(ru)* accept the guilt of another
8 事 *nuregoto* love affair
10 荷 *nureni* sea-damaged goods
12 場 *nureba* love scene
13 鼠 *nurenezumi* drowned rat; a person soaked to the skin
15 縁 *nureen* open veranda

B 濫 〔3366 J4d74 M18521〕 RAN overflow; spread over. *mida(ri) ni* without authority, without reason, arbitrarily,

4

心 忄 小 戈 戸 手 扌 支 攴 攵 文 斗 斤 方 无 日 曰 月 木 欠 歹 殳 毋 比 毛 氏 气 水 氵 氺 【火 灬】。爪 爫 父 爻 爿 丬 片 牙 牛 犬 犭

unnecessarily, indiscriminately, recklessly. *midari(gamashii)* morally corrupt.

5 用 *ran'yō* abuse, misuse, misappropriation
6 伐 *rambatsu* indiscriminate deforestation
7 作 *ransaku* overproduction; excessive writing
9 造 *ranzō* overproduction, careless manufacture
発 *rampatsu* excessive money issue
14 読 *randoku* indiscriminate reading
18 觴 *ranshō* origin, source, beginning

───── **15** ─────

瀆 3373 / J-X / M18591 TOKU, DOKU blasphemc. *kega(su)* vt defile, pollute, stain. *kega(reru)* vi be defiled, be polluted, be soiled.

───── **16** ─────

瀧 3376 / J426d / M18671 See 滝 3273.

瀦 3377 / J4375 / M-X CHO puddle; pool; swamp.

瀞 3380 / J-X / M18659 SEI. SHŌ. *toro* pool (in a river).

瀕 3381 / J494e / M18636 HIN shore, brink; near. *hin(suru)* be on the verge of.
6 死 *hinshi* on the verge of death

瀬 3384 / J4025 / M18672' RAI. *se* current, torrent, rapids, shallows, shoal.
B
4 戸 *seto* strait, channel
戸内海 *Setonaikai* Inland Sea
戸物 *setomono* porcelain; pottery
戸際 *setogiwa* crucial moment, crisis, threshold, brink, eleventh hour
15 踏 *sebu(mi)* wading to test depth; first trial, trial balloon, making inquiries

───── **17** ─────

灌 3390 / J5e75 / M18759 KAN. *soso(gu)* vt pour into, pour on, irrigate, sprinkle; shed (tears). *soso(gu)* vi (rain) falls; flow into; pay attention to, concentrate on.
4 木 *kamboku* shrub, shrubbery
13 腸 *kanchō* enema
15 漑 *kangai* irrigation, watering

───── **19** ─────

灘 3391 / J4667 / M18784 TAN. *nada* open sea.

════ **RAD. 火 86** ════

Hi or *ka* fire. At left: *hi hen.* At bottom: ⼩ *yotsu ten* four dots or *renga* or *rekka* (*ka* "fire" in a *retsu* "row"). Nickname: Fire.

火 3394 / J3250 / M18850 KA fire; Tuesday. *hi*
A
fire, flame, blaze. *(toro)bi* low fire. *ho* fire.
2 力 *karyoku* steam power; heating power; force of the flames
口 *hokuchi* tinder. *kakō* crater. *higuchi* burner; muzzle (of a gun); origin of a fire
口原 *kakōgen* crater basin
山 *kazan* volcano
山灰 *kazambai* volcanic ash
山岩 *kazangan* lava, igneous rock
山活動 *kazan katsudō* volcanic activity
山脈 *kazammyaku* volcanic range
山帯 *kazantai* volcanic zone
4 手 *hi(no)te* flames, blaze, fire. *kashu* stoker
水 *himizu* fire and water; discord
元 *himoto, hi (no) moto* origin of a fire
5 加減 *hikagen* condition of the fire
打石 *hiu(chi)ishi* flint stone
気厳禁 *Kaki-Genkin* Inflammable— Keep Out.

4

心 忄 小 戈 手 扌 支 攴 文 斗 斤 方 无 日 曰 月 木 欠 止 歹 殳 毋 比 毛 氏 气 水 氵 氺 【火 灬】 爪 爫 父 爻 爿 丬 片 牙 牛 犬 犭

---

⁷見櫓 *hi(no)mi yagura* fire tower
花 *hibana* spark
災 *kasai* conflagration, fire
災保険 *kasai hoken* fire insurance
災報知器 *kasai hōchiki* fire-alarm box
災警報 *kasai keihō* fire alarm
⁸炎 *kaen* flames, blazes
炎瓶 *kaembin* Molotov cocktail
事 *kaji* conflagration, fire
⁹急 *kakyū* urgency, emergency
星 *Kasei* Mars
¹⁰砲 *kahō* gun, cannon
¹¹遊 *hiaso(bi)* playing with fire; playing with love
達磨 *hidaruma* mass of flames
¹²焔 *kaen* flame, blaze
葬 *kasō* cremation
¹³傷 *yakedo, kashō* burn, scald
煙 *kaen* fire and smoke
鉢 *hibachi* brazier
勢 *kasei* force of the flames
照 *hote(ru)* feel hot, flush, burn. *hote(ri)* glow, heat; burning sensation
蓋切 *hibuta (o) ki(ru)* open fire
¹⁴種 *hidane* live coals (for starting a fire); remains of a fire
¹⁵箸 *hibashi* tongs
器 *kaki* firearms
縄銃 *hinawajū, hinawazutsu* matchlock, harquebus
¹⁶燵 *kotatsu* charcoal brazier in a floor well; heat source under a table and quilt
薬 *kayaku* gunpowder
¹⁸曜 *Kayō* Tuesday
曜日 *Kayōbi* Tuesday

--- 2 ---

灯 $\frac{3395}{\text{J4574}}$ 燈 $\frac{3476}{\text{J4575}}$ TEI. CHŌ. TŌ
A $\frac{}{\text{M18855}}$ $\frac{}{\text{M19402}}$ lamp, light; counter for lights. *akari, akashi, tomoshibi, hi* a light.
³下 *tōka* beneath the lamp
⁴火 *tōka* a light, lamplight. *tōka ni* by lamplight
⁵台 *tōdai* lighthouse, beacon; lampstand
台守 *tōdaimori* lighthouse keeper
芯 *tōshin* wick
⁸油 *tōyu, toboshi abura* lamp oil
明 *tōmyō* light offered to a god

---

²²籠 *tōrō* garden lantern, votive lantern
籠流 *tōrōnaga(shi)* setting afloat the *Bon* Festival lanterns

灰 $\frac{3396}{\text{J3325}}$ KAI. *hai* ashes. *aku*
A $\frac{}{\text{M18859}}$ puckery juice. *hai ni suru* burn up; cremate. *hai ni naru* be reduced to ashes; be cremated.
⁵皿 *haizara* ash tray
汁 *aku* lye; harsh taste
汁抜 *akunu(ki)* removal of the harsh taste in vegetables. *akunu(ke), akunu(keta)* refined, elegant, urbane
⁶色 *hai iro* ashen, ash color, gray
¹³搔 *haika(ki)* poker, ash rake
¹⁸燼 *kaijin* complete destruction

--- 3 ---

灼 $\frac{3398}{\text{J3c5e}}$ SHAKU. *arata(kana)*
$\frac{}{\text{M18878}}$ miraculous.
¹⁵熱 *shakunetsu* incandescence, red heat, scorching heat

灸 $\frac{3399}{\text{J3564}}$ KYŪ moxa cautery,
$\frac{}{\text{M18872}}$ chastisement. *yaito* moxa cautery.

災 $\frac{3400}{\text{J3a52}}$ SAI. *wazawai* calamity,
A $\frac{}{\text{M18879}}$ misfortune, woe, evil, curse.
⁴厄 *saiyaku* calamity, disaster, accident
¹⁰害 *saigai* disaster, calamity, accident
¹³禍 *saika* accident, calamity, disaster, misfortune
¹⁸難 *sainan* calamity, disaster, accident, misfortune

--- 4 ---

炉 $\frac{3403}{\text{J4f27}}$ RO furnace, kiln, hearth;
B $\frac{}{\text{M18902}}$ (nuclear) reactor.
⁴辺 *robata, rohen* fireside, hearth
¹⁴端 *robata* fireside, hearth

炎 $\frac{3404}{\text{J316a}}$ EN inflammation. *honō,*
B $\frac{}{\text{M18910}}$ *honoho, homura* flame, blaze.
³上 *enjō* blazing up; destruction (of a large building) by fire
⁴天 *enten* blazing heat, scorching sun

⁸ 炎 *en'en(taru)* blazing, fiery
¹⁰ 症 *enshō* inflammation
¹² 暑 *ensho* intense heat, heat wave
¹⁵ 熱 *ennetsu* sweltering heat

B 炊 3405 J3f66 M18904 SUI. *ta(ku), kashi(gu)* cook, boil.
⁵ 出 *takida(shi)* emergency rice feeding
⁸ 事 *suiji* cooking, culinary affairs
事係 *suijigakari* cook, chef
事場 *suijiba* kitchen, cookhouse, field kitchen, galley
¹² 飯 *suihan* cooking rice
飯器 *suihanki* electric rice cooker

─────── **5** ───────

B 為 3411 J3059 M18981 I *na(ru)* change; be of use; reach to. *na(su)* do. *su(ru)* do; try; play; practice; cost; serve as; pass, elapse. *ni su(ru)* make (something) of (a person); turn into (money). *tame* good, advantage, benefit, welfare, sake; to, in order to; because of, as a result of. *tame ni* for, for the sake of, to one's advantage, in favor of, on behalf of.
² 人 *hitotonari* temperament
⁹ 政者 *iseisha* statesman
¹² 替 *kawase* money order; exchange
替手形 *kawase tegata* draft
替相場 *kawase sōba* exchange rates

A 点 3412 J4540 M18980 TEN point; mark; score, run; speck; stain; defect; a detail; standpoint; items, pieces; decimal point; vote. *ten(jiru), ten(zuru)* drop; light, kindle; make tea. *tomo(ru), tobo(ru)* burn, be lighted. *tomo(su), tobo(su)* light, turn on. *tsu(ku)* (electricity) comes on. *tsu(keru)* turn on (electricity), light up. *sa(su)* light (a fire); apply moxa cautery.
⁴ 心 *tenshin, tenjin* Zen monk's snack; Chinese dessert; dim sum
火 *tenka* lighting, ignition
火栓 *tenkasen* spark plug
⁶ 灯 *tentō* lighting
字 *tenji* Braille
在 *tenzai suru* be dotted with
⁸ 呼 *tenko* roll call, muster
取虫 *tento(ri)mushi* derisive term for a diligent student

⁹ 点 *tenten* here and there, sporadically, scattered; in drops; little by little; dot, spot
¹¹ 描 *tembyō* sketch
眼 *tengan suru* drop medicine in the eyes
¹² 検 *tenken* inspection, examination; roll calling
¹³ 滅 *temmetsu* turning a light on and off
滅器 *temmetsuki* electric switch
数 *tensū* marks, credits, points; score, runs; number of items
¹⁴ 滴 *tenteki* falling drops, raindrops; intravenous drip, IV
¹⁵ 線 *tensen* dotted line; perforated line

A 炭 3413 J433a M18953 TAN charcoal; coal. *sumi* charcoal.
⁴ 火 *sumibi, tanka* charcoal fire; coals of fire
化 *tanka* carbonization
化水素 *tanka suiso* hydrocarbon
化物 *tankabutsu* carbide
水 *tansui* coal and water; carbon and hydrogen
水化物 *tansuikabutsu* carbohydrates
⁷ 坑 *tankō* coal mine
¹⁰ 素 *tanso* carbon
¹² 焼 *sumiya(ki)* charcoal making; charcoal maker
¹³ 鉱 *tankō* coal mine
¹⁴ 酸 *tansan* carbonic acid
酸水 *tansansui* carbonated water
酸瓦斯 *tansan gasu* carbon dioxide
²⁰ 礦 *tankō* coal mine

─────── **6** ───────

B 烈 3420 J4e75 M18987 RETSU. *hage(shii)* violent, vehement, furious, severe, acute, intense, extreme, passionate, heated, stormy (applause); tempestuous (temperament); mighty.
³ 士 *resshi* patriot, hero
女 *retsujo* heroine
⁴ 火 *rekka* raging fire
⁹ 風 *reppū* violent wind, hurricane, gale
¹⁵ 震 *resshin* violent earthquake

烏 3421 J3128 M18998 U. O. *karasu* crow, raven.

心 忄 小 戈 戸 手 扌 支 攴 攵 文 斗 斤 方 旡 日 曰 月 木 欠 止 歹 殳 毋 比 毛 氏 气 水 氵 氺 【火 灬】6 爪 爫 父 爻 爿 丬 片 牙 牛 犬 犭

³口 *karasuguchi* ruling pen
⁶行水 *karasu (no) gyōzui* a quick bath
合衆 *ugō(no)shū* disorderly crowd, mob
⁷貝 *karasugai* fresh-water mussel
¹⁰竜茶 *ūroncha* oolong tea
¹²帽子 *eboshi* noble's court headgear
¹³賊 *ika* squid, cuttlefish

────── 7 ──────

焔 3423 / J316b / M-X EN. *honoo, homura* flame, blaze.

⁶色 *enshoku* flame color, flame scarlet, bright reddish orange

烹 3425 / J4b23 / M19049 HŌ. *ni(ru)* vt boil, cook.

────── 8 ──────

煉 3428 / J4e7b / M-X Nonstandard for 煉 3455.

焚 3434 / J4a32 / M19100 FUN. *ta(ku)* burn, kindle, build a (fire); boil, cook. *ya(ku)* vt set fire to, burn, fire; bake, roast (over a fire), toast, broil, parch; char, scorch, singe; cremate; print (photos); be envious of.
⁴火 *takibi* blazing fire, bonfire
⁵付 *ta(ki)-tsu(keru)* light, kindle, build a fire); instigate, stir up. *takitsu(ke)* kindling, fire lighter

然 3435 / J4133 / M19149 ZEN. NEN. *sō, sa* so.
A *shika(rashimeru)* to decree. *sō(shite), so(shite)* and. *sa(ri)towa* if so, well. *sa(ru)* a certain, such. *shika(raba)* if so, in that case. *shika(razu)* no, it is not so. *shika(redomo)* but. *shika(ri)* yes, you are right. *shika(rubeki)* due, proper, reasonable, respectable, justifiable. *shika(ru)* ni however, nevertheless, on the contrary. *shika(shi), sare(do)* but, however. *shika(mo)* moreover, nevertheless. *shika* so, in that way. *-zen* resembling.

焦 3436 / J3e47 / M19119 SHŌ. *ko(geru)* vi burn, scorch, singe, char. *ko(gasu)*
B

vt burn, scorch, char, singe; pine for. *koga(reru)* pine for, yearn for; be deeply in love with; be scorched. *ase(ru)* be in a hurry, be hasty, be impatient, be overzealous. *ji(reru)* be irritated. *ji(rasu)* irritate. *ji(rettagaru)* be impatient. *ko(gashi)* parched-barley flour. *ji(rettai)* irritating, provoking; impatient, vexed.
³土 *shōdo* burnt ground; scorched earth
⁹眉 *shōbi* emergency, urgency, imminence
点 *shōten* focus
臭 *kogekusa(i), kinakusa(i)* smelling burnt
茶 *kogecha* dark brown
¹⁵慮 *shōryo* impatience, worry
熱 *shōnetsu* scorching heat; scorching
¹⁷燥 *shōsō* impatience, irritation, uneasiness

煮 3437 / J3c51 / M19165′ SHA. *ni(eru)* boil, cook,
B be cooked, be boiled. *ni(ru)* vt boil, cook. *ni* cooking.
²〆 *ni-shi(meru)* boil up thoroughly
³干 *nibo(shi)* small dried sardines
⁴込 *ni-ko(mu)* cook together. *niko(mi)* meat and vegetable stew
⁵立 *ni-ta(teru)* boil up, bring to a boil. *ni-ta(tsu)* boil up, bring to a boil; begin to boil
汁 *nijiru, nitsuyu, nishiru* gravy, stock, broth
出 *ni-da(su)* vt boil down, decoct, extract. *nida(shi)* stock, broth
⁸炊 *nita(ki)* boiling
物 *nimono* cooking; cooked food
沸 *shafutsu suru, ni(e)-ta(giru)* boil up
⁹染 *ni-shi(meru)* boil hard
¹⁰凍 *nikogo(ri)* boiled-down food
¹¹魚 *nizakana* boiled fish
¹²湯 *ni(e)yu* boiling water
¹⁶麺 *nyūmen* boiled vermicelli

焼 3438 / J3e46 / M19166′ SHŌ. burning. *ya(ku)* vt
A set fire to, burn, fire; bake, roast (over a fire), toast, broil, parch; char, scorch, singe; cremate; print (photos); be envious of. *ya(keru)* vi be burnt, be burnt down; be roasted, be toasted, be grilled, be broiled; be scorched; be sunburnt; warm up, heat up (as a motor); be tarnished,

fade; have heartburn; be jealous of; glow, be illuminated. *ya(ki)* baking, toasting, roasting, broiling; roast; porcelain; tempering; discipline.

² 入 *ya(ki)i(re)* hardening, tempering. *ya(ki) (o) i(reru)* torture

⁵ 付 *ya(ki)-tsu(keru)* join by baking; bake (porcelain); enamel; glaze; plate; stain (glass); fuse together; print (pictures). *ya(ki)-tsu(ku)* scorch. *yakitsu(ke)* baking; enamelling; plating; annealing; (photographic) printing

払 *ya(ki)-hara(u)* burn up, consume. *ya(ki)hara(i)* violent burning of unwanted goods

打 *yakiu(chi)* setting on fire, attacking and burning

⁶ 肉 *ya(ki)niku* roast meat, roast fowl

尽 *ya(ki) tsuku(su)* burn up, consume, reduce to ashes. *ya(ke)-tsu(kiru)* burn out

印 *ya(ki)in* brand, branding iron; stigma

芋 *ya(ki)imo* baked or roasted sweet potato

夷弾 *shōidan* incendiary bomb, incendiary shell

死 *shōshi, ya(ke)ji(ni)* death by fire

死体 *shōshitai* charred body

⁷ 却 *shōkyaku* destruction by fire, incineration

戻 *ya(ki)-modo(su)* anneal, temper

⁸ 物 *ya(ki)mono* pottery, porcelain

⁹ 香 *shōkō* incense offering

畑 *ya(ki)bata, ya(ke)bata, ya(ki)batake, ya(ke)batake* burnt-over fields

¹⁰ 酒 *ya(ke)zake* drowning one's cares in saké

討 *ya(ki)u(chi)* an attack with fire

酎 *shōchū* a low-grade alcoholic drink

¹¹ 魚 *ya(ki)zakana* broiled fish

鳥 *ya(ki)tori* fried chicken, roast fowl, yakitori

野原 *ya(ke)nohara, ya(ke)no(ga)hara* burnt-out area

¹² 飯 *ya(ki)meshi* fried rice

焦 *ya(ke)ko(ge), ya(ke)koga(shi)* hole made by burning

¹³ 滅 *shōmetsu sasu, ya(ki)-horobo(su)* vt destroy by fire. *shōmetsu suru* vi be destroyed by fire

腹 *ya(ke)bara* despair, desperation

¹⁴ 増 *yakima(shi)* an extra print

網 *ya(ki)ami* toasting grill, broiling grill

餅 *ya(ki)mochi* toasted rice cake

¹⁵ 蕎麦 *ya(ki)soba* fried noodles

A 無 $\frac{3439}{J4c3.5}$ MU, BU nothing, nil, M19113 negation. *na(i), na(shi)* none. *na(kattara)* if there were none; were it not for; unless. *mu ni suru* make worthless. *na(ku) naru* be lost; run short, be used up; disappear; die. *naku(su), na(ku) suru* lose; run out of; remove; absorb. *na(kute)* without; for want of; in the absence of. *na(sasōna)* unlikely, improbable. *na(kumogana)* needless, useless. *na(shi) ni, na(shi) de* without.

¹ 一文 *muichimon* penniless

一物 *muichibutsu, muichimotsu* penniless

² 二無三 *munimusan* recklessly, furiously, desperately, forcibly

力 *muryoku* helpless, incompetent; lack of funds

人 *bunin, mujin* shortage of help; unmanned. *mujin, munin* uninhabited

人島 *mujintō* uninhabited island

³ 口 *mukuchi* reticence

下 *muge ni* flatly, squarely, point-blank

上 *mujō no* supreme, best, greatest

⁴ 心 *mushin* request. *mushin no* innocent; insentient; involuntary

比 *muhi no* peerless, unparalleled

双 *musō* peerless, unparalleled

分別 *mufumbetsu* rashness, indiscretion

欠 *muketsu* perfection

辺 *muhen na* limitless, boundless, infinite

⁵ 生物 *museibutsu* inanimate object; lifeless thing

主 *mushu* ownerless

礼 *burei* discourtesy, rudeness

礼講 *bureikō* informal party, unrestrained revelry

用 *muyō* useless; unwanted; unnecessary; prohibited; without business

用心 *buyōjin* insecurity, carelessness

⁶ 色 *mushoku* colorless, achromatic

休 *mukyū* no holiday

地 *muji* solid color

血 *muketsu* bloodless

尽 *mujin* infinity, endless, unfathomable; lottery savings system

4

心 忄 小 戈 戸 手 扌 支 攴 攵 文 斗 斤 方 无 日 曰 月 木 欠 止 歹 殳 母 比 毛 氏 气 水 氵 氺 【火 灬】 爪 爫 父 爻 爿 丬 片 牙 牛 犬 犭

尽蔵 *mujinzō* inexhaustible supply

気力 *mukiryoku* lethargy, enervation

気味 *bukimi* ill-feeling

防備 *mubōbi* unfortified, open, defenseless

名 *mumei* unnamed, anonymity, obscurity; unjustifiable

名戦士 *mumei senshi* the unknown soldier

⁷私 *mushi* unselfishness, impartiality

芸 *mugei no* uncultured, unaccomplished

邪気 *mujaki* innocence, artlessness

沙汰 *busata* silence, neglect to write or call

作法 *busahō* bad manners, discourtesy, rudeness

体 *mutai* forcibly

形 *mukei no* abstract, incorporeal, immaterial; moral, spiritual; invisible, intangible

形文化財 *mukei-bunkazai* intangible cultural asset

言 *mugon* silence

我 *muga* selflessness; ecstasy

我夢中 *muga-muchū* unconsciousness; ecstasy

条件 *mujōken* unconditional

声 *musei* voiceless, noiseless, silent

⁸届 *mutodo(ke)* without permission; without notice

性 *musei* asexual. *mushō* thoughtless, rash, indiscreet; immoderate; unnecessary

効 *mukō* void, invalid; ineffective

制限 *museigen* unlimited, unrestricted

表情 *muhyōjō na* expressionless

免許 *mumenkyo* unlicensed

味 *mumi* tasteless, flat, insipid

味乾燥 *mumi-kansō na* dry as dust, uninteresting

抵抗 *muteikō* nonresistance, passive resistance

法 *muhō* injustice; wrong; unlawfulness; outrage; violence

知 *muchi* ignorance, illiteracy, stupidity

知蒙昧 *muchi-mōmai* unenlightenment

念 *munen* regret; resentment; chagrin; impassive state of mind

念無想 *munen-musō* impassive state of mind

定見 *muteiken* lack of principle, inconstant

実 *mujitsu* falsehood; innocence

学 *mugaku* ignorance; illiteracy

事 *buji* safety, security; peace, tranquility; good health; boredom

事故 *mujiko* no accident, no trouble; safety (week)

所属 *mushozoku* free, independent, nonaffiliated, nonpartisan

限 *mugen* infinite, endless, unfathomable; infinity, eternity

⁹垢 *muku* purity, innocence; plain-colored suit; an all-white garb

臭 *mushū* odorless

造作 *muzōsa* easiness; simplicity; artlessness

神経 *mushinkei* callousness, apathy, stolidity

神論 *mushinron* atheism

茶 *mucha na* absurd, unreasonable; reckless, wanton; excessive, immoderate

茶苦茶 *muchakucha* confused; absurd, unreasonable; reckless, mad

為 *bui, mui* idleness, inaction

¹⁰根 *mukon* groundless, unfounded, false

残 *muzan* cruel, merciless, pitiful

粋 *busui na* inelegant, unromantic, lacking in polish

恥 *muchi* shamelessness, impudence

益 *mueki* futility, uselessness, carelessness

害 *mugai* harmless, innocent, inoffensive

記名 *mukimei* blank (endorsement), unregistered, uninscribed (shares)

差別 *musabetsu, mushabetsu* indifference; making no discrimination

挨拶 *buaisatsu* impoliteness, incivility

病息災 *mubyō-sokusai* perfect health

配当 *muhaitō* nondividend

骨 *bukotsu* uncouth, clumsy, brusque

料 *muryō* no charge, free

能 *munō* inefficiency, incompetence

¹¹疵 *mukizu* flawless, faultless, sound, without blemish

道 *budō, mudō* tyranny; atrocity; wickedness

惨 *muzan* cruel, merciless; pitiful

情 *mujō* heartlessness, cruelty

視 *mushi suru* disregard; defy, set aside, ignore

聊 *buryō, muryō* boredom, tediousness

欲 *muyoku* not covetous

常 *mujō no* uncertain, evanescent, transient

責任 *musekinin* irresponsibility

断 *mudan* unannounced; unauthorized

断欠勤 *mudan kekkin* absent without permission, AWOL

宿 *mushuku* homeless

産政党 *musan seitō* proletarian party

産階級 *musan kaikyū* proletarians, property-less class

理 *muri* unreasonable, unjustifiable, unnatural; impossible, beyond one's strength; overwork; extravagance. *muri(karanu)* reasonable, natural. *muri ni* forcibly, against one's will

理矢理 *muriyari ni* forcibly, against one's will

理心中 *muri shinju* forced double suicide

理押 *murio(shi)* pushing things too far

理強 *murijii* coercion

¹² 税 *muzei* duty-free, tax-free

給 *mukyū* unpaid, nonsalaried

辜 *muko no* innocent, harmless

策 *musaku* resourcelessness

智 *muchi* ignorance, illiteracy, stupidity

統制 *mutōsei* uncontrolled

着陸 *muchakuriku* nonstop (flight)

遠慮 *buenryo* forwardness, impertinence, audacity, boldness, frankness

期 *muki* unlimited, perpetual, indefinite

期限 *mukigen* unlimited, perpetual, indefinite

¹³ 数 *musū* innumerable

鉄砲 *muteppō na* reckless, thoughtless

頓着 *mutonchaku, mutonjaku* nonchalance, indifference

慈悲 *mujihi na* cruel, merciless

暗 *muyami na, muyami(yatarana)* thoughtless, rash, indiscreet; immoderate; unnecessary

暗矢鱈 *muyami-yatara na* thoughtless, rash, indiscreet; immoderate; unnecessary

節操 *musessō* unchastity, inconstancy

電 *muden* wireless, radio

勢 *buzei, muzei* shortage of people, numerical inferiority

愛想 *buaisō* rudeness; unsociability

罪 *muzai* innocent, not guilty

蓋 *mugai no* open, uncovered

意味 *muimi* meaningless, nonsensical, to no purpose

意識 *muishiki* unconsciousness; involuntariness

資格 *mushikaku* disqualification; incapacity

¹⁴ 様 *buzama na* unshapely, unsightly, unpresentable; uncouth, clumsy

精 *bushō* sloth, laziness

雑作 *muzōsa* easiness; simplicity; artlessness

関心 *mukanshin* unconcern, indifference, apathy

駄 *muda* futility, uselessness, waste

¹⁵ 論 *muron* of course, naturally

敵 *muteki* invincible, unrivaled

器用 *bukiyō* clumsiness, unskillfulness

縁 *muen* no surviving relatives

線 *musen* wireless; no electricity service; no need for electricity

¹⁶ 謀 *mubō na* reckless, thoughtless

頼 *burai* villainy

頼漢 *buraikan* villain, scoundrel, outlaw

機物 *mukibutsu* inorganic substance; minerals (in food)

¹⁷ 償行為 *mushō (no) kōi* volunteer service

¹⁸ 難 *bunan* safety, security; faultlessness; no difficulty

類 *murui* choicest, finest

職 *mushoku* unemployed, no occupation

———————— 9 ————————

煤 ³⁴⁵²／J4761／M19220 BAI. *susu* soot. *susu(keru), susuba(mu), susu(buru)* get sooty, be sooty, get smoked up; be smoke-dried.

¹³ 煙 *baien* soot and smoke, smoke

煎 ³⁴⁵³／J4079／M19184 SEN. *i(ru)* broil, parch, roast, fire (tea), boil down (in oil). *sen(jiru)* boil, decoct, infuse.

⁵ 玉子 *iritamago* scrambled eggs

⁹ 茶 *sencha* green tea

¹⁵ 餅 *sembei* Japanese rice cracker; wafer

¹⁶ 薬 *sen(ji)gusuri, sen'yaku* (medical) decoction, infusion

B 煩 ³⁴⁵⁴／J4851／M19229 BON. HAN trouble, worry. *wazura(u)* be ill; worry, be

4

心 忄 小 戈 戸 手 扌 支 攴 攵 文 斗 斤 方 无 日 日 月 木 欠 歹 殳 毋 比 毛 氏 气 水 氵 氺 【火 灬】 爪 爫 父 爻 爿 丬 片 牙 牛 犬 犭

afflicted, be in pain, be troubled.
wazura(wasu), *wazura(waseru)* trouble,
keep (someone) busy, disturb, annoy.
uru(sagaru) feel annoyed by, regard as a
nuisance. *uru(sai)* annoying,
troublesome, irksome, inquisitive,
importunate. *wazura(i)* agony, anxiety;
illness; involvement, trouble.
wazura(washii) troublesome,
complicated, confused.

⁶ 忙 *hambō* pressure of business
¹⁰ 悩 *bonnō* evil passions, carnal desire
¹² 悶 *hammon* anguish, worry, trouble
¹⁴ 雑 *hanzatsu* complexity, trouble,
complication, intricacy

煉 <u>3455</u> J-X M19178 REN. *ne(ru)* refine (metals).
neri kneading over fire.

⁵ 瓦 *renga* brick
⁶ 合 *ne(ri)-a(waseru)* knead together;
compound
⁸ 固 *ne(ri)-kata(meru)* harden by kneading
⁹ 炭 *rentan* briquette
¹⁴ 獄 *rengoku* purgatory

煙 <u>3456</u> B J316c M19203 EN smoke. *kemu(ru)*,
kebu(ru) smoke, smolder,
be smoky, appear dim. *kemu(rasu)*
smoke up, fumigate. *kemu(i)*, *kebu(i)*
smoky. *kemuri, kemu, kebu, keburi*
smoke; fumes; spray. *kemu(tagaru)* be
sensitive to smoke; feel awkward.
kebu(tai), kemu(tai) smoky; feeling
awkward.

⁴ 火 *enka* rocket, beacon. *hanabi*
fireworks, firecrackers
⁸ 雨 *en'u* misty, fine, or drizzling rain
突 *entotsu* chimney, smokestack, funnel,
stovepipe
⁹ 草 *tabako* tobacco, cigar, cigarette
¹² 筒 *entō* chimney, smokestack, funnel,
stovepipe
¹³ 幕 *emmaku* smoke screen
¹⁴ 管 *enkan* chimney. *kiseru* (tobacco)
pipe; stolen train ride
¹⁹ 霧 *emmu* haze, mist, smog

照 <u>3457</u> A J3e48 M19226 SHŌ. *te(ru)* shine. *te(rasu)*
shine on, shed light on,
illuminate; compare with. *te(reru)* be
bashful. *te(ri)* sunshine; dry weather,
drought; gloss, luster.

⁶ 返 *te(ri)-kae(su)* reflect
合 *te(ri)-a(waseru)*, *te(rashi)-a(waseru)*,
te(rashi)-a(wasu), *shōgō* (*suru*)
verify, check, compare
会 *shōkai* inquiry
⁸ 明 *shōmei* illumination, lighting, flare
⁹ 度 *shōdo* (intensity of) illumination
¹⁰ 射 *shōsha* shining
¹³ 照坊主 *te(ru)te(ru)bōzu* paper doll used
in praying for good weather
準 *shōjun* aim, aiming, sight

—————— **10** ——————

熔 <u>3458</u> J4d50 M19319 See 鎔 6327.

熊 <u>3468</u> J3727 M19294 YŪ. *kuma* bear.

⁴ 手 *kumade* rake, fork

煽 <u>3469</u> J407a M19272 SEN. *ao(ru)* fan, flap;
instigate, agitate; bolster up;
gulp down, quaff. *ao(gu)* fan; instigate.
oda(teru) stir up, instigate; flatter.

⁵ 立 *ao(ri)-ta(teru)*, *ao(gi)-ta(teru)*
instigate, stir up
¹¹ 動 *sendō* instigation, agitation
情的 *senjōteki* lascivious, sensational,
suggestive

—————— **11** ——————

熟 <u>3472</u> A J3d4f M19332 JUKU. *u(reru)*, *juku(suru)*,
juku(su) ripen, mellow,
mature; acquire skill; be ripe for; become
popular (as a word). *u(mu)* ripen.
kona(reru) be digested; combine; be
skilled; be pulverized. *na(reru)* get used
to, become experienced; be tamed; get too
familiar, mature. *jit(to)* firmly, intently,
patiently.

⁶ 成 *jukusei suru* ripen, mature; cure;
ferment
考 *jukukō, jukkō* due consideration,
deliberation, mature reflection
年 *jukunen* middle age
⁸ 知 *jukuchi* thorough knowledge
¹¹ 視 *jukushi* steady gaze, scrutiny
¹³ 睡 *jukusui* sound sleep
¹⁴ 語 *jukugo* a word of two or more
characters; a set phrase

読 *jukudoku* careful reading
練 *jukuren* skill, mastery, practice
15 慮 *jukuryo* mature deliberation

A 熱 3473 J472e M19360 NETSU heat, warmth; temperature; fever; mania, fad; enthusiasm; passion. *nes(suru)* vt heat, make hot; burn, boil. vi become warm; become excited; become earnest. *atsu(garu)* feel the heat, swelter. *iki(ru)* be hot and sultry. *hotō(ru), hotobo(ru)* get heated; get angry. *atsu(i)* hot. *hotobo(ri)* warmth, heat; sensation, furore; enthusiasm, energy, momentum; reputation. *atsu(gari)* person sensitive to heat.
2 力学 *netsurikigaku* thermodynamics
4 中 *netchū* enthusiasm, zeal, mania
心 *nesshin* earnestness, enthusiasm
5 弁 *netsuben* fervent speech
気 *netsuke* feverishness. *nekki* heat, hot air; enthusiasm
気球 *nekkikyū* hot-air balloon
血漢 *nekketsukan* a hot-blooded man
7 狂 *nekkyō* enthusiasm, frenzy, rage, mania, excitement
9 風 *neppū* fiery-hot wind
10 烈 *netsuretsu na* ardent, passionate, vehement
病 *netsubyō* fever
帯 *nettai* torrid zone, tropics
帯雨林 *nettai urin* tropical rain forest
帯魚 *nettaigyo* tropical fish
11 情 *netsujō* fervor, warmth, ardent love, passion
望 *netsubō* fervent hope, longing
12 湯 *nettō* boiling water
量 *netsuryō* heat value, caloric value
13 愛 *netsuai* ardent love, devotion
意 *netsui* zeal, enthusiasm
14 演 *netsuen* enthusiastic performance
16 燗 *atsukan* hot saké

───── **12** ─────

燈 3476 J4575 M19402 See **灯** 3395.

燕 3489 J316d M19429 EN *tsubame, tsubakura, tsubakuro* the swallow.
7 尾服 *embifuku* swallow-tailed coat
11 雀 *enjaku* small birds

A 燃 3490 J4733 M19394 NEN. *mo(su), mo(yasu)* burn. *mo(yuru), mo(eru)* burn, blaze, glow.
3 上 *mo(e)-a(garu)* blaze up, burn up
10 料 *nenryō* fuel
11 盛 *mo(e)-saka(ru)* burn fiercely
12 焼 *nenshō* combustion

───── **13** ─────

B 燥 3493 J4167 M19467 SŌ dry up. *kawa(ku), hasha(gu)* vi dry up, parch.

燭 3496 J3f24 M19480 SOKU, SHOKU light; candle power.
5 台 *shokudai* candlestick, candlestand
6 光 *shokkō* candle power; candlelight

燦 3498 J3b38 M19468 SAN brilliance. *san(taru)* brilliant.
12 然 *sanzen* brilliance, radiance
17 燦 *sansan(taru)* brilliant, bright
21 爛 *sanran(taru)* brilliant, bright, radiant

燐 3499 J4e55 M19417 RIN phosphorus.
3 寸 *matchi* match
4 火 *rinka* phosphorescence
6 光 *rinkō* phosphorescence
14 酸 *rinsan* phosphoric acid

───── **15** ─────

B 爆 3505 J477a M19540 BAKU. *ha(zeru)* burst open, pop, split.
6 竹 *bakuchiku* firecracker
9 音 *bakuon* buzzing, whirr; explosion, detonation
風 *bakufū* bomb blast, shell blast, explosion blast
発 *bakuhatsu* explosion, blasting
10 笑 *bakushō* roar of laughter
破 *bakuha* explosion, blasting
12 弾 *bakudan* bomb
裂 *bakuretsu* explosion, blasting
13 煙 *bakuen* the smoke of an explosion
雷 *bakurai* depth bomb
15 撃 *bakugeki* bombing
撃機 *bakugekiki* bombing plane
16 薬 *bakuyaku* blasting power, explosive compound

4
心忄小戈戸手扌
支攴攵文斗斤方
无日曰月木欠
止歹殳毋比毛氏气
水氵氺【火灬】15
爪爫父爻爿丬片
牙牛犬犭

■■■■■■■■■■ RAD. 爪 87 ■■■■■■■■■■

Tsume nail, claw. At top: 爫 or 爪 *tsume kammuri* or *no-tsu* (the katakana *no* plus the katakana *tsu*). Nickname: Claw.

爪 $\frac{3509}{\frac{J445e}{M19653}}$ Sō. *tsume* nail, claw, talon, hoof; hook, catch; plectrum.
- ⁴ 切 *tsumeki(ri)* nail clipper
- ⁶ 先 *tsumasaki* tiptoe, tip of the toe
- ¹¹ 痕 *tsume ato* scratch; pinch mark
- ¹³ 楊枝 *tsumayōji* toothpick

────── 13 ──────

B 爵 $\frac{3514}{\frac{J3c5f}{M19710'}}$ SHAKU peerage, court rank
- ⁷ 位 *shakui* peerage, court rank

■■■■■■■■■■ RAD. 父 88 ■■■■■■■■■■

Chichi father. Nickname: Father.

A 父 $\frac{3516}{\frac{J4963}{M19721}}$ FU. *chichi* father. *(o)tō(chan)* papa, daddy (juvenile).
- ³ 子 *fushi* father and child
- ⁵ 母 *chichihaha, fubo, tete-haha* father and mother
- 兄 *fukei* parents and older brothers; guardians

- 兄会 *fukeikai* parents' association
- ⁹ 祖 *fuso* ancestors, forefathers
- ¹⁶ 親 *chichi oya, tete oya* father

────── 8 ──────

爺 $\frac{3517}{\frac{J4c6c}{M19734}}$ YA. *jii, jii(ya)* old man. *jijii* old man, grandpa.

■■■■■■■■■■ RAD. 爻 89 ■■■■■■■■■■

Majiwaru to mix. Variant: 爻. Nickname: Double X.

────── 7 ──────

爽 $\frac{3520}{\frac{J4156}{M19746}}$ Sō. *sawa(yakana)* refreshing, bracing; clear, resonant, sweet (voice); fluent.
- ⁷ 快 *sōkai na* refreshing, exhilarating

────── 10 ──────

爾 $\frac{3521}{\frac{J3c24}{M19750}}$ JI. NI. *nanji* thou, you. *shika* so, in that way.
- ⁷ 来 *jirai* since then
- ⁹ 後 *jigo* thereafter

■■■■■■■■■■ RAD. 爿 90 ■■■■■■■■■■

Hidari kata (a left-hand *kata* "side," to distinguish it from Rad. 91). Variant: 丬 (3 strokes) *shō hen*. Nickname: Left Side.

RAD. 片 91

Migi kata (a right-hand *kata* "side," to distinguish it from Rad. 90)
or *kata hen*. Nickname: Right Side.

片 3525 J4a52 M19813 HEN *hira* leaf, sheet, petal, flake. *kata-* one (eye, etc.); single (shift, etc.); one-way; one-sided.

⁴ 方 *katappō, katahō, katakata* one side; one party; the other side; the other party; mate to (a shoe)

片 *hempen* pieces, scraps

手 *katate* one hand. *katate no* single-handed, one-handed

手仕事 *katate shigoto* side job

手間 *katadema, katatema* spare time

手落 *katateo(chi)* partiality, unfairness

⁵ 目 *katame* one eye. *mekkachi* one-eyed person

付 *katazu(keru)* put in order; put away; dispose of, solve, finish; marry off, get married. *katazu(ku)* be put in order; be settled, be disposed of; marry (a man)

田舎 *katainaka* backwoods

⁶ 帆 *kataho* close-hauled sail

仮名 *kaiukana, katakanna* the square syllabary

肌脱 *katahada nu(gu)* bare one

⁷ 足 *kataashi* one leg; one foot

言 *hengen* a word, a few words. *katakoto* lisp, babble; one side of a story

言隻句 *hengen-sekku* just a word

⁹ 思 *kataomo(i)* unrequited love

¹⁰ 流 *katanaga(re)* a shed roof

栗粉 *katakuriko* an edible starch (from dogtooth violet)

¹¹ 道 *katamichi* one way

隅 *katasumi* nook, corner

寄 *katayo(ri)* inclination; offset; polarization. *katayo(ru)* lean, incline; be biased

側 *katagawa, katakawa* one side

¹² 割 *katawa(ri)* half. *katawa(re)* fragment; one of the group; the other half; the accomplice

¹³ 意地 *kataiji na* narrow-minded, uncompromising, stubborn

腹痛 *katahara-ita(i)* absurd, ridiculous, contemptible

¹⁴ 端 *kata(p)pashi, katahashi* an end, an edge, a side; smattering; fag end; petty official

¹⁶ 親 *kataoya* one parent

²⁴ 鱗 *henrin* a (fish) scale; a part, a particle; a glimpse

— 4 —

版 3526 J4847 M19817 HAN printing block or plate; printing; edition, impression; board; label.

⁴ 木 *hangi* (printing) block, woodcut, engraving block

元 *hammoto* publisher

⁵ 本 *hampon* wood-block book; printed book

⁷ 図 *hanto* dominion, territory

⁸ 画 *hanga* woodcut print

¹⁵ 権 *hanken* copyright

— 8 —

牌 3528 J4757 M19854 HAI label, signboard; medal. *pai* mahjong playing tiles.

— 9 —

牒 3529 J442d M19871 CHŌ label; genealogy; circular. *chō(zu)* circularize, notify.

4

心 忄 小 戈 戸 手 扌 支 攴 攵 文 斗 斤 方 无 日 日 月 木 欠 止 歹 殳 毋 比 毛 氏 气 水 氵 氺 火 灬 爪 爫 父 爻 爿 片 【牙】 牛 犬 犭

RAD. 牙 92

Kiba tusk or *kiba hen*. Variant: 牙 (5 strokes).
Do not confuse with Rad. 71. Nickname: Tusk.

牙 3531 / J3267 / M19909 GA. GE. *kiba* tusk, fang, canine tooth, eyetooth.

⁹城 *gajō* stronghold, inner citadel

RAD. 牛 93

Ushi cow. At left: 牛 *ushi hen*. Nickname: Cow.

A 牛 3532 / J356d / M19922 GO. GYŪ beef, cow. *ushi* cattle, cow, bull, ox.

⁶耳 *gyūji(ru)* control, lead, command; direct. *gyūji* ox ears
肉 *gyūniku* beef
⁸追 *ushio(i)* cattle herder
⁸舍 *gyūsha* cow barn, cow shed
歩 *gyūho, ushi (no) ayumi* snail's pace
乳 *gyūnyū* (cow's) milk
¹³蒡 *gobō* burdock
¹⁷鍋 *gyūnabe* popular Japanese beef-and-vegetable dish, sukiyaki

--- 2 ---

牟 3533 / J4c36 / M19928 BŌ. MU pupil of the eye; mooing of a cow.

牝 3534 / J4c46 / M19925 HIN *mesu, men, me-* female.

--- 3 ---

牢 3535 / J4f34 / M19934 RŌ prison, jail; hardness.

⁸固 *rōko(taru)* firm, strong, inflexible, steadfast
⁹屋 *rōya* prison, jail
¹⁰破 *rōyabu(ri)* jailbreak
¹⁴獄 *rōgoku* prison, jail

牡 3536 / J3234 / M19933 BO. *osu, on-, o-* male.

⁴丹 *botan* tree peony
丹雪 *botan yuki* large snowflakes
²⁰蠣 *kaki* edible oyster

--- 4 ---

A 牧 3537 / J4b52 / M19950 BOKU. *boku(suru)* care for, shepherd, feed. *maki* pasture.

⁹草 *bokusō, makigusa* grass, pasture
¹⁰畜 *bokuchiku* cattle raising
師 *bokushi* pastor, minister, priest
¹²場 *bokujō* stock farm, pasture. *makiba* pasture, grazing land
童 *bokudō* cowboy, shepherd
¹⁴歌 *bokka* pastoral song

A 物 3538 / J4a2a / M19959 BUTSU. MOTSU. *mono* thing, object, matter; somebody, something, success; reason. *mono no* about, nearly, a matter of. *mono(suru)* do, perform; write (poetry).
²力 *butsuryoku* the power of material things; the power of wealth
³乞 *monogoi* begging ⌈clothes
干 *monoho(shi)* a frame for drying
⁴心 *monogokoro* judgment, discretion. *busshin* matter and mind
分 *monowaka(ri)* understanding
busshoku suru look for; select
件 *bukken* thing, article ⌈whim
好 *monozu(ki)* curiosity, eccentricity,
⁷足 *monota(razu), monota(rinai)* unsatisfying; unsatisfactory; something missing
体 *buttai* body, solid, object, substance. *mottai* overemphasis
狂 *monoguru(i)* insanity; mad person (in plays). *monoguru(oshii), monoguru(shii), monoguru(washii)* crazy, wild, desperate

別 *monowaka(re)* rupture (of relations)

忘 *monowasu(re)* forgetfulness

売 *monou(ri)* peddler, vendor; peddling

言 *mono-i(u)* speak; talk. *mono-i(wazu)* saying nothing; a quiet person; a dumb person. *mono-i(i)* way of speaking; speech, language; dispute; objection

見高 *monomidaka(i)* burning with curiosity

見遊山 *monomi yusan* pleasure-seeking

見櫓 *monomi yagura* watchtower

8 怪 *mokke* something unexpected. *mono(no)ke* specter, evil spirit

知 *monoshi(razu)* ignorant person. *monoshi(ri)* extensive knowledge; well-informed person, scholar

事 *monogoto* things, matters

物交換 *butsubutsu-kōkan* barter

的 *butteki* material, physical

価 *bukka* prices

価指数 *bukka shisū* price index

9 音 *monooto* sound, noise

指 *monosashi* ruler, measure, yardstick

珍 *monomezu(rashii)* curious

故 *bukko suru* die; be dead

思 *monoomo(u)* worry; be buried in grief. *monoomo(i)* reverie, meditation; anxiety. *monoomo(washige) na* pensive, meditative

臭 *monogusa* laziness; idler. *monogusa(na), monogusa(i)* lazy

品 *buppin* goods, article, commodity

10 凄 *monosugo(i)* ghastly, lurid, weird; terrible, tremendous. *monosusama(jii)* dreadful, alarming

恥 *monohazuka(shii)* shy, bashful

陰 *monokage* cover, hiding

笑 *monowara(i)* laughingstock, joke

差 *monosa(shi)* ruler, measure, yardstick

真似 *monomane, monomanebi* imitating (sounds or gestures)

納 *butsunō* payment in kind

11 情 *butsujō* public feeling; state of affairs

惜 *monoo(shimi)* stinginess

淋 *monosabi(shii)* lonely, lonesome, dreary

欲 *butsuyoku* worldly desire

産 *bussan* produce, product

理 *butsuri* natural law; physics

理学 *butsurigaku* physics

12 量 *butsuryō* material resources

悲 *monogana(shii)* sad, plaintive, melancholy

覚 *monoobo(e)* memory

象 *busshō* an object; material phenomena ⌈demeanor

13 腰 *monogoshi* manner, bearing,

置 *monooki* storeroom

資 *busshi* commodities, resources

14 静 *monoshizu(kana)* quiet, still; serene

語 *monogatari* story, legend, romance, narrative. *monogata(ru)* tell, narrate

15 質 *busshitsu* matter, substance

18 騒 *bussō na* disturbed, troublous, unsettled, dangerous. *monosawaga(shii)* noisy, boisterous

20 議 *butsugi* public discussion, public criticism

--- 5 ---

性

B
3539
J4037
M19986

SEI. *ikenie, nie* sacrifice, offering, gift.

--- 6 ---

特

A
3541
J4643
M20013

TOKU special. *toku ni* especially, particularly.

3 大 *tokudai* oversize

上 *tokujō no* finest, highest grade

6 色 *tokushoku* characteristic, peculiarity, idiosyncrasy

有 *tokuyū* characteristic of, peculiar to

7 技 *tokugi* special skill, specialty

売 *tokubai* special sale

別 *tokubetsu* special, extraordinary

8 例 *tokurei* special case, exception

使 *tokushi* special envoy, special messenger

性 *tokusei* characteristic, peculiarity

典 *tokuten* special favor, privilege

長 *tokuchō* distinctive feature; strong point, forte, merit

効 *tokkō* special efficacy

命 *tokumei* special appointment

定 *tokutei suru* specify

価 *tokka* special price

9 級 *tokkyū* extra-special class or grade

点 *tokuten* special favor, privilege

心 忄 小 戈 戸 手 扌 支 攴 攵 文 斗 斤 方 无 日 曰 月 木 欠 止 歹 殳 毋 比 毛 氏 气 水 氵 氺 火 灬 爪 爫 父 爻 爿 丬 片 牙 牛 【犬 犭】

急 *tokkyū* limited express
約 *tokuyaku* special contract
待生 *tokutaisei* scholarship student
派 *tokuha suru* dispatch
派員 *tokuhain* delegate; special correspondent
¹⁰ 記 *tokki* special mention
殊 *tokushu na* special, characteristic, typical, individual, unique
¹¹ 設 *tokusetsu* special installation
赦 *tokusha* amnesty, special pardon
産 *tokusan* specialty, special product
異 *tokui* peculiar, unique
許 *tokkyo* patent, (company) charter, concession, license, special permission
許庁 *Tokkyochō* Patent Agency
¹² 筆 *tokuhitsu* special mention
集 *tokushū* special edition; special collection
¹⁴ 選 *tokusen* special selection; recognition; special make
徴 *tokuchō* distinctive feature
製 *tokusei* special make
¹⁵ 賞 *tokushō* special commendation; special reward
質 *tokushitsu* characteristic, special ⌐quality
権 *tokken* privilege, special rights, prerogative; (civil) liberties; chartered rights

---

7

牽 $\frac{3544}{\substack{J3823\\M20025}}$ KEN. *hi(ku)* vt draw, pull, haul, tug, jerk, drag, trail, bend, attract; lead (horses or captives); draw (lines); admit; install (utilities); quote, refer to; look up (words); subtract, reduce; apply, daub on; blunt (a sword); patronize; choose; catch (a cold). vi retreat, withdraw, retire; subside.
⁴ 引│ *ken'in suru* haul, tow, pull, drag
引車 *ken'insha* tractor
⁸ 制 *kensei* check, restraint, constraint; diversion, feint, screen
¹¹ 強付会 *kenkyō-fukai no* farfetched, distorted

8

犀 $\frac{3546}{\substack{J3a54\\M20045}}$ SAI rhinoceros.

13

犠 $\frac{3550}{\substack{J553e'\\M20190'}}$ GI sacrifice.
⁹ 牲 *gisei* (animal) sacrifice, offering; self-sacrifice

RAD. 犬 94

Inu dog. At left: 犭 (3 strokes) *kemono hen* left-hand "animal." Nickname: Dog.

犬 $\frac{3553}{\substack{J3824\\M20234}}$ KEN dog. *inu* dog; spy. A *inu(koro)* puppy.
³ 小屋 *inugoya* kennel
⁶ 死 *inuji(ni) suru* die a dog's death; die in vain
¹⁰ 釘 *inukugi* spike
¹² 歯 *kenshi* cuspid, eyetooth, canine tooth
¹³ 搔 *inukaki* dog paddle
²³ 鷲 *inuwashi* golden eagle

犯 $\frac{3554}{\substack{J4848\\M20238}}$ BON. HAN offense, crime; counter for criminal offenses. *oka(su)* commit, sin against; violate, break; defy, disregard; attack, assault; seduce, rape.
A
² 人 *hannin* criminal, offender
⁶ 行 *hankō* crime, offense
⁹ 則 *hansoku* transgression; default
¹³ 意 *han'i* criminal intent; malice
罪 *hanzai* crime, offense ⌐convict
罪者 *hanzaisha* offender, criminal,

2

3

状 3556 J3e75 M20257 Jō condition, circumstances; form, appearances; letter.

A

- [8] 況 *jōkyō* circumstances
- [10] 差 *jōsa(shi)* simple letter file, letter rack
- [13] 勢 *jōsei* state of affairs, condition, indication, appearance
- [14] 態 *jōtai* state of affairs, situation

———— 4 ————

狂 3562 J3638 M20287 Kyō lunatic. *kyō(suru)* go insane; be beside oneself with. *kuru(u)* go insane; lose one's head; run amuck, rave; be madly in love; go haywire, break down; be upset; warp; fluctuate; miss the mark; (winds) howl. *kuru(waseru), kuru(wakasu), kuru(wasu)* derange, dislocate; drive mad; upset, discomfit, disturb. *fu(reru)* go mad, be crazy. *kuru(i)* madness, insanity; confusion; warp; going wide of the mark; fluctuations. *kuruo(shi)* about crazy. *kuru(washii)* appearing to be crazy. -*kyō* maniac, enthusiast, fan.

B

- [2] 人 *kyōjin* lunatic, maniac
- [4] 犬病 *kyōkembyō* rabies
- [6] 死 *kyōshi, kuru(i)ji(ni)* death from madness
- 気 *kyōki* madness, insanity
- [7] 乱 *kyōran* fury, frenzy, madness
- 言 *kyōgen* play, drama; program; noh comedy; trick, make-believe
- [8] 的 *kyōteki* insane; frantic; fanatic
- 奔 *kyōhon suru* rush around, run wild; bestir oneself
- [9] 信 *kyōshin* fanaticism
- [12] 喜 *kyōki* wild joy, ecstasy
- [13] 想曲 *kyōsōkyoku* rhapsody
- [15] 暴 *kyōbō* rage, frenzy

———— 5 ————

狗 3565 J3669 M20345 Ku pup, dog.

- [6] 肉 *kuniku* dog flesh

狛 3566 J397d M20349 Haku lion-dog shrine guardians. *koma* part of ancient Korea.

- [4] 犬 *koma inu* lion-dog (stone) shrine guardians

狙 3567 J4140 M20347 So. *nera(u)* aim at, sight; watch for, shadow, stalk. *nera(i)* aim.

- [15] 撃 *neraiu(chi), sogeki* shooting, sniping

狐 3568 J3851 M20333 Ko. *kitsune* fox.

- [6] 色 *kitsune iro* tan, light brown
- [13] 嫁入 *kitsune (no) yomei(ri)* a line of will-o'-the-wisps; sudden shower during sunshine

———— 6 ————

狭 3572 J3639 M20406 Kyō. *seba(meru) vt* narrow, contract, reduce. *seba(maru) vi* narrow, become narrow, contract. *sema(i)* narrow, small (area), limited, tight. *sa-* honorary prefix.

B

- [3] 小 *kyōshō na* narrow, cramped; limited
- [4] 心症 *kyōshinshō* heart attack, angina pectoris
- [9] 軌 *kyōki* narrow gauge
- [10] 窄 *kyōsaku* constriction; strangulation
- [12] 間 *hazama* interval; interstice; ravine, glen; loophole (in a castle)
- 隘 *kyōai na* narrow, cramped; narrow-minded
- 量 *kyōryō* narrow-mindedness
- [13] 義 *kyōgi* narrow sense
- [19] 霧 *sagiri* light fog, mist, haze

狩 3573 J3c6d M20390 Shu. *ka(ru)* hunt. *ka(ri)* hunting; raiding; gathering (mushrooms); viewing (maples).

B

- [2] 人 *kariudo, karyūdo* hunter
- [4] 込 *ka(ri)ko(mi)* round-up, arrest
- [11] 猟 *shuryō* hunting

独 3574 J4648 M20406 Doku alone. *hitori, hitori(botchi)* alone, on one's own *hitori(deni)* of itself, spontaneously, automatically. -*Doku*-Germany.

A

- [2] 力 *dokuryoku* one's own effort
- [5] 白 *dokuhaku* monologue, soliloquy
- 占 *dokusen, hitoriji(me)* exclusive possession; monopoly; brushing everyone else aside

4

心 忄 小 戈 戸 手 扌 支 攵 文 斗 斤 方 无 日 曰 月 木 欠 止 歹 殳 母 比 毛 氏 气 水 氵 氺 火 灬 爪 爫 父 爻 爿 片 牙 牛 【犬 犭】

6 犭

立 *dokuritsu* independence, freedom; self-support; separation, isolation. *hitorida(chi)* standing alone, independence

6 自 *dokuji no* original, peculiar, characteristic; personal, individual

7 走 *dokusō* running alone; sailing alone (ships)

身 *dokushin, hitorimi* single life, celibacy

8 居 *dokkyo* solitude, solitary life

8 学 *dokugaku* self study

房 *dokubō* solitary cell

9 奏 *dokusō* instrumental solo

10 逸 *Doitsu* Germany

修 *dokushū* studying by oneself

特 *dokutoku* peculiarity, uniqueness

11 得 *dokutoku* peculiarity, uniqueness

唱 *dokushō* vocal solo

断 *dokudan* arbitrary decision; dogmatism

習 *dokushū* studying by oneself

12 善 *hitoriyo(gari), dokuzen* self-importance, self-conceit, self-complacency, self-gratification

創 *dokusō* originality, invention

裁 *dokusai* autocracy, dictatorship

13 禁法 *dokkinhō* antitrust law

楽 *koma* top

14 語 *dokugo* talking to oneself, monologue, soliloquy. *Dokugo* German language

演 *dokuen* solo recital; solo performance

16 壇場 *dokudanjō* one's unrivaled field, unchallenged position

───── 7 ─────

狽 <u>3576</u> <u>J4762</u> <u>M20433</u> Bai wolf; be flurried.

狸 <u>3578</u> <u>J432c</u> <u>M20427</u> Ri. *tanuki* badger; cunning person.

13 寝入 *tanuki ne-i(ri)* feigned sleep

狼 <u>3579</u> <u>J4f35</u> <u>M20432</u> Rō. *ōkami* wolf.

10 狽 *urota(eru)* get confused, lose one's head. *rōbai* consternation, dismay, panic

13 煙 *rōen, noroshi* signal fire, beacon, rocket

17 藉 *rōzeki* confusion, disorder, violence, riot

───── 8 ─────

猪 <u>3585</u> <u>J4376</u> <u>M20511'</u> Cho. *i, inoshishi, shishi* wild boar.

3 口 *choko, choku* saké cup

8 突 *chototsu* recklessness

猫 <u>3586</u> <u>J4f2d</u> <u>M20535</u> Byō. *neko* cat.
B

6 舌 *nekojita* aversion to hot food

9 背 *nekoze* stoop, round shoulders

10 被 *nekokaburi* hypocrisy, false modesty, feigned innocence; hypocrite; wolf in sheep's clothing

15 撫声 *nekonadegoe* coaxing voice, insinuating voice

17 糞 *nekobaba* embezzlement, misappropriation

猟 <u>3587</u> <u>J4e44</u> <u>M20512'</u> Ryō shooting, hunting;
B game, take, bag. *kari* hunting; raiding.

2 人 *kariudo, karyūdo, ryōjin* hunter, sportsman

4 犬 *ryōken, kari inu* hunting dog

6 色 *ryōshoku* lewdness, debauchery

8 官 *ryōkan* office-seeking

奇 *ryōki* hunting for the bizarre

10 師 *ryōshi* hunter

14 銃 *ryōjū* shotgun, hunting gun

猛 <u>3588</u> <u>J4c54</u> <u>M20498</u> Mō wildness, fierceness;
B strength. *take(ru)* become furious, rush, rage, rave. *take(ku), mō ni* valiantly, bravely, fiercely.

4 火 *mōka* raging flames; heavy gunfire

犬 *mōken* fierce dog

7 攻 *mōkō* fierce attack

8 毒 *mōdoku* deadly poison

者 *mosa* veteran; man of valor

9 威 *mōi* violence, fierceness

勇 *mōyū* bravery

省 *mōsei* serious reflection

10 進 *mōshin suru* dash forward, drive on

烈 *mōretsu na* violent, furious, fierce, keen (competition), intense, awful

訓練 *mōkunren* hard training
[11] 猛 *takedake(shii)* fierce, ferocious; audacious
[12] 然 *mōzen to* fiercely, resolutely, savagely
[13] 禽 *mōkin* bird of prey
[14] 練習 *mōrenshū* intensive practice
[16] 獣 *mōjū* fierce animal

———————— **9** ————————

猷 | 3590 / J4d32 / M20558 | YŪ measure; plan, scheme.

猶 | 3593 / J4d31 / M20557 | B YŪ. Yu. *nao* further, furthermore, still, still more, yet; just like.
[4] 予 *yūyo* postponement, grace, extension (of time); reprieve, stay; delay, slackness
予期間 *yūyo kikan* renewal period, period of grace, legal delay, cooling-off period

献 | 3596 / J3825 / M20539 | B KEN, KON counter for drinks. *sasa(geru), ken(jiru), ken(zuru), tatematsu(ru)* present, dedicate, offer.
[3] 上 *kenjō suru* present to
[5] 本 *kempon* presentation (copy)
立 *kondate* menu, program, schedule
[7] 言 *kengen* memorial, petition, proposal
呈 *kentei* presentation
身 *kenshin* devotion, dedication
身的 *kenshinteki* self-sacrificing, devoted
[8] 金 *kenkin* offering, donation, collection
[10] 納 *kennō* presentation, donation
[12] 策 *kensaku* suggestion, recommendation

———————— **10** ————————

獅 | 3599 / J3b62 / M20609 | SHI lion. *shishi* lion.

[3] 子 *shishi* lion
子奮迅 *shishi funjin* rushing ahead at full tilt

猿 | 3600 / J316e / M20584 | B EN monkey. *mashira* monkey. *saru* monkey, ape; mimic; sly person; door bolt; fastener.
[2] 人 *enjin* ape man
[5] 芝居 *saru shibai* monkey show
[8] 知恵 *sarujie* shallow cleverness
[10] 真似 *sarumane* indiscriminate imitation
[13] 楽 *sarugaku* noh-drama prototype
[22] 轡 *sarugutsuwa* (mouth) gag

———————— **11** ————————

獄 | 3602 / J3976 / M20603 | B GOKU prison, jail. *hitoya* prison, jail.
[4] 中 *gokuchū* in prison, imprisoned
[8] 舎 *gokusha* prison house, jail
[11] 窓 *gokusō* prison window; prison

———————— **12** ————————

獣 | 3606 / J3d43 / M20714 | B JŪ. *kedamono, kemono* animal, beast.
[6] 行 *jūkō* bestiality, assault (on a woman)
[7] 医 *jūi* veterinarian
医学 *jūigaku* veterinary science
[11] 欲 *jūyoku* carnal desire, lust, bestiality

———————— **13** ————————

獲 | 3609 / J334d / M20758 | B KAKU. *e(ru), u(ru)* get, acquire, find, earn, win, gain, receive; can, be able to, may; commit (sin).
[8] 物 *emono* game, bag, catch, spoils, prize, trophy, booty, prey
[11] 得 *kakutoku* acquisition, possession

5

〔玄〕玉王瓜瓦甘生用田疋疒癶白皮皿目矛矢石示ネ内禾穴立

5-STROKE RADICALS

■■■■■ RAD.  玄 95 ■■■■■

Gen blackness. Nickname: Dark (cf. Rad. 203).

玄 $\frac{3616}{\text{J383c}}$ $\overline{\text{M20814}}$ GEN occultness, mystery, black.

B

² 人 *kurōto* professional, expert; geisha, prostitute
⁶ 米 *gemmai* unpolished rice, whole-grained rice, brown rice
⁷ 妙 *gemmyō na* abstruse, occult, mysterious, miraculous
¹⁴ 関 *genkan* porch, entranceway, vestibule, front door
関払 *genkambara(i)* refusing a visitor saying no one is at home

─────── 6 ───────

率 $\frac{3618}{\text{J4e28}}$ $\overline{\text{M20817'}}$ SOTSU. RITSU rate, percentage; proportion; coefficient, factor; constant; index. *hiki(iru)* lead, spearhead (a group), command (troops).

A

⁶ 先 *sossen* taking the initiative
⁸ 直 *sotchoku* frankness, openheartedness
¹² 然 *sotsuzen* suddenly, unexpectedly

■■■■■ RAD. 玉 96 ■■■■■

Tama jewel. Variant: 王 (4 strokes) *ō* king. At left: 王 (4 strokes) *tama hen* or *ō hen*.
At bottom: 壬 (4 strokes). Nickname: Jewel.

王 $\frac{3619}{\text{J3226}}$ $\overline{\text{M20823}}$ Ō *kimi* king, rule, magnate, baron.

A

³ 女 *ōjo* princess
子 *ōji* prince
⁴ 手 *ōte* check, checkmate
⁵ 立 *ōritsu* royal
⁶ 妃 *ōhi* queen
⁷ 位 *ōi* the throne, the crown
⁸ 国 *ōkoku* kingdom, monarchy
者 *ōja, ōsha* king, ruler, monarch, sovereign; royalty
⁹ 候 *ōkō* princes, royalty, crowned heads
冠 *ōkan* crown, diadem; bottle cap
室 *ōshitsu* ruling family
¹⁰ 座 *ōza* throne; God's throne; championship
家 *ōke* royal family
宮 *ōkyū* royal palace
¹¹ 道 *ōdō* rule of right; principles of royalty
¹² 朝 *ōchō* dynasty

玉 $\frac{3620}{\text{J364c}}$ $\overline{\text{M20821}}$ GYOKU gem, jewel, precious stone, jade. *tama*

A

ball, bowl, sphere, bulb; lens; gem, jewel, bullet, shot, shell; billiards; tool, cat's-paw; pretty girl; person; margin (in stocks); testicles. *tama-* beautiful; round.

³ 子 *tamago* egg; spawn, roe; (an expert) in the making
⁴ 手箱 *tamatebako* Pandora's box; treasured casket
⁵ 石混淆 *gyokuseki-konkō* a mixture of good and bad
⁶ 虫色 *tamamushi iro* iridescence
⁸ 杯 *gyokuhai* jade cup
突 *tamatsu(ki)* billiards
⁹ 砕 *gyokusai* honorable death, honorable defeat
冠 *gyokukan* jeweled crown; beautiful crown, ceremonial crown
姿 *gyokushi* beautiful figure
砂利 *tamajari* pebbles, gravel
¹⁰ 座 *gyokuza* imperial throne, throne
¹² 葱 *tamanegi* onion
¹³ 蜀黍 *tōmorokoshi* corn, maize
¹⁵ 器 *gyokki* jeweled utensil

¹⁷ 輿 *tama (no) koshi* jeweled palanquin
¹⁹ 璽 *gyokuji* the seal of a sovereign
²¹ 露 *gyokuro* refined green tea

— 3 —

玖 | 3621 / J366a / M20846 | KYŪ. KU beautiful black gem; nine.

— 4 —

玩 | 3622 / J3461 / M20872 | GAN. *mochiaso(bu)*, *moteaso(bu)* play; take pleasure in; play (on an instrument); play with; make sport of; trifle with (affections).
⁷ 弄 *ganrō suru* make sport of, toy with, play with
⁸ 味 *gammi suru* taste, enjoy, appreciate
具 *gangu, omocha* toy

— 5 —

珂 | 3625 / J3251 / M20906 | KA jewel.

玲 | 3626 / J4e68 / M20888 | REI sound of jewels.

珊 | 3630 / J3b39 / M20917 | SAN stagger; loneliness. *senchi* centimeter.
¹³ 瑚 *sango* coral
瑚礁 *sangoshō* coral reef

珍 | 3631 / J4441 / M20920 | CHIN rare, curious, strange. *mezura(shigaru)* think (something is) strange. *mezura(shigatte)* out of curiosity. *mezura(shii)* new, novel, rare, strange, curious, unusual; nice (gift).
⁷ 妙 *chimmyō* queerness, oddity
⁸ 味 *chimmi* delicacy
奇 *chinki* novelty, curiosity
宝 *chimpō* valuables, treasure
事 *chinji* marvel, rare event
⁹ 重 *chinchō suru* prize, value highly
品 *chimpin* curio, rare article

— 6 —

班 | 3636 / J4849 / M20976 | HAN corps, unit, squad; party, companions, group; order.

珠 | 3637 / J3c6e / M20956 | SHU. JU. *tama* gem, jewel.
⁵ 玉 *shugyoku* gem, jewel, jewelry
¹³ 数 *juzu, zuzu* a string of beads; a (Buddhist) rosary
¹⁴ 算 *shuzan* abacus calculation

珪 | 3638 / J373e / M20972 | KEI jade tablet or scepter (as symbol of authority); silicon.

— 7 —

琢 | 3640 / J4276 / M-X | Nonstandard for 琢 3650.

琉 | 3642 / J4e30 / M20978 | RYŪ, RU lapis lazuli.
¹¹ 球 *Ryūkyū* the Ryukyu islands

球 | 3643 / J3565 / M21011 | KYŪ globe, sphere, ball; bulb; (radio) tube. *tama* ball, bowl, sphere, bulb.
孔 *kyūkō* golf-green cup
⁶ 団 *kyūdan* baseball team
⁷ 技 *kyūgi* any game where a ball is used
状 *kyūjō* globular shape
形 *kyūkei* globular form
⁹ 面 *kyūmen* spherical surface
¹⁰ 根 *kyūkon* tuber, bulb, rhizome
¹² 場 *kyūjō* baseball field, a ballpark

理 | 3644 / J4d7d / M21014 | RI reason, justice, truth, principle. *kotowari* reason.
⁴ 不尽 *rifujin na* unreasonable, unfair, absurd
化学 *rikagaku* physics and chemistry
⁵ 由 *riyū* reason, cause; pretext, excuse; consideration, motive
⁸ 屈 *rikutsu* theory; reason, logic; argument; pretext. *rikutsu(ppoi)* argumentative
念 *rinen* idea; ideology
性 *risei* reason, reasoning power
知 *richi* intellect, intelligence
事 *riji* director, trustee
事会 *rijikai* board of directors;
⁹ 科 *rika* science
¹⁰ 財 *rizai* economy, finance
容 *riyō* tonsorial art

¹³ 解 *rikai* understanding, comprehension; appreciation

路整然 *riro-seizen toshita* logical

想 *risō* ideal

¹⁴ 髪 *rihatsu* haircutting

髪店 *rihatsuten* barbershop

¹⁵ 論 *riron* theory

論的 *rironteki* theoretical; argumentative

A 現 3645 / J383d / M21004 GEN present, existing, actual. *gen(zu)* reveal; be revealed. *ara(wasu)* show, indicate, display, prove, disclose, express; represent; distinguish oneself. *ara(wareru)* appear, emerge, come in sight, show up; be revealed, be discovered; be mentioned; become famous. *gen ni* actually, really. *utsutsu* reality; reverie; ecstasy, absent-mindedness; vision. *ara(ware)* manifestation, expression. *ara(wa) ni* openly, publicly; frankly, clearly.

³ 下 *genka* the present time

⁴ 今 *genkon* the present time, today

⁵ 世 *gensei, gense, genze, utsu(shi)yo* present world, this life, this transient world

代 *gendai* present age, today, modern times

代語 *gendaigo* living language, present-day language

⁶ 存 *genson, genzon* living, existing, extant; the Real Presence

有 *gen'yū* existing, present, in actual possession

地 *genchi* the actual place. *genchi no* local

行 *genkō no* present, existing, current, in force, in operation

行犯 *genkōhan* flagrant crime, crime seen by a police officer

在 *genzai* the present time, now; present tense; actually; the Real Presence

在地 *genzaichi* place where one is now located

⁷ 状 *genjō* existing state of affairs, present situation, status quo

状維持 *genjō-iji* preserving the status quo

住所 *genjūsho* present address

役 *gen'eki* active service; commissioned (battleship)

⁸ 況 *genkyō* present condition

物 *gembutsu* the actual article

金 *genkin* cash, specie, money in hand, down payment. *genkin na* mercenary

実 *genjitsu* actuality, reality

実的 *genjitsuteki* realistic, materialistic, pragmatic, actual, real

⁹ 品 *gempin* the actual articles, stock on hand

¹² 象 *genshō* phenomenon, occurrence, appearance

場 *gemba, genjō* the scene, the spot. *gemba* the construction site

¹³ 業 *gengyō* outdoor service, field work

¹⁴ 像 *genzō* developing (a film)

¹⁸ 職 *genshoku* present position

———— 8 ————

琳 3646 / J4e56 / M21077 RIN a kind of jewel; blue jewel; ringing sound of gems when struck.

瑛 3647 / J314d / M21127 EI, YŌ jewel's sparkle; a kind of quartz.

琶 3649 / J474a / M21081 HA, BE lute.

琢 3650 / J-X / M21058 TAKU polish.

¹⁶ 磨 *takuma* diligent application

琵 3653 / J487c / M21080 BI glissando on strings; a lute.

¹² 琶 *biwa* lute

琵湖 *Biwako* Lake Biwa

B 琴 3654 / J3657 / M21079 GON, KIN harp. *koto* long horizontal Japanese harp, a koto; lyre. *kinnokoto* a seven-stringed koto.

¹⁵ 線 *kinsen* heartstrings

———— 9 ————

瑚 3662 / J386a / M21126 KO, GO ancestral-offering receptacle.

瑞 3665 J3f70 M21131 ZUI congratulations.
⁶ 兆 *zuichō* good omen
¹⁰ 祥 *zuishō* good omen
¹³ 瑞 *mizumizu(shii)* young and vivacious
¹⁵ 穂 *mizuho* young heads of rice
穂国 *Mizuho(no)kuni* Japan, the Land of Abundant Rice

——————— 10 ———————

瑳 3667 J3a3c M21170 SA polish.

璃 3669 J4d7e M21196 RI lapis lazuli.

瑠 3673 J4e5c M21143 RU lapis lazuli.

■ RAD. 瓜 97 ■
Uri melon. Nickname: Melon.

瓜 3686 J313b M21371 KA. *uri* melon.

——————— 11 ———————

瓢 3688 J493b M21419 BYŌ. HYŌ *hisago* gourd.

———————

¹⁴ 璃 *ruri* lapis lazuli

——————— 13 ———————

環 3680 J3444 M-X KAN ring. *wa* circle, ring, B link, wheel, hoop, loop. *tamaki* circle, ring.
⁷ 状 *kanjō* ring, loop, circle
状線 *kanjōsen* loop line, belt line
¹¹ 視 *kanshi* concentrated attention
¹⁴ 境 *kankyō* environment, circumstances

——————— 14 ———————

璽 3683 J3c25 M21309 JI emperor's seal.
B

———————

¹⁸ 箪 *hyōtan* gourd, bottle gourd

——————— 14 ———————

瓣 3689 J6122 M21425 See 弁 1664.

■ RAD. 瓦 98 ■
Kawara tile. As enclosure: 瓦. Nickname: Tile.

瓦 3690 J3424 M21438 GA. *kawara* tile. *guramu* gram.
⁸ 版 *kawaraban* printing from impressions on baked tiles
⁹ 屋根 *kawara yane* tiled roof
¹² 斯 *gasu* gas
¹³ 解 *gakai* collapse, overthrow, fall, breakdown
²⁰ 礫 *gareki* rubble; rubbish

——————— 6 ———————

瓶 3699 J4953 M21486 HEI, BIN bottle, vial, B jar, flask. *kame* jar, jug, vat, urn, vase.
¹³ 詰 *binzume* bottling; canning in jars

——————— 11 ———————

甑 3706 J3979 M-X SŌ *koshiki* pottery rice steamer.

玄玉王瓜【瓦】¹¹ 甘生用田疋疒癶白皮皿目矛矢石示礻内禾穴立

5

玄玉王瓜瓦〔甘〕生用田疋疒癶白皮皿目矛矢石示礻禸禾穴立

RAD. 甘 99

Amai sweet. Nickname: Sweet.

B 甘 3710 J3445 M21643 KAN. *ama(eru)*, *ama(ttareru)* presume upon, take advantage of; coax. *ama(nzuru)*, *ama(njiru)* be content with, be resigned to. *ama(yakasu)* pamper, be indulgent, coddle. *ama(i)* sweet; honeyed (words); lenient; half-witted; easy-going; soft, mild; loose; trashy, sentimental. *ama(ttarui)* sugary, sentimental. *uma(i)* delicious, appetizing; skillful, clever, expert; wise; successful; fortunate; splendid; promising. *ama-* sugared, sweet; slightly salted.

³ 口 *amakuchi* sweet flavor; mildness; sweet tooth; flattery; stupidity. *umakuchi* clever talking

⁴ 心 *kanshin* satisfaction

⁷ 言 *kangen* flattery, blarney

⁸ 受 *kanju suru* submit to, put up with

苦 *kanku* joys and sorrows, ups and downs

味 *kammi, amami* sweetness, lusciousness

⁹ 美 *kambi* sweetness

草 *kanzō* licorice

¹⁰ 酒 *amazake* sweet saké

党 *amatō* person with a sweet tooth

栗 *amaguri* broiled sweet chestnuts

納豆 *amanattō* sweet red-bean candy

¹⁴ 蔗 *kansho, kansha, satōkibi* sugar cane

²¹ 露 *kanro* nectar, sweetness

——— 4 ———

B 甚 3711 J3f53 M21648 JIN exceedingly. *hanaha(da)* very, greatly, exceedingly. *hanaha(dashii)* extreme, excessive, intense, severe, serious, terrible, tremendous, heavy (damage). *ita(ku)* exceedingly.

³ 大 *jindai na* very great, enormous; serious

⁵ 句 *jinku* lively song; lively dance

——— 6 ———

甜 3712 J453c M21656 TEN sweet.

RAD. 生 100

Umareru to be born. Nickname: Birth.

A 生 3715 J4038 M21670 SHŌ, SEI birth; life, existence, living; subsistence; student. *ha(eru)* grow, spring up; cut (teeth). *ha(yasu)* grow, cultivate, wear (a beard). *i(kasu)* revive, resuscitate; restore to life; let live, spare a life; make the most of; give life to; stet. *i(keru)* keep alive; arrange flowers (in a vase); living (adj.). *i(kiru)* live, subsist, exist; be enlivened; stet; be safe (on first). *na(rasu)* cause to bear (fruit). *na(ru)* grow (on a plant), bear (fruit). *na(su)* bear (a child). *o(u)* grow. *shō(jiru)*, *shō(zuru)* produce, yield, create, give rise to, bear, breed; happen, result from.

u(mareru) be born. *u(mu)* bear, give birth to, breed, spawn; produce, yield (interest). *nama* raw, uncooked, fresh; unripe; half-boiled; rare; hard cash; impertinent, conceited; inexperienced; (beer) on tap; crude (rubber), unprocessed. *i(ki)* living; freshness; stetting. *u(mare)* birth, origin, lineage; birthplace. *u(mi)* childbirth, bearing a child. *-fu* grassy place; woods. *ki-* pure, undiluted, genuine; raw, crude.

¹ 一本 *kiippon no* pure, unadulterated; simple, honest

⁴ 方 *i(ki)kata* way of life, how to live

化学 *seikagaku* biochemistry

⁵母 *seibo* one's real mother

生 *seisei* lively, vividly. *namanama(shii)* green, raw, fresh; unripe; still warm (game birds, etc.); reeking (of blood). *i(ki)i(ki) toshita* lively, vivid, graphic

付 *u(mare)-tsu(ku)* be endowed with. *u(mi)-tsu(keru)* give birth to, lay, deposit, spawn. *u(maremo)tsu(kanu)* not congenital. *u(mare)tsu(kī)* nature, character, disposition; by nature, naturally

写 *i(ki)utsu(shi), shōutsu(shi)* close resemblance

半可 *namahanka na* superficial, half-baked

甲斐 *i(ki)gai* (something) worth living (for)

⁶糸 *kiito* raw silk thread

色 *seishoku* animated look, energetic appearance

気 *seiki* animation, life, spirit, vitality

字引 *i(ki) jibiki* walking dictionary, living dictionary

地 *seichi* birthplace. *kiji* one's true colors; ground; body (of porcelain); cloth, suiting

年 *u(mare)doshi, seinen* year of birth; age. *shōnen* the years of one's life, age.

年月日 *seinengappi* date of birth

死 *seishi, i(ki)shi(ni), shōshi, shōji* life or death, life and death

存 *i(ki)-naga(raeru)* live on, enjoy longevity; survive (a disaster); outlive (someone). *seizon* existence, being, life, survival

存中 *seizonchū* during one's lifetime

存者 *seizonsha* survivor

存競争 *seizon kyōsō* struggle for existence

⁷身 *i(ki)mi, namami* living flesh, flesh and blood, the quick; raw meat, raw fish

花 *i(ke)bana* flower arrangement. *seika* flower arrangement; natural flower

来 *shōrai no, seirai no* natural, innate, inborn. *seirai* by nature, naturally, by birth

体 *seitai* living body

⁸易 *namayasa(shii)* easy, simple

茂 *o(i)-shi(geru)* grow luxuriantly

命 *seimei* life; soul

命工学 *seimei kōgaku* biotechnology

命保険 *seimei hoken* life insurance

命線 *seimeisen* lifeline

物 *i(ki)mono, seibutsu* living creature, life. *na(ri)mono* farm products. *namamono* uncooked food, raw fish, unbaked pastry

物学 *seibutsugaku* biology

物界 *seibutsukai* plants and animals, animate creation, life

物兵器 *seibutsu heiki* biological weapon

⁹保 *seiho* life insurance

後 *seigo* after birth

前 *seizen* during one's lifetime; lifetime

計 *seikei* livelihood, living

臭 *namagusa(i)* smelling of fish; bloody

活 *seikatsu* life, livelihood

活水準 *seikatsu suijun* standard of living

活費 *seikatsuhi* living expenses

活様式 *seikatsu yōshiki* mode of living

¹⁰起 *seiki* occurrence of phenomena

娘 *kimusume* maiden, virgin, innocent girl

徒 *seito* student, pupil

粋 *kissui* purity

家 *seika* the house of one's birth

真面目 *kimajime* too serious; a person who is too serious; honesty, sincerity

残 *i(ki)-noko(ru)* survive, outlive. *i(ki)noko(ri), seizon* survival

殺与奪 *seisatsu-yodatsu* killing and letting live; giving and taking away

息 *seisoku suru* live, subsist; multiply

¹¹得 *seitoku, shōtoku* nature; naturally; capturing alive. *shōtoku no* natural, inborn, inherent, congenital

涯 *shōgai* life, career, lifetime; for life

彩 *seisai* beautiful light, luster

理 *seiri* physiology, menstruation

理学 *seirigaku* physiology

理的 *seiriteki* physiological

産 *seisan* production

産力 *seisanryoku* productive capacity, productivity

産地 *seisanchi* producing area

産物 *seisambutsu* produce, product

産高 *seisandaka* yield, production, output ⌈mild

¹²温 *namanuru(i)* lukewarm; half-hearted;

5

玄
玉
王
瓜
瓦
甘
生
[用]
田
疋
扩
癶
白
皮
皿
目
矛
矢
石
示
礻
禸
禾
穴
立

殖 *seishoku* reproduction, procreation, generation
¹³ 暖 *namaatataka(i)* lukewarm
業 *seigyō, sugiwai, nariwai* occupation, calling, living, livelihood
意気 *namaiki* conceit, impertinence
¹⁴ 憎 *ainiku, ayaniku* unfortunately, unluckily; too bad, a pity
態 *seitai* mode of life, ecology
態系 *seitaikei* ecosystem
態学 *seitaigaku* ecology
¹⁵ 誕 *seitan* birth, nativity
蕎麦 *kisoba* buckwheat noodles
還 *seikan* returning alive; scoring a run
¹⁷ 鮮 *seisen na* fresh
¹⁸ 類 *shōrui, seirui* living creatures

───────── 6 ─────────

A 産 ³⁷¹⁶ J3b3a M21684' SAN childbirth; product; native (of a place); fortune, property. *san(suru)* vi and vt produce, yield, bring up, bear (a child); appear; be born; be brought up. *u(mu)* bear, give birth to, breed, spawn; produce, yield (interest). *u(mareru)* be born. *u(mi)* childbirth, bearing a child.
⁵ 出 *sanshutsu* output, yield, production
出高 *sanshutsudaka* output, yield,

production
⁶ 米 *sammai* the rice production
地 *sanchi* producing area
気付 *sankezu(ki)* premonition of labor pains
⁷ 別 *sambetsu* industrial union
声 *ubugoe* baby's first cry
児制限 *sanji seigen* birth control
卵 *sanran* egg-laying, spawning
⁸ 物 *sambutsu* product, production, produce; result
⁹ 後 *sango* after childbirth
院 *san'in* maternity hospital
前 *sanzen* before delivery (of the baby)
前産後 *sanzen-sango* before and after childbirth
科 *sanka* obstetrics
科医 *sankai* obstetrician
¹¹ 婦 *sampu* woman in childbirth
婦人科 *sanfujinka* obstetrics and gynecology
婆 *samba* midwife
¹³ 業 *sangyō* industry
¹⁵ 褥 *sanjoku* confinement; labor bed
¹⁸ 額 *sangaku* production, yield, output

───────── 7 ─────────

甥 ³⁷¹⁹ J3179 M21689 SEI. Sō . *oi* nephew.

■■■■■■■■■ RAD. 用 101 ■■■■■■■■■
Mochiiru to use. Nickname: Using.

A 用 ³⁷²¹ J4d51 M21703 YŌ business, work; function; errand; engagement; use, service; expenses; call of nature. *yō(zuru), mochi(iru)* use; adopt (a method); employ. *-yō* for, used for.
² 人 *yōnin* steward, factotum
⁴ 心 *yōjin* care, caution, discretion
心深 *yōjimbuka(i)* careful, thoughtful, cautious, scrupulous, alert
心棒 *yōjimbō* cudgel; bodyguard, protector

水 *yōsui* city water; water for fire; irrigation water; cistern water
水路 *yōsuiro* flume; water system
⁵ 立 *yōda(teru)* lend, advance (money). *yōda(te)* accommodation (in business). *yō (ni) ta(tsu)* be useful
⁶ 件 *yōken* business, matter, items
⁷ 言 *yōgen* declinable word
足 *yōta(shi)* performing an errand; taking care of nature's call
兵 *yōhei* tactics, troop manipulation
材 *yōzai* materials; lumber, timber

⁸ 例 *yōrei* example, illustration

法 *yōhō* directions, how to use

命 *yōmei* command, order, request

事 *yōji* errand, business, appointment

具 *yōgu* tool, instrument; machinery; apparatus; utensils; appliances; (sporting) goods; (teaching) aids

⁹ 度 *yōdo* expenses; supplies

途 *yōto* use, service

品 *yōhin* supplies

便 *yōben* defecation ⌈paper

¹⁰ 紙 *yōshi* blank form; stationery, writing

¹¹ 務員 *yōmuin* clerks

¹² 量 *yōryō* dosage, dose

¹³ 意 *yōi* preparation, arrangement

意周到 *yōi-shūtō* prudence, cautiousness, thorough preparation

¹⁴ 聞 *yōki(ki)* taking orders

箋 *yōsen* form, blank, stationery, writing pad

語 *yōgo* term, terminology, vocabulary, diction

¹⁵ 談 *yōdan* business talk

器 *yōki* tool, instrument; chamber pot; using tools

───────── 2 ─────────

甫 [3722] [J4a63] [M21706] HO. FU. *haji(mete)* for the first time; not until.

━━━━━ RAD. 田 102 ━━━━━

Ta rice paddy. At left: *ta hen.* Nickname: Rice Field.

A 由 [3724] [J4d33] [M21724] YU, YU. *yo(ru)* depend on. *yoshi* reason, cause, significance; means, way; effect; point; intent. *yo(tte)* therefore, consequently.

⁵ 由 *yuyu(shii)* grave, serious, alarming

⁷ 来 *yurai suru* derive from, originate in. *yurai* reason; origin, destiny; history; derivation, source; originally, naturally

¹⁴ 緒 *yuisho* history, lineage

¹⁵ 縁 *yuen* acquaintance; relation; affinity; reason

B 甲 [3725] [J3943] [M21725] KAN high (voice). Kō A, first class; former; back (of the hand); instep; armor; shell, tortoise shell, carapace. *kōra* shell (of turtle or crab). *yoroi* suit of armor. *kinoe* first calendar sign.

¹ 乙 *kōotsu* A and B, excellent and good; discrimination

⁶ 虫 *kōchū, kabutomushi* a beetle

⁷ 状腺 *kōjōsen* thyroid gland

⁹ 冑 *katchū, kōchū* armor and helmet

¹⁰ 高 *kōdaka na* high-backed; high in the instep. *kandaka(i)* shrill, high-pitched

¹² 斐 *kai* effect, result; use, avail, worth

斐性 *kaishō* resourcefulness, ability

¹⁴ 種 *kōshu* grade A, first grade

¹⁵ 論乙駁 *kōron-otsubaku* pros and cons

¹⁹ 羅 *kōra* shell, carapace

A 申 [3726] [J3f3d] [M21726] SHIN. *mō(su)* have the honor to; say, tell, talk, speak, declare; call, term, name. *saru* 3–5 p.m; ninth zodiac sign; monkey.

² 入 *mō(shi)-i(reru)* propose, suggest. *mō(shi)i(re)* proposal, offer; notice, report

³ 上 *mō(shi)-a(geru)* say, tell, state (humble)

⁴ 込 *mō(shi)-ko(mu)* propose (marriage); offer (mediation); make an overture (of peace); challenge; lodge (objections); request (an interview); apply for (a job); subscribe for; book, reserve. *mōshiko(mi)* proposal, offer, overture; challenge

込書 *mōshikomisho* application blank; written application

⁵ 立 *mō(shi)ta(teru)* declare; plead

付 *mō(shi)-tsu(keru)* order, instruct

出 *mō(shi)-de(ru)* report to, tell; suggest; submit; request. *mō(shi)-i(de), mōshide* proposal; request, claim; report, notice

⁶ 合 *mō(shi)-a(waseru)* arrange; appoint; agree upon

5

玄玉王瓜瓦甘生用〔田〕疋疒癶白皮皿目矛矢石示礻内禾穴立

---

⁷ 述 *mō(shi)-no(beru)* say, tell, state
告 *shinkoku* report, statement, notification; filing a return
⁸ 送 *mō(shi)-oku(ru)* write to; send word to; hand over (official business)
受 *mō(shi)-u(keru)* accept; ask for; charge (a price)
¹¹ 添 *mō(shi)-so(eru)* add to what has been said.
訳 *mō(shi)wake* excuse, apology
¹² 越 *mō(shi)-ko(su)* send word to, write to
開 *mō(shi)-hira(ku)* explain, justify
渡 *mō(shi)-wata(su)* tell, announce, declare, order
¹⁵ 請 *shinsei* application, petition
請書 *shinseisho* written application

田 $\frac{3727}{\text{J4544}}$ M21723 DEN *ta* rice field, paddy field.

A

⁶ 虫 *tamushi* ringworm
地 *denchi, denji* land, farm, rice fields
⁸ 舎 *inaka* the country, the provinces, rural areas. *inaka(meku)* wear a rustic air
舎者 *inakamono* a rustic
⁹ 畑 *tahata, dempata, tahatake* fields and rice paddies
¹⁰ 圃 *tambo* rice field
¹¹ 野 *den'ya* cultivated fields
¹² 植 *taue* rice transplanting
楽 *dengaku* ancient music and dancing; tofu baked with miso
園 *den'en* fields and gardens; rural districts

--- 2 ---

町 $\frac{3729}{\text{J442e}}$ M21735 CHŌ town; block; street; 2.45 acres; 119 yards. *machi* town; quarters; street.

A

² 人 *chōnin* merchant
⁴ 内 *chōnai* in the town; in the block; the neighborhood
民 *chōmin* townspeople
⁶ 会 *chōkai* town council, town-block association
⁷ 角 *machikado* street corner
役場 *machi yakuba* town office
⁸ 長 *chōchō* town mayor
並 *machina(mi)* row of houses along the street
歩 *chōbu* hectare (2.45 acres)
²⁰ 議 *chōgi* town councilmember

男 $\frac{3731}{\text{J434b}}$ M21730 DAN baron; man, male. NAN counter for sons. *otoko, onoko* man; male; fellow; adult; manhood; male servant; paramour. *otoko(rashii)* manly, manful. *otoko(datera) ni* unmanly.

A

³ 子 *danshi* man, male, boy, son. *o(no)ko, otoko (no) ko* boy, boy baby, son
女 *danjo, nannyo* men and women, both sexes. *otoko-onna* hermaphrodite
女共学 *danjo kyōgaku* coeducation
女合唱 *danjo gasshō* mixed chorus
女同権 *danjo dōken* equality of the sexes
⁶ 色 *danshoku, nanshoku, okama* sodomy, male homosexual
児 *danji* boy, son ⌐manliness
⁸ 性 *dansei* male, male sex; masculinity,
性的 *danseiteki* manly
前 *otokomae* man's looks; good bearing
¹⁰ 根 *dankon, nankon* penis; phallus
¹² 装 *dansō* male attire
尊女卑 *danson-johi* subjection of women
¹⁶ 親 *otoko oya* father
¹⁷ 優 *dan'yū* actor
爵 *danshaku* baron

--- 3 ---

画 $\frac{3733}{\text{J3268}}$ M21739 GA, E picture, drawing, painting, sketch. KAKU stroke (in a character). *kaku(suru)* draw, demarcate, mark, divide, map out. *ega(ku)* draw, paint, sketch, describe.

A

¹ 一 *kakuitsu* uniformity, standardization
一主義 *kakuitsu shugi* standardization
² 人 *gajin* painter, artist
³ 才 *gasai* artistic talent
⁵ 布 *gafu* canvas for oil painting
用紙 *gayōshi* drawing paper
⁶ 匠 *gashō* painter, artist
⁷ 伯 *gahaku* artist, master painter
⁸ 板 *gaban* drawing board, drafting board
法 *gahō* art of drawing and painting
⁹ 面 *gamen* scene, picture, the screen (in TV); photo
風 *gafū* style of painting
架 *gaka* easel
¹⁰ 家 *gaka* painter, artist
竜点睛 *garyō-tensei* adding the eyes to the dragon; the finishing touch

¹¹ 廊 *garō* picture gallery
商 *gashō* picture dealer
¹² 策 *kakusaku suru* plan, scheme, formulate a program, maneuver
報 *gahō* illustrated news magazine, pictorial
期的 *kakkiteki* epoch-making
¹⁴ 像 *gazō* portrait, picture
¹⁵ 鋲 *gabyō* thumbtack, drawing pin
¹⁶ 壇 *gadan* artists' world, painting circles
¹⁸ 題 *gadai* subject of a painting, motif, theme

──────── **4** ────────

界 3739 J3326 M21775 | **堺** 1045 J3a66 M5289 | KAI circle, world, boundary, limits. *sakai* boundary, border, frontier; place.
A
¹¹ 隈 *kaiwai* neighborhood; district

畑 3741 J482a M21797 (国字) *hata, hatake* field, farm, plantation, garden; one's specialty.
A
⁶ 地 *hatachi* farmland
⁷ 作 *hatasaku* upland farming

畏 3742 J305a M21778 I. *oso(reru)* fear, be overawed, be appehensive. *kashiko(mu)* fear. *kashiko(maru)* obey respectfully; sit respectfully. *kashiko(i)* august, majestic. *kashiko(kumo)* graciously.
⁸ 怖 *ifu* awe, fear, fright

──────── **5** ────────

畔 3746 J484a M21801 HAN. *aze, kuro* rice-paddy ridge, levee.
B

畠 3747 J482b M21827 (国字) *hatake, hata* garden, field, farm, plantation.

畝 3748 J4026 M21815 BŌ. Ho ridge, furrow, rib (in cloth). *se* thirty *tsubo*. *une* ridge (in a field), furrow, rib or cord (in cloth). *u(neru)* undulate, meander, surge, swell, roll.
B

畜 3749 J435c M21814 CHIKU domesticated fowl and animals.
B

⁵ 生 *chikushō* beast, brute; angry exclamation of disgust
¹¹ 産 *chikusan* animal husbandry

留 3750 J4e31 M21808 RYŪ. RU. *to(maru)* stop, halt, stand still, pull up; cease, be interrupted, be discontinued; be choked; alight on, perch, roost; be held in position. *to(meru)* stop; check; allay (pain); fasten; turn off; detain; forbid to do; dissuade. *todo(maru)* stop, halt, stay, remain, stay behind; be limited to. *todo(meru)* stop, cease, detain, put an end to; leave; fix; remain in (a certain condition); content oneself with. *to(me)* stopping; prohibition; end; a stop.
A
⁶ 任 *ryūnin* remaining in office
年 *ryūnen suru* (student) stay back a year, be held back a year
守 *rusu* absence, being away from home; watching a house; neglecting (responsibilities)
守番 *rusuban* caretaker; watching a house
守番電話 *rusuban denwa* a telephone answering machine
⁸ 学 *ryūgaku* studying abroad
学生 *ryūgakusei* overseas student
⁹ 保 *ryūho* reserving, withholding, saving, protection
¹³ 意 *ryūi* attention, heed, consideration
置 *to(me)-o(ku)* lock up, detain, retain; leave till called for, quarantine. *ryūchi* detention, custody, retention
置場 *ryūchijō* house of detention; police cell; guardhouse

──────── **6** ────────

畢 3754 J492d M21829 HITSU. *owa(ru)* end, terminate, adjourn, be over, die, finish, complete. *owa(ri)* end, conclusion, expiration.
¹¹ 竟 *hikkyō* after all, in short, virtually

略 3755 J4e2c M21839 RYAKU abbreviation, abridgment; omission; outline. *ryaku(su), ryaku(suru)* abridge, omit, shorten, abbreviate; capture, seize, plunder. *hobo* almost, nearly.
A
⁵ 史 *ryakushi* brief history
⁶ 式 *ryakushiki* informality

5

玄玉王瓜甘生用〔田〕⁶疋疒癶白皮皿目矛矢石示礻内禾穴立

玄玉王瓜瓦甘生用［田］正疒癶白皮皿目矛矢石示礻内禾穴立

5

字 *ryakuji* simplified characters; abbreviation

名 *ryakumei* initials; initialing

⁷図 *ryakuzu* outline map; rough plan

⁸画 *ryakuga* rough sketch

¹⁰称 *ryakushō* abbreviation; abbreviated name

¹⁴歴 *ryakureki* brief personal history, brief biography

語 *ryakugo* abbreviation

奪 *ryakudatsu* pillage, plunder, looting, depredation

異 $\frac{3757}{\text{J305b}}$ M21854 A I uncommonness, strangeness, queerness; difference. *i na* strange, wonderful, curious. *koto(naru)* differ, vary; be unusual. *koto (ni) suru* differ, vary.

²人 *ijin* foreigner; different person

³才 *isai* genius, prodigy

口同音 *ikudōon ni* with one accord, by common consent, unanimously

⁴心 *ishin* treachery, intrigue

分子 *ibunshi* alien elements, outsider

⁶色 *ishoku* different color; novelty

存 *izon* objection

同 *idō* difference

邦人 *ihōjin* foreigner, stranger, gentile

⁷見 *iken* different opinion; objection

状 *ijō* something wrong, accident, change, abnormality

体 *itai* different shape or form; a nonstandard character form

⁸例 *irei* exception; illness

性 *isei* the opposite sex   ⌐body

物 *ibutsu* foreign substance, foreign

国 *ikoku, kotokuni* foreign country. *ikoku no* foreign

⁹変 *ihen* accident, disaster

臭 *ishū* offensive smell

¹¹動 *idō* change, shifting

彩 *isai* conspicuous color. *isai(aru)* conspicuous, brilliant, resplendent

教徒 *ikyōto* heathen, pagans, heretics

常 *ijō* anything unusual; abnormality

¹⁴聞 *ibun* another story; a strange tale

境 *ikyō* foreign country

様 *iyō na* strange, quaint, outlandish

種 *ishu* different kind, different species; variety

端 *itan* heresy

¹⁵論 *iron* different opinion; objection

質 *ishitsu* heterogeneity

¹⁸類 *irui* varieties, different kinds

²⁰議 *igi* objection, protest

7

番 $\frac{3762}{\text{J4856}}$ M21858 A BAN watch, guard; duty; number; order; size, game, round, turn, bout. *ban(suru)* keep watch, guard. *tsuga(u)* pair, mate, join, copulate. *tsuga(eru)* mate; pair; notch (an arrow); exchange (promises). *tsugai* pair, couple, brace (of ducks); joint.

²人 *bannin* watchman, guard; caretaker, janitor

⁴犬 *banken* watchdog

⁵付 *banzuke* graded list; program

号 *bangō* number

外 *bangai* outside; extra

⁶地 *banchi* number

⁷狂 *bankuru(wase)* program change; upset; surprise

兵 *bampei* sentry, guard, sentinel

⁹茶 *bancha* coarse tea

¹¹組 *bangumi* program

¹²傘 *bangasa* coarse oilpaper umbrella

¹⁶頭 *bantō* clerk, secretary, attendant; steward, manager

畳 $\frac{3763}{\text{J3e76}}$ M21875´ B CHŌ. JŌ mat counter. *tata(mu)* fold, fold up, furl, shut up, shut; wind up (affairs); do away with, kill; bear in mind. *tata(maru)* be folded (up). *tatami* straw mat, straw matting. *tata(mi)-* folding, collapsible.

²入 *tata(mi)-i(reru)* fold up, fold in

³上 *tata(mi)-a(geru)* fold up

⁴込 *tata(mi)-ko(mu)* fold in; fold up; bear in mind   ⌐maker

⁹屋 *tatamiya* straw mat dealer, straw mat

8

畷 $\frac{3766}{\text{J466d}}$ M21892 TETSU. TEI. SEI. *nawate* rice-field ridge path.

10

畿 $\frac{3768}{\text{J3526}}$ M21925 KI capital; capital suburbs.

⁴内 *Kinai* the Five Capital Provinces around Kyoto

■■■ RAD. 疋 103 ■■■

Hiki (counter for animals). At left: ⻊ *hiki hen*. Nickname: Animal Counter.

疋 $\frac{3774}{\substack{J4925 \\ M21994}}$ HITSU. *hiki* head (animal counter); roll of cloth.

────── **7** ──────

NOTE: Characters 3775 and 3776 are sometimes used interchangeably. It is therefore necessary to look under both for definitions and compounds.

疏 $\frac{3775}{\substack{J4141 \\ M22000}}$ So estrangement; sparseness; neglect. (See note above.)

疎 $\frac{3776}{\substack{J4142 \\ M22002}}$ So rough; sparseness;
B uto(mu), uto(njiru), uto(nzuru) neglect, alienate. maba(ra) na sparse, thin (hair); scattered, sporadic, straggling (village). oro(ka) making light of; ...to say nothing of ... oroso(ka) na negligent, careless. uto(i) distant, estranged; disinterested, ignorant of. uto(mashii) disagreeable. (See note above.)

⁴ 水 *sosui* drainage; canal
⁵ 外 *sogai* estrangement, indifference, neglect
⁸ 放 *sohō* carelessness, fault, oversight
⁹ 通 *sotsū* drainage; mutual understanding
¹¹ 略 *soryaku na* crude, rough, plain, humble, shabby; careless, rude
密 *somitsu* sparseness and luxuriant growth
¹² 遠 *soen* estrangement, neglect (to write), long silence
隔 *sokaku* alienation, estrangement
開 *sokai* dispersal, evacuation, deployment
¹⁴ 漏 *sorō* carelessness, negligence
雑 *sozatsu na* coarse, rough, crude

────── **9** ──────

疑 $\frac{3777}{\substack{J353f \\ M22007}}$ GI. *utaga(u), utagu(ru)*
A doubt; distrust; be suspicious of. *utaga(i), utagu(ri)* doubt, question, uncertainty, skepticism; suspicion; distrust. *utaga(washii)* doubtful, questionable, uncertain, disputable; suspicious.
⁴ 心 *gishin* doubt, suspicion, fear, apprehension
⁶ 似 *giji-* suspected, quasi-, pseudo-, sham
⁸ 念 *ginen* doubt, suspicion, misgivings, scruples
¹¹ 問 *gimon* question, problem, doubt
問文 *gimombun* interrogative sentence
¹² 惑 *giwaku* doubt, misgivings, distrust, suspicion
¹³ 義 *gigi* doubt
¹⁴ 獄 *gigoku* scandal, graft case

■■■ RAD. 疒 104 ■■■

Yamaidare trailing "sickness." Nickname: Sick.

────── **4** ──────

疫 $\frac{3783}{\substack{J3156 \\ M22069}}$ YAKU, EKI epidemic.
B
¹⁰ 病 *ekibyō, yakubyō* pestilence, plague, epidemic

────── **5** ──────

疹 $\frac{3788}{\substack{J3f3e \\ M22097}}$ SHIN, CHIN measles; sickness

症 $\frac{3795}{\substack{J3e49 \\ M22140}}$ SHŌ illness; condition of a
B patient; nature of a disease, symptoms.
⁷ 状 *shōjō* symptoms; condition of the illness
⁸ 例 *shōrei* a case (a patient)

5

[10] 候 *shōkō* symptoms

疲 $\frac{3796}{J4868}$ M22084 B Hɪ. *tsuka(reru)* get tired, grow weary. *tsuka(rakasu), · tsuka(rasu)* tire (a horse), weary (one's mind), exhaust (one's energy).

[4] 切 *tsuka(re)-ki(ru)* be tired out
[7] 労 *hirō* fatigue
[8] 果 *tsuka(re)-ha(teru)* be tired out
[15] 弊 *hihei* impoverishment, exhaustion

疾 $\frac{3797}{J3c40}$ M22112 B Sнɪтsu illness, disease. *to(kku)* fast, swiftly; early. *to(kku) kara* since long ago. *to(u) ni, to(kku) ni* long ago; already. *to(u) kara* for a long time. *haya(i)* fast. *yama(shii)* ashamed, painful, having a guilty conscience, sickly.

[7] 走 *shissō suru* scamper, dash along. *shissō* a sprint, a dash
[9] 風 *shippū, hayate* squall, gale, hurricane, fresh breeze
[10] 病 *shippei* sickness
[11] 患 *shikkan* disease, ailment
[14] 駆 *shikku suru* scamper, speed, dash along

病 $\frac{3798}{J4942}$ M22127 A Bʏō. Hᴇɪ. *ya(mu)* get sick, be sick, suffer from. *ya(meru)* be sick, be in ill health. *yamai* illness; bad habit; weakness; passion. - *ya(mi)* sufferer of (a disease). *ya(mi)*- diseased.

[2] 人 *byōnin* patient, invalid
[4] 中 *byōchū* during an illness
[6] 因 *byōin* cause of the disease, etiology
死 *byōshi* natural death, death from illness
名 *byōmei* name of a disease
虫害 *byōchūgai* insect damage
気 *byōki* sickness, disease, ailment; fault; infirmity
気見舞 *byōki mima(i)* calling on the sick
[7] 没 *byōbotsu* death from illness, natural death
状 *byōjō* patient's condition
床 *byōshō* sickbed
[8] 臥 *byōga suru* be sick in bed, be bedridden
毒 *byōdoku* virus, germ

的 *byōteki* morbid, abnormal, unsound
[9] 室 *byōshitsu* sickroom, ward, sick bay, infirmary
院 *byōin* hospital, infirmary
[10] 症 *byōshō* nature of a disease
根 *byōkon* cause of the disease; root of an evil
害 *byōgai* health impairment from illness; crop damage due to disease
弱 *byōjaku* delicate constitution
原菌 *byōgenkin* virus, germ
[11] 菌 *byōkin* bacteria
巣 *byōsō* focus (of an infection)
理学 *byōrigaku* pathology
[12] 棟 *byōtō* ward
[13] 勢 *byōsei* progress of the disease
[14] 歴 *byōreki* patient's case history
[15] 弊 *byōhei* evil, vice, abuse; harmful influence; bad effect
[21] 魔 *byōma* disease, demon of ill health

――――― **6** ―――――

痕 $\frac{3803}{J3a2f}$ M22171 Kᴏɴ. *ato* mark; footprint.
[13] 跡 *konseki* traces, vestiges, evidences

痔 $\frac{3804}{J3c26}$ M22167 Jɪ piles, hemorrhoids.
[10] 疾 *jishitsu* hemorrhoids

――――― **7** ―――――

痩 $\frac{3806}{J4169}$ M-X See 瘦 3832.

痢 $\frac{3810}{J4e21}$ M22213 B Rɪ diarrhea.
[10] 病 *ribyō* diarrhea

痘 $\frac{3813}{J4577}$ M22185 B Tō smallpox.
[15] 瘡 *tōsō* smallpox

痛 $\frac{3814}{J444b}$ M22195 A Tsū pain. *ita(mu)* feel a pain, hurt; be hurt, be damaged, be spoiled, be bruised, wear out, be worn out. *ita(meru)* hurt, injure, impair, spoil, worry, bother, afflict, cause pain. *ita(mi)* pain, ache. *ita(garu)*

complain of pain. *ita(i)* painful, sore; trying. *ita(mashii), ita(washii)* sad, pitiful, wretched, pathetic.

⁴ 手 *itade* serious wound; hard blow
切 *tsūsetsu ni* keenly, acutely
⁵ 付 *ita(me)-tsu(keru)* rebuke, reprove, scold severely
打 *tsūda* painful blow; grand-slam hit
⁷ 快 *tsūkai* thrill, keen pleasure. *tsūkai na* extremely delightful, very gratifying; merciless incisive
⁹ 恨 *tsūkon* great sorrow, bitterness
¹⁰ 烈 *tsūretsu na* severe, bitter, scathing
¹¹ 痒 *tsūyō* interest, concern; pain and tickling. *ita(shi)kayu(shi) no* delicate, ticklish (question)
¹² 飲 *tsūin* carousal
覚 *tsukaku* sense of pain
¹³ 感 *tsūkan suru* feel keenly; fully realize
¹⁵ 憤 *tsūfun* great indignation
論 *tsūron* vehement argument
罵 *tsūba* condemnation, denunciation
撃 *tsūgeki* hard blow, severe attack

—— 8 ——

痴 3823 / J4354 / M22257 B CHI foolish.
² 人 *chijin* dunce, fool, idiot
⁷ 呆症 *chihōshō* dementia
¹¹ 情 *chijō* blind love
話喧嘩 *chiwagenka* lovers' quarrel
¹⁴ 態 *chitai* silliness

—— 10 ——

痩 3832 / J-X / M22415 SŌ. SHŪ. SHU. *yase(ru)* get thin.
⁷ 身 *sōshin* slender body, thin body
¹⁸ 駆 *sōku* a lean figure

—— 12 ——

癌 3840 / J3462 / M22538 GAN cancer; cancerous evil; stumbling block.

療 3842 / J4e45 / M22500 B RYŌ heal, cure.
⁸ 法 *ryōhō* medical treatment, remedy
治 *ryōji* medical treatment, remedy
¹⁵ 養 *ryōyō* recuperation, medical care

—— 13 ——

癒 3847 / J4c7e / M22545 B YU. *i(yasu)* heal, cure; quench (thirst); wreak (vengeance). *i(eru), nao(ru)* recover, be healed, heal.
¹² 着 *yuchaku suru* adhere, knit, unite, heal up. *yuchaku* adhesion

癖 3848 / J4a4a / M22550 B HEKI habit. *kuse* habit, peculiarity, vice, trait, fault; curl, kink; mannerism. *-kuse ni* and yet, when, though.

玄玉王瓜瓦甘生用田疋疒〔疋〕白皮皿目矛矢石示ネ内禾穴立

■■■ RAD. 火 105 ■■■

Hatsugashira (crown like that on *hatsu* "to depart"). Nickname: Dotted Tent.

—— 4 ——

発 3860 / J482f / M22662 A HOTSU, HATSU departure; discharge (of a gun). *has(suru)* discharge, fire; emit, emanate, radiate, give out; publish; utter, give vent to; give rise to; originate in, spring from; emanate from; start from; flow from; send out, dispatch, forward; leave, start, take off, announce; break out (a disease). *aba(ku)* unearth, disclose, divulge, reveal; open (a grave). *-hatsu* departure; round, shot; dated.
⁴ 火 *hakka* ignition, combustion, discharge, firing
⁵ 刊 *hakkan* publication

5

玄玉王瓜瓦甘生用田疋疒【宀】白皮皿目矛矢石示礻内禾穴立

令 *hatsurei* official announcement
布 *happu* proclamation; issuance; promulgation
生 *hassei* occurrence, outbreak; genesis; production, growth, development, rise
⁶光 *hakkō* radiation, luminescence
行 *hakkō* publication; flotation; issue
⁷見 *hakken* discovery, detection, revelation
走 *hassō* starting; first race
足 *hossoku, hassoku* starting, inauguration
車 *hassha* departure of a vehicle
狂 *hakkyō* madness, insanity
作 *hossa* fit, spasm, an attack of
売 *hatsubai* sale
言 *hatsugen* speaking, speech, proposal
声 *hassei* utterance, exclamation, speaking
⁸送 *hassō* sending, forwarding, shipping
注 *hatchū* ordering (goods)
効 *hakkō* coming into effect
券 *hakken* note issuing
表 *happyō* announcement, communique
明 *hatsumei* invention, innovation
明者 *hatsumeisha* inventor
明家 *hatsumeika* inventor
育 *hatsuiku* growth, development, progress
⁹信 *hasshin* sending a letter or telegram
信音 *hasshinon* dial tone
音 *hatsuon* pronunciation, enunciation, articulation
¹⁰病 *hatsubyō* onset of a disease, stroke
破 *happa* blasting
祥 *hasshō* ancestral origin; appearance of a good omen
祥地 *hasshōchi* cradle, birthplace
射 *hassha* discharge, firing; emanation, radiation
案 *hatsuan* suggestion, proposition, motion
起 *hokki* promotion (of a plan); proposition, suggestion
起人 *hokkinin* originator, promoter, sponsor
砲 *happō* firing, discharge
展 *hatten* expansion, extension, development, growth; dissipation
展途上国 *hatten tojōkoku* developing countries
¹¹達 *hattatsu* growth, development,

progress, advancement
掘 *hakkutsu* excavation; disinterring, exhuming
現 *hatsugen* revelation, manifestation
情 *hatsujō* sexual excitement, heat (in animals)
動 *hatsudō* motion, activity; exercise (of power)
動機 *hatsudōki* motor, engine
¹²揮 *hakki* exhibition, demonstration
散 *hassan* exhalation; emanation; diffusion; radiation; evaporation; divergence
着 *hatchaku* departure and arrival
覚 *hakkaku* detection, disclosure
¹³想 *hassō* expression (in music); conception (of an idea)
禁 *hakkin* banned, sale prohibited
電 *hatsuden* generation of electricity; dispatch of a telegram
電所 *hatsudensho* powerhouse, generating plant
電機 *hatsudenki* dynamo, generator
¹⁴端 *hottan, hattan* origin, commencement
酵 *hakkō* fermentation
¹⁵憤 *happun suru* be enraged; be inspired
熱 *hatsunetsu* attack of fever; generation of heat
¹⁶奮 *happun suru* be enraged; be inspired
¹⁷癌性 *hatsugansei* carcinogenic
癌物質 *hatsugan busshitsu* carcinogen
²⁰議 *hatsugi, hotsugi* proposal, motion
²¹露 *hatsuro* expression, manifestation, revelation

---- 7 ----

A 登 ₃₈₆₂ J4550 M22668 Tō. To. *nobo(ru)* rise, ascend, go up, climb; go to (the capital); add up to; be promoted; advance (in price); sail up; come up (on the agenda). *nobo(ri)* ascent; up train (toward the capital).
³山 *tozan* mountain climbing, mountain ascent
⁵用 *tōyō* appointment; promotion
庁 *tōchō* attendance at the office
⁷坂 *nobo(ri)zaka* ascent, upgrade
⁸板 *tōban suru* step into the pitcher's box
¹⁰竜門 *tōryūmon* the only gateway to eminence

玄
玉
王
瓜
甘
生
用
田
疋
扩
癶
【白】⁰
皮
皿
目
矛
矢
石
示
ネ
内
禾
穴
立

校 *tōkō* attending school
校拒否 *tōkōkyohi* refusal to attend school
記 *tōki* registry, registration
¹¹道 *nobo(ri)michi* uphill road, road up a mountain
頂 *tochō, tōchō* ascent (of a mountain)
¹²場 *tōjō suru* enter the stage; appear on the scene

場人物 *tōjō jimbutsu* cast of a play
¹³載 *tōsai suru* register, record, enter
¹⁶壇 *tōdan* ascending the platform
録 *tōroku* registration, entry, record, enrollment
録商標 *tōroku shōhyō* registered trademark
¹⁹攀 *tōhan suru* climb up, ascend

━━ RAD. 白 106 ━━

Shiroi white. Nickname: White.

λ 白 3863 / J4772 / M22678 HAKU, BYAKU white. *shiro(mu), shira(mu)* grow light; turn gray, whiten; weaken. *shiro* white; innocence. *shiro(i)* white; fair (skin); gray (hair); blank (paper); spotless; innocent. *shiro(ppoi)* whitish. *shiro* feigned ignorance. *serifu* speech, words, lines, remarks. *shiro(meru)* vt. whiten. *shira(keru)* become cheerless; become chilled; be spoiled (as a child). *shira-* white.

²人 *hakujin* white person, Caucasian
³刃 *hakujin, shiraha* naked sword, drawn sword
⁴内障 *hakunaishō* white cataract
日 *hakujitsu* daytime, broad daylight
日夢 *hakujitsumu* daydream
木 *shiraki* plain wood, unfinished woodwork
⁵白 *shirojiro* pure, white. *shirajira* dawning. *hakuhaku* very clear. *shirajira(shii)* barefaced (lie). *shirajira(shiku)* with feigned ignorance; under false premises
玉 *hakugyoku* white jade. *shiratama* white gem, pearl; rice-flour dumplings
⁶衣 *byakui, byakue, hakui* white robe
地 *shiroji* white cloth; white ground
地図 *hakuchizu* outline map, contour map ⌈sail
帆 *shiraho* white sail; boat with a white
百合 *shirayuri* Easter lily, white lily
米 *hakumai* polished rice
羽 *shiraha* white feather
羽矢立 *shiraha(no)ya (o) ta(teru)* choose

a human sacrifice; select someone
血病 *hakketsubyō* leukemia
色 *hakushoku* white
⁷身 *shiromi* white of an egg; white meat; sap; sapwood
状 *hakujō* confession, acknowledgment
亜 *hakua* chalk, chalkstone
兵戦 *hakuheisen* hand-to-hand fight
⁸金 *hakkin* platinum
波 *shiranami* white-capped waves; thief
夜 *hakuya, byakuya* white (arctic) night, short night
⁹面 *hakumen* unpainted face; pale face; fair skin; inexperience. *shirafu* sobriety, soberness
星 *shiroboshi* white dot; victory mark
昼 *hakuchū* daytime, broad daylight, midday
砂青松 *hakusa-seishō* white sand and green pines; beautiful seashore scene
¹⁰馬 *hakuba, shirouma, shirauma* white horse
骨 *hakkotsu* skeleton, bleached bones
書 *hakusho* a white paper, a white book
紙 *shirakami, hakushi* white paper; blank paper; flyleaf; clean slate
粉 *oshiroi* face powder, face paint
¹¹魚 *shirauo* whitebait
鳥 *hakuchō* swan
黒 *shirokuro* black and white; good and bad; right or wrong; guilty or innocent ⌈cabbage
菜 *hakusai* Chinese cabbage; celery
票 *hakuhyō* white (affirmative) vote; blank vote; favorable vote

5

玄玉王瓜瓦甘生用田疋疒灬【白】皮皿目矛矢石示衤禸禾穴立

雪 *hakusetsu, shirayuki* (white) snow
眼視 *hakuganshi suru* look coldly at, look askance at, frown upon
12 湯 *sayu* plain hot water
晢 *hakuseki* white (race), white complexion
雲 *hakuun, shirakumo* white clouds, fleecy clouds
13 痴 *hakuchi* imbecility
蓮 *byakuren* white lotus
14 旗 *hakki, shirahata* white flag; flag of truce
樺 *shirakaba, shirakamba* white birch
磁 *hakuji* white chinaware
銀 *shirogane* silver
墨 *hakuboku* chalk
熊 *shirokuma* polar bear
銅 *hakudō* nickel
髪 *hakuhatsu, shiraga* white hair, gray hair
15 線 *hakusen* white line, white tape
熱 *hakunetsu* white heat, incandescence; climax
檀 *byakudan* sandalwood, almug wood
18 襟 *shiroeri* white collar
19 蟻 *shiroari* white ant, termite
24 鷺 *shirasagi* snowy heron

───────── 1 ─────────

百 ₃₈₆₄ Byaku. Hyaku
A ─── J4934
M22679 hundred; a great number; all. *momo* hundred; a great number, great amount.
人一首 *hyakunin'isshu* 100 poems by 100 famous poets; the poem card game
3 万長者 *hyakumanchōja* millionaire; multimillionaire
4 方 *hyappō* in every way
分率 *hyakubunritsu* percentage
日紅 *sarusuberi* crape myrtle
日草 *hyakunichisō* zinnia
5 出 *hyakushutsu suru* arise in great numbers
合 *yuri* lily
7 足 *mukade* centipede
花繚乱 *hyakka-ryōran* blooming in profusion; a gathering of many beautiful women

8 官 *hyakkan* all the officials
姓 *hyakushō* farmer, peasant. *hyakusei* the common people
9 点 *hyakuten* hundred points, perfect mark
面相 *hyakumensō* life's many phases
発百中 *hyappatsu-hyakuchū* always hitting the bull's-eye; infallibility
科事典 *hyakka jiten* encyclopedia
10 般 *hyappan no* all, every, all kinds of
害 *hyakugai* great damage
鬼夜行 *hyakki-yagyō, hyakki-yakō* pandemonium, scandalous scene
11 済 *Kudara* an ancient Korean kingdom, Paekche
貨店 *hyakkaten* department store
16 薬長 *hyakuyaku (no) chō* the best medicine, i.e., saké

───────── 3 ─────────

的 ₃₈₆₇ Teki. *mato* mark, target;
A ─── J452a
M22692 object; the point. *-teki* adjective ending.
4 中 *tekichū suru* hit the mark, come true, guess right
5 外 *matohazu(re)* wide of the mark; out of focus
15 確 *tekkaku, tekikaku* precision, accuracy, infallibility

───────── 4 ─────────

皆 ₃₈₆₉ Kai. *mina, minna* all,
B ─── J3327
M22699 everybody, everything.
5 目 *kaimoku* altogether; (not) at all
10 殺 *minagoro(shi)* massacre, annihilation
既 *kaiki* total eclipse, totality
12 無 *kaimu* nothing
勤 *kaikin* perfect attendance
14 様 *minasama, minasan* all of you, all the people

皇 ₃₈₇₀ Kō. Ō. *sumeragi, sumera*
A ─── J3944
M22701 emperor.
3 上 *kōjō* emperor
4 太子 *kōtaishi* crown prince
太子妃 *kōtaishihi* the crown princess
太后 *kōtaikō, kōtaigō* empress dowager, queen mother
6 后 *kōgō* empress, queen
7 位 *kōi* imperial throne

居 *kōkyo* Imperial Palace
⁹室 *Kōshitsu* the Imperial Household, the reigning line
帝 *kōtei* emperor
¹⁰宮 *kōgū* imperial palace
¹¹族 *kōzoku* member of the Imperial Family

6

皋 [3873 J3b29 M22727] Kō swamp, shore.

RAD. 皮 107

Kegawa animal hide or *hi no kawa* (*kawa* "leather" or "skin" written with the character read *hi*) as distinguished from Rad. 177. Nickname: Skin.

A 皮 [3878 J4869 M22823] Hɪ. *kawa* skin; hide; leather; fur, pelt; bark; peeling, husk, shell; film, cream.

³下注射 *hika chūsha* hypodermic injection
⁶肉 *hiniku(ru)* be sarcastic. *hiniku* sarcasm, irony

⁹皮 *hikaku* hides, leather
相 *hisō na* apparent, outward, surface, superficial
¹⁴製 *kawasei* made of leather
算用 *kawazan'yō, kawasan'yō* counting one's unhatched chickens
¹⁵膚 *hifu* skin

RAD. 皿 108

Sara dish or *shitazara* bottom "dish." Nickname: Dish.

A 皿 [3885 J3b2e M22941] Bᴇɪ. Mʏō. *sara* dish; a helping; a course.

⁶回 *saramawa(shi)* dish-spinning trick
⁹洗 *saraara(i)* dishwashing; dishwasher

4

盃 [3887 J4756 M22955] See 杯 2586.

盈 [3888 J314e M22961] Eɪ. *mi(chiru), mi(tsuru)* be full; rise (tides); mature, expire.

B 盆 [3889 J4b5f M22959] Bᴏɴ Lantern Festival, Festival of the Dead; tray.

⁶地 *bonchi* round valley, hollow, basin
¹⁰栽 *bonsai* miniature tray landscape
¹¹祭 *Bon Matsu(ri)* the *Bon* Festival

¹²景 *bonkei* tray landscape
¹⁴踊 *Bon Odo(ri)* the *Bon* Festival Dance
暮 *Bon-ku(re) Bon* and year-end seasons

5

A 益 [3891 J3157 M22972] Eᴋɪ, Yᴀᴋᴜ gain, benefit, profit, use, advantage. *eki(suru)* be beneficial, useful, profitable, or valuable. *ma(su)* vt increase, add to, augment, gain; promote (health); enlarge, extend. *vi* increase.

⁶虫 *eikichū* beneficial insect
¹⁰益 *masumasu* increasingly, more and more
¹¹鳥 *eichō* beneficial bird

6

B 盗 [3894 J4570 M23000] Tō thief. *nusu(mu)* steal, rob, pilfer.

² 人 *nusubito, nusutto* thief

⁵ 用 *tōyō* embezzlement; surreptitious use

⁷ 見 *nusu(mi)-mi(ru)* steal a glance

作 *tōsaku* plagiarism

⁸ 取 *nusu(mi)-to(ru)* steal

⁹ 品 *tōhin* stolen article, stolen goods

¹⁰ 笑 *nusu(mi)wara(i)* laughing up one's sleeve

¹³ 賊 *tōzoku* thief, robber, burglar

¹⁴ 聞 *nusu(mi)gi(ki)* eavesdropping, wire tapping

読 *nusu(mi)yo(mi)* surreptitious reading

¹⁷ 聴 *tōchō* wire tapping; unlicensed radio listening

¹⁸ 癖 *tōheki* kleptomania

難 *tōnan* robbery, burglary, theft

難品 *tōnanhin* stolen goods

盛 ³⁸⁹⁵ J4039 M23001ᵗ SHŌ. SEI. JŌ. *sakae(ru)* prosper, flourish; copulate (animals). *mo(ru)* serve, fill; heap up; prescribe or give (medicine); poison; mark out, graduate. *mo(ri)* quantity; good measure, liberal serving. *saka(n) na* prosperous; successful (meeting); energetic; enthusiastic; popular; furious (attack); keen (competition); extensive, large. *saka(ri)* height, peak; prime, bloom; heat (in animals).

³ 土 *mo(ri)tsuchi* raising the ground level

大 *seidai na* prosperous, grand, magnificent, successful (meeting), enthusiastic (welcome)

上 *mo(ri)-a(garu)* rise, swell. *mo(ri)-a(geru)* pile up, heap up

⁴ 込 *mo(ri)-ko(mu)* incorporate in

⁶ 会 *seikai* successful meeting

名 *seimei* fame, reputation

⁷ 花 *mo(ri)bana* flowers arranged in a basin or tray

沢山 *moridakusan* many, a lot of, all kinds of; crowded (program)

⁸ 況 *seikyō* prosperity, success, boom

事 *seiji* grand event; splendid enterprise

¹⁰ 夏 *seika* midsummer

衰 *seisui* rise and fall, ups and downs, vicissitudes; welfare

¹² 場 *saka(ri)ba* pleasure resort; busiest quarters (of a town), crowded place

装 *seisō* best clothes, beautiful attire, full regalia, full armor

──────── 8 ────────

盟 ³⁸⁹⁹ J4c41 M23024 MEI oath; alliance.

⁴ 友 *meiyū* staunch friend

⁵ 主 *meishu* leader, leading power (of an alliance)

⁹ 約 *meiyaku* pledge, pact, alliance

──────── 9 ────────

監 ³⁹⁰¹ J3446 M23032 KAN *asa* office, government office; director, head official.

⁶ 守 *kanshu* custody, surveillance

⁸ 房 *kambō* cell, ward

⁹ 査 *kansa* inspection; auditing; auditor

査役 *kansayaku* inspector, controller, auditor

¹⁰ 修 *kanshū* (editorial) supervision

¹¹ 視 *kanshi* guarding, observation, inspection, supervision, surveillance

¹³ 禁 *kankin* imprisonment

督 *kantoku* supervision, surveillance, jurisdiction; inspector, superintendent; direction; (film) director; manager; bishop

¹⁴ 獄 *kangoku* prison, jail, penitentiary, place of detention

製 *kansei* controlled manufacturing

察 *kansatsu* inspection; inspector

──────── 10 ────────

盤 ³⁹⁰² J4857 M23036 BAN, HAN shallow bowl, platter, tray, tub; board; phonograph record.

⁵ 石 *banjaku* huge rock. *banseki* the *go* board and its stones

⁹ 面 *bammen* face of a record or board

¹⁵ 踞 *bankyo suru* lurk in the way; proudly occupy (territory), be dominant, hold sway

RAD. 目 109

Me eye. At left: *me hen*. Nickname: Eye.

目 A — 3906 J4c5c M23105 — **MOKU** item, division, class; order (of plants or animals). *me* eye; look, gaze; notice, attention; viewpoint; discrimination, insight; experience; treatment; care, favor, pity; texture, weave; mesh; grain, square; sight, vision; tooth (of a saw); weight; momme (0.1325 oz.); eye (of a needle). *moku(suru)* regard as. *me(boshii)* attractive, conspicuous, notable; valuable. *me(magurushii)* dizzy, bewildering; bustling. *ma* eye. *me* ordinal ending, -st, -nd, -rd, -th; point; degree, extent.

³ 下 *meshita* subordinate, junior, inferior
上 *meue* seniors, superiors

⁴ 方 *mekata* weight
分量 *mebunryō* eye measurement

⁵ 立 *meda(tsu)* be conspicuous. *me (ni) ta(tsu)* be prominent. *meta(te)* setting (a saw)
処 *medo* aim, goal; outlook; eye (of a needle)
尻 *mejiri* the outside corner of the eye
打 *meu(chi)* perforation
礼 *mokurei* nod (in greeting)
白押 *mejiroo(shi)* jostling, milling
出度 *medeta(i)* happy, auspicious; stupid, half-witted. *(o)medeto(u) (gozaimasu)* congratulations. *medeta(ku)* happily, successfully, auspiciously
玉 *me (no) tama, medama* eyeball; scolding
玉焼 *medamaya(ki)* eggs sunny side up
付 *metsu(ki)* look, eye expression. *metsu(karu), me(kkaru)* be found; be found out, be discovered. *me(kkeru)* find; find out; discover; locate; catch sight of; notice; recognize; hunt for, get used to seeing, be familiar to. *metsu(ke)* feudal overseer, public censor ⌐mark

⁶ 印 *mejirushi* landmark, pylon, guide,
次 *mokuji* table of contents
安 *meyasu* standard, criterion; aim
当 *mea(te)* guide (as a star); aim. *ma(no)a(tari)* face to face, on the spot, in one's presence, with ones own eyes

先 *mesaki* before one's eyes, under one's nose; immediate future; foresight, acumen; appearance

⁷ 利 *meki(ki)* judging; judge, connoisseur, virtuoso. *me (ga) ki(ku)* have good judgement; be a good superintendent
余 *me (ni) ama(ru)* scandalous, intolerable
医者 *meisha* oculist
抜通 *menu(ki)dō(ri)* principal street

⁸ 明 *mea(ki)* one who can see, educated person. *mea(kashi)* detective, (police) spy
注 *me (o) soso(gu)* examine carefully
肥 *me (ga) koe(ru)* have good judgement
毒 *me(no)doku* something tempting
的 *mokuteki* aim, purpose, intention
的地 *mokutekichi* destination

⁹ 途 *mokuto* aim, goal
通 *medō(ri)* an audience (with); height of the eyes. *me (o) tō(su)* glance through
指 *meza(su)* aim at; spot or eye (someone)
映 *mabayu(i)* glaring; dazzling, blinding
前 *me (no) mae* in one's presence, close at hand. *mokuzen* under one's nose, before one's eyes; immediate (gain). *mesaki* before one's eyes, under one's nose; immediate future; foresight, acumen; appearance
星 *meboshi* objective

¹⁰ 高 *me (ga) taka(i)* have good judgement
眩 *mekurume(ku)* be dazzled. *me (ga) kura(mu)* be dizzy. *memai* dizziness.
紛 *memaguru(shii)* dizzy, bewildering, dazzled, confused
配 *mokuba(se) suru* wink significantly at. *mekuba(ri)* vigilance, surveillance
敏 *mezato(i), mebashiko(i)* quick-eyed, sharp-eyed
差 *meza(su)* aim at; spot (someone). *manaza(shi)* a glance, a look

¹¹ 張 *meba(ri) suru* paste paper over, seal up (a window)

5

玄
玉
王
瓜
瓦
甘
生
用
田
疋
疒
癶
白
皮
皿
【目】
矢
矢
石
示
礻
内
禾
穴
立

移 *meutsu(ri)* distraction, difficulty in choosing

許 *memoto* the eyes

盛 *memo(ri)* scale, graduation

¹² 測 *mokusoku* measuring with the eye

覚 *meza(masu)* vt rouse, awaken. *meza(meru)* vi wake up, awake to (reality). *meza(me)* waking, awakening, conversion. *meza(mashii)* remarkable, conspicuous, brilliant. *meza(mashi)* eye-opener (a drink)

¹³ 隠 *mekaku(shi)* eye bandage, blindfold; blinkers; a (board) screen

障 *mezawa(ri)* eyesore, disfigurement, unsightly object, unsightly area

新 *meatara(shii)* novel, original

蓋 *mabuta* eyelid

¹⁴ 算 *mokusan* anticipation, calculation

鼻立 *mehanada(chi)* looks, features

¹⁵ 標 *mokuhyō* sign, mark; target; objective; standard

論 *mokuro(mu)* plan, scheme, contemplate

論見 *mokuromi* plan, scheme; aim, intention; frame up.

撃 *mokugeki* observation

撃者 *mokugekisha* eyewitness

¹⁶ 録 *mokuroku* contents, list, inventory, catalog

薬 *megusuri* eye medicine. *me (no) kusuri* a treatment for sore eyes

───── **3** ─────

盲 ³⁹⁰⁷ J4c55 M23132 Bō. Mō blindness. *mekura, meshii* blindness; blind person; ignorance, ignoramus.

² 人 *mōjin* blind person

⁵ 目 *mōmoku* blindness

⁸ 学校 *mōgakkō* school for the blind

⁹ 信 *mōshin* blind belief, credulity

点 *mōten* blind spot

¹⁰ 従 *mōjū* blind obedience

¹¹ 動 *mōdō, bōdō* acting blindly

¹³ 腸 *mōchō* appendix; caecum

腸炎 *mōchōen* appendicitis

¹⁴ 導犬 *mōdōken* seeing-eye dog

直 ³⁹⁰⁸ J443e M23136 Jiki, Choku honesty, frankness; simplicity; correctness; being straight; night duty.

nao(ru) be mended; get well; be restored; return to normal; be installed (as a legal wife); change (from third to second class). *nao(su)* mend, repair, put in order, reform, correct; revise, amend; re-do, alter; cure; restore; adjust, regulate; convert (money). *jika ni* directly, firsthand, in person. *jiki* direct, in person; soon; at once; just; near by. *jiki ni* soon; immediately; easily. *ne* price, cost, value. *su(gu)* immediately; easily; right (near). *su(gu) na* honest, upright. *tada(chi) ni* immediately, directly, in person. *hita to* close to. *nao(ki)* straight, upright. *nao(shi)* correction; repair; person making repair. *tada* direct; close; straight; immediately; *nao* straight; mischief; ordinary, common.

hita earnestly; immediately; exactly.

³ 下 *chokka* directly under. *chokka suru* fall perpendicularly.

下型地震 *chokkagata jishin* shallow earthquake centered beneath populated area

⁴ 方体 *chokuhōtai* right-angled parallelepiped

⁵ 立 *chokuritsu* vertical, perpendicular, upright, erect. *chokuritsu suru* stand erect, rise perpendicularly

⁶ 行 *chokkō* through, non-stop

伝 *jikiden* direct transmission (of mysteries or skill); initiation

列 *chokuretsu* series wiring

⁷ 角 *chokkaku* right angle

言 *chokugen* plain speaking

系 *chokkei* lineal descendant, direct line

売 *chokubai suru* sell directly

⁸ 送 *chokusō* direct delivery

径 *chokkei* diameter

直 *jikijiki no* personal, direct

⁹ 面 *chokumen suru* face, confront, be confronted by

通 *chokutsū* direct communication, through service

後 *chokugo* immediately after, right behind

前 *chokuzen* just before

¹⁰ 進 *chokushin suru* go right on, go straight ahead

流 *chokuryū* direct current

¹¹ 視 *chokushi suru* look straight at, face squarely

訳 *chokuyaku* literal translation

情径行 *chokujokeikō* frankness; impulsiveness

接 *chokusetsu* direct, immediate, personal, firsthand

¹² 属 *chokuzoku* direct control

結 *chokketsu* direct connection

訴 *jikiso* direct appeal

営 *chokuei* direct management

¹³ 腸 *chokuchō* rectum

感 *chokkan* intuition

¹⁵ 線 *chokusen* straight line, air line, beeline

談判 *jika dampan* direct talks

撃 *chokugeki* direct hit

輸入 *chokuyunyū, jiki yunyū* direct import

輸出 *chokuyushutsu, jiki yushutsu* direct export

¹⁷ 轄 *chokkatsu* direct control

¹⁸ 観 *chokkan* intuition, insight

———— 4 ————

盾 B ³⁹¹² ^{J3d62} ^{M23171} JUN. *tate* shield, buckler, escutcheon; pretext.

冒 B ³⁹¹⁵ ^{J4b41} ^{M-X} BŌ. *oka(su)* risk, face, defy, dare; (diseases) attack; damage; desecrate; assume (a name).

¹⁰ 険 *bōken* risk, venture, adventure

¹⁶ 頭 *bōtō* opening paragraph or statement

¹⁸ 瀆 *bōtoku* blasphemy, profanity, desecration, sacrilige

省 A ³⁹¹⁶ ^{J3e4a} ^{M23179} SEI. SHŌ ministry, department; province (in China). *habu(ku)* omit, eliminate; curtail, economize. *kaeri(miru)* look back; turn around, look back upon, review; examine oneself; take notice of. *tsukasa* office, government office; director, head official.

¹¹ 略 *shōryaku* abbreviation, abridgment, omission ⌈consideration

¹⁴ 察 *seisatsu, shōsatsu* reflection,

眉 ³⁹¹⁷ ^{J487d} ^{M23190} BI. MI. *mayu* eyebrow.

⁴ 毛 *mayuge* eyebrows

⁵ 目 *bimoku* face, looks, features

¹¹ 唾物 *mayutsubamono* fake

¹² 間 *miken* brow, middle forehead

¹⁴ 墨 *mayuzumi* blackened eyebrows; eyebrow pencil

県 A ³⁹¹⁸ ^{J3829} ^{M23210'} KEN prefecture; district (in China). *agata* ancient demarcated cultivated areas.

² 人 *kenjin* native of a prefecture

人会 *kenjinkai* an association of people from the same province

³ 下 *kenka* in or under the prefecture, throughout the prefecture

⁵ 立 *kenritsu* prefectural (institution)

庁 *kenchō* prefectural office

外 *kengai* outside the prefecture

⁶ 会 *kenkai* prefectural assembly

⁸ 知事 *ken chiji* prefectural governor

¹² 税 *kenzei* prefectural tax

営 *ken'ei* prefectural operation

²⁰ 議 *kengi* prefectural assembly member

議会 *kengikai* prefectural assembly

看 A ³⁹¹⁹ ^{J3447} ^{M23196} KAN. *mi(ru)* see.

⁶ 守 *kanshu* jailer

⁸ 取 *mi-to(ru)* care for the sick. *kanshu suru* see through, perceive, notice, get wind of

板 *kamban* sign, signboard, doorplate; poster, billboard; appearance; figurehead; policy; attraction; closing time

⁹ 点 *kanten* viewpoint

¹⁰ 破 *mi-yabu(ru), kampa suru* see through, penetrate, fathom

病 *kambyō* nursing (a patient)

¹¹ 過 *kanka* connivance, shutting one's eyes to

做 *mi-na(su)* consider as

²⁰ 護 *kango* nursing

護士 *kangoshi* (male) nurse

護学 *kangogaku* nursing science

護婦 *kangofu* (female) nurse

相 A ³⁹²⁰ ^{J416a} ^{M23151} SŌ aspect, phase, physiognomy. SHŌ minister of state, councilor. *ai-* together, each other; mutually, reciprocally; fellow-;

5

玄
玉
王
瓜
瓦
甘
生
用
田
疋
疒
癶
白
皮
皿
【目】
矛
矢
石
示
礻
内
禾
穴
立

emphatic verbal prefix.

⁴反 *aihan suru* be contrary to, disagree with

手 *aite* companion, mate, date, partner; the other party, opponent, adversary; object

手取 *aitedo(ru)* take on (opponents); sue

互 *sōgo* mutual, reciprocal. *aitagai ni* mutually, each other, one another

互会社 *sōgogaisha* mutual insurance company

互作用 *sōgo sayō* reciprocal action, interaction

互扶助 *sōgo fujo* mutual aid

互条約 *sōgo jōyaku* bilateral treaty, treaty of reciprocity

互組合 *sōgo kumiai* cooperative society, mutual-aid association

互援助 *sōgo enjo* mutual assistance

互銀行 *sōgo ginkō* mutual-financing bank

互関係 *sōgo kankei* reciprocity, interrelationship

⁵打 *aiu(chi)* striking each other simultaneously

加平均 *sōka heikin* arithmetical mean

⁶次 *aitsu(gu)* follow in succession. *aitsu(ide)* in succession

好 *sōgō* looks, features, countenance

交 *aimaji(waru)* associate with. *tsuru(mu)* mate, copulate

年 *aidoshi* the same age

争 *aiaraso(u)* quarrel, dispute

合傘 *aia(i)gasa de* under the same umbrella

似 *sōji* resemblance, similarity, analogy

伝 *sōden* inheritance, heirship; conferring of priestly orders

当 *sōtō na* suitable, proper, corresponding, reasonable; respectable; sufficient, adequate, passable. *sōtō suru* befit, be worthy of; deserve, merit; correspond to; be proportionate to

⁷応 *fusawa(shii)* suitable, becoming, fitting, worthy of, proper, adequate, appropriate. *sōō* suitability, fitness

伴 *aitomona(u)* accompany. *shōban* participation

克 *sōkoku* rivalry

身互 *aimitaga(i)* mutual assistance

対 *aitai suru* face each other, lie opposite. *sōtai* relativity, reciprocity, symmetry. *aitai de* personally, directly

対立 *aitairitsu suru* oppose; face each other

対的 *sōtaiteki* relative, reciprocal

対性 *sōtaisei* relativity

⁸性 *aishō* affinity, compatibility

定 *aisada(meru)* ordain, decide on

⁹連 *aitsurana(ru)* be joined

持 *aimo(chi)* cooperation, interdependence, mutual help; common possession; sharing (expenses)

計 *aihaka(ru)* plan together

客 *aikyaku* roommate; fellow passenger; one sharing a seat

乗 *aino(ri)* riding together. *sōjō* multiplication

変 *aikawa(razu)* as usual

剋 *sōkoku* rivalry

思 *sōshi* mutual love

思相愛 *sōshisōai* mutual love

¹⁰称 *sōshō* symmetry

殺 *sōsatsu, sōsai* offset, cancellation (of obligations)

容 *aii(renai)* contrary, incompatible

¹¹接 *aises(uru)* meet, get together

宿 *aiyado(ri), aiyado* lodging together

¹²棒 *aibō* pal, partner, accomplice

等 *sōtō* equality

集 *aiatsu(maru), aitsudo(u)* *vi* gather together

場 *sōba* market price; speculation; estimation

違 *sōi* difference, disparity, gap, discrepancy, disagreement, variation, contrast

違無 *sōina(i)* no doubt that. *sōina(ku)* without fail, surely

¹³携 *aitazusa(ete)* together with, hand-in-hand, in couples

愛 *sōai* mutual love

槌 *aizuchi, ai (no) tsuchi* chiming in with another's conversation

槌打 *aizuchi (o) u(tsu)* chime in with, echo (someone)

続 *sōzoku* succession, inheritance, descent

続人 *sōzokunin* heir

続税 *sōzokuzei* inheritance tax

続権 *sōzokuken* heirship, right of inheritance

[14] 貌 *sōbō* features, looks, physiognomy

関 *sōkan* mutual relationship, interdependence

関的 *sōkanteki* correlative

[15] 撲 *sumō* sumo, wrestling; wrestling match; sumo wrestler

撲取 *sumōtori* sumo wrestler

談 *sōdan* consultation, conversation, talk; bargain; offer, proposal; agreement, arrangement. *sōdan(zuku)* mutual agreement

談役 *sōdan'yaku* counselor, consultant

[16] 謀 *aihaka(ru)* plan together; plot together

整 *aitotono(u)* be prepared, be arranged. *aitotono(eru)* prepare, arrange

[17] 償 *aitsuguna(u)* recompense each other

[19] 識 *sōshiki* acquaintance

———————— 5 ————————

B 眠 $\frac{3925}{\substack{J4c32 \\ M23240}}$ Mɪɴ sleep. *nebu(ru)*, *nemu(ru)* sleep, die. *nemu(ri‑kokeru)* feel sleepy. *nemu(ri‑kokeru)* sleep soundly. *nemu(i)*, *nebu(tai)*, *nemu(tai)*, *nemu(ge) ni*, *nemu(tage) ni*, *nemu(sō) ni*, *nemu(tasō) ni* sleepy, drowsy, lethargic.

[6] 気 *nemuke* sleepiness, drowsiness

A 真 $\frac{3926}{\substack{J3f3f \\ M23236}}$ Sʜɪɴ truth; reality; genuineness; Buddhist sect originating in the thirteenth century. *makoto* sincerity, honesty, fidelity; truth. *shin ni, hon ni* truly, actually, really. *ma‑* just, right, due (east); pure, genuine, true.

[1] 一文字 *maichimonji* straight, as the crow flies

[2] 人間 *maningen* an honest man, a good citizen

[4] 心 *magokoro* sincerity, devotion

水 *mamizu* fresh water

中 *manaka, ma(n)naka* center, middle, midway

[5] 平 *ma(t)taira na* perfectly level. *ma(p)pira* (not) by any means; humbly, sincerely

冬 *mafuyu* dead of winter

只中 *ma(t)tadanaka* right in the midst of, right at the height of

白 *ma(s)shiro, mashiro* pure white

正 *shinsei* genuine, authentic, true, pure

正直 *mashōjiki, ma(s)shōjiki* perfectly honest

正面 *mashōmen, ma(s)shōmen* directly opposite, right in front

[6] 因 *shin'in* true reason, true motive

近 *maji(ka) ni* nearness, proximity. *majika(i)* near at hand

向 *ma(k)kō* brow; front. *mamuka(i), mamu(ki)* face to face, straight ahead, just in front of. *hitamu(ki) na* earnest; single‑handed

先 *ma(s)saki* the head, the foremost; beginning

似 *mane(ru)* imitate, mimic, mock, follow suit. *mane* mimicry, imitation; behavior, pretense

似事 *manegoto* sham, make‑believe, mere form

[7] 言 *Shingon* Buddhist sect originating in the eighth century

赤 *ma(k)ka* deep red, crimson

否 *shimpi* true or false

[8] 青 *ma(s)sao na* deep blue; ghastly pale

直 *ma(s)sugu na* straight, direct, upright, erect; honest; frank

夜中 *mayonaka* dead of night, midnight

逆様 *ma(s)sakasama ni* headlong, head over heels

実 *shinjitsu* truth, reality, fact; in reality, truly

実性 *shinjitsusei* fidelity, truth, authenticity, credibility

空 *shinkū* vacuum. *shinkū no* hollow, empty

空管 *shinkūkan* vacuum tube

[9] 面目 *majime* serious, earnest, honest. *shimmemmoku* one's true character, oneself; seriousness, earnestness

相 *shinsō* the truth, the facts, the real situation

昼 *mahiru* broad daylight, midday

昼間 *ma(p)piruma* broad daylight

[10] 夏 *manatsu* midsummer

剣 *shinken* real sword; earnestness

剣勝負 *shinkenshōbu* fighting with real swords; game played in real earnest

珠 *shinju* pearl

珠養殖 *shinju yōshoku* pearl cultivation

[11] 黒 *ma(k)kuro na* jet black

偽 *shingi* truth or error, authenticity

玄 玉 王 瓜 瓦 甘 生 用 田 疋 疒 癶 白 皮 皿 【目】 矛 矢 石 示 礻 内 禾 穴 立

5

玄玉王瓜瓦甘生用田疋扩癶白皮皿【目】矛矢石示礻内禾穴立

情 *shinjō* true feeling
理 *shinri* truth
盛 *ma(s)saka(ri), masaka(ri)* height of, middle of; full bloom
¹² 筆 *shimpitsu* autograph; one's own handwriting; personal note
最中 *ma(s)saichū* midst; height
¹³ 新 *maatara(shii)* brand new
暗 *makkura* total darkness; shortsightedness
暗闇 *makkurayami* total darkness
意 *shin'i* real intention, true motive; true meaning
¹⁴ 綿 *mawata* silk floss, silk wadding
¹⁷ 鍮 *shinchū* brass
¹⁸ 髄 *shinzui* essence, pith, spirit, soul, essentials, core, kernel, the life blood
鯉 *magoi* black carp
顔 *magao* serious look
¹⁹ 鯛 *madai* red sea bream

───────── 6 ─────────

B 眺 3933 J442f M23314 CHŌ . *naga(meru)* watch, look at, see; scrutinize. *naga(me)* view, scene.
¹¹ 望 *chōbō* prospect, view, outlook

A 眼 3935 J3463 M23318 GAN. GEN. *me* eye; look, gaze; notice, attention; viewpoint, discrimination, insight; experience; treatment; care, favor, pity; texture, weave; mesh; grain, square; sight, vision; tooth (of a saw); weight; eye (of a needle). *manako* eye.
² 力 *ganriki, ganryoku* insight, power of observation
³ 下 *ganka* (a view) below one's eyes
⁴ 辺 *ma (no) ata(ri)* in one's presence, before one's eyes
中 *ganchū ni* in one's eyes; in one's view
⁵ 玉 *medama* eyeball
目 *gammoku* core, point, gist, essence, main object
⁶ 光 *gankō* glint of the eye; discernment, insight
⁷ 医者 *meisha* oculist
⁹ 前 *ganzen* before one's eyes
科 *ganka* ophthalmology
¹⁰ 病 *gambyō, meya(mi)* eye disease;

person with sore eyes
差帯 *manaza(shi)* a look (at someone)
帯 *gantai* eye bandage
¹¹ 球 *gankyū* eyeball. *medama, me (no) tama* eyeball; scolding
¹⁴ 精疲労 *gansei hirō* eyestrain
鏡 *gankyō, megane* spectacles, glasses

───────── 7 ─────────

A 着 3938 J4365 M23339 CHAKU arrival, finish (in a race); suit counter. *ki(ru), chaku(suru)* put on, wear. *ki(seru)* clothe, dress, put on; cover, plate, coat, gild; veneer; blame for, impute a crime to. *ki(konasu)* wear, dress. *tsu(ku), chaku(suru)* arrive at, reach, attain to. *ki(se)* dish cover. *ki(gonashi)* style of dress. *ki(nikui)* uncomfortable or awkward to wear. *-ki* wearing; clothes.
³ 工 *chakkō* starting construction
⁴ 手 *chakushu* start, commencement
火 *chakka* igniting
水 *chakusui* alighting on water
心地 *kigokochi* fit and feel (of clothes)
⁵ 用 *chakuyō suru* wear, have on
目 *chakumoku* viewpoint, observation
付 *kitsu(ke)* dressing (someone); attire
⁶ 衣 *chakui* dressing (oneself); one's clothes
任 *chakunin* arrival at one's post
色 *chakushoku* color, coloration, coloring; embellishment
⁷ 身着儘 *ki(no)mi-ki(no)mama de* (sleep) in one's clothes; without changing one's clothes; with only the clothes on one's back
⁸ 物 *kimono* clothes, kimono
服 *chakufuku* dressing (oneself); embezzlement, misappropriation
実 *chakujitsu na* trustworthy, sober-minded, steady
⁹ 信 *chakushin* arrival of mail
¹⁰ 席 *chakuseki* taking a seat
座 *chakuza* taking a seat
倒 *kidao(re)* extravagance in dress
流 *kinaga(shi)* not dressed up
剣 *chakken, tsu(ke)ken* fixed bayonet
陸 *chakuriku* landing, alighting
¹¹ 船 *chakusen* ship arrival
道楽 *kidōraku* love of dress; lover of fine clothes

眼 *chakugan* viewpoint, observation
¹² 港 *chakkō* arrival at port
着 *chakuchaku* steadily
替 *kiga(e)* changing clothes; change of clothes
¹³ 飾 *ki-kaza(ru)* dress up; wear fine clothes
想 *chakusō* conception, idea
¹⁴ 駅 *chakueki* destination station
²⁰ 艦 *chakkan* deck landing

——————— **8** ———————

睦 _{3945 J4b53 M23460} Boku. *mutsu(majii)* friendly, intimate, harmonious. *mutsu(mu), mutsu(bu)* get along well together.
⁴ 月 *mutsuki* first lunar month
⁷ 言 *mutsugoto* lovers' talk, words of friendship

督 _{3946 J4644 M23457} Toku. *toku(suru)* command, lead, supervise; urge.
⁷ 励 *tokurei* encouragement
⁹ 促 *tokusoku suru* urge, dun, press (a person for action)

B 睡 _{3948 J3f67 M23448} Sui. *nemu(ru), nebu(ru)* sleep, die. *nemu(garu)* feel sleepy. *nemu(gari), nemu(gariya)* sleepyhead.
¹⁰ 眠 *suimin* sleep
眠不足 *suimimbusoku, suimin fusoku*

lack of sleep
眠剤 *suiminzai* sleeping drug, narcotic
¹³ 蓮 *suiren* water lily
²¹ 魔 *suima* sleepiness, drowsiness; sandman

——————— **12** ———————

瞥 _{3959 J4a4d M23672} Betsu glance at.
⁷ 見 *bekken* glance, glimpse

瞭 _{3960 J4e46 M23697} Ryō clear.
¹² 然 *ryōzen(taru)* obvious, clear, plain

瞳 _{3961 J4637 M23707} Dō. *hitomi* pupil of the eye.
⁴ 孔 *dōkō* pupil of the eye

——————— **13** ———————

B 瞬 _{3969 J3d56 M23694} Shun. *mabata(ku), majiro(gu)* wink, blink. *matata(ku)* wink, twinkle, flicker. *shibatata(ku), shibata(ku)* wink, blink. *mebata(ki), mabata(ki)* wink, blink. *matata(ki)* wink; twinkling (of stars).
¹⁰ 時 *shunji* instant, moment, second, minute
¹² 間 *shunkan* instant, moment, second. *mabata(ku)ma ni, matata(ku)ma ni* in the twinkling of an eye

━━━━━━━ **RAD.** 矛 **110** ━━━━━━━

Hoko spear. At left: *hoko hen*. Nickname: Spear (cf. Rad. 62).

B 矛 _{3974 J4c37 M23846} 鉾 _{6255 J4b48 M40353} Mu. Bō. *hoko* halberd; arms, festival car, float.
⁶ 先 *hokosaki* the point of a sword;

spearhead; the brunt (of an argument); the aim (of an attack)
⁹ 盾 *mujun* contradiction

玄玉王瓜瓦甘生用田疋疒癶白皮皿目矛【矢】石示礻内禾穴立

━━━ RAD. 矢 111 ━━━

Ya arrow. At left: *ya hen*. Nickname: Arrow.

A 矢 $\frac{3976}{\text{J4c70}}$ M23929 SHI. *ya* arrow.

⁶印 *yajirushi* a direction arrow

先 *yasaki* arrowhead; the point; the moment

⁹面 *yaomote* thick of the fight; front line of archers; face of the enemy

¹¹張 *ya(p)pari, yahari* too, also, as well, likewise, like the rest, still, just the same, after all, nevertheless

━━━ 3 ━━━

A 知 $\frac{3978}{\text{J434e}}$ M23935 CHI knowledge, acquaintance, sense. *shi(ru)* know; understand; appreciate recognize; realize; notice, sense, feel; remember; infer, gather; be concerned with. *shi(reru)* become known, be disclosed, be found out, turn out to be. *shi(rasu)* rule (a country). *shi(raseru)* inform, give notice. *shi(rase)* information, report, news; omen. *shi(reta)* obvious; negligible. *-(kamo)shi(renai)* maybe, perhaps, one can't tell. *-(ka)shi(ra)* I wonder if ... *-shi(razu)* unconsciously, unknowingly; free from (hot weather).

² 人 *chijin* acquaintance

力 *chiryoku* wisdom, intellectual power, mental capacity, intellect, mentality, brains ⌐friend

³ 己 *chiki* acquaintance, appreciative

⁶ 合 *shi(ri)-a(u)* know each other. *shiria(i)* an acquaintance

名 *chimei no* noted, well-known

⁷ 見 *chiken* knowledge, information; view, opinion

⁸ 性 *chisei* intellect, intelligence, mentality

育 *chiiku* mental training

事 *chiji* governor

的 *chiteki* mental, intellectual

¹⁰ 振 *shi(ranu)fu(ri)* feigned ignorance; indifference. *shi(tta)fu(ri)* pretending to know

恵 *chie* wisdom, sense, sagacity, intelligence, resourcefulness

恵袋 *chiebukuro* brain trust, close

advisers ⌐faculties

能 *chinō* intellect, intelligence, mental

能犯 *chinōhan* the crimes of forgery, deception, etc.

能指数 *chinō shisū* intelligence quotient, I.Q.

能検査 *chinō kensa* mental test

¹¹遇 *chigū* favor, friendship, appreciation

略 *chiryaku* ingenuity, talents

悉 *chishitsu* complete knowledge of

¹²覚 *chikaku* perception, sensation

¹⁶謀 *chibō* ingenuity, resourcefulness

¹⁹識 *chishiki* knowledge, information, learning, attainments, understanding

識人 *chishikijin* a highbrow, an intellectual

━━━ 4 ━━━

矧 $\frac{3979}{\text{J476a}}$ M23938 SHIN. *ha(gu)* feather (an arrow), fletch.

矩 $\frac{3980}{\text{J366b}}$ M23947 KU. *kane* ruler, carpenter's square.

⁷形 *kukei* rectangle

━━━ 7 ━━━

A 短 $\frac{3982}{\text{J433b}}$ M23978 TAN shortness, brevity; fault, defect, demerit, weak point. *mijika(i)* short, brief.

²刀 *tantō* short sword, dagger

³小 *tanshō na* small, stunted

⁴文 *tambun* short sentence; short composition

日月 *tanjitsugetsu* short period of time

⁵册 *tanzaku, tanjaku* small vertical poem

⁶気 *tanki* quick temper, card⌐ irritability, impatience

⁷見 *tanken* shortsightedness, narrow view

兵急 *tampeikyū na* impetuous; sudden

⁸所 *tansho* shortcoming, defect, fault

命 *tammei* short life

波 *tampa* short-wave (length)

⁹音階 *tan'onkai* minor scale

¹⁰針 *tanshin* hour hand

剣 *tanken* dagger; hour hand

時間 *tanjikan* short time
¹¹ 距離 *tankyori* shortdistance race, dash, sprint
¹² 絡 *tanraku* short circuit
期大学 *tanki daigaku* junior college
期間 *tankikan* short time
¹⁴ 銃 *tanjū* pistol, revolver
歌 *tanka* 31-syllable poem, tanka
¹⁵ 慮 *tanryo* hot temper; shallowness; narrow-mindedness
編 *tampen* short story, short novel
調 *tanchō* minor key

篇小説 *tampen shōsetsu* short story, short novel
¹⁷ 縮 *tanshuku* shortening, curtailment, reduction, abridgment, abbreviation

——————— **12** ———————

矯 _{3984 / J363a / M24015} KYŌ. *ta(meru)* straighten;
B correct, reform, cure; control (one's feelings); pretend, falsify; aim.
⁵ 正 *kyōsei* reform, correction, training

======= RAD. 石 112 =======

Ishi stone. At left: *ishi hen.* Nickname: Stone.

石 _{3985 / J4050 / M24024} SEKI. SHAKU. *ishi* stone,
A pebble, rock; jewel; the go playing stones. *koku* 4.96 bushels; 10 cubic feet (of lumber).
³ 工 *ishiku, sekkō* stonemason, stonecutter
⁴ 化 *sekka* petrifaction
切場 *ishiki(ri)ba* quarry, stone pit
⁶ 臼 *ishi usu* stone mortar, stone mill
灯籠 *ishidōrō* stone lantern
灰 *ishibai, sekkai* lime
材 *sekizai* stone, building stone
⁸ 版 *sekiban* lithography; lithograph
英 *sekiei* quartz
油 *sekiyu* kerosene, petroleum
⁹ 屋 *ishiya* stone merchant, stonemason
造 *ishizuku(ri), sekizō* masonry; made of stone
垣 *ishigaki* stone wall
柱 *sekichū* stone pillar
段 *ishidan* stone step, stone steps
炭 *sekitan* coal; carboniferous
¹⁰ 高 *kokudaka* crop, yield; stipend, salary; amount of rice
¹² 塀 *ishibei* stone wall
塔 *sekitō* tombstone, stone slab, stone monument
棺 *sekkan, sekikan* sarcophagus, stone coffin
畳 *ishidatami* stone pavement, stone flooring; checkered pattern
¹³ 塊 *sekkai, ishikoro, ishikure* stones, pebbles, piece of stone

窟 *sekkutsu* stone cave
¹⁴ 像 *sekizō* stone image; stone statue
碑 *sekihi* tombstone, stone slab, stone monument
綿 *ishiwata, sekimen* asbestos
膏 *sekkō* gypsum, satin spar, alabaster, plaster of Paris
榴 *zakuro* pomegranate
¹⁵ 器 *sekki* stonework; stone implement
器時代 *Sekki Jidai* Stone Age
¹⁶ 頭 *ishi atama* hardhead, obstinate person
²⁴ 鹸 *sekken* soap

——————— **4** ———————

砕 _{3990 / J3a55 / M24080} SAI. *kuda(ku)* break, smash,
B crush; pulverize; tax (one's ingenuity); explain simply. *kudake(ru)* break, crumble, be crushed, go to pieces; become familiar. *kuda(keta)* broken, crushed; familiar, popular, friendly.
⁵ 石 *saiseki* broken stone, rubble; something worthless; crushing rock
氷船 *saihyōsen* icebreaker

研 _{3991 / J3826 / M24080} KEN. *to(gu)* sharpen,
A grind, scour, hone, polish; wash (rice).
⁷ 究 *kenkyū* study, research, investigation
究会 *kenkyūkai* research society

5

玄
玉
王
瓜
瓦
甘
生
用
田
疋
疒
癶
白
皮
皿
目
矛
矢
【石】
示
礻
内
禾
穴
立

究所 *kenkyūjo, kenkyūsho* laboratory, research institute

究科 *kenkyūka* postgraduate course, seminar

究室 *kenkyūshitsu* laboratory, seminar room

究員 *kenkyūin* researcher

9 屋 *togiya* polisher, grinder, sharpener

10 修 *kenshū* study and training

15 摩 *kemma* grinding, polishing; studying

16 磨 *kemma* grinding, polishing; studying

23 鑽 *kensan* study

砂 _{3992 J3a3d M24046} **SA. SHA.** *isago, suna* sand. A

3 山 *sunayama* sand hill, sand bank

5 丘 *sakyū* sand dune, sand hill

6 地 *sunaji* sandy soil

防 *sabō* erosion control

州 *sasu* sandbar, sandbank, reef

7 利 *jari, zari* gravel, ballast, pebbles

8 岩 *sagan, shagan* sandstone

金 *sakin, shakin* gold dust, alluvial gold, placer gold

9 洲 *sasu* sandbar, sandbank, reef

10 原 *sunahara* desert, sandy plain

浜 *sunahama, sahin* sandy beach

時計 *sunadokei* sand clock, hourglass

11 粒 *suna tsubu* grain of sand

12 場 *sunaba* sand pit

13 漠 *sabaku* desert

鉄 *satetsu, shatetsu* iron sand, magnetic sand

14 塵 *sajin* dust storm

糖 *satō* sugar

18 囊 *sanō, shanō, sunabukuro* sandbag

20 礫 *sareki, shareki* gravel, pebbles

砺 _{3993 J4557 M-X} Nonstandard for 礪 4056.

砆 _{3994 J395c M-X} See 鉱 6252.

砧 _{3996 J354e M24099} **CHIN.** *kinuta* fulling block.

砥 _{3997 J4556 M24093} **SHI.** *to* whetstone, grindstone.

5 石 *toishi* whetstone, grindstone, hone

砲 _{3998 J4b24 M24120} **HŌ** gun, cannon, battery; gunnery, ordnance, artillery. B *tsutsu* gun.

3 口 *hōkō* caliber, muzzle (of gun)

丸 *hōgan* cannonball

4 手 *hōshu* gunner

火 *hōka* gunfire, shellfire

5 台 *hōdai* battery, fort

声 *hōsei* sound of firing, roar of a gun

兵 *hōhei* artillery; gunner

8 門 *hōmon* embrasure; battleship porthole; gun

10 座 *hōza* gun platform

12 弾 *hōdan* projectile

塁 *hōrui* battery, fort

13 煙 *hōen* cannon smoke

煙弾雨 *hōen-dan'u* the smoke of guns and a hail of bullets

15 撃 *hōgeki* bombardment, cannonade

20 艦 *hōkan* gunboat

破 _{3999 J474b M24124} **HA.** *ya(buru)* vt tear, rip, A rend; break, crush, destroy; violate, transgress; defeat; baffle, frustrate. *yabu(ku)* vt tear, rip, rend. *yabu(reru), yabu(keru)* vi be torn, tear, rip open; be broken, burst; rupture, collapse; be worn out; be defeated; be frustrated. *yabu(re)* rupture, breach, rent, tear, breakdown, collapse. *yabu(rekabure)* desperation.

4 片 *hahen* fragment, splinter; scrap, broken piece

天荒 *hatenkō* unprecedented, record-breaking

竹勢 *hachiku (no) ikio(i)* violent force

7 戒 *hakai* breaking the Buddhist commandments

却 *hakyaku* destruction, demolition

局 *hakyoku* catastrophe, cataclysm, collapse

8 門 *hamon* excommunication, expulsion

9 風 *hafu* gable

砕 *hasai* crushing, smashing, splintering

約 *hayaku* breach of contract

10 格 *hakaku* exception

---

¹¹ 産 *hasan* bankruptcy

¹² 裂 *haretsu* explosion, bursting, rupture, eruption

¹³ 損 *hason* damage, breakage, breach

滅 *hametsu* ruin, destruction, collapse

毀 *haki* destruction; reversal (by a court)

棄 *haki* breaking (a treaty), revocation, annulment, downfall

廉恥 *harenchi* shamelessness, infamy

¹⁴ 綻 *hatan* failure, ruin, bankruptcy (of business or character)

算 *hasan* checking, refiguring; doing over again

¹⁵ 談 *hadan* cancellation, annulment, rupture, breaking off, rejection

¹⁶ 壊 *hakai* destruction, demolition, collapse

───────── 6 ─────────

砦 $\frac{4002}{\text{J3a56}}$ M24098 SAI. *toride* fort, stronghold, entrenchments.

───────── 7 ─────────

硲 $\frac{4004}{\text{J4823}}$ M24243 (国字) *hazama* gorge, ravine, gap, valley. *sako* valley, ravine.

硯 $\frac{4005}{\text{J3827}}$ M24233 KEN. *suzuri* inkstone.

¹⁵ 箱 *suzuribako* inkstone case

硫 $\frac{4006}{\text{J4e32}}$ M24229 B RYŪ sulphur.

⁶ 安 *ryūan* ammonium sulphate

¹¹ 黄 *iō, yuō* sulphur, brimstone

¹⁴ 酸 *ryūsan* sulphuric acid

硝 $\frac{4007}{\text{J3e4b}}$ M24201′ B SHŌ saltpeter.

³ 子 *garasu* glass, pane

¹³ 煙 *shōen* gunpowder smoke

¹⁴ 酸 *shōsan* nitric acid

硬 $\frac{4008}{\text{J3945}}$ M24230 B KŌ. *kata(i)* hard, solid; tough, rigid; tight; steady, firm; strict; safe, reliable, upright; chaste, constant; stiff; bookish; classical; stubborn.

⁴ 水 *kōsui* hard water

化 *kōka* hardening; vulcanization; sclerosis; stiffening

⁶ 式 *kōshiki* hard, rigid

⁹ 派 *kōha* tough elements

度 *kōdo* hardness, solidity

¹⁰ 骨 *kōkotsu* hard bone; firmness, inflexibility, stubbornness

骨漢 *kōkotsukan* sturdy individual, man of will power

¹¹ 貨 *kōka* metallic money, coin

───────── 8 ─────────

碓 $\frac{4012}{\text{J3130}}$ M24294 TAI, TE a foot-driven mortar, a foot-driven mill.

碗 $\frac{4014}{\text{J4f52}}$ M24306 WAN porcelain bowl, teacup.

碕 $\frac{4015}{\text{J3a6c}}$ M24296 KI. *saki* cape, spit, promontory.

碍 $\frac{4016}{\text{J3337}}$ M24283 GE. GAI obstacle.

³ 子 *gaishi* insulator

碇 $\frac{4019}{\text{J4476}}$ M24275 TEI *ikari* anchor, grapnel.

⁸ 泊 *teihaku* anchorage, moorings

碁 $\frac{4020}{\text{J386b}}$ M24261 B GO go, Japanese checkers.

⁵ 石 *goishi* a go stone, a checker

¹⁵ 盤 *goban* checkerboard, go board

───────── 9 ─────────

碩 $\frac{4026}{\text{J4059}}$ M24338 SEKI large; eminent; great.

⁸ 学 *sekigaku* profound scholar

碧 $\frac{4027}{\text{J4a4b}}$ M24334 HEKI blue; green.

⁵ 玉 *hekigyoku* jasper

⁸ 空 *hekikū, aozora* azure sky

碑 $\frac{4028}{\text{J486a}}$ M24364′ B HI monument, tombstone. *ishibumi* stone monument.

玄玉王瓜瓦甘生用田疋扩兴白皮皿目矛矢【石】示礻内禾穴立

⁴文 *hibun* epitaph, inscription
⁵石 *hiseki* tombstone, stone slab, stone monument

磁 $\frac{4029}{\text{J3c27}}$ M24364 Jı magnetism; porcelain.

A

²力 *jiryoku* magnetism
⁴化 *jika* magnetization
⁵石 *jishaku, jiseki* magnet, compass
⁶気 *jiki* magnetism
⁹界 *jikai* magnetic field
¹⁰針 *jishin* magnetic needle
¹²場 *jijō, jiba* magnetic field
極 *jikyoku* magnetic pole
¹³鉄鉱 *jitekkō* lodestone, magnetite
¹⁵器 *jiki* porcelain

―――― 10 ――――

磐 $\frac{4037}{\text{J4858}}$ M24401 HAN, BAN wall (in a mine). *iwa* rock, crag; reef.

確 $\frac{4039}{\text{J334e}}$ M24366 KAKU firm, tight, hard, solid. *tashi(kameru)* ascertain, confirm, verify. *kaku(taru), tashi(ka) na* sure, positive; accurate; reliable; sound, firm; clear, evident; genuine; able, competent; sober, sane; I think; if I remember right. *tashi(ka) ni* certainly, doubtless. *tashi(ka) niwa* for certain. *shika to* certainly, definitely, exactly, firmly, fully.

A

⁵立 *kakuritsu* establishment
乎 *kakko(taru)* firm, determined, indomitable
⁷言 *kakugen* positive statement
⁸固 *kakko(taru)* sure, firm
実 *kakujitsu* certainly, authenticity, reliability
定 *kakutei* decision, confirmation
⁹保 *kakuho suru* secure, ensure, assure, guarantee, maintain
信 *kakushin* conviction, confidence, assurance
約 *kakuyaku* definite promise
¹¹率 *kakuritsu* probability
執 *kakushitsu, kakushū* discord, antagonism
¹²答 *kakutō* definite answer
然 *kakuzen(taru)* definite, positive
報 *kakuhō* definite news, authentic report

証 *kakushō* conclusive evidence, assurance, confirmation, corroboration
¹⁴認 *kakunin suru* verify, certify, confirm, validate

―――― 11 ――――

磨 $\frac{4045}{\text{J4b61}}$ M24449' MA. *miga(ku)* polish, scour; shine (shoes); brush (teeth); improve (skill), cultivate (character), train (the mind). *su(ru)* rub, chafe, file; lose. *su(reru)* rub, chafe, wear; become sophisticated. *to(gu)* sharpen, grind, scour, hone, polish; wash (rice).

B

⁶合 *su(ri)-a(waseru)* fit by rubbing together
¹⁰耗 *mamō* abrasion, wear
¹¹崩 *su(ri)-kuzu(su)* rub to pieces
¹²減 *su(ri)-he(rasu)* wear away, rub down, abrade
減 *mametsu* wear and tear; defacement; crushing (a nerve)
¹⁵潰 *su(ri)-tsubu(su)* pulverize; mash; deface; lose (a fortune)

―――― 12 ――――

礁 $\frac{4048}{\text{J3e4c}}$ M24502 SHŌ sunken rock.

B

磯 $\frac{4049}{\text{J306b}}$ M24465 KE. KI. *iso* seashore, beach.

⁴辺 *isobe* seashore, beach
⁶伝 *isozuta(i)* following the beach
⁸松 *isomatsu* seashore pines
波 *isonami* breakers
¹¹釣 *isozuri* beach fishing

―――― 13 ――――

礎 $\frac{4054}{\text{J4143}}$ M24522 SO. *ishizue* foundation stone, cornerstone.

B

⁵石 *soseki* cornerstone, foundation stone, footstone

―――― 14 ――――

礪 $\frac{4056}{\text{J626a}}$ M24571 REI. whetstone; polish

RAD. 示 113

Shimesu to show. At left: 礻 or ネ (4 strokes) *shimesu hen*. Nickname: Showing.

A 示 $\frac{4060}{\text{J3c28}}$ Jɪ. Sʜɪ indication.
M24623 *shime(su)* show, indicate,
point out, give (an example), signify,
display, express. *shime(shi)* (parental)
discipline; revelation.

⁶ 合 *shime(shi)-a(u)* inform one another;
show one another. *shime(shi)-a(waseru), shime(shi)-a(wasu)*
inform one another; plan together; plot
together

⁹ 威 *jii* demonstration (against something)

¹⁰ 唆 *shisa* suggestion

¹¹ 教 *shikyō* instruction, information

¹⁵ 談 *jidan* settlement out of court

--- 1 ---

A 礼 $\frac{4061}{\text{J4e69}}$ Rᴀɪ, Rᴇɪ salutation,
M24626 salute, bow, courtesy,
propriety, ceremony, thanks, appreciation,
remuneration, return present. *uya*
courtesy.

⁶ 式 *reishiki* etiquette, manners

⁷ 状 *reijō* letter of thanks

⁸ 金 *reikin* honorarium, remuneration,
reward, fee ⌈decorum

法 *reihō* courtesy, propriety, manners,

服 *reifuku* full dress, dress suit,
ceremonial dress, evening dress, dress
uniform, vestments ⌈sacraments

典 *reiten* ceremony, ritual, rite,

拝 *reihai, raihai* worship; adoration;
church service

¹⁰ 砲 *reihō* gun salute

¹² 装 *reisō* ceremonial dress, full dress

¹³ 節 *reisetsu* courtesy, etiquette, propriety,
manners

¹⁵ 賛 *raisan* worship, adoration,
admiration, praise ⌈decorum

儀 *reigi* courtesy, propriety, manners,

儀止 *reigitada(shii)* courteous

儀作法 *reigisahō* courtesy, propriety,
manners, decorum

²² 讃 *raisan* worship, adoration,
admiration, praise

--- 2 ---

祁 $\frac{4063}{\text{J3737}}$ Kɪ. Gɪ big, large;
M24634 excessive; quiet; plentiful.

--- 3 ---

A 社 $\frac{4065}{\text{J3c52}}$ Sʜᴀ Shinto shrine;
M24637 association; firm,
company, office. *yashiro* Shinto shrine.

⁴ 内 *shanai* in the shrine; in the company

⁵ 用 *shayō* for company business

用族 *shayōzoku* persons living high on
their firm's expense account

外 *shagai* outside the company

⁶ 寺 *shaji* shrines and temples

宅 *shataku* company living quarters

名 *shamei* company name

団法人 *shadan hōjin* corporate person

交 *shakō* society; social life

交界 *shakōkai* society circles

会 *shakai* society, community, the
world; social (service)

会人 *shakaijin* a member of society

会主義 *shakai shugi* socialism

会生活 *shakai seikatsu* social life,
community life ⌈sociobiology

会生物学 *shakai seibutsugaku*

会学 *shakaigaku* sociology

会制度 *shakai seido* social system

会事業 *shakai jigyō* social service,
public-welfare work

会面 *shakaimen* society page, local
news page

会科 *shakaika* social studies

会福祉 *shakai fukushi* social welfare

⁸ 長 *shachō* company (firm) president

⁹ 屋 *shaoku* company building

是 *shaze* company policy

風 *shafū* company customs

¹⁰ 員 *shain* company personnel, clerk

¹¹ 務所 *shamusho* shrine office

¹³ 殿 *shaden* main shrine building

¹⁴ 説 *shasetsu* an editorials

--- 4 ---

祇 $\frac{4068}{\text{J3540}}$ Gɪ national god, local
M-X god; peaceful; great.

5

玄玉王瓜瓦甘生用田疋疒癶白皮皿目矛矢石【示ネ】内禾穴立

5

B 祉 4069 / J3b63 / M24641′ SHI happiness.

B 祈 4071 / J3527 / M24640′ KI. ino(ru) pray; wish. ino(ri) prayer, grace.

⁷ 求 ino(ri)-moto(meru) pray for
¹¹ 祷 kitō prayer; devotions; grace; exorcism
¹⁹ 願 kigan suru, ino(ri)-nega(u) pray, implore. kigan prayer, supplication

——————— 5 ———————

祢 4074 / J472a / M-X See 禰 4115.

祐 4079 / J4d34 / M24652′ YŪ help.

A 祖 4083 / J4144 / M24664′ SO ancestor, founder, originator, pioneer.

⁴ 父 sofu grandfather. ōji an old man
父母 sofubo grandparents
⁵ 母 sobo, baba, ōba, oba grandmother
⁶ 先 sosen ancestors
先崇拝 sosen sūhai ancestor worship
⁷ 述 sojutsu exposition, propagation
⁸ 国 sokoku fatherland, native country
¹³ 業 sogyō a business kept in the family for many generations

A 祝 4085 / J3d4b / M24672′ SHUKU, SHŪ celebration, congratulations.
shuku(suru) celebrate, congratulate, bless. iwa(u) congratulate, celebrate, commemorate. iwa(i) celebration, festival, congratulations.

⁴ 日 iwa(i)bi, shukujitsu holiday, festival day, feast day ⌐wedding
⁷ 言 shūgen congratulations; celebration;
⁸ 杯 shukuhai congratulatory cup, a toast
典 shukuten celebration, festival
事 iwa(i)goto, hogigoto auspicious occasion, celebration
¹⁰ 宴 shukuen congratulatory banquet, feast
¹¹ 祭日 shukusaijitsu festivals, feasts
¹² 賀 shukuga celebration, congratulations
賀会 shukugakai congratulatory party
¹³ 福 shukufuku blessing; benediction
辞 shukuji congratulatory address
電 shukuden congratulatory telegram
¹⁵ 儀 shūgi congratulations; celebration;

congratulatory gift; tip

A 神 4087 / J3f40 / M24673′ JIN, SHIN god, deity; mind, soul. kami God, god, Allah. kami(sabita), kan(sabita) venerable, hallowed. kan-, kamu- god.

⁴ 父 shimpu priest, father ⌐Buddhas
仏 shimbutsu, kami-hotoke gods and
⁵ 主 kannushi Shinto priest
出鬼没 shinshutsu-kibotsu elusiveness
代 jindai, shindai, kamiyo age of the gods
仙 shinsen wizard, Taoist hermit-wizard
⁶ 式 shinshiki Shinto rites
色 shinshoku the heart and the countenance; attitude
⁷ 佑 shin'yū providence, divine help
体 shintai god-body in a Shinto shrine
妙 shimmyō na, shimbyō na mysterious, marvelous; admirable; docile, tame, meek; faithful
技 shingi consummate skill
社 jinja, jinsha Shinto shrine
⁸ 官 shinkan Shinto priest
学 shingaku theology
学的 shingakuteki theological
学校 shingakkō theological seminary
⁹ 速 shinsoku speed, promptness, quickness
通力 jintsūriki, shintsūriki occult, supernatural, or divine power
風 kamikaze providential wind; suicide plane. shimpū providential wind
前 shinzen at the shrine, before the god
¹⁰ 酒 miki, shinshu sacred wine, wine offering
託 shintaku divine message, oracle
宮 jingū Shinto shrine; Ise Shrines
格化 shinkakuka deification
秘 shimpi mystery ⌐miraculous
秘的 shimpiteki mystic, mysterious,
¹¹ 道 Shintō, Kami (no) Michi, Kan(nagara) (no) Michi, Shindō Shinto
経 shinkei nerves
経学 shinkeigaku neurology
経症 shinkeishō nervous disease, neurosis ⌐exhaustion
経衰弱 shinkei suijaku nervous
経質 shinkeishitsu nervousness, nervous temperament
¹² 棚 kamidana Shinto household shrine
童 shindō prodigy, child wonder

無月 *kannazuki, kaminazuki, kamina(shi)zuki,* tenth lunar month (the month the gods are all away at the Izumo shrine)

¹³意 *shin'i* divine will, divine decree, providence

殿 *shinden* temple, shrine, sanctuary

話 *shinwa* myth; mythology

楽 *kagura* Shinto dance

聖 *shinsei* divine nature; sacredness, sanctity, holiness; godliness; dignity. *shinsei na* sacred, divine

様 *kamisama* god; God

¹⁶頼 *kamidano(mi)* calling on a god in distress

¹⁷輿 *mikoshi, shin'yo* palanquin of a Shinto god, portable shrine

¹⁸職 *shunshoku* Shinto priest

髄 *shinzui* true meaning, mystery

――――― 6 ―――――

票 $\frac{4089}{\text{J493c}}$ Hyō label; ballot; ticket;
A $\overline{\text{M24694}}$ sign.

⁷決 *hyōketsu* vote, voting

¹³数 *hyōsū* number of votes

祥 $\frac{4090}{\text{J3e4d}}$ Jō, Shō happiness.
B $\overline{\text{M24689}}$ *saga* good omen.

祭 $\frac{4092}{\text{J3a57}}$ Sai. *matsu(ru)* offer
A $\overline{\text{M24700}}$ prayers; celebrate; deify; enshrine; worship. *matsu(ri)* festival, feast. *-sai* festival.

⁴日 *saijitsu* national holiday, festival day, feast day

⁵礼 *sairei* festival, feast, rituals

司 *saishi* priest

⁸典 *saiten* festival, rite

事 *saiji* sacred rites, festival

⁹神 *saijin, saishin* the enshrined deity

¹²場 *saijō* place of a ceremony

¹³殿 *saiden* shrine, sanctuary

¹⁶壇 *saidan* altar

――――― 7 ―――――

祷 $\frac{4093}{\text{J4578}}$ Nonstandard for 禱 4114.
$\overline{\text{M-X}}$

――――― 8 ―――――

禄 $\frac{4096}{\text{J4f3d}}$ Roku fief, allowance,
$\overline{\text{M24741}}$ pension, grant; happiness.

禁 $\frac{4098}{\text{J3658}}$ Kin prohibition, ban,
A $\overline{\text{M24743}}$ embargo; law. *kin(jiru), kin(zuru)* prohibit, ban, forbid, repress, restrain; abstain from.

⁴中 *kinchū* the Court, Imperial Palace, Imperial Household

止 *kinshi* prohibition, ban, taboo, embargo

⁵句 *kinku* tabooed word

札 *kinsatsu* prohibition notice board

令 *kinrei* ban, embargo, interdict, prohibition

⁷足 *kinsoku* confinement

忌 *kinki* taboo, contraindication

⁸固 *kinko* imprisonment

物 *kimmotsu* taboo, forbidden thing, injurious thing, something to avoid

治産者 *kinchisansha* a person adjudged incompetent

制 *kinsei* prohibition, ban, embargo

¹⁰酒 *kinshu* prohibition, temperance, abstinence

¹¹断 *kindan* prohibition

欲 *kin'yoku* self-denial, asceticism; abstinence, continence, mortification

猟 *kinryō* prohibition of hunting; No Hunting

¹³煙 *kin'en* prohibition of smoking; No Smoking

¹⁴漁 *kinryō, kingyo* prohibition of fishing; No Fishing

――――― 9 ―――――

禎 $\frac{4099}{\text{J4477}}$ Tei happiness.
$\overline{\text{M24767}}$

禍 $\frac{4102}{\text{J3252}}$ Ka calamity, misfortune.
B $\overline{\text{M24766}}$ *maga, wazawai* calamity, misfortune, woe, evil, curse.

¹⁰根 *kakon* root of evil

¹³福 *kafuku* weal or woe; ups and downs

禅 $\frac{4104}{\text{J4135}}$ Zen silent meditation;
B $\overline{\text{M24787}}$ Buddhist sect originating in the twelfth century.

⁶寺 *zendera* Zen temple

宗 *zenshū* Zen sect

¹³僧 *zensō* Zen priest

5

玄 玉 王 瓜 瓦 生 用 田 疋 疒 癶 白 皮 皿 目 矛 矢 石 示 礻 [内] 禾 穴 立

²⁰ 讓 *zenjō* abdication

福 4105 / J4a21 / M24768' FUKU fortune, blessing,
A luck, wealth;
food which has been offered to gods.

⁴ 引 *fukubiki* lottery
⁷ 利 *fukuri* prosperity, welfare, well-being
寿 *fukuju* prosperity and longevity
⁸ 祉 *fukushi* prosperity, welfare, well-being
⁹ 神 *fukujin, fuku (no) kami* god of wealth, god of good fortune
音 *fukuin* gospel, good news, glad tidings
¹¹ 運 *fukuun* happiness and good fortune
¹⁴ 徳 *fukutoku* good fortune, happiness and prosperity; good deeds and the resultant prosperity

———— **11** ————

穎 4109 / J3150 / M24824 See **穎** 4173.

———— **12** ————

禦 4111 / J357a / M24820 GYO. *fuse(gu)* defend, protect; resist; keep away, shut out, ward off; prevent.

———— **14** ————

禱 4114 / J-X / M24852 TŌ. *ino(ru)* pray.

禰 4115 / J-X / M24851 **禰** 4116 / J4729 / M-X NE ancestral shrine.
⁸ 宜 *negi* Shinto priest of lower rank

■■■■ RAD. **内** 114 ■■■■
Jū or *ashiato* footprint. Note that this is a 5-stroke radical and is so counted whenever it appears. Nickname: Footprint.

———— **8** ————

¹⁶ 獣 *kinjū* birds and animals

禽 4120 / J3659 / M24893 KIN bird; captive; capture.
tori bird.

■■■■ RAD. **禾** 115 ■■■■
Nogi the katakana *no* plus *ki* "tree." At left: *nogi hen.*
Nickname: 2-Branch Tree (cf. Rads. 75 and 127).

禾 4121 / J3253 / M24906 KA rice; grain; sprouts; straw.

———— **2** ————

禿 4122 / J4645 / M24910 TOKU. *ha(geru)* become bald; become bare. *chibi(ru)* wear out, waste away. *hage* baldness, bald person. *kaburo* baldhead. *kamuro* little girl employed in a brothel as an attendant.

³ 山 *hageyama* bare mountain
¹⁶ 頭 *hageatama, tokutō* baldness, bald head; baldheaded person

秀 4123 / J3d28 / M24911 SHŪ excellence; beauty.
B *hii(deru), sugu(reru)* surpass, excel, tower above, rise to eminence.
³ 才 *shūsai* genius, person of great talents, prodigy
⁷ 抜 *shūbatsu* excellence, pre-eminence

¹⁰ 逸 *shūitsu* supreme excellence; masterpiece

¹⁹ 麗 *shūrei na* graceful, beautiful

A 私 <u>4124</u> / J3b64 / M24913 Sнι I; private affairs. *watakushi, watashi, washi* I, myself, private (affairs). *watakushi suru* think only of one's own gain. *hiso(ka) na* secret, private, stealthy, hushed.

² 人 *shijin* private individual
³ 大 *shidai* private college
小説 *watakushi shōsetsu, shishōsetsu* a first-person novel; an "I" novel
⁴ 心 *shishin* selfishness, private interest
文書 *shibunsho* private document
⁵ 用 *shiyō* personal use; private business, misappropriation, embezzlement
立 *shiritsu* private, nongovernment
生児 *shiseiji* illegitimate child
生活 *shiseikatsu* one's private life
⁶ 有 *shiyū* private ownership
有権 *shiyūken* right of private property
⁷ 見 *shiken* personal opinion
利 *shiri* self-interest, personal gain
⁸ 版 *shihan* private publication
物 *shibutsu* private property, personal effects
的 *shiteki* private, personal
事 *shiji, watakushigoto* personal affairs
服 *shifuku* ordinary clothes; plain-clothes police officer
⁹ 室 *shishitsu* private room
¹⁰ 書函 *shishokan, shishobako* post-office box
書箱 *shishobako* post-office box
¹¹ 道 *shidō* private road, private path
達 *watakushitachi* we
淑 *shishuku suru* adore, look up to, pattern after
設 *shisetsu* private
¹² 費 *shihi* private expense, one's own expense
¹³ 鉄 *shitetsu* private railway line
腹 *shifuku* one's own pocket
腹肥 *shifuku (o) ko(yasu)* line one's own pockets
¹⁴ 塾 *shijuku* private school

─────── 4 ───────

A 秒 <u>4129</u> / J4943 / M24952 Bγō one-sixtieth of a minute (of time, latitude,

degree, etc.).
⁹ 速 *byōsoku* speed per second
¹⁰ 針 *byōshin* second hand (of a watch)
読 *byōyomi* countdown

A 科 <u>4130</u> / J324a / M24950 Ka course, branch, department, faculty, school, college; arm (of defense); family (in biology). *ka(suru), ka(su)* inflict (punishment), fine. *toga* fault, blame; charge, offense, sin, transgressions, trespasses. *shina* actions, deportment. *shigusa* acting, gestures.

⁵ 白 *serifu, kahaku* speech, words, lines, remarks
目 *kamoku* subdivision (in scientific classification)
⁷ 条 *kajō* laws; assortment, category
⁸ 学 *kagaku* science
¹⁰ 料 *karyō* minor fine
挙 *kakyo* the (ancient) Chinese higher civil-service examinations

A 秋 <u>4131</u> / J3d29 / M24940 Sнū *aki* autumn. *aki(meku), aki(sabu)* feel like fall.

刀魚 *samma* saury, skipper, mackerel, pike
³ 口 *akiguchi* early fall
山 *akiyama* mountains in the fall
⁴ 日和 *akibiyori* clear fall weather
分 *shūbun* fall equinox
⁶ 色 *shūshoku, aki (no) iro* autumn scenery, fall colors
⁷ 冷 *shūrei* autumn chill, cool fall weather
⁸ 雨 *shūu, akisame* autumn rain
波 *shūha* amorous glance, wink
空 *akizora* autumn sky
季 *shūki* autumn
¹² 晴 *akiba(re)* clear fall weather
期 *shūki* autumn
¹⁷ 霜烈日 *shūsō-retsujitsu* withering frost and scorching sun; severe punishment

─────── 5 ───────

A 秦 <u>4133</u> / J3141 / M24995 Sнιν Qin dynasty. *hata* name given anciently to naturalized foreigners.

A 秤 <u>4134</u> / J4769 / M24993 Sнō. *hakari* balances, scales, steelyard.
¹² 量 *hyōryō* estimation, weighing

5

玄玉王瓜甘生用田疋疒癶白皮皿目矛矢石示衤内〔禾〕穴立

B 秩 <u>4135</u> J4361 M24998 CHITSU salary; order.

⁷序 *chitsujo* order, system, discipline, regularity, method

B 租 <u>4138</u> J4145 M24988 SO crop tax; borrowing.

⁹界 *sokai* concession, settlement
¹⁰借 *soshaku suru* lease
借地 *soshakuchi* leased territory, leasehold
借権 *soshakuken* lease, leasehold
¹²税 *sozei* taxes, taxation

B 称 <u>4139</u> J3e4e M25016′ SHŌ name, title; fame; praise. *tona(eru), shō(suru)* name, entitle; claim, plead, pretend to be; praise, admire. *tona(eru)* recite, chant; call upon; cry, yell *(banzai)*; advocate, preach; quote (prices). *tata(eru)* praise, admire.

⁵号 *shōgō* title, degree
⁸呼 *shōko* appellation, name, title
¹²揚 *shōyō* praise, admiration
¹⁵賛 *shōsan* praise, admiration
²²讃 *shōsan* praise, admiration

A 秘 <u>4140</u> J486b M24977 HI secret. *hi(meru), hi(suru)* conceal, keep a secret. *hisoka ni* secretly.

⁴中 *hichū* in secret
⁵史 *hishi* secret history
本 *hihon* treasured book, tabooed book
⁶伝 *hiden* secret, mystery, secret formula
⁸法 *hihō* secret formula, secret process
宝 *hihō* treasure, treasured article
事 *hiji* secret; mystery; private affairs. *hi(me)goto* secret. *misokagoto* secret; clandestine relationship
¹⁰書 *hisho* private secretary
¹¹術 *hijutsu* secret art; the mysteries
訣 *hiketsu* secret; the mysteries; the key to
密 *himitsu* secrecy, privacy, mystery, secret
密話 *himitsubanashi* confidential talk
¹²策 *hisaku* a secret plan
¹³話 *hiwa* secret story; secret history
¹⁴蔵 *hizō* treasuring
¹⁶録 *hiroku* confidential document, secret memoirs
薬 *hiyaku* nostrum, secret medicine

6

A 移 <u>4141</u> J305c M25045 I. *utsu(ru)* move, change, shift, pass into, drift; soak in; be infected, catch (a cold); catch fire, spread. *utsu(su)* move, transfer; pour into, divert (attention), give (a disease to someone). *utsu(rou)* change, shift, fade, decline.

²入 *inyū* import
⁵民 *imin* immigration; emigration; immigrant; emigrant; settler, colonist
⁶行 *ikō suru* veer to, shift to, switch over to. *utsu(ri)-yu(ku)* change, shift, come and go
⁷住 *ijū* migration; emigration; immigration; moving
住民 *ijūmin* emigrant; immigrant; settler; colonist
住者 *ijūsha* emigrant; immigrant
⁸送 *isō* transfer, transport, remove
⁹変 *utsu(ri)-kawa(ru)* change, shift, come and go. *utsu(ri)kawa(ri)* change, transition
¹¹転 *iten* moving; transfer; demise
動 *idō* movement, transfer, migration, turnover, locomotion
¹²植 *ishoku* transplanting; naturalization (of plants); (skin) grafting
¹⁴管 *ikan* transfer of control
²⁰籍 *iseki* changing one's domiciliary registry

7

A 程 <u>4144</u> J4478 M25081′ TEI degree; law; formula; distance. *hodo* limits, limit, extent, degree; moderation; social status; distance; time; amount. *-hodo* about, more or less, as, to the degree.

⁶合 *hodoa(i)* limit, limits
⁷良 *hodoyo(i)* good, favorable, proper; moderate, temperate; vague (answer)
⁹度 *teido* degree, extent, limit, level, standard
¹²程 *hodohodo ni* properly, judiciously, temperately, moderately

A 稀 <u>4145</u> J3529 M25058 KI. KE. *mare na* rare, phenomenal, few. *ki-* dilute (acid).

⁴元素 *kigenso* rare element
少 *kishō* scarcity

5 代 *kidai no, kitai no* uncommon, rare; remarkable, matchless; notorious

6 有 *keu* rare, extraordinary

8 金属 *kikinzoku* rare metals

11 釈 *kishaku* dilution

16 薄 *kihaku na* thin, lean, rare, diluted, sparse, weak

17 覯本 *kikōbon* rare book

稅 | 4146 J4047 M25070' | ZEI tax, duty.

A

4 込 *zeiko(mi)* (salary) before tax is taken out

引 *zeibi(ki)* after taxes

5 収 *zeishū* tax revenue

8 金 *zeikin* tax, duty

法 *zeihō* tax law, taxation scheme

制 *zeisei* tax system

11 率 *zeiritsu* tax rates; tariff

務署 *zeimusho* tax office

14 関 *zeikan* customs; customs house

18 額 *zeigaku* tax amount

──────── 8 ────────

稔 | 4149 J4c2d M25107 | JIN, NIN, NEN harvest; ripen.

稗 | 4151 J-X M25713 | 稗 | 4156 J4923 M-X | HAI humble. *hie* deccan grass, a barnyard grass.

5 史 *haishi* legend, fiction, romance

稜 | 4152 J4e47 M25123 | RYŌ angle, edge, corner; power, majesty.

15 線 *ryōsen* mountain-ridge line

稚 | 4154 J4355 M25120 | CHI young. *itokena(i)* young (child).

B

6 気 *chiki* childishness

7 児 *chigo* baby, child; page; festive children

8 拙 *chisetsu na* unskillful, childish

11 魚 *chigyo* young fish

──────── 9 ────────

稗 | 4156 J4923 M-X | See 稗 4151.

穀 | 4157 J3972 M25188' | KOKU cereals, grain.

A

8 物 *kokumotsu* cereals, grain

倉 *kokugura, kokusō* granary, grain

15 潰 *gokutsubu(shi)* idler, drone

18 類 *kokurui* grains

稲 | 4158 J3070 M25187' | TŌ. *ine, ina-* rice plant.

B

4 刈 *ineka(ri)* rice reaping

5 田 *inada* rice field

6 光 *inabikari* lightning

7 作 *inasaku* rice crop; rice cultivation

8 妻 *inazuma* lightning

10 荷 *Inari* harvest god; fox god

17 藁 *inawara* rice straw

種 | 4159 J3c6f M25174 | SHU kind, class, variety; seed; species. *tane* seed, kernel; kind, species; quality, tone; material; breed; topic; cause, source; trick; data; inside story; secret; leaven. *kusa* materials, origins.

A

3 子 *shushi* seed, pit, stone

子島 *tanegashima* matchlock gun, arquebus

5 目 *shumoku* item; lot; event (as a race)

7 別 *shubetsu* classification, assortment

8 明 *taneaka(shi)* exposure of a trick; exposing a secret

11 族 *shuzoku* race, tribe, family, caste; genus, species

12 無 *tanena(shi)* seedless

痘 *shutō* vaccination, inoculation

13 蒔 *tanemaki* sowing, seeding, planting

14 種 *shuju* variety. *kusagusa* various

種様様 *shuju-samazama* great variety

18 類 *shurui* kind, variety, class, species

──────── 10 ────────

稽 | 4163 J374e M25218 | See 稽 4174.

稿 | 4166 J3946 M25220 | KŌ copy, manuscript, draft; straw.

B

10 料 *kōryō* payment for a manuscript

穂 | 4168 J4466 M25236' | SUI. *ho* ear, head (of grain); crest (of waves).

B

6 先 *hosaki* beard of grain; head of grain; spearhead

116

5

玄玉王瓜瓦甘生用田疋疒癶白皮皿目矛矢石示⻂肉 [ⁱ⁰禾] 穴立

B 稼 4169 J3254 M25217 KA. *kase(gu)* work; earn money. *kasegi* work; income.
⁴ 手 *kasegite* breadwinner, hard worker
¹⁰ 高 *kasegidaka* earnings
¹¹ 動 *kadō* operation, actual work

───── **11** ─────

穐 4170 J302c M25281 Nonstandard for 龝 4184.

穆 4171 J4b54 M25251 BOKU, MOKU respect; sincerity; politeness; beauty; gentleness.

穎 4173 J314f M25267 潁 4109 J3150 M24824 EI heads of grain; point (of an instrument); cleverness.

稽 4174 J-X M-X KEI think, consider; quarrel.
⁵ 古 *keiko* practice, training, study, instruction
古着 *keikogi* gym suit, practice suit

B 穏 4175 J323a M25280′ ON. *oda(yaka)* calm, quiet, peace; moderation. *oda(yakanaranu)* disquieting, alarming, serious, threatening.
⁶ 当 *ontō na* proper, reasonable, just, right, moderate
⁸ 和 *onwa* moderation
⁹ 便 *ombin na* gentle, quiet, peaceable; private, out of court
¹¹ 健 *onken na* quiet, dependable, uniform

A 積 4176 J4051 M25266 SEKI product (in math); acreage, contents, measurement. *tsu(mu)* vt pile up, stack, lay; load, ship, take on; accumulate, amass, save. *tsu(moru)* vi accumulate, be piled up, be amassed; lie on, be covered (with snow); amount to; estimate,

calculate, measure. *tsu(mori)* intention, purpose; belief; motive; expectation; idea; estimate. *tsu(mi)* loading; shipment; capacity. *-zu(mi)* shipment, loading, burden, capacity.
³ 上 *tsu(mi)-a(geru)* pile up, accumulate
⁴ 木 *tsu(mi)ki* toy blocks; piled timber
込 *tsu(mi)-ko(mu)* load, take on, ship. *tsu(mi)ko(mi)* shipping, loading; shipment
分 *sekibun* integral calculus
⁵ 立 *tsu(mi)-ta(teru)* save, reserve, amass. *tsu(mi)ta(te)* reserve funds
立金 *tsumitatekin* reserve fund
⁶ 年 *sekinen* (many) years
⁷ 乱雲 *sekiran'un* cumulo-nimbus clouds
⁸ 金 *tsu(mi)gane, tsu(mi)kin* reserve funds, savings
⁹ 重 *tsu(mi)-kasa(naru)* vi be piled up, accumulate. *tsu(mi)-kasa(neru)* vt pile up, accumulate
¹⁰ 荷 *tsu(mi)ni* load, freight, cargo, shipment
¹¹ 雪 *sekisetsu* drifted snow, deep snow, snowdrift
極 *sekkyoku* the positive
極的 *sekkyokuteki* positive, active, constructive, progressive
¹³ 載 *sekisai* lading, loading, carrying
載量 *sekisairyō* carrying capacity, load
¹⁴ 算 *sekisan* addition, estimate

───── **13** ─────

穰 4179 J3e77 M25335′ JŌ good crops; prosperity.

B 穫 4180 J334f M25334′ KAKU harvest; reap. *to(ru)* to harvest.

───── **16** ─────

龝 4184 J6354 M25381 See 秋 4131.

━━━ **RAD.** 穴 **116** ━━━

Ana kammuri "hole" crown. Variants: 穴, ⽳. Nickname: Cave.

穴 ―――4187――― KETSU, *ana* hole, aperture,
   J376a
   M25406 slit; gap, stop (of musical
instrument); eyelet; cavity; socket; cave;
den; hiding place; pit; fault, defect; deficit;
grave; dark horse.

³ 子 *anago* sea eel, conger eel
⁸ 居 *kekkyo* cave dwelling
¹⁰ 埋 *anau(me)* filling a hole; stopgap;
   covering a deficit
¹¹ 掘 *anaho(ri)* excavation, digging a hole;
   novice, bungler
¹⁴ 蔵 *anagura* cellar
   熊 *anaguma* badger

――――――― **2** ―――――――

究 ―――4189――― KYŪ. *kiwa(meru)*
A   J3566
   M25409 investigate thoroughly,
master; carry to extremes.

⁸ 明 *kyūmei* investigation, inquiry

¹² 極 *kyūkyoku* eventuality, extremity,
   desperate situation

――――――― **3** ―――――――

突 ―――4191――― TOTSU protruding,
B   J464d
   M25424 thrusting. *tsu(ku)*
thrust, pierce, spear, stab, prick; gore;
lunge at; push, poke; strike (a bell); attack;
strike (at the heart); brave (a storm); be
pungent; strike against; (words) rush (to
one's lips). *tsutsu(ku)* poke, pick at, peck,
elbow. *tsun-, tsu(ki)-* prefix meaning
tsu(ku).

² 入 *totsunyū suru* plunge into, rush in, cut
   in between. *tsu(ki)-i(ru)* rush into.
   tsu(ki)-i(reru) thrust into
³ 上 *tsu(ki)-a(geru)* push up; toss up;
   nauseate
⁴ 止 *tsu(ki)-to(meru)* make sure of
   込 *tsu(ki)-ko(mu), tsu(k)ko(mu)* thrust
   into, poke into; plunge into, dip;
   penetrate, pierce; ram in; close in on;
   give (one) a thrust
   切 *tsu(ki)-ki(ru)* break through, go right
   across
⁵ 付 *tsu(ki)-tsu(keru)* point (a gun at); put
   right under one's nose
   出 *tsu(ki)-da(su), tsunda(su)* push out,
   stick out, stretch out, jut out. *tsu(ki)-*

de(ru) project, stick out, jut, bulge
out. *tsu(ki)da(shi)* protrusion; start;
newcomer; hors d'oeuvre. *tosshutsu*
projection, protrusion, prominence
⁶ 返 *tsu(ki)-kae(su)* thrust in return; refuse
   to accept
   如 *totsujo, totsujo toshite* suddenly,
   unexpectedly
   合 *tsu(ki) a(u)* poke each other, thrust
   each other. *tsu(ki)-a(waseru), tsu(ki)-*
   a(wasu) confront (someone) with,
   bring face to face; compare with.
   tsu(ki)a(i) thrusting one another
   当 *tsu(ki)-ata(ru)* collide; come to the end
   of a street. *tsu(ki)-a(teru)* dash against,
   run against. *tsu(ki)ata(ri)* collision;
   dead end of a street or hallway
⁷ 走 *tsu(p)pashi(ru)* run swiftly
   抜 *tsu(ki)-nu(keru)* vi pierce through,
   break through. *tsu(ki)-nu(ku)* vt
   pierce, shoot through, penetrate
⁸ 放 *tsu(p)pana(su), tsu(ki)-hana(su)*
   throw off, forsake
   刺 *tsu(ki)-sa(saru)* vi stick, pierce.
   tsu(ki)-sa(su) vt pierce, penetrate
⁹ 風 *toppū* squall, sudden gust
   発 *toppatsu* burst, gust, outbreak
¹⁰ 起 *tokki* protuberance, prominence,
   projection
   進 *tosshin* rush, onrush, dash, charge
   倒 *tsu(ki)-tao(su)* knock (a person)
   down
   破 *toppa suru* break through; overcome.
   tsu(ki)-yabu(ru) break through,
   pierce, pass (an exam); exceed, go
   over (a goal)
¹¹ 張 *tsu(p)pa(ru)* stretch (an arm)
   against, plant (one's foot) on; insist
   on. *tsu(p)pa(ri)* prop, brace,
   support, bolster, strut, buttress, (door)
   bar
   貫作業 *tokkan sagyō* rush work
¹² 堤 *tottei* pier, breakwater
   落 *tsu(ki)-o(tosu)* push off, thrust down.
   tsu(ki)oto(shi) sag (in the stock
   market)
   然 *totsuzen* suddenly, unexpectedly
   然変異 *totsuzen hen'i* mutation
¹³ 傷 *tsu(ki)kizu* stab wound
¹⁴ 端 *toppana, tottan* tip of a headland.
   toppashi extreme end
¹⁵ 撃 *totsugeki* charge, assault

5
玄 玉 王 瓜 瓦 甘 生 用 田 疋 疒 癶 白 皮 皿 目 矛 矢 石 示 礻 内 禾 【穴】³ 立

5

玄玉王瓜瓦甘生用田疋疒癶白皮皿目矛矢石示礻内禾【穴】立

³【穴】立

A 空 ⸻4192⸻ J3675 M25415 KŪ air, sky; emptiness; vanity, unreality; hollow; void. *su(ku), a(ku)* vi become empty, be less crowded. *a(keru)* vt empty. *a(ita)* open; empty, vacant. *a(ki)* gap, opening, aperture; space, blank, vacancy. *kara* emptiness, vacancy, hollowness, vacuum. *kara, kara(ppo)* empty. *muna(shii)* void, empty, vain; ineffective; lifeless. *sora* sky, heavens, air, weather, memory, absent-mindedness. *utsu(ro)* hollow, cavity, void; emptiness. *utsuke, ukke* emptiness; dumbness. *kū ni* vainly, ineffectively. *a(ki)-* empty, vacant, unoccupied, spare (hours). *sora-* pretended, sham, mock.

⁴ 文 *kūbun* dead letter, scrap of paper
手 *karate de, kūshu de* empty-handed; with bare fists. *karate* barehanded fighting, karate
手形 *kara tegata* bad check; empty promise
中 *kūchū* air, sky, space. *kūchū no* aerial, air
⁵ 母 *kūbo* aircraft carrier
白 *kūhaku* blank space, vacuum, void
出張 *skarashutchō* collecting travel funds for a trip not taken
⁶ 色 *sora iro* sky blue; weather
回 *karamawa(ri)* racing (of a propeller); skidding (of a car); profitless business activity; fruitless effort
地 *akichi, kūchi* vacant lot, open space, room
缶 *akikan* empty can
気 *kūki* air, atmosphere
車 *karaguruma, kūsha* empty conveyance
冷 *kūrei* air cooled
⁸ 所 *kūsho* space, open space, blank space
⁹ 洞 *kūdō* cave, hollow, cavity
軍 *kūgun* air force
室 *kūshitsu* vacant room
前 *kūzen no* unprecedented, record-breaking
前絶後 *kūzen-zetsugo* unparalleled
¹⁰ 席 *kūseki* vacant seats, vacancy
振 *karabu(ri)* missing a ball, strike
砲 *kūhō* blank shot
家 *akiya* vacant house
挺隊 *kūteitai* airborne unit
¹¹ 転 *kūten, karamawa(ri)* racing (an engine)

瓶 *akibin* empty bottle
虚 *kūkyo* emptiness; hollow; without content; fruitlessness. *kūkyo na* empty, vacant, hollow; inane
巣 *akisu* sneak thief, prowler
¹² 間 *akima* vacant room. *kūkan* space; room; air space
港 *kūkō* airfield, airport
雇用 *koyō* putting a fictitious person on the payroll
費 *kūhi* wastefulness
閑地 *kūkanchi* an open (unused) field
¹³ 漠 *kūbaku(taru)* vast; boundless; vague, dreamy
路 *kūro* air lane
隙 *kūgeki* vacant space, aperture, gap
腹 *kūfuku, sukihara, suki(p)para* hunger, empty stomach
想 *kūsō* daydream, air castle, fancy, imagination, vision
¹⁴ 模様 *sora moyō* looks of the sky, weather
¹⁵ 論 *kūron* abstract or impracticable theory
¹⁶ 輸 *kūyu* air transportation
¹⁹ 爆 *kūbaku* bombing
²² 襲 *kūshū* air raid

⸻ 4 ⸻

B 窃 ⸻4195⸻ J4060 M25453 SETSU. *nusu(mu)* steal. *hiso(ka)na* secret, private, stealthy, hushed.
¹¹ 盗 *settō* theft, larceny

⸻ 5 ⸻

窄 ⸻4197⸻ J3a75 M25455 SAKU. narrow. *subo(mu), subo(maru)* narrow, get narrower. *subo(meru)* make narrower; shut (an umbrella); fold; furl; shrug; pucker up. *tsubo(mu), tsubo(maru)* vi shut, close, get narrower. *tsubo(meru)* vt shut, close; fold; make narrower; gather up (skirts); shrug; pucker up.

穿 ⸻4198⸻ J407c M25436 SEN. *ha(ku)* put on (the feet or legs). *uga(tsu)* dig, cut through, pierce, drill, penetrate; put on, wear. *hojiku(ru), hoji(ru)* dig up; pick (ears or teeth); examine closely; worm

out; pick at (a person). *uga(tta)* happy (expression), witty (remark).

¹¹ 掘 *senkutsu* excavation ⌈footwear
¹² 替 *ha(ki)-ka(eru)* change socks or
²⁸ 鑿 *sensaku* excavation, boring, search, inquiry, investigation

──────── **6** ────────

窒 4200 J4362 M25493 CHITSU plug up, obstruct.
B

¹⁰ 息 *chissoku* suffocation, asphyxiation
素 *chisso* nitrogen

窓 4201 J416b M25494 SŌ window. *mado* window, windowpane.
A

³ 口 *madoguchi* window
⁵ 外 *sōgai* out of the window; outside the window
⁸ 明 *madoaka(ri)* window light
枠 *madowaku* window frame or sash
¹³ 際 *madogiwa ni* at the window

──────── **8** ────────

窟 4206 J3722 M25552 KUTSU. *iwaya* cavern.

──────── **9** ────────

窪 4209 J3726 M25580 A. *kubo(mu)* cave in, sink, become hollow. *kubo(mi)* hollow, cavity, dent, pit. *kubo* depression, hollow. ⌈ground

⁶ 地 *kubochi* hollow, depression, low

──────── **10** ────────

窯 4210 J4d52 M25594 YŌ. *kama* kiln, oven, furnace, stove.
B

¹³ 業 *yōgyō* ceramics, brickmaking, glassmaking, and cement manufacture

窮 4212 J3567 M25593 KYŪ. *kyū(suru)* be destitute; suffer; be perplexed;
B
be cornered. *kiwa(maru)* terminate; reach an extreme; be in a dilemma. *kiwa(meru)* investigate thoroughly, master; carry to extremes.

³ 乏 *kyūbō* poverty
⁵ 民 *kyūmin* poor people
⁶ 死 *kyūshi* dying of distress and poverty
地 *kyūchi* dilemma, predicament
⁷ 迫 *kyūhaku* financial difficulty, distress
状 *kyūjō* distress, sad plight
余 *kyūyo* desperation
余一策 *kyūyo (no) issaku* the last resort
⁸ 屈 *kyūkutsu* narrowness; being cramped; formality, strictness; restraint, oppressiveness
¹² 極 *kyūkyoku* eventuality, extremity
¹⁴ 境 *kyūkyō* dilemma, predicament, extremity

──────── **11** ────────

窺 4215 J312e M25633 KI. *ukaga(u)* watch for (a chance), lie in wait, spy on, reconnoiter; see, discover.

──────── **12** ────────

竈 4216 J3376 M-X See 竈 4221.

──────── **16** ────────

竈 4221 J635e M25703 SŌ. *kamado, kama* kitchen stove, furnace, oven; household. *hettsui* hearth; kitchen stove.

════════ **RAD.** 立 **117** ════════

Tatsu to stand. At left: 𧾷 *tatsu hen*. Nickname: Standing.

立 4223 J4e29 M25721 RYŪ, RITSU standing.
A *ta(tsu)* stand, rise, rouse oneself; be built, be established; go up (smoke); burn out; depart; take flight; run

high (waves); stick into; be worked out; be maintained; save (face); establish oneself, begin life; spread (rumors); shut (doors); be active; open (markets); be excited;

5

玄玉王瓜瓦甘生用田疋疒癶白皮皿目矛矢示礻肉禾穴 【立】⁰

come (seasons); makes (a total of thirty).
ta(teru) stand something up, set up, raise;
put up; set on edge; prick up (one's ears);
build, erect; close (a door); establish;
institute, enact; lay (plans); map out; set
forth, lay down (a proposition); formulate;
render (services), perform; look up to,
respect; be loyal to; do justice to; circulate
(rumors); have (an aim); establish
(oneself), make (a success); support
(oneself); make (an oath); sharpen, set (a
saw); put up (a candidate); make (tea);
save (face). *ta(taseru)* make stand, set
upright, raise, lift up; rouse (to activity).
ta(chi) start, departure; (a charcoal fire)
burning out. *ta(tchi)* standing up
(juvenile). *ta(te)* leading part; leading
actor. *ta(chi-hadakaru)* stand in one's
way, confront. *rittoru* liter. *-ta(teru)* up
(as in stir up noise). *ta(chi)-* standing;
emphatic prefix.

² 入 *ta(chi)-i(ru)* enter, penetrate; interfere
in, be inquisitive
入検査 *tachii(ri) kensa* spot inspection
入禁止 *Tachiiri Kinshi* Keep Out
³ 上 *ta(chi)-a(garu)* stand up, rise, spring
up, regain one's feet, stand erect.
ta(chi)-nobo(ru) rise, ascend. *ta(chi)-*
a(gari) starting; beginning. *ta(chi)-*
a(ge) initialization process
⁴ 木 *ta(chi)ki* standing tree, standing
timber
止 *ta(chi)-do(maru)* stop, halt, stand still
方 *rippō* cube
方体 *rippōtai* a cube
⁵ 札 *ta(te)fuda* notice board, signboard
冬 *rittō* setting in of winter
⁶ 尽 *ta(chi)-tsuku(su)* continue standing
向 *ta(chi)-mu(kau)* face, confront; fight
against; head for
地 *ritchi* location of industry
合 *ta(chi)-a(u)* attend, be present at, take
part in, witness; be pitted against.
tachia(i) presence, attendance;
conference, session; witnessing
会 *tachia(i)* attendance, presence,
witnessing
⁷ 身出世 *risshin-shusse* success in life
役者 *ta(te)yakusha* leading actor;
protagonist; leading spirit
売 *tachiu(ri)* street peddling; street
peddler

志伝 *risshiden* success story
見 *ta(chi)mi* viewing from the gallery
while standing
体 *rittai* solid, solid body
⁸ 所 *ta(chi)dokoro ni* immediately, in an
instant, on the spur of the moment, in
no time; impromptu
並 *ta(chi)-nara(bu)* stand in a row, line
up; be equal to
直 *ta(te)-nao(ru) vi* recover, rally, pick
up. *ta(te)-nao(su) vt* recover, rally;
make over; recover (one's energy);
reorganize, reshuffle. *ta(chi)nao(shi)*
rebuilding as before. *tachinao(ri)*
recovery, restoration
往生 *ta(chi)ōjō suru* make a last stand;
be stalled, be stranded; be nonplused;
be at a standstill
退 *ta(chi)-no(ku)* leave, depart, vacate,
evacuate; take refuge
法 *rippō* legislation, lawmaking
法機関 *rippō kikan* legislative body
⁹ 食 *tachigui(i), risshoku* eating while
standing
派 *rippa na* fine, handsome, excellent,
grand; imposing, commanding,
honorable, respectable; commendable,
noble; prominent; honest; legal,
legitimate; sufficient, justifiable
秋 *risshū* setting in of fall
姿 *ta(chi)sugata* standing pose, standing
position
春 *risshun* setting in of spring
看板 *ta(te)kamban* standing signboard
¹⁰ 消 *tachigi(e)* going out, dying out,
flickering out
夏 *rikka* the official first day of summer
党 *rittō* formation of a new party
候補 *rikkōho* announcing one's
candidacy
案 *ritsuan* plan, design, draft
¹¹ 寄 *ta(chi)-yo(ru)* get near; call at, drop
in, look (someone) up; stop over
脚 *rikkyaku suru* be based on
脚点 *rikkyakuten* position, standpoint,
viewpoint
¹² 場 *tachiba* standpoint, position, footing,
station; attitude; situation; viewpoint;
standing room. *ta(te)ba* stopping
place, stage; cab stand; wholesaler
証 *risshō* proof, demonstration,
substantiation

飲 *ta(chi)no(mi)* drinking while standing

替 *ta(te)-ka(eru)* advance money; pay for another; lend

¹³ 続 *ta(te)tsuzu(ke)* succession, continuation

腹 *rippuku* anger, indignation

話 *ta(chi)banashi* standing and chatting

¹⁴ 像 *ritsuzō* a standing image

¹⁵ 論 *ritsuron* argument; argumentation

稽古 *ta(chi)geiko* rehearsal

¹⁶ 錐余地 *rissui (no) yochi* standing room

憲 *rikken* adopting a constitution

----------- 5 -----------

竜 ₄₂₃₂ J4e35 M25751 龍 ₇₁₀₃ J4e36 M48818 Ryū, Ryō dragon; imperial. *tatsu* dragon.

巻 *tatsuma(ki)* waterspout

¹⁰ 骨 *ryūkotsu* keel

宮 *ryūgū* sea god's dragon palace

¹⁶ 頭 *ryūzu* watch stem

頭蛇尾 *ryūtōdabi* fast start and slow finish; ending in an anticlimax

----------- 6 -----------

章 ₄₂₃₅ J3e4f M25761 Shō chapter; composition; poem; badge, mark, sign; design.

¹³ 節 *shōsetsu* chapter and verse

----------- 7 -----------

竣 ₄₂₃₈ J3d57 M25773 Shun end, finish.

³ 工 *shunkō* completion

童 ₄₂₃₉ J4638 M25775 Dō child. *warawa, warabe* child.

³ 女 *dōjo, dōnyo* girl, maiden, lass

子 *dōji* child, boy

⁴ 心 *dōshin* child's mind, naïveté

⁹ 貞 *dōtei* chastity; (Catholic) nun

¹³ 話 *dōwa* nursery tale, fairy tale, juvenile tale

¹⁶ 謡 *dōyō* children's song, nursery rhyme

¹⁸ 顔 *dōgan* boyish face

----------- 8 -----------

竪 ₄₂₄₀ J4328 M25790 Ju. *tate* length; height; warp.

⁵ 穴 *tateana* pit, hole; mine shaft; site of ancient pit dwelling

¹² 琴 *tategoto* harp; lyre

----------- 9 -----------

端 ₄₂₄₃ J433c M25806 Tan origin; end; point. *hashi, haji, ha* end, tip; edge, border, one side; corner; beginning; scrap of cloth. *hana* beginning, inception; end, edge, verge, point, extremity, cape. *hashita* fraction, odd sum, fragment, scrap. *hashitana(i)* uncouth, rude. *hata* side, edge. *tsuma* end. *hashi kara* one after another. *hashi(kure), hashi(kkure)* scrap, piece, bit. *tan* tip, extremity.

³ 子 *tanshi* terminal (in electricity)

午 *Tango* Boy's Festival (May 5)

⁵ 正 *tansei* correct, just, orderly, proper

末機 *tammatsuki* computer terminal

⁷ 役 *hayaku* minor post; minor role

坐 *tanza suru* sit erect

⁸ 物 *hamono* incomplete set; odds and ends

的 *tanteki na* direct, blunt, frank

¹⁰ 倪 *tangei* limit; from beginning to end; mountain tops and river banks; guess, conjecture

¹² 無 *hashitana(i)* rude. *hashina(ku) mo* suddenly, unexpectedly, accidentally

¹³ 艇 *tantei* boat

数 *hasū* fraction, odd sum

¹⁴ 境期 *hazakaiki* between harvests, lean period

¹⁹ 麗 *tanrei* grace, beauty

----------- 15 -----------

競 ₄₂₄₄ J3625 M25831 Kyō. Kei. *kiso(u), kio(u)* emulate, compete with. *se(ru)* compete, vie, bid; sell at auction. *seri* auction. *-kura* race, bout, contest.

³ 上 *se(ri)-a(geru)* auction off

⁶ 合 *se(ri)-a(u)* compete with, vie for. *araso(i)-a(u)* contend with, quarrel. *kyōgō* concurrence, conflict, competition

争 *kyōsō* rivalry, contest, competition

争相手 *kyōsō aite* competitor, rival

玄玉王瓜瓦甘生用田疋疒癶白皮皿目矛矢石示礻肉禾穴〔立〕¹⁵

6

⁷ 走 *kiso(i)-hashi(ru)* to race. *kyōsō* race
技 *kyōgi* contest, sporting event, tournament, race
技場 *kyōgijō* stadium
売 *seriu(ri)* auction; auctioneer. *kyōbai* auction
⁸ 泳 *kyōei* swimming race
歩 *kyōho* walking race

¹⁰ 馬 *keiba* horse race; horse racing
馬場 *keibajō* racetrack
馬騎手 *keiba kishu* jockey
¹² 落 *se(ri)-o(tosu)* bid successfully, knock down. *kyōraku* auctioning, bidding
¹³ 艇 *keitei, kyōtei* boat race
¹⁴ 演 *kyōen* recital contest
¹⁵ 輪 *keirin* bicycle race

6-STROKE RADICALS

RAD. 竹 118

Take bamboo. Variant: ⺮ *take kammuri* "bamboo" crown. Nickname: Bamboo.

A 竹 | 4246 / J435d / M25841 | CHIKU bamboo. *take* bamboo; bamboo wind instrument.
² 刀 *chikutō, shinai* fencing stick
³ 子 *take (no) ko* bamboo shoots
⁸ 林 *chikurin, takebayashi* bamboo grove
⁹ 垣 *takegaki* bamboo fence, bamboo hedge
竿 *takezao* bamboo pole
¹⁰ 馬 *takeuma, chikuba* bamboo horse; stilts
¹¹ 細工 *takezaiku* bamboo work, bamboo ware
¹² 筒 *takezutsu* bamboo pipe
¹⁸ 藪 *takeyabu* bamboo grove

A 笑 | 4256 / J3e50 / M25885 | SHŌ laughter. *wara(u)* laugh, smile; ridicule; be in full bloom. *e(mu)* smile, bloom; split, open, crack. *emi* smile. *wara(i)* laughing, smile; derision.
⁴ 止千万 *shōshi-semban* extremely funny
⁷ 声 *wara(i)goe, shōsei* laughter, laugh; laughing voice
⁸ 物 *wara(i)mono* object of ridicule
事 *wara(i)goto* laughing matter
¹⁰ 納 *shōnō* your acceptance; receiving
¹³ 話 *wara(i)banashi, shōwa* humorous story
¹⁸ 顔 *egao, wara(i)gao* smiling face, radiant look

—— 2 ——

竺 | 4247 / J3c33 / M25842 | JIKU, CHIKU bamboo.

—— 3 ——

笈 | 4249 / J3568 / M25869 | KYŪ portable bookcase carried on the back.

竿 | 4250 / J3448 / M25854 | KAN. *sao* pole, rod; beam (of scales); (well) sweep; neck (of a violin).
⁶ 竹 *saodake* bamboo pole
¹⁶ 頭 *kantō* top of a pole

—— 4 ——

筥 | 4265 / J3f5a / M25934 | SU, SHI *ke* lunch box; food box; clothes chest.

A 笛 | 4268 / J452b / M25917 | TEKI flute. *fue* flute, pipe, clarinet, whistle, fife, pitch pipe, bagpipe, piccolo.
⁷ 吹 *fue-fu(ku)* play a flute. *fuefu(ki)* flute player, clarinetist

笠 | 4269 / J335e / M25924 | RYŪ. *kasa* bamboo hat; one's influence; lampshade; (chimney) hood.

B 符 | 4270 / J4964 / M25935 | FU sign, mark, tally; charm, amulet.

—— 5 ——

² 丁 *fuchō* sign, mark, token, symbol; code; secret (price) mark; password, countersign

⁵ 号 *fugō* mark, sign, symbol, code

⁶ 合 *fugō* agreement, coincidence, correspondence, conformity

⁹ 点 *futen* dot (in music)

¹³ 牒 *fuchō* sign, mark, token, symbol; code; secret (price) mark; password, countersign

節 *fusetsu* tally, check

笹 `4271 / J3a7b / M25968` (国字) *sasa* bamboo grass.

⁶ 舟 *sasabune* toy bamboo-leaf boat

¹⁰ 原 *sasawara* field of bamboo grass

¹⁸ 藪 *sasayabu* bamboo-grass brush

A 第 `4272 / J4268 / M25943` TEI, DAI residence. DAI- number (1, 2, 3, etc.).

¹ 一 *dai-ichi ni* first, in the first place. *dai-ichi no* first, foremost, primary, initial, principal, chief. *dai-ichi* the first, the best, number one, the greatest

一人者 *dai-ichininsha* an authority, tops (in one's field)

一次 *dai-ichiji* first

一印象 *dai-ichi inshō* first impression

一線 *dai-issen* front line

³ 三者 *dai-sansha* third party, disinterested person

三国 *dai-sangoku* third power

⁴ 六感 *dai-rokkan* the sixth sense

--- 6 ---

筈 `4277 / J4826 / M25990` KATSU. *hazu* notch of an arrow; something that ought to, must, or should be; something to be expected; be due to.

筑 `4280 / J435e / M26002` CHIKU an ancient musical instrument,

¹² 紫 *Tsukushi* Kyushu

筏 `4282 / J4835 / M26000` BATSU. *ikada* raft.

B 筒 `4283 / J457b / M26004` TŌ pipette, tube. *tsutsu* pipe, tube, case, gun barrel, sleeve, well curb.

---

⁷ 抜 *tsutsunu(ke) ni* directly, clearly, just as told

A 策 `4284 / J3a76 / M26009` SAKU plan, scheme, policy; step, means; whip. *saku(suru)* plan.

³ 士 *sakushi* schemer, tactician, man of resources

⁷ 応 *sakuō* cooperation, concert, collusion

¹¹ 略 *sakuryaku* stratagem, scheme, plan, policy, frame-up

動 *sakudō* scheming, maneuvering, manipulation

¹³ 源地 *sakugenchi* base of operations

¹⁶ 謀 *sakubō* artifice, stratagem, frame-up

A 答 `4285 / J457a / M26006` TŌ answer. *kota(eru)* answer; respond; solve. *kota(e)* answer; solution.

⁵ 弁 *tōben* reply, explanation, defense

申 *tōshin* a report

礼 *tōrei* return salute, return courtesye

¹⁰ 案 *tōan* examination paper

¹³ 辞 *tōji* formal reply, response

A 筋 `4286 / J365a / M25994` KIN muscle, sinew, tendon. *suji* muscle; sinew, tendon; vein; fiber; string; line; stripe, streak; plot, plan; reason, logic; circumstances; thread, sequence; quarters, sources, authorities; lineage, strain, stock, descent; grain, texture. *suji(darake)* sinewy; stringy.

² 力 *kinryoku* physical strength

⁶ 交 *sujika(i)* diagonal, oblique; brace

合 *sujiai* reason

肉 *kinniku* muscles, sinews

⁸ 金 *sujigane* metal reinforcement

¹⁰ 骨 *kinkotsu, sujibone* sinews and bones

書 *sujiga(ki)* synopsis, outline; scenario, plot, story; plan, program, schedule

¹¹ 道 *sujimichi* reason, logic, thread, chain (of reasoning); method, system

¹² 違 *sujichiga(i)* cramp, sprain, absurdity; intersection. *sujikai* diagonal, oblique; brace

---

A 等 `4287 / J4579 / M25992` TŌ class, grade, degree; and so forth; equality. *hito(shii)* equal, similar, alike, equivalent. *-nado* and so forth. *-ra* and others, and the like; a plural ending.

6

〔竹〕
米
糸
缶
网
罒
羊
羽
老
耂
而
耒
耳
聿
肉
月
臣
自
至
臼
舌
舛
舟
艮
色
艸
艹
虍
虫
血
行
衣
衤
西

⁴分 *tōbun* division into equal parts; equal parts
比 *tōhi* proportion
辺 *tōhen* equal sides
⁵外 *tōgai* inferior grades
号 *tōgō* the sign of addition
圧線 *tōatsusen* isobar
⁶式 *tōshiki* equality
⁷角 *tōkaku* equal angles
身 *tōshin* life-size
⁸価 *tōka* equivalence, parity
⁹級 *tōkyū* class, grade, order, rank, magnitude, rating, classification
¹⁰高線 *tōkōsen* contour line
差 *tōsa* difference; equal difference
¹¹距離 *tōkyori* equal distances; equidistance
¹²閑 *naozari, tōkan* neglect, disregard
量 *tōryō no* equivalent
等 *tōtō* etc., and so forth
温線 *tōonsen* isotherm
¹⁵質 *tōshitsu* homogeneity

筆 _{4288 J492e M25987} **A** HITSU. *fude* writing brush, paintbrush; writing, drawing, painting; the pen; handwriting, penmanship; literary work.
² 入 *fudei(re)* writing-brush holder. *fude (o) i(reru)* correct a document
力 *hitsuryoku* power of the pen
⁴太 *fudebuto ni* in bold strokes, in a bold hand, in bold lettering
不精 *fudebushō* poor correspondent
⁵写 *hissha* copying
⁶舌 *hitsuzetsu* the pen and the tongue
名 *hitsumei* pen name, pseudonym
⁸使 *fudezuka(i)* penmanship; writing technique, stroke of the pen
者 *hissha* writer, author
¹⁰記 *hikki* taking notes; notes, copying
記試験 *hikki shiken* written examination
¹²順 *hitsujun* stroke order
¹³跡 *hisseki* holograph; handwriting (specimen)
置 *fude (o) o(ku)* leaving off writing
勢 *hissei* power of the pen; penmanship
¹⁴算 *hissan* calculation
墨 *hitsuboku* pen and ink
¹⁵談 *hitsudan* conversation by writing
¹⁶録 *hitsuroku* recording
頭 *hittō* head of a brush; first in the list

7

節 _{4299 J4061 M26102} **A** SETSU season, period, occasion, time; verse, clause, paragraph, section, stanza; integrity, honor. *ses(suru)* be temperate, be moderate; control, restrain; save, be sparing. *fushi* joint, knuckle; knob, lump, knot; tune, melody; point (in a talk). *notto* knot, nautical mile.
⁴水 *sessui* water economy
介 *sekkai* untimely interference
分 *setsubun* last day of winter
⁵用 *setsuyō* frugality, economy
目 *fushime* knots in lumber
穴 *fushiana* knothole
句 *sekku* annual festival
⁶回 *fushimawa(shi)* melody, intonation
⁸制 *sessei* temperance, moderation, self-restraint ⌈diet
⁹食 *sesshoku* moderation in eating, spare
度 *setsudo* rule, standard; instructions; moderation
約 *setsuyaku* economy
¹²減 *setsugen* curtailment, economy, retrenchment
¹³節 *fushibushi* joints; points (in a talk)
電 *setsuden* economy of electricity
¹⁶操 *sessō* constancy, integrity, honor, chastity

8

箸 _{4301 J4824 M-X} Nonstandard for 箸 4328.

箕 _{4307 J4c27 M26143} KI winnowing device. *mi* winnow, winnowing fan, winnowing fork.

箆 _{4310 J4a4f M26114} HEI, HAI. *hera* spatula. *no* arrow shaft; arrow-shaft bamboo.

箔 _{4312 J4773 M26142} BAKU, HAKU foil, leaf, tinsel, gilt.

箇 _{4315 J3255 M26116} **B** KA, KO counter for things.
⁷条書 *kajōgaki* itemization, items
⁸所 *kasho* place, spot, point, section, part, passage (in a book)

¹⁴箇 *koko* one by one; individuals. *koko ni* individually, separately

算 ⁴³¹⁶ J3b3b M26146 SAN divining (block); calculation; number; abacus; plan; probability. *kazo(eru), san(suru)* number, count, calculate.

A

² 入 *sannyū* inclusion in the calculation
⁴ 木 *sangi* divining block; calculating device
⁵ 出 *sanshutsu* computation, calculation
用 *san'yō, sannyō* calculation, computation
用数字 *san'yō sūji* Arabic numerals
⁸ 定 *santei* calculation, estimate, assessment, amount
⁹ 段 *sandan suru* try, contrive, manage
¹¹ 術 *sanjutsu* arithmetic
¹³ 数 *sansū* calculation, computation; arithmetic, mathematics
¹⁵ 盤 *soroban* abacus; account

管 ⁴³¹⁷ J3449 M26162 KAN pipe, tube; (brush) holder; wind instrument. *kuda* pipe, tube; drunken talk.

A

³ 下 *kanka* jurisdiction, control
⁴ 区 *kanku* jurisdictional area; parish
内 *kannai* within the jurisdiction of
⁵ 外 *kangai* outside the jurisdiction
⁷ 見 *kanken* narrow view; view; personal views
⁸ 制 *kansei* control
弦楽 *kangengaku* orchestra; orchestral ⌐music
¹⁰ 財人 *kanzainin* trustee, custodian, administrator, receiver
¹¹ 絃楽 *kangengaku* orchestra; orchestral music
理 *kanri* managing, administration, supervision, control
理人 *kanrinin* steward, manager, supervisor, executor, caretaker, trustee, steward
¹³ 楽器 *kangakki* wind instruments
¹⁷ 轄 *kankatsu* jurisdiction, control

———— 9 ————

箪 ⁴³²¹ J433d M-X Nonstandard for 簞 4357.

篇 ⁴³²⁴ J4a53 M26257 HEN volume, book; chapter, section, part;

compilation, editing.

箭 ⁴³²⁵ J407d M26193 SEN. *ya* arrow.

箸 ⁴³²⁸ M26224 箸 ⁴³⁰¹ J4824 M-X DO. CHO. JAKU. CHAKU. *hashi* chopsticks.
¹³ 置 *hashio(ki)* chopstick rest

範 ⁴³³⁰ J484f M26253 HAN example, model, pattern; limit.

B

⁷ 囲 *han'i* extent, scope, limits, sphere, range; purview
¹⁹ 疇 *hanchū* category

箱 ⁴³³¹ J4822 M26209 SŌ. *hako* box, case, chest, bin, coffer, railway car.

A

² 入娘 *hakoi(ri) musume* innocent maiden, well-protected daughter
⁶ 舟 *hakobune* an ark; (Noah's) ark
¹⁰ 庭 *hako niwa* miniature garden
¹³ 詰 *hakozume* boxed, cased

———— 10 ————

篭 ⁴³³² J4f36 M26371 籠 See 籠 4376.

篤 ⁴³⁴² J4646 M26344 TOKU. *atsu(i)* kind, cordial, fervent, affectionate; serious (illness). *toku to* deliberately, carefully, seriously.

B

⁷ 志 *tokushi* benevolence; zeal; volunteering
志家 *tokushika* volunteer, self-sacrificing person
⁸ 実 *tokujitsu* sincerity, faithfulness
学 *tokugaku* love of learning
¹³ 農 *tokunō* conscientious farmer

築 ⁴³⁴³ J435b M26298 CHIKU. *kizu(ku)* build, construct.

A

¹ 上 *kizu(ki)-a(geru)* build up
⁶ 地 *tsukiji* reclaimed land. *tsukiji, tsuiji* a roofed mud wall
⁹ 造 *chikuzō* building, construction
城 *chikujō* fortification; castle construction
¹² 堤 *chikutei* embankment, banking
港 *chikkō, chikukō* harbor construction

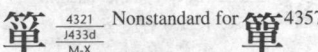

6

竹
【米】
糸
缶
网
皿
羊
羽
老
耂
而
耒
耳
聿
肉
月
臣
自
至
臼
舌
舛
舟
艮
色
艸
艹
虍
虫
血
行
衣
衤
西

11

篠 4352 / J3c44 / M-X — Zō. *shino* a small bamboo. *sasa* bamboo grass.
6 竹 *shinodake* small bamboo

12

簞 4357 / J-X / M26509 — TAN bamboo rice basket.
11 笥 *tansu* chest of drawers, dresser, buffet, cupboard

A 簡 4358 / J344a / M26520' — KEN, KAN brevity; simplicity. *fuda* tag, placard; nameplate; check; charm, (playing) card; tender, bid.
8 明 *kammei* brevity, conciseness
易 *kan'i* simplicity, easiness
易保険 *kan'i hoken* post-office life insurance
9 便 *kamben* simplicity; convenience; expediency
約 *kan'yaku* conciseness, brevity, simplification, abbreviation
要 *kan'yō na* brief and to the point
単 *kantan* brevity, simplicity
10 素 *kanso* simplicity
11 略 *kanryaku* simplicity; brevity, conciseness; informality
15 潔 *kanketsu* brevity, conciseness, simplicity

13

簸 4363 / J4876 / M26609 — HA. *hi(ru)* winnow, fan.

B 簿 4364 / J4a6d / M26623' — BO. HAKU. *-bo* record book.
10 記 *boki* bookkeeping

簾 4365 / J4e7c / M26616 — REN a screen. *sudare, su* bamboo screen, rattan blind.

14

B 籍 4368 / J4052 / M26676 — SEKI domiciliary register; membership.

16

籠 4376 / J6446 / M26752 — RŌ. *ko(mu)* be crowded; requiring (a lot of work). *ko(meru)* include; load (a gun); concentrate on; devote oneself to. *komo(ru)* seclude oneself, be confined in; be implied; be stuffy; be filled with (smoke). *kago* cage, coop; basket. *ko* basket, bamboo containers.
9 城 *rōjō* siege, confinement (indoors). *rōjō suru* be besieged
11 球 *rōkyū* basketball
12 絡 *rōraku suru* cajole, inveigle, entice

RAD. 米 119

Kome rice. At left: *kome hen*. Nickname: Rice.

A 米 4380 / J4a46 / M26832 — BEI. MAI *kome, yone* rice. *-Bei-* U.S.A. *bei-* rice. *mētoru* meter.
7 麦 *beibaku* rice and barley; grain
作 *beisaku* rice culture, rice crop
寿 *beiju* 88th birthday
8 国 *Beikoku* U.S.A.
価 *beika* the price of rice
9 屋 *komeya* rice merchant
軍 *Beigun* U.S. armed forces
10 俵 *komedawara* straw rice bag

11 粒 *kome tsubu, beiryū* a grain of rice
14 穀 *beikoku* rice

3

粂 4382 / J3729 / M26860 — (国字) *kume* used in proper names.

粁 4383 / J364e / M26858 — (国字) *kiromētoru* kilometer, 1000 meters.

籾 4384 J4c62 M26857 (国字) *momi* unhulled rice.

――― 4 ―――

粍 4387 J4c30 M26881 (国字) *mirimētoru* millimeter, one-thousandth of a meter.

粋 B 4389 J3f68 M26875 SUI purity, essence, pith, cream, pick, elite, choice; elegance; fashion; taste; gracefulness; considerateness. SAI. *iki* chic, style.

² 人 *suijin* refined man, romantic man, man about town

粉 A 4390 J4a34 M26872 FUN dust, powder. *ko, kona* flour, meal, powder.

⁵ 末 *fummatsu* powder, dust

石鹸 *kona sekken* powdered soap

⁸ 乳 *funnyū* powdered milk

⁹ 糾 *funkyū* disorder, entanglement, confusion

砕 *funsai* pulverization, smashing, crushing

¹⁰ 骨砕身 *funkotsu-saishin suru* do one's very best

¹¹ 雪 *kona yuki* powder snow

¹³ 飾 *funshoku* makeup, showy ornaments; embellishment

微塵 *kona mijin, komijin* smithereens, fragments

¹⁴ 塵 *funjin* flour and dust; inconsequential things; mundane things

――― 5 ―――

粕 4391 J4774 M26891 HAKU. *kasu* scrap, waste.

¹⁴ 漬 *kasuzuke* vegetables pickled in saké lees

粒 B 4392 J4e33 M26084 RYŪ grain; drop. *tsubu* grain, drop; counter for tiny particles.

³ 子 *ryūshi* particle (of matter); corpuscle

⁷ 状 *ryūjō no* granular

¹¹ 粒辛苦 *ryūryū-shinku no* strenuous, painstaking, assiduous

¹² 揃 *tsubuzoroi* uniformly good

¹⁴ 選 *tsubuyori* the pick of the lot

粘 B 4393 J4734 M26901 NEN. *neba(ru)* be sticky, be glutinous, be greasy; persevere. *ne(ru)* knead. *neba(ri)* stickiness, viscosity; tenacity, perseverance. *neba(i), neba(tta)* sticky.

³ 土 *nendo, nebatsuchi* clay, slime

⁶ 気 *neba(ri)ke, neba(rik)ke* stickiness, viscosity; tenacity, perseverance

⁹ 度 *nendo* viscosity

¹¹ 強 *neba(ri)zuyo(i)* tenacious, persevering

液 *nen'eki* mucus, phlegm; slime

¹² 着 *neba(ri)-tsu(ku)* be sticky, adhere to. *nenchaku* adhesion

¹⁴ 膜 *nemmaku* mucous membrane

粗 B 4394 J4146 M26898 SO roughness, coarseness; not fine; neglect; carelessness. *ara(i), ara(ppoi)* coarse, rough, rugged; loose (fabric); large (meshes). *ara* defect, flaw, blemish. *ara-* rough, coarse, natural, sparse, crude.

³ 大 *sodai na* coarse, rough

⁵ 末 *somatsu na* crude, rough, plain, humble, shabby; careless, rude. *somatsu ni suru* waste

⁸ 忽 *sokotsu* carelessness, rashness, absent-mindedness; blunder, fault, error

⁹ 食 *soshoku* coarse fare, plain food, poor diet

品 *soshina, sohin* trifling gift; inferior goods

茶 *socha* coarse tea

相 *sosō* carelessness, oversight

¹¹ 探 *arasaga(shi)* faultfinding

略 *soryaku na, zonzai na* crude, rough, plain, humble, shabby; careless, rude

野 *soya na* rustic, rude, vulgar

悪 *soaku na* coarse, crude, inferior

¹² 筋 *arasuji* outline, summary, synopsis

¹⁴ 雑 *sozatsu na* coarse, rough, rude

製 *sosei* crude manufacture

製濫造 *sosei-ranzō* mass production of poor articles

¹⁵ 暴 *sobo na* wild, rude, violent, hard, fierce

¹⁶ 餐 *sosan* plain meal

6
竹
【米】₅
糸
缶
网
罒
羊
羽
老
耂
而
耒
耳
聿
肉
月
臣
自
至
白
舌
舛
舟
艮
色
艸
艹
虍
虫
血
行
衣
衤
西

6

竹
【米】
⁶
糸
缶
网
罒
羊
羽
老
耂
而
耒
耳
聿
肉
月
臣
自
至
臼
舌
舛
舟
艮
色
艸
艹
虍
虫
血
行
衣
衤
西

─────── 6 ───────

B 粧 ₄₄₀₀ J3e51 M26945 SHŌ. *yosōu* adorn (one's person).

粥 ₄₄₀₂ J3421 M26938 IKU. JUKU. *kayu, kai* rice gruel.

粟 ₄₄₀₃ J3040 M26922 ZOKU. *awa* millet.

⁵ 立 *awada(tsu)* have goose flesh (from cold or horror)

─────── 8 ───────

A 精 ₄₄₁₁ J403a M26997 SHŌ. SEI spirit, ghost, fairy; energy, vitality; white rice; details; excellence; purity; skill. *shira(geru)* refine, polish. *kuwa(shii)* full, detailed, minute, accurate; versed in, well informed.

¹ 一杯 *seiippai* with all one's might
² 力 *seiryoku* energy, vigor, vitality
³ 子 *seishi* sperm
⁵ 巧 *seikō na* elaborate, exquisite, delicate
出 *seida(su)* exert oneself, be diligent, work hard
白米 *seihakumai* polished rice
⁶ 肉 *seiniku* fresh meat
気 *seiki* energy, spirit; essence
米 *seimai* white rice
⁷ 励 *seirei* diligence; industry
妙 *seimyō na* fine, exquisite; subtle
⁸ 油 *seiyu* refined oil
⁹ 通 *seitsū suru* be versed in, be conversant with, be posted on
神 *seishin* mind, spirit, soul, heart; intention, motive; the spirit (of the thing)
神分析 *seishin bunseki* psychoanalysis
神分裂症 *seishin bunretsushō* schizophrenia
神的 *seishinteki* mental, spiritual
神病 *seishimbyō* insanity, mental disease
神病院 *seishin byōin* mental hospital, insane asylum
神異状 *seishin ijō* mental derangement
神障害 *seishin shōgai* mental derangement
神衛生 *seishin eisei* mental therapy
神論 *seishinron* idealism; spiritualism

神薄弱 *seishin hakujaku* weak-mindedness
¹⁰ 悍 *seikan na* intrepid, fierce
根 *seikon* energy, vitality
酒 *seishu* refined saké
粉 *seifun* fine powder
華 *seika* essence; brilliance
進 *shōjin* concentration, diligence, devotion; purification; abstinence
進料理 *shōjin ryōri* vegetarian diet, vegetarian food
¹¹ 液 *seieki* semen, sperm
細 *seisai* minuteness, precision, accuracy
彩 *seisai* luster, brilliance; vividness
密 *seimitsu* precision, accuracy; minuteness
¹² 勤 *seikin* diligence, good attendance
¹⁴ 精 *seizei* to the utmost, as far as possible; at most; at best
読 *seidoku* careful reading, discriminate reading
魂尽 *seikontsu(kiru)* lose all one's energy
選 *seisen* careful selection
練 *seiren* refining, smelting, tempering
算 *seisan* exact calculation, accurate account; adjustment; settlement of accounts
製 *seisei* careful manufacture; refining
確 *seikaku* accuracy, precision
¹⁵ 鋭 *seiei na* very powerful; highly efficient (weapons). *seiei* picked (troops)
霊 *seirei* spirit, soul (of the deceased). *shōryō* spirits of the dead, spirit visitor
¹⁶ 緻 *seichi na* nice, fine, minute, subtle, delicate, exquisite, elaborate
糖 *seitō* sugar refining; refined sugar
¹⁸ 髄 *seizui* essence, pith, spirit, soul, essentials, core, kernel, the lifeblood

─────── 9 ───────

糎 ₄₄₁₃ J4138 M27057 (国字) *senchimētoru* centimeter, one-hundredth of a meter.

糊 ₄₄₁₅ J3852 M27037 KO. *nori* paste, glue; starch; sizing.
³ 口 *kokō* bare existence, livelihood, living on others
¹³ 塗 *koto suru* patch up, gloss over

── 10 ──

A **糖** 4420 / J457c / M27070 Tō sugar.
⁴ 分 *tōbun* sugar content
⁶ 衣錠 *tōijō* sugar-coated pill
⁷ 尿病 *tōnyōbyō* diabetes
¹³ 業 *tōgyō* sugar industry
¹⁸ 類 *tōrui* sugars

── 11 ──

糟 4423 / J416c / M27104 Sō. *kasu* dregs, grounds, refuse, sediment, scum, dross.
¹⁷ 糠妻 *sōkō (no) tsuma* a wife married in poverty, a faithful companion

糠 4424 / J3947 / M27105 Kō. *nuka* rice bran.
⁸ 雨 *nukaame* drizzle

油 *nuka abura* rice-bran oil
味2 *nuka miso* salted rice bran paste (for pickling)
¹² 喜 *nuka yoroko(bi)* premature rejoicing

糞 4425 / J4a35 / M27102 Fun excrement. *kuso* feces, excrement, droppings.
² 力 *kusojikara* brute force, great strength
⁷ 尿 *funnyō* excreta, feces and urine
⁹ 便 *fumben* excrement, night soil, stools
¹⁰ 真面目 *kusomajime* absurd seriousness

── 12 ──

B **糧** 4426 / J4e48 / M27132 Ryō. Rō. *kate* food, provisions, bread.
⁹ 食 *ryōshoku* provisions, food, victuals, rations
¹⁰ 秣 *ryōmatsu* provisions and fodder
¹¹ 道 *ryōdō* supply of provisions

▌ RAD. 糸 120 ▐

Ito thread. At left: *ito hen.* Nickname: Long Thread (cf. Rad. 52).

A **糸** 4431 / J3b65 / M27221 Shi thread; one ten-thousandth of a hair.
ito thread, yarn; gut; string (of a violin); (fish) line.
³ 口 *itoguchi* thread end; beginning; clue
⁴ 切歯 *itoki(ri)ba* eyetooth, canine tooth
⁵ 瓜 *hechima* snake gourd
⁷ 車 *itoguruma* spinning wheel
⁸ 雨 *itosame* fine rain
底 *itozoko* bottom rim line (of porcelain)
⁹ 巻 *itomaki* spool, bobbin, reel; beam (in weaving); turning peg
¹⁶ 鋸 *itonoko* scroll saw; jeweler's saw

── 1 ──

A **系** 4433 / J374f / M27223 Kei system; lineage; faction, group; zone; corollary; connection.
⁶ 列 *keiretsu* order, succession
⁷ 図 *keizu* genealogy, pedigree
¹² 統 *keitō* system; geological formation; lineage, ancestry
統的 *keitōteki* systematic

¹⁹ 譜 *keifu* genealogy, lineage

── 3 ──

A **級** 4437 / J3569 / M27258' Kyū grade, class, rank; steps; decapitated head.
⁴ 友 *kyūyū* classmate
⁷ 別 *kyūbetsu* grading
¹³ 数 *kyūsū* series or progression (in math)

B **糾** 4438 / J356a / M-X Kyū. *tada(su)* ask, demand, question; investigate, ascertain, verify. *azana(u)* twist (rope).
⁶ 合 *kyūgō suru* rally, muster
⁸ 明 *kyūmei* arraignment; searching examination
¹¹ 問 *kyūmon* cross-examination; arraignment
¹² 弾 *kyūdan* impeachment, censure

A **紀** 4439 / J352a / M27234 Ki account, narrative, history, annals, geological period.

6

⁴元 *kigen* era, epoch; imperial era; A.D., C.E.
元前 *kigenzen* B.C., B.C.E
元後 *kigengo* A.D., C.E.
⁶行文 *kikōbun* travelogue
⁹要 *kiyō* memoirs, bulletin

約 [4440 / J4c73 / M27242] A. YAKU promise, vow; approximately; abridgment. *yaku(suru)* promise; economize. *tsuzu(maru)* shrink; be summarized. *tsuzu(meru)* condense, reduce, shorten, curtail, abridge; economize. *tsuzu(mari)* conclusion. *tsuzu(mayakana)* neat and small, modest, unpretentious; concise; frugal.
⁴手 *yakute* promissory note
分 *yakubun* reduction of a fraction to lowest terms
⁷言 *yakugen* contraction; summary
束 *yakusoku* pledge, promise; appointment, date; contract, agreement, bargain, betrothal, covenant; condition; convention, rule, destiny
束手形 *yakusoku tegata* promissory note
⁸定 *yakujō* promise, agreement, contract
¹²款 *yakkan* stipulation, agreement, article
¹³数 *yakusū* a measure; a divisor
¹⁴説 *yakusetsu* summary

紅 [4441 / J3948 / M27243] A. GU. KU. Kō red, crimson. *beni* red, crimson; rouge, lipstick. *kurenai* deep red, crimson. *momi* red silk cloth.
¹一点 *kōitten* one red flower in the foliage; sole woman in a men's party; a touch of color
⁴毛 *kōmō* red hair
⁵生姜 *beni shōga* red pickled ginger
玉 *kōgyoku* ruby, carbuncle (gem); Jonathan apple
白 *kōhaku* red and white
⁶色 *kōshoku* red
⁹海 *Kōkai* Red Sea
茶 *kōcha* black tea
¹⁰梅 *kōbai* red-blossom plum tree
¹¹殻 *benigara* Indian red, red-ocher rouge, red oxide of iron
¹²葉 *kōyō* fall colors. *momiji* maple; autumnal foliage; venison
¹³蓮焔 *guren (no) honō* roaring flames

¹⁵潮 *kōchō suru* blush, redden, be rosy; be flushed with drink; menstruate

───── **4** ─────

紘 [4445 / J3949 / M27289] Kō large.

紗 [4446 / J3c53 / M27287] SA. SHA gauze, gossamer.

紐 [4448 / J4933 / M27268] CHŪ. JŪ. *himo* string, cord, braid, lace, band, tape, strap, thong, ribbon; restrictions, conditions.
⁵付 *himotsu(ki)* encumbrance, strings, conditions
¹⁰帯 *jūtai, chūtai* band, bond, tie

索 [4449 / J3a77 / M27306] B. SAKU rope, cord. *tsuna* rope, cord, string, line, hawser, cable; morality. *moto(meru)* search for.
⁴引 *sakuin* index
⁷条 *sakujō* cable, rope
条鉄道 *sakujō tetsudō* cable railway
⁸具 *sakugu* rigging, gear, tackle
¹⁰莫 *sakubaku(taru)* desolate, bleak, dreary
¹¹道 *sakudō* overhead freight-carrying cable
¹²然 *sakuzen(taru)* dry, desolate
¹⁵敵 *sakuteki* searching for the enemy

紡 [4450 / J4b42 / M27305] B. BŌ. *tsumu(gu)* spin, make yarn.
¹⁶錘 *bōsui, tsumu* spindle
¹⁷績 *bōseki* spinning
¹⁸織 *bōshoku* spinning and weaving

紋 [4451 / J4c66 / M27262] B. MON crest; (textile) figures.
⁴切型 *monki(ri)gata no* conventional, hackneyed, stereotyped
⁵付 *montsu(ki)* crested kimono
⁸所 *mondokoro* crest
服 *mompuku* crested kimono
¹¹章 *monshō* crest; coat of arms
¹⁴様 *mon'yō* crest pattern

紛 [4452 / J4a36 / M27295] B. FUN. *magi(reru)*, *magu(reru)* be mistaken

for, be confused with; go astray; be diverted from. *magi(rawasu), magi(rasu)* divert, distract; beguile; evade; conceal. *maga(u)* be mistaken for; become confused. *magi(rawashii)* misleading, ambiguous. *magi(remonai)* obvious, certain. *-magi(re) ni* in a fit of (anger); under the influence of (alcohol).

⁴ 込 *magi(re)-ko(mu), magu(re)-ko(mu)* get lost with; disappear in (the crowd)

⁵ 失 *funshitsu* loss

⁶ 争 *funsō* dispute, quarrel, complications

⁹ 糾 *funkyū* complication, entanglement, confusion

¹⁰ 紛 *fumpun* confusedly, pell-mell

²⁰ 議 *fungi* dissension, controversy, dispute

納 ⁴⁴⁵³ / J473c / M27264 Nō. Tō. Na. *osa(meru)* A obtain, reap; dedicate, consecrate; pay; supply; store; finish; collect; restore; replace; accept (a present); bury; gather; rally (troops); sheathe (the sword). *osa(maru)* be paid; be restored; stay (in the stomach); look composed; be contented; be satisfied; be settled. *osa(mari)* end, settlement, conclusion. *osa(me)* tax; the end.

² 入 *nōnyū* payment; delivery

⁴ 戸 *nando* closet, back room, storeroom

⁵ 付 *nōfu* payment, delivery

⁶ 会 *nōkai* the last meeting (of the period)

⁷ 豆 *nattō* fermented soy beans

⁸ 金 *nōkin* payment; money due; money paid

⁹ 屋 *naya* shed, barn

品 *nōhin* delivery; delivered goods

¹⁰ 骨 *nōkotsu* depositing the ashes (of the dead)

骨堂 *nōkotsudō* ossuary, crypt

¹¹ 得 *nattoku* assent, agreement, consent, compliance

涼 *nōryō* enjoying the cool of the evening

¹² 期 *nōki* payment date, delivery date

税 *nōzei* tax payment

純 ⁴⁴⁵⁴ / J3d63 / M27277 Jun purity, innocence; net A (profit). *jun na* pure, innocent, chaste, natural, genuine.

⁴ 心 *junshin* purity, sincerity

毛 *jummō* all-wool

文学 *jumbungaku* pure literature

⁵ 白 *jumpaku* pure white

正 *junsei na* pure, genuine

⁶ 朴 *jumboku* simplicity and honesty

血 *junketsu no* purebred, thoroughbred

⁷ 良 *junryō* pure, genuine

⁸ 金 *junkin* pure gold, solid gold

国産 *junkokusan* an all-Japanese product

⁹ 度 *jundo* purity

¹⁰ 真 *junshin* purity, sincerity

粋 *junsui* purity, genuineness

益 *jun'eki* clear profit

¹¹ 情 *junjō* pure heart; naïveté; self-sacrificing devotion

¹² 然 *junzen(taru)* pure, sheer, veritable, absolute, perfect

¹⁴ 銀 *jungin* pure silver, solid silver

¹⁵ 潔 *junketsu* purity, integrity, innocence

紙 ⁴⁴⁵⁵ / J3b66 / M27293 Shi *kami* paper. A

¹ 一重 *kami hitoe* tiny crack; something very thin; very slight difference

² 入 *kamii(re)* purse, wallet

³ 上 *shijō de* on paper; by letter; in the newspaper or magazine

⁴ 片 *shihen* piece of paper

切 *kamiki(re), kamigi(re)* piece of paper. *kamiki(ri)* paper knife; paper cutter

⁵ 芝居 *kami shibai* picture-story show

⁹ 面 *shimen* (newspaper) space; letter; newspaper

挟 *kamibasami* paper clip

巻煙草 *kamimaki tabako* cigarette

¹⁰ 屑 *kamikuzu* waste paper

屑籠 *kamikuzu kago* wastebasket

¹¹ 魚 *shimi, shigyo* clothes moth, silverfish, bookworm

袋 *kamibukuro, kambukuro* paper sack or bag

¹² 幅 *shifuku* paper width

¹³ 数 *shisū* number of pages

¹⁵ 幣 *shihei* paper money

素 ⁴⁴⁵⁶ / J4147 / M27300 So principle; element. Su A naked, uncovered, simple. *moto* beginning, origin; foundation, basis, source; cause; root (of a tree); (raw) material, base, capital, principal; cost; forebears; formerly. *moto(yori)* from the beginning; of course.

6

竹
米
〔糸〕⁴
缶
网
罒
羊
羽
老
耂
而
耒
耳
聿
肉
月
臣
自
至
臼
舌
舛
舟
艮
色
艸
⺾
虍
虫
血
行
衣
⻂
西

² 人 *shiröto, shiroto* amateur; layman; novice; outsider; unskilled hand; decent woman

³ 子 *soshi* device

⁴ 手 *sude* empty hands, bare hands. *sude de* barehanded, unarmed, with naked fists

⁶ 行 *sokō* conduct, behavior

地 *sochi, soji* grain of wood; plain wood; foundation, groundwork

朴 *soboku* simplicity, artlessness

肌 *suhada* bare skin; stark naked

早 *subaya(i)* quick, agile

⁷ 足 *suashi* bare feet

材 *sozai* raw materials; matter, material, subject matter

⁸ 性 *sujō* birth, parentage, lineage; identity, personal history

的 *suteki* grand, cute, fine, big, splendid, remarkable, superb

直 *sunao na* gentle, meek; obedient; tame; honest, frank

知顔 *soshi(ranu) kao* innocent look

⁹ 面 *shirafu* sobriety, soberness. *sumen* sober face, unmasked face

通 *sudō(ri)* passing through without stopping

透 *sudō(shi) no* transparent; plain glass (spectacles)

封家 *sohōka* rich family; rich person

¹⁰ 振 *sobu(ri)* manner, behavior, attitude, bearing, look

¹¹ 描 *sobyō, sugaki* rough sketch

粒子 *soryūshi* the tiniest particle of matter, elemental (subatomic) particles

¹² 晴 *suba(rashii)* splendid, magnificent, glorious, excellent, superb, remarkable

焼 *suya(ki)* unglazed pottery

¹³ 裸 *suhadaka* nudity

数 *sosū* indivisible numbers

¹⁴ 読 *sodoku* reading without getting the meaning

¹⁵ 膚 *suhada* stark naked

敵 *suteki* grand, cute, fine, big, splendid, remarkable, superb

養 *soyō* elementary attainments

質 *soshitsu* temperament, character, nature; constitution; quality; predisposition

¹⁶ 麺 *sōmen* somen, vermicelli

¹⁸ 顔 *sugao* unpainted face; sober face

───── 5 ─────

紬 ₄₄₆₂ _{J445d} _{M27338} CHŪ. *tsumugi* pongee.

紹 ₄₄₆₅ _{J3e52} _{M27361} SHŌ inherit; help. B

⁴ 介 *shōkai* introduction, presentation

介状 *shōkaijō* letter of introduction

紺 ₄₄₆₆ _{J3a30} _{M27362} KON dark blue, navy blue. B

¹⁴ 碧 *kompeki* dark blue

紳 ₄₄₆₇ _{J3f42} _{M27348} SHIN good belt; gentleman. B

³ 士 *shinshi* gentleman

士服 *shinshifuku* men's wear

士録 *shinshiroku* who's who, directory

絃 ₄₄₆₈ _{J383e} _{M27373} GEN string, chord. *ito* string (on a violin); samisen music.

¹³ 楽 *gengaku* string music

楽器 *gengakki* stringed instruments

累 ₄₄₆₉ _{J4e5f} _{M27343} RUI involvement, trouble; tie up; pile up; continually. B

⁵ 代 *ruidai* successive generations; from generation to generation

犯者 *ruihansha* repeat offender

⁹ 計 *ruikei* total

¹⁰ 進 *ruishin* successive promotions; graduated increase

¹¹ 累 *ruirui(taru)* piled up; in heaps

¹⁶ 積 *ruiseki* accumulation, pile, heap

組 ₄₄₇₀ _{J4148} _{M27374} SO. *kumi(suru)* take part in; be implicated in; side with; support. *ku(mu)* braid, plait; construct; assemble; cross (legs); fold (arms); unite with, cooperate with; grapple with. *kumi* class, party, group; set; pack (of cards); suit; assortment; typesetting. *-gumi* group, gang; company. A

² 入 *ku(mi)-i(reru)* include, insert, enroll

³ 上 *ku(mi)-a(geru)* compose; build up. *ku(mi)-a(garu)* be composed (in printing); be framed (in construction)

⁴込 *ku(mi)-ko(mu)* cut in (in printing); insert, include

分 *kumiwa(ke)* sorting, separation into groups

⁵立 *ku(mi)-ta(teru)* construct, erect, frame, assemble. *kumita(te)* construction, framework, organization, composition, assembly, erection

⁶成 *sosei* composition, formation, constitution

伏 *ku(mi)-fu(seru)* get or hold (a person) down

合 *ku(mi)-a(u)* form a partnership; grapple with; be pitted against. *ku(mi)-a(wasu), ku(mi)-a(waseru)* combine; intertwine; dovetail. *kumiai* association, league, fraternity, union, partnership, guild, trust, cartel, syndicate. *ku(mi)a(i)* grapple, scrimmage. *kumiawa(se)* combination; assortment; braid; matching, pairing; schedule

⁸長 *kumichō* group leader, foreman

版 *ku(mi)han* typesetting, composition

¹⁰紐 *ku(mi)himo* braid

¹⁴閣 *sokaku* formation of a cabinet

¹⁵敷 *ku(mi)-shi(ku)* get or hold (a person) down

¹⁸織 *soshiki* organization, inauguration, composition, structure, setup; anatomy, texture, tissue, organism; system

A 終 $\frac{4471}{J3d2a}$ $\frac{}{M27372}$ SHŪ end. *owa(ru) vi* end, terminate, adjourn, be over; die. *vt* end, finish, complete. *o(eru) vt* end, finish, complete. *owa(ri)* end, conclusion, expiration. *tsui ni* finally, after all.

²了 *shūryō* end, termination, signing off, expiration, conclusion, completion

⁴日 *shūjitsu, hinemosu, himosugara, hisugara* all day

止 *shūshi* termination, cessation, stop

止符 *shūshifu* full stop, period, end

⁵生 *shūsei* all through life; a lifetime

末 *shūmatsu* end, conclusion, termination, settlement, result

⁶年 *shūnen* the whole year; the whole life

⁷局 *shūkyoku* end, conclusion, finale

決 *shūketsu* settlement

身刑 *shūshinkei* life sentence

身雇用 *shūshin koyō* lifetime employment

⁸夜 *shūya, yomosugara* all night

始 *shūshi* beginning and end; from first to last; always

始一貫 *shūshi-ikkan shita* constant, consistent

⁹点 *shūten* terminus

¹⁰息 *shūsoku* cessation, eradication

¹¹焉 *shūen* last moments, death

¹²結 *shūketsu* conclusion, termination

着駅 *shūchaku eki* terminal station

¹³幕 *shūmaku* end, close, curtain; closing scene, closing drama

電 *shūden* the last train or streetcar for the day

電車 *shūdensha* the last train or streetcar for the day

業 *shūgyō* close of work, end of a school term

業式 *shūgyōshiki* closing ceremony

戦 *shūsen* end of the war, termination of hostilities

¹⁵盤 *shūban* nearing the end of the (chess or checker) game

盤戦 *shūbansen* the ending of a campaign

A 細 $\frac{4472}{J3a59}$ $\frac{}{M27344}$ SAI. *hoso(ru)* get thin; taper off. *hoso(meru)* make narrow. *hoso(i)* fine (line); thin (voice); slender; narrow (trousers). *koma(ka) na, koma(kai), koma(i)* small, fine; detailed; minor, trifling; elaborate, delicate; stingy, frugal; small (change). *koma(kashii)* very small. *koma(yakana)* warm, tender, close; minute; deep (color). *(ka)boso(i)* slender, slim, feeble, delicate. *sasa(yakana)* small. *isasa* small. *sazare-* small. *sasa-* small; a few.

³大洩 *saidaimo(rasazu)* absolutely everything

工 *saiku* work, craftsmanship, ware; artifice, device, tactics, trick

⁴心 *saishin* carefulness, discretion

切 *komagi(re)* small pieces of cloth; chopped meat. *komagi(ri)* chopped meat

分 *saibun suru* divide into small parts

6

竹米【糸】缶网罒羊羽老耂而耒耳聿肉月臣自至臼舌舛舟艮色艸⺿虍虫血行衣⻂西

⁵目 *saimoku* details, specifications, items. *hosome* narrow eyes; narrow openings

⁷身 *hosomi* narrow blade

⁸長 *hosonaga(i)* slender, lanky, linear, long and narrow

事 *saiji* minor affair; trifle; details

⁹則 *saisoku* bylaws, detailed rules

胞 *saibō, saihō* cell

¹⁰部 *saibu* details

¹¹道 *hosomichi* path, narrow lane

細 *komagoma* in pieces, in detail. *hosoboso(shita)* slender, delicate, scanty (living). *sasayaka na* small; poor, humble

密 *saimitsu* minuteness

菌 *saikin* germ, microbe, bacteria, bacillus

¹²腕 *hosoude* thin arm; slender means; poor ability

¹³節 *saisetsu* minor details

A 経 4473 J3750 M27392 KEI longitude; sutra; warp. KYŌ sutra. *he(ru)* pass, elapse; pass through; experience. *ta(tsu)* pass, elapse, expire. *he(te)* through, by way of, via. *tate* length; height; warp. *ta(teba)* (a few days) hence. *tateito* warp (in weaving).

⁴文 *kyōmon* sutras

⁵由 *keiyu* via. *keiyu suru* go by way of

世 *keisei* government, administration; statesmanship, statecraft

⁸国 *keikoku* administration, government

典 *kyōten, keiten* sacred books; sutras; the Bible; the canon; the Scriptures

⁹度 *keido* longitude

¹⁰師 *kyōji* paperhanger

¹¹過 *keika* progress, course, development; interim; lapse; expiration; transit (of a moon)

略 *keiryaku* governing (a country)

常 *keijō* ordinary, current (budget)

理 *keiri* management, accounting

理士 *keirishi* public accountant

済 *keizai* economy; economics; finance; thrift

済的 *keizaiteki* financial; economic; economical

済学 *keizaigaku* economics; political economy

¹²費 *keihi* expenses, cost, outlay

営 *keiei* construction; management, operation; development; project

¹³路 *keiro* the road one has traveled; channel; circumstances

¹⁴綸 *keirin* government, administration, statesmanship

歴 *keireki* personal history, career; pilgrimage

¹⁶緯 *keii* longitude and latitude, position; warp and woof; particulars. *ikisatsu* complication, troubles. *tateyoko* length and breadth; every direction; right and left; warp and woof

¹⁸験 *keiken* experience

験談 *keikendan* personal-experience narrative

--- 6 ---

絢 4481 J303c M27427 KEN kimono design.

²¹爛 *kenran(taru)* dazzling, gorgeous, flowery, gaudy

B 絡 4484 J4d6d M27426 RAKU. *kara(mu)* vi coil around, get twisted; stick to; pick a quarrel. *kara(meru)* vt twine around. *shigara(mu), kara(maru)* twist around; get caught in; be urged on by. *mato(u)* wear; wind around.

⁵付 *kara(mi)-tsu(ku)* twist about, entwine; cling to; be caught in

⁶合 *kara(mi)-a(u)* get or be intertwined, be in gear with

¹⁹繰 *karaku(ri)* mechanism, contrivance, scheme, makeshift

B 絞 4485 J394a M27421 KŌ. *shi(meru)* strangle, constrict, wring. *shibo(ru)* wring, squeeze, press, extract; milk; close tight; extort; scold. *shibo(ri)* dapple, white-spotted cloth; stop, diaphragm.

³上 *shibo(ri)-a(geru)* gather up (a curtain); squeeze (money) out of

⁵出 *shibo(ri)-da(su)* press out, squeeze out, drain out. *shibo(ri)da(shi)* (toothpaste) tube

⁹首刑 *kōshukei* death by hanging

¹⁰殺 *kōsatsu* hanging, strangulation. *shi(me)-koro(su)* strangle to death

B 紫 4486 J3b67 M27337 SHI purple, violet. *murasaki* purple, violet; soy sauce.

⁵外線 *shigaisen* ultraviolet rays
¹¹陽花 *ajisai* hydrangea
¹³煙 *shien* tobacco smoke; purple smoke; purple haze
電 *shiden* flashes of lightning
¹⁷檀 *shitan* red sandalwood, rosewood
¹⁹蘇 *shiso* beefsteak plant

A 統 4487 J457d M27447 TŌ relationship; lineage; beginning. *su(beru)* control, supervise, govern. *sube(te)* all, the whole; entirely; in general.

¹一 *tōitsu* unity, unification, consolidation, uniformity, coherence; standardization; rule, dominance; concentration
⁸合 *tōgō suru* integrate, combine, unify
⁸治 *tōchi suru, tōji suru, su(be)-osa(meru)* reign over, rule
制 *tōsei* control, regulation
⁹括 *tōkatsu* generalization. *su(be)kuku(ru)* generalize
帥 *tōsui* high command
計 *tōkei* statistics
¹¹率 *tōsotsu suru* command, lead
¹²御 *tōgyo suru* rule, control, administer
¹⁴領 *tōryō* chief, manager, dictator
¹⁷轄 *tōkatsu* control

A 絵 4488 J3328 M27464 KAI. *e* picture, drawing, painting, sketch, illustration, cut, print.

²入 *ei(ri)* illustrated, pictorial
⁴心 *egokoro* artistic taste
文字 *emoji* picture writing, hieroglyphics
⁵札 *efuda* picture card
本 *ehon* picture book
⁷図 *ezu* drawing, illustration, diagram, plan, design, sketch, map, chart
⁸具 *e(no)gu* paints, colors, oils, pigments
画 *kaiga* picture, painting, drawing
⁹草紙 *ezoshi* picture book
巻 *emaki* picture scroll
¹⁰馬 *ema, euma* votive picture (originally of a horse)
¹¹描 *eka(ki)* painter, artist; painting
¹²筆 *efude* paintbrush
葉書 *ehagaki* picture postcard

A 給 4489 J356b M27432 KYŪ wage; gift; wage grade. *kyū(suru)* allow, grant, supply; favor. *tama(waru), tama(u), tamo(u)* deign to, grant, give, bestow on, honor with.

³与 *kyūyo* grant, ration; compensation, allowance
⁴水 *kyūsui* water supply, water distribution
水車 *kyūsuisha* water wagon
水所 *kyūsuijo* water station
水管 *kyūsuikan* water pipe
⁵付 *kyūfu suru* present, pay, deliver, furnish
仕 *kyūji* office boy or girl, page, bellhop; waiter, waitress; table service
⁷助 *kyūjo* charity, alms
⁸金 *kyūkin* wages
油 *kyūyu* supply of oil; refueling
⁹食 *kyūshoku* providing with food, supplying (school) lunches
¹⁰料 *kyūryō* wages, salary, payroll
¹²費 *kyūhi* scholarship, student support
¹³電 *kyūden* supply of electricity
¹⁵養 *kyūyō* rations, provisions, allowance

A 絶 4490 J4064 M-X ZETSU. *zes(suru)* be beyond (words). *ta(tsu)* sever, cut off; shut off, interrupt; abstain from; eradicate; suppress. *ta(eru)* become extinct, die out, discontinue, end, fail, peter out. *ta(yasu)* exterminate, eradicate, root out; run out of (stock); let (a fire) go out. *ta(ete)* (with neg.) never. *ta(ezaru)* unceasing, continual. *ta(ezu)* constantly, unceasingly; always.

³大 *zetsudai na* tremendous, immense
⁵句 *zekku suru* forget one's lines. *zekku* a style of Chinese poetry
世 *zessei* peerless, unrivaled, unequaled
⁶叫 *zekkyō* scream, exclamation
好 *zekkō no* splendid, grand, first-rate
交 *zekkō* breaking off friendship; breaking off diplomatic relations
⁷妙 *zetsumyō no* most admirable, exquisite, superb
体絶命 *zettai-zetsumei* desperate situation, last extremity
対 *zettai no* absolute, positive, categorical, unconditional
対 的 *zettaiteki* absolute, positive, imperative

6

竹
米
【糸】⁶
缶
网
皿
羊
羽
老
耂
而
耒
耳
聿
肉
月
臣
自
至
臼
舌
舛
舟
艮
色
艸
艹
虍
虫
血
行
衣
衤
西

6
竹 米 【糸】
⁶【糸】
缶 网 皿 羊 羽 老 耂 而 耒 耳 聿 肉 月 臣 自 至 臼 舌 舛 舟 艮 色 艸 艹 虍 虫 血 行 衣 衤 西

⁸ 佳 *zekka no* superb
命 *zetsumei* death
果 *ta(e)-ha(teru)* be extinguished, be exterminated, die out
版 *zeppan* out of print
⁹ 海 *zekkai* distant seas
品 *zeppin* rare article, masterpiece
食 *zesshoku* fasting
¹⁰ 倫 *zetsurin* excellence, superiority
¹¹ 唱 *zesshō* fine poem; excellent song
頂 *zetchō* summit, peak, climax, acme, zenith
望 *zetsubō* hopelessness, despair
¹² 絶 *ta(e)da(e)* faint, almost exhausted
勝 *zesshō* fine scenery
景 *zekkei* superb view
筆 *zeppitsu* one's last literary work
無 *zetsumu* nothing, naught, nil
間無 *ta(e)mana(ku)* continually, unceasingly
¹³ 滅 *ta(e)-horo(bosu)* quench, put out. *zetsumetsu* eradication, extermination
¹⁵ 賛 *zessan* great praise
縁 *zetsuen* insulation; isolation; breaking off relations; dissociating oneself from
¹⁶ 壁 *zeppeki* precipice, cliff, bluff
²² 讃 *zessan* great praise

結 A
⁴⁴⁹² J376b M27398
KETSU. *musu(bu)* tie, bind; tie a knot; make (contracts, treaties, and friendships); join; finish, wind up; unite with; organize. *musu(boreru)* tangle, knot, kink, get twisted; get complicated. *yu(u), i(u)* do up (the hair); make (a braided fence). *iwa(eru), yuwa(eru)* bind, fasten, tie, tie up. *su(ku)* make (a net). *musu(bi)* knot; end, conclusion.
³ 上 *yu(i)-a(geru)* do up (the hair)
⁵ 石 *kesseki* calculus, stones (in the biliary or urinary tracts)
句 *kekku* conclusion; after all; the last line of a poem
付 *musu(bi)-tsu(keru)* vt tie up, join together, link together. *musu(bi)-tsu(ku)* vi join with, ally with
氷 *keppyō* freezing; frost
末 *ketsumatsu* end, conclusion, termination, settlement, result
⁶ 成 *kessei* formation, organization

合 *ketsugō suru, musu(bi)-a(waseru)* tie together, unite, combine. *musu(bi)-a(u)* unite with, cleave to. *ketsugō* union, fusion, cohesion, joint, coupling, link
⁷ 局 *kekkyoku* after all, in conclusion
社 *kessha* association, society
束 *kessoku* union, unity
⁸ 実 *ketsujitsu* fruit bearing; success
果 *kekka* consequences, result, effect
¹⁰ 託 *kettaku* conspiracy, collusion, complicity
党 *kettō* formation of a party
納 *yuinō* engagement present
核 *kekkaku* tubercle; tuberculosis
¹¹ 婚 *kekkon* marriage
婚式 *kekkonshiki* wedding
¹² 着 *ketchaku* conclusion, settlement
集 *kesshū* concentration; regimentation; the editing of Gautama's works by his disciples
晶 *kesshō* crystal; crystallization
¹³ 節 *kessetsu* knot; tubercle; nodule
¹⁴ 語 *ketsugo* conclusion
構 *kekkō* structure; architecture; setup; quite sufficient; very well; fairly well. *kekkō na* splendid, excellent
¹⁵ 論 *ketsuron* conclusion
²¹ 露 *ketsuro* formation of dew

――――― 7 ―――――

絹 A
⁴⁴⁹⁹ J3828 M27470
KEN silk. *kinu* silk, silk thread.
⁶ 地 *kinuji* silk fabrics
糸 *kinu ito, kenshi* silk thread
¹⁸ 織物 *kinu orimono* silk goods

続 A
⁴⁵⁰⁰ J4233 M27533
ZOKU continuation, second series. *tsuzu(ku)* vi continue; be contiguous. *tsuzu(keru)* vt continue. *tsuzu(ki)* continuation, succession; another installment, sequel; series; row. *-tsuzu(ki)* row; continuity; succession.
⁵ 出 *zokushutsu* frequent occurrence, series of events
⁶ 行 *zokkō suru* go on, continue, resume
⁹ 柄 *tsuzu(ki)gara* family relationship
発 *zokuhatsu* frequent occurrence, series of events
¹² 報 *zokuhō* further news

¹³続 *zokuzoku* successively, one after another
¹⁴様 *tsuzu(ke)sama ni* successively, consecutively, in a row
¹⁵篇 *zokuhen* sequel, continuation, supplementary volume

継 B
4501
J4751
M27531
KEI. *tsu(gu)* succeed to, inherit; follow; patch; graft (trees); tell. *tsu(gi)* patch. *mama(shii)* fostered (child). *mama-* step-(child, etc.).
³子 *mamako, keishi* stepchild
⁴父 *mamachichi, keifu* stepfather
⁵母 *mamahaha, keibo* stepmother
目 *tsu(gi)me* joint, seam, suture
⁶合 *tsu(gi)-a(wasu), tsu(gi)-a(waseru)* join together, patch, splice, dovetail, glue together
当 *tsugia(te)* patchwork
⁷足 *tsu(gi)-ta(su)* add to, extend, piece. *tsu(gi)ta(shi)* adding to
⁸承 *keishō* succession, accession, inheritance
¹³嗣 *keishi* successor, heir

──── **8** ────

綬
4510
J3c7a
M27565
JU cordon, ribbon (a decoration).

綻
4514
J433e
M27587
TAN. *hokoro(biru)* be rent, be ripped; unravel, run; begin to smile; smile. *hokoro(basu), hokoro(baseru)* tear, rip; smile.

維 B
4516
J305d
M27568
I tie; rope.
⁹持 *iji* upkeep, support, maintenance
¹³新 *Ishin* 1868 Imperial Restoration

緋
4517
J486c
M27604
HI scarlet, cardinal.

綜
4520
J416e
M27533
SŌ rule.
⁶合 *sōgō* synthesis, coordination, composite
⁹括 *sōkatsu* synthesis, summarization, recapitulation

緒 B
4521
J3d6f
M27632
SHO, CHO beginning, inception; end. *itoguchi*

thread end; beginning; clue. *o* cord, strap, thong; clog cord; string.
⁷言 *chogen, shogen* forward, preface, introduction
¹⁵論 *choron, shoron* introduction, preface

綾
4523
J303d
M27591
RYŌ. *aya* design, figured cloth, twill.
⁸取 *ayato(ru)* tie across (the back). *ayato(ri)* string play (cat's cradle, etc.)
¹³絹 *ayaginu* figured silk
¹⁸織 *ayao(ri)* twill

緊 B
4524
J365h
M27603
KIN hard, solid; reliable; tight. *shi(maru)* vi be tightened. *shi(meru)* vt tighten.
⁷迫 *kimpaku* tension, strain
⁹要 *kin'yō* important, momentous
急 *kinkyū* crisis, emergency; urgency, rush
¹¹密 *kimmitsu* rigor, closeness; compactness
張 *kinchō* strain, tension, seriousness
¹⁷縮 *kinshuku* shrinkage, contraction, constriction; strict economy, retrenchment

綱 B
4525
J394b
M27576
KŌ class (in zoology). *tsuna* rope, cord, string, line, hawser, cable; morality.
⁴引 *tsunahi(ki)* tug-of-war; forward puller
⁵目 *kōmoku* gist, outline, main points
⁹要 *kōyō* outline, summary, essentials
紀 *kōki* ropes; law and order, administration, official discipline
紀粛正 *kōki shukusei* enforcement of official discipline
¹²渡 *tsunawata(ri)* tightrope walking, tightrope walker; danger. *tsunawata(shi)* rope ferry
¹⁴領 *kōryō* general plan; main points, summary

綴
4526
J4456
M27579
TEI. TETSU. SETSU. *tsuzu(ru)* spell; compose, write; bind; patch. *to(jiru)* bind, file, sew up. *tsuzuri* spelling, orthography; binding, patching. *tsuzu(re)* rags, tatters. *to(ji)* binding, sewing.

6

竹米【糸】

⁸糸

缶网罒羊羽老耂而耒耳聿肉月臣自至臼舌舛舟艮色艸艹虍虫血行衣衤西

---

⁴方 *tsuzu(ri)kata* composition, theme; spelling, how to spell. *tojikata* binding, how to bind

込 *to(ji)-ko(mu)* file; interleave, insert. *tojiko(mi)* file

⁶字 *setsuji, teiji, tsuzuriji* spelling, orthography

網 _BA 4527 J4c56 M27577 Mō net; network. *ami* net, netting.

⁴戸 *amido* screen door

元 *amimoto* head fisher

⁵目 *amime, ami (no) me* net meshes

⁷状 *mōjō* net form

¹²棚 *amidana* baggage rack

¹⁴膜 *mōmaku* retina

¹⁹羅 *mōra suru* include, contain; collect

緑 A 4528 J4e50 M27541 RYOKU, ROKU. *midori* green; verdure.

⁴化 *ryokka, ryokuka* tree planting, afforestation

内障 *ryokunaishō* glaucoma

⁶色 *midori iro* green. *ryokushoku* green, verdure

地 *ryokuchi* green stretch of land; oasis

地帯 *ryokuchitai* green belt

⁸青 *rokushō* green rust, copper rust

⁹茶 *ryokucha* green tea, Japanese tea

草 *ryokusō* green grass

¹⁰陰 *ryokuin* tree shade, shady nook

¹¹野 *ryokuya* green field

練 A 4530 J4e7d M27631 REN. *ne(ru)* gloss, soften; train, drill; polish; refine. *ne(reru)* be docile, be teachable; become dependable. *ne(reta)* mellowed. *ne(ri)* kneading; glossing (silk).

⁷兵 *rempei* military drill, parade

⁸乳 *rennyū* condensed milk

⁹炭 *rentan* briquette

¹¹習 *renshū* training, practice, rehearsal

習帳 *renshūchō* exercise book, workbook

¹⁶磨 *remma* exercise, training, drilling

綿 A 4531 J4c4a M27592 MEN cotton; cotton thread; cotton cloth. *wata* cotton, cotton wool.

²入 *watai(re)* padded clothes; cotton-quilted bedclothes

⁴毛 *watage* fluff, nap, fuzz, down, pile, fleece

⁶糸 *menshi* cotton thread or yarn

⁷花 *menka* raw cotton

⁹屋 *wataya* cotton dealer

¹¹密 *memmitsu na* minute, detailed; careful, meticulous

¹⁴綿 *memmen(taru)* endless, continuous

製品 *menseihin* cotton goods

¹⁸織物 *men'orimono* cotton goods

総 A 4532 J416d M27620 Sō - whole, all, general, gross, total, full. *su(beru)* control, supervise. *fusa* tuft, tassel, fringe, lock (of hair); cluster, bunch, segment (of an orange). *sō(jite)* in general, as a rule. *sato(i)* clever, intelligent; keen, quick. *sube(te)* all, the whole; entirely; in general.

²力 *sōryoku* full strength

⁴元締 *sōmotoji(me)* general manager

支配人 *sōshihainin* general manager

⁵代 *sōdai* representative, delegate

出 *sōde* full force

目 *sōmoku* catalog; table of contents

本山 *sōhonzan* sectarian headquarters temple

⁶会 *sōkai* general meeting, annual conference, assembly, synod

会屋 *sōkaiya* a gangster who extorts money in return for not causing trouble at a shareholders' meeting

合 *sōgō* synthesis, coordination, composite

合大学 *sōgō daigaku* university

⁷身 *sōmi, sōshin* the whole body

局 *sōkyoku* overseas (newspaper) headquarters

決算 *sōkessan* complete financial statements

攻撃 *sōkōgeki* general attack, general offensive

花 *sōbana* tips to all, rewards for everyone

花的 *sōbanateki* across-the-board, pleasing everyone

体 *sōtai* all, the whole. *sōtai ni* on the whole, in general

体的 *sōtaiteki ni* generally

⁸長 *sōchō* (college) president; secretary-general

和 *sōwa* total

画 *sōkaku* complete number of strokes (in a character)

所得 *sōshotoku* gross income

⁹帥 *sōsui* commander, leader

計 *sōkei* total

則 *sōsoku* general rules, general provisions

括 *su(be)-kuku(ru)* generalize. *sōkatsu* synthesis, summarization, recapitulation

括的 *sōkatsuteki* all-inclusive, all-embracing, lump-sum, general

¹⁰称 *sōshō* general term. *sōshō suru* speak in general terms

員 *sōin* full force, all hands, the entire staff

¹¹菜 *sōzai* daily fare, plain food, ordinary side dish

動員 *sōdōin* general mobilization

理 *sōri* president; leader; prime minister

理大臣 *sōri daijin* prime minister

理府 *sōrifu* prime minister's office

務 *sōmu* general affairs; manager

¹²統 *sōtō* leader, president, generalissimo

裁 *sōsai* president, governor (of a bank)

¹³数 *sōsū* total number

意 *sōi* consensus of opinion

勢 *sōzei* the whole army; all members

辞職 *sōjishoku* resignation en masse

督 *sōtoku* governorship; governor; governor-general

¹⁴選挙 *sōsenkyo* general election

領 *sōryō* ruling; heir, eldest son, eldest child, family head

領事 *sōryōji* consul-general

領事館 *sōryōjikan* consulate-general

¹⁵論 *sōron* general remarks, introduction

¹⁸額 *sōgaku* total amount

────── 9 ──────

緬 4542 J4c4b M27674 MEN fine thread.

⁶羊 *men'yō* sheep

縄 4547 J466c M27729 B JŌ . *nawa* rope, cord.

⁴文 *jōmon* straw-rope pattern

⁹飛 *nawato(bi)* skipping rope

¹¹張 *nawaba(ri)* stretching a rope; cordon; sphere of influence, jurisdiction

線 4548 J407e M27641 A SEN line; track, route; wire.

⁴分 *sembun* line segment

引 *sembi(ki)* ruling lines

⁸画 *senga* line drawing, line engraving

⁹香 *senkō* incense stick

¹³路 *senro* railway track

締 4549 J1479 M27651 B TEI . *shi(meru)* tie, tighten; wring, constrict, strangle; shut; total; control strictly; rebuke. *shi(maru)* be shut, be locked, be fastened; be tight, be firm; become sober, reform; be thrifty. *shi(mete)* total.

⁴切 *shi(me)-ki(ru)* close, close up, keep closed. *shimeki(ri)* closing, closing up; deadline; cutoff; cofferdam

⁵付 *shi(me)-tsu(keru)* bind, throttle; strangle, choke; press hard, compress; control strictly

出 *shi(me)-da(su)* shut out, lock out

⁸具 *shi(me)gu* clamp, fastener

⁹括 *shi(me)-kuku(ru)* hold together, bind; supervise, control. *shi(me)kuku(ri)* supervision, control; completion

約 *teiyaku suru* make a treaty. *teiyaku* treaty, agreement

¹²結 *teiketsu suru* conclude, contract

縫 4550 J4b25 M27805 B HŌ . *nu(u)* sew, stitch, embroider. *nu(i)* sewing; embroidery.

⁴込 *nu(i)-ko(mu)* sew in, tuck

⁵目 *nu(i)me* seam, suture

付 *nu(i)-tsu(keru)* sew on

代 *nu(i)shiro* the margin left for a seam; a seam

包 *nu(i)guru(mi)* actors' clothing to imitate animals; stuffed toys

⁶糸 *nuiito* sewing thread

合 *nu(i)-a(waseru)* sew up, sew together. *hōgō* suturing, stitching

⁸物 *nuimono* sewing, needlework

緩 4551 J344b M27669 B KAN . *yuru(mu)* vi loosen, lessen; relax; be unguarded; be moderate. *yuru(meru)* vt loosen, unbend, unfasten; relax, ease, slacken; mitigate. *yuru(yakana)* loose; easy (grade); gentle, lenient, generous; slow (stream). *yukku(ri)* slowly, gently,

6

竹
米
【糸】
缶
网
罒
羊
羽
老
耂
而
耒
耳
聿
肉
月
臣
自
至
臼
舌
舛
舟
艮
色
艸
艹
虍
虫
血
行
衣
衤
西

leisurely. *yuru(i)* loose, slack; lenient, generous, slow.

⁶行 *kankō* going slowly

⁸和 *kanwa* relief; mitigation; alleviation; pacification

⁹急 *kankyū* high and low speed; tempo; emergency, circumstances

¹⁴慢 *kamman* slow moving; inactivity

¹⁵緩 *yuruyuru* slowly, leisurely, gently

衝 *kanshō* buffer

A **編** 4552 J4a54 M27665 HEN compilation, editing; completed poem; a book; a part of a book. *a(mu)* knit, plait, braid, net, weave, twist, crochet; compile, edit, frame. *a(mi)-* braided, knitted.

²入 *hennyū* entry, incorporation, enlistment, enrollment

⁴戸 *a(mi)do* braided door

⁵目 *a(mi)me* knitting stitch

出 *a(mi)-da(su)* invent, devise, originate, work out

⁶成 *hensei* formation, organization, composition

曲 *henkyoku* arrangement (in music)

合 *a(mi)-a(wasu), a(mi)-a(waseru)* intertwine, knit together

年史 *hennenshi* annals, chronicle

年体 *hennentai* chronological order

⁷述 *henjutsu* gathering materials and writing a book

⁸物 *amimono* knitting, crocheting

制 *hensei* formation, organization, composition

者 *hensha* editor, compiler

¹⁰修 *henshū* compilation, editing

¹¹隊 *hentai* formation (flight)

¹²集 *henshū* editing, compilation

¹⁶輯 *henshū* editing, compilation

²⁰纂 *hensan* compilation, editing

B **縁** 4553 J316f M27656 EN relation, connection, affinity, ties, bond; blood relation; karma relation; fate, destiny; chance; marriage; acquaintance; marriage alliance; veranda, balcony. *fuchido(ru)* add a border. *enishi* relation, connection, affinity, ties, bond; blood relation, karma relation; fate, destiny; chance; marriage; acquaintance; marriage alliance. *fuchi* edge, verge, shore, side, brink, margin, brim, rim, flange, frill,

frame, bank, fringe, border. *heri* edge, verge, brink, margin, border, fringe, rim, brim, hem, limb (of the sun). *yukari* acquaintance; relation; affinity. *yosuga* way, means.

⁴日 *ennichi* a fair; temple festival

辺 *empen* connections, relatives, kith and kin

切 *enki(ri)* separation, divorce, severing of connections

⁵台 *endai* bench

⁸取 *fuchito(ri), herito(ri)* bordering, hemming

者 *enja* relative

⁹故 *enko* relation, connection, affinity

¹⁰起 *engi* history, origin, legend; omen; luck; portent

¹¹側 *engawa* veranda, porch, balcony, open corridor

組 *engumi* betrothal, wedding, marriage; alliance; adoption; fraternization, affiliation

¹²遠 *endōi* late marriage

結 *emmusu(bi)* marriage, marriage tie, love knot

¹³続 *entsuzu(ki)* relationship, connection

¹⁵談 *endan* marriage proposal, offer of marriage, marriage engagement

──────── **10** ────────

B **緯** 4566 J305e M27682 I woof; horizontal; left and right; parallels of latitude; latitude. *nuki* woof.

⁹度 *ido* latitude

B **縛** 4567 J477b M27771 BAKU arrest, binding. *shiba(ru)* bind, tie, fasten, truss, fetter, restrain, chain; arrest, catch. *imashi(me)* binding, bonds.

³上 *shiba(ri)-a(geru)* tie up; truss up

⁵付 *shiba(ri)-tsu(keru)* tie up, fasten to

縞 4569 J3c4a M27777 KŌ. *shima* stripe.

⁹柄 *shimagara* striped pattern

¹⁰馬 *shima uma* zebra

¹⁴模様 *shima moyō* striped pattern

B **繁** 4570 J484b M27803' HAN frequency, complexity, trouble. *shige(ru)* grow thick, be overgrown, be

luxuriant. *shige(ku)* thickly, densely; frequently. *shige(ri), shige(mi)* thicket, bush.

⁴文繡礼 *hambun jokurei* red tape, officialism

⁶忙 *hambō* pressure of business

多 *hanta* very numerous; many things to do

⁸昌 *hanjō* prosperity, success

茂 *hammo* luxuriant growth

⁹栄 *han'ei* prosperity

¹⁰華 *hanka* prosperity, bustle

華街 *hankagai* a busy street

¹¹盛 *hanjō, hansei* prosperity

¹²殖 *hanshoku suru* breed, propagate, increase, multiply

¹⁴雑 *hanzatsu* complexity, intricacy, trouble

縦 A `4571` `J3d44` `M27804` SHŌ. JŪ length, height. *hoshiimama* self-indulgent, wayward, selfish, arbitrary. *tate* length; height; warp. *yoshi* a hesitant OK; if, if by any chance. *tatoe, tatoi* if, even if, though, although.

⁶列 *jūretsu* column, file, queue

⁷走 *jūsō* following a mountain ridge

¹⁰書 *tatega(ki)* vertical writing

¹¹断 *jūdan* cutting vertically

貫 *jūkan suru* traverse from end to end

¹²揺 *tateyu(re)* pitch (of a ship)

¹⁵横 *tate-yoko, jūō* length and breadth; every direction; right and left; warp and woof. *jūō ni* vertically and horizontally

横無尽 *jūō-mujin* rush of business

¹⁶縞 *tatejima* vertical stripes; striped fabric

覧 *jūran* inspection; reading

--- **11** ---

繍 `4572` `J3d2b` `M-X` Nonstandard for 繡 4600.

繋 `4573` `J3752` `M-X` Nonstandard for 繫 4601.

繢 A `4579` `J4053` `M27845` SEKI exploits; unreeling cocoons.

縮 A `4585` `J3d4c` `M27815` SHUKU. *chiji(kamu), chiji(mu), chiji(komaru)*

shrink, contract, shrivel, wrinkle. *chiji(masu), chiji(meru), chiji(komeru)* shorten, contract, shrink, reduce, boil down, simplify, abbreviate, abridge, condense, compress, crumple, wrinkle, withdraw. *chiji(keru), chiji(maru)* be shortened, be contracted, be reduced, be abridged; be abbreviated, shrink, shrivel, wrinkle. *chijiku(reru), chiji(kamaru)* curl up; squeeze into; shrink, shorten, contract, be abridged. *chiji(reru)* be wavy, curl; shrink; be corrugated, be wrinkled. *chiji(rakasu), chiji(rasu), chiji(raseru)* vt curl, crinkle, crimp. *chiji(mi)* crepe, shrunken cloth.

³小 *shukushō* reduction, retrenchment, cut

上 *chiji(mi)-a(garu)* shrink up; quail, flinch, wince, cower

⁴毛 *chiji(re)ge* curly, wavy, or fuzzy hair

尺 *shukushaku* reduced scale

⁵写 *shukusha* copying on a small scale; reduced copy

⁷図 *shukuzu* reduced drawing, miniature copy; epitome

⁸刷版 *shukusatsuban* small-type edition, pocket edition

¹²減 *shukugen suru* reduce

繊 B `4586` `J4121` `M27874` SEN fine, slender; thin kimono.

¹¹細 *sensai na* fine, nice; delicate; subtle

¹⁴維 *sen'i* fiber, textiles, strand

--- **12** ---

繕 B `4594` `J4136` `M27893` ZEN. *tsukuro(u)* repair, mend, darn; trim, tidy up, adjust.

繭 B `4595` `J4b7a` `M27944` KEN. *mayu* cocoon.

織 A `4596` `J3l25` `M27892` SHOKU, SHIKI weaving. *o(ru)* weave *o(ri)* fabric, weave.

⁴込 *o(ri)-ko(mu)* weave into

⁵交 *o(ri)-maji(eru)* weave into

⁸物 *orimono* cloth; textiles

物業 *orimonogyō* textile manufacturing

¹⁶機 *shokki* weaving machine, loom

6

竹 米 糸 [缶] 网 罒 羊 羽 老 耂 而 耒 耳 聿 肉 月 臣 自 至 臼 舌 舛 舟 艮 色 艸 艹 虍 虫 血 行 衣 衤 西

繡 `4600` `J-X` `M27913` SHŪ sew; figured cloth.

繋 `4601` `J-X` `M27940` 繫 `4573` `J3752` `M-X` KEI. *tsuna(gu)* tie, fasten, chain, hitch, tether; moor; keep on a leash; connect, join; sustain, preserve (life). *tsuna(garu)* be connected, be tied up, be fastened to; be related to, follow closely. *kaka(ru)* anchor, lie at anchor. *tsuna(gi)* connection, bond, tie; stopgap, substitute.

⁵ 目 *tsuna(gi)me* joint
⁶ 合 *tsuna(gi)-a(waseru)* connect, join
  争 *keisō* dispute, contention
¹⁰ 索 *keisaku* mooring ropes
  留 *keiryū* mooring, anchorage
¹¹ 累 *keirui* encumbrances, dependents
  船 *keisen* mooring (a ship)
¹² 属 *keizoku* relationship

繰 `4602` `J372b` `M27953` SŌ. *ku(ru)* reel (thread); B wind; gin (cotton); spin; turn (pages); look up (a word, etc.); refer to; count (the days); open (shutters).

² 入 *ku(ri)-i(reru)* deposit, transfer (money)
³ 下 *ku(ri)-sa(geru)* move ahead (an appointment). *ku(ri)-oro(su)* gradually lower
  上 *ku(ri)-a(geru)* advance (a date)
⁴ 込 *ku(ri)-ko(mu)* deposit, transfer; assign; march in ; rush in; turn out
⁵ 広 *ku(ri)-hiro(geru)* unroll; spread (a rug)

出 *ku(ri)-da(su)* pay out (rope); call out (troops); go forth; disburse
⁶ 返 *ku(ri)-kae(su)* do over, repeat, duplicate
⁷ 言 *ku(ri)goto* tedious talk; repetition; complaint
⁸ 延 *ku(ri)-no(beru)* postpone, defer
¹² 越 *ku(ri)-ko(su)* transfer, carry forward

纂 `4608` `J3b3c` `M28012` SAN editing, compiling.

纈 `4612` `J453b` `M28043` See 纏 4617. *kōkechi, kōketsu* tie-dyeing

纏 `4617` `J6575` `M28058` 纈 `4612` `J453b` `M28043` TEN. *mato(u)* wear; wrap up, tie up. *mato(maru), matsu(waru)* coil around; follow about; dangle after. *mato(meru)* settle, complete, agree upon, arrange; collect; put in order; unify, coordinate. *mato(maru)* be settled, be completed; be collected; be in order; be coherent; be united. *kuru(mu)* wrap up, tuck in. *kuru(meru)* lump together, include, sum up; quibble. *mato(matta)* round, large, definite, coherent. *mato(i)* fireman's standard.

³ 上 *mato(me)-a(geru)* sum up, unite

▬▬▬▬▬▬ RAD. 缶 121 ▬▬▬▬▬▬

Mizugame water jar. At left: *hodogi hen* left-side "earthen jar." Nickname: Jar.

缶 `4624` `J344c` `M28108` KAN can. *kama* steam B boiler.

⁴ 切 *kanki(ri)* can opener

¹³ 詰 *kanzume* canning, canned goods; confining

6

Amigashira "net" crown. Variant: 罒 (5 strokes) *ami me* ("net" shaped like *me* "eye"), *megashira* "eye" crown, or *yoko me* sideways "eye." Nickname: Net.

罫 | 4642 / J3753 / M28295 | KAI. KE, KEI ruled line.

¹⁵ 線 *keisen* ruled line

署 | 4643 / J3070 / M28311 | SHO government
A office, (police) station.
sho(suru) sign, write one's name. *tsukasa* office, government office; director, head official.

⁶ 名 *shomei* signature, autograph ⌐seal
名捺印 *shomei-natsuin* signature and
⁸ 長 *shochō* government office chief; police chief
¹⁰ 員 *shoin* an official attached to an office

罪 | 4644 / J3a61 / M28293 | ZAI. *tsumi* sin, crime,
A offense, guilt, blame, fault,
misconduct. *tsumi suru* charge; sentence; punish.

² 人 *tsumibito* sinner. *zainin* criminal
⁷ 作 *tsumitsuku(ri)* sinfulness; sinner
状 *zaijō* nature of an offense, charges
⁹ 科 *zaika* crime; wickedness; punishment
¹¹ 過 *zaika* offense, sin, fault
深 *tsumibuka(i)* sinful, guilty
悪 *zaiaku* crime, sin, vice ⌐conscience
悪感 *zaiakukan* sense of wrong, guilty
¹² 証 *zaishō* evidence of guilt
¹³ 滅 *tsumihorobo(shi)* amends, expiation, penance, conscience money
業 *zaigō* sin, iniquity, crime
¹⁴ 罰 *zaibatsu* crime, offense

置 | 4645 / J4356 / M28298 | CHI. *o(ku)* vt place, put,
A set, deposit, lay; leave
behind; keep, have, leave; establish; employ; appoint; post, station; pawn; skip (one day). *vi* be formed (dew). *o(keru)* go on (this way); keep (over night). *o(itekibori)*, *o(itekebori)* leaving behind, giving the slip to. -*o(ki)* every other (day). *o(ki)-* standing, placed.

⁴ 手紙 *o(ki)tegami* letter left behind
⁵ 石 *o(ki)ishi* garden landscaping stone
去 *o(ki)za(ri)* deserting (someone)
⁷ 忘 *o(ki)-wasu(reru)* mislay; leave

behind, forget
⁸ 物 *okimono* ornament for display (in *tokonoma*), objet d'art
¹⁰ 時計 *o(ki)dokei* table clock ⌐something
¹² 場 *o(ki)ba* storehouse, yard, place to put

— 9 —

罰 | 4647 / J4833 / M28315 | BATSU punishment,
B penalty. BACHI retribution,
divine punishment. *bas(suru)* punish.
⁸ 金 *bakkin* fine, penalty
⁹ 則 *bassoku* penal regulations
点 *batten* demerit marks

— 10 —

罵 | 4649 / J474d / M28333 | BA. *nonoshi(ru)* abuse,
insult, speak ill of.
⁷ 言 *bagen* abuse, insult, slander, evil
¹⁰ 倒 *batō* denunciation, abuse ⌐speaking
¹² 詈雑言 *barizōgon* abusive language

罷 | 4650 / J486d / M28336 | HI. *ya(mu)* vi end, stop,
B cease; subside, calm down,
pass; die out, be extinguished; leave, go off; be abandoned. *ya(meru)* vt end, discontinue; give up, abandon; abolish; resign, retire. *maka(ru)* leave, withdraw, go. *ya(me)* end, discontinuance, stop.
⁸ 免 *himen* dismissal
⁹ 通 *maka(ri)-tō(ru)* pass
¹² 間違 *maka(ri)-machiga(u)* make a mistake. *maka(ri)-machiga(ttemo)* at the worst. *maka(ri)-machiga(eba)* if worse comes to worst
¹³ 業 *higyō* strike, walkout

— 14 —

羅 | 4655 / J4d65 / M28397 | RA silk gauze, thin silk.
B
⁶ 列 *raretsu* marshalling; an array.
raretsu suru arrange, enumerate, itemize.
¹⁰ 針盤 *rashimban* compass

竹米糸缶【网罒】羊羽老耂而耒耳聿肉月臣自至臼舌舛艮色艸艹虍虫血行衣衤西 ₁₄

6

RAD. 羊 123

Hitsuji sheep. At left: 𦍌 *hitsuji hen*. At top: 龷. Nickname: Sheep.

A 羊 <u>4658 / J4d53 / M28425</u> Yō. *hitsuji* sheep.
- ⁴水 *yōsui* amniotic fluid
- 毛 *yōmō* wool
- ⁵皮紙 *yōhishi* parchment, sheepskin
- ⁶肉 *yōniku* mutton
- ¹⁹羹 *yōkan* sweet bean jelly

─────── 3 ───────

A 美 <u>4660 / J487e / M28435</u> BI beauty, grace, charm. *utsuku(shii)* beautiful, lovely, fine, good-looking; picturesque; sweet (voice); noble, pure.
- ²人 *bijin* a beautiful woman
- ³女 *bijo* beautiful woman
- ⁴化 *bika* beautification, idealization
- ⁶名 *bimei* good name, fame, high reputation
- ⁷妙 *bimyō* elegance, grace, exquisiteness
- 声 *bisei* beautiful voice
- 男 *binan, bidan* handsome man
- 男子 *binanshi, bidanshi* handsome man
- ⁸味 *bimi* relish, good flavor, delicacy, rich dishes, deliciousness. *oi(shii)* delicious
- 的 *biteki* esthetic
- 事 *migoto* splendid, beautiful. *biji* commendable act
- 学 *bigaku* esthetics
- ⁹点 *biten* good point, virtue, merit
- 美 *bibi(shii)* beautiful, splendid
- 食 *bishoku* dainty food; lavish diet
- ¹⁰酒 *bishu, umazake* quality saké
- 称 *bishō* euphemism
- 容 *biyō* beautiful face; beauty
- 容院 *biyōin* beauty parlor
- ¹¹術 *bijutsu* art, fine arts
- ¹³感 *bikan* sense of beauty
- 意識 *biishiki* art appreciation
- ¹⁴徳 *bitoku* virtue, fine trait; good deed
- 貌 *bibō* good looks
- ¹⁵談 *bidan* praiseworthy anecdote, story
- ¹⁷醜 *bishū* personal appearance, beauty or ugliness
- ¹⁸観 *bikan* lovely view, beautiful sight
- 顔術 *biganjutsu* facial treatment, the beautician's art
- ¹⁹麗 *birei* beautiful; clean, pure

─────── 7 ───────

羨 <u>4665 / J4122 / M28503</u> SEN. *uraya(mu)* be envious, be jealous, covet. *uraya(mashii)* enviable.
- ¹¹望 *sembō* envy

A 群 <u>4666 / J3732 / M28498</u> GUN group, crowd, gang, herd, swarm, flock; common run. *mu(reru), mura(garu)* crowd, flock, swarm. *mu(re)* group, crowd, flock, herd, bevy, school, swarm; cluster (of stars); clump. *mura* crowd; swarming.
- ⁵生 *gunsei* all animate creation; many people; gregariousness
- ⁶臣 *gunshin* the whole body of officials
- ⁸青 *gunjō* ultramarine, navy blue
- ⁹発地震 *gumpatsu jishin* swarm earthquakes
- ¹⁰島 *guntō* archipelago, group of islands
- ¹²落 *gunraku* many communities; a cluster of plants
- 衆 *gunshū* crowd, multitude
- 雄 *gun'yū* rival chiefs
- 集 *mure-atsu(maru)* gather in large groups. *gunshū* crowd, multitude, group
- ¹⁴像 *gunzō* sculptured group

A 義 <u>4668 / J3541 / M28504</u> GI justice, righteousness, morality; humanity; integrity, honor, loyalty, chivalry, devotion; meaning, significance. *gi to suru* justify. *gi-* in-law; artificial.
- ³士 *gishi* loyal retainer; righteous person; martyr
- ⁴手 *gishu* artificial arm; artificial hand
- 父 *gifu* father-in-law; foster father; stepfather
- 太夫 *gidayū* ballad-drama music

⁵ 母 *gibo* mother-in-law, foster mother, stepmother

兄弟 *gikyōdai* brother-in-law, stepbrother, sworn brother

⁶ 気 *giki* chivalrous spirit, chivalry, heroism

⁷ 足 *gisoku* artificial leg

⁸ 肢 *gishi* artificial limb

⁹ 侠 *gikyō* chivalry, generosity, heroism

侠心 *gikyōshin* chivalrous spirit, public spirit

勇 *giyū* heroism, loyalty and courage

勇軍 *giyūgun* volunteer corps

¹⁰ 挙 *gikyo* worthy undertaking; heroic deed

捐金 *gienkin* donation, contribution

¹¹ 眼 *gigan* artificial eye

務 *gimu* duty, obligation, responsibility, liability

務的 *gimuteki* obligatory, binding, compulsory

務者 *gimusha* debtor, responsible person

務教育 *gimu kyōiku* compulsory education

理 *giri* sense of duty, sense of honor, obligation, justice, courtesy, debt of gratitude

理人情 *giri-ninjō* justice and charity, duty and humanity

¹² 歯 *gishi* artificial tooth, false tooth

¹⁵ 憤 *gifun* righteous indignation

RAD. 羽 124

Hane feather, wing. At top: *hane kammuri.* Variant: 羽. Nickname: Wing.

A 羽 — 4675 J3129 M28614' — U. *ha* feather. *hane* feather, plumage, wing; blade, paddle, fan. *wa* bird counter.

² 二重 *habutae* habutae silk

³ 子板 *hagoita* battledore

⁴ 毛 *umō* feathers, plumage, down

⁵ 目 *hame* panel, wainscoting; predicament, plight

⁸ 突 *hanetsu(ki)* battledore and shuttlecock

¹⁰ 振 *habu(ri)* plumage; influence, power

¹³ 搏 *habata(ku)* flap, flutter. *habata(ki)* flapping, fluttering

¹⁷ 翼 *uyoku* wings; assistance

¹⁸ 織 *haori* Japanese half-coat. *hao(ru)* put on, slip over

--- **4** ---

B 翁 — 4677 J3199 M28635' — Ō old man; venerable. *okina* old man.

--- **5** ---

A 翌 — 4679 I4d62 M28657' — YOKU. *akuru* next, following.

⁴ 日 *yokujitsu* the next day

月 *yokugetsu* the next month

⁶ 年 *yokutoshi, yokunen* the next year

¹¹ 翌日 *yokuyokujitsu* two days after

翌年 *yokuyokunen* year after next

朝 *yokuchō, yokuasa* the next morning

A 習 — 4681 J3d2c M28672' — SHŪ. *nara(u)* learn, be taught, take lessons, practice. *nara(wasu)* have children study or practice. *nara(i)* habit, custom, usage; the way, the lot. *nara(washi)* custom, usage, tradition.

⁶ 字 *shūji* penmanship, calligraphy

⁷ 作 *shūsaku* a practice project

⁸ 性 *shūsei* habit, second nature

⁹ 俗 *shūzoku* usage, convention

¹¹ 得 *shūtoku* learning, acquirement

¹⁴ 慣 *shūkan* custom, habit, way, usage, practice

¹⁵ 熟 *shūjuku* mastery, proficiency

¹⁸ 癖 *shūheki* habit

--- **8** ---

翠 — 4685 J3169 M28732 — SUI. *midori* green, verdure.

⁶ (side column, vertical) 竹 米 糸 缶 网 罒 羊 【羽】⁸ 老 耂 而 耒 耳 聿 肉 月 臣 自 至 臼 舌 舛 舟 艮 色 艸 艹 虍 虫 血 行 衣 衤 西

6

竹 米 糸 缶 网 皿 羊 羽 【老耂】 而 耒 耳 聿 肉 月 臣 自 至 臼 舌 舛 舟 艮 色 艸 卅 虍 虫 血 行 衣 衤 西

0

━━━━━ **9** ━━━━━

翫 <u>4689</u> J3465 M28766 GAN. *moteaso(bu)* play; take pleasure in; play (on an instrument); play with; make sport of; trifle with (affections).

━━━━━ **10** ━━━━━

翰 <u>4690</u> J344d M28780 KAN letter; writing brush.

━━━━━ **11** ━━━━━

翼 B <u>4692</u> J4d63 M28801' YOKU wing; plane; flank. *tsubasa* wings.
[14] 端 *yokutan* wing tip
[15] 賛 *yokusan* support, approval, countenance

━━━━━ **12** ━━━━━

翻 B <u>4694</u> J4b5d M28814 HON. HAN. *hirugae(ru)* vi turn over, wave, flutter. *hirugae(su)* vt change (one's mind); turn, reverse; wave, flutter; dodge. *kobo(reru)* vi spill, overflow, be scattered. *kobo(su)* vt spill; grumble over. *hirugae(tte)* on second thought.
[7] 弄 *honrō suru* toss (a ship) about; flirt with; make fun of
[8] 刻 *honkoku, hankoku* reprint
[10] 案 *hon'an* an adaptation
[11] 訳 *hon'yaku* translation, version
[12] 然 *honzen to* suddenly
[13] 意 *hon'i suru* change one's mind

━━━━━ **14** ━━━━━

耀 <u>4695</u> J4d54 M28828 YŌ. *kagaya(ku)* shine, sparkle, gleam, twinkle; brilliant, radiant, bright. *kagaya(kasu)* vt light up, brighten, illumine. *kagaya(kashii)* bright (future); brilliant (achievement).

◼◼◼ **RAD.** 老 **125** ◼◼◼

Rō or *oi* old. Variant: 耂 (4 strokes) *oi kammuri* or *oigashira*. Nickname: Old Man.

老 A <u>4696</u> J4f37 M28842 RŌ aging, old age, old people. *o(iru), oiba(mu)* grow old. *fu(keru)* grow old. *o(iraku)* old age. *o(i)* old age; old person. *o(i)-* old, aging.
[2] 人 *rōjin* old person; old folks
[3] 女 *rōjo* old woman; senior lady-in-waiting
  大家 *rōtaika* veteran authority
[4] 木 *rōboku, o(i)ki* an old tree
  父 *rōfu* one's aged father
  夫婦 *rōfūfu* an old couple
[5] 母 *rōbo* an aged mother
  幼 *rōyō* old people and children, young and old
[6] 死 *rōshi suru* die of old age
  朽 *rōkyū* superannuation, decrepitude. *o(i)-ku(chiru)* grow old and useless
  年 *rōnen* old age, declining years
[7] 体 *rōtai* old body, an aged person
[8] 若 *rōjaku, rōnyaku* old and young
  妻 *rōsai* aged wife
[9] 後 *rōgo* old age, declining years
[10] 骨 *rōkotsu* old bones, old man
  師 *rōshi* an aged teacher; aged priest
  衰 *o(i)-otoro(eru)* grow old and weak. *rōsui* senility, old-age infirmity
  耄 *o(i)-bo(reru)* to age and weaken. *rōmō, o(i)bo(re)* second childhood; senile person; age and weakness
[11] 眼鏡 *rōgankyō* glasses for older people
  婆 *rōba* an old woman
  婆心 *rōbashin* grandmotherly concern, excessive solicitude
  躯 *rōku* old age; enfeebled body
[12] 爺 *oyaji, rōya* elderly man, old man
  廃物 *rōhaibutsu* waste matter, waste products
[14] 境 *rōkyō* old age, declining years
  練 *rōren na* experienced, veteran, skilled
[15] 舗 *rōho, shinise* long-established shop
[16] 樹 *rōju* an old tree
  獪 *rōkai na* crafty, astute, wily
[17] 齢 *rōrei* old age

2

考 A 4697 J394d M28843 **Kō** thought, consideration; research, treatise. *kanga(eru)* think, consider, believe, suspect; be of the opinion; intend; expect, hope, fear; judge; conclude; imagine, suppose; regard as; be discreet; ponder over; reconsider; be prepared for; invent. *kanga(e)* thought; idea; opinion; intention; discretion; consideration; deliberation; resolution; plan; expectation; imagination.

⁴方 *kanga(e)kata* way of thinking; point of view; solution
込 *kanga(e)-ko(mu)* be absorbed in thought, meditate ⌈invent
⁵付 *kanga(e)-tsu(ku)* recall, remember;
出 *kanga(e)-da(su)* think out, invent; recall, remember; begin to think
古学 *kōkogaku* archeology

⁷究 *kōkyū* investigation, research
⁸事 *kanga(e)goto* something to think about; concern, preoccupation, worry
⁹査 *kōsa* consideration; test; quiz
¹⁰案 *kōan suru* contrive, plan, originate. *kōan* idea, plan; project; scheme; device, gadget ⌈mistake
¹²違 *kanga(e)chiga(i)* misconception,
¹⁴様 *kanga(e)yō* way of thinking, viewpoint
察 *kōsatsu* consideration, inquiry
¹⁵慮 *kōryo* careful thought, consideration, deliberation
課 *kōka* studying students' or personnel records (for placement purposes)

4

者 A 4698 J3c54 M28852 **SHA** person; thing. *mono* person, somebody. *-sha* agent, actor.

■■■ RAD. 而 126 ■■■

Shikashite and then. Nickname: Rake.

而 4704 J3c29 M28871 **JI**. *shika(shite)* but, however. *shika(mo)* moreover, nevertheless. *sōshi(te), soshi(te)* and.

3

耐 B 4705 J4251 M28879 **TAI** enduring. *ta(eru)* endure; support; withstand, resist, brave, weather; be fit for, be equal to.
³乏 *taibō* austerity, voluntary privation

久 *taikyū* endurance, persistence, permanence, durability
⁴水 *taisui* waterproof, watertight
火 *taika* fireproof
⁷忍 *ta(e)-shino(bu)* patiently endure. *tainin* patience, perseverance, fortitude
¹²湿 *taishitsu* moistureproof
寒 *taikan* coldproof
¹⁵熱 *tainetsu* heat-resisting
震 *taishin* earthquake-proof

■■■ RAD. 耒 127 ■■■

Suki hen left side "plow" or *rai-suki* (*rai* being the *on* both of *suki* "plow" and 來 or 耒 *kuru* "come"). Nickname: 3-Branch Tree (cf. Rads. 75 and 115).

4

耗 B 4709 J4c57 M28909 **Mō** , **Kō** *he(ru)* decrease.

耕 A 4710 J394c M28907 **Kō**. *tagaya(su)* plow, cultivate.
⁶地 *kōchi* arable land; farm land
⁷作 *kōsaku* cultivation, farming
¹¹運機 *kōunki* farm tractor

竹米缶网皿羊羽老耂而耒【耳】聿肉月臣自至白舌舛舟艮色艸屮虍虫血行衣衤西

RAD. **耳** 128

Mimi ear. At left: *mimi hen*. Enclosure: 耳. Nickname: Ear.

耳 A 〔4715 J3c2a M28999〕 JI ear. *mimi* ear; edge, border; loop; selvage; bread crusts.

⁴元 *mimimoto de* around one's ears

⁵目 *jimoku* eye and ear; one's attention; informer

打 *mimiu(chi) suru* whisper in another's ear

⁶朶 *mimitabu* earlobe. *jida* earlobe, ears

⁸学問 *mimi gakumon* learning by ear, picked-up knowledge

¹¹殻 *jikaku* auricle, external ear

寄 *mimiyo(ri) na* welcome, encouraging

¹²遠 *mimidō(i)* strange, uncommon; deaf. *mimi (ga) tō(i)* to be deaf

¹³傾 *mimi (o) katamu(keru)* listen

搔 *mimikaki* earpick

障 *mimizawa(ri) na* discordant, harsh

飾 *mimikaza(ri)* ear ornament; earring

¹⁴鳴 *jimei, mimina(ri)* ringing in the ears

慣 *mimina(reru)* get used to hearing

鼻咽喉科 *jibiinkōka* otorhinolaryngology

--- **2** ---

耶 〔4716 J4c6d M29008〕 YA. JA. *ya, ka* question mark.

--- **4** ---

耽 〔4721 J433f M29024〕 TAN. *fuke(ru)* be addicted to; be absorbed in.

⁹美主義 *tambi shugi* estheticism

¹³溺 *tandeki* addiction, dissipation

¹⁴読 *tandoku suru* read avidly

--- **7** ---

聖 A 〔4727 J403b M29074〕 SHŌ, SEI saint; sage; great master; holiness, sacredness, holy. *hijiri* high-ranking priest; emperor; sage; saint; a master. *sei(naru)* holy, sacred. *sei (to) suru* keep holy. *sei-* holy.

²人 *shōnin, seijin* sage, saint, holy man, great religious leader

³山 *seizan* sacred mountain, holy mountain

上 *seijō* the emperor

⁴水 *seisui* holy water

火 *seika* sacred fire, sacred torch

⁵母 *seibo* the emperor's mother; a sage's mother; the Virgin Mary

⁶地 *seichi* Holy Land; sacred ground

⁸夜 *seiya* the holy night; the night Christ was born, Christmas Eve

典 *seiten* a sage's writings, the sacred books of a religion; the Bible, the Buddhist Scriptures, the Koran; rites, sacraments

者 *shōja, seija* saint, holy man; Holy One

¹⁰恩 *seion* imperial favor

書 *Seisho* Bible, Scriptures

¹¹域 *seiiki* sacred precincts

断 *seidan* imperial decision

堂 *seidō* Confucian temple; temple; sanctuary

¹³戦 *seisen* holy war, crusade

¹⁴像 *seizō* sacred image; icon; the image of a saint; an image of Confucius

歌 *seika* sacred song, hymn, chant

¹⁵賢 *seiken* the sages and saints

¹⁸職 *seishoku* ministry, clergy, holy orders

--- **8** ---

聡 〔4730 J416f M29109〕 SŌ. *sato(i)* wise; having a quick memory. *mimizato(i)* excellent hearing; quick understanding.

⁸明 *sōmei* wisdom, sagacity

聞 A 〔4732 J4a39 M29104〕 BUN. MON. *ki(ku)* hear, listen to; learn of; inquire; follow advice. *ki(kasu), ki(kaseru)* inform; secure acquiescence; read to, play for, sing to; give the tune. *ki(koeru)* hear, be heard; sound, ring, seem;

be well known; be reasonable.
ki(kareru) be overheard; be tolerable;
be fairly good. *ki(kitagaru)* be
inquisitive, be curious. *ki(koenai)* be
unreasonable, be cruel. *ki(koe)*
reputation, fame, notoriety, publicity.
ki(koegashi) ni within hearing; wanting to
be heard.

² 入 *ki(ki)-i(reru)* comply with, grant
(a request), accept (a resignation),
assent to. *ki(ki)-i(ru)* listen
attentively

⁴ 手 *ki(ki)te* listener, audience

⁵ 出 *ki(ki)-da(su), ki(ki)-ida(su)* find out,
hear

⁶ 返 *ki(ki)-kae(su)* be told again, inquire
again

耳 *ki(ki)mimi* attentive ears

⁷ 役 *ki(ki)yaku* official who hears
people's complaints

⁸ 知 *bunchi suru ki(ki)-shi(ru)* hear of, be
informed of

苦 *ki(ki)guru(shii)* offensive to the ear,
hard to grasp the meaning of;
scandalous; objectionable

取 *ki(ki)-to(ru)* catch, follow,
understand. *ki(ki)to(ri)* hearing,
audition

⁹ 洩 *ki(ki)-mo(rasu)* miss hearing. *ki(ki)-
mo(re)* something one missed
hearing

¹⁰ 流 *ki(ki)-naga(su)* pay no
attention to

納 *kikiosa(me)* the last time we heard
(him)

書 *kikiga(ki)* verbatim notes

¹¹ 惚 *ki(ki)-ho(reru)* listen with rapt
interest

捨 *ki(ki)-su(teru)* ignore,
overlook

¹³ 飽 *ki(ki)-a(kiru)* be tired of hearing, get
tired of

馴 *ki(ki)-na(reru)* get used to
hearing

置 *ki(ki)-o(ku)* hear, keep in mind

¹⁴ 漏 *ki(ki) mo(rasu)* miss hearing.
ki(ki)-mo(re) something one missed
hearing

¹⁸ 嚙 *ki(ki)-kaji(ru)* have a smattering of
knowledge

──────── **11** ────────

聯 4737 J4e7e M29153 REN set; party, company,
gang, clique. See 連 6062
for compounds.

聴 B 4740 J4430 M29173 CHŌ careful inquiry.
ki(kanai) headstrong,
naughty. *ki(ku)* hear, listen to, learn of;
inquire; follow advice.

² 力 *chōryoku* hearing ability

⁸ 取 *chōshu* listening, hearing, audition,
radio reception

取料 *chōshuryō* radio license fee

¹¹ 問会 *chōmonkai* public hearing

視 *chōshi* viewing and listening
(to TV)

¹² 衆 *chōshū* audience

覚 *chōkaku* sense of hearing

診器 *chōshinki* stethoscope

¹⁴ 聞会 *chōmonkai* public hearing

¹⁷ 講 *chōkō* lecture attendance, auditing

──────── **12** ────────

職 A 4742 J3f26 M29183 SHOKU employment, work,
job, office. SHIKI
occupation, handicraft. *tsukasa* office,
government office; director, head official.

² 人 *shokunin* worker, mechanic,
craftsperson

³ 工 *shokkō* factory worker

⁶ 安 *shokuan* employment security office

名 *shokumei* occupation name; official
title

⁸ 制 *shokusei* office organization; holy
orders; ministry

¹⁰ 能 *shokunō* work efficiency

員 *shokuin* staff, personnel, faculty; staff
member, employee

¹¹ 責 *shokuseki* official duties

務 *shokumu* office, job, duties

務質問 *shokumu shitsumon* police
check-up (on a criminal)

¹² 場 *shokuba* place of work, workshop

掌 *shokushō* duties, functions, office

¹³ 業 *shokugyō* occupation, business, trade,
vocation, profession

業安定所 *shokugyō anteijo, shokugyō
anteisho* employment security office

¹⁴ 歴 *shokureki* one's occupational
history

種 *shokushu* occupation category

¹⁵ 権 *shokken* official authority

6
竹 米 糸 缶 网 罒 羊 羽 老 耂 而 耒 【耳】¹²
聿 肉 月 臣 自 至 臼 舌 舛 舟 艮 色 艸 艹 虍 虫 血 行 衣 衤 西

竹
米
糸
缶
网
罒
羊
羽
老
耂
而
耒
耳
【聿】
肉
月
臣
自
至
白
舌
舛
舟
艮
色
艸
艹
虍
虫
血
行
衣
衤
西

———— 16 ————

聿 聾 | 4745 / J4f38 / M29212 | Rō deafness. *rō(suru)* deafen. *tsumbo, mimishii*

deafness; deaf person.
[8] 者 *rōsha* deaf person
[10] 唖 *rōa* deaf-mute

■■■■ RAD. 聿 129 ■■■■

Fude writing brush. At right: *fudezukuri*. Variant: 聿. Nickname: Brush.

———— 6 ————

B 肅 | 4747 / J3d4d / M29223' | SHUKU. *shuku toshite* quietly, softly, solemnly.

[5] 正 *shukusei* regulation, enforcement
[11] 清 *shukusei* purge, cleanup, liquidation
肅 *shukushuku to* softly, quietly,

solemnly
[12] 然 *shukuzen to* softly, quietly, solemnly

———— 8 ————

肇 | 4751 / J4825 / M29228 | CHŌ beginning.

[8] 国 *chōkoku* founding a nation

■■■■ RAD. 肉 130 ■■■■

Niku flesh, meat. Variants: 肉 and 月 or 月 (4 strokes) *nikuzuki* ("flesh" written like character for *tsuki* "moon"). These variants may often belong to Rad. 74, but except for "moon" itself, are treated herein as Rad. 130. Nickname: Meat.

A 肉 | 4753 / J4679 / M29236 | 宍 | 1312 / J3c35 / M7084 | NIKU flesh, meat; the flesh; seal pad, ink pad; thickness, succulence. *shishi* muscles; meat. (Today 宍 is only read *shishi*.)

太 *nikubuto* bold-faced (type)
[5] 付 *nikuzu(ku)* put on flesh. *nikuzu(ki), nikutsu(ki)* one's build. *nikuzu(ke)* modeling (in clay, etc.)
[7] 迫 *nikuhaku suru* close in on, press hard, compete fiercely
声 *nikusei* natural voice, lifelike tone
身 *nikushin* the flesh, the body; kindred, blood relationship
体 *nikutai* the flesh, the body
体的 *nikutaiteki* corporal, concerning the body
体美 *nikutaibi* physical beauty
[9] 食 *nikushoku, nikujiki* meat diet
屋 *nikuya* butcher shop; butcher
[11] 眼 *nikugan* naked eye
欲 *nikuyoku* animal passions, lusts of the flesh

[12] 弾 *nikudan* human bullet
筆 *nikuhitsu* autograph, one's own painting, one's own handwriting
[13] 塊 *nikukai, nikkai* piece of flesh; the flesh, the body
感的 *nikukanteki* carnal
[16] 親 *nikushin* kindred, blood relationship
薄 *nikuhaku suru* close in on, press hard, compete fiercely

———— 2 ————

肋 | 4754 / J4f3e / M29239 | ROKU. *abara* rib.

[7] 材 *rokuzai* framing timbers (as in a ship)
[10] 骨 *rokkotsu, abarabone* ribs
[14] 膜 *rokumaku* pleura

B 肌 | 4755 / J4829 / M29242 | KI. *hada, hadae* skin, body; grain, texture; disposition.

[6] 色 *hada iro* flesh color
合 *hadaa(i)* disposition

⁷ 身 *hadami* the body
¹² 寒 *hadasamu(i), hadazamu(i)* chilly
着 *hadagi* underwear

有 4756 / J4d2d / M14332 **YŪ** possession. **U** being, existence. *yū(suru)* have, possess. *a(ru)* there is, have, exist; occur; be located, be contained in; (it) measures; happen; be found; be held; consist of. *a(ramashi)* approximately, almost. *a(rayuru), a(ritoarayuru)* all, every. *a(risōna)* probable. *a(rimoshinai)* imaginary, nonexistent. [月]

² 力 *yūryoku na* influential
⁵ 用 *yūyō na* useful, available, serviceable; *yūyō(sa)* usefulness, helpfulness
史 *yūshi* historical
⁶ 色人種 *yūshoku jinshu* colored race
名 *yūmei na* famous; notorious; proverbial
名無実 *yūmei-mujitsu* nominal, titular
⁷ 利 *yūri na* advantageous, profitable, better
余 *a(ri)-ama(ru)* be superfluous, be in excess. *yūyo* excess
形 *yūkei* material, concrete, visible
志 *yūshi* sympathy, interest; volunteer
⁸ 金 *a(ri)gane* ready cash
毒 *yūdoku* poisonous
事 *yūji* emergency, unusual event
刺鉄線 *yūshi tessen* barbed wire
価証券 *yūka shōken* valuable securities
限 *a(ru)kagi(ri)* as long as we have some. *a(ran)kagi(ri)* all, to the utmost. *a(ri)kiri* only that, only that much; as much as possible. *yūgen* limited, finite
限会社 *yūgengaisha* limited company, ltd.
効 *yūkō* effectiveness, efficiency; validity; availability
効期限 *yūkō kigen* term of validity
⁹ 為 *ui* vicissitudes of life; perpetual change in destiny caused by karma. *yūi no* capable, efficient, promising
為転変 *ui-tempen* vicissitudes of life
¹⁰ 益 *yūeki na* beneficial, profitable, instructive, edifying
能 *yūnō na* capable, efficient
畜農業 *yūchiku nōgyō* diversified farming

害 *yūgai na* harmful, noxious, destructive
料 *yūryō* toll; charge
¹¹ 望 *yūbō* good prospects
頂天 *uchōten* exaltation, rapture, ecstasy
終美 *yūshū (no) bi* perfection, crowning glory
産階級 *yūsan kaikyū* propertied class
¹² 象無象 *uzō-muzō* riffraff, rabble
閑階級 *yūkan kaikyū* the leisure class
給 *yūkyū* salaried
無 *umu, yūmu* existence; presence; yes or no. *a(ri)na(shi)* whether there is any or not
¹³ 数 *yūsū no* prominent, distinguished; very few
蓋車 *yūgaisha* covered wagon
意 *yūi no* conscious, voluntary, intentional
意義 *yūigi na* significant
罪 *yūzai* guilt, criminality
¹⁴ 様 *a(ri)sama, a(ri)yō* situation, circumstances; sight; the (naked) truth
¹⁵ 権者 *yūkensha* qualified person; eligible voter; franchise holder; constituent body, electorate
線 *yūsen* wire (as opposed to wireless)
¹⁶ 機 *yūki* organic
¹⁷ 償 *yūshō* compensation, consideration
¹⁸ 難 *a(ri)gata(garu)* be thankful. *a(ri)gata(i)* thankful, grateful, blessed. *a(ri)gato(u)* thank you
難迷惑 *a(ri)gatameiwaku* embarrassing favor
¹⁹ 識者 *yūshikisha* intellectual person, learned person

──── 3 ────

肖 4760 / J3e53 / M29263 **SHŌ** resemble. *ayaka(ru)* resemble.
¹⁴ 像 *shōzō* portrait, picture

肘 4761 / J492a / M29268 **CHŪ** . *hiji* elbow; arm (of something).
⁸ 枕 *hiji makura (o) suru* use the elbow for a pillow
突 *hijitsu(ki)* elbow rest
¹¹ 掛 *hijika(ke)* elbow rest; bay window
鉄砲 *hijideppō* rebuff

6

竹米糸缶网罒羊羽老耂而耒耳聿【肉月】臣自至臼舌舛舟艮色艸艹虍虫血行衣衤西

肝 4762 / J344e / M29273 **B** KAN liver. *kimo* liver; pluck, courage, nerve.

² 入 *kimoiri* assisting

³ 小 *kimo (ga) chii(sai)* cowardly

⁴ 心 *kanjin na* essential, important, fundamental ⌈nerve

⁵ 玉 *kimo(t)tama, kimodama* courage,

⁹ 要 *kan'yō* import; importance; necessity

胆相照 *kantan'aite(rasu)* become intimate

¹² 腎 *kanjin na* fundamental, important, essential

¹⁴ 魂 *kimodama, kimotama, kimodamashii, kimo(t)tama* courage, nerve

¹⁸ 臓 *kanzō* liver

———— 4 ————

肪 4766 / J4b43 / M29302 **B** BŌ fat.

肴 4767 / J3a68 / M29322 KŌ . *sakana* fish, a side dish.

肢 4768 / J3b68 / M29285 **B** SHI limbs, arms and legs.

⁷ 体 *shitai* limbs, members; body

朋 4769 / J4a7e / M14340' HŌ friend, companion. [月]

⁴ 友 *hōyū* friend, companion

¹⁵ 輩 *hōbai* comrade, friend, associate, fellow apprentice

肱 4770 / J394f / M29315 KŌ . *kaina* arm; ability, talent. *hiji* elbow; arm (of something).

肯 4771 / J394e / M29311 **B** KŌ . *ukega(u), gae(njiru), gae(nzuru)* agree to, consent, comply with, undertake.

⁸ 定 *kōtei suru* affirm, acknowledge

定文 *kōteibun* affirmative sentence

定的 *kōteiteki* affirmative

股 4772 / J3854 / M29284 KO thigh, crotch; yarn; strand; ply. *mata* crotch, thigh, groin. *momo* thigh, femur.

¹⁴ 関節 *kokansetsu* hip joint

育 4773 / J3069 / M29318 **A** IKU . *soda(tsu)* be raised, be brought up, grow, grow up. *soda(teru), haguku(mu)* raise, rear, bring up. *soda(te)* bringing up, raising. *soda(chi)* breeding, growth.

³ 上 *soda(te)-a(geru)* raise, rear, bring up, train, educate

⁶ 成 *ikusei* rearing, training

⁷ 児 *ikuji* care of children

⁸ 苗 *ikubyō* raising seedlings

英会 *ikueikai* scholarship society; educational society

¹⁴ 種 *ikushu* (plant) breeding

肥 4774 / J486e / M29290 **A** HI . *ko(eru)* get fat; get fertile. *ko(yasu)* fertilize, enrich; fatten; feather one's nest; pamper one's taste. *futo(ru)* get fat, gain, fill out. *koyashi* manure, fertilizer. *koe* night soil; manure.

³ 大 *hidai* corpulence, hypertrophy

⁴ 太 *ko(e)-futo(ru)* grow fat, be well fed

⁵ 立 *hida(tsu)* grow up; get well. *hida(chi)* convalescence after childbirth, growth of an infant

⁷ 沃 *hiyoku* fertility

¹⁰ 料 *hiryō* fertilizer, compost, manure

¹² 満 *himan suru* become obese

服 4775 / J497e / M14345' **A** FUKU dress, costume, clothes, garment, suit, uniform. *fuku(suru)* yield to, obey; abide by; be devoted to, acknowledge, admit; serve (in the army); discharge (duties). *matsuro(u)* obey. [月]

⁵ 用 *fukuyō suru* take (medicine, etc.), use internally; dress (oneself)

⁶ 地 *fukuji* cloth, suiting, dress materials

⁷ 役 *fukueki* servitude, military service

⁸ 制 *fukusei* dress regulations, costume

毒 *fukudoku* taking poison

¹⁰ 従 *fukujū* obedience, submission

¹¹ 務 *fukumu* duties, public service

務年限 *fukumu nengen* tenure of office

¹² 属 *fukuzoku suru* become a retainer; yield allegiance to

装 *fukusō* dress, garments, costume, attire

喪 *fukumo* mourning

¹³ 飾 *fukushoku* dress and its ornaments, attire, personal appearance

¹⁶ 薬 *fukuyaku* taking medicine

B 肩 4776 J382a M29299 KEN. *kata* shoulder.

2 入 *katai(re)* assistance. *kata (o) i(reru)* assist, sponsor, participate

5 代 *katagawa(ri)* relief palanquin bearer; one who shoulders another's debt or business proposition

甲骨 *kenkōkotsu* shoulder blade

6 当 *kataa(te)* shoulder pad

7 身 *katami* shoulder and body; face (that one loses), honor

車 *kataguruma* (riding) on the shoulders

8 並 *kata (o) nara(beru)* stand or walk in a row; run neck and neck

9 透 *katasuka(shi)* dodging

持 *kata (o) mo(tsu)* assist, flatter

胛骨 *kenkōkotsu* shoulder blade

10 書 *kataga(ki)* title, degree; address (on a letter); criminal record

11 掛 *kataka(ke)* shawl

章 *kenshō* shoulder strap, epaulette

12 越 *katago(shi)* over the shoulder

幅 *katahaba* breadth of one's shoulders

替 *katagawa(ri)* relief palanquin bearer; one who shoulders another's debt or business proposition

貸 *kata (o) ka(su)* assist, sponsor, participate

13 馴 *katanara(shi)* light training, warming up, workout

――――― 5 ―――――

胤 4786 J307d M29405 IN descendant. *tane* issue, offspring; paternal blood.

B 胞 4788 J4b26 M29396 HŌ theca, sac, sheath, case; placenta.

3 子 *hōshi* spore

B 胎 4789 J425b M29369 TAI womb, uterus.

4 内 *tainai* interior of the womb. *tainai kara* from the mother's womb

7 児 *taiji* fetus

15 盤 *taiban* placenta, afterbirth

B 胆 4790 J4340 M29354 TAN gall bladder; courage. *i* gall bladder. *kimo* liver; pluck, nerve, courage.

2 力 *tanryoku* courage, nerve, grit

5 汁 *tanjū* bile, gall

汁質 *tanjūshitsu* bilious or choleric temperament

石 *tanseki* gallstones

18 囊 *tannō* gall bladder

A 肺 4791 J4759 M29422 HAI lung.

8 炎 *haien* pneumonia

9 活量 *haikatsuryō* lung capacity

10 病 *haibyō* pulmonary tuberculosis, consumption

12 結核 *hai kekkaku* pulmonary tuberculosis

腑 *haifu* lungs; (one's inmost) heart; important point

17 癌 *haigan* lung cancer

18 臓 *haizo* lungs

胡 4792 J3855 M29400 U. GO. KO barbarian, foreign.

5 瓜 *kyūri* cucumber

10 桃 *kurumi* walnut; nut

11 麻 *goma* sesame, sesame seed

麻擂 *gomasu(ri)* apple polisher, brown-noser; sycophant

12 椒 *koshō* pepper

15 蝶 *kochō* butterfly

A 胃 4793 J305f M29348 I stomach; paunch, crop, craw.

8 炎 *ien* gastritis

10 病 *ibyō* stomach trouble

11 袋 *ibukuro* stomach; paunch, crop, craw

液 *ieki* gastric juice

13 腸 *ichō* stomach and intestines

14 酸 *isan* stomach acid

15 潰瘍 *ikaiyō* stomach ulcer

17 癌 *igan* stomach cancer

A 背 4794 J4758 M29363 HAI back, behind. *somu(ku)* act contrary to, go back on, disobey, defy, rebel against, turn one's back on. *somu(keru)* look away from, avert. *se* back, back side; stature, height; ridge. *sei* stature, height. *sobira, sena* back.

3 丈 *setake, seitake* height, stature

4 反 *haihan suru* contradict, be contrary to, interfere with

水陣 *haisui (no) jin* last stand

中 *senaka* back

竹 米 糸 缶 网 ⺱ 羊 羽 老 耂 而 耒 耳 聿 【肉 月】 5 臣 自 至 臼 舌 舛 舟 艮 色 艸 ⺾ 虍 虫 血 行 衣 衤 西

6

竹
米
糸
缶
网
罒
羊
羽
老
耂
而
耒
耳
聿
【肉
月】
⁵
臣
自
至
白
舌
舛
舟
艮
色
艸
艹
虍
虫
血
行
衣
衤
西

⁵広 *sebiro* business suit
⁶向 *haikō* facing toward the back; obedience and disobedience. *se (o) mu(keru)* turn the back on; pretend not to see; not cooperate with
任 *hainin* breach of trust
⁷伸 *seno(bi) suru* stretch oneself, stand on tiptoe
⁸泳 *haiei, seoyo(gi)* backstroke swimming
⁹面 *haimen* rear, back, reverse
信 *haishin* breach of faith, betrayal, apostasy
後 *haigo* back, rear; backing
負 *seo(u), sho(u)* carry on the back, shoulder, be burdened with
負子 *sho(i)ko, seo(i)go* pack frame
¹⁰骨 *sebone* backbone, spinal column, spine
¹²景 *haikei* background; scenery, setting; backing, pull
筋 *sesuji* line of the backbone; seam down the back. *haikin* the muscles of the back
番号 *sebangō* number on a player's back
¹⁴徳 *haitoku* immorality, corruption
¹⁸嚢 *hainō* knapsack, pack

——————— 6 ———————

朕 ⁴⁷⁹⁷ J443f M14361
B CHIN imperial we. [月]

脆 ⁴⁸⁰⁰ J4048 M29468
ZEI. *moro(i)* brittle, fragile; easy (to beat); sentimental, susceptible. *moro(ku)* easily.
¹⁰弱 *zeijaku na* fragile, frail, delicate, tender, flimsy, brittle

朔 ⁴⁸⁰¹ J3a73 M14359
SAKU conjunction (in astronomy). *tsuitachi* first day of the month. [月]
⁵北 *sakuhoku* north
⁹風 *sakufū* north wind

朗 ⁴⁸⁰² J4f2f M14362
A RŌ. *hogara(ka) na* clear, bright, serene; melodious; cheerful, sunny. [月]
¹⁰朗 *rōrō(taru)* sonorous, silvery (voice or moon)
¹²詠 *rōei* recitation

報 *rōhō* good news
¹⁴読 *rōdoku* reading aloud

脅 ⁴⁸⁰³ J363c M29466
B KYŌ. *obiya(kasu)* threaten; coerce.
⁷迫 *kyōhaku* threat, menace, terrorism, coercion
迫状 *kyōhakujō* intimidating letter
迫罪 *kyōhakuzai* intimidation
⁹威 *kyōi* threat, menace

脊 ⁴⁸⁰⁴ J4054 M29472
SEKI. *se, sei* stature, height.
⁹柱 *sekichū* spine, spinal column, backbone
¹¹梁 *sekiryō* spine, spinal column
¹²椎 *sekitsui* spinal column, spine; vertebra
椎動物 *sekitsui dōbutsu* vertebrates
¹⁸髄 *sekizui* spinal cord

脈 ⁴⁸⁰⁵ J4c2e M29470
A MYAKU. vein (of ore); blood vessel; pulse; pulsation; hope.
⁵打 *myakuu(tsu)* (the heart) pounds
⁸拍 *myakuhaku* pulsation
¹⁰脈 *myakumyaku* continuous
¹¹動 *myakudō* pulsating motion
¹²絡 *myakuraku* context, logical connection
¹³搏 *myakuhaku* pulsation. *myakuu(tsu)* pulsate

脇 ⁴⁸⁰⁷ J4f46 M29467
KYŌ. *waki* the other way; another place; side, armpit, flank; supporting role.
⁵目 *wakime* onlooker's eyes; looking aside
⁷見 *wakimi suru* look aside, look off, look away
役 *wakiyaku* supporting role
¹⁰差 *wakiza(shi)* short sword
息 *kyōsoku* armrest
¹¹道 *wakimichi* side road, branch road; digression
¹³腹 *wakibara* side of the chest, flank

脂 ⁴⁸⁰⁸ J3b69 M29463
B SHI fat; rouge. *abura* fat, grease, tallow, blubber, lard, suet. *abura(gitta)* greasy, oily; fleshy. *yani* resin, rosin, gum; nicotine, tar; earwax, eye discharge.

⁷ 身 *aburami* fat meat

⁸ 肪 *shibō* fat, grease, blubber, suet, lard

¹⁰ 粉 *shifun* cosmetics

A 能 4809 J473d M29454 Nō ability, talent, skill, capacity; noh play, classical drama. *ato(u)* can, be able to; be possible; be done, be finished, be ready; be made of; be established, be set up; be formed; come into being; grow, be produced; break out; be good at; be versed in; become intimate with. *yoku(suru)* be skilled in. *yo(ku)* skillfully, thoroughly.

² 力 *nōryoku* ability, faculty, capacity

⁵ 弁 *nōben* eloquence, oratory

弁家 *nōbenka* orator

⁶ 吏 *nōri* able official

⁷ 狂言 *nō kyōgen* noh farce, noh interlude

⁹ 面 *nōmen* noh mask

¹⁰ 書 *nōga(ki)* advertising the excellence of one's wares; boasting. *nōsho* excellent calligraphy; calligraphy

¹¹ 動的 *nōdōteki* active

率 *nōritsu* efficiency

率的 *nōritsuteki* efficient

¹³ 楽 *nōgaku* noh drama

B 胴 4810 J4639 M29436 Dō torso, trunk (of a body); body armor; body (of a suit); drum (of a machine); barrel (of a horse); cylinder (of a drum); bulge (of a bucket); hull (of a ship); hub (of a wheel).

⁶ 回 *dōmawa(ri)* girth

⁷ 体 *dōtai* body, torso, trunk; hull; fuselage

乱 *dōran* wallet, grip, collecting case

⁸ 長 *dōnaga* long-torsoed

¹² 揚 *dōa(ge)* congratulatory tossing of a person

着 *dōgi* undergarment; vest, waistcoat

間声 *dōmagoe* thick voice; deep resonant voice

A 胸 4811 J363b M29442 Kyō. *mune* chest, breast, bosom; heart, mind, feelings. *muna-* breast.

³ 三寸 *munesanzun* heart, mind, feelings

⁴ 中 *kyōchū* one's heart, mind, or intentions

元 *munamoto* breast; pit of the stomach

⁶ 回 *munemawa(ri)* chest measurement

⁷ 囲 *kyōi* chest measurement

⁸ 板 *manaita* the breast

苦 *munaguru(shii)* feeling heavy in the chest

¹⁰ 部 *kyōbu* chest, breast

郭 *kyōkaku* the chest wall

倉 *munagura* the breast

¹² 焼 *muneya(ke), munaya(ke)* heartburn, sour stomach

腔 *kyōkō, kyōkū* thorax, thoracic cavity

¹⁴ 像 *kyōzō* bust

算用 *munazan'yō* mental arithmetic; expectation

¹⁸ 騒 *munasawa(gi)* uneasiness; (heart) flutter; emotional upset

襟 *kyōkin* heart, bosom

襟開 *kyōkin (o) hira(ite)* frankly

———— 7 ————

A 望 4819 J4b3e M14368 Mō. Bō full moon; hope. *nozo(mu)* desire; aspire to; expect, hope for; like, choose; see, command (a view of). *nozo(mashii)* desirable, welcome, advisable. *nozo(mi)* desire, hope, expectation; ambition; prospects; preference. *mochi* full moon. [月]

⁴ 月 *mochizuki, bōgetsu* full moon

⁵ 外 *bōgai no* unexpected

⁷ 見 *nozo(mi)-mi(ru)* scan (the scene); look into (the future). *bōken* watching from afar

¹⁰ 郷 *bōkyō* homesickness, nostalgia

¹² 遠鏡 *bōenkyō* telescope; binoculars

¹³ 楼 *bōrō* watchtower

B 脚 4820 J3553 M29502 KAKU, KYAKU leg, skid; undercarriage. *ashi* foot; leg; paw; flipper, tentacles, arms; walk, step, pace, speed; footing; draft (of a ship); foot (of a mountain); trace; deficit, shortage. *-kyaku* chair counter.

² 力 *kyakuryoku, kyakuriki* walking ability

³ 下 *kyakka ni* at one's feet

⁴ 元 *ashimoto* gait, pace, step

⁵ 立 *kyatatsu* footstool; stepladder

本 *kyakuhon* play, drama, script

⁶ 光 *kyakkō* footlights

色 *kyakushoku* plot, dramatization; stage or screen version

気 *kakke* beriberi
[8] 注 *kyakuchū* footnotes
[10] 部 *kyakubu* leg
[11] 絆 *kyahan* leggings, gaiters
[19] 韻 *kyakuin* rhyme

A 脳 <u>4821</u> / J473e / M29567 Nō brain; memory.
[4] 天 *nōten* scalp, pate, crown of the head; head; brain
[5] 出血 *nōshukketsu* apoplexy, cerebral hemorrhage, stroke
[6] 死 *nōshi* brain death
[8] 炎 *nōen* brain inflammation, encephalitis
卒中 *nōsotchū* apoplexy
味噌 *nōmiso* gray matter, brains
[13] 裏 *nōri* brain; mind; memory; in the mind; in the heart
溢血 *nōikketsu* apoplexy, cerebral hemorrhage, stroke
[14] 膜炎 *nōmakuen* meningitis
[18] 髄 *nōzui* brain

B 脱 <u>4822</u> / J4326 / M29539 DATSU removing. *das(suru)* vi escape from; get rid of; be omitted, be left out. vt take off (clothes); omit; rise above. *nu(gu)* take off (clothes), undress. *nu(geru)* come off, slip off, slip down. *nu(gasu), nu(gaseru)* strip off clothes, undress (someone). *nu(keru)* come off, fall out, slip out; be omitted; be missing; be rid of; pass through; escape; be captured; withdraw; be less than. *to(reru)* can be held, can take; come off, come apart, be off, be removed; be relieved (of pain); be obtained; be produced; be caught; be earned; come out (well) (a photo); require (time); be interpreted as; can get; let (light) in; take (one's measure); can feel (the pulse); take (a pen and write).
[2] 力感 *datsuryokukan* feeling of exhaustion
[4] 毛 *datsumō, nu(ke)ge* falling out of hair; depilation; shed feathers
[5] 皮 *dappi* shedding, molting, emergence
出 *dasshutsu* escape, extrication; prolapse. *nu(ke)-da(su)* leave; escape
[6] 臼 *dakkyū* dislocation
色 *dasshoku* decoloration, bleaching
衣 *datsui* undressing

[7] 却 *dakkyaku suru* get rid of, extricate oneself from, emerge from
兎 *datto* dashing away; tremendous speed
走 *dassō* escape, flight, desertion, abscondence
[8] 退 *dattai* secession, withdrawal
[9] 臭 *dasshū* deodorization
俗 *datsuzoku* becoming a hermit; separating oneself from the world
[10] 脂綿 *dasshimen* absorbent cotton
[11] 殻 *dakkaku* shedding, molting, casting off. *nu(ke)gara* cast-off skin
[12] 帽 *datsubō* removing the headgear; hats off
税 *datsuzei* tax evasion
落 *datsuraku* molting, falling off; omission; defection, desertion, apostasy
[14] 漏 *datsurō* omission
獄 *datsugoku* jail-breaking
穀 *dakkoku* threshing
[15] 稿 *dakkō* completion of writing
線 *dassen* derailment; deviation, aberration, digression

––––––––– **8** –––––––––

腔 <u>4826</u> / J3950 / M29630 Kō body cavity.

B 脹 <u>4832</u> / J4431 / M29570 CHŌ. *fuku(ramu)* vi distend, bulge, fill out, swell dilate. rise. *fuku(reru)* vi swell, fill out, get big, bulge, expand, dilate, distend, rise, be inflated. *fuku(ramasu), fuku(rakasu), fuku(raseru)* vt dilate, expand, distend, swell, blow up, puff out, inflate, pump up, raise (bread). *fuku(yokana)* plump, fat, well-rounded.

腎 <u>4834</u> / J3f55 / M29621 JIN kidney.
[18] 臓 *jinzō* kidney

B 腐 <u>4835</u> / J4965 / M29625 FU. *kusa(ru), kusa(reru)* rot, decay; turn sour; fester; corrode; be corrupted; feel gloomy. *kusa(rasu), kusa(raseru), kusa(rakasu)* vt let spoil, rot, corrode, addle. *kuta(su)* let rot, spoil; slander. *kusa(su)* ridicule. *kusare-* spoiled, decayed, rotten.

⁴心 *fushin* pains, trouble, hard work, diligence, intense application

⁶肉 *funiku* tainted meat, putrid flesh; carrion; gangrene

朽 *fukyū* decay, decomposition, putrefaction

⁷乱 *furan* inflammation, festering, decomposition

⁹食 *fushoku* corrosion, erosion, rot, rust

¹¹敗 *fuhai* decay, decomposition, rottenness, putrefaction; necrosis; corruption, degeneration, depravity

¹²葉土 *fuyōdo* leaf mold

植 *fushoku* humus, leaf mold

¹⁵縁 *kusa(re)en* mismated marriage; unpleasant relationships

蝕 *fushoku* corrosion, erosion, rot, rust

²¹爛 *furan* putrefaction

期 4836 J347c M14378 KI, Go time, date, period, term; an age; season; session; a stage; opportunity. *ki(suru)* expect, anticipate, hope for, rely on; appoint (a day). *go(suru)* wait expectantly for. *ki(sezu) shite* unexpectedly, accidentally. [月]

⁴日 *kijitsu, kinichi* date; time limit

⁵末 *kimatsu* term end

⁶成 *kisei* realization (of a plan)

成同盟 *kisei dōmei* uniting to carry out a plan

⁸限 *kigen* term, period, time limit

⁹待 *kitai* expectation, hope, anticipation, contemplation

腕 4837 J4f53 M29631 WAN arm. *ude* arm; abilty, talent. *kaina* arm.

²力 *wanryoku* muscular strength, brute force, brawn

⁴木 *udegi* bracket, crosspiece, roof truss, armrest

⁵白 *wampaku* naughtiness, mischief

⁶尽 *udezu(ku) de* by main force. *udezu(ku) no* forcible, strong-arm

⁷利 *udeki(ki)* man of ability

⁹首 *udekubi* wrist

前 *udemae* ability, skill, capacity

相撲 *udezumō* arm wrestling

¹⁰時計 *udedokei* wristwatch

¹¹組 *udegu(mi)* folding one's arms

章 *wanshō* armband, arm badge, chevron, stripes

¹³試 *udedame(shi)* trial of strength

飾 *udekaza(ri)* bracelet

節 *udebushi, ude(p)pushi* arm joint, muscular strength

¹⁵輪 *udewa* bracelet

朝 4838 J442b M14374' CHŌ dynasty; reign, regime; period, epoch; the court. *asa* morning, forenoon. *ashita* morn, morning. *chō(suru)* proceed to the palace; empty into (the sea). [月]

³夕 *asayū, chōseki* day and night, morning and evening; always; daily. *asa(na)-yū(na)* morning and evening

⁴方 *asagata* toward morning; during the morning

日 *asahi* morning sun, rising sun

⁵立 *asada(chi)* early-morning departure

刊 *chōkan* morning paper

礼 *chōrei* morning meeting, morning exercises

市 *asa ichi* morning market

令暮改 *chōrei-bokai* the issue of an order in the morning and its repeal in the evening; lack of principle

⁶臣 *chōshin* courtier; the court. *ason* a high-ranking noble

衣 *chōi* court dress

凪 *asanagi* morning calm (at sea)

⁷見 *chōken* imperial audience

廷 *chōtei* imperial court

⁸明 *asaa(ke)* daybreak, dawn

⁹風呂 *asaburo* morning bath

食 *chōshoku* breakfast

¹⁰貢 *chōkō suru* bring tribute

¹¹野 *chōya* government and the people; the whole nation

¹²晩 *asaban* morning and evening; always

焼 *asaya(ke)* sunrise colors

賀 *chōga* congratulating the emperor

飯 *asameshi, asahan* breakfast

飯前 *asameshimae* before breakfast; something so simple it can be done before breakfast, a piece of cake

¹³寝坊 *asanebō* late rising; late riser

¹⁴駆 *asaga(ke)* attack in the morning; departure in the morning

6

竹米糸缶网罒羊羽老耂而耒耳聿【肉月】臣自至臼舌舛舟艮色艸艹虍虫血行衣衤西

⁸

——————— 9 ———————

腿 4846 J425c M29747 TAI. *momo* thigh, femur.

腺 4847 J4123 M29746 SEN. gland.

¹⁰ 病質 *sembyōshitsu* weak constitution

腫 4848 J3c70 M29697 SHU tumor, swelling. *ha(reru)* swell, become swollen. *ha(rebottai)* beginning to swell. *ha(rasu)* inflame, cause to swell. *ha(re)* swelling, dropsy.

³ 上 *ha(re)-a(garu)* swell up
¹⁴ 瘍 *shuyō* tumor, neoplasm

腸 A 4849 J4432 M29721 CHŌ intestines, bowels, entrails; digestive system in lower animals. *harawata* intestines, bowels, entrails, viscera; the heart. *wata* entrails.

¹³ 詰 *chōzume* sausage

腰 B 4850 J3978 M29705 YŌ. *koshi* hips, loins, waist, pelvic region; small of the back; haunch; lower-panel wainscoting (lower wall only); stem (of a wine glass).

³ 巾着 *koshiginchaku* belt purse; one's shadow; a henchman
⁴ 元 *koshimoto* woman working for a noble family; the hips
⁶ 回 *koshimawa(ri)* hip measurement
⁷ 抜 *koshinu(ke)* cowardice; coward; cripple. *koshi (ga) nu(keru)* be very much surprised
  低 *koshi (ga) hiku(i)* humble
  折 *koshio(re)* poor poem, doggerel; stooped over (old people). *koshi (o) o(ru)* bow; surrender; interrupt (someone)
⁸ 板 *koshiita* panels; wainscoting (lower wall only)
  物 *koshi (no) mono* sword worn at the side
⁹ 砕 *koshikuda(ke)* weakening, hips giving way (and falling)

巻 *koshima(ki)* underskirt; loincloth, flannel waistband
¹⁰ 骨 *koshibone, yōkotsu* hipbone; perseverance
¹¹ 強 *koshi (ga) tsuyo(i)* firm (character); strong (paste); stiff (paper)
  掛 *koshika(keru)* sit down. *koshikake* seat, chair, bench, stool, pew, bleachers; steppingstone to something higher
¹² 痛 *yōtsū, koshiita* lumbago, pain in the hip, pain in the back
  椎 *yōtsui* lumbar vertebrae
¹⁵ 縄 *koshinawa* waist cord (for tying prisoners)

腹 A 4851 J4a22 M29722 FUKU. *(o)naka* belly, stomach. *hara* abdomen, belly, bowels, stomach; heart, mind; intention; courage, spirit, pluck; anger; womb; thickest or widest part.

³ 下 *harakuda(ri)* diarrhea. *harakuda(shi)* diarrhea; laxative
⁴ 心 *fukushin* trusted friend; trusted retainer
  切 *haraki(ri)* suicide by disembowelment
⁵ 立 *harada(tsu)* get angry, take offense. *harada(tashii)* irritating, exasperating
  立紛 *harada(chi)magi(re)* beside oneself with anger
⁶ 虫 *hara (no) mushi* intestinal worms; heart, intention; courage
⁷ 芸 *haragei* a person of strong personality
⁹ 巻 *haramaki* waistband
  背 *fukuhai* front and back; close relative
  這 *harabai, hara(m)bai* lying on the stomach. *haraba(u)* crawl
¹⁰ 部 *fukubu* abdomen, belly
  案 *fukuan* plan, scheme, idea
  帯 *haraobi, fukutai* health band, bellyband, saddle girth
¹¹ 黒 *haraguro(i)* evilhearted, crafty. *haraguro* schemer
  探 *hara (o) sagu(ru)* probe another's feelings
  据 *hara (o) su(eru)* make a decision
¹² 痛 *fukutsū, haraita, haraita(mi)* stomachache, colic, abdominal pain

減 *hara (ga) he(ru)* be hungry
割 *hara (o) wa(ru)* make an abdominal incision; tell everything
筋 *hara suji, fukukin* abdominal muscles
違 *harachiga(i)* born of a different mother
¹³ 話術 *fukuwajutsu* ventriloquy
¹⁴ 蔵無 *fukuzōna(ku)* freely, frankly, plainly
¹⁸ 癒 *haraise* retaliation. *hara (ga) i(reru)* be satisfied with one's revenge

──────── **10** ────────

膜 | 4854 J4b6c M29808' | B MAKU membrane.

膏 | 4860 J3951 M29800 | KŌ paste, ointment, plaster. *abura* fat, grease, tallow, lard, suet, blubber.
¹⁶ 薬 *kōyaku* salve, ointment, plaster

──────── **11** ────────

膚 | 4867 J4966 M29829 | B FU. *hada, hadae* skin, body; grain, texture; disposition.

膝 | 4868 J4928 M29837 | SHITSU. *hiza* knee; lap.
³ 下 *shikka* paternal home; at the knees. *hizamoto* with one's parents; with one's lord close by; ruler's capital city
小僧 *hizakozō* kneecap
⁴ 元 *hizamoto* with one's parents; with one's lord close by; ruler's capital city
⁵ 正 *hiza (o) tada(su)* sit (on the floor) correctly
⁶ 交 *hiza (o) maji(eru)* have a frank talk
⁸ 枕 *hizamakura* using someone's lap for a pillow
¹⁰ 栗毛 *hizakurige* a hike; traveling on foot, shank's mare
¹¹ 掛 *hizaka(ke)* lap robe
崩 *hiza (o) kuzu(su)* relax one's squatting position
¹⁶ 頭 *hizagashira* kneecap

──────── **12** ────────

膳 | 4873 J4137 M29891 | ZEN small low table; tray.
⁵ 立 *zenda(te)* setting the table; preparations, program, scheme
¹⁰ 部 *zembu* tray of food

膨 | 4874 J4b44 M29861 | B BŌ get fat; get thick, swell. *fuku(reru)* swell.
³ 大 *bōdai* swelling, expansion
¹¹ 張 *bōchō* swelling; inflation; expansion; growth, increase
¹² 満 *bōman suru* be inflated
脹 *bōchō* swelling; inflation; expansion; growth, increase

──────── **13** ────────

臀 | 4880 J673d M29939 | DEN. *shiri* buttocks, hips; rear or back of a person; bottom (of a kettle); tail end, tag end.
¹⁰ 部 *dembu* buttocks, hips, haunch

臆 | 4883 J3232 M29951 | OKU timidity; breast, heart, mind. *oku(suru)* fear, hesitate, be nervous, be cowardly, be timid.
⁹ 面 *okumen* shy face
¹⁰ 病 *okubyō* cowardice, timidity
¹¹ 断 *okudan* guess, hypothesis, supposition
¹² 測 *okusoku* guess, hypothesis, supposition
¹⁴ 説 *okusetsu* conjecture, hypothesis

膿 | 4884 J473f M29938 | NŌ pus, discharge. *u(mu)* form pus, fester, suppurate. *umi* pus, discharge.
¹⁴ 瘍 *nōyō* boil, abscess

──────── **14** ────────

臓 | 4886 J4221 M29995' | A ZŌ viscera, bowels.
⁸ 物 *zōmotsu, harawata* entrails, giblets
¹⁵ 器 *zōki* intestines, internal organs, viscera, bowels

6

竹 米 糸 缶 网 罒 羊 羽 老 耂 而 耒 耳 聿 肉 月 【臣】 自 至 臼 舌 舛 舟 艮 色 艸 艹 虍 虫 血 行 衣 衤 西

RAD. 臣 131

Shin or *kerai* retainer, minister, subject. As a radical this is always counted as 6 strokes even though it often seems to have 7.
Nickname: Minister (of State).

A 臣 4894 / J3f43 / M30068 SHIN *omi* retainer, subject.
³下 *shinka* subject, retainer, vassal
⁵民 *shimmin* subject, national

--- 2 ---

臥 4896 / J3269 / M30071 GA. *fu(su), ga(su)* bend down, bow down,
lie prostrate. *fu(seru)* lie down, retire, go to bed.
⁷床 *gashō* confined to bed. *fushido* a bed
⁸所 *fushido* bed, cot, place to sleep

--- 11 ---

A 臨 4899 / J4e57 / M30087 RIN. *nozo(mu)* face, front on, border on; meet; be

confronted by; be on the verge of; attend, assist at; deal with; rule over; command a view of; deign to; visit, call on; come upon; come up to.
⁴月 *ringetsu* last month of pregnancy
⁷床 *rinshō* clinical
床医学 *rinshō igaku* clinical medicine
⁹界 *rinkai* limit; critical (temperature)
海 *rinkai* marine, seaside
¹⁰席 *rinseki* presence, attendance, those present
時 *rinji* temporary, special, extraordinary
¹¹終 *rinjū* dying hour, deathbed, one's last hour
¹²検 *rinken* inspection visit, raid, domiciliary search
¹⁶機応変 *rinki-ōhen* adaptation to circumstances

RAD. 自 132

Mizukara oneself. Nickname: Dotted Eye (cf. Rad. 109).

A 自 4900 / J3c3b / M30095 SHI, JI oneself. *mizuka(ra)* oneself, personally.
onozuka(ra), ino(zuto) naturally, of itself.
²力 *jiryoku* self-reliance, one's own efforts, self-help. *jiriki* (Buddhist) salvation by works
力更生 *jiriki-kōsei* attaining success by overcoming difficulties
³己 *jiko* oneself, ego. *jiko-* self-, auto-
⁴分 *jibun* self, oneself. *jibun no* one's own, personal
分自身 *jibun-jishin* oneself (emphatic)
分勝手 *jibun-katte* selfishness, egoism
⁵白 *jihaku* confession, acknowledgment
他 *jita* oneself and others; transitive and intransitive
弁 *jiben* paying one's own expenses
失 *jishitsu* absent-mindedness; stupor,

daze; unconsciousness; apathy
立 *jiritsu* independence, self-reliance, self-support
主 *jishu* independence, autonomy independence
主的 *jishuteki* independent, autonomous
由 *jiyū* independence, freedom, liberty; liberal; voluntary
由平等 *jiyū-byōdō* freedom and equality before the law
由自在 *jiyū-jizai na* free, unrestricted
⁶尽 *jijin* suicide
伝 *jiden* autobiography
任 *jinin* pretension, bragging
存 *jizon, jison* self-existence
宅 *jitaku* one's home, private residence
在 *jizai ni* freely, at will
⁷足 *jisoku* self-sufficiency, satisfaction

with what one possesses

身 *jishin* self, oneself, itself, yourself. *jishin de* by oneself, in person, personally

戒 *jikai* self-discipline

体 *jitai* one's own body, oneself, itself; originally

決 *jiketsu* self-determination; resignation; suicide

作 *jisaku* one's own work

我 *jiga* self, the ego

⁸供 *jikyō* confession

明 *jimei* self-evidence

炊 *jisui* cooking for oneself

制心 *jiseishin* self-control

国 *jikoku* one's own country. *jikoku no* native, domestic

画自賛 *jiga-jisan* praising one's own picture

画像 *jigazō* self-portrait

治 *jichi* self-government

⁹首 *jishu* surrender (to police)

活 *jikatsu* self-support

前 *jimae de* at one's own expense. *jimae no* independent (geisha)

信 *jishin* self-confidence

叙伝 *jijoden* autobiographyt

負 *jifu* bragging about one's ability; conceit

発 *jihatsu* spontaneousness

律 *jiritsu* autonomy, self-control, self-determination

¹⁰称 *jishō* self-styled, would-be; first person

害 *jigai* suicide

殺 *jisatsu* suicide

家用 *jikayō* private use

¹¹著 *jicho* one's own publication

粛 *jishuku* self-control, self-discipline

堕落 *jidaraku* depravity

販機 *jihanki* vending machine

閉症 *jiheishō* autism

問 *jimon suru* question oneself

問自答 *jimon-jitō* soliloquy, monologue, answering one's own question

惚 *unubo(reru)* be conceited, flatter oneself

転 *jiten* rotation

転車 *jitensha* bicycle

習 *jishū* studying by oneself

責 *jiseki* self-condemnation

動 *jidō* automatic action

動車 *jidōsha* automobile

¹²筆 *jihitsu* one's own handwriting

営 *jiei* self-management

給 *jikyū* self-support

給自足 *jikyū-jisoku* self-support, self-sufficiency

尊心 *jisonshin* self-respect; self-esteem, conceit

覚 *jikaku* consciousness; self-consciousness; insight; realization

費 *jihi* one's own expense

然 *shizen, jinen* nature. *shizen no* natural; unaffected; spontaneous, automatic

¹³滅 *jimetsu* natural decay; self-ruin, suicide, self-destruction

愛 *jiai* self-love, selfishness, egoism, self-regard

意識 *jiishiki* self-consciousness

業自得 *jigō-jitoku* reaping what one sows

棄 *jiki, yake* despair; desperation

¹⁴説 *jisetsu* one's own view

認 *jinin* admission

慢 *jiman* pride, boasting

¹⁵賛 *jisan* self-praise

縄自縛 *jijōjibaku* caught in one's own trap

暴自棄 *jibōjiki* despair, desperation

¹⁶衛 *jiei* self defense; bodyguard

衛隊 *Jieitai* Self-Defense Force

²²讃 *jisan* praising oneself

───── 3 ─────

臭 $\frac{4901}{\text{J3d2d}}$ SHŪ odor, savor,
B $\frac{}{\text{M30103}}$ fragrance. *kusa(i)*
ill-smelling; suspicious-looking. *nio(i)*
smell, odor, scent; stench; fragrance,
aroma, perfume. *-kusa(i)* smelling;
smacking of; looking (suspicious).

⁶気 *shūki* offensive odor, stench

¹⁰素 *shūso* bromine

¹⁴聞 *shūbun* scandal, ill-fame

6

RAD. 至 133

Itaru to arrive. Nickname: Arriving.

A 至 $\frac{4903}{\substack{J3b6a \\ M30142}}$ SHI. *ita(ru)* go, proceed, come; arrive, reach, attain; result in, lead to. *ita(ri)* the utmost, the height of, climax; on account of. *ita(ru made)* to, until. *ita(ranai)* imperfect, incompetent, careless. *ita(tte)* very, exceedingly. *ita(tte) wa* as for, as to.

³ 上 *shijō* supremacy
上命令 *shijōmeirei* a supreme (inviolable) command; the categorical imperative
⁶ 尽 *ita(reri)-tsu(kuseri)* complete, thorough
近 *shikin* very, very near
⁷ 言 *shigen* wise saying
⁹ 便 *shiben* very convenient
急 *shikyū* urgent
¹⁰ 高 *shikō* supremacy, sublimity
¹² 極 *shigoku* very, quite, exceedingly

¹³ 福 *shifuku* beatitude, supreme bliss, highest good
誠 *shisei* sincerity, faith, devotion; one's true heart
¹⁸ 難 *shinan* extreme difficulty

4

B 致 $\frac{4904}{\substack{J4357 \\ M30149}}$ CHI. *ita(su)* do; send, forward; cause, incur; render (assistance); exert (oneself); engage, call in (a doctor).

⁴ 方 *ita(shi)kata* way, method, means, help, course, resource
方無 *ita(shi)katana(ku)* unavoidably
⁶ 死 *chishi no* fatal, deadly, lethal, mortal
⁸ 命的 *chimeiteki* fatal, deadly, lethal, mortal
命傷 *chimeishō* fatal injury

RAD. 臼 134

Usu mortar. Nickname: Mortar.

臼 $\frac{4907}{\substack{J3131 \\ M30173}}$ KYŪ. *usu* mortar, hand mill.
¹² 歯 *kyūshi, usuba* molar

9

A 興 $\frac{4913}{\substack{J363d \\ M30226}}$ KŌ. KYŌ interest, entertainment, pleasure. *kyō(garu)* be amused or interested in. *kyō(jiru), kyō(zuru)* amuse oneself, make merry. *oko(ru)* rise, flourish. *oko(su)* revive, retrieve (fortunes), raise up.

³ 亡 *kōbō* rise and fall, ups and downs
⁶ 行 *kōgyō* entertainment industry

⁸ 味 *kyōmi* interest
味津津 *kyōmi-shinshin(taru)* of great interest
味深 *kyōmibuka(i), kyōmifuka(i)* very interesting
⁹ 信所 *kōshinjo* detective agency
¹⁰ 隆 *kōryū* rise, prosperity
¹³ 業 *kōgyō* industrial enterprise
¹⁵ 趣 *kyōshu* interest (in something)
¹⁶ 醒 *kyōza(meru)* lose interest. *kyōza(mashi), kyōza(me)* a killjoy, a wet blanket
奮 *kōfun* excitement, agitation, stimulation

RAD. 舌 135

Shita tongue. At left: *shita hen*. Nickname: Tongue.

6

竹
米
糸
缶
网
羊
羽
老 耂
而
耒
耳
聿
肉
月
臣
自
至
白
舌
舛【舟】
艮
色
艸 ⺾
虍
虫
血
行
衣 ⻂
西

A

舌 4917 / J4065 / M30277 ZETSU. *shita* tongue; reed; clapper. *shita(tarui)* lisping.

5 代 *zetsudai, shitadai* notice, announcement

打 *shitau(chi)* smacking one's lips; clicking the tongue; hissing; saying "tut-tut"

9 巻 *shita (o) ma(ku)* be astonished

13 鼓 *shitatsuzumi* smacking one's lips

(when eating)

触 *shitazawa(ri)* taste

戦 *zessen* a war of words

禍 *zekka* an unfortunate slip of the tongue

──── **10** ────

舘 4923 / J345c / M30326 See 館 6701.

──────────────

RAD. 舛 136

Mai ashi dancing "legs" (i.e., the lower element in *mau* "to dance") or *masu* (i.e., the right-hand element in the character for *masu* "a measure"). As commonly printed and written, this rather rare element actually has 7 strokes and it is normally so counted herein. Nickname: Dancing.

舛 4924 / J4124 / M30338 SEN. *somu(ku)* go against, disobey; rebel. *masu* a measuring box.

──── **6** ────

舜 4925 / J3d58 / M30339 SHUN. morning glory; rose of Sharon, althea.

──── **8** ────

B

舞 4926 / J4971 / M30342 BU. *ma(u)* dance; flutter about, flit; circle, wheel.

mai dancing; dance.

3 子 *maiko* dancing girl

上 *ma(i)-a(garu)* soar, fly high, be whirled up

6 曲 *bukyoku* musical dance, music and dancing

7 戻 *ma(i)-modo(ru)* find one's way back, return

妓 *ma(i)ko, bugi* dancing girl

9 姫 *maihime* dancing girl

14 踊 *ma(i)-odo(ru)* dance *buyō* dancing; dance

15 踏 *butō* dancing

──────────────

RAD. 舟 137

Fune hen left-side "ship." Variant: 舟. Nickname: Ship.

B

舟 4927 / J3d2e / M30350 SHŪ. boat. *fune* boat, ship, vessel, steamer, liner, barge; shipping; tank, trough, cistern, vat.

2 人 *funabito, shūjin* a seaman, a ship passenger

6 行 *shūkō* navigation; going by ⌈by ship

11 運 *shūun* ship transportation, freighting

遊 *funaaso(bi), shūyū* boating

13 艇 *shūtei* boat, craft

──── **4** ────

般 4931 / J484c / M30388 HAN. carry; all.

8 若 *hannya* wisdom personified; demoness

航 4933 / J3952 / M30385 KŌ. navigation; cross over.

A

kō(suru) sail, cruise, navigate; fly.

6 行 *kōkō* navigation, cruise

8 空 *kōkū* aviation, flight, air navigation

空便 *kōkūbin* airmail

4917–4933

竹米糸缶网罒羊羽老耂而耒耳聿肉月臣自至臼舌舛舟【艮】色艸艹虍虫血行衣衤西

⁹海 *kōkai* voyage, ocean navigation
¹³跡 *kōseki* wake of a ship
続力 *kōzokuryoku* cruising range; flying range
路 *kōro* sea route, steamer lane, service

─────── 5 ───────

舶 [4936 J4775 M30402] B HAKU ship.
⁵用 *hakuyō* marine
⁷来 *hakurai* importation; imported goods

舵 [4937 J4249 M30400] 柁 [2597 J4248 M14599] DA rudder. *kaji* rudder, helm, wheel.
⁴手 *dashu* helmsman, coxswain
⁸取 *kajito(ri)* steering; helmsman; coxswain; guidance, leadership; leader
¹⁵輪 *darin* steering wheel, helm

舷 [4938 J383f M30403] GEN gunwale. *funaberi, funabata* ship's side, gunwale.
⁶灯 *gentō* running light, side light
⁸門 *genmon* gangway (to a ship)
¹¹窓 *gensō* porthole
側 *gensoku* ship's side, broadside

船 [4939 J4125 M30407] A SEN ship. *fune* boat, ship, vessel, steamer, liner, barge; shipping; tank, trough, cistern, vat. *-sen* ship, vessel.
⁵主 *funanushi, senshu* shipowner
出 *funade* ship's departure
外機 *sengaiki* outboard motor
⁶団 *sendan* fleet of vessels
⁷足 *funaashi* draft; speed (of a ship)
尾 *sembi* ship's stern
体 *sentai* hull, ship
⁸長 *senchō* ship's captain

底 *funazoko, sentei* ship's bottom; bilge
⁹首 *senshu, miyoshi* bow, prow
便 *funabin, sembin, funadayo(ri)* shipping service, sea mail
乗 *funano(ri)* sailor, seaman, mariner; traveling by ship
客 *senkyaku, senkaku* ship passenger
室 *senshitsu* stateroom, cabin
¹⁰旅 *funatabi* voyage
員 *sen'in* crew, ship's company, sailors
荷 *funani* ship's cargo, freight
¹¹酔 *funayo(i)* seasickness
舶 *sempaku* ship, vessel, bottoms
¹²着場 *funatsukiba* harbor, wharf, anchorage
¹³路 *funaji, funamichi, senro* course, channel; sea route; voyage; wake
¹⁴端 *funabata* ship's side, gunwale
¹⁶積 *funazu(mi)* shipment, shipping, loading, lading
頭 *sendō* boatman, seaman, mariner
¹⁷齢 *senrei* ship's age

─────── 7 ───────

艇 [4941 J447a M30440] B TEI small boat.

─────── 14 ───────

艦 [4950 J344f M30571] B KAN warship.
³上機 *kanjōki* carrier-based plane
⁸長 *kanchō* captain of a warship
¹⁰砲 *kampō* ship's guns
¹¹隊 *kantai* squadron, fleet
船 *kansen* ships and warships
¹³艇 *kantei* naval vessels
載機 *kansaiki* carrier-based plane
¹⁶橋 *kankyō* bridge of a warship

████ RAD. 艮 138 ████

Nezukuri (the right-hand side of *ne* "root"). Variant: 艮 (5 strokes).
Nickname: Good (as in 良 *yoi* "good").

艮 [4953 J3a31 M30596] GON, KON stopping. *ushitora* northeast.

─────── 1 ───────

6

A 良 4954 J4e49 M30597 Ryō good, fine. *i(i)*, *yo(i)* good, good-natured; pleasing; precious, noble; lovely, beautiful, fine; lucky; efficacious; right; suitable; justifiable; appropriate, satisfactory; better; all right; unnecessary; no objection; intimate, friendly; easy; well; desirous. *yo(ku) suru* be skilled in. *yo(sa)* goodness, virtue, merit. *yo(shi)* good, all right, well, so.

⁴ 心 *ryōshin* conscience
⁶ 好 *ryōkō na* good, favorable, satisfactory

⁷ 否 *ryōhi* good or bad; quality
妻賢母 *ryōsai-kembo* good wife and wise mother
⁹ 俗 *ryōzoku* good customs
品 *ryōhin* superior article
風 *ryōfū* good custom
¹⁰ 家 *ryōka* good family
案 *ryōan* good idea
¹² 策 *ryōsaku* good plan, good policy
¹⁵ 縁 *ryōen* happy (marital) match
質 *ryōshitsu* good quality
¹⁶ 薬 *ryōyaku* good medicine
¹⁹ 識 *ryōshiki* good sense

RAD. 色 139

Iro color. Nickname: Color.

A 色 4956 J3f27 M30602 SHOKU, SHIKI color. *iro* color, tint, tinge; complexion; countenance, look; sensual pleasure; sweetheart; charms; fall colors; embellishment; slight concession; kind. *iro(meku)* color, be tinged, liven, become active, be stirred; begin to waver (in battle). *iro(zuku)* color, color up. *iro(ppoi)*, *iro(mekashii)* amorous, fascinating, seductive. *iro(nna)* various.

⁵ 白 *irojiro* light complexion; white
⁶ 色 *iroiro na* various
合 *iroa(i)* coloring, tint, shade, tone. *iroa(wase)* color matching
気 *iroke* coloring, shade, tone; coquetry; passion; romance; inclination, interest
⁸ 刷 *irozu(ri)* color print; color printing
取 *irodo(ru)* color, paint, make up. *irodori* coloring, coloration; color scheme; makeup
盲 *shikimō* color blindness
直 *ironao(shi)* changing wedding garments for ordinary clothes; redyeing
事 *irogoto* love affair; love scene
¹⁰ 紙 *irogami* colored paper. *shikishi* square drawing paper

素 *shikiso* coloring matter, pigment
弱 *shikijaku* slight color blindness
¹¹ 黒 *iroguro* dark complexion
欲 *shikiyoku* sexual passion, lust
情 *shikijō* sexual passion, lust
¹⁵ 調 *shikichō* color tone

13

艶 4957 J3f70 M30632 EN luster, glaze, polish; charm. *tsuya(meku)* be glossy, be charming, be colorful. *nama(meku)* be charming, be colorful, be of excellent quality, be beautiful. *tsuya(yakana)* glossy and beautiful. *nama(mekashii)* charming, captivating. *tsuya* gloss, luster, glaze, polish, brightness; charm, romance, love. *tsuya(ppoi)* romantic, spicy, amorous. *ade(yakana)* charming, fascinating.

¹⁰ 消 *tsuyake(shi)* frosted (glass)
¹³ 福 *empuku* good fortune in love; beau, gallant
¹⁴ 聞 *embun* love affair, love rumor
¹⁹ 艶 *tsuyatsuya shita* glossy, bright, slick
麗 *enrei* beauty, charm

艸 RAD. 140

Kusa grass. At top: ⺿ (4 strokes) or ⺾ (3 strokes) *kusa kammuri* or *sōkō* "grass" crown. These variants are here always counted as 3 strokes. Do not confuse with 廾 Rad. 55, which has longer verticals. Nickname: Grass.

3

B **芝** 4961 / J3c47 / M30699' SHI. *shiba* lawn, sod, turf.
5 生 *shibafu, shibau* lawn, turf, grass plot
8 居 *shibai* play, drama, show

B **芋** 4964 / J3072 / M30670' U. *imo* potato.
6 虫 *imomushi* a green caterpillar

4

芙 4966 / J4967 / M30694 FU. *hasu* water lily.

苅 4969 / J3423 / M30771 KAI cutting (grass).

芹 4970 / J365c / M30742 KIN. *seri* parsley.

芭 4974 / J474e / M30730 BA banana.
15 蕉 *bashō* banana plant

芦 4975 / J3032 / M30716 RO. *ashi, yoshi* reed,
11 笛 *roteki* reed flute

芯 4976 / J3f44 / M30732 SHIN wick.

芥 4977 / J3329 / M30715 KAI. KE. *karashi* mustard. *karashina* mustard (plant), rape. *gomi, akuta* dust, trash, rubbish.
3 子 *karashi* mustard. *keshi* poppy

A **芸** 4978 / J375d / M30741' GEI art, craft; artistic accomplishment; performance, acting; trick, stunt, feat.
2 人 *geinin* player, performer, entertainer, actor
6 当 *geitō* an art, trick, feat, stunt, performance
名 *geimei* stage name, screen name
7 妓 *geigi* geisha
8 者 *geisha* geisha, singing girl, entertainer
10 能 *geinō* public entertainment; accomplishments, attainments
能人 *geinōjin* star, entertainer
11 術 *geijutsu* art, the arts

B **芳** 4979 / J4b27 / M30736' HŌ fragrance. *kōba(shii), kamba(shii)* fragrant; balmy; favorable. *kamba(shikunai)* poor, unfavorable; disgraceful. *hō-* a prefix of respect.
9 香 *hōkō* perfume, fragrance
紀 *hōki* age (of a young lady)

A **花** 4980 / J3256 / M30734' KE. KA flower. *hana* flower, blossom; cherry blossoms; essence, spirit, pride; pearl; youth; best days; beautiful woman, flower arrangement; flower-card game. *hana(yakana)* gay, showy, brilliant, gorgeous. *hanaya(gu)* become brilliant.
4 木 *kaboku* flowers and trees; flowering trees. *hana (no) ki* flowering tree
火 *hanabi* fireworks, firecrackers
5 卉 *kaki* flowering plant
7 形 *hanagata* floral pattern; flourish; ornament; star actor; a popular person
花 *hanabana(shii)* brilliant, magnificent, spectacular
束 *hanataba* bouquet
見 *hanami* flower viewing
8 実 *kajitsu* flowers and fruit; exterior and interior
9 畑 *hanabatake* flower bed, flower garden
紅葉 *hana-momiji* flowers and maples; fine spring and autumn leaves
屋 *hanaya* flower store
柳 *karyū* blossoms and willows; geisha; prostitutes; red-light district
10 紛 *kafun* pollen
紛症 *kafunshō* hay fever
11 道 *kadō* flower arrangement. *hanamichi*

passage through the audience to the stage

瓶 *kabin*, *hanagame* vase

盛 *hanazaka(ri)* flowers in full bloom

祭 *Hanamatsuri* Buddha's birthday festival (April 8)

崗岩 *kakōgan* granite

鳥風月 *kachōfūgetsu* beauties of nature; elegant pursuits

¹² 婿 *hanamuko* bridegroom

¹³ 園 *hanazono*, *kaen* flower garden

嫁 *hanayome* bride

¹⁴ 模様 *hana moyō* floral design

¹⁵ 輪 *hanawa* wreath

器 *kaki* flower vase

¹⁶ 壇 *kadan* flower bed, flower garden

¹⁷ 環 *hanawa* wreath

5

苓 4981 / J4e6a / M30777 REI, RYŌ cocklebur, burrweed.

茎 B 4991 / J3754 / M30861' KEI, KYŌ *kuki* stem, stalk.

茄 4995 / J3258 / M30835 KA eggplant.

³ 子 *nasu*, *nasubi* eggplant

苑 4996 / J3171 / M30774 EN garden, farm, yard. *sono* park, garden.

茂 B 4998 / J4c50 / M30833' MO. *shige(ru)* grow thick, be overgrown, be luxuriant.

苧 5000 / J4377 / M30798 CHO. *o* hemp, flax; hemp thread. *karamushi* ramie.

苔 5001 / J425d / M30778 TAI moss. *koke* moss; lichen; incrustation; fur (on the tongue). *kokera* moss. ⌈spreads

⁵ 生 *kokemu(su)* the moss grows or

芽 A 5002 / J326a / M30860' GA. *me* sprout, spear, germ. *megu(mu)* bud, sprout.

⁵ 生 *mebae* bud, sprout, seedling. *meba(eru)* sprout, bud

苫 5003 / J4651 / M30802 SEN. *toma* rush matting.

⁹ 屋 *tomaya* a hut roofed and walled with rushes

苗 B 5004 / J4944 / M30781' BYŌ, MYŌ. *nae* seedling, sapling, shoot.

⁴ 木 *naegi* sapling, seedling ⌈bed

⁵ 代 *nawashiro*, *naeshiro* rice-seedling

⁶ 字 *myōji* surname

茅 5005 / J337d / M30836 BŌ. *kaya*, *chigaya*, *chi* miscanthus reed.

⁹ 屋 *bōoku* thatched cottage, hovel, my humble cottage

¹² 葺 *kayabuki* miscanthus-thatched

苛 5006 / J3257 / M30785 KA. *iji(meru)*, *saina(mu)* torment, scold, chastise.

⁵ 立 *irada(teru)* irritate, exasperate. *irada(tsu)* be irritated, be exasperated

⁸ 苛 *iraira suru* get nervous, be irritated, fret

性 *kasei* caustic

¹⁴ 酷 *kakoku* rigor, severity, cruelty

¹⁷ 斂誅求 *karen-chūkyū* exaction, extortion

若 A 5007 / J3c63 / M30796' JAKU. NYA. *mo(shi)*, *mo(shimo)* if. *moshi (kashitara)*, *moshi(ka) suru to* perhaps, possibly. *mo(shikuwa)* or, otherwise. *mo(shiya)* by any chance, perchance. *waka-*, *waka(i)* young, juvenile, youthful; younger, junior; immature, inexperienced; low number. *waka(yagu)* grow young again, look young. *shi(ku)* be equal to, compare with.

² 人 *wakōdo*, *waka(i)hito* young person, young man, young woman

³ 干 *jakkan*, *sokobaku*, *sokubaku* some, a number of

⁴ 手 *wakate* young person; young official

⁵ 布 *wakame* an edible seaweed

⁶ 返 *wakagae(ru)* grow young again

年 *jakunen* youth

⁷ 作 *wakazuku(ri)* makeup to look younger

君 *wakagimi* young lord

⁸ 者 *wakamono*, *waka(i)mono* young person; young manservant; young apprentice, young man, lad, youth

⁹ 造 *wakazō* youngster, stripling

¹² 葉 *wakaba* new leaves, fresh verdure

6

竹米糸缶网罒羊羽老耂耒耳聿肉月臣自至臼舌舛舟艮色【艸⼨】虍虫血行衤西

6

衆 *wakashū, waka(i)shū* young person; young manservant; young apprentice, young man, lad, youth

15 輩 *jakuhai* young people; novice

A 英 5008 J3151 M30808 EI England, Britain; gifted person; wit. *-Ei, Ei-* English.

3 才 *eisai* brilliant intellect, talent, genius

4 文 *Eibun* English, English composition

文学 *Eibungaku* English literature

文和訳 *Eibun-Wayaku* English-to-Japanese translation

6 米 *Ei-Bei* England and America

気 *eiki* excellent talent

名 *eimei* fame, glory, reputation

会話 *Eikaiwa* English conversation

字 *Eiji* English letter

8 知 *eichi* wisdom, intelligence; intellect

和 *Ei-Wa* English-Japanese

明 *eimei na* clever, intelligent, clear-sighted

国 *Eikoku* England, Great Britain, United Kingdom

11 断 *eidan* prompt decision, resolution, drastic steps

12 雄 *eiyū* hero

13 傑 *eiketsu* an outstanding person

誉 *eiyo* fame, great praise

14 語 *Eigo* the English language

15 邁 *eimai* wise and brave, great, talented

霊 *eirei* spirits of the war dead; great men

A 苦 5009 J366c M30797 KU suffering, trial, worry, trouble, hardship, difficulty, toil. *kuru(shimu), kuru(shigaru)* suffer; groan; be troubled, be worried, be perplexed; strive, try hard. *kuru(shimeru)* torment; harass, worry; persecute, inflict pain. *niga(mu), niga(ru)* feel bitter; scowl. *ku ni suru* worry. *kuru(shii)* painful; distressing, embarrassing, difficult, bitter; straitened; farfetched; stiff (climb). *niga(i)* bitter; hard, trying. *kuru(shimi)* pain, agony, torment, trouble, distress; mortification.

4 心 *kushin* pains, trouble, anxiety; hard work, diligence

手 *nigate* weak point; ugly customer

5 汁 *kujū* bitterness of life; a hard time. *nigari* brine

6 肉 *kuniku* countermeasure at personal sacrifice

行 *kugyō* penance, austerities, mortification

7 言 *kugen* frank advice, exhortation

役 *kueki* hard labor, drudgery; penal servitude

労 *kurō* hardships, difficulties, trials; toil; anxiety

8 杯 *kuhai* bitter cup, ordeal

況 *kukyō* hard circumstances, trouble, predicament, crisis

苦 *niganiga(shii)* unpleasant, disgusting, loathsome, shameful, scandalous

味 *kumi, nigami* bitter taste

味走 *nigamibashi(tta)* sternly handsome

学 *kugaku* studying under adversity

9 界 *kukai, kugai* this world of suffering; life of prostitution

衷 *kuchū* distress

10 悩 *kunō* distress, suffering. *kuru(shimi)-naya(mu)* be in distress

紛 *kuru(shi)magi(re) ni* out of desperation, driven by distress, under pressure

笑 *kushō, nigawara(i)* bitter smile, forced smile

11 渋 *kujū* bitter and puckery; drenched; sentences hard to understand

情 *kujō* complaint, objections, troubles

12 痛 *kutsū* pain, suffering, agony

悶 *kumon* agony, anguish

13 戦 *kusen* hard fighting; tight game

節 *kusetsu* fidelity in adversity

楽 *kuraku* pleasure and pain

14 境 *kukyō* hard circumstances, trouble, predicament, crisis

15 慮 *kuryo* pains, trouble, anxiety; hard work, diligence

18 闘 *kutō suru* fight hard; struggle (for a living)

難 *kunan* suffering, hardship; passion (of Christ)

————— **6** —————

茨 5017 J3071 M30896 SHI. *ibara* thorn, briar.

茜 5019 J302b M30871 SEN. *akane* madder, red dye, madder red, Turkey red.

荏 5022 / J3141 / M30950 JIN bean.

⁸荏苒 *jinzen to* procrastinatingly

茸 5026 / J427b / M30918 JŌ. *take* mushroom.

荊 5027 / J3755 / M-X KEI thorn; whip. *ibara* thorn, briar.

B 荘 5031 / J4171 / M30890 SŌ villa, inn. SHŌ villa, cottage, feudal manor.

重 *sōchō* solemnity, gravity, impressiveness

¹³園 *shōen, sōen* manor

¹⁷厳 *sōgon* solemnity, sublimity, impressiveness, magnificence, majesty

A 草 5032 / J4170 / M30945' SŌ. *kusa* grass; grass hand(writing); weeds; herbs, plants; pasture. *sō(suru)* write, draft. *kusa(ikire)* hot and humid feeling when walking through tall summer grass.

³子 *sōshi* storybook; copybook

⁴分 *kusawa(ke)* going through deep grass; founding a village; village founder; pioneer

双紙 *kusazōshi* picture book

刈 *kusaka(ri)* grass cutting, mowing

木 *sōmoku, kusaki* vegetation, trees and plants

⁵本 *sōhon* herbs; draft, manuscript

⁶地 *sōchi* steppes. *kusachi* meadow, grassland

⁷花 *sōka, kusabana* flowering plant

⁸枕 *kusamakura* traveling

臥 *kutabi(reru)* be tired, be exhausted. *kusabushi* lying on the grass; sleeping in the field

⁹食 *sōshoku no* herbivorous

草 *sōsō* brevity; rudeness; hurry; the closing words of a letter

¹⁰原 *sōgen* prairie, grassy plain, steppe. *kusawara, kusahara* meadow, grass plot

紙 *sōshi* shadow of the grass

案 *sōan* draft (of a law or manuscript)

書 *sōsho* cursive script, grass hand

根木皮 *sōkombokuhi* roots and bark; Chinese medicinal materials. *sōkommokuhi* medicinal plants

¹¹庵 *kusa(no)iori, kusa(no)io, sōan* hut, hermitage, thatched cottage

笛 *kusabue* reed whistle

¹²葺 *kusabuki* grass thatch

創 *sōsō* inauguration, beginning, origination

葉蔭 *kusaba (no) kage (de)* under the sod, in the grave

¹⁵稿 *sōkō* lecture notes, outline, draft, manuscript

履 *zōri* sandals, zori

鞋 *waraji* straw sandals

¹⁸叢 *kusamura* clump of bushes, grassy place, thicket, jungle, the bush

A 茶 5033 / J4363 / M30915' SA, CHA tea; tea plant; tea leaves; light brown. *cha(gakatta)* brownish. *cha (ni) suru* make fun of. *cha(ppoi)* brownish, light brown.

⁴化 *chaka(su)* laugh away, make fun of

⁶色 *cha iro* light brown, tawny

托 *chataku* teacup holder

会 *chakai, cha(no)e* tea party, tea ceremony

⁷呑 *chanomi* teacup; tea lover; tea drinking

⁸房 *sabō* refreshment parlor

⁹室 *chashitsu* tea arbor; tea cottage; tearoom

屋 *chaya* teahouse; tea dealer

¹⁰席 *chaseki* tea arbor, tea cottage; tea-ceremony seat

釜 *chagama* teakettle

¹¹匙 *chasaji* teaspoon

道 *chadō, sadō* Way of Tea, tea ceremony

菓子 *chagashi* teacakes

¹²間 *cha(no)ma* family living room

湯 *cha(no)yu* tea ceremony, Way of Tea

筒 *chazutsu* tea container

飯事 *sahanji* everyday occurrence

番劇 *chabangeki* burlesque, low comedy

飲 *chano(mi)* teacup; tea lover; tea drinking

¹³碗 *chawan* rice bowl; teacup

褐色 *chakasshoku* yellowish brown

話会 *chawakai, sawakai* tea party

¹⁴摘 *chatsumi* tea picking; tea picker

6

竹 米 糸 缶 网 ⴿ 羊 羽 老 耂 而 耒 耳 聿 肉 月 臣 自 至 臼 舛 舟 艮 色 【艸 艹】⁶ 虍 虫 血 行 衣 衤 西

6

竹
米
糸
缶
网
罒
羊
羽
老
耂
而
耒
耳
聿
肉
月
臣
自
至
臼
舌
舛
舟
艮
色
【艸
艹】
6
虍
虫
血
行
衣
衤
西

漬 *chazuke* simple meal; tea poured on boiled rice
15 箪笥 *chadansu* tea cupboard
16 濁 *cha (o) nigo(su)* cover up one's mistakes

荒 A ⟨5034 / J3953 / M30953⟩ Kō. *ara(i)* rough, rude, wild, harsh, violent, gruff, fierce. *ara(ppoi)* rough, rude, violent, wild. *sabi(reru), a(reru)* be ruined, become stormy; tear around; get chapped. *a(rabiru), a(raburu)* get rough, be insolent. *susa(bu), susa(mu)* get desolate, go wild; decline; get rough. *a(rasu)* lay waste. *a(rarageru)* raise voice in anger. *a(rekure)* daredevil, rowdy, a tough. *are* storm, stormy weather; chapping, roughness. *arara(ka) ni* violently, roughly. *ara-* wild, rough, fierce, wild; drastic. *-ara(shi)* robbery, robber.
4 天 *kōten* stormy weather
5 立 *arada(tsu)* be excited, be exasperated, be agitated. *arada(teru)* aggravate, exasperate
仕事 *arashigoto* rough work, hard work; robbery, burglary; a big haul; heavy manual labor
6 地 *arechi* waste land, wilderness, desert
肌 *arehada* rough skin
7 作 *arazuku(ri)* spadework, preliminary arrangements
狂 *a(re)-kuru(u)* get stormy, rage; get angry
8 波 *aranami* stormy seas, raging waves
果 *a(re)-ha(teru)* be dilapidated, be ruined, lie waste, be desolate
武者 *aramusha* daredevil, rowdy, a tough
放題 *a(re)hōdai* left to go to ruin
9 海 *araumi* rough sea
削 *arakezu(ri)* roughing, rough planing, rough hewing, rough turning
荒 *araara(shii)* rough, wild, violent, rude, harsh, gruff, fierce
巻 *aramaki* fresh slightly-salted salmon; a gift of fish wrapped in bamboo leaves
10 馬 *arauma, a(re)uma* untamed horse, restive horse
唐無稽 *kōtōmukei* absurdity, nonsense
11 涼 *kōryō(taru)* desolate, dreary
野 *arano, areno, kōya* wilds, wilderness, desert

12 廃 *a(re)-suta(reru)* become desolate, be dilapidate. *kōhai* desolation, ruin, dilapidation
14 寥 *kōryō na* desolate and lonely
模様 *a(re)moyō* threatening sky
15 稼 *arakase(gi)* robbery, burglary; a big haul; heavy manual labor
縄 *aranawa* rough straw rope
蕪地 *kōbuchi* deserted and desolate place

———— 7 ————

莱 ⟨5039 / J4d69 / M-X⟩ See 莱 5073.

莞 ⟨5052 / J3450 / M31063⟩ Kan. reed used for *tatami* covers.
14 爾 *kanji toshite* with a smile

荻 ⟨5054 / J322e / M31005⟩ Teki. *ogi* reed.
10 原 *ogihara* reedy field

莫 ⟨5057 / J477c / M31078⟩ Baku. Bo. *naka(re)* must not, do not, be not.
3 大 *bakudai na* vast, immense, enormous

華 B ⟨5058 / J325a / M31119⟩ Ge. Ka flower; petal; shining, luster; appearance; ostentation. *hanaya(gu)* become brilliant. *hana* flower. *hana(yakana)* gay, showy, brilliant, gorgeous. -Ka- China.
4 氏 *kashi* Fahrenheit
9 美 *kabi* pomp, splendor; gaudiness, colorfulness
11 道 *kadō* flower arrangement
族 *kazoku* noble, peer
12 奢 *kasha* luxury, pomp, extravagance. *kyasha na* delicate, slender; fragile
14 僑 *Kakyō* overseas Chinese
17 厳 *Kegon* Buddhist sect originating in the eighth century
燭典 *kashoku (no) ten* wedding ceremony
19 麗 *karei* splendor, magnificence

荷 A ⟨5059 / J3259 / M31000⟩ Ka shoulder-pole load. *nina(u)* carry, bear (a burden), shoulder (a gun). *ni* load,

baggage, freight, cargo; burden.
⁵ 札 *nifuda* tag, label
⁷ 車 *niguruma* cart, wagon
役 *niyaku* handling cargo
⁸ 物 *nimotsu* baggage; load
送 *nioku(ri)* consignment
担 *katan* support; conspiracy, complicity. *nikatsu(gi)* carrying; laden
受 *niu(ke)* receipt of goods
⁹ 重 *kajū* load
造 *nizuku(ri)* packing, baling, crating
¹⁶ 積 *nizu(mi)* loading

——————— 8 ———————

葛 ┌ 5060 ┐ Nonstandard for 葛 5126.
    │ J336b │
    └ M-X ┘

萊 ┌ 5073 ┐ 萊 ┌ 5039 ┐ RAI
    │ J-X │   │ J4d69 │ goosefoot,
    └ M31262 ┘   └ M-X ┘
pigweed.

萄 ┌ 5075 ┐ Dō, Tō grape vine, wild
    │ J463a │ grape.
    └ M31252 ┘

菟 ┌ 5077 ┐ To, Tsu dodder (plant).
    │ J-X │
    └ M31189 ┘

菰 ┌ 5079 ┐ Ko. *komo* a reed used for
    │ J3856 │ matting.
    └ M31217 ┘

菖 ┌ 5085 ┐ Shō iris.
    │ J3e54 │
    └ M31174 ┘
¹³ 蒲 *ayame* Japanese iris. *shōbu* iris, flag

萎 ┌ 5087 ┐ I. *na(eru)* wither, droop,
    │ J3060 │ weaken; be paralyzed, be
    └ M31269 ┘
lame. *shibo(mu), shio(reru), shina(biru)*
droop, wither, wilt, fade; be downcast.
¹⁷ 縮 *ishuku* withering, contraction, atrophy

菅 ┌ 5090 ┐ KAN *suge* sedge.
    │ J3f7b │
    └ M31142 ┘

菌 ┌ 5091 ┐ KIN fungus, germ, bacteria.
B   │ J365d │
    └ M31156' ┘

菱 ┌ 5092 ┐ Ryō. *hishi* water chestnut;
    │ J4929 │ diamond (shape).
    └ M31219 ┘

⁷ 形 *ryōkei, hishigata* rhombus shape; diamond shape

菩 ┌ 5093 ┐ Bo kind of grass; sacred
    │ J4a6e │ tree.
    └ M31205 ┘
¹² 提 *bodai* Buddhahood; supreme
提樹 *bodaiju* bo tree; lime tree; linden tree
¹⁶ 薩 *bosatsu* bodhisattva; Buddhist saint

萌 ┌ 5094 ┐ Hō. Bō. *moe(ru)* sprout,
    │ J4b28 │ bud. *moya(su)* to malt,
    └ M31265 ┘
cause to sprout artificially. *kiza(su)* show
signs or symptoms of. *moya(shi)* malt;
artificially sprouted beans or grains.
kiza(shi) signs, omen, symptoms;
germination.
⁵ 立 *moe-ta(tsu)* sprout, bud
出 *moe-de(ru)* sprout, bud
⁸ 芽 *hōga* germination; germ, sprout
¹¹ 黄色 *moegi iro* light green

菓 ┌ 5095 ┐ KA cakes; fruit.
B   │ J325b │
    └ M31168' ┘
³ 子 *kashi* confectionery, pastry, candy

菊 ┌ 5096 ┐ KIKU chrysanthemum.
B   │ J3546 │
    └ M31153' ┘
⁴ 月 *kikuzuki* ninth lunar month
⁷ 判 *kikuban* small octavo

菜 ┌ 5097 ┐ SAI side dish; greens;
A   │ J3a5a │ vegetables. *na* greens;
    └ M31184' ┘
vegetables; the rape or mustard plant.
⁷ 花 *na (no) hana* mustard flowers, rape blossoms
⁹ 食 *saishoku* vegetarian diet; plain food
¹⁴ 種 *natane* rapeseed
¹⁵ 箸 *saibashi* chopsticks for cooking

著 ┌ 5098 ┐ CHO literary work.
A   │ J4378 │ *ara(wasu)* write, publish.
    └ M31302 ┘
ichijiru(shii) remarkable, phenomenal.
⁶ 名 *chomei* eminence, celebrity, fame
⁷ 述 *chojutsu* literary work
作 *chosaku* literary work, book; authorship
作権 *chosakuken* copyright
⁸ 者 *chosha* author, writer
¹⁰ 書 *chosho* literary work, book

6
竹
米
糸
缶
网
罒
羊
羽
老
耂
而
耒
耳
聿
肉
月
臣
自
至
臼
舌
舛
艮
色
【艸
艹】
8
虍
虫
血
行
衤
衣
西

左余白（部首索引）:
竹 米 糸 缶 网 罒 羊 羽 老 耂 而 耒 耳 聿 肉 月 臣 自 至 臼 舌 舛 舟 艮 色 【艸⺾】 ⺾⁹ 虍 虫 血 行 衣 衤 西

6 ——— 9 ———

蓬 5099 / J4b29 / M-X — Nonstandard for 蓬 5157.

蒐 5102 / J4551 / M-X — Nonstandard for 蒐 5077.

蓮 5105 / J4f21 / M-X — Nonstandard for 蓮 5158.

葎 5111 / J4e2a / M31397 — RITSU. *mugura* creeper; trailing plants.

董 5118 / J4621 / M31433 — TŌ correct.

葵 5120 / J302a / M31458 — KI. *aoi* hollyhock.

萱 5121 / J337e / M31345 — KEN. *kaya* miscanthus reed.

萩 5122 / J476b / M31333 — SHŪ. *hagi* bush clover.

葱 5123 / J472c / M31454 — SŌ. *negi* stone leek, Welsh onion, long onion.

葺 5125 / J4978 / M31465 — SHŪ. *ashi* reed, rush. *fu(ku)* to thatch, cover, shingle, tile.

葛 5126 / J-X / M31420 — KATSU. *tsuzura* arrowroot, a strong-fiber vine. *kuzu* kudzu, arrowroot; arrowroot starch.
¹⁸ 藤 *kattō* complications, dissension

葡 5127 / J4972 / M31430 — BU, Ho wild grape.
¹¹ 萄 *budō* grapes, grapevine
萄酒 *budōshu* wine

B 葬 5128 / J4172 / M31448 — SŌ. *hōmu(ru)* bury; shelve. *tomura(u)* mourn for; hold a memorial service for; condole. *tomura(i)* funeral, burial, condolence.
⁶ 式 *sōshiki* funeral ceremony
列 *sōretsu* funeral procession
⁸ 送 *sōsō* attendance at a funeral
¹¹ 祭 *sōsai* funerals and festivals

---

¹⁵ 儀 *sōgi* funeral service
儀場 *sōgijō* funeral parlor

A 葉 5129 / J4d55 / M31387 — YŌ leaf; plane; lobe; counter for flat things. *ha, ha(ppa)* leaf, foliage, needle, blade, spear, frond.
⁴ 月 *hazuki* eighth lunar month
⁹ 巻 *hamaki* cigar
¹⁰ 書 *hagaki* postcard
¹⁴ 緑素 *yōryokuso* chlorophyll

A 落 5130 / J4d6e / M31362 — RAKU. *o(chiru)* fall, drop, come down, go down; drip; collapse, cave in; sink; fail (in exams); be missing; come off, come out; flee; lose popularity; abate; flow into; be inferior; fall unconscious; fade; be captured, be carried away by. *o(tosu)* drop, let fall; throw down; throw (a shadow); miss (a ball), fumble; lose; capture; omit; degrade; depreciate, detract from; decrease; make worse; drive away, exorcise; leave behind; knock down (an article); cause abortion; entrap; end (a story) with a punch; remove (stains). *o(chibureru)* be ruined, sink into poverty. *o(chi)* error, fault, slip; point (of a joke); outcome. *o(toshi)* trap; false bottom; ashpan; chute; brazier. *-o(chi)* off, less, minus; flight. *o(chi)-* lower, low; fallen (fruit); defeated.
² 人 *ochūdo, ochibito, ochiudo* refugee; deserter; fugitive
入 *o(chi)-i(ru)* fall into, get into, slide into, lapse into; cave in, sink; fall (a fort)
丁 *rakuchō* missing pages
³ 下 *rakka* falling, descent
下傘 *rakkasan* parachute
⁴ 手 *rakushu* receiving
日 *rakujitsu* setting sun
込 *o(chi)-ko(mu)* fall in; sink, subside; decline (of prices); come in
⁵ 目 *o(chi)me* declining fortune, adversity
穴 *o(toshi)ana* pitfall, trap
札 *rakusatsu* successful bid. *o(chi)fuda* prize-winning ticket
⁶ 合 *o(chi)-a(u)* meet, come upon, rendezvous. *o(chi)a(i)* meeting; confluence
成 *rakusei* completion of construction
伍 *rakugo* straggling, dropping out; losing out (in the struggle for

existence)

7 花生 *rakkasei* peanuts

花狼藉 *rakkarōzeki suru* fall off, pass away, scatter

8 物 *o(toshi)mono* lost article

命 *rakumei* death

9 胆 *rakutan* discouragement

度 *o(chi)do* fault, error, slip, lapse, oversight; blame, guilt

10 馬 *rakuba* a fall from a horse. *rakuba suru* fall from a horse, be thrown from a horse

涙 *rakurui suru* shed tears

差 *rakusa* water level, head, fall

書 *rakuga(ki)* scribbling in public places, graffiti. *rakusho* anonymous critical broadsides

11 陽 *rakuyō* setting sun; Loyang (in China)

第 *rakudai* failure in an examination

12 款 *rakkan* writer's or artist's signature

掌 *rakushō* receiving

着 *o(chi)-tsu(keru)* calm (oneself). *o(chi)-tsu(ku)* calm down; settle down; keep cool; subside (pain); be steady; harmonize with. *ochitsu(ki)* calmness, serenity; stability. *rakuchaku* settlement, end, conclusion

葉 *o(chi)ba* fallen leaves. *rakuyō* fall of leaves; fallen leaves

13 雷 *rakurai suru* be struck by lightning

14 選 *rakusen* election defeat; rejection

語 *rakugo* humorous story

15 盤 *rakuban* cave-in

穂拾 *o(chi)bohiro(i)* gleaning; gleaner

———— 10 ————

蒋 [5132 / J3e55 / M-X] See 蔣 5177.

蓉 [5135 / J4d56 / M31648] Yō lotus.

蔀 [5138 / J3c43 / M31748] Hō. *shitomi* latticed shutters.

蓑 [5143 / J4c2c / M31661] Sa. *mino* straw raincoat.

蒜 [5144 / J4947 / M31562] San. *ninniku* garlic.

蔭 [5151 / J307e / M31840] In. *kage* shade; backing, (your) assistance.

蒔 [5153 / J3c2c / M31546] Shi. Ji. *ma(ku)* sow (seed).

12 絵 *makie* gold or silver lacquer work

蒙 [5154 / J4c58 / M31555] Mō ignorance; darkness. *kōmu(ru)* get, receive, be subjected to, sustain (damage), suffer (loss). *kōmu(rasu)* cause (damage); inflict on; subject to.

5 古 *Mōko* Mongolia

9 昧 *mōmai* ignorance

14 塵 *mōjin suru* flee from the palace (the emperor)

蓋 [5155 / J3338 / M31652] Gai cover. *futa* cover, lid, flap, hood. *keda(shi)* probably; after all; in the long run.

12 然性 *gaizensei* probability

蒲 [5156 / J3377 / M31611] Fu. Bo. Ho. Bu. *gama* flag, cattail, bulrush. *kaba* bulrush.

4 公英 *tampopo* dandelion

6 団 *futon* bedding; mattress; pallet

14 鉾 *kamaboko* boiled fish paste

蓬 [5157 / J-X / M31720] Hō. *yomogi* sagebrush, wormwood, mugwort; an edible weed.

11 莱 *hōrai* isle of eternal youth; fairyland; Elysian fields; eternal youth ornament

14 髪 *hōhatsu* unkempt hair

蓮 [5158 / J-X / M31722] Ren. *hasu, hachisu* lotus.

10 根 *renkon* lotus root

華 *renge* lotus, lotus flower

12 葉 *hasuha, hasu(p)pa* lotus leaf. *hasuha na, hasu(p)pa na* wanton, loose, coquettish

蒐 [5159 / J3d2f / M31539] Shū gather.

12 集 *shūshū* collection, accumulation

葦 [5160 / J3031 / M31437] I. *ashi, yoshi* reed, bulrush.

6

竹米糸缶网罒羊羽耂而耒耳聿肉月臣自至臼舌舛舟艮色【艸⺾】虍虫血行衣⻂西

6

蓄 ₅₁₆₁ J435f M31642' CHIKU. *takuwa(e)* store,
B hoard, savings.
takuwa(eru) store, lay in stock, save,
keep, wear (a mustache).
⁹ 音器 *chikuonki* phonograph
¹⁰ 財 *chikuzai* amassing of wealth
¹³ 電 *chikuden* charging with electricity
電池 *chikudenchi* storage battery
電器 *chikudenki* electric condenser
¹⁶ 積 *chikuseki* accumulation, amassing

蒼 ₅₁₆₂ J4173 M31627 SŌ. *ao* blue, pale.
⁴ 天 *sōten* blue sky
⁵ 白 *aojiro(i), sōhaku na* pale, pallid,
livid
⁸ 穹 *sōkyū* blue sky
空 *sōkū* blue sky
氓 *sōbō* the people
⁹ 海 *sōkai* blue sea

蒸 ₅₁₆₃ J3e78 M31618' JŌ. SHŌ. *mu(su)* steam,
A heat up (with steam); be
close, be sultry; foment, poultice.
mu(reru) be stuffy, get musty; moulder,
heat. *mu(rasu)* steam, cook by steam.
fu(kasu) steam. *fu(keru)* be steamed, be
boiled. *mu(shi)-* steamed (dish).
⁶ 気 *jōki* steam, vapor; steamship
気船 *jōkisen* steamship
気機関車 *jōki kikansha* steam
locomotive
⁹ 発 *jōhatsu* evaporation, volatilization
¹⁰ 留 *jōryū* distillation
留水 *jōryūsui* distilled water
留酒 *jōryūshu* distilled liquor
¹² 暑 *mu(shi)atsu(i)* sultry, sweltering
焼 *mu(shi)ya(ki)* baking in covered
casseroles
蒸 *mu(shi)mu(shi) suru* be sultry, be
close
¹³ 溜 *jōryū* distillation
²² 籠 *seiro, seirō* steamer, basket for
steaming rice

――――― **11** ―――――

蒋 ₅₁₇₇ J-X M31820 SHŌ a reed.

蔦 ₅₁₇₈ J4455 M31828' CHŌ. *tsuta* ivy.

蔑 ₅₁₇₉ J4a4e M31781 BETSU. *naigashiro (ni)*
suru ignore, despise,
neglect, ridicule. *nami(suru)* set at
naught, ridicule. *sagesu(mu), sageshi(mu)*
despise, ridicule.
¹¹ 視 *besshi* contempt, derision; slight

蔓 ₅₁₈₀ J4c22 M31784 MAN. *habiko(ru)* spread,
sprawl; overgrow; thrive;
be rampant, become powerful. *tsuru*
vine, tendril, runner; influence,
connections, medium, good offices.
⁸ 延 *habiko(ru), man'en suru* spread,
diffuse, prevail, be widespread, gain
headway

蔚 ₅₁₈₁ J3136 M31805 I, UTSU thick growth.
otokoyomogi (a kind of)
mugwort; thick growth, thicket.

蔵 ₅₁₈₂ J4222 M31885' SŌ. ZŌ. *kura* storehouse,
A warehouse, godown;
cellar; depository; treasury; granary,
elevator. *zō(suru)* hide; accumulate;
have, own, keep, cherish. *osa(meru)*
obtain, reap; dedicate, consecrate; pay;
supply; store; finish; collect; restore,
replace. *-zō* possession.
⁴ 元 *kuramoto* warehouse superintendent
⁵ 本 *zōhon* one's library, one's private
collection of books
⁹ 相 *zōshō, zōsō* finance minister
屋敷 *kura yashiki* daimyo's city
storehouse
¹⁰ 書 *zōsho* one's library, book collection

――――― **12** ―――――

蕊 ₅₁₈₈ J3c49 M31939 ZUI. *shibe* pistil; stamen.

蕉 ₅₁₉₁ J3e56 M31937 SHŌ banana.

蔽 ₅₁₉₃ J4a43 M31888 HEI. *ō(i)* cover, covering;
shade; mantle, coat; hood,
bonnet; casing; awning. *ō(u)* cover, veil;
hang over; brood over; conceal; overlap;
shelter; screen; disguise; wrap; obscure;
shade; overshadow.

左margin: 竹 米 糸 缶 网 罒 羊 羽 老 耂 而 耒 耳 聿 肉 月 臣 自 至 臼 舌 舛 舟 艮 色 【艸 艹】 虍 虫 血 行 衣 衤 西

蕨 5194 / J4f4f / M32001 KETSU. *warabi* bracken, fernbrake.

蕪 5196 / J4973 / M32004 BU. *kabu, kabura* turnip.

蕎 5197 / J363e / M31946 KYŌ buckwheat.
7 麦 *soba* buckwheat; buckwheat noodles

蕩 5198 / J4622 / M32002 TŌ. *toro(kasu)* vt melt, fuse; charm, captivate.
toro(keru) vi melt, fuse; charm, captivate.
6 尽 *tōjin* squandering
7 児 *tōji* debauchee, libertine

蕃 5199 / J4859 / M31906 BAN, HAN grow luxuriously.
2 人 *banjin* aborigine
11 族 *banzoku* savage tribe

――――― 13 ―――――

薗 5200 / J3172 / M32119 See 園 962.

薮 5201 / J4c79 / M-X Nonstandard for 藪 5240.

薯 5202 / J3d72 / M-X Nonstandard for 薯 5230.

蕗 5203 / J4979 / M31964 RO. *fuki* a butterbur, a big rhubarb, a coltsfoot.

薩 5217 / J3b27 / M32189' SATSU Buddha.
15 摩薯 *satsuma imo* sweet potato

薦 5219 / J4126 / M32143' SEN. *susu(me)* recommendation, advice, encouragement. *susu(meru)* recommend, advise, encourage; offer (wine). *komo* mat.

薙 5221 / J4665 / M32121 TEI. *na(gu)* mow down (the enemy).
2 刀 *naginata* halberd

薪 5222 / J3f45 / M32149' SHIN. *maki* firewood.
takigi firewood, kindling, fuel.

4 水 *shinsui* fuel and water; cooking; salary; board
9 炭 *shintan* wood and charcoal, fuel

薫 5223 / J3730 / M32173 KUN. *kun(zuru)* send forth fragrance, be scented, impregnate with. *kao(ru)* smell, be fragrant. *kuyu(rasu)* smoke (tabacco); burn (incense). *kao(ri)* fragrance, perfume, aroma, odor, scent, smell.
9 風 *kumpū* balmy breeze
10 陶 *kuntō* education, training, instruction, discipline

薬 5224 / J4c74 / M32188' YAKU medicine. *kusuri* medicine; glaze, enamel; chemical; gunpowder; benefit.
5 代 *kusuridai, yakudai* medical fee, doctor's fee, charge for medicine
用 *yakuyō* medicinal use
石 *yakuseki* medical treatment
6 缶 *yakan* teakettle
7 局 *yakkyoku* dispensary, medical office, pharmacy
8 店 *yakuten* drugstore
価 *yakuka, yakka* medical charge
味 *yakumi* spices, flavor, seasoning; the taste of a medicine
効 *yakkō* medicinal value, remedial result
物 *yakubutsu* medicines, drugs, *materia medica*
学 *yakugaku* pharmacology
9 屋 *kusuriya* drug store
指 *kusuriyubi* third finger, ring finger
品 *yakuhin* medicines, drugs, chemicals
草 *yakusō* medicinal plants
10 剤 *yakuzai* medicine, drugs, compounded medicines
剤師 *yakuzaishi* pharmacist
11 液 *yakueki* liquid medicine
15 箱 *kusuribako* medicine chest
22 籠 *yakurō* medicine chest

薄 5225 / J4776 / M32083' HAKU. *usu(i)* thin, weak (tea), light, pale, faint, scanty, ungenerous. *usu(meru)* dilute, weaken. *usu(ragu), usu(rogu), usu(reru)* thin, thin out, fade, grow pale, be toned down, get dim, cool (emotions), abate,

6

lessen, decline. *usu(ppera) na* thin; shallow-minded, superficial, frivolous. *-usu, usu-* thin, weak, scanty, slightly, light (color).

⁴切 *usugi(ri)* slicing thin
　化粧 *usugeshō* light makeup
⁵目 *usume* rather light, comparatively thin; half-closed eyes
　氷 *hakuhyō, usugōri* thin ice; danger
⁶地 *usuji* thin cloth; thin metal
　汚 *usugitana(i)* filthy, dirty, bedraggled
　気味悪 *usukimi (no) waru(i), usukimiwaru(i)* weird, uncanny, eerie, unearthly; ominous
⁷利 *hakuri* small profits, narrow margin, low interest
　利多売 *hakuri-tabai* small profits and large sales
⁸明 *hakumei, usuaka(ri)* twilight, dawn. *usuakaru(i)* dim; gloomy, somber.
　命 *hakumei* evil fate, misfortune
　幸 *hakkō* misfortune, bad luck
¹⁰笑 *usuwara(i)* faint smile
　弱 *hakujaku* flimsiness, weakness; feebleness, infirmity
　荷 *hakka* mint, peppermint
¹¹黒 *usuguro(i)* dark, dusky, dingy
　情 *hakujō* poor sense of duty; unkindness; cruelty; coldheartedness
¹²給 *hakkyū* meager salary
　寒 *usu(ra)samu(i)* chilly
　着 *usugi* thin clothing, scanty clothes
　紫 *usumurasaki* light purple, orchid
¹³塩 *usujio* slightly salted
　暗 *usugura(i)* dim; gloomy, somber. *usukura(gari)* dim light, gloom, dusk
¹⁴暮 *hakubo* nightfall, dusk, twilight
¹⁶曇 *usugumo(ri)* slightly cloudy
¹⁷謝 *hakusha* small token of gratitude

─────── **14** ───────

薯 | 5230 / J-X / M32191 | SHO. *imo* potato.

藍 | 5233 / J4d75 / M32258 | RAN. *ai* indigo (blue); indigo plant.

藁 | 5234 / J4f4e / M32222 | KŌ. *wara* straw.

⁵半紙 *warabanshi* a low-grade paper
⁹屋根 *wara yane* straw roof

¹²葺 *warabuki* straw thatch
¹⁵縄 *wara nawa* straw rope

─────── **15** ───────

藷 | 5237 / J3d73 / M-X | Nonstandard for 藷 5247.

藪 | 5240 / J692e / M32348 | SŌ. *yabu* thicket, bush, underbrush, grove.

⁷医者 *yabu isha* quack doctor
¹¹蛇 *yabuhebi* boomerang, hornet's nest, stirring up unnecessary trouble

藤 | 5241 / J4623 / M32340' | TŌ. *fuji* wisteria.

⁶色 *fuji iro* light purple, lilac, mauve, lavender
¹²棚 *fujidana* wisteria trellis
　壺 *fujitsubo* barnacle
　紫 *fuji murasaki* dark lilac, smalt, powder blue

藩 | 5242 / J484d / M32346' | B HAN feudal clan; enclosure.

³士 *hanshi* retainer
⁵主 *hanshu* feudal lord, daimyo
⁷邸 *hantei* daimyo's estate; daimyo's Edo estate
⁹政 *hansei* clan government
¹¹屏 *hampei* bulwark, pillar

─────── **16** ───────

藷 | 5247 / J-X / M32391 | SHO. *imo* potato.

蘇 | 5252 / J4149 / M32427 | SO. SU. *yomigae(ru)* be resurrected, be revived, be resuscitated, be rehabilitated. *yomigae(ri)* resurrection; reviving, resuscitation; rehabilitation. *-So-* Soviet Union.

⁵生 *sosei* revival, resuscitation; resurrection

藻 | 5254 / J4174 / M32401 | B SŌ. *mo* duckweed, seaweed.

蘭 | 5255 / J4d76 / M32477' | RAN orchid; Dutch.

⁸学 *Rangaku* study of the Dutch language

竹
米
糸
缶
网
罒
羊
羽
老
耂
而
耒
耳
聿
肉
月
臣
自
至
臼
舌
舛
舟
艮
色
艸
艹
虍
[虫]₀
血
行
衣
衤
西

RAD. 虍 141

Tora kammuri or *toragashira* "tiger" top—really an enclosure. Nickname: Tiger.

— 2 —

虎 5265 / J3857 / M32675 Ko. *tora* tiger, drunkard.

³ 口 *kokō* very dangerous place; tiger's den

⁵ 穴 *koketsu* tiger's den; dangerous place

⁹ 巻 *tora (no) maki* pony, answer book; trade secrets; the trump card; the authority; the open sesame and wolf; wild beast; cruel man, brute

¹¹ 視耽耽 *koshi-tantan* on the alert; gloatingly; with vigilant hostility

— 4 —

B 虐 5267 / J3554 / M32678 GYAKU. *shiita(geru)*, *shiita(geru)* oppress, tyrannize.

⁹ 待 *gyakutai* mistreatment, abuse, cruelty

¹⁰ 殺 *gyakusatsu* massacre, butchery, carnage

— 5 —

B 虚 5269 / J3575 / M32708 KYO, Ko emptiness; unpreparedness; crack, fissure; unguarded position; untruth. *muna(shiku) suru* make empty. *uro* cavity, hollow, hole. *ukke* emptiness. *muna(shii)* void, empty, vain; ineffective; lifeless.

⁴ 心 *kyoshin* disinterestedness, lack of prejudice

心坦懐 *kyoshin tankai* frankness

⁵ 礼 *kyorei* formalities, empty forms

⁶ 妄 *kyomō, kyobō* falsehood, something unsubstantiated; delusion, superstition

仮 *koke* dunce, idiot

⁸ 実 *kyojitsu* truth and falsehood; preparedness and unpreparedness; the situation

空 *kokū* empty space, empty sky

⁹ 栄 *kyoei* vanity, vainglory

栄心 *kyoeishin* vanity, vainglory

¹⁰ 弱 *kyojaku* feebleness, weakness; imbecility

¹¹ 偽 *kyogi* falsehood, fiction, fallacy

脱 *kyodatsu* prostration, collapse

¹² 報 *kyohō* false alarm

無 *kyomu* nothingness

¹³ 飾 *kyoshoku* ostentation, show, affectation

勢 *kyosei* bluff

¹⁴ 像 *kyozō* virtual image, ghost image (in optics)

構 *kyokō* fabrication, falsehood

— 7 —

B 虞 5272 / J3673 / M32723 GU. *osore* fear; anxiety; concern; uneasiness.

⁹ 美人草 *gubijinsō* field poppy, red poppy

B 虜 5273 / J4e3a / M32720 RYO captive; barbarian; low epithet for the enemy. *toriko* captive, victim, slave.

⁵ 囚 *ryoshū* captive, prisoner

RAD. 虫 142

Mushi insect. At left: *mushi hen*. Nickname: Bug.

A 虫 5275 / J436e / M32804 CHŪ. *mushi* worm, vermin, bug, insect; temper; nervousness, peevishness; bad company.

³ 干 *mushibo(shi)* airing (clothes and books)

⁹ 食 *mushiku(i)* worm-eaten spot

除 *mushiyo(ke)* insect powder, charm against insects

¹⁰ 害 *chūgai* insect pests, insect damage, blight

¹² 歯 *mushiba* decayed tooth

²² 籠 *mushikago* insect case

虻 5277 J303a M32835 Bō . *abu* horsefly, gadfly.

虹 5279 J467a M32830 Kō . *niji* rainbow.
¹¹ 彩 *kōsai* iris (of the eye)

蚤 5287 J4742 M32893 Sō . *nomi* flea.

蚊 5288 J3263 M32849 **B** Bun . *ka* mosquito.
⁸ 取線香 *katori senkō* mosquito incense
¹¹ 帳 *kaya, kachō* mosquito net
¹² 遣 *kayari* mosquito smudge

蚕 5290 J3b3d M32869 **A** San . *kaiko* silkworm.
⁶ 糸 *sanshi* silk thread, silk yarn
⁹ 食 *sanshoku* encroachment, aggression, inroad, invasion

蛎 5291 J3342 M-X Nonstandard for 蠣 5399.

蛋 5301 J4341 M32977 Tan barbarian; egg.
⁵ 白質 *tampakushitsu* protein; albumen

蛍 5302 J3756 M32983 **B** Kei . *hotaru* firefly.
⁶ 光 *keikō* fluorescence. *hotaru (no) hikari* light of a firefly
光灯 *keikōtō* fluorescent light
¹¹ 雪 *keisetsu* diligent study

蛇 5303 J3c58 M32964 **B** Ja, Da (large) snake, serpent; hard drinker. *hebi, kuchinawa* snake.
³ 口 *jaguchi* faucet, hydrant; drain
⁵ 目傘 *ja(no)megasa* umbrella with a bulls-eye design
⁶ 行 *dakō suru* crawl meanderingly. *dakō* meandering

⁷ 足 *dasoku* superfluity, redundancy, padding
¹³ 腹 *jabara* bellows; cornice

蛭 5308 J4948 M33048 Shitsu . *hiru* leech.

蛤 5312 J483a M33023 Kō . *hamaguri* clam.

蛙 5313 J333f M32997 A . *kaeru, kawazu* frog.

蛮 5314 J485a M33044 **B** Ban barbarian.
² 人 *banjin* savage, barbarian
⁶ 行 *bankō* barbarism, brutality
⁷ 声 *bansei* rough voice
⁹ 勇 *ban'yū* brute courage, reckless valor, foolhardiness
¹¹ 族 *banzoku* savage tribe

蛾 5325 J326b M33082 Gi . Ga moth.
⁹ 眉 *gabi* arched eyebrows; a beauty

蛸 5330 J427d M33072 Sō . Shō . *tako* octopus, devilfish; pile driver; dirt tamper.
¹² 壺 *takotsubo* octopus trap; foxhole

蜂 5331 J4b2a M33088 Hō . *hachi* bee, wasp, hornet.
¹⁰ 起 *hōki* insurrection; disturbance
¹⁴ 蜜 *hachimitsu* honey

蝋 5332 J4f39 M-X Nonstandard for 蠟 5403.

蝕 5333 J3f2a M-X Nonstandard for 蝕 5358.

蜘 5342 J4358 M33134 Chi spider.
¹² 蛛 *kumo* spider

蜜 5343 J4c2a M33143 MITSU honey, nectar, molasses, honeydew.

4 月 *mitsugetsu* honeymoon
9 柑 *mikan* tangerine, mandarin orange
13 蜂 *mitsubachi* honeybee

──────── 9 ────────

蠅 5344 J4768 M-X Nonstandard for 蠅 5394.

蝉 5349 J4066 M-X Nonstandard for 蟬 5388.

蝕 5358 J-X M33264 SHOKU eclipse, occultation; be defective. *mushiba(mu)* be wormy.

蝶 5363 J4433 M33333 CHŌ butterfly.

12 結 *chōmusu(bi)* bowknot
番 *chōtsugai, chōban* hinge, hinge joint
15 蝶 *chōchō* butterfly

蝦 5364 J325c M33299 KA. GE. *ebi* lobster, shrimp, prawn.

6 夷 *Ezo* Ainu; Hokkaido. *Emishi, Emisu*
16 蟇 *gama* toad, bullfrog   Ainu」

──────── 10 ────────

融 5371 J4d3b M33384 B YŪ. *to(keru)* vi, *to(kasu)* vt dissolve, melt.

4 込 *to(ke)-ko(mu)* melt into, merge into
化 *yūka suru* soften, dissolve
6 合 *yūgō* fusion, union
8 和 *yūwa* melting; softening; conciliation; soothing
9 通 *yūzū* accommodation, financing, loan; circulation; transfer; elasticity, adaptability, versatility
11 雪 *yūsetsu* thaw, melting snow
13 解 *yūkai* fusing, melting, dissolving

資 *yūshi* financing

──────── 11 ────────

螺 5382 J4d66 M33512 RA. *nina, nishi* a small edible spiral river shell.

3 子 *neji, rashi* screw, faucet, (watch) spring
11 旋 *rasen* screw; spiral; spiral spring
13 鈿 *raden* mother-of-pearl

──────── 12 ────────

蟬 5388 J-X M33616 SEN. *semi* cicada, locust.

10 時雨 *semi shigure* an outburst of cricket chirping

──────── 13 ────────

蠅 5394 J6a24 M33690 YŌ. *hae, hai* fly.

5 叩 *haitataki* flyswatter

蟹 5395 J332a M33668 KAI. *kani* crab.

3 工船 *kanikōsen* crab-canning ship

蟻 5397 J3542 M33672 GI. *ari* ant.

6 地獄 *arijigoku* ant lion
12 塚 *arizuka* anthill

──────── 14 ────────

蠣 5399 J695a M33799 REI oyster.

──────── 15 ────────

蠟 5403 J-X M33786 RŌ wax.

17 燭 *rōsoku* candle

═══════ **RAD.** 血 **143** ═══════

Chi blood. At left: 血 *chi hen.* Nickname: Dotted Dish (cf. Rad. 108).

血 5411 J376c M33964 A KETSU blood. *chi* blood, consanguinity. *chi(bamu)* become bloody. *chi(darake)* bloody, bloodstained.

6

竹米糸缶网罒羊羽老耂而耒耳聿肉月臣自至臼舌舛舟艮色艸⺾虍虫血〔行〕衣衤西

⁴友病 *ketsuyūbyō* bleeders' affliction, hemophilia
⁵圧 *ketsuatsu* blood pressure
⁶肉 *ketsuniku* flesh and blood
　行 *kekkō* circulation of the blood
　色 *kesshoku* complexion
　色素 *kesshikiso* hemoglobin
　気盛 *kekkizaka(ri) no* vigorous, sanguine
⁷豆 *chimame* blood blister
　沈 *ketchin* precipitation of blood
　判 *keppan* seal of blood
⁸雨 *chi(no)ame* bloodshed
　迷 *chimayo(u)* lose control of oneself, run wild, be out of one's head
⁹相 *kessō* expression, looks
¹⁰涙 *chi (no) namida, ketsurui* tears of blood; bitter tears
　脈 *ketsumyaku* blood vessel; blood relationship
　書 *kessho* writing in blood
¹¹痕 *kekkon* bloodstain
　清 *kessei* blood serum, lymph
　祭 *chimatsu(ri)* blood offering, offering to the war god
　族 *ketsuzoku* blood relative
　液 *ketsueki* blood
　液型 *ketsuekigata* blood type
¹²税 *ketsuzei* blood tax, heavy taxation; conscription

統 *kettō* lineage, pedigree, family line
筋 *chisuji* blood relationship, lineage, stock, strain
¹³路 *ketsuro* a way out, the way through, a way of escape
¹⁴管 *kekkan* blood vessel
¹⁵潮 *chishio* the blood
　縁 *ketsuen* blood relative; blood relationship

──────── 6 ────────

A 衆 [5417 / J3d30 / M33981] SHU, SHŪ great numbers, multitude, populace; companions.
⁵生 *shujō* mankind, human beings; all living beings
　目 *shūmoku* public attention
⁸知 *shūchi* the wisdom of all
⁹院 *Shūin* House of Representatives, the Lower House
　怨 *shūen* public hatred, public grievance
¹¹望 *shūbō* the hope of many people; popular sentiment
¹²智 *shūchi* the wisdom of many
²⁰議 *shūgi* deliberation, public discussion
　議院 *Shūgiin* Lower House

⁰〔行〕

RAD. 行 144

Yukigamae or *gyōgamae* "going" enclosure. With the exception of the radical character itself, shown below, all characters historically belonging to this radical are herein treated under Rad. 60. Nickname: Going.

A 行 [5419 / J3954 / M34029] AN. Kō party, suite; journey; expedition; line, row. Gyō line, row; religious austerities. *i(ku), yu(ku)* go; run (water). *gyō(suru)* act, conduct oneself. *i(keru)* can go; can drink; can speak (a language); good. *oko(nau)* do, act, conduct oneself; carry out; perform, conduct (school); exercise (control); hold (a ceremony). *okona(wareru)* be practiced; become operative; take place; prevail, obtain; come into use; continue. *ya(ru)* give, let have, bestow on, present; send; do, perform, undertake; do for; act; study; row; operate; hold (a meeting), give (a dinner); eat, drink, smoke, find solace in. *yu(ki), i(ki)* going; travel. *i(ttakiri), yu(kikkiri)* gone for good. *oko(nai)* act, action, deed, conduct, behavior, religious austerities. *kudari* column of print; sentence. *-yuki* bound for.
²人 *kōjin* passerby, pedestrian
⁴手 *yukute* destination, route, objective
　止 *yu(ki)do(mari), i(ki)do(mari)* no passage, dead end, blind alley
　水 *gyōzui* tub bath

方 *yu(ki)gata* the direction one is to go. *yu(ki)kata* way of doing. *yukue* whereabouts

方不明 *yukue-fumei* missing; unaccounted for

⁵付 *i(ki)tsu(ke), yu(ki)tsu(ke) no* habitual, regular, favorite

末 *yu(ku)sue* one's future, fate

司 *gyōji* sumo referee

⁶列 *gyōretsu* procession, parade, queue

灯 *andon* paper-enclosed oil light

交 *yu(ki)-ka(u)* come and go. *yu(ki)kō, yu(ki)ka(i)* coming and going; street traffic; swing (of a pendulum); social intercourse

当 *yu(ki)-a(taru), i(ki)-a(taru)* come up against, be struck by. *i(ki)a(tari-battari)* haphazard, happy-go-lucky

年 *gyōnen* age at death. *kōnen* age, number of years

先 *yu(ki)saki, yu(ku)saki, i(ki)saki, i(ku)saki* destination, whereabouts, address. *yu(ku)saki* one's future, fate

在 *anzai* emperor's temporary headquarters

⁷状 *gyōjō* behavior, conduct, deportment, manners

李 *kōri* wicker telescope trunk; baggage; travel preparations

⁸届 *yu(ki)-todo(ku)* be scrupulous, be attentive, be careful, be prudent, be thorough, be hospitable

使 *kōshi suru* use; exercise (rights); put in circulation

幸 *gyōkō, miyuki* journey, visit, or attendance of the emperor

事 *gyōji* event, function, observance

⁹軍 *kōgun* march, marching

為 *kōi* act, deed, conduct, transaction, practices. *yu(ki)na(ri)* leaving things to chance

政 *gyōsei* administration

政改革 *gyōsei kaikaku* administrative reform

政指導 *gyōsei shidō* administrative guidance

¹⁰倒 *ikidao(re), yukidao(re)* falling ill on the road; falling dead on the road

旅 *kōryo* travel; traveler

員 *kōin* bank clerk

宮 *angū* emperor's temporary palace

書 *gyōsho* semicursive writing

進 *kōshin* advance; march; parade

¹¹過 *i(ki)-su(giru), yu(ki)-su(giru)* go too far, go to extremes, go beyond. *yu(ki)su(gi)* going too far, going to extremes; overdoing

啓 *gyōkei* visit or attendance of an empress or a crown prince

脚 *angya* pilgrimage; (a priest's) walking tour; tour

商 *gyōshō* peddling, itinerant trade; peddler

動 *kōdō* action, conduct, movements, operations

¹²場 *yu(ki)ba* place to go, resort, destination

渡 *yu(ki)-wata(ru), i(ki)-wata(ru)* extend; prevail; spread; penetrate; reach

程 *kōtei* distance; journey; march; itinerary; stroke (of a piston)

着 *i(ki)-tsu(ku), yu(ki)-tsu(ku)* arrive at, reach

違 *yu(ki)-chiga(eru)* mistake one's direction. *yu(ki)chiga(i), i(ki)chiga(i)* crossing; missing each other; misunderstanding, disagreement; error

雲流水 *kōun-ryūsui* moving clouds and running water; taking life easy

間 *gyōkan* between the lines

¹³詰 *yu(ki)-zu(maru), i(ki)-zu(maru), yu(ki)-tsu(maru)* be deadlocked, come to a standstill, be reduced to the last extremity, go to the wall; be tongue-tied

跡 *gyōseki* conduct, behavior

路 *kōro* path, road, course, career

楽 *kōraku* picnic, excursion; having a good time

楽地 *kōrakuchi* pleasure resort

¹⁵儀 *gyōgi* behavior, manners, deportment

6

竹米糸缶网罒羊羽老耂而耒耳聿肉月臣自至臼舌舛舟艮色艸虍虫血行【衣衤】西

Koromo clothes. At left: 衤 (5 strokes), *koromo hen*. Nickname: Clothing.

A **衣** 5420 / J3061 / M34091 E, I garment. *koromo* clothes, robe; dressing; frosting; coating. *kinu* clothing, kimono.

8 服 *ifuku* clothes, clothing
9 食住 *ishokujū* food, clothing, and shelter; necessities of life
冠束帯 *ikan-sokutai* full traditional ceremonial court dress; Shinto priest's garb
10 桁 *ikō* clothes rack
料 *iryō* clothing
紋掛 *emonka(ke)* coat hanger
12 替 *koromoga(e)* seasonal change of clothes
装 *ishō* clothes, wardrobe, costume
13 鉢 *ihatsu, ehatsu* assuming the mantle of
14 裳 *ishō* clothes, costume, wardrobe
18 類 *irui* clothing

———————— **3** ————————

A **表** 5422 / J493d / M34105 Hyō table, schedule, diagram, chart, list. *ara(wasu), hyō(suru)* express, show, manifest. *arawa(reru)* appear, emerge, come in sight, show up; be revealed, be discovered, be mentioned; become famous. *omote* surface, right side, face; exterior, outside; front; the street; mat covers; head (of a coin); first half (of an inning).

3 口 *omoteguchi* front door
土 *hyōdo* topsoil
4 日本 *Omote Nihon* Pacific seaboard of 「Japan
5 白 *hyōhaku* expression, confession
皮 *hyōhi* epidermis; bark, rind, peel, husk
立 *omoteda(tsu)* become public, be known. *omoteda(tta)* public, open; formal, official. *omoteda(tte)* publicly, openly; ostensibly; formally
札 *hyōsatsu* nameplate, door plate
出 *hyōshutsu* expression, presentation
示 *hyōji* indication, expression
6 向 *omotemu(ki)* publicly, openly; ostensibly; formally
7 芸 *omotegei* main accomplishments

沙汰 *omotezata* publicity, lawsuit
8 明 *hyōmei* indication, manifestation, demonstration, expression, announcement
具屋 *hyōguya* paperer, picture framer
9 通 *omotedō(ri)* main street
看板 *omote kamban* sign out in front; a front (for someone)
音文字 *hyōon moji* phonetic symbol
面 *hyōmen* surface, face, outside; appearance
10 紙 *hyōshi* cover, binding
記 *hyōki suru* publish (information); list (prices); declare (the value); write; address (a package)
11 情 *hyōjō* facial expression
現 *hyōgen* expression, presentation
12 装 *hyōsō* mounting
13 意文字 *hyōi moji* hieroglyph, ideograph
14 彰 *hyōshō* commendation, awarding
18 題 *hyōdai* title (of a book or lecture); index

———————— **4** ————————

衿 5431 / J365e / M34149 KIN. *eri* neck, neckband, collar, lapel.

B **衰** 5432 / J3f6a / M34127 SUI. *otoro(eru)* decline, wane, weaken, abate, decay, wither, waste away.

3 亡 *suibō* ruin, downfall, collapse
8 退 *suitai* decline, decadence, waning; ebb tide
10 弱 *suijaku* weakness, debility, prostration, breakdown
11 運 *suiun* declining fortunes, decadence
13 微 *suibi* decline, decadence, waning; ebb tide 「decline
勢 *suisei* downward tendency, decay,

———————— **5** ————————

袈 5442 / J3736 / M34166 KE a coarse camlet.

13 裟 *kesa* Buddhist priest's stoal, sacred shoulder scarf

袋 $\frac{5443}{\text{J425e}}$ $\frac{}{\text{M34171}}$ TEI. TAI bag; bag counter.
B *fukuro* bag, sack, pouch.
(o)fukuro mama.
³ 小路 *fukurokōji* blind alley
⁵ 叩 *fukurodataki* sound thrashing, beating

袖 $\frac{5444}{\text{J4235}}$ $\frac{}{\text{M34192}}$ SHŪ. *sode* sleeve; sleeve
pocket; wing (of a
building); extension (of a table). *sode ni suru* jilt, cold shoulder (someone).
³ 口 *sodeguchi* cuff, sleeve band
下 *sode(no)shita* bribe
丈 *sode take* sleeve length
⁹ 珍 *shūchin* pocket (edition)
珍本 *shūchimbon* pocket-size book; manual

被 $\frac{5445}{\text{J486f}}$ $\frac{}{\text{M34222}}$ HI receiving. *kabu(ru) vi*
B and *vt* wear, put on; take
(the blame); pour on; be covered with; ship (a wave); have (labor pains); be accidentally exposed (a film). *kabu(seru)* cover with; put on; pour on, play (a stream of water) on; fix (blame) on; shift (responsibility) on. *kabu(saru)* get covered; overlap; hang over. *ō(u)* cover, veil; hang over; brood over; conceal; overlap; shelter; screen; disguise; wrap, envelop; obscure; shade; overshadow. *hi-* recipient or victim of (an action). *kōmu(ru)* get, receive, sustain (an injury), be subjected to (criticism). *kazu(ku)* put on, wear. *kazu(keru)* blame. *ō(i)* cover, covering; shade; mantle, coat; hood, bonnet; casing; awning.
⁵ 写体 *hishatai* the one being photographed
⁷ 災 *hisai* suffering (from a calamity); affliction
災者 *hisaisha* victim, sufferer
告 *hikoku* defendant
告人 *hikokunin* defendant
¹⁰ 害 *higai* damage, harm, casualties, injury
害地 *higaichi* stricken area
害妄想 *higaimōsō* persecution complex
害者 *higaisha* victim, injured party, sufferer
¹² 弾 *hidan* being bombed
¹⁴ 疑者 *higisha* a suspect
¹⁸ 覆 *hifuku* covering, mantle, insulation
¹⁹ 爆 *hibaku* being bombed
爆地 *hibakuchi* bombed area

爆者 *hibakusha* bombing victims

———— 6 ————

袴 $\frac{5448}{\text{J3853}}$ $\frac{}{\text{M34236}}$ KO. *hakama* men's formal
divided skirt, women's
pleated skirt.

袷 $\frac{5449}{\text{J3041}}$ $\frac{}{\text{M34240}}$ KŌ. KYŌ. *awase* lined;
lined kimono.

裂 $\frac{5453}{\text{J4e76}}$ $\frac{}{\text{M34260}}$ RETSU. *sa(ku) vt* split,
B rend, tear, burst, rip, crack.
sa(keru) vi split, rend, tear, burst, rip, crack.
⁵ 目 *sa(ke)me* rent, tear, crack, fissure, split, slit, cleft, rip, rift

裁 $\frac{5454}{\text{J3a5b}}$ $\frac{}{\text{M34258}}$ SAI. *saba(ku)* judge.
A *ta(tsu)* cut out (a suit);
sever, cut off; shut off, interrupt; abstain from; eradicate; suppress. *saba(ki)* judgment, decision, verdict. *ta(chi)* cutting, cut.
⁵ 可 *saika* sanction, approval
⁷ 決 *saiketsu* decision, judgment, ruling
決書 *saiketsusho* written verdict
判 *saiban* trial; adjudication
判沙汰 *saibanzata* lawsuit, litigation
判長 *saibanchō* presiding judge
判所 *saibansho* a court; courthouse
判官 *saibankan* the judge
⁸ 定 *saitei* decision, ruling, award, arbitration
¹¹ 断 *saidan suru* cut off; cut out (clothes); decide, judge
¹² 量 *sairyō* discretion
¹⁵ 縫 *saihō* sewing. *ta(chi)-nu(u)* cut and sew

装 $\frac{5455}{\text{J4175}}$ $\frac{}{\text{M34283}}$ SŌ. SHŌ. *yosō(u)*
A dress; spruce up;
pretend, disguise; profess. *yosō(i)* array, dress, equipment.
² 丁 *sōtei* binding, format
⁵ 甲 *sōkō* armor, armor plate
甲車 *sōkōsha* armored car
⁷ 束 *sōzoku, shōzoku* costume (of ancient nobles), personal appearance; clothing; interior decoration; landscaping; household furniture

6

竹米糸缶网罒羊羽老耂而耒耳聿肉月臣自至臼舌舛舟艮色艸艹虍虫血行〔衣⁶衤〕西

竹
米
糸
缶
网
罒
羊
羽
老
耂
而
耒
耳
聿
肉
月
臣
自
至
臼
舌
舛
舟
艮
色
艸
艹
虍
虫
血
行
【衣
衤】
西

身具 *sōshingu* personal ornaments

8 具 *sōgu* equipment; harness; trappings; furnishings, fittings

12 備 *sōbi* equipment; outfit, rigging

幀 *sōtei* binding, format

着 *sōchaku suru* equip, fit, install, lay, lay down, place

13 填 *sōten* gun charge

置 *sōchi* equipment, installation, plant, apparatus, device

飾 *sōshoku* ornament, ornamentation, decoration, adornment

7

裟 5457 / J3a40 / M34325 SA surplice (Buddhist).

裕 5461 / J4d35 / M34305 YŪ. *yutaka* abundant, rich, fruitful, fertile.

B

13 福 *yūfuku* prosperity, affluence

裏 5462 / J4e22 / M34294 ／ 裡 5463 / J4e23 / M34295 RI inside. *uchi ni* amidst, in. *ura* reverse, wrong side; undersurface, inside; palm, sole; opposite; back, rear; lining, last half (of an inning).

A

3 山 *urayama* the hill back of one's home; a hill back from the seashore

口 *uraguchi* back door, rear entrance

4 日本 *Ura-Nippon, Ura-Nihon* Japan Sea coast areas

切 *uragi(ri)* treachery, betrayal, perfidy. *uragi(ru)* betray

切者 *uragirimono* betrayer, traitor, turncoat, informer

5 付 *urazu(keru)* support; endorse; substantiate. *urazu(ke)* backing, security; proof, foundation; lining (something); something lined. *urazu(ki)* lined; something lined

打 *urau(chi)* lining, backing; vouching for

6 返 *uragae(su)* turn inside out; turn the other way, turn (something) over. *uragae(ru)* be turned inside out. *uragae(shi)* inside out; upside down

地 *uraji* lining

7 作 *urasaku* second crop, interim crop

町 *uramachi* back street, back alley, slums

声 *uragoe* falsetto

8 門 *uramon* back gate

表 *ura-omote* wrong side out; both sides; reverse, opposite; double-dealing

表紙 *urabyōshi* back cover

9 通 *uradō(ri)* back street, side street, alley

面 *rimen* back, reverse, other side, inside, tails (of coins), background

10 庭 *ura niwa* rear garden, backyard

書 *uragaki* endorsement; proof; note on back of the scroll

11 側 *uragawa* the reverse, the lining

13 腹 *urahara* opposite, reverse, contrary

話 *urabanashi* a story not generally known

補 5464 / J4a64 / M34320 HO assistant, learner. *ogina(u)* supply, make good, make up (losses), stop (a gap), offset, piece out; compensate for; supplement. *ho(suru)* appoint, select. *-ho* assistant.

A

4 欠 *hoketsu* filling a vacancy; making up a shortage

5 正 *hosei* revision; correction; compensation (in machines); supplementary (budget)

6 任 *honin suru* appoint to office; take up one's duties

充 *hojū* supplement, complement, draft, replacement

7 足 *hosoku* replenishment, complement, amendment

佐 *hosa* assistance; assistant; counselor

助 *hojo* assistance; subsidy; supplement; auxiliary

助金 *hojokin* subsidy, grant, appropriation, bounty

10 修 *hoshū* repair, mending; correction

11 強 *hokyō suru* strengthen the weak places

習 *hoshū* supplementary study materials

12 遺 *hoi* supplement, appendix

給 *hokyū* supply, replenishment

13 填 *hoten suru* fill, supply (a deficiency), make up (a loss)

14 語 *hogo* complement (in grammar)

導 *hodō* guidance

17 講 *hokō* supplementary lecture

聴器 *hochōki* hearing aid

償 *hoshō* indemnity, compensation, reparation

— 8 —

裳 ₅₄₇₂ J3e58 M34357 SHŌ . *mo* ancient skirt.

B 褐 ₅₄₇₃ J336c M-X KATSU woolen kimono.
⁶色 *kasshoku* brown. *kachi iro* dark blue

裾 ₅₄₇₄ J3f7e M34382 KYO. *suso* cuff (of trousers); hem (of a skirt); foot (of a mountain).
⁴分 *susowa(ke)* distribution of a gift; sharing
¹¹野 *susono* foot (of a mountain)
¹⁴模様 *susomoyō* skirt design

B 裸 ₅₄₇₅ J4d67 M34371 RA. *hadaka* naked body, nude; uncovered, only partially clothed, undressed; without investing; leafless; unpreparedness (for a wedding); unsaddled; denuded, bare.
¹一貫 *hadaka ikkan* starting from scratch; bankrupt
⁴火 *hadakabi* open fire
⁷足 *hadashi* bare feet
体 *ratai* naked body, nakedness, nudity
¹¹婦 *rafu* nude woman

A 製 ₅₄₇₆ J403d M34380 SEI. *sei(suru)* make, manufacture. -*sei* make, manufacture.
⁵出 *seishutsu* production
氷 *seihyō* ice manufacture
本 *seihon* bookbinding
⁶糸 *seishi* silk-thread manufacture
⁷図 *seizu* drafting; cartography, mapmaking; drawing
作 *seisaku* manufacture, production
作者 *seisakusha* manufacturer, maker; producer
材 *seizai* sawing, lumbering
⁸法 *seihō* method of manufacture, process, recipe
油 *seiyu* oil refining
版 *seihan* platemaking (printing)
⁹品 *seihin* manufactured goods, products
造 *seizō* manufacture, production, making
造業 *seizōgyō* manufacturing industry

¹⁰粉 *seifun* milling flour
紙 *seishi* paper manufacture
¹¹産 *seisan* production
菓 *seika* confectionery
¹³鉄 *seitetsu* iron manufacture
靴 *seika* shoemaking
¹⁶錬 *seiren* refining, smelting
糖 *seitō* sugar manufacture
鋼 *seikō* steel manufacturing
薬 *seiyaku* medicine manufacture; manufactured medicine

— 9 —

B 褒 ₅₄₈₃ J4b2b M34437 HŌ. *ho(mechigiru), ho(mesoyasu)* praise, extol. *ho(meru)* praise, commend.
⁷言葉 *ho(me)kotoba* eulogy, compliment
⁹美 *hōbi* prize, reward
¹¹章 *hōshō* medal
¹⁵賞 *hōshō* prize, reward

A 複 ₅₄₈₄ J4a23 M34417 FUKU double, compound, composite, multiple. *futatabi, mata* again.
⁴文 *fukubun* compound sentence
⁵写 *fukusha* copying, duplication; duplicate, copy, facsimile
⁶合 *fukugō* composite, complex, compound
⁷利 *fukuri* compound interest
¹¹眼 *fukugan* compound eye (of an insect)
習 *fukushū* review
¹²葉 *fukuyō* biplane; compound leaf
¹³数 *fukusū* plural
試合 *fukushiai* doubles (in tennis)
¹⁴製 *fukusei* reproduction, duplication, reprinting
雑 *fukuzatsu* complexity, complication, intricacy; maze, labyrinth
¹⁵縁 *fukuen* conjugal reconciliation
線 *fukusen* double track

— 12 —

襖 ₅₄₉₈ J3228 M-X See 襖 5503.

嚢 ₅₄₉₉ J4739 M-X Nonstandard for 嚢 933.

6

竹米糸缶网罒羊羽老耂而耒耳聿肉月臣自至臼舌舛舟艮色艸虍虫血行衣衤[西]

─────── 13 ───────

襖 `5503` `J-X` `M34629`   襖 `5498` `J3228` `M-X`   Ō. *fusuma* sliding paper door. opaque

B 襟 `5504` `J365f` `M34647`   KIN. *eri* neck, neckband, collar, lapel.
⁴ 元 *erimoto* front of neck
⁷ 足 *eriashi* border of the hair in back
⁹ 首 *erikubi* nape of the neck
  巻 *erimaki* muffler, scarf, neckpiece

¹¹ 章 *erishō* badge

─────── 16 ───────

B 襲 `5510` `J3d31` `M34717`   SHŪ attack. *oso(u)* attack, advance on; succeed to; call unexpectedly. *kasa(ne)* pile, heap, layer; suits; set; course (of stones).
⁶ 名 *shūmei* succession to another's professional name
⁷ 来 *shūrai* invasion, raid, attack; visitation (of a calamity)
¹⁵ 撃 *shūgeki* attack, charge, raid

─────── RAD. **西** 146 ───────

Nishi west. Variants: 覀 , 襾 . Nickname: West.

A 西 `5514` `J403e` `M34763`   SEI, SAI *nishi* west.
³ 下 *saika suru* start for Kansai or western Japan
⁴ 方 *seihō* west, western, westward; the West. *Saihō* Western Paradise
  方浄土 *Saihō Jōdo* Western Paradise
⁵ 半球 *nishi hankyū* Western Hemisphere
  瓜 *suika* watermelon
⁸ 国 *saikoku, saigoku* the western countries; western Japan
  欧 *Seiō* Western Europe; the West, the Occident
⁹ 洋 *Seiyō* the West, the Occident; the western ocean
  洋人 *Seiyōjin* Westerner, European
¹⁰ 部 *seibu* the west, western part
  部劇 *seibugeki* a Western (film)
¹¹ 域 *seiiki* India and lands to the west of China
  経 *seikei* west longitude
¹⁴ 暦 *Seireki* Christian Era, Current Era, Common Era

⁴ 心 *yōjin* care, caution, discretion
⁵ 目 *yōmoku* principal items
  石 *kaname ishi* keystone
⁶ 因 *yōin* primary factor, main cause, prerequisite
  件 *yōken* requisite, important matter; qualification; essentials
  旨 *yōshi* gist, point, essentials; argument; summary; fundamental principles
⁷ 求 *yōkyū* request, demand, requirement
⁸ 所 *yōsho* important position, strategic point
⁹ 約 *yōyaku* summary, digest
  点 *yōten* gist, essentials, substance
¹⁰ 員 *yōin* necessary personnel
  害 *yōgai* fort, stronghold
  素 *yōso* element, essential, requisite, constituent
¹¹ 略 *yōryaku* choosing the important sections and omitting the rest; digest of an article; gist, summary
  望 *yōbō suru* cry for, demand, long for
¹² 項 *yōkō* gist, synopsis, important point
¹³ 路 *yōro* important road, main artery; responsible position; the authorities
  塞 *yōsai* fort, stronghold, fortification
¹⁴ 綱 *yōkō* outline, summary; general idea; general plan, prospectus
  領 *yōryō* the point, gist, essentials, outline, summary
  領良 *yōryōyo(ku)* pointedly, sensibly, practically
¹⁵ 請 *yōsei* demand, request, requirement

─────── 3 ───────

A 要 `5515` `J4d57` `M34768`   YŌ main point, essence; aim; secret; need. *yō(suru)*, *i(ru)* require, need; waylay, ambush. *yō(suru) ni* in the last analysis, in short. *i(ranu)* unwanted, useless, unnecessary. *kaname* pivot; the main point; the key (to).
² 人 *yōjin* leading personage, important man

¹⁶諦 *yōtei* secret (of success)
覧 *yōran* survey, summary, outline; handbook, directory, catalog
¹⁸職 *yōshoku* responsible post

12

覆 ₅₅₁₇ _{J4a24} _{M34/89'} FUKU. FU. *kutsuga(eru)*
B overturn, capsize; fall; be ruined. *kutsuga(esu)* overturn, capsize; overthrow; undermine; frustrate; veto; disprove (a theory). *ō(u)* cover, veil; hang over; brood over; conceal; overlap; shelter; screen; disguise; wrap, envelop; obscure; shade; overshadow. *ō(i)* cover, covering; shade; mantle, coat; hood, bonnet; casing; awning.
⁴水 *fukusui* spilt water

⁷没 *fukubotsu suru* capsize and sink; suffer a serious defeat or a serious reversal in family fortunes
⁸刻 *fukkoku* reproducing a book from identical plates
⁹面 *fukumen* mask, veil, disguise
¹³滅 *fukumetsu* overthrow, destruction
¹⁴蔵無 *fukuzōna(ku)* freely, frankly, plainly

13

覇 ₅₅₁₉ _{J4746} _{M34790} HA supremacy,
B leadership, domination, hegemony; supreme ruler; champion.
⁶気 *haki* ambition
⁸者 *hasha* supreme ruler; champion
¹⁵権 *haken* domination, supremacy, leadership

7-STROKE RADICALS

RAD. 見 147
Miru to see. Nickname: Seeing.

見 ₅₅₂₂ _{J382b} _{M34796} KEN, GEN hopes, chances;
A ideas, opinion. *mi(ru)* see, look at, witness, observe; regard as; sightsee; look through; examine; consult (a lexicon); tell (one's future); estimate; care for; try, test. *mi(eru)* see, be seen, be visible, be in sight; look like, seem, appear; come, show up; be found. *mi(seru)* show, let see, display; make look like, pretend. *mami(eru)* see, be presented to, have an audience with. *mi(sebirakasu)* display, flaunt, parade. *mi(seshime)* object lesson, warning, example. *mi(ttomonai)* indecent, unbecoming, scandalous; unsightly, ugly. *mi(e)* ostentation. *mi(tekure)* appearance.
³下 *mi-kuda(su)* command a view of; look down on, despise. *mi-o(rosu)* overlook, command a view of. *mi-sa(geru)* look down over; look down on

⁴方 *mikata* viewpoint, way of looking
込 *mi-ko(mu)* expect, anticipate; estimate; trust; mark (as a victim). *miko(mi)* hope, prospects, possibility, forecast, expectation
分 *mi-wa(keru)* distinguish, recognize; judge; identify. *miwa(ke)* distinction; discrimination, judgment; identification, recognition
⁵失 *mi-ushina(u)* lose sight of, miss
付 *mitsu(karu)* be found; be found out, be discovered. *mitsu(keru)* find; find out; discover, locate; catch sight of; notice, recognize; hunt for, get used to seeing, be familiar to. *mitsuke* approach (to a castle gate)
出 *mi-ida(su)* discover, detect, select, find out. *mida(shi)* heading, caption, subtitle, index
本 *mihon* sample, pattern, specimen, copy, model, example

⁷【見】₀
角言谷豆豕豸貝赤走足身車辛辰辵邑阝釆里

7

[見]

角言谷豆豕豸貝赤走足身車辛辰辵邑阝釆里

本市 *mihon ichi* industrial fair

世物 *misemono* show, exhibition, circus

目 *mi(ru)me* the sight; power of observation. *mi(ta)me ni* to look at. *mime* looks, features, face, form

目麗 *mime-uruwa(shii)* beautiful (woman)

6 向 *mi-mu(ku)* look around, look toward (us)

地 *kenchi* standpoint, viewpoint

守 *mi-mamo(ru)* watch over

劣 *mioto(ri)* unfavorable comparison

合 *mi-a(u)* exchange glances; counterbalance. *mi-a(waseru)* exchange glances; postpone. *mia(i)* marriage interview

当 *mi-ata(ru)* be found. *kentō* aim, mark; estimate, guess; direction; approximation

当違 *kentōchiga(i)* wrong guess, miscalculation

初 *mi-so(meru)* see for the first time, fall in love at first sight

8 届 *mi-todo(keru)* ascertain, verify

逃 *mi-noga(su)* miss, overlook, let pass; wink at, leave at large

送 *mi-oku(ru)* see off, bid farewell; follow with one's eyes; escort (home); care for until death; let pass; wait and see

所 *midokoro* merit, promise. *mi(ta) tokoro* to all appearances

放 *mi-sa(ku)* look afar.

限 *mi-kagi(ru)* forsake, desert, abandon, despair of

直 *mi-nao(su)* look again; take a turn for the better; think better of

定 *mi-sada(meru)* ascertain, make sure of

苦 *miguru(shii)* disgraceful; unsightly; indecent; clumsy

学 *kengaku* study and observation

事 *migoto* beautiful, splendid

知 *kenchi suru, mi-shi(ru)* know by inspection, knowing by sight. *mishiri* an acquaintance. *mi-shi(ranu), mi(zu)-shi(razu) no* strange, unknown

取図 *mitorizu* rough sketch, sketch map

物 *mimono* sight, spectacle, attraction. *kembutsu* sightseeing. *mi(se)mono*

show, circus

9 透 *mi(e)-su(ku)* be transparent. *mi-su(kasu)* see through. *mi-tō(su)* get an unobstructed view; see through

通 *mi-tō(su)* get an unobstructed view; see through. *mitō(shi)* perspective, unobstructed view; outlook, forecast

映 *miba(e)* outward appearance

栄 *mie* appearance; show, display

10 破 *mi-yabu(ru)* see through

納 *miosa(me)* farewell look

殺 *migoro(shi)* letting (someone) die before one's eyes without helping

11 過 *mi-su(gosu), mi-su(gusu)* miss, overlook, let pass, wink at, leave at large

做 *mina(su)* regard as, consider, presume

頃 *migoro* the time to see

惚 *mi-to(reru), mi-ho(reru)* be charmed by, gaze in rapture

捨 *mi-su(teru)* forsake, desert, abandon, leave desolate

掛 *mi-ka(keru)* see, meet; perceive, notice. *mika(ke)* appearance; apparent

習 *mi-nara(u)* receive training; learn by observation; follow an example. *minarai* apprenticeship; apprentice, learner

習生 *minaraisei* trainee

張 *miha(ru)* watch, stand guard, picket; strain (one's eyes). *miha(ri)* guard, lookout, picket; floorwalker

12 違 *mi-chiga(eru)* mistake, cannot recognize. *michiga(i), michiga(e)* misperception, mistake

場 *miba* looks, appearance. *mi(se)ba* highlight (of a play)

晴 *mi-ha(rasu)* command a view of. *miha(rashi)* view, outlook, visibility

極 *mi-kiwa(meru)* see through, discern, probe, make sure of

渡 *mi-wata(su)* look out over, survey (the scene)

落 *mi-o(tosu)* miss seeing, overlook, lose sight of

覚 *mi-obo(eru)* remember, recognize

間違 *mi-machiga(eru)* mistake, cannot recognize

13 損 *mi-sokona(u)* misjudge, mistake, miss seeing. *mi-son(zuru), mi-son(jiru)* make a mistake in observation

解 *kenkai* opinion, view
詰 *mi-tsu(meru)* gaze at, stare at, behold
飽 *mi-a(kiru)* be tired of looking at
馴 *mi-na(reru)* get used to seeing, be familiar to
14 聞 *kemmon, kembun, miki(ki)* information; experience, observation
境 *misakai* distinction, discrimination
慣 *mi-na(reru)* get used to seeing, be familiar to (me)
15 舞 *mi-ma(u)* inquire about a sick person. *mima(i)* inquiry, expression of sympathy
舞品 *mima(i)hin* gift to a sick person
舞客 *mima(i)kyaku* hospital visitors
16 積 *mi-tsu(moru)* estimate at, value at, assess (damage). *mitsumo(ri)* estimate, quotation
積書 *mitsumorisho* written estimate
19 識 *kenshiki* views, discernment, knowledge; dignity, self-respect

───────── 4 ─────────

規 $\frac{5524}{J352c}$ M34810 KI standard; measure.
A
8 制 *kisei* regulation, control
定 *kitei* bylaws, provisions, regulations
9 律 *kiritsu suru* govern (a program). *kiritsu* regulations; order; discipline; system; regularity
約 *kiyaku* agreement, pact, rules, code, bylaws, articles
則 *kisoku* regulation, rule
10 格 *kikaku* standard, norm, gauge, rule
13 準 *kijun* standard, basis
14 模 *kibo* scale, scope, plan, structure
15 範 *kihan* standard, norm, criterion

視 $\frac{5525}{J3b6b}$ M34827 SHI regard as. *mi(ru)*
A see, look at; guard. *-shisuru* regard as, look upon as. *shi-* apparent (in astronomy).
2 力 *shiryoku* eyesight, visual power
7 角 *shikaku* angle of vision; optic angle; viewpoint
9 点 *shiten* viewpoint
界 *shikai* range of vision, visibility
10 差 *shisa* parallax
11 野 *shiya* field of vision
12 程 *shitei* visibility, visual range
覚 *shikaku* sense of sight, vision

14 察 *shisatsu* inspection, observation
15 線 *shisen* line of vision
17 聴率 *shichōritsu* audience rating
聴覚 *shichōkaku* visual and auditory senses, sight and hearing, audiovisual

───────── 5 ─────────

覗 $\frac{5528}{J4741}$ M34839 SHI. *nozo(ku)* peep, peek; come in sight.
4 込 *nozo(ki)-ko(mu)* look into, peer into, peep in
5 穴 *nozoki ana* peephole, sky hole

覚 $\frac{5529}{J3350}$ M34846 KAKU. *obo(eru)*
A remember, memorize; learn, perceive; feel, experience, know; expect. *sato(ru)* perceive, discern, realize, understand, comprehend; attain enlightenment, find one's philosophy. *sa(masu)* vt awake, wake up. *sa(meru)* vi awake, be disillusioned; sober up. *obo(ezu)* involuntarily, unwittingly, instinctively. *obo(shii)* looking like a, apparently a (foreigner). *obo(e)* feeling, learning; memory, recollection; esteem, memo.
10 書 *oboegaki* memo, note; memorial, protocol; book of remembrance
悟 *kakugo* resolution, readiness, expectation, resignation; perception (of truth)
16 醒 *kakusei* awakening, disillusionment
醒剤 *kakuseizai* stimulant

───────── 9 ─────────

覧 $\frac{5533}{J4d77}$ M34928 RAN. *mi(ru)* see.
A

親 $\frac{5534}{J3f46}$ M34918 SHIN intimacy; parents;
A relative. *oya* parent; dealer (in card games); banker (in gambling). *chika(i), shita(shii)* intimate, familiar, friendly. *shita(shimu)* be intimate with; have a liking for; take habitually. *shita(shimi)* intimacy, familiarity, friendship. *mizukara* oneself, personally. *shin-* pro-(American).
3 子 *oyako* parent and child; bowl of rice topped with chicken and eggs. *shinshi* parent and child

7

見【角】
0
言谷豆豕豸貝赤走足身車辛辰辵邑阝酉釆里

---

⁴心 *oyagokoro* parental love, parent's heart

方 *oyakata* boss, foreman

父 *shimpu* father. *oyaji* (in familiar talk) governor, judge, father

元 *oyamoto ni* at home, with one's parents

友 *shin'yū* close friend, chum, pal

王 *shinnō* imperial prince

切 *shinsetsu* kindness

分 *oyabun* boss, chief, head

⁶会社 *oyagaisha*, *oya kaisha* parent company; holding corporation; assembly plant

近 *shinkin* familiarity; personal attendants

近感 *shinkinkan* feeling of familiarity

任 *shinnin* personal imperial appointment

⁷身 *shimmi* relative. kind, cordial, sincere

孝行 *oya-kōkō* filial piety

⁸和力 *shinwaryoku* chemical attraction, affinity

⁹指 *oyayubi* thumb; the boss

¹⁰書 *shinsho* autographed letter

馬鹿 *oyabaka* parental overindulgence

展 *shinten* confidential, personal (letter)

¹¹許 *oyamoto* parental roof; parents; home; banker for gamblers

密 *shimmitsu* intimacy, close friendship

戚 *shinseki* relative

族 *shinzoku* relatives

¹²筆 *shimpitsu* one's own writing

善 *shinzen* friendship, amity, goodwill

¹³愛 *shin'ai* affection, love

睦 *shimboku* friendship, reunion

¹⁶衛隊 *shin'eitai* bodyguard troops

¹⁸類 *shinrui* relative

— 11 —

観 A
5538
J3451
M34955
KAN look, appearance; spectacle; condition; view, outlook. *kan(zuru)* view, contemplate. *mi(ru)* see, look at, witness, observe; regard as; sight-see; look through; examine; consult (a lexicon); tell (one's fortune); estimate; care for; try, test.

⁶光 *kankō* sightseeing

⁸念 *kannen* meditation; idea; intention; sense (of duty); resignation to, preparation; conviction

⁹点 *kanten* viewpoint, angle of vision

客 *kankaku*, *kankyaku* visitors, spectators, audience

音 *Kannon* Bodhisattva of mercy, Kannon

¹²衆 *kanshū* audience, spectators

測 *kansoku* observation, survey; thinking, opinion

¹³戦 *kansen suru* witness a battle or a game

¹⁴察 *kansatsu* observation, survey, investigation, supervision; view

¹⁵劇 *kangeki* theatergoing

賞 *kanshō* admiration, enjoyment

¹⁶覧 *kanran* inspection, viewing

RAD. 角 148

Tsuno horn. At left: *tsuno hen*. Nickname: Horn.

角 A
5543
J3351
M35003
KAKU angle; corner; square; squared timber; target. *kado* corner; angle; edge; angularity; harshness. *kaku(na)* square, four-cornered. *tsuno* horn, antlers; feeler, tentacle. *tsuno(gumu)* sprout. *sumi* corner, nook.

²力 *sumō* sumo wrestling; wrestler

⁵立 *tsunoda(teru)*, *kadoda(teru)* be sharp,

be pointed; be rough; sound harsh. *kado (ga) ta(tsu)* sound harsh

⁷材 *kakuzai* squared timber, lumber

⁹度 *kakudo* angle

逐 *kakuchiku suru* compete with, vie with

砂糖 *kakuzatō* cube sugar

¹²帽 *kakubō* square college cap

¹⁴膜 *kakumaku* cornea

¹⁵ 質 *kakushitsu* keratin, horniness

6

触 ₅₅₄₇ _{J3f28} _{M35070} SHOKU touching. *fu(reru)* touch, feel,
B hit, strike, graze; announce, proclaim,
mention, refer to; conflict with, be
contrary to. *sawa(ru)* touch, feel. *fu(re)*
touch, contact; official notice. *sawa(ri)*
touch, feel; point (of a story); good mixer.

⁶ 回 *fu(re)-mawa(su)*, *fu(re)-mawa(ru)*
spread (a rumor), noise abroad,
broadcast

合 *fu(re)-a(u)* touch, come in contact
with

⁷ 角 *shokkaku* feeler, antenna, tentacle
⁸ 官 *shokkan* the organ of touch
⁹ 発 *shokuhatsu* contact detonation
¹¹ 接 *shokusetsu* touching
¹² 媒 *shokubai* catalyst
診 *shokushin* palpation, manipulation,
manual examination
覚 *shokkaku* sense of touch
¹³ 感 *shokkan* touch sensation

解 ₅₅₄₈ _{J3272} _{M35067} GE, KAI explanation,
A notes; key; excuse;
understanding. *kai(suru)* understand,
comprehend, interpret. *to(ku)* untie,
undo, loosen, unpack; unravel,
disentangle, unsew; dismantle; solve,
answer; dispel; cancel; absolve; release;
dismiss (a person); explain. *to(ku)*,
to(kasu) comb out. *to(keru)* get loose,
come untied; relent; be solved, be
dispelled; be relieved (of a job). *hodo(ku)*
vi and *vt* undo, untie, unpack, unfasten,
loosen, unlace, unravel, get untied.
hogu(reru), *hodo(keru)* get loose, get
untied. *hogu(su)*, *hogo(su)* untie,
unfasten, loosen, fray, unknit, unravel,
disentangle. *hogo(reru)* get loose, get

untied; fray, get disentangled. *hotsu(reru)*
fray, ravel, stray, become loose. *waka(ru)*
understand, comprehend; know, be
known, be identified; be open to reason,
be sensible; can tell (what will happen);
appreciate; be announced; be discovered;
recognize. *ge(senai)* (it) passes
understanding.

氷 *kaihyō* thaw; thawing
⁶ 任 *kainin* dismissal, release
合 *to(ke)-a(u)* be melted together, be
reconciled. *to(ke)a(i)* compromise
⁷ 体 *kaitai* dismantling, dissolution,
liquidation; autopsy
決 *kaiketsu* solution, settlement
⁸ 明 *to(ki)-a(kasu)*, *kaimei suru* explain,
elucidate
毒剤 *gedokuzai* antidote
析 *kaiseki* analysis
放 *to(ki)-hana(tsu)*, *kaihō suru* release,
deliver, liberate, emancipate
⁹ 約 *kaiyaku* cancellation of a contract
除 *kaijo* cancellation, rescinding;
release; exoneration
¹⁰ 消 *kaishō* dissolution, liquidation;
cancellation; settlement
剖 *kaibō* dissection; autopsy; analysis
¹¹ 脱 *gedatsu* (Buddhist) salvation,
emancipation, deliverance
釈 *kaishaku* explanation,
interpretation
¹² 雇 *kaiko* discharge, dismissal
散 *kaisan* dispersion, disbanding,
dissolution, dismissal
答 *kaitō* solution
¹³ 禁 *kaikin* lifting a ban or embargo
¹⁴ 読 *kaidoku* deciphering, decoding
説 *kaisetsu* explanation, commentary
¹⁵ 熱 *genetsu* alleviation of fever
¹⁸ 職 *kaishoku* discharge, dismissal
題 *kaidai* synopsis, review of a
subject
²⁷ 纜 *kairan* sailing, leaving

7

見
角
[言]⁰

谷
豆
豕
豸
貝
赤
走
足
身
車
辛
辰
辵
辶
邑
阝
酉
釆
里

■ **RAD.** 言 **149** ■

Kotoba word. At left: *gomben* left-side "speaking." Nickname: Speaking.

言 ₅₅₅₂ _{J3840} _{M35205} GEN, GON word; phrase;
A speech; statement. *yu(u)*,

i(u) say, tell, talk, speak, declare; call,
term, name. *kotoba* word, term; phrase;

7

見
角
[言]
谷
豆
豕
豸
貝
赤
走
足
身
車
辛
辰
辵
邑
阝
西
釆
里

language; a language; dialect; statement. *i(i-konasu)* express correctly. *i(i-sobireru)* fail to tell, miss a chance of telling. *i(waba)* so to speak, in a sense. *(to) i(eba)* speaking of. *(towa) i(u) monono, (towa)i(e)* but, still, however. *i(ikonashi)* an expression. *i(wambakari)* as much as to say. *i(wazumogana)* better left unsaid. *-koto* word.

³ 及 *i(i)-oyo(bu)* refer to, mention. *genkyū* reference

上 *gonjō suru* relate, inform, report (to a higher person)

下 *genka ni, gonka ni* promptly, readily

⁴ 切 *i(i)-ki(ru)* declare, say definitely; tell all

分 *i(i)bun* one's say, one's point; objection, complaint; excuse, explanation; case

文一致 *gembun itchi* unification of the written and spoken languages

⁵ 外 *gengai no* unexpressed, implied, implicit

出 *i(i)-da(su), i(i)-ida(su)* start talking; break the ice, speak out; propose

付 *i(i)-tsu(karu)* have orders (to do). *i(i)-tsu(keru)* order (to do). *kotozu(karu)* be entrusted with; be asked to send word. *kotozu(ke)* message. *kotozu(keru)* entrust with (a message). *i(i)tsu(ke)* order, instructions

⁶ 回 *i(i)-mawa(su)* express (well). *iimawa(shi)* an expression; phraseology

伝 *i(i)-tsuta(eru)* hand down, circulate, inform. *iitsuta(e)* tradition, legend. *kotozuta(e), kotozu(te)* declaration, hearsay, message

交 *i(i)-kawa(su)* pledge one's love; talk together

合 *i(i)-a(u)* quarrel, argue. *i(i)-a(waseru)* arrange beforehand

争 *i(i)-araso(u)* quarrel, dispute

行 *genkō* speech and conduct, profession and practice

成 *i(i)na(ri)* being submissive, saying yes to all

⁷ 抜 *i(i)-nu(keru)* give an evasive answer, excuse oneself, explain away, quibble. *iinu(ke)* evasion, excuse, prevarication

含 *i(i)-fuku(meru)* instruct, inculcate

⁸ 逃 *i(i)noga(re)* evasion, excuse, prevarication

¹⁰ 残 *i(i)-noko(su)* leave word; leave unsaid. *i(i)noko(ri)* something left unsaid

¹¹ 過 *i(i)-su(giru), i(i)-su(gosu)* overstate, say too much. *i(i)-ayama(tsu)* misstate, make a slip

張 *i(i)-ha(ru)* insist on, maintain

淀 *i(i)-yodo(mu)* hesitate in saying

渋 *i(i)-shibu(ru)* hesitate to say, falter

訳 *i(i)wake* apology, excuse, explanation, justification

動 *gendō* speech and conduct

¹² 換 *i(i)-ka(eru)* say in other words

渡 *i(i)-wata(su)* sentence, condemn; order, instruct, announce

違 *i(i)-chiga(eru)* misstate, make a slip. *iichiga(i)* misstatement

葉 *koto(no)ha* words; a tanka poem. *kotoba* words, language

葉使 *kotobazuka(i)* speech, diction

葉遣 *kotobazuka(i)* speech, diction

¹³ 損 *i(i)-sokona(u), i(i)-son(jiru)* make a slip; fail to tell, misstate

辞 *genji* words, speech, language, expression

触 *i(i)-fu(rasu)* spread a report or rumor

¹⁴ 漏 *i(i)-mo(rasu)* disclose; leave unsaid

説 *gensetsu* remark, opinion, statement

語 *gengo, gongo* language, speech, words. *i(wazu)-kata(rasu)* tacitly, by implication

語学 *gengogaku* philology; linguistics

語道断 *gongo-dōdan* unmentionable, outrageous, unpardonable

¹⁵ 質 *genshitsu, genchi* pledge, commitment, promise

論 *genron* speech, discussion

───────── 2 ─────────

訂 ₅₅₅₃ J447b M35211 **TEI** correct; decide.
B

⁵ 正 *teisei* correction; revision

計 ₅₅₅₅ J3757 M35220 **KEI** plan, scheme, trick; total; meter, gauge.
A
haka(ru) measure, gauge, weigh; fathom, sound; compute, estimate. *haka(ru)* plan, devise, scheme; counsel with; have in

mind; aim at; deceive, impose on; measure. *haka(rau)* manage, arrange, dispose of, see about, talk over.
³ 上 *keijō suru* add up, appropriate
⁸ 画 *keikaku* plan, scheme, project; intention
画的 *keikakuteki* planned, intentional, premeditated
¹⁰ 時 *keiji* timing (in races)
¹¹ 略 *keiryaku* plan, trick, stratagem
¹² 量 *keiryō* measuring, weighing, computation, measurement
¹³ 数 *keisū* calculation, computation
¹⁴ 算 *keisan* computation, calculation
算器 *keisanki* calculator, computer
¹⁵ 器 *keiki* meter, gauge

————— 3 —————

訊 $\frac{5559}{\text{J3f56}}$ $\frac{}{\text{M35224}}$ JIN request; question, investigate. *ki(ku)*, *tazu(neru)* ask, inquire.

B 託 $\frac{5560}{\text{J4277}}$ $\frac{}{\text{M35243}}$ TAKU requesting, entrusting with. *taku(suru)* entrust with, charge with; pretend; hint. *kotozu(karu)* be requested. *kako(tsu)*, *kakotsu(keru)*, *kotozu(keru)* pretend; plead; make excuses. *kako(chi)* complaining, grumbling.
⁷ 児所 *takujisho* day nursery; nursery school
⁸ 送 *takusō suru* consign, send by (someone), check (baggage)
⁹ 宣 *takusen* (Buddhist or Shinto) oracle

A 討 $\frac{5561}{\text{J4624}}$ $\frac{}{\text{M35231}}$ TŌ. *u(tsu)* attack, defeat, destroy, conquer.
² 入 *u(chi)-i(ru)* break into, raid
⁴ 手 *u(chi)te, u(t)te* attacking party, punitive force, pursuers; shooter, murderer
⁶ 伐 *tōbatsu* subjugation, suppression
¹⁵ 論 *tōron* debate, discussion, contention, argumentation
²⁰ 議 *tōgi* debate, discussion

A 訓 $\frac{5562}{\text{J3731}}$ $\frac{}{\text{M35238}}$ KIN, KUN Japanese reading (of a character); explanation of a character; lesson; regulation; rule. *oshi(eru)* instruct. *yo(mu)* read.

kun(zuru) read; read in the *kun* .
⁵ 示 *kunji* instruction
令 *kunrei* directive, instructions
⁷ 戒 *kunkai* admonition, warning
告 *kunkoku*
⁸ 育 *kun'iku* education, discipline
¹² 詁 *kunko* exegesis, interpretation of old words
¹³ 辞 *kunji* address to students
話 *kunwa* fable, moral tale
電 *kunden* telegraphic instructions
¹⁴ 読 *kundoku, kun'yo(mi)* reading characters with Japanese sounds
練 *kunren* training, practice, drill, discipline, schooling

A 記 $\frac{5563}{\text{J352d}}$ $\frac{}{\text{M35244}}$ KI account, narrative, history, annals; remembering; writing; the *Kojiki*. *ki(suru)* write down, record, describe; remember. *shiru(su)* write down; inscribe; mention, give an account of. *shirushi* record.
² 入 *kinyū* entry (in a record)
⁵ 号 *kigō* mark, sign, symbol
⁶ 名 *kimei* signature
⁷ 述 *kijutsu* description, account
⁸ 者 *kisha* journalist, reporter
者会見 *kisha kaiken* news conferences, press interview
事 *kiji* description, statement, news item, article
念 *kinen* remembrance, commemoration
念日 *kinembi* memorial day, anniversary
念品 *kinenhin* souvenir, memento
⁹ 紀 *Kiki* the *Kojiki* and the *Nihonshoki*
¹¹ 章 *kishō* medal, badge, insignia
帳 *kichō* registry; entry, posting, bookkeeping; signature
¹³ 載 *kisai* statement, publication; entry
¹⁶ 憶 *kioku* memory, remembrance, recollection
録 *kiroku* record, document, archives, minutes, proceedings, chronicle

————— 4 —————

B 訟 $\frac{5565}{\text{J3e59}}$ $\frac{}{\text{M35266}}$ SHŌ accuse.

訣 $\frac{5567}{\text{J376d}}$ $\frac{}{\text{M35272}}$ KETSU separation; part; secret.

7

見
角
【言】
⁴ 谷
豆
豕
豸
貝
赤
走
足
身
車
辛
辰
辵
之
邑
阝
酉
釆
里

⁷ 別 *ketsubetsu* separation, farewell

許 ₅₅₆₉ _{J3576} _{M35298} Kyo. Ko. *yuru(su)* permit, approve; authorize; acknowledge; confide in; forgive, pardon; release, acquit; overlook. *moto* (parental) roof, a person's house. *-bakari* approximately; only, merely, alone; degree; almost, practically; absorbed in; continue doing; just now; be about to do; be ready for; have no alternative; now or never.

A

⁵ 可 *kyoka* permission, approval, license, permit, authorization, admission
⁷ 否 *kyohi* permission, sanction
¹⁰ 容 *kyoyō* permission, approval; pardon
¹³ 嫁 *iinazuke* fiancee
¹⁵ 諾 *kyodaku* consent, approval, permit

設 ₅₅₇₀ _{J405f} _{M35293} Setsu. *mō(keru)* prepare, provide; establish, found, set up, organize; enact, lay down (rules); get (a child).

A

⁵ 立 *setsuritsu suru* establish, found, organize, promote, incorporate
⁸ 定 *settei* establishment, creation
⁹ 計 *sekkei* plan, design
¹¹ 問 *setsumon* question
¹² 備 *setsubi* equipment, fixtures, installations, arrangements, accommodations, convenience, facilities
　営 *setsuei* construction, arrangements
¹³ 置 *setchi suru* establish, found

訪 ₅₅₇₁ _{J4b2c} _{M35284} Hō. *otozu(reru)* visit, call on. *tazu(neru)* call on, visit, look up. *tobura(u), to(u)* call on, visit, offer sympathy.

A

¹¹ 問 *hōmon* visit, interview, call

訳 ₅₅₇₂ _{J4c75} _{M35324}ʻ Yaku translation. Eki. *yaku(su), yaku(suru)* translate. *wake* meaning, sense; reason, cause; circumstances, the case; understanding (between them). *yaku* translation, version; interpretation.

A

² 了 *yakuryō suru* finish translating
⁴ 文 *yakubun* translation, version, rendering
⁵ 出 *yakushutsu* translation
　本 *yakuhon* translated book

⁷ 述 *yakujutsu suru* translate and explain. *yakujutsu* translation
⁸ 注 *yakuchū* translation with notes
　者 *yakusha* translator
¹⁰ 書 *yakusho* a translation, a version, translated book
¹⁴ 語 *yakugo* word used in translation, an equivalent

―――――― **5** ――――――

詑 ₅₅₇₉ _{J4242} _{M35374} I. Ta deceive, delude. *wa(biru)* apologize. *wa(bi)* apology.

詔 ₅₅₈₁ _{J3e5b} _{M35379} Shō imperial edict. *mikotonori* imperial edict, decree.

B

⁹ 勅 *shōchoku* imperial proclamation
¹⁰ 書 *shōsho* imperial edict

詞 ₅₅₈₂ _{J3b6c} _{M35394} Shi words; poetry. *kotoba* words.

A

¹⁹ 藻 *shisō* figure of speech, rhetorical flourishes; prose and poetry

註 ₅₅₈₃ _{J4370} _{M35340} Chū notes, comment. *chū(suru)* comment on; annotate.

⁴ 文 *chūmon* an order
¹⁰ 記 *chūki suru* make entries; write down
¹¹ 釈 *chūshaku* notes, comment, exegesis
¹³ 解 *chūkai* notes, comment; commentary

詠 ₅₅₈₄ _{J3153} _{M35409} Ei poem; song; singing; composing. *yo(mu)* recite, chant. *ei(suru)* write poems; recite poems.

B

⁷ 吟 *eigin* reciting poetry
¹³ 嘆 *eitan* exclamation, admiration
¹⁴ 誦 *eishō* reciting poetry
　歌 *eika* composition of a poem or song; poem; song; Buddhist pilgrim's song
¹⁵ 歎 *eitan* exclamation, admiration

詐 ₅₅₈₅ _{J3a3e} _{M35373} Sa. *itsuwa(ru)* lie, falsify; deceive; pretend; deceive, cheat.

B

⁸ 取 *sashu* fraud, swindle
¹⁰ 称 *sashō* misrepresentation, false statement, impersonation

¹¹ 偽 *sagi* lie, falsehood
術 *sajutsu* deceptive means
¹² 欺 *sagi* fraud, swindling

診 5586 / J3f47 / M35337 B SHIN seeing; diagnosing. *mi(ru)* diagnose, examine.
¹¹ 断 *shindan* diagnosis
¹⁴ 察 *shinsatsu* medical examination
¹⁷ 療 *shinryō* examination and treatment
療所 *shinryōjo* clinic, medical office

評 5587 / J493e / M35383 A HYŌ criticism, comment. *hyō(suru)* criticize, comment on.
⁷ 決 *hyōketsu* decision, verdict
判 *hyōban* fame, reputation, popularity; sensation; rumor
⁸ 注 *hyōchū* commentary
定 *hyōjō* conference, consultation. *hyōtei* rating, evaluation
者 *hyōsha* critic, reviewer
価 *hyōka* appraisal, valuation, assessment; appreciation
¹¹ 釈 *hyōshaku* annotation, commentary
¹² 註 *hyōchū* commentary
¹⁴ 語 *hyōgo* critical remark; mark; epithet
¹⁵ 論 *hyōron* criticism, review, comment, editorial
論家 *hyōronka* critic, commentator, reviewer
²⁰ 議 *hyōgi* consultation, discussion, conference, deliberation

訴 5588 / J41ca / M35325 B SO. *utta(eru)* sue; complain of (pain); appeal to; have recourse to. *utta(e)* lawsuit, complaint, accusation, charge, indictment; appeal, petition.
⁷ 状 *sojō* petition, written complaint
¹¹ 訟 *soshō* lawsuit, litigation
訟事件 *soshō jiken* case, lawsuit

証 5589 / J3e5a / M35341 A SHŌ proof, evidence; certificate. *shō(suru)* prove, guarantee. *akashi suru* witness. *akashi* proof, evidence, vindication, witnessing.
² 人 *akashibito, shōnin* witness
⁴ 文 *shōmon* deed, bond, promissory note
⁵ 左 *shōsa* proof, evidence, testimony
⁷ 言 *shōgen* testimony, evidence

⁸ 明 *shōmei* proof, evidence; testimony, witness; certification
明書 *shōmeisho* certificate
券 *shōken* securities, bonds, deed, certificate
拠 *shōko* proof, evidence, testimony
拠物件 *shōko bukken* material evidence
¹⁰ 書 *shōsho* bond, deed, certificate

———— 6 ————

詣 5594 / J3758 / M35412 KEI. *kei(suru)* visit a temple or shrine. *mai(ru), mō(deru)* go; come; call, visit; visit a shrine. *mō(de), mai(ri)* temple or shrine visit.

詫 5598 / J4f4d / M35431 TA. *wa(biru)* apologize, make an excuse. *wabi* apology, excuse, intercession.
⁷ 言 *wabigoto* apology
状 *wabijō* written apology

該 5601 / J333a / M35445 B GAI the said.
⁶ 当 *gaitō* pertinence, relevance
当者 *gaitōsha* the person concerned or qualified
¹² 博 *gaihaku na* profound, extensive (knowledge)

誉 5602 / J4d40 / M35498 B YO. *home(ru)* praise. *homa(re)* honor, glory.
⁷ 言葉 *homekotoba* words of praise
¹¹ 望 *yobō* fame

詮 5604 / J4127 / M35435 SEN discussion; selection; methods called for; result, effect. *sen(zuru)* think over; discuss. *kai* effect, result, use.
¹⁰ 索 *sensaku* search, inquiry, investigation
²⁰ 議 *sengi* discussion, investigation, inquiry, examination

誇 5605 / J3858 / M35474 B KO. *hoko(ru)* boast of, be proud of. *hoko(rakasu)* take a boastful attitude. *hoko(rashii)* proud. *hoko(rashige ni)* proudly, triumphantly. *hoko(ri)* pride.

7

見
角
⁶【言】
谷
豆
豕
豸
貝
赤
走
足
身
車
辛
辰
辵
邑
阝
西
釆
里

³大 *kodai* exaggeration, hyperbole, bombast
⁵示 *koshi, koji* ostentation, display
¹¹張 *kochō* exaggeration

誠 A
5606
J403f
M35497

SEI. *imashi(meru)* admonish, warm; prohibit. *makoto* sincerity, honesty, fidelity; truth. *makoto no* true, genuine, actual. *makoto ni* really; extremely. *makoto(shiyakana)* plausible.
⁴心 *seishin* sincerity
心誠意 *seishin-seii* sincerity, wholehearted devotion; sincerely, devotedly
⁸実 *seijitsu* sincerity, honesty, truthfulness, faithfulness
¹³意 *seii* sincerity, good faith

詳 B
5607
J3e5c
M35446

SHŌ. *tsumabira(kana), kuwa(shii)* full, detailed, minute, accurate; versed in, well-informed on.
⁷述 *shōjutsu* detailed explanation
¹¹細 *shōsai* details, particulars
密 *shōmitsu na* detailed
¹²報 *shōhō* particulars, full report

話 A
5608
J4f43
M35441

WA. *hana(su)* talk, speak, converse; tell; explain. *hana(seru)* sensible, intelligent, agreeable. *hanashi tsuide ni* in the course of the conversation. *hanashi* talk, chat, conversation; story; rumor; news; consultation; negotiations; facts, reasons.
⁴手 *hana(shi)te* speaker
⁵半分 *hanashi-hambun* a statement to be taken at half its face value
甲斐 *hana(shi)gai* effect of a speech
⁶合 *hana(shi)-a(u)* discuss, talk over, consult with. *hanashia(i)* consultation; agreement
⁷言葉 *hana(shi)kotoba* speech, spoken language
⁹柄 *wahei* topic of conversation
相手 *hanashi aite* adviser, someone to talk to
¹¹術 *wajutsu* storyteller's art
掛 *hana(shi)-ka(keru)* accost, speak to
¹⁶頭 *watō* topic of conversation
¹⁸題 *wadai* topic of conversation

詰 B
5609
J354d
M35440

KITSU. *tsu(mu)* be pressed in, be packed, become close; be checkmated. *tsu(meru) vt* stuff, fill, pack, plug; place closely; write closely; sit closely; shorten; curtail; checkmate; keep doing; hold (one's breath). *vi* attend (office). *tsu(maru)* be stopped up, be blocked; be full, be stuffed; be shortened, contract; be hard up; be held up, be deadlocked. *naji(ru)* reprove, rebuke, blame. *tsu(me)* stuffing, packing, stopper; end, foot of, edge; checkmate; appointment to. *tsu(maranai)* trifling, insignificant, small, of no account, worthless, trashy, foolish, despicable, uninteresting, cheerless, monotonous. *tsu(mari)* after all, eventually; in short, to sum up; in other words. *-zu(me)* packed in, bottled in; boxed in; kept (standing); on duty at.
⁴込 *tsu(me)-ko(mu)* stuff, pack, jam into; crowd into; tamp
⁶合 *tsu(me)-a(waseru)* assort, pack an assortment. *tsumeawa(se)* assortment (of cakes). *tsumia(i)* working at the same place; coworker; arguing
⁸所 *tsumesho* office; guard room; crew room; side room. *tsu(maru)tokoro* after all
¹¹問 *kitsumon* grilling, cross-examination

詩 A
5610
J3b6d
M35427

SHI poem, poetry.
²人 *shijin* poet; minstrel
³才 *shisai* poetic genius
⁴心 *shishin* poetic sentiment
文 *shibun* prose and poetry, literature
⁵句 *shiku* verse, stanza
⁷吟 *shigin* reciting Chinese poems
⁸的 *shiteki* poetical, poetic
¹¹情 *shijō* poetic sentiment, poetic interest
¹²集 *shishū* anthology of poetry
¹⁴歌 *shika, shiika* Chinese and Japanese poetry

試 A
5611
J3b6e
M35415

SHI testing. *kokoro(miru)* try, attempt. *tame(su)* attempt, try, experiment, test, sample. *kokoro(mi)* trial, test, attempt, experiment; ordeal, temptation.

⁵用 *shiyō* trial

写 *shisha* preview, private showing

⁶行錯誤 *shikō-sakugo* trial and error

合 *shiai* contest, match, game, bout, tournament, joust

⁷作 *shisaku* trial manufacture, first production, trial production

⁸金石 *shikinseki* touchstone; test, test case

⁹食 *shishoku* sampling food

乗 *shijō* trial ride

¹⁰案 *shian* draft, tentative plan

射 *shisha* test firing

¹¹問 *shimon* question, interview, test, quiz, examination

運転 *shiunten* trial run, test run

掘 *shikutsu* prospecting

¹²飲 *shiin suru* sampling beverages

¹³煉 *shiren* test, trial, probation, ordeal

¹⁴錬 *shiren* test, trial, probation, ordeal

算 *shisan* preliminary calculation; auditing accounts

¹⁵論 *shiron* preliminary essay, sketch

¹⁸験 *shiken* examination; experiment; test, trial; demonstration

験官 *shikenkan* examiner

験勉強 *shiken-benkyō* cramming for examinations

験管 *shikenkan* test tube

——— 7 ———

誌 A
5620
J3b6f
M35501
SHI records; document; magazine. *shiru(su)* write down; inscribe; mention; give an account of. *shirushi* record. *-shi* magazine.

³上 *shijō* in a magazine

⁹面 *shimen* a page of a magazine

誓 B
5622
J4040
M35514
SEI. *chika(u)* swear, pledge, vow. *chika(i)* oath, pledge, vow. *chika(tte)* positively, surely.

⁴文 *seibun, seimon* written oath

⁹約 *seiyaku* a written vow

約書 *seiyakusho* written pledge, covenant

¹⁹願 *seigan* oath, pledge, vow

認 A
5623
J4727
M35502
NIN. *mito(meru)* witness; sight; discern, authorize, recognize; appreciate; approve of; judge, conclude; believe; regard as.

shitata(meru) write, draw up; eat. *mito(me)* approval; private seal.

⁵可 *ninka* approval, license, permission

⁶印 *mito(me)in, nin'in* personal seal, signet

合 *mito(me)-a(u)* see another's viewpoint

⁷否 *nimpi* approval or disapproval

⁸知 *ninchi* recognition, acknowledgment

定 *nintei* authorization, recognition, acknowledgment, presumption, permission; identification

¹⁰容 *nin'yō* admission, tolerance, acknowledgment

¹¹許 *ninkyo* consent, recognition

¹²証 *ninshō* approval, validation, confirmation, certification

¹⁹識 *ninshiki* recognition, understanding, knowledge

誘 B
5625
J4d36
M35525
YŪ. *saso(u)* invite, ask; call for; provoke, cause; bring (tears); allure, tempt, seduce. *izana(u)* invite; lead, tempt. *obi(ku)* decoy, entice, lure.

⁴引 *yūin suru* entice, invite, beguile, induce, attract, allure

⁶因 *yūin* immediate cause; incentive, motive

⁸拐 *yūkai* kidnapping, abduction

⁹発 *yūhatsu suru* cause, induce, lead up to, give advice to

¹⁰致 *yūchi suru* lure, entice, invite, bring about

¹²惑 *yūwaku* temptation, seduction

¹⁴導 *yūdō* induction, incitement, inducement, encouragement

導訊問 *yūdō jimmon* leading question

誤 A
5626
J386d
M35546
GO. *ayama(ru)* vi and vt err, be mistaken; do wrong; mislead. *ayama(ri)* mistake, error. *ayama(tte)* by mistake, accidentally.

⁵用 *goyō* misapplication, misuse, abuse

写 *gosha* scribal error, error in copying

⁶伝 *goden* misinformation, incorrect report

字 *goji* wrong character, wrong word, misprint

⁹信 *goshin* mistaken belief

¹⁰記 *goki* clerical error, misentry, error in writing

7

見角【言】谷豆豖豸貝赤走足身車辛辰辵邑阝酉釆里

⁷

配 *gohai* misdelivery (of letters)
差 *gosa* error, aberration
¹¹訳 *goyaku* mistranslation
¹²植 *goshoku* typographical error, erratum, misprint
診 *goshin* wrong diagnosis
報 *gohō* misinformation, incorrect report
¹³解 *gokai* misunderstanding, misconception, delusion
¹⁴認 *gonin* misunderstanding, misconception, mistake
読 *godoku* misreading
説 *gosetsu* mistaken theory
算 *gosan* miscalculation
¹⁵審 *goshin* wrong refereeing
¹⁸謬 *gobyū* error, fallacy, mistake
²¹魔化 *gomaka(su)* cheat, deceive, camouflage, hoodwink, prevaricate; gloss over, cover up; tamper with, doctor up; patch up; quibble; embezzle

A 説 ⁵⁶²⁷ J4062 M35556 ZEI. ETSU. SETSU opinion, view, assertion; comment; theory; rumor, report; version. *to(ku)* explain, expound, advocate, preach, teach, persuade.
⁶伏 *to(ki)-fu(seru), to(ki)-fu(su)* confute, argue down, convince; prevail on, persuade to do. *seppuku* persuading, persuasion, convincing
⁸法 *seppō* (Buddhist) sermon
服 *seppuku* persuading, convincing
明 *setsumei suru, to(ki)-aka(su)* explain, interpret, illustrate, solve (a riddle). *setsumei, tokiaka(shi)* explanation, interpretation, description
明書 *setsumeisho* explanatory note
¹⁰起 *to(ki)-o(kosu)* begin to explain
¹¹得 *settoku* persuasion
教 *to(ki)-oshi(eru)* propound, preach. *sekkyō* sermon; preaching; admonition; scolding
¹³話 *setsuwa* story, narrative
¹⁶諭 *setsuyu suru, to(ki)-sato(su)* convince, persuade; reprove

A 語 ⁵⁶²⁸ J386c M35533 Go word, speech, language, term. GYO. *kata(ru)* talk, tell, narrate, recite. *kata(rau)* talk, chat; pledge one's troth; invite, entice; win; conspire with.

kata(rai) talk, chat; lovers' vow. *kata(ri)* narrative (in the noh); reciter. *-go* (technical) term; language.
⁴手 *kata(ri)te* speaker, narrator, reciter
⁵句 *goku* words, phrases
⁶気 *goki* tone of voice, manner of speaking
⁷尾 *gobi* word ending, the inflected end of a word
呂 *goro* the sound, euphony
⁸法 *gohō* diction, phraseology, grammar, syntax
学 *gogaku* language study; linguistics
¹¹族 *gozoku* a family of languages
釈 *goshaku* explanation of words
¹³源 *gogen* derivation, etymology
継 *kata(ri)-tsu(gu)* transmit, hand down
彙 *goi* vocabulary, glossary
義 *gogi* meaning of a word
感 *gokan* the impression of words
幹 *gokan* stem, root of a word
¹⁵調 *gochō* accent, tone, rhythm
幣 *gohei* unhappy expression, faulty expression, misleading statement, misunderstanding
¹⁶録 *goroku* analects, book of aphorisms

A 読 ⁵⁶²⁹ J4649 M35580 TŌ. TOKU, DOKU reading. *yo(mu)* read, peruse; understand, read (one's heart), guess, divine. *yo(meru)* can read; be legible, be readable; read well; be decipherable; understand, perceive, see through. *yo(mi-konasu)* read thoroughly. *yo(mi)* reading; Japanese rendering of a Chinese character. *yo(mide)* worthwhile reading.
²了 *dokuryō suru* finish reading
³上 *yo(mi)-a(geru)* read aloud, read off, read out (the names)
⁵本 *tokuhon* reader. *yomihon* reader, storybook
⁸物 *yomimono* reading matter, a reading
取 *yo(mi)-to(ru)* read (someone's) mind, guess, divine
者 *dokusha* reader, subscriber
⁹点 *tōten* comma
後感 *dokugokan* impression of a book
¹⁰破 *dokuha suru, yo(mi)-yabu(ru)* read through
耽 *yo(mi)-fuke(ru)* be absorbed in reading

唇術 *dokushinjutsu* lip reading
書 *yo(mi)ka(ki)* reading and writing.
dokusho, tokusho reading books
書人 *dokushojin* a reader of books, a
scholar; the intelligentsia
書家 *dokushoka* well-read person
¹¹ 経 *dokyō, dokkyō* chanting Buddhist
sutras
¹³ 解 *dokukai* reading and explaining a
book

───── **8** ─────

諫 5630 / J3452 / M35642　See 諫 5664.

諏 5632 / J3f5b / M35648　SHU, SU, SŌ consult.

誼 5634 / J3543 / M35605　GI friendship, intimacy,
good will. *yoshi(mi)*
friendship, intimacy, good will.

B 謁 5637 / J315a / M35690'　ETSU audience (with a
ruler). *es(suru)*
have an audience with.
⁷ 見 *ekken* an audience (with someone)

B 諾 5638 / J427a / M35687　DAKU assent, consent,
agreement. *daku(suru)*
agree to. *ubena(u)* agree to; follow.
⁷ 否 *dakuhi* definite answer, yes or no,
acceptance or refusal

誹 5639 / J4870 / M35601　HI ridicule, slander.
¹⁷ 謗 *hibō* slander; abuse

A 誕 5640 / J4342 / M35692'　TAN be born; deceive; lie;
be arbitrary.
⁵ 生 *tanjō* birth, nativity
生日 *tanjōbi* birthday

諒 5641 / J4e4a / M35653　RYŌ fact, reality. *ryō (to)*
suru understand;
appreciate; excuse.
⁷ 承 *ryōshō* acknowledgment
¹³ 解 *ryōkai* understanding, comprehension

誰 5642 / J432f / M35586　SUI *dare, tare* who.
dare(ka) someone,
somebody. *dare mo, dare(shimo)*
everyone; (neg.) no one.
⁴ 方 *donata* who
⁷ 何 *suika suru* challenge, question

A 談 5643 / J434c / M35633　DAN conversation,
talk. *dan(jiru), dan(zuru)*
discuss, talk (with or about); negotiate
with.
⁶ 合 *dan(ji)-a(u)* negotiate with, consult
together. *dangō* consultation,
conference
⁷ 判 *dampan* negotiation, conference,
parley, discussion
¹⁰ 笑 *danshō* friendly chat
¹³ 話 *danwa* conversation, talk, chat,
speaking
¹⁵ 論 *dunron* discussion, argument,
discourse
論風発 *danron-fūhatsu* eloquence;
ready controversialist
²⁰ 議 *dangi* lecture, lesson, sermon
(Buddhist)

A 課 5644 / J325d / M35589　KA lesson; section,
department; allotment,
division. *ka(suru), ka(su)* levy, assess;
assign (a task); charge with.
⁵ 目 *kamoku* subject, course, curriculum;
items
外 *kagai* extracurricular
外活動 *kagai katsudō* extracurricular
activities
⁸ 長 *kachō* section head
¹² 程 *katei* course, curriculum, routine
税 *kazei* taxation, assessment, tax, duty,
levy
¹³ 業 *kagyō* schoolwork, lessons
¹⁸ 題 *kadai* subject, theme, problem,
homework

B 請 5645 / J4041 / M35640'　SHIN. SHŌ. JŌ. SEI
requesting, inviting.
shō(jiru), shō(zuru) invite, usher in. *ko(u)*
ask, request; invite; pray for; beg, solicit.
u(keru) receive, accept, take, get, obtain;
face, front on, inherit; catch the public's
fancy.
⁶ 合 *u(ke)-a(u)* undertake; promise,
guarantee. *u(ke)a(i)* guarantee,
assurance
⁷ 求 *ko(i)-moto(meru)* ask for, beg. *seikyū*
demand, claim, application

7

見
角
[言]⁸·
谷
豆
豕
豸
貝
赤
走
足
身
車
辛
辰
辵
邑
阝
西
釆
里

求書 *seikyūsho* application, written claim

⁹ 負 *u(ke)-o(u)* contract for, undertake. *ukeoi* contract

¹⁰ 託 *seitaku* request, secret request

訓 *seikun* request for instructions

¹⁹ 願 *seigan* petition

願書 *seigansho* (written) petition

論 A ‖5646 J4f40 M35658‖ RON argument; discourse. *agetsura(u)*, *ron(jiru)*, *ron(zuru)* discuss, argue, comment on, deal with, consider.

³ 及 *ronkyū suru* touch on, refer to, enter into

⁴ 文 *rombun* dissertation, thesis, article, paper, treatise, essay

⁵ 外 *rongai* beside the point, irrelevant

功行賞 *ronkō kōshō* distribution of awards

⁶ 旨 *ronshi* point of an argument

考 *ronkō* a study

争 *ronsō* dispute, controversy, argument

争点 *ronsōten* point of dispute

⁷ 述 *ronjutsu* statement, enunciation

告 *ronkoku* stating one's belief; prosecution; prosecutor's address

⁸ 拠 *ronkyo* basis of an argument, data

法 *rompō* argument, reasoning, logic

⁹ 陣 *ronjin* argument

点 *ronten* point at issue, disputed point

客 *ronkaku, ronkyaku* disputant, controversialist

¹⁰ 破 *rompa suru* refute, argue against. *rompa* rebuttal

¹¹ 理 *ronri* logic

理学 *ronrigaku* logic

¹² 評 *rompyō* criticism, review, comment

証 *ronshō* proof, demonstration

¹³ 戦 *ronsen* verbal battle, argument

¹⁴ 語 *Rongo* Confucian Analects

説 *ronsetsu* discourse, dissertation; editorial

駁 *rombaku suru* refute, argue against

¹⁵ 調 *ronchō* tone of the argument

敵 *ronteki* opponent (in debate), adversary

¹⁶ 壇 *rondan* world of criticism; lecture platform

¹⁸ 難 *ronnan* denunciation, criticism, censure

題 *rondai* subject, theme, topic for debate

叢 *ronsō* collection of treatises

²⁰ 議 *rongi* discussion, controversy, argument

調 A ‖5647 J4434 M35609‖ CHŌ tune, tone, meter; key (in music); style of writing; tax in kind. *chō(zuru)* investigate, scrutinize; provide; prepare; make; curse, exorcise; ridicule. *shira(beru)* test, examine, investigate, survey, check up; inspect, overhaul; search for; look up (a word); refer to (a book); interrogate; correct (papers); play (on an instrument). *totono(eru)* prepare, arrange; fill (orders); supply; raise (money); put in order, tidy up, adjust (clothes); regulate; settle; purchase. *totono(u)* be prepared, be arranged, be in order, be adjusted, be well regulated; be settled. *mitsugi* tribute. *shira(be)* melody, tune; notes.

³ 子 *chōshi* tune, tone, key, note, pitch; time, rhythm; accent; vein; manner, style; condition, state (of health); trend

⁶ 印 *chōin* signature, signing, sealing

合 *chōgō* mixing, compound

⁸ 法 *chōhō* convenience, usefulness. *chōhō(garu)* find useful, think highly of

和 *chōwa* harmony, accord, agreement; symphony; symmetry; conformity

味料 *chōmiryō* condiments, seasoning, relishes, dressing

⁹ 速機 *chōsokuki* governor, speed regulator

度 *chōdo* furniture, appliances, utensils, supplies

度品 *chōdohin* furniture, appliances, utensils, supplies

律師 *chōritsushi* piano tuner

査 *chōsa* investigation, examination, inquiry, survey, research

¹⁰ 書 *chōsho* protocol, preliminary memorandum, record

剤 *chōzai* compounding medicines

¹¹ 達 *chōtatsu, chōdatsu* supply, procurement, provision

教 *chōkyō* breaking or training (animals)

停 *chōtei* arbitration, conciliation, mediation, intercession, intervention

理 *chōri* cooking
13 節 *chōsetsu* regulation, adjustment, control, modulation, governing, tempering, tuning, tuning in
14 製 *chōsei* manufacture, preparation
16 整 *chōsei* regulation, adjustment, governing, control, coordination, correction, modulation, tuning

A 諸 5648 J3d74 M35691' SHO- many, several, various, all. *moro-* every; many; two; together.
3 子 *shoshi* you; sage, master
刃 *moroha no* double-edged
4 手 *morote, shote* with both hands
方 *shohō* every direction, all sides, everywhere
5 外国 *shogaikoku* many foreign countries
民族 *shominzoku* many nations or races
7 君 *shokun* gentlemen, ladies and gentlemen, my friends, you
8 事 *shoji* various matters, everything
国 *shokoku* all countries, various countries; all provinces
10 般 *shohan no* various, several, all, every
島 *shotō* group of islands, archipelago
11 経費 *shokeihi* costs, expenses
問題 *shomondai* all questions, various questions
14 説 *shosetsu* various views, various theories
15 諸 *moromoro no* all, all kinds of, various

───── **9** ─────

謂 5656 J3062 M35759 I. *iwa(re)* reason; origin; a history; oral tradition. *i(i)* meaning. *yu(u), i(u)* say, tell, talk, speak, declare; call, term, name.

諺 5659 J3841 M-X GEN. *kotowaza* maxim, priverb.

B 諮 5660 J3b70 M35728 SHI. *haka(ru)* consult with.
11 問 *shimon* question, inquiry
13 詢 *shijun* question, inquiry

謎 5661 J4666 M35800 MEI. *nazo* riddle, puzzle, enigma; hint, tip.

諦 5663 J447c M35716 TEI. TAI. *akira(meru)* abandon, give up, resign to, be reconciled to.
8 念 *teinen* a heart that understands truth
18 観 *teikan* clear vision; resignation (to)

諫 5664 J6b5d M35724 諫 5630 J3452 M35642 KAN. *isa(meru)* remonstrate with, admonish, dissuade.
7 言 *kangen* remonstrance; admonition

諜 5665 J4435 M35697 CHŌ. *chō(zuru)* spy out, reconnoiter.
8 者 *chōja* spy
12 報 *chōhō* intelligence, secret information

B 謡 5666 J4d58 M35779' YŌ. *uta(u)* chant. *utai* chanting of the noh; noh singer.
6 曲 *yōkyoku* noh chant

諭 5667 J4d21 M35727' YU. *sato(su)* admonish, charge, remonstrate with, counsel, persuade, warn; make known to. *sato(shi)* advice, reproof, admonition; oracle.
6 旨 *yushi* explanation, reasoning

B 謀 5671 J4b45 M35756 BŌ. MU. *haka(ru)* plan, devise, scheme; counsel with; have in mind; aim at; deceive, impose on. *tabaka(ru)* cheat, impose on. *hakarigoto* plan, scheme, policy, stratagem, plot, trick.
4 反 *muhon* rebellion, insurrection, treason
9 叛 *muhon, bōhan* rebellion, insurrection, treason
10 殺 *bōsatsu* premeditated murder
11 略 *bōryaku* strategy, scheme, plot
20 議 *bōgi* consultation; conspiracy

───── **10** ─────

B 謄 5685 J4625 M35780' TŌ copy.
5 本 *tōhon* certified copy, transcript, duplicate; domiciliary registration copy
写 *tōsha* copy, reproduction; mimeographing

7
見
角
[10] [言]
谷
豆
豕
豸
貝
赤
走
足
身
車
辛
辰
辵
邑
阝
酉
釆
里

B 謙 5686 J382c M35821' KEN. *herikuda(ru)* humble oneself, condescend, be modest.
11 虚 *kenkyo* modesty, humility
13 遜 *kenson* humility, modesty
20 譲 *kenjō* modesty, humility

A 謝 5687 J3c55 M35827 SHA. *sha(suru)* thank; apologize; decline, refuse; take one's leave. *ayama(ru)* apologize; be floored. *ayama(ri)* apology, excuse.
5 礼 *sharei* thanks; remuneration, honorarium
10 恩 *shaon* repaying a kindness, expression of gratitude
12 絶 *shazetsu suru* refuse, decline (to see)
13 辞 *shagi* address of thanks; apology
意 *shai* gratitude, thanks; apology
罪 *shazai* apology

B 謹 5688 J3660 M35850' KIN. *tsutsushi(mu)* be discreet, be careful, be prudent, be cautious; restrain oneself, be moderate. *tsutsushi(mi)* prudence, modesty, discretion, self-control. *tsutsushi(nde)* respectfully, reverently, humbly.
12 賀新年 *Kinga Shinnen* Happy New Year
13 慎 *kinshin* penitence; discipline; domiciliary confinement
14 製 *kinsei* carefully produced by
17 厳 *kingen na* stern, serious, solemn, austere

A 講 5689 J3956 M35824 KŌ club, association; lecture. *kō(jiru), kō(zuru)* read aloud; lecture on; read with; study; practice; conceive, devise.
7 究 *kōkyū* research, investigation
8 和 *kōwa suru* make peace with
10 座 *kōza* lectureship; correspondence course; course of study
師 *kōshi* speaker, lecturer, instructor
11 堂 *kōdō* lecture hall, auditorium
釈 *kōshaku* lecture, storytelling
習 *kōshū* short training course
習所 *kōshūjo* training school
12 評 *kōhyō* criticism, review
13 義 *kōgi* lecture, exposition
14 読 *kōdoku suru* read and explain

演 *kōen* lecture, address
15 談 *kōdan* storytelling; narrative
16 壇 *kōdan* lecture platform, rostrum, pulpit

---- **11** ----

謬 5695 J4935 M35872 BYŪ. *ayamari* mistake.
14 説 *byūsetsu* fallacy, mistaken opinion, false report

---- **12** ----

B 譜 5703 J4968 M35990 FU music, note, staff, score; album, record, table; genealogy.

A 識 5704 J3c31 M35974 SHIKI know, discriminate, write.
7 見 *shikken* knowledge, judgment, discernment, vision, intelligence
別 *shikibetsu* discrimination, discernment, identification
8 者 *shikisha* intelligent people, thinkers, intelligentsia

A 警 5705 J3759 M35989 KEI. *imashi(meru)* admonish, warn, prohibit. *imashime* precept, exhortation, instruction, commandment.
7 告 *keikoku* warning, advice
戒 *keikai* warning, admonition; vigilance
8 官 *keikan* police officer
部 *keibu* police inspector
11 視 *keishi* police superintendent
視庁 *Keishichō* Metropolitan Police Headquarters
12 報 *keihō* warning, alarm
報器 *keihōki* warning bell or siren
備 *keibi* defense, guard, policing
14 察 *keisatsu* police (force); police station
察庁 *Keisatsuchō* National Police Agency
察署 *keisatsusho* police station
15 衛 *keiei* guard, patrol, escort
20 鐘 *keishō* fire bell, alarm bell
護 *keigo* guard, escort, convoy, patrol
22 邏 *keira* patrol officer

---- **13** ----

B 讓 5714 / J3e79 / M36037 Jō. *yuzu(ru)* turn over, hand over, transfer, convey, assign, deed, bequeath, give away, give up; sell, dispose of; yield to; be inferior to; defer, postpone.

³ 与 *jōyo* cession, transfer; concession
⁶ 合 *yuzu(ri)-a(u)* compromise, concede
⁸ 歩 *jōho* concession, conciliation, compromise, condescension
¹² 渡 *yuzu(ri)-wata(su)* turn over, hand over, convey, cede. *jōto* transfer, conveyance, delivery, grant

A 護 5715 / J386e / M36038 Go. *mamo(ru)* defend, protect; keep, observe, obey; abide by; stick to; be true to.

⁷ 身 *goshin* self-protection, self-defense, self-preservation
身術 *goshinjutsu* art of self-defense
⁸ 送 *gosō* convoy, escort
岸 *gogan* sea wall; river dike
⁹ 持 *goji* defense, protection, maintenance, retention; prayer
¹⁵ 衛 *goei* guard, convoy, escort

A 議 5716 / J3544 / M36027 Gi consultation, deliberation, debate; consideration, proposal, suggestion. *gi(suru)* discuss, deliberate on, consider.

⁶ 会 *gikai* deliberative assembly
会政治 *gikai seiji* parliamentary government
⁷ 決 *giketsu* decision, resolution
⁸ 長 *gichō* chair, speaker, president (of the senate)

定書 *giteisho, gijōsho* protocol; written agreement
事 *giji* proceedings
事堂 *gijidō* assembly hall, capitol, diet building
事録 *gijiroku* minutes, proceedings, report, journal
⁹ 院 *giin* the House, the Diet Chamber
院制度 *giin seido* parliamentary system
院政治 *giin seiji* parliamentary government
¹⁰ 席 *giseki* parliamentary seat, the floor
案 *gian* bill, measure
員 *giin* member of an assembly
¹⁵ 論 *giron* argument, discussion, controversy, debate
¹⁸ 題 *gidai* topic for discussion, agenda

——— 15 ———

讃 5720 / J3b3e / M36110 See 讚 5729.

——— 16 ———

讐 5722 / J3d32 / M36125 SHŪ enemy. *ada* enemy; revenge.

——— 19 ———

讚 5729 / J6c2d / M36163 讃 5720 / J3b3e / M36110 SAN praise; title or brief inscription on a picture.

RAD. 谷 150

Tani valley. At left: *tani hen*. Nickname: Valley.

A 谷 5730 / J432b / M36182 KOKU. *tani* valley, dale, ravine; trough (of a wave); trough (in atmospheric pressure). *-ya* valley.

³ 口 *taniguchi* mouth of a valley
川 *tanigawa* valley stream, mountain stream
⁸ 底 *tanizoko, tanisoko* bottom of a ravine; valley bottom
¹² 間 *tanima, taniai* ravine, chasm, dell, valley

7

見
角
言
谷
0 【豆】
豕
豸
貝
赤
走
足
身
車
辛
辰
辵
辶
邑
阝
酉
釆
里

RAD. 豆 151

Mame bean. At left: 豆 *mame hen*. Nickname: Bean.

A 豆 5735 J4626 M36245 Tō. Zu. *mame* beans, peas, pulse. *mame-* miniature, midget, pocket (battleship), small.

⁵ 本 *mame hon* miniature book
⁸ 乳 *tōnyū* soybean milk
¹³ 電球 *mame denkyū* miniature light bulb
¹⁴ 腐 *tōfu* bean curd, tofu

--- 6 ---

A 豊 5737 J4b2d M36263 Hō. *yuta(kana)* abundant; rich; fruitful. *toyo-* excellent, rich.

⁶ 年 *hōnen* fruitful year
⁷ 作 *hōsaku* abundant harvest
¹² 満 *hōman* stout, corpulent
富 *hōfu* abundance, wealth
¹⁴ 漁 *hōryō, hōgyo* big catch (of fish)
¹⁵ 潤 *hōjun* rich and prosperous; luxurious (fruit)
²¹ 饒 *hōjō* fertility

RAD. 豕 152

Buta or *inoko* pig. At left: *inoko hen*. Variant: 豕 (6 strokes). Nickname: Pig.

--- 4 ---

B 豚 5743 J465a M36352 Ton hog. *buta* pig, hog, swine.

⁵ 汁 *tonjiru, butajiru* pork broth soup
⁶ 肉 *butaniku, tonniku* pork, hog meat
児 *tonji* my son (humble)
⁸ 舎 *tonsha* pigsty

--- 5 ---

A 象 5744 J3e5d M36372 Shō image; shape; sign (of the times). Zō elephant. *katado(ru)* pattern after, imitate; symbolize.

⁵ 牙 *zōge* ivory
⁷ 形 *shōkei* copying the form (of something); hieroglyphics
形文字 *shōkei monji, shōkei moji* hieroglyphics, Chinese characters; a type of characters resembling pictures (e.g. 馬, 魚, and 鳥)
¹⁴ 徴 *shōchō suru* symbolize, foreshadow. *shōchō* symbol, emblem

--- 7 ---

B 豪 5749 J396b M36406 Gō great, powerful, excelling.

⁶ 気 *gōki* sturdy spirit
壮 *gōsō* splendor, magnificence, grandeur
⁷ 快 *gōkai na* exciting, stirring, lively; heroic; largehearted; splendid
⁸ 放 *gōhō na* largehearted, frank, unaffected
雨 *gōu* heavy rain, downpour, cloudburst
⁹ 勇 *gōyū* bravery, prowess
¹⁰ 華 *gōka* splendor, pomp, extravagance
¹¹ 遊 *gōyū* wild merrymaking
族 *gōzoku* powerful family or clan
商 *gōshō* wealthy merchant
¹² 傑 *gōketsu* hero, outstanding person
奢 *gōsha* luxury, magnificence, extravagance
¹³ 勢 *gōsei* luxury, magnificence, extravagance
農 *gōnō* wealthy farmer
¹⁴ 語 *gōgo* bombast, boasting, big talk

RAD. 豸 153

Mujina badger or *ashinakimushi* reptiles. At left: *mujina hen*.
Nickname: Clawed Dog (cf. Rads. 87 & 94).

3

豹 5753 J493f M36499 HYŌ leopard, panther.

⁹変 *hyōhen* sudden change

7

貌 5762 J4b46 M36556 BŌ form, appearance; countenance.

RAD. 貝 154

Kai shell or *kogai* small "shell" (to distinguish it from Rad. 181).
At left: *kai hen*. Nickname: Small Shell.

A 貝 5766 J332d M36656 BAI shellfish. *kai* shell; shellfish.

⁹柱 *kaibashira* shell ligament
¹²殻 *kaigara* sea shell
¹³塚 *kaizuka* shell mound, kitchen midden
¹⁸類 *kairui* shellfish

2

B 貞 5768 J4467 M36658 JŌ. TEI chastity; constancy; righteousness.

¹¹淑 *teishuku* chastity, feminine modesty
¹³節 *teisetsu* fidelity, constancy, virginity
¹⁵潔 *teiketsu* chastity, purity
¹⁶操 *teisō* chastity, virginity

B 負 5769 J4969 M-X FU negative, minus; minus sing. *ma(keru)* be defeated; get the worst of it; be overcome with; yield to; be inferior to; lower the price; be poisoned with lacquer. *ma(kasu)* overcome, outrival, defeat. *ma(karu)* reduce the price. *ma(kesaseru)* knock the price down. *o(u)* bear, carry on the back; owe; assume, bear (a responsibility); be accused of, sustain (an injury). *o(wasu), o(waseru)* make carry, burden with, entrust with, charge with, blame. *o(mbu), o(buu)* carry on the back. *o(busaru)* ride on the back; rely on, be dependent on. *ma(ke)* defeat. *(o)ma(ke)* a small discount; a little extra thrown in;

exaggeration, embellishment. *(o)ma(ke) ni* in addition, besides.

⁸担 *futan* encumbrance, burden, load, responsibility, obligation, liability
¹⁰荷 *fuka* burden, load (electricity)
¹¹惜 *ma(ke)o(shimi)* unwillingness to admit defeat
¹²越 *ma(ke)ko(shi)* more losses than wins
¹³債 *fusai* debt, liabilities, loan
傷 *fushō* injury, wound, bruise, cut
傷者 *fushōsha* wounded or injured person

3

B 貢 5772 J3957 M36665 KŌ. KU. *mitsugi* tribute. *mitsu(gu)* support, finance. *kō(suru)* bear tribute.

⁸物 *mitsugimono, kōbutsu, kōmotsu* tribute
¹⁰献 *kōken* contribution, service

A 財 5773 J3a62 M36664 ZAI, SAI money, wealth, assets; property; commodities.

²力 *zairyoku* financial ability, competence; resources, assets; solvency
⁵布 *saifu* purse
⁶団 *zaidan* foundation, financial group, consortium, syndicate, endowment
団法人 *zaidan hōjin* incorporated foundation; juridical person

7

³【貝】

赤走足身車辛辰辵邑阝酉釆里

⁸物 *zaibutsu, zaimotsu* property, goods
宝 *zaihō* wealth, treasure, valuables
⁹界 *zaikai* financial world, money market
政 *zaisei* public financial affairs; economy
¹¹欲 *zaiyoku* greed for wealth
貨 *zaika* commodities, property, wealth
務 *zaimu* financial affairs
産 *zaisan* property, estate, fortune, assets
¹³源 *zaigen* source of funds, resources, finances
¹⁴閥 *zaibatsu* financial clique, giant family trust

─────── 4 ───────

貫 B | 5778 / J3453 / M36681 | KAN 8⅓ pounds. *tsuranu(ku)* pierce, penetrate, perforate; shoot through; attain (one's object). *nuki* brace.
⁵目 *kamme* 8⅓ pounds; weight
⁹通 *kantsū suru* pierce, penetrate, perforate, tunnel through
¹⁰流 *kanryū suru* flow through
¹³禄 *kanroku* weight, dignity
¹⁵徹 *kantetsu* accomplishment, realization, fulfillment; penetration

販 B | 5779 / J484e / M36679 | HAN sell, trade.
⁷売 *hambai* sale, selling
¹³路 *hanro* market, outlet

責 A | 5780 / J4055 / M36682 | SEKI. SHAKU. *se(meru)* condemn, blame, censure, criticize, take to task; torture, persecute; urge, tease (to do something). *se(me)* responsibility, liability, blame, guilt, censure; torture, torment.
⁶任 *sekinin* responsibility, liability
⁸苦 *semeku* torture, torment, cruelty
¹¹務 *sekimu* duty, obligation

貨 A | 5781 / J325f / M36678 | KA freight; goods, property.
⁷車 *kasha* freight car; van
⁸物 *kamotsu, kabutsu* freight, cargo, goods
物列車 *kamotsu ressha* freight train
物自動車 *kamotsu jidōsha* truck
物船 *kamotsusen* freighter

¹⁵幣 *kahei* money, currency, coin, coinage

貧 A | 5782 / J494f / M36677 | HIN, BIN poverty. *hin(suru)* become poor, live in poverty. *mazu(shii)* poor, destitute; meager.
³乏 *bimbō* poverty
⁵民 *himmin* poor people
⁶血 *hinketsu* anemia
⁷困 *hinkon* poverty; lack
⁸苦 *hinku* hardship, serious poverty
⁹相 *hinsō na* poor looking
¹⁰弱 *hinjaku na* poor, meager, scanty
¹²富 *himpu* rich and poor; wealth and poverty
¹⁵窮 *hinkyū* great poverty
窮化 *hinkyūka suru* impoverish

─────── 5 ───────

費 A | 5786 / J4871 / M36717 | HI expenses, cost. *tsuiya(su)* spend, consume, waste. *tsui(eru)* become less; be wasted. *tsuie* expenses.
⁵用 *hiyō* expenses, cost
目 *himoku* expense item
¹⁰消 *hishō* embezzlement, misappropriation

貼 | 5787 / J453d / M36718 | CHŌ counter for medicine packages. *ha(ru)* stick, paste, affix, post, paper, apply (tile, etc.).
⁵付 *ha(ri)-tsu(keru)* stick on, paste up, affix (stamps). *chōfu suru* affix, stick, attach, apply, paste
札 *ha(ri)fuda* placard, bill, poster; tag
出 *ha(ri)-da(su)* put up a notice. *harida(shi)* bill, poster, notice
¹⁰紙 *ha(ri)gami* sticker, bill, tag, label

貿 | 5788 / J4b47 / M36721 | BŌ exchange.
⁸易 *bōeki* trade, commerce
易風 *bōekifū* trade wind
易摩擦 *bōeki masatsu* trade friction

貰 | 5789 / J4c63 / M36699 | SEI *mora(u)* get, have, obtain, receive, accept; get (him) to do (it). *morai* tip, gratuity; geisha's call from another entertainment. *(o)morai* beggar.

⁴手 *moraite* recipient, receiver
火 *moraibi* a neighbor's fire that spreads to one's home
⁸泣 *mora(i)na(ki)* weeping in sympathy
物 *moraimono* present, gift
受 *mora(i)-u(keru)* receive (something)
¹⁰涙 *morai namida* tears of sympathy

賀 A ⟨5790 / J326c / M36725⟩ GA congratulations, felicitations, compliments, joy of the occasion. *ga(suru)* celebrate, congratulate, compliment, approve of.
⁵正 *Gashō* New Year's congratulations, Happy New Year
⁷状 *gajō* greeting card

貯 A ⟨5791 / J4379 / M36698⟩ CHO. *takuwa(eru)* store, lay in stock, save, keep, wear (a mustache). *ta(meru)* vt accumulate, pile up, store, save, collect. *takuwa(e)* store, hoard, savings.
⁴木場 *chomokujō* log-storage place
水 *chosui* storage of water
水池 *chosuichi* reservoir
水槽 *chosuisō* water tank
⁸金 *chokin* savings, deposit
金通帳 *chokin tsūchō* bank book
金箱 *chokimbako* savings box, bank
¹³蓄 *chochiku* savings
¹⁴蔵 *chozō* storage, preservation
蔵品 *chozōhin* stock, supplies
蔵庫 *chozōko* storehouse

貸 A ⟨5792 / J425f / M36709⟩ TAI. *ka(su)* lend; hire out, rent, lease; give credit to. *ka(shi)* loan, lending; bill, account, debt; hire, renting; for rent, for hire.
³与 *kashi-ata(eru)* let out, lease, lend. *taiyo* loan, lending
⁴手 *ka(shi)te* creditor, lender; landlord
方 *kashikata* creditor; how to lend; credit side
切 *kashi-ki(ru)* reserve, book. *kashiki(ri)* reserved; reservation
⁵付 *kashi-tsu(keru)* lend, advance. *kashitsu(ke)* lending
出 *ka(shi)-da(su)* lend. *kashida(shi)* loan, lending; advance; credit
出金 *kashidashikin* a loan
⁸金 *kashikin* loan
金庫 *ka(shi) kinko* safety deposit box

¹⁰席 *kashiseki* hall for rent, room for rent
¹⁰借 *taishaku* loan, debit and credit, lending and borrowing. *ka(shi)ka(ri)* loan; lending and borrowing
倒 *kashidao(re)* bad debts
家 *ka(shi)ie, kashiya* house for rent
¹²越 *kashiko(shi)* overdraft; outstanding account
間 *kashima* room for rent
¹³賃 *ka(shi)chin* rent, hire

買 A ⟨5793 / J4763 / M36708⟩ BAI buying. *ka(u)* buy, invest in; incur; appreciate; call in (geisha). *ka(i)* buying.
²入 *ka(i)-i(reru)* purchase, lay in
⁴手 *kaite* buyer
方 *ka(i)kata* purchaser; way to buy
込 *ka(i)-ko(mu)* purchase, buy up
⁵付 *kaitsu(ke)* buying
収 *baishū* buying up, purchasing
占 *ka(i)-shi(meru)* buy up, corner (the market)
⁷言葉 *ka(i) kotoba* a sharp response to a cutting remark
⁸物 *kaimono* purchase; shopping; bargain
¹⁰値 *kaine* cost price
掛金 *ka(i)ga(ke)kin* debt, accounts payable
¹³置 *ka(i)o(ki)* hoarding

貴 A ⟨5794 / J352e / M36704⟩ KI. *tōto(bu), tatto(bu), tōto(mu), tatto(mu)* value, prize, esteem; respect, honor, revere. *tōto(i), tatto(i)* valuable, precious; noble, exalted, venerable. *ki-* your.
²人 *kijin* noble, nobleman, man of rank, dignitary; the nobility
³下 *kika* you
⁴方 *anata, anta, kihō* you
公子 *kikōshi* young noble
⁵兄 *kikei* you
⁷社 *kisha* your company
⁸金属 *kikinzoku* precious metals
国 *kikoku* your country
⁹重 *kichō na* precious, priceless
重品 *kichōhin* valuables; treasure
¹¹婦人 *kifujin* lady. *kifujin(rashii)* ladylike
族 *kizoku* nobility
¹³殿 *kiden* you (at present a term of ridicule)

7

見角言谷豆豕豕豸【貝】赤走足身車辛辰辵邑阝酉釆里

5

¹⁴ 様 *kisama* you (vulgar)
¹⁵ 賓 *kihin* a noble visitor
賓席 *kihinseki* distinguished visitors' gallery
¹⁶ 翰 *kikan* your letter
¹⁸ 顕 *kiken* men of distinction, dignitaries
簡 *kikan* your letter

--------- 6 ---------

賤 | 5796 / J4128 / M-X | Nonstandard for 賤

賂 | 5799 / J4f28 / M36738 | RO. *mainai* bribe.

賄 | B | 5800 / J4f45 / M36745 | WAI. KAI. *makana(u)* board; supply; finance. *makana(i)* board, meals; catering, feeding.
¹³ 賂 *wairo* bribe, bribery

賊 | B | 5801 / J4231 / M36759 | ZOKU rebel; traitor; robber. *zoku(suru)* injure, kill.
⁹ 軍 *zokugun* insurgents, rebel army
¹⁰ 徒 *zokuto* rebels, traitors

賃 | A | 5802 / J4442 / M36743 | CHIN hire, rent, wages; fare, freight, charge, fee.
³ 上 *chin'a(ge)* wage increase
⁵ 仕事 *chinshigoto* piecework
⁷ 労働 *chinrōdō* working for wages
⁸ 金 *chingin* wages, pay. *chinkin* wages; fare; (freight) rates
¹⁰ 借 *chinshaku, chinga(ri)* hiring, renting, leasing, hire
¹² 貸 *chintai, chingashi* lease, hire

資 | A | 5803 / J3b71 / M36750 | SHI resources, capital, funds; materials; data; quality, disposition; help. *shi(suru)* be conducive to, contribute to, assist.
² 力 *shiryoku* means, resources, funds
⁵ 本 *shihon* capital; fund
本主義 *shihon shugi* capitalism
本金 *shihonkin* capital, capital stock
⁷ 材 *shizai* materials, supplies
⁸ 金 *shikin* fund, capital
¹⁰ 料 *shiryō* materials, data
財 *shizai* property, means, assets
格 *shikaku* qualifications, requirements, capabilities

¹¹ 産 *shisan* property, means, assets
¹³ 源 *shigen* resources
¹⁵ 質 *shishitsu* nature, disposition

--------- 7 ---------

賑 | 5806 / J4678 / M36785 | SHIN. *nigi(wau)* flourish, be bustling. *nigi(wai)* prosperity, bustle, crowd. *nigi(washii), nigi(yakana)* lively, gay, cheerful; bustling, populous; noisy; prosperous.

--------- 8 ---------

賓 See 1365.

賭 | 5807 / J4552 / M-X | See 賭 5819.

賠 | B | 5810 / J4765 / M36818 | BAI indemnify.
¹⁷ 償 *baishō* reparation, indemnity, compensation

賦 | B | 5811 / J496a / M36800 | FU ode, prose poem; poetical prose; tribute; exacted service; installment. *fu(suru)* compose, write; allot.
³ 与 *fuyo suru* give
⁷ 役 *fueki* forced labor; exacted service
¹⁵ 課 *fuka* tax, levy, assessment

賜 | B | 5812 / J3b72 / M36809 | SHI. *tama(waru), tamo(u), tama(u)* deign to, grant, give, bestow on, honor with. *tamamono* gift, boon; results.
⁸ 杯 *shihai* trophy from the imperial family

賤 | 5813 / J6c4d / M36826 賤 | 5796 / J4128 / M-X | SEN. *iya(shimu)* despise. *iya(shii)* humble; base, mean, vile, vulgar; greedy. *shizu* low-rank person; poverty.
⁵ 民 *semmin* the lowly, the poor, the outcasts, serfs, peasants
¹³ 業 *sengyō* mean occupation; shameful calling

賛 | A | 5814 / J3b3f / M36841 | SAN praise; title or brief inscription on a picture;

agreement. *san(su)* assist, agree with, support; praise.

⁶ 同 *sandō* approval, endorsement

成 *sansei* approval, agreement, support, favor

⁷ 助 *sanjo* support, backing, approval

否 *sampi* approval or disapproval, yes and no, for and against

⁹ 美 *sambi* praise, adoration

美歌 *sambika* hymn

¹³ 嘆 *santan* praise, admiration

辞 *sanji* eulogy, compliment

意 *san'i* approval

¹⁴ 歌 *sanka* praise, admiration

賞 A 5815 / J3e5e / M36813 SHŌ prize, reward; praise. *shō(suru)*, *home(ru)* praise, commend, admire, enjoy (beauty). *me(deru)* love; appreciate.

³ 与 *shōyo* reward, prize, bonus

⁷ 状 *shōjō* honorable mention, certificate of merit

⁸ 金 *shōkin* prize, monetary reward

味 *shōmi* relish, gusto, appreciation

⁹ 品 *shōhin* (nonmonetary) prize

美 *shōbi* praise, admiration

¹⁴ 罰 *shōbatsu* rewards and punishments; praise and blame; justice

¹⁵ 賛 *shōsan* praise, admiration, commendation

²² 讃 *shōsan* praise, admiration, commendation

賢 B 5816 / J382d / M36822 KEN wisdom, cleverness. *kashiko(i)* wise, intelligent. *saka(shirana)* pert, impertinent. *saka(shii)* clever, bright, intelligent, wise.

² 人 *kenjin* wise man

⁴ 夫人 *kempujin* wise lady

⁸ 明 *kemmei* wisdom, intelligence, advisability, prudence

者 *kenja* wise man

¹² 策 *kensaku* wise policy

¹⁴ 察 *kensatsu* your discernment, judgment, understanding, or sympathy

---

質 A 5817 / J3c41 / M36803 SHITSU substance, matter, quality, temperament. SHICHI hostage, pawn, pledge, hock. *tada(su)* ask, demand, question; investigate, ascertain, verify. *tachi* nature (of a person); quality.

² 入 *shichii(re)* pawning

⁶ 朴 *shitsuboku* simplicity

⁸ 店 *shichiten* pawnshop

的 *shitsuteki* qualitative

実 *shitsujitsu* plainness, simplicity

実剛健 *shitsujitsu-gōken* frugal and courageous

⁹ 屋 *shichiya* pawnshop

¹⁰ 素 *shisso* simplicity, modesty, frugality

¹¹ 問 *shitsumon* question; interrogation

¹² 量 *shitsuryō* mass (in physics)

¹⁴ 疑 *shitsugi* question, inquiry, interpellation

疑応答 *shitsugi-ōtō* questions and answers

--- **9** ---

賭 5819 / J-X / M36847 **賭** 5807 / J4552 / M-X TO gambling. *to(suru)* wager, bet; risk, stake, hazard. *ka(keru)* wager, place a bet. *kake* a bet, wager, gambling.

⁸ 金 *kakekin* stakes, bet

¹² 場 *toba* gambling place

博 *tobaku* gambling

--- **10** ---

購 B 5823 / J3958 / M36885 KŌ. *agana(u)* buy.

² 入 *kōnyū* purchase, buying

¹² 買 *kōbai* purchasing

買部 *kōbaibu* shopping service

¹⁴ 読 *kōdoku* subscription

読者 *kōdokusha* subscriber

--- **11** ---

贈 B 5827 / J4223 / M36920 ZŌ, SŌ presenting (something). *oku(ru)* send, give to, award to, confer on.

³ 与 *zōyo* donation, presentation

与税 *zōyozei* gift tax

⁵ 収賄 *zōshūwai* corruption, bribery

呈 *zōtei* presentation

⁸ 物 *oku(ri)mono* present, gift

¹² 答 *zōtō* exchange of presents

¹³ 賄 *zōwai* bribery, corruption, graft

見角言谷豆豕豸貝【赤】走足身車辛辰疋辵邑阝酉釆里

12

贋 5830 / J3466 / M36993 GAN counterfeit. *nise* sham, counterfeit, forgery, imitation, false (prophet). *ni(seru)* copy, imitate, counterfeit, forge.

[7] 作 *gansaku* sham, counterfeit
[8] 物 *nisemono, gambutsu* imitation, forgery, counterfeit, sham
[9] 造 *ganzō* counterfeiting, forgery, fabrication

RAD. 赤 155

Aka red. Nickname: Red.

A 赤 5840 / J4056 / M36993 SEKI. SHAKU. *aka, aka(i)* red, crimson, scarlet. *aka* Communist, Red. *aka(bamu)* redden, color up, blush. *aka(ramu)* become red. *aka(rameru), aka(meru), aka(mu)* blush, redden. *aka(chan)* baby. *aka-* complete, entirely.

[2] 十字 *sekijūji* red cross; Red Cross
[3] 子 *akago* baby. *sekishi* baby; subjects
[4] 心 *sekishin* sincerity, true heart
  毛 *akage* red hair
  札 *akafuda* goods sold; clearance goods
  他人 *aka (no) tanin* strangers
  外線 *sekigaisen* infrared rays
[6] 肌 *akahada* plucked (chicken) skin; abraded skin; nakedness; bareness
  字 *akaji* red figures, deficit
  血球 *sekkekkyū* red corpuscle
[7] 坊 *aka(m)bō, aka(m)bo* baby
[9] 面 *sekimen* a blush, shamefacedness. *akatsura* red face
  信号 *aka shingō* red light, red danger signal
  茶色 *akacha iro* russet, reddish brown
[10] 恥 *akahaji* public disgrace, open shame
  剥 *akamu(ke)* skin abrasion

[11] 道 *sekidō* equator
  貧 *sekihin* extreme poverty
[12] 痢 *sekiri* dysentery
  帽 *akabō* redcap
  飯 *akameshi, sekihan* rice and red-bean dish
[13] 裸 *akahadaka* stark naked. *sekira* stark naked; open, frank
  裸裸 *sekirara* nakedness, nudity; frankness
[14] 銅色 *shakudō iro* brown color

4

B 赦 5841 / J3c4f / M36999 SHA forgiveness. *yuru(su)* permit, approve; authorize; acknowledge; confide in; forgive, pardon; release, acquit; overlook.

[8] 免 *shamen* pardon, amnesty, absolution, clemency

7

赫 5843 / J3352 / M37010 KAKU. *kat(to)* suddenly. *kagaya(kasu)* light up, brighten, illumine.

[14] 赫 *kakukaku, kakkaku(taru)* bright, brilliant, distinguished

---
RAD. 走 156

Hashiru to run. Variant: 走 *sōnyō* "running" enclosure. Nickname: Running.

A 走 5845 / J4176 / M37034 SŌ. *hashi(ru)* run, rush, flee; turn to; become; go to excess. *hashi(rakasu), hashi(raseru)* make (someone or something) run. *hashi(ri)* first of the season; first supplies.

⁸使 *hashi(ri)zuka(i)* errand boy, messenger

狗 *sōku* hunting dog; tool, cat's paw

者 *sōsha* (base) runner, (track) runner

⁹査 *sōsa* scanning (in TV)

¹⁰破 *sōha suru* run through

¹⁰書 *hashi(ri)ga(ki)* cursive writing, scrawl, hasty writing

¹³路 *sōro* race track, course; escapee's trail

— 2 —

赴 _{5847 / J496b / M37040} **FU.** *omomu(ku)* proceed to; get, become, tend toward.

B

⁶任 *funin suru* proceed to a new appointment. *funin* (new) appointment

任地 *funinchi* place of appointment

— 3 —

起 _{5849 / J352f / M37048} **KI.** *o(kiru)* get up, rise, awake; occur; (a fire) is kindled. *oko(su)* raise up, set up, pick up (someone); open, begin; promote, organize; generate; get sick; awaken; establish; plow; kindle (a fire). *oko(ru)* happen; break out; originate in; rise, flourish, spring up; be produced; have an attack of. *ta(tsu)* stand, rise; rouse oneself; be built, be established; go up (smoke); burn out; depart; take flight; run high (waves); stick into; be worked out; be maintained; save (face); establish oneself, begin life; spread (rumors); shut (doors); be active; open (markets); be excited; come (seasons); makes (a total of thirty). *ta(taseru)* make stand, set upright, raise, lift up; rouse (to activity). *oko(ri)* origin, source, beginning; cause.

A

³工 *kikō* breaking ground

⁵用 *kiyō* appointment, employment

立 *oko(ri)-ta(tsu)* rise up. *o(ki)-ta(tsu)* rise, get up. *kiritsu* rising, standing

⁶因 *kiin suru* originate in; be attributable to

伏 *kifuku* ups and downs, undulations; relief (map). *o(ki)fu(shi)* getting

around; rising and lying down; morning and evening, daily life

死回生 *kishi kaisei* revival, resuscitation; entering great happiness

⁷床 *kishō* getting up, rising

承転結 *kishō-tenketsu* rules for composing Chinese poetry

⁸居 *kikyo* state of health; daily life. *tachii* one's movement

⁹点 *kiten* starting point; terminus; home port

重機 *kijūki* crane, derrick

草 *kisō* drafting

¹⁰案 *kian suru* draft, draw up

¹¹動 *kidō* starting

¹²結 *kiketsu* beginning and end

訴 *kiso* prosecution, indictment, accusation, litigation

¹³債 *kisai* bond issue, loan flotation

源 *kigen* origin, beginning

業 *kigyō* starting a business, promotion of an enterprise

¹⁴算 *kisan* starting point in reckoning

¹⁹爆 *kibaku* priming (in explosives)

— 5 —

越 _{5851 / J315b / M37110} **OTSU. ETSU.** *ko(su)* cross; pass; spend; tide over; outrun; exceed; surpass; move; go; come. *ko(eru)* cross; go beyond; exceed; clear (an obstacle); overstep (authority). *ko(ezaru)* not more than (two months). *(o)ko(shi)* coming. *-go(shi)* over, across, long-standing, beyond.

B

⁵冬 *ettō* passing the winter

⁶年 *etsunen suru, otsunen suru* ring out the old year; tide over the year end; pass the winter, hibernate

¹⁴境 *ekkyō* border transgression

¹⁵権 *ekken no* unauthorized. *ekken, okken* arrogation, abuse of confidence, going beyond one's authority

超 _{5852 / J4436 / M37096} **CHŌ.** super-, ultra-. *ko(eru)* cross; go beyond; exceed; clear (an obstacle); overstep (authority).

B

²人 *chōjin* superhuman

人的 *chōjinteki* superhuman

7

⁹ 音波 *chōompa* supersonic waves
音速 *chōonsoku* supersonic speed
¹⁰ 党派 *chōtōha* bipartisanship
高速度 *chōkōsokudo* super high speed
特急 *chōtokkyū* super express
¹¹ 現実主義 *chōgenjitsu shugi* surrealism
過 *chōka* excess. *chōka suru* exceed
¹² 越 *chōetsu suru* be superior, excel, surpass, stand above, stand aloof. *chōetsu* superiority, excellence, pre-eminence, transcendency
短波 *chōtampa* ultrashort wave, ultrahigh frequency
然 *chōzen(taru)* transcendental, standing aloof, with a detached air
絶 *chōzetsu* transcendence; superiority, excellence

8

趣 $\frac{5854}{\substack{J3c71 \\ M37207}}$ SHU. *omomu(ku)* proceed to; become; tend toward. *omomuki* import, meaning, contents, tenor, gist; tone, touch, sentiment, charm; aspect, appearance.
⁶ 向 *shukō* plan, idea, device, plot
旨 *shushi* opinion, idea; meaning, gist, tenor; aim, motive, purpose ⌐hobby
⁸ 味 *shumi* taste, charm; zest, interest,
¹³ 意 *shui* opinion, idea; meaning, gist, tenor; aim, motive, purpose

---

10

趨 $\frac{5855}{\substack{J3I76 \\ M37258}}$ SŪ, SHU run; go; quick; tend towards.
¹³ 勢 *sūsei* trend, tendency

RAD. 足 157

Ashi leg, foot. At left: 𧾷 *ashi hen*. Nickname: Foot.

足 $\frac{5856}{\substack{J422d \\ M37365}}$ SOKU foot; leg; counter for pairs of footwear. *ashi* foot; leg; paw; flipper, tentacles, arms; walk, step, pace, speed; footing; draft (of a ship); foot (of a mountain); trace; deficit, shortage. *ashi, (o)ashi* money. *ta(ru), ta(riru)* be sufficient, suffice; serve; answer, will do (for something); be worth, deserve; be satisfied; qualify. *ta(su)* add to, add up; make up for; make good; supply, supplement. *ta(rinai), ta(ranai), ta(ranu), ta(razu)* be insufficient, lack; be missing; be unworthy, be not worth it; be beneath notice; dull, stupid. *ta(rinasa)* insufficiency, shortcomings. *ta(shi)* complement, supplement; making up; supply; help. *-soku* pair (a counter).
³ 下 *ashimoto* gait, pace, step. *ashimoto ni, sokka ni* at one's feet. *sokka* you (familiar and polite)
⁴ 止 *ashido(me)* confinement; inducement
手纏 *ashitemato(i), ashidemato(i)* encumbrance, hindrance, impediment
⁵ 代 *ashidai* traveling expenses
⁶ 早 *ashibaya* quick, swift-footed

並 *ashina(mi)* pace, step
⁹ 音 *ashioto* sound of footsteps
首 *ashikubi* ankle
拵 *ashigoshira(e)* footgear
枷 *ashigase, ashi kase* fetters, shackles, irons, hobbles
¹⁰ 弱 *ashiyowa* poor walker
¹¹ 掛 *ashiga(kari)* scaffolding; foothold; clue. *ashika(ke)* footing, foothold; pedal, footboard; step; going on (about so many years)
袋 *tabi* foot gloves, Japanese socks, tabi
¹² 場 *ashiba* scaffold; footing, foothold; situation
軽 *ashigaru* footman, foot soldier; lowest samurai ⌐flounder
¹³ 搔 *aga(ku)* paw, struggle, wriggle,
溜 *ashidamari* stand, foothold, footing; stopping place; center of activity
腰 *ashikoshi* legs and loins
跡 *ashiato, sokuseki* footprint
馴 *ashina(rashi)* walking practice
¹⁵ 踏 *ashibu(mi), ashifu(mi)* stepping, stamping; step; stalemate, marking time; treadle machine

7

¹⁶ 繁 *ashishige(ku)* frequently
¹⁹ 蹴 *ashige* kicking

──────── 4 ────────

B 距 5866 J3577 M37481 KYO. *heda(taru)* be distant.
¹⁹ 離 *kyori* distance, range, interval; gap

──────── 6 ────────

B 跨 5872 J3859 M37504 KO. KA. *mataga(ru)* be, sit, or stand astride; extend over; be laid across. *mata(gu)* straddle, bestride.

B 践 5873 J4129 M37547 SEN. *fu(mu)* step on, trample on, stamp on; carry through, practice; appraise; set foot on; evade payment.
¹⁰ 祚 *senso* accession to the throne

B 跡 5875 J4057 M37493 SEKI. *ato* mark, print, impression; trace, track, trail; wake; marks, traces, evidence; scar; ruins, precedent.
⁴ 片付 *atokatazu(ke)* cleaning up, putting things in order
⁵ 目 *atome* heir, successor
⁷ 形 *atokata* traces, marks, vestiges, evidence
　形無 *atokatana(i)* no traces
⁸ 取 *atoto(ri)* heir, successor
　始末 *atoshimatsu* settlement, liquidation, clearing up
¹³ 継 *atotsu(gi)* heir, successor

A 路 5876 J4129 M37524 RO road, route, path. *-ji* route, road; distance. *michi* road, path, lane, way, street, highway, route; journey; distance; course, way, means; duty, morality, moral doctrine; teachings; specialty; an art; reason, justice.
³ 上 *rojō* on the road; road
⁵ 用 *royō* traveling expenses
⁶ 地 *roji* alley, lane, garden path
⁹ 面 *romen* road surface
¹² 程 *rotei* distance, mileage
　傍 *robō* roadside, wayside
¹⁵ 線 *rosen* route, way
　盤 *roban* roadbed
¹⁶ 頭 *rotō* wayside, roadside

B 跳 5877 J4437 M37533 CHŌ. *ha(neru)* leap, spring up, hop; jerk, prance, buck; bound; spatter, splash; snap, crack, sputter; close, be over. *odo(ru)* dance; leap, skip; throb (the heart); act as a cat's-paw; double (the interest on a debt). *to(bu)* jump, leap, spring, bound, vault, hop. *ha(ne)* splashes (of mud).
³ 下 *tobio(ri)* jumping off a (moving vehicle)
⁴ 反 *ha(ne)-kae(ru)* vi rebound, recoil, bounce, spring back. *ha(ne)-kae(su)* vt kick back, throw off
¹² 越 *to(bi)-ko(eru)* jump over, fly over, fly across
²¹ 躍 *ha(ne)-odo(ru)* prance around. *chōyaku suru* jump, leap, skip, bounce, spring

──────── 7 ────────

B 踊 5882 J4d59 M37587 YŌ. *odo(ru)* dance; leap, skip; throb (the heart); act as a cat's-paw; double (the interest on a debt). *odo(ri)* dance; dancing; step.
³ 子 *odo(ri)ko* dancer, dancing girl
¹² 場 *odo(ri)ba* dance hall; stair landing

──────── 8 ────────

B 踏 5889 J4627 M37602 TŌ. *fu(mu)* step on, trample on, stamp on; carry through, practice; appraise; set foot on; evade payment. *fu(maeru)* step on, stand on.
² 入 *fu(mi)-i(reru), fu(mi)-i(ru)* walk in on, step in, tread upon
⁴ 止 *fu(mi)-todo(maru)* stand one's ground, hold one's own; stay in office. *fu(mi)-todo(meru)* bring oneself to a stop
　込 *fu(mi)-ko(mu), fu(n)go(mu)* step into; break into, raid
　切 *fu(mi)-ki(ru)* cross; push off (in jumping). *fungi(ru)* proceed with decision. *fumikiri* railway crossing
⁵ 石 *fu(mi)ishi* steppingstone
　付 *fu(mi)-tsu(keru), fu(n)-zu(keru)* step on and scatter, tread on, trample; spurn, despise, slight

7

見
角
言
谷
豆
家
豕
豸
貝
赤
走
足
【**身**】
車
辛
辰
辵
辶
邑
阝
酉
釆
里

台 *fu(mi)dai* footstool, step, steppingstone, springboard

外 *fu(mi)-hazu(su)* miss one's footing, make a false step

⁸迷 *fu(mi)-mayo(u)* lose the way, go astray

⁹段 *fu(mi)dan* step, stair, carriage step, footboard

査 *tōsa* survey, exploration, investigation

¹⁰破 *fu(mi)-yabu(ru)* walk across; travel on foot. *tōha suru* crush underfoot; travel on foot

¹¹張 *fu(m)ba(ru)* stretch (the legs); straddle; hold out, persist in; exert oneself

¹²越 *fu(mi)-ko(eru), fu(mi)-ko(su)* step over, step across

場 *fu(mi)ba* footing, place to step

絵 *fu(mi)e* crucifix plaque to be stepped on as evidence of faith

¹³跡 *fu(mi)ato* footprint

¹⁵潰 *fu(mi)-tsubu(su)* crush under foot

締 *fu(mi)-shi(meru)* step firmly, step cautiously

――――――― **9** ―――――――

蹄 5894 / J447d / M37724 TEI. *hizume* hoof.

⁷形 *teikei* U shape, horseshoe shape

¹³鉄 *teitetsu* horseshoe

――――――― **11** ―――――――

蹟 5905 / J4058 / M37814 SEKI, SHAKU remains (of something), footprint, traces.

――――――― **12** ―――――――

蹴 5913 / J3d33 / M37876 SHUKU. SHŪ. *ke(ru)* kick.

³上 *ke-aga(ru)* jump up. *ke-age(ru)* kick up. *kea(ge)* step riser

⁹飛 *ke-to(basu)* kick off; kick down; turn down

破 *ke-yabu(ru), ke(ri)-yabu(ru)* kick open

¹¹球 *shūkyū* football

¹²散 *ke-chi(rasu)* kick around, rout

落 *ke-oto(su)* kick down; kick overboard

――――――― **14** ―――――――

B 躍 5921 / J4c76 / M37955¹ YAKU. *odo(ru)* dance; leap, skip; throb (the heart); act as a cat's-paw; double (the interest on a debt).

³上 *odo(ri)-a(geru)* jump up, dance for joy

¹⁰起 *yakki* excitement; jumping up and down; desperation; enthusiasm, zeal

進 *yakushin* rush, dash; onslaught; prancing, dancing ahead

¹¹動 *yakudō suru* move lively

■■■■■■■■■■■■■■ RAD. **身** 158 ■■■■■■■■■■■■■■

Mi body. At left: *mi hen*. Nickname: Body.

A 身 5928 / J3f48 / M38034 SHIN. *mi, karada* body; person; the quick; one's station in life; self; heart, soul, mind; ability; flesh, meat; life; blade; container; garment width. *mi(jirogu)* stir (oneself) slightly. *mi(gonashi)* deportment.

³上 *shinjō* merit; body; one's fortune, one's history; estate; social position. *shinshō* one's fortune, one's history; one's property; social position. *mi(no)ue* one's fortune, one's future, one's lot; one's history

上相談 *mi(no)ue sōdan* consultation about personal affairs

⁴心 *shinshin* body and mind

辺 *shimpen* one's person

内 *miuchi* one's whole body; relatives; friends, followers

支度 *mijitaku* dress, outfit (for a trip)

元 *mimoto* one's birth, identity, history, career; character

元保証 *mimoto hoshō* personal references

分 *mibun* status, social position, identity, birth, circumstances

分不相応 *mibun fusōō* beyond one's means

分証明書 *mibun shōmeisho* identification document

⁵代 *shindai* property, estate, wealth. *migawa(ri)* vicarious substitute. *mi(no)shiro* ransom money

代金 *mi(no)shirokin* ransom money

⁶近 *miji(ka) ni* near oneself

回品 *mi(no)mawa(ri)hin, mimawa(ri)hin* personal belongings

⁷売 *miu(ri)* selling oneself for a term of service

体検査 *shintai kensa* physical examination; searching a person

体障害者 *shintai shōgaisha* the physically handicapped, cripple

⁸長 *mitake, shinchō, mi (no) take* stature, height

命 *shimmei* the body and life; life

⁹柄 *migara* one's person

重 *miomo* pregnancy

持 *mimo(chi)* conduct, morals; pregnancy

¹⁰振 *miburu(i)* shivering, shuddering.

mibu(ri) gesture

粉 *mi (o) ko ni suru* work assiduously

窄 *misubora(shii)* shabby, poor, miserable

¹¹動 *miugo(ki)* moving around

寄 *miyo(ri)* a relative

¹²軽 *migaru na* light, agile

勝手 *migatte* selfishness, egotism

程 *mi(no)hodo* social standing

程知 *mi(no)hodo shi(razu)* not knowing one's place

¹³嗜 *midashina(mi)* care of personal appearance, grooming

¹⁴構 *migama(eru), migama(e) suru* stand ready, stand on guard

¹⁵震 *miburu(i)* shivering, trembling, shuddering

¹⁸繕 *mizukuro(i) suru* dress up

²²籠 *migomo(ru)* conceive, become pregnant; hide

4

躯 $\frac{5930}{\text{J366d}}$ Nonstandard for 軀 5935.
M-X

11

軀 $\frac{5935}{\text{J-X}}$ KU body. *mukuro, karada* body; corpse; tree with M38137 rotten heart.

■■■ RAD. **車** 159 ■■■

Kuruma vehicle. At left: *kuruma hen*. Nickname: Car.

A 車 $\frac{5939}{\text{J3c56}}$ SHA vehicle; a vehicle M38172 load. *kuruma* wheel; vehicle, carriage, wagon; cart, wheelbarrow; go-cart; jinricksha; van, automobile.

³上 *shajō* on the train, in the car

⁴止 *kurumado(me)* wheel block; railway buffer stop; Closed to Vehicles.

内 *shanai* inside the car

中 *shachū* in a vehicle

⁵外 *shagai* outside the car

台 *shadai* chassis

⁶両 *sharyō* vehicles, rolling stock

⁷体 *shatai* chassis, car body

¹⁰庫 *shako* carbarn, garage

馬 *shaba* horses and vehicles

¹¹道 *shadō* roadway, driveway

窓 *shasō* car window

¹²軸 *shajiku* axle

検 *shaken* vehicle inspection

掌 *shashō* conductor

¹⁵輪 *sharin* wheel

輛 *sharyō* heavy vehicles; rolling stock

7

見
角
言
谷
豆
豕
豸
貝
赤
走
足
身
【車】
2
辛
辰
辵
辶
邑
阝
酉
釆
里

軌 5941 / J3530 / M38176 B **KI** wheel track; railway; orbit; rut; rule; model; road; road; way of doing.

7 条 *kijō* rails
11 道 *kidō* railway, tramway; orbit; beaten track
12 間 *kikan* railway-track gauge
13 跡 *kiseki* wagon tracks

軍 5943 / J3733 / M38179 A **GUN** army, force, troops. *ikusa* war; battle; campaign; army.

2 人 *gunjin* soldier, member of the military
4 手 *gunte* army cotton gloves
5 功 *gunkō* meritorious war service
令 *gunrei* military command
用 *gun'yō* military use
6 団 *gundan* army corps
7 役 *gun'eki, gun'yaku* military service
医 *gun'i* military surgeon
8 門 *gummon* camp gate; a general (polite)
服 *gumpuku* military or naval uniform
制 *gunsei* military system military organization
法会議 *gumpō kaigi* court-martial
国主義 *gunkoku shugi* militarism
国色 *gunkokushoku* military character
事 *gunji* naval and military affairs; military
事裁判 *gunji saiban* court martial
9 律 *gunritsu* martial law; articles of war; military discipline; military law
政 *gunsei* military government
10 記 *gunki* war chronicle
配 *gumbai* stratagem, tactics; (ancient) military leader's fan; sumo umpire's fan
部 *gumbu* military authorities, army circles
11 略 *gunryaku* strategy, tactics
務 *gummu* military and naval affairs; military service
曹 *gunsō* sergeant
隊 *guntai* army, troops, corps
12 属 *gunzoku* civilian in military employ
港 *gunkō* naval port, naval station
装 *gunsō* soldier's equipment
備 *gumbi* armaments, military preparations

13 勢 *gunzei* military forces, host, troops
資金 *gunshikin* war funds; campaign
楽隊 *gungakutai* military or naval band
14 閥 *gumbatsu* army clique, militarist party
旗 *gunki* battle flag, colors, ensign
歌 *gunka* war song
需 *gunju* munitions, military stores
17 縮 *gunshuku* disarmament, limitation of arms
20 籍 *gunseki* military or naval register, muster roll
艦 *gunkan* warship, battleship

軒 5944 / J382e / M38187 B **KEN** house counter. *noki* eaves.

3 下 *nokishita* under the eaves
6 先 *nokisaki* edge of the eaves; house frontage
8 並 *nokinara(bi), nokina(mi)* row of houses
9 昂 *kenkō* climbing high; high spirits, full of energy

軟 5947 / J4670 / M38213 B **NAN.** *yawaraka(i)* soft.

4 化 *nanka* softening, mollification; weakening (of a market)
水 *nansui* soft water
6 式野球 *nanshiki yakyū* softball
7 体動物 *nantai dōbutsu* mollusca
9 風 *nampū* gentle breeze, zephyr
派 *nampa* moderate party
10 骨 *nankotsu* cartilage, gristle
弱 *nanjaku* weakness, effeminacy
13 禁 *nankin* internment; house arrest
14 膏 *nankō* soft ointment

転 5948 / J453e / M38234 A **TEN** turn, remove, change. *ten(jiru), ten(zuru)* vt and vi revolve, rotate, turn around; turn, shift; alter, change; move, be transferred. *koro(bu), maro(bu)* fall down, tumble. *koro(geru), koro(garu)* roll over, tumble; lie down (on the lawn); be convulsed (with laughter). *koro(gasu), koro(basu), maro(basu), maro(bakasu)* knock down, roll over. *utata* more and more,

increasingly; somehow; indeed.

²入 *tennyū* transfer into, moving into. *maro(bi)-i(ru)* roll into

入学 *tennyūgaku* transferring from another school

⁴化 *tenka suru* change, be transformed

⁵用 *ten'yō suru* divert, convert

写 *tensha suru* transfer, transcribe, copy

出 *tenshutsu* transfer, moving out; transfer (of a ration record or church membership)

⁶回 *koro(bi)-mawa(ru)* wallow, welter, tumble about. *koro(ge)-mawa(ru)* tumble about; writhe. *tenkai* revolution, rotation

任 *tennin* change of post

向 *tenkō* turn, conversion, about-face

地 *tenchi* change of air, change of climate

⁷身 *tenshin* changing one's status or occupation

売 *tembai* resale

⁸居 *tenkyo* moving, changing quarters

送 *tensō suru* transmit; refer back (to a committee); translate (a cable); forward (mail)

⁹変 *tempen* mutation, change, vicissitude

¹⁰倒 *koro(bi)-tao(reru)* fall down. *tentō suru* turn over, turn upside down, fall down violently; invert; reverse

校 *tenkō* changing schools

記 *tenki* posting (in bookkeeping)

¹¹移 *ten'i* change, transition

訛 *tenka* corruption (of a word)

¹²属 *tenzoku suru* be transferred

勤 *tenkin suru* be transferred to another office

落 *maro(bashi)-o(tosu), koro(bashi)-o(tosu)* roll (something) down (a hill). *tenraku suru, koro(ge)-o(chiru)* fall off, tumble down

換 *tenkan suru* convert; divert, distract; reconvert; switch; transpose

¹³嫁 *tenka* blame another for one's mistake

戦 *tensen suru* take part in various battles, fight here and there

置 *tenchi suru* transpose, displace, dislocate

業 *tengyō suru* change one's employment

載 *tensai* reproduction, reprinting in another publication

¹⁵調 *tenchō* changing the key in the midst of a musical piece

¹⁶機 *tenki* turning point

¹⁸覆 *tempuku* overthrow, overturn; subvert; upset, capsize

職 *tenshoku* change of post; change of occupation

¹⁹轍機 *tentetsuki* railway switch

───────── 5 ─────────

B 軸 | 5952 / J3c34 / M38269 | JIKU axis; axle; spindle; shaft; pivot; stem, stalk; (pen) holder; scroll picture.

⁸受 *jikuu(ke)* bearing

A 軽 | 5953 / J375a / M38281 | KEI. *karu(i), karo(i)* light; trifling, unimportant; simple, easy; plain or light (meal); undignified. *karo(njiru), karo(nzuru)* slight, make light of; neglect; belittle; underrate; pay no attention to. *karu(ku) suru* lighten, relieve. *karu(yakana)* light, easy. *kei-* light.

³口 *karukuchi, karuguchi* joke; talkativeness

工業 *keikōgyō* light industry

⁴水炉 *keisuiro* light water reactor

⁵石 *karuishi* pumice stone

犯罪 *keihanzai* minor offense

⁶合金 *keigōkin* light alloy

自動車 *keijidōsha* a light car

⁷快 *keikai* nimbleness; lighteartedness; convalescence

⁸侮 *keibu* contempt, scorn

油 *keiyu* light fuel oil

易 *keii* easy, light, simple

佻浮薄 *keichō-fuhaku* irresponsibility; frivolity

⁹食 *keishoku* light meal

重 *keijū, keichō* relative importance; relative seriousness; relative weight

便 *keiben* convenience, simplicity

¹⁰症 *keishō* minor illness

挙妄動 *keikyo-mōdō* rash behavior

¹¹視 *keishi suru* despise, slight, ignore, neglect

率 *keisotsu* rashness, hastiness

¹²減 *keigen* reduction, alleviation, commutation

見角言谷豆豕豸貝赤走足身【車】辛辰辷辶邑阝酉釆里

7

5

見角言谷豆家豕豸貝赤走足身【車】辛辰辵辶邑阝酉釆里

5

7 軽 *karugaru(shii)* indiscreet, thoughtless, careless; frivolous. *karugaru to* easily. *keikei ni* carelessly, rashly

装 *keisō* lightweight equipment; lightweight dress

量 *keiryō* light weight

13 傷 *keishō* minor injury

微 *keibi na* insignificant, minor, slight, light (illness)

業 *karuwaza* acrobatics; risky undertaking

14 蔑 *keibetsu* contempt, slight, scorn

16 薄 *keihaku* insincerity; untruthfulness; frivolity; inconstancy; flattery

--- 6 ---

B 較 | 5959 J3353 M38297 | KAKU. KŌ. *kura(beru)* compare, balance, contrast. contrast.

B 載 | 5960 J3a5c M38309 | SAI. *no(ru)* ride, board, mount; get up on; spread (paints); be taken in; share in, join; be found in (a dictionary); feel like doing; be mentioned in; be in harmony with. *no(seru)* place, put, lay, set; let (one) take part; impose on; record, mention

16 録 *sairoku suru* record

--- 7 ---

輔 | 5964 J4a65 M38342 | HO helping; helper. *tasu(keru)* help.

--- 8 ---

B 輩 | 5971 J475a M38398 | HAI fellow, people, companion; line. *tomogara, yakara* fellows, companions, set.

5 出 *haishutsu suru* (people with talent) appear successively; come crowding on

B 輝 | 5972 J3531 M38372 | KI. *kagaya(ku)* shine, sparkle, gleam, twinkle; brilliant, radiant, bright. *kagaya(kasu)* vt light up, brighten, illumine. *kagaya(ki)* brilliancy, radiance, splendor, glitter. *kagaya(kashii)* bright (future); brilliant (achievement).

A 輪 | 5973 J4e58 M38400 | RIN ring, circle; wheel; corolla; wheel counter. *wa* circle, ring, link, wheel, hoop, loop.

4 切 *wagi(ri)* round slices

7 作 *rinsaku* crop rotation

9 廻 *rinne* transmigration

姦 *rinkan suru* rape by turns, gang rape

10 郭 *rinkaku* outlines, contours, profile, skyline; sketch, outline

11 唱 *rinshō* a round (in music)

転機 *rintenki* cylinder press; mimeograph

12 軸 *rinjiku* wheel and axle

番 *rimban* turn, rotation; executive committee chairman (of a Buddhist sect)

13 禍 *rinka* traffic accident

廓 *rinkaku* outlines, contours, profile, skyline; sketch, outline

14 読 *rindoku* reading by turns

舞 *rimbu* round dance

--- 9 ---

輯 | 5976 J3d34 M38420 | SHŪ gather, collect, compile.

A 輸 | 5978 J4d22 M38438' | YU send, transport. *yu(suru)* be inferior to.

5 出 *yushutsu* exports; exportation

出入 *yushutsunyū* exporting and importing

6 血 *yuketsu* blood transfusion

8 送 *yusō* transportation

--- 10 ---

B 轄 | 5981 J336d M38482' | KATSU. *kusabi* wedge.

輿 | 5983 J4d41 M38468 | YO. *kago, koshi* palanquin; bier.

11 望 *yobō* popularity, esteem, reputation; confidence

15 論 *yoron* public opinion

--- 12 ---

轍 | 5988 J4532 M38524 | TETSU *wadachi* rut, wheel track.

¹⁵ 踏 *tetsu (o) fu(mu)* follow the footsteps of one's predecessor

report

然 *gōzen(taru)* roaring, deafening, thunderous

───── **14** ─────

轟 ⁵⁹⁹¹ J396c M38577 Gō. *todoro(ku)* roar, thunder, boom, resound, ring; become well-known; throb.
⁹ 音 *gōon* deafening roar, loud

───── **15** ─────

轡 ⁵⁹⁹² J3725 M38587 Hi. *kutsuwa* (horse's) bit.
⁶ 虫 *kutsuwa mushi* a noisy cricket

══════ **RAD. 辛 160** ══════

Karai bitter. Variant: 牟. Nickname: Bitter.

辛 ⁵⁹⁹⁶ J3f49 M38630 B SHIN H, eighth. *kara(i)* hot, acrid, sharp; salty; bitter, trying; harsh, severe. *kara(kumo), karō(jite)* barely. *tsura(i)* painful, trying, bitter, cruel. *kanoto* eighth calendar sign.
³ 口 *karakuchi* salty tooth; dry (saké); bitterness, acrimony
⁶ 気臭 *shinkikusa(i)* feeling depressed, having the blues
⁷ 労 *shinrō* hardship, toil, trouble
⁸ 抱 *shimbō* patience, perseverance, endurance
苦 *shinku* hardship, toil, trouble
味 *karami* salty, hot, or sharp taste
¹⁰ 党 *karatō* drinker
¹² 勝 *shinshō* narrow victory
¹⁴ 辣 *shinratsu na* bitter, sharp, acrimonious
酸 *shinsan* hardships, privations

───── **6** ─────

辞 ⁶⁰⁰⁰ J3c2d M38638 A JI word, term, expression; sentence; an address.

ji(suru) resign, leave, decline. *ya(meru)* resign. *ina(mu)* refuse, decline; deny.
⁵ 令 *jirei* written appointment, government order; commission; wording
去 *jikyo suru* leave, quit, retire
世 *jisei* passing away; last words; deathbed poem
⁶ 任 *jinin* resignation
⁸ 退 *jitai* refusal, declining
典 *jiten* dictionary
表 *jihyō* written resignation
¹⁰ 書 *jisho* dictionary, glossary
¹⁸ 職 *jishoku* resignation

───── **9** ─────

辨 ⁶⁰⁰² J517e M38657   辧 ⁶⁰⁰³ J5221 M38656 See 弁 1665.

───── **14** ─────

辯 ⁶⁰⁰⁵ J6d67 M38677 See 弁 1666.

══════ **RAD. 辰 161** ══════

Tatsu dragon or, commonly, *shin no tatsu* (the character for "dragon" that is also read *shin*, as distinguished from Rad. 212).

辰 ⁶⁰⁰⁶ J4324 M38682 SHIN. *tatsu* 7-9 a.m.; fifth zodiac sign; dragon.

辱 ⁶⁰⁰⁷ J3f2b M38686 B JOKU. *hazuka(shimeru)* humiliate, put to shame, disgrace, insult; rape, assault. *katajikena(i)* thankful, indebted. *haji* shame, dishonor, disgrace, humiliation, insult.

───── **3** ─────

7

見
角
言
谷
豆
豕
豸
貝
赤
走
足
身
車
辛
辰
【辵辶】
邑阝
酉
釆
里

—————— **6** ——————

農 6008 J4740 M38688 **B** Nō agriculture; farmers.
⁴夫 *nōfu* farmer, farmhand
水省 *Nōrinshō* Ministry of Agriculture, Forestry, and Fisheries
⁵民 *nōmin* peasants, farmers
⁶地 *nōchi* farmland
地改革 *nōchi kaikaku* agrarian reform
⁷作 *nōsaku* land cultivation
作物 *nōsakubutsu* crops, farm produce
村 *nōson* farm village, rural community, agricultural district
芸 *nōgei* agricultural technology
⁸協 *nōkyō* agricultural cooperative
具 *nōgu* farm implements
事 *nōji* agriculture
林 *nōrin* agriculture and forestry

⁹相 *Nōshō* Minister of Agriculture, Forestry, and Fisheries
科 *nōka* agriculture department; agricultural course
政 *nōsei* agricultural administration
¹⁰家 *nōka* farmhouse; farmers
耕 *nōkō* farming; farm labor
¹¹道 *nōdō* agricultural road
婦 *nōfu* woman farmer
産 *nōsan* agricultural products
産物 *nōsambutsu* agricultural products
¹²場 *nōjō* farm, ranch, plantation
閑期 *nōkanki* farmers' slack season
¹³園 *nōen* farm, plantation
業 *nōgyō* agriculture
¹⁶機具 *nōkigu* farm equipment
薬品 *nōyakuhin* agricultural chemicals
繁期 *nōhanki* the farmers' busy season

■■■■ **RAD.** 辵 **162** ■■■■

Always used as an enclosure in the modified form 辶 (2 strokes) or 辶 (3 strokes).
Shinnyū "advancing" enclosure (like that of *shin, susumu* "to advance").
Nickname: Road (as in 道 *michi* road).

—————— **2** ——————

込 6010 J397e M38712 **B** (国字) *ko(mu)* be crowded; requiring (a lot of work). *ko(meru)* include; load (a gun); concentrate on; devote oneself to. -*ko(mu)* (get) into, (slip) into, (fall) into. *ko(mi)* mixture; a line of plants. -*ko(mi) de* in bulk; included.
²入 *ko(mi)-i(ru)* be complicated
³上 *ko(mi)-a(geru)* feel nauseated, feel like vomiting; be filled (with anger)

辺 6011 J4a55 M38710' **A** Hen side; boundary, border; beach; region, district, rural areas; vicinity; approximation. *ata(ri), hoto(ri), he* vicinity. -*be* vicinity.
⁶地 *henchi* remote place
¹³鄙 *hempi na* remote, secluded
¹⁴境 *henkyō* frontier, remote region

辻 6012 J4454 M38711 (国字) *tsuji* crossroad, street crossing, street corners; streets; roadside.
¹³褄 *tsujitsuma* consistency, coherence, reasonableness

—————— **3** ——————

迄 6013 J4b78 M38724 Kitsu. *made* to, till, until, up to; as far as; to the extent of; limited to. *made ni* by, before, not later than.

迅 6014 J3f57 M38727' **B** Jin. *haya(i)* fast.
⁹速 *jinsoku* swiftness, promptness

迪 6015 J4329 M38718 Ten. *tado(ru)* follow (a road), pursue (a course), follow up.

迂 6016 J312a M38722 U roundabout way.
⁶回 *ukai* detour, roundabout way
¹²遠 *uen na* roundabout; devious; circumlocutory

¹⁷ 闊 *ukatsu* carelessness, stupidity

------- **4** -------

B 迎 _{6019 / J375e / M38748'} GEI. *muka(eru)* meet, greet, welcome; invite, engage. *muka(e)* meeting; person sent to meet.

² 入 *muka(e)-i(reru)* usher in, welcome
⁵ 打 *muka(e) u(tsu)* await and attack an approaching enemy
⁶ 合 *geigō* flattery, ingratiation
⁹ 春 *geishun* welcoming the new year
¹⁰ 酒 *muka(e)zake* drinking again (the next day), hair of the dog
¹⁵ 賓 *geihin* welcoming guests
賓館 *geihinkan* reception hall

A 返 _{6020 / J4a56 / M38758'} HEN answer. *kae(ru)* go back; return to former employer; (colors) fade. *kae(su)* return, give back; repay; put back; overturn; requite (favors); take vengeance; turn around; answer; regurgitate. *kae(shi)* return gift; (money) change; return poem; answer; change of scene. *(o)kae(shi)* return; reply.

³ 上 *henjō suru* send back, return, resign
⁵ 礼 *henrei* return gift
⁷ 却 *henkyaku* return, repayment
⁸ 金 *henkin* repayment
送 *hensō suru* send back, return
事 *henji* reply
⁹ 咲 *kae(ri)za(ku)* bloom a second time. *kae(ri)za(ki)* second bloom; a comeback (in business)
品 *hempin* returned goods
信 *henshin* reply
¹¹ 済 *hensai* payment, refunding, redemption, repayment
¹² 答 *hentō* reply
¹³ 辞 *henji* reply
¹⁵ 還 *henkan* return, restoration, repayment

A 近 _{6021 / J3661 / M38752'} KIN. *chika(i)* early, immediate; near, short (road), close by; akin to; nearby, bordering on, verge of, tantamount to; intimate, friendly. *chika(zuku)* approach, get acquainted with, associate with. *chika(zukeru)* allow to approach, associate with. *chika(zuki)* acquaintance, friendship. *chika(ku)* before long; nearby, neighborhood, vicinity; approximately. *chika(shii)* intimate, friendly.

⁴ 辺 *kimpen* neighborhood, vicinity
日 *kinjitsu* soon, in a few days
⁵ 刊 *kinkan* recent issue; forthcoming book
世 *kinsei* recent times
代 *kindai* modern times
代化 *kindaika* modernization
⁶ 回 *chikamawa(ri)* neighborhood, vicinity; shortcut
因 *kin'in* immediate cause
在 *kinzai* neighboring villages, suburban districts
似 *kinji* approximation; very similar
⁷ 来 *kinrai* recently
⁸ 況 *kinkyō* recent condition
郊 *kinkō* suburbs
東 *Kintō* Near East
所 *kinjo* neighborhood, vicinity
⁹ 海 *kinkai* coastal waters, adjacent seas
¹⁰ 時 *kinji* recently
¹¹ 道 *chikamichi* short cut
頃 *chikagoro* recently, nowadays
接 *kinsetsu* neighboring, adjacent
寄 *chikayo(ru)* approach. *chikayo(seru)* allow to approach, associate with
距離 *kinkyori* short distance, close range
視 *kinshi* nearsightedness, shortsightedness
眼 *chikame, kingan* nearsightedness, shortsightedness
眼鏡 *kingankyō* glasses for the nearsighted
¹² 傍 *kimbō* vicinity, neighborhood, environs
着 *kinchaku* recent arrival
¹⁴ 隣 *kinrin* neighborhood, vicinity
¹⁵ 影 *kin'ei* recent portrait
畿 *Kinki* the Osaka-Kyoto area, the prefectures of Hyogo, Kyoto, Osaka, Mie, Nara, Shiga, and Wakayama
¹⁶ 衛 *konoe* imperial guards; bodyguards
親 *kinshin* near relative

------- **5** -------

迚 _{6022 / J4676 / M38793} See 邇 6122.

迦 _{6027 / J3260 / M38789} KA, KE (used phonetically).

見
角
言
谷
豆
豕
豸
貝
赤
走
足
身
車
辛
辰
[走
辶]
邑
阝
酉
釆
里

迭 _{6029 J4533 M38800'} TETSU alternation. **B**

述 _{6030 J3d52 M38803'} JUTSU state, speak, relate. *nobe(ru)* state, speak, recite, relate, mention. **A**

⁷ 作 *jutsusaku* writing a book, literary work
¹⁴ 語 *jutsugo* predicate
¹⁶ 懐 *jukkai* recollections, reminiscences; *shukkai* lament

迫 _{6031 J4777 M38797'} HAKU. *se(maru)* press for, urge, force, spur on; approach; gain on, close in on; be on the verge of; be imminent. *se(ru)* urge on. **B**

² 力 *hakuryoku* force; intensity; appeal
¹⁰ 真 *hakushin* truthfulness to life, verisimilitude
¹⁰ 害 *hakugai* oppression, persecution
¹⁵ 撃砲 *hakugekihō* mortar, mine thrower

───── **6** ─────

迷 _{6037 J4c42 M38825'} MEI. *mayo(u)* be perplexed, be in doubt, hesitate, vacillate, go astray, err; be tempted; be infatuated; be misguided. *mayo(wakasu), mayo(wasu)* perplex; mislead, deceive; tempt; seduce; charm, infatuate. *samayo(u)* wander around, stray, loiter. *mayo(i)* perplexity; doubt; ignorance; illusion, delusion, infatuation, skepticism. **A**

³ 子 *maigo, mayo(i)go* lost child
⁴ 込 *mayo(i)-ko(mu)* go astray, lose one's way
⁶ 妄 *meimō* illusion, fallacy, delusion
⁹ 信 *meishin* superstition
¹⁰ 宮 *meikyū* maze, labyrinth; mystery
¹¹ 彩 *meisai* camouflage
¹² 惑 *meiwaku* trouble, annoyance
¹³ 路 *meiro* maze, labyrinth, blind alley
夢 *meimu* illusion, fallacy, delusion
想 *meisō* fallacy

逃 _{6038 J4628 M38845'} TŌ. *nige(ru)* flee, run away, escape; shirk, evade, back out. *noga(su), niga(su)* let go, set free, let escape, miss (a chance). *noga(reru)* escape, avoid, evade, shirk. **B**

³ 口 *ni(ge)guchi* way of escape, loophole

口上 *ni(ge)kōjō* excuse, evasion, quibbling
亡 *tōbō* flight, escape, abscondence, desertion
⁴ 込 *ni(ge)-ko(mu)* run into, seek shelter
⁷ 足 *ni(ge)ashi* flight; preparation to flee
走 *ni(ge)-hashi(ru)* flee, run away. *tōsō* flight, desertion, escape
走者 *tōsōsha* fugitive, deserter
⁹ 後 *ni(ge)-oku(reru)* fail to escape
¹¹ 道 *ni(ge)michi* way of escape; way out (of a difficulty)
¹² 場 *ni(ge)ba* place of refuge; means of escape; exit. *noga(re)ba* refuge, shelter, asylum
¹³ 腰 *ni(ge)goshi* preparation to flee; evasive attitude
¹⁵ 避 *tōhi* escape, evasion, flight

送 _{6039 J4177 M38842'} SŌ sending. *oku(ru)* send, ship; transmit; remit; see off; see home, escort; spend (one's time), live (a life); add *okurigana* (*kana* showing inflection). **A**

⁴ 込 *oku(ri)-ko(mu)* see (someone) home; usher in. *oku(ri)ko(mi)* feeding (a machine)
⁵ 付 *sōfu* sending, forwarding, remitting
主 *oku(ri)nushi* sender
出 *oku(ri)-da(su)* forward, send out; see (a person) out, send away
⁶ 返 *oku(ri)-kae(su)* send back, repatriate
先 *oku(ri)saki* forwarding address, cosignee ⌈inflection
仮名 *oku(ri)gana* suffixed *kana* showing
迎 *sōgei, oku(ri)muka(e)* seeing (someone) off and meeting upon return
⁷ 状 *oku(ri)jō* invoice
呈 *sōtei* presentation
別 *sōbetsu* farewell, send-off
別会 *sōbetsukai* farewell party
⁸ 金 *sōkin* remittance; remitting
⁹ 風 *sōfū* air blast, forced draft, ventilation
信 *sōshin* transmission of a message
¹⁰ 料 *sōryō* postage, shipping cost
¹¹ 達 *sōtatsu* delivery, dispatch
¹² 検 *sōken* sending to the prosecutor
葬 *sōsō* funeral
¹³ 電 *sōden* transmission of electricity
話 *sōwa* transmission (of a telephone message)

¹⁵ 還 *sōkan* repatriation

A 退 _{6040 / J4260 / M38839'} TAI. *shirizo(ku), shisa(ru), shiza(ru), susa(ru)* retreat, withdraw; retire, resign. *shirizo(keru)* repel, drive away, expel; depose; keep away; reject, turn down. *no(ku)* get out of the way; go away. *no(keru), do(keru)* get rid of, remove; finish; omit, exclude. *hi(ku)* retreat, withdraw, retire; subside, abate, ebb. *do(ku)* get out of the way, move aside.

⁴ 化 *taika* degeneration, retrogression, depravation, atrophy
⁵ 去 *taikyo* evacuation, withdrawal, removal, exodus, departure
出 *taishutsu* leaving, withdrawal
⁶ 色 *taishoku* fading; faded color
行 *taiko* regression (in psychoanalysis)
任 *tainin* retirement from office
会 *taikai* withdrawal from membership
⁷ 却 *taikyaku* retreat, withdrawal
位 *taii* abdication
社 *taisha* retirement from a firm; leaving the office
役 *taieki* retirement from military service
⁸ 治 *taiji* subjugation; extermination; crusade (against); control
官 *taikan* retirement from office
歩 *taiho suru* retrograde, degenerate; deteriorate
学 *taigaku* dropping out of school
屈 *taikutsu* tedium, boredom
⁹ 院 *taiin* leaving the hospital
¹⁰ 席 *taiseki suru* leave one's seat; withdraw, retire
¹¹ 敗 *taihai* defeat
¹² 場 *taijō suru* leave, walk out, exit, withdraw
散 *taisan suru* disperse, break up (a crowd)
廃 *taihai* deterioration, degeneration, laxness, corruption, decadence, ruin
廃的 *taihaiteki* corrupt
¹³ 路 *tairo* path of retreat
勢 *taisei* downward tendency, decline, decay
¹⁴ 蔵 *taizō* hoarding
¹⁵ 避 *taihi* taking refuge, evacuation
潮 *taichō* ebb tide, low tide
¹⁷ 嬰的 *taieiteki* conservative, negative, passive, destructive

¹⁸ 職 *taishoku* retirement (from office)
職金 *taishokukin* retirement allowance

A 逆 _{6041 / J3555 / M38849'} GYAKU, GEKI reverse, inverse, opposite, unnatural; wicked; traitorous. *saka(rau)* oppose, act contrary to; offend. *gyaku ni* conversely, inversely, contrariwise, on the other hand, vice versa. *saka(sa), saka(sama), saka(shima)* reverse, inversion, upside down.

³ 上 *nobo(seru)* be dizzy, be feverish, get excited, be enthusiastic over. *gyakujō, nobose* rush of blood to the head, dizziness; madness; distraction
⁴ 心 *gyakushin* treachery, perfidy, treason
手 *gyakute* foul trick, dirty trick. *sakate ni* with point downward, (holding) upside down
比例 *gyakuhirei* inverse proportion
⁵ 立 *sakada(teru)* vt stand on end (hair), bristle up, ruffle up (feathers). *sakada(tsu)* vi stand on end, stand up, bristle up, oppose. *saka(rai)-ta(tsu)* rise against. *sakada(chi)* handstand, standing on one's head
⁶ 行 *gyakkō, gyakukō* retrogression, backward movement; countermarch
光 *gyakkō* backlighting (in photography)
⁷ 作用 *gyaku sayō* reaction, adverse effect
⁸ 効果 *gyakkōka, gyakukōka* reverse effect
⁹ 風 *gyakufū* adverse wind, head wind
¹⁰ 徒 *gyakuto* rebel, traitor, insurgent
¹¹ 転 *gyakuten* (sudden) change, reversal, retrogression; loop; reverse
¹³ 賊 *gyakuzoku* rebel, traitor, insurgent
¹⁴ 境 *gyakkyō* reverses, adversity, unfavorable circumstances
算 *gyakusan* counting backwards
説 *gyakusetsu* paradox
¹⁵ 撫 *sakana(de)* rubbing against the grain
¹⁶ 輸入 *gyaku yunyū* reimportation
²² 襲 *gyakushū* counterattack, sortie
²³ 鱗 *gekirin* imperial wrath

A 追 _{6042 / J4449 / M38836'} TSUI. *o(u)* drive away; chase; drive (cattle); follow, pursue (pleasure). *o(tte)* later on, soon after. *o(kkake)* meanwhile, presently. *o(i)-* follow-up. *-o(i)* herder.

見角言谷豆冢豕豸貝赤走足身申辛辰【走⻌】邑⻏酉釆里

見角言谷豆家豕貝赤走足身車辛辰〔辵・辶〕邑阝酉釆里

7

6

³ 及 *tsuikyū suru* gain on; overtake, carry out; solve (a crime)
⁴ 手 *otte, o(i)te* tail wind; pursuer
込 *o(i)-ko(mu)* corner, drive into; run on (a certain page-in printing); strike inward (a disease)
⁵ 立 *o(i)-ta(teru), o(t)ta(teru)* hurry off, urge on, drive away, evict
付 *o(i)-tsu(ku), o(t)tsu(ku)* overtake
打 *o(i)u(chi),* pursuit, attack
払 *o(p)para(u), o(i)-hara(u)* drive away, rout. *o(i)bara(i)* later payment
出 *o(i)-da(su)* expel, put out, eject, dismiss
加 *tsuika* addition, appendix, supplement
⁷ 尾 *tsuibi* pursuit
伸 *tsuishin* postscript
抜 *o(i)-nu(ku)* pass (a car), outdistance, outsail, outstrip
究 *tsuikyū* investigation, inquiry
求 *o(i)-moto(meru), tsuikyū suru* pursue; follow up, seek for
⁸ 送 *tsuisō suru* send promptly afterwards
突 *tsuitotsu* rear-end collision, bump
放 *o(i)-hana(tsu)* chase away. *tsuihō* exile, banishment, excommunication, deportation; purge
⁹ 風 *o(i)kaze, o(i)te* tail wind
¹⁰ 従 *tsuijū suru* follow; imitate; be servile to. *tsuishō* flattery
記 *tsuiki* postscript
随 *tsuizui suru* follow in the wake of
討 *tsuitō, o(i)u(chi)* subjugation, chastisement
¹¹ 掛 *o(i)-ka(keru), o(k)ka(keru)* chase, run after
悼 *tsuitō* mourning; memorial (address)
¹² 越 *o(i)-ko(su)* pass (a car), outdistance, outsail, outstrip
訴 *tsuiso* supplementary suit
¹³ 想 *tsuisō* recollection, reminiscence
試験 *tsuishiken* supplementary exam
跡 *tsuiseki* pursuit
¹⁴ 認 *tsuinin* ratification, confirmation
慕 *tsuibo suru* cherish the memory of, yearn for
徴 *tsuichō* additional collection, supplementary charge
¹⁵ 撃 *tsuigeki, o(i)u(chi)* pursuit, attack
¹⁶ 懐 *tsuikai* recollection, reminiscence
憶 *tsuioku* recollection, reminiscence

録 *tsuiroku* supplement, postscript, addendum
¹⁸ 贈 *tsuizō* posthumous conferment of court rank

——————— 7 ———————

逝 ⁶⁰⁵¹ / J4042 / M38895 SEI. *yu(ku)* die, pass away.
⁵ 去 *seikyo* death

逗 ⁶⁰⁵³ / J3160 / M38887 TŌ. stop.
¹⁰ 留 *tōryū* stay, sojourn

逢 ⁶⁰⁵⁴ / J3029 / M38901 HŌ. *a(u)* meet, interview. *a(waseru)* introduce, expose to, subject to.
⁴ 引 *aibi(ki)* date, rendezvous, clandestine courting
¹² 着 *hōchaku* face, encounter
¹⁹ 瀬 *ōse* meeting, tryst, date

逓 ⁶⁰⁵⁵ / J447e / M38881¹ TEI in turn; sending (parcels) in feudal time.
⁶ 伝 *teiden* relaying a message; the post horse; the post rider
⁸ 送 *teisō* forwarding
¹² 減 *teigen* successive diminution
¹⁴ 増 *teizō* gradual increase

逐 ⁶⁰⁵⁶ / J4360 / M38877¹ CHIKU. *o(u)* drive away; chase; drive (cattle); follow, pursue (pleasure). *to(geru)* accomplish, attain; commit (suicide).
¹ 一 *chikuichi* one by one, in detail, minutely
⁶ 次 *chikuji* one by one, point by point, in order, in succession, successively, gradually
年 *chikunen* annually, year by year
⁷ 条 *chikujō* section by section, point by point
¹³ 電 *chikuden* flight, abscondence
¹⁴ 語的 *chikugoteki* literal, word for word
語訳 *chikugoyaku* literal translation

途 ⁶⁰⁵⁷ / J4553 / M38882¹ TO, ZU way, road. *michi* road, path, lane, way, street, highway; route; journey; distance; course, way, means.

³ 上 *tojō* on the way; on the road
⁴ 切 *togi(reru)* break, pause, be interrupted
方 *tohō* way, destination, direction, reason
方暮 *tohō (ni) ku(reru)* be at one's wit's end
中 *tochū* on the way, enroute
⁶ 次 *toji* on the way
¹² 絶 *toda(eru)* cease, stop, end. *tozetsu* suspension, interruption
¹⁴ 端 *totan ni* in the act of, just as

這 ⁶⁰⁵⁸ J4767 M38889 SHA. *ha(u)* crawl, creep; grovel; trail (vines).
³ 上 *ha(i)-a(garu)* crawl up, climb up
⁵ 出 *ha(i)-de(ru), ha(i)-da(su)* crawl out
⁶ 回 *ha(i)-mawa(ru)* crawl about

B 透 ⁶⁰⁵⁹ J4587 M38876 TŌ. *tō(ru)* permeate, penetrate. *su(ku)* be transparent; be seen through; be thin; leave a gap. *su(kasu)* leave a space; thin (trees); make transparent; look through. *su(kashi)* watermark; openwork; transparent. *su(ki)* time; leisure; gap, crack; room space; chance; unpreparedness, unguarded moment. *su(kasazu)* at once, right away. *tō(su)* let (light) through, penetrate.
⁵ 写 *tōsha, su(ki)utsu(shi)* tracing, copy
⁸ 明 *tōmei* transparency
¹¹ 過 *tōka* permeability
視 *tōshi* seeing through; clairvoyance
視図 *tōshizu* cutaway view
視画 *tōshiga* perspective drawing
¹² 間 *su(ki)ma* crevice, gap, opening, space
¹⁵ 徹 *su(ki)-tō(ru)* be transparent, be clear, be seen through. *tōtetsu suru* penetrate, pierce, permeate; be transparent; prevail; penetrating; coherent. *tōtetsu(shita)* transparent, clear; pure

A 速 ⁶⁰⁶⁰ J422e M38897 SOKU. *haya(i),* *sumi(yakana)* speedy, prompt, swift. *haya(meru)* vt hasten, precipitate, accelerate, expedite; advance (the date).
² 力 *sokuryoku* speed, velocity, rate
⁶ 成 *sokusei* quick training, short course instruction ⌐course
⁸ 刻 *sokkoku* instantly, immediately
効 *sokkō* immediate effect

⁹ 度 *sokudo* speed, velocity, pace, rate; tempo (in music), time
¹⁰ 座 *sokuza* prompt, impromptu
記 *sokki* shorthand
¹¹ 断 *sokudan* prompt decision; hasty conclusion, snap judgment
達 *sokutatsu* special delivery
¹² 答 *sokutō* prompt answer
報 *sokuhō* urgent message
¹⁴ 読 *sokudoku* rapid reading

A 造 ⁶⁰⁶¹ J4224 M38898 ZŌ. *tsuku(ru)* make, create, manufacture, prepare, draw up, write, compose; build; coin; cultivate; organize, establish; make up (a face), trim (a tree); fabricate; prepare food; commit (sin). *tsuku(ri)* make, structure, construction; physique, build; workmanship; (a woman's) makeup; cultivation; a mounting. *-zuku(ri)* made of; work; architectural style.
⁴ 反 *zōhan* revolution
化 *zōka* creation, nature
⁵ 本 *zōhon* bookbinding
⁶ 成 *tsuku(ri)-na(su), zōsei* create
⁷ 花 *tsuku(ri)bana, zōka* artificial flower
形 *zōkei* modeling, molding
作 *zōsaku* making; house fixtures; facial features. *zōsa* trouble, difficulty
⁸ 林 *zōrin* forestation; reforestation
物主 *Zōbutsushu* Creator, Maker, God
物者 *Zōbutsusha* Creator, Maker, God
⁹ 型 *zōkei* modeling, molding
¹¹ 船 *zōsen* shipbuilding
¹² 営 *zōei* building, construction
¹³ 詣 *zōkei* scholarship, erudition
園 *zōen* landscape gardening
¹⁴ 語 *zōgo* coined word
¹⁵ 幣 *zōhei* minting, coinage
幣局 *zōheikyoku* the mint

A 連 ⁶⁰⁶² J4f22 M38902 REN. ream; set; party, company, gang, clique; series counter. *tsura(naru)* range, be connected with, join; stand in a row; attend; join one's people (in death). *tsura(neru)* put in a row, join. *tsu(reru)* take (someone) along. *tsu(re)* companion. *(ni) tsu(rete)* in proportion to; accompanied by; to the accompaniment of.
³ 山 *renzan* mountain range

7

見角言谷豆豕豸貝赤走足身車辛辰【辵⻌】邑⻏酉釆里

7 辵⻌

⁴日 *renjitsu* day after day, every day

中 *renchū, renjū* party, company, clique

⁵用 *ren'yō* continuous use

立 *tsu(re)da(tsu)* accompany. *renritsu* alliance, coalition, union

⁶行 *tsu(re)-yu(ku)* take (someone) along. *renkō suru* walk a suspect to the police

休 *renkyū* consecutive holidays

年 *rennen* every year; many years

名 *remmei* joint signature

邦 *rempō* federated states, union, commonwealth, federal state; federation

合 *tsu(re)-a(u)* keep company with, get married. *rengō* union, combination, federation, alliance. *tsure(ai)* spouse, mate

⁷戻 *tsu(re)-modo(su)* take back, bring back, lead back

判状 *rempanjō, rembanjō* jointly sealed compact

⁸夜 *ren'ya* night after night, nightly

呼 *renko* repeated calls

⁹係 *renkei* connection, liaison, contact

発 *rempatsu* occurring continually; running fire, volley

¹⁰座 *renza* implication, complicity; sitting in the same seat

破 *rempa* a succession of victories (in games)

帯 *rentai* joint responsibility, solidarity

¹¹敗 *rempai* successive defeats

動 *rendō* gearing, linkage, drive

累 *renrui* implication, involvement, complicity

隊 *rentai* regiment

¹²勝 *renshō* series of victories

絡 *renraku* connection, contact, liaison, communication

結 *renketsu* coupling, connection, joint; combination

¹³携 *renkei* cooperation, collaboration, association

続 *renzoku* continuation, succession, sequence, series

想 *rensō* association of ideas

盟 *remmei* league, federation, union

載 *rensai suru* publish serially

¹⁴関 *renkan* connection, relation, association

綿 *remmen(taru)* consecutive, continuous

歌 *renga* linked haiku poems

¹⁶濁 *rendaku* a euphonic change of an unvoiced to a voiced sound

¹⁸鎖 *rensa* chain, series, links

鎖反応 *rensa hannō* chain reaction

¹⁹覇 *rempa* successive championships

A 通 ⁶⁰⁶³ ᴶ⁴⁴⁴ᶜ ᴹ³⁸⁸⁹²ⁱ Tsū. Tō. Tsū pass; expert. *tsū(zuru), tsū(jiru)* pass, run; be opened (to traffic); prevail, pervade, transmit (electricity); be well versed in; be understood; become intimate with; communicate secretly with; send in (one's card). *tō(ru)* walk along, pass by; pass through; pass (exams); be known as; be admissible; come in; be understood; reach; draw (on a pipe); drain (as a sink); be consistent. *tō(su)* let (someone) pass; pass (something) through; make way for; let in, admit; usher in; cut through; pierce; permeate, penetrate; carry one's point; persist in; look over (a book); keep on doing, continue; pose as; pass (a law); order (a meal). *kayo(u)* commute; attend (school); ply between; frequent (a place); go (for treatments); circulate; breathe; be charged with. *kayo(wasu), kayo(waseru)* send (to school); charge (with electricity); circulate. *tsū(garu)* make a show of knowledge. *tō(risugari)* on the way. *tsū(jite)* through, via; throughout, all over; total, together with; in collusion with. *tō(shite)* through, through the medium of, through the good offices of; for (five days). *tō(shi)* consecutive (pages). *tō(tte)* via, by way of. *tsū(ji)* bowel evacuation, stool; effect. *tō(ri)* road, street, thoroughfare; street traffic; drainage; penetration (of a voice); kind; suite, set (of furniture); way, manner; reputation, favor; understanding; like, the same. *kayo(i)* daily attendance; living out; plying; a line, a run; bankbook; chit book. *tō(shi) de* straight through, without stopping. *(o)tō(shi) suru* usher in. *tō(shi)* hors d'oeuvre. *tō(shi)-* through (bill of lading). *-tsū* thorough knowledge of, authority on, expert judge, connoisseur; knowledge of the world; occult powers; part, copy; counter for cables, letters, or copies. *-dō(ri)* street; in accordance with; according to; just as, as. *-dō(shi)* all

through (the night); all the time.

⁴分 *tsūbun* reduction of fractions to common denominator

⁵用 *tsūyō* common use, circulation, currency

用口 *tsūyōguchi* service entrance, side door

⁶気 *tsūki* ventilation, draft, airing

行 *tō(ri)-yu(ku)* pass by. *tsūkō* passing, passage, transit, traffic

行人 *tsūkōnin* passerby, pedestrian, wayfarer

行止 *Tsūkōdo(me)* No Thoroughfare, road blocked

⁷抜 *tō(ri)-nu(keru)* pass through

告 *tsūkoku* notification, announcement

⁸例 *tsūrei* usually, customarily

念 *tsūnen* common sense, generally accepted idea

夜 *tsuya* deathwatch, wake. *tsūya* all night

学 *tsūgaku* attending school

知 *tsūchi* notification, information

知簿 *tsūchibo* school report card

⁹則 *tsūsoku* general rules

院中 *tsūinchū* coming for treatments

風 *tsūfū* ventilation, airing, draft

俗 *tsūzoku* popularity, conventionality

信 *tsūshin* correspondence, communication, intelligence, information, news, dispatch, report

信社 *tsūshinsha* news agency

信販売 *tsūshin hambai* mail-order business; mail-order sale

信教育 *tsūshin kyōiku* education by correspondence

信衛星 *tsūshin eisei* communication satellite

信講座 *tsūshin kōza* correspondence course

信簿 *tsūshimbo* report card

¹⁰称 *tsūshō* popular name, alias

航 *tsūkō suru* navigate, sail, ply

¹¹道 *tō(ri)michi* passage, path, route; one's way; (cattle) runway

達 *tsūtatsu, tsūdatsu* communication, notification; proficiency, mastery, skill

帳 *kayo(i)chō, tsūchō* bankbook; chit book

過 *tō(ri)-su(giru)* to pass, pass through. *tsūka* passage, transit. *tsūka suru* to pass, pass through

過駅 *tsūka eki* a station at which the train does not stop

運 *tsūun* express, transportation, forwarding

産相 *Tsūsanshō* Minister of International Trade and Industry

産省 *Tsūsanshō* Ministry of International Trade and Industry

貨 *tsūka* currency

訳 *tsūyaku* interpreting; interpreter

商 *tsūshō* commerce, trade

常 *tsūjō* normally, generally, ordinarily; regular (meeting)

¹²越 *tō(ri)-ko(su)* go beyond; pass through; be more than

勤 *tsūkin, kayo(i)zuto(me)* living away from one's work

¹³路 *tō(ri)michi, kayo(i)michi, kayo(i)ji* route, path. *tsūro* passageway, path, thoroughfare, entranceway, aisle, catwalk

牒 *tsūchō* notification

話 *tsūwa* phone call

話料 *tsūwaryō* phone-call charge

¹⁴関 *tsūkan* customs clearance

説 *tsūsetsu* common opinion

読 *tsūdoku suru* read through

算 *tsūsan* totaling

¹⁵弊 *tsūhei* common evil

¹⁸観 *tsūkan* general view

─────── **8** ───────

逮 $\frac{6069}{J4261}$ M38931' TAI chase.
B

¹⁰捕 *taiho* arrest, capture

捕状 *taihojō* arrest warrant

週 $\frac{6070}{J3d35}$ M38937' SHŪ week.
A

⁴日 *shūjitsu* week day

⁵刊 *shūkan* weekly publication

刊誌 *shūkanshi* weekly publication

末 *shūmatsu* weekend

⁶休 *shūkyū* weekly holiday

¹²間 *shūkan* week

給 *shūkyū* weekly pay

逸 $\frac{6071}{J306f}$ M38951' ITSU idleness, leisure.
B

is(suru) midd (a chance); let escape; deviate from. *so(reru)* miss the mark, deviate from, diverge, glance

見
角
言
谷
豆
豕
豸
貝
赤
走
足
身
車
辛
辰
【辵
辶】
邑
⻏
西
釆
里

7

off, go astray; be off (the tune).
so(raseru), so(rasu) look away, evade,
elude, parry. *hagu(reru)* go astray,
become separated from. *haya(ru)* be
hasty, be rash.

7 材 *itsuzai* outstanding talent
8 物 *itsubutsu* excellent person, superb
    article. *ichimotsu* excellent animal
  事 *itsuji* anecdote; unknown fact
9 速 *ichihaya(ku)* promptly
  品 *ippin* superb article
11 脱 *itsudatsu* deviation, omission
13 話 *itsuwa* anecdote

進 | 6073 / J3f4a / M38943 | SHIN advancing.

A *shin(zuru), shin(jiru),
shin(zeru)* give, present. *susu(mu) vi*
advance, proceed, progress; be promoted;
be in an advanced stage; (watches) gain;
feel like (doing). *susu(meru) vt* move
forward; set (watches) ahead; promote,
elevate; stimulate; speed up; present.

2 入 *shinnyū(suru), susu(mi)-i(ru)* go on
    into, penetrate, enter
4 化 *shinka* evolution; progress
  化論 *shinkaron* theory of evolution
  化論者 *shinkaronja* evolutionist
  水 *shinsui* launching (a ship)
6 行 *shinkō suru, susu(mi)-yu(ku)* go
    forward, advance
7 言 *shingen* advice, memorial, proposal
  攻 *shinkō* attack, drive
  呈 *shintei* presentation
8 物 *shimmotsu* present, gift
  取 *shinshu* enterprise
  退 *shintai* advance or retreat; movement;
    course of action; conduct; attitude;
    resigning or carrying on
  学 *shingaku* entrance to a higher school
  歩 *shimpo* advance, progress
9 度 *shindo* progress
  級 *shinkyū* (school) promotion
  軍 *shingun* a march, an advance
10 捗 *shinchoku* progress, advance
  展 *shinten* development, progress
11 運 *shin'un* progress, advancement
13 路 *shinro* course, way, route
14 境 *shinkyō* progress, improvement
15 撃 *shingeki* assault, charge, attack,
    advance
  駐 *shinchū* occupation, stationing
  駐軍 *shinchūgun* occupation army

9

遥 | 6075 / J4d5a / M-X | Nonstandard for 遙 6097.

遇 | 6083 / J3678 / M38991 | **B** GŪ. GU. *gū(suru)* treat,
entertain, receive, deal with.
ashira(u) receive, entertain; deal with,
treat, manage, manipulate. *a(u)* meet,
interview.

遂 | 6084 / J3f6b / M38985 | **B** SUI. *to(geru)* accomplish,
attain, commit (suicide).
tsui ni finally, after all.

6 行 *suikō* accomplishment, execution,
    prosecution (of a war)

逼 | 6085 / J492f / M38973 | FUKU. HITSU. *sema(ru)*
press for, urge, force, spur
on; approach; gain on, close in on; be on
the verge of, be imminent.

7 迫 *hippaku* (money) stringency
13 塞 *hissoku* poverty-stricken and slipping
    into obscurity; house arrest

遍 | 6086 / J4a57 / M39001 | **B** HEN times. *amane(ku)*
widely, generally,
everywhere.

6 在 *henzai* omnipresence, ubiquity
13 路 *henro* pilgrim
14 歴 *henreki* travels, pilgrimage

遁 | 6087 / J465b / M38982 | TON. *noga(reru)* escape,
avoid, evade, shirk.

5 世 *tonsei* seclusion from the world,
    escape from life
7 走 *tonsō* flight
13 辞 *tonji* excuse, evasion, prevarication

達 | 6088 / J4323 / M39011 | **A** TATSU. *tas(suru)* reach,
arrive at, attain; amount
to; become expert, be versed in;
accomplish; notify. *tat(te)* forcibly,
unreasonably. *tas(shinai)* fall short of; be
uncompleted. *tas(shi)* government notice.
-tachi plural ending.

2 人 *tatsujin* expert, master, master mind,
    great character, philosopher
6 成 *tassei* achievement, accomplishment
8 者 *tassha na* healthy, strong; skillful;
    free (in a language)
12 筆 *tappitsu* facile pen, skillful hand;

---

speedy writing

¹³意 *tatsui* intelligibility, perspicuity

¹⁸観 *takkan* farsighted view; philosophic view

遅 ⁶⁰⁸⁹ J4359 M38989 CHI. *oku(reru)* be late, be delayed, be overdue; lag **B** behind; (clocks) lose. *oku(rasu), oku(raseru)* retard, delay, defer. *oso(nawaru)* be late. *oso(i)* late; slow. *oso(kutomo)* at the latest. *oso-* slow, late.

⁶早 *oso(kare)-haya(kare)* sooner or later

⁸延 *chien* delay, retardation, procrastination

参 *chisan* lateness, tardiness

知恵 *osojie* retarded development of understanding

刻 *chikoku* tardiness, lateness

¹⁰配 *chihai* delay in rationing

¹¹遅 *chichi* slow, lagging

過 *ososu(giru)* be too late

¹³滞 *chitai* delay, procrastination, arrearage

¹⁴疑 *chigi* hesitation, vacillation, indecision

過 ⁶⁰⁹⁰ J3261 M39002 KA error; excess. *su(giru)* **A** pass, go past; elapse; exceed. *su(gosu)* pass, spend; tide over; go through; live, (eat) too much. *yo(giru)* pass by, cross, go across. *ayama(tsu)* err. *ayama(chi)* fault, error, indiscretion. *ayama(tte)* by mistake, accidentally. *su(ginai)* nothing more than, merely. *-su(giru)* over-, too; to a fault, in excess. *-su(gi)* past, after; over; too; excessive.

³大 *kadai na* excessive; unreasonable; too large

大評価 *kadai hyōka* overvaluation

小 *kashō* too small

小評価 *kashō hyōka* undervaluation

⁴日 *kajitsu* recently, the other day

分 *kabun na* excessive; unmerited; generous

不足 *kafusoku* excess or deficiency

⁵半 *kahan* the greater part

半数 *kahansū* majority, plurality, greater part

去 *su(gi)-sa(ru)* pass. *kako* the past; previous life; previous existence; past tense

失 *kashitsu* error, blunder; accident;

negligence

⁶当 *katō na* excessive, undeserved, unreasonable, exorbitant

多 *kata* excess, superabundance

⁷労 *karō* overwork, strain

労死 *karōshi* death due to overwork

⁹食 *kashoku* overeating

信 *kashin suru* trust too much; overestimate (ability); be overconfident

負荷 *kafuka* overload (in electricity)

重 *kajū* overweight

度 *kado* excess

¹⁰料 *karyō* correctional fine

敏 *kabin* nervousness, oversensitiveness

¹¹剰 *kajō* excess, surplus

¹²程 *katei* process, course

給器 *kakyūki* supercharger

渡 *kato* crossing; ferry; changing from the old (to the new)

渡期 *katoki* transition period

¹⁴誤 *kago* mistake, fault

酷 *kakoku* rigor, severity, cruelty

¹⁶激 *kageki na* extreme, radical

道 ⁶⁰⁹¹ J463b M39010 DŌ district, province, **A** prefecture; road. *michi* road, path, lane, way, street, highway, route; journey; distance; course, way, means; duty, morality, moral doctrine; teachings; specialty; an art; reason, justice. *michi(naranu)* improper, illicit. *michi(sugara)* on the way.

⁴中 *dōchū* during the journey

化 *dōke(ru)* jest, clown. *dōke* clowning, antics, tomfoolery, pleasantry

⁷床 *dōshō* roadbed

⁸学者 *dōgakusha* moralist

具 *dōgu* tool, instrument, implement, utensil, appliance; furniture; (stage) scenery; instrumentality, means, vehicle; steppingstone

⁹連 *michizu(re)* traveling companion

¹⁰案内 *michi annai* guidance; guide; signpost

¹¹教 *Dōkyō* Taoism ⌈reason

理 *dōri* reason, right, truth. *kotowari*

¹²場 *dōjō* gymnasium, arena; Buddhist seminary

順 *michijun* route, itinerary

程 *dōtei, michinori* distance; journey; process

見角言谷豆豕豸貝赤走足身車辛辰【辵辶】₉ 邑阝酉采里

7

筋 *michisuji* path, way, route, itinerary; reason

¹³ 路 *dōro* road, way, street, route, highway, thoroughfare

義 *dōgi* morality, moral principles

楽 *dōraku* dissipation, prodigality, hobby

¹⁴ 端 *michibata* roadside

徳 *dōtoku* morals, morality, virtue

¹⁵ 標 *michi shirube, dōhyō* road marker

A 運 6092 J313f M38998' UN destiny, fate, lot, fortune, luck. *hako(bu)* carry, transport; progress, advance. *megu(ru)* *vi* and *vt* turn, go around; revolve, rotate, spin, gyrate; patrol, tour; take effect (medicine); be transferred. *megu(rasu)* enclosed, surround; turn, turn around; ponder; devise. *hako(bi)* carrying; arrangements, managing, paving the way; progress; stage; step, pace.

⁵ 用 *un'yō suru* make use of, employ (capital), enforce (laws); invest, put in practice

⁶ 行 *unkō* motion, movement, revolution. *unkō suru* ply between, run

気 *unki* fate, fortune

休 *unkyū* service suspended (trains, etc.)

⁸ 河 *unga* canal, waterway

命 *ummei* destiny, fate

送 *unsō* shipping, transportation, forwarding

¹¹ 転 *unten* operation; motion; running, working; driving (a car)

転手 *untenshu* driver, engineer, chauffeur, operator (of a machine)

動 *undō* motion, movement; exercise; sports, games; campaign; agitation; lobbying

動会 *undōkai* athletic meet

動神経 *undō shinkei* motor nerves

動場 *undōjō* playing field

動靴 *undōgutsu* sports shoes

動選手 *undō senshu* athlete, sportsman

¹² 筆 *umpitsu* strokes of the brush, handling the brush

営 *un'ei* operation, management, administration

¹³ 勢 *unsei* fate, fortune

賃 *unchin* shipping charges

搬 *umpan* transportation, transfer

¹⁶ 輸 *un'yu* transportation

輸省 *Un'yushō* Ministry of Transportation

A 遊 6093 J4d37 M38994' YŪ. YU. *aso(bu)* play; enjoy oneself; visit; take a holiday; be out of use, be unemployed, be idle; study under; go on a spree. *aso(baseru), aso(basu)* amuse, entertain; let play; be pleased to. *aso(bi)* play, game, sport, amusement, recreation, fun, outing; play (of a wheel); gambling; dissipation; dull business; idle time; light (literature). *susa(bi)* amusement, recreation.

³ 子 *yūshi* wanderer, traveler, capital

山 *yusan* excursion, outing, picnic

弋 *yūyoku* cruise

女 *aso(bi)me, yūjo* harlot, prostitute

⁴ 友達 *aso(bi) tomodachi* playmate, companion in play

⁵ 民 *yūmin* idle people, idlers; the unemployed; unemployment

半分 *aso(bi)hambun* half in fun

⁶ 仲間 *aso(bi)nakama* playmate, companion

休 *yūkyū* idle, unused

⁷ 里 *yūri* red-light district

芸 *yūgei* the polite accomplishments

⁸ 歩 *yūho* walk, stroll, ramble

学 *yūgaku* traveling to study

泳 *yūei* swimming

牧 *yūboku* nomadism

牧民 *yūbokumin* nomads

侠 *yūkyō* chivalrous man; gangster

⁹ 星 *yūsei* planet

¹⁰ 郭 *yūkaku* red-light district

時間 *aso(bi) jikan* recess, playtime

¹¹ 道具 *aso(bi) dōgu* plaything, toy

船 *yūsen* yacht, pleasure boat

猟 *yūryō* hunting

¹² 場 *aso(bi)ba* playground

¹³ 廓 *yūkaku* red-light district

楽 *yūraku* amusement, pleasure,

園地 *yūenchi* amusement park, recreation area, playground

¹⁴ 歴 *yūreki* tour, pleasure trip

説 *yūzei* electioneering tour, oratorical campaign, agitation tour; campaign speech

¹⁵ 戯 *aso(bi)-tawamu(reru)* play, frolic. *yūgi* games, sport, play, entertainment, amusement, pastime

蕩 *yūtō* dissipation, profligacy
16 覽 *yūran* excursion, sightseeing
興 *yūkyō* pleasure-seeking, amusement, spree
19 離 *yūri* separation, isolation

――――― **10** ―――――

遡 6094 / J414c / M39048 See 溯 3272.

遙 6097 / J7423 / M39035 Yō. *haru(ka) ni* far off, in the distance; a long time ago; by far. *haru(keshi)* distant.
8 拜 *yōhai* worshipping from afar
13 遙 *harubaru* from afar, all the way, far out over (the sea)

遜 6098 / J423d / M39038 Son. *herikuda(ru)* humble oneself, condescend, be modest.
6 色 *sonshoku* inferiority

違 6099 / J3063 / M39067 B I. *chiga(u)* differ, vary; disagree with; be mistaken; cross or pass (someone); No (negation). *chiga(eru)* change, alter, vary, disguise; make a mistake; break (a promise); sprain, dislocate; cross (two sticks). *taga(u)* differ from, vary; violate, break, transgress. *taga(eru)* break (a promise or a law), violate. *chiga(i)* difference, divergence, disparity, discrepancy. *chiga(inai)* I am sure.
4 反 *ihan* violation, infringement, breach (of contract)
法 *ihō* unlawfulness; foul (play)
9 背 *ihai* violation, transgression
約 *iyaku* breach of contract, default
16 憲 *iken* unconstitutionality

遣 6100 / J382f / M39052 B Ken. *tsuka(wasu)* send, dispatch; give, donate, bestow on; do for (someone). *ya(ru)* give, let have, bestow on, present; send; do, perform, undertake; do for; act; study; row; operate; hold (a meeting), give (a dinner); eat, drink, smoke; find solace in. *yoko(su)* send, forward, deliver. *ya(ri-konasu)* manage a difficult task. *tsuka(u)* use; handle, manipulate; employ; need, want; spend, consume; speak (English); practice (fencing); take (one's lunch); circulate (bad money).
3 口 *yarikuchi* procedure, policy, way of doing
4 手 *yarite* person with talent, tactician, performer
込 *ya(ri)-ko(meru)* snub, refute, corner
方 *ya(ri)kata* way of doing, method, manner of doing means, arrangement, management
切 *ya(ri)-ki(renai)* cannot stand, cannot go on, cannot make ends meet, be intolerable
5 外 *kengai* sent abroad
6 尽 *ya(ri)-tsuku(su)* do all in one's power
返 *ya(ri)-kae(su)* try again, make over; refute, answer back
合 *ya(ri) a(u)* do something) against each other, quarrel, argue
8 直 *ya(ri)-nao(su)* do over, remake, resume, begin again
10 唐使 *kentōshi* envoy to Tang China
11 過 *ya(ri)-su(giru)* overdo, carry too far, drink too much, give too much.
ya(ri)-su(gosu) let a person go past
遂 *ya(ri)-to(geru)* accomplish, fulfill, finish
12 場 *ya(ri)ba* disposal; use; place (to put a thing)
繰 *ya(ri)-ku(ru)* proceed in spite of shortages. *ya(ri)ku(ri)* tiding over, makeshift, manipulation

遠 6101 / J3173 / M39047 A En. On. *tō(i)* far, distant, remote; hard (of hearing). *tō(ku)* far away, in the distance. *tō(zakaru) vi* become more distant, recede; die away; keep away, stand aloof, be estranged. *tō(zakeru) vt* keep away, keep at a distance, shun, abstain from; alienate. *tō(karazu), tō(karazu) shite* soon, in the near future. *tō-* far, distant.
3 大 *endai na* far-reaching, grand, lofty
4 方 *empō* great distance, long way; distant place
心力 *enshinryoku* centrifugal force
5 出 *tōde* going afar; changing a geisha registry to another city
6 回 *tōmawa(ri)* roundabout way, detour. *tōmawa(shi)* roundabout expression ⌜predisposing
因 *en'in* remote, underlying, or

7

見角言谷豆豕豸貝赤走足身車辛辰【辵⻌】邑⻏酉釆里

近 *enkin* distance, far and near, perspective. *ochikochi* here and there

7 足 *ensoku* trip, hike, picnic, excursion, outing

来 *enrai* foreign visitor, visitor from afar

8 退 *tōno(keru)* keep (someone) at a distance. *tōno(ku)* stay at a distance; recede, fade away

泳 *en'ei* long-distance swim

征 *ensei* expedition, invasion, campaign; a tour (by a team of performers)

9 浅 *tōasa* a wide shallow beach; a shoal

乗 *tōno(ri)* a long ride

巻 *tōma(ki)* surrounding at a distance

海 *enkai* deep sea, ocean

洋 *en'yō* ocean, deep sea

洋航海 *en'yō kōkai* ocean navigation

洋漁業 *en'yō gyogyō* deep-sea fishing

10 島 *entō, tōjima* a distant island. *entō* exile to an island

11 望 *embō* vista, distant view, perspective

距離 *enkyori* long distance, great distance, long-range

視 *enshi* farsightedness

12 景 *enkei* distant view, vista, perspective, background

隔 *enkaku* distant, remote, isolated

13 路 *enro* long road, long journey; roundabout way, detour, long distance

雷 *enrai* distant thunder

15 縁 *tōen* distant relative

慮 *enryo* reserve, modesty, deference, restraint, discretion; forethought, prudence

慮深 *enryobuka(i)* reserved, backward, bashful, shy, modest

16 謀 *embō* forethought, foresight

——— **11** ———

遭 $\frac{6105}{\substack{J4178 \\ M39082}}$ Sō . *a(u)* meet, interview. *a(waseru)* introduce, expose to, subject to.

B

11 遇 *sōgū* an encounter, meeting someone

18 難 *sōnan* disaster, accident, shipwreck, distress

遮 $\frac{6106}{\substack{J3c57 \\ M39086}}$ Sha. *saegi(ru)* interrupt, obstruct, intercept.

B

2 二無二 *shanimuni* recklessly, furiously, desperately, forcibly

6 光 *shakō suru* shade, darken, cut off the light

11 断 *shadan* interception, isolation

断器 *shadanki* circuit breaker

断機 *shadanki* railroad crossing gate

15 蔽 *shahei* cover, shelter

蔽物 *shaheibutsu* cover, shelter

適 $\frac{6107}{\substack{J452c \\ M39076}}$ Teki suitable. *teki(suru)* fit, suit, agree with, be adapted to, be qualified for. *kana(u)* suit, be capable of; measure up to expectations; suit, be capable of; measure up to expectations; match, rival, keep up to expectations; rival, keep up with; stand (the work); bear (the heat). *kana(eru)* grant, hear, answer. *tama no* occasionally, rare. *tamasaka* occasionally. *tamatama* casually, unexpectedly; few.

A

4 中 *tekichū suru* hit the mark, guess right, come right

切 *tekisetsu na* pertinent, appropriate, adequate, timely

5 用 *tekiyō suru* apply ⌈normal

正 *tekisei na* proper, right, reasonable,

6 地 *tekichi* suitable site

合 *tekigō* conformity, compatibility, adaptation

当 *tekitō na* suitable, proper, right; adequate; competent, qualified; reasonable, timely

任 *tekinin* suitability, competence

7 役 *tekiyaku* suitable post

材 *tekizai, tekisai* the right person

材適所 *tekizai-tekisho* the right person in the right place

応 *tekiō* adaptation, accommodation, adjustment, conformity

応性 *tekiōsei* adaptability, flexibility

8 例 *tekirei* good example, typical instance

法 *tekihō* legality, lawfulness

宜 *tekigi* suitableness

性 *tekisei* adaptability

9 度 *tekido ni* moderately, in moderation, temperately

10 時 *tekiji* timely, at any time, at all times

格 *tekikaku, tekkaku* competency, fitness

12 量 *tekiryō* proper quantity, proper dose

17 齢 *tekirei* marriageable age; conscription age

18 職 *tekishoku* an appropriate occupation (for a certain person)

──────── **12** ────────

遼 6111 J4e4b M39137 RYŌ distant.

¹² 遠 *ryōen na* distant, remote

遵 6112 J3d65 M39118' JUN follow, obey; learn.

B

⁶ 守 *junshu suru* obey, observe
⁸ 奉 *jumpo suru* obey, observe
法 *jumpō na* law-abiding

遷 6113 J412b M39123' SEN. *utsu(ru)* move,
change, shift; pass into,
drift; soak in; be infected, catch (a cold);
catch fire, spread. *utsu(su)* move,
transfer; pour into, divert (attention), give
(a disease to someone).

B

⁸ 延 *sen'en* delay, procrastination,
postponement
都 *sento* moving the capital
¹¹ 移 *sen'i* transition, change

選 6114 J412a M39127' SEN selection, choice.
*yo(ru), era(bu), e(ru),
era(mu)* choose, select; cull out; elect;
prefer; decide on. *sugu(ru)* choose,
select, cull out.

A

⁴ 手 *senshu* athlete, player
手権 *senshuken* championship title
⁵ 出 *e(ri)-da(su), era(bi)-da(su)* select,
pick out, cull out. *senshutsu*
election
⁶ 考 *senkō* selection, evaluation (of
people)
⁷ 別 *era(bi)-wa(katsu)* set apart. *sembetsu*
selection, separation, concentration (in
mining)
良 *senryō* the people's choice; diet
member
択 *sentaku* selection, choice, option,
selectivity
抜 *e(ri)-nu(ku)* choose, select, pick out,
sort out. *sembatsu* selection, choice
⁸ 定 *era(bi)-sada(meru)* appoint. *sentei*
selection, choice
¹⁰ 挙 *senkyo* election
挙区 *senkyoku* election district, precinct,
constituency
挙演説 *senkyo enzetsu* campaign speech
挙権 *senkyoken* suffrage, franchise, right
to vote

¹² 集 *senshū* selection, anthology

遺 6115 J3064 M39134' I. YUI. *noko(su)* leave
behind; bequeath; save,
reserve.

A

⁵ 失 *ishitsu* loss
失物 *ishitsubutsu* lost article
失品 *ishitsuhin* lost article
⁶ 臣 *ishin* surviving retainer
存 *ison* extant, still existing
伝 *iden* heredity
伝子 *idenshi* gene
伝学 *idengaku* genetics
⁷ 作 *isaku* posthumous works
体 *itai* corpse, remains
児 *iji* orphan
言 *yuigon, igen, igon* will, testament,
last request
言状 *yuigonjō* will, testament
⁸ 物 *yuimotsu* keepsake; inheritance,
bequest. *ibutsu* relic, (old) remains,
memento
⁹ 恨 *ikon* grudge, ill-will, enmity
品 *ihin* articles of the deceased
¹⁰ 骨 *ikotsu* remains, ashes of the
deceased
書 *isho* posthumous work; note left by
the dead
留 *iryū suru* bequeath
留品 *iryūhin* lost articles
¹¹ 族 *izoku* bereaved family
産 *isan* inheritance, bequest, heritage
産相続 *isan sōzoku* succession to
property
¹³ 跡 *iseki, yuiseki* (historic) ruins, remains,
relics
棄 *iki* abandonment, desertion
¹⁴ 徳 *itoku* benefit from ancestors' virtue
漏 *irō* omission, negligence, oversight
髪 *ihatsu* hair of the deceased
¹⁵ 稿 *ikō* posthumous manuscript
¹⁶ 骸 *igai, yuigai* remains, corpse, (dead)
body
憾 *ikan na* regrettable, unsatisfactory
¹⁸ 蹟 *iseki* (historic) ruins

──────── **13** ────────

避 6120 J4872 M39163' HI. *yo(keru), sa(keru)*
avoid, avert, ward off, keep
aloof from, stay away from; evade, shirk,
shun.

B

7

見
角
言
谷
豆
豕
豸
貝
赤
走
足
身
車
辛
辰
辵
辶
【邑 阝】
西
釆
里

⁷ 妊 *hinin* contraception
¹² 寒 *hikan* wintering, hibernation
暑 *hisho* summering; going to a summer resort
暑地 *hishochi* summer resort
¹³ 雷針 *hiraishin* lightning rod
¹⁸ 難 *hinan* shelter, refuge, evacuation
難民 *hinammin* refugees
難所 *hinanjo* shelter structures

B 還 6121 J3454 M39174' Kan. Gen. *kae(ru)* return; take one's leave; come again; come around (time). *kae(su)* send

(someone) back.
⁴ 元 *kangen* restoration; reduction (chemistry)
⁵ 付 *kampu* return, restitution, restoration
⁹ 俗 *genzoku* quitting the priesthood, return to secular life
¹⁴ 暦 *kanreki* one's 61st birthday

———————— 14 ————————

邇 6122 J6d6e M39193 Ji approach; near.

———————— RAD. 邑 163 ————————

Ōzato large village (in contradistinction to Rads. 166 & 170). Except for the radical character itself, always used at right in the modified form 阝 (2 strokes) *ōzatozukuri*. Nickname: Right Village.

邑 6127 J4d38 M39269 Yū village, rural community, town; dominion.

———————— 4 ————————

那 6129 J4661 M39305 Na what?

B 邦 6130 J4b2e M39310 Hō country. *kuni* country.
² 人 *hōjin* fellow countryman; a Japanese
⁴ 文 *hōbun* Japanese language
⁶ 字 *hōji* Japanese characters
⁸ 画 *hōga* a Japanese movie or painting
¹¹ 訳 *hōyaku* translation into Japanese
¹³ 楽 *hōgaku* Japanese music

———————— 5 ————————

B 邸 6134 J4521 M39347 Tei *yashiki* mansion, residence.
⁶ 内 *teinai* grounds, premises
⁶ 宅 *teitaku* mansion, residence

B 邪 6135 J3c59 M39357' Sa. Ja injustice, unrighteousness, wickedness. *yokoshima* wickedness, wrong, injustice.

⁴ 心 *jashin* sinister design
⁶ 気 *jaki* miasma, poison, pestilential vapor; malice, evil; a cold
⁸ 念 *janen* sinister design, evil intention
¹⁰ 険 *jaken* cruelty, hardheartedness
¹¹ 道 *jadō* evil course; heresy
推 *jasui* unjust suspicion, distrust
教 *jakyō* heresy, paganism, heathenism
悪 *jaaku* wickedness, viciousness, vice
²¹ 魔 *jama* hindrance, obstacle, barrier, inconvenience, encumbrance, interference, disturbance

———————— 6 ————————

郁 6136 J306a M39371 Iku cultural progress; perfume.

B 郊 6137 J3959 M39392 Kō suburbs; rural area.
⁵ 外 *kōgai* suburbs, outskirts
¹¹ 野 *kōya* suburban fields

B 郎 6138 J4f3a M39405' Rō man; husband; counter for sons.
¹⁰ 党 *rōtō, rōdō* retainers, vassals

———————— 7 ————————

A 郡 6143 / J3734 / M39436 GUN *kōri* county, district.

---------- **8** ----------

B 郭 6144 / J3354 / M39474 KAKU enclosure; quarters. *kuruwa* enclosure, fortification; quarters; red-light district.

A 郷 6145 / J363f / M39498 KYŌ village, native place. GŌ country, district, village.

³ 土 *kyōdo* one's birthplace, one's old home
土色 *kyōdoshoku* local color
土愛 *kyōdoai* local patriotism
⁷ 里 *kyōri* one's old home, native place
村 *gōson* villages
¹⁰ 党 *kyotō* one's fellow villagers; one's village
¹³ 愁 *kyōshū* nostalgia, homesickness

A 部 6146 / J4974 / M39460 BU department, bureau, section; faculty; division, class, category; part, portion, region; copy, volume, set. *be* the large ancient family.

³ 下 *buka* subordinate, follower; under one's command
⁴ 分 *bubun* part, portion, section. *buwa(ke)* classification
⁷ 位 *bui* part (of the body), region
⁸ 長 *buchō* head of a division, department, or section
門 *bumon* class, group, department, section, category; branch, line, field; genus, order, type
所 *busho* one's post of duty
⁹ 首 *bushu* radical (of a character)
活 *bukatsu* club activities
品 *buhin* parts, accessories
屋 *heya* room, apartment
¹⁰ 員 *buin* staff; staff member, member,
¹¹ 族 *buzoku* tribe
隊 *butai* unit, corps, squad, detachment; club members
¹² 落 *buraku* community, settlement, village
¹³ 数 *busū* number of copies, circulation
署 *busho* one's post of duty
¹⁸ 類 *burui* class, heading, group, category, order, division

A 郵 6147 / J4d39 / M39485 YŪ stagecoach stop; mail.

⁸ 送 *yūsō* mailing
送料 *yūsōryō* postage
⁹ 政省 *Yūseishō* Ministry of Postal Services
便 *yūbin* mail
便切手 *yūbin kitte* postage stamp
便局 *yūbinkyoku* post office
便物 *yūbimbutsu* mail matter
便函 *yūbimbako* mailbox
便受 *yūbin u(ke)* mailbox
便屋 *yūbin'ya* mail carrier
便配達 *yūbin haitatsu* mail delivery, mail carrier
便貯金 *yūbin chokin* postal savings
便葉書 *yūbin hagaki* postcard
便箱 *yūbimbako* mailbox
¹¹ 船 *yūsen* mail steamer
袋 *yūtai* maibag

A 都 6148 / J4554 / M39497 TO, TSU *miyako* capital, metropolis.

³ 下 *toka* throughout the capital, in the metropolis
大路 *miyako ōji* main thoroughfare of the metropolis
⁴ 心 *toshin* heart of the city
内 *tonai* within the capital
⁵ 立 *toritsu* metropolitan, municipal
庁 *Tochō* Tokyo Metropolitan Government Office
民 *Tomin* Tokyo citizens
市 *toshi* cities; towns and cities
⁶ 合 *tsugō* circumstances, conditions, reasons; convenience; opportunity; occasion; arrangement, management; accommodation; in all
会 *Tokai* Tokyo Metropolitan Assembly. *tokai* city, town
会人 *tokaijin* townsmen, city residents
⁸ 制 *tosei* metropolitan government
知事 *To chiji* Tokyo governor
⁹ 度 *tsudo* each time, whenever, as often as
城 *tojō* castle town
¹¹ 鳥 *miyakodori* sea gull
道府県 *to-dō-fu-ken* urban and rural prefectures
¹² 営 *Toei* operated by Tokyo
²⁰ 議会 *To Gikai* Tokyo Metropolitan Assembly

7

見角言谷豆豕豸貝赤走足身車辛辰辵〔邑阝〕⁸西釆里

─────── 12 ───────   ⁹重 *teichō* courtesy

鄭 6155 / J4522 / M39647   TEI an ancient Chinese province.

■■■■■■■■ 酉 RAD. 164 ■■■■■■■■

Tori or *hiyori no tori* ("the bird of the zodiac," as distinguished from the common bird of Rad. 196). At left: *tori hen*. In combinations this element connotes liquid and hence in any position is generally called *sakezukuri* (i.e., the right-hand element of the character for saké). Nickname: Saké.

酉 6157 / J4653 / M39763   YŪ . *tori* 5-7 p.m., tenth zodiac sign; bird; west.
⁵市 *tori (no) ichi* year-end fair

─────── 2 ───────

酋 6159 / J3d36 / M39765   SHŪ chieftain.
⁸長 *shūchō* chief, chieftain

酒 A 6160 / J3c72 / M39776   SHU *sake* saké, rice wine; alcoholic liquor.
⁴手 *sakate* drink money, tip
⁶色 *shushoku* wine and women, debauchery
 気 *sakake, shuki* smell of liquor
⁷乱 *shuran* drunken frenzy; vicious drinker
⁸店 *saketen, sakamise* saké shop
 杯 *shuhai* wine glass
 肴 *shukō, sake-sakana* food and drink
⁹屋 *sakaya* wine shop; wine merchant
 保 *shuho* canteen, post exchange, PX
 造 *shuzō, sakezuku(ri), sakazuku(ri)* saké brewing
¹⁰席 *shuseki* banquet, feast
¹¹盛 *sakamo(ri)* carousal, revelry
¹²場 *sakaba* bar, barroom
 量 *shuryō* drinking capacity
¹⁴豪 *shugō* heavy drinker
 蔵 *sakagura* wine cellar, wineshop
 精 *shusei* alcohol, spirits, hard liquor
¹⁶樽 *sakadaru* wine barrel
¹⁸癖 *sake kuse, sakaguse, shuheki* drinking habits

─────── 3 ───────

酌 6161 / J4371 / M39772   CHŪ saké.

酌 B 6162 / J3c60 / M39768   SHAKU serving saké; the server. *ku(mu)* draw (water), ladle, dip, scoop, pump; consider; sympathize with; drink; think.

配 A 6163 / J475b / M39771   HAI distribute; spouse; exile; rationing. *hai(suru)* allot; arrange; match (a couple); exile; subordinate. *kuba(ru)* distribute; serve (food); allocate; keep (your eyes) on. *ashira(u)* arrange, decorate; garnish; accompany (a singer).
³下 *haika* subordinates, followers, adherents
⁴分 *haibun* distribution, apportionment
⁵付 *haifu* distribution, apportionment
 布 *haifu* distribution, apportionment
 本 *haihon* distribution, apportionment
⁶色 *haishoku* color scheme
 列 *hairetsu* arrangement, grouping, disposition
 合 *haigō* composition, combination, distribution, arrangement, harmony, match, (color) scheme; mixture
 当 *haitō* dividend, share, quota, allotment
 当金 *haitōkin* share, dividend
⁷車 *haisha* car allocation
 役 *haiyaku* cast (of a play)
¹¹遇 *haigū* combination; spouse; marriage
 遇者 *haigūsha* spouse, consort
 達 *haitatsu* delivery, distribution; delivery person

達人 *haitatsunin* delivery person, mail carrier, person who delivers milk

達料 *haitatsuryō* delivery charge

[12] 属 *haizoku* attached to, assigned to

備 *haibi* arrangement, disposition, stationing

給 *haikyū* distribution, rationing

[13] 置 *haichi* arrangement, disposition (of troops)

電 *haiden* distribution of electricity

電盤 *haidemban* switchboard

[14] 管 *haikan* plumbing, piping

[15] 慮 *hairyo* consideration, solicitation, care, concern, anxiety, trouble

線 *haisen* (electric) wiring

――――― 4 ―――――

酔 6166 / J3f6c / M39807 **B** SUI. *yo(u)* get drunk; feel sick; be poisoned; be elated, be spellbound. *yo(pparau)* get drunk. *yo(i), ei* intoxication. *yo(idore)* drunkard.

[4] 心地 *yo(i)gokochi, eigokochi* a gloriously drunk feeling

[5] 払 *yoppara(i)* drunkard

[11] 眼 *suigan* bleary eyes

眼朦朧 *suigammōrō(taru)* (eyes) dimmed with drunk

漢 *suikan* drunkard

[14] 態 *suitai* intoxication, drunkenness

[15] 潰 *yo(i)-tsubu(reru)* be dead drunk. *yo(i)-tsubu(su)* make someone dead drunk

――――― 5 ―――――

酢 6169 / J3f5d / M39824 **B** SAKU. SO. *su* vinegar. *su(i), su(ppai)* sour, acid, tart.

[14] 酸 *sakusan* acetic acid

――――― 6 ―――――

酬 6171 / J3d37 / M39850 **B** SHŪ. *mukui* reward; retribution.

酪 6172 / J4d6f / M39847 **B** RAKU whey; broth; fruit juice.

[13] 農 *rakunō* dairy farming

農家 *rakunōka* dairy farmer

農場 *rakunōjō* dairy farm

酵 6175 / J395a / M39868 **B** KŌ fermentation. *moto* materials for making saké.

[5] 母 *kōbo* yeast, leaven

母菌 *kōbokin* yeast fungus

[10] 素 *kōso* enzyme, ferment

酷 6176 / J3973 / M39870 **B** KOKU severity, cruelty. *hido(i), mugo(i)* cruel, harsh, merciless, atrocious; unjust, unfair; severe, intense, bitter, serious, terrible, outrageous, unreasonable. *hanahada* very, greatly, exceedingly.

[5] 目 *hido(i)me* rough handling, maltreatment

[6] 似 *kokuji* close resemblance

吏 *kokuri* exacting official

[8] 使 *kokushi* hard-driving, abuse, exploitation

[10] 烈 *kokuretsu no* severe, intense, rigorous

[12] 税 *kokuzei* severe taxes

寒 *kokkan* intense cold; depth of winter

暑 *kokusho* intense heat

評 *kokuhyō* severe criticism

[15] 熱 *kokunetsu* intense heat

[16] 薄 *kokuhaku* brutality, atrocity

酸 6177 / J3b40 / M39871 **B** SAN acid; bitterness. *su(i), su(ppai)* sour, acid, tart.

[4] 化 *sanka* oxidation

化物 *sankabutsu* oxide

[8] 味 *su(i)mi, sammi* acidity, sourness

性 *sansei* acidity

[10] 素 *sanso* oxygen

[14] 鼻 *sambi* extreme pain; deep sorrow

――――― 8 ―――――

醇 6181 / J3d66 / M39901 JUN pure saké; purity; affection.

[4] 化 *junka suru* refine, purify, chasten, sublimate; be refined, be chastened

[5] 平 *junko no* pure, sheer, unalloyed

[6] 朴 *jumboku* simplicity and honesty

[9] 厚 *junkō no* kindhearted, courteous

風 *jumpū* good custom

風美俗 *jumpū bizoku* good customs

7

見角言谷豆豕豸貝赤走足身車辛辰辵邑阝酉【釆】0里

—— 9 ——

醶 6182 / J4830 / M-X — Nonstandard for 醱 6194.

酥 6183 / J386f / M39930 — Go a kind of cream obtained from boiling butter.

醍 6184 / J4269 / M39924 — DAI whey; good Buddhist teaching.
16 醍味 *daigomi* sweet taste; zest for life; Buddha's excellent teachings

醒 6185 / J4043 / M39936 — SEI . *sa(meru)* vi awake; be disillusioned; sober up. *sa(masu)* vt wake up, awake.

—— 10 ——

醤 6186 / J3e5f / M-X — Nonstandard for 醬 6192.

醜 6189 / J3d39 / M39969 — B SHŪ ugliness; uncleanness; shame. *miniku(i)* bad-looking, ugly; unsightly; indecent, disgraceful.
3 女 *shūjo, shikome* homely woman, plain-looking woman
6 名 *shūmei* scandal, ill fame. *shikona*

true name; nickname; wrestler's name
9 美 *shūbi* beauty or ugliness, personal appearance
11 悪 *shūaku* unsightliness, ugliness, meanness, offensiveness
14 聞 *shūbun* scandal, ill fame
態 *shūtai* shameful conduct; ugly scene

—— 11 ——

醬 6192 / J-X / M40011 — 醤 6186 / J3e5f / M-X — SHŌ . *hishio* a kind of *miso*.
8 油 *shōyu* soy sauce

—— 12 ——

醱 6194 / J-X / M40041 — HATSU fermentation, brewing.
14 酵 *hakkō* fermentation

—— 13 ——

醸 6197 / J3e7a / M40064' — B JŌ . *kamo(su)* brew; cause, give rise to.
5 出 *kamo(shi)-da(su)* cause, bring about
6 成 *jōsei suru* brew; foment, breed, cause, create
9 造 *jōzō* brewing, distilling
造酒 *jōzōshu* brewage

RAD. 釆 165

Nogome (i.e., the katakana *no* plus Rad. 119 *kome* "rice").
At left: *nogome hen*. Nickname: Topped Rice.

釆 6201 / J3a53 / M40116 — 釆 6202 / J4850 / M40115 — SAI dice; form, appearance. *to(ru)* take. *irodori* coloring.
10 配 *saihai* baton of command; duster

—— 4 ——

釈 6203 / J3c61 / M40120' — B SHAKU, SEKI explanation. *to(ku)* explain.

8 放 *shakuhō* release, liberation, acquittal
明 *shakumei* explanation; vindication
迦 *Shaka* Gautama, Sakyamuni
迦牟尼 *Shakamuni* Sakyamuni, Gautama, Buddha
迦如来 *Shaka Nyorai* Sakyamuni
12 尊 *Shakuson* Buddha, Gautama
然 *shakuzen toshite* with sudden awakening, well satisfied with (an explanation)
13 義 *shakugi* commentary, exposition

RAD. 里 166

Sato village or *ri* two and a half miles. At left: 里 *sato hen*. Nickname: Village.

A 里 ^{6206 J4e24 M40131} Rɪ village; a Japanese league, 2.44 miles. *sato* village, hamlet, the country; parents' home.

² 人 *rijin, satobito* villagers, countryfolk

³ 子 *satogo* child put out to nurse, foster child

⁴ 心 *satogokoro* homesickness, nostalgia

方 *satokata* wife's home, wife's folks; childhood home of an adopted son

⁶ 芋 *satoimo* taro

¹⁰ 帰 *satogae(ri)* bride's first visit to her old home ⌜ri

¹² 程標 *riteihyō* posts marking distances in

¹⁶ 親 *satooya* foster parent

— 2 —

A 重 ^{6207 J3d45 M40132} Chō . Jū nest of boxes. *kasa(neru)* pile up, heap up, add, repeat. *kasa(naru)* pile up, be piled; lie on one another. *omo(ru)* get heavy; grow serious. *omo(njiru), omo(nzuru)* honor, respect, esteem, prize. *omo(i), omo(tai)* heavy; massive; serious; important; severe; oppressed. *omo(mi)* importance, weight, dignity. *omo(sa)* weight. *kasa(ne)* pile, heap, layer; suits; set; course (of stones). *kasa(nete)* repeatedly, again. *omo(na), omo(naru)* main, principal, important. *jū-* heavy; double. *-e* -fold, ply. *-jū* -fold.

² 力 *jūryoku* gravity

³ 工業 *jūkōgyō* heavy industry

大 *jūdai na* important, serious

大化 *jūdaika* aggravation

大性 *jūdaisei* importance, seriousness

大視 *jūdaishi* taking (something) seriously

⁴ 心 *jūshin* center of gravity

火器 *jūkaki* heavy weapons

⁵ 用 *jūyō suru* appoint to a responsible post

石 *omoshi, omo(shi) ishi* stone weights on pickle-tub covers

圧 *jūatsu* pressure

犯 *jūhan, chōhan* felony; felon; old offender

⁶ 臣 *jūshin* chief vassal; senior statesman

任 *jūnin* heavy responsibility, important post; re-election, reappointment

刑 *jūkei* heavy sentence

⁷ 体 *jūtai* seriously ill

役 *omoyaku* heavy responsibilities; director. *jūyaku* director, directorate

労働 *jūrōdō* heavy labor; hard labor (in prison)

⁸ 味 *omomi* weight; importance; emphasis; dignity

油 *jūyu* crude oil; fuel oil

版 *jūhan* additional printing, literary piracy

宝 *chōhō(garu)* find useful; think lightly of. *chōhō* convenience, usefulness. *chōhō, jūhō* priceless treasure

苦 *omokuru(shii)* heavy, cumbrous; gloomy, oppressive, leaden; awkward (expression)

金属 *jūkinzoku* heavy metals

⁹ 厚 *jūkō* thickness; composure and dignity. *chōkō* composure and dignity

重 *kasa(ne)gasa(ne)* frequently; sincerely; exceedingly. *omoomo(shii)* serious, grave, dignified. *jūjū no* repeated, manifold. *jūjū ni* extremely. *jūjū nimo* repeatedly

点 *jūten* colon; emphasis, importance

要 *jūyō na* important, momentous; essential; principal, major

要視 *jūyōshi suru* regard highly

¹⁰ 病 *jūbyō* serious illness

砲 *jūhō* heavy artillery

症 *jūshō* serious illness

¹¹ 視 *jūshi* serious consideration

陽 *chōyō* Chrysanthemum Festival (the ninth day of the ninth lunar month)

曹 *jūsō* sodium bicarbonate, baking soda

責 *jūseki* heavy responsibility

商主義 *jūshō shugi* mercantilism

婚 *jūkon* bigamy

¹² 税 *jūzei* heavy taxation

畳 *chōjō* piled one upon another; excellent, splendid

7

見
角
言
谷
豆
豕
豸
貝
赤
走
足
身
車
辛
辰
辵
辶
邑
阝
酉
釆
【里】
2

着 *kasa(ne)gi* wearing one garment over another
量 *jūryō* weight; heavyweight boxer
量挙 *jūryōa(ge)* weight lifting
量感 *jūryōkan* thick and heavy
¹³罪 *jūzai* felony, serious crime
農主義 *jūnō shugi* emphasizing agriculture
傷 *jūshō, omode* serious wound or injury
¹⁴罰 *jūbatsu* heavy punishment
態 *jūtai* seriously ill
複 *chōfuku, jūfuku* duplication, overlapping, repetition, redundancy
¹⁵箱 *jūbako* nest of boxes
箱読 *jūbako yo(mi)* mixed *on-kun* pronunciation
¹⁶篤 *jūtoku na* serious (illness)
機 *jūki* heavy machine gun
¹⁸職 *jūshoku* responsible position
鎮 *jūchin* leader, authority, mainstay

──────── 4 ────────

野 [6208 / J4c6e / M40133] A YA field, plain; the Opposition; civilian life; rustic. *no* field, plain. *ya-, no-* wild.
³山 *noyama* hills and fields
⁴牛 *noushi, yagyū* wild ox, bison, buffalo
犬 *yaken* stray dog
心 *yashin* ambition, aspiration, sinister design, intrigue, treachery
⁵史 *yashi* an unauthorized history
生 *yasei* wildness; wild
生動物 *yasei dōbutsu* wild animals
生植物 *yasei shokubutsu* wild plants
外 *yagai* the fields, the open air, outdoors; suburbs
外運動 *yagai undō* a field sport, outdoor exercises
⁶合 *yagō* cohabitation without marriage
⁷良 *nora* the fields; laziness
良犬 *nora inu* stray dog
良仕事 *nora shigoto* farm work, field work
良猫 *nora neko* stray cat
良着 *noragi* farm field smock
⁸郎 *yarō* fellow, guy, rogue
性 *yasei* wild nature, uncouthness
性的 *yaseiteki* wild, rough, mean, rude
放 *nobana(shi)* posturing; pasture; leaving things to themselves

放図 *nohōzu na* haphazard, wild, proud
⁹面 *nozura* the field
卑 *yahi na* rode, coarse, vulgar
草 *yasō* wild grass, wild pants. *nogusa* grass in a field
¹⁰原 *nohara* plain, field, moor, wilderness, prairie
晒 *nozara(shi) no* weatherworn
党 *yatō* opposition party
倒死 *notareji(ni)* dying of exposure
砲 *yahō* field gun; field artillery
¹¹鳥 *yachō* wild fowl, wild bird
遊 *noaso(bi)* picnic, outing
道 *nomichi* road across a field
宿 *nojuku* camping out
望 *yabō* ambition, aspiration, sinister design, intrigue, treachery
菜 *yasai* vegetables
球 *yakyū* baseball
¹²焼 *noya(ki)* winter burning of the fields
景 *yakei* view of open fields; landscape views
蛮 *yaban* heathenism, barbarism
蛮人 *yabanjin* barbarian, savage
営 *yaei* camping, camp, bivouac
¹³戦 *yasen* open warfare, field operations
¹⁴暮 *yabo na* rustic, unrefined; stupid, unfeeling; stale; conventional
¹⁵趣 *yashu* rural beauty, rural air, rusticity
¹⁶積 *nozu(mi)* piling up (supplies) outside
獣 *yajū* wild animal, wild game

──────── 5 ────────

量 [6209 / J4e4c / M40138] A RYŌ quantity, amount, volume; magnanimity; a measure. *haka(ru)* measure, gauge, weigh; fathom, sound; compute, estimate.
⁴水器 *ryōsuiki* water meter
⁵目 *ryōme* weight
⁶刑 *ryōkei* weighing an offense
⁷売 *haka(ri)u(ri)* selling by measure
⁸的 *ryōteki* quantitative
¹¹産 *ryōsan* mass production
¹²感 *ryōkan* volume (in a painting)

8-STROKE RADICALS

■■■ RAD. 金 167 ■■■

Kane metal, money, gold. At left: 金 *kane hen*. Nickname: Metal.

A 金 ⁶²¹¹ ^{J3662} ^{M40152} KON. KIN gold; money; Friday. *kane* money, metal. *kana-* metal.

¹ 一封 *kin'ippū* a wrapped gift of money
² 力 *kinryoku* the power of wealth
³ 子 *kinsu* money, funds
山 *kanayama* metal mine. *kinzan* gold mine; mountain fortress
⁴ 欠病 *kinketsubyō* sick from shortage of lays the golden egg
目 *kaneme* monetary value
本位制 *kinhon'isei* gold standard
⁶ 回 *kanemawa(ri)* money circulation; financial condition
糸 *kinshi* gold thread, spun gold
字塔 *kinjitō* a pyramid; a monumental work
色 *kinshoku, kin iro, konjiki* golden color
⁷ 言 *kingen* maxim, golden rule, aphorism
利 *kinri* interest rate, bank rate
⁸ 杯 *kimpai* gold cup
具 *kanagu* metal fittings or fixtures
物 *kanamono* hardware
物屋 *kanamonoya* hardware store
⁹ 廻 *kanemawa(ri)* money circulation; financial condition
持 *kanemochi* person of wealth
品 *kimpin* money and valuables
星 *Kinsei* Venus. *kimboshi* splendid victory
型 *kanegata* metal pattern
科玉条 *kinka-gyokujō* one's watchword; a consuming principle; an excellent law
城湯池 *kinjō-tōchi* a impregnable castle
¹⁰ 粉 *kimpun, kinko* gold dust
脈 *kimmyaku* gold vein
庫 *kinko, kanegura* safe, vault; cashbox; depository; treasure house; financier
剛 *kongō* diamond; great strength; strong man; emery powder

剛石 *kongōseki* diamond
¹¹ 堂 *kondō* main temple structure
魚 *kingyo* goldfish
魚鉢 *kingyobachi* goldfish bowl
貨 *kinka* gold coin
¹² 歯 *kimba* gold tooth
遣 *kanezuka(i)* way of spending
策 *kinsaku suru* raise money, get a loan. *kinsaku* means of raising money
無垢 *kimmuku* pure gold
満家 *kimmanka* wealthy person, millionaire
棒 *kanabō* iron rod, metal rod, bar; crowbar; iron club; horizontal bar
貸 *kaneka(shi)* moneylender; moneylending
属 *kinzoku* metal
属疲労 *kinzoku hirō* metal fatigue
属製 *kinzokusei* made of metal
属製品 *kinzoku seihin* hardware
¹³ 搔 *kanaga(ki)* farmer's hoeing fork
詰 *kanezuma(ri), kinzuma(ri)* shortage of money
槌 *kanazuchi* hammer, sledge
鉱 *kinkō* gold ore
¹⁴ 網 *kanaami* wire netting, screen
蔵 *kanegura* treasure house; financier, backer
蔓 *kanezuru* source of money, a "gold mine"
髪 *kimpatsu* fair hair; blonde; golden hair, auburn hair
製 *kinsei* made of gold
管楽器 *kinkan gakki* brass musical instrument
銀 *kingin* gold and silver; money
箔 *kimpaku* gold leaf, gold foil
銭 *kinsen* money, cash
銭登録器 *kinsen tōrokuki* cash register
¹⁵ 縁 *kimbuchi* gold rims, gilt frame, gilt edges; gold-rimmed (glasses)
輪際 *konrinzai* never, by no means

8

⁰〔金〕

長門阜阝隶隹雨青非

権 *kinken* almighty dollar, financial influence

権政治 *kinken seiji* plutocracy

16 盥 *kanadarai* metal basin, washbowl

融 *kin'yū* money (market); credit situation, money circulation; financial

融業 *kin'yūgyō* financial operations, banking business

融機関 *kin'yū kikan* banking facilities

17 鎚 *kanazuchi* hammer, sledge

環食 *kinkanshoku* annular solar eclipse

環蝕 *kinkanshoku* annular solar eclipse

18 額 *kingaku* amount of money

儲 *kanemōke* money-making

曜 *Kin'yō* Friday

曜日 *Kin'yōbi* Friday

20 簪 *kin kanzashi, kinsan* gold hairpin

22 襴 *kinran* gold brocade

─────── **2** ───────

釜 6215 J3378 M40164 Fu. *kama* kettle, cauldron, iron pot; boiler. *kanae* three-legged kettle.

12 飯 *kamameshi* rice served in the kettle

釘 6217 J4523 M40159 Tei. Chō. *kugi* nail, spike, tack; rivet; peg.

針 6218 J3f4b M40165 Shin needle. *hari* needle, pin; staple; fishhook; stinger; spine (of a fish); thorn; stitch; (watch) hand; (phonograph) needle; (hypodermic) needle; sting; molehill; acupuncture. *(o)hari* needlework, sewing; seamstress. A

3 山 *hariyama* pincushion

小棒大 *shinshō-bōdai* exaggeration, hyperbole

5 目 *harime* seam

仕事 *hari shigoto* needlework, sewing

8 刺 *harisa(shi)* pincushion

金 *harigane* wire

12 葉樹 *shin'yōju* coniferous tree, needle-leaf tree

13 路 *shinro* direction, compass bearing

15 箱 *haribako* needlecase, sewing box

─────── **3** ───────

釧 6222 J367c M40176 Sen bracelet.

鈕 6223 J4b55 M40175 Kō. *botan* button.

鈎 6224 J4460 M40172 Chō. *tsu(ru)* angle, fish, catch; decoy, allure. *tsu(reru)* be caught; have a cramp. *tsu(ri)* change (for a dollar); (rod) fishing. B

3 下 *tsu(ri)-sa(geru)* suspend from

上 *tsu(ri)-a(geru)* pull in (a fish); raise (one's eyes); boost (prices). *tsu(ri)-a(garu)* be hung up, be lifted up, turn up

6 糸 *tsuri ito* fishing line

合 *tsu(ri)-a(u)* match, suit, balance, be in harmony, be in proportion. *tsuriai* balance, equilibrium, proportion, symmetry, harmony, match

8 具 *tsurigu* fishing tackle

9 竿 *tsurizao* fishing rod

10 師 *tsurishi* angler

針 *tsuribari* fishhook

11 堀 *tsuribori* fishpond

船 *tsuribune* fishing boat; boat-shaped vase

梯子 *tsuribashigo* rope ladder

道具 *tsuri dōgu* fishing tackle

魚 *tsuriuo* game fish. *chōgyo* angling, fishing

瓶 *tsurube* well bucket

12 場 *tsuriba* fishing place

棚 *tsuridana* hanging shelf

14 銭 *tsurisen* change (for a dollar)

16 橋 *tsuribashi* suspension bridge

20 鐘 *tsurigane* hanging bell; temple bell

22 籠 *tsuri kago* fisherman's basket; hanging basket

─────── **4** ───────

鈎 6226 J3343 M40220 See 鉤 6250.

鈍 6235 J465f M40219 Don dullness, slowness, foolishness. *nibu(ru)* become dull, weaken. *nibu(rasu)*, *nibu(raseru)* dull, blunt, take the edge off, weaken. *nama(ru)* get dull. *nama(kura)* blunt sword, lazy fellow. *noro(i)* slow, dilatory, dull; flirtatious. *nibu(i)* dull, slow; blunt (tool); dim (light); thick (voice). *noro* dullness. B

3 才 *donsai* dullness, stupidity

⁶行 *donkō* ordinary train
⁷角 *donkaku* obtuse angle
⁸重 *donjū* dull-witted, stolid, phlegmatic
¹²痛 *dontsū* dull pain
¹³感 *donkan* stolidity, thickheadedness
¹⁵器 *donki* dull weapon, blunt sword

――――― 5 ―――――

鈷 [6236 / J385a / M40270] Ko Buddhist weapon; cobalt, sky blue, navy blue. *hinoshi* an iron, a flatiron.

鉦 [6246 / J3e60 / M40322] SEI, SHŌ gong. *kane* bell, gong, chimes, carillon.

B 鈴 [6247 / J4e6b / M40267] REI, RIN bell, hand bell, buzzer. *suzu* bell.
⁵生 *suzuna(ri)* abundance of fruit (on a tree)
¹⁹蘭 *suzuran* lily-of-the-valley

B 鉢 [6249 / J482d / M40317] HATSU, HACHI bowl, rice tub, pot; crown, brainpan.
⁶合 *hachia(wase)* bumping of heads, collision
⁹巻 *hachimaki* (towel) headband, hatband, frontlet
¹²植 *hachiu(e)* potted plant

鉤 [6250 / J6e6c / M40319] 鈎 [6226 / J3343 / M40220] Kō. *kagi* hook, barb, gaff; brackets (in punctuation).
²十字 *kagi jūji* swastika
⁴手 *kagi(no)te* right angle; bend; bend in the road; kleptomaniac
¹⁰針 *kagibari* hook, crochet hook
¹²裂 *kagiza(ki)* tear, rent (in one's clothes)
¹⁴鼻 *kagibana* hooked nose
縄 *kagi nawa* hooked rope

B 鉛 [6251 / J3174 / M40310] EN. *namari* lead (metal).
⁸直 *enchoku* perpendicular, plumb
毒 *endoku* lead poisoning
¹²筆 *empitsu* lead pencil
¹⁴管 *enkan* lead pipe

A 鉱 [6252 / J395b / M40340] 砿 [3994 / J395c / M-X] Kō ore.
³工業 *kōkōgyō* mining and manufacturing
山 *kōzan, kanayama* mine

⁴夫 *kōfu* miner
⁵石 *kōseki* ore, mineral, (radio) crystal
⁸毒 *kōdoku* mine pollution; copper poisoning
物 *kōbutsu* minerals, inorganic substances
物学 *kōbutsugaku* mineralogy
物質 *kōbutsushitsu* mineral matter
⁹泉 *kōsen* mineral springs
¹⁰脈 *kōmyaku* vein of ore
¹³業 *kōgyō* mining industry

A 鉄 [6253 / J4534 / M40285] TETSU iron, steel; reddish black, iron blue. *kurogane* iron. *kana-, kane-* metal.
²人 *tetsujin* a very robust man
³工 *tekkō* ironworker, blacksmith
⁴火 *tekka* red-hot iron; ordeal; gunfire; swords and guns; brave heart
火巻 *tekkamaki* tuna slices rolled in rice and covered with laver
火場 *tekkaba* gambling room; battlefield
⁶血 *tekketsu* blood and iron; war preparations; military strength
⁷材 *tetsuzai* iron or steel material
条網 *tetsujōmō* barbed-wire entanglement
⁸板 *teppan, tetsu ita, tetsuban* steel plate, sheet of iron ⌈plate
板焼 *teppan'yaki* meat roasted on a hot
⁹則 *tessoku* ironclad rule
面皮 *tetsumempi* impudence, audacity
¹⁰屑 *tetsu kuzu* scrap iron
扇 *tessen* iron-ribbed fan
格子 *tetsugōshi* iron-barred window, iron grating
拳 *tekken* clenched fist
骨 *tekkotsu* steel frame
砲 *teppō* gun, firearms; bath fire-pipe
¹¹瓶 *tetsubin* iron teakettle
道 *tetsudō* railway, railroad
道線路 *tetsudō senro* railroad track; right-of-way
¹²塔 *tettō* steel tower
筋 *tekkin* ferro-(concrete), iron bar
腕投手 *tetsuwan tōshu* cannon-ball pitcher
棒 *kanabō, tetsubō* iron rod, metal rod, bar; crowbar; iron club; horizontal bar
¹³路 *tetsuro* railroad
槌 *tettsui* iron hammer; large hammer; hammer (in sports)

8
⁵【金】

長門阜阝隶隹雨青非

鉱 *tekkō* iron ore
14 管 *tekkan* iron pipe
製 *tessei* made of iron or steel
15 器 *tekki* ironware, hardware; grill, gridiron; iron tool
器時代 *Tekki Jidai* Iron Age
16 橋 *tekkyō* steel bridge
蹄 *tettei* horseshoe
壁 *teppeki* iron wall; impregnable fortress
鋼 *tekkō* iron and steel
鋼業 *tekkōgyō* iron-and-steel industry
18 鎖 *tessa* iron chain

──────── 6 ────────

鉾 $\frac{6255}{J4b48}$ See 矛 3974.
M40353

銚 $\frac{6260}{J4438}$ CHŌ saké bottle.
M40387
3 子 *chōshi* saké dipper; saké bottle

銑 $\frac{6263}{J412d}$ SEN. *zuku* pig iron.
B M40376
13 鉄 *sentetsu, zukutetsu* pig iron

銭 $\frac{6264}{J412c}$ SEN. *one*-hundredth of a
A M40413 yen; coin. *zeni* money.
8 金 *zenikane* money
12 湯 *sentō* bathhouse, public bath

銘 $\frac{6265}{J4c43}$ MEI inscription, signature
B M40385 (of an artisan); precept, motto. *mei(jiru), mei(zuru)* engrave, impress upon.
9 柄 *meigara* brand, name, description
茶 *meicha* refined tea
10 記 *meiki suru* impress upon
酒 *meishu* superior saké
銘 *meimei ni* apiece, to each
銘伝 *meimeiden* lives, biographies

銅 $\frac{6266}{J463c}$ DŌ copper. *aka, akagane*
A M40361 copper.
3 山 *dōzan* copper mine
8 版 *dōban* copperplate
11 貨 *dōka* copper coin
14 像 *dōzō* bronze statue, bronze image
15 器 *dōki* bronze or copper utensil, copperware
器時代 *Dōki Jidai* Bronze Age

19 鏡 *dōkyō* bronze mirror
21 鐸 *dōtaku* bronze bell
27 鑼 *dora* gong, tom-tom
鑼声 *doragoe* gruff voice

銃 $\frac{6267}{J3d46}$ JŪ gun, arms. *tsutsu* gun.
B M40359
3 口 *jūkō, tsutsuguchi* gun muzzle
4 火 *jūka* gunfire
7 身 *jūshin* gun barrel
床 *jūshō* gun stock
声 *jūsei* a shot, gun report
9 後 *jūgo* home front
10 殺 *jūsatsu* shooting to death, execution by shooting
剣 *jūken* bayonet, side arms
11 眼 *jūgan* loophole
猟 *jūryō* hunting
12 弾 *jūdan* bullet
15 撃 *jūgeki* rifle shooting
器 *jūki* small arms

銀 $\frac{6268}{J3664}$ GIN silver. *shirogane*
A M40355 silver. *gim(bura)* a stroll along the Ginza.
3 山 *ginzan* silver mine
5 世界 *gin sekai* silvery world, vast snowy scene
本位制 *gin hon'isei* silver standard
6 色 *gin iro, ginshoku* silver color, silvery
行 *ginkō* bank
行員 *ginkōin* bank clerk, bank staff
7 杏 *ginnan* gingko nut. *ichō* gingko tree, maidenhair tree
8 杯 *gimpai* silver cup
河 *Ginga* Milky Way; the Galaxy
9 盃 *gimpai* silver cup
10 座 *ginza* silver mint; the Ginza
紙 *gingami* silver paper
11 貨 *ginka* silver coin
12 牌 *gimpai* silver medal
筋 *ginsuji* silver line
13 鼠 *ginnezumi, ginnezu* silver grey
幕 *gimmaku* silver screen
14 髪 *gimpatsu* silver hair
製 *ginsei* made of silver
製品 *ginseihin* silverware, silver utensil
15 盤 *gimban* skating rink; ice surface; large silver platter
器 *ginki* silver utensils

─────── **7** ───────

鋪 _{6269 J4a5f M40491} See 舖 322.

舖

鋒 _{6275 J4b2f M40455} Hō dagger, sword's point. *hoko* halberd; arms; festival car, float.

鋲 _{6277 J4946 M40503} (国字) *byō* rivet, tack, thumbtack, hobnail.

鋤 _{6278 J3d7b M40480} Jo. *su(ku)* spade up, plow. *suki* spade for cultivation, plow.
¹⁷ 鍬 *suki-kuwa* plows and hoes, farm tools

鋭 B _{6279 J3154 M40418} Eɪ sharpness; edge; (sharp) weapon; picked men (soldiers), the pick. *surudo(i)* pointed, sharp; violent, scathing; keen (sense); sharp (ear); penetrating (eye); shrewd.
⁶ 気 *eiki* courage, ardor, high spirits
⁷ 角 *eikaku* acute angle
利 *eiri* sharpness, keenness
¹⁰ 敏 *eibin* sharpness, keenness, sensitiveness; mental acumen
¹³ 意 *eii* eagerly, earnestly
¹⁵ 鋒 *eihō* brunt of an attack or argument

鋳 B _{6280 J4372 M40503'} SHU. SHŪ, CHŪ casting. *i(ru)* cast, mint, coin.
⁴ 込 *i-ko(mu)* cast in a mold
⁸ 金 *chūkin* casting
物 *imono* cast metal; casting
⁹ 型 *igata* mold; pig bed; matrix; die
造 *chūzō* casting, founding; minting, coining
¹¹ 掛屋 *ika(ke)ya* tinner ⌈casting
鉄 *itetsu, chūtetsu, igane* cast iron, iron
¹⁴ 像 *chūzō* molten image
¹⁵ 潰 *i-tsubu(su)* melt down
¹⁶ 鋼 *chūkō* steel casting; cast steel

─────── **8** ───────

鎚 _{6281 J444a M-X} Nonstandard for 鎚 6310.

鎚

錘 B _{6291 J3f6e M40547} Suɪ. *omori* weight, plumb bob, sinker, sounding lead. *tsumu* spindle.

錫 _{6292 J3c62 M40573} Sekɪ, Shaku copper; gold-copper alloy. *suzu* tin.

錠 B _{6293 J3e7b M40559} Chō. Teɪ. Jō lock, padlock, latch; pill; close up; counter for pills.
⁹ 前 *jōmae* lock
¹⁰ 剤 *jōzai* pill, lozenge, tablet

錐 _{6294 J3f6d M40536} Suɪ pyramid; cone; gimlet. *kiri* auger, drill, awl, gimlet.
¹² 揉 *kirimo(mi)* drilling, boring; tailspin

錨 _{6295 J4945 M40598} Byō. Myō. *ikari* anchor, grapnel.
⁶ 地 *byōchi* anchorage
⁸ 泊 *byōhaku* anchorage, anchoring
¹⁸ 鎖 *byōsa* chain cable

錆 _{6296 J3b2c M40523} Shō. *sabi(ru)* get rusty, rust; mature and die (fish). *sabi* rust, tarnish.
⁴ 止 *sabido(me)* rust preventative
⁶ 色 *sabi iro* rust color, reddish brown

鋸 _{6297 J3578 M40505} Kyo. *nokogiri, noko* saw.
¹² 歯 *nokogiriba, kyoshi* saw tooth; indentation

録 A _{6298 J4f3f M40519} Roku. *shiru(su)*, *roku(suru)* record.
⁸ 画 *rokuga* television recording
⁹ 音 *rokuon* sound recording, transcription

錯 B _{6299 J3a78 M40579} Saku mix; be in disorder. *ma(zeru)* mix, blend, mingle; include, let in on. *ma(jiru)* be mixed, be blended; mingle with.
⁷ 乱 *sakuran* confusion, distraction, derangement
¹² 覚 *sakkaku* optical illusion; hallucination
¹⁴ 綜 *sakusō* complication, intricacy
誤 *sakugo* mistake
雑 *sakuzatsu* complication, intricacy

錬 B _{6300 J4f23 M40576} Ren. *ne(ru)* refine (metals); drill, train; polish (sentences). *ne(ri)* tempering.

8
【金】₈
長門阜阝隶隹雨青非

8
【金】

長門阜阝隶隹雨青非

⁶成 *rensei* training, drilling
⁸金術 *renkinjutsu* alchemy
¹³鉄 *rentetsu, ne(ri)kurogane* wrought iron

錦 6301 / J3653 / M40569 KIN. *nishiki* brocade; fine dress; honors.
¹²絵 *nishikie* woodblock color print

A 鋼 6302 / J395d / M40509 KŌ steel. *hagane* steel.
⁷材 *kōzai* rolled steel; steel materials
⁸板 *kōhan, kōban* steel sheet, steel plate
¹⁰索 *kōsaku* wire rope or cable
¹³鉄 *kōtetsu* steel
鉄板 *kōtetsuban* steel plate
鉄製 *kōtetsusei* made of steel
¹⁴管 *kōkan* steel tubing

———— 9 ————

鎚 6310 / J-X / M40715 TSUI. *tsuchi* hammer, mallet.

鍾 6311 / J3e61 / M40672 SHŌ gather, collect.

鍍 6312 / J4555 / M40607 TO plating, gilding.
⁸金 *mekki, tokin* gilt; gilding, plating; gold plating; gold filled

鍔 6313 / J4457 / M40617 GAKU. *tsuba* sword guard; supporting brim of a kettle.
⁷迫合 *tsubazeria(i)* close fighting

鍬 6314 / J372d / M40643 SHŌ. *kuwa* hoe with long blade set at an acute angle.

鍋 6315 / J4669 / M40603 KA. *nabe* pan, pot, kettle.
¹²焼 *nabeya(ki)* scalloped; cooked in a casserole

鍵 6317 / J3830 / M40654 KEN (piano) key. *kagi* key.
⁵穴 *kagi ana* keyhole
¹⁵盤 *kemban* keyboard

B 鍛 6318 / J4343 / M40625 TAN. *kita(eru)* forge, temper; drill, train, practice.
³上 *kita(e)-a(geru)* temper thoroughly; train well
⁷冶 *tan'ya* forging. *kaji* blacksmith
冶工 *kajikō* metalworker, blacksmith
冶屋 *kajiya* blacksmith
⁹造 *tanzō* forging
¹³鉄 *tantetsu* tempering iron; wrought iron, malleable iron
¹⁶錬 *tanren* temper, forging; hardening; discipline, training

———— 10 ————

鎗 6320 / J4179 / M40709 SŌ. *yari* spear, lance, javelin.

鎧 6324 / J333b / M40735 GAI. *yoro(u)* put on armor; arm oneself. *yoroi* suit of armor.
⁴戸 *yoroido* Venetian blinds
¹⁰袖一触 *gaishū-isshoku* easy victory

B 鎖 6325 / J3a3f / M40708 SA. *kusari* chain; irons; connection. *to(zasu)* shut, close, lock, fasten; plunge (in grief).
⁷状 *sajō* chainlike
⁸国 *sakoku* national isolation, exclusion of foreigners
¹⁰骨 *sakotsu* clavicle, collarbone

鎌 6326 / J3379 / M40693 REN. *kama* sickle, scythe; trick.
⁹首 *kamakubi* gooseneck

鎔 6327 / J6f30 / M40704 ‖ 熔 3458 / J4d50 / M19319 YŌ. *to(keru) vi* fuse, melt. *to(kasu) vt* fuse, melt, smelt.
⁸岩 *yōgan* lava
岩流 *yōganryū* lava flow
⁹点 *yōten* melting point
¹¹接 *yōsetsu* welding
¹³鉱炉 *yōkōro* blast furnace
解 *yōkai* melting, fusing
鉄 *yōtetsu* ingot iron, ingot steel
¹⁶融 *yōyū* fusion, melting, smelting, flux
融点 *yōyūten* melting point

B 鎮 6328 / J4443 / M40745 CHIN ancient garrisons for peace-preservation.

shizu(maru) vi get quiet, calm down, grow still; subside, die down; be suppressed.
shizu(meru) vt calm, pacify; soothe, alleviate; appease; suppress, quell.
shizu(me) pillar (of society).

⁴ 火 *chinka suru* be extinguished, be brought under control
⁵ 圧 *chin'atsu* suppression, subjugation
⁶ 守 *chinju* local Shinto deity, tutelary god
⁸ 定 *chintei suru* suppress, repress, subdue, pacify
¹⁰ 座 *chinza suru* be enshrined
¹² 痛 *chintsū* relieving pain
痛剤 *chintsūzai* painkiller, sedative
¹⁴ 静 *chinsei* calm, quiet, tranquillity; appeasement, pacification
魂 *chinkon* repose of souls

鐙 6348 J462a M40904 Tō. *abumi* stirrup.

B 鐘 6352 J3e62 M40902 Shō. Shu. *kane* bell, gong, chimes, carillon.
⁸ 乳洞 *shōnyūdō* stalactite cave
¹³ 楼 *shōrō, shurō* belfry, bell tower
¹⁵ 撞堂 *kanetsukidō* bell tower, belfry

--- **13** ---

鐸 6356 J4278 M40951 Taku large hand bell.

鑓 6357 J-X M40998 (国字) *yari* spear, lance, javelin.

--- **11** ---

A 鏡 6341 J3640 M40812 Kyō. *kagami* mirror; speculum; barrelhead. round rice-cake offering.
⁵ 台 *kyōdai* dresser, mirror stand
¹² 開 *kagamibira(ki)* cutting the New Year's rice cakes
¹⁵ 餅 *kagamimochi* round glutenous-rice cakes (often used as offerings)

--- **12** ---

鑓 6343 J4c7a M-X Nonstandard for 鑓 6357.

--- **14** ---

B 鑑 6361 J3455 M40988 Kan. *kanga(miru)* take warning from, learn a lesson from. *kagami* mirror, pattern, example. *kanga(mite)* in view of, learning a lesson from.
⁵ 札 *kansatsu* license, permit
⁷ 別 *kambetsu* discrimination, judgment
⁸ 定 *kantei* judgment, expert opinion, legal advice, appraisal, criticism
定書 *kanteisho* expert's report
⁹ 査 *kansa* inspection; inspector
¹⁵ 賞 *kanshō* appreciation
¹⁹ 識 *kanshiki* judgment, discernment, discrimination, appreciation

---

RAD. 長 168

Nagai long. At left; 镸 (7 strokes) *nagai hen*. Nickname: Long.

A 長 6379 J4439 M41100 Chō head, chief, headman, commander, director, manager; merit, forte, advantage; superiority; length. *chō(jiru), chō(zuru)* grow up; be one's senior; excel in. *naga(raeru)* live long, live on. *naga(meru)* lengthen, prolong. *ta(keru)* excel in, be proficient in; grow older. *naga(i)* long, lengthy. *naga(ki)* length, long period. *naga(ku)* long, a long time, eternally. *naga(sa)* length. *naga(tarashii)* lengthy, long and boring. *osa* chief, head. *naga(no)* long, eternal. *tokoshi(e) ni* forever. *naga(raku)* long, a long time. *chō-* long; deep.
³ 女 *chōjo* eldest daughter
子 *chōshi* eldest son; first child

8

金 長 【門】
阜 阝 隶 隹 雨 青 非

久 *chōkyū* permanence, endurance; eternity, perpetuity

上 *chōjō* a senior, one's elder, a superior

⁴月 *nagatsuki* ninth lunar month

引 *nagabi(kaseru)* prolong, drag out. *nagabi(ku)* be prolonged, drag out

方形 *chōhōkei* rectangle, oblong

文 *chōbun* long letter, long document

⁵生 *chōsei, nagaiki* long life, longevity

幼 *chōyō* young and old

兄 *chōkei* eldest brother

広舌 *chōkōzetsu* eloquence; long-windedness

⁶江 *chōkō* long river; Yangzi Jiang

老 *chōrō* an elder, a senior, a superior; priest, presbyter

年 *naganen* a long time, many years

⁷足 *chōsoku* rapid strides, leaps and ⌐ bounds

身 *chōshin* great stature

男 *chōnan* eldest son

寿 *chōju* longevity, long life

⁸長 *naganaga(shii)* long-drawn-out. *naganaga to* very long, at great length; tediously

雨 *nagaame* a long rain

居 *nagai* a long visit, overstaying

所 *chōsho* one's forte, strong point; advantages

命 *chōmei* a long life, longevity

官 *chōkan* magistrate, chief, governor, president, secretary, administrator, director

者 *chōja* millionaire, rich person. *chōsha* one's superior, one's senior

波 *chōha* a long wave

⁹屋 *nagaya* tenement building, long apartment house ⌐distance

途 *chōto, nagamichi* a long way, a great 逝 *chōsei suru* die, pass away

持 *nagamo(chi)* oblong chest; durability, endurance

音 *chōon* a long sound, a long vowel, long tone, dash

¹⁰唄 *nagauta* song accompanied by the samisen

旅 *nagatabi* a long trip

袖 *nagasode, chōshū* long-sleeved kimono or its wearer; courtiers

針 *chōshin* the long hand, the minute hand

時間 *chōjikan* a long time; long-playing

¹¹蛇 *chōda* a long snake; a long line, a long queue; a hero

距離 *chōkyori* a long distance, a long range

¹²閑 *nodo(kana), nodo(yakana)* tranquil, mild, peaceful, balmy. *nodo(kesa)* tranquility, serenity, calmness

湯 *nagayu* staying in the bath a long time

椅子 *nagaisu* couch, settee

短 *chōtan* length; long and short, merits and demerits. *naga(shi)-mijika(shi)* either too long or too short

期 *chōki* a long period

期予報 *chōki yohō* long-range forecasting

期戦 *chōkisen* prolonged war

¹³煩 *nagawazura(i)* a long illness

話 *nagabanashi* a long talk, tedious talk

靴 *nagagutsu* boots; high shoes. *chōka* high shoes

嘆息 *chōtansoku* a deep sigh

¹⁴駆 *chōku suru* ride a long distance; pursue the enemy a long distance

歌 *chōka, nagauta* a long epic poem

髪 *chōhatsu* long hair

¹⁵調 *chōchō* major key

編 *chōhen* a long story; a long poem; a long film

篇 *chōhen* a long story; a long poem; a long film

¹⁹襦袢 *nagajuban* long underwear

RAD. 門 169

Mon or *kado* gate. As enclosure: *mongamae* or *kadogamae*. Nickname: Gate.

A 門 6381 J4c67 M41208 MON gate, gateway; private school; class; counter for cannon. *kado* gate, door.

²人 *monjin* disciple, pupil

³口 *kadoguchi* gateway, entrance, front door

下 *monka* vicinity of the gate; disciple, pupil; discipleship

下生 *monkasei* disciple, pupil

⁴戸 *monko* door, entrance; pedigree, lineage

⁵生 *monsei* pupil, disciple

付 *kadozu(ke)* strolling singer, street musician

札 *monsatsu, kado fuda* name plate

出 *kadode, kadoide* departure

外 *mongai* outside the gate; outside one's speciality; another matter

外漢 *mongaikan* outsider, layperson, someone outside the field

⁶灯 *montō* gate light

⁷弟 *montei* pupil, disciple

⁸松 *kadomatsu* New Year's pine-and-bamboo decorations

限 *mongen* closing time, curfew

⁹柱 *monchū, mombashira* gatepost

前 *monzen* before the gate

前払 *monzembara(i)* turning people away at the gate

前町 *monzemmachi* a temple town, a shrine town

¹⁰徒 *monto* believer, adherent; student

¹²扉 *mompi* leaves of a gate

番 *momban* doorkeeper

¹³跡 *monzeki* priest prince; temple whose head is a prince; Honganji Temple

¹⁴閥 *mombatsu* pedigree, lineage

¹⁶衛 *mon'ei* guard, porter, gatekeeper

─────── 2 ───────

閃 <u>6383</u> <u>J412e</u> <u>M41214</u> SEN. *hirame(kasu)* brandish, flash, display. *hirame(ku)* flash, flicker; flutter, wave.

⁶光 *senkō* flash, glint

─────── 3 ───────

A 閉 <u>6385</u> <u>J4a44</u> <u>M41222</u> HEI. *to(jiru), shi(meru)* shut, close. *to(zasu)* shut, close, lock, fasten; plunge (in grief).

³口 *heikō suru* be dumbfounded, be stumped, be silent

⁴込 *to(ji)-ko(meru)* lock up, shut in, confine. *ta(te)-ko(meru)* shut up (the house)

⁶会 *heikai* adjournment, closing

⁷廷 *heitei* court adjournment

⁸門 *heimon* closing the gate; house imprisonment

店 *heiten* closing the shop; going out of business

¹³塞 *to(ji)-fusa(geru)* close up, cover over. *heisoku* blockade

幕 *heimaku* falling of the curtain

¹⁶館 *heikan suru* close the doors (of a hall)

¹⁸鎖 *heisa* closing, closure, lockout

²²籠 *to(ji)-komo(ru)* confine oneself, remain indoors

─────── 4 ───────

閏 <u>6389</u> <u>J313c</u> <u>M41244</u> JUN intercalation. intercalary month; illegitimate throne. *urū* intercalation.

⁶年 *urūdoshi, junnen* leap year; intercalary year

B 閑 <u>6390</u> <u>J3457</u> <u>M41247</u> KAN. *hima* leisure.

⁵古鳥 *kankodori* cuckoo

⁷却 *kankyaku* negligence, oversight

⁸居 *kankyo* leisurely life; quiet retreat

¹¹寂 *kanjaku* quiet; tranquillity

¹²散 *kansan* leisure; quiet, inactivity

¹⁴静 *kansei* quietness, tranquillity

¹⁸職 *kanshoku* an easy job; a leisurely task

A 間 <u>6391</u> <u>J3456</u> <u>M41249</u> KAN interval; space; between; among; discord; favorable opportunity. KEN six feet. *ai* interval; between, medium; crossbred. *aida, awai* space, interval, gap; between, among; midway; on the way; distance; time, period; relationship. *ma* space, room; interval; pause; rest (in music); time; a while; leisure; luck; timing, harmony. *ma(monaku)* soon.

¹一髪 *kan'ippatsu* a hair's breadth

³口 *maguchi* frontage; width

⁴手 *ai(no)te* interlude; accompaniment; sideshow; strain of music

欠 *kanketsu* intermittence; intermittent

尺 *mashaku* measurement; accounting

引 *mabi(ku)* thin out. *mabi(ki)* thinning out (plants); killing unwanted children

⁵仕切 *majiki(ri)* partition, division

⁶近 *majika* nearness, proximity. *majika(i)* near at hand

合 *ma(ni)a(u)* be in time for; serve the purpose; can do without.

8

金長【門】
阜阝隶隹雨青非

ma(ni)a(waseru) make (something) do; get (something) ready.
ma(ni)a(wase) makeshift, expedient.
maa(i) interval

⁷投詞 kantōshi interjection

抜 ma (ga) nu(keru) be stupid; be funny; be out of harmony. manu(ke) disharmony; stupidity; simpleton, moron. manu(kesa) stupidity

⁸取 mado(ri) plan of the house, room arrangement

者 kanja spy

⁹食 kanshoku, aidagu(i) eating between meals

柄 aidagara relation, relationship

奏曲 kansōkyoku interlude

¹⁰借 maga(ri) renting a room

¹¹道 kandō secret path, side road, short cut

悪 ma(ga)waru(i) be embarrassed, feel self-conscious

断 kandan interruptions; intervals

接 kansetsu indirect

¹²遠 madō ni at long intervals

違 machiga(u) vi mistake.
machiga(eru) vt mistake.
machiga(tta) wrong, mistaken.
machiga(e), machiga(i) mistake; fault, failure; indiscretion, dispute

隔 kankaku space

無 ma(mo)na(ku) soon, in a moment

貸 maga(shi) renting out a room

¹³隙 kangeki gap, aperture, opening, space, interstice, crevice. ma(gana)-suki(gana) always, constantly

際 magiwa ni just before, on the verge of, at the eleventh hour

歇 kanketsu intermittence; intermittent

歇泉 kanketsusen geyser; intermittent hot-water service (at hot springs)

¹⁶諜 kanchō spy, secret agent

A 開 ⁶³⁹³ J332b M41233 KAI opening. hira(ku) open, unfold, unroll, uncover, unpack, untie, unseal; establish; clear (land); pioneer; clear the way; convene; enlighten (a country); bloom; differ, have a margin; widen (the space between). hira(keru) become civilized, become modernized, become sensible; be opened to traffic; feel relief; be open; grow, develop (a town). a(keru) open; empty, vacate; leave (a space); clear (the table); make (a hole); reserve (a seat), stay away from; dawn; end, expire, be over; open, begin. a(ku) open, be opened; start, begin, commence; become vacant, become empty, be disengaged, be free; expire, be over. a(karu) vi open. a(ita) open; empty, vacant. hira(keta) open, clear, commodious; civilized, modernized; sociable. hira(ki) opening; cupboard; difference; margin; aperture; breaking up (of a meeting).

³山 kaizan, kaisan (sect) founder; pioneer

⁴化 kaika civilization, enlightenment

⁶帆 kaihan suru set sail

会 kaikai opening a meeting

⁷廷 kaitei court session; trial

花 kaika flowering, blossoming

⁸門 kaimon opening of the gate

国 kaikoku founding of a country; opening of a country

店 kaiten opening of a new shop

始 kaishi commencement, inauguration

明 kaimei civilization, enlightenment

拓 kaitaku clearing, reclamation, exploitation, opening up land

拓者 kaitakusha cultivator; settler, colonist, pioneer

放 kaihō suru, hira(ki)-hana(tsu) open, throw open; leave open. a(ke)-hana(su) throw open; leave open. a(kep)pana(shi) no frank, openhearted; leaving (a door) wide open

放的 kaihōteki frank candid, openhearted

⁹通 kaitsū opening to traffic

城 kaijō capitulation (of a fort)

削 kaisaku cutting through (a road); digging a canal; clearing (land, for farming)

封 kaifū suru break the seal, open. hira(ki)fū, kaifū unsealed letter

巻 kaikan opening a book and reading; first part of a book

発 kaihatsu colonization; development; enlightenment

発途上国 kaihatsu tojōkoku developing country

¹⁰陳 kaichin suru express (opinions). kaichin statement

¹¹運 kaiun better fortune

帳 kaichō exhibiting a Buddhist image; opening a gambling game

設 *kaisetsu* establishment, inauguration, opening; installation (of telephones)

基 *kaiki* laying a foundation; founding; a founder

眼 *kaigan, kaigen* enlightenment, spiritual awakening; opening the eyes (investing a new image with sacred qualities)

票 *kaihyō* counting the ballots

閉 *kaihei* opening and shutting; (electrical) make and break. *a(ke)ta(te)* opening and shutting

¹² 場 *kaijō* opening

港 *kaikō* opening a port; open port

¹³ 幕 *kaimaku* rising of the curtain

催 *kaisai* holding (a meeting)

戦 *kaisen* outbreak of war

業 *kaigyō* opening a business or a practice

業医 *kaigyōi* doctor in private practice

¹⁴ 演 *kaien* opening of a play; opening of a lecture

¹⁶ 館 *kaikan* opening of a new hall

墾 *kaikon* cultivating new land

墾地 *kaikonchi* cultivated land

¹⁷ 講 *kaikō* opening of a lecture course

豁 *kaikatsu na* open (land); magnanimous

¹⁸ 襟 *kaikin* open-collared (shirt)

²¹ 闢 *kaibyaku* beginnings, creation, founding (of an empire)

²⁸ 鑿 *kaisaku* clearing (land, for farming); cutting through (a road); digging (a canal)

──────── **6** ────────

閤 [6397 / J395e / M41301] Kō small side gate.

B 閥 [6398 / J4836 / M41308] BATSU lineage, pedigree; clique, faction, clan, combine.

A 閣 [6401 / J3355 / M41300] KAKU tower, tall building, palace; cabinet (of a government).

³ 下 *Kakka* Your Excellency

⁴ 内 *kakunai* within the cabinet

⁵ 外 *kakugai* outside the cabinet

¹⁰ 員 *kakuin* cabinet member

¹⁴ 僚 *kakuryō* cabinet members

²⁰ 議 *kakugi* cabinet meeting

A 関 [6402 / J3458 / M41297] KAN barrier, gateway. *kan(suru)* related to, be connected with, concern, affect, involve, pertain to. *kaka(waru)* concern oneself in, have to do with; affect, influence; stick to (opinions). *(ni) kan(shite)* concerning. *kaka(wari)* relation, connection. *seki* barrier, checking station.

³ 山 *seki (no) yama* one's utmost.

与 *kan'yo* participation

⁴ 心 *kanshin* concern, interest, regard

⁵ 白 *kampaku* (ancient) chief advisor to the emperor; a domineering husband

⁸ 門 *kammon* barrier, gateway; Shimonoseki Moji

所 *sekisho* barrier, checking station

知 *kanchi* concern

取 *sekitori* sumo wrestler in top two divisions

⁹ 連 *kanren* connection, relation, association

係 *kankei* relation, connection, concern, participation; influence, effect; illicit relations. *kankei(naku)* regardless of

係者 *kankeisha* participant; interested party, the person concerned

¹² 税 *kanzei* customs, duty, tariff

¹³ 節 *kansetsu* joint

節炎 *kansetsuen* arthritis

¹⁶ 頭 *kantō* turning point; parting of the ways; place of execution

──────── **7** ────────

B 閲 [6404 / J315c / M41341] ETSU inspection, revision. *es(suru)* review, revise. *kemi(suru)* read, look, over; examine; pass, elapse.

⁷ 兵 *eppei* parade, review, inspection of troops

¹⁴ 歴 *etsureki* career, personal history

読 *etsudoku* reading, perusal

¹⁶ 覧 *etsuran* perusal, inspection, reading

覧室 *etsuranshitsu* reading room

──────── **9** ────────

闇 [6414 / J3047 / M41421] AN, *kura(garu)* get dark, get gloomy. *yami* darkness; grief, gloom; disorder, black

8

金 長 門 【阜 阝】 隶 隹 雨 青 非

market. *kura(i)* dark, gloomy, somber; dim, faint; ignorant.

⁵打 *yamiu(chi)* assassination, foul murder

市 *yamiichi* black market

⁸夜 *yamiyo, an'ya* dark night

取引 *yami torihiki* black-market dealings, undercover dealings

⁹屋 *yamiya* black marketeer

相場 *yami sōba* black-market price

¹⁰値 *yamine* black-market price

¹¹商人 *yami shōnin* black marketeer

¹²雲 *yamikumo ni* thoughtlessly, haphazardly, at random

───── **10** ─────

B 闘 [6418 / J462e / M45649] Tō fighting. *tataka(u)* wage war; fight; engage in a contest; struggle against.

³士 *tōshi* fighter, boxer, combatant; champion (of truth)

⁴犬 *tōken* dogfight; a fighting dog

牛 *tōgyū* bullfight; fighting bull

牛士 *tōgyūshi* matador, bullfighter

⁶争 *tōsō* fight, combat, conflict; labor strife

⁷志 *tōshi* fighting spirit

¹⁰病 *tōbyō suru* fight against an illness

¹⁴魂 *tōkon* fighting spirit

¹⁹鶏 *tōkei* cockfight; cockfighting; fighting cock

─────────── **RAD. 阜 170** ───────────

Kozato small village (i.e., in contradistinction to Rads. 163 & 166). Except for the radical character itself, it is always used as the left in the modifed form 阝 (2 strokes) *kozato hen*. Nickname: Left Village.

阜 [6423 / J496c / M41534] Fu hill; mound.

───── **4** ─────

阪 [6428 / J3a65 / M41562] Han slope. *saka* incline.

⁹神 *Hanshin* Osaka-Kobe

A 防 [6429 / J4b49 / M41576] Bō *fuse(gu)* defend, protect; resist; keep away, shut out, ward off; prevent.

²人 *sakimori* ancient military guards

⁴止 *bōshi* prevention

水 *bōsui* waterproof, watertight; holding back flood waters ⌐proof

火 *bōka* fire prevention, fire fighting, fire

⁵犯 *bōhan* crime prevention

⁶虫剤 *bōchūzai* insecticide

⁸波堤 *bōhatei* breakwater

空 *bōkū* air defense

空壕 *bōkūgō* air-raid shelter

⁹音 *bōon* soundproof; soundproofing

風 *bōfū* wind protection

風林 *bōfūrin* windbreak

砂林 *bōsarin* trees holding drifting sand

臭 *bōshū* deodorization

臭剤 *bōshūzai* deodorant, deodor-izer

疫 *bōeki* prevention of epidemics, disinfection, quarantine

¹¹雪 *bōsetsu* snowbreak ⌐guarding

¹²備 *bōbi* defense, defense works,

湿 *bōshitsu* dampproofing

弾 *bōdan* bulletproof; bombproof

寒 *bōkan* protection against the cold

寒具 *bōkangu* cold-protection outfit

御 *bōgyo* defense, protection

¹³戦 *bōsen* defensive war

¹⁴塵 *bōjin* dustproof

腐 *bōfu* preservation; embalmment; antisepsis

腐剤 *bōfuzai* antiseptic, preservative

¹⁶壁 *bōheki* barrier, bulwark, wall of defense

衛 *bōei* defense, protection

衛庁 *Bōeichō* Defense Agency

¹⁷禦 *bōgyo* defense, protection

²⁰護 *bōgo* protection, custody

───── **5** ─────

陀 [6432 / J424b / M41600] Ta, Da steep.

附 B | 6433 J496d M41606 | FU. *fu(suru)* give to, submit to, refer to; affix, attach, append. *tsu(keru) vt* attach, join, stick, glue, fasten; sew on; furnish (a house with); wear, put on; make an entry; appraise, set (a price); apply (ointment); bring alongside; place (under guard or a doctor); follow, shadow; add, append; affix; load; give (courage to); keep (an eye on); establish (relations or understanding). *tsu(ku) vi* be connected with; be dyed; be stained; be scarred; be recorded; be attached to; accompany; study with; increase, be added to. (For compounds, see 付 124).

阻 B | 6434 J414b M41593 | SO separate from; prevent, stop. *haba(mu)* obstruct, prevent, impede, deter, hinder, thwart, resist, frustrate.
⁴ 止 *soshi* obstruction, check, hindrance, prevention
¹⁰ 害 *sogai* hindrance, check, deterrent, obstruction, interference
¹² 隔 *sokaku* alienation, estrangement, separation
喪 *sosō* loss of power, loss of energy, dejection

阿 | 6435 J3024 M41599 | A. O. *omone(ru)*, *hetsura(u)* flatter, fawn upon. *kuma* corner, nook, recess; indentation, bend, turn; shade, shading; makeup.
⁴ 片 *ahen* opium
⁷ 呆 *ahō* fool, simpleton. *ahora(shii)* foolish
⁸ 房 *ahō* fool, simpleton
弥陀 *Amida* Amida (Buddha); lottery; wearing a hat on the back of the head
弥陀仏 *Amida Butsu* Amida Buddha

─────── 6 ───────

限 A | 6439 J3842 M41627 | GEN. *kagi(ru)* limit, restrict, confine. *kagi(ri)* limit(s); as far as possible, as much as possible, to the best of (one's ability). *(ni) kagi(tte)* of all (days, persons, etc.); alone. *-kagi(ri)* insofar as; this time only. *-kiri* (June) delivery.

⁸ 定 *gentei* limitation, qualification, definition, determination
⁹ 界 *genkai* boundary, limit, limits, bounds
度 *gendo* limit, limits, limitation

─────── 7 ───────

陛 A | 6444 J4a45 M41654 | HEI. *kizahashi* steps (of the throne).
³ 下 *Heika* His or Her Majesty

陥 B | 6446 J3459 M41676 | KAN. *ochii(ru)* fall into, get into, slide into, lapse into; cave in, sink; fall (a fort). *otoshii(reru)* ensnare, tempt.
⁷ 没 *kambotsu* a cave-in; subsidence
¹² 落 *kanraku* fall, sinking, a cave-in; surrender; giving in

院 A | 6447 J3121 M41665 | IN mansion; temple; palace; hospital; school; institution; congress; ex-emperor.
⁴ 内 *innai* inside congress; within the institution
⁵ 外 *ingai* outside congress; nonparliamentary; outside of the institution
外団 *ingaidan* lobbying group
⁸ 長 *inchō* head of a hospital, court, or school

陣 B | 6448 J3f58 M41667 | JIN battle array, ranks; camp; position. *jin(suru)* set up (an army) camp.
⁴ 中 *jinchū ni* in the field, in camp
⁶ 地 *jinchi* encampment; position
⁷ 没 *jimbotsu* death in action
形 *jinkei* battle array
⁸ 殁 *jimbotsu* death in action
取 *jindo(ru)* encamp, take up a position. *jindo(ri)* battle array; playing war
¹⁰ 容 *jin'yō* battle array
¹² 痛 *jintsū* labor pains
営 *jin'ei* camp; barracks
¹⁶ 頭 *jintō* the head of an army; the field of battle
頭指揮 *jintō shiki* a commander personally leading his army into battle

除 A | 6449 J3d7c M41669 | JI. JO division (in math). *jo(suru)* divide (in math);

8

金 長 門 【阜 阝】 隶 隹 雨 青 非

₇

exclude. *nozo(ku)* remove, abolish, cancel; exclude, except. *no(keru)* get rid of, remove; finish; omit, exclude. *nozo(ite)*, *nozo(ite wa)* except, exclusive of. *-yoke* protection, shelter, charm.

⁵去 *nozo(ki)-sa(ru)* remove, take away. *jokyo* removal, exclusion

外 *jogai* exclusive, exception

⁶名 *jomei* disfellowshipping, expulsion, dropping a name, excommunication

⁸者 *no(ke)mono* outcast

夜 *joya* New Year's Eve

夜鐘 *joya (no) kane* New Year's midnight bells

⁹草 *josō* weeding

¹¹隊 *jotai* military discharge

雪 *josetsu* snow removal

¹³幕式 *jomakushiki* unveiling (ceremony)

¹⁷霜 *josō* defrosting, deicing

²⁰籍 *joseki suru* remove a name, expel, denationalize; decommission (warships)

降 [6450 / J395f / M41620] A

Kō going down; surrender. *fu(ru)* fall, drop, come down (rain, etc.). *kuda(su)* let down; get down, descend; be given; be less than; have diarrhea; retire; leave the capital. *o(riru)* come down, go down, step down, descend; get off; land. *o(rosu)* take down, lower, pull down, lift down, let down, drop; launch; let off (passengers); wear (for the first time); cause (abortion); grate; invoke; exercise; borrow (in subtraction); lock. *ku(daru)* surrender. *ku(dasu)*, *fu(rasu)* make it rain. *kuda(tte)* on down; as for me (humble).

³下 *kōka* fall, descent; losing altitude; outpouring; (plane) landing; (atmospheric) depression

下部隊 *kōka butai* parachute troops

⁶伏 *kōfuku* surrender, submission

⁷車 *kōsha* alighting

車口 *kōshaguchi* way out, station exit

⁸服 *kōfuku* surrender, submission

参 *kōsan* surrender; giving in; being nonplussed

雨 *kōu* rain, rainfall

雨量 *kōryō* amount of precipitation

¹¹雪 *kōsetsu* snow; a snowfall

¹⁵誕 *kōtan* birth, nativity

¹⁷臨 *kōrin* advent, descent

———— 8 ————

陵 [6454 / J4e4d / M41704] B

Ryō *misasagi* imperial tomb.

¹³墓 *ryōbo* imperial tomb

隆 [6455 / J4e34 / M41720'] B

Ryū high; noble; prosperity.

⁸昌 *ryūshō* energy, vitality; prosperity

¹⁰起 *ryūki* protuberance, bulging, upheaval, elevation

隆 *ryūryū(taru)* prosperous, thriving; brawny

¹¹盛 *ryūsei* prosperity

険 [6456 / J3831 / M41721'] A

KEN inaccessible place, impregnable pass, strategic position; steep place; sharp (eyes); sinister (look). *kewa(shii)* steep; severe, angry.

⁷阻 *kenso* steepness; precipice

¹¹悪 *ken'aku na* dangerous; inclement; serious, gloomy

陳 [6457 / J4444 / M41698] B

CHIN. *no(beru)*, *chin(zuru)*, *chin(jiru)* state, relate, explain. *hineku(reru)* get warped, become distorted. *hine* old grain; old goods; precocity.

⁵弁 *chimben* explanation, defense, justification

⁶列 *chinretsu* exhibition, display, show

⁷述 *chinjutsu* statement, declaration

¹¹情 *chinjō* petition, appeal

¹⁴腐 *chimpu na* trite, commonplace, worn out, old-fashioned, out-of-date, stereotyped

¹⁷謝 *chinsha* apology

陪 [6458 / J4766 / M41680] B

BAI follow, accompany, attend on.

⁹食 *baishoku* dining with a superior

¹⁰席 *baiseki* sitting with a superior

¹⁵審 *baishin* jury

審員 *baishin'in* jury, juror

陶 [6459 / J462b / M41705] B

Tō. *sue* porcelain, pottery.

³土 *tōdo* potter's clay, porcelain clay

⁷芸 *tōgei* ceramic art

冶 *tōya* training, education; culture

¹¹酔 *tōsui* intoxication; fascination; rapture

¹²然 *tōzen* gloriously drunk

---

¹³ 業 *tōgyō* porcelain industry
¹⁴ 磁器 *tōjiki* porcelain, pottery
¹⁵ 器 *tōki* porcelain, pottery

隨 B — 6460 J3f6f M41764 — ZUI. *manimani* at the mercy of (the waves). *mama* as it is; as one likes; because. - *naga(ra)* though, notwithstanding; while, during; both, all. *shitaga(u)* obey, submit to, comply with, observe (a law); follow; accompany.

¹ 一 *zuiichi* the first, the best, number one, the greatest
⁴ 分 *zuibun* very, extremely; tolerably; cruel, terrible; many
⁵ 処 *zuisho ni* everywhere, anywhere, here and there
⁶ 行 *zuikō* attendant, follower. *zuikō suru* attend on, accompany, follow
⁷ 伴 *zuihan suru* attend on, accompany
⁸ 所 *zuisho* everywhere
¹⁰ 時 *zuiji* any time, at all times; whenever required
員 *zuiin* attendants, suite
¹² 喜 *zuiki* adoration, idolization
筆 *zuihitsu* essays, miscellaneous writings
¹³ 想 *zuisō* occasional thoughts
意 *zuii* voluntary, optional. *manimani* at the mercy of

陸 A — 6461 J4e26 M41708 — ROKU. RIKU *oka, kuga* land.

³ 上 *rikujō* on shore, land (events)
上自衛隊 *Rikujō Jieitai* Ground Self-Defense Force
⁶ 地 *rikuchi* land
⁸ 岸 *rikugan* shore; land
⁹ 風 *rikufū* land breeze
海軍 *rikukaigun, rikkaigun* army and navy
軍 *rikugun* army
¹¹ 運 *rikuun* land transportation
¹² 揚 *rikua(ge)* landing, unloading
棲 *rikusei* land (animal), terrestrial
¹³ 続 *rikuzoku to* continuously, successively
路 *rikuro, kugaji* land route
戦 *rikusen* land battle, land warfare
¹⁴ 稲 *rikutō, okabo* upland rice, dry-land rice
¹⁶ 橋 *rikkyō* overpass; viaduct; land bridge

陰 B — 6462 J3122 M41691 — ON. AN. IN the yin principle; negative; melancholy; north side of a mountain; sex organs; secret; shadow; south side of a river; negative electrode; earth; bottom; back; inactivity; nighttime; moon. *kage(ru)* darken; cloud up; be obscured. *kage* shade; back; (your) assistance. *(o)kage* indebtedness, favor, help, patronage, support. *hisoka ni, in ni* secretly.

³ 口 *kageguchi* malicious gossip
干 *kagebo(shi)* drying in the shade
⁴ 日向 *kage-hinata* light and shade
⁶ 気 *inki* gloom, melancholy
⁸ 門 *immon* vagina
雨 *in'u* dark and rainy
画 *inga* a negative
茎 *inkei* penis
性 *insei* dormant; negative
¹⁰ 険 *inken na* tricky, wily, treacherous
陰 *in'in* gloomy and lonely
部 *imbu* pubic region
¹¹ 惨 *insan* sadness and gloom
陽 *in'yō, on'yō* cosmic dual forces, positive and negative principles, active and passive, male and female, shade and light, sun and moon. *in(ni)-yo(ni)* publicly and privately
¹² 湿 *inshitsu* the dampness of shady places
極 *inkyoku* negative pole
¹⁴ 暦 *inreki* lunar calendar
徳 *intoku* secret charity
¹⁵ 影 *in'ei* shadow; shading; gloom
¹⁶ 謀 *imbō* plot, intrigue, conspiracy
¹⁷ 翳 *in'ei* shadow; shading; gloom

— 9 —

隈 — 6466 J3728 M41748 — WAI. *kuma* corner, nook, recess; indentation, bend, turn; shade, shading; make-up. *kuma(naku)* everywhere; universally.
¹² 無 *kumana(ku)* completely

隅 B — 6467 J3679 M41743 — GŪ corner. *sumi, sumi(kko)* corner, nook.
¹¹ 隅 *sumizumi* every nook and corner

隊 A — 6468 J4262 M41750 — TAI party, company, corps, squad, crew, band, posse, force, unit.

8

金長門【阜阝】隷隹雨青非

⁹

⁶ 伍 *taigo* the ranks, a line, procession
⁶ 列 *tairetsu* ranks, file, procession
⁷ 形 *taikei* battle formation, disposition of troops
⁸ 長 *taichō* captain, leader, commander
¹⁰ 員 *taiin* members of the group
¹¹ 商 *taishō* caravan

階 ⁶⁴⁶⁹ J332c M41755 **A** KAI stair, staircase; round; step; grade; story, floor; counter for stories (in a building). *kizahashi, kidahashi* stairway; ladder; order.

³ 下 *kaika* lower floor, downstairs; under the stairway
上 *kaijō* upper floor; the head of the stairs
⁹ 段 *kaidan, kizahashi* steps, stairway
級 *kaikyū* class, estate, caste, rank, grade
¹⁴ 層 *kaisō* classes of people

陽 ⁶⁴⁷⁰ J4d5b M41725 **A** YŌ yang principle, positive; male; heaven; daytime; sun; top; movement; facing the sun; sunshine; south face of a mountain; north side of a river; pride; positive electrode. *arawa ni* openly, publicly; frankly, clearly. *yō ni* openly, publicly.

³ 子 *yōshi* proton
⁶ 気 *yōki* season, weather; vivacity, cheerfulness, gaiety
光 *yōkō* sunshine, sunlight; the sun
当 *hiata(ri)* sunny place; exposure to the sun
⁸ 画 *yōga* positive photographic print
炎 *yōen, kagerō, kageroi* simmering of the air
性 *yōsei no* positive, plus
物 *yōbutsu* phallus; penis
⁹ 春 *yōshun* spring, springtime
¹⁰ 差 *hizashi* sunlight, sun's height
¹¹ 転 *yōten* positive (TB) test
動作戦 *yōdō sakusen* feint operation
¹² 極 *yōkyoku* anode, positive pole
¹⁴ 暦 *yōreki* solar calendar; Julian calendar

─────── **10** ───────

隙 ⁶⁴⁷¹ J3764 M41792 See 隙 6477.

隔 ⁶⁴⁷⁵ J3356 M-X **B** KAKU every other, alternate; distance. *heda(teru)* separate, interpose; screen, shield; estrange. *hedata(ru)* be distant from, be separated from, become estranged. *heda(tari)* distance; interval; gap; gulf, difference, disparity; distance; coolness. *heda(te)* partition; interval; barrier; distinction; discrimination; reserve, coolness.

⁴ 日 *kakujitsu* alternate days
月 *kakugetsu* alternate months
⁵ 世 *kakusei* a distant age; a different world
世遺伝 *kakusei iden* atavism
⁶ 年 *kakunen* alternate years
¹⁰ 週 *kakushū* biweekly
¹² 絶 *kakuzetsu* isolation, separation, blockade
¹³ 意 *kakui* reserve, estrangement, alienation
¹⁶ 壁 *kakuheki* partition; bulkhead; septum
¹⁹ 離 *kakuri* isolation, separation

─────── **11** ───────

隙 ⁶⁴⁷⁷ J-X M41813 隙 ⁶⁴⁷¹ J3764 M41792 GEKI crevice, fissure, chink; discord; opportunity. *su(kasu)* leave a space, thin (trees); make transparent; look through. *hima* time; leisure; poor business; leave of absence; dismissal; divorce; opening. *suki* time; leisure; gap, crack; room, space; chance; unpreparedness, unguarded moment.

¹² 間 *sukima* crevice, gap, opening, space
間風 *sukimakaze* draft

際 ⁶⁴⁷⁸ J3a5d M41820 **A** SAI time, occasion; when. *kiwa* side, edge, verge. *sai(suru)* meet, encounter. *kiwa(doi)* dangerous; adventurous; delicate; indecent. *(ni) sai(shite)* at that time.

⁵ 立 *kiwada(tsu)* be prominent, be conspicuous
⁶ 会 *saikai suru* meet, face, confront
⁸ 限 *saigen* limits, end, bounds
¹¹ 涯 *saigai* extremity

障 ⁶⁴⁷⁹ J3e63 M41821 **A** SHŌ. *sawa(ru)* hinder, interfere with; affect; hurt, harm. *sawa(ri)* hindrance, interference;

harm, bad aftereffects; menses.
³ 子 *shōji* translucent sliding paper door
¹⁰ 害 *shōgai* obstacle, hindrance, difficulty, handicap; hurdles
害物 *shōgaibutsu* obstacle, obstruction
¹⁶ 壁 *shōheki* enclosing wall, barrier

隠 B $\frac{6480}{\text{J3123}}$ M41836 IN. ON. *kaku(su)* hide, conceal, cover, veil, cloak, disguise. *kaku(reru)* hide, disappear; pass away; be anonymous; lurk. *komo(ru)* seclude oneself, be confined in; be implied; be stuffy, be filled with (smoke). *kaku(renaki)* well-known, open (secret).
⁴ 元豆 *ingen mame* kidney bean
⁵ 処 *kaku(re)ga* hiding place
⁷ 見 *inken* appearance and disappearance
坊 *kaku(rem)bō, kaku(rem)bo* hide-and-seek.
芸 *kaku(shi)gei* stunt, trick; an accomplishment unknown to others
忍 *innin* patience, endurance
⁸ 居 *inkyo* retirement; retired person; old person
者 *inja* hermit, recluse
事 *kaku(shi)goto, inji* secret
退 *intai* retirement, seclusion
¹⁰ 匿 *intoku* concealment
逸 *in'itsu* retirement, seclusion
栖 *insei* secluded life
家 *kaku(re)ga* retreat, refuge
¹¹ 道 *kaku(re) michi* secret passage
密 *ommitsu, immitsu* privacy, secrecy; detective; spy, secret agent

¹² 遁 *inton* retirement, seclusion
喩 *in'yu* metaphor
棲 *insei* secluded life
然 *inzen toshite* in reality, actually; in secret
場 *kaku(re)ba* refuge, hiding place
¹³ 微 *imbi* obscurity, abstruseness, mystery
¹⁴ 語 *ingo* secret language; password
¹⁵ 蔽 *impei* concealment, suppression, hiding
¹⁸ 顕 *inken* appearance and disappearance

——————— **13** ———————

隣 B $\frac{6484}{\text{J4e59}}$ M41847 RIN neighboring. *tona(ru)* adjoin. *tonari* next-door neighbor; adjoining.
² 人 *rinjin, tonaryūdo,* neighbor
人愛 *rinjin'ai* love of one's neighbors
⁵ 付合 *tonarizu(ki)a(i)* neighborliness
⁶ 地 *rinchi* adjoining land
邦 *rimpō* neighboring country
合 *tona(ri)-a(u)* adjoin, be next to. *tona(ri)a(i), tona(ri)a(wase)* adjoining
近所 *tonari kinjo* neighborhood
同士 *tonaridōshi* next door to each other
⁸ 国 *ringoku, tonariguni* neighboring country
⁹ 室 *rinshitsu* the next room
県 *rinken* neighboring prefectures
¹⁰ 家 *rinka* neighboring house
¹¹ 接 *rinsetsu(shita)* adjacent, adjoining, neighboring; related

■■■■■■■■ RAD. 隶 **171** ■■■■■■■■

Reizukuri (i.e., the right-hand element of the character for *rei* "servant, slave"). Nickname: Slave.

——————— **8** ———————

隷 B $\frac{6490}{\text{J4e6c}}$ M41928 REI servant; criminal; prisoner, follower.

¹⁰ 従 *reijū* slavery
書 *reisho* ancient squared character
¹² 属 *reizoku* subordination, dependency

8

金
長
門
阜
阝
隶
【隹】
雨
青
非

2

RAD. 隹 172

Furutori old "bird" (i.e., the less complicated "bird," as distinguished from the "long-tailed" bird of Rad. 196). Nickname: Old Bird.

———— **2** ————

隼
6493
J483b
M41943
JUN. *hayabusa* a peregrine (falcon).

B 隻
6494
J4049
M41941
SEKI. counter for ships, fish, birds, arrows, etc., and one of a pair.

¹¹ 眼 *sekigan* one eye; an eye (for pictures, etc.)

¹⁴ 語 *sekigo* just a word

———— **3** ————

雀
6496
J3f7d
M41954
JAKU. *suzume* sparrow.

¹² 斑 *sobakasu* freckles

¹³ 蜂 *suzumebachi* wasp, hornet

²¹ 躍 *jakuyaku suru* leap for joy, exult

———— **4** ————

B 雇
6497
J385d
M41976
KO. *yato(u)* employ, hire. *yatoi* employee.

² 人 *yatoinin* employee

⁵ 主 *yatoinushi* employer

用 *koyō* employment

¹⁰ 員 *koin* employee

¹³ 傭 *koyō* employment

雁
6498
J3467
M41960
GAN *kari, karigane* wild goose.

⁴ 木 *gangi* stepped pier; toothing gear; escapement; hooked stick; zigzag

⁵ 皮紙 *gampishi* rice paper, tissue paper

⁶ 行 *gankō* the flight formation of geese; lining up shoulder to shoulder like flying geese; leading out

字搦 *ganjigarami ni, ganjigarame ni* (bind) firmly, truss up

⁹ 首 *gankubi* pipe bowl; head, neck. *gankubi (o soroete)* lined up (in a straight line). *karikubi* goose neck

B 雄
6499
J4d3a
M41972
YŪ. male; hero; great leader; superiority,

excellence. *osu, on-, o-* male.

³ 大 *yūdai na* grand, majestic, sublime

才 *yūsai* talents

⁴ 心 *yūshin, ogokoro* manly spirit, ambition, aspiration, gallant spirit

牛 *oushi* bull, steer

⁵ 弁 *yūben* oratory, eloquence

⁶ 叫 *otake(bi), osake(bi)* war cry; courageous shout; roar of an animal

壮 *yūsō* bravery, heroism

⁹ 飛 *yūhi* flying jump; great achievement

途 *yūto* a courageous departure

勁 *yūkei na* pithy, vigorous (style)

姿 *yūshi* gallant figure

¹¹ 断 *yūdan* a manly decision

¹² 偉 *yūi no* imposing, grand, magnificent

渾 *yūkon na* magnificent, sublime; vigorous, virile, sturdy, bold

¹⁵ 蕊 *oshibe, yūzui* stamen

A 集
6500
J3d38
M41974
SHŪ. collection, gathering. *atsu(maru), tsudo(u)* meet, assemble, congregate; swarm, flock or gather together; be collected, be gathered together; converge. *atsu(meru)* gather, collect; focus (something on). *atsu(mari), tsudo(i)* assembly, meeting; collection; gathering.

³ 大成 *shūtaisei* compilation

⁴ 中 *shūchū* concentration, convergence, centralization, integration

中治療室 *shūchū chiryōshitsu* intensive care unit

中豪雨 *shūchū gōu* a localized torrential downpour

⁶ 成 *shūsei* collection, compilation

合 *shūgō* gathering, meeting, group; collection

会 *shūkai* meeting, assembly

会所 *shūkaijo* meeting place, assembly hall

団 *shūdan* group, body, mass, crowd, host

団心理 *shūdan shinri* mass psychology

団的自衛権 *shūdanteki jieiken* right of collective self-defense

団意識 *shūdan ishiki* group consciousness
⁸金 *shūkin* collecting money
⁹約 *shūyaku suru* intensify
計 *shūkei* total
¹⁰荷 *shūka* collection of freight
配 *shūhai* collection and delivery
¹¹貨 *shūka* collection of freight
魚灯 *shūgyotō* fish-luring light
¹²落 *shūraku* centers of population, towns and villages
結所 *shūketsujo* concentration center
散 *shūsan* collection and distribution
¹⁶録 *shūroku* compilation, editing
積 *shūseki* accumulation, pile
積回路 *shūseki kairo* integrated circuit

―――――― 5 ――――――

雅 ᴮ ₆₅₀₅ _{J326d} _{M41973} Gᴀ elegance, refined taste. *miya(bita), miya(biyakana)* graceful, refined.
⁴文 *gabun* elegant style, classic style
⁵号 *gagō* pen name, pseudonym
⁹俗 *gazoku* the refined and the vulgar; the classical and the colloquial
¹²量 *garyō* magnanimity, generosity, tolerance, liberality, broad-mindedness, capacity
¹³楽 *gagaku* ceremonial court music
¹⁴語 *gago* polite expression, refined diction
¹⁵趣 *gashu* artistry, elegance, taste

―――――― 6 ――――――

雌 ᴮ ₆₅₀₆ _{J3b73} _{M41998} Sʜɪ female. *mesu, men-, me-* female.
⁶伏 *shifuku suru* remain in obscurity
¹⁵蕊 *meshibe, shizui* pistil

雑 ᴬ ₆₅₀₇ _{J3b28} _{M42022} Zō. Zᴀᴛsᴜ miscellany; miscellaneous. *ma(zeru)* mix, blend, mingle; include, let in on. *ma(zaru), ma(jiru)* be mixed, be blended; mingle with. *maji(eru)* mix; converse with; cross (swords). *zatsu na* rough, coarse, rude; miscellaneous.
³巾 *zōkin* mop, scrubbing cloth
巾掛 *zōkinga(ke)* scrubbing
⁴木 *zōki, zōboku, zatsuboku* miscellaneous trees

木林 *zōkibayashi, zōbokurin* grove of miscellaneous trees
⁵用 *zatsuyō* miscellaneous business. *zōyō* miscellaneous business, miscellaneous expenses
⁶色 *zasshoku* various colors.
件 *zakken* miscellaneous affairs
多 *zatta na* miscellaneous, various
⁷芸 *zatsugei* miscellaneous accomplishments
役 *zatsueki* odd jobs, sundry services
⁸炊 *zōsui* medley soup; hodgepodge
念 *zatsunen, zōnen* worldly thoughts
学 *zatsugaku* wide knowledge
事 *zatsuji* miscellaneous affairs
居 *zakkyo suru* live together (in the same room, area, or country)
⁹音 *zatsuon* noise, static, jamming; (heart) murmur
食 *zasshoku no* omnivorous
草 *zassō* weeds
¹⁰記 *zakki* miscellaneous notes
記帳 *zakkichō* notebook; exercise book
¹¹務 *zatsumu* miscellaneous business
魚 *zako, jako* small fish; various kinds of small fish ⌈group
魚寝 *zakone suru* sleep together in a
貨 *zakka* sundries, notions; general cargo; miscellaneous goods
貨店 *zakkaten* emporium, variety store
¹²然 *zatsuzen to* promiscuously, in confusion
煮 *zōni* glutenous rice cakes boiled with vegetables
費 *zappi* miscellaneous expenses
報 *zappō* miscellaneous news
¹³感 *zakkan* miscellaneous impressions
¹⁴種 *zasshu* mixed breed, hybrid, mongrel; various kinds
駁 *zappaku na* confused, incoherent, desultory, hazy
誌 *zasshi* magazine, periodical
穀 *zakkoku* minor grains
¹⁵踏 *zattō* congestion, traffic jam, throng
談 *zatsudan* chitchat, gossip
¹⁶録 *zatsuroku* miscellaneous notes

―――――― 10 ――――――

雛 ₆₅₁₄ _{J3f77} _{M42121} Sū. *hina* chick, squab, duckling; doll. *hiyoko* chick; stripling.

8
金長門阜阝隶【隹】雨青非

8

金
長
門
阜
阝
隶
【隹】
雨
青
非

[10]

² 人形 *hina ningyō* festival dolls
⁷ 形 *hinagata* pattern, model, sample, specimen, form, copy, miniature
¹¹ 鳥 *hinadori* chick, young bird
菊 *hinagiku* daisy
祭 *Hinamatsu(ri)* Girls' Festival
¹⁶ 壇 *hinadan* doll stand; musicians' platform; state ministers' gallery (on the doll stands)

難 $\frac{6515}{\text{J4671}}$ NAN trouble, difficulty; accident, disaster; defect;
A M42128' criticism. *kata(i)* difficult; impossible. *muzuka(shii), mutsuka(shii)* hard, difficult; delicate; troublesome; doubtful; hopeless; stern; sullen; hard to please; serious; technical. *nan(zuru)* criticize. *haba(mu)* obstruct, prevent, impede, deter, hinder, thwart, resist, frustrate. *nan(naku)* easily, successfully. *-niku(i)* difficult, awkward. *-gata(i)* difficult (to do). *-ka(neru)* cannot; hesitate to; be impatient.
⁵ 民 *nammin* needy people, sufferers; displaced persons, refugees
⁶ 色 *nanshoku* hesitation; disapproval
行苦行 *nangyō-kugyō* penance, austerities
⁷ 局 *nankyoku* difficult situation, crisis
攻不落 *nankō-furaku* impregnability
⁸ 所 *nansho, nanjo* steep, difficult, or dangerous places
物 *nambutsu* hard customer
易 *nan'i* relative difficulty; difficulty and ease
事 *nanji* difficult matter; hardship
⁹ 点 *nanten* difficult point
¹⁰ 病 *nambyō* serious illness
航 *nankō* stormy voyage; rough flight; rough sledding
破 *nampa* shipwreck
破船 *nampasen* shipwreck
¹¹ 渋 *nanjū* suffering, distress, hardship
船 *nansen* shipwreck
産 *nanzan* difficult delivery (in childbirth)
問 *nammon* difficult question
¹² 無 *nanna(ku)* easily
¹³ 解 *nankai na* hard to understand; unintelligible; illegible
詰 *nankitsu* blame, censure
路 *nanro* difficult road
¹⁴ 関 *nankan* strong barrier, obstacle, difficulty

読 *nandoku* difficult reading
¹⁵ 儀 *nangi* hardship, trouble
¹⁷ 聴 *nanchō* hard of hearing
¹⁸ 癖 *nankuse* fault, bad habit
題 *nandai* difficult topic; hard question; unreasonable charge; unreasonable demand

───── **11** ─────

離 $\frac{6517}{\text{J4e25}}$ RI separation. *hana(reru),*
B M42140 *saka(ru) vi* and *vt* separate, part from; come off; become disjoined; digress; get free; become estranged; be (three miles) away; be separated (by three years); leave, quit, depart from. *hana(su) vt* separate, disconnect, sever; detach; keep apart; alienate; isolate; let go, release, set free. *hana(re)* detached (building).
⁴ 日 *ri-Nichi* departure from Japan
反 *rihan* estrangement, alienation, desertion, revolt
⁶ 任 *rinin* leaving one's position
合 *rigō* meeting and parting
⁷ 別 *ribetsu* divorce; dissolution of adoption
⁸ 岸 *rigan* setting sail
乳 *rinyū* weaning
乳食 *rinyūshoku* a baby's weaning meal
¹⁰ 島 *hana(re)jima, ritō* outlying island
宮 *rikyū* detached palace
党 *ritō* withdrawal from a party
陸 *ririku* takeoff; pulling out from the shore
¹¹ 脱 *ridatsu* secession; separation; abolition; giving up (one's membership)
婚 *rikon* divorce
¹² 散 *risan* dispersion, scattering, breakup
着 *richaku* taking off and landing
間 *rikan* estrangement, separation, rupture
¹³ 業 *hana(re)waza* stunt, feat
¹⁵ 縁 *rien* divorce; separation of an adopted son
¹⁸ 職 *rishoku* quitting one's job, loss of employment
¹⁹ 離 *hana(re)bana(re)* scattered, dispersed, separated, disconnected
²⁰ 籍 *riseki* removal of a name from a registry

右 金長門阜阝隶隹【雨】⁴青非

RAD. 雨 173

Ame rain. At top: 雲 or 雨 *ame kammuri*. Nickname: Rain.

A 雨 6518 J312b M42210 U. *ame* rain, rainfall. *ama-* rain.

³ 上 *ameaga(ri), amaaga(ri)* after the rain
⁴ 乞 *amagoi* praying for rain
  戸 *amado* shutter, storm door
  水 *amamizu, usui* rainwater
  天 *uten* rainy weather
  天順延 *uten'jun'en* in case of rain postponed to the next good day
⁶ 合羽 *amagappa* raincoat, oilcoat
⁸ 具 *amagu* rain gear
  季 *uki* rainy season
  垂 *amadare* raindrops, eavesdrops
⁹ 音 *amaoto* sound of falling rain
¹¹ 脚 *amaashi, ame ashi* a passing shower
  宿 *amayado(ri)* taking shelter from the rain
  笠 *amagasa* rain hat
¹² 期 *uki* rainy season
  傘 *amagasa* umbrella
  雲 *amagumo* rain cloud
  量 *uryō* rain, rainfall
¹³ 靴 *amagutsu* overshoes
¹⁴ 樋 *amadoi* eaves trough
  漏 *amamo(ri)* roof leak
  滴 *uteki* raindrop
  模様 *amamoyō, ame moyō* signs of rain
¹⁶ 曇 *amagumo(ri)* overcast weather
²¹ 露 *uro* rain and dew

---------- **3** ----------

雫 6519 J3c36 M42219 DA. DAN. *shizuku* drop, trickle, dripping.

A 雪 6520 J4063 M42216 SETSU. *yuki* snow, snowfall. *susu(gu), soso(gu)* rinse, wash, pour on.

³ 下 *yukioro(shi)* snowy wind; shoveling snow off the roof
  女 *yuki onna* snow demon, snow fairy
  上 *setsujō* on the snow
  上車 *setsujōsha* snow tractor
⁴ 片 *seppen* snowflake
⁵ 目 *yukime* snow blindness
  氷 *seppyō* snow ice

⁶ 合戦 *yuki gassen* snowball fight
⁷ 庇 *seppi* overhanging snow
  見 *yukimi* snow viewing
  見酒 *yukimizake* drinking saké at a snow scene
⁸ 国 *yukiguni* snowy country
  明 *yukiaka(ri)* snow light
  夜 *yukiyo* snowy night
⁹ 除 *yukiyo(ke)* snow guard, snowshed, roof guards (to prevent snow sliding off)
¹⁰ 原 *setsugen* snow field, frozen waste
  留 *yukidama(ri)* snowdrift, snowbank
  辱 *setsujoku* vindication of honor, making up for a loss, revenge
¹¹ 道 *yukimichi* snowy road
  遊 *yukiaso(bi)* playing with snow
  崩 *nada(reru)* incline toward, give way and fall. *nadare, yuki nadare* snowslide, snow avalanche
  達磨 *yuki daruma* snowman
¹² 焼 *yukiya(ke)* snow tan
  景色 *yukigeshiki* snow scene
¹³ 傾 *yukinada(re)* snowslide, avalanche
  掻 *yukikaki* snow shoveling, snow removal; snow shovel, snow scraper; snowplow
  隠 *setchin, setsuin* lavatory, toilet
¹⁴ 模様 *yuki moyō* snowflake pattern; threatening to snow
¹⁵ 線 *sessen* snow line
¹⁷ 嶺 *setsurei* snow-capped peak

---------- **4** ----------

B 霧 6521 J4a37 M42231 FUN fog.

⁷ 囲気 *fun'iki* atmosphere, environment, surroundings

A 雲 6522 J3140 M42235 UN. *kumo* cloud.

³ 上人 *unjōbito, kumo(no)uebito* nobles
⁴ 水 *unsui* itinerant priest; clouds and
  丹 *uni* sea urchin
⁵ 母 *ummo, umbo, kirara* isinglass, mica water

8

金
長
門
阝
隶
隹
【⁴雨】
青
非

⁶行 *kumoyu(ki)* cloud movements; situation, turn of events; progress; signs

⁷助 *kumosuke* palanquin bearer, coolie, wandering robber

⁸泥差 *undei (no) sa* a wide difference

⁹海 *unkai* sea of clouds; sea of clouds meeting the great ocean

¹¹梯 *untei* scaling ladder

脚 *unkyaku* cloud movements; overhanging clouds

雀 *hibari* skylark

¹²散霧消 *unsan-mushō* vanishing like clouds and mist

集 *unshū suru* swarm, throng, gather in crowds

¹³煙 *un'en* clouds and smoke; a landscape; a beautiful picture

隠 *kumogaku(re)* demise, passing; disappearance

¹⁷霞 *unka* clouds and haze. *kumo-kasumi* clouds and fog; disappearance, fleeing

霧 *ummu* clouds and fog

───── 5 ─────

零 6524 J4e6d M42242 REI zero, nothing, cipher; fall. *kobo(reru)* vi spill, overflow, be scattered. *kobo(su)* vt spill; grumble over.

B

³下 *reika* below zero, subzero

⁹度 *reido* zero, freezing point

点 *reiten* zero; freezing point; zero grade

¹⁰時 *reiji* twelve o'clock; noon; midnight

¹¹細 *reisai na* petty, small, infinitesimal

細企業 *reisai kigyō* a small business

雷 6525 J4d6b M42245 RAI *ikazuchi* thunder. *kaminari* thunder; thunderbolt.

B

⁴文 *raimon* zigzag

⁶同 *raidō* blindly following the crowd

光 *raikō* lightning

名 *raimei* renown, fame; your famous name

⁸雨 *raiu* thunderstorm

⁹神 *raijin* the god of thunder

¹²雲 *raiun* thunderhead

¹³電 *raiden* thunder and lightning, thunderbolt

¹⁴鳴 *raimei* thunder

管 *raikan* percussion cap, detonator

¹⁵撃 *raigeki* torpedo attack

電 6526 J4545 M42253 DEN electricity. *inazuma* lightning.

A

²力 *denryoku* electric power

³子 *denshi* electron

子工学 *denshi kōgaku* electronics

子会議 *denshi kaigi* teleconference

子顕微鏡 *denshi kembikyō* electron microscope

⁴文 *dembun* telegram, telegraphic message

化 *denka* electrification

⁵圧 *den'atsu* voltage

⁶池 *denchi* electric battery

光 *denkō* electric light; lightning

光石火 *denkō-sekka* an instant, a flash

灯 *dentō* electric light

気 *denki* electricity; electric light

気工 *denkikō* electrician

気工学 *denki kōgaku* electrical engineering

気通信 *denki tsūshin* telecommunication

⁷車 *densha* electric car, streetcar, tramcar, electric train, trolley

車賃 *denshachin* carfare

⁸卓 *dentaku* electronic calculator

送 *densō* electrical facsimile transmission

波 *dempa* electric wave, radio wave

波望遠鏡 *dempa bōenkyō* radio telescope

⁹柱 *denchū* telephone pole

信 *denshin* telegraph, telegram, wire, cable, cablegram

信柱 *denshimbashira* telegraph pole

¹⁰流 *denryū* electric current

¹¹探 *dentan* radar

球 *denkyū* electric-light bulb

動力 *dendōryoku* electromotive power

動機 *dendōki* electric motor

¹²極 *denkyoku* electrode, pole, terminal

報 *dempō* telegram

¹³源 *dengen* source of electricity

路 *denro* electric circuit

鉄 *dentetsu* electric railway

飾 *denshoku* illumination; electric decorations

話 *denwa* telephone 「operator

話交換手 *denwa kōkanshu* telephone

話帳 *denwachō* telephone directory

¹⁴ 磁気 *denjiki* electromagnetism
磁波 *denjiha* electromagnetic waves
¹⁵ 撃 *dengeki* electric shock
熱 *dennetsu* electric heat
線 *densen* electric wire, electric line, telegraph wire, telephone wire, electric cord, cable
¹⁹ 離層 *denrisō* ionosphere
²⁷ 纜 *denran* electric cable

------- 6 -------

需 ₆₅₂₈ _{J3c7b} _{M42275} Ju request; need.
B
⁹ 要 *juyō* demand (for commodities); requirements
要者 *juyōsha* user
要供給 *juyo-kyōkyū* supply and demand
¹² 給 *jukyū* supply and demand

------- 7 -------

震 ₆₅₃₁ _{J3f4c} _{M42300} SHIN. *furu(eru), furu(u)* shake, tremble, quiver, shiver, shudder; vibrate. *furu(i), furu(e)* shivering, shaking, trembling, shuddering.
B
³ 上 *furu(e)-a(garu)* tremble, shiver; be frightened, be intimidated
⁷ 災 *shinsai* earthquake disaster
災地 *shinsaichi* earthquake disaster area
⁹ 度 *shindo* earthquake magnitude
¹¹ 動 *furu(e)-ugo(ku)* quake, tremble, shake, reel, rock. *shindō* tremor, shock, concussion, vibration
¹³ 源 *shingen* earthquake center; center of a disturbance
源地 *shingenchi* earthquake center; center of a disturbance
¹⁶ 撼 *shinkan* terror, alarm, fright

霊 ₆₅₃₂ _{J4e6e} _{M42309} REI soul, spirit; Holy Spirit. RYŌ spirits who possess humans. *tamashii, tama* soul, spirit.
B
³ 山 *reizan* sacred mountain
⁶ 気 *reiki* an atmosphere (feeling) of mystery
安室 *reianshitsu* morgue
⁷ 妙 *reimyō na* wonderful, marvelous, miraculous
⁸ 的 *reiteki* spiritual

長類 *reichōrui* primates, man
⁹ 前 *reizen* before a god; before the spirit of the deceased
界 *reikai* spiritual world; psychic world
枢 *reikyū* coffin, casket
枢車 *reikyūsha* hearse
¹² 場 *reijō* hallowed ground, sacred place
媒 *reibai* spirit medium
¹³ 園 *reien* cemetery park
感 *reikan* inspiration; sacred intuition
¹⁴ 魂 *reikon* soul, spirit
¹⁵ 廟 *reibyō* mausoleum, shrine
¹⁸ 験 *reigen, reiken* miracle, miraculous virtue

------- 9 -------

霞 ₆₅₄₁ _{J3262} _{M42365} KA. *kasu(mu)* be hazy; grow dim (eyes), be blurred. *kasumi* haze, mist; dimness of sight.
B
¹⁴ 関 *Kasumigaseki* Foreign Ministry (Japan)

霜 ₆₅₄₂ _{J417a} _{M42363} SŌ. *shimo* frost.
B
⁴ 月 *shimotsuki* 11th lunar month
⁹ 柱 *shimobashira* frost columns, ice needles
除 *shimoyo(ke)* frost protection
降 *shimofu(ri)* frosting; gray, salt-and-pepper color
枯 *shimoga(reru)* be killed by the frost. *shimoga(re) no* wintry, bleak, frost-nipped
¹⁰ 害 *sōgai* frost damage
¹² 焼 *shimoya(ke)* chilblains; frostbite

------- 11 -------

霧 ₆₅₄₅ _{J4c38} _{M42418} MU. *kiri* mist, fog, spray. *ki(ru)* get foggy, get cloudy.
B
⁵ 氷 *muhyō* fog freezing on vegetation; frost flowers
⁷ 吹 *kirifu(ki)* atomizer, sprayer, vaporizer
⁸ 雨 *kiriame, kirisame* drizzle
¹¹ 笛 *muteki* fog horn
¹² 散 *musan suru* dissipate, be dispelled

8
金長門阜阝隶隹【雨】¹¹青非

─────── 13 ───────

露 $\frac{6549}{\text{J4f2a}}$ Ro dew; Russia. *tsuyu*
B $\overline{\text{M42463}}$ dew; dewdrops; tears;
mortality, flimsiness; (with neg.) not a bit.
ara(wa) ni openly, publicly; frankly,
clearly. *tsuyu, tsuyu (hodo mo)* (not) in
the least, (not) a particle. *tsuyu(keshi)*
dampness. -*Ro*- Russia.

⁴天 *roten* open air
天掘 *rotembo(ri)* strip mining
⁵台 *rodai* outside balcony
出 *roshutsu* exposure; disclosure;

outcrop; (photographic) exposure
⁶地 *roji* farming fields
光 *rokō* exposure (in photography)
⁷見 *roken* discovery, detection
呈 *rotei* exposure, disclosure
⁸命 *romei* transient life
店 *roten* roadside stand
¹⁰骨 *rokotsu na* plain, frank, undisguised;
conspicuous, acute; lewd
座 *roza* sitting out in the open
¹¹悪 *roaku* boasting of one's wickedness
¹²営 *roei* bivouac, camping out
¹⁸顕 *roken* discovery, detection

███ RAD. **青** 174 ███

Aoi blue. Variant: 靑. Nickname: Blue.

青 $\frac{6557}{\text{J4044}}$ SEI. SHŌ. *ao* blue, green;
A $\overline{\text{M42425'}}$ green light. *ao(mu)*
turn green. *ao(bamu)* turn greenish,
be tinged with green. *ao(i)* blue, green;
pale; unripe, green, inexperienced.
ao- unripe; new; immature; novice; blue,
green.
³山 *aoyama, seizan* blue mountain, green
hills. *seizan* cemetery
⁴少年 *seishōnen* youth, younger
generation
天 *seiten* blue sky
⁵白 *aojiro(i)* pale, pallid; bluish white
史 *seishi* history, annals
写真 *aojashin, aoshashin* blueprint
田 *aota, aoda* green rice fields
田刈 *aotaga(ri)* a green crop
田買 *aotaga(i)* buying unharvested rice;
making offers to recruits still in
school
⁶虫 *aomushi* green caterpillar, grub
竹 *aodake* green bamboo
年 *seinen* youth, young people
年男女 *seinen danjo* young men and
women
年期 *seinenki* adolescence
⁸空 *aozora, seikū* blue sky
物 *aomono* greens, vegetables
⁹臭 *aokusa(i)* smelling grassy or unripe;
inexperienced, unskilled
信号 *aoshingō* a green light
春 *seishun* springtime of life, youth.

seishun no youthful, adolescent
春期 *seishunki* puberty, adolescence
海苔 *aonori* green edible seaweed
¹⁰書 *seisho* a "blue book" (government
report)
息吐息 *aoiki-toiki* pitiful dejection
¹²畳 *aodatami* new mat, green mat
葉 *aoba* foliage, greenery, green leaves
雲志 *seiun (no) kokorozashi*
determination to succeed
¹⁴磁 *seiji* celadon porcelain
酸 *seisan* hydrocyanic acid, prussic acid
銅 *seidō, karakane* bronze
銅器 *seidōki* bronze ware

─────── 5 ───────

靖 $\frac{6559}{\text{J4c77}}$ SEI. *yasu(i)* peaceful.
$\overline{\text{M42570'}}$

─────── 6 ───────

静 $\frac{6560}{\text{J4045}}$ JŌ, SEI quiet, peace,
A $\overline{\text{M42574'}}$ inactivity. *shizu(maru) vi*
get quiet, calm down, grow still; subside,
die down, be suppressed. *shizu(meru) vt*
calm, pacify; soothe, alleviate; appease;
suppress, quell. *shizu(kana)* quiet, still,
silent; calm, placid; serene, peaceful; soft
(rain); gentle (voice); graceful; slow
(walk); deserted. *shizu(kesa), shizu(kasa)*
stillness, silence, hush; calm, serenity.

⁴ 止 *seishi* stillness, repose, standing still

止衛星 *seishi eisei* geostationary satellite

水 *seisui* still water, stagnant water

⁸ 的 *seiteki* static

物 *seibutsu* object at rest; still life

⁹ 思 *seishi* meditation, contemplation

¹⁰ 脈 *jōmyaku* vein

¹¹ 粛 *seishuku* silence, quiet

寂 *seijaku* silence, quiet, hush

¹³ 電気 *seidenki* static electricity

¹⁵ 養 *seiyō* rest, recuperation, convalescence

¹⁶ 穏 *seion* calm, tranquility

¹⁷ 聴 *seichō* quietly listening; attention

謐 *seihitsu* peace, tranquility

¹⁸ 観 *seikan* serene contemplation; watchful waiting

RAD. 非 175
Arazu not. Nickname: Negative.

A 非 $\frac{6563}{\text{J4873}}$ M42585 HI mistake; misdeed; injustice; wrong; non-, un-, anti-. *ara(zu)* not, not so, not to be. *ara(zaru)* other than. *ara(zareba)* unless, except. *hi (to) suru* condemn, denounce, disapprove.

² 力 *hiriki* disability, incompetence

人 *hinin* beggar; outcast; criminal

人間的 *hiningenteki* inhuman

³ 凡 *hibon na* extraordinary, unusual

⁴ 公式 *hikōshiki* informal, unofficial, exhibition (game)

公開 *hikōkai* closed (meeting)

⁵ 礼 *hirei* impoliteness

⁶ 行 *hikō* misdemeanor, evil deed, immoral act

合法 *higōhō* illegal; out of order

⁷ 売品 *hibaihin* articles not for sale

⁸ 命 *himei* untimely death

金属 *hikinzoku* nonmetal

武装 *hibusō* demilitarization

⁹ 政府機構 *hiseifu kikō* non-governmental organizations

科学的 *hikagakuteki* unscientific

¹⁰ 核地帯 *hikakuchitai* nuclear weapon free zone

¹¹ 情 *hijō* inanimate nature

道 *hido(i)* cruel, harsh, merciless, atrocious; unjust, unfair; severe, intense, bitter, serious, terrible, outrageous, unreasonable. *hidō* tyranny, cruelty, injustice, lawlessness, unfairness

常 *hijō* emergency, unforeseen occurrence, calamity. *hijō na* remarkable, unusual. *hijō ni* exceedingly, extremely, remarkably, unusually

常口 *hijōguchi* emergency exit

常灯 *hijōtō* emergency light

常事態 *hijō jitai* state of emergency

常勤 *hijōkin* part-time work

常線 *hijōsen* cordon

常識 *hijōshiki* lack of common sense, absurdity, thoughtlessness

¹² 番 *hiban* off duty, off guard

¹³ 鉄金属 *hitetsu kinzoku* nonferrous metals

¹⁴ 認 *hinin* denial, disapproval, repudiation, veto, nonrecognition

関税障壁 *hikanzei shōheki* non-tariff barrier

¹⁵ 課税 *hikazei* tax exemption

論理的 *hironriteki* irrational, illogical

¹⁸ 難 *hinan* criticism, denunciation

9
[面]
革韋韭音頁風飛食首香

9-STROKE RADICALS

RAD. 面 176

Men face. Nickname: Face.

A 面 6566 J4c4c M42618 MEN face features; mask; face guard; surface; plane; side, facet; aspect, phase, corner (of a board); page. *men(suru)* face, border, front on. *omo, omote* face, honor, reputation. *tsura* face, surface.

³ 子 *mentsu* face, honor
⁵ 目 *memmoku, memboku* face, honor, dignity; credit; appearance, aspect
目無 *membokuna(i)* ashamed
白 *omoshiro(i)* interesting; entertaining; delightful, amusing, comical, queer, promising; favorable. *omoshiro(garu)* amuse oneself, be amused. *omoshiro(garaseru)* amuse, entertain
⁶ 汚 *tsurayogo(shi)* disgrace, dishonor, shame
当 *tsuraa(te)* mean words, innuendo
会 *menkai* interview, meeting
⁷ 妖 *men'yō na* strange, mysterious
⁹ 面 *memmen* each one, all; every direction
食 *menku(rau)* be confused, be bewildered, be embarrassed. *menku(i)* emphasizing looks in choosing a mate

持 *omomo(chi)* countenance, look, features
映 *omoha(yui)* bashful, ashamed, coy; disgraceful, shameful
相 *mensō* countenance, looks, features
前 *menzen* presence; before one's eyes
¹⁰ 倒 *mendō* trouble, difficulty, complications; care, attention. *mendō na, mendō(i)* troublesome, complicated
倒臭 *mendōkusa(i)* troublesome, tiresome ⌈resistance
従腹背 *menjū-fukuhai* passive
¹¹ 舵 *omokaji* starboard; turning to starboard
接 *mensetsu* interview
¹² 喰 *menku(rau)* be confused, be bewildered, be embarrassed
¹⁴ 構 *tsuragama(e)* expression, look
¹⁵ 談 *mendan* personal conversation, interview, talk
影 *omokage* visage, face; trace, shadow; memory ⌈face
罵 *memba suru* abuse (someone) to his
¹⁶ 積 *menseki* area
¹⁹ 識 *menshiki* acquaintance

RAD. 革 177

Tsukuri kawa tanned hide or *kaku no kawa* (*kawa* "leather" written with the character read *kaku* as distinguished from Rad. 107). At left: *kawa hen.* Nickname: Shoe Leather (as in 靴 *kutsu* shoe).

A 革 6570 J3357 M42710 KAKU tanned leather. *arata(maru)* become serious (illness). *kawa* skin; hide; leather; fur, pelt; bark; peeling, husk, shell; film, cream.

⁸ 命 *kakumei* revolution
命的 *kakumeiteki* revolutionary, radical
¹³ 靴 *kawagutsu* leather shoes or boots

新 *kakushin* reform, innovation
新的 *kakushinteki* reformatory
¹⁴ 製 *kawasei* made of leather

─── 3 ───

鞝 6573 J3f59 M-X JIN soft, pliable. NIN. *utsubo, utsuo* quiver.
¹⁰ 帯 *jintai* ligament

6566–6573

——————— 4 ———————

靴 6576 / J3724 / M42729 B Kᴀ shoes. *kutsu* shoes; boots.

³ 下 *kutsushita* socks, stockings
⁸ 底 *kutsuzoko* shoe sole
  直 *kutsunao(shi)* shoe repair; cobbler
⁹ 屋 *kutsuya* shoemaker, shoe store
¹⁰ 紐 *kutsuhimo* shoelaces
¹⁴ 篦 *kutsubera* shoehorn
  墨 *kutsuzumi* shoe polish; bootblack
¹⁶ 磨 *kutsumigaki* shoe polish; bootblack
¹⁷ 擦 *kutsuzure* shoe sore

——————— 5 ———————

鞄 6582 / J33/3 / M42781 Hᴀᴋᴜ. Hō. Bʏō. *kaban* suitcase, briefcase, bag.

⁹ 持 *kabammo(chi)* private secretary

——————— 6 ———————

鞍 6586 / J3048 / M42815 Aɴ *kura* saddle.

¹⁰ 部 *ambu* col, saddle (between mountains)

¹² 替 *kuraga(e)* changing quarters (by jobs geisha or prostitutes); changing
壺 *kura tsubo* seat of a saddle

——————— 7 ———————

鞘 6587 / J3e64 / M42850 Sʜō. *saya* (sword) sheath, case, cap; margin, difference, brokerage; spread; (bean)
⁶ 当 *sayaa(te)* courtship rivalry   shells.⌋

——————— 8 ———————

鞠 6589 / J3547 / M42892 Kɪᴋᴜ. Kʏū. *mari* ball.

¹⁰ 躬 *kikkyū* bowing respectfully

——————— 9 ———————

鞭 6595 / J4a5c / M42937 Bᴇɴ *muchi* whip, rod. *muchiu(tsu)* whip, flog; urge on, encourage.

⁵ 打 *muchiu(tsu)* whip, flog; urge on, encourage
  打症 *muchiuchishō* whiplash injury
¹⁵ 撻 *bentatsu* urging, spurring on; whipping

═══════════ RAD. **韋** 178 ═══════════

Nameshigawa tanned leather. This rare radical is traditionally a 9-stroke element.
Its more common variant 韋 has 10 strokes.
(as in 違 *chigau* differ).

——————— 8 ———————

韓 6602 / J345a / M43159 Kᴀɴ *Kara* Korea.

⁸ 国 *Kankoku, Karakuni* Korea

═══════════ RAD. **韭** 179 ═══════════

Nira leek. Nickname: Leek.

——————— 3 ———————

韮 6605 / J4723 / M43237 Kʏū. *nira* leek.

RAD. 音 180

Oto sound. Variant: 音. At left: *oto hen*. Nickname: Noisy.

A 音 6607 / J323b / M43265 ON sound; noise; pronunciation. IN sound, tone. *oto* sound, noise, roar; fame. *ne* sound, tone, note, voice, chirping.

⁶色 *neiro, onshoku* tone color, tone quality

曲 *ongyoku, onkyoku* songs accompanied by the samisen; musical performance

⁷沙汰 *otosata* news, letter

声 *onsei, onjō* voice

声学 *onseigaku* phonetics

⁸波 *ompa* sound wave

⁹速 *onsoku* speed of sound

便 *ombin* euphony, euphonic change

信 *onshin, inshin, otozure* correspondence, message, news, tidings

¹⁰訓 *onkun* Chinese and Japanese pronunciations of characters

¹¹域 *on'iki* voice range

訳 *on'yaku* transliteration

階 *onkai* musical scale

符 *ompu* note, score, notation

¹³痴 *onchi* tone deafness, no ear for music

節 *onsetsu* syllable

感 *onkan* sense of sound

楽 *ongaku* music

楽会 *ongakkai, ongakukai* concert, musicale

楽家 *ongakka, ongakuka* musician

¹⁴読 *ondoku* reading aloud. *on'yo(mi)* the *on* or Chinese reading of a character or a compound

¹⁵調 *onchō* tune, tone, rhythm, melody, harmony, euphony

質 *onshitsu* tone quality

標文字 *ompyō monji, ompyō moji* phonetic symbols

¹⁶頭 *ondo* songs where someone takes the lead and others sing or dance in response; a song leader

¹⁹譜 *ompu* music, notes, notation

韻 *on'in* vocal sound

響 *onkyō* sound, noise, echo

— 10 —

B 響 6610 / J3641 / M43318 KYŌ. *hibi(ku)* sound, resound, reverberate, echo, ring, vibrate; grate on; affect, find an echo in; become known. *hibi(ki)* sound, noise, peal, boom, crash, explosion; echo, reverberation; influence, effect; vibration, shock.

B 韻 6611 / J3124 / M43307 IN rhyme; elegance; tone.

⁹律 *inritsu* rhythm

RAD. 頁 181

Ōgai big "shell" (to distinguish it from Rad. 154), *ichi no kai* (i.e., the character *ichi* "one" plus *kai* "shell"), or *pēji* "page." Nickname: Big Shell.

頁 6614 / J4a47 / M43333 KETSU. *pēji* page, leaf.

— 2 —

頃 6615 / J3a22 / M43338 KEI. *koro* time, period. *koro(shimo)* just at that time. *-goro, -koro* about (regarding time).

⁶合 *koroa(i)* suitable time; propriety;

moderation

A 頂 6616 / J443a / M43335 CHŌ. *itadaki* head; top of the head; top, summit, peak; spire. *itada(ku)* be crowned with, wear; live under (a ruler); install (a president); receive, accept; buy; take, eat, drink. *unaji* nape of the neck.

³上 *chōjō* top, summit, crest, peak, apex; climax, acme

⁹点 *chōten* apex, vertex, peak, climax, acme, top, height

¹⁷戴 *chōdai suru* accept, receive; take, eat, enjoy. *chōdai* please, be good enough to

━━━━━ **3** ━━━━━

項 6617 J3960 M43343 **B** Kō clause, paragraph; item; term (in math); argument (in math or linguistics). *unaji* nape of the neck.

⁵目 *kōmoku* head, item, provision, clause

須 6618 J3f5c M43352 Su. Shu. *subeka(raku)* by all means, necessarily.

順 6619 J3d67 M43349 **A** Jun order; turn; right; docility, obedience; occasion.

⁵次 *junji* gradually. *junji ni* in order, successively

当 *juntō na* proper, right, regular, normal

⁷位 *jun'i* order, rank, precedence

応 *junnō* adaptation; sympathy

序 *junjo* order; system; procedure

⁸延 *jun'en* postponement

逆 *jungyaku* obedience and disobedience, right and wrong

⁹風 *jumpū* favorable wind, tail wind

¹²順 *junjun ni* in order, in turn

番 *jumban* order, turn

¹³路 *junro* regular route; itinerary

¹⁵調 *junchō* smoothness, favorable condition

¹⁹繰 *jungu(ri) ni* in turn, in order

━━━━━ **4** ━━━━━

頒 6621 J4852 M43378 **B** Han. *waka(tsu)* divide, separate; share with; distinguish between.

⁵布 *hampu* distribution, circulation, dissemination

頓 6623 J465c M43381 Ton. *tomi ni, niwaka ni* suddenly, in a hurry, immediately. *ton to* entirely; (neg.) not in the least.

⁸知 *tonchi* ready wit, tact

⁹珍漢 *tonchinkan* absurdity, contradiction

¹⁰馬 *tomma* dunce, simpleton. *tomma na* silly

挫 *tonza* setback, rebuff, standstill, impasse, deadlock

¹²着 *tonjaku, tonchaku* care, heed, concern, anxiety

頑 6624 J3468 M43374 **B** Gan stubborn; foolish. *gan(toshite)* firmly, stubbornly, resolutely. *kataku(na)* obstinate, stubborn.

³丈 *ganjō na* solid, firm, stout

⁸固 *ganko* obstinacy, stubbornness, persistence, bigotry

迷 *gammei* obstinacy, perversity, bigotry

¹¹健 *ganken* robust health

張 *gamba(ru)* persist in, insist on, be inflexible

強 *gankyō* obstinacy, persistence

預 6625 J4d42 M43373 **A** Yo. *azu(keru)* vt place in custody, deposit, leave with, entrust with, commit to, give. *azu(karu)* vi take charge of; receive on deposit; undertake to do; call off (as a tie); refrain from; receive, enjoy. *azu(kari)* depositing; custody. *azu(ke)* entrusting to, committing to. *(o)azu(ke)* not carrying out a promise; making a dog wait for a command to eat.

²入 *azu(ke)-i(reru)* make a deposit

⁷言 *yogen* prophecy

言者 *yogensha* prophet

⁸物 *azu(ke)mono* checked article, article left in charge of someone. *azu(kari)mono* a thing on deposit; consignment

金 *azu(ke)kin* key money. *yokin* deposit, bank account, credit

金通帳 *yokin tsūchō* bankbook

¹⁰託 *yotaku suru* deposit

¹²貯金 *yochokin* deposit, bank account

━━━━━ **5** ━━━━━

頚 6626 J375b M43434 See 頸 6638.

頸

頗 6627 J3f7c M43415 Ha be prejudiced. *sukobu(ru)* exceedingly, extremely.

9

面革韋韭音【頁】風飛食首香

5

A 領 6628 J4e4e M43423 Ryō dominion, territory possession, fief; suit (of armor). *ryō(suru)* govern, reign, be in possession of.

3 土 *ryōdo* territory, dominion, possession
4 内 *ryōnai* domains, territory
5 分 *ryōbun* territory, dominion, possession; domain, sphere, field
5 主 *ryōshu* lord of a fief, daimyo
  収 *ryōshū* receipt, voucher
  収書 *ryōshūsho* receipt, voucher
  収証 *ryōshūshō* receipt, voucher
6 地 *ryōchi* territory, dominion, possession; fief
  有 *ryōyū* possession
7 承 *ryōshō* acknowledgment
8 空 *ryōkū* territorial air
  事 *ryōji* consul
  事館 *ryōjikan* consulate
9 海 *ryōkai* territorial waters
10 袖 *ryōshū* leader, chief, boss
11 域 *ryōiki* territory, dominion, possession, domain, sphere

─────── 6 ───────

頬 6629 J4b4b M-X Nonstandard for 頰 6637.

頰

─────── 7 ───────

B 頼 6635 J4d6a M43529 RAI. *tano(mu)* ask, request, entreat, appeal; entrust to, commission; employ, call in; depend on, have recourse to, trust in. *tayo(ru)* rely on, have recourse to. *tano(moshii)* reliable, trustworthy; hopeful. *tayo(rinai)* forlorn, helpless; vague; unreliable. *tano(mō)* hello there.

頰 6637 J-X M43496 頬 6629 J4b4b M-X KYŌ. *hō, hoo, hoho* cheek.

7 杖突 *hōzue (o) tsu(ku)* rest the chin on one's hands
9 紅 *hōbeni* rouge
10 骨 *hōbone, kyōkotsu* cheekbone
  被 *hōkabu(ri)* tying a cloth around the cheeks; affecting ignorance
11 張 *hōba(ru)* take (food); take a big mouthful
15 髯 *hōhige* sideburns

頸 6638 J7074 M43515 KEI. *kubi* neck, head.

10 骨 *keikotsu* neckbone
  部 *keibu* neck (region)
11 動脈 *keidōmyaku* carotid artery
12 椎 *keitsui* cervical vertebrae
14 静脈 *keijōmyaku* jugular vein

A 頭 6639 J462c M43490 TŌ head, counter for large mammals. ZU head. *atama* head; brain, mind, intellect; leader; top; head (of boil); idea; hair; idea, point of view, consideration. *kashira* head; hair; leader, chief. *kōbe, kaburi, kabu, tsumuri* head. *atama kara* from the beginning; (not) at all. *atama(dekkachi)* top-heaviness. *atama(gonashi) ni* unsparingly, categorically. *-gashira* the very moment; the beginning.

3 巾 *zukin* hood, turban
  上 *zujō* overhead
4 文字 *kashira moji* capital letter; initials; first word
5 目 *tōmoku* chief, head, leader
7 角 *tōkaku* top of the head
8 金 *atamakin* down payment, key money
  取 *tōdori* (private bank) president; manager
10 骨 *tōkotsu* skill
  株 *atamakabu* leader, executives
  部 *tōbu, zubu* the head
11 脳 *zunō* head, brain
12 寒足熱 *zukan-sokunetsu* keeping the head cool and the feet warm
  痛 *zutsū, tōtsū* headache; worry
13 蓋骨 *zugaikotsu* skull, cranium
14 髪 *tōhatsu* hair, head of hair
19 韻 *tōin* alliteration

─────── 8 ───────

B 頻 6641 J4951 M-X HIN. *shiki(ru) vi* repeat, occur repeatedly. *shiki(ri) ni* repeatedly, incessantly, insistently, intently.

5 出 *hinshutsu* frequent appearance
9 発 *himpatsu* frequent occurrence, frequent
  度 *hindo* frequency
13 数 *hinsū* frequency
16 繁 *himpan* frequency
17 頻 *himpin to, shikushiku to* frequently

─────── **9** ───────

顎 6643 J335c M43590 GAKU jaw. *ago* jaw, chin. *agito* gill.
²² 顎 *agohige* beard

額 6644 J335b M43586 GAKU tablet, plaque,
A framed picture; sum, quantity, amount, volume; denomination. *hitai* forehead, brow. *nuka(zuku)* bow, kowtow, prostrate oneself.
⁹ 面 *gakumen* face value; par; denomination; mere outlook
¹⁵ 縁 *gakubuchi* picture frame

題 6645 J426a M43584 DAI subject, theme, topic;
A title, caption, heading; question, problem. *dai(suru)* give a title to.
⁵ 目 *daimoku* title (of a book); heading
号 *daigō* book title
⁶ 字 *daiji* preface of a book or title
名 *daimei* title
⁷ 材 *daizai* subject matter, theme

顕 6646 J3832 M43609 KEN. *ara(wareru)* appear,
B emerge, come in sight, show up; be revealed, be discovered; be mentioned; become famous. *ara(wasu)* show, indicate, display, prove, disclose, express; represent; distinguish oneself.
⁵ 示 *kenji suru* show, unfold, unveil, uncover
⁶ 在 *kenzai suru* reveal
⁷ 花植物 *kenka shokubutsu* flowering plant
⁸ 官 *kenkan* dignitary, high official
¹¹ 現 *kengen* manifestation
著 *kencho na* remarkable, striking, obvious
¹³ 微鏡 *kembikyō* microscope
¹⁴ 彰 *kenshō suru* manifest, display, exalt, honor
¹⁸ 職 *kenshoku* important post

類 6647 J4e60 M43608 RUI kind, variety, class,
A genus; description; parallel case, an equal. *rui(suru)* be similar to, be akin to. *tagu(eru)* compare with. *tagui* kind, sort, class; match, equal. *-rui* resembling.
² 人猿 *ruijin'en* anthropoid ape, orangutan

⁵ 句 *ruiku* synonymous expression; similar haiku poems
⁶ 同 *ruidō* similarity; same kind
名 *ruimei* generic name
似点 *ruijiten* points of similarity
似品 *ruijihin* an imitation
⁷ 伴 *ruiban* same kind; companion; accomplice
別 *ruibetsu* classification
⁸ 例 *ruirei* similar example; analogy
⁹ 型 *ruikei* similar type
¹⁰ 書 *ruisho* similar books
¹¹ 推 *ruisui* analogy
¹² 焼 *ruishō* spreading fire
¹⁴ 語 *ruigo* synonym
¹⁵ 縁 *ruien* affinity, family relationship
¹⁸ 題 *ruidai* similar question

顔 6648 J3469 M43591 GAN. *kambase* face,
A countenance, expression; honor, prestige. *kao* face, countenance, expression; honor, prestige.
⁵ 立 *kaoda(chi)* facial features. *kao (ga) ta(tsu)* save face
付 *kaotsu(ki)* countenance, looks, features
出 *kaoda(shi) suru* visit, put in an appearance
⁶ 色 *kao iro, ganshoku* complexion, countenance, expression, color
向 *kaomu(ke)* facing the public
合 *kaoa(wase)* meeting, presentation, being matched against or paired with
⁷ 役 *kaoyaku* leader, boss
利 *kao (ga) ki(ku)* be influential
売 *kao (o) u(ru), kao (ga) u(reru)* become famous
見世 *kaomise* debut, first stage appearance
見知 *kaomishi(ri)* one whose face one recognizes
⁹ 負 *kaoma(ke) suru* be outshone, be made to blush
面 *gammen* the face
¹⁰ 料 *ganryō* cosmetics
¹³ 触 *kaobure* personnel, line-up
¹⁹ 繋 *kaotsuna(gi)* getting acquainted

─────── **10** ───────

顚 6651 J-X M43628 顛 6652 J453f M-X TEN overturn;
summit; origin.

9

面革韋韭音頁【風】飛食首香

⁵ 末 *temmatsu* circumstances, facts, details

A 顧 `6653 J346a M43623` GAN prayer, petition, vow. *nega(u)* desire, wish, hope; beg, implore. *nega(i)* desire, wish, request, prayer; petition, application. *nega(wakuwa)* I pray. *nega(washii)* desirable.

³ 下 *nega(i)-sa(geru)* withdraw a request
⁵ 出 *nega(i)-de(ru)* apply for. *nega(i)de* application, petition
⁸ 事 *nega(i)goto* prayer, one's desire
¹⁰ 書 *gansho* written application or petition
¹¹ 掛 *ganka(ke)* Shinto or Buddhist prayer

望 *gambō, gammō* desire, wish, aspiration
¹³ 意 *gan'i* object of an application

──────── **12** ────────

A 顧 `6655 J385c M43689` KO. *kaeri(miru)* look back; turn around, look back upon, review; examine oneself; take notice of.

⁹ 客 *kokyaku, kokaku* customer, patron, client
¹¹ 望 *kobō suru* look around; hesitate
問 *komon* adviser, consultant

━━━━━━━━ RAD. 風 182 ━━━━━━━━

Kaze wind. Variant: 凬 *fūnyō* "wind" enclosure. Nickname: Wind (cf. Rad. 16).

A 風 `6663 J4977 M43756` FU, FŪ wind; air, look, appearance, bearing, mien, deportment; manners, custom; trend, tone, tendency; way, fashion, manner; style, type; disposition, turn of mind; kind; vein; state, condition. *kaze* wind, storm, breeze, draft, current of air; a cold. *furi* form; condition; deportment; pretense; discipline; custom. *kaza-* wind.

² 力 *fūryoku* wind force
³ 下 *kazashimo, kazashita* leeward
上 *kazakami* windward
土 *fūdo* climate, topography, natural feature
土病 *fūdobyō* endemic disease
土記 *fudoki* topography, description of natural features
⁴ 月 *fūgetsu* wind and moon; beauties of
水 *fūsui* wind and flowing water
水害 *fūsuigai* storm and flood damage
化 *fūka* weathering; efflorescence; influence of a ruler on the governed
⁵ 圧 *fūatsu* wind pressure, air pressure; leeway, driftage
⁶ 向 *fūkō, kazamu(ki), kazemu(ki)* wind direction; situation; tendency
当 *kazaa(tari), kazea(tari)* force of the wind; fierce criticism; oppression
防 *fūbō* windshield, windbreak
⁷ 車 *fūsha* windmill. *kazaguruma*

windmill; pinwheel
体 *fūtei, fūtai* appearance, looks, dress, posture, attitude
邪 *fūja, kaze* a cold
見 *kazami* weather vane
来坊 *fūraibō* wanderer, vagabond, waif, tramp
呂 *furo* bath; bathtub
呂屋 *furoya* bathhouse, public bath
呂桶 *furooke* bathtub
呂場 *furoba* bathroom
呂敷 *furoshiki* wrapping cloth, kerchief
⁸ 味 *fūmi* taste, flavor
波 *fūha* wind and waves; rough seas; discord, quarrel
刺 *fūshi* sarcasm, innuendo, irony
采 *fūsai* appearance, mien, bearing
物 *fūbutsu* natural objects, nature, scenery, landscape; scenes and manners
⁹ 通 *kazetō(shi), kazatō(shi), kazetō(ri)* ventilation
洞 *fūdō* wind tunnel
紀 *fūki* discipline, public morals
変 *fūgawa(ri)* eccentricity, peculiarity
姿 *fūshi* appearance, looks, mien
速 *fūsoku* wind velocity
前灯 *fūzen (no) tomoshibi* flickering light; dangerous situation; verge of death

俗 *fūzoku* manners, customs, morals
俗営業 *fūzoku eigyō* business affecting public morals
¹⁰ 格 *fūkaku* character, personality, appearance, style
浪 *fūrō* wind and waves, heavy seas
流 *fūryū* taste, elegance, refinement
致 *fūchi* taste, elegance; scenic beauty
致地区 *fūchi chiku* scenic zone
¹¹ 情 *fuzei* appearance, air; taste; elegance; entertainment, hospitality
船 *fūsen* balloon
習 *fūshū* manners, customs, usage
雪 *fūsetsu* snowstorm, blizzard
¹² 評 *fūhyō* rumor
媒花 *fūbaika* wind-pollinated flower

景 *fūkei* landscape, scenery, view
雲児 *fūunji* a lucky adventurer
¹³ 雅 *fūga* taste, elegance, refinement; literature, poetry
鈴 *fūrin* wind bell
¹⁴ 聞 *fūbun, kaze (no) ki(koe)* report, rumor
説 *fūsetsu* rumor, report, hearsay
貌 *fūbō* looks, features, appearance
¹⁵ 趣 *fūshu* import, meaning, contents, tenor, gist; tone, touch, sentiment, charm; aspect, appearance
潮 *fūchō* lee tide; current (of the times), fashion, trend
¹⁹ 靡 *fūbi suru* overwhelm, conquer, dominate, sway

RAD. 飛 183

Tobu to fly. Nickname: Flying.

飛 6672 J4874 M44000 Hᵢ. *to(bu)* fly; skip (pages). *to(basu)* fly (a kite); let fly; blow away; scatter; splash; drive fast; skip over, omit; issue, send out. *ton(da)* surprising, extraordinary, shocking, terrible, tremendous, strange, serious. *to(ndemonai)* absurd; unexpected; fantastic; strange, extraordinary.
⁴ 火 *to(bi)hi* flying sparks; leaping flames; repercussions
切 *tobiki(ri)* top quality, beyond comparison; a flying shot (at a bird)
込 *to(bi)-ko(mu)* jump into; dive in; fly into; thrust oneself into
込自殺 *tobiko(mi) jisatsu* committing suicide by jumping in front of a train
⁶ 交 *to(bi)-ka(u)* fly about, flit about
行 *hikō* flight, flying, aviation
行士 *hikōshi* aviator
行船 *hikōsen* airship, dirigible
行場 *hikōjō* airfield, airport
行艇 *hikōtei* flying boat, hydroplane
行機 *hikōki* airplane, aircraft
行機雲 *hikōkigumo* a vapor trail, a

condensation trail, a contrail
⁷ 来 *hirai suru* come flying; come by air. *to(bi)-kita(ru)* come flying, come running, come in a hurry
⁸ 沫 *himatsu* splash, spray
⁹ 降 *to(bi)o(ri)* jumping off a moving vehicle
降自殺 *to(bi)o(ri) jisatsu* committing suicide by jumping off a building
乗 *to(bi)-no(ru)* jump on (a horse); jump on a moving vehicle
¹⁰ 起 *to(bi)-o(kiru)* jump out of bed; start up, spring to one's feet
¹¹ 魚 *to(bi)uo* flying fish
鳥 *hichō* flying bird. *Asuka* Asuka Era (593-710)
¹² 越 *to(bi)-ko(su)* jump over, fly cross. *to(bi)ko(shi)* leapfrog
翔 *hishō* flight, flying, soaring
散 *hisan suru, to(bi)-chi(ru)* scatter, disperse
¹³ 跳 *to(bi)-ha(neru)* jump up; fly away
²¹ 躍 *hiyaku* leap; activity; rapid progress; flight (of imagination); maneuvers
躍的 *hiyakuteki* rapid

9

面革韋韭音頁風飛【食】首香

Shoku food. Variant: 食. At left: 飠 or 𩙿 (8 strokes) *shoku hen*. Nickname: Food.

A 食 6674 J3f29 M44014 SHI, JIKI food. SHOKU food, provisions; eating, meal; appetite. *ta(beru), shoku(suru)* eat. *ku(u)* eat; subsist on; support oneself; consume; get (a scolding); encroach; bite at, gnaw at; (shoes) pinch; be cheated. *ku(rau)* eat, drink; receive (a blow). *ku(rawasu)* feed; strike (someone). *ha(mu)* eat, feed on, graze on, live on, prey on, receive (an allowance). *ku(i-chigiru)* eat off, bite off. *ku(enai)* inedible; hard to get along; cunning, crafty. *ku(eru)* edible; can get along. *shoku(pan)* bread.

³ 下 *ku(i)-sa(garu)* hang on to; hold on to (convictions)

⁴ 方 *ta(be)kata, ku(i)kata* manner of eating; how to eat, table manners

止 *ku(i)-to(meru)* restrain, resist, prevent. *ku(i)sa(shi)* food remnants. *ku(i)sa(shi) no* half-eaten

込 *ku(i)-ko(mu)* eat into, eat up; bore into; cut into; be deep-seated; erode, corrode; drain (funds). *kura(i)-ko(mu)* go to jail; shoulder a debt or other load; be deceived; abandon oneself to vice; fall heir to (trouble). *ku(i)ko(mi)* thrust; intrusion; deficit

中 *shokuata(ri)* food poisoning, food disagreement

中毒 *shoku chūdoku* food poisoning

⁵ 生活 *shoku seikatsu* eating habits, dietary life

用 *shokuyō no* edible, used for food

用品 *shokuyōhin* foodstuffs, groceries

⁶ 合 *ku(i)-a(waseru)* eating two things together; dovetail. *ku(i)-a(u)* bite each other; engage (gears); fit together exactly. *ku(i)a(i)* fighting; biting each other

肉 *shokuniku* meat eating

⁷ 坊 *ku(ishim)bō* gourmand; gluttony

扶持 *ku(i)buchi* food expenses

⁸ 味 *shokumi* flavor (of a food)

逃 *ku(i)ni(ge)* run off without paying for food

券 *shokken* meal ticket

放題 *ta(be)hōdai, ku(i)hōdai* overeating

卓 *shokutaku* dining table

事 *shokuji* meal, diet, board

物 *ta(be)mono, ku(i)mono* food, provisions; victim, prey. *ku(u)mono* food, feed. *shokumotsu* food, provisions; diet; feed. *ku(wase)mono* imitation, counterfeit, fraud; impostor, hypocrite, crook (a person)

物連鎖 *shokumotsu rensa* food chain

物繊維 *shokumotsu sen'i* dietary fiber

⁹ 通 *shokutsū* connoisseur of food

後 *shokugo* after eating; after a meal

指 *shokushi* forefinger, index finger

前 *shokuzen* before meals; at the dinner table

品 *shokuhin* foodstuffs, groceries

品加工 *shokuhin kakō* food processing

品店 *shokuhinten* grocery store

品衛生 *shokuhin eisei* food sanitation

¹⁰ 倒 *ku(i)-tao(su)* sponge on. *ku(i)dao(re)* wasting one's money on food

残 *ta(be)-noko(su), ku(i)-noko(su)* leave half-eaten. *ta(be)noko(shi)* leftover food

料 *shokuryō* food; main article of diet

¹¹ 頃 *ta(be)goro, ku(i)goro* time to eat; season for; done to a turn; period of big appetite

盛 *ta(be)zaka(ri)* growing period. *ku(i)zaka(ri)* time to eat; season for; done to a turn; period of big appetite

堂 *shokudō* dining hall, mess hall

習慣 *shokushūkan* dietary habits

道 *shokudō* alimentary canal, esophagus

道楽 *ku(i)dōraku* epicureanism; gourmet

欲 *shokuyoku* appetite

欲不振 *shokuyoku-fushin* poor appetite

¹² 違 *ku(i)-chiga(u)* cross, interlock; run counter to, clash with; go amiss

費 *shokuhi* food expense, board charge

¹³ 傷 *shokushō* food poisoning; food disagreement; surfeiting

塩 *shokuen* table salt, sodium chloride

詰 *ku(i)-tsu(meru)* fail, go broke, lose one's job, be in penury

¹⁵ 器 *shokki* tableware, dinner set

潰 *ku(i)-tsubu(su)* sponge on.
ku(i)tsubu(shi) parasite, hanger-on
餌療法 *shokuji ryōhō* diet therapy
16 膳 *shokuzen* dining table
18 糧 *shokuryō* food, provisions, rations

the influence of alchohol
料 *no(mi)ryō* drink money; drink reserved for oneself. *inryō* a drink, beverage
料水 *inryōsui* drinking water

─────── 2 ───────

飢 B 6675 / J3532 / M44023' KI. *u(eru)* be hungry, starve.
6 死 *ueji(ni)* starving to death
11 渇 *kikatsu* hunger and thirst, starvation
15 餓 *kiga* hunger, starvation, famine
20 饉 *kikin* famine

─────── 4 ───────

飯 A 6679 / J4853 / M44064' HAN cooked rice; food; meal. *meshi* cooked rice; meal; food, livelihood. *mamma, mama* cooked rice (a child's word). *ii* cooked grains.
8 炊 *meshita(ki)* cooking rice
事 *mamagoto* (children) playing house
9 屋 *meshiya* eating house
11 盒 *hangō* mess tin, canteen
12 場 *hamba* worker's temporary quarters

飲 A 6680 / J307b / M44063' IN drinking; feast. *no(mu)* drink, taste, take; swallow, devour; smoke; conceal (a weapon); accept (an idea); despise. *no(meru)* can drink; be good to drink; drinkable. *non(dakureru)* be dead drunk. *no(mikko)* drinking contest.
3 干 *no(mi)-ho(su)* drink up, drain (the cup)
4 込 *no(mi)-ko(mu)* swallow, gulp down; understand
水 *no(mi)mizu* drinking water
5 用 *in'yō* drinking
用水 *in'yōsui* drinking water
6 仲間 *no(mi) nakama* drinking companion
8 物 *nomimono* beverage, drinks
9 屋 *no(mi)ya* tavern, grogshop
食 *no(mi)ku(i), inshoku* food and drink, eating and drinking
食店 *inshokuten* restaurant
食物 *inshokubutsu* food and drink
10 酒 *inshu* drinking saké
酒運転 *inshu unten* drioing while under

─────── 5 ───────

飴 6682 / J303b / M44080 I. *ame* rice jelly, candy.

飾 B 6683 / J3e7e / M44111' SHOKU. *kaza(ru)* ornament, decorate, adorn, embellish; exhibit; be ostentatious; whitewash. *kaza(ri)* adornment, decoration, ornament.
5 立 *kaza(ri)-ta(teru)* adorn, dress up; play up. *kaza(ri)ta(te)* ornamentation, decoration
付 *kaza(ri)-tsu(keru)* decorate, arrange
6 気 *kaza(ri)ke* showing off, affectation
8 物 *kaza(ri)mono* ornament, decoration; figurehead
11 窓 *kaza(ri) mado* show window
12 棚 *kaza(ri)dana* display shelves

飽 B 6684 / J4b30 / M44109' HŌ. *a(kiru), a(ku)* get tired of, lose interest in, have enough. *a(kasu)* vt satiate, surfeit; bore, tire, weary. *a(kumademo)* to the utmost, to the bitter end, persistently, strictly. *a(kunaki)* insatiable, rapacious. *a(kanu)* untiring, reluctant, unwilling, inseparable. *aki(ppoi)* fickle; soon tired of (something).
6 迄 *a(ku)made* to the bitter end, tenaciously, persistently, strictly, exceedingly
気味 *a(ki)gimi* weariness, being tired of
8 和 *hōwa* saturation
和点 *hōwaten* saturation point
易 *a(ki)yasu(i)* fickle, soon tired of
9 食 *hōshoku* satiety; gluttony

飼 A 6685 / J3b74 / M44107' SHI raising (animals). *ka(u)* raise, keep, feed.
4 犬 *ka(i)inu* pet dog
5 主 *ka(i)nushi* (dog) owner; shepherd
8 育 *shiiku suru* breed, raise, rear, keep
10 料 *shiryō* fodder, feed
11 猫 *ka(i)neko* pet cat
12 葉 *ka(i)ba* fodder

¹⁵養 *shiyō* breeding, raising, keeping

───────── 6 ─────────

餅 6689 / J4c5f / M44133 HEI. *mochi, mochii* rice cake.
⁶肌 *mochihada* soft white skin
¹³搗 *mochitsu(ki)* making rice cake

餌 6690 / J3142 / M44146 JI food. *e, eba, esa* feed, food; bait; prey; tempting profit.
⁹食 *eba(mu)* feed. *ejiki* food, bait, prey, victim

養 6691 / J4d5c / M44144 A YŌ. *yashina(u)* bring up, rear; adopt, foster; support; promote (health); cultivate, develop. *yashina(i)* nutrition, nurture; rearing; sustenance; manure.
³女 *yōjo* adopted daughter; stepdaughter; daughter-in-law
子 *yashina(i)go* foster child. *yōshi* adopted son
⁴分 *yōbun* nourishment, sustenance
父 *yōfu* foster father
父母 *yōfubo* adopted parents
⁵母 *yōbo* foster mother
生 *yōjō* health care, hygiene; recuperation
⁶成 *yōsei* training, education
老 *yōrō* provision for the aged
老年金 *yōrō nenkin* endowment annuity, old-age pension
⁸育 *yōiku suru, yashina(i)-soda(teru)* bring up, rear; cultivate
¹⁰蚕 *yōsan* silkworm culture
¹¹豚 *yōton* hog raising, hogs
魚 *yōgyo* fish farming, fish breeding
¹²殖 *yōshoku* culture, raising, breeding
¹³蜂 *yōhō* beekeeping

¹⁹鶏 *yōkei* poultry
²⁰護 *yōgo* protection, care
護学校 *yōgo gakkō* school for handicapped children
護教諭 *yōgo kyōyu* nurse-teacher

───────── 7 ─────────

餐 6696 / J3b71 / M44160 SAN eat; drink; swallow.

餓 6697 / J326e / M44168 B GA. *u(eru), katsu(eru)* be hungry, starve, thirst. *himo(jii)* hungry.
⁶死 *gashi, ueji(ni), katsu(e)ji(ni)* death from starvation
¹⁰鬼 *gaki* hungry ghost; urchin, brat, mischievous child

───────── 8 ─────────

館 6701 / J345b / M44237' 舘 4923 / J345c / M30326 A KAN mansion, large building, hall. *tachi* mansion; small castle; government housing. *tate* mansion, palace, fort. *yakata* mansion; temporary residence.

───────── 10 ─────────

饗 6705 / J3642 / M-X Nonstandard for 饗 6715. 饗

───────── 12 ─────────

饗 6715 / J-X / M44431 饗 6705 / J3642 / M-X KYŌ banquet. *kyō(suru)* banquet, treat.
⁷応 *kyōō* treat, feast, banquet
¹⁰宴 *kyōen* banquet, dinner

━━━━━━ RAD. 首 185 ━━━━━━

Kubi neck. Nickname: Neck.

首 6719 / J3c73 / M44489 A SHU head; neck; beginning; the first; poem and song counter. *kubi* neck, head. *kōbe* the head. *kubi ni suru* dismiss (someone). *kubi ni* *naru* be dismissed.
⁴引 *kubi(p)pi(ki)* tug of war using necks; constantly using reference books
⁶曲 *kubimaga(ri)* crooked neck; person

吊 *kubitsu(ri)* hanging oneself, with a crooked neck
⁷位 *shui* first place, head position
尾 *shubi* issue, course (of events), arrangements, result; beginning and end; head and tail; attitude; rendezvous
⁸長 *shuchō* leader, chief, head. *kubi (o) naga(ku) suru* wait expectantly
府 *shufu* capital
肯 *shukō* assent, consent
実検 *kubi jikken* inspection of a severed head; identification of a suspect
⁹相 *shushō* prime minister
¹⁰席 *shuseki* head seat, head, chief, president, governor, chair
班 *shuhan* head position; prime minister
都 *shuto* capital
釣 *kubitsuri* hanging oneself
唱 *shushō* advocacy, promotion
脳 *shunō* head, brains, leading spirit
¹²筋 *kubisuji* nape of the neck
¹³飾 *kubikaza(ri)* necklace
¹⁴魁 *shukai* leader, ringleader
領 *shuryō* head, chief, boss, leader
導 *shudō* main leadership
¹⁶謀 *shubō* planning; plotting; main planner, ringleader
¹⁸題 *shudai* the first paragraph

RAD. 香 186

Nioi odor or *kaori* fragrance. Nickname: Perfume.

B 香 <u>6722 / J3961 / M44518</u> Kō incense, fragrance. *ka* smell, scent, odor; aroma, perfume, fragrance, flavor. *kao(ru)* smell, be fragrant. *kōba(shii), kamba(shii)* fragrant; balmy; favorable. *kao(ri)* fragrance, perfume, aroma, odor, scent, smell. *nioi* smell, odor, scent; stench; fragrance, aroma, perfume.
⁴木 *kōboku* aromatic tree, scented wood
水 *kōsui* perfume
⁶気 *kōki* fragrance, aroma, perfume
⁷辛料 *kōshinryō* spices, seasoning
⁸油 *kōyu* pomade, balm, perfumed oil
炉 *kōro* censer, incense burner
典 *kōden* condolence gift
典返 *kōdengae(shi)* return present for a condolence gift
⁹草 *kōsō* aromatic grasses
¹⁰料 *kōryō* spices; perfumes; condolence gift
華 *kōge* (Buddhist) flowers and incense
¹²奠 *kōden* condolence gift
奠返 *kōdengae(shi)* return present for a condolence gift

11

馨 <u>6724 / J333e / M44559</u> KEI. *kao(ru)* be fragrant. *kamba(shii), kōba(shii)* fragrant; balmy; favorable.

10-STROKE RADICALS

RAD. 馬 187

Uma horse. At left: *uma hen*. Nickname: Horse.

A 馬 <u>6725 / J474f / M44572</u> ME, BA, MA horse. *uma* horse; horseflesh; stepladder.
²力 *bariki* horsepower; energy; cart, wagon
³子 *mago* pack-horse driver

10
【馬】
0馬
骨
高
髟
鬥
鬯
鬲
鬼

上 *bajō* horseback, mounted
小屋 *umagoya* horse barn
4 方 *umakata* pack-horse driver, wagon driver
匹 *bahitsu* horses
6 肉 *baniku* horse meat
耳東風 *baji-tōfū* utter indifference
7 車 *basha* carriage, coach; cart, wagon
8 券 *baken* pari-mutuel ticket
具 *bagu* harness, saddlery
9 乗 *umano(ri)* horse riding; horseman; astraddle
10 骨 *uma (no) hone* person of doubtful origin, a nondescript
11 術 *bajutsu* horsemanship
脚 *bakyaku* horse's legs; true character. *uma (no) ashi* human horse; poor actor
鹿 *baka* dunce, fool; folly, farce, nonsense; benumbed; dull. *baka(geta)* foolish. *baka ni* extremely. *baka(rashii)* foolish, ridiculous
鹿丁寧 *baka-teinei* excessively polite
鹿正直 *baka-shōjiki* simple honesty, foolishly honest, credulity
鹿者 *bakamono* fool
鹿馬鹿 *bakabaka(shii)* silly, absurd
鹿野郎 *bakayarō* fool, simpleton, idiot
12 喰 *bakurō* horse trader
場 *baba* riding ground, racecourse
13 鈴薯 *bareisho* Irish potato, white potato
16 蹄 *batei* horse's hoof
17 齢 *barei* one's age (humble), insignificant years
糞 *bafun, maguso* horse manure
20 籍 *baseki* horse registration

───── 3 ─────

馴 $\frac{6729}{J466b}$ M44595 JUN. *na(reru)* get used to, become experienced; be tamed; get too familiar, mature. *na(rasu)* tame, charm (snakes); train, exercise, drill; habituate, accustom to. *nara(u)* experience; become a habit. *na(re)* practice, habit, skill, experience. *na(rekko)* being used to.
4 化 *junka suru* acclimate
6 合 *na(re)-a(u)* conspire with, be intimate. *narea(i)* collusion, conspiracy; illicit intercourse

9 染 *naji(mu)* become familiar with. *najimi* intimacy; friend
10 致 *junchi suru* tame, domesticate; pave the way for
13 馴 *na(re)na(reshii)* familiar, too free, unceremonious

馳 $\frac{6730}{J435a}$ M44593 CHI. *ha(seru)* run, gallop; sail; drive (a wagon); win (fame); dispatch.
7 走 *chisō* treat, banquet, entertainment, feast, dinner; hospitality; good things to eat
8 参 *ha(se)-san(zuru)* hurry to

───── 4 ─────

駁 $\frac{6733}{J477d}$ M44619 HAKU, BAKU refutation, contradiction. *buchi* spots, specks, patches.

B 駄 $\frac{6734}{J424c}$ M44633 TA, DA horse load; pack hotse; sending by horses.
4 文 *dabun* poor piece of writing
5 目 *dame* useless; impossible; ruined; unsuccessful, hopeless; must not
弁 *dabe(ru)* jabber, chatter, chat with. *daben* foolish talk
7 作 *dasaku* poor piece of writing
9 洒落 *dajare* poor joke
10 馬 *daba* draft horse, pack horse; poor horse
11 菓子 *dagashi* cheap sweets
13 賃 *dachin* carriage or horse charge; reward, tip
14 駄 *dada* fretfulness, disobedience

A 駅 $\frac{6735}{J3158}$ M44633¹ EKI post town; stage; station.
5 弁 *ekiben* station lunch
6 伝 *ekiden* stagecoach, post horse; cross-country relay race
8 長 *ekichō* stationmaster
舎 *ekisha* station building
前 *ekimae* in front of the station
10 員 *ekiin* station employee, station staff
16 頭 *ekitō* station; front of the station

B 駆 $\frac{6736}{J366e}$ M44634 KU. *ka(keru)* run, gallop; advance. *ka(ru)* drive

(a car); spur on, prompt, actuate, inspire, sway, impel. *ka(rareru)* be carried away by, be actuated by. *ka(kezuru)* run around, bustle around. *ka(kekko), ka(kekkura), ka(kekura)* foot race.
⁴込 *ka(ke)-ko(mi)* dash into, seek refuge in, run into
引 *ka(ke)hi(ki)* bargaining, maneuvering; advancing and retreating; dickering
⁵巡 *ku(ke)-megu(ru)* run around, bustle around
付 *ka(ke)-tsu(keru)* hurry to (the place)
出 *ka(ke)-da(su)* run out, start running. *ka(ri)-da(su)* chase away. *kakeda(shi)* beginner; amateur
⁷足 *ka(ke)ashi* running fast, double time
抜 *ka(ke)-nu(keru)* run through (a gate)
⁸使 *kushi suru* order around; use freely
⁹逐 *kuchiku* expulsion, extermination
逐艦 *kuchikukan* destroyer
除 *kujo* extermination, destruction
¹¹動 *kudō* driving (force)
動装置 *kudō sōchi* running gear
¹²落 *kakeo(chi)* defeat and flight; disappearance without a trace; elopement

───── 5 ─────

駒 6742 J3670 M44663 KU. *koma* horse; colt, pony; chessman; frame (of a film); bridge (of a violin).
¹¹鳥 *komadori* robin

駕 6743 J3261 M44667 KA, GA vehicle. *kago* palanquin, litter. *ga(suru)* hitch up an animal.
²²籠 *kago* palanquin, litter

駈 6744 J366f M44636 KU. *ka(keru)* run, gallop, advance. *ka(ru)* drive, urge on; prompt; inspire.

駐 6745 J4373 M44660 CHŪ. *todo(maru)* stop; B reside in. *chū-* resident in.
⁴屯 *chūton* stationing (troops), occupation
⁶在 *chūzai* residence, stay
在所 *chūzaisho* police substation
⁷車 *chūsha* parking
車場 *chūshajō* parking area
¹⁰留 *chūryū* retention, stationing (of troops)

留軍 *chūryūgun* army of occupation
¹⁴劄 *chūsatsu* resident at
¹⁵輪場 *chūrinjō* public parking area for bicycles

───── 7 ─────

駿 6754 J3d59 M44775 SHUN a good horse; speed; a fast person.
³才 *shunsai* talented person, genius, prodigy
⁷足 *shunsoku* swift horse; talented person
¹⁰馬 *shumme, shumba* swift horse

───── 8 ─────

験 6758 J3833 M44835 KEN effect; tesing. A GEN beneficial effect (of austerities). *tame(su), ken(suru)* test, attempt. *shirushi* sign, indication, omen.

騒 6760 J417b M44834' SŌ. *sawa(gu)* make a B noise, be boisterous, shout, clamor; raise an uproar; be excited, be agitated; bustle around; make a fuss about; make merry, go on a spree. *sawa(gaseru)* disturb, trouble, agitate, excite, create a sensation. *sawa(gareru)* be made much of. *zawame(ku), zawatsu(ku)* be noisy, be boisterous. *zome(ku), some(ku)* be noisy. *sawa(gashii)* noisy, boisterous; tumultuous, troubled, agitated. *sawa(gi)* noise, uproar; turmoil, trouble, agitation; fuss, ado; affair; dispute; excitement; sensation; merrymaking, spree.
⁷乱 *sōran* commotion, riot
⁹音 *sōon* noise, cacophony
¹¹動 *sōdō* disturbance, strife, riot, rebellion
¹²然 *sōzen(taru)* noisy, confused, uproarious
¹⁸騒 *sōzō(shii), zawazawa(toshita)* noisy, boisterous, turbulent
擾 *sōjō* disturbance, commotion, riot

騎 6761 J3533 M44817 KI riding on horses; B counter for horsemen.
³士 *kishi* horseman, equestrian, knight
士道 *kishidō* knighthood, chivalry
⁴手 *kishu* rider, horseman, jockey

10

馬
[骨]

0

高
髟
鬥
鬯
鬲
鬼

⁶ 行 *kikō* horseback riding
⁷ 兵 *kihei* cavalry; cavalryman, horseman
⁹ 乗 *kijō no* mounted, on horseback
¹⁰ 馬 *kiba* riding on a horse; the rider

───────── 9 ─────────

驔 | 6762 / J424d / M-X | DAN. DA. dappled horse; white horse with black mane.

───────── 10 ─────────

騰 | 6767 / J462d / M44915' | B TŌ rising; price rise. *a(gari)* advancing, going up.

¹² 貴 *tōki* rise (in prices)

───────── 12 ─────────

驚 | 6774 / J3643 / M45013' | B KYŌ. KEI. *odoro(ku)* be surprised; be frightened, be taken aback; be appalled; be amazed. *odoro(kasu)* surprise; frighten; create a stir. *odoro(kubeki)* amazing, surprising, wonderful.

⁴ 天動地 *kyōten-dōchi* world-shaking, astounding, tremendous
⁷ 呆 *odoro(ki)-aki(reru)* be appalled
¹¹ 異 *kyōi* wonder, miracle
異的 *kyōiteki* wonderful, phenomenal
¹² 愕 *keigaku, kyōgaku* surprise, fright, shock
喜 *kyōki* pleasant surprise
¹³ 嘆 *kyōtan* wonder, admiration
¹² 然 *shūzen toshite* suddenly

━━━━━━━━━ RAD. 骨 188 ━━━━━━━━━

Hone bone. At left: *hone hen.* Nickname: Bone.

骨 | 6784 / J397c / M45098 | A KOTSU bone; remains; knack. *hone* bone; skeleton; frame; rib (of an umbrella); grit, backbone; effort, pains.

³ 子 *kosshi* bones; marrow; essentials, gist
⁴ 片 *koppen* pieces of bone
⁶ 肉 *kotsuniku* one's own flesh and blood; flesh and blood
休 *honeyasu(mi), honeyasu(me)* relaxation, recreation
⁷ 材 *kotsuzai* aggregate
折 *honeo(ru)* take pains, exert oneself. *kossetsu* broken bone, bone fracture. *honeo(ri)* pains, exertion. *hone (ga) ore(ru)* be difficult
抜 *honenu(ki) no* boned; mutilated; watered down
¹⁰ 格 *kokkaku* physique, build, frame
¹¹ 惜 *honeo(shimi)* sparing oneself, laziness
粗鬆症 *kotsusoshōshō* osteoporosis
組 *honegu(mi)* skeleton; framework

¹² 無 *honena(shi)* rickets; spineless person; an invertebrate
董 *kottō* curios, antiques
董品 *kottōhin* curios, antiques
¹³ 節 *kossetsu, honebushi* joint. *hone(p)pushi* joint; strong character, spirit
幹 *kokkan* physique, build, frame
盤 *kotsuban* pelvis; pelvic bone
¹⁸ 髄 *kotsuzui* marrow; true spirit

───────── 6 ─────────

骸 | 6789 / J333c / M45164 | GAI bone, body. *mukuro* body; corpse.

¹⁰ 骨 *gaikotsu* skeleton

───────── 8 ─────────

髄 | 6791 / J3f71 / M45240 | B ZUI marrow, pith.

━━━━━━━━━ RAD. 高 189 ━━━━━━━━━

Takai high. Variant: 髙 (11 strokes). Nickname: High.

A 高 ⟨6796 J3962 M45313⟩ Kō high. *taka(i)* high, tall, lofty, raised, elevated, eminent; exalted, noble; loud, stentorian; expensive; widely known. *taka* quantity, volume, amount, sum; rise (in prices); high; fief. *taka(maru)* rise; swell; be elevated, be promoted; increase. *taka(meru)* raise, lift, promote, elevate; improve, enhance; ennoble; heighten; boost. *taka(buru)* be proud, be arrogant; be high. *taka(mi)* height, eminence. *taka(raka ni)* loudly. *(o)taka(ku)* proudly (in a bad sense). *taka(ga)* only, merely, at best, after all. *kō(jiru), kō(zuru)* increase; be proud.

山 *kōzan* high mountain, lofty peak
山病 *kōzambyō* mountain sickness
山植物 *kōzan shokubutsu* alpine flora
⁴水準 *kōsuijun* high level
⁵圧 *kōatsu* high tension, high voltage; high handedness
圧線 *kōatsu densen* high-tension line
⁶地 *kōchi* high ground, plateau, heights
名 *kōmyō* reknown, fame; your name. *kōmei* fame, good reputation
血圧 *kōketsuatsu* high blood pressure
気圧 *kōkiatsu* high atmospheric pressure
⁷見 *kōken* your opinion; excellent idea
弟 *kōtei* best student; senior disciple
低 *kōtei, takahiku* unevenness, undulations; fluctuations; modulation; height; pitch
位 *kōi* honors, high rank
利 *kōri* high interest
利貸 *kōriga(shi)* usury; usurer
⁸所 *kōsho* elevation, height; altitude; long view (of things).
炉 *kōro* blast furnace
官 *kōkan* high office; high official, dignitary
尚 *kōshō na* high noble, refined, advanced
空 *kōkū* high altitude. *takazora* clear sky
学年 *kōgakunen* upper grades in school
周波 *kōshūha* high frequency
性能 *kōseinō* high (explosives); high efficiency; high fidelity
価 *kōka* high price
⁹度 *kōdo* altitude, height; high degree;

high power; intense; advanced (stage)
飛 *takato(bi)* high jump; dancing and jumping; abscondence; flying high; skipping the country.
飛車 *takabisha na* highhanded
音 *takane, kōon* high tone; high key; loud sound
架 *kōka* elevated (line)
架鉄道 *kōka tetsudō* elevated railway
速 *kōsoku* high speed, high gear
速炉 *kōsokuro* fast reactor
速度 *kōsokudo* high speed
速道路 *kōsoku dōro* expressway
速増殖炉 *kōsoku zōshokuro* fast breeder reactor
級 *kōkyū* high rank, seniority; high grade, high class
級品 *kōkyūhin* high-grade goods
¹⁰原 *kōgen* tableland, plateau
峰 *kōhō* lofty peak
配 *kōhai* your good offices, your trouble
校 *kōkō* senior high school
校生 *kōkōsei* senior-high-school student
高 *takadaka* very high; at most, at best. *takadaka to* aloft, very high; loudly
¹¹率 *kōritsu* high rate
望 *takanozo(mi)* viewing from the heights; high hopes
¹²遠 *kōen na* high and distant; high, lofty, noble; hard to understand
揚 *kōyō suru* enhance, exhalt, promote
温 *kōon* high temperature
給 *kōkyū* high salary
貴 *kōki* nobility
等 *kōtō* high class, high grade
等学校 *kōtō gakkō* senior high school
等教育 *kōtō kyōiku* higher education
等裁判所 *kōtō saibansho* higher court
¹³僧 *kōsō* high priest, prelate; virtuous priest
¹⁴慢 *kōman* pride, insolence, arrogance. *kōman(chiki) na* haughty, arrogant
説 *kōsetsu* valuable opinion; your views
層 *kōsō* high altitude, upper (atmospheric) strata; tall (building)
層建築 *kōsō kenchiku* skyscraper
¹⁵邁 *kōmai na* high, lofty, noble
潔 *kōketsu* purity, nobility
熱 *kōnetsu* high fever
潮 *kōchō, takashio* spring tide, flood tide. *kōchō* high tide; climax, acme

10

馬骨高〔髟〕鬥鬯鬲鬼

4

踏 *kōtō* living a holy life aloof from the world
踏的 *kōtōteki* transcendent; high-toned; highbrowed
16 覧 *kōran* your perusal
17 齢 *kōrei* advanced age
齢化社会 *kōreika shakai* aging society
齢者 *kōreisha* senior citizen, old person

嶺 *takane* lofty peak
嶺花 *takane (no) hana* flowers on inaccessible heights; unattainable object
18 額 *kōgaku* high price, expensiveness
19 麗 *Kōrai, Koma* Koguryo (ancient Korean kingdom)
20 欄 *kōran* railing, balcony
騰 *kōtō* sudden price jump

髟 RAD. 190

Kami hair. At top: *kamigashira* or *kami kammuri*. Nickname: Long Hair (cf. Rad. 59).

4

髪 6804 / J4831 / M45387 B **HATSU**. *kami* the hair.
9 型 *kamigata* hairstyle
12 結 *kamiyu(i)* combing the hair; hairdressing; hairdresser
13 飾 *kamikaza(ri)* hair ornament

6

髭 6812 / J4926 / M45399 **SHI**. *hige* beard; moustache; hairspring. *hige(zemmai)* hairspring.
9 面 *higezura* unshaven face, hairy face
剃 *higesori* shaving

鬥 RAD. 191

Tō or *tatakai* fighting. As enclosure: *tōgamae* or *tatakaigamae*. Nickname: Broken Gate (cf. Rad. 169).

鬯 RAD. 192

Kaorigusa fragrant herbs. Nickname: Herb.

鬲 RAD. 193

Ashi kamae tripod. Nickname: Tripod.

鬼 RAD. 194

Oni devil. Variant: 鬼 *kinyō* "devil" enclosure. Nickname: Devil.

11

鬼 ⁶⁸³³ J3534 M45758 **KI** devil, demon; spirits of the dead. *oni* devil, demon, ghost; spirits of the dead; fiend; creditor; the one who is "it" (in games). *oni-* sharp, relentless, crack (detective), tough, extremely competent. *oni(gokko)* tag games.
³ 才 *kisai* genius, wizard, prodigy
子母神 *kishimojin, kishibojin* goddess of children
⁵ 瓦 *onigawara* ridge-end tile; gargoyle
⁶ 気 *kiki* weirdness, ghastliness
⁸ 門 *kimon* unlucky quarter (northeast); anathema; defect, weakness; undesirable person
⁹ 神 *kishin, kijin, onigami* terrible god, fierce god; departed spirit; demon, ghost, monster, goblin
¹⁰ 畜 *kichiku* a devil
哭 *kikoku* wail of a ghost
¹¹ 婆 *onibaba* witch, hag
²⁰ 籍 *kiseki* record of the dead

──────── **4** ────────

魁 ⁶⁸³⁴ J3321 M45785 **KAI** *sakigake* charging ahead of others.
¹² 偉 *kaii na* brawny, muscular, impressive

魂 ⁶⁸³⁵ J3a32 M45787 **KON** *tamashii, tama* soul, spirit.
⁹ 胆 *kontan* soul; plot, intrigue
¹⁰ 消 *tamage(ru)* be startled, be astonished
¹⁵ 魄 *kompaku* soul, spirit

──────── **5** ────────

魅 ⁶⁸³⁸ J4c25 M45811 **MI** *mi(suru)* charm, fascinate, bewitch, enchant. *baka(su)* bewitch, confuse, enchant, delude.
² 力 *miryoku* charm, glamor, appeal
了 *miryō suru* charm, fascinate
¹² 惑 *miwaku* fascination, enchantment, charm

──────── **11** ────────

魔 ⁶⁸⁴³ J4b62 M45906 **MA** demon, devil, evil spirit.
² 力 *maryoku* magical power, charm
³ 女 *majo* witch, sorceress
⁴ 手 *mashu* evil influence
王 *maō* the devil
⁸ 性 *mashō* devilishness
物 *mamono* goblin, apparition
法 *mahō* magic, sorcery, witchcraft
法使 *mahōtsukai* magician, sorcerer
法鑵 *mahōbin* thermos bottle
⁹ 神 *mashin, majin* devil, evil spirit
除 *mayo(ke)* charm against evil spirits, talisman, amulet
界 *makai* world of spirits, infernal regions, hell
¹¹ 術 *majutsu* magic, sorcery, witchcraft, augury
術師 *majutsushi* magician, conjurer
¹² 訶不思議 *maka-fushigi* profound mystery
¹³ 窟 *makutsu* den (of thieves); brothel, redlight district

11-STROKE RADICALS

──────── **RAD. 魚 195** ────────

Sakana or *uo* fish. At left: *uo hen*. Nickname: Fish.

魚 ⁶⁸⁴⁵ J357b M45956 **GYO** *uo, sakana* fish.
⁴ 介 *gyokai* marine products, sea food
⁵ 市場 *uoichiba* fish market
⁶ 肉 *gyoniku* fish meat
⁸ 河岸 *uogashi* riverside fish market
⁹ 屋 *sakanaya* fish shop, fish peddler
¹¹ 釣 *uotsuri* fishing

10

₀【魚】

鳥
鹵
鹿
麥
麦
麻

眼写真 *gyogan shashin* fish eye (180-degree) photo

¹³ 群 *gyogun* school of fish
雷 *gyorai* torpedo
¹⁸ 類 *gyorui* the fishes

───────── 4 ─────────

魯 | 6848 / J4f25 / M46013 | Ro foolish; Russia.

¹² 鈍 *rodon* foolishness, stupidity

───────── 5 ─────────

鮒 | 6854 / J4a2b / M46075 | Ho. Fu. *funa* carp.

鮎 | 6855 / J303e / M46070 | Den. Nen. *ayu* fresh-water trout, sweet smelt.

───────── 6 ─────────

鮪 | 6858 / J4b6e / M46126 | Ki. Yū. *maguro, shibi* tuna, tunny.

鮭 | 6859 / J3a7a / M46132 | Kai. Kei. *sake, shake* salmon.

鮫 | 6863 / J3b2d / M46127 | Kō. *same* shark.

⁶ 肌 *samehada* goose flesh (due to cold, etc.)

鮮 | 6864 / J412f / M46133 | B Sen Korea. *azaya(ka) na* vivid, clear, brilliant, fresh, graceful, splendid, beautiful.

⁶ 血 *senketsu* lifeblood; flowing blood
⁸ 明 *semmei* clearness, distinctness
⁹ 度 *sendo* (degree of) freshness
¹¹ 魚 *sengyo* fresh fish
¹⁹ 麗 *senrei na* gorgeous, vivid

───────── 7 ─────────

鯉 | 6874 / J3871 / M46182 | Ri. *koi* carp.

¹⁵ 幟 *koinobori* carp streamer

───────── 8 ─────────

鯵 | 6875 / J3033 / M-X | Nonstandard for 鰺 6912.

鰺

鯖 | 6883 / J3b2a / M46210 | Sei. *saba* mackerel.

¹⁴ 読 *saba (o) yo(mu)* cheat in counting

鯛 | 6884 / J4264 / M46226 | Chō. *tai* sea bream, red snapper.

鯨 | 6886 / J375f / M46257 | B Gei. *kujira* whale.

⁸ 波 *geiha* raging waves; tidal wave; shout of victory. *toki* war cry
¹² 飲 *geiin suru* drink hard, drink like a fish

───────── 9 ─────────

鰍 | 6895 / J3362 / M46331 | Shū. Shu. *kajika* bullhead.

鰐 | 6901 / J4f4c / M46337 | Gaku. *wani* crocodile, alligator.

───────── 10 ─────────

鰯 | 6904 / J3073 / M46413 | (国字) *iwashi* sardine.

鰭 | 6907 / J4949 / M46400 | Ki. Gi. *hire* fin.

───────── 11 ─────────

鰺 | 6912 / J724d / M46442 | Sō. *aji* horse mackerel.

鰻 | 6914 / J3137 / M46443 | Man. *unagi* eel.

鰹 | 6915 / J336f / M46437 | Ken. *katsuo* bonito, skipjack.

¹³ 節 *katsuobushi, katsubushi* dried bonito

鱈 | 6916 / J432d / M46470 | (国字) Setsu. *tara* codfish.

³ 子 *tarako* cod roe

───────── 12 ─────────

鱒 | 6921 / J4b70 / M46492 | Son. Zon. Sen. Zan. *masu* trout.

鱗 | 6923 / J4e5a / M46502 | Rin. *uroko, koke, kokera* (fish) scales.

RAD. 鳥 196

Tori bird. Nickname: Bird.

鳥 6931 J443b M466234 CHŌ bird. *tori* bird; chicken; fowl.
A
⁶ 肌 *torihada* goose flesh (due to cold, etc.)
⁸ 居 *torii* Shinto shrine gateway
¹² 葬 *chōsō* Parsee burial (in a tower leaving the body to be defleshed by carnivorous birds)
¹⁶ 獣 *chōjū, tori-kedamono* birds and animals
¹⁷ 瞰図 *chōkanzu* bird's-eye view
¹⁸ 類 *chōrui* the birds, fowls
²² 籠 *torikago* bird cage

──── 2 ────

鳩 6936 J4837 M46648 KYŪ. *hato* dove, pigeon.
⁷ 麦 *hatomugi* pearl barley
尾 *kyūbi, mizoochi, mizuochi* solar plexus, pit of the stomach
⁹ 首 *kyūshu suru* go into a huddle
¹⁰ 胸 *hatomune* pigeon breast, deformed protruding chest

──── 3 ────

鳳 6937 J4b31 M46671 HŌ male phoenix bird.
⁵ 仙花 *hōsenka* balsam
¹¹ 凰 *hōō* mythical phoenix bird

鳶 6938 J4650 M46674 EN. *tobi* black kite; fire fighter; hook. *tombi* black kite; cloak; pilferer.
³ 口 *tobiguchi* fire ax, fire hook
¹⁸ 職 *tobishoku* casual laborer, construction laborer

鳴 6939 J4L44 M46672 MEI. *na(ku)* (animals and birds) cry, bark, chirp, etc. *na(ru)* sound, ring, roar; (thunder) rumbles; (clocks) strike; boom; resound, echo; be famous; (fingers) itch for; sonorous, ringing, squeaky. *na(rasu) vt* ring, sound, blow (a whistle), beat (drums), clank, clink, clap, crack (a whip),
A
smack (lips), cluck (one's tongue), honk; air (grievances); attain (celebrity). *na(ri)* sound, ringing.
³ 子 *naruko* clapper
⁷ 声 *na(ki)goe* sound of a bird or animal
⁸ 門 *naruto* whirlpool, maelstrom
物 *na(ri)mono* music; musical instruments
物入 *na(ri)monoi(ri)* loud proclamation, bombastic announcement
¹¹ 動 *meidō* rumbling
¹² 渡 *na(ri)-wata(ru)* resound, re-echo
¹⁹ 響 *na(ri)-hibi(ku)* reverberate, echo, resound, be sonorous

──── 4 ────

鴎 6941 J322a M-X Nonstandard for 鷗 6998.

鴇 6943 J463e M46730 HŌ. *nogan* Siberian bustard; bustard; grey horse; procuress. *toki* Japanese crested ibis.

──── 5 ────

鴬 6945 J3229 M-X Nonstandard for 鶯 6994.

鴫 6948 J3c32 M46831 (国字) *shigi* snipe.

鴛 6953 J3175 M46795 EN male mandarin duck.
¹⁶ 鴦 *oshidori, en'ō* mandarin duck

鴨 6955 J337b M46823 Ō. *kamo* wild duck; easy mark.
⁸ 居 *kamoi* lintel

──── 6 ────

鴻 6963 J3963 M46874 KŌ large, great; large bird. *ōtori* large wild goose.
⁴ 毛 *kōmō* goose feathers; something very light

11

魚
鳥
【鹵】
⁸
鹿
麥
麦
麻

━━━━ 7 ━━━━

鵠 6968 / J3974 / M46961 KOKU swan.

鵜 6971 / J312d / M46952 TEI. *u* cormorant.
⁵ 目鷹目 *u(no)me-taka(no)me de* with sharp eyes
⁶ 匠 *ushō* cormorant fisher
¹² 飲 *uno(mi)* swallowing whole
¹³ 飼 *uka(i)* cormorant fishing

━━━━ 8 ━━━━

鵡 6974 / J4c39 / M46963 BU, MU cockatoo.

鵬 6979 / J4b32 / M47005 HŌ phoenix, huge mythical bird. *ōtori* fabulous bird.

鶏 6980 / J375c / M47074 B KEI. *niwatori* chicken.
⁶ 肉 *keiniku* chicken (meat)
⁷ 卵 *keiran* hen egg

━━━━ 10 ━━━━

鶯 6994 / J7274 / M47169 Ō. *uguisu* nightingale, bush warbler.
⁶ 色 *uguisu iro* greenish brown

鶴 6995 / J4461 / M47185 KAKU. *tsuru* crane, stork.

⁹ 首 *kakushu suru* stretch out the neck
¹¹ 亀 *tsurukame* crane and tortoise; congratulations
¹⁶ 嘴 *tsuruhashi, tsurubashi* pick, pickax, mattock

━━━━ 11 ━━━━

鷗 6998 / J-X / M47268 Ō. *kamome* sea gull.

━━━━ 12 ━━━━

鷲 7004 / J4f49 / M47345 SHŪ. JU. *washi* eagle.
¹¹ 掴 *washizuka(mi)* clutch, grab
¹⁴ 鼻 *washibana* aquiline nose, Roman nose

━━━━ 13 ━━━━

鷺 7006 / J3a6d / M47362 RO. *sagi* heron.

鷹 7007 / J426b / M47377 YŌ. Ō. *taka* hawk.
⁶ 匠 *takajō* falconer, hawker
⁹ 狩 *takaga(ri)* hawking, falconry
¹² 揚 *ōyō* generosity, largeheartedness; easy-going

━━━━━ RAD. 鹵 197 ━━━━━

Shio salt. Nickname: Salt.

━━━━ 8 ━━━━

鹹 7013 / J3834 / M-X Nonstandard for 鹹 7016.

━━━━ 13 ━━━━

鹹 7016 / J-X / M47576 KEN saltiness; lye; salt.
⁴ 化 *kenka* saponification

━━━━━ RAD. 鹿 198 ━━━━━

Shika deer. At left: *shika hen*. As enclosure: 鹿. Nickname: Deer.

鹿 7017 J3c2f M47586 ROKU. *shika* deer.

fine, serene. *uruwa(shii)* beautiful, lovely, graceful.
²人 *reijin* beauty, belle

──── 8 ────

麓 7023 J4f3c M47658 ROKU. *fumoto* foot of a mountain.

B 麗 7026 I4e6f M47663 REI. RAI. *urara(ka) na* beautiful, bright and clear,

──── 12 ────

麟 7028 J4e5b M47690 RIN giraffe.

━━━━━━ RAD. 麥 199 ━━━━━━

Mugi wheat. Variant: 麦 (7 strokes). Variants: 麦 and 麦 *bakunyō* "wheat" enclosure. Nickname: Wheat.

A 麦 7030 J477e M47718 BAKU. *mugi* wheat, barley, oats, rye.
⁸芽 *bakuga* malt
⁹畑 *mugibatake, mugibata* wheat field; barley field
秋 *mugiaki, mugi (no) aki, bakushū* wheat harvest
茶 *mugicha* parched-barley tea
¹⁰酒 *bakushu, bīru* beer
粉 *mugiko* (wheat) flour
¹⁷藁 *mugiwara* wheat straw
藁帽子 *mugiwara bōshi* straw hat

麹 7036 J396d M-X 麴 7037 J-X M47818 KIKU. *kōji* malt, leaven, yeast.

──── 9 ────

麺 7038 J4c4d M-X 麵 7039 J-X M47827 MEN noodles; wheat flour.
¹²棒 *membō* rolling pin
¹⁸類 *menrui* noodles

──── 8 ────

━━━━━━ RAD. 麻 200 ━━━━━━

Asa hemp. Variants: 麻 and 麻 *asa kammuri,* used as an enclosure. Nickname: Hemp.

B 麻 7040 J4b63 M47888 MA. *asa* flax, hemp, ramie, jute, linen.
⁵布 *mafu, asa nuno* hemp cloth, linen
¹¹雀 *majan* mahjong
酔 *masui* anesthesia
¹³痺 *mahi* paralysis, palsy, numbness, stupor, anesthesia

¹⁵縄 *asa nawa* hemp rope
¹⁶薬 *mayaku* anesthetic; narcotic

──── 7 ────

麿 7044 J4b7b M47909 (国字) *maro* I; you.

【黄】黍黑黑黹

12-STROKE RADICALS

RAD. 黄 201

Kiiroi yellow. Variant: 黄 (11 strokes). Nickname: Yellow.

黄 7045 J322b M47926 KŌ. Ō. *ki* yellow.
A *ki(bamu)* turn yellow.
ki(bami) yellow tint.

³ 土 *ōdo* yellow ocher. *kōdo* the earth; yellow soil, loess; hades ⌐yellow

⁶ 色 *kiiro, kiiro(i), kōshoku, ōshoku*
色人種 *ōshoku jinshu* yellow race
色声 *kiiro(i) koe* shrill voice

⁷ 身 *kimi* yolk of an egg

⁸ 昏 *kōkon, tasogare* dusk, twilight
金 *kogane* gold. *ōgon* gold; gold pieces; money

金時代 *ōgon jidai* the golden age

⁹ 海 *Kōkai* Yellow Sea
泉 *kōsen* underground spring. *kōsen, yomi* hades, realm of the dead

¹⁰ 粉 *kinako* soybean flour

¹¹ 道 *ōdo, kōdō* ecliptic

¹⁴ 塵 *kōjin* dust (in the air); this dusty world

¹⁵ 熱病 *ōnetsubyō, kōnetsubyō* yellow fever

RAD. 黍 202

Kibi millet. Nickname: Millet.

黍 7048 J3550 M47991 SHO. *kibi* millet.

⁶ 団子 *kibi dango* millet dumplings

RAD. 黑 203

Kuroi black. Variant: 黒 (11 strokes). Nickname: Black (cf. Rad. 95).

黒 7052 J3975 M48040 KOKU. *kuro* black; dark.
A *kuro(zumu), kuro(zuku)* blacken, darken. *kuro(bamu), kuro(maru) vi* blacken, become black. *kuro(meru) vt* blacken; talk wrong into right. *kuro(raka)* blackness, deep black. *kuro(ku) suru vt* blacken. *kuro(i)* black; dark, swarthy, browned; dirty. *kuro(ppoi)* dark, blackish.

² 人 *Kokujin* Black person

³ 子 *kokushi* face mole; mite. *kurogo* prompter, stagehand. *hokuro* dark mole; beauty spot
山 *kuroyama* a large crowd

⁵ 白 *kokuhaku, kokubyaku, kuro-shiro* black and white; right and wrong

⁶ 字 *kuroji* black figures, profit

⁸ 板 *kokuban* blackboard

⁹ 海 *Kokkai* Black Sea
点 *kokuten* black spot, dark spot; sunspot
砂糖 *kurozatō* unrefined sugar

¹¹ 黒 *kuroguro* deep black
船 *kurofune* the black ships (of the Westerners)
眼鏡 *kuromegane* dark glasses

¹² 焦 *kuroko(ge)* something burnt black
雲 *kokuun, kurokumo* dark clouds, black clouds

¹³ 煙 *kokuen, kurokemuri* black smoke
鉛 *kokuen* black lead, graphite
幕 *kuromaku* black curtain; wirepuller

塗 *kuronu(ri)* blackening; blackened thing; *kuronu(ri)* black-lacquered, black-colored
[15] 潮 *Kuroshio* Japan Current

──────── **4** ────────

黙 ⁷⁰⁵⁵ J4c5b M48063ⁱ MOKU keeping silence. *moku(suru)* be silent. *moda(su)* be silent; leave as it is. *dama(ru), moda(su)* become silent, stop speaking, say nothing. *damma(ri)* silence, reticence.
[5] 礼 *mokurei suru* bow silently
示録 *Mokujiroku, Mokushiroku* Revelation
[6] 考 *mokkō* contemplation, meditation
[8] 念 *mokunen* remaining silent
[9] 約 *mokuyaku* tacit understanding
思 *mokushi* contemplation
契 *mokkei* secret understanding without speaking

[10] 殺 *mokusatsu suru* ignore
秘 *mokuhi* secrecy, silence
秘権 *mokuhiken* the right to keep silent
[11] 過 *mokka* overlooking, connivance
視 *mokushi suru* wink at, overlook, tolerate
許 *mokkyo* tacit permission, connivance
梼 *mokutō* silent prayer; silent tribute
[12] 然 *mokuzen(taru)* silent, tacit, mute
[13] 想 *mokusō* meditation, reverie
[14] 読 *mokudoku* silent reading
認 *mokunin* tacit approval, admission, connivance
[15] 黙 *mokumoku(taru)* silent, tacit, mute

──────── **5** ────────

黛 ⁷⁰⁶⁰ J4263 M48075 TAI blackened eyebrows; blue-black. *mayuzumi* blackened eyebrows.

──────── RAD. 黹 **204** ────────

Nuu to embroider, sew. Nickname: Sewing.

13-STROKE RADICALS

──────── RAD. 黽 **205** ────────

Aogaeru tree frog. Nickname: Frog.

──────── RAD. 鼎 **206** ────────

Kamae kettle. This is actually a 12-stroke radical but is placed here in its traditional place among the 13-stroke radicals. Nickname: Kettle.

鼎 ⁷⁰⁷⁴ J4524 M48315 TEI. *kanae* three-legged kettle.
[5] 立 *teiritsu* triangular position; three-cornered (contest)

電
鼎
〔鼓〕
鼠
鼻
齊
齒
歯
龍
竜
龜
亀
龠

14-STROKE RADICALS

鼓 RAD. 207

Tsuzumi hand-drum. Variant: 皷 (14 strokes). Nickname: Drum.

鼓 B | 7076 J385d M48330 | Ko *tsuzumi* drum. *ko(su)* beat; rouse, muster (courage). *tsuzumi* hand drum.

⁷吹 *kosui* inspiration; advocacy; encouragement

¹¹動 *kodō* beat, palpitation, pulsation,

throbbing

笛隊 *kotekitai* drum-and-fife band

¹⁴膜 *komaku* eardrum

¹⁵樓 *korō* drum tower (at a temple)

舞 *kobu* inspiration, stimulation, encouragement

鼠 RAD. 208

Nezumi rat. As enclosure: 鼡. Nickname: Rat.

鼠 | 7078 J414d M48390 | So. *nezumi, nezu* rat, mouse; dark gray.

⁶色 *nezumi iro* dark gray, slate

⁸取 *nezumitor(i)* rat poison;

mousetrap

¹⁴算 *nezumizan* multiplying like rats

¹⁷蹊部 *sokeibu* the groin

鼻 RAD. 209

Hana nose. Variant: 鼻. Nickname: Nose.

鼻 A | 7082 J4921 M48498 | BI nasal. *hana* nose; snout, muzzle.

hana(ppashi) bridge of the nose.

³下 *bika* under the nose

⁴毛 *hanage* nostril hairs

水 *hanamizu* nasal discharge

孔 *bikō* nostrils

⁵白 *hanajiro(mu)* feel let down; feel ashamed

汁 *hanajiru* nasal discharge

⁶血 *hanaji* nosebleed

先 *hanasaki* tip of the nose.

hanasaki ni under one's nose; imminent

⁷声 *hanagoe, bisei* nasal voice

⁸炎 *bien* nasal inflammation

⁹面 *hanazura* muzzle, snout

音 *bion* a nasal sound

柱 *hana(p)pashira, hanabashira* septum, bridge of the nose

風邪 *hanakaze* head cold

¹⁰唄 *hanauta* humming, crooning

紙 *hanagami* handkerchief paper

高 *hana (ga) taka(i)* proud. *hana (o) taka(ku) suru* be proud

息 *hanaiki* nasal breathing; a person's pleasure

¹¹梁 *biryō* bridge of the nose

¹²腔 *bikō, bikū* nasal cavity

¹³詰 *hanatsuma(ri), hanazuma(ri)* nose being clogged up

¹⁴摘 *hanatsuma(mi)* uncouth person, bore

緒 *hanao* geta thong

歌 *hanauta* humming, crooning

¹⁶薬 *hanagusuri* bribe, hush money

¹⁷糞 *hana kuso* nasal discharge

齊 **RAD.** 齊 210

Sai or *hitoshii* alike. Variant: 斉 (8 strokes). Nickname: Mr. Saito
(i.e., the first character of this common surname).

15-STROKE RADICALS

齒 **RAD.** 齒 211

Ha tooth. Variant: 歯 (12 strokes). Nickname: Tooth.

———— 5 ————

B 齡 $\frac{7093}{\text{J4e70}}$ REI. *yowai*
$\overline{\text{M48632}'}$ age.

16-STROKE RADICALS

龍 **RAD.** 龍 212

Tatsu dragon. Variants: 竜 (10 strokes). Nickname: Big Dragon (cf. Rad. 161).

龍 $\frac{7103}{\text{J4e36}}$ See 竜 4232.
$\overline{\text{M48818}}$

龜 **RAD.** 龜 213

Kame turtle. Variant: 亀 (11 strokes). Nickname: Turtle.

17-STROKE RADICALS

龠 **RAD.** 龠 214

Fue flute. Nickname: Flute.

APPENDIX 1. HOW TO FIND A CHARACTER

Some three centuries ago the Chinese evolved a system of classifying their characters according to 214 basic elements or radicals. The system was based partially on the character's shape and composition and partially on the meaning of the character. Thus, although most characters involving the enclosure 門 (Rad. 169-gate) are to be found under that radical, 聞 4732 is classified under 耳 (Rad. 128-ear), presumably because hearing is done with the ear. This system is still used today in Chinese, Korean, and Japanese character dictionaries and is followed in the present dictionary also. There have been a large number of attempts to reclassify the characters, either under a new radical system or under a redistribution of the characters within the traditional system. One drawback of these attempts is that it is difficult for one who has learned one of the revised systems to use a traditional Japanese, Korean, or Chinese character dictionary; another in that it separates different versions of the same character that differ only in the arrangement of their component elements. Finding the radical, then, is not a deterministic process and may require some trial and error.

1. Determine the radical of the character (see Appendices 3, 4, 5, and 6), count the strokes of the radical, and find the radical number on the chart inside the front covers.

2. Spin the pages of the dictionary till you come to that radical number in the upper, outer corners of the pages.

Another method, replacing the foregoing two steps (this short cut is recommended only for those familiar enough with the radicals to realize immediately that, for example, the common 3-stroke grass radical is actually a variant of the 6-stroke grass radical—No. 140—and is to be looked for under the larger stroke-count): Having determined the radical and without worrying about its number, spin immediately to the place where all the radicals of the same stroke-count appear in the marginal radical strings, the stroke-count being shown by the large numeral at the head of each string. (*In case of a variant radical, use the stroke-count of its parent radical.*) Now find your radical in the radical string and spin the pages slowly one way or the other till the brackets moving up and down the string reach your radical.

3. Count the number of strokes in the non-radical part of the character and then, as a guide to the eye, place your thumb near the proper radical in the radical string and slowly spin the pages one way or the other till the tiny numeral opposite your radical reaches your stroke-count.

4. Glance through the main-character entries nearby to find the one you want; it will be somewhere in those pages with the proper non-radical stroke-count as indicated either by the tiny marginal numeral or the large numerals in the column-wide dividers. Within any given stroke-count section, the main character entries are arranged with cross-reference and rarer characters first, followed by the more familiar characters in the ascending order of the number of compounds listed under each.

APPENDIX 2. HOW TO FIND A COMPOUND

1. Find the first character of the compound by the procedure described in the preceding appendix.

3. How to Determine the Radical of a Character

2. Count the total number of strokes in the second character and then glance down the series of superscript numerals immediately to the left of the list of compounds till you find the proper second-character stroke-count.

3. Look for the second character of your compound among those with this stroke-count. In listing each compound, its first character has been omitted since it is the same as the character shown in the main entry above it. Note also that the character-repetition sign (々) has not been used; since the first character is omitted in listing compounds, in such cases it was felt better to repeat the full character.

4. If there are many compounds listed under the same second-character stroke-count, time can be saved by keeping in mind that within such a grouping the compounds have been arranged in the following order: (a) 2-character compounds, (b) 3-character compounds, (c) 4-character compounds, and (d) "families" of compounds, i.e., a group of compounds whose second characters, as well as the first, are identical.

5. If you cannot find your compound, possible reasons and remedies are:

(a) You may have miscounted the strokes of the second character. So look for it up and down the adjacent stroke-count groups.

(b) The second character of your compound may be in a variant form that differs in shape, and probably in stroke-count as well, from the standard form used in the compounds of this dictionary. For example, it may be a Jōyō Kanji given in its older form, while in our lists of compounds all Jōyō Kanji appear only in their newer forms. Or again, it may be a non-Jōyō Kanji in which, according to the unauthorized usage of some printers, one element has been simplified by analogy with the same element in a Jōyō Kanji, while in our lists non-Jōyō Kanji usually appear only in their original forms. To have included such variations in our lists would have led to endless duplication of entries. But we do give the important variants in our main-character entries. Hence, the surest remedy, which is unfortunately also the most time-consuming, is to look up the second character of your compound in the main-character entries, there ascertain its standard form, and then look for such standard form in your list of compounds. But we recommend first checking quickly through the same stroke-count group and the immediately adjacent groups for a character that looks almost the same as the one you are looking for. This method will usually work when the variation is slight.

(c) The word may be one of the less frequently used ones which do not appear in this dictionary. So either look for it in one of the large Japanese character dictionaries (the M numbers provide ready reference to Morohashi's dictionary) or determine its probable reading by looking up the individual characters of which it is composed and then consult a Japanese-English romanized dictionary like Kenkyūsha's.

(d) In the case of a compound of three or more characters, it may be a "compound compound." So try, for example, in the case of four characters, looking for separate compound forms of the first two and the last two.

APPENDIX 3. HOW TO DETERMINE THE RADICAL OF A CHARACTER

Those who are familiar with character dictionaries know how difficult it often is to decide which is the radical of a character. This is due to the fact that nearly every character, excepting only a few, contains from two to seven or eight radicals. The character 裁, for example, contains the following seven elements, each of which hap-

3. How to Determine the Radical of a Character

pens to be a radical (the radical numbers are shown in parentheses): 一 (1), 丨 (2), 丶 (3), 丿 (4), 十 (24), 戈 (62), 隹 (172). So it is anybody's guess as to which of these is the traditional radical under which this character would be listed. (In fact, it is listed under 戈 62.) The process of deciding under which radical to search is far too often a time-wasting and discouraging trial-and-error process. We believe that we have solved this problem with the introduction of the **Universal Radical Index**, Appendix 15. The URI allows character look-ups based on virtually any reasonable radical element found in the character. Aimed primarily at the novice user, but useful to anyone frustrated by obscure radicals and difficult-to-remember "radical priorities," the URI lists characters (including characters which consist of one and only one radical) under multiple alternative radicals and plausible miscounts of residual strokes. The following 12 steps run from most likely to least likely radical placement. The rules are not absolute, but are guidelines that will generally lead the user to the correct location. If the character is not found in the first or second try, the user may wish to resort to the Universal Radical Index.

THE 12 STEPS. If you follow these steps, you will be able to choose the radical correctly in most cases and, after a little practice, almost instantaneously. (The numerals given below in parentheses show the numbers of the radicals.)

N.B. If there are two radicals in the same designated position, always take the one with the GREATER stroke-count.

STEP 1. ALL? *Is ALL the character a radical?* For a complete listing, see Appendix 13. Here are a few examples:

土(32), 方(70), 生(100), 米(119), 辛(160), 高(189), 鼻(209).

STEP 2. LONE? *Does it have only one lone radical?*

乂 (丶 3), 乃 (丿 4), 久 (丿 4), 了 (亅 6)

STEP 3. ENCLOSURE? *Does it have a completely exterior ENCLOSURE radical?* The enclosure may cover two, three, or four sides.

Examples of characters containing all the radicals that *enclose two sides* (the radicals and their numbers shown in parentheses):

勿 (勹 20), 原 (厂 27), 局 (尸 44), 度 (广 53), 廻 (廴 54), 式 (弋 56), 成 (戈 62), 房 (戶 63), 死 (歹 78), 毯 (毛 82), 气 (气 84), 爬 (爪 87), 甌 (瓦 98), 病 (疒 104), 虎 (虍 141), 起 (走 156), 辱 (辰 161), 速 (辶 162), 颮 (風 182), 魁 (鬼 194), 麝 (鹿 198), 麪 (麥 199), 磨 (广 200), 鼬 (鼠 208)

Examples of all the radicals that *enclose three sides*:

円 (冂 13), 凶 (凵 17), 医 (匚 22), 閉 (門 169), 齎 (齊 210)

Example of the one radical that *encloses four sides*: 国 (囗 31)

STEP 4. LEFT? *Is there a clearly defined LEFT radical?* By "clearly defined" we mean a radical that completely dominates the left side, i.e., one that is unobstructed both above and below, such as 十 in 協. It follows that in the character 截, for example, neither 十 nor 隹 can be chosen as a left radical. Some other examples:
偉—both left and right are radicals; take the left, 亻 (9).
准—both left and right are radicals; take the left, 冫 (15).
杉—both left and right are radicals; take the left, 木 (75).

3. How to Determine the Radical of a Character

釣—right not a radical, take the left, 金 (167).

STEP 5. RIGHT? *Is there a clearly defined* RIGHT *radical?*
和—both left and right are radicals; take the right, 口 (30).
彤—left not a radical; take the right, 彡 (59).
欧—left not a radical; take the right, 欠 (76). Note that we ignore any slight interference with the left by a left-tapering stroke.
頂—left not a radical; take the right, 頁 (181).

STEP 6. TOP? *Is there a clear* TOP *radical?* Examples:
空—take the top, 穴 (116). Note that we take this in place of 宀 (40) because in general it is advantageous to take the more complex of two similarly placed radicals.
云—take 二 (7).
公—both top and bottom are radicals; take the top, 八 (12). Note that Rad. 12 appears in three forms 八, 丷, and 丷.
兼—take 八 (12).
套—take 大 (37).
安—both top and bottom are radicals; take the top, 宀 (40).
男—both top and bottom are radicals; take the top, 田 (102).

Note that many top radicals are closed canopies like 人, 冖, 大, 宀, or 穴.

STEP 7. BOTTOM? *Is there a clear* BOTTOM *radical?* Note that this may or not be resting under a canopy. Examples:
急—top not a radical; take the bottom, 心 (61).
思—both top and bottom are radicals; take the bottom, 心 (61).
学—top not a radical; take the bottom, 子 (39).
嚮—top not a radical; take 口 (30) at the bottom under the canopy.
劈—top not a radical; take the bottom, 刀 (18).
朵—top not a radical; take the bottom, 木 (75).

STEP 8. NW? *Is there a radical in the* NORTHWEST *corner?* Examples:
報—Going down our table of steps, we find this is neither ALL, LONE, ENCLOSURE, LEFT, RIGHT, TOP, nor BOTTOM. So we start around the corners clockwise beginning in the NORTHWEST, and there sits 土 (32). This is our radical. There is also 十 (24) in that same corner; but remember, we generally take the more complex of two possible radicals.
梵—The character is not a radical in its own right, has no enclosures, and does not divide into left and right portions. It does divide into top and bottom, but the top as a whole is not a radical, nor is the bottom. Take 木 (75) at the upper left (NW) corner.

STEP 9. NE? *Is there a radical in the* NORTHEAST *corner?* Example: 吳—bottom is also a radical, but take the upper right (NE) corner, 口 (30).

STEP 10. SE? *Is there a radical in the* SOUTHEAST *corner?* Example: 君—Here again we find that 口 (30) is the radical in the SE corner. Note that this is not the case of a lone radical because we also have radicals 丿 (4), 一 (1), 尸 (44), and 彐 (58).

STEP 11. SW? *Is there a radical in the* SOUTHWEST *corner?* Examples:
糶 The upper right, lower right, and lower left (southwest) corners are all radicals; take the lower left, 米, (119)

羅—All four corners are radicals; here, too, take the southwest corner radical, 米, (119).

虱 At first glance, the upper right element may look like an enclosure, however, it is not a radical and we are lead to the lower left corner, 虫 (142).

STEP 12. INSIDE? *Is there a radical in the INTERIOR of the character?* Examples:

周 One would expect the enclosure 冂 (13) to be the relevant radical, but the character is to be found under the bottom inside, 口 (30). In the URI, this character is listed under 冂, 口, and 土.

巡 The obvious radical is ⻌ (162), but the character is traditionally classified under 巛 (47).

APPENDIX 4. MORE ABOUT RADICALS

MISCELLANEOUS EXAMPLES OF RADICALS. The following table, arranged by the twelve steps given above, illustrates the process of finding the radical for a given character. In general, following the eleven steps will lead to finding the character quickly and easily. Usually a top radical will be preferred to a bottom one, a left radical to a right one, and an enclosure to the inside, but not every time. When in doubt, consult the Universal Radical Index, where each character is listed under all of its likely radicals.

STEP 1. ALL

木 2531 → 木 75
欠 2928 → 欠 76
高 6796 → 高 189
黒 7052 → 黑 203

STEP 2. LONE

乃 42 → 丿 4
久 47 → 丿 4
了 67 → 亅 6

STEP 3. ENCLOSURE

凩 434 → 几 16
函 446 → 凵 17
匍 575 → 勹 20
匪 592 → 匚 22
厭 662 → 厂 27
園 962 → 囗 31
履 1434 → 尸 44
座 1619 → 广 53
建 1660 → 廴 54

弍 1673 → 弋 56
或 2030 → 戈 62
疱 3791 → 疒 104
趁 5850 → 走 156
途 6057 → 辶 162
間 6391 → 門 169
鬮 6823 → 鬥 191

STEP 4. LEFT

俐 208 → 人 9
冲 413 → 冫 15
加 523 → 力 19
協 617 → 十 24
味 766 → 口 30
址 982 → 土 32
奴 1174 → 女 38
孩 1294 → 子 39
柱 2584 → 木 75
灯 3395 → 火 86
牾 3543 → 牛 93
疏 3775 → 疋 103

眈 3911 → 目 109
硯 4005 → 石 112
訴 5588 → 言 149
販 5779 → 貝 154
軋 5940 → 車 159
麒 7025 → 鹿 198
馹 7083 → 鼻 209
齯 7099 → 齒 211

STEP 5. RIGHT

刦 462 → 刀 18
勛 542 → 力 19
卸 641 → 卩 26
彬 1717 → 彡 59
欧 2931 → 欠 76
殳 2994 → 殳 79
状 3556 → 犬 94
視 5525 → 見 147
韓 6602 → 韋 178
頂 6616 → 頁 181
鳩 6935 → 鳥 196

STEP 6. TOP

丁 2 → 一 1
主 38 → 丶 3
乖 53 → 丿 4
交 90 → 亠 8
今 112 → 人 9
分 370 → 八 12
宣 1328 → 宀 40
彙 1709 → 彑 58
登 3862 → 癶 105
笑 4256 → 竹 118
要 5515 → 襾 146
魯 6848 → 魚 195

STEP 7. BOTTOM

兄 344 → 儿 10
兵 374 → 八 12
分 454 → 刀 18
午 601 → 十 24
吞 737 → 口 30
弄 1668 → 廾 55

4. More about Radicals

当 1706 → ヨ 58

志 1785 → 心 61

擘 2290 → 手 64

泉 3095 → 水 85

砦 4002 → 石 112

綮 4447 → 糸 120

靡 6565 → 非 175

鶩 6984 → 鳥 196

黶 7066 → 黒 203

龕 7104 → 龍 212

STEP 8. NORTHWEST

報 1059 → 土 32

巽 1546 → 己 49

幾 1601 → 幺 52

競 4244 → 立 117

靉 6556 → 雨 173

STEP 9. NORTHEAST

整 2360 → 攵 66

耀 4695 → 羽 124

STEP 10. SOUTHEAST

友 672 → 又 29

君 746 → 口 30

将 1379 → 寸 41

左 1535 → 工 48

幹 1596 → 干 51

炭 3413 → 火 86

産 3716 → 生 100

STEP 11. SOUTHWEST

旬 2415 → 日 72

帰 2966 → 止 77

STEP 10. SOUTHEAST

羅 4430 → 米 119

羅 4429 → 米 119

虱 5276 → 虫 142

鬱 6830 → 鬯 192

STEP 12. INSIDE

夙 1126 → 夕 36

夾 1144 → 大 37

嬲 1275 → 女 38

県 3918 → 目 109

聞 4732 → 耳 128

輿 5983 → 車 159

IMPORTANT RADICALS. Here are the 67 radicals that you will most often encounter. They are classified by stroke-count and arranged by their numbers. It will definitely be worth your while to memorize their numbers and recommended "nicknames" which accompany them. Note that only the parent form of each radical is shown here; consult Appendix 5 and the chart inside the cover for important variant forms.

ONE STROKE
一 1—one
｜ 2—rod
丶 3—dot
丿 4—*kana no*

TWO STROKES
亠 8—lid
人 9—man
八 12—eight
刀 18—sword
力 19—strong
十 24—cross
厂 27—cliff

THREE STROKES
口 30—mouth
囗 31—box
土 32—earth
女 38—woman
宀 40—*kana u*
小 42—little
尸 44—flag
山 46—mountain
巾 50—cloth
广 53—dotted cliff
弓 57—bow

彳 60—going man

FOUR STROKES
心 61—heart
手 64—hand
支 66—folding chair
日 72—sun
木 75—tree
水 85—water
火 86—fire
牛 93—cow
犬 94—dog

FIVE STROKES
玉 96—jewel
田 102—rice field
疒 104—sick
皿 108—dish
目 109—eye
石 112—stone
示 113—showing
禾 115—2-branch tree
立 117—standing

SIX STROKES
竹 118—bamboo

米 119—rice
糸 120—thread
耳 128—ear
肉 130—meat
舟 137—ship
艸 140—grass
虫 142—bug
衣 145—clothing

SEVEN STROKES
見 147—seeing
言 149—speaking
貝 154—small shell
足 157—foot
車 159—car
辵 162—road
邑 163—right village

EIGHT STROKES
金 167—metal
門 169—gate
阜 170—left village
隹 172—old bird
雨 173—rain

4. More about Radicals

NINE STROKES
頁 181—big shell
食 184—food

TEN STROKES
馬 187—horse

ELEVEN STROKES
魚 195—fish
鳥 196—bird

WARNINGS ON UNUSUAL RADICALS. It is well, occasionally, to look over the Step-1 table of Appendix 13 in the book to refresh your memory as to which current characters are their own radicals.

Remember that 彑 is a variety of 彐 (Rad. 58).

Note the distinct difference between Rads. 71 and 92 as shown on the chart inside the front cover. 牙 is a 5-stroke variant of the 4-stroke 牙 (92) and it is encountered more often than the parent. 无 is a 5-stroke variant of the 4-stroke 无 (71) and it is also encountered more often than the parent.

Note that 内 (114) is a 5-stroke, not a 4-stroke, radical and is always counted as 5 whenever it appears in any character.

Remember that 彑 is a 6-stroke variant of the 7-stroke 豕 (152).

Glance over the chart inside the front cover beginning with Rad. 187 and note the many radicals in the 10- to 17-stroke categories. You will encounter them more or less frequently.

Let us repeat that it is very important to be able to recognize a radical when you see one, even though you may not be able to recall its name nor its number.

When you are not sure whether an element of a character is a radical or not, consult the chart inside the front cover or the tables in Appendix 13.

LOST RADICALS. In the simplification of characters by the Japanese Government, some have actually lost their traditional radicals, making them most difficult to find in ordinary dictionaries. These have been reclassified according to the standard practice of Japanese character dictionaries and have been entered into the Universal Radical Index.

The following table gives a representative list of characters that have lost their radicals. Each entry shows, first, the original form of the character followed by its traditional radical (now lost) and radical number; and then, following an arrow, are given the present simplified form of the character, the number under which it is entered in this dictionary, and the radical and radical number under which we classify it.

兩	入 (12)	→	両 (23)	一 (1)
豫	豕 (152)	→	予 (68)	亅 (6)
會	曰 (72)	→	会 (143)	人 (9)
處	虍 (141)	→	処 (435)	几 (16)
醫	酉 (164)	→	医 (590)	匚 (22)
單	口 (30)	→	単 (620)	十 (24)
嚴	口 (30)	＞	厳 (663)	厂 (27)
營	火 (86)	→	営 (857)	口 (30)
聲	耳 (128)	→	声 (989)	士 (32)
壽	士 (32)	→	寿 (1374)	寸 (41)
盡	皿 (108)	→	尽 (1408)	尸 (44)
貳	貝 (154)	→	弍 (1675)	弋 (56)

5. The Radicals Classfied by Position

當	田 (102)	→	当 (1706)	ヨ (58)
舊	臼 (134)	→	旧 (2412)	日 (72)
來	人 (9)	→	来 (2565)	木 (75)
爲	爪 (87)	→	為 (3411)	火 (86)
縣	糸 (120)	→	県 (3918)	目 (109)

APPENDIX 5. THE RADICALS CLASSIFIED BY POSITION

The charts which follow are arranged in the same order as the steps suggested above for finding the radical of a character. Only the first seven steps are illustrated because the radicals appearing in the corners and inside are not limited to a definable set.

STEP 1. ALL
The Characters Which Are Also Radicals

1	一 1	乙 5	**2**	二 7	人 9	入 11	八 12	刀 18	力 19	匕 21	十 24
卜 25	厶 28	又 29	**3**	口 30	土 32	士 33	夕 36	大 37	女 38	子 39	寸 41
小 42	尸 44	山 46	川 47	工 48	己 49	已 49	巳 49	巾 50	干 51	廾 55	弋 56
弓 57	彳 60	**4**	心 61	戸 63	戸 63	手 64	文 67	斗 68	斤 69	方 70	日 72
曰 73	月 74	木 75	欠 76	止 77	毋 80	比 81	毛 82	氏 83	水 85	火 86	爪 87
父 88	片 91	牙 92	牛 93	犬 94	王 [96]	**5**	母 [80]	牙 [92]	玄 95	玉 96	瓜 97
瓦 98	甘 99	生 100	用 101	田 102	疋 103	白 106	皮 107	皿 108	目 109	矛 110	矢 111
石 112	示 113	穴 116	立 117	**6**	竹 118	米 119	糸 120	缶 121	羊 123	羽 124	羽 124
老 125	而 126	耒 127	耳 128	肉 130	臣 131	自 132	至 133	臼 134	舌 135	舟 137	色 139
虫 142	血 143	行 144	衣 145	西 146	**7**	臣 [131]	見 147	角 148	言 149	谷 150	豆 151

豕 152	貝 154	赤 155	走 156	足 157	身 158	車 159	辛 160	辛 160	辰 161	邑 163	酉 164
釆 165	里 166	麦 [199]	8	金 167	長 168	門 169	阜 170	雨 173	雨 173	青 174	青 174
非 175	9	面 176	革 177	韭 179	音 180	音 180	頁 181	風 182	飛 183	食 184	食 184
首 185	香 186	10	馬 187	骨 188	高 189	鬼 194	11/17	魚 195	鳥 196	鹵 197	鹿 198
麥 199	麻 200	麻 200	黃 [201]	黑 [203]	黃 201	黍 202	黑 203	鼎 206	鼓 207	鼠 208	鼔 [207]
鼻 209	鼻 209	齊 210	齒 211	龍 212	龜 213	龠 214					

STEP 2. LONE
The Common Characters Having But OneRadical
(each followed by Its rad. & rad. no.)

| 乂 → 丶 3 | 乃 → 丿 4 | 久 → 丿 4 | 了 → 亅 6 |

STEP 3. ENCLOSURE
The Radicals Found as Enclosures

1 乚 5	**2** 冂 13	刀 13	卩 13	刀 13	几 16	凡 16	凵 17	勹 20	匚 22
匸 22	厂 27	辶 [162]	**3**	口 31	夂 34	尸 44	广 53	夂 54	弋 56	辶 [162]
4 戈 62	戶 63	戶 63	支 65	歹 78	毛 82	气 84	爪 87	**5**	瓦 98	疒 104
6 耳 128	虍 141	**7**	走 156	辰 161	麦 [199]	**8**	門 169	**9**	風 182	
10 鬥 191	鬼 194	**11**	鹿 198	夒 199	麻 200	13/14	鼠 208	齊 210		

STEP 4. LEFT
The Radicals Found at the Left

1 丨 2	丨 2	丿 4	**2** 亻 9	冫 15	力 19	十 24	又 29	ㄨ 29	阝 [170]
3 口 30	土 32	夕 36	女 38	子 39	山 46	川 47	工 48	己 49	巾 50	干 51
幺 52	弓 57	彡 59	彳 60	忄 [61]	扌 [64]	氵 [85]	丬 [90]	犭 [94]		
4 戸 63	戸 63	手 64	文 67	斤 69	方 70	日 72	木 75	止 77	歹 78	火 86
爻 89	爿 90	片 91	牙 92	牛 93	王 [96]	礻 [113]	月 [130]	月 [130]		
5 牙 [92]	玄 95	瓦 98	甘 99	生 100	田 102	疋 103	白 106	皮 107	目 109	矛 110
矢 111	石 112	示 113	禾 115	立 117	艮 [138]	衤 [145]	**6** 米 119	糸 120	缶 121	羊 123
羽 124	羽 124	而 126	耒 127	耒 127	耳 128	臣 131	至 133	舌 135	舟 137	虫 142	血 143
7 臣 [131]	角 148	言 149	谷 150	豆 151	豕 152	豸 153	貝 154	赤 155	足 157	身 158
車 159	辛 160	酉 164	釆 165	里 166	镸 [168]	**8** 金 167	隹 172	靑 174	青 174	食 [184]
斉 [210]	**9** 面 176	革 177	韋 178	音 180	音 180	飠 [184]	首 185	香 186		
10 韋 [178]	馬 187	骨 188	鬲 193	鬼 [195]	**11** 魚 195	鳥 196	鹵 197	鹿 198	麥 199
黄 [201]	黑 [203]	**12/17**	黄 201	黍 202	黑 203	歯 [211]	鼠 208	鼻 209	齊 210	齒 211	龍 212

STEP 5. RIGHT
The Radicals Found at the Right

1	｜ 2	｜ 2	乚 5	2	人 9	几 16	刀 18	刂 18	力 19	匕 21	十 24
卜 25	卩 26	又 29	阝 [163]	3	口 30	子 39	寸 41	彡 59	4	戈 62	支 65
攴 66	攵 66	斗 68	斤 69	欠 76	殳 79	比 81	毛 82	犬 94	月 [130]	月 [130]	
5	尢 [71]	爪 97	瓦 98	甘 99	皮 107	冃 109	立 117	6	羊 123	羽 124	羽 124
耳 128	聿 129	艮 138	色 139	虫 142	7	見 147	角 148	谷 150	豕 152	辛 160	辛 160
酉 164	里 166	8	隶 171	隹 172	青 174	青 174	9	韋 178	頁 181	風 182	飛 183
10	韋 [178]	鬼 194	11	鳥 196							

STEP 6. TOP
The Radicals Found at the Top

1	一 1	一 1	、 3	一 4	ノ 4	2	二 7	亠 8	亠 8	人 9	入 11
八 12	八 12	丷 12	冖 14	刀 18	力 19	匕 21	十 24	卜 25	厶 28	又 29	
3	口 30	土 32	士 32	夂 34	夕 36	大 37	女 38	子 39	宀 40	小 42	屮 42
山 46	巛 47	工 48	己 49	彐 58	彐 58	彐 58	毌 58	廿 [140]	4	戈 62	攵 66
文 67	日 72	曰 72	木 75	止 77	冊 80	比 81	氏 83	水 85	火 86	罒 87	灬 87

5. The Radicals Classfied by Position

父 88	牛 93	王 [96]	艹 [140]	**5**	玄 95	甘 99	田 102	火 105	白 106	目 109	柔 110
石 112	禾 115	穴 116	究 116	究 116	立 117	皿 [122]	**6**	竹 118	米 119	羊 123	羽 124
羽 124	老 125	而 126	耳 128	聿 129	自 132	臼 134	虫 142	血 143	衣 145	西 146	襾 146
7	貝 154	車 159	辰 161	釆 165		**8**	隹 172	雨 173	非 175		
9	音 180	音 180	**10**	馬 187	高 189	髟 190	**11**	魚 195	鳥 196	鹿 198	麻 200
麻 200	黒 [203]		**12**		黑 203		**13/16**		鼓 207	齊 210	龍 212

STEP 7. BOTTOM
The Radicals Found at the Bottom

1	一 1	丶 3	**2**	二 7	儿 10	八 12	冫 15	几 16	刀 18	力 19
十 24	巳 26	厶 28	又 29	又 29	**3**	口 30	土 32	夂 34	夊 34	夕 36
大 37	女 38	子 39	寸 41	小 42	山 46	工 48	己 49	巾 50	干 51	廾 55	弓 57
彐 58	彡 59	**4**	心 61	小 61	手 64	斤 69	方 70	日 72	曰 72	木 75
止 77	母 80	比 81	毛 82	水 85	火 86	灬 86	牛 93	犬 94	王 [96]	壬 [96]	月 [130]
5	母 [80]	氺 [85]	玉 96	瓦 98	甘 99	用 101	田 102	疋 103	白 106	皿 108	目 109
矢 111	石 112	示 113	禾 115	**6**	米 119	糸 120	缶 121	羊 123	羽 124	羽 124
而 126	耳 128	聿 129	肉 130	至 133	臼 134	舌 135	舛 136	艮 138	虫 142	衣 145	豕 [152]

7	舛 [136]	見 147	角 148	言 149	豆 151	豕 152	貝 154	足 157	車 159	辛 160	辛 160
辰 161	酉 164	里 166	**8**	金 167	隹 172	非 175		**9**	面 176	革 177	
韭 179	音 180	音 180	風 182	食 184	食 184	香 186		**10**	馬 187	高 193	鬼 194
11	魚 195	鳥 196	鹿 198		**12**	黃 201	黑 203		**16**	龍 212	

APPENDIX 6. HOW TO COUNT STROKES

Nothing will so much speed up your dictionary work as skill and accuracy in counting strokes, whether of whole characters, radicals, or non-radical elements. Therefore, every effort has been made in this dictionary to make this process free of guesswork. In this connection, some knowledge of how to write characters is needed; such a study is outside the scope of this dictionary, but an excellent treatment can be found in *A Guide to Reading and Writing Japanese* edited by Florence Sakade (Tuttle, 1959).

ACCURACY. The general rule is: No matter how a line may twist and turn nor how complex its printed form, if it is written without lifting your pencil, count it as a single stroke. Examples:

2 strokes: 乃, 辶, 阝
3 strokes: 及, 与, 辶, 弓

STROKE DETAILS TO BE IGNORED. Because of variations in type fonts and other practical considerations the following details are ignored in counting strokes:

1. *Ignore* the little flip at the bottom of the element 亅 as found in such characters as the following, thus giving them the stroke-counts shown in parentheses; in handwritten characters, such a little flip is a mere continuation of the vertical member above it and even in printed form it seldom touches or cuts through the next element to the right: 良 (7), 卯 (5), 留 (10), 以 (4), 似 (6), 民 (5), and especially in characters traditionally belonging to the 6-stroke radical 衣, such as 衾 (10), 裂 (11), and 袋 (11), and 裂 (12). It also follows logically not to count the similarly situated flip in such characters as 表 (8), 喪 (12), or 畏 (9). *However*, we do count a similar stroke in the following three pairs of characters as the said stroke either cuts through or takes a firm grip on the next element to the right: 叫 or 叫 (6); 収 (5) or 收 (7); and 糾 (9).

2. *Ignore* the little protrusion in the elements 勹 and 勹 in such characters as the following, counting these as 1 and 乙 strokes respectively, especially so since in some type fonts the protrusion is scarcely visible: 考 (6), 顎 (18), 互 (4), and 祿 (12).

3. *Ignore* the downward protrusion of 口 as found in characters like the following in some fonts: 啼, 鳴, @ . We still consider the left member the radical, i.e., 口 (30). The element 书 is counted as three strokes, in 韋 (Rad. 178), but it is usually counted as four strokes.

4. *Ignore* any interference with another member of a character (usually a left radical) by a left-tapering stroke as such vary in length. These usually involve the radical 口 and examples follow: 吸, 呎, 吹, 呱, 喫, 咯, 每.

7. Hints for Speed

5. *Ignore* the slight left interference with a left radical of an ichi (一) stroke at the bottom of such characters as 岨, 阻, 組, and 粗.

6. *Ignore* any interference of any slightly hooked stroke like the horizontal element in the character 予, where we take 亅 (6) as the radical.

COUNTING STROKES OF PARENT RADICALS AND THEIR VARIANTS.

1. The stroke-count of a *parent radical* is always that shown in the chart inside the front cover. Thus the following radicals whose stroke-count, at least in the printed form, appears to differ from that historically assigned to them are always given the stroke-count indicated in the following examples: 廴 (3), 厶 (2). Thus when the element 厶 appears in the character 宏, it is counted as 2 and not 3 strokes, making this character one of 7 strokes, not 8.

2. *Radical variants*, however, always carry their natural stroke-count wherever they appear. Thus the parent radical 水 is always a 4-stroke element but it has the following variants which carry the indicated stroke-counts: 氵 (3), 氺 (5). Similarly:

Rad. 92, a parent radical of 4 strokes (牙), has a 5-stroke variant in 牙.

Rad. 64, a parent radical of 4 strokes (手), has a 3-stroke variant in 扌.

Rad. 61, a parent radical of 4 strokes (心), has a 3-stroke variant in 忄.

Rad. 125, a parent radical of 6 strokes (老), has a 4-stroke variant in 耂.

Rad. 152, a parent radical of 7 strokes (豕), has a 6-stroke variant in 豕.

Rad. 140, a parent radical of 6 strokes (艸) has a 3-stroke variant in 艹 and a 4-stroke variant in ⁺⁺. The latter, however, is always counted as 3 strokes as it is often impossible to detect the space between the two crosses.

APPENDIX 7. HINTS FOR SPEED

Much has been done in the arrangement of this dictionary to speed up the process of finding a character. But much will also depend upon the user, and here a little effort will pay great dividends. When one is reading a Japanese book or magazine, speed in looking up a new word is of the essence if the chain of thought is not to be interrupted. Several suggestions to this end:

Spinning the pages of this book, which has been made strong and flexible for this very purpose, will often get you to your character almost immediately. Many of you will soon have memorized many radical numbers and you will spin quickly to the correct radical area. Some of you will prefer to spin to the proper radical string and locate your radical there. Having located your radical in its proper string, you will now spin again, and perhaps more slowly, until the heavy brackets scurrying up and down the strings crawl around your radical. Spinning further and a bit more slowly, you will see the tiny numeral beside the radical change to the stroke-count of the non-radical part of your character and your compound will not be far away. For you have now arrived at the proper stroke-count group, wherein the characters are arranged in the ascending order of the number of their compounds.

Quick stroke-counting is important in the speeding-up process. You will soon learn the stroke-counts of the more common radicals as you will be using them frequently, and you should also make an effort to memorize the stroke-counts of other elements which, though not radicals, reoccur frequently. Then make a habit of counting the strokes by mentally adding up the number of strokes of their larger components. For example, in 截 you should not laboriously count the strokes one by one but as follows: 2(十) + 4(戈) + 8(隹) = 14.

A good magnifying glass is most helpful in counting strokes, especially when reading type that is small or not clear.

All *cross references are in the Arabic notation* and refer to the serial numbers of

the 7107 numbered character entries. These character numbers also appear conveniently at the lower outer corners of the pages, a contribution to speed.

Whenever you are not sure whether an element of a character is a radical or not, consult *the chart inside the front cover* or Appendix 13.

By all means familiarize yourself with the 214 historic radicals as given inside the front cover so that you can always recognize a radical when you see one. And if you wish to quadruple your speed in dictionary work, memorize their numbers. Missionaries in China used to do this as a matter of course during their first year of language study. A few brave souls in Japan have also done so. You should at least memorize the 67 more important radicals as given in Appendix 4.

APPENDIX 8. THE *KANA* SYSTEMS

There are two syllabaries in Japan, called *kana*. One of these is *katakana*, or the squared form, and the other is *hiragana*, or the cursive. They are arranged in two ways, one the A-I-U-E-O, or systematic, arrangement, and the other, the I-RO-HA arrangement, which forms a poem on the Buddhist theme of the transitoriness of life. This latter arrangement is still occasionally used in indices, outlines, and the like, much as the alphabet is used in the West; however, it is rapidly giving way to the easily remembered A-I-U-E-O arrangement.

Katakana are used much like italics are used in English. However, *katakana* are also used to write foreign names and most foreign words that have entered the Japanese language. Additionally, many plant and animal names, as well as onomatopoeia, are usually written in *katakana*. *Hiragana*, however, are more widely used, particularly as *okurigana* to indicate the inflections of verbs and other words whose stems are written in characters. With the limitation of the use of characters since WWII, many words previously written in *kanji* are now written in *hiragana*. Formerly, and to some extent today, *hiragana* have been used along the side of the text to indicate the pronunciation of the characters. When used in this way, they are called *furigana* or *rubi*.

THE HIRAGANA A-I-U-E-O ARRANGEMENT

あ a	か ka	さ sa	た ta	な na	は ha	ま ma	や ya	ら ra	わ wa	
い i	き ki	し shi	ち chi	に ni	ひ hi	み mi	[1]い (y)i	り ri	[2]ゐ (w)i	
う u	く ku	す su	つ tsu	ぬ nu	ふ fu	む mu	ゆ yu	る ru	[1]う (w)u	
え e	け ke	せ se	て te	ね ne	へ he	め me	[1]え e	れ re	[2]ゑ (w)e	
お o	こ ko	そ so	と to	の no	ほ ho	も mo	よ yo	ろ ro	[3]を (w)o	ん n

[1] Pronounced as a simple vowel. A repetition of the corresponding kana in the first column.

[2] Pronounced as a simple vowel. Not used in approved postwar orthography, having been replaced by the corresponding *kana* in the first column.

[3] Pronounced as a simple vowel. In approved orthography, now used only for the particle *o*.

8. The Kana System

THE KATAKANA A-I-U-E-O ARRANGEMENT

ア	カ	サ	タ	ナ	ハ	マ	ヤ	ラ	ワ	
a	*ka*	*sa*	*ta*	*na*	*ha*	*ma*	*ya*	*ra*	*wa*	
イ	キ	シ	チ	ニ	ヒ	ミ	[1]イ	リ	[2]ヰ	
i	*ki*	*shi*	*chi*	*ni*	*hi*	*mi*	*(y)i*	*ri*	*(w)i*	
ウ	ク	ス	ツ	ヌ	フ	ム	ユ	ル	[1]ウ	
u	*ku*	*su*	*tsu*	*nu*	*fu*	*mu*	*yu*	*ru*	*(w)u*	
エ	ケ	セ	テ	ネ	ヘ	メ	[1]エ	レ	[2]ヱ	
e	*ke*	*se*	*te*	*ne*	*he*	*me*	*e*	*re*	*(w)e*	
オ	コ	ソ	ト	ノ	ホ	モ	ヨ	ロ	[3]ヲ	ン
o	*ko*	*so*	*to*	*no*	*ho*	*mo*	*yo*	*ro*	*(w)o*	*n*

[1,2,3] See footnotes for *hiragana*.

THE I-RO-HA ARRANGEMENT

The Poem	Romanization	Kana Represented
色は匂へど	Iro wa nioedo	I-ro ha ni-ho-he-to
散りぬるを	Chirinuru o	Chi-ri-nu-ru (w)o
我世誰ぞ	Waga yo tare zo	Wa-ka yo ta-re so
常ならむ	Tsune naran	Tsu-ne na-ra-mu
有為の奥山	Ui no okuyama	U-(w)i no o-ku-ya-ma
今日越えて	Kyō koete	Ke-fu ko-e-te
浅き夢見じ	Asaki yume miji	A-sa-ki yu-me mi-shi
酔もせず	Ei mo sezu.	(W)e-hi mo se-su

A roughly literal paraphrase might run as follows: "Colors are fragrant, but they fade away. In this world of ours none lasts forever. Today cross the high mountain of life's illusions [i.e., rise above this physical world], and there will be no more shallow dreaming, no more drunkeness [i.e., there will be no more uneasiness, no more temptations]."

SOUND CHANGES. The sounds of the basic *kana* given above, as well as of the *kana* combinations treated hereafter, may be changed in any one of three ways, or in a combination of these ways. (Note that, although all the examples below are given in *hiragana*, the same remarks apply to *katakana* unless otherwise indicated.) The three ways are listed below.

1) By lengthening the vowels. This is done in *hiragana* by adding the appropriate vowel *kana* to sounds ending in *a, i, e,* or *u.* In the case of sounds ending in *o*, usually the *kana u* is added, but for certain words, it is the *kana o* that is added. For example, か *ka* becomes かあ *kā*; き *ki*, きい *kī*; く *ku*, くう *kū*; ね *ne*, ねえ *nē*; and と *to*, とう *tō* or とお *tō*. In *katakana*, the lengthening of a vowel is indicated by a dash-like symbol in place of the additional *kana*. For example, カ *ka* becomes カー *kā*, etc.

2) By inserting a small っ *tsu* before a *kana* beginning with *k, s, t,* or *p*, thereby doubling that consonant. For example, また *mata* becomes まった *matta*.

3) By adding two kinds of diacritical marks to certain of the *kana*, to represent other sounds. The first of these two, ゛, is called *dakuten* (literally, "voice marks"),

and the second, ˚ , is called *handakuten* (literally, "half voice marks"). Their use is illustrated below.

が ga	ざ za	だ da	ば ba	ぱ pa
ぎ gi	じ ji	ぢ ji	び bi	ぴ pi
ぐ gu	ず zu	づ zu	ぶ bu	ぷ pu
げ ge	ぜ ze	で de	べ be	ぺ pe
ご go	ぞ zo	ど do	ぼ bo	ぽ po

KANA COMBINATIONS. Certain *kana* clusters represent given combinations of sounds. The modern combinations are shown below. Note that the preceding sound change rules also apply here.

きゃ kya	しゃ sha	ちゃ cha	ひゃ hya	みゃ mya	りゃ rya
きゅ kyu	しゅ shu	ちゅ chu	ひゅ hyu	みゅ myu	りゅ ryu
きょ kyo	しょ sho	ちょ cho	ひょ hyo	みょ myo	りょ ryo

In addition to the modern *kana* combinations given above, there are certain histori-cal combinations which were used in pre-WWII writing. Though no longer approved, they are still occasionally encountered. Following is a list of many such historical *kana* combinations, in the A-I-U-E-O arrangement, and likewise subject to the sound change rules; also included are a few single *kana* which had special pronunciations in certain words, instead of the standard modern pronunciations shown in parentheses.

あう	ō	けう	kyō	そふ	sō	なふ	nō
あふ	ō	けふ	kyō	たう	tō	にふ	nyū
いふ	yū (iu)	こふ	kō	たふ	tō	ぬふ	nū
おふ	ō	さふ	sō	ちう	chū	ねう	nyō
かう	kō	しう	shū	ちふ	chū	のふ	nō
かふ	kō	しふ	shū	づふ	zū	はう	hō
きう	kyū	すふ	sū	てう	chō	はふ	hō
きふ	kyū	せう	shō	てふ	chō	ひ	i (hi)
くふ	kū	せふ	shō	なう	nō	ひう	hyū

8. The Kana System

ふ	u,o (fu)	む	n (mu)	らふ	rō	わう	ō
へ	e (he)	めう	myō	りう	ryū	ゐ	i
へう	hyō	もふ	mō	りふ	ryū	ゑ	e
ほ	o (ho)	やう	yō	るふ	rū	ゑふ	yō
ほふ	hō	ゆふ	yū	れう	ryō	をう	ō
まう	mō	よふ	yō	れふ	ryō	をふ	ō
まふ	mō	らう	rō	ろふ	rō		

Kana Derivations. Both *hiragana* and *katakana* were derived from *kanji*. *Hiragana* were developed from cursive writing of characters; *katakana* were mostly made from parts of characters. Both sets of *kana* and their parent characters are listed below.

HIRAGANA

あ 安	か 加	さ 左	た 太	な 奈	は 波	ま 末	や 也	ら 良	わ 和
い 以	き 幾	し 之	ち 知	に 仁	ひ 比	み 美		り 利	ゐ 爲
う 宇	く 久	す 寸	つ 川	ぬ 奴	ふ 不	む 武	ゆ 由	る 留	
え 衣	け 計	せ 世	て 天	ね 祢	へ 部	め 女		れ 礼	ゑ 惠
お 於	こ 己	そ 曾	と 止	の 乃	ほ 保	も 毛	よ 與	ろ 呂	を 遠	ん 无

KATAKANA

ア 阿	カ 加	サ 散	タ 多	ナ 奈	ハ 八	マ 末	ヤ 也	ラ 良	ワ 和
イ 伊	キ 幾	シ 之	チ 千	ニ 仁	ヒ 比	ミ 三		リ 利	ヰ 井
ウ 宇	ク 久	ス 須	ツ 川	ヌ 奴	フ 不	ム 牟	ユ 由	ル 流	
エ 江	ケ 介	セ 世	テ 天	ネ 祢	ヘ 部	メ 女		レ 礼	ヱ 慧
オ 於	コ 己	ソ 曾	ト 止	ノ 乃	ホ 保	モ 毛	ヨ 與	ロ 呂	ヲ 乎	ン 尔

APPENDIX 9. JŌYŌ KANJI LISTS

For convenience, particularly when studying characters, we have gathered into this appendix a complete listing of all the Jōyō Kanji as established by the Japanese Government, arranging them under three headings: essential characters, general use characters, and additions for proper names. Also shown, for purpose of speedy reference, is the number under which each character has been listed in the body of this dictionary.

1006 ESSENTIAL CHARACTERS. These have been marked with a small capital A in the body of this dictionary and are here arranged according to the elementary school grades in which they are taught; within each grade the characters are arranged in the order in which they appear in this dictionary.

GRADE ONE — 80 CHARACTERS

一	七	三	下	上	中	九	二	五	人	休
1	3	8	9	10	28	57	72	77	99	142
先	入	八	六	円	出	力	十	千	口	右
350	366	369	371	385	445	521	598	599	685	700
名	四	土	夕	大	天	女	子	字	学	小
716	938	966	1123	1133	1138	1173	1281	1285	1294	1389
山	川	左	年	手	文	日	早	月	木	本
1439	1526	1535	1593	2060	2364	2410	2419	2530	2531	2536
村	林	校	森	正	気	水	火	犬	王	玉
2564	2590	2669	2749	2955	3025	3030	3394	3553	3619	3620
生	田	町	男	白	百	目	石	空	立	竹
3715	3727	3729	3731	3863	3864	3906	3985	4192	4223	4246
糸	耳	花	草	虫	見	貝	赤	足	車	金
4431	4715	4980	5032	5275	5522	5766	5840	5856	5939	6211
雨	青	音								
6518	6557	6607								

GRADE TWO — 160 CHARACTERS

万	丸	交	京	今	会	体	作	何	元	兄
7	34	90	93	112	143	165	167	169	343	344
光	公	内	冬	刀	切	分	前	北	午	半
349	372	386	410	448	453	454	490	581	604	608
南	原	友	台	古	合	同	回	図	国	園
619	652	672	699	702	715	717	941	947	950	962
地	声	売	場	夏	外	多	夜	太	妹	姉
976	989	990	1058	1120	1125	1127	1129	1137	1199	1201
室	家	寺	少	岩	工	市	帰	広	店	弓
1327	1337	1373	1390	1461	1532	1549	1564	1604	1613	1678
引	弟	弱	強	当	形	後	心	思	戸	才
1681	1685	1692	1695	1706	1713	1742	1780	1824	2048	2059

Essential Kanji

9. Jōyō Kanji Lists

教 2345	数 2353	新 2387	方 2389	明 2435	昼 2450	星 2452	春 2453	時 2462	書 2463	晴 2488
曜 2522	来 2565	東 2596	楽 2790	歌 2945	止 2954	歩 2958	母 3005	毎 3006	毛 3013	池 3042
汽 3068	活 3132	海 3133	点 3412	父 3516	牛 3532	理 3644	用 3721	画 3733	番 3762	直 3908
矢 3976	知 3978	社 4065	科 4130	秋 4131	答 4285	算 4316	米 4380	紙 4455	組 4470	細 4472
絵 4488	線 4548	羽 4675	考 4697	聞 4732	肉 4753	朝 4838	自 4900	船 4939	色 4956	茶 5033
行 5419	西 5514	親 5534	角 5543	言 5552	計 5555	記 5563	話 5608	語 5628	読 5629	谷 5730
買 5793	走 5845	近 6021	通 6063	週 6070	道 6091	遠 6101	里 6206	野 6208	長 6379	門 6381
間 6391	雪 6520	雲 6522	電 6526	頭 6639	顔 6648	風 6663	食 6674	首 6719	馬 6725	高 6796
魚 6845	鳥 6931	鳴 6939	麦 7030	黄 7045	黒 7052					

GRADE THREE — 200 CHARACTERS

丁 2	世 20	両 23	主 38	乗 54	予 68	事 71	他 122	仕 123	代 125	全 145
住 164	使 196	係 217	倍 252	具 376	写 400	列 460	助 530	勉 543	動 549	勝 553
化 580	区 585	医 590	去 665	反 674	受 678	取 679	号 692	向 712	君 746	味 766
命 767	和 770	品 792	員 808	問 830	商 832	坂 985	夫 1136	始 1203	委 1204	守 1310
安 1311	定 1323	実 1324	客 1329	宮 1336	宿 1344	寒 1350	対 1375	局 1412	屋 1421	岸 1459
島 1476	州 1529	帳 1568	平 1590	幸 1595	度 1616	庫 1617	庭 1618	式 1676	役 1726	待 1741
急 1823	息 1850	悪 1873	悲 1897	想 1922	意 1926	感 1928	所 2054	打 2063	投 2095	拾 2149
持 2151	指 2152	放 2333	整 2360	旅 2396	族 2399	曲 2418	昔 2433	昭 2446	暑 2484	暗 2503
板 2595	柱 2631	根 2670	植 2751	業 2789	様 2821	横 2854	橋 2879	次 2929	歯 2961	死 2968
氷 3032	決 3070	泳 3090	波 3101	注 3103	油 3106	洋 3130	消 3158	流 3160	深 3206	湖 3240
港 3242	湯 3245	温 3246	漢 3281	炭 3413	物 3538	球 3643	由 3724	申 3726	界 3739	畑 3741
病 3798	発 3860	登 3862	皮 3878	皿 3885	県 3918	相 3920	真 3926	着 3938	短 3982	研 3991

礼 4061	神 4087	祭 4092	福 4105	秒 4129	究 4189	章 4235	童 4239	笛 4268	第 4272	等 4287
筆 4288	箱 4331	級 4437	終 4471	緑 4528	練 4530	羊 4658	美 4660	習 4681	者 4698	有 4756
育 4773	服 4775	期 4836	苦 5009	荷 5059	葉 5129	落 5130	薬 5224	血 5411	表 5422	詩 5610
談 5643	調 5647	豆 5735	負 5769	起 5849	路 5876	身 5928	転 5948	軽 5953	農 6008	返 6020
送 6039	追 6042	速 6060	進 6073	運 6092	遊 6093	部 6146	都 6148	酒 6160	配 6163	重 6207
鉄 6253	銀 6268	開 6393	院 6447	階 6469	陽 6470	集 6500	面 6566	題 6645	飲 6680	館 6701
駅 6735	鼻 7082									

GRADE FOUR — 200 CHARACTERS

不 13	争 69	以 109	令 121	付 124	仲 140	伝 141	位 162	低 166	例 193	便 219
信 221	候 250	倉 255	借 259	停 273	側 275	健 278	働 297	億 321	兆 346	児 355
共 373	兵 374	典 375	冷 419	利 466	別 467	初 469	刷 479	副 503	功 522	加 523
努 527	労 531	勇 541	包 572	卒 615	協 617	単 620	博 621	印 630	参 666	史 697
司 698	各 714	告 744	周 768	唱 829	喜 858	器 898	囲 945	固 949	型 1010	堂 1037
塩 1075	士 1117	変 1119	央 1140	失 1141	好 1180	季 1292	孫 1296	完 1315	官 1322	害 1333
察 1360	差 1537	希 1553	席 1561	帯 1563	府 1611	底 1612	康 1621	建 1660	径 1730	徒 1746
得 1755	街 1759	必 1781	念 1800	愛 1927	成 2025	戦 2037	折 2094	挙 2150	改 2332	敗 2343
救 2344	散 2352	料 2374	旗 2402	昨 2449	景 2487	最 2492	札 2533	末 2534	未 2535	束 2559
材 2561	松 2592	果 2594	栄 2635	梅 2666	案 2667	械 2685	巣 2705	極 2753	標 2852	機 2880
欠 2928	歴 2964	残 2976	殺 2994	毒 3007	氏 3020	民 3021	求 3036	治 3100	泣 3104	法 3107
浅 3129	浴 3153	清 3205	満 3248	漁 3309	灯 3395	然 3435	焼 3438	無 3439	照 3457	熱 3473
牧 3537	特 3541	産 3716	的 3867	省 3916	祝 4085	票 4089	種 4159	積 4176	競 4244	笑 4256
節 4299	管 4317	粉 4390	紀 4439	約 4440	給 4489	結 4492	続 4500	置 4645	老 4696	胃 4793

9. Jōyō Kanji Lists

脈 4805	望 4819	腸 4849	臣 4894	航 4933	良 4954	芸 4978	芽 5002	英 5008	菜 5097	衣 5420
要 5515	覚 5529	観 5538	訓 5562	試 5611	説 5627	課 5644	議 5716	象 5744	貨 5781	費 5786
貯 5791	賞 5815	軍 5943	輪 5973	辞 6000	辺 6011	連 6062	達 6088	選 6114	郡 6143	量 6209
録 6298	鏡 6341	関 6402	陸 6461	隊 6468	静 6560	順 6619	類 6647	願 6653	飛 6672	飯 6679
養 6691	験 6758									

GRADE FIVE — 185 CHARACTERS

久 47	仏 111	件 130	任 136	似 138	仮 144	余 168	価 188	舎 189	保 222	俵 243
個 258	修 260	備 284	像 308	再 391	刊 456	判 465	券 473	制 481	則 487	効 535
務 546	勢 558	厚 651	句 693	可 701	営 857	因 939	団 940	圧 970	在 975	均 988
基 1040	報 1059	墓 1073	境 1085	増 1088	夢 1131	妻 1200	婦 1243	容 1335	寄 1345	富 1349
導 1388	居 1416	属 1430	布 1548	師 1562	常 1569	幹 1596	序 1607	弁 1663	張 1694	往 1733
術 1754	復 1760	徳 1767	衛 1776	志 1785	応 1789	快 1802	性 1822	恩 1851	情 1898	態 1947
慣 1970	承 2088	技 2092	招 2124	授 2208	採 2209	接 2213	提 2237	損 2255	支 2324	故 2334
政 2335	敵 2359	断 2385	旧 2412	易 2432	暴 2511	条 2563	枝 2591	査 2630	桜 2664	格 2668
検 2752	構 2823	武 2959	比 3010	永 3031	河 3102	液 3199	混 3204	測 3244	減 3249	準 3278
演 3310	潔 3332	災 3400	燃 3490	版 3526	犯 3554	状 3556	独 3574	率 3618	現 3645	留 3750
略 3755	益 3891	眼 3935	破 3999	確 4039	示 4060	祖 4083	禁 4098	移 4141	程 4144	税 4146
築 4343	精 4411	素 4456	経 4473	統 4487	絶 4490	綿 4531	総 4532	編 4552	績 4579	織 4596
罪 4644	群 4666	義 4668	耕 4710	職 4742	肥 4774	能 4809	興 4913	舌 4917	製 5476	複 5484
規 5524	解 5548	許 5569	設 5570	評 5587	証 5589	謝 5687	講 5689	識 5704	護 5715	豊 5737
財 5773	責 5780	貧 5782	貿 5788	賀 5790	貸 5792	資 5803	賛 5814	質 5817	輸 5978	述 6030
迷 6037	退 6040	逆 6041	造 6061	過 6090	適 6107	酸 6177	鉱 6252	銭 6264	銅 6266	防 6429

限	険	際	雑	非	預	領	額	飼
6439	6456	6478	6507	6563	6625	6628	6644	6685

GRADE SIX — 181 CHARACTERS

並	乱	乳	亡	仁	供	俳	値	傷	優	党
24	60	61	86	110	195	254	257	301	334	363

冊	処	刻	創	割	劇	勤	危	卵	厳	収
389	435	478	506	507	517	552	629	632	663	675

后	吸	否	呼	善	困	垂	城	域	奏	奮
704	713	742	769	859	946	999	1011	1030	1156	1172

姿	存	孝	宅	宇	宙	宝	宗	宣	密	寸
1216	1284	1289	1308	1309	1318	1320	1321	1328	1343	1372

専	将	射	尊	就	尺	届	展	層	己	巻
1377	1379	1380	1386	1401	1404	1413	1425	1432	1540	1545

幕	干	幼	庁	座	延	律	従	忘	忠	憲
1578	1589	1599	1603	1619	1657	1740	1745	1784	1801	1988

我	批	拡	担	拝	捨	探	推	揮	操	敬
2028	2086	2118	2121	2126	2205	2211	2212	2229	2296	2351

映	晩	暖	暮	机	枚	染	株	棒	模	権
2448	2491	2502	2508	2543	2582	2636	2665	2750	2825	2853

樹	欲	段	泉	沿	派	洗	済	源	潮	激
2878	2936	2991	3095	3096	3126	3131	3197	3274	3336	3350

灰	熟	片	班	異	疑	痛	皇	盛	盟	看
3396	3472	3525	3636	3757	3777	3814	3870	3895	3899	3919

砂	磁	私	秘	穀	穴	窓	策	筋	簡	糖
3992	4029	4124	4140	4157	4186	4201	4284	4286	4358	4420

系	紅	納	純	絹	縦	縮	署	翌	聖	肺
4433	4441	4453	4454	4499	4571	4585	4643	4679	4727	4791

背	朗	胸	脳	腹	臓	臨	至	若	著	蒸
4794	4802	4811	4821	4851	4886	4899	4903	5007	5098	5163

蔵	蚕	衆	裁	装	裏	補	視	覧	討	訪
5182	5290	5417	5454	5455	5462	5464	5525	5533	5561	5571

訳	詞	誠	誌	認	誤	誕	論	諸	警	貴
5572	5582	5606	5620	5623	5626	5640	5646	5648	5705	5794

賃	遺	郷	郵	針	鋼	閉	閣	陛	除	降
5802	6115	6145	6147	6218	6302	6385	6401	6444	6449	6450

障	難	革	頂	骨
6479	6515	6570	6616	6784

939 GENERAL-USE CHARACTERS. These are the rest of the 1945 Jōyō Kanji, which have been marked with a small capital B in the body of this dictionary. They are arranged here in the order of their appearance in this dictionary.

丈	与	丙	且	丘	衷	丹	乏	乙	乾	了
5	6	16	17	19	31	36	46	56	63	67

互 75	井 76	亜 81	享 92	亭 96	介 108	仙 120	伐 132	企 135	仰 137	伏 139
但 154	佐 155	伺 156	伴 157	伯 158	伸 163	侮 187	併 190	依 191	侍 192	佳 194
侯 211	促 212	俊 216	侵 218	俗 220	傲 235	倫 246	倹 248	俸 249	倒 256	偵 270
偶 274	偽 276	偏 277	傘 283	偉 285	傍 286	傑 293	債 296	催 298	傾 299	僧 300
僕 313	僚 314	舗 322	儀 324	儒 330	償 333	充 348	克 354	免 361	兼 381	冗 399
冠 401	准 426	凍 427	凝 431	凡 433	凶 442	凸 443	凹 444	刃 449	刈 452	刑 461
到 477	刺 480	削 488	剖 492	剤 493	剛 497	剣 498	剰 501	劣 524	励 528	劾 534
勅 540	勘 548	募 551	勧 559	勲 560	勺 565	匁 566	匹 584	匠 588	匿 591	升 603
卓 616	卑 618	占 624	却 631	即 633	卸 641	厄 646	厘 650	又 668	及 670	双 673
叔 677	叙 681	召 695	吏 706	叫 708	吐 709	吉 711	呈 734	吟 740	呉 741	含 743
吹 747	咲 790	哀 791	唆 803	唇 807	哲 811	唐 812	喝 824	啓 828	唯 831	喚 852
喪 853	喫 855	嗣 868	嘆 872	嘱 894	噴 900	嚇 915	囚 937	圏 960	壮 974	壱 983
坊 986	坑 987	坪 998	垣 1009	埋 1020	培 1032	堕 1033	堀 1036	堅 1038	執 1039	塚 1048
塀 1051	塔 1052	堤 1054	塁 1056	堪 1057	塑 1068	塊 1070	塗 1074	墜 1082	塾 1083	墨 1086
墳 1095	墾 1097	壌 1098	壇 1101	壊 1102	壁 1103	奔 1148	奉 1149	奇 1150	契 1155	奥 1165
奨 1167	奪 1171	奴 1174	妃 1176	妄 1177	如 1178	妨 1187	妥 1188	妊 1189	妙 1191	姓 1196
姻 1215	姫 1217	威 1219	娠 1224	娘 1230	娯 1231	婆 1240	婚 1242	婿 1246	媒 1247	嫁 1256
嫌 1257	嫡 1263	嬢 1270	孔 1282	孤 1293	宜 1317	宰 1330	宴 1332	宵 1334	寂 1342	寛 1352
寝 1353	寧 1361	寡 1363	賓 1365	寮 1366	審 1367	寿 1374	封 1376	尉 1383	尋 1385	尚 1395
尼 1405	尽 1408	尿 1410	尾 1411	屈 1415	履 1434	屯 1438	岐 1447	岳 1457	岬 1458	峠 1464
峡 1465	峰 1473	崎 1485	崇 1490	崩 1491	巡 1528	巧 1533	巨 1534	帆 1551	帥 1559	帝 1560
帽 1573	幅 1574	幣 1585	幻 1598	幽 1600	幾 1601	床 1608	廊 1622	庸 1624	庶 1625	廃 1630

廉 1634	廷 1654	弊 1670	弐 1675	弔 1680	弧 1687	弦 1688	弾 1699	彩 1718	彫 1719	彰 1721
影 1722	征 1731	彼 1732	徐 1744	循 1758	御 1761	微 1765	徴 1768	徹 1771	衝 1772	衡 1775
忙 1783	忌 1786	忍 1787	怖 1817	怠 1818	怒 1820	怪 1821	恨 1842	恭 1845	恥 1846	恵 1847
悔 1848	恒 1849	恋 1852	恐 1853	悩 1867	悦 1868	悟 1870	患 1871	悠 1872	悼 1891	惑 1892
惜 1894	惨 1896	慌 1917	愉 1920	惰 1921	愁 1923	慈 1924	愚 1925	慨 1944	慎 1945	慕 1948
慮 1962	慶 1967	慢 1968	憎 1969	憂 1971	慰 1972	憩 1980	憤 1990	憾 1999	憶 2001	懇 2002
懐 2003	懲 2006	懸 2011	戒 2027	戯 2041	戻 2051	房 2053	扇 2056	扉 2058	払 2062	扱 2070
択 2082	把 2083	拒 2084	抄 2087	扶 2089	抑 2090	抗 2091	抜 2093	拐 2107	抹 2112	拠 2113
拍 2114	拓 2115	披 2116	抽 2119	抵 2120	拙 2122	拘 2123	抱 2125	押 2128	拷 2142	括 2143
挑 2145	挟 2146	挿 2167	捜 2168	捕 2170	振 2171	措 2190	掲 2194	据 2195	描 2196	掌 2200
控 2202	掘 2204	掃 2207	排 2210	掛 2214	搭 2228	援 2230	握 2232	換 2233	揺 2235	揚 2236
搬 2249	搾 2251	摂 2252	携 2253	摩 2264	撃 2265	摘 2266	撲 2274	撤 2280	撮 2282	擁 2294
擦 2306	擬 2307	攻 2331	敏 2337	敢 2350	敷 2357	斉 2366	斎 2368	斗 2373	斜 2376	斤 2379
斥 2380	施 2391	旋 2400	既 2407	旨 2414	旬 2415	更 2422	昆 2430	昇 2434	是 2451	曹 2477
晶 2482	暁 2485	替 2486	普 2489	暇 2501	暦 2507	暫 2510	曇 2518	朴 2544	朽 2545	朱 2546
杉 2562	析 2574	枠 2585	杯 2586	枢 2588	柄 2627	某 2628	柳 2629	架 2632	柔 2633	枯 2634
栓 2649	栽 2654	桟 2658	核 2660	桑 2661	桃 2663	棋 2744	植 2746	棟 2747	棚 2748	楼 2785
棄 2787	概 2824	槽 2844	欄 2914	欧 2931	款 2938	欺 2939	歓 2948	歳 2962	殉 2974	殊 2975
殖 2981	殴 2990	殻 2996	殿 3001	汁 3035	江 3045	汗 3046	汚 3047	沢 3062	沖 3065	没 3066
沈 3069	況 3086	沼 3091	泌 3092	泡 3093	沸 3094	泰 3098	泊 3099	泥 3105	津 3122	洪 3123
洞 3125	浄 3128	浜 3152	涙 3154	浪 3155	浦 3156	浸 3157	浮 3159	涯 3181	渉 3190	淑 3191
渇 3195	渓 3196	涼 3198	渋 3200	添 3201	淡 3202	滋 3238	湾 3239	渦 3241	湿 3243	渡 3247

Essential Kanji

漠	滝	溝	溶	滅	滞	滑	滴	潰	漂	漆
3268	3273	3275	3277	3279	3280	3282	3299	3301	3303	3304
漸	漏	漫	潟	澄	潤	潜	濁	濃	濯	濫
3305	3307	3308	3328	3333	3334	3337	3348	3349	3360	3366
瀬	炉	炎	炊	為	烈	焦	煮	煩	煙	燥
3384	3403	3404	3405	3411	3420	3436	3437	3454	3456	3493
爆	爵	牲	犠	狂	狭	狩	猫	猟	猛	猶
3505	3514	3539	3550	3562	3572	3573	3586	3587	3588	3593
献	猿	獄	獣	獲	玄	珍	珠	琴	環	璽
3596	3600	3602	3606	3609	3616	3631	3637	3654	3680	3683
瓶	甘	甚	甲	畔	畝	畜	畳	疎	疫	症
3699	3710	3711	3725	3746	3748	3749	3763	3776	3783	3795
疲	疾	痢	痘	痴	療	癒	癖	皆	盆	盗
3796	3797	3810	3813	3823	3842	3847	3848	3869	3889	3894
監	盤	盲	盾	冒	眠	眺	督	睡	瞬	矛
3901	3902	3907	3912	3915	3925	3933	3946	3948	3969	3974
矯	砕	砲	硫	硝	硬	碁	碑	磨	礁	礎
3984	3990	3998	4006	4007	4008	4020	4028	4045	4048	4054
祉	祈	祥	禍	禅	秀	秩	租	称	稚	稲
4069	4071	4090	4102	4104	4123	4135	4138	4139	4154	4158
稿	穂	稼	穏	穫	突	窃	窒	窯	窮	竜
4166	4168	4169	4175	4180	4191	4195	4200	4210	4212	4232
端	符	筒	箇	範	篤	簿	籍	粋	粒	粘
4243	4270	4283	4315	4330	4342	4364	4368	4389	4392	4393
粗	粧	糧	糾	索	紡	紋	紛	紹	紺	紳
4394	4400	4426	4438	4449	4450	4451	4452	4465	4466	4467
累	絡	絞	紫	継	維	緒	緊	綱	網	縄
4469	4484	4485	4486	4501	4516	4521	4524	4525	4527	4547
締	縫	緩	縁	緯	縛	繁	繊	繕	繭	繰
4549	4550	4551	4553	4566	4567	4570	4586	4594	4595	4602
缶	罰	罷	羅	翁	翼	翻	耐	耗	聴	粛
4624	4647	4650	4655	4677	4692	4694	4705	4709	4740	4747
肌	肖	肝	肪	肢	肯	肩	胞	胎	胆	朕
4755	4760	4762	4766	4768	4771	4776	4788	4789	4790	4797
脅	脂	胴	脚	脱	脹	腐	腕	腰	膜	膚
4803	4808	4810	4820	4822	4832	4835	4837	4850	4854	4867
膨	臭	致	舞	舟	般	舶	艇	艦	芝	芋
4874	4901	4904	4926	4927	4931	4936	4941	4950	4961	4964
芳	茎	茂	苗	荘	荒	華	菌	菓	菊	葬
4979	4991	4998	5004	5031	5034	5058	5091	5095	5096	5128
蓄	薦	薪	薫	薄	藩	藻	虐	虚	虞	虜
5161	5219	5222	5223	5225	5242	5254	5267	5269	5272	5273
蚊	蛍	蛇	蛮	融	衰	袋	被	裂	裕	褐
5288	5302	5303	5314	5371	5432	5443	5445	5453	5461	5473

裸 5475	褒 5483	襟 5504	襲 5510	覆 5517	覇 5519	触 5547	訂 5553	託 5560	訟 5565	詔 5581
詠 5584	詐 5585	診 5586	訴 5588	該 5601	誉 5602	誇 5605	詳 5607	詰 5609	誓 5622	誘 5625
謁 5637	諾 5638	請 5645	諮 5660	謡 5666	諭 5667	謀 5671	謄 5685	謙 5686	謹 5688	譜 5703
譲 5714	豚 5743	豪 5749	貞 5768	貢 5772	貫 5778	販 5779	賄 5800	賊 5801	賠 5810	賦 5811
賜 5812	賢 5816	購 5823	贈 5827	赦 5841	赴 5847	越 5851	超 5852	趣 5854	距 5866	践 5873
跡 5875	跳 5877	踊 5882	踏 5889	躍 5921	軌 5941	軒 5944	軟 5947	軸 5952	較 5959	載 5960
輩 5971	輝 5972	轄 5981	辛 5996	辱 6007	込 6010	迅 6014	迎 6019	迭 6029	迫 6031	逃 6038
逝 6051	逓 6055	逐 6056	途 6057	透 6059	逮 6069	逸 6071	遇 6083	遂 6084	遍 6086	遅 6089
違 6099	遣 6100	遭 6105	遮 6106	遵 6112	遷 6113	避 6120	還 6121	邦 6130	邸 6134	邪 6135
郊 6137	郎 6138	郭 6144	酌 6162	酔 6166	酢 6169	酬 6171	酪 6172	酵 6175	酷 6176	醜 6189
醸 6197	釈 6203	釣 6224	鈍 6235	鈴 6247	鉢 6249	鉛 6251	銑 6263	銘 6265	銃 6267	鋭 6279
鋳 6280	錘 6291	錠 6293	錯 6299	錬 6300	鍛 6318	鎖 6325	鎮 6328	鐘 6352	鑑 6361	閑 6390
閥 6398	閲 6404	闘 6418	附 6433	阻 6434	陥 6446	陣 6448	陵 6454	隆 6455	陳 6457	陪 6458
陶 6459	随 6460	陰 6462	隅 6467	隔 6475	隠 6480	隣 6484	隷 6490	隻 6494	雇 6497	雄 6499
雅 6505	雌 6506	離 6517	雰 6521	零 6524	雷 6525	需 6528	震 6531	霊 6532	霜 6542	霧 6545
露 6549	靴 6576	響 6610	韻 6611	項 6617	頒 6621	頑 6624	頼 6635	頻 6641	顕 6646	顧 6655
飢 6675	飾 6683	飽 6684	餓 6697	香 6722	駄 6734	駆 6736	駐 6745	騒 6760	騎 6761	騰 6767
驚 6774	髄 6791	髪 6804	鬼 6833	魂 6835	魅 6838	魔 6843	鮮 6864	鯨 6886	鶏 6980	麗 7026
麻 7040	黙 7055	鼓 7076	齢 7093							

284 ADDITIONS FOR PROPER NAMES. The following characters, in addition to the 1945 Jōyō Kanji, have been approved by the Government for use in proper names.

丑 12	丞 22	乃 42	之 48	也 58	亀 62	亘 79	亦 88	亥 89	亨 91	亮 95

伍 131	伎 133	伊 134	伶 149	佑 150	伽 159	侑 177	侃 182	倖 228	倭 242	偲 266
允 342	冴 417	冶 418	凌 424	凜 429	凪 437	凱 440	勁 538	匡 587	尭 614	卯 628
叡 683	叶 689	只 694	呂 728	吾 733	哉 779	啄 793	唄 802	喬 841	嘉 887	圭 973
奈 1147	奎 1152	媛 1244	嬉 1267	孟 1291	宏 1314	宥 1326	寅 1341	峻 1475	峯 1480	嵐 1496
嵯 1500	嵩 1502	嶺 1517	巌 1521	已 1538	巴 1541	巽 1546	庄 1605	弘 1682	弥 1689	彗 1708
彦 1714	彪 1716	彬 1717	怜 1812	恕 1834	悌 1861	惇 1887	惣 1889	惟 1890	慧 1964	憧 1982
拳 2148	捺 2189	捷 2198	敦 2349	斐 2370	於 2390	旦 2411	旭 2416	昂 2424	旺 2427	昌 2428
昴 2441	晋 2455	晃 2458	晏 2460	晟 2472	晨 2476	智 2490	暉 2499	暢 2506	曙 2519	李 2549
杏 2554	杜 2560	柊 2614	柾 2619	柚 2622	栞 2645	桐 2655	桂 2659	栗 2662	梓 2688	梢 2695
梨 2697	梧 2700	椋 2725	椰 2739	椎 2742	楓 2777	楠 2779	椿 2782	楊 2784	榛 2811	樺 2817
槙 2819	槻 2845	橘 2868	檀 2895	欣 2930	欽 2940	毅 3003	毬 3016	汀 3034	汐 3041	汰 3055
沙 3063	洸 3113	洵 3116	洲 3120	浩 3147	渚 3164	淳 3189	湧 3207	渥 3224	滉 3257	漱 3293
澪 3342	熙 3465	熊 3468	燎 3483	燦 3498	燿 3500	爽 3520	爾 3521	猪 3585	玖 3621	玲 3626
琢 3640	琳 3646	瑛 3647	瑶 3656	瑚 3662	瑞 3665	瑳 3667	璃 3669	瑠 3673	甫 3722	皐 3873
皓 3875	眉 3917	眸 3932	睦 3945	瞭 3960	瞳 3961	矩 3980	碩 4026	碧 4027	磯 4049	祐 4079
禄 4096	禎 4099	秦 4133	稀 4145	稔 4149	稜 4152	穣 4179	竣 4238	笙 4264	笹 4271	紘 4445
紗 4446	紬 4462	絃 4468	絢 4481	緋 4517	綸 4519	綜 4520	綺 4522	綾 4523	翔 4683	翠 4685
耀 4695	耶 4716	聡 4730	肇 4751	朋 4769	胤 4786	胡 4792	朔 4801	脩 4815	舜 4925	艶 4957
芙 4966	芹 4970	茉 4994	茄 4995	苑 4996	茅 5005	茜 5019	莉 5044	莞 5052	菖 5085	菫 5086
萌 5094	蓮 5105	葵 5120	萩 5122	蓉 5135	蒔 5153	蒼 5162	蔦 5178	蕉 5191	蕗 5203	藍 5233
藤 5241	蘭 5255	虎 5265	虹 5279	蝶 5363	衿 5431	袈 5442	裟 5457	詢 5593	誼 5634	諄 5635
諒 5641	趙 5848	輔 5964	辰 6006	迪 6026	遥 6075	遼 6111	邑 6127	那 6129	郁 6136	酉 6157

醇	采	錦	鎌	阿	隼	雛	霞	靖	鞠	須
6181	6201	6301	6326	6435	6493	6514	6541	6559	6589	6618

頌	颯	馨	駒	駿	魁	鮎	鯉	鯛	鳩	鳳
6622	6665	6724	6742	6754	6834	6855	6874	6884	6936	6937

鴻	鵬	鶴	鷹	鹿	麟	麿	黎	黛
6963	6979	6995	7007	7017	7028	7044	7049	7060

APPENDIX 10. THE ON-KUN INDEX

This *on-kun* index is a romanized listing of all the *on* (Sino-Japanese) and *kun* (native Japanese and foreign) readings of all the individual characters in alphabetical order. Also included are unpredictable compound readings (e.g., *asu* for 明日). The compounds listed here are only those with readings that are unpredicatable given the readings listed in this dictionary. In many cases, there are other compounds that are used to write the words spelled out by these unpredicatable compounds using predictable readings of their component characters. These common, predictable compounds may be found in any large Japanese-English dictionary. The order of each entry is as follows: the ON (in small capitals) or *kun* (in italics) followed by the various characters having that reading and the Nelson number of each character. Compounds are indexed by Nelson number followed by the stroke-count of the second member of the compound (e.g., 明日 2435.4). In this index, okurigana have not been marked by parentheses, as was done in the entries in the body of the dictionary. As in the body of the dictionary, prefixes, suffixes, verbs, and phrases are printed in italics along with the *kun* readings for simplicity's sake, even though they may contain *on* readings within them.

— A —

A	亜	81
	唖	827
	娃	1213
	窪	4209
	蛙	5313
	阿	6435
a-	亜	81
-A-	亜	81
abaku	暴	2511
	発	3860
abara	肋	4754
abareru	暴	2511
abiru	浴	3153
abiseru		
	浴	3153
abu	虻	5277
abuku	泡	3093
abumi	鐙	6348
abunagaru		
	危	629
abunai	危	629
abunakkashii		
	危	629
abura	油	3106
	脂	4808
	膏	4860
aburagiru		
	油	3106
aburagitta		
	脂	4808
aburakke		

	油気	3106.6
aburakkoi		
	油濃	3106.16
achi	彼方	1732.4
achira	彼方	1732.4
ada	仇	106
	徒	1746
	讐	5722
adakamo		
	恰	1838
adashi	徒	1746
adeyakana		
	艶	4957
aemono	和物	770.8
aenai	敢	2350
aete	敢	2350
afureru	溢	3270
agaku	足掻	5856.13
agameru		
	崇	1490
aganau	購	5823
agari	上	10
	騰	6767
-agari	上	10
agaru	上	10
	挙	2150
	揚	2236
agata	県	3918
agattari	上	10
age	揚	2236
ageru	上	10
	挙	2150
	揚	2236

agete	挙	2150
agetsurau		
	論	5646
-agezu	上	10
agito	顎	6643
ago	顎	6643
agumu	倦	251
	厭	662
ahōdori		
	信天翁	
		221.4
AI	哀	791
	娃	1213
	愛	1927
	挨	2160
ai	藍	5233
	間	6391
ai-	合	715
ai-	相	3920
aida	間	6391
ainiku	生憎	3715.14
airashii	愛	1927
aisuru	愛	1927
aita	空	4192
	開	6393
aite	対手	1375.4
aitsu	彼奴	1732.5
aji	味	766
	鯵	6912
aji na	味	766
ajisai	紫陽花	
		4486.11
ajiwai	味	766

ajiwau	味	766
aka	垢	1008
	朱	2546
	赤	5840
	銅	6266
aka-	赤	5840
akabamu		
	赤	5840
akachan		
	赤	5840
akagane		
	銅	6266
akai	赤	5840
akambo	赤坊	5840.7
akambō	赤坊	5840.7
akameru		
	赤	5840
akamu	赤	5840
akane	茜	5019
akanu	飽	6684
akarameru		
	赤	5840
akaramu		
	赤	5840
akari	明	2435
	灯	3395
akaru	開	6393
akarui	明	2435
akashi	明	2435
	灯	3395
	証	5589
akashi suru		
	証	5589

akasu	厭	662	*ama*	尼	1405	*anego*	姐御	1195.12	*arasu*	荒	5034

asa	朝	4838	atama	頭	6639	atsukamashii			aya	彪	1716

asa	朝	4838
	麻	7040
asa-	浅	3129
asahakana		
	浅	3129
asahi	旭	2416
asai	浅	3129
asamashii		
	浅	3129
asaru	漁	3309
asatte	明後日	
		2435.9
ase	汗	3046
asebamu		
	汗	3046
asedaku	汗	3046
asekkaki		
	汗掻	3046.13
asemizuku		
	汗	3046
aseru	急	1823
	焦	3436
ase suru	汗	3046
ashi	脚	4820
	芦	4975
	葺	5125
	葦	5160
	足	5856
ashii	悪	1873
ashikarazu		
	悪	1873
ashirau	遇	6083
	配	6163
ashita	明日	2435.4
	朝	4838
asobaseru		
	遊	6093
asobasu	遊	6093
asobi	遊	6093
asobu	遊	6093
asoko	彼処	1732.5
ason	朝臣	4838.6
assuru	圧	970
asu	明日	2435.4
Asuka	飛鳥	6672.11
asuko	彼処	1732.5
ata	仇	106
ataeru	与	6
atai	価	188
	値	257
atai suru		
	価	188
	値	257
atakamo	宛	1319
	恰	1838

atama	頭	6639
atamadekkachi		
	頭	6639
atamagonashi ni		
	頭	6639
atama kara		
	頭	6639
ataranai	当	1706
atarashigaru		
	新	2387
atarashii		
	新	2387
atari	当	1706
	辺	6011
-atari	当	1706
ataru	当	1706
atatakai	暖	2502
	温	3246
atatamaru		
	暖	2502
	温	3246
	暖	2502
atatameru		
	暖	2502
	温	3246
atchi	彼方	1732.4
ate	当	1706
-ate	宛	1319
atedo	当所	1706.8
atekko	当	1706
aterareru		
	当	1706
ateru	充	348
	宛	1319
	当	1706
atezuppō		
	当	1706
ato	後	1742
	痕	3803
	跡	5875
ato ni	後	1742
ato no	後	1742
atou	能	4809
ATSU	圧	970
	幹	2378
atsubottai		
	厚	651
atsugari	暑	2484
	熱	3473
atsugaru		
	暑	2484
	熱	3473
atsui	厚	651
	惇	1887
	暑	2484
	熱	3473
	篤	4342

atsukamashii		
	厚	651
atsukau	扱	2070
atsumari		
	集	6500
atsumaru		
	集	6500
atsumeru		
	集	6500
atsusa	厚	651
	暑	2484
atsusaatari		
	暑中	2484.4
attakai	暖	2502
	温	3246
attamaru		
	暖	2502
	温	3246
attameru	暖	2502
	温	3246
au	会	143
	合	715
	逢	6054
	遇	6083
	遭	6105
awa	沫	3085
	泡	3093
	粟	4403
awai	淡	3202
	間	6391
aware	哀	791
awaremi		
	憐	1987
awaremu		
	哀	791
	憐	1987
awareppoi		
	哀	791
awasaru	併	190
	合	715
awase	袷	5449
awase-	合	715
awaseru	会	143
	併	190
	合	715
	逢	6054
	遭	6105
awasete	併	190
awasu	合	715
awatadashii		
	慌	1917
awatefutameku		
	慌	1917
awateru	周章	768.11
	慌	1917

aya	彪	1716
	文	2364
	綾	4523
ayabumu		
	危	629
ayadoru	操	2296
ayakaru	肖	4760
ayamachi		
	過	6090
ayamari	誤	5626
	謝	5687
	謬	5695
ayamaru		
	誤	5626
	謝	5687
ayamatsu		
	過	6090
ayamatte		
	誤	5626
	過	6090
ayame	菖蒲	5085.13
ayameru	危	629
ayashigena		
	怪	1821
ayashii	怪	1821
ayashimu		
	怪	1821
ayatsu	彼奴	1732.5
ayatsuru	操	2296
ayaui	危	629
ayu	鮎	6855
ayumu	歩	2958
aza	字	1285
azamuku		
	欺	2939
azana	字	1285
azanau	糾	4438
azayakana		
	鮮	6864
aze	畔	3746
azekura	校倉	2669.10
azukari	預	6625
azukaru	与	6
	預	6625
azuke	預	6625
azukeru	預	6625
azuki	小豆	1389.7
azuma	東	2596
azumaya	四阿	938.7
azusa	梓	2688

— B —

BA	婆	1240
	罵	4649

Reading	Kanji	No.
	芭	4974
	馬	6725
ba	場	1058
baba	婆	1240
	祖母	4083.5
babā	婆	1240
BACHI	罰	4647
BAI	倍	252
	唄	802
	売	990
	培	1032
	媒	1247
	枚	2582
	梅	2666
	煤	3452
	狽	3576
	貝	5766
	買	5793
	賠	5810
	陪	6458
baisuru	倍	252
-bakari	斗	2373
	許	5569
bakasu	化	580
	魅	6838
bakeru	化	580
BAKU	博	621
	幕	1578
	暴	2511
	曝	2524
	漠	3268
	爆	3505
	箔	4312
	縛	4567
	莫	5057
	駁	6733
	麦	7030
BAN	万	7
	伴	157
	挽	2169
	播	2273
	晩	2491
	板	2595
	番	3762
	盤	3902
	磐	4037
	蕃	5199
	蛮	5314
-ban	判	465
bansuru	番	3762
bara	散	2352
barasu	散	2352
-bari	張	1694
bassuru	罰	4647
Bateren	伴天連	157.4
BATSU	伐	132
	抜	2093
	末	2534
	筏	4282
	罰	4647
	閥	6398
bāya	婆	1240
BE	琶	3649
	部	6146
-be	辺	6011
BEI	吠	739
	皿	3885
	米	4380
	米	4380
bei-	米	4380
-Bei-	米	4380
bekarazu	可	701
-beki	可	701
BEN	便	219
	勉	543
	娩	1233
	弁	1664
	弁	1665
	弁	1666
	鞭	6595
beni	紅	4441
benjiru	便	219
	弁	1665
	弁	1666
benzuru	便	219
	弁	1665
	弁	1666
-beshi	可	701
besshite	別	467
BETSU	別	467
	瞥	3959
	蔑	5179
-betsu	別	467
betsu ni	別	467
betsu no	別	467
BI	備	284
	尾	1411
	弥	1689
	微	1765
	枇	2580
	梶	2699
	琵	3653
	眉	3917
	美	4660
	鼻	7082
bīru	麦酒	7030.10
biki	引	1681
bikkuri suru	吃驚	707.22
	喫驚	855.22
BIN	便	219
	敏	2337
	瓶	3699
	貧	5782
Bishamon	毘沙門	3011.7
biwa	琵琶	3653.12
BO	慕	551
	墓	1073
	姥	1212
	慕	1948
	戊	2020
	暮	2508
	模	2825
	母	3005
	牡	3536
	簿	4364
	莫	5057
	菩	5093
	葡	5127
	蒲	5156
-bo	簿	4364
BŌ	乏	46
	亡	86
	傍	286
	剖	492
	卯	628
	呆	738
	坊	986
	妄	1177
	妨	1187
	帽	1573
	忙	1783
	忘	1784
	房	2053
	暴	2511
	某	2628
	棒	2750
	牟	3533
	畝	3748
	盲	3907
	冒	3915
	矛	3974
	紡	4450
	肪	4766
	望	4819
	膨	4874
	茅	5005
	萌	5094
	虻	5277
	謀	5671
	貌	5762
	貿	5788
boke	防	6429
	呆	738
	惚	1893
bokeru	惚	1893
boko	凹	444
BOKU	僕	313
	卜	622
	墨	1086
	撲	2274
	朴	2531
	木	2544
	牧	3537
	睦	3945
	穆	4171
boku suru	卜	622
	牧	3537
BON	凡	433
	煩	3454
	犯	3554
	盆	3889
bossuru	没	3066
botan	釦	6223
botchan	坊	986
BOTSU	勃	539
	没	3066
botsu	没	3066
bōya	坊	986
BU	不	13
	亡	86
	侮	187
	分	454
	奉	1149
	捕	2170
	撫	2281
	歩	2958
	武	2959
	無	3439
	舞	4926
	蒲	5156
	蕪	5196
	部	6146
	鵡	6974
buchi	斑	2371
	駁	6733
BUN	分	454
	文	2364
	聞	4732
	蚊	5288
bun-	分	454
-buri	振	2171
buta	豚	5743
BUTSU	仏	111
	勿	569
	物	3538

Reading	Kanji	No.
	壊	1102
	恵	1847
	歪	2960
	画	3733
	衣	5420
e	枝	2591
	柄	2627
	江	3045
	絵	4488
	餌	6690
-e	方	2389
	重	6207
eba	餌	6690
ebamu	餌食	6690.9
ebaru	威張	1219.11
ebi	海老	3133.6
	蝦	5364
ebisu	夷	1143
	戎	2024
eboshi	烏帽子	3421.12
eda	枝	2591
Edokko	江戸子	3045.4
egaku	描	2196
	画	3733
ehō	吉方	711.4
EI	叡	683
	営	857
	嬰	1273
	影	1722
	衛	1776
	曳	2417
	映	2448
	栄	2635
	永	3031
	泳	3090
	洩	3118
	瑛	3647
	盈	3888
	穎	4173
	英	5008
	詠	5584
	鋭	6279
ei	酔	6166
-Ei	英	5008
Ei-	英	5008
eijiru	映	2448
eisuru	詠	5584
eizuru	映	2448
EKI	亦	88
	役	1726
	易	2432
	液	3199
	疫	3783
	益	3891
	訳	5572
	駅	6735
ekisuru	役	1726
	益	3891
emi	笑	4256
Emishi	蝦夷	5364.6
Emisu	蝦夷	5364.6
emu	笑	4256
EN	俺	240
	円	385
	厭	662
	咽	788
	員	808
	園	962
	圧	970
	垣	1009
	堰	1055
	塩	1075
	奄	1146
	媛	1244
	宛	1319
	宴	1332
	延	1657
	怨	1819
	掩	2192
	援	2230
	沿	3096
	淵	3237
	演	3310
	炎	3404
	煙	3456
	燄	3485
	燕	3489
	猿	3600
	縁	4553
	艶	4957
	苑	4996
	遠	6101
	鉛	6251
	鳶	6938
	鴛	6953
enishi	縁	4553
enjiru	演	3310
	榎	2810
enzuru	怨	1819
	演	3310
erabu	択	2082
	撰	2277
	選	6114
eragaru	偉	285
erai	偉	285
eramu	撰	2277
	選	6114
eri	衿	5431
	襟	5504
erigui	撰食	2277.9
eru	得	1755
	択	2082
	獲	3609
	選	6114
esa	餌	6690
ese-	似而非	138.6
essuru	謁	5637
	閲	6404
esuru	会	143
etagaru	得	1755
etari	得	1755
ete	得	1755
ETSU	咽	788
	悦	1868
	説	5627
	謁	5637
	越	5851
	閲	6404
eyō	栄耀	2635.20
Ezo	蝦夷	5364.6

— F —

Reading	Kanji	No.
FU	不	13
	付	124
	埠	1029
	夫	1136
	婦	1243
	富	1349
	布	1548
	府	1611
	怖	1817
	扶	2089
	敷	2357
	斧	2382
	普	2489
	楓	2777
	浮	3159
	父	3516
	甫	3722
	符	4270
	腐	4835
	膚	4867
	芙	4966
	蒲	5156
	覆	5517
	譜	5703
	負	5769
	賦	5811
	赴	5847
	釜	6215
	阜	6423
	附	6433
	風	6663
	鮒	6854
fu	二	72
	斑	2371
	歩	2958
-fu	生	3715
FŪ	夫	1136
	富	1349
	封	1376
	楓	2777
	風	6663
fū	二	72
fubuki	吹雪	747.11
fubuku	吹雪	747.11
fuchi	淵	3237
	縁	4553
fuchidoru	縁	4553
fuda	札	2533
	簡	4358
fude	筆	4288
fue	笛	4268
fueru	増	1088
	殖	2981
fugu	河豚	3102.11
fuji	藤	5241
fūjiru	封	1376
fukai	深	3206
fukamaru	深	3206
fukameru	深	3206
fukami	深	3206
fukasu	吹	747
	更	2422
	深	3206
	蒸	5163
fukeru	化	580
	更	2422
	深	3206
	老	4696
	耽	4721
	蒸	5163
	蕗	5203
fukki	富貴	1349.12
FUKU	伏	139
	副	503
	幅	1574
	復	1760
	福	4105
	服	4775
	腹	4851
	複	5484

	覆	5517	*funaberi*	舷	4938	*fusegu*	拒	2084		我	2028

— H —

HA	巴	1541
	把	2083
	播	2273
	杷	2575
	波	3101
	派	3126
	琶	3649
	破	3999
	簸	4363
	覇	5519
	頗	6627
ha	刃	449
	歯	2961
	端	4243
	羽	4675
	葉	5129
haba	巾	1547
	幅	1574
habamu	阻	6434
	難	6515
habataki	羽搏	4675.13
habataku	羽搏	4675.13
haberu	侍	192
habikoru	蔓	5180
	蔓延	5180.8
habuku	省	3916
HACHI	八	369
	捌	2162
	鉢	6249
hachi	蜂	5331
hachisu	蓮	5158
hada	肌	4755
	膚	4867
hadae	肌	4755
	膚	4867
hadaka	裸	5475
hadare	斑	2371
hadashi	裸足	5475.7
hae	映	2448
	栄	2635
	蠅	5394
haearu	栄	2635
haeru	映	2448
	栄	2635
	生	3715
hagane	鋼	6302
hage	禿	4122
hagemasu	励	528
hagemi	励	528

hagemu	励	528
hageru	禿	4122
hageshii	劇	517
	激	3350
	烈	3420
hagi	接	2213
	萩	5122
hagu	接	2213
	剥	3979
hagukumu	育	4773
hagureru	逸	6071
haha	母	3005
HAI	俳	254
	吠	739
	廃	1630
	拝	2126
	排	2210
	敗	2343
	杯	2586
	牌	3528
	稗	4151
	箆	4310
	肺	4791
	背	4794
	輩	5971
	配	6163
hai	灰	3396
	蠅	5394
hai ni naru	灰	3396
hai ni suru	灰	3396
hairu	入	366
haisuru	廃	1630
	拝	2126
	排	2210
	配	6163
haji	恥	1846
	端	4243
	辱	6007
hajikeru	弾	1699
hajiki	弾	1699
hajiku	弾	1699
hajimaranai	始	1203
hajimari	始	1203
hajimaru	始	1203
hajime	初	469
	始	1203
-hajime	初	469

hajimemashite	始	1203
hajimeru	初	469
	創	506
	始	1203
hajimete	初	469
	始	1203
	甫	3722
hajirau	恥	1846
hajiru	恥	1846
haka	墓	1073
hakadoru	捗	2161
hakama	袴	5448
hakanai	果敢	2594.12
	果無	2594.12
hakarau	計	5555
hakarazu	図	947
hakarazu mo	図	947
hakari	秤	4134
	量	6209
hakarigoto	謀	5671
hakaru	図	947
	測	3244
	計	5555
	諮	5660
	謀	5671
	量	6209
hakase	博士	621.3
hake	刷毛	479.4
hakeru	捌	2162
hako	函	446
	箱	4331
hakobi	運	6092
hakobu	運	6092
hakobune	方舟	2389.6
HAKU	伯	158
	博	621
	拍	2114
	柏	2623
	泊	3099
	狛	3566
	白	3863
	箔	4312
	簿	4364
	粕	4391
	舶	4936
	薄	5225
	迫	6031

	鞄	6582
	駁	6733
haku	吐	709
	履	1434
	掃	2207
	穿	4198
-haku	博	621
hakusuru	博	621
hama	浜	3152
hamaguri	蛤	5312
hamu	食	6674
HAN	伴	157
	凡	433
	判	465
	半	608
	反	674
	叛	680
	坂	985
	帆	1551
	幡	1584
	搬	2249
	播	2273
	斑	2371
	板	2595
	氾	3033
	汎	3043
	煩	3454
	版	3526
	犯	3554
	班	3636
	畔	3746
	盤	3902
	磐	4037
	範	4330
	繁	4570
	翻	4694
	般	4931
	蕃	5199
	藩	5242
	販	5779
	阪	6428
	頒	6621
	飯	6679
han	榛	2811
hana	端	4243
	花	4980
	華	5058
	鼻	7082
hanabi	煙火	3456.4
hanahada		
	太	1137
	孔	1282
	甚	3711

Reading	Kanji	No.
hiromeru	広	1604
hirou	拾	2149
hiroyakana	広	1604
hiru	干	1589
	昼	2450
	簸	4363
	蛭	5308
hirugaeru	翻	4694
hirugaesu	翻	4694
hirugaette	翻	4694
hirumu	怯	1816
hisago	瓢	3688
hisashi	庇	1606
hisashii	久	47
	尚	1395
hisashiku	久	47
hishi	菱	5092
hishio	醤	6192
hisoka na	密	1343
	私	4124
	窃	4195
hisoka ni	潜	3337
	秘	4140
	陰	6462
hisomaru	潜	3337
hisomeru	潜	3337
hisomu	潜	3337
hisoyakana	密	1343
hissageru	提	2237
hisugara	終日	4471.4
hisuru	比	3010
	秘	4140
hita	直	3908
hita to	直	3908
hitai	額	6644
hitamuki	真向	3926.6
hitaru	浸	3157
	漬	3301
hitasu	浸	3157
	漬	3301
hitasura	只管	694.14
hito	人	99

Reading	Kanji	No.
hito-	一	1
hitoe	単	620
hitoe ni	偏	277
hitomi	瞳	3961
hitorashii	人	99
hitori	一人	1.2
	独	3574
hitoribotchi	独	3574
hitori de	孤	1293
hitorideni	独	3574
hitorikko	一人子	1.2
hitoshii	均	988
	斉	2366
	斎	2368
	等	4287
hi to suru	非	6563
hitotonari	人	99
	為人	3411.2
hitotsu	一	1
hitotsu ni	一	1
hitotsu ni wa	一	1
hitotsu wa	一	1
hitoya	獄	3602
HITSU	匹	584
	弼	1697
	必	1781
	泌	3092
	畢	3754
	正	3774
	筆	4288
	逼	6085
hitsugi	棺	2746
hitsuji	未	2535
	羊	4658
hiuo	乾魚	63.11
hiya	冷	419
hiyakasu	冷	419
hiyari to shita	冷	419
hiyasu	冷	419
hiyayakana	冷	419
hiyoko	雛	6514
hiyori	日和	2410.8
hiyowai	弱	1692
hiza	膝	4868

Reading	Kanji	No.
hizakana	乾魚	63.11
hizashi	陽差	6470.10
hizume	蹄	5894
hizumu	歪	2960
HO	保	222
	舗	322
	圃	954
	布	1548
	捗	2161
	捕	2170
	歩	2958
	浦	3156
	甫	3722
	畝	3748
	葡	5127
	蒲	5156
	補	5464
	輔	5964
	鮒	6854
ho	帆	1551
	火	3394
	穂	4168
ho-	芳	4979
-ho	補	5464
HŌ	保	222
	傲	235
	俸	249
	傍	286
	剖	492
	包	572
	呆	738
	培	1032
	報	1059
	奉	1149
	妨	1187
	宝	1320
	封	1376
	峰	1473
	崩	1491
	庖	1610
	抱	2125
	捧	2199
	放	2333
	方	2389
	棚	2748
	泡	3093
	法	3107
	烹	3998
	縫	4550
	朋	4769
	胞	4788
	芳	4979
	萌	5094

Reading	Kanji	No.
	蔀	5138
	蓬	5157
	蜂	5331
	褒	5483
	訪	5571
	豊	5737
	達	6054
	邦	6130
	鋒	6275
	鞄	6582
	飽	6684
	鳳	6937
	鴇	6943
	鵬	6979
hō	朴	2544
	頬	6637
hō-	芳	4979
hobo	略	3755
hodo	程	4144
-hodo	程	4144
hodokeru	解	5548
hodokoshi	施	2391
hodokosu	施	2391
hodoku	解	5548
hoeru	吠	739
hofuru	屠	1429
hogaraka na	朗	4802
hogigoto	祝事	4085.8
hogo	反古	674.5
	反故	674.9
hogoreru	解	5548
hogosu	解	5548
hogu	反古	674.5
	反故	674.9
hogureru	解	5548
hogusu	解	5548
hoho	頬	6637
hojikuru	穿	4198
hojiru	穿	4198
hōjiru	報	1059
	崩	1491
hoka	他	122
	外	1125
hoka naranu	外	1125
hoka no	外	1125
Hokekyō	法華経	3107.10
hokeru	惚	1893
hoko	戟	2035

Reading	Kanji	No.
	矛	3974
hokorakasu		
	誇	5605
hokorashigeni		
	誇	5605
hokorashii		
	誇	5605
	誇	5605
hokorippoi		
	埃	1017
hokorobaseru		
	綻	4514
hokorobasu		
	綻	4514
hokorobiru		
	綻	4514
hokoru	誇	5605
HOKU	北	581
hokuro	黒子	7052.3
homare	誉	5602
homechigiru		
	褒	5483
homeru	褒	5483
	誉	5602
	賞	5815
homesoyasu		
	褒	5483
homura	炎	3404
	焔	3485
hōmura	葬	5128
HON	反	674
	叛	680
	品	792
	奔	1148
	幡	1584
	本	2536
	翻	4694
hone	骨	6784
hon ni	真	3926
honō	炎	3404
honoho	炎	3404
honokana		
	側	275
honoo	焔	3485
hoo	頬	6637
hora	法	3107.17
	洞	3125
horeru	惚	1893
hori	堀	1036
	壕	1108
	濠	3363
horo	幌	1577
horobiru	亡	86
	滅	3279
horobosu	亡	86

Reading	Kanji	No.
	滅	3279
horu	刻	478
	彫	1719
	掘	2204
	放	2333
hoshi	星	2452
hoshi-	乾	63
hoshigaru		
	欲	2936
hoshii	欲	2936
hoshiimama		
	縦	4571
hosoi	細	4472
hosomeru		
	細	4472
hosoru	細	4472
Hossō	法相	3107.9
hossuru	欲	2936
hosu	乾	63
	干	1589
hosuru	保	222
	補	5464
hotaru	蛍	5302
Hotei	布袋	1548.11
hotobori	熱	3473
hotoboru	熱	3473
hotohoto	幾	1601
	殆	2972
Hotoke	仏	111
hotondo	殆	2972
hotori	辺	6011
hoōtoru	熱	3473
hototogisu		
	杜鵑	2560.18
HOTSU	発	3860
hotsureru		
	解	5548
hottarakasu		
	放	2333
hottategoya		
	掘建小屋	
		2204.9
hōzuru	報	1059
	奉	1149
	封	1376
	崩	1491
HYAKU	柏	2623
	百	3864
HYŌ	俵	243
	兵	374
	坪	998
	平	1590
	彪	1716
	拍	2114
	標	2852

Reading	Kanji	No.
	氷	3032
	漂	3303
	瓢	3688
	票	4089
	表	5422
	評	5587
	豹	5753
hyōryō	秤量	4134.12
hyōsuru	表	5422
	評	5587
HYŪ	彪	1716

— I —

Reading	Kanji	No.
I	易	2432
	維	4516
	井	76
	以	109
	伊	134
	位	162
	依	191
	偉	285
	医	590
	唯	831
	囲	945
	夷	1143
	委	1204
	威	1219
	尉	1383
	惟	1890
	意	1926
	慰	1972
	椅	2737
	為	3411
	猪	3585
	畏	3742
	異	3757
	移	4141
	緯	4566
	胆	4790
	胃	4793
	萎	5087
	葦	5160
	蔚	5181
	衣	5420
	訛	5579
	謂	5656
	違	6099
	遺	6115
	飴	6682
-i	位	162
-I	伊	134
I-	伊	134
ibara	茨	5017
	荊	5027

Reading	Kanji	No.
ibari	尿	1410
ibitsu no	歪	2960
ICHI	壱	1
		983
ichi	市	1549
ichi-	一	1
ichihayaku		
	逸速	6071.9
ichijirushii		
	著	5098
		372.10
ichō	公孫樹	
	銀杏	6268.7
idaku	抱	2125
idasu	出	445
ideyu	温泉	3246.9
idomu	挑	2145
ie	否	742
	家	1337
	癒	3847
igameru	歪	2960
igami	歪	2960
igamu	歪	2960
ii	佳	194
	可	701
	善	859
	好	1180
	宜	1317
	良	4954
	謂	5656
	飯	6679
iie	否	742
ii-konashi	言	5552
iinazuke	言	5569.11
	許	5569.13
ii-sobireru		
	言	5552
iiya	否	742
ijikuru	弄	1668
ijimeru	苛	5006
ijiru	弄	1668
ika	墨	1086.11
	如何	1178.7
	柔	2633.11
	烏	3421.13
	紙	4455.14
ikada	筏	4282
ikade	争	69
ikaga	如何	1178.7
ikameshii		
	厳	663
ikan	奈何	1147.7
	如何	1178.7
ikana	如何	1178.7

Reading	Kanji	No.
jo-	助	530
-jo	所	2054
JŌ	丈	5
	上	10
	丞	22
	乗	54
	冗	399
	剰	501
	城	1011
	場	1058
	壌	1098
	娘	1230
	嬢	1270
	定	1323
	帖	1558
	常	1569
	情	1898
	成	2025
	承	2088
	擾	2314
	杖	2555
	条	2563
	浄	3128
	状	3556
	畳	3763
	盛	3895
	祥	4090
	穣	4179
	縄	4547
	蒸	5163
	請	5645
	譲	5714
	貞	5768
	醸	6197
	錠	6293
	静	6560
jō	尉	1383
jō-	定	1323
-jō	条	2563
-jō-	上	10
jōgo	漏斗	3307.4
jōjiru	乗	54
JOKU	濁	3348
	辱	6007
jōro	如雨露	1178.8
josuru	叙	681
	恕	1834
	除	6449
jōzuru	乗	54
JU	儒	330
	入	366
	受	678
	呪	764
	嬬	1271

Reading	Kanji	No.
	寿	1374
	就	1401
	従	1745
	授	2208
	樹	2878
	濡	3365
	珠	3637
	堅	4240
	綬	4510
	需	6528
	鷲	7004
ju-	従	1745
JŪ	什	105
	住	164
	充	348
	十	598
	廿	1662
	従	1745
	戎	2024
	拾	2149
	柔	2633
	汁	3035
	渋	3200
	獣	3606
	紐	4448
	縦	4571
	重	6207
	銃	6267
jū-	重	6207
-jū	中	28
	重	6207
JUKU	塾	1083
	熟	3472
	粥	4402
jukusu	熟	3472
jukusuru		
	熟	3472
JUN	准	426
	巡	1528
	循	1758
	惇	1887
	旬	2415
	楯	2776
	殉	2974
	淳	3189
	準	3278
	潤	3334
	盾	3912
	純	4454
	遵	6112
	醇	6181
	閏	6389
	隼	6493
	順	6619
	馴	6729

Reading	Kanji	No.
jun-	準	3278
junjiru	准	426
	殉	2974
jun na	純	4454
junzuru	准	426
	殉	2974
	準	3278
jūsuru	住	164
JUTSU	術	1754
	述	6030
juzu	数珠	2353.10
	珠数	3637.13

— K —

Reading	Kanji	No.
KA	下	9
	仮	144
	伽	159
	何	169
	価	188
	佳	194
	個	258
	加	523
	化	580
	卦	625
	可	701
	和	770
	嘩	861
	嘉	887
	夏	1120
	嫁	1256
	家	1337
	寡	1363
	暇	2501
	果	2594
	架	2632
	榎	2810
	樺	2817
	歌	2945
	河	3102
	渦	3241
	火	3394
	珂	3625
	瓜	3686
	禍	4102
	禾	4121
	科	4130
	稼	4169
	箇	4315
	花	4980
	茄	4995
	苛	5006
	華	5058
	荷	5059

Reading	Kanji	No.
	菓	5095
	蝦	5364
	課	5644
	貨	5781
	跨	5872
	迦	6027
	過	6090
	鍛	6306
	鍋	6315
	霞	6541
	靴	6576
	駕	6743
-ka	乎	49
	耶	4716
	蚊	5288
	香	6722
	鹿	7017
-ka	処	435
	化	580
	家	1337
	日	2410
-ka-	下	9
	華	5058
kaba	樺	2817
	蒲	5156
kaban	鞄	6582
kabane	姓	1196
kabau	庇	1606
kabe	壁	1103
kabocha	南瓜	619.5
kabosoi	細	4472
kabu	株	2665
	蕪	5196
	頭	6639
kabura	蕪	5196
kaburi	頭	6639
kaburo	禿	4122
kaburu	被	5445
kabusaru		
	被	5445
kabuseru	被	5445
kabuto	兜	364
kachi	勝	553
	徒	1746
kachide	徒歩	1746.8
kachi iro	徒	1746
	褐色	5473.6
kado	廉	1634
	角	5543
	門	6381
kae-	替	2486
kaede	替	2486
	楓	2777
kaeri	帰	1564

kaerigake ni
帰 1564
kaerimiru
省 3916
顧 6655
kaerishina ni
帰 1564
kaeru
代 125
反 674
変 1119
帰 1564
換 2233
替 2486
蛙 5313
返 6020
還 6121
kaerusa ni
帰 1564
kaeshi
返 6020
kaesu
反 674
帰 1564
返 6020
還 6121
kaette
却 631
反 674
kagamaru
屈 1415
kagameru
屈 1415
kagami 鏡 6341
鑑 6361
kagamu 屈 1415
kagashi 案山子
2667.3
kagayakashii
耀 4695
輝 5972
kagayakasu
耀 4695
赫 5843
輝 5972
kagayaki
輝 5972
kagayaku
耀 4695
輝 5972
kage 影 1722
蔭 5151
陰 6462
kagerō 陽炎 6470.8
kageroi 陽炎 6470.8
kageru 陰 6462
kagi 鉤 6250
鍵 6317
kagiri 限 6439

-kagiri 限 6439
kagiru 限 6439
kago 籠 4376
興 5983
駕 6743
kagomu 屈 1415
kagura 神楽 4087.13
KAI
介 108
会 143
刈 452
回 941
塊 1070
壊 1102
届 1413
廻 1659
街 1759
快 1802
怪 1821
恢 1843
悔 1848
懐 2003
戒 2027
拐 2107
掛 2214
改 2332
晦 2478
械 2685
檜 2894
海 3133
潰 3335
灰 3396
界 3739
皆 3869
絵 4488
苅 4642
苅 4969
芥 4977
蟹 5395
解 5548
賄 5800
開 6393
階 6469
魁 6834
鮭 6859
粥 4402
詮 5604
貝 5766
貫 5793
蚕 5290
kaiko
kaimamiru
垣間見
1009.12
kaina 胘 4770
腕 4837
kairi 浬 3142

kaishite 介 108
kaisuru 介 108
会 143
解 5548
kaji 梶 2699
舵 4937
鍛冶 6318.7
kajika 鰍 6895
kakae 抱 2125
kakaeru 抱 2125
kakageru 掲 2194
kakari 係 217
掛 2214
kakaru 係 217
懸 2011
掛 2214
斯 2386
繋 4601
kakashi 案山子
2667.3
kakasu 欠 2928
kakawarazu
拘 2123
kakawari
係 217
関 6402
kakawaru
係 217
拘 2123
関 6402
kake 掛 2214
欠 2928
賭 5819
-kake 掛 2214
kakekko 駆 6736
kakekkura
駆 6736
kakekura
駆 6736
kakeru 懸 2011
掛 2214
架 2632
欠 2928
賭 5819
駆 6736
駈 6744
-kakeru 掛 2214
-kaketewa
掛 2214
kakezuru
駆 6736
kaki 垣 1009
柿 2624
牡蠣 3536.20

kaki- 掻 2256
kako 水夫 3030.4
kakochi 託 5560
kakoi 囲 945
kakomi 囲 945
kakomu 囲 945
kakotsu 託 5560
kakotsukeru
託 5560
kakou 囲 945
KAKU 劃 513
各 714
嚇 915
塙 1063
客 1329
廓 1633
拡 2118
掴 2263
攪 2322
核 2660
格 2668
殻 2996
獲 3609
画 3733
確 4039
穫 4180
脚 4820
覚 5529
角 5543
赫 5843
較 5959
郭 6144
閣 6401
隔 6475
革 6570
鶴 6995
kaku 描 2196
掻 2256
斯 2386
書 2463
欠 2928
kaku- 各 714
客 1329
kakumau 匿 591
kakuna 角 5543
kaku no 核 2660
kakurega
隠処 6480.5
kakurembō
隠坊 6480.7
kakurenaki
隠 6480
kakureru
隠 6480

karasu	枯	2634
	烏	3421
kare	彼	1732
kare-	枯	2634
karebamu		
	枯	2634
kareru	枯	2634
kari	借	259
	狩	3573
	猟	3587
	雁	6498
karigane		
	雁	6498
kari ni	仮	144
kari nimo		
	仮	144
kari no	仮	144
kariru	借	259
kariudo	狩人	3573.2
	猟人	3587.2
karoi	軽	5953
karōjite	辛	5996
karonjiru		
	軽	5953
karonzuru		
	軽	5953
karu	借	259
	刈	452
	狩	3573
	駆	6736
	駈	6744
karui	軽	5953
karuku suru		
	軽	5953
karuyakana		
	軽	5953
kariudo	狩人	3573.2
	猟人	3587.2
kasa	傘	283
	嵩	1502
	笠	4269
kasamu	嵩	1502
kasanaru		
	重	6207
kasane	襲	5510
	重	6207
kasaneru		
	重	6207
kasanete	重	6207
kasegi	稼	4169
kasegu	稼	4169
kaseru	乾	63
kashi	樫	2849
	河岸	3102.8
	貸	5792

kashigeru		
	傾	299
kashigu	傾	299
	炊	3405
kashiko	彼処	1732.5
kashikoi	畏	3742
	賢	5816
kashikokumo		
	畏	3742
kashikomaru		
	畏	3742
kashikomu		
	畏	3742
kashimashii		
	姦	1218
kashira	頭	6639
-kashira	知	3978
kashiwa	柏	2623
kashiwade		
	拍手	2114.4
kassen	合戦	715.13
kassuru	渇	3195
kasu	化	580
	嫁	1256
	科	4130
	粕	4391
	糟	4423
	課	5644
	貸	5792
kasukana		
	幽	1600
	微	1765
kasumeru		
	掠	2191
kasumi	霞	6541
kasumu	霞	6541
kasureru		
	掠	2191
	擦	2306
kasuri	掠	2191
kasuru	化	580
	嫁	1256
	掠	2191
	擦	2306
	架	2632
	科	4130
	課	5644
kata	型	1010
	形	1713
	方	2389
	渇	3328
	肩	4776
kata-	片	3525
-kata	方	2389
katabuku		

	傾	299
katachi	容	1335
	形	1713
katadoru	模	2825
	象	5744
katageru		
	傾	299
	担	2121
katagi	気質	3025.15
katagu	傾	299
katai	固	949
	堅	1038
	硬	4008
	難	6515
katajikenai		
	辱	6007
kataki	仇	106
	敵	2359
katakuna na		
	頑	6624
katamari		
	固	949
	塊	1070
katamaru		
	固	949
katame	固	949
katameru		
	固	949
katami ni		
	互	75
katamukeru		
	傾	299
katamuki		
	傾	299
katamuku		
	傾	299
katana	刀	448
katarai	語	5628
katarau	語	5628
katari	語	5628
katarogu		
	型録	1010.16
kataru	語	5628
katawara		
	側	275
	傍	286
katawara ni		
	傍	286
katawara no		
	傍	286
katayori	偏	277
katayoru	偏	277
katazu o nomu		
	固唾飲	

		949.11
kate	糧	4426
KATSU	割	507
	喝	824
	憩	1980
	括	2143
	活	3132
	渇	3195
	滑	3282
	筈	4277
	葛	5126
	褐	5473
	轄	5981
katsu	且	17
	克	354
	勝	553
katsubushi		
	鰹節	6915.13
katsueru	餓	6697
katsugi	担	2121
katsugu	担	2121
katsuo	鰹	6915
katsura	桂	2659
katsute	嘗	878
	曾	2483
katte	曾	2483
katto	赫	5843
kau	支	2324
	買	5793
	飼	6685
kawa	側	275
	川	1526
	河	3102
	皮	3878
	革	6570
kawaii	可愛	
		701.13
kawaisō	可哀想	
		701.9
kawakasu		
	乾	63
kawaki	乾	63
	渇	3195
kawaku	乾	63
	渇	3195
	燥	3493
kawappa		
	河童	3102.12
kawara	瓦	3690
	川原	1526.10
kawarake		
	土器	966.15
kawaranu		
	変	1119
kawari	代	125

reading	kanji	no.
kisezu shite	期	4836
kishi	岸	1459
kishikata	来方	2565.4
kisou	競	4244
kissaki	切先	453.6
kissui	生粋	3715.10
kissuru	喫	855
kisuru	帰	1564
	期	4836
	記	5563
kita	北	581
kitaeru	鍛	6318
kitanai	汚	3047
kitaru	来	2565
kitasu	来	2565
ki to suru	奇	1150
KITSU	乞	59
	吃	707
	吉	711
	喫	855
	桔	2653
	橘	2868
	詰	5609
	迄	6013
kitsune	狐	3568
kitsutsuki	啄木鳥	821.4
-kitte no	切	453
kiwa	際	6478
kiwadoi	際	6478
kiwamarinai	極	2753
kiwamaru	極	2753
	窮	4212
kiwameru	極	2753
	究	4189
	窮	4212
kiwamete	極	2753
kiwami	極	2753
kiyoi	浄	3128
	清	3205
kiyomaru	浄	3128
	清	3205
kiyomawaru	浄	3128
	清	3205
kiyome	清	3205
kiyomeru	浄	3128
	清	3205
kiyorakana	清	3205
kiyuru	消	3158
kiza	刻	478
	段	2991
kizahashi	段階	2991.11
	陛	6444
	階	6469
	階段	6469.9
kizami	刻	478
kizamu	刻	478
kizashi	兆	346
	萌	5094
kizasu	兆	346
	萌	5094
kizu	傷	301
	創	506
kizuku	築	4343
KO	乎	49
	個	258
	去	665
	古	702
	呼	769
	固	949
	壷	1034
	姑	1194
	孤	1293
	居	1416
	巨	1534
	己	1540
	庫	1617
	弧	1687
	戸	2048
	拠	2113
	故	2334
	枯	2634
	湖	3240
	火	3394
	狐	3568
	瑚	3662
	箇	4315
	糊	4415
	股	4772
	胡	4792
	菰	5079
	虎	5265
	虚	5269
	袴	5448
	許	5569
	誇	5605
	跨	5872
	鈷	6236
	鋼	6285
	雇	6497
	顧	6655
	鼓	7076
ko	九	57
	仔	119
	児	1281
	子	1281
	木	2531
	籠	4376
	粉	4390
ko-	子	1281
	小	1389
	故	2334
KŌ	互	80
	交	90
	亨	91
	仰	137
	佼	175
	侯	211
	倖	228
	候	250
	光	349
	公	372
	功	522
	劫	529
	効	535
	勾	568
	厚	651
	口	685
	叩	693
	后	696
	向	704
	喉	712
	坑	854
	垢	987
	塙	1008
	壕	1063
	好	1108
	孔	1180
	孝	1282
	宏	1289
	尻	1314
	岬	1407
	岡	1458
	工	1460
	巧	1532
	巷	1533
	幌	1543
	幸	1577
	広	1595
	庚	1604
	康	1609
		1621
	弘	1682
	後	1742
	衡	1775
	恰	1838
	恒	1849
	慌	1917
	抗	2091
	拘	2123
	拷	2142
	控	2202
	攪	2322
	攻	2331
	更	2422
	昂	2447
	晃	2458
	杭	2583
	桁	2656
	格	2668
	校	2669
	梗	2698
	構	2823
	江	3045
	洪	3123
	浩	3147
	港	3242
	溝	3275
	甲	3725
	皇	3870
	皐	3873
	硬	4008
	稿	4166
	糠	4424
	紅	4441
	紘	4445
	絞	4485
	綱	4525
	縞	4569
	考	4697
	耗	4709
	耕	4710
	肴	4767
	肱	4770
	肯	4771
	腔	4826
	膏	4860
	興	4913
	航	4933
	荒	5034
	薨	5234
	虹	5279
	蛤	5312
	行	5419
	裕	5449
	講	5689
	貢	5772

ON-KUN INDEX

-kyaku	脚	4820
kyahan	脚絆	4820.11
kyan	俠	213
kyatatsu	脚立	4820.5
kyatsu	彼奴	1732.5
KYO	去	665
	嘘	885
	居	1416
	巨	1534
	拒	2084
	拠	2113
	挙	2150
	据	2195
	渠	3230
	虚	5269
	裾	5474
	許	5569
	距	5866
	鋸	6297
KYŌ	亨	91
	亨	92
	京	93
	佼	175
	供	195
	俠	213
	僑	307
	兄	344
	兜	347
	共	373
	凶	442
	劫	529
	匡	587
	協	617
	卿	643
	叶	689
	叫	708
	向	712
	喬	841
	境	1085
	峡	1465
	強	1695
	彊	1702
	怯	1816
	恭	1845
	恐	1853
	慶	1967
	挟	2146
	教	2345
	敬	2351
	杏	2554
	校	2669
	梗	2698
	橋	2879
	橿	2889
	況	3086

	狂	3562
	狭	3572
	矯	3984
	競	4244
	経	4473
	脅	4803
	脇	4807
	胸	4811
	興	4913
	茎	4991
	喬	5197
	裕	5449
	郷	6145
	鏡	6341
	響	6610
	頬	6637
	饗	6715
	驚	6774
kyō	今日	112.4
-kyō	強	1695
	狂	3562
kyōgaru	興	4913
kyōjiru	興	4913
KYOKU	局	1412
	旭	2416
	曲	2418
	極	2753
kyōsuru	供	195
	狂	3562
	饗	6715
kyōzuru	興	4913
KYŪ	丘	19
	久	47
	九	57
	仇	106
	休	142
	厩	660
	及	670
	吸	713
	宮	1336
	弓	1678
	急	1823
	扱	2070
	救	2344
	旧	2412
	朽	2545
	求	3036
	汲	3064
	泣	3104
	灸	3399
	玖	3621
	球	3643
	究	4189
	窮	4212
	笈	4249

	級	4437
	絆	4438
	給	4489
	白	4907
	鞠	6589
	韮	6605
	鳩	6936
kyū na	急	1823
kyū ni	急	1823
kyūri	胡瓜	4792.5
kyūsuru	休	142
	窮	4212
	給	4489

— M —

MA	摩	2264
	磨	4045
	馬	6725
	魔	6843
	麻	7040
ma	目	3906
	間	6391
ma-	真	3926
mabara na	疎	3776
mabataki	瞬	3969
mabataku	瞬	3969
maboroshi	幻	1598
mabureru	塗	1074
mabusu	塗	1074
machi	街	1759
	町	3729
machiagumu	待	1741
mada	未	2535
madara	斑	2371
made	迄	6013
made ni	迄	6013
mado	窓	4201
madoi	惑	1892
madoka na	円	385
madoki ni		
madou	惑	1892
madowakasu	惑	1892
madowasu	惑	1892
mae	前	490

-mae	前	490
mae ni	前	490
maga	禍	4102
magai	擬	2307
magari-kuneru	曲	2418
magarinari ni	曲	2418
magaru	曲	2418
magatama	勾玉	568.5
magatta	曲	2418
magau	紛	4452
mageru	曲	2418
magirasu	紛	4452
magirawashii	紛	4452
magirawasu	紛	4452
magiremonai	紛	4452
-magire ni	紛	4452
magireru	紛	4452
mago	孫	1296
magureru	紛	4452
maguro	鮪	6858
MAI	売	990
	埋	1020
	妹	1199
	昧	2444
	枚	2582
	毎	3006
	米	4380
mai	舞	4926
mai-	毎	3006
-mai	枚	2582
maigo	迷子	6037.3
mainai	賂	5799
mairaseru	参詣	666
mairi	詣	5594
mairu	参	666
	哩	805
	詣	5594
mājan	麻雀	7040.11
majieru	交	90
	雑	6507
majime	真面目	3926.9
majinai	呪	764
majinau	呪	764

majirogu 瞬 3969	*mama* 任 136	*marobakasu* 転 5948	3926.5
majiru 交 90	儘 327	*marobasu* 転 5948	*massugu na* 真直 3926.8
混 3204	随 6460	*marobu* 転 5948	*masu* 升 603
錯 6299	飯 6679	*marōdo* 客人 1329.2	増 1088
雑 6507	*mama-* 継 4501	*maroyaka na* 円 385	枡 2587
majiwaru 交 90	*mamashii* 継 4501	*maru* 丸 34	益 3891
makanai 賄 5800	*mame* 忠実 1801.8	円 385	舛 4924
makanau 賄 5800	豆 5735	*maru de* 丸 34	鱒 6921
makaru 罷 4650	*mume-* 豆 5735	*marui* 丸 34	*masuru* 摩 2264
負 5769	*mameyaka na* 忠実 1801.8	円 385	*mata* 亦 88
makaseru 任 136	*mamieru* 見 5522	*marukkoi* 丸 34	俣 202
委 1204	*mamireru* 塗 1074	*marumeru* 丸 34	又 668
makasu 任 136	*mamma* 飯 6679	*masa* 柾 2619	復 1760
委 1204	*mamonaku* 間 6391	*masaki* 柾 2619	股 4772
負 5769	*mamori* 守 1310	*masame* 柾 2619	複 5484
make 負 5769	*mamoru* 守 1310	*masa ni* 将 1379	*matagaru* 跨 5872
makeru 負 5769	護 5715	当 1706	*matagu* 跨 5872
makesaseru 負 5769	MAN 万 7	応 1789	*matamoya* 又 668
maki 巻 1545	慢 1968	方 2389	*mataseru* 待 1741
槇 2818	満 3248	正 2955	*mata shitemo* 又 668
牧 3537	漫 3308	*masaru* 優 334	*matataki* 瞬 3969
薪 5222	蔓 5180	勝 553	*matataku* 瞬 3969
makka 真赤 3926.7	*man-* 満 3248	増 1088	*mata to* 復 1760
makkō 真向 3926.6	*mana-* 愛 1927	*masashiku* 正 2955	*mata wa* 又 668
makkura 真暗 3926.13	*manabi* 学 1294	*maseta* 老成 4696.6	*matchi* 燐寸 3499.3
makkuro na 真黒 3926.11	*manabu* 学 1294	*mashi* 増 1088	*mato* 的 3867
makoto 信 221	*manaita* 胸板 4811.8	*mashi na* 増 1088	*matoi* 纏 4617
実 1324	*manako* 眼 3935	*mashira* 猿 3600	*matomaru* 纏 4617
真 3926	*manazashi* 目差 3906.10	*mashite* 況 3086	*matomatta* 纏 4617
誠 5606	*mane* 真似 3926.6	*massaichū* 真最中 3926.12	*matomeru* 纏 4617
makoto ni 誠 5606	*maneki* 招 2124	*massakari* 真盛 3926.11	*matomo* 正面 2955.9
makoto no 誠 5606	*maneku* 招 2124	*massakasama ni* 真逆様 3926.8	*matou* 絡 4484
makotoshiyakana 誠 5606	*maneru* 真似 3926.6	*massaki* 真先 3926.6	纏 4617
MAKU 幕 1578	*manimani* 随 6460	*massao na* 真青 3926.8	MATSU 抹 2112
膜 4854	随意 6460.13	*masshiro* 真白 3926.5	末 2534
maku 巻 1545	*manoatari* 眼辺 3935.4	*masshōjiki* 真正直 3926.5	沫 3085
捲 2193	*manugareru* 免 361	*masshōmen* 真正面	*matsu* 待 1741
播 2273	*manukareru* 免 361		松 2592
撒 2279	*mappira* 真平 3926.5		*-matsu* 末 2534
蒔 5153	*mappiruma* 真昼間 3926.9		*matsuri* 祭 4092
makura 枕 2589	*mare na* 希 1553		*matsurigoto* 政 2335
makure 捲 2193	稀 4145		*matsurou* 服 4775
makureru 捲 2193	*mari* 鞠 6589		
makuru 捲 2193	*maro* 麿 7044		

ON-KUN INDEX

Reading	Kanji	No.
nuku	抜	2093
	抽	2119
	擢	2303
nukui	温	3246
nukumaru		
	温	3246
nukumeru		
	温	3246
nukumi	温	3246
nukumori		
	温	3246
nukumoru		
	温	3246
nukutoi	温	3246
numa	沼	3091
numerakasu		
	滑	3282
numeri	滑	3282
numeru	滑	3282
nuno	布	1548
nurasu	濡	3365
nureru	濡	3365
nuri	塗	1074
nuru	塗	1074
nusa	幣	1585
nushi	主	38
nusumu	盗	3894
	窃	4195
nusutto	盗人	3894.2
nuu	縫	4550
NYA	若	5007
NYO	女	1173
	如	1178
NYŌ	女	1173
	尿	1410
NYU	嬬	1271
NYŪ	乳	61
	入	366
	柔	2633
nyūmen	煮麺	3437.16

— O —

Reading	Kanji	No.
O	悪	1873
	於	2390
	汚	3047
	烏	3421
	阿	6435
o	尾	1411
	緒	4521
	芋	5000
o-	小	1389
	御	1761
	牡	3536
	雄	6499
ō	凹	444
	央	1140
	奥	1165
	始	1208
	往	1733
	応	1789
	押	2128
	旺	2427
	桜	2664
	横	2854
	欧	2931
	殴	2990
	王	3619
	皇	3870
	翁	4677
	襖	5503
	鴨	6955
	鶯	6994
	鴎	6998
	鷹	7007
	黄	7045
ō-	大	1133
oashi	足	5856
oazuke	預	6625
oba	伯母	158.5
	叔母	677.5
	祖母	4083.5
ōba	大	4083.5
obake	化	580
obashima		
	欄	2914
obi	帯	1563
obieru	怯	1816
obiku	誘	5625
ōbira ni	大	1133
obiru	帯	1563
obiyakasu		
	劫	529
	脅	4803
oboe	覚	5529
oboeru	覚	5529
oboezu	覚	5529
oborakasu		
	溺	3271
oborasu	溺	3271
oboreru	溺	3271
oboshii	覚	5529
obusaru	負	5769
obuu	負	5769
ochi	落	5130
ochi-	落	5130
-ochi	落	5130
ōchi	樗	2841
ochibureru		
	落	5130
ochiiru	陥	6446
ochikochi		
	遠近	6101.6
ochiru	落	5130
ochiudo	落人	5130.2
ochūdo	落人	5130.2
odateru	煽	3469
odayaka	穏	4175
odayakanaranu		
	穏	4175
odokasu	嚇	915
odoke	滑稽	3282.15
odokeru	戯	2041
odomu	沈澱	3069.16
odori	踊	5882
odorokasu		
	驚	6774
odoroku	驚	6774
odorokubeki		
	驚	6774
odoru	跳	5877
	踊	5882
	躍	5921
odoshi	威	1219
odosu	嚇	915
	威	1219
oeru	終	4471
ofukuro	袋	5443
ofuru	古	702
ogakuzu	大鋸屑	
		1133.16
ogamu	拝	2126
ogi	荻	5054
ōgi	扇	2056
oginau	補	5464
ogosokana		
	厳	663
ohako	十八番	
		598.2
oharai	払	2062
ohari	針	6218
ohayō	早	2419
ohitashi	浸	3157
ohiya	冷	419
oi	甥	3719
	老	4696
oi-	追	6042
-oi	追	6042
ōi	多	1127
	蔽	5193
	被	5445
	覆	5517
oibamu	老	4696
oide	出	445
oideninaru		
	出	445
ōinaru	大	1133
	巨	1534
ōi ni	大	1133
oira	俺等	240.12
oiraku	老	4696
oiru	老	4696
ōisa	大	1133
oishii	美味	4660.8
oite	追風	6042.9
oitekebori		
	置	4645
oitekibori		
	置	4645
oji	伯父	158.4
	叔父	677.4
ōji	祖父	4083.4
ojikeru	怖	1817
ojiru	怖	1817
ōjiru	応	1789
oka	丘	19
	岡	1460
	陸	6461
okabo	陸稲	6461.14
okaerinasai		
	帰	1564
okaeshi	返	6020
okagami		
	鏡	6341
okage	陰	6462
okama	男色	3731.6
okamai nashi ni		
	構	2823
okami	女将	1173.10
ōkami	狼	3579
okāsan	母	3005
okashii	可笑	701.10
okasu	侵	218
	犯	3554
	冒	3915
oke	桶	2694
okeru	置	4645
oki	沖	3065
oki-	置	4645
-oki	置	4645
ōkii	大	1133
	巨	1534
okimari	決	3070
okina	翁	4677
ōkini	大	1133
ōkiru	起	5849
ōkisa	大	1133
okitsu	沖	3065

	烈	3420		露	6549	*ryakusu*	略	3755
	裂	5453		魯	6848	*ryakusuru*		
RI	利	466		鷺	7006		略	3755
	吏	706		露	6549	RYO	侶	205
	哩	805	*Ro-*				呂	728
	履	1434	RŌ	労	531		慮	1962
	李	2549		妻	1235		旅	2396
	梨	2697		廊	1622		虜	5273
	犂	3547		弄	1668	RYŌ	両	23
	狸	3578		榔	2766		了	67
	理	3644		楼	2785		亮	95
	璃	3669		浪	3155		令	121
	痢	3810		滝	3273		僚	314
	裏	5462		漏	3307		凌	424
	里	6206		牢	3535		寮	1366
	離	6517		狼	3579		嶺	1517
	鯉	6874		籠	4376		料	2374
RICHI	律	1740		糧	4426		梁	2702
RIKI	力	521		老	4696		椋	2725
-riki	力	521		聾	4745		涼	3198
rikimu	力	521		朗	4802		漁	3309
RIKU	六	371		荊	5403		猟	3587
	陸	6461		郎	6138		療	3842
RIN	倫	246	ROKU	六	371		瞭	3960
	厘	650		瀧	3300		稜	4152
	林	2590		禄	4096		竜	4232
	淋	3194		緑	4528		糧	4523
	燐	3499		肋	4754		綾	4523
	琳	3646		録	6298		良	4954
	臨	4899		陸	6461		苓	4981
	輪	5973		鹿	7017		菱	5092
	鈴	6247		麓	7023		諒	5641
	隣	6484	*rokusuru*				遼	6111
	鱗	6923		録	6298		量	6209
	麟	7028	RON	乱	60		陵	6454
rinne	輪廻	5973.9		論	5646		霊	6532
rissuru	律	1740	*ronjiru*	論	5646		領	6628
risu	栗鼠	2662.13	*ronzuru*	論	5646	RYOKU	力	521
risuru	利	466	*rōsuru*	労	531		緑	4528
RITSU	律	1740		弄	1668	*-ryoku*	力	521
	栗	2662		聾	4745	*ryōsuru*	了	67
	率	3618		妻	1235		領	6628
	立	4223	RU	屢	1431	*ryō to suru*		
	葎	5111		流	3160		了	67
Ritsu	律	1740		琉	3642		諒	5641
rittoru	立	4223		瑠	3673	RYŪ	劉	515
RO	侶	205		留	3750		柳	2629
	呂	728		畧	1056		流	3160
	櫓	2908	RUI	涙	3154		溜	3276
	櫨	2910		累	4469		琉	3642
	炉	3403		類	6647		留	3750
	芦	4975	*-rui*	類	6647		硫	4006
	蕗	5203	*ruisuru*	類	6647		立	4223
	略	5799	RYAKU	掠	2191		竜	4232
	路	5876		暦	2507		笠	4269
				略	3755			

	粒	4392
	隆	6455
-ryū	流	3160

— S —

SA	乍	50
	些	84
	佐	155
	作	167
	叉	669
	唆	803
	嵯	1500
	左	1535
	差	1537
	早	2419
	查	2630
	沙	3063
	搓	3667
	砂	3992
	紗	4446
	茶	5033
	蓑	5143
	裟	5457
	詐	5585
	邪	6135
	鎖	6325
sa	然	3435
sa-	小	1389
	狭	3572
saba	鯖	6883
sabakeru		
	捌	2162
sabaketa		
	捌	2162
sabaki	審	1367
	裁	5454
sabaku	審	1367
	捌	2162
	裁	5454
sabi	寂	1342
	錆	6296
sabireru	淋	3194
	荒	5034
sabiru	寂	1342
	錆	6296
sabishigaru		
	寂	1342
sabishii	寂	1342
	淋	3194
sachi	幸	1595
sadakana		
	定	1323
sadamari		
	定	1323

sadamaru			財	5773	崎	1485	*samisen*	三味線
	定	1323	賽	5822	碕	4015		8.8
sadame	定	1323	載	5960	-*saki* 咲	790	*samishii*	寂 1342
sadameru			采	6201	*sakigake*			淋 3194
	定	1323	際	6478	魁	6834	*samma*	秋刀魚
sadameshi			*sai-*	391	*sakimori*			4131.2
	定	1323	再	2492	防人	6429.2	*sampu*	撒布 2279.5
sadamete			-*sai* 才	2059	*saki ni* 先	350	*samugari*	
	定	1323	歳	2962	前	490		寒 1350
saegiru	遮	6106	祭	4092	*sakinjiru*		*samugaru*	
saga	性	1822	*sainamu*		先	350		寒 1350
	祥	4090	苛	5006	*saki no* 先	350	*samui*	寒 1350
sagari	下	9	*saisuru* 際	6478	*sakinzuru*		*samurai*	侍 192
sagaru	下	9	*saiwai* 幸	1595	先	350		士 1117
sagasu	捜	2168	*saji* 匙	582	*sako* 硲	4004	*samushii*	
	探	2211	*sajiki* 桟敷	2658.15	SAKU 作	167		淋 3194
sageru	下	9	*saka* 坂	985	促	212	SAN	三 8
	提	2237	阪	6428	冊	389		傘 283
sageshimu			*saka-* 酒	6160	削	488		参 666
	蔑	5179	*sakae* 栄	2635	捉	2159		山 1439
sagesumu			*sakaeru* 栄	2635	搾	2251		惨 1896
	蔑	5179	*sakai* 境	1085	数	2353		撰 2277
sagi	鷺	7006	界	3739	昨	2449		散 2352
saguri 探	2211		*sakaki* 榊	2808	柵	2620		杉 2562
saguru 探	2211		*sakan* 壮	974	溯	3272		桟 2658
SAI	偲	266	旺	2427	窄	4197		燦 3498
	債	296	*sakana* 肴	4767	策	4284		珊 3630
	催	298	魚	6845	索	4449		産 3716
	再	391	*sakan na*		朔	4801		算 4316
	切	453	盛	3895	酢	6169		簒 4608
	哉	779	*sakanoboru*		錯	6299		蒜 5144
	塞	1069	溯	3272	*saku* 割	507		蚕 5290
	妻	1200	*sakarau* 逆	6041	咲	790		讃 5729
	宰	1330	*sakaru* 盛	3895	裂	5453		賛 5814
	彩	1718	離	6517	*saku-* 昨	2449		酸 6177
	才	2059	*sakasa* 倒	256	*sakura* 桜	2664		餐 6696
	採	2209	逆	6041	*sakusuru*		-*san* 散	2352
	斎	2368	*sakasama*		策	4284	*sanagara*	
	晒	2461	倒	256	*sama* 様	2821	宛	1319
	最	2492	逆	6041	*samasu* 冷	419	*sanaka ni*	
	栽	2654	*sakashii* 賢	5816	覚	5529	最中	2492.4
	柴	2657	*sakashima*		醒	6185	*sane*	実 1324
	歳	2962	倒	256	*samatage*			核 2660
	殺	2994	逆	6041	妨	1187	*sanjiru*	参 666
	済	3197	*sakashirana*		*samatageru*			散 2352
	災	3400	賢	5816	妨	1187	*sansu*	賛 5814
	犀	3546	*sakazuki* 杯	2586	*samayou*		*sansui*	撒水
	砕	3990	*sake* 酒	6160	迷	6037		2279.4
	砦	4002	鮭	6859	*same* 鮫	6863	*sansuru*	産 3716
	祭	4092	*sakebu* 叫	708	*sameru* 冷	419		算 4316
	粋	4389	*sakeru* 裂	5453	覚	5529	*santaru*	惨 1896
	細	4472	避	6120	醒	6185		燦 3498
	菜	5097	*saki* 先	350	*samidare*		*sanzuru*	参 666
	裁	5454	埼	1028	五月雨			散 2352
	西	5514	岬	1458		77.4	*sao*	竿 4250

星	2452	鐘	6352	趣	5854	淑	3191
晶	2482	障	6479	趨	5855	祝	4085
松	2592	青	6557	酒	6160	縮	4585
梢	2695	鞘	6587	鋳	6280	粛	4747
樟	2851	*shō-* 小	1389	鐘	6352	蹴	5913
橡	2863	*-shō* 床	1608	須	6618	*shuku suru*	
樵	2871	*shōjiru* 生	3715	首	6719	祝	4085
正	2955	請	5645	鰍	6895	*shuku toshite*	
沼	3091	*shokiatari*		SHŪ 主	38	粛	4747
消	3158	暑気中		修	260	*shumoku*	
渉	3190		2484.6	収	675	撞木	2276.4
清	3205	SHOKU 嘱	894	周	768	SHUN 俊	216
湘	3216	埴	1031	囚	937	峻	1475
瀟	3380	属	1430	執	1039	春	2453
焦	3436	拭	2144	宗	1321	瞬	3969
焼	3438	植	2751	就	1401	竣	4238
照	3457	殖	2981	崇	1490	舜	4925
生	3715	燭	3496	州	1529	駿	6754
症	3795	織	4596	愁	1923	*shun* 旬	2415
盛	3895	職	4742	拾	2149	*shutaru* 主	38
省	3916	色	4956	揖	2222	*shūto* 姑	1194
相	3920	蝕	5358	摺	2262	*shūtome* 姑	1194
硝	4007	触	5547	柊	2614	*shu toshite*	
礁	4048	食	6674	栖	2769	主	38
祥	4090	飾	6683	汁	3035	SHUTSU 出	445
秤	4134	*shokuatari*		洲	3120	帥	1559
称	4139	食中	6674.4	渋	3200	SO 塑	1068
章	4235	*shokusuru*		痩	3832	姐	1195
笑	4256	嘱	894	祝	4085	岨	1456
粧	4400	食	6674	秀	4123	所	2054
精	4411	*shosuru* 処	435	秋	4131	措	2190
紹	4465	書	2463	終	4471	曾	2483
縦	4571	著	4643	繍	4600	杵	2581
聖	4727	*shōsuru* 抄	2087	習	4681	柘	2626
肖	4760	称	4139	臭	4901	楚	2771
荘	5031	証	5589	舟	4927	溯	3272
菖	5085	賞	5815	萩	5122	狙	3567
蒸	5163	*shotchū* 始終	1203.11	葺	5125	疏	3775
醮	5177	*shōzuru* 生	3715	蒐	5159	疎	3776
蕉	5191	請	5645	衆	5417	礎	4054
蛸	5330	SHU 主	38	袖	5444	祖	4083
装	5455	修	260	襲	5510	租	4138
裳	5472	取	679	讐	5722	粗	4394
訟	5565	守	1310	蹴	5913	素	4456
詔	5581	手	2060	輯	5976	組	4470
証	5589	朱	2546	週	6070	蘇	5252
詳	5607	柊	2614	酋	6159	訴	5588
請	5645	株	2665	酬	6171	酢	6169
象	5744	殊	2975	醜	6189	阻	6434
賞	5815	狩	3573	鋳	6280	鼠	7078
醤	6192	珠	3637	集	6500	*-So* 蘇	5252
鉦	6246	種	4159	鰍	6895	*So-* 蘇	5252
鐘	6311	腫	4848	鷲	7004	sō 争	69
鍬	6314	衆	5417	夙	1126	倉	255
		諏	5632	SHUKU 宿	1344	僧	300

takaraka ni		弾	1699	但	154
高 6796		玉	3620	単	620
take		珠	3637	嘆	872
丈 5		球	3643	坦	997
岳 1457		霊	6532	担	2121
竹 4246		魂	6835	探	2211
茸 5026	tama-	玉	3620	旦	2411
takeku 猛 3588	tamageru			椴	2772
takeru 猛 3588	魂消	6835.10	檀	2895
長 6379	tamago 卵	632	歎	2947
takeshi 武 2959	tamaki 環	3680	段	2991
taki 滝 3273	tamamono		淡	3202
takigi 薪 5222	賜	5812	湛	3234
tako 凧 434	tama no 偶	274	灘	3391
蛸 5330	適	6107	炭	3413
TAKU 卓 616	tamaranai		短	3982
啄 821	堪	1057	端	4243
宅 1308	tamari 溜	3276	綻	4514
度 1616	tamaru 溜	3276	耽	4721
托 2069	tamasaka		胆	4790
択 2082	偶	274	蛋	5301
拓 2115	適	6107	誕	5640
擢 2303	tamashii		鍛	6318
沢 3062	霊	6532	tan 反	674
濯 3360	会	143	-tan 端	4243
琢 3650	偶	274	tana 店	1613
託 5560	適	6107	棚	2748
鐸 6356	tamatsuki		tanabata	
taku 炊 3405	撞球	2276.11	七夕	3.3
焚 3434	tamau 給	4489	tanagokoro	
takumanai	賜	5812	掌	2200
巧 1533	tamawaru		tane 種	4159
takumanu	給	4489	胤	4786
巧 1533	賜	5812	tanegashima	
takumi 匠 588	tame 溜	3276	種子島	
工 1532	為	3411		4159.3
巧 1533	tame ni 為	3411	tani 渓	3196
takumi na	tameru 溜	3276	谷	5730
巧 1533	矯	3984	tanjiru 嘆	872
takumu 工 1532	貯	5791	tannaru 単	620
takurami	tameshi 例	193	tan ni 単	620
企 135	tamesu 試	5611	tannō 堪能	1057.10
takuramu	験	6758	tanomō 頼	6635
企 135	tami 民	3021	tanomoshii 頼	6635
takushi-ageru	tamotsu 保	222	tanomu 頼	6635
手繰上	tamou 給	4489	tanoshibi	
2060.19	賜	5812	楽	2790
takusuru	tampopo		tanoshibu	
托 2069	蒲公英		楽	2790
託 5560		5156.4	tanoshige na	
takuwae 蓄 5161	tamuke 手向	2060.6	楽	2790
貯 5791	tamukeru		tanoshii 愉	1920
takuwaeru	手向	2060.6	楽	2790
蓄 5161	tamuro 屯	1438		
貯 5791	TAN 丹	36		
tama 丸 34				

tanoshimi	
楽	2790
tanoshimu	
愉	1920
楽	2790
tanuki 狸	3578
tanzuru 嘆	872
弾	1699
taore 倒	256
taoreru 倒	256
taoru 手折	2060.7
taosu 倒	256
tara 鱈	6916
taranai 足	5856
taranu 足	5856
tarasu 垂	999
誑	5619
tarazu 足	5856
tare 垂	999
誰	5642
tareru 垂	999
tarinai 足	5856
tarinasu 足	5856
tariru 足	5856
taru 樽	2875
足	5856
tarumeru 弛	1684
tarumu 弛	1684
tashi 足	5856
tashika 確	4039
tashika ni	
確	4039
tashika niwa	
確	4039
tashikameru	
確	4039
tasogare	
黄昏	7045.8
tasshi 達	6088
tasshinai	
達	6088
tassuru 達	6088
tasu 足	5856
tasukaru 助	530
tasuke 助	530
tasukeru 助	530
扶	2089
援	2230
輔	5964
tataeru 湛	3234
称	4139
tatakai 戦	2037
tatakau 戦	2037
闘	6418

杜 2560	納 4453	留 3750	*toki niwa*	
渡 3247	統 4487	駐 6745		時 2462
登 3862	萄 5075		*toki to shite*	
菟 5077	董 5118	椴松 2772.8		時 2462
賭 5819	蕩 5198	*todome* 止 2954	*toki toshite*	
途 6057	藤 5241	*todomeru*		時 2462
都 6148	討 5561	停 273	*tokimeku*	
鍍 6312	読 5629	止 2954		時 2462
to 十 598	膽 5685	留 3750	*tokinaranu*	
砥 3997	豆 5735	*todoroku*		時 2462
-to 人 99	踏 5889	轟 5991	*tokishimo*	
tō 丁 2	逃 6038	*toga* 科 4130		時 2462
倒 256	逗 6053	*togarakasu*	*tokishimoare*	
党 363	透 6059	尖 1393		時 2462
兜 364	通 6063	*togarasu*	*tokitama*	
冬 410	鐙 6348	尖 1393		時 2462
凍 427	闘 6418	*togari* 尖 1393	*tokkakaru*	
刀 448	陶 6459	*togaru* 尖 1393		取掛 679.11
到 477	頭 6639	*toge* 刺 480	*tokku kara*	
吋 703	騰 6767	*tōge* 峠 1464		疾 3797
唐 812	*tō* 十唐 598	*togeru* 逐 6056	*tokku ni* 疾 3797	
塔 1052	*Tō-* 十唐 812	遂 6084	*toko* 床 1608	
塘 1066	*tō-* 当 1706	*togi* 伽 159	所 2054	
套 1161	遠 6101	*togu* 研 3991	*toko-* 常 1569	
宕 1316	*tobari* 帳 1568	磨 4045	*tokō* 左右 1535.5	
島 1476	幌 1577	*toi* 問 830	*tokoro* 処 435	
当 1706	幕 1578	樋 2816	所 2054	
悼 1891	*tobasu* 飛 6672	*tōi* 遠 6101	*tokoro de*	
憧 1982	*tobi* 鳶 6938	*to ieba* 言 5552	所 2054	
投 2095	*tobira* 扉 2058	*toji* 綴 4526	*tokoro ga*	
搭 2228	*toboru* 点 3412	*tōji* 杜氏 2560.4	所 2054	
撞 2276	*toboshi abura*	*tojiru* 綴 4526	*tokoshie* 永久 3031.3	
東 2596	灯油 3395.8	閉 6385	*tokoshie ni*	
桐 2655	*toboshii*	*tōjiru* 投 2095		長 6379
桃 2663	乏 46	*tōka* 十日 598.4	TOKU 匿 591	
桶 2694	*toboso* 枢 2588	*tōkarazu*	得 1755	
棟 2747	*tobosu* 点 3412	遠 6101	徳 1767	
樋 2816	*tobu* 跳 5877	*tōkarazu shite*	瀆 3373	
檮 2897	飛 6672	遠 6101	特 3541	
沓 3060	*toburai* 弔 1680	*tokasu* 溶 3277	督 3946	
洞 3125	*toburau* 弔 1680	融 5371	禿 4122	
淘 3187	訪 5571	解 5548	篤 4342	
湯 3245	*tochi* 栃 2613	鎔 6327	読 5629	
濤 3361	橡 2863	*tokei* 時計 2462.9	*toku* 溶 3277	
灯 3395	*todokōri*	*tokeru* 溶 3277	疾 3797	
痘 3813	滞 3280	融 5371	解 5548	
登 3862	*todokōru*	解 5548	説 5627	
盗 3894	滞 3280	鎔 6327	釈 6203	
禱 4114	*todoke* 届 1413	*toki* 斎 2368	*tōku* 遠 6101	
稲 4158	*todokeru*	時 2462	*toku ni* 特 3541	
筒 4283	届 1413	鯨波 6886.8	*tokusuru*	
答 4285	*todoku* 届 1413	鴾 6943		得 1755
等 4287	*todomaru*	*toki ni* 時 2462		督 3946
糖 4420	停 273	*toki ni totte*	*toku to* 篤 4342	
	止 2954	時 2462	*toma* 苫 5003	

ON-KUN INDEX

tomare 止 2954
tomari 止 2954 / 泊 3099
tomaru 停 273 / 止 2954 / 泊 3099 / 留 3750
tomasu 鳶 1349
tombi 鳶 6938
tome 止 2954 / 留 3750 / 富 1349
tomeru 止 2954 / 泊 3099 / 留 3750
tomi 富 1349
tomi ni 頓 6623
tomo 伴 157 / 供 195 / 侶 205 / 共 373 / 友 672
tomoe 巴 1541
tomogara 輩 5971
tomokakumo 左右 1535.5
tomonau 伴 157
tomo ni 倶 245 / 共 373
tomo ni suru 共 373
tōmorokoshi 玉蜀黍 3620.13
tomoru 点 3412
tomoshibi 灯 3395
tomoshii 乏 46
tomosu 点 3412
tomu 富 1349
tomurai 弔 1680 / 葬 5128
tomurau 弔 1680 / 葬 5128
TON 噸 910 / 団 940 / 屯 1438 / 惇 1887 / 敦 2349 / 沌 3054 / 豚 5743 / 遁 6087 / 頓 6623

tonaeru 唱 829 / 称 4139
tonari 隣 6484
tonaru 隣 6484
tōnasu 南瓜 619.5
tonda 飛 6672
tondemonai 飛 6672
tongarakaru 尖 1393
tongarasu 尖 1393
tongari 尖 1393
tongaru 尖 1393
tonikakuni 左右 1535.5
tono 殿 3001
tō no 当 1706
tonoi 宿直 1344.8
tonomo 外面 1125.9
ton to 頓 6623
ton'ya 問屋 830.9
tora 寅 1341 / 虎 5265
toraeru 囚 937 / 捉 2159 / 捕 2170
toramaeru 捉 2159 / 捕 2170
torawareru 囚 937 / 捕 2170
toreru 取 679 / 捕 2170 / 採 2209 / 脱 4822
tori 禽 4120 / 酉 6157 / 鳥 6931
tōri 通 6063
toride 砦 4002
toriko 虜 5273
tōrisugari 通 6063
toro 瀞 3380
torobi 火 3394
torokasu 蕩 5198
torokeru 蕩 5198
toru 取 679 / 執 1039 / 把 2083 / 捕 2170 / 採 2209 / 摂 2252 / 撮 2282 / 穫 4180 / 采 6201

tōru 亨 91 / 徹 1771 / 透 6059 / 通 6063
toshi 年 1593 / 歳 2962
tōshi 通 6063
tōshi- 通 6063
tōshi de 通 6063
tōshite 通 6063
tōsu 徹 1771 / 透 6059 / 通 6063
tosuru 賭 5819
tōsuru 党 363
totchimeru 取 679
tōtobu 尊 1386 / 貴 5794
tōtoi 尊 1386 / 貴 5794
to tomo ni 共 373
tōtomu 尊 1386 / 貴 5794
totonoeru 整 2360 / 斉 2366 / 調 5647
totonou 整 2360 / 調 5647
TOTSU 凸 443 / 突 4191
totsugu 嫁 1256
totsukuni 外国 1125.8
totte 取 679
tōtte 通 6063
tottoku 取 679
tottsuki 取付 679.5
tou 問 830 / 訪 5571
tou kara 疾 3797
tou ni 疾 3797
towa 常 1569 / 永 3031
towa ie 言 5552
towa iu monono 言 5552
-towazu 問 830

採 2209 / 摂 2252 / 撮 2282 / 采 6201
toyo- 豊 5737
tōzakara 遠 6101
tōzakeru 遠 6101
tozama 外様 1125.14
tozasu 鎖 6325 / 閉 6385
tōzuru 投 2095
TSU 菟 5077 / 通 6063 / 都 6148
tsu 津 3122
TSŪ 痛 3814 / 通 6063
-tsū 通 6063
tsuba 唾 826 / 鍔 6313
tsubaki 唾 826 / 椿 2782
tsubakura 燕 3489
tsubakuro 燕 3489
tsubame 燕 3489
tsubasa 翼 4692
tsubo 坪 998 / 壷 1034 / 歩 2958
tsubomaru 窄 4197
tsubomeru 窄 4197
tsubomu 窄 4197
tsubone 局 1412
tsubu 粒 4392
tsubura na 円 385
tsubureru 潰 3335
tsubusa ni 備 284 / 具 376 / 悉 1864
tsubusu 潰 3335
tsuchi 土 966 / 地 976 / 椎 2742 / 槌 2767 / 鎚 6310
tsuchikau 培 1032
tsuchinoe 戊 2020

tsuchinoto		東	2559	*-tsuke*	付	124	*tsumaranai*			
	己	1540	柄	2627	*tsukeken*	着剣	3938.10		詰	5609
tsudoi	集	6500	*tsukaeru*	事	71	*tsukeru*	付	124	*tsumari*	詰	5609
tsudou	集	6500		仕	123		漬	3301	*tsumaru*	詰	5609
tsue	杖	2555		使	196		点	3412	*tsumasaki*		
tsuga	栂	2618		支	2324		附	6433		爪先	3509.6
tsugaeru	番	3762	*tsukai*	使	196	*tsuketari*			*tsumashii*		
tsugai	番	3762	*tsukai-konasu*				付	124		倹	248
tsūgaru	通	6063		使	196	*tsuki*	付	124		爪楊枝	
tsugau	番	3762	*tsukai suru*				月	2530			3509.13
tsuge	告	744		使	196		槻	2845	*tsumbo*	聾	4745
tsugeru	告	744	*tsukamaeru*			*tsuki-*	突	4191	*tsume*	爪	3509
tsugi	次	2929		捉	2159	*-tsuki*	付	124		詰	5609
	継	4501		捕	2170	*tsukiji*	築地	4343.6	*tsumeru*	詰	5609
tsugi ni	次	2929		掴	2263	*tsukimashite wa*			*tsumetai*		
tsugomori			*tsukamaru*				就	1401		冷	419
	晦	2478		捉	2159	*tsukinami*			*tsumi*	積	4176
tsugu	亜	81		捕	2170		月次	2530.6		罪	4644
	嗣	868		掴	2263	*tsukiru*	尽	1408	*tsumi suru*		
	接	2213	*tsukamaseru*			*tsukiyama*				罪	4644
	次	2929		掴	2263		築山	4343.3	*tsumigoe*		
	注	3103	*tsukamatsuru*			*tsuku*	付	124		堆肥	1035.8
	継	4501		仕	123		即	633	*tsumori*	積	4176
tsugunau			*tsukami*	掴	2263		吐	709		心算	1780.14
	償	333	*tsukamu*	掴	2263		就	1401	*tsumoru*	積	4176
TSUI	墜	1082	*tsukaneru*				衝	1772	*tsumu*	摘	2266
	椎	2742		束	2559		撞	2276		積	4176
	槌	2767	*tsukarakasu*				点	3412		紡錘	4450.16
	追	6042		疲	3796		着	3938		詰	5609
	鎚	6310	*tsukarasu*				突	4191	*tsumugi*	紬	4462
tsui	対	1375		疲	3796		附	6433	*tsumugu*		
tsuibamu			*tsukareru*			*tsukuda*	佃	151		紡	4450
	啄	821		疲	3796	*tsukue*	机	2543	*tsumuji*	旋毛	2400.4
tsuide	尋	1385	*tsukaru*	浸	3157	*tsukuri*	作	167	*tsumuri*	頭	6639
	序	1607		漬	3301		造	6061	*tsun-*	突	4191
	次	2929	*tsukasa*	司	698	*tsukurou*			*tsuna*	索	4449
tsuide ni	序	1607		台	699		繕	4594		綱	4525
tsuie	弊	1670		坊	986	*tsukuru*	作	167	*tsunagaru*		
	費	5786		官	1322		造	6061		繋	4601
tsuieru	潰	3335		寮	1366	*Tsukushi*			*tsunagi*	繋	4601
	費	5786		府	1611		筑紫	4280.12	*tsunagu*	繋	4601
tsuiji	築地	4343.6		監	3901	*tsukusu*	尽	1408	*tsune*	常	1569
tsui ni	終	4471		省	3916		悉	1864	*tsune ni*	常	1569
	遂	6084		署	4643	*tsuma*	夫	1136		恒	1849
tsuitachi				職	4742		妻	1200	*tsune no*	常	1569
	一日	1.4	*tsukasadoru*				端	4243	*tsunenaranu*		
	朔	4801		司	698	*tsumabiraka*				常	1569
tsuite wa				掌	2200		審	1367	*tsuno*	角	5543
	就	1401	*tsukau*	使	196	*tsumabirakana*			*tsunogumu*		
tsuiyasu	費	5786		遣	6100		詳	5607		角	5543
tsuji	辻	6012	*tsukawasu*			*tsumami*			*tsunoru*	募	551
tsūji	通	6063		使	196		撮	2282	*tsura*	面	6566
tsūjiru	通	6063		遣	6100	*tsumamu*	摘	2266	*tsurai*	辛	5996
tsūjite	通	6063	*tsuke*	付	124		撮	2282	*tsuramaeru*		
tsuka	塚	1048	*tsuke-*	付	124					捉	2159

— U —

Reading	Kanji	No.
	遣	6100
yasa-	優	334
yasashige na	優	334
yasashii	優	334
yaseru	痩	3832
yashiki	邸	6134
yashinai	養	6691
yashinau	養	6691
yashiro	社	4065
yasu	安	1311
yasui	安	1311
	廉	1634
	易	2432
	靖	6559
-yasui	易	2432
yasumaru	休	142
	安	1311
yasumaseru	休	142
yasumeru	休	142
yasumi	休	142
yasumu	休	142
yasunjiru	安	1311
yasunzuru	安	1311
yasupika	安	1311
yasuppoi	安	1311
yasurakana	安	1311
yasurau	休	142
	安	1311
yatoi	雇	6497
yatou	傭	295
	雇	6497
yatsu	八	369
	奴	1174
yatsusu	扮	2080
yattsu	八	369
yawai	柔	2633
yawara	柔	2633
yawarageru	和	770
	柔	2633
yawaragu	和	770
	柔	2633
yawarakai	柔	2633
	軟	5947
yawarakan	柔	2633
yayamosureba	動	549
yayatomosureba	動	549
yayoi	弥生	1689.5
YO	与	6
	予	68
	余	168
	誉	5602
	輿	5983
	預	6625
yo	世	20
	代	125
	四	938
YŌ	傭	295
	厭	662
	妖	1190
	容	1335
	幼	1599
	庸	1624
	揺	2235
	揚	2236
	擁	2294
	曜	2522
	桶	2694
	楊	2784
	様	2821
	洋	3130
	涌	3150
	溶	3277
	瑛	3647
	用	3721
	窯	4210
	羊	4658
	耀	4695
	腰	4850
	葉	5129
	蓉	5135
	蠅	5394
	要	5515
	謡	5666
	踊	5882
	遙	6097
	鎔	6327
	陽	6470
	養	6691
	鷹	7007
yō-	洋	3130
-yō	用	3721
-yobawari suru	呼	769
yobawaru	呼	769
yobu	呼	769
	喚	852
yodo	淀	3182
	澱	3347
yōdo	沃度	3061.9
yodomu	淀	3182
	澱	3347
yogiru	過	6090
yogore	汚	3047
yogoreru	汚	3047
yogoreta	汚	3047
yogosu	汚	3047
yoi	佳	194
	可	701
	善	859
	好	1180
	宜	1317
	宵	1334
	良	4954
	酔	6166
yoidore	酔	6166
yōka	八日	369.4
yōkan	羊羹	4658.19
-yoke	除	6449
yokeru	避	6120
yokka	四日	938.4
yoko	横	2854
yokoshima	邪	6135
yōkoso	善	859
yokosu	寄	1345
	遣	6100
yokotaeru	横	2854
yokotawaru	横	2854
YOKU	抑	2090
	欲	2936
	沃	3061
	浴	3153
	翌	4679
	翼	4692
	能	4809
yoku	克	354
	能	4809
yoku suru	善	859
	良	4954
yokusuru	浴	3153
	能	4809
yome	嫁	1256
yomeru	読	5629
yomi	読	5629
	黄泉	7045.9
yomide	読	5629
	蘇	5252
yomigaeri	蘇	5252
yomigaeru	蘇	5252
yomi-konasu	読	5629
yomisuru	嘉	887
yomo	四方	938.4
yomogi	蓬	5157
yomosugara	夜	1129
	終夜	4471.8
yomu	訓	5562
	詠	5584
	読	5629
yon	四	938
yō na	様	2821
yone	米	4380
yō ni	様	2821
	陽	6470
yo no	余	168
yopparau	酔	6166
yoreru	撚	2278
yori	寄	1345
	撚	2278
-yori	寄	1345
yoroi	甲	3725
	鎧	6324
yorokobashii	喜	858
	悦	1868
yorokobasu	喜	858
yorokobi	喜	858
	悦	1868
	歓	2948
yorokobu	喜	858
	悦	1868
	慶	1967
	欣	2930
	歓	2948
Yōroppa	欧羅巴	2931.19
yoroshiku	宜	1317
yorou	鎧	6324

zasuru	座	1619	*zeni*	銭	6264		賊	5801	ZUI	瑞	3665
ZATSU	雑	6507					鏃	6336		蕊	5188
zatsu na				善悪	859.11	*zokuppoi*				随	6460
	雑	6507	*zessuru*	絶	4490		俗	220		髄	6791
zawameku			ZETSU	絶	4490	*zokusu*	属	1430	*-zuke*	付	124
	騒	6760		舌	4917	*zokusuru*			*-zuki*	付	124
zawatsuku			ZŌ	像	308		属	1430		好	1180
	騒	6760		嘈	889		賊	5801	*zuku*	銑	6263
ZE	是	2451		増	1088	*-zome*	染	2636	*-zuku*	就	1401
ZEI	税	4146		憎	1969	*zomeku*	騒	6760	*-zuku de*	尽	1408
	脆	4800		曹	2477	ZON	存	1284	*-zukuri*	造	6061
	説	5627		篠	4352		鱒	6921	*-zukushi*	尽	1408
ZEN	全	145		臓	4886	*zonjiru*	存	1284	*-zume*	詰	5609
	前	490		蔵	5182	*zonzai*	粗略	4394.11	*-zumi*	済	3197
	善	859		象	5744	*zonzuru*	存	1284		積	4176
	漸	3305		贈	5827	*zōri*	草履	5032.15	*-zure*	擦	2306
	然	3435		造	6061	*zōsuru*	蔵	5182	*zūtai*	図体	947.7
	禅	4104		雑	6507	ZU	厨	657	*-zutai ni*	伝	141
	繕	4594	*-zō*	蔵	5182		図	947	*-zutsu*	宛	1319
	膳	4873	ZOKU	俗	220		杜	2560	*-zuyoi*	強	1695
zen-	全	145		属	1430		豆	5735	*zuzu*	数珠	2353.10
	前	490		族	2399		途	6057		珠数	3637.13
-zen	前	490		粟	4403		頭	6639	*zūzūshii*		
	然	3435		続	4500	*-zu*	不	13		図図	947.7

One of the innovative features of this dictionary inherited from the revised Nelson's character dictionary is the **Universal Radical Index**, which allows character look-ups based on virtually any reasonable radical element found in the character. Aimed primarily at the novice user, but useful to anyone frustrated by obscure radicals and difficult-to-remember 'radical priorities,' the URI lists characters (including characters which consist of one and only one radical) under multiple alternative radicals and plausible miscounts of residual strokes. To further facilitate look-ups, three nonce radicals "frequently recurring graphical elements that do not have official status" have been added to the traditional 214 radicals. These three have been added at the end of the traditional list and consist of Rad. 301 ク *kana ku*, Rad. 302 マ *kana ma*, and Rad. 303 *santengammuri*, (as in the three dots on top of characters such as 覚 and 巣); the numbering serves to clearly distinguish these three as artificial classifiers.

Using the URI requires the reader to identify a salient radical or radical-like element in a character and to count the residual strokes as if doing a traditional character look-up. Each character is then referenced to the place it occurs in the body of the dictionary, which follows traditional radical and stroke-count order. For example, the character 稲 can be found by five means: Rad. 115 plus 9 residual strokes (its traditional listing), Rad. 2 plus 13 residual strokes, Rad. 87 plus 10 residual strokes, and either Rad. 72 or 73 plus 10 residual strokes. The one-radical character 黒 can be accessed not only via the traditional Rad. 203 plus 0 residual strokes, but also by Rad. 86 plus 7 residual strokes , Rad. 102 plus 6 or 7 residual strokes, Rad. 32 plus 8 or 9 residual strokes, and Rad. 166 plus 4 residual strokes. The URI also facilitates searches in cases where unsuspected traditional radicals might frustrate even the experienced user: 聞 is listed under both Rad. 128 plus 8 residual strokes and also under Rad. 169 plus 6 residual strokes.

Attention to detail and a forgiving attitude toward inexperienced users has resulted in an index in excess of 10,000 individual listings, or roughly four to five for any given character. Certain constraints had to be observed, however, to keep the size (and reasonableness) of the index manageable. Not every horizontal line means a character gets listed under Rad. 1, nor is every vertical considered an occurrence of Rad. 2. Attention has also been paid to the relative prominence of radicals and the likelihood of their being recmnized as such. Thus, while Rad. 120 characters are never crosslisted under Rad. 52, Rad. 95 characters consl stently are.

For each entry the JIS code and the Morohashi index number have been given, together with the Nelson number. Each entry includes the JIS code prefixed with J, and the Morohashi index number with M. For example, the entry 立 is followed by $\frac{J4267}{M38703}$ 2610.

In general, the compilation of the index has followed these conventions:

· Use of single-stroke radicals has been limited to cases where the radical either does not touch any other element in the character or extends all the way through the character. Despite these constraints, many hundreds of characters can be located by keying to these simple radicals.

· Characters containing radicals which overlap completely or nearly completely in form with another radical (cf. Rad. 22 & Rad. 23; Rad. 72 & 73; Rad 74 &

130) are usually listed under both possible radicals in the index.

· Characters listed in the index under their traditional "correct" radical have **bold** Nelson numbers.

· Within each radical group in the index, subheadings for residual stroke counts (see Appendix 6) have been provided, with characters listed in Nelson number order under these subheadings. In some cases, a range of residual stroke counts has been combined into a single subgrouping. Here, too, Nelson number order is used within the subgrouping.

Rad. 1 一

0 residual stroke

一	J306c / M1	**1**

1 residual strokes

丁	J437a / M2	**2**
七	J3c37 / M6	**3**
二	J4673 / M247	72
十	J3d3d / M2695	598

2 residual strokes

丈	J3e66 / M11	**5**
与	J4d3f / M20	**6**
万	J4b7c / M10	**7**
三	J3b30 / M12	**8**
下	J323c / M14	**9**
上	J3665 / M13	**10**
千	J4046 / M2697	599
土	J455a / M4867	966
士	J3b4e / M5638	1117
大	J4267 / M5831	1133
女	J3d77 / M6036	1173
子	J3b52 / M6930	1281
寸	J4023 / M7411	1372
工	J3929 / M8714	1532
干	J3433 / M9165	1589

廿	J467b / M9586	1662
才	J3a4d / M11769	2059

3 residual strokes

与	J4d3f / M20	**6**
丑	J312f / M23	**12**
不	J4954 / M19	**13**
世	J4024 / M31	**20**
丞	J3e67 / M40	**22**
丹	J4330 / M99	36
云	J313e / M254	74
互	J385f / M255	75
井	J3066 / M258	76
五	J385e / M257	77
元	J3835 / M1340	343
六	J4f3b / M1453	371
升	J3e23 / M2702	603
午	J3861 / M2703	604
友	J4d27 / M3119	672
壬	J3f51 / M5639	968
夫	J4957 / M5835	1136
太	J4240 / M5834	1137
天	J4537 / M5833	1138
尤	J4c60 / M7543	1399
廿	J467b / M9586	1662
弓	J355d / M9692	1678
尸	J304d / M11696	2048
手	J3c6a / M11768	2060

木	J4c5a / M14415	2531
止	J3b5f / M16253	2954
氏	J3b61 / M17026	3020
牛	J356d / M19922	3532
王	J3226 / M20823	3619
瓦	J3424 / M21438	3690
甘	J3445 / M21643	3710

4 residual strokes

丏	J5022 / M22	**11**
丑	J312f / M23	**12**
丙	J4a3a / M16	**16**
且	J336e / M29	**17**
丕	J5022 / M30	**18**
丘	J3556 / M33	**19**
世	J4024 / M31	**20**
丞	J3e67 / M40	**22**
丼	J5027 / M101	37
乎	J3843 / M131	49
互	J385f / M255	75
五	J385e / M257	77
令	J4e61 / M387	121
兮	J5142 / M1455	370
冉	J5147 / M1514	388
冊	J3a7d / M1515	389
册	J5146 / M1516	390
写	J3c4c / M1570	400
弁	J5243 / M2706	606

半	J483e / M2707	608
叮	J525a / M3244	690
号	J3966 / M3256	692
右	J3126 / M3250	700
可	J3244 / M3245	701
央	J317b / M5040	1140
失	J3c3a / M5844	1141
孕	J5554 / M6938	1283
巧	J3a38 / M8721	1533
左	J3a38 / M8720	1535
平	J4a3f / M9167	1590
厅	J4423 / M9223	1603
弁	J4a5b / M9588	1663
弁	J4a5b / M9588	1664
弁	J4a5b / M9588	1665
弁	J4a5b / M9588	1666
弐	J5031 / M9661	1673
弓	J355d / M9692	1678
打	J4247 / M11781	2063
旦	J4336 / M13734	2411
末	J4b76 / M14420	2534
未	J4c24 / M14419	2535
本	J4b5c / M14421	2536
正	J4035 / M16255	2955
毋	J5d59 / M16721	3004
母	J4a6c / M16723	3005
氏	J3b61 / M17026	3020
民	J4c31 / M17028	3021
汀	J4475 / M17103	3034

牙	J3267 / M19909	3531
玉	J4c70 / M20821	3620
瓦	J3424 / M21438	3690
甘	J3445 / M21643	3710
生	J4038 / M21670	3715
皿	J3b2e / M22941	3885
矢	J4c70 / M23929	3976
石	J4050 / M24024	3985
示	J3c28 / M24623	4060
立	J4e29 / M25721	4223
迂	J312a / M38722	6016

5 residual strokes

且	J336e / M29	**17**
世	J4024 / M31	**20**
丞	J3e67 / M40	**22**
両	J4e3e / M46	**23**
争	J4168 / M236	69
亘	J4f4b / M262	79
互	J4f4a / M265	80
光	J483d / M1923	349
先	J4068 / M1349	350
共	J3626 / M1458	373
再	J3a46 / M1524	391
写	J3c4c / M1570	400
号	J3966 / M3256	692
吏	J4d79 / M3299	706
合	J3967 / M3287	715

Rad.1: 5 residual strokes

	J	M	No.
同	J4631	M3294	717
在	J3a5f	M4881	975
妄	J4c51	M6063	1177
存	J4238	M6943	1284
字	J3b7a	M6942	1285
宇	J3127	M7067	1309
巧	J392a	M8721	1533
弐	J4675	M-X	1675
式	J3c30	M9663	1676
戎	J3d3f	M11539	2024
朽	J3560	M14439	2545
朱	J3c6b	M14424	2546
死	J3b60	M16365	2968
母	J4a6c	M16723	3005
毎	J4b68	M16724	3006
民	J4c31	M17028	3021
気	J3524	M17046	3025
求	J3561	M17105	3036
汚	J3178	M17133	3047
灯	J4574	M18855	3395
百	J4934	M22679	3864
羊	J4d53	M28425	4658
而	J3c29	M28871	4704
耳	J3c2a	M28899	4715
至	J3b6a	M30142	4903
舌	J4065	M30277	4917
舟	J3d2e	M30350	4927
血	J376c	M33964	6411
行	J3954	M34029	5419
西	J403e	M34763	5514
迂	J312a	M38722	6016

6 residual strokes

	J	M	No.
両	J4e3e	M46	23

	J	M	No.
亘	J4f4b	M262	79
亙	J4f4a	M265	80
亜	J3021	M272	81
但	J4322	M495	154
伺	J3b47	M483	156
克	J396e	M1355	354
兵	J4a3c	M1462	374
冷	J4e64	M1622	419
励	J4e65	M2326	528
司	J3b4a	M3257	698
吾	J3863	M3379	733
呑	J465d	M3329	737
吟	J3633	M3330	740
呉	J3862	M3365	741
否	J485d	M3340	742
含	J345e	M3350	743
囲	J304f	M4722	945
坐	J3a41	M4931	978
夷	J3050	M5852	1143
宏	J3928	M7086	1314
完	J3430	M7079	1315
寿	J3c77	M7419	1374
弄	J4f2e	M9596	1668
形	J3741	M9969	1713
扶	J4953	M11840	2089
拔	J4834	M11901	2093
更	J3939	M14283	2422
杇	J3560	M14439	2545
杖	J3e73	M14469	2555
束	J422b	M14480	2559
材	J3a60	M14463	2561
汚	J3178	M17133	3047

6 residual strokes

	J	M	No.
汽	J3525	M17177	3068
甫	J4962	M21706	3722
町	J442e	M21735	3729

	J	M	No.
芦	J3032	M30716	4975
芸	J375d	M30741	4978
表	J493d	M34105	5422
言	J3840	M35205	5552
豆	J4626	M36245	5735
車	J3c56	M38172	5939
辰	J4324	M38682	6006
邸	J4521	M39347	6134
邪	J3c59	M39357	6135
酉	J4653	M39763	6157
釆	J4850	M40115	6202
長	J4439	M41100	6379
阻	J414b	M41593	6434
麦	J477e	M44718	7030

7 residual strokes

	J	M	No.
並	J4a42	M54	24
事	J3b76	M241	71
亜	J3021	M272	81
価	J3241	M628	188
使	J3b48	M573	196
典	J4535	M1473	375
具	J4236	M1473	376
其	J4236	M1472	378
函	J4821	M1826	446
尭	J3646	M-X	614
味	J4c23	M3456	766
命	J4c3f	M3473	767
坦	J4333	M4971	997
垂	J3f62	M5012	999
奈	J4660	M5893	1147
奔	J4b5b	M-X	1148
奉	J4a74	M5894	1149
奇	J3471	M5892	1150

	J	M	No.
姐	J3039	M6172	1195
妹	J4b65	M6138	1199
妻	J3a4a	M6140	1200
宜	J3539	M7111	1317
定	J446a	M7109	1323
実	J3c42	M7124	1324
姐	J413b	M7984	1456
岳	J3359	M8001	1457
岩	J3464	M7985	1461
底	J446c	M9122	1612
征	J402c	M10077	1731
念	J4730	M10390	1800
怡	J4e61	M10461	1812
怖	J495d	M10450	1817
或	J303f	M11563	2030
戻	J4c61	M11707	2051
房	J4b3c	M11714	2053
抹	J4b75	M11926	2112
抵	J4471	M11921	2120
担	J4334	M11941	2121
拝	J4752	M11969	2126
昔	J403e	M13816	2433
昇	J3e3a	M13993	2434
枡	J5b46	M14577	2587
東	J456c	M14499	2596
武	J4027	M16273	2959
毒	J4647	M17235	3007
沫	J4b77	M17235	3085
炉	J4f27	M18902	3403
狙	J4140	M20347	3567
画	J3268	M21739	3733
肴	J3a68	M29322	4767
肱	J394f	M29315	4770
肩	J3826	M29299	4776
苔	J4e6a	M30777	4981

	J	M	No.
苧	J4377	M30798	5000
苛	J3257	M30785	5006
若	J3c63	M30796	5007
表	J493d	M34105	5422
辰	J4324	M38682	6006
郁	J306a	M39371	6136
長	J4439	M41100	6379
雨	J312b	M42210	6518

8 residual strokes

	J	M	No.
乗	J3e68	M153	54
便	J4a58	M659	219
尭	J3646	M-X	614
卑	J485c	M2751	618
垣	J3340	M5060	1009
夷	J3050	M5852	1143
奏	J4155	M5915	1156
始	J3028	M6242	1208
宥	J4d28	M7137	1326
宣	J406b	M7132	1328
専	J406b	M-X	1377
屍	J3b53	M7688	1420
峠	J463d	M8068	1464
峡	J362e	M8068	1465
巻	J342c	M8759	1545
恰	J3366	M10603	1838
悔	J3279	M10617	1848
恒	J3931	M10527	1849
抵	J4471	M11921	2120
挟	J3634	M-X	2146
拳	J377d	M11996	2148
拾	J3c2f	M12014	2149
政	J402f	M13135	2335
昧	J4b66	M13846	2444

Char	Code	M-No.	No.
昼	J436b	M13886	2450
春	J3d55	M13844	2453
柾	J4b6f	M14675	2619
柵	J3a74	M14665	2620
柄	J4a41	M14603	2627
査	J3a3a	M14643	2630
歪	J4f44	M16286	2960
毒	J4647	M16730	3007
洪	J393l	M17402	3123
洞	J4636	M17386	3125
浅	J4075	M17452	3129
海	J3324	M17450	3133
狭	J3639	M20406	3572
玲	J4e68	M20888	3626
珊	J3b39	M20917	3630
甚	J3f53	M21648	3711
発	J482f	M22662	3860
盃	J4756	M22955	3887
研	J3826	M24080	3991
祐	J4d34	M24652	4079
祖	J4144	M24664	4083
胆	J4340	M29354	4790
衿	J365e	M34149	5431
訂	J447b	M35211	5553
計	J3757	M35220	5555
逗	J3f60	M38887	6053
逐	J4360	M38877	6056
重	J3d45	M40132	6207
院	J3121	M41665	6447
面	J4c4c	M42618	6566
革	J3357	M42710	6570
頁	J4a47	M43333	6614

9 residual strokes

Char	Code	M-No.	No.
倫	J4e51	M793	246
検	J3770	M823	248
兼	J3773	M1483	381
冥	J4c3d	M1588	405
唖	J3022	M3743	795
唇	J3f30	M3697	807
圃	J4a60	M4774	954
夏	J3a5e	M5720	1120
套	J4565	M5926	1161
峨	J3265	M8071	1471
峰	J4a76	M8094	1473
峯	J4a77	M8093	1474
島	J4567	M8108	1476
師	J3b55	M8916	1562
帯	J4253	M8929	1563
恵	J3743	M10618	1847
悟	J3867	M10680	1870
扇	J4070	M11743	2056
挙	J3573	M12081	2150
挿	J415e	M12119	2167
振	J3f36	M12093	2171
晋	J3f38	M13899	2455
晃	J3938	M13891	2458
桧	J4930	M-X	2637
栢	J4259	M14714	2638
栩	J4073	M14737	2651
桓	J343c	M14774	2652
栽	J3a5f	M14750	2654
桐	J364d	M14770	2655
泰	J4259	M17325	3098
海	J3324	M17450	3133
涛	J4573	M-X	3138
浜	J494d	M17462	3152
浦	J313a	M17475	3156
烏	J3128	M18998	3421

Char	Code	M-No.	No.
瓶	J4953	M21486	3699
畏	J305a	M21778	3742
畔	J484a	M21801	3746
畢	J492d	M21829	3754
病	J4942	M22127	3798
益	J3157	M22972	3891
真	J3f3f	M23236	3926
砥	J4556	M24093	3997
秦	J3f41	M24995	4133
租	J4145	M24988	4138
笹	J3a7b	M25968	4271
紐	J4933	M2/268	4448
耕	J3943	M28907	4710
朕	J443f	M14361	4797
脊	J4054	M29472	4804
胴	J4639	M29436	4810
莱	J4d69	M-X	5039
莞	J3450	M31063	5052
華	J325a	M31119	5058
蚕	J3b3d	M32869	5290
衰	J3f6a	M34127	5432
袴	J3853	M34236	5448
訊	J3f56	M35243	5559
託	J4277	M35243	5560
討	J4624	M35231	5561
訓	J3731	M35238	5562
記	J352d	M35244	5563
財	J3a62	M36664	5773
辱	J3f2b	M38686	6007
逗	J3f60	M38887	6053
逐	J4360	M38877	6056
郵	J4d39	M39485	6147
酒	J3c72	M39776	6160
釘	J4523	M40159	6217
険	J3831	M41721	6456

Char	Code	M-No.	No.
随	J3f6f	M41764	6460
陰	J3122	M41691	6462

10 residual strokes

Char	Code	M-No.	No.
冨	J495a	M1592	406
副	J497b	M2097	503
唇	J3f30	M3697	807
啄	J-X	M3801	821
唾	J4243	M3785	826
啞	J-X	M3835	827
壷	J445b	M5657	1034
基	J3470	M5197	1040
寅	J4652	M7204	1341
寄	J3473	M7203	1345
崎	J3a6a	M8169	1485
師	J3b55	M8916	1562
得	J4640	M10137	1755
悪	J302d	M10717	1873
振	J3f36	M12093	2171
捷	J3e39	M12216	2198
捧	J4a7b	M12189	2199
捻	J4731	M12222	2201
斜	J3c50	M13509	2376
曹	J4162	M14297	2477
梗	J393c	M14849	2698
淑	J3d4a	M17634	3191
爽	J4156	M4276	3520
琢	J4276	M19746	3640
瓶	J4953	M21486	3699
畏	J305a	M21778	3742
畢	J305b	M21854	3754
異	J305b	M21854	3757
皐	J3b29	M22727	3873
票	J493c	M24694	4089

Char	Code	M-No.	No.
祷	J4578		4093
笥	J3f5a	M25934	4265
笹	J3a7b	M25968	4271
粗	J4146	M26898	4394
組	J4148	M27374	4470
葉	J4d55	M31387	5129
虚	J3575	M32708	5269
袴	J3853	M34236	5448
袷	J3041	M34240	5449
訟	J3e59	M35266	5565
訣	J376d	M35272	5567
許	J3576	M35298	5569
設	J405f	M35293	5570
訪	J4b2c	M35271	5571
訳	J4c75	M35324	5572
貫	J3763	M36699	5789
辱	J3f2b	M38686	6007
遂	J3f6b	M38985	6084
逼	J492f	M38973	6085
遍	J4b29	M39011	6086
道	J463b	M39010	6091
閉	J4a44	M41771	6385
随	J3f6f	M41764	6460
陽	J4d5b	M41725	6470
零	J3c36	M42219	6519
頃	J3a22	M42338	6615
鳥	J443b	M46634	6931

11 residual strokes

Char	Code	M-No.	No.
偉	J304e	M837	285
勝	J3e21	M2409	553
博	J476e	M2761	621
厨	J3f05	M3005	657
喋	J437d	M3917	850

喪 J4153 M3985 853
喧 J3776 M3976 856
善 J4131 M3904 859
塚 J444d M-X 1048
塔 J4563 M5332 1052
場 J3e6c M5278 1058
富 J4959 M7230 1349
寒 J3428 M7239 1350
巽 J4327 M8765 1546
幅 J497d M8995 1574
惹 J3c66 M10866 1886
愉 J4c7c M10905 1920
惰 J4246 M10855 1921
扁 J4070 M11743 2056
捲 J377e M12208 2193
搭 J456b M12508 2228
援 J3167 M12407 2230
揚 J4d48 M12355 2236
敢 J343a M13260 2350
斌 J494c M13468 2369
斯 J3b5b M13563 2386
替 J4258 M14300 2486
普 J4961 M13982 2489
棲 J4033 M14980 2743
棋 J347d M14922 2744
棒 J4b40 M14929 2750
検 J3821 M15065 2752
極 J364b M15181 2753
湊 J4c2c M17822 3226
湛 J4339 M17846 3234
滋 J3c22 M17919 3238
港 J3941 M17783 3242
湿 J3c3e M17920 3243
湯 J4572 M17874 3245
満 J4b7e M17921 3248

減 J383a M17759 3249
滞 J425a M18067 3280
焼 J3e46 M19166 3438
無 J4c35 M19113 3439
牒 J442d M19871 3529
琢 J-X M21058 3650
琴 J3657 M21079 3654
畳 J3e76 M21875 3763
痘 J4577 M22185 3813
登 J4550 M22668 3862
短 J433b M23978 3982
硬 J3945 M24230 4008
稀 J3529 M25058 4145
筒 J457b M26004 4283
答 J457a M26006 4285
紐 J4933 M27268 4448
絵 J3328 M27464 4488
給 J356b M27432 4489
期 J347c M14378 4835
董 J4621 M31433 5118
萱 J337e M31345 5121
葬 J4172 M31448 5128
葉 J4d55 M31387 5129
蒸 J372 M31618 5163
蛤 J3436 M33023 5312
補 J4a64 M34320 5464
覗 J4741 M34839 5528
詫 J4242 M35374 5579
詔 J3e5b M35379 5581
詞 J3b6c M35394 5582
註 J4370 M35340 5583
詐 J3a3e M35373 5585
診 J3f47 M35337 5586
評 J493e M35383 5587
訴 J414a M35325 5588

証 J3e5a M35341 5589
賞 J4c63 M36699 5789
貯 J4379 M36698 5791
貴 J352e M36704 5794
逼 J492f M39010 6085
道 J463b M39010 6091
遣 J382f M39052 6100
量 J4e4c M40138 6209
開 J332b M41223 6393
隔 J3356 M-X 6475
雇 J385b M41976 6497
雄 J4d3a M41972 6499
雲 J3140 M42235 6522
韮 J4723 M43237 6605
項 J3960 M43343 6617

12 residual strokes

喪 J4153 M3985 853
嗣 J3b4c M4109 868
塔 J4563 M5332 1052
塞 J3a49 M5349 1069
廉 J4e77 M9436 1634
愈 J4c7c M10904 1909
感 J3436 M10953 1928
慎 J3f35 M11024 1945
暖 J4348 M14064 2502
暢 J4242 M14095 2506
極 J364b M15181 2753
楢 J424a M15133 2780
椿 J4458 M15090 2782
楊 J4d4c M15112 2784
業 J3648 M15170 2789
溢 J306e M17944 3207
溝 J3942 M17944 3275

滞 J425a M18067 3280
漢 J3441 M18068 3281
潅 J4433 M18216 3287
煩 J4851 M19229 3454
牒 J442d M19871 3529
獅 J3b62 M20606 3599
瑞 J3f70 M21131 3665
睡 J4851 M23448 3948
碕 J3337 M24973 4016
碁 J386b M24261 4020
福 J4a21 M24768 4105
稔 J4c2d M25107 4149
組 J4148 M42374 4470
腫 J3c70 M29697 4848
腸 J4432 M29721 4849
糞 J312c M31661 5143
蔭 J307e M31840 5151
蒙 J4c58 M31555 5154
蒲 J3377 M31611 5156
葦 J3031 M31437 5160
蒼 J4173 M31627 5162
虞 J3673 M32723 5272
詣 J3758 M35412 5594
詫 J372 M35431 5598
該 J333a M35445 5601
誉 J4d40 M35602 5602
詮 J4127 M35435 5604
誇 J3858 M35474 5605
誠 J403f M35497 5606
詳 J3e5c M35497 5607
話 J4f43 M35441 5608
詰 J354a M35440 5609
詩 J3648 M35415 5611
試 J492c M10299 1781
豊 J4b2d M36263 5737

賄 J4f45 M36745 5800
跨 J3859 M37504 5872
践 J4129 M37547 5873
農 J4740 M38688 6008
遺 J382f M39052 6100
鉦 J3e60 M40322 6246
鈴 J4e6b M40267 6247
鉢 J482d M40317 6249
雅 J326d M41973 6505
零 J4e6d M42242 6524
頑 J3468 M43374 6624
飼 J3b74 M44107 6685

13 residual strokes

劃 J3344 M2193 513
喪 J4153 M3985 853
嘘 J3133 M-X 886
寧 J472b M7296 1361
寡 J3249 M7286 1363
旗 J3446 M13687 2402
榎 J315d M15219 2810
榛 J3f3a M15240 2811
樺 J3372 M15497 2817
槙 J4b6a M-X 2819
槍 J4164 M15319 2822
構 J393d M15317 2823
潅 J4433 M18216 3287
漕 J4166 M18131 3306
演 J3069 M18130 **3310**
爾 J3c24 M19750 3521
監 J3446 M23032 3901
端 J433c M25806 4243
箕 J4c27 M26143 4307
絵 J3328 M27464 4488

- 給 J356b / M27432 4489
- 罰 J4833 / M28315 4647
- 肇 J4825 / M29228 4751
- 蓑 J4c2c / M31661 5143
- 蝶 J4433 / M33333 5363
- 該 J333a / M35445 5601
- 誇 J3858 / M35474 5605
- 誌 J3b6f / M35501 5620
- 誓 J4040 / M35514 5622
- 認 J4727 / M35502′ 5623
- 誘 J4d36 / M35525 5625
- 誤 J386d / M35546′ 5626
- 説 J4062 / M35556′ 5627
- 語 J386c / M35533 5628
- 誕 J4342 / M35692′ 5640
- 跨 J3859 / M37504 5872
- 農 J4740 / M38688 6008
- 銅 J463c / M40361 6266
- 閣 J395e / M41301 6397
- 関 J3458 / M41297 6402
- 需 J3c7b / M42275 6528
- 頗 J3f7c / M43415 6627
- 領 J4e4e / M43423 6628
- 飼 J3b74 / M44107′ 6685
- 餅 J4c5f / M44133 6689
- 髪 J4831 / M45387′ 6804
- 魂 J3a32 / M45787 6835
- 鳳 J4b31 / M46671 6937

14 residual strokes

- 舗 J4a5e / M30323′ 322
- 嘘 J-X / M4206 885
- 賚 J4950 / M-X 1365
- 憂 J4d2b / M11170 1971
- 撲 J4b50 / M12755 2274
- 撰 J4071 / M12753 2277
- 撒 J3b35 / M12697 2279
- 撫 J496f / M12743 2281
- 槽 J4165 / M15393 2844
- 槻 J4450 / M15390 2845
- 権 J3822 / M15484 2853
- 横 J3223 / M15484′ 2854
- 澄 J4021 / M18315 3333
- 潰 J4459 / M18281 3335
- 監 J3446 / M23032 3901
- 篇 J4a53 / M26257 4324
- 緬 J4c4b / M27674 4542
- 緩 J344b / M27669 4551
- 翫 J3465 / M28766 4689
- 舞 J4971 / M30342′ 4926
- 蕪 J4973 / M32004 5196
- 蕩 J4622 / M32002 5198
- 蝶 J4433 / M33333 5363
- 誘 J4d36 / M35525 5625
- 諌 J3452 / M35642 5630
- 諏 J3f5b / M35648 5632
- 誼 J3543 / M35605 5634
- 諾 J427a / M35687 5638
- 誹 J4870 / M35601 5639
- 誕 J4342 / M35692′ 5640
- 諒 J4e4a / M35653 5641
- 誰 J432f / M35586 5642
- 談 J434c / M35633 5643
- 課 J325d / M35589 5644
- 請 J4041 / M35640′ 5645
- 論 J4f40 / M35658 5646
- 調 J4434 / M35640′ 5647
- 諸 J3d74 / M35691′ 5648
- 謎 J4666 / M35800 5661
- 諜 J4435 / M35697 5665
- 賦 J496a / M36800 5811
- 賛 J3b3f / M36841 5814
- 輪 J4e58 / M38400 5973
- 還 J3454 / M39174′ 6121
- 鋲 J4946 / M40503 6277
- 震 J3f4c / M42300 6531
- 霊 J4e6e / M42309′ 6532
- 頬 J4b4b / M-X 6629
- 餅 J4c5f / M44133 6689
- 駈 J366f / M44636 6744
- 魅 J4c25 / M45811 6838

15 residual strokes

- 儒 J3c74 / M1220 330
- 叡 J3143 / M3214 683
- 壇 J4345 / M5528 1101
- 彊 J3630 / M9872 1702
- 憂 J4d2b / M11170 1971
- 憾 J3438 / M11312 1999
- 曇 J465e / M14172 2518
- 滋 J3c22 / M17919′ 3238
- 澱 J4543 / M18410 3347
- 濃 J473b / M18442 3349
- 燈 J4575 / M19402 3476
- 獣 J3d43 / M20714′ 3606
- 稽 J-X / M-X 4174
- 窺 J312e / M25633 4215
- 縛 J477b / M27771 4567
- 興 J363d / M30226 4913
- 舞 J4971 / M30342 4926
- 融 J4d3b / M33384 5371
- 覧 J4d77 / M34928 5533
- 諺 J3841 / M-X 5659
- 諮 J3b70 / M35728 5660
- 謎 J4666 / M35800 5661
- 蝶 J4435 / M35697 5665
- 諭 J4d21 / M35727′ 5667
- 輸 J4d22 / M38438′ 5978
- 還 J3454 / M39174′ 6121
- 醗 J4830 / M-X 6182
- 醍 J4269 / M39924 6184
- 錘 J3f6e / M40547 6291
- 鋼 J395d / M40509 6302
- 頭 J462c / M43490 6639
- 麺 J4c4d / M-X 7038

16 residual strokes

- 儲 J4c59 / M-X 331
- 優 J4d25 / M1261 334
- 彊 J3630 / M9872 1702
- 徽 J-X / M10267 1778
- 戴 J4257 / M11685 2045
- 橿 J3360 / M15629 2889
- 檜 J5b58 / M15676 2894
- 檀 J4349 / M15632 2895
- 濃 J473b / M18442 3349
- 濤 J5e39 / M18508 3361
- 濠 J396a / M18502 3363
- 濡 J4728 / M18504 3365
- 濫 J4d74 / M18521 3366
- 犠 J353e / M20190′ 3550
- 糟 J416c / M27104 4423
- 糞 J4a35 / M27102 4425
- 緬 J4c4b / M27674 4542
- 緩 J344b / M27669 4551
- 縮 J3d4c / M27815 4585
- 翼 J4d63 / M28801′ 4692
- 膿 J473f / M29938 4884
- 興 J363d / M30226 4913
- 藍 J4d75 / M32258 5233
- 謄 J4625 / M35780′ 5685
- 謙 J382c / M35821′ 5686
- 講 J3956 / M35824 5689
- 購 J3958 / M36885 5823
- 輿 J4d41 / M38468 5983
- 邇 J6d6e / M39193 6122
- 鍔 J4457 / M40617 6313
- 鮪 J4b6e / M46126 6858

17 residual strokes

- 儲 J-X / M1284 335
- 叢 J4151 / M3220 684
- 彊 J3630 / M9872 1702
- 擾 J3e71 / M12920 2314
- 濫 J4d74 / M18521 3366
- 癒 J4c7e / M22545 3847
- 禰 J4729 / M-X 4116
- 糧 J4e48 / M27132 4426
- 縛 J477b / M27771 4567
- 膿 J473f / M29938 4884
- 藍 J4d75 / M32258 5233
- 藷 J3d73 / M32391 5237
- 藤 J4623 / M32340′ 5241
- 観 J3451 / M34955 5538
- 輿 J4d41 / M38468 5983
- 邇 J6d6e / M39193 6122
- 鍔 J4457 / M40617 6313
- 鎗 J4179 / M40709 6320
- 鎧 J333b / M40735 6324
- 鎌 J3379 / M40693 6326
- 鎮 J4443 / M40745 6328

Red.1: 17 residual strokes

鬪 J462e / M45649° 6418
難 J4671 / M42128° 6515
鞭 J4a5c / M42937 6595
顎 J335c / M43590 6643
驗 J3833 / M44835 6758
騎 J3533 / M44817 6761
髓 J3f71 / M45240° 6791

18 residual strokes

徽 J-X / M10267 1778
曝 J4778 / M14239 2524
檮 J5b6d / M15713 2897
瀬 J4025 / M18672° 3384
爆 J477a / M19540 3505
璽 J3c25 / M21309 3683
燾 J-X / M24852 4114
襧 J-X / M24851 4115
簣 J4876 / M26609 4363
簿 J4a6d / M26623° 4364
簾 J4e7c / M26616 4365
縮 J3d4c / M27815 4585
艷 J3170 / M30632 4957
藷 J-X / M32391 5247
蟻 J3542 / M33672 5397
覇 J4746 / M34790 5519
蹴 J3d33 / M37876 5913
顎 J335c / M43590 6643
顛 J453f / M-X 6652
髓 J3f71 / M45240 6791
鵑 J4c39 / M46963 6974
鷄 J375c / M47074 6980
鯨 J3834 / M-X 7013
麗 J4e6f / M47663 7026

19 residual strokes

瀬 J494e / M18636 3381
艦 J344f / M30571 4950
鐙 J462a / M40904 6348
騰 J462d / M44915° 6767
鰐 J4f4c / M46337 6901
麗 J4e6f / M47663 7026
齡 J4e70 / M48632° 7093

20-24 sresidual strokes

囊 J-X / M4633 933
攬 J5a30 / M13046 2322
艦 J344f / M30571 4950
囊 J4739 / M-X 5499
讚 J3b3e / M36110 5720
鑑 J3455 / M40988 6361
饗 J-X / M44431 6715
鰐 J4f4c / M46337 6901
鷲 J4f49 / M47345 7004
鹹 J-X / M47576 7016

Rad. 2 丨

1 residual stroke

十 J3d3d / M2695 598
卜 J4b4e / M2774 622

2 residual strokes

下 J323c / M14 9
上 J3e65 / M13 10
也 J4c69 / M171 58

千 J4069 / M2697 599
口 J387d / M3227 685
土 J455a / M4867 966
山 J3b33 / M7869 1439
川 J406e / M8673 1526
工 J3929 / M8714 1532
巾 J3652 / M8771 1547
干 J3433 / M9165 1589

3 residual strokes

不 J4954 / M19 13
世 J4024 / M31 20
中 J4366 / M73 **28**
井 J3066 / M258 76
介 J3270 / M359 108
内 J4662 / M1512 386
升 J3e23 / M2702 603
午 J3861 / M2703 604
口 J387d / M3227 685
弔 J4l4c / M9698 1680
引 J307a / M9699 1681
斗 J454d / M13489 2373
斤 J3654 / M13534 2379
日 J467c / M13733 2410
木 J4c5a / M14415 2531
止 J3b5f / M16253 2954
爪 J445e / M19653 3509
牛 J356d / M19922 3532
王 J3226 / M20823 3619
甘 J3445 / M21643 3710

4 residual strokes

且 J336e / M29 17

丘 J3556 / M33 19
世 J4024 / M31 20
主 J3c67 / M100 38
乍 J4663 / M130 50
五 J385e / M257 77
以 J304a / M388 109
内 J4662 / M1512 386
冊 J3a7d / M1515 389
凸 J464c / M1809 443
凹 J317c / M1810 444
出 J3d50 / M1811 445
北 J4b4c / M2574 581
半 J483e / M2707 608
卯 J312c / M2847 628
収 J3c7d / M3128 675
史 J3b4b / M3249 697
四 J3b4d / M4682 938
央 J317b / M5840 1140
巨 J3570 / M8722 1534
市 J3b54 / M8775 1549
平 J4a3f / M9167 1590
弗 J4a26 / M9708 1683
旧 J356c / M13737 2412
未 J4b76 / M14420 2534
末 J4c24 / M14419 2535
本 J4b5c / M14421 2536
正 J4035 / M16255 2955
玉 J364c / M20821 3620
甘 J3445 / M21643 3710
用 J4d51 / M21703 3721
由 J4d33 / M21724 3724
甲 J3943 / M21725 3725
申 J3f3d / M21726 3726
田 J4544 / M21723 3727

皿 J3b2e / M22941 3885
目 J4c5c / M23105 3906

5 residual strokes

且 J336e / M29 17
世 J4024 / M31 20
両 J4e3e / M46 23
仲 J4367 / M403 140
凸 J464c / M1809 443
凹 J317a / M1810° 444
卯 J312c / M2847 628
印 J3075 / M3240 630
叫 J362b / M3240 708
向 J387e / M3301 712
壮 J4154 / M5642 974
在 J3a5f / M4881 975
地 J434f / M4802 976
存 J4238 / M6943 1284
州 J3d23 / M8678 1529
巨 J3570 / M8722 1534
年 J472f / M9168 1593
弗 J4a26 / M9708 1683
曳 J3148 / M14282 2417
曲 J364a / M14280 2418
民 J4c31 / M17028 3021
池 J4353 / M1714T 3042
祁 J3737 / M24634 4063
竹 J435d / M25841 4246
羊 J4d53 / M28425 4658
耳 J3c2a / M28999 4715
白 J3131 / M30173 4907
虫 J436e / M32804 5275
那 J4661 / M39305 6129
邦 J4b2e / M39310 6130

6 residual strokes		
両	J4e3e M46	23
串	J367a M80	**30**
亜	J3021 M272	81
伸	J3f2d M481	163
児	J3b79 M1364	355
凸	J464c M1809	443
凹	J317a M1810	444
判	J483d M1923	465
否	J485d M3340	742
囲	J304f M4722	945
弗	J4a26 M9708	1683
形	J3741 M9969	1713
束	J422b M14480	2559
沖	J322d M17209	3065
状	J3e75 M20257	3556
甫	J4a63 M21706	3722
臣	J3f43 M30068	4894
臼	J3131 M30173	4907
芥	J3329 M30715	4977
車	J3c56 M38172	5939
采	J4850 M40115	6202
長	J4439 M41100	6379
7 residual strokes		
並	J4a42 M54	24
亜	J3021 M272	81
典	J4535 M1474	375
其	J4236 M1472	378
凸	J464c M1809	443
卵	J4d71 M2857	632
咋	J3a70 M3488	751
味	J4c23 M3456	766

坤	J3a25 M4969	996
坪	J445a M4976	998
垂	J3f62 M5012	999
奉	J4a74 M5894	1149
姐	J3039 M6172	1195
妹	J4b65 M6138	1199
宙	J4368 M7108	1318
官	J3431 M7107	1322
屈	J367e M7669	1415
岬	J4c28 M7992	1458
忠	J4369 M10353	1801
抽	J436a M11930	2119
拙	J405b M11965	2122
拝	J4752 M11969	2126
押	J3221 M11929	2128
斉	J4046 M13454	2366
昇	J3e3a M13794	2434
枡	J5b46 M14577	2587
果	J324c M14556	2594
東	J456c M14499	2596
沫	J4b77 M17235	3085
沸	J4a28 M17251	3094
油	J4c7d M17253	3106
画	J3268 M21739	3733
直	J443e M23136	3908
耶	J4c6d M29008	4716
服	J497e M14345	4775
良	J4e49 M30597	4954
追	J4439 M38836	6042
長	J4439 M41100	6379
門	J4c67 M41208	6381
雨	J312b M42210	6518
非	J3773 M42585	6563

8 residual strokes		
乗	J3e68 M153	54
単	J4331 M2752	620
峠	J463d M8068	1464
帥	J3f63 M8886	1559
幽	J4d29 M9205	1600
律	J4a27 M10097	1740
施	J3b5c M13629	2391
昨	J3a72 M13847	2449
歪	J4f44 M16286	2960
段	J434a M16619	2991
洲	J3d27 M17413	3120
津	J4445 M17396	3122
派	J4749 M17428	3126
甚	J3f53 M21648	3711
界	J3326 M21775	3739
矧	J476a M23978	3979
研	J3826 M24080	3991
神	J3f40 M24673	4087
糾	J356a M-X	4438
追	J4449 M38836	6042
重	J3d45 M40132	6207
陥	J3459 M41676	6446
降	J395f M41620	6450
面	J4c4c M42618	6566
飛	J4874 M44000	6672
9 residual strokes		
衷	J436f M-X	**31**
候	J3875 M775	250
兼	J3773 M1483	381
唖	J3022 M3743	795
唐	J4562 M3709	812

将	J3e2d M7437	1379
峰	J4a76 M8094	1473
峯	J4a77 M8093	1474
師	J3b55 M8916	1562
悌	J4470 M10642	1861
挿	J415e M12119	2167
旅	J4e39 M-X	2396
書	J3d71 M14294	2463
涌	J4d30 M17534	3150
浦	J313a M17475	3156
烏	J3128 M18998	3421
瓶	J4953 M21486	3699
畔	J4a34 M21801	3746
畢	J492d M21825	3754
窄	J3a75 M25455	4197
耕	J394c M28907	4710
華	J325a M31119	5058
袖	J4235 M34192	5444
郵	J4d39 M39485	6147
針	J3f4b M40165	6218
馬	J474f M44572	6725
10 residual strokes		
剰	J3e6a M2107	501
壺	J445b M5657	1034
堀	J4b59 M5205	1036
師	J3b55 M8916	1562
庸	J4d47 M9378	1624
患	J3435 M10691	1871
悠	J4d2a M10681	1872
悪	J302d M10717	1873
排	J4753 M12256	2210
断	J4347 M13557	2385
巣	J4163 M8696	2705

梯	J4474 M14881	2706
淵	J4a25 M17692	3237
焔	J316b M-X	3423
瓶	J4953 M21486	3699
笛	J452b M25917	4268
第	J4268 M25943	4272
糾	J356a M-X	4438
紳	J3f42 M27348	4467
粛	J3d4d M29223	4747
菅	J3f7b M31142	5090
雫	J3c36 M42219	6519
11 residual strokes		
偉	J304e M837	285
善	J4431 M3904	859
悲	J4d2a M10720	1897
扉	J4862 M11750	2058
斐	J4865 M13469	2370
棺	J343d M14993	2746
淵	J4a25 M17692	3237
湿	J3c3e M17251	3243
無	J4c35 M19113	3439
痩	J4169 M-X	3806
筆	J4934 M25987	4288
葦	J4e2a M31397	5111
装	J4175 M34283	5455
補	J4a64 M34320	5464
詐	J353a M35373	5585
費	J4871 M26717	5786
軸	J3c34 M38269	5952
酢	J3f5d M39824	6169
開	J332b M41233	6393

12 residual strokes

幽 J4d29 / M9205 1600
廉 J4e77 / M9436 1634
暢 J442a / M14095 2506
椴 J464e / M15075 2772
獅 J3b62 / M20609 3599
睡 J3f67 / M23448 3948
碁 J386b / M24261 4020
紳 J3f42 / M27348 4467
罪 J3a61 / M28293 4644
腫 J3c70 / M29697 4848
蜂 J4b2a / M33088 5331
蝸 J4f39 / M-X 5332
裝 J4175 / M34283 5455
酬 J3d37 / M39850 6171
馴 J466b / M44595 6729
馳 J435a / M44593 6730

13 residual strokes

旗 J347a / M13687 2402
榊 J-X / M15352 2808
漕 J4166 / M18131 3306
爾 J3c24 / M19750 3521
稲 J3070 / M25187 4158
種 J3c6f / M25174 4159
箕 J4c27 / M26143 4307
管 J3449 / M26162 4317
肇 J4825 / M29228 4751
餅 J4c5f / M44133 6689

14 residual strokes

痩 J-X / M22415 3832

舞 J4971 / M30342 4926
蝦 J325c / M33299 5364
輦 J475a / M38398 5971
靈 J4e6e / M42309 6532
餅 J4c5f / M44133 6689

15 residual strokes

舘 J345c / M30326 4923
舞 J4971 / M30342 4926
鎚 J444a / M-X 6281
錘 J3f6e / M40547 6291
鴨 J337b / M46823 6955

16 residual strokes

環 J3444 / M-X 3680
篠 J3c44 / M-X 4352
謙 J382c / M35821 5686
邁 J6d6e / M39193 6122
鎚 J444a / M-X 6281
鎰 J-X / M40715 6310
鍾 J3e61 / M40672 6311
鍛 J4343 / M40625 6318
霞 J3262 / M42365 6541

17 residual strokes

襑 J4729 / M-X 4116
繭 J4b7a / M27944 4595
蟬 J-X / M33616 5388
邁 J6d6e / M39193 6122
鎚 J444a / M-X 6280
鎰 J-X / M40715 6310
鎌 J3379 / M40693 6326

顕 J3832 / M43609 6646
鶫 J312d / M46952 6971

18–20 residual strokes

璽 J3c25 / M21309 3683
襷 J-X / M24851 4115
簾 J4e7c / M26616 4365
繭 J4b7a / M27944 4595
繍 J-X / M27913 4600
嚢 J4739 / M-X 5499

Rad. 3 、

1 residual stroke

⺍ J213a / M116 **33**
メ J2561 / M115 40
之 J4737 / M125 48

2 residual strokes

丸 J345d / M94 **34**
々 J2139 / M97 45
乏 J4b33 / M133 46
之 J4737 / M125 48
亡 J4b34 / M287 86
凡 J4b5e / M1739 433
刃 J3f4f / M1850 449
勺 J3c5b / M2495 565
叉 J3a35 / M3116 669
夕 J4d3c / M5749 1123
寸 J4023 / M7411 1372

---

3 residual strokes

不 J4954 / M19 13
丹 J4330 / M99 **36**
乏 J4b33 / M-X 46
之 J4737 / M125 48
以 J304a / M388 109
六 J4f3b / M1453 371
双 J4150 / M3125 673
太 J4240 / M5834 1137
尤 J4c60 / M7543 1399
心 J3f34 / M10295 1780
斗 J454a / M13489 2373
火 J3250 / M18850 3394
瓦 J3424 / M21438 3690

4 residual strokes

主 J3c67 / M100 **38**
乏 J4b33 / M133 46
乎 J3843 / M131 49
以 J304a / M388 109
半 J483e / M2707 608
外 J3330 / M5750 1125
市 J3b54 / M8775 1549
庁 J4423 / M9223 1603
広 J392d / M9224 1604
必 J492c / M10299 1781
斥 J404d / M13535 2380
永 J314a / M17088 3031
氷 J4939 / M17087 3032
玉 J364c / M20821 3620
瓦 J3424 / M21438 3690

---

5 residual strokes

互 J4f4a / M265 80
亦 J4b72 / M293 88
兎 J4546 / M-X 358
団 J4344 / M4703 940
夙 J3d48 / M5755 1126
多 J423f / M5756 1127
尽 J3f54 / M7642 1408
州 J3d23 / M8678 1529
帆 J4841 / M8787 1551
式 J3c30 / M9663 1676
忙 J4b3b / M10334 1783
求 J3561 / M17105 3036
汎 J4846 / M17120 3043

6 residual strokes

互 J4f4a / M265 80
住 J3d3b / M505 164
吠 J4b4a / M3331 739
寿 J3c77 / M7419 1374
忍 J4726 / M10312 1787
我 J3266 / M11545 2028
汰 J4241 / M17160 3055
灼 J3c5e / M18878 3398
甫 J4a63 / M21706 3722

---

7 residual strokes

卵 J4d71 / M2857 632
国 J3971 / M4752 950
往 J317d / M10073 1733
於 J3177 / M13628 2390
泳 J314b / M17328 3090

注	J436d M17316	3103

8 residual strokes

亭	J4462 M303	96
変	J4a51 M5703	1119
帝	J446b M8865	1560
柱	J436c M14660	2631
洲	J3d27 M17413	3120
為	J3059 M18981	3411
籽	J4c62 M26857	4384

9 residual strokes

圃	J4a60 M4774	954
峨	J3265 M8071	1471
恐	J3632 M10552	1853
烏	J3128 M18998	3421
蚤	J4742 M32893	5287
豹	J493f M36499	5753
酌	J3c60 M39768	6162

10 residual strokes

啄	J-X M3801	821
域	J3068 M5158	1030
術	J3d51 M34046	1754
救	J355f M13221	2344
率	J4e28 M20817	3618

11 residual strokes

塁	J4e5d M5316	1056
就	J3d22 M7599	1401
筑	J435e M26002	4280

詠	J3153 M35409	5584

12–15 residual strokes

舗	J4a5e M30323	322
楽	J335a M15213	2790
築	J435b M26298	4343
賭	J-X M36847	5819
酬	J3d37 M39850	6171
霊	J4e6e M42309	6532
駄	J424c M44633	6734
駐	J4373 M44660	6745
鼠	J414d M48390	7078

Rad. 4 丿

1 residual stroke

乂	J213a M116	33
乃	J4735 M113	**42**
九	J3665 M167	57
入	J467e M1415	366
八	J482c M258	369
刀	J4561 M1845	448
力	J4e4f M2288	521

2 residual strokes

丈	J3e66 M11	5
万	J4b7c M10	7
丸	J345d M94	34
乃	J4735 M113	**42**
々	J2139 M97	**45**
乏	J4b33 M133	**46**
久	J3557 M118	**47**

乞	J3870 M170	59
凡	J4b5e M1739	433
凧	J427c M1749	434
刃	J3f4f M1850	449
千	J4069 M2697	599
又	J4b74 M115	668
叉	J3a35 M3116	669
及	J355a M3118	670
夕	J4d3c M5749	1123
大	J4267 M5831	1133
夫	J4957 M5835	1136
女	J3d77 M6036	1173
川	J406e M8673	1526
才	J3a4d M11769	2059

3 residual strokes

不	J4954 M19	13
丹	J4330 M99	36
乏	J4b33 M133	**46**
之	J4737 M125	**48**
乞	J3870 M170	59
井	J3066 M258	76
仇	J3558 M355	106
介	J3270 M359	108
刈	J3422 M1859	452
匁	J4c68 M2502	566
勿	J4c5e M2501	569
区	J3668 M2674	585
升	J3e23 M2702	603
午	J3861 M2703	604
及	J355a M3118	670
友	J4d27 M3119	672
双	J4150 M3125	673
反	J483f M3127	674

壬	J3f51 M5639	968
夫	J4957 M5835	1136
太	J4240 M5834	1137
天	J4537 M5833	1138
少	J3e2f M7475	1390
尤	J4c60 M7543	1399
尺	J3c5c M7632	1404
屯	J4656 M7828	1438
戸	J384d M11696	2048
文	J4a30 M13450	2364
斤	J3654 M13534	2379
方	J4a77 M13620	2389
木	J4c5a M14415	2531
欠	J3767 M15991	2928
水	J3f65 M17083	3030
火	J3250 M18850	3394
爪	J445e M19653	3509
片	J4a52 M19762	3525
牛	J356d M19922	3532

4 residual strokes

丞	J3e67 M40	22
乏	J4b33 M133	**46**
乎	J3843 M131	**49**
乍	J4663 M130	**50**
冬	J455f M1610	410
処	J3d68 M1745	435
区	J3668 M2674	585
卯	J312c M2847	628
叱	J3c38 M3247	691
史	J3b4b M3249	697
右	J3126 M3250	700
外	J3330 M5750	1125
央	J317b M5840	1140

失	J3c3a M5844	1141
尻	J3f2c M7634	1407
左	J3a38 M8720	1535
布	J495b M8778	1548
弗	J4a26 M9708	1683
必	J492c M10299	1781
戊	J4a6a M11532	2020
斥	J404d M13535	2380
末	J4b76 M14420	2534
未	J4c24 M14419	2535
本	J4b5c M14421	2536
毛	J4c53 M16772	3013
水	J3f65 M17083	3030
牙	J3267 M19909	3531
瓜	J313b M21371	3686
生	J4038 M21670	3715
疋	J4925 M21994	3774
皮	J4869 M22823	3878
矛	J4c37 M23846	3974
矢	J4c70 M23929	3976
石	J4050 M24024	3985
禾	J3253 M24906	4121
辷	J4b78 M38724	6013

5 residual strokes

丞	J3e67 M40	22
亦	J4b72 M293	88
亥	J3067 M292	89
伊	J304b M432	134
兆	J437b M1349	346
先	J4068 M1349	350
刑	J3861 M1886	461
劣	J4e74 M2302	524
卯	J312c M2847	628

Red.4: 5 residual strokes

危	J346d / M2849	629	
及	J355a / M3118	670	
后	J3921 / M3298	704	
更	J4d79 / M3299	706	
吃	J3549 / M3280	707	
吸	J355b / M3372	713	
在	J3a5f / M4881	975	
存	J4238 / M6943	1284	
宅	J4076 / M7064	1308	
州	J3d23 / M8678	1529	
年	J472f / M9168	1593	
弗	J4a26 / M9708	1683	
弟	J446f / M9737	1685	
戎	J3d3f / M11539	2024	
托	J4271 / M11793	2069	
旭	J3030 / M13747	2416	
曳	J3148 / M14282	2417	
朱	J3c6b / M14424	2546	
每	J4b68 / M16724	3006	
永	J314a / M17088	3031	
汲	J3562 / M17163	3064	
竹	J435d / M25841	4246	
缶	J344c / M28108	4624	
老	J4f37 / M28842	4696	
考	J394d / M28843	4697	
有	J4d2d / M14332	4756	
辿	J4b78 / M38724	6013	
那	J4661 / M39305	6129	
邦	J4b2e / M39310	6130	

6 residual strokes

丞	J3e67 / M40	22	
亥	J3067 / M292	89	
兎	J4546 / M-X	358	

冴	J3a63 / M-X	417	
吸	J355b / M3372	713	
呂	J4f24 / M3386	728	
吻	J4a2d / M3375	729	
呑	J465d / M3329	737	
呆	J4a72 / M3395	738	
否	J485d / M3340	742	
告	J3970 / M3381	744	
君	J372f / M3323	746	
囲	J304f / M4722	945	
図	J3f5e / M4734	947	
夷	J3050 / M5852	1143	
妊	J4725 / M6072	1189	
妖	J4d45 / M6086	1190	
妙	J4c2f / M6090	1191	
孝	J3927 / M6952	1289	
宏	J3928 / M7086	1314	
寿	J3c77 / M1374	1374	
対	J4250 / M719	1375	
希	J3475 / M8813	1553	
弗	J4a26 / M9708	1683	
弟	J446f / M9737	1685	
形	J3741 / M9969	1713	
我	J3266 / M11545	2028	
抄	J3e36 / M11863	2087	
抜	J4834 / M11901	2093	
更	J3939 / M14283	2422	
杖	J3e73 / M14469	2555	
東	J422b / M14480	2559	
材	J3a60 / M14463	2561	
来	J4d68 / M14489	2565	
沌	J4659 / M17193	3054	
沃	J4d60 / M17184	3061	
沙	J3a3b / M17212	3063	
汲	J3562 / M17163	3064	

沈	J4440 / M17189	3069	
灸	J3564 / M18872	3399	
玖	J366a / M20846	3621	
秀	J3d28 / M24911	4123	
究	J3566 / M25409	4189	
系	J374f / M27223	4433	
考	J394d / M28843	4697	
苅	J3423 / M30771	4969	
芥	J3329 / M30715	4977	
赤	J4056 / M36993	5840	
身	J3f48 / M38034	5928	
迚	J4676 / M38793	6022	
邪	J3c59 / M39357	6135	

7 residual strokes

並	J4a4a / M54	24	
兎	J4546 / M-X	358	
免	J4c48 / M-X	361	
刷	J3a7e / M1964	479	
制	J4029 / M1961	481	
卵	J4d71 / M2857	632	
咋	J3a70 / M3488	751	
呼	J3846 / M3471	769	
垂	J3c62 / M5012	999	
姓	J402b / M6178	1196	
威	J3052 / M6259	1219	
岩	J3464 / M7985	1461	
延	J3164 / M-X	1657	
弟	J446f / M9737	1685	
忽	J397a / M10405	1799	
怖	J495d / M10450	1817	
承	J3e35 / M11852	2088	
斉	J4046 / M13454	2366	
易	J3057 / M13814	2432	

昇	J3e3a / M13794	2434	
枠	J4f48 / M14576	2585	
枡	J5b46 / M14577	2587	
果	J324c / M14556	2594	
東	J456c / M14499	2596	
欧	J3224 / M16024	2931	
殴	J3225 / M16618	2990	
泌	J423a / M17279	3092	
沸	J4a2a / M17251	3094	
物	J4a2a / M19959	3538	
秀	J3d28 / M24911	4123	
者	J3c54 / M28852	4698	
肴	J3a64 / M29322	4767	
肱	J394f / M29315	4770	
若	J3c63 / M30796	5007	
迚	J4676 / M38793	6022	
郁	J306a / M39371	6136	
采	J3a53 / M40116	6201	
非	J4873 / M42585	6563	

8 residual strokes

乗	J3e68 / M153	54	
係	J3738 / M663	217	
卑	J485c / M2751	618	
卸	J3237 / M2666	641	
叛	J4840 / M3166	680	
咳	J3331 / M3555	789	
垢	J3924 / M5058	1008	
型	J373f / M5030	1010	
城	J3e6b / M4889	1011	
奏	J4155 / M5915	1156	
姥	J3138 / M6216	1212	
宥	J4d28 / M7137	1326	
拷	J3969 / M12006	2142	

栃	J464a / M14687	2613	
柳	J4c78 / M14662	2629	
染	J4077 / M14621	2636	
歪	J4f44 / M16286	2960	
洩	J314c / M17401	3118	
派	J4749 / M17428	3126	
洗	J4076 / M17379	3131	
為	J3059 / M18981	3411	
界	J3326 / M21775	3739	
盃	J4756 / M22955	3887	
盈	J314e / M22961	3888	
盾	J3d62 / M23171	3912	
省	J3a4a / M23179	3916	
看	J3447 / M23196	3919	
研	J3826 / M24080	3991	
砂	J3a3d / M24046	3992	
称	J472x / M-X	4074	
祐	J4d34 / M24652	4079	
秒	J4943 / M24952	4129	
笈	J3568 / M25869	4249	
級	J4d6x / M27258	4437	
胤	J307d / M29405	4786	
軌	J3530 / M38176	5941	
逅	J447e / M38881	6055	
透	J4629 / M38876	6059	
郡	J3734 / M39436	6143	
重	J3d45 / M40132	6207	
面	J4c4c / M42618	6566	
飛	J4874 / M44000	6672	

9 residual strokes

兼	J3773 / M1483	381	
卿	J362a / M2878	642	
咳	J3331 / M3555	789	

漢	J	M	No.
夏	J3246	M5720	1120
娩	J4a5a	M6337	1233
孫	J4239	M6987	1296
峨	J3265	M8071	1471
差	J3a3a	M8732	1537
怠	J4255	M10469	1818
悌	J4470	M10642	1861
悩	J473a	M10716	1867
拷	J3969	M12006	2142
捗	J-X	M12160	2161
挿	J415e	M12119	2167
教	J3635	M13213	2345
旅	J4e39	M-X	2396
既	J347b	M13721	2407
柳	J4c78	M14662	2629
栴	J4073	M14737	2651
核	J334b	M14743	2660
株	J3374	M14723	2665
殺	J3b26	M16629	2994
涛	J4573	M-X	3138
浩	J3940	M17479	3147
班	J4849	M20976	3636
珠	J3c6e	M20956	3637
瓶	J4953	M21486	3699
盈	J314e	M22961	3888
秩	J4361	M24998	4135
称	J3e4e	M25016	4139
秘	J486b	M24977	4140
窄	J3a75	M25455	4197
筅	J3568	M25869	4249
粋	J3f68	M26875	4389
級	J3569	M27258	4437
紘	J3949	M27289	4445
紗	J3c53	M27287	4446
耕	J394c	M28907	4710

漢	J	M	No.
耽	J433f	M29024	4721
胤	J307d	M29405	4786
託	J4277	M35243	5560
財	J3062	M36664	5773
逋	J447e	M38881	6055
透	J4629	M38876	6059
郵	J4d39	M39485	6147
都	J4554	M39497	6148
釜	J3378	M35298	6215
随	J3f6f	M41764	6460

10 residual strokes

漢	J	M	No.
剰	J3e6a	M2107	501
卿	J362a	M2878	642
咳	J3331	M3555	789
唾	J4243	M3785	826
執	J3c39	M5193	1039
孫	J4239	M6987	1296
密	J4c29	M7205	1343
廻	J3276	M9575	1659
惣	J397b	M10811	1893
捗	J443d	M-X	2173
排	J4753	M12256	2210
教	J3635	M13213	2345
既	J347b	M13721	2407
核	J334b	M14743	2660
梼	J456e	M14911	2672
梗	J393c	M14849	2698
巣	J4163	M8659	2705
梯	J4474	M14881	2706
渚	J3d6d	M-X	3164
渉	J456a	M17749	3190
済	J3a51	M17749	3197
添	J453a	M17698	3201

漢	J	M	No.
淵	J4a25	M17692	3237
猪	J4376	M20511	3585
瓶	J4953	M21486	3699
祷	J4578	M-X	4093
第	J4268	M25943	4272
級	J3569	M27258	4437
胤	J307d	M29405	4786
著	J4378	M31302	5098
許	J3576	M35298	5569
躯	J366d	M-X	5930
逸	J306f	M38951	6071
遁	J465b	M38982	6087
酔	J3f6c	M39807	6166
閉	J4a44	M41222	6385
随	J3f6f	M41764	6460
陽	J4d5b	M41725	6470
雀	J3f7d	M41954	6496
集	J3d38	M41974	6500

11 residual strokes

漢	J	M	No.
卿	J-X	M2880	643
喬	J362c	M3990	841
堵	J4548	M-X	1021
堋	J4d3a	M5316	1051
堵	J-X	M5279	1053
媛	J4932	M6516	1244
孫	J4239	M6987	1296
屠	J-X	M7761	1429
属	J4230	M7754	1430
廃	J4751	M9425	1630
惹	J3c66	M10866	1886
惣	J4a3a	M10829	1889
悲	J4861	M10872	1897
惰	J4246	M10855	1921

漢	J	M	No.
扉	J4862	M11750	2058
援	J3167	M12407	2230
揚	J4d48	M12355	2236
斐	J4865	M13469	2370
既	J347b	M13721	2407
暑	J3d6b	M14031	2484
渚	J-X	M17758	3228
淵	J4a25	M17692	3237
湯	J4572	M17874	3245
煮	J3c51	M19165	3437
着	J4365	M23339	3938
硬	J4d47	M24230	4008
稀	J3529	M25058	4145
級	J3569	M27258	4437
紘	J3949	M27289	4445
紗	J3c53	M27287	4446
衆	J3d30	M33981	5417
詐	J3a3e	M35373	5585
象	J3e5d	M36372	5744
費	J4871	M36717	5786
遁	J465b	M38982	6087
酢	J3f5d	M39824	6169
鈍	J465f	M40219	6235
開	J4123	M41233	6393
雄	J4d3a	M41972	6499
集	J3d38	M41974	6500
雑	J3b28	M42022	6507
順	J3d42	M43349	6619
鼎	J4524	M48315	7074

12 residual strokes

漢	J	M	No.
園	J3160	M4818	962
塾	J3d4e	M5402	1083
嵯	J3a37	M8363	1500

漢	J	M	No.
携	J3748	M12529	2253
暖	J4348	M14064	2502
楯	J3d5d	M15173	2776
楕	J424a	M15133	2780
業	J3648	M15170	2789
潅	J3443	M18216	3287
牌	J4757	M-X	3528
牒	J4d87	M19871	3529
睡	J3f67	M23448	3948
稗	J-X	M25113	4151
署	J3d70	M28311	4643
罪	J3061	M28293	4644
群	J3732	M28498	4666
該	J333a	M35445	5601
賎	J4128	M-X	5796
賄	J445	M36745	5800
跡	J4057	M37493	5875
酬	J3d37	M37837	6171
鉄	J4534	M40285	6253
隙	J-X	M41813	6477
雅	J326d	M41973	6505
頓	J465c	M41973	6623
馴	J466b	M44595	6729
鳩	J4a64	M46648	6936

13 residual strokes

漢	J	M	No.
僑	J3623	M1088	307
塾	J3d4e	M5402	1083
携	J3748	M12529	2253
潅	J3443	M18216	3287
瑳	J3a3c	M21170	3667
碑	J486a	M24364	4028
稗	J-X	M25113	4151
稗	J4923	M-X	4156

Red.4: 13 residual strokes

種 J3c6f M25174 4159
箸 J4824 M-X 4301
緒 J3d6f M27632 4521
蜜 J4c2a M33143 5343
該 J333a M35445 5601
酷 J3973 M39870 6176
銑 J412d M40376 6263
餅 J4c5f M44133 6689
駁 J477d M44619 6733
髪 J4831 M45387 6804

14 residual strokes

嘱 J3e7c M4249 894
賓 J4950 M-X 1365
衝 J3e57 M34069 1772
戯 J353a M11665 2041
権 J3822 M15484 2853
歓 J343f M16197 2948
畿 J3526 M21925 3768
稽 J374e M25218 4163
箸 J-X M26224 4328
緩 J344b M27669 4551
諸 J427a M35687 5638
諸 J3d74 M35691 5648
賭 J4552 M-X 5807
輩 J475a M38398 5971
鋳 J4372 M40503 6280
餅 J4c5f M44133 6689

15 residual strokes

嘸 J4655 M4429 910
熱 J472e M19360 3473
稽 J-X M-X 4174

緒 J3d6f M27632 4521
薯 J3d72 M-X 5202
賭 J3f6e M36847 5819
錘 J3f6e M40547 6291
錫 J3c62 M40573 6292

16 residual strokes

儲 J4c59 M-X 331
曙 J3d6c M-X 2519
環 J3444 M-X 3680
矯 J363a M24015 3984
緩 J344b M27669 4551
謙 J382c M35821 5686
鍾 J3e61 M40672 6311
鮪 J4b6e M46126 6858

17 residual strokes

儲 J-X M1284 335
曖 J-X M14220 2523
諸 J3d73 M32391 5237
観 J3451 M34955 5538
輌 J-X M38137 5935
鎌 J3379 M40693 6326
鞭 J4a5c M46595 6595
髄 J3f71 M45240 6791
鵯 J3974 M46961 6968
鴉 J312d M46952 6971

18 residual strokes

簾 J4e7c M26616 4365
藷 J-X M32391 5247
蹴 J3d33 M37876 5913

霧 J4c38 M42418 6545
願 J346a M43623 6653
髄 J3f71 M45240 6791

19–22 residual strokes

瀕 J494e M18636 3381
鰭 J4949 M46400 6907
鶴 J4461 M47185 6995
鷺 J4f49 M47345 7004

Rad. 5 乙

0 residual strokes

乙 J3235 M161 **56**

1 residual strokes

七 J3c37 M6 3
九 J3665 M167 **57**

2 residual strokes

丸 J345d M94 34
也 J4c69 M171 **58**
乞 J3870 M170 **59**
亡 J4b34 M287 86
巳 J4c26 M8744 1538
己 J384a M8742 1540

3 residual strokes

孔 J3926 M6933 1282
尤 J4c60 M7543 1399

屯 J4656 M7828 1438
巴 J4743 M8745 1541

4 residual strokes

他 J423e M370 122
叱 J3c38 M3247 691
必 J492c M10299 1781
札 J3b25 M14422 2533
毛 J4c53 M16772 3013
礼 J4e69 M24626 4061
迄 J4b78 M38724 6013

5 residual strokes

兆 J437b M1347 346
吃 J3280 M3280 707
地 J434f M4890 976
妃 J485e M6061 1176
宅 J4270 M7064 1308
弛 J492c M9724 1684
托 J4271 M11793 2069
旭 J3030 M13747 2416
曳 J3148 M14282 2417
池 J4353 M17141 3042
色 J3f27 M30602 4956
迄 J4b78 M38724 6013

6 residual strokes

乱 J4d70 M187 **60**
乳 J467d M190 **61**
吾 J3353 M3379 733
売 J4764 M5647 990
弛 J4350 M9724 1684

沌 J4659 M17193 3054

7 residual strokes

乳 J467d M190 **61**
奄 J3162 M5881 1146
庖 J4a79 M9266 1610
弛 J4350 M9724 1684

8 residual strokes

乳 J467d M190 **61**
施 J3b5c M13629 2391
染 J4077 M14621 2636
胤 J307d M29405 4786

9 residual strokes

竜 J4e35 M25751 4232
粍 J4c30 M26881 4387
胤 J307d M29405 4786
託 J4277 M35243 5560

10 residual strokes

亀 J3535 M210 **62**
乾 J3425 M204 **63**
庵 J3043 M9369 1623
掩 J3166 M12285 2192
胤 J307d M29405 4786
酔 J3f6c M39807 6166

12 residual strokes

塾 J3d4e M5402 1083

滝 J426c M18067 3273	手 J3c6a M11768 2060	序 J3d78 M9253 1607	釘 J4523 M40159 6217		**2 residual strokes**	
詫 J4f4d M35411 5598	水 J3f65 M17083 3030	我 J3266 M11545 2028			云 J313e M254 **74**	
跳 J4437 M37533 5877		材 J3a60 M14463 2561	**10 residual strokes**		互 J385f M255 **75**	
電 J4545 M42253 6526	**4 residual strokes**	町 J442e M21735 3729	埼 J3a6b M5201 1028		井 J3066 M258 **76**	
馳 J435a M44593 6730	丞 J3e67 M40 22	羽 J3129 M28614 4675	崎 J3a6a M8169 1485		五 J385e M257 **77**	
鳩 J4837 M46648 6936	争 J4168 M236 **69**	身 J3f48 M38034 5928	康 J392f M9376 1621		仁 J3f4e M349 110	
	可 J3244 M3245 701	邪 J3c59 M39357 6135	救 J355f M13221 2344		元 J3835 M1340 343	
13–16 residual strokes	庁 J4423 M9223 1603	阿 J3024 M41599 6435	貯 J4379 M36698 5791		午 J3861 M2703 604	
塾 J3d4e M5402 1083	打 J4247 M11781 2063		逮 J4261 M38931 6069		夫 J4957 M5835 1136	
穡 J302c M25281 4170	氷 J4939 M17087 3032	**7 residual strokes**	閉 J4a44 M41222 6385		天 J4537 M5833 1138	
竃 J3376 M-X 4216	汀 J4475 M17103 3034	事 J3b76 M241 **71**	頂 J443a M43335 6616		牛 J356d M19922 3532	
篭 J4f36 M26371 4332	牙 J3267 M19909 3531	亨 J357c M295 **91**				
縄 J466c M27729 4547	矛 J4c37 M23846 3974	奇 J3471 M5892 1150	**11–19 residual strokes**		**3 residual strokes**	
蝿 J4768 M-X 5344	迂 J312a M38722 6016	学 J3358 M6974 1294	尊 J423a M7445 1386		丑 J312f M23 12	
		承 J3e35 M11852 2088	厳 J3460 M8624 1521		互 J385f M255 **75**	
Rad. 6 亅	**5 residual strokes**	泳 J314b M17328 3090	瀞 J-X M18659 3380		五 J385e M257 **77**	
1 residual stroke	丞 J3e67 M40 22	河 J322f M17245 3102	編 J-X M38137 5935		刊 J3429 M1865 456	
丁 J437a M2 2	宇 J3127 M7067 1309	苧 J4377 M30798 5000	雅 J326d M41973 6505		半 J483e M2707 608	
了 J4e3b M226 **67**	永 J314a M17088 3031	苛 J3257 M30785 5006	静 J4045 M42574 6560		失 J3c38 M5844 1141	
	求 J3561 M17105 3036	閂 J4c67 M41208 6381			平 J4a3f M9167 1590	
2 residual strokes	灯 J4574 M18855 3395		**Rad. 7 二**		未 J4b76 M14420 2534	
子 J3b2c M6930 1281	竹 J435d M25841 4246	**8 residual strokes**	**0 residual strokes**		末 J4c24 M14419 2535	
寸 J4023 M7411 1372	芋 J3072 M30670 4964	亭 J4462 M303 **96**	二 J4673 M247 **72**		正 J4035 M16255 2955	
小 J3e2e M7473 1389	行 J3954 M34029 5419	浄 J3e74 M17451 3128			示 J3c28 M24623 4060	
才 J3a4d M11769 2059	迂 J312a M38722 6016	珂 J3251 M20906 3625	**1 residual stroke**		迂 J312a M38722 6016	
水 J3f65 M17083 3030		除 J3d7c M41669 6449	三 J3b30 M12 8			
	6 residual strokes		工 J3929 M8711 1532		**4 residual strokes**	
3 residual strokes	亨 J357c M295 **91**	**9 residual strokes**	干 J3433 M9165 1589		亘 J4f4b M262 **79**	
予 J4d3d M231 **68**	何 J323f M511 169	峨 J3265 M8071 1471			瓦 J4f4a M265 **80**	
少 J3e2f M7475 1390	冴 J3a63 M-X 417	烹 J4b23 M19049 3425			伝 J4541 M462 141	
	司 J3b4a M3257 698	財 J3662 M36664 5773			会 J3271 M460 143	
	尿 J4722 M7651 1410	逮 J4261 M38931 6069			宇 J3127 M7067 1309	

弐 J4675 M-X 1675
朱 J3c6b M14424 2546
汚 J3178 M17133 3047
缶 J344c M28108 4624
芋 J3072 M30670 4964
行 J3954 M34029 5419
迂 J312a M38722 6016

5 residual strokes

亘 J4f4b M262 79
亙 J4f4a M265 80
亜 J3021 M272 81
伝 J4541 M462 141
会 J3271 M460 143
吾 J3863 M3379 733
囲 J304f M4722 945
坐 J3a41 M4931 978
完 J3430 M7079 1315
形 J3741 M9969 1713
政 J402f M13135 2335
汚 J3178 M17133 3047
芸 J375d M30741 4977

6 residual strokes

並 J4a42 M54 24
亜 J3021 M272 81
些 J3a33 M268 84
其 J4236 M1472 378
味 J4c23 M3456 766
坪 J445a M4976 998
奈 J4660 M5893 1147
奉 J4573 M5894 1149
妹 J4b65 M6138 1199

歩 J4a62 M16284 2958
玩 J3461 M20872 3622
岌 J3c33 M25842 4247

7 residual strokes

咲 J3a69 M3554 790
垣 J3340 M5060 1009
奏 J4155 M5915 1156
巻 J342c M8759 1545
怜 J4e67 M10461 1812
恒 J3931 M10527 1849
看 J3447 M23196 3919
院 J3121 M41665 6447

8 residual strokes

唖 J3022 M3743 795
峯 J4a77 M8093 1474
徐 J3d79 M10110 1744
恭 J3633 M10596 1845
悟 J3867 M10680 1870
晋 J3f38 M13899 2455
桧 J4930 M-X 2637
桓 J343c M14774 2652
殊 J4642 M16451 2975
泰 J4259 M17325 3098
莞 J3450 M31063 5052
蚕 J3b3d M32869 5290
袴 J3853 M34236 5448

9 residual strokes

基 J3470 M5197 1040
崇 J3f72 M8152 1490

悪 J302d M10717 1873
斜 J3c50 M13509 2376
票 J493c M24694 4089
袴 J3853 M34236 5448
転 J453e M38234 5948

10 residual strokes

廃 J4751 M9425 1630
普 J4961 M13982 2489
款 J343e M16107 2938
湊 J4c2b M17822 3226
無 J4c51 M19113 3439
開 J332b M41233 6393
雲 J3140 M42235 6522

11–20 residual strokes

暖 J4348 M14064 2502
曇 J465e M14172 2518
灘 J4775 M18784 3391
甑 J3465 M28766 4689
隷 J4e6c M41928 6490
霊 J4e6e M42309 6532
頑 J3468 M43374 6624
顎 J335c M43590 6643
魂 J3a32 M45787 6835
鰐 J4f4c M46337 6901

Rad. 8 亠

1 residual stroke

之 J4737 M125 48
亡 J4b34 M287 86

2 residual strokes

之 J4737 M125 48
六 J4f3b M1453 371
文 J4638 M13450 2364
方 J4a7d M13620 2389

3 residual strokes

主 J3c67 M100 38
市 J3b54 M8775 1549
玄 J383c M20814 3616
立 J4e29 M25721 4223

4 residual strokes

亦 J4b72 M293 88
亥 J3067 M292 89
交 J3872 M291 90
充 J3d3c M1345 348
妄 J4c51 M6063 1177
忙 J4b3b M10334 1783
衣 J3061 M34091 5420

5 residual strokes

亥 J3067 M292 89
亨 J357c M295 91
享 J357d M298 92
住 J3d3b M505 164
坊 J4b37 M4924 986
坑 J3923 M4932 987
妨 J4b38 M6111 1187
宛 J3c35 M7084 1312
対 J4250 M7419 1375

忘 J4b3a M10333 1784
抗 J3933 M11889 2091
玄 J383c M20814 3616
衣 J3061 M34091 5420
辛 J3f49 M38630 5996

6 residual strokes

亨 J357c M295 91
享 J357d M298 92
京 J357e M299 93
俠 J3873 M570 175
依 J304d M607 191
刻 J396f M1970 478
劾 J332f M2342 534
劫 J387a M2334 535
卒 J4234 M2740 615
夜 J4c6b M5763 1129
姜 J3e2a M6147 1198
妻 J3a4a M6140 1200
姉 J3b50 M6165 1201
弦 J3839 M9754 1688
斉 J4046 M13454 2366
杭 J393a M14494 2583
泣 J3563 M17309 3104
盲 J4c55 M23132 3907
育 J3069 M29318 4773
郊 J3959 M39392 6137

7 residual strokes

亨 J357c M295 91
亮 J4e3c M304 95
亭 J4462 M303 96
依 J304d M607 191

劾	J332f M2342	534	高	J3962 M45313	6796	景	J374a M13983	2487

墊 J3d4e M5402 1083 | 賠 J4765 M36818 5810

咳 J3331 M3555 789 | 椋 J4c3o M15020 2725 | 境 J362d M5409 1085 | 醇 J3d66 M39901 6181

哀 J3025 M3580 791 | 湾 J4f51 M17920 3239 | 嫡 J4364 M6656 1263

変 J4a51 M5703 1119 | **9 residual strokes** | 疏 J4141 M22000 3775 | 摘 J4526 M12582 2266 | **14 residual strokes**

帝 J446b M8865 1560 | 停 J4464 M864 273 | 硫 J4e32 M24229 4006 | 棄 J347e M14913 2787 | 僻 J4a48 M1166 323

弦 J3839 M9754 1688 | 割 J3364 M2112 507 | 禽 J3659 M24893 4120 | 滴 J4529 M18084 3299 | 嘯 J4838 M4433 903

柿 J3341 M14681 2624 | 商 J3e26 M3803 832 | 童 J4638 M25775 4239 | 熟 J3d4f M19332 3472 | 壊 J3e6d M-X 1098

育 J3069 M29318 4773 | 培 J475d M5195 1032 | 絞 J394a M27421 4485 | 璃 J4d7e M21196 3669 | 嬢 J3e6e M6807 1270

肺 J4759 M29422 4791 | 弦 J3839 M9754 1688 | 統 J457d M27447 4487 | 絞 J394a M27421 4485 | 憶 J3231 M11295 2001

荒 J3953 M30953 5034 | 惇 J4657 M10759 1887 | 蛮 J485a M33044 5314 | 統 J457d M27447 4487 | 擁 J4d4a M12781 2294

虹 J303a M32835 5277 | 掠 J4e2b M12273 2191 | | 網 J4c56 M27577 4527 | 檎 J3869 M15657 2888

音 J323b M43265 6607 | 敦 J4658 M13276 2349 | **11 residual strokes** | 翠 J3f69 M28732 4685 | 網 J4c56 M27577 4527

斎 J3a50 M13467 2368 | 膏 J3951 M29800 4860 | 縞 J3c4a M27777 4569

8 residual strokes | 核 J334b M14743 2660 | 喪 J4153 M3985 853 | 蓑 J4c2c M31661 5143 | 親 J3f46 M34918 5534

衷 J436f M-X 31 | 梓 J3034 M14845 2688 | 塙 J4839 M5341 1063 | 該 J333a M35445 5601 | 諺 J396b M-X 5659

剖 J4b36 M2034 492 | 淳 J3d5f M17690 3189 | 塘 J4564 M5340 1066 | 豪 J36ab M36406 5749 | 諦 J452c M35716 5663

剤 J3a5e M2076 493 | 涼 J4e43 M17606 3198 | 塾 J3d4e M5402 1083 | 適 J452c M39076 6107 | 蹄 J447d M37724 5894

咳 J3331 M3555 789 | 液 J3155 M17599 3199 | 嵩 J3f73 M8348 1502 | 醇 J3d66 M39901 6181 | 辨 J517e M38657 6002

哀 J3025 M3580 791 | 烹 J4b23 M19049 3425 | 廊 J3347 M9461 1633 | 銃 J3d46 M40359 6267 | 辧 J5221 M38656 6003

変 J4a51 M5703 1119 | 牽 J3823 M20025 3544 | 意 J3055 M10921 1926 | | 骸 J333c M45164 6789

宰 J3a4b M7160 1330 | 率 J4e28 M20817 3618 | 新 J3f37 M13572 2387 | **13 residual strokes**

恋 J4e78 M10537 1852 | 琉 J4e30 M20978 3642 | 暗 J3045 M14065 2503 | 影 J3146 M10019 1722 | **15 residual strokes**

惇 J4657 M10759 1887 | 産 J3b3a M21684 3716 | 棄 J347e M14913 2787 | 徹 J4530 M10245 1771 | 壇 J4345 M5528 1101

核 J334b M14743 2660 | 翌 J4d62 M28657 4679 | 禽 J3659 M24893 4120 | 撤 J4531 M12726 2280 | 壕 J3968 M5559 1108

校 J393b M14713 2669 | 望 J4b3e M14368 4819 | 蓑 J4c2c M31661 5143 | 敵 J4528 M13354 2359 | 擁 J4d4a M12781 2294

流 J4e2e M17572 3160 | 郭 J3354 M39474 6144 | 蓄 J435f M31642 5161 | 棄 J347e M14913 2787 | 檎 J3869 M15657 2888

淳 J3d5f M17690 3189 | | 裏 J4e22 M34294 5462 | 毅 J3523 M16673 3003 | 檀 J4349 M15632 2895

烹 J4b23 M19049 3425 | **10 residual strokes** | 該 J333a M35445 5601 | 熟 J3d4f M19332 3472 | 濠 J396a M18502 3363

猷 J4026 M21815 3748 | 傍 J4b35 M948 286 | 跡 J4057 M37493 5875 | 璃 J4d7e M21196 3669 | 締 J4479 M27651 4549

竜 J4e35 M25751 4232 | 就 J3d22 M7599 1401 | 較 J3353 M38297 5959 | 稿 J3946 M25220 4166 | 藁 J4f4e M32222 5234

航 J3952 M30385 4933 | 慌 J3932 M11057 1917 | 適 J452c M39076 6107 | 締 J4479 M27651 4549 | 骸 J333c M45164 6789

蚊 J3263 M32849 5288 | 敦 J4658 M13276 2349 | | 蓄 J435f M31642 5161 | 鮫 J3b2d M46127 6863

衰 J3f6a M34127 5432 | 斐 J4865 M13469 2370 | **12 residual strokes** | 褒 J4b2b M34437 5483

郭 J3354 M39474 6144 | 斑 J4843 M13470 2371 | 喪 J4153 M3985 853 | 諒 J4e4a M35653 5641

16 residual strokes		
穰	J3e77 / M25335'	4179
縞	J3c4a / M27777	4569
離	J4e25 / M42140	6517
顔	J3469 / M43591'	6648

17 residual strokes		
籠	J437e / M7368	1370
瀧	J426d / M18671	3376
蹴	J3d33 / M37876	5913
轍	J4532 / M38524	5988
鏑	J452d / M40790	6334
離	J4e25 / M42140	6517
鯨	J375f / M46257	6886

18–21 residual strokes		
讓	J3e79 / M36037'	5714
讌	J6d67 / M38677	6005
釀	J3e7a / M40064'	6197
鸞	J4f49 / M47345	7004

Rad. 9 人

0 residual strokes		
人	J3f4d / M344	99

1 residual stroke		
及	J355a / M3118'	670
大	J4267 / M5831	1133

2 residual strokes		
久	J3557 / M118	47
什	J3d3a / M348	105
仇	J3558 / M355	106
介	J3270 / M359	108
以	J304a / M388	109
仁	J3f4e / M349	110
仏	J4a29 / M364	111
今	J3a23 / M358	112
仔	J3b46 / M367	119
内	J4662 / M1512	386
化	J323d / M2572	580
及	J355a / M3118'	670
太	J4240 / M5834	1137
火	J3250 / M18850	3394

3 residual strokes		
丙	J4a3a / M35	16
以	J304a / M388	109
仏	J4a29 / M364	111
全	J2138 / M378	114
仔	J3b46 / M367	119
仙	J4067 / M374	120
令	J4a61 / M387	121
他	J423e / M370	122
仕	J3b45 / M368	123
付	J4955 / M373	124
代	J4265 / M386	125
囚	J3c7c / M4680	937

4 residual strokes		
亥	J3067 / M292	89

件	J376f / M410	130
伍	J3860 / M435	131
伐	J4832 / M439	132
伎	J346c / M436	133
伊	J304b / M432	134
企	J346b / M422	135
任	J4724 / M416	136
仰	J3644 / M400	137
似	J3b77 / M485	138
伏	J497a / M438	139
仲	J4367 / M403	140
伝	J4541 / M462'	141
休	J3559 / M440	142
会	J3271 / M398	143
仮	J323e / M398	144
全	J4134 / M1424	145
住	J3d3b / M505	164
低	J4463 / M504	166
何	J323f / M511	169
及	J355a / M3118'	670
吸	J355b / M3372'	713
合	J3967 / M3287	715
扱	J3037 / M-X	2070
汲	J3562 / M17163	3064
肉	J4679 / M29236	4753

5 residual strokes		
亥	J3067 / M292	89
仰	J3644 / M400	137
似	J3b77 / M485	138
伝	J4541 / M462'	141
会	J3271 / M460	143
伶	J4e62 / M478	149
佑	J4d24 / M507	150

佃	J4451 / M492	151
但	J4322 / M495	154
佐	J3a34 / M506	155
伺	J3b47 / M483	156
伴	J483c / M475	157
伯	J476c / M466	158
伽	J3240 / M486	159
位	J304c / M503	162
伸	J3f2d / M481	163
住	J3d3b / M505	164
体	J424e / M509	165
低	J4463 / M504	166
作	J3a6b / M518	167
余	J4d3e / M515	168
何	J323f / M511	169
冷	J4e64 / M1622	419
吸	J355b / M3372'	713
吟	J3663 / M3330	740
含	J345e / M3350	743
坐	J3a41 / M4931	978
扱	J3037 / M-X	2070
汲	J3562 / M17163	3064
芥	J3329 / M30715	4977
花	J3256 / M30734'	4980
谷	J432b / M36182	5730
附	J496d / M41606	6433

6 residual strokes		
低	J4463 / M504	166
佐	J4b79 / M-X	170
侠	J3622 / M625	171
佼	J3873 / M570	175
侃	J3426 / M577	182
侮	J496e / M629'	187

価	J3241 / M628'	188
舎	J3c4b / M30278'	189
併	J4a3b / M561	190
依	J304d / M607	191
侍	J3b78 / M589	192
例	J4e63 / M587	193
佳	J3242 / M557	194
供	J3621 / M605	195
使	J3b48 / M573	196
刻	J396f / M1970	478
卒	J4234 / M2740	615
命	J4c3f / M3473	767
夜	J4c6b / M5763	1129
奉	J4a74 / M5894	1149
岱	J4252 / M7997	1452
府	J495c / M9283	1611
念	J4730 / M10390	1800
怜	J4e67 / M10461	1812
於	J3177 / M13628	2390
臥	J3269 / M30071	4896
苔	J4e6a / M30777	4981
金	J3662 / M40152	6211

7 residual strokes		
侮	J496e / M629'	187
依	J304d / M607	191
俣	J4b73 / M718	202
侶	J4e37 / M647	205
侯	J3874 / M633	211
促	J4225 / M664	212
俄	J3264 / M665	215
俊	J3d53 / M674	216
係	J3738 / M663	217
侵	J3f2f / M646	218

Char	J-code	M-code	No.
便	J4a58	M659	219
俗	J422f	M695	220
信	J3f2e	M707	221
保	J4a5d	M702	222
倣	J4a6f	M785	235
修	J3d24	M721	260
叙	J3d76	M3163	681
咳	J3331	M3555	789
始	J3028	M6242	1208
恰	J3366	M10603	1838
拾	J3d26	M12014	2149
柄	J4a41	M14603	2627
玲	J4e68	M20888	3626
珍	J4441	M20920	3631
界	J3326	M21775	3739
臥	J3269	M30071	4896
茌	J3141	M30950	5022
茶	J4363	M30915	5033
衿	J365e	M34149	5431
途	J4553	M38882	6057
除	J3d7c	M41669	6449
食	J3f29	M44014	6674

8 residual strokes

Char	J-code	M-code	No.
俊	J3d53	M674	216
倖	J3876	M771	228
倣	J4a6f	M785	235
俺	J3236	M736	240
倭	J4f41	M796	242
俵	J4936	M730	243
俱	J3666	M724	245
倹	J3770	M823	248
倬	J4a70	M734	249
候	J3875	M775	250

Char	J-code	M-code	No.
倦	J3771	M788	251
倍	J475c	M760	252
俳	J4750	M726	254
倉	J4152	M756	255
倒	J455d	M767	256
値	J434d	M758	257
個	J3844	M758	258
借	J3c5a	M781	259
修	J3d24	M721	260
偶	J3676	M899	274
剣	J3775	M2076	498
咳	J3331	M3555	789
容	J4d6d	M7172	1335
座	J3a42	M9319	1619
挫	J3a43	M12087	2163
桧	J4930	M-X	2637
栓	J4072	M14689	2649
浴	J4d61	M17496	3153
疹	J3f3e	M22097	3788
病	J4942	M22127	3798
納	J473c	M27264	4453
脊	J4054	M29472	4804
荷	J3259	M31000	5059
途	J4553	M38882	6057
釘	J4523	M40159	6217
針	J3f4b	M40165	6218
閃	J412e	M41214	6383
険	J3831	M41721	6456
陰	J3122	M41691	6462
食	J3f29	M44014	6674
飢	J3532	M44023	6675

9 residual strokes

Char	J-code	M-code	No.
俵	J4936	M730	243

Char	J-code	M-code	No.
値	J434d	M786	257
偲	J3c45	M898	266
偵	J4465	M898	270
停	J4464	M864	273
偶	J3676	M899	274
側	J4226	M897	275
偽	J3536	M927	276
偏	J4a50	M848	277
健	J3772	M875	278
偉	J304e	M837	285
堺	J3a66	M5289	1045
宿	J3d49	M7195	1344
悠	J4d2a	M10681	1872
捻	J4731	M12222	2201
捨	J3c4e	M12191	2205
斜	J3c50	M13509	2376
糀	J3371	M15065	2683
欲	J4d6f	M16080	2936
液	J3155	M17586	3199
符	J4964	M25935	4270
袋	J425e	M34171	5443
袷	J3041	M34240	5449
貨	J325f	M36678	5781
釧	J367c	M40171	6222
釦	J4b55	M40175	6223
釣	J4460	M40172	6224
飢	J3532	M44023	6675

10 residual strokes

Char	J-code	M-code	No.
偶	J3676	M899	274
傘	J3b31	M966	283
備	J4877	M967	284
偉	J304e	M837	285
傍	J4b35	M948	286

Char	J-code	M-code	No.
傑	J3766	M955	293
傾	J3739	M1038	299
創	J414f	M2127	506
喰	J3674	M4015	849
喉	J3922	M3913	854
塔	J4563	M5332	1052
幾	J3476	M9208	1601
愉	J4c7b	M10905	1920
搭	J456b	M12508	2228
検	J3821	M15065	2752
欽	J3656	M16104	2940
琴	J2f09	M21079	3654
磁	J4823	M24243	4004
禽	J3669	M24893	4120
筏	J4835	M26000	4282
答	J457a	M26006	4285
納	J473c	M27264	4453
絵	J3328	M27464	4488
給	J356b	M27432	4489
葛	J-X	M31420	5126
蓉	J4d56	M31648	5135
蛤	J483a	M33023	5312
衆	J3d30	M33981	5417
袋	J425e	M34171	5443
裕	J4d35	M34305	5461
診	J3f47	M35337	5586
貸	J425f	M36709	5792
鈎	J3343	M40220	6226
鈍	J465f	M40219	6235
雁	J4534	M41960	6498
飯	J4853	M44064	6679
飲	J307b	M44063	6680
黍	J3550	M47991	7048

11 residual strokes

Char	J-code	M-code	No.
僅	J364f	M-X	279
僅	J-X	M1048	292
傑	J3766	M955	293
傭	J4d43	M1007	295
債	J3a44	M1006	296
働	J462f	M1079	297
催	J3a45	M1005	298
傾	J3739	M1038	299
僧	J414e	M1076	300
傷	J3d7d	M1029	301
塔	J4563	M5332	1052
幹	J3434	M9183	1596
愈	J4c7c	M10904	1909
溶	J4d4f	M17983	3277
禽	J3659	M24893	4120
稔	J4c2d	M25107	4149
蔭	J307e	M31840	5151
蒼	J4173	M31627	5162
該	J333a	M35445	5601
詮	J3f36	M35435	5606
賃	J4442	M36743	5802
鉆	J385a	M40270	6236
鉦	J3e60	M40322	6246
鈴	J4a66	M40267	6247
鉢	J482d	M40317	6249
鉛	J3174	M40310	6251
鉱	J395b	M40340	6252
鉄	J4534	M40285	6253
零	J4e6d	M42242	6524
靴	J3724	M42729	6576
飯	J4853	M44064	6679
飲	J307b	M44063	6680
飴	J303b	M44080	6682

飾 J3e7e M41111' 6683
飽 J4b30 M44109' 6684
飼 J3b74 M44107' 6685

12 residual strokes

償 J3a44 M1022 296
僑 J3623 M1088 307
像 J417c M1084 308
僕 J4b4d M1094 313
僚 J4e3d M1100 314
斡 J3036 M13522 2378
槍 J4164 M15319 2822
漆 J3c3f M18108 3304
熔 J4d50 M19319 3458
箟 J4a4f M26114 4310
絵 J3328 M27464' 4488
給 J356b M27432 4489
翠 J3f69 M28732 4685
腐 J4965 M29625 4835
蝕 J3f2a M-X 5333
該 J333a M35445 5601
鉾 J4b48 M40353 6255
銚 J4438 M40387 6260
銑 J412d M40376 6263
銭 J412c M40413 6264
銘 J4c43 M40385 6265
銅 J463c M40361 6266
銃 J3d46 M40359 6267
銀 J3664 M40355 6268
閣 J395e M41301 6397
閥 J4836 M41308 6398
領 J4e4e M43423 6628
飴 J302b M44080 6682
飾 J3e7e M44111' 6683

飽 J4b30 M44109' 6684
飼 J3b74 M44107' 6685
餅 J4c5f M44133 6689
餌 J4d21 M44146 6690

13 residual strokes

億 J322f M1178 321
舗 J4a5e M30323' 322
僻 J4a48 M1166 323
儀 J3537 M1172 324
劉 J4e2d M2224 515
懲 J4d5d M11163 1951
篤 J4a4f M26114 4310
膝 J4928 M29837 4868
蝕 J3f2a M-X 5333
蝕 J4b2b M33264 5358
褒 J4b2b M34437 5483
論 J4f40 M35658 5646
輸 J4e58 M38400 5973
舗 J4a5f M40491 6269
鋒 J4a5f M40455 6275
鋏 J4946 M40503 6277
鋤 J3d7b M40480 6278
鋭 J3154 M40418' 6279
鋳 J4372 M40503' 6280
餅 J4c5f M44133 6689
餌 J3142 M44146 6690
餓 J326e M44168' 6697

14 residual strokes

盡 J5056 M1234 327
儒 J3c74 M1220 330
叡 J3143 M3214 683

橢 J3869 M15657 2888
翰 J344d M28780 4690
舘 J345c M30326 4923
諭 J35727' M35727' 5667
輸 J4d22 M38438' 5978
鎚 J444a M-X 6281
錘 J3f6e M40547 6291
錫 J3c62 M40573 6292
錠 J4a5e M40559 6293
錐 J3f6d M40536 6294
錨 J4945 M40598 6295
錆 J3b2c M40523 6296
鋸 J4d5d M40505 6297
録 J4f3f M40519' 6298
錯 J3a78 M40579 6299
錬 J4f23 M40576 6300
錦 J3653 M40569 6301
鋼 J395d M40509 6302
鍵 J3830 M40654 6317
餐 J3b41 M44160 6696
餓 J4a5f M44168 6697
館 J345b M44237' 6701
骸 J333c M45164 6789
鮒 J4a2b M46075 6854

15 residual strokes

儲 J4c59 M-X 331
償 J3d7e M1245 333
優 J4d25 M1261 334
嶺 J4e66 M8553 1517
橢 J3869 M15657 2888
檜 J5b58 M15676 2894
篠 J3c44 M-X 4352
縮 J3d4c M27815 4585

鎚 J444a M-X 6281
鎚 J-X M40715 6310
鐘 J3e61 M40672 6311
鍍 J4555 M40607 6312
鍔 J4457 M40617 6313
鍬 J372d M40643 6314
鍋 J4669 M40603 6315
鍵 J3830 M40654 6317
鍛 J4343 M40625 6318
餐 J3b41 M44160 6696
館 J345b M44237' 6701
骸 J333c M45164 6789
黛 J4263 M48075 7060

16 residual strokes

儲 J-X M1284 335
嚙 J-X M4516 921
癒 J4c7e M22545 3847
謬 J4935 M35872 5695
鎚 J444a M-X 6281
鎚 J-X M40715 6310
鍔 J4457 M40617 6313
鎗 J4179 M40709 6320
鎧 J333b M40735 6324
鎖 J3a3f M40708' 6325
鎌 J3379 M40693 6326
鎮 J4443 M40745 6328
鞭 J4a2c M42937 6595
験 J3833 M44835 6758

17 residual strokes

縮 J3d4c M27815 4585
贋 J3466 M36943 5830

鏑 J452d M40790 6334
鏡 J3640 M40812 6341
饗 J3642 M-X 6705
鹸 J3834 M-X 7013
麹 J-X M47818 7037

18 residual strokes

鐙 J4c7a M-X 6343
鐙 J462a M40904 6348
鐘 J3e62 M40902 6352
饗 J3642 M-X 6705
麺 J-X M47827 7039

19 residual strokes

鏈 J4c7a M-X 6343
鐸 J4278 M40951 6356
鐙 J-X M40998 6357
饗 J3642 M-X 6705
饗 J-X M44431 6715

20–22 residual strokes

鑪 J4c7a M-X 6343
鑽 J-X M40998 6357
鑑 J3455 M40988 6361
饗 J-X M44431 6715
鱶 J724d M46442 6912
鷹 J426b M47377 7007
鹹 J-X M47576 7016

Rad. 10 儿

2 residual strokes

允 J3074 M1338 **342**
元 J3835 M1340 **343**
冗 J3e69 M1566 399
匹 J4924 M2673 584
尤 J4c60 M7543 1399

3 residual strokes

兄 J373b M1343 **344**
四 J3b4d M4682 938

4 residual strokes

兆 J437b M1347 **346**
兌 J3624 M1348 **347**
充 J3d3c M1345 **348**
光 J3077 M1350 **349**
先 J4068 M1349 **350**
西 J403e M34763 5514

5 residual strokes

克 J396e M1355 **354**
児 J3b79 M1364 **355**
兎 J4546 M1364 **358**
売 J4764 M5647' 990
完 J3430 M7079 1315
沈 J4440 M17189 3069
禿 J4645 M24910 4122
究 J3566 M25409 4189
見 J382b M34796 5522
酉 J4653 M39763 6157

---

6 residual stroke

兎 J4546 M-X **358**
免 J4c48 M-X **361**
尭 J3646 M-X 614
呪 J3c76 M3443 764
枕 J4b6d M14546 2589
況 J3637 M17264 3086
玩 J3b61 M20872 3622
虎 J3857 M32675 5265
逃 J4628 M38845 6038

7 residual strokes

亮 J4e3c M304 95
冠 J3427 M1580 401
尭 J3646 M-X 614
挑 J4429 M12055 2145
洗 J4076 M17379 3131
甚 J3f53 M21648 3711
発 J482f M22662 3860
祝 J3d4b M24672' 4085
荒 J3953 M30953' 5034
逃 J4628 M38845 6038
酋 J3d36 M39765 6159
院 J3121 M41665 6447

8 residual strokes

党 J455e M1381 **363**
凌 J4e3f M1669 424
勉 J4a59 M2384' 543
唆 J3a36 M3696 803
娩 J4e?? M6337 1233
峻 J3d54 M8116 **1475**

悦 J3159 M10629' 1868
挽 J-X M12111 2169
挽 J4854 M-X 2172
晃 J3938 M13891 2458
桃 J456d M14757 2663
浣 J4642 M-X 3134
莞 J3450 M31063 5052
逸 J306f M38951' 6071
陵 J4e4d M41704 6454
陸 J4e26 M41708 6461
鬼 J3534 M45758 6833

9 residual strokes

兜 J3375 M1386 **364**
勘 J342a M2393 548
商 J3e26 M3803 832
挽 J4854 M-X 2172
控 J3935 M12283 2202
探 J4335 M12276 2211
琉 J4e30 M20978 3642
現 J383d M21004 3645
眺 J442f M23314 3933
脱 J4326 M29539' 4822
菱 J4929 M31219 5092
規 J352c M34810 5524
視 J3b6b M34827' 5525
逸 J306f M38951' 6071

10 residual strokes

兜 J3375 M1386 **364**
喚 J342d M3953 852
堪 J342e M5266 1057
尊 J423a M7445 1386

就 J3d22 M7599 1401
廃 J4751 M9425 1630
換 J3439 M12358 2233
曉 J3647 M14031 2485
晚 J4855 M14030' 2491
溌 J482e M-X 3209
湛 J4339 M17846 3234
焼 J3e46 M19166' 3438
疏 J4141 M22000 3775
硯 J3827 M24233 4005
硫 J4e32 M24229 4006
税 J4047 M25070' 4146
竣 J3d67 M25773 4238
統 J457d M27447 4487
腔 J3950 M29630 4826
莵 J4551 M-X 5102
覘 J4741 M34839 5528
覚 J3350 M34846 5529
隔 J3356 M X 6475

11 residual strokes

兜 J3375 M1386 **364**
堪 J342e M5266 1057
塊 J3274 M5319 1070
寛 J3432 M7276 1352
幌 J4b5a M9022 1577
微 J4879 M10203 1765
搾 J3a71 M12553 2251
睦 J4e53 M23460 3945
稜 J4e47 M25123 4152
続 J4233 M27533 4500
蒐 J3d2f M31539 5159
頑 J4368 M43374 6624

---

12 residual strokes

境 J362d M5409 **1085**
統 J457d M27447 4487
綾 J303d M27591 4523
説 J4062 M35556 5627
読 J4649 M35580' 5629
貌 J4b46 M36556 5762
酸 J3d61 M39871 6177
銑 J412d M40376 6263
銃 J3d46 M40359 6267
魁 J3321 M45785 6834
魂 J3a32 M45787 6835

13 residual strokes

噂 J313d M4286 896
撹 J3349 M-X 2267
槻 J4450 M15290 2845
続 J4233 M27533 4500
甌 J3531 M28766 4689
輝 J38372 ... 5972
鋭 J3154 M40418' 6279
閣 J315c M41341' 6404
魅 J4c25 M45811 6838

14 residual strokes

橘 J354c M15551 2868
窯 J312e M25633 4215
綾 J303d M27591 4523
融 J4d3b M-X 5371
覧 J4d77 M34928 5533
親 J3f46 M34918 5534
醒 J4830 M-X 6182

15–18 residual strokes

潰 J-X / M18591 3373
競 J25831 / M25831 4244
耀 J4d54 / M28828 4695
観 J3451 / M34955 5538
醜 J3d39 / M39969 6189
鏡 J3640 / M40812 6341
駿 J3d59 / M44775 6754

19–26 residual stroke

魘 J4b62 / M45906' 6843
攬 J5978 / M13041 2322
纏 J453b / M28043 4612
鷙 J4f49 / M47345 7004
讚 J6c2d / M36163 5729

Rad. 11 入

0 residual strokes

入 J467e / M1415 **366**

1–4 residual strokes

久 J3557 / M118 **47**
仝 J2138 / M378 114
全 J4134 / M1424 145
内 J4662 / M1512 386
込 J397e / M38712' 6010

9–11 residual stroke

堺 J3a66 / M5289 1045
塔 J4563 / M5332 1052
塗 J4549 / M5338 1074
愈 J4c7c / M10904 1909

Rad. 12 八

0 residual strokes

八 J482c / M1450 **369**

2 residual strokes

六 J4f3b / M1453 **371**
公 J3878 / M1452 **372**
分 J4a2c / M1853 454
少 J3e2f / M475 1390
父 J4963 / M19721 3516

3 residual strokes

半 J483e / M2707 608
只 J427e / M3239 694
平 J4a3f / M9167 1590
必 J492c / M10299 1781
穴 J236 / M25406 4186
立 J4e29 / M25721 4223

4 residual strokes

共 J3626 / M1458 **373**
劣 J4e74 / M2302 524
尽 J3f54 / M7642 1408
米 J4a46 / M26832 4380
羊 J4d53 / M28425 4658
辛 J3f49 / M38630 5996

---

5 residual strokes

伴 J483c / M475 157
余 J4d3e / M515 168
兵 J4a3c / M1462 **374**
判 J483d / M1923 465
呉 J3862 / M3365' 741
宗 J3c35 / M7084 1312
弟 J446f / M9737 1685
扮 J4a31 / M11830 2080
来 J4d68 / M14489 2565
谷 J432b / M36182 5730
豆 J4626 / M36245 5735
貝 J322d / M36656 5766
述 J3d52 / M38803' 6030
逆 J3555 / M38849' 6041

6 residual strokes

並 J4a42 / M54 24
併 J3621 / M561 190
供 J3621 / M605 195
典 J4535 / M174 **375**
具 J3671 / M1473 **376**
其 J4236 / M1472 **378**
券 J3774 / M1966 473
呼 J3846 / M3471 769
岡 J322c / M7962 1460
幸 J392c / M9176 1595
弟 J446f / M9737 1685
斧 J4960 / M13539 2382
松 J3e3e / M14516 2592
沿 J3168 / M17260 3096
述 J3d52 / M38803 6030
送 J4177 / M38842' 6039

逆 J3555 / M38849' 6041
金 J3662 / M40152 6211

7 residual stroke

俊 J3d53 / M674 216
俗 J422f / M695 220
剃 J4466 / M1989 489
前 J4130 / M2011 490
南 J466e / M2750 619
叛 J4840 / M3166 680
呉 J3862 / M3365' 741
咲 J3069 / M3554 790
巷 J392b / M-X 1543
巻 J342c / M8759' 1545
弟 J446f / M9737 1685
挟 J3634 / M-X 2146
拳 J377d / M11996 2148
洪 J393f / M17402 3123
洋 J4d4e / M17363 3130
狭 J3639 / M20406' 3572
盆 J4b5f / M22959 3889
省 J3e4a / M23179 3916
美 J487e / M28435 4660
茶 J4363 / M30915' 5033
負 J4969 / M-X 5769
送 J4177 / M38842' 6039
逗 J3f60 / M38887 6053
酋 J392c / M39765 6159
頁 J3227 / M43333 6614
首 J3c73 / M44489 6719

8 residual strokes

俊 J3d53 / M674 216

俱 J3666 / M724 245
倦 J3771 / M781 251
兼 J3773 / M1483 **381**
冥 J4c3d / M1588 405
剃 J4466 / M1989 489
剛 J3964 / M2042 497
唄 J3134 / M3694 802
員 J3077 / M3633 808
娯 J3864 / M6307' 1231
宰 J3a4b / M7160 1330
容 J4d46 / M7172 1335
差 J3a39 / M8732 1537
従 J3d3e / M10133 1745
恭 J3633 / M10596 1845
悌 J4470 / M10642 1861
悦 J3159 / M10629' 1868
拳 J377d / M12081' 2150
晋 J3f38 / M13899 2455
浜 J494d / M17462 3152
浴 J4d61 / M17496 3153
狼 J4762 / M20433 3576
瓶 J4953 / M21486 3699
畔 J484a / M21801 3746
益 J3157 / M22972' 3891
真 J3f3f / M23236 3926
祥 J3e4d / M24689' 4090
秤 J4769 / M24993 4134
粉 J4a34 / M26872 4390
紛 J4a36 / M27295 4452
翁 J3227 / M28635' 4677
朕 J443f / M14361 4797
朔 J3a73 / M14359 4801
貢 J3957 / M36665 5772
財 J3a62 / M36664 5773
逗 J3f60 / M38887 6053

Char			No.
釜	J3378	M40164	6215
釘	J4523	M40159	6217
針	J3f4b	M40165	6218

9 residual strokes

Char			No.
執	J3c39	M5193	1039
基	J3470	M5197	1040
寅	J4652	M7204	1341
敗	J4754	M13227	2343
曾	J413e	M-X	2464
梯	J4474	M14881	2706
欲	J4d5f	M16080	2936
瓶	J4953	M21486	3699
異	J305b	M21854	3757
翌	J4d62	M28657	4679
脱	J4326	M29539	4822
船	J4125	M30407	4939
訟	J3e59	M35266	5565
販	J484e	M36679	5779
責	J4055	M36682	5780
貨	J325f	M36678	5781
貧	J494f	M36677	5782
貫	J4c63	M36699	5789
遂	J3f6b	M38985	6084
達	J463b	M39011	6088
道	J163b	M39010	6091
釧	J367c	M40176	6222
鈕	J4b55	M40175	6223
釣	J4460	M40172	6224
隊	J4262	M41750	6468
雀	J3f7d	M41954	6496
頃	J3a22	M43338	6615
頂	J443a	M43335	6616
黄	J322b	M47926	7045

10 residual strokes

Char			No.
傾	J3739	M1038	299
勝	J3e21	M2409	553
厨	J2f5f	M3005	657
喜	J346e	M3957	858
善	J4131	M3904	859
圏	J3777	M4815	960
嫌	J3779	M6618	1257
寒	J3428	M7239	1350
尊	J423a	M7445	1386
屡	J3c48	M7770	1428
巽	J4417	M8765	1546
捲	J377e	M12208	2193
揃	J4237	M12319	2226
斯	J3b5b	M13563	2386
曾	J413d	M14299	2483
普	J4961	M13982	2489
棋	J347d	M14922	2744
欺	J353d	M16097	2939
欽	J3656	M16104	2940
滋	J3c22	M17919	3238
港	J3941	M17783	3242
測	J422c	M17780	3244
爺	J4c6c	M19734	3517
猶	J4d31	M20557	3593
献	J3825	M20539	3596
痘	J4577	M22185	3813
登	J4550	M22668	3862
着	J4365	M23339	3938
短	J433b	M23978	3982
碯	J4823	M24243	4004
税	J407c	M25070	4146
紛	J4a36	M27295	4452
腔	J3950	M29630	4826

Char			No.
期	J347c	M14378	4835
蓉	J4d56	M31648	5135
裕	J4d35	M34305	5461
評	J493e	M35383	5587
貫	J3453	M36681	5778
費	J4871	M36717	5786
貼	J453d	M36718	5787
貿	J4b47	M36721	5788
貫	J4c63	M36699	5789
賀	J326c	M36725	5790
貯	J4379	M36698	5791
貸	J425f	M36709	5792
買	J4763	M36708	5793
貴	J352e	M36704	5794
遂	J3f6b	M38985	6084
達	J4323	M39011	6088
道	J463b	M39010	6091
遡	J414c	M39048	6094
鈞	J3343	M40220	6226
鈍	J465f	M40219	6235
雰	J4a37	M42231	6521
項	J3960	M33343	6617
須	J3f5c	M33352	6618
順	J3d67	M43349	6619

11 residual strokes

Char			No.
僧	J414e	M1076	300
塞	J3a49	M5349	1069
嫌	J3779	M6618	1257
嵯	J3a37	M8363	1500
廉	J4e77	M9436	1634
愈	J4d50	M10904	1909
慈	J3b7c	M10980	1924
慎	J3f35	M11024	1945

Char			No.
損	J423b	M12459	2255
新	J3f37	M12387	2387
楢	J466a	M15154	2769
楠	J466f	M15152	2779
業	J3648	M15170	2789
殿	J4542	M16651	3001
溢	J306e	M17951	3270
溯	J5e6a	M17975	3272
溶	J4d4f	M17983	3277
煎	J4079	M19184	3453
煩	J4851	M19229	3454
献	J4d32	M20558	3590
碁	J386b	M24261	4020
禎	J4477	M24767	4099
羨	J4122	M28503	4665
群	J3732	M28498	4666
義	J3541	M28504	4668
虞	J3673	M32723	5272
誉	J4d40	M35498	5602
詳	J3e5c	M35446	5607
豊	J4b2d	M36263	5737
賎	J4128	M-X	5796
賂	J4f28	M	5799
賄	J4f45	M36745	5800
賊	J4231	M36759	5801
賃	J4442	M36743	5802
資	J3b71	M24364	5803
遡	J414c	M39048	6094
鈷	J385a	M40270	6236
鉦	J3e60	M40322	6246
鈴	J4e6b	M40267	6247
鉢	J482d	M40317	6249
鉛	J3174	M40310	6251
鉱	J395b	M40340	6252
鉄	J4534	M40285	6253

Char			No.
頒	J4852	M43378	6621
頓	J465c	M43381	6623
頑	J3468	M43374	6624
預	J4d42	M43373	6625
鼓	J385d	M48330	7076

12 residual strokes

Char			No.
僕	J4b4d	M1094	313
噌	J4139	M-X	873
噓	J3133	M-X	886
嘉	J3245	M4176	887
増	J417d	M5448	1088
嫡	J4364	M6656	1263
寡	J3249	M7286	1363
導	J4633	M7463	1388
層	J4158	M-X	1432
摘	J4526	M12582	2266
旗	J347a	M13687	2402
槇	J7422	M15310	2818
慎	J6b6a	M-X	2819
様	J4d4d	M5352	2821
潰	J4452	M	3301
演	J3169	M18130	3310
熔	J4d50	M19319	3458
瑳	J3a3c	M	3667
磁	J3c27	M24364	4029
箕	J4c27	M26143	4307
網	J394b	M27576	4525
網	J4c56	M27577	4527
総	J416d	M27620	4532
聡	J416f	M29109	4730
誤	J386d	M35546	5626
説	J395b	M35556	5627
賑	J4678	M36785	5806

遵 J3d65/M39118′ 6112
選 J412a/M39127′ 6114
遺 J3064/M39134′ 6115
鄭 J4522/M39647 6155
鉾 J4b48/M40353 6255
銚 J4438/M40387 6260
銑 J412d/M40376 6263
銭 J412c/M40413 6264
銘 J4c43/M40385 6265
銅 J463c/M40361 6266
銃 J3d46/M40359 6267
銀 J3664/M40355 6268
関 J3458/M41297 6402
頚 J375b/M43434 6626
頗 J3f7c/M43415 6627
領 J4e4e/M43423 6628
餅 J4c5f/M44133 6689

13 residual strokes

儀 J3537/M1163 324
噌 JX/M4303 889
噂 J313d/M4286 896
噴 J4a2e/M4345 900
嬉 J3472/M6736 1267
賓 J4950/M-X 1365
寮 J4e40/M7325 1366
導 J4633/M7463′ 1388
慾 J4d5d/M11163 1951
憎 J417e/M11188′ 1969
慣 J3437/M11111 1970
撲 J4b50/M12755 2274
撰 J4071/M12753 2277
敵 J4528/M13354 2359
暴 J4b3d/M14137 2511
様 J4d4d/M15352′ 2821
横 J3223/M15484′ 2854
澄 J4021/M18315 3333
潰 J4459/M18281 3335
甑 J3979/M-X 3706
箭 J407d/M26193 4325
蕨 J4f4f/M32001 5194
賭 J4552/M-X 5807
賠 J4765/M36818 5810
賦 J496a/M36800 5811
賜 J3b72/M36809 5812
賎 J6c4d/M36826 5813
賛 J3b3f/M36841 5814
賢 J382d/M36822 5816
質 J3c41/M36833 5817
遵 J3d65/M39118′ 6112
選 J412a/M39127′ 6114
遺 J3064/M39134′ 6115
鋪 J4a5f/M40491 6269
鋒 J4b2f/M40455 6275
鋲 J4946/M40503 6277
鋤 J3d7b/M40480 6278
鋭 J3154/M40418′ 6279
鋳 J4372/M40503′ 6280
閲 J315c/M41341′ 6404
頬 J4b4b/M-X 6629
餅 J4c5f/M44133 6689
養 J4d5c/M44144 6691

14 residual strokes

叡 J3143/M3214 683
嘶 J4838/M4433 903
噸 J4655/M4429 910
壌 J3e6d/M-X 1098
嬢 J3e6e/M6807′ 1270
慣 J3437/M11111 1970
憤 J4a30/M11239 1990
樽 J432e/M15500 2875
樹 J3c79/M15496 2878
滋 J3c22/M17919′ 3238
澱 J4543/M18410 3347
熱 J472e/M19360 3473
燈 J4575/M19402 3476
甑 J3979/M-X 3706
瞥 J4a4d/M23672 3959
頴 J3150/M24824 4109
穎 J314f/M25267 4173
積 J4051/M25266 4176
綱 J394b/M27576 4525
網 J4c56/M27577 4527
総 J416d/M27620 4532
縦 J3d44/M27804′ 4571
膳 J4137/M29891 4873
膨 J4b44/M29861 4874
興 J363d/M30226 4913
諺 J3841/M-X 5659
賢 J382d/M36822 5816
賭 J-X/M36847 5819
蹄 J447d/M37724 5894
辨 J517e/M38657 6002
辧 J5221/M38656 6003
鎚 J444a/M-X 6281
錘 J3f6e/M40547 6291
錫 J3c62/M40573 6292
錠 J3e7b/M40559 6293
錐 J3f6d/M40536 6294
錨 J4945/M40598 6295
錆 J3b2c/M40523 6296
鋸 J3578/M40505 6297
録 J4f3f/M40519′ 6298
錯 J3a78/M40579 6299
錬 J4f23/M40576 6300
錦 J3653/M40569 6301
鋼 J395d/M40509 6302
鍵 J3830/M40654 6317
頼 J4d6a/M43529′ 6635
頭 J462c/M43490 6639
養 J4d5c/M44144 6691

15 residual strokes

償 J3d7e/M1245 333
嬰 J3145/M6828 1273
嶺 J4e66/M8553 1517
慈 J3b7c/M10980′ 1924
檜 J5b58/M15676 2894
犠 J353e/M20190′ 3550
療 J4e45/M22500 3842
瞥 J4a4d/M23672 3959
瞭 J4e46/M23697 3960
糞 J4a35/M27102 4425
績 J4053/M27845 4579
翼 J4d63/M28801′ 4692
興 J363d/M30226 4913
謄 J4625/M35780′ 5685
謙 J382c/M35821′ 5686
購 J3958/M36885 5823
輿 J4d41/M38468 5983
邇 J6d6e/M39193 6122
鎚 J444a/M-X 6281
鎚 J-X/M40715 6310
鍾 J3e61/M40672 6311
鍍 J4555/M40607 6312
鍔 J4457/M40617 6313
鍬 J372d/M40643 6314
鍋 J4669/M40603 6315
鍵 J3830/M40654 6317
鍛 J4343/M40625 6318
頻 J4951/M-X 6641
鮮 J412f/M46133 6864

16 residual strokes

瀆 J-X/M18591 3373
磁 J3c27/M24364 4029
禰 J4729/M-X 4116
穣 J3e77/M25335′ 4179
縦 J3d44/M27804′ 4571
繕 J4136/M27893 4594
藤 J4623/M32340′ 5241
贈 J4223/M36920′ 5827
蹟 J4058/M37814 5905
輿 J4d41/M38468 5983
邇 J6d6e/M39193 6122
鎚 J444a/M-X 6281
鎚 J-X/M40715 6310
鍔 J4457/M40617 6313
鎗 J4179/M40709 6320
鎧 J333b/M40735 6324
鎖 J3a3f/M40708′ 6325
鎌 J3379/M40693 6326
鎮 J4443/M40745 6328
闘 J462e/M45649′ 6418
顎 J335c/M43590 6643
額 J335b/M43586 6644
顕 J3822/M43609′ 6646
類 J4e60/M43608′ 6647
顔 J3469/M43591′ 6648
鵜 J312d/M46952 6971

17 residual strokes

籠 J437e/M7368 1370
曝 J4778/M14239 2524
瀧 J426d/M18671 3376
瀬 J4025/M18672′ 3384
爆 J477a/M19540 3505
禰 J-X/M24851 4115
簸 J4876/M26609 4363
簾 J4e7c/M26616 4365
績 J4053/M27845 4579
艶 J3170/M30632 4957
蟻 J3542/M33672 5397
譜 J4968/M35990 5703
鏑 J452d/M40790 6334
鏡 J3640/M40812 6341
韻 J3124/M43307 6611
顎 J335c/M43590 6643
顚 J-X/M43628 6651
顛 J453f/M-X 6652

18 residual strokes

瀕 J494e/M18636 3381
繕 J4136/M27893 4594
譲 J3e79/M36037′ 5714
議 J3544/M36027 5716
醸 J3e7a/M40064′ 6197
鑓 J4c7a/M-X 6343
鐙 J462a/M40904 6348
鐘 J3e62/M40902 6352
騰 J462d/M44915′ 6767

19 residual strokes

纏 J453b/M28043 4612
譲 J3e79/M36037′ 5714
辯 J6d67/M38677 6005
鑓 J4c7a/M-X 6343
鐸 J4278/M40951 6356
鑓 J-X/M40998 6357

20 residual strokes

嚢 J4739/M-X 5499
讃 J3b3e/M36110 5720
鑓 J4c7a/M-X 6343
鑓 J-X/M40998 6357
鑑 J3455/M40988 6361

21 residual strokes

纏 J453b/M28043 4612
鑑 J3455/M40988 6361
鰤 J4b70/M46492 6921

Rad. 13 冂

1 residual stroke

巾 J3652/M8771 1547

2 residual strokes

丹 J4330/M99 36
円 J315f/M1513 **385**
内 J4662/M1512 **386**
月 J376b/M14330 2530

3 residual strokes

丙 J4a3a/M35 16
冊 J3a7d/M1515 **389**
用 J4d51/M21703 3721

4 residual strokes

両 J4e3e/M46 23
再 J3a46/M1524 **391**
向 J387e/M3301 712
同 J4631/M3294 717
而 J3c29/M28871 4704
肉 J4679/M29236 4753
舟 J3d2e/M30350 4927

5 residual strokes

両 J4e3e/M46 23
甫 J4a63/M21706 3722
角 J3351/M35003 5543

6 residual strokes

周 J3c7e/M3441′ 768
尚 J3e30/M7493 1395
岡 J322c/M7962 1460
雨 J312b/M42210 6518

7 residual strokes

南 J466e/M2750 619
柵 J3a74/M14665 2620
柄 J4a41/M14603 2627
洞 J4636/M17386 3125
珊 J3b39/M20917 3630

8 residual strokes

倫 J4e51/M793 246
凋 J437c/M1668 423
剛 J3964/M2042 497
圃 J4a60/M4774 954
栴 J4073/M14737 2651
桐 J364d/M14770 2655
病 J4942/M22127 3798
納 J473c/M27264 4453
胴 J4639/M29436 4810
般 J484c/M30388 4931
航 J3952/M30385 4933
週 J3d35/M38937′ 6070
高 J3962/M45313 6796

9 residual strokes

商 J3e26/M3803 832
彫 J4426/M9995 1719
舶 J4775/M30402 4936
舵 J4249/M30400 4937
舷 J383f/M30403 4938
船 J4125/M30407 4939
週 J3d35/M38937′ 6070
遇 J3678/M38991′ 6083
遍 J4a57/M39001′ 6086
過 J3261/M39002′ 6090
隅 J3679/M41743 6467

10 residual strokes

喬 J362c/M3990 841
喚 J342d/M3953 852
寓 J3677/M7243 1348
属 J4230/M7754 1430
換 J3439/M12358 2233
渦 J3132/M17771 3241
満 J4b7e/M17921′ 3248
献 J3825/M20539 3596
筒 J457b/M26004 4283
策 J3a76/M26009 4284
納 J473c/M27264 4453
艇 J447a/M30440 4941
遇 J3678/M38991′ 6083
遍 J4a57/M39001′ 6086
過 J3261/M39002′ 6090
隔 J3356/M-X 6475

11 residual strokes

嗣 J3b4c/M4109 868
塙 J4839/M5341 1063
嵩 J3f73/M8348 1502
愚 J3672/M10946 1925
楠 J466f/M15152 2779
溝 J3942/M17944 3275
瑞 J3f70/M21131 3665
禍 J3252/M24766′ 4102
舷 J383f/M30403 4938
艇 J447a/M30440 4941
適 J452c/M39076′ 6107

12 residual strokes

僑 J3623/M1088 307
嫡 J4364/M6656 1263
摘 J4526/M12582 2266
構 J393d/M15317 2823
滴 J4529/M18084 3299

Red.13: 12 residual strokes

爾 J3c24 M19750 3521	綱 J394b M27576 4525	艦 J344f M30571 4950	**8 residual strokes**
璃 J4d7e M21196 3669	網 J4c56 M27577 4527	鏑 J452d M40790 6334	党 J455e M1381 363
端 J433c M25806 4243	縞 J3c4a M27777 4569	離 J4e25 M42140 6517	冥 J4c3d M1588 **405**
綱 J394b M27576 4525	融 J33384 M33384 5371	鯛 J4264 M46226 6884	帯 J4253 M8929 1563
網 J4c56 M27577 4527	鋼 J395d M40509 6302		帰 J3522 M8930 1564
蔽 J4a43 M31888 5193		**Rad. 14 ⌁**	洗 J4642 M-X 3134
製 J403d M34380 5476		**1–4 residual strokes**	浸 J3f3b M17505 3157
適 J452c M39076 6107	**15 residual strokes**	冗 J3e69 M1566 399	索 J3a77 M27306 4449
銅 J463c M40361 6266	橋 J3869 M15657 2888	写 J3c4c M1570 **400**	耽 J433f M29024 4721
需 J3c7b M42275 6528	濡 J4728 M18504 3365		骨 J397c M45098 6784
	瞥 J4a4d M23672 3959	**5 residual strokes**	

13 residual strokes

嘱 J3e7c M4249 894	矯 J363a M24015 3984	労 J4f2b M2329 531	**9 residual strokes**
幣 J4a3e M9088 1585	編 J4a54 M27665 4552	壱 J306d M5647 983	停 J4464 M864 273
廠 J3e33 M9490 1643	薬 J4f4e M32222 5234	売 J4764 M5647 990	富 J495a M1592 **406**
敵 J4528 M13354 2359	講 J3956 M35824 5689		壷 J445b M5657 1034
璃 J4d7e M21196 3669	購 J3958 M36885 5823	**6 residual strokes**	堂 J4632 M5207 1037
稿 J3946 M25220 4166	邁 J6d6e M39193 6122	勃 J4b56 M2351 539	婦 J4958 M6432 1243
篇 J4a53 M26257 4324	鍋 J4669 M40603 6315	受 J3c75 M3159 678	常 J3e6f M8955 1569
綱 J3946 M27576 4525		学 J3358 M6974 1294	掃 J415d M12237 2207
編 J4a54 M27665 4552	**16 residual strokes**	枕 J4b6d M14546 2589	授 J3c78 M12242 2208
蔽 J4a43 M31888 5193	礪 J626a M24571 4056		探 J4335 M12276 2211
蕎 J363e M31946 5197	襦 J4729 M-X 4116	**7 residual strokes**	深 J3f3c M17687 3206
製 J403d M34380 5476	縞 J3c4a M27777 4569	亮 J4e3c M304 95	牽 J3823 M20025 3544
論 J4f40 M35658 5646	繭 J4b7a M27944 4595	亭 J4462 M303 96	蛍 J3756 M32983 5302
輪 J4e58 M38400 5973	邁 J6d6e M39193 6122	侵 J3f2f M646 218	運 J313f M38998 6092
	離 J4e25 M42140 6517	冠 J3427 M1580 **401**	

14 residual strokes

儒 J3c74 M1220 330	**17–19 residual strokes**	帝 J446b M8865 1560	**10 residual strokes**
橘 J354c M15551 2868	璽 J3c25 M21309 3683	栄 J3149 M14687 2635	営 J3144 M857
橋 J3636 M15526 2879	礪 J626a M24571 4056	軍 J3733 M38179 5943	塚 J444d M-X 1048
橋 J3869 M15657 2888	襦 J-X M24851 4115		掌 J444d M12248 2200
瞥 J4a4d M23672 3959	繭 J4b7a M27944 4595		揮 J3478 M12394 2229
			殻 J334c M-X 2996

Red.13: 12 residual strokes (continued)

滞 J425a M18067 3280	
畳 J3e76 M21875 3763	
索 J3a77 M27306 4449	
覚 J3350 M34846 5529	
運 J313f M38998 6092	

11 residual strokes

夢 J4c34 M5801 1131
寝 J3f32 M7278 1353
愛 J3026 M10947 1927
滞 J425a M18067 3280
滑 J336a M18032 3281
続 J4233 M27533 4500
舞 J3d58 M30339 4925
蒙 J4c58 M31555 5154

12 residual strokes

嘗 J3e28 M4205 878
穀 J3972 M25188 4157
綬 J3c7a M27565 4510
裳 J3e58 M34357 5472
読 J4649 M35580 5629
豪 J396b M36406 5749

13 residual strokes

憂 J4d2b M11170 1971
撹 J3349 M-X 2267
確 J334e M24366 4039
続 J4233 M27533 4500
締 J4479 M27651 4549
賞 J3e5e M36813 5815
輝 J3531 M38372 5972

14 residual strokes

叡	J3143 / M3214	683
憂	J4d2b / M11170	1971
綏	J3c7a / M27565	4510
諦	J447c / M35716	5663
蹄	J447d / M37724	5894
鴬	J3229 / M-X	6945

15 residual strokes

償	J3d7e / M1245	333
優	J4d25 / M1261	334
壕	J3968 / M5559	1108
濠	J396a / M18502	3363
瞬	J3d56 / M-X	3969
締	J4479 / M27651	4549

16–23 residual strokes

襄	J-X / M4633	933
擾	J3e71 / M12920	2314
攬	J5978 / M13041	2322
瞬	J3d56 / M23694	3969
鶴	J4461 / M47185	6995

Rad. 15 冫

3 residual strokes

| 冬 | J455f / M1610 | 410 |

4 residual strokes

| 兆 | J437b / M1347 | 346 |

次	J3c21 / M15992	2929
求	J3561 / M17105	3036
状	J3e75 / M20257	3556
羽	J3129 / M28614	4675

5–7 residual strokes

冴	J3a63 / M-X	417
冶	J4c6a / M1621	418
冷	J4e64 / M1622	419
准	J3d5a / M1661	426
姿	J6257 / M6257	1216
挑	J4429 / M12055	2145
茨	J3071 / M30896	5017

8 residual strokes

凋	J437c / M1668	423
凌	J4e3f / M1669	424
凄	J4028 / M1657	425
准	J3d5a / M1661	426
凍	J4560 / M1749	427
弱	J3c65 / M9791	1692
桃	J456a / M14757	2663

9–10 residual strokes

弱	J3c65 / M9791	1692
盗	J4570 / M23000	3894
眺	J442f / M23314	3933
装	J4175 / M34283	5455

11 residual strokes

楽	J335a / M15213	2790
溺	J452e / M17990	3271
装	J4175 / M34283	5455
資	J3b71 / M36750	5803
跳	J4437 / M37533	5877

12–20 residual strokes

凝	J3645 / M1720	431
薬	J4c74 / M32188	5224
譜	J3b70 / M35728	5660
鰯	J3073 / M46413	6904

Rad. 16 几

1 residual stroke

| 凡 | J4b5e / M1739 | 433 |

3 residual strokes

凧	J427c / M1749	434
処	J3d68 / M1745	435
尻	J3f2c / M7634	1407

4 residual strokes

凪	J4664 / M1758	437
夙	J5755 / M5755	1126
帆	J4841 / M8787	1551
机	J3479 / M14435	2543
汎	J4977 / M17120	3043
肌	J4829 / M29242	4755

---

5 residual strokes

坑	J3923 / M4932	987
役	J4c72 / M10057	1726
抗	J3933 / M11889	2091
投	J456a / M11887	2095
没	J4b57 / M17233	3066

6 residual strokes

抛	J3572 / M11985	2113
杭	J393a / M14494	2583
殴	J3225 / M16618	2990
股	J3854 / M29284	4772

7 residual strokes

段	J434a / M16619	2991
疫	J3156 / M22069	3783
風	J4977 / M43756	6663

8 residual strokes

恐	J3632 / M10552	1853
殺	J3b26 / M16629	2994
般	J484c / M30388	4931
航	J3952 / M30385	4933
訊	J3f56 / M35224	5559
飢	J3532 / M44023	6675

9 residual strokes

猶	J4e44 / M20512	3587
設	J405f / M35293	5570
飢	J3532 / M44023	6675

10–12 residual strokes

凱	J332e / M1790	**440**
嵐	J4d72 / M8289	1496
搬	J4842 / M12507	2249
椴	J464e / M15075	2772
楓	J4976 / M15126	2779
殻	J334c	2996
殿	J4542 / M16651	3001
穀	J3972 / M25188	4157
筑	J435e / M26002	4280
蝋	J4f39	5332
鳳	J4b31 / M46671	6937

13–15 residual strokes

撃	J3762 / M12674	2265
毅	J3523 / M16673	3003
潑	J-X / M18225	3325
澱	J4543 / M18410	3347
盤	J4857 / M23036	3902
磐	J4858 / M24401	4037
築	J435b / M26298	4343
繋	J3752 / M-X	4573
鍛	J4343 / M40625	6318

17–19 residual strokes

繋	J3752 / M-X	4573
繋	J-X / M27940	4601
醗	J-X / M40041	6194
馨	J333e / M44559	6724

麗 J4e6f M47663 7026

Rad. 17 凵

1 residual stroke

山 J3b33 M7869 1439

2 residual strokes

凶 J3627 M1803 **442**
屯 J4656 M7828 1438

3 residual strokes

凸 J464c M1809 **443**
凹 J317a M1810 **444**
出 J3d50 M1811 **445**

4 residual strokes

兜 J3624 M1348 347
凸 J464c M1809 **443**
凹 J317a M1810 **444**
臼 J3131 M30173 4907

5–10 residual strokes

凸 J464c M1809 **443**
凹 J317a M1810 **444**
函 J4821 M1826 **446**
幽 J4d29 M9205 1600
悩 J473a M10716ʹ 1867
齒 J3b75 M16323 2961
画 J3268 M21739 3733
胸 J363b M29442 4811

脳 J473e M29567 4821

11–18 residual strokes

嚙 J337a M-X 888
幽 J4d29 M9205 1600
橢 J3869 M15657 2888
離 J4e25 M42140 6517
齡 J4e70 M48632ʹ 7093

Rad. 18 刀

0 residual strokes

刀 J4561 M1845 **448**

1–4 residual stroke

刃 J3f4f M1850 **449**
刈 J3422 M1859 **452**
切 J405a M1858 **453**
分 J4a2c M1853 **454**
刊 J3429 M1865 **456**
列 J4e73 M1901 **460**
刑 J373a M1886 **461**
刄 J4c68 M2502 566
召 J3e24 M3241 695
辺 J4a55 M38710ʹ 6011

5 residual strokes

判 J483d M1923 **465**
利 J4d78 M1932 **466**
別 J4a4c M767 **467**
初 J3d69 M1911 **469**

忍 J4726 M10312ʹ 1787
扮 J4a31 M11830 2080
苅 J3423 M30771 4969

6 residual strokes

例 J4e63 M587 193
券 J3774 M1966 **473**
到 J457e M1950 **477**
刻 J396f M1970 **478**
刷 J3a7e M1964 **479**
刺 J3b49 M1969 **480**
制 J4029 M1961 **481**
拐 J327d M11955 2107
招 J3e37 M11968 2124
沼 J3e42 M17257 3091

7 residual strokes

則 J4227 M1994 **487**
削 J3a6f M2000 **488**
剃 J4466 M1989 **489**
前 J4130 M2011 **490**
型 J373f M5030 1010
契 J3740 M5917 1155
昭 J3e3c M13855 2446
盆 J4b5f M22959 3889
窃 J4060 M25453 4195
籾 J4c62 M26857 4384
荊 J3755 M-X 5027

8 residual strokes

倒 J455d M767 256
剃 J4466 M1989 **489**

剖 J4b36 M2034 **492**
剤 J3a5e M2076 **493**
剥 J476d M48939 **496**
剛 J3964 M2042 **497**
剣 J3775 M2076 **498**
帰 J3522 M8930 1564
捌 J3b2b M12141 2162
烈 J4e2b M18987 3420
留 J4e31 M21808 3750
粉 J4a34 M26872 4390
紛 J4a36 M27295 4452

9 residual strokes

側 J4226 M897 275
剰 J3e6a M2107 **501**
副 J497b M2097 **503**
梨 J4d7c M14873 2697
梁 J4e42 M14825 2702
紹 J3e52 M27361 4465
貧 J494f M36677 5782

10 residual strokes

創 J414f M2127 **506**
割 J3364 M2112ʹ **507**
喫 J354a M3987 855
愉 J4c7b M10905ʹ 1920
揃 J4237 M12319 2226
測 J422c M17780 3244
痢 J4e21 M22213 3810
紛 J4a36 M27295 4452
裂 J4e76 M34260 5453
詔 J3e5b M35415 5581
試 J3b6e M35415 5611

貿 J4b47 M36721 5788
超 J4436 M37096 5852
雰 J4a37 M42231 6521
鞄 J3f59 M-X 6573

11 residual strokes

溜 J4e2f M17943 3276
煎 J4079 M19184 3453
照 J3e48 M19226 3457
紹 J3e52 M27361 4465
裂 J4e76 M34260 5453
解 J3272 M35067 5548
頒 J4852 M43378 6621

12 residual strokes

劃 J3344 M2193 **513**
劇 J3760 M2218 **517**
寡 J3249 M7286 1363
瑠 J4e5c M21143 3673
罰 J4833 M28315 4647
製 J403d M34380 5476
認 J4727 M35502ʹ 5623

13 residual strokes

劉 J4e2d M2224 **515**
劇 J3760 M2218 **517**
潔 J3769 M18231 3332
箭 J407d M26193 4325
製 J403d M34380 5476

14 residual strokes

諭	J4d21 M35727	5667
輸	J4d22 M38438	5978
辨	J517e M38657	6002
辦	J5221 M38656	6003

15–17 residual strokes

潔	J3769 M18231	3332
癒	J4c7e M22545	3847
蟹	J332a M33668	5395

Rad. 19 力

0 residual strokes

力	J4e4f M2288	521

3 residual strokes

功	J3879 M2295	522
加	J3243 M2297	523
屍	J3f2c M7634	1407
幼	J4d44 M9193	1599

4 residual strokes

劣	J4e74 M2302	524
肋	J4f3e M29239	4754

5 residual strokes

伽	J3240 M486	159
努	J4558 M2314	527
励	J4e65 M2326	528
劫	J3965 M2316	529

助	J3d75 M2313	530
労	J4f2b M2329	531
男	J434b M21730	3731
迦	J3260 M38789	6027

6 residual strokes

劾	J332f M2342	534
効	J387a M2334	535
協	J3628 M2742	617
茄	J3258 M30835	4995
迦	J3260 M38789	6027

7 residual strokes

劾	J332f M2342	534
勃	J4b56 M2351	539
勅	J443c M2354	540
勇	J4d26 M2360	541
架	J324d M14586	2632

8 residual strokes

勃	J4b56 M2351	539
勉	J4a59 M2384	543
務	J4c33 M2394	546
砺	J4557 M-X	3993
脅	J363c M29466	4803
脇	J4f46 M29467	4807

9 residual strokes

務	J4c33 M2394	546
勘	J342a M2393	548
動	J4630 M2390	549

袈	J3736 M34166	5442

10 residual strokes

募	J4a67 M2416	551
勤	J3650 M2415	552
勝	J3e21 M2409	553
湧	J4d2f M17862	3207
甥	J3179 M21689	3719
筋	J365a M25994	4286
袈	J3736 M34166	5442
賀	J326c M36725	5790

11–17 residual strokes

働	J462f M1079	297
勢	J402a M2422	558
勧	J342b M2433	559
勲	J372e M2463	560
嘉	J3245 M4176	887
虜	J4e3a M32720	5273
鋤	J3d7b M40480	6278
霧	J4c38 M42418	6545
駕	J326f M44667	6743

Rad. 20 勹

1 residual stroke

勺	J3c5b M2495	565

2 residual strokes

勼	J4c68 M2502	566
匀	J4677 M2503	567

勾	J387b M2500	568
勿	J4c5e M2501	569

3–4 residual strokes

包	J4a71 M2506	572
句	J3667 M3234	693
旬	J3d5c M13746	2415

5 residual strokes

吻	J4a2d M3375	729
均	J3651 M4916	988
局	J3649 M7653	1412
杓	J3c5d M14466	2558
灼	J3c5e M18878	3398
灸	J3564 M18872	3399

6 residual strokes

庖	J4a79 M9266	1610
忽	J397a M10405	1799
拘	J3934 M11963	2123
抱	J4a7a M11917	2125
易	J3057 M13814	2432
泡	J4b22 M17307	3093
物	J4a2a M19959	3538
狗	J3669 M20345	3565
的	J452a M22692	3867

7 residual strokes

約	J4c73 M27242	4440
胞	J4b26 M29396	4788
陥	J3459 M41676	6446

8 residual strokes

挽	J-X M12111	2169
殉	J3d5e M16448	2974
砲	J4b24 M24120	3998
胸	J363b M29442	4811
豹	J493f M36499	5753
酌	J3c60 M39768	6162
陶	J462b M41705	6459

9 residual strokes

喝	J3365 M-X	824
惚	J397b M10811	1893
揭	J3747 M12311	2194
掬	J3545 M12290	2197
淘	J4571 M17642	3187
約	J4c73 M-X	4440
葛	J336b M-X	5060
萄	J463a M31252	5075
菊	J3546 M31153	5096
鈎	J4460 M40172	6224
陽	J4d5b M41725	6470

10 residual strokes

惣	J415a M10829	1889
揚	J4d48 M12355	2236
敬	J3749 M13285	2351
湯	J4572 M17874	3245
絢	J303c M27427	4481
葱	J472c M31454	5123
葛	J-X M31420	5126
葡	J4972 M31430	5127
鉤	J3343 M40220	6226

11 residual strokes

暢 J442a M14095 2506
楊 J4d4c M15112 2784
腸 J4432 M29721 4849
褐 J336c M-X 5473
飽 J4b30 M44109 6684

12 residual strokes

絢 J303c M27427 4481
鞄 J3373 M42781 6582
飽 J4b30 M44109 6684

13 residual strokes

潟 J3363 M18247 3328
蕩 J4622 M32002 5198
謁 J315a M35690 5637
賜 J3b72 M36809 5812
駒 J3670 M44663 6742
麹 J396d M-X 7036

14–20 residual strokes

濁 J4279 M18440 3348
爛 J3f24 M19480 3496
警 J3256 M35989 5705
趨 J3f76 M37258 5855
錫 J3c62 M40573 6292
雛 J3f77 M42121 6514
鞠 J3759 M42892 6589
驚 J3643 M45013 6774
麹 J-X M47818 7037

Rad. 21 ヒ

2 residual strokes

匂 J4677 M2503 567
化 J323d M2572 **580**
比 J4866 M16743 3010

3 residual strokes

北 J4b4c M2574 **581**
叱 J3c38 M3247 691
尼 J4674 M7635 1405
比 J4866 M16743 3010

4 residual strokes

庇 J485f M9239 1606
旨 J3b5d M13738 2414
此 J3a21 M16259 2956
死 J3b60 M16365 2968
牝 J4c46 M19925 3534
老 J4f37 M28842 4696

5 residual strokes

壱 J306d M5647 983
庇 J485f M9239 1606
批 J4863 M11845 2086
花 J3256 M30734 4979
陀 J424b M41600 6432

6 residual strokes

些 J3a33 M268 84
批 J4863 M11845 2086

昆 J3a2b M13792 2430
枇 J487a M14528 2580
泥 J4525 M17311 3105
虎 J3857 M32675 5265

7 residual strokes

姥 J3138 M6216 1212
屍 J3b53 M7688 1420
指 J3b58 M12034 2152
昆 J3a2b M13792 2430
枇 J487a M14528 2580
枳 J4248 M14599 2597
毘 J487b M16753 3011
皆 J3327 M22699 3869
窃 J4060 M25453 4195
背 J4758 M29363 4794
虐 J3554 M32678 5266
陛 J4a45 M41654 6444

8 residual strokes

柴 J3c46 M14664 2657
毘 J487b M16753 3011
皆 J3327 M22699 3869
脂 J3b69 M29463 4808
能 J473d M29454 4809
陛 J4a45 M41654 6444

9 residual strokes

匙 J3a7c M2590 **582**
喝 J3365 M-X 824
揭 J3747 M12311 2194
椛 J3371 M15065 2683

渴 J3369 M17748 3195
混 J3a2e M17694 3204
砦 J4525 M24098 4002
舵 J4249 M30400 4937
葛 J336b M-X 5060
蛇 J3c58 M32964 5303
貨 J325f M36678 5781
階 J332c M41755 6469
頃 J3a22 M43338 6615
鹿 J3c2f M47586 7017

10 residual strokes

傾 J3739 M1038 299
卿 J-X M2880 643
混 J3a2e M17694 3204
琵 J487c M21080 3653
紫 J3b67 M22337 4486
葬 J4172 M31448 5128
詫 J3b60 M35374 5579
階 J332c M41755 6469
鹿 J3c2f M47586 7017

11 residual strokes

傾 J3739 M1038 299
厩 J3139 M-X 654
塡 J4536 M-X 1072
琵 J487c M21080 3653
虞 J3673 M32723 5272
虜 J4e3a M32720 5273
褐 J336c M-X 5473
詣 J3758 M35412 5594
靴 J3724 M42729 6576

---

12 residual strokes

厩 J-X M3006 660
嘗 J3e28 M4205 878
塵 J3f50 M5388 1087
態 J4256 M11052 1947
滬 J3977 M18112 3300
熊 J3727 M19294 3468
疑 J353f M22007 3777
箇 J4a4f M26114 4310
紫 J3b67 M27337 4486
雌 J3b73 M41998 6506

13 residual strokes

嘘 J-X M4206 885
塵 J3f50 M5388 1087
態 J4256 M11052 1947
慮 J4e38 M11132 1962
戯 J353a M11665 2041
滬 J3977 M18112 3300
稽 J374e M25218 4163
箇 J4a4f M26114 4310
罷 J486d M28336 4650
膚 J4966 M29829 4867
謁 J315a M35690 5637
鴿 J463e M46730 6943

14 residual strokes

凝 J3645 M1720 431
燕 J316d M19429 3489
頴 J3150 M24824 4109
穎 J314f M24824 4173
髭 J4926 M45399 6812

15–23 residual strokes

擬	J353c M12870	2307
鰭	J4949 M46400	6907
麓	J4f3c M47658	7023
麗	J4e6f M47663	7026
麟	J4e5b M47690	7028

Rad. 22 匚

2 residual strokes

匹	J4924 M2673	**584**
区	J3668 M2674	**585**
巨	J3570 M8722	1534

3–5 residual strokes

匝	J4159 M2599	**586**
匡	J3629 M2606	**587**
匠	J3e22 M2605	**588**
医	J3065 M2680	**590**
巨	J3570 M8722	1534
拒	J3571 M-X	2084
臣	J3f43 M30068	4894

6 residual strokes

枢	J3f75 M14577	2588
欧	J3224 M16024	2931
殴	J3225 M16618	2990

7 residual strokes

姬	J4931 M6229	1217

甚	J3f53 M21648	3711
矩	J366b M23947	3980
虜	J3554 M32678	5267
虹	J303a M32835	5277

8 residual strokes

匿	J463f M2690	**591**
匪	J485b M2629	**592**

9 residual strokes

勘	J342a M2393	548
脈	J4c2e M29470	4805
距	J3577 M37481	5866
躯	J366d M-X	5930

10–21 residual strokes

堰	J3161 M5274	1055
輌	J-X M38137	5935
駆	J366e M44634	6736
鴎	J322a M-X	6941

Rad. 23 匸

2–4 residual strokes

匹	J4924 M2673	584
区	J3668 M2674	585
匝	J4159 M2599	586
匡	J3629 M2606	587
匠	J3e22 M2605	588
妄	J4c51 M6063	1177
巨	J3570 M8722	1534

5–9 residual strokes

医	J3065 M2680	590
匿	J463f M2690	591
匪	J485b M2629	592

Rad. 24 十

0 residual strokes

十	J3d3d M2695	**598**

1 residual stroke

千	J4069 M2697	**599**
土	J455a M4867	966
士	J3b4e M5638	1117
干	J3433 M9165	1589
廿	J467b M9586	1662

2 residual strokes

丑	J312f M23	12
井	J3066 M258	76
什	J3d3a M348	105
升	J3c6a M2702	**603**
午	J3861 M2703	**604**
壬	J3f51 M5639	968
廿	J467b M9586	1662
支	J3b59 M13061	2324
斗	J454d M13489	2373
辻	J4454 M38711	6012

3 residual strokes

丑	J312f M23	12

半	J483e M2707	**608**
叶	J3370 M3255	689
古	J3845 M3233	702
平	J4a3f M9167	1590
汁	J3d41 M17104	3035
辻	J4454 M38711	6012
迅	J3f57 M38727	6014

4 residual strokes

伎	J346c M436	133
年	J472f M9168	1593
早	J4161 M13742	2419
缶	J344c M28108	4624
迅	J3f57 M38727	6014

5 residual strokes

克	J396e M1355	354
妓	J3538 M6083	1185
岐	J3474 M7936	1447
技	J353b M11855	2092
述	J3d52 M38803	6030

6 residual strokes

勃	J4b56 M2351	539
尭	J3646 M-X	**614**
卒	J4234 M2740	**615**
卓	J426e M2741	**616**
協	J3628 M2742	**617**
固	J3847 M745	949
坪	J445a M4976	998
垂	J3b62 M5012	999
奔	J4b5b M-X	1148

姑	J3848 M6174	1194
居	J356f M7663	1416
昇	J3e3a M13794	2434
杵	J354f M14503	2581
柿	J4f48 M14576	2585
枝	J3b5e M14557	2591
直	J443e M23136	3908
肢	J3b68 M29285	4768
苦	J366c M30797	5009
述	J3d52 M38803	6030
阜	J496c M41534	6423

7 residual strokes

乗	J3e68 M153	54
勃	J4b56 M2351	539
尭	J3646 M-X	**614**
卑	J485c M2751	**618**
南	J466e M2750	**619**
単	J4331 M2752	**620**
哉	J3d48 M3596	779
専	J406c M-X	1377
括	J3367 M11988	2143
故	J384e M13161	2334
枯	J384f M14579	2634
盾	J3d62 M23171	3912
砕	J3a55 M24080	3990
粋	J364e M26858	4383
胡	J3855 M29400	4792
草	J4170 M30945	5032
茶	J4363 M30915	5033
計	J3757 M35220	5555
重	J3d45 M40132	6207
革	J3357 M42710	6570

8 residual strokes

値	J434d M786	257
単	J4331 M2752	**620**
峰	J4a76 M8094	1473
恵	J3743 M10618	1847
挿	J415e M12119	2167
捕	J4a61 M12157	2170
栽	J3a4f M14750	2654
真	J3f3f M23236	3926
粋	J3f68 M26875	4389
索	J3a77 M27306	4449
針	J54b M40165	6218
隼	J483b M41943	6493

9 residual strokes

乾	J3425 M204	63
唾	J4243 M3785	826
埠	J4956 M5161	1029
埴	J3e7d M5188	1031
婁	J4f2c M6383	1235
術	J3d51 M34046	1754
悼	J4569 M10738	1891
捕	J4a61 M12157	2170
据	J3f78 M12204	2195
率	J4e28 M20817	3618
皐	J3b29 M22727	3873
章	J3e4f M25761	4235
許	J3576 M35298	5569
遁	J465b M38982	6087
酔	J3f6c M39807	6166

10 residual strokes

傘	J3b31 M966	283
博	J476e M2761	**621**
循	J3d5b M10187	1758
戟	J3761 M11606	2035
暁	J3647 M14031	2485
植	J3f22 M15023	2751
湖	J3850 M17836	3240
焼	J3e46 M19166	3438
牌	J4757 M-X	3528
献	J3825 M25053	3596
索	J3a77 M27306	4449
朝	J442b M14374	4838
裁	J3a5b M34258	5454
遁	J465b M38982	6087
靭	J3f59 M-X	6573

11 residual strokes

嘩	J325e M-X	861
填	J4536 M-X	1072
幹	J3434 M9183	1596
弾	J4346 M9836	1699
慎	J3f35 M11024	1945
戦	J406f M11631	2037
楢	J3d5d M15173	2776
楠	J466f M15152	2779
準	J3d60 M17934	3278
牌	J4757 M-X	3528
瑚	J386a M21126	3662
禅	J4135 M24787	4104
稗	J-X M25113	4151
置	J4356 M28298	4645
裾	J4231 M34382	5474
賊	J4231 M36759	5801
載	J3a5c M38309	5960

適	J452c M39076	6107
鉆	J385a M40270	6236
障	J3e63 M41821	6479
靴	J3724 M42729	6576
鼓	J385d M48330	7076

12 residual strokes

嫡	J4364 M6656	1263
彰	J3e34 M10015	1721
徳	J4641 M10237	1767
摘	J4526 M12582	2266
幹	J3036 M13522	2378
樺	J3472 M15497	2817
槙	J4b6a M-X	2819
滴	J4529 M18084	3299
碑	J486a M24364	4028
稗	J4923 M-X	4156
箇	J3255 M26116	4315
翠	J3f69 M28732	4685
適	J452c M39076	6107
鞄	J3373 M42781	6582

13 residual strokes

噴	J4a2e M4345	900
墳	J4a2f M5488	1095
廟	J4940 M9489	1645
衝	J3e57 M34069	1772
敷	J495f M13359	2357
敵	J4528 M13354	2359
樟	J3e40 M15451	2851
潮	J442c M18277	3336
穂	J325e M25236	4168
箪	J433d M26297	4321

糊	J3852 M27037	4415
蝉	J4066 M-X	5349
鞍	J3048 M42815	6586
鴇	J463e M46730	6943

14 residual strokes

壊	J3275 M5541	1102
憩	J3746 M11246	1980
憤	J4a30 M11239	1990
懐	J327b M11351	2003
穂	J-X M25236	4168
箪	J433d M26297	4321
翰	J344d M28780	4690
舘	J345c M30326	4923
蝉	J4066 M-X	5349
醐	J386f M39930	6183
鋸	J3578 M40505	6297
鞘	J3e64 M42850	6587
韓	J345a M43159	6602

15 residual strokes

懐	J327b M11351	2003
戴	J4257 M11685	2045
聡	J4430 M29173	4740
鞠	J3547 M42892	6589
韓	J345a M43159	6602

16 residual strokes

簞	J-X M26509	4357
蟬	J33616	5388
鎮	J4a5c M40745	6328
鞭	J4a5c M42937	6595

17-20 residual strokes

嚢	J-X M4633	933
簞	J-X M26509	4357
蟬	J-X M33616	5388
覇	J4746 M34790	5519
鏑	J452d M40790	6334
顛	J453f M-X	6652
驊	J424d M-X	6762
麺	J-X M47827	7039

Rad. 25 卜

0 residual strokes

卜	J4b4e M2774	**622**

1-2 residual stroke

下	J323c M14	9
上	J3e65 M13	10
止	J3b5f M16253	2954

3 residual strokes

占	J406a M2780	**624**
外	J3330 M5750	1125
正	J4035 M16255	2955
疋	J4925 M21994	3774

4 residual strokes

朴	J4b51 M14428	2544
正	J4035 M16255	2955
此	J3a21 M16259	2956

5 residual strokes

帖 J4421 / M8849 1558
走 J4176 / M37034 5845
足 J422d / M37365 5856

6 residual strokes

些 J3a33 / M268 84
卓 J426e / M2741 616
卦 J3735 / M2798 **625**
叔 J3d47 / M3154 677
定 J446u / M7109 1323
庇 J485f / M9239 1606
店 J4539 / M9267 1613
延 J3164 / M-X 1657
步 J4a62 / M16284 2958
祖 J3b63 / M24641 4069
肯 J394e / M29311 4771
苦 J4651 / M30802 5003
虎 J3857 / M32675 5265

7 residual strokes

峠 J463d / M8068 1464
是 J4027 / M13859 2451
柾 J4b6f / M14675 2619
歪 J4f44 / M16286 2960
点 J4540 / M18980 3412
虐 J3554 / M32678 5267
貞 J4467 / M36658 5768
赴 J496b / M37040 5847

8 residual strokes

捉 J422a / M12136 2159
症 J3e49 / M22140 3795
砧 J354e / M24099 3996
起 J352f / M37048 5849
越 J315b / M37110 5851

9 residual strokes

偵 J4465 / M898 270
寂 J3c64 / M7200 1342
彪 J4937 / M9993 1716
悼 J4569 / M10738 1891
戚 J404c / M11594 2032
捗 J443d / M-X 2173
捷 J3e39 / M12216 2198
掛 J335d / M12267 2214
淀 J4d64 / M17610 3182
涉 J3f44 / M17749 3190
淑 J3d4a / M17634 3191
渋 J3d42 / M17750 3200
粘 J4734 / M26901 4393
虚 J3575 / M32708 5269
蛋 J4341 / M32977 5301
雫 J3c36 / M42219 6519

10 residual strokes

提 J4473 / M12344 2237
疏 J4141 / M22000 3775
疎 J4142 / M22002 3776
証 J3e5a / M35341 5589
貼 J453d / M36718 5787
越 J315b / M37110 5851
超 J4436 / M37096 5852

11 residual strokes

楚 J413f / M15141 2771
歳 J3a50 / M16326 2962
碇 J4476 / M24275 4019
禎 J4477 / M24767 4099
罫 J3753 / M28295 4642
虞 J3673 / M32723 5272
虜 J4e3a / M32720 5273
越 J315b / M37110 5851
跨 J3859 / M37504 5872
践 J4129 / M37547 5873
跡 J4057 / M37493 5875
路 J4f29 / M37524 5876
跳 J4437 / M37533 5877
鉦 J3e60 / M40322 6246

12 residual strokes

劇 J3760 / M2218 517
歴 J4e72 / M16334 2964
疑 J353f / M22007 3777
綻 J433e / M27587 4514
跨 J3859 / M37504 5872
踊 J4d75 / M37587 5882

13 residual strokes

劇 J3760 / M2218 517
嘘 J-X / M4206 885
嘘 J3133 / M-X 886
慮 J4e38 / M11132 1962
膚 J4966 / M29829 4867
趣 J3c71 / M37207 5854
踏 J4627 / M37602 5889

14 residual strokes

叡 J3143 / M3214 683
整 J4030 / M13394 2360
稽 J-X / M-X 4174
綻 J433e / M27587 4514
縦 J3d44 / M27804 4571
醍 J4e7b / M39924 6184
錠 J3b41 / M40559 6293
餐 J3b41 / M44160 6696
鮎 J303e / M46070 6855

15–22 residual strokes

囓 J-X / M4516 921
櫃 J4827 / M15844 2910
燦 J3b38 / M19468 3498
縦 J3d44 / M27804 4571
趨 J3f76 / M37258 5855
餐 J3b41 / M44160 6696
魔 J4b62 / M45906 6843
鹸 J3834 / M-X 7013
鹹 J-X / M47576 7016

Rad. 26 卩

2 residual strokes

厄 J4c71 / M2893 646

3 residual strokes

卯 J312c / M2847 **628**
叩 J4321 / M3238 696
氾 J4845 / M17101 3033

犯 J4848 / M20238 3554

4 residual strokes

仰 J3644 / M400 137
卯 J312c / M2847 **628**
危 J346d / M2849 **629**
印 J3075 / M2848 **630**
迎 J375e / M38748 6019

5 residual strokes

仰 J3644 / M400 137
却 J3551 / M2856 **631**
即 J4228 / M2855 **633**
抑 J4d5e / M11883 2089
迎 J375e / M38748 6019

6 residual strokes

卵 J4d71 / M2857 **632**
即 J4228 / M2855 **633**
抑 J4d5e / M11883 2090
昂 J3937 / M13783 2424
服 J497e / M14345 4775
苑 J3171 / M30774 4996

7–9 residual strokes

卸 J3237 / M2861 **641**
卿 J362a / M2878 **642**
怨 J3165 / M10479 1819
昂 J-X / M13885 2447
柳 J4c78 / M14662 2629
脆 J4048 / M29468 4800

10–21 residual strokes

卿 J-X M2880 **643**
報 J4a73 M5275 1059
御 J3866 M10157 1761
椀 J4f50 M15001 2732
櫛 J367b M-X 2884
渡 J454f M17765 3247
碗 J4f52 M24306 4014
禦 J357a M24820 4111
節 J4061 M26102 4299
範 J484f M26253 4330
腕 J4f53 M29631 4837
鶯 J3175 M46795 6953

Rad. 27 厂

2 residual strokes

厄 J4c71 M2893 **646**
反 J483f M3127 674
斤 J3654 M13534 2379

3 residual strokes

圧 J3035 M4879 970

4 residual strokes

仮 J323e M398 144
危 J346d M2849 **629**
后 J3921 M3298 704
成 J402e M11542 2025
灰 J3325 M18859 3396
返 J4a56 M38758 6020

阪 J3a65 M41562 6428

5 residual strokes

励 J4e65 M2326 528
坂 J3a64 M4910 985
辰 J4324 M38682 6006
返 J4a56 M38758 6020

6 residual strokes

厚 J387c M2949 **651**
岸 J345f M8009 1459
底 J446c M9262 1612
彼 J4860 M10066 1732
板 J4844 M14518 2595
版 J4847 M19817 3526
茂 J402a M30833 4998
虎 J3857 M32675 5265
辰 J4324 M38682 6006

7 residual strokes

厘 J4e52 M2946 **650**
厚 J387c M2949 **651**
叛 J484d M3166 680
垢 J3924 M5058 1008
城 J3e6b M5086 1011
威 J3052 M6259 1219
彦 J4927 M9981 1714
恢 J327a M10577 1843
栃 J464a M14687 2613
炭 J433a M18953 3413
盾 J3d62 M23171 3912
虐 J3554 M32678 5267

8 residual strokes

原 J3836 M2973 **652**
唇 J3f30 M3697 807
娠 J3f31 M6322 1224
振 J3f36 M12093 2171
砺 J4557 M-X 3993
脆 J4048 M29468 4800
脈 J4c2e M29470 4805
辱 J3f2b M38686 6007

9 residual strokes

厩 J3139 M-X **654**
唇 J3f30 M3697 807
崖 J3333 M8180 1488
彪 J4937 M9993 1716
戚 J404c M11594 2032
振 J3f36 M12093 2171
涯 J3336 M17582 3181
産 J3b3a M21684 3716
盛 J4039 M23001 3895
虚 J3575 M32708 5269
蛎 J3342 M-X 5291
販 J484e M36679 5779
辱 J3f2b M38686 6007

10 residual strokes

備 J4877 M967 284
厩 J3139 M-X **654**
厨 J3f5f M3005 **657**
循 J3d5b M10187 1758
減 J383a M17759 3249
雁 J3467 M41960 6498

飯 J4853 M44064 6679

11 residual strokes

厩 J3139 M-X **654**
嫉 J3c3b M6611 1255
惑 J3436 M10953 1928
楯 J3d5d M15173 2776
歳 J3a50 M16326 2962
源 J383b M17926 3274
滅 J4c47 M18008 3279
虞 J3673 M32723 5272
虜 J3727 M32720 5273
誠 J403f M35497 5606
農 J4740 M38688 6008
飯 J4853 M44064 6679

12 residual strokes

厭 J315e M3025 **662**
嘘 J3133 M-X 886
暦 J4e71 M14111 2507
歴 J4e72 M16334 2964
蔑 J4a4e M31781 5179
蔵 J4222 M31885 5182
賑 J3466 M36785 5806
農 J4740 M38688 6008

13 residual strokes

噓 J-X 885
慮 J4e38 M11132 1962
糧 J4138 M27057 4413
膚 J4966 M29829 4867
蔵 J4222 M31885 5182

蕨 J4f4f M32001 5194
震 J3f4c M42300 6531

14 residual strokes

憾 J3438 M11312 1999
濃 J473b M18442 3349
薩 J3b27 M32189 5217
諺 J3841 M-X 5659

15–18 residual strokes

厳 J3837 M3048 **663**
濃 J473b M18442 3349
礦 J626a M24571 4056
臆 J3538 M29938 4884
臓 J4221 M29995 4886
顔 J3469 M43591 6648
贋 J3466 M36943 5830
願 J346a M43623 6653
巌 J3460 M8624 1521

Rad. 28 厶

2 residual strokes

云 J313e M254 74
仏 J4a29 M364 111
允 J3074 M1338 342
公 J3878 M1452 372
勾 J387b M2500 568
去 J356e M3070 **665**
弘 J3930 M9709 1682

3 residual strokes

去	J356e / M3070	**665**
台	J4266 / M3246	699
広	J392d / M9224	1604
弁	J4a5b / M9588	1663
弁	J4a5b / M9588	1664
弁	J4a5b / M9588	1665
弁	J4a5b / M9588	1666
弘	J3930 / M9709	1682
払	J4a27 / M11784	2062

4 residual strokes

伝	J4541 / M462	141
会	J3271 / M460	143
充	J3d3c / M1345	348
弘	J3930 / M9709	1682
牟	J4c36 / M19928	3533
至	J3b6a / M30142	4903

5 residual strokes

冶	J4c6a / M1621	418
劫	J3965 / M2316	529
却	J3551 / M2856	631
宏	J3928 / M7086	1314
私	J3b64 / M24913	4124
芸	J375d / M30741	4978

6 residual strokes

到	J457e / M1950	477
参	J3b90 / M3090	**666**
始	J3b4f / M6166	1203

怯	J3631 / M10491	1816
拡	J3348 / M11985	2118
松	J3e3e / M14516	2592
治	J3c23 / M17256	3100
法	J4b21 / M17290	3107
肱	J394f / M29315	4770
育	J3069 / M29318	4773
苔	J425d / M30778	5001

7 residual strokes

俊	J3d53 / M674	216
室	J3c3c / M7136	1327
屋	J3230 / M7684	1421
怠	J4255 / M10469	1818
殆	J4b58 / M16430	2972
胎	J425b / M29369	4789

8 residual strokes

俊	J3d53 / M674	216
唆	J3a36 / M3696	803
套	J4565 / M5926	1161
峻	J3d54 / M8116	1475
挨	J3027 / M12082	2160
桧	J4930 / M-X	2637
流	J4e2e / M17572	3160
砂	J395c / M-X	3994
紘	J3949 / M27289	4445
翁	J3227 / M28635	4677
能	J473d / M29454	4809
致	J4357 / M30149	4904
陰	J3122 / M41691	6462
鬼	J3534 / M45758	6833

9 residual strokes

強	J362f / M9815	1695
惨	J3b34 / M10850	1896
棄	J347e / M14913	2787
琉	J4e30 / M20978	3642
窒	J4362 / M25493	4200
窓	J416b / M25494	4201
脚	J3553 / M29502	4820
訟	J3e59 / M35266	5565
転	J453e / M38234	5948

10 residual strokes

幾	J3476 / M9208	1601
強	J362f / M9815	1695
握	J302e / M12366	2232
棄	J347e / M14913	2787
渥	J302f / M17770	3224
滋	J3c22 / M17919	3238
疏	J4141 / M22000	3775
硫	J4e32 / M24229	4006
竣	J3d57 / M25773	4238
紘	J3949 / M27289	4445
統	J457d / M27447	4487
絵	J3328 / M27464	4488
蛭	J4948 / M33048	5308
鈎	J3343 / M40220	6226
雄	J4d3a / M41972	6499
雲	J3140 / M42233	6522

11 residual strokes

塊	J3274 / M5319	1070
強	J362f / M9815	1695

慈	J3b7c / M10980	1924
棄	J347e / M14913	2787
蔭	J307e / M31840	5151
蓋	J3338 / M31652	5155
蒐	J3d2f / M31539	5159
鉱	J395b / M40340	6252
飴	J303b / M44080	6682

12 residual strokes

態	J4256 / M11052	1947
熊	J3727 / M19294	3468
璃	J4d7e / M21196	3669
統	J457d / M27447	4487
絵	J3328 / M27464	4488
総	J416d / M27620	4532
聡	J416f / M29109	4730
酸	J3b40 / M39871	6177
鉾	J4b48 / M40353	6255
銃	J3d46 / M40359	6267
飴	J303b / M44080	6682
髪	J4831 / M45387	6804
魁	J3321 / M45755	6834
魂	J3a32 / M45787	6835

13 residual strokes

徹	J4530 / M10245	1771
撤	J4531 / M12726	2280
璃	J4d7e / M21196	3669
畿	J3526 / M21925	3768
罷	J486d / M28336	4650
魅	J4c25 / M45811	6838

14 residual strokes

曡	J465e / M14172	2518
檎	J3869 / M15657	2888
総	J416d / M27620	4532
髭	J4926 / M45399	6812

15–17 residual strokes

檎	J3869 / M15657	2888
瓣	J6122 / M21425	3689
轍	J4532 / M38524	5988
醜	J3d39 / M39969	6189
駿	J3d59 / M44775	6754
鯵	J3033 / M-X	6875

Rad. 29 又

0 residual strokes

又	J4b74 / M3115	**668**

1 residual strokes

叉	J3a35 / M3116	**669**

2 residual strokes

及	J355a / M3118	**670**
友	J4d27 / M3119	**672**
双	J4150 / M3125	**673**
反	J483f / M3127	**674**
支	J3b59 / M13061	2324

3 residual strokes

冬	J455f / M1610	410
処	J3d68 / M1745	435
収	J3c7d / M3128	**675**
奴	J455b / M6039	1174
皮	J4869 / M22823	3878

4 residual strokes

伎	J346c / M436	133
仮	J323e / M398	144
各	J3346 / M3281	714
返	J4a56 / M38758	6020
阪	J3a65 / M41562	6428

5 residual strokes

努	J4558 / M2314	527
吸	J355b / M3372	713
坂	J3a64 / M4910	985
妓	J3538 / M6083	1185
岐	J3474 / M7936	1447
役	J4c72 / M10057	1726
技	J353b / M11855	2092
抜	J4834 / M11901	2093
投	J456a / M11887	2095
条	J3e72 / M14486	2563
没	J4b57 / M17233	3066
返	J4a56 / M38758	6020
麦	J477e / M47718	7030

6 residual strokes

叔	J3d47 / M3154	**677**

受 J3c75 / M3159 **678**
取 J3c68 / M3158 **679**

径	J3742 / M10080	1730
彼	J4860 / M10066	1732
怪	J3278 / M10483	1821
披	J4864 / M11909	2116
枝	J3b5e / M14557	2591
板	J4844 / M14518	2595
殴	J3225 / M16618	2990
波	J4748 / M17308	3101
版	J4847 / M19817	3526
肢	J474c / M29285	4768
股	J3854 / M29284	4772
服	J497e / M14345	4775
茎	J3754 / M30861	4990

7 residual strokes

侵	J3f2f / M646	218
叛	J4840 / M3166	**680**
叙	J3d76 / M3163	**681**
度	J4559 / M9313	1616
怒	J455c / M10439	1820
段	J434a / M16619	2991
疫	J3156 / M22069	3783
盈	J314e / M22961	3888

8 residual strokes

夏	J3246 / M5720	1120
寂	J3c64 / M7200	1342
捜	J415c / M12179	2168
桑	J372c / M14772	2661
殺	J3b26 / M16629	2994
浸	J3b3b / M17505	3157

疲	J4868 / M22084	3796
盈	J314e / M22961	3888
破	J474b / M24124	3999
般	J484c / M30388	4931
蚤	J4742 / M32893	5287
被	J486f / M34222	5445
隻	J4049 / M41941	6494

9 residual strokes

堅	J3778 / M5210	1038
婆	J474c / M6390	1240
寂	J3c64 / M7200	1342
掻	J415f / M-X	2175
授	J3c78 / M12242	2208
淑	J3d4a / M17634	3191
経	J3750 / M27392	4473
設	J405f / M35293	5570
販	J484e / M36679	5779

10 residual strokes

堅	J3778 / M5210	1038
報	J4a73 / M5275	1059
媛	J4932 / M6516	1244
援	J3167 / M12407	2230
最	J3a47 / M14301	2492
極	J364b / M15181	2753
殻	J334c / M-X	2996
痩	J4169 / M-X	3806
督	J4644 / M23457	3946
腎	J3f55 / M29621	4834
軽	J375a / M38281	5953
飯	J4853 / M44064	6679

11 residual strokes

寝	J3f32 / M7278	1353
搬	J4842 / M12507	2249
掻	J-X / M12477	2256
暖	J324b / M14036	2501
暖	J4348 / M14064	2502
極	J364b / M15181	2753
椴	J4e15 / M15075	2772
殿	J4542 / M16651	3001
暖	J466d / M21892	3766
督	J4644 / M23457	3946
竪	J4328 / M25790	4240
経	J3750 / M27392	4473
腎	J3f55 / M29621	4834
飯	J4853 / M44064	6679
鼓	J385d / M48330	7076

12 residual strokes

漫	J4c21 / M18166	3308
穀	J3972 / M20758	4157
竪	J4328 / M25790	4240
綏	J3c7a / M27565	4510
緊	J365b / M27603	4524
綴	J4456 / M27579	4526
蔓	J4c22 / M31784	5180
頚	J375b / M43434	6626
頗	J47c7 / M43415	6627
髪	J4831 / M45387	6804

13 residual strokes

慢	J4b71 / M11110	1968
憂	J4d2b / M11170	1971

撃 J3762 / M12674 2265

撮	J3b23 / M12748	2282
樫	J335f / M15485	2849
毅	J3523 / M16673	3003
潑	J-X / M18225	3325
痩	J-X / M22415	3832
盤	J4857 / M23036	3902
磐	J4858 / M24401	4037
緊	J365b / M27603	4524
緩	J344b / M27669	4551
蝦	J325c / M33299	5364
諏	J3f5b / M35648	5632
賢	J382d / M36822	5816
趣	J3c71 / M37207	5854

14 residual strokes

叡 J3143 / M3214 **683**

樫	J335f / M15485	2849
澱	J4543 / M18410	3347
獲	J334d / M20758	3609
綬	J3c7a / M27565	4510
緊	J365b / M27603	4524
縅	J4456 / M27579	4526
賢	J382d / M36822	5816
餐	J3b41 / M44160	6696

15 residual strokes

燦	J3b38 / M19468	3498
緩	J344b / M27669	4551
繋	J3752 / M-X	4573
鍍	J4555 / M40607	6312
鍛	J4343 / M40625	6318
霞	J3262 / M42365	6541

餐 J3b41 / M44160 **6696**

16–26 residual strokes

叢 J4151 / M3220 **684**
穫 J334f / M25334 **4180**
籔 J4876 / M26609 **4363**
繋 J3752 / M-X **4573**
覆 J4a24 / M34789 **5517**
護 J386e / M36038 **5715**
醶 J-X / M40041 **6194**
馨 J333e / M44559 **6724**
騷 J417b / M44834 **6760**
鰻 J3137 / M46443 **6914**

Rad. 30 口

0 residual strokes

口 J387d / M3227 **685**
巳 J4c26 / M8744 **1538**

1 residual stroke

中 J4366 / M73 **28**
巳 J4c26 / M8744 **1538**

2 residual strokes

兄 J373b / M1343 **344**
加 J3243 / M2297 **523**
占 J406a / M2780 **624**
叶 J3370 / M3255 **689**
叱 J3c38 / M3247 **691**
号 J3966 / M3256 **692**

句 J3667 / M3234 **693**
只 J427e / M3239 **694**
召 J3e24 / M3241 **695**
叩 J4321 / M3238 **696**
史 J3b4b / M3249 **697**
司 J3b4a / M3257 **698**
台 J4266 / M3246 **699**
右 J3126 / M3250 **700**
可 J3244 / M3245 **701**
古 J3845 / M3233 **702**
田 J4544 / M21723 **3727**
石 J4050 / M24024 **3985**

3 residual strokes

仲 J4367 / M403 **140**
号 J3966 / M3256 **692**
吋 J3125 / M3292 **703**
后 J3921 / M3298 **704**
更 J4d79 / M3299 **706**
吃 J3549 / M3280 **707**
叫 J362b / M3240 **708**
吐 J4547 / M3300 **709**
吊 J445f / M3291 **710**
吉 J3548 / M3289 **711**
向 J387e / M3301 **712**
吸 J355b / M3372 **713**
各 J3346 / M3281 **714**
合 J3967 / M3287 **715**
名 J4c3e / M3297 **716**
同 J4631 / M3294 **717**
吹 J3f61 / M3373 **747**
回 J3273 / M4690 **941**
如 J4721 / M6060 **1178**
舌 J4065 / M30277 **4917**

虫 J436e / M32804 **5275**
西 J403e / M34763 **5514**

4 residual strokes

串 J367a / M00 **30**
乱 J4d70 / M187 **60**
亨 J357c / M295 **91**
享 J357d / M298 **92**
佑 J4d24 / M507 **150**
伺 J3b47 / M483 **156**
伽 J3240 / M486 **159**
何 J323f / M511 **169**
克 J396e / M1355 **354**
冶 J4c6a / M1621 **418**
別 J4a4c / M1924 **467**
司 J3b4a / M3257 **698**
吸 J355b / M3372 **713**
呂 J4f25 / M3386 **728**
吻 J4a2d / M3375 **729**
吾 J3863 / M3379 **733**
呈 J4468 / M3401 **734**
吞 J465d / M3329 **737**
呆 J4a72 / M3395 **738**
吠 J4b4a / M3331 **739**
吟 J3663 / M3330 **740**
呉 J3862 / M3365 **741**
否 J485d / M3340 **742**
含 J345e / M3343 **743**
告 J3970 / M3381 **744**
君 J372f / M3323 **746**
吹 J372f / M3373 **747**
局 J3649 / M7653 **1412**
杏 J3049 / M14461 **2554**
束 J422b / M14480 **2559**

沖 J322d / M17209 **3065**
言 J3840 / M35205 **5552**
谷 J432b / M36182 **5730**
豆 J4626 / M36245 **5735**
足 J422d / M37365 **5856**
迦 J3260 / M38789 **6027**
邑 J4d38 / M39269 **6127**
酉 J4653 / M39763 **6157**
阿 J3024 / M41599 **6435**

5 residual strokes

事 J3b76 / M241 **71**
亨 J357c / M295 **91**
享 J357d / M298 **92**
京 J357e / M299 **93**
侃 J3426 / M577 **182**
舍 J3c4b / M30278 **189**
使 J3b48 / M573 **196**
兎 J4546 / M-X **358**
吾 J3863 / M3379 **733**
咋 J3a70 / M3488 **751**
呪 J3c76 / M3443 **764**
味 J4c23 / M3456 **766**
命 J4c3f / M3473 **767**
周 J3c7e / M3441 **768**
呼 J3846 / M3471 **769**
和 J4f42 / M3490 **770**
固 J3847 / M4745 **949**
命 J3471 / M5892 **1150**
姑 J3848 / M6174 **1194**
姉 J454a / M6121 **1197**
始 J3b4f / M6166 **1203**
宕 J4566 / M7103 **1316**
尚 J3e30 / M7493 **1395**

屈 J464f / M7667 **1413**
居 J356f / M7663 **1416**
岩 J3840 / M7985 **1461**
帖 J4421 / M8849 **1558**
店 J4539 / M9267 **1613**
廻 J3276 / M9575 **1659**
忠 J303f / M10353 **1801**
或 J303f / M11563 **2030**
拐 J327d / M11955 **2107**
拓 J4273 / M11958 **2115**
拘 J3934 / M11963 **2123**
招 J3e37 / M11968 **2124**
況 J3637 / M17224 **3086**
沼 J3e42 / M17257 **3091**
沿 J3168 / M17260 **3096**
治 J3c23 / M17256 **3100**
河 J324f / M17245 **3102**
狗 J3669 / M20345 **3565**
知 J434e / M23935 **3978**
茄 J3258 / M30835 **4995**
苔 J425d / M30778 **5001**
苦 J4651 / M30802 **5003**
苛 J3257 / M30785 **5006**
若 J3c63 / M30796 **5007**
苦 J366c / M30802 **5009**
迦 J3260 / M38789 **6027**
阜 J496c / M41534 **6423**

6 residual strokes

亭 J357c / M295 **91**
亮 J4e3c / M304 **95**
亭 J4462 / M303 **96**
俣 J4b73 / M718 **202**
侶 J4e37 / M647 **205**

促	J4225 / M664	212
俗	J422f / M695	220
保	J4a5d / M702	222
勅	J443c / M2354	540
呉	J3862 / M3365*	741
哉	J3a48 / M3596	779
咽	J3076 / M3577	788
咳	J3331 / M3555	789
咲	J3a69 / M3554	790
哀	J3025 / M3580	791
品	J494a / M3581	792
垢	J3924 / M5058	1008
始	J3028 / M6242	1208
客	J3552 / M7128	1329
帥	J3f63 / M8886	1559
息	J4255 / M10469	1818
恰	J3366 / M10603	1838
括	J3367 / M11988	2143
拾	J3d26 / M12014	2149
挽	J-X / M12111	2169
故	J384e / M13161	2334
昭	J3e3c / M13855	2446
昼	J436b / M13886	2450
柘	J4453 / M14626	2626
架	J324d / M14586	2632
枯	J384f / M14579	2634
殆	J4b58 / M16430	2972
洛	J4d6c / M17383	3119
洞	J4636 / M17386	3125
活	J3368 / M17423	3132
点	J4540 / M18980	3412
独	J4648 / M20406	3574
珂	J3251 / M20406	3625
祐	J4d34 / M24652*	4079
祝	J3d4b / M24672*	4085

胎	J425b / M29369	4789
胡	J3855 / M29400	4792
虹	J3a2d / M32835	5277
虹	J467a / M32830	5279
訂	J447b / M35211	5553
計	J3757 / M35220	5555
逗	J3f60 / M38887	6053
這	J4767 / M38889	6058
速	J422e / M38897	6060
造	J4224 / M38898	6061
郡	J3734 / M39436	6143
郭	J3354 / M39474	6144
革	J3357 / M42710	6570
風	J4977 / M43756	6663

7 residual strokes

衷	J436f / M-X	31
倹	J3770 / M823	248
倍	J475c / M760	252
倉	J4152 / M756	255
個	J3844 / M758	258
党	J455e / M1381	363
富	J495a / M1592	406
凋	J437c / M1668	423
剖	J4b36 / M2034	492
剣	J3775 / M2076	498
匿	J463f / M2690	591
咳	J3331 / M3555	789
哀	J3025 / M3580	791
啄	J426f / M-X	793
唖	J3022 / M3743	795
唄	J3134 / M3694	802
峻	J3a36 / M3696	803
哩	J4b69 / M3649	805

唇	J3f30 / M3697	**807**
員	J3077 / M3633	**808**
哨	J3e25 / M3646	**809**
哲	J452f / M3667	**811**
唐	J4562 / M3709*	**812**
娯	J3864 / M6307*	1231
婉	J4a5a / M6337	1233
害	J3332 / M7165	1333
容	J4d46 / M7172	1335
宮	J355c / M7156	1336
帥	J3f63 / M8886	1559
師	J3b55 / M8916	1562
廻	J3276 / M9575	1659
息	J4255 / M10469	1818
恕	J3d7a / M10560	1834
恩	J3238 / M10591	1851
悦	J3159 / M10629*	1868
悟	J3867 / M10680	1870
悼	J4657 / M10759	1887
捉	J422a / M12136	2159
捌	J3b2b / M12141	2162
挽	J4854 / M-X	2172
桔	J354b / M14777	2653
桐	J364d / M14770	2655
格	J334a / M14749	2668
浩	J3940 / M17479	3147
浴	J4d61 / M17496	3153
淳	J3d5f / M17690	3189
烏	J3128 / M18998	3421
烹	J4b23 / M19049	3425
砺	J4557 / M-X	3993
砧	J354e / M24099	3996
胴	J4639 / M29436	4810
荷	J3259 / M31000	5059
蚤	J4742 / M32893	5287

蚊	J3263 / M32849	5288
衰	J3f6a / M34127	5432
訊	J3e25 / M35224	5559
託	J4277 / M35243	5560
討	J4624 / M35231	5561
訓	J3731 / M35238	5562
記	J352d / M35244	5563
逗	J3f60 / M38887	6053
這	J4767 / M38889	6058
速	J422e / M38897	6060
造	J4224 / M38898	6061
週	J3d35 / M38937*	6070
郭	J3354 / M39474	6144
部	J4974 / M39460	6146
険	J3831 / M41721*	6456
陪	J4766 / M41680	6458
高	J3962 / M45313	6796

8 residual strokes

停	J4464 / M864	273
副	J497b / M2097	503
匿	J463f / M2690	591
啄	J426f / M-X	**793**
唇	J3f30 / M3697	**807**
啄	J-X / M3801	**821**
喝	J3365 / M-X	**824**
唾	J4243 / M3785	**826**
啓	J373c / M3820	**828**
唱	J3e27 / M3765	**829**
問	J4c64 / M3814	**830**
唯	J4d23 / M3761	**831**
商	J3e26 / M3803	**832**
埼	J306b / M5201	1028
城	J3068 / M5158	1030

培	J475d / M5195	1032
壷	J445b / M5657	1034
堂	J4632 / M5207	1037
婁	J4f2c / M6383	1235
寄	J3473 / M7203	1345
崎	J3a6a / M8169	1485
常	J3e6f / M8955	1569
廻	J3276 / M9575	1659
強	J362f / M9815	1695
彫	J4426 / M9995	1719
患	J3435 / M10691	1871
悪	J302d / M10717	1873
悼	J4657 / M10759	1887
挽	J4854 / M-X	2172
掻	J415f / M-X	2175
掠	J4e2b / M12273	2191
据	J3f78 / M12204	2195
捨	J3c4e / M12191*	2205
敦	J4658 / M13276	2349
梧	J3868 / M14872	2700
欲	J4d5f / M16080	2936
淳	J3d5f / M17690	3189
涼	J4e43 / M17605	3198
烹	J4b23 / M19049	3425
甜	J453c / M21656	3712
略	J4e2c / M21839	3755
筥	J3f5a / M25934	4265
粘	J4734 / M26901	4393
紹	J3e52 / M27361	4465
脱	J4326 / M29539*	4822
船	J4125 / M30407	4939
菟	J-X / M31189	5077
菩	J4a6e / M31205	5093
蛎	J3342 / M-X	5291
蛋	J4341 / M32977	5301

蛍	J3756	M32983	5302
蛇	J3c58	M32964	5303
袈	J3736	M34166	5442
袷	J3041	M34240	5449
訟	J3e59	M35266	5565
訣	J376d	M35272	5567
許	J3576	M35298	5569
設	J405f	M35293	5570
訪	J4b2c	M35284	5571
訳	J4c75	M35324′	5572
距	J3577	M37481	5866
週	J3d35	M38937′	6070
逼	J492f	M38973	6085
過	J3261	M39002′	6090
釦	J4b55	M40175	6223

9 residual strokes

偉	J304e	M837	285
創	J414f	M2127	506
割	J3364	M2112′	507
勤	J3650	M2415′	552
厨	J3f5f	M3005	657
喬	J362c	M3990	**841**
喰	J3674	M4015	**849**
喋	J437d	M3917	**850**
喚	J342d	M3953	**852**
喪	J4153	M3985	**853**
喉	J3922	M3913	**854**
喫	J354a	M3987	**855**
喧	J3776	M3976	**856**
営	J3144	M4025	**857**
喜	J346e	M3957	**858**
善	J4131	M3904	**859**
塔	J4563	M5332	1052
富	J4959	M7230	1349
尋	J3f52	M7447	1385
就	J3d22	M7599	1401
属	J4230	M7754	1430
幅	J497d	M8995	1574
強	J362f	M9815	1695
惹	J3c66	M10866	1886
惑	J4f47	M10789	1892
掌	J3e38	M12248	2200
揖	J4d2c	M12351	2222
搭	J456b	M12508	2228
敦	J4658	M13276	2349
敬	J3749	M13285′	2351
景	J374a	M13983	2487
智	J4352	M14010	2490
椋	J4c3a	M15020	2725
椅	J3058	M15009	2737
検	J3821	M15065′	2752
極	J364b	M15101	2753
湖	J3850	M17836	3240
渦	J3132	M17771	3241
減	J383a	M17759	3249
疎	J4142	M22002	3776
痘	J4577	M22185	3813
登	J4550	M22668	3862
短	J433b	M23978	3982
硲	J4823	M24243	4004
程	J4478	M25081′	4144
税	J4047	M25070′	4146
筈	J4826	M25990	4277
筒	J457b	M26004	4283
答	J457a	M26006	4285
絡	J4d6d	M27426	4484
給	J356b	M27432	4489
結	J376b	M27398	4492
菟	J4551	M-X	5102
葺	J4978	M31465	5125
落	J4d6e	M31362	5130
蓉	J4d56	M31648	5135
蛭	J4948	M33048	5308
蛤	J483a	M33023	5312
蛙	J333f	M32997	5313
袈	J3736	M34166	5442
裕	J4d35	M34305	5461
覗	J4741	M34839	5528
詑	J4242	M35374	5579
詔	J3e5b	M35379	5581
詞	J3b6c	M35394	5582
註	J4370	M35340	5583
詐	J3a3e	M35373	5585
診	J3f47	M35337	5586
評	J493e	M35383	5587
訴	J414a	M35325	5588
証	J3e5a	M35341	5589
象	J3e5d	M36372	5744
貼	J453d	M36718	5787
賀	J326c	M36725	5790
貴	J352e	M36704	5794
超	J4436	M37096	5852
距	J3577	M37481	5866
逼	J492f	M38973	6085
過	J3261	M39002′	6090
違	J3063	M39067′	6099
遺	J382f	M39052′	6100
遠	J3173	M39047′	6101
隔	J3356	M-X	6475
靭	J3f59	M-X	6573

10 residual strokes

僅	J-X	M1048	292
喪	J4153	M3985	**853**
嘩	J325e	M-X	**861**
嗣	J3b4c	M4109	**868**
嘆	J4332	M4138′	**872**
園	J3160	M4818	962
塔	J4563	M5332	1052
塙	J4839	M5341	1063
塘	J4564	M5340	1066
塩	J3176	M5382	1075
塾	J3d4e	M5402	1083
嵩	J3f73	M8348	1502
廓	J3347	M9461	1633
強	J362f	M9815	1695
感	J3436	M10953	1928
損	J423b	M12459	2255
搔	J-X	M12477	2256
極	J364b	M15181	2753
溶	J4d4f	M17983	3277
漢	J3441	M18068′	3281
煉	J-X	M19178	3455
照	J3e48	M19226	3457
猿	J316e	M20584	3600
獄	J3976	M20603	3602
瑚	J386a	M21126	3662
痴	J4354	M22257	3823
碕	J3a6c	M24296	4015
禍	J3252	M24766′	4102
福	J4a21	M24768′	4105
紹	J3e52	M27361	4465
絹	J3828	M27470	4499
群	J3732	M28498	4666
聖	J403b	M29074	4727
蒔	J3c43	M31748	5138
蓑	J4c2c	M31661	5143
葦	J3031	M31437	5160
蒼	J4173	M31627	5162
虜	J3673	M32723′	5272
蛾	J326b	M33082	5325
蛸	J427d	M33072	5330
蜂	J4b2a	M33088	5331
裾	J3f7e	M34382	5474
触	J3f28	M35070	5547
詣	J3758	M35412	5594
詫	J4f4d	M35431	5598
該	J333a	M35445	5601
誉	J4d40	M35498	5602
詮	J4127	M35435	5604
誇	J3858	M35474	5605
誠	J403f	M35497′	5606
詳	J3e5c	M35446	5607
話	J4f43	M35441	5608
詰	J354d	M35440	5609
詩	J3b6d	M35427	5610
試	J3b6e	M35415	5611
豊	J4b2d	M36263	5737
賂	J4f28	M36738	5799
跨	J3859	M37504	5872
践	J4129	M37547′	5873
跡	J4057	M37493	5875
路	J4f29	M37524	5876
辞	J3c2d	M38638	6000
違	J3063	M39067′	6099
遺	J382f	M39052′	6100
遠	J3173	M39047′	6101
適	J452c	M39076′	6107
酪	J4d6f	M39847	6172
鈷	J385a	M40270	6236
鉛	J3174	M40310	6251
靴	J3724	M42729	6576

飴 J303b M44080 6682
飼 J3b74 M44107 6685
鼓 J385d M48330 7076

11 residual strokes

僑 J3623 M1088 307
喪 J4153 M3985 **853**
噌 J4139 M-X **873**
嘗 J3e28 M4205 **878**
噓 J-X M4206 **885**
嘘 J3133 M-X **886**
嘉 J3245 M4176 **887**
塾 J3d4e M5402 1083
嫡 J4364 M6656 1263
屢 J-X M7787 1431
摑 J4 M12572 2263
摘 J4526 M12582 2266
槍 J4164 M15319 2822
歌 J324e M16167 2945
歎 J4337 M16182 2947
滴 J4529 M18084 3299
熔 J4d50 M19319 3458
熟 J3d4f M19332 3472
箇 J3255 M26116 4315
絡 J4d6d M27426 4484
給 J356b M27432 4489
結 J376b M27398 4492
罰 J4833 M28315 4647
膏 J3951 M29800 4859
蕘 J4c2c M31661 5143
蜩 J4f39 M-X 5332
蜘 J4358 M33134 5342
蜜 J4c2a M33143 5343
蝶 J4433 M33333 5363

裳 J3e58 M34357 5472
該 J333a M35445 5601
誇 J3858 M35474 5605
誌 J3b6f M35501 5620
誓 J4040 M35514 5622
認 J4727 M35502 5623
誘 J4d36 M35525 5625
誤 J386d M35546 5626
説 J4062 M35556 5627
語 J386c M35533 5628
読 J4649 M35580 5629
誕 J4342 M35692 5640
豪 J396b M36406 5749
跨 J3859 M37504 5872
踊 J4d59 M37587 5882
適 J452c M39076 6107
遺 J3064 M39134 6115
酷 J3973 M39870 6176
醇 J3d66 M39901 6181
銘 J4c43 M40385 6265
銅 J463c M40361 6266
閣 J395e M41301 6397
閤 J3355 M41300 6401
鞄 J3373 M42781 6582
飴 J303b M44080 6682
飼 J3b74 M44107 6685
鳴 J4c44 M46672 6939

12 residual strokes

舖 J4a5e M30323 322
僻 J4a48 M1166 323
噓 J-X M4206 **885**
噌 J-X M4303 **889**
嘱 J3e7c M4249 **894**

噂 J313d M4286 **896**
器 J346f M4349 **898**
噴 J4a2e M4345 **900**
嬉 J3472 M6736 1267
廝 J3e33 M9490 1643
影 J3146 M10019 1722
衛 J3152 M34073 1776
慾 J4d5d M11163 1951
敷 J495f M13359 2357
敵 J4528 M13354 2359
澄 J4021 M18315 3333
潰 J4459 M18281 3335
熟 J3d4f M19332 3472
稿 J3946 M25220 4166
糊 J3852 M27037 4415
絹 J3828 M27470 4499
緯 J305e M27682 4566
蕎 J363e M31946 5197
蝿 J4768 M-X 5344
蝉 J4066 M-X 5349
蝕 J-X M33264 5358
蝶 J4433 M33333 5363
蝦 J325c M33299 5364
褒 J4b2b M34437 5483
誘 J4d36 M35525 5625
諌 J3452 M35630 5630
諷 J3f5b M35648 5632
誼 J3543 M35605 5634
謁 J315a M35690 5637
諸 J427a M35687 5638
誹 J4870 M35601 5639
誕 J4342 M35692 5640
諒 J4e4a M35653 5641
誰 J432f M35586 5642
談 J434c M35633 5643

課 J325d M35589 5644
請 J4041 M35640 5645
論 J4f40 M35658 5646
調 J4434 M35609 5647
諸 J3d74 M35691 5648
謎 J4666 M35800 5661
賠 J4765 M36818 5810
賞 J3e5e M36813 5815
踏 J4627 M37602 5889
遵 J3064 M39134 6115
避 J4872 M39163 6120
還 J3841 M39174 6121
醇 J3d66 M39901 6181
鋭 J3154 M40418 6279
関 J315c M41341 6404
鞍 J3048 M42815 6586
駒 J3670 M44663 6742
駕 J326f M44667 6743

13 residual strokes

噛 J4838 M4433 **903**
嗅 J4655 M4429 **910**
壇 J4345 M5528 1101
壁 J4a49 M5516 1103
憩 J3746 M11246 1980
憾 J3438 M11312 1999
操 J4160 M12806 2296
整 J4030 M13394 2360
橡 J464b M15564 2863
橘 J354c M15551 2868
樹 J3c79 M15496 2878
橋 J3636 M15526 2879
濁 J4279 M18440 3348
燈 J4575 M19402 3476

燕 J316a M19429 3489
獣 J3d43 M20714 3606
糖 J457c M27070 4420
緯 J305e M27682 4566
縞 J3c4a M27777 4569
膳 J4137 M29891 4873
膨 J4b44 M29861 4874
薗 J3172 M32119 5200
蕗 J4979 M31964 5203
融 J4d3b M33384 5371
諛 J3062 M35759 5656
諺 J3841 M-X 5659
諮 J3b72 M35728 5660
謎 J4666 M35800 5661
蹄 J447d M37724 5894
輯 J3d34 M38420 5976
避 J4872 M39163 6120
還 J3454 M39174 6121
醐 J386f M39930 6183
鋸 J3578 M40505 6297
鞘 J3e64 M42850 6587
韓 J345a M43159 6602
頼 J4d6a M43529 6635
頭 J462c M43490 6639
鮎 J303e M46070 6855

14 residual strokes

儲 J4c59 M-X 331
償 J3d7e M1245 333
嚇 J3345 M4459 **915**
壕 J3968 M5559 1108
檜 J5b58 M15676 2894
檀 J4349 M15632 2895
濤 J5e39 M18508 3361

濠 J396a M18502 3363
燦 J4167 M19467 3493
燭 J3f24 M19480 3496
環 J3444 M-X 3680
癌 J3462 M22538 3840
矯 J363a M24015 3984
緯 J305e M27682 4566
臨 J4e57 M30087 4899
舘 J345c M30326 4923
藁 J4f4e M32222 5234
螺 J4d66 M33512 5382
謹 J3660 M35850 5688
轄 J336d M38482 5981
鍔 J4457 M40617 6313
鍋 J4669 M40603 6315
霞 J3262 M42365 6541
鞠 J3547 M42892 6589
韓 J345a M43159 6602

15 residual strokes

儲 J-X M1284 335
囁 J-X M4516 921
癖 J4a4a M22550 3848
箪 J-X M26509 4357
緯 J305e M27682 4566
縞 J3c4a M27777 4569
繕 J4136 M27893 4594
臨 J4e57 M30087 4899
諸 J3d73 M32391 5237
蝉 J-X M33616 5388
蹟 J4058 M37814 5905
軀 J-X M38137 5935
轡 J3725 M38587 5992
鍔 J4457 M40617 6313

鎗 J4179 M40709 6320
鎧 J333b M40735 6324
闘 J462e M45649 6418
難 J4671 M42128 6515
鞭 J4d5c M42937 6595
顎 J335c M43590 6643
額 J335b M43586 6644
験 J3833 M44835 6758
騒 J417b M44834 6760
騎 J3533 M44817 6761
鵲 J3974 M46961 6968
麿 J4b7b M47909 7044

16 residual strokes

瀬 J4025 M18672 3384
疇 J-X M24852 4114
繰 J372b M27953 4602
艶 J3170 M30632 4957
藷 J4174 M32391 5247
藻 J4174 M32401 5254
螺 J4d66 M33512 5382
蟹 J332a M33668 5395
蟻 J3542 M33672 5397
覇 J4746 M34790 5519
警 J3759 M35989 5705
蹴 J3d33 M37876 5913
鏑 J4264 M40790 6334
韻 J3124 M43307 6611
顛 J335c M43590 6643
鯛 J4264 M46226 6884
鯨 J375f M46257 6886
鹸 J3834 M-X 7013

17 residual strokes

灌 J5e75 M18759 3390
競 J3625 M25831 4244
繍 J4136 M27893 4594
蠣 J695a M33799 5399
鐙 J4264 M40904 6348
鰐 J4f4c M46337 6901

18–21 residual strokes

嚢 J-X M4633 933
繰 J372b M27953 4602
蠟 J-X M33786 5403
躍 J4c76 M37955 5921
轡 J3725 M38587 5992
鑢 J4c7a M-X 6343
鑢 J-X M40998 6357
露 J3643 M42463 6549
驚 J4264 M45013 6774
鴎 J-X M47268 6998
鷲 J4f49 M47345 7004
鷺 J3a6d M47362 7006
鹸 J-X M47576 7016

Rad. 31 口

2 residual strokes

囚 J3c7c M4680 937
四 J3b4d M4682 938
田 J4544 M21723 3727

3 residual strokes

因 J3078 M4693 939
団 J4344 M4703 940
回 J3273 M4690 941

4 residual strokes

囲 J304f M4722 945
困 J3a24 M4717 946
図 J3f5e M4734 947

5–10 residual strokes

個 J3844 M758 258
咽 J3076 M3577 788
回 J3273 M4690 941
固 J3847 M4745 949
国 J3971 M4752 950
囤 J4a60 M4774 954
圏 J3777 M4815 960
園 J3160 M4818 962
姻 J3079 M6250 1215
恩 J3238 M10591 1851
捆 J444f M-X 2174
梱 J-X M14883 2696
菌 J365d M31156 5091
面 J4c4c M42618 6566

11–23 residual strokes

壇 J4345 M5528 1101
摑 J-X M12572 2263
檀 J4349 M15632 2895
箇 J3255 M26116 4315
緬 J4c4b M27674 4542

蘭 J3172 M32119 5200
蠟 J-X M33786 5403
鹸 J3834 M-X 7013
鹹 J-X M47576 7016

Rad. 32 土

0 residual strokes

土 J455a M4867 966
士 J3b4e M5638 1117

1 residual stroke

壬 J3f51 M5639 968

2 residual strokes

主 J3c67 M100 38
仕 J3b45 M368 123
去 J356e M3070 665
圧 J3035 M4879 970
生 J4038 M21670 3715

3 residual strokes

任 J4724 M416 136
先 J4068 M1349 350
吐 J4547 M4300 709
吉 J354g M3289 711
圭 J373d M4887 973
壮 J4154 M5642 974
在 J3a5f M4881 975
地 J434f M4890 976
寺 J3b7b M7414 1373

Rad.32: 3 residual strokes

庄 J3e31 / M9234	1605	
老 J4f37 / M28842	4696	
考 J394d / M28843	4697	
至 J3b6a / M30142	4903	

4 residual strokes

劫 J3965 / M2316 529
却 J3551 / M2856 631
告 J3970 / M3381 744
坐 J3a41 / M4931 978
壱 J306d / M5647 983
坂 J3a64 / M4910 985
坊 J4b37 / M4924 986
坑 J3923 / M4932 987
均 J3651 / M4916 988
声 J403c / M5645 989
売 J4764 / M5647 990
孝 J3927 / M6952 1289
志 J3b56 / M10331 1785
杜 J454e / M14477 2560
牡 J3234 / M19933 3536
社 J3c52 / M24631 4065
考 J394d / M28843 4697
赤 J4056 / M36993 5840
走 J4176 / M37034 5845
里 J4e24 / M40131 6206

5 residual strokes

舎 J3c4b / M30278 189
侍 J3b78 / M589 192
佳 J3242 / M557 194
到 J457e / M1950 477
尭 J3646 / M-X 614

卦 J3735 / M2798 625
周 J3c7e / M3441 768
坤 J3a25 / M4969 996
坦 J4333 / M4971 997
坪 J445a / M4976 998
垂 J3f62 / M5012 999
幸 J392c / M9176 1595
径 J3742 / M10080 1730
怯 J3631 / M10491 1816
怪 J3278 / M10483 1821
性 J402d / M10478 1822
法 J3a41 / M17290 3107
者 J3c54 / M28852 4698
茎 J3754 / M30861 4991
里 J4e24 / M40131 6206

6 residual strokes

厘 J4e52 / M2946 650
哉 J3a48 / M3596 779
垢 J3924 / M5058 1008
垣 J3340 / M5060 1009
型 J373f / M5030 1010
城 J3b6b / M5086 1011
姪 J4c45 / M6226 1209
姥 J3138 / M6216 1212
娃 J3023 / M6262 1213
室 J3c3c / M7136 1327
封 J4975 / M7426 1376
屋 J3230 / M7684 1421
待 J4254 / M10085 1741
拷 J3969 / M12006 2142
持 J3b7c / M12019 2151
洗 J4076 / M17379 3131
荘 J4171 / M30890 5031

赴 J496b / M37040 5847
造 J4224 / M38898 6061
陞 J4a45 / M41654 6444

7 residual strokes

俸 J3876 / M771 228
凌 J4e3f / M1669 424
厘 J4e52 / M2946 650
哩 J4b69 / M3649 805
埋 J4b64 / M5116 1020
座 J3a43 / M9319 1619
徒 J454c / M10121 1746
拷 J3969 / M12006 2142
挫 J3a43 / M12087 2163
教 J3635 / M13213 2345
時 J3b7e / M13890 2462
桔 J354b / M14777 2653
栽 J3a4f / M14750 2654
桂 J374b / M14755 2659
洸 J4642 / M-X 3134
浬 J333d / M17485 3142
浩 J3940 / M17479 3147
特 J46d3 / M20013 3541
狸 J432c / M20427 3578
致 J4357 / M30149 4904
起 J352f / M37048 5849
造 J4224 / M38898 6061
週 J3d35 / M38937 6070
都 J4554 / M39497 6148
重 J3d45 / M40132 6207
陛 J4a45 / M41654 6444
陵 J4e4d / M41704 6454
陸 J4e26 / M41708 6461

---

8 residual strokes

堵 J4548 / M-X 1021
塾 J4738 / M5154 1022
埼 J3a6b / M-X 1028
埠 J4956 / M5161 1029
域 J3068 / M5158 1030
埴 J3e7d / M5188 1031
培 J475d / M5195 1032
堕 J4244 / M-X 1033
壷 J445b / M5657 1034
堆 J424f / M5211 1035
堀 J4b59 / M5205 1036
堂 J4632 / M5207 1037
堅 J3778 / M5210 1038
執 J3c39 / M5193 1039
基 J3470 / M5197 1040
屠 J454b / M-X 1426
崖 J3333 / M8180 1488
彫 J4426 / M9995 1719
捨 J3c4e / M12191 2205
掛 J335d / M12267 2214
教 J3635 / M13213 2345
渚 J3d6d / M-X 3164
涯 J3336 / M17582 3181
狸 J432c / M20427 3578
猪 J4376 / M20511 3585
理 J4d7d / M21014 3644
畦 J374d / M21842 3753
痔 J3c26 / M22167 3804
窒 J4362 / M25493 4200
経 J3553 / M27392 4473
脚 J3553 / M29502 4820
菱 J4929 / M31219 5092
著 J4378 / M31302 5098

赦 J3c4f / M36999 5841
週 J3d35 / M38937 6070
達 J4323 / M39011 6088
黒 J3975 / M48040 7052

9 residual strokes

喜 J346e / M3957 858
堕 J4244 / M-X 1033
堅 J3778 / M5210 1038
堺 J3a66 / M5289 1045
塚 J444d / M-X 1048
塀 J4a3d / M5316 1051
塔 J4563 / M5332 1052
堵 J-X / M5279 1053
堤 J4469 / M5259 1054
堰 J3161 / M5274 1055
塁 J4e5d / M5316 1056
堪 J342e / M5266 1057
場 J3a6c / M5278 1058
報 J4a73 / M5291 1059
屠 J-X / M7761 1429
街 J3339 / M34051 1759
握 J302e / M12366 2232
暑 J3d6b / M14031 2484
款 J343e / M16107 2938
殻 J334c / M-X 2996
渥 J302f / M17770 3224
渚 J-X / M17758 3228
煮 J3c51 / M19165 3437
珪 J373e / M20972 3638
理 J4d7d / M21014 3644
童 J4638 / M25775 4239
等 J4579 / M25992 4287
粧 J3e51 / M26945 4400

結 J376b M27398 4492
董 J4621 M31433 5118
蛭 J4948 M33048 5308
蛙 J333f M32997 5313
裁 J3a5b M34258 5454
装 J4175 M34283 5455
越 J315b M37110 5851
超 J4436 M37096 5852
軽 J375a M38281 5953
達 J4323 M39011 6088
遠 J3173 M39047 6101
野 J4c6e M40133 6208
量 J4e4c M40138 6209
黒 J3975 M48040 7052

10 residual strokes

勢 J402a M2422 558
園 J3160 M4818 962
塔 J4563 M5332 1052
堪 J342e M5266 1057
塙 J4839 M5341 1063
塘 J4564 M5340 1066
塑 J413a M5328 1068
塞 J3a49 M5349 1069
塊 J3274 M5319 1070
填 J4536 M-X 1072
墓 J4a68 M5431 1073
塗 J4549 M5338 1074
塩 J3176 M5382 1075
塾 J3d4e M5402 1083
煙 J316c M19203 3456
猿 J316e M20584 3600
睦 J4b53 M23460 3945
稜 J4e47 M25123 4152

童 J4638 M25775 4239
経 J3750 M27392 4473
罫 J3753 M28295 4642
蒔 J3c2c M31546 5153
蓋 J3338 M31652 5155
装 J4175 M34283 5455
裡 J4e23 M34295 5463
詰 J354d M35440 5609
詩 J3d6b M35427 5610
越 J315b M37110 5851
載 J3a5c M38309 5960
遠 J3173 M39047 6101
酵 J395a M39868 6175
量 J4e4c M40138 6209
鼓 J385d M48330 7076

11 residual strokes

嘉 J3245 M4176 887
墜 J4446 M5451 1082
塾 J3d4e M5402 1083
境 J362d M5409 1085
墨 J4b4f M-X 1086
塵 J3f50 M5388 1087
増 J417d M5448 1088
窪 J3726 M25580 4209
箸 J4824 M-X 4301
結 J376b M27398 4492
緒 J3d6f M27632 4521
綾 J303d M27591 4523
誌 J3b6f M35501 5620
読 J4649 M35580 5629
赫 J3352 M37010 5843
酵 J195a M39868 6175
酷 J3973 M39870 6176

銑 J412d M40376 6263
頸 J375b M43434 6626

12 residual strokes

舗 J4a5e M30323 322
墜 J4446 M5451 1082
墳 J3f50 M5388 1087
墳 J4a2f M5488 1095
嬉 J3472 M6736 1267
衝 J3e57 M34069 1772
憧 J4634 M11242 1982
撞 J4635 M12717 2276
樫 J335f M15485 2849
熱 J472e M19360 3473
種 J3c6f M25174 4159
箸 J-X M26224 4328
糧 J4138 M27057 4413
調 J4434 M35609 5647
諸 J3d74 M35691 5648
賭 J4552 M-X 5807
趣 J3c71 M37207 5854

13 residual strokes

墾 J3a26 M5509 1097
壌 J3e6d M-X 1098
壇 J4345 M5528 1101
壊 J3275 M5541 1102
壁 J4a49 M5516 1103
憧 J4634 M11242 1982
撞 J4635 M12717 2276
樫 J335f M15485 2849
樹 J3c79 M15496 2878
糧 J4138 M27057 4413

緒 J3d6f M27632 4521
綾 J303d M27591 4523
膨 J4b44 M29861 4874
薗 J3172 M32119 5200
薯 J3d72 M-X 5202
薫 J3730 M32173 5223
賭 J-X M36847 5819
隷 J4e6c M41928 6490
黙 J4c5b M48063 7055
黛 J4263 M48075 7060

14 residual strokes

儲 J4c59 M-X 331
嚇 J3345 M4459 915
壕 J3968 M5559 1108
戴 J4257 M11685 2045
曙 J3d6c M-X 2519
濤 J5e39 M18508 3361
瞳 J4637 M23707 3961
穀 J3972 M25188 4157
竃 J3376 M-X 4216
繊 J4121 M27874 4586
薫 J3730 M32173 5223
薯 J-X M32191 5230
趨 J3f76 M37258 5855
鍾 J3e61 M40672 6311
鮭 J3a7a M46132 6859
黛 J4263 M48075 7060

15 residual strokes

儲 J-X M1284 335
曙 J-X M14220 2523
潰 J-X M18591 3373

瞳 J4637 M23707 3961
糧 J4e48 M27132 4426
諸 J3d73 M32391 5237
鍾 J3e61 M40672 6311
鯉 J3871 M46182 6874
鵠 J3974 M46961 6968

16 residual strokes

樽 J5b6d M15713 2897
禱 J-X M24852 4114
糧 J4e48 M27132 4426
繊 J4121 M27874 4586
諸 J-X M32391 5247
鯉 J3871 M46182 6874
鯛 J4264 M46226 6884

17–20 residual strokes

纏 J453b M28043 4612
鐘 J3e62 M40902 6352
鐸 J4278 M40951 6356
馨 J333e M44559 6724
鰭 J4949 M46400 6907
鰹 J336f M46437 6915

Rad. 33 士

0 residual strokes

士 J3b4e M5638 1117

1 residual stroke

壬 J3f51 M5639 968

3 residual strokes		
吉	J3548 M3289	711
壮	J4154 M5642	974
4 residual strokes		
壱	J306d M5647	983
声	J403c M5645	989
売	J4764 M5647	990
志	J3b56 M10331	1785
6–8 residual strokes		
壷	J445b M5657	1034
桔	J354b M14777	2653
洗	J4642 M-X	3134
荘	J4171 M30890	5031
週	J3d35 M38937	6070
9 residual strokes		
喜	J346e M3957	858
結	J376b M27398	4492
装	J4175 M34283	5455
10 residual strokes		
続	J4233 M27533	4500
装	J4175 M34283	5455
詰	J354d M35440	5609
鼓	J385d M48330	7076
11 residual strokes		

嘉	J3245 M4176	887
結	J376b M27398	4492
誌	J3b6f M35501	5620
読	J4649 M35580	5629
12 residual strokes		
嬉	J3472 M6736	1267
続	J4233 M27533	4500
調	J4434 M35609	5647
13–16 residual strokes		
檮	J5b6d M15713	2897
濤	J5e39 M18508	3361
瀆	J-X M18591	3373
禱	J-X M24852	4114
膨	J4b44 M29861	4874
隷	J4e6c M41928	6490
鯛	J4264 M46226	6884

Rad. 34 夂

1–5 residual strokes		
冬	J455f M1610	410
処	J3d68 M1745	435
各	J3346 M3281	714
拠	J3572 M11985	2113
条	J3e72 M14486	2563
麦	J477e M47718	7030
6 residual strokes		

俊	J3d53 M674	216
変	J4a51 M5703	1119
客	J3552 M7128	1329
後	J3865 M10098	1742
柊	J4922 M14610	2614
洛	J4d6c M17383	3119
粂	J3729 M26860	4382
達	J3029 M38901	6054
降	J395f M41620	6450
7 residual strokes		
凌	J4e3f M1669	424
唆	J3a36 M3696	803
夏	J3246 M-X	1120
峰	J4a76 M8094	1473
峯	J4a77 M8093	1474
峻	J3d54 M8116	1475
格	J334a M14749	2668
達	J3029 M38901	6054
陵	J4e4d M41704	6454
陸	J4e34 M41720	6455

Rad. 34 夂

8 residual strokes		
夏	J3246 M5720	1120
略	J4e2c M21839	3755
終	J3d2a M27372	4471
菱	J4929 M31219	5092
9 residual strokes		
復	J497c M10183	1760
竣	J3d57 M25773	4238
絡	J4d6d M27426	4484

蓬	J4b29 M-X	5099
落	J4d6e M31362	5130
10 residual strokes		
愛	J3026 M10947	1927
稜	J4e47 M25123	4152
終	J4c.. M27372	4471
腹	J4a22 M29722	4851
蓬	J4b29 M-X	5099
蓬	J-X M31720	5157
蜂	J4b2a M33088	5331
賂	J4f28 M36738	5799
路	J4f29 M37524	5876
酪	J4d6f M39847	6172
11 residual strokes		
榎	J315d M15219	2810
絡	J4d6d M27426	4484
綾	J303d M27591	4523
蓬	J4b29 M-X	5099
蓬	J-X M31720	5157
複	J4a23 M34417	5484
酸	J3b40 M39871	6177
閣	J3355 M41300	6401
12 residual strokes		
履	J4d7a M7799	1434
慶	J3744 M11145	1967
憂	J4d2b M11170	1971
縫	J4b25 M27805	4550
鋒	J4b2f M40455	6275
麹	J396d M-X	7036

13 residual strokes		
綾	J303d M27591	4523
縫	J4b25 M27805	4550
蕗	J4979 M31964	5203
麺	J4c4d M-X	7038
14–22 residual strokes		
優	J4d25 M1261	334
擾	J3e71 M12920	2314
縫	J4b25 M27805	4550
露	J4f2a M42463	6549
額	J335b M43586	6644
駿	J3d59 M44775	6754
鷺	J3d6d M47362	7006
麹	J-X M47818	7037

Rad. 35 夂

Rad. 36 夕

0 residual strokes		
夕	J4d3c M5749	1123
2 residual strokes		
外	J3330 M5750	1125
3 residual strokes		
列	J4e73 M1901	460
名	J4c3e M3297	716

夙 J3d48/M5755 **1126**
多 J423f/M5756 **1127**
死 J3b60/M16365 2968
汐 J3c2e/M17122 3041
舛 J4124/M30338 4924

4–5 residual strokes

夜 J4c6b/M5763 **1129**
宛 J3038/M7110 1319
舛 J4124/M30338 4924
苑 J3171/M30774 4996

6 residual strokes

屍 J3b53/M7688 1420
怨 J3165/M10479 1819
拶 J3b22/M12004 2134
殆 J4b58/M16430 2972

7 residual strokes

桝 J4b71/M-X 2673
殉 J3d5e/M16448 2974
殊 J3c6c/M16451 2975
残 J3b44/M16459 2976
烈 J4e75/M18987 3420

8 residual strokes

桝 J4b71/M-X 2673
液 J3155/M17586 3199
祭 J3a57/M24700 4092
移 J305c/M25045 4141

9 residual strokes

傑 J3766/M955 293
椀 J4733/M15001 2732
殖 J3f23/M16502 2981
然 J4133/M19149 3435
腕 J4l53/M29631 4837
葬 J4172/M31448 5128
裂 J4e76/M34260 5453

10 residual strokes

夢 J4c34/M5801 **1131**
碗 J4f52/M24306 4014
舜 J3d58/M30339 4925
裂 J4e76/M34260 5453
遙 J7423/M39035 6097
際 J3a5d/M41820 6478

11 residual strokes

察 J3b21/M7283 1360
蓬 J-X/M31720 5157
遙 J7423/M39035 6097
銘 J4c43/M40385 6265
隣 J4e59/M41847 6484

12 residual strokes

憐 J4e79/M11206 1987
撚 J4732/M12713 2278
舞 J4971/M30342 4926
隣 J4e59/M41847 6484

13 residual strokes

憐 J4e79/M11206 1987
燃 J4733/M19394 3490
燐 J4e55/M19417 3499
舞 J4971/M30342 4926
餐 J3b41/M44160 6696
駑 J3175/M46795 6953

14 residual strokes

擦 J3b24/M12862 2306
燦 J3b38/M19468 3498
燐 J4e55/M19417 3499
瞬 J3d56/M23694 3969
餐 J3b41/M44160 6696

15–22 residual strokes

瞬 J3d56/M23694 3969
醤 J-X/M40011 6192
鱗 J4e5a/M46502 6923
麟 J4e5b/M47690 7028

Rad. 37 大

0 residual strokes

大 J4267/M5831 **1133**

1 residual stroke

夫 J4957/M5835 **1136**
太 J4240/M5834 **1137**
天 J4537/M5833 **1138**

犬 J3824/M20234 3553

2 residual strokes

央 J317b/M5840 **1140**
失 J3c3a/M5844 **1141**
矢 J4c70/M23929 3976

3 residual strokes

因 J3078/M4693 939
尖 J406d/M7480 1393

4 residual strokes

医 J3065/M2680 590
呑 J465d/M3329 737
吠 J4b4a/M3331 739
夷 J3050/M5852 **1143**
妖 J4d45/M6086 1190
快 J3277/M10369 1802
扶 J495e/M11840 2089
汰 J4241/M17160 3055
沃 J4d60/M17184 3061
決 J3768/M17174 3070
状 J3e75/M20257 3556
芙 J4967/M30694 4966

5 residual strokes

侠 J3622/M625 171
券 J3774/M1966 473
医 J3065/M2680 590
参 J3b32/M3090 666
奄 J3162/M5881 **1146**

奈 J4660/M5893 **1147**
奔 J4b5b/M-X **1148**
奉 J4a74/M5894 **1149**
奇 J3471/M5892 **1150**
実 J3c42/M7124 1324
庚 J392e/M-X 1609
戻 J4c61/M11707 2051
突 J464d/M25424 4191
英 J3151/M30808 5008
迭 J4533/M38800 6029
送 J4177/M38842 6039

6 residual strokes

侯 J4b73/M718 202
俠 J-X/M706 213
咽 J3076/M3577 788
夷 J3050/M5852 **1143**
契 J3740/M5917 **1155**
奏 J4155/M5915 **1156**
姻 J3079/M6250 1215
峡 J362e/M8068 1465
挟 J3634/M-X 2146
拳 J377d/M11996 2148
映 J3147/M13838 2448
春 J3d55/M13844 2453
狭 J3639/M20406 3572
美 J487e/M28435 4660
臭 J3d2d/M30103 4901
迭 J4533/M38800 6029
送 J4177/M38842 6039

7 residual strokes

俺 J3236/M736 240

Rad.37: 7 residual strokes

俸 J4a70/M734 249	勝 J3e21/M2409 553	僕 J4b4d/M1094 313	衡 J3955/M34078 1775
倦 J3771/M788 251	喬 J362c/M3990 841	僚 J4e3d/M1100 314	橋 J3636/M15526 2879
套 J4565/M5926 **1161**	喚 J342d/M3953 852	厭 J315e/M3025 662	燃 J4733/M19394 3490
恩 J3238/M10591 1851	喫 J354a/M3987 855	墓 J4a68/M5431 1073	窺 J312e/M25633 4215
泰 J4259/M17325 3098	圏 J3777/M4815 960	奪 J4325/M5994 **1171**	頻 J-X/M43496 6637
涙 J4e5e/M17573 3154	奥 J317c/M5981 **1165**	慕 J4a69/M11088 1948	

3 residual strokes

疾 J3c40/M22112 3797	捲 J377e/M12208 2193	暮 J4a6b/M14128 2508	
秦 J3f41/M24995 4133	換 J3439/M12358 2233	榛 J3f3a/M15240 2811	妃 J485e/M6061 **1176**

14 residual strokes

秩 J4361/M24998 4135	替 J4330/M14300 2486	模 J4c4f/M15453 2825	妄 J4c51/M6063 **1177**
笑 J3e50/M25885 4256	椅 J3058/M15009 2737	膜 J4b6c/M29808 4854	如 J4721/M6060 **1178**
朕 J443f/M14361 4797	棒 J4b40/M14929 2750	誇 J3858/M35474 5605	好 J3925/M6053 **1180**
莫 J477c/M31078 5057	湊 J4c2c/M17822 3226	跨 J3859/M37504 5872	安 J3042/M7072 1311
蚕 J3b3d/M32869 5290	然 J4133/M19149 3435	遼 J4e4b/M39137 6111	汝 J4672/M17138 3040
	瑛 J314d/M21127 3647	遷 J412b/M39123 6113	

療 J4a25/M22500 3842
瞭 J4e46/M23697 3960
矯 J363a/M24015 3984
襖 J3228/M-X 5498
膾 J4625/M35780 5685

4 residual strokes

8 residual strokes — 葵 J302a/M31458 5120 / 鄭 J4522/M39647 6155 / 努 J4558/M2314 527

	袴 J3853/M34236 5448	関 J3458/M41297 6402	妓 J3538/M6083 **1185**
埼 J3a6b/M5201 1028		駄 J424c/M44633 6734	妨 J4b38/M6111 **1187**
套 J4565/M5926 **1161**			妥 J4245/M6107 **1188**
寄 J3473/M7203 1345	**10 residual strokes**		妊 J4725/M6072 **1189**
崎 J3a6a/M8169 1485	嘆 J4332/M14138 872	**12 residual strokes**	妖 J4d45/M6086 **1190**
庵 J3043/M9369 1623	奨 J3e29/M5990 **1167**	器 J346f/M4349 898	妙 J4c2f/M6090 **1191**
惨 J3b34/M10850 1896	幕 J4b6b/M9051 1578	寮 J4e40/M7325 1366	
掠 J4668/M12221 2189	摸 J4c4e/M12644 2250	撲 J4b50/M12755 2274	**5 residual strokes**
掩 J3166/M12285 2192	椿 J4458/M15090 2782	槻 J4450/M15390 2845	姑 J3848/M6174 **1194**
捧 J4a7b/M12189 2199	漠 J4779/M18149 3267	潜 J4078/M18241 3337	姐 J3039/M6172 **1195**
渓 J374c/M-X 3196	漢 J3441/M31946 3281	蕎 J363e/M31946 5197	姓 J402b/M6178 **1196**
添 J453a/M17698 3201	献 J4d32/M20558 3590	贅 J3b3f/M36841 5814	姉 J454a/M6121 **1197**
爽 J4156/M19746 3520	碕 J3a6c/M24296 4015	遼 J4e4b/M39137 6111	妾 J3e2a/M6147 **1198**
袴 J3853/M34236 5448	誇 J3858/M35474 5605	遷 J412b/M39123 6113	妹 J4b65/M6138 **1199**
規 J352c/M34810 5524	跨 J3859/M37504 5872	頬 J4b4b/M-X 6629	妻 J3a4a/M6140 **1200**
訣 J376d/M35272 5567	鉄 J4534/M40285 6253	黙 J4c5b/M48063 7055	姉 J3b50/M6165 **1201**

15–19 residual strokes

灘 J4667/M18784 3391
纂 J3b3c/M28012 4608
藤 J4623/M32340 5241
讃 J3b3e/M36110 5720
難 J4671/M42128 6515
類 J4a60/M43608 6647
騎 J3533/M44817 6761
騰 J4544/M44915 6767
鰺 J3033/M- 6875
鶏 J375c/M47074 6980

9 residual strokes — 募 J4a67/M2416 551

11 residual strokes — 僑 J3623/M1088 307

13 residual strokes — 奮 J4a33/M6012 **1172**

Rad. 38 女

0 residual strokes

女 J3d77/M6036 **1173**

2 residual strokes

奴 J455b/M6039 **1174**
好 J3925/M6053 **1180**

始 J3b4f/M6166 **1203**
委 J3051/M6181 **1204**

6 residual strokes

始 J3028 / M6242 **1208**
姪 J4c45 / M6226 **1209**
姥 J3138 / M6216 **1212**
娃 J3023 / M6262 **1213**
姻 J3079 / M6250 **1215**
姿 J3b51 / M6257 **1216**
姬 J4931 / M6229 **1217**
姦 J342f / M6217 **1218**
威 J3052 / M6259 **1219**
怒 J455c / M10439 1820
按 J3044 / M12038 2147
要 J4d57 / M34768 5515

7 residual strokes

倭 J4f41 / M796 242
凄 J4028 / M1657 425
姫 J4931 / M6229 **1217**
娠 J3f31 / M6322 **1224**
娘 J4c3c / M6304 **1230**
娟 J3864 / M6307 **1231**
娩 J4a5a / M6337 **1233**
宴 J3163 / M7166 **1332**
恕 J3d7a / M10560 1834
桜 J3a79 / M14796 2664
案 J3046 / M14762 2667

8 residual strokes

娠 J3f31 / M6322 **1224**
娘 J4c3c / M6304 **1230**
娟 J3864 / M6307 **1231**
娩 J4a5a / M6337 **1233**

婁 J4f2c / M6383 **1235**
婆 J474c / M6390 **1240**
娼 J3e2b / M6376 **1241**
婚 J3a27 / M6418 **1242**
婦 J4958 / M6432 **1243**
接 J405c / M12280 2213
萎 J3060 / M31269 5087

9 residual strokes

堰 J3161 / M5274 1055
媛 J4932 / M6516 **1244**
婿 J4c3b / M6470 **1246**
媒 J475e / M6498 **1247**
嫌 J3779 / M6618 **1257**
屡 J3c48 / M7770 1428
棲 J4033 / M14980 2743

10 residual strokes

媛 J4932 / M6516 **1244**
嫉 J3c3b / M6611 **1255**
嫁 J3247 / M6602 **1256**
嫌 J3779 / M6618 **1257**
数 J3874 / M13319 2353
楼 J4f30 / M15212 2785
腰 J3978 / M29705 4850

11–14 residual strokes

嫡 J4364 / M6656 **1263**
嬉 J3472 / M6736 **1267**
嬢 J3e6e / M6807 **1270**
嬬 J445c / M6821 **1271**

嬰 J3145 / M6828 **1273**
屢 J-X / M7787 **1431**
薇 J4c79 / M-X 5201
鞍 J3048 / M42815 6586

Rad. 39 子

0 residual strokes

子 J3b52 / M6930 **1281**

1 residual stroke

孔 J3926 / M6933 **1282**

2 residual strokes

仔 J3b46 / M367 119

3 residual strokes

好 J3925 / M6053 1180
存 J4238 / M6943 **1284**
字 J3b7a / M6942 **1285**

4 residual strokes

孜 J3b5a / M6951 **1287**
孝 J3927 / M6952 **1289**
李 J4d7b / M14459 2549

5 residual strokes

享 J357d / M298 92
孟 J4c52 / M6960 **1291**
季 J3528 / M6965 **1292**

孤 J3849 / M6966 **1293**
学 J3358 / M6974 **1294**

6 residual strokes

勃 J4b56 / M2351 539
厚 J387c / M2949 651
孤 J3849 / M6966 **1293**

7 residual strokes

孫 J4239 / M6987 **1296**
浮 J4962 / M17487 3159
郭 J3354 / M39474 6144

8 residual strokes

孫 J4239 / M6987 **1296**
悼 J4657 / M10759 1887
教 J3635 / M13213 2345
淳 J3d5f / M17690 3189
猛 J4c54 / M20498 3588
菰 J3856 / M31217 5079
遊 J4d37 / M38994 6093

9 residual strokes

孫 J4239 / M6987 **1296**
敦 J4658 / M13276 2349
遊 J4d37 / M38994 6093
遜 J423d / M39038 6098

10–12 residual strokes

塾 J3d4e / M5402 1083
廓 J3347 / M9461 1633
熟 J3d4f / M19332 3472
遜 J423d / M39038 6098
醇 J395a / M39868 6175
醇 J3d66 / M39901 6181

Rad. 40 宀

2 residual strokes

穴 J376a / M25406 4186

3 residual strokes

字 J3b7a / M6942 1285
宅 J4270 / M7064 **1308**
宇 J3127 / M7067 **1309**
守 J3c69 / M7071 **1310**
安 J3042 / M7072 **1311**

4 residual strokes

宍 J3c35 / M7084 **1312**
宋 J4157 / M7078 **1313**
宏 J3928 / M7086 **1314**
完 J3430 / M7079 **1315**
牢 J4f34 / M19934 3535
究 J3566 / M25409 4189
陀 J424b / M41600 6432

5 residual strokes

宕 J4566 / M7103 **1316**
宜 J3539 / M7111 **1317**
宙 J4368 / M7108 **1318**

Rad.40: 5 residual strokes

宛 J3038 M7110 **1319**	穿 J407c M25436 4198	
宝 J4a75 M7122 **1320**	莞 J3450 M31063 5052	
宗 J3d21 M7106 **1321**		
官 J3431 M7107 **1322**	**8 residual strokes**	
定 J446a M7109 **1323**	寅 J4652 M7204 **1341**	
実 J3c42 M7124 **1324**	寂 J3c64 M7200 **1342**	
突 J464d M25424 4191	密 J3d45 M7205 **1343**	
空 J3675 M25415 4192	宿 J3d49 M7195 **1344**	
苧 J4377 M30798 5000	寄 J3473 M7203 **1345**	
	崇 J3f72 M8152 1490	

6 residual strokes

宥 J4d28 M7137 **1326**
室 J3c3c M7136 **1327**
宣 J406b M7132 **1328**
客 J3552 M7128 **1329**
按 J3044 M12038 2147
柂 J4248 M14599 2597
狩 J3c6d M20390 3573
窃 J4060 M25453 4195
穿 J407c M25436 4198
院 J3121 M41665 6447

常 J3e6f M8955 1569
控 J3935 M12283 2202
淀 J4d64 M17610 3182
窒 J4362 M25493 4200
窓 J416b M25494 4201
舵 J4249 M30400 4937
菅 J3f7b M31142 5090
蛇 J3c58 M32964 5303

7 residual strokes

宰 J3a4b M7160 **1330**
宴 J3163 M7166 **1332**
害 J3332 M7165 **1333**
宵 J3e2c M7168 **1334**
容 J4d46 M7172 **1335**
宮 J355c M7156 **1336**
家 J3248 M7169 **1337**
寂 J3c64 M7200 **1342**
案 J3046 M14762 2667
窄 J3a75 M25455 4197

9 residual strokes

割 J3364 M2112 507
喧 J3776 M3976 856
寓 J3677 M7243 **1348**
富 J4959 M7230 **1349**
寒 J3428 M7239 **1350**
椀 J4f50 M15001 2732
棺 J343d M14993 2746
腔 J3950 M29630 4826
腕 J4f53 M29631 4837
萱 J4e40 M31345 5121
記 J4242 M35374 5579
貯 J4379 M36698 5791

10 residual strokes

塞 J3a49 M5349 1069
嫁 J3247 M6602 1256
寛 J3432 M7276 **1352**
寝 J3f32 M7278 **1353**
搾 J3a71 M12553 2251
溶 J4d4f M17983 3277
碗 J4f52 M24306 4014
碇 J4476 M24275 4019
窟 J3722 M25552 4206
蓉 J4d56 M31648 5135
詫 J4f4d M35431 5598

11 residual strokes

察 J3b21 M7283 **1360**
寧 J472b M7296 **1361**
寡 J3249 M7286 **1363**
審 J3f33 M7316 **1367**
演 J3169 M18130 3310
熔 J4d50 M19319 3458
窪 J3726 M25580 4209
管 J3449 M26162 4317
綻 J433e M27587 4514
綜 J416e M27535 4520
蜜 J4c2a M33143 5343

12 residual strokes

賓 J4950 M-X 1365
寮 J4e40 M7325 1366
審 J3f33 M7316 **1367**
稼 J3254 M25217 4169
窯 J4d52 M25594 4210

13 residual strokes

窮 J3567 M25593 4212
誼 J3543 M35605 5634
鞍 J3048 M42815 6586

憲 J377b M11269 1988
確 J334e M24366 4039
窺 J312e M25633 4215
綻 J433e M27587 4514
綜 J416e M27535 4520
錠 J3b7b M40559 6293
館 J345b M44237 6701

14 residual strokes

擦 J3b24 M12862 2306
竈 J3376 M-X 4216
縮 J3d4c M27815 4585
舘 J3a5c M30326 4923
轄 J384d M38482 5981
館 J345b M44237 6701

15–18 residual strokes

寵 J437e M7368 **1370**
縮 J3d4c M27815 4585
鎔 J6f30 M40704 6327
額 J335b M43586 6644
鶴 J4461 M47185 6995

Rad. 41 寸

0 residual strokes

寸 J4023 M7411 **1372**

2 residual strokes

付 J4955 M373 124

3 residual strokes

吋 J3125 M3292 703
団 J4344 M4703 940
守 J3c69 M7071 1310
寺 J3b7b M7414 **1373**

4 residual strokes

寿 J3c77 M7419 **1374**
対 J4250 M7419 **1375**
村 J423c M14464 2564
肘 J492a M29268 4761
附 J496d M41606 6433

5 residual strokes

侍 J3b78 M589 192
府 J495c M9283 1611

6 residual strokes

冠 J3427 M1580 401
封 J4975 M7426 **1376**
専 J406c M-X **1377**
待 J4254 M10085 1741
持 J3b7d M12019 2151
狩 J3c6d M20390 3573
耐 J4251 M28879 4705

7 residual strokes

将 J3e2d M7437 **1379**
射 J3c4d M7434 **1380**
時 J3b7e M13890 2462
涛 J4573 M-X 3138
特 J4643 M20013 3541
討 J4624 M35231 5561
辱 J3f2b M38686 6007
酎 J4371 M39772 6161

8 residual strokes

尉 J3053 M7440 **1383**
得 J4640 M10137 1755
梼 J456e M14911 2672
痔 J3c26 M22167 3804
祷 J4578 M-X 4093
符 J4964 M25935 4270
辱 J3f2b M38686 6007

9 residual strokes

博 J476e M2761 621
厨 J3f5f M3005 657
尋 J3f52 M7447 **1385**
尊 J423a M7445 **1386**
等 J4579 M25992 4287

10 residual strokes

奨 J3e29 M5990 1167
碍 J3337 M24283 4016
蒋 J3e55 M-X 5132
蒔 J3c2c M31546 5153

詩 J3b6d M35427 5610

11 residual strokes

奪 J4325 M5994 1171
導 J4633 M7463 **1388**
腐 J4965 M29625 4835
醗 J-X M31820 5177
蔚 J3136 M31805 5181
遵 J3d65 M39118 6112

12 residual strokes

噂 J313d M4286 896
導 J4633 M7463 **1388**
慰 J3056 M11135 1972
遵 J3d65 M39118 6112
鋳 J4372 M40503 6279

13 residual strokes

奮 J4a33 M6012 1172
樽 J432e M15500 2875
樹 J3c79 M15496 2878
縛 J477b M27771 4567
薄 J4776 M32083 5225
醤 J3e5f M-X 6186
鮒 J4a2b M46075 6854

14 residual strokes

濤 J5e39 M18508 3361
爵 J3c5f M19710 3514
謝 J3c55 M35827 5687

15 residual strokes

爵 J3c5f M19710 3514
縛 J477b M27771 4567
醤 J-X M40011 6192
闘 J462e M45649 6418

16–23 residual strokes

檮 J5b6d M15713 2897
爵 J3135 M-X 2924
爵 J-X M15978 2926
禱 J-X M24852 4114
簿 J4a6d M26623 4364
鱒 J4b70 M46492 6921

Rad. 42 小

0 residual strokes

小 J3e2e M7473 **1389**

1 residual stroke

少 J3e2f M7475 **1390**

2 residual strokes

示 J3c28 M24623 4060

3 residual strokes

光 J3877 M1350 349
劣 J4e74 M2302 524
尖 J406d M7480 **1393**

当 J4576 M9913 1706
糸 J3b65 M27221 4431

4 residual strokes

余 J4d3e M515 168
妙 J4c2f M6090 1191
抄 J3e36 M11863 2087
沙 J3a3b M17212 3063
系 J374f M27223 4433
肖 J3e53 M29263 4760
迩 J4676 M38793 6022

5 residual strokes

京 J357e M299 93
叔 J3d47 M3154 677
尚 J3e30 M7493 **1395**
弥 J4c6f M9753 1689
歩 J4a62 M16284 2958
糸 J3b65 M27221 4431
迹 J4676 M38793 6022

6 residual strokes

削 J3a6f M2000 488
叙 J3d76 M3163 681
省 J3e4a M23179 3916
県 J3829 M23210 3918
砂 J3a3d M24046 3992
祢 J472a M-X 4074
秒 J4943 M24952 4129
途 J4553 M38882 6057
除 J3d7c M41669 6449

7 residual strokes

党 J455e M1381 363
原 J3836 M2973 652
哨 J3e25 M3646 809
宵 J3e2c M7168 1334
屑 J367d M7709 1424
徐 J3d79 M10110 1744
晃 J3938 M13891 2458
消 J3e43 M17529 3158
称 J3e4e M25016 4139
紗 J3c53 M27287 4446
途 J4553 M38882 6057

8 residual strokes

堂 J4632 M5207 1037
寂 J3c64 M7200 1342
常 J3e6f M8955 1569
戚 J404c M11594 2032
捗 J443d M-X 2173
掠 J4e2b M12273 2191
斎 J3a58 M13467 2368
斜 J3c50 M13509 2376
梢 J3e3f M14866 2695
渉 J3e44 M17749 3190
淑 J3d4a M17634 3191
涼 J4e43 M17606 3198
雀 J3f7d M41954 6496

9 residual strokes

就 J3d22 M7599 1401
掌 J3e38 M12248 2200
景 J374a M13983 2487

Rad.42: 9 residual strokes

椋 $\frac{J4c3a}{M15020}$ 2725

硝 $\frac{J3e4b}{M24201}$ 4007

紗 $\frac{J3c53}{M27287}$ 4446

隙 $\frac{J3764}{M41792}$ 6471

遼 $\frac{J4e4b}{M39137}$ 6111

13 residual strokes

穆 $\frac{J4b54}{M25251}$ 4171

鞘 $\frac{J3e64}{M42850}$ 6587

10 residual strokes

塗 $\frac{J4549}{M5338}$ 1074

幌 $\frac{J4b5a}{M9022}$ 1577

源 $\frac{J383b}{M17926}$ 3274

督 $\frac{J4644}{M23457}$ 3946

蛸 $\frac{J427d}{M33072}$ 5330

裟 $\frac{J3a40}{M34325}$ 5457

隔 $\frac{J-X}{M41813}$ 6477

11 residual strokes

僚 $\frac{J4e3d}{M1100}$ 314

嘗 $\frac{J3e28}{M4205}$ 878

幣 $\frac{J4a3e}{M9088}$ 1585

裟 $\frac{J3a40}{M34325}$ 5457

裳 $\frac{J3e58}{M34357}$ 5472

遼 $\frac{J4e4b}{M39137}$ 6111

12 residual strokes

賓 $\frac{J4950}{M-X}$ 1365

寮 $\frac{J4e40}{M7325}$ 1366

幣 $\frac{J4a3e}{M9088}$ 1585

廠 $\frac{J3e33}{M9490}$ 1643

影 $\frac{J3146}{M10019}$ 1722

蔽 $\frac{J4a43}{M31888}$ 5193

諒 $\frac{J4e4a}{M35653}$ 5641

賞 $\frac{J3e33}{M36813}$ 5815

輝 $\frac{J3531}{M38372}$ 5972

14 residual strokes

償 $\frac{J3d7e}{M1245}$ 333

擦 $\frac{J3b24}{M12862}$ 2306

療 $\frac{J4e45}{M22500}$ 3842

瞥 $\frac{J4a4d}{M23672}$ 3959

瞭 $\frac{J4e46}{M23697}$ 3960

頻 $\frac{J4951}{M-X}$ 6641

15–22 residual strokes

瀬 $\frac{J494e}{M18636}$ 3381

耀 $\frac{J4d54}{M28828}$ 4695

蹴 $\frac{J3d33}{M37876}$ 5913

鎖 $\frac{J3a3f}{M40708}$ 6325

願 $\frac{J346a}{M43623}$ 6653

鯨 $\frac{J375f}{M46257}$ 6886

鷲 $\frac{J4f49}{M47345}$ 7004

Rad. 43 尢

1–16 residual strokes

尤 $\frac{J4c60}{M7543}$ 1399

就 $\frac{J3d22}{M7599}$ 1401

蹴 $\frac{J3d33}{M37876}$ 5913

Rad. 44 尸

1 residual stroke

尺 $\frac{J3c5c}{M7632}$ **1404**

戸 $\frac{J384d}{M11696}$ 2048

2–3 residual strokes

伊 $\frac{J304b}{M432}$ 134

尼 $\frac{J4674}{M7635}$ **1405**

尻 $\frac{J3f2c}{M7634}$ **1407**

尽 $\frac{J3f54}{M7642}$ **1408**

4 residual strokes

声 $\frac{J403c}{M5645}$ 989

尿 $\frac{J4722}{M7651}$ **1410**

尾 $\frac{J4878}{M7650}$ **1411**

局 $\frac{J3649}{M7653}$ **1412**

択 $\frac{J4272}{M11902}$ 2082

沢 $\frac{J4274}{M17234}$ 3062

芦 $\frac{J3032}{M30716}$ 4975

5 residual strokes

侭 $\frac{J4b79}{M1964}$ 170

刷 $\frac{J3a7e}{M1964}$ 479

届 $\frac{J464f}{M7667}$ **1413**

屈 $\frac{J367e}{M7669}$ **1415**

居 $\frac{J356f}{M7663}$ **1416**

戻 $\frac{J4c61}{M11707}$ 2051

房 $\frac{J4b3c}{M11714}$ 2053

泥 $\frac{J4525}{M17311}$ 3105

炉 $\frac{J4f27}{M18902}$ 3403

肩 $\frac{J382a}{M29299}$ 4776

6 residual strokes

屍 $\frac{J3b53}{M7688}$ **1420**

屋 $\frac{J3230}{M7684}$ **1421**

昼 $\frac{J3886}{M13886}$ 2450

眉 $\frac{J487d}{M23190}$ 3917

7 residual strokes

屑 $\frac{J367d}{M7709}$ **1424**

展 $\frac{J4538}{M7715}$ **1425**

扇 $\frac{J4070}{M11743}$ 2056

涙 $\frac{J4e5e}{M17573}$ 3154

8 residual strokes

堀 $\frac{J4b59}{M5205}$ 1036

尉 $\frac{J3053}{M7440}$ 1383

展 $\frac{J4538}{M7715}$ **1425**

屠 $\frac{J454b}{M-X}$ **1426**

据 $\frac{J4164}{M12204}$ 2195

掘 $\frac{J3721}{M12264}$ 2204

梶 $\frac{J3361}{M14889}$ 2699

訳 $\frac{J4c75}{M35324}$ 5572

遍 $\frac{J4a57}{M39001}$ 6086

遅 $\frac{J4359}{M38989}$ 6089

秩 $\frac{J3c61}{M40120}$ 6203

9 residual strokes

堺 $\frac{J4a3d}{M5316}$ 1051

屠 $\frac{J454b}{M-X}$ **1426**

屢 $\frac{J3c48}{M7770}$ **1428**

属 $\frac{J4230}{M7754}$ **1430**

扇 $\frac{J4070}{M11743}$ 2056

扉 $\frac{J4862}{M11750}$ 2058

握 $\frac{J302e}{M12366}$ 2232

渥 $\frac{J302f}{M17770}$ 3224

犀 $\frac{J3c54}{M20045}$ 3546

遍 $\frac{J4a57}{M39001}$ 6086

遅 $\frac{J4359}{M38989}$ 6089

雇 $\frac{J385b}{M41976}$ 6497

10 residual strokes

殿 $\frac{J4542}{M16651}$ 3001

窟 $\frac{J3722}{M25552}$ 4206

蒼 $\frac{J4173}{M31627}$ 5162

裾 $\frac{J3f7e}{M34382}$ 5474

11 residual strokes

啓 $\frac{J373c}{M3820}$ 828

屢 $\frac{J-X}{M7787}$ **1431**

層 $\frac{J4158}{M-X}$ **1432**

槍 $\frac{J4158}{M15319}$ 2822

漏 $\frac{J4f33}{M18120}$ 3307

煽 $\frac{J407a}{M19272}$ 3469

肇 $\frac{J4825}{M29228}$ 4751

蔚 $\frac{J3136}{M31805}$ 5181

駅 $\frac{J3158}{M44633}$ 6735

12 residual strokes

僻 $\frac{J4a48}{M1166}$ 323

嘱 $\frac{J3e7c}{M4249}$ 894

履 $\frac{J4d7a}{M7799}$ **1434**

慰 $\frac{J3056}{M11135}$ 1972

篇 $\frac{J4a53}{M26257}$ 4324

編 $\frac{J4a54}{M27665}$ 4552

避 J4872/M39163' 6120

13 residual strokes
壁 J4a49/M5516 1103
澱 J4543/M18410 3347
避 J4872/M39163' 6120
鋸 J3578/M40505 6297

14–18 residual strokes
癖 J4a4a/M22550 3848
編 J4a54/M27665 4552
臀 J673d/M29939 4880
鎗 J4179/M40709 6320
顧 J385c/M43689 6655
馨 J333e/M44559 6724

Rad. 45 屮
1–7 residual strokes
屯 J4656/M7828 **1438**
純 J3d63/M27277 4454
朔 J3a73/M14359 4801
逆 J3555/M38849 6041

9 residual strokes
純 J3d63/M27277 4454
遡 J414c/M39048 6094
鈍 J465f/M40219 6235

10–16 residual strokes
顐 J4655/M4429 910
塑 J413a/M5328 1068
蕨 J4f4f/M32001 5194
趨 J3f76/M37258 5855
遡 J414c/M39048 6094
雛 J3f77/M42121 6514
頓 J465c/M43381 6623

Rad. 46 山
0 residual strokes
山 J3b33/M7869 **1439**

1–2 residual stroke
仙 J4067/M374 120
屯 J4656/M7828 1438
迪 J4329/M38718 6015

3 residual strokes
両 J4e3e/M46 23
缶 J344c/M28108 4624
迪 J4329/M38718 6015

4 residual strokes
両 J4e3e/M46 23
岐 J3474/M7936 **1447**

5 residual strokes

屈 J367e/M7669 1415
岱 J4252/M7997 **1452**
岨 J413b/M7984 **1456**
岳 J3359/M8001 **1457**
岬 J4c28/M7992 **1458**
岸 J345f/M8009 **1459**
岡 J322c/M7962 **1460**
若 J3464/M7985 **1461**
拙 J405b/M11965 2122

6 residual strokes
峠 J463d/M8068 **1464**
峡 J362e/M8068' **1465**
幽 J4d29/M9205 **1600**
炭 J433a/M18953 3413

7 residual strokes
剛 J3964/M2042 497
峨 J3265/M8071 **1471**
峰 J4a76/M8094 **1473**
峯 J4a77/M8093 **1474**
峻 J3d54/M8116 **1475**
島 J4567/M8108 **1476**
陶 J462b/M41705 6459

8 residual strokes
堀 J4b59/M5205 1036
密 J4c29/M7205 1343
崎 J3a6a/M8169 **1485**
崖 J3333/M8180 **1488**
崇 J3f72/M8152 **1490**
崩 J4a78/M8212 **1491**

掘 J3721/M12264 2204
淘 J4571/M17642 3187
萄 J463a/M31252 5075
遥 J4d5a/M-X 6075

9 residual strokes
凱 J332e/M1790 440
堀 J4b59/M5205 1036
嵐 J4d72/M8289 **1496**
揺 J4d49/M12445' 2235
満 J4b7e/M17921' 3248
遥 J4d5a/M-X 6075

10 residual strokes
催 J3a45/M1005 298
嵯 J3a37/M8363 **1500**
嵩 J3f73/M8348 **1502**
幽 J4d29/M9205 1600
微 J4879/M10203 1765
溯 J5e6a/M17975 3272
瑞 J3f70/M21131 3665
窟 J3722/M25552 4206
遙 J7423/M39035 6097

11 residual strokes
嶋 J4568/M8434 **1503**
徴 J4427/M10238' 1768
溯 J5e6a/M17975 3272
窟 J3722/M25552 4206
端 J433c/M25806 4243
綱 J394b/M27576 4525
遙 J7423/M39035 6097

13 residual strokes
綱 J394b/M27576 4525
謡 J4d58/M35779' 5666
鋼 J395d/M40509 6302

14 residual strokes
嶺 J4e66/M8553 **1517**
徽 J352b/M-X 1773
徽 J-X/M10267 1778
癌 J3462/M22538 3840

15–18 residual strokes
巌 J3460/M8624' **1521**
徽 J-X/M10267 1778
戀 J4428/M11399' 2006
繋 J-X/M27940 4601
鎧 J333b/M40735 6324

Rad. 47 川
0 residual strokes
川 J406e/M8673 **1526**

2–4 residual strokes
巡 J3d64/M8690 **1528**
州 J3d23/M8678 **1529**
災 J3a52/M18879 3400

6–8 residual strokes

Rad.47: 8 residual strokes

拶 J3b22 / M12004 2134
巢 J4163 / M8696ʼ 2705
洲 J3d27 / M17413 3120
流 J4e2e / M17572ʼ 3160
琉 J4e30 / M20978 3642
荒 J3953 / M30953 5034
訓 J3731 / M35238 5562
釧 J367c / M40176 6222

9 residual strokes

慌 J3932 / M11057 1917
巢 J4163 / M8696ʼ 2705
疏 J4141 / M22000 3775
硫 J4e32 / M24229 4006
順 J3d67 / M43349 6619

10–18 residual strokes

酬 J3d37 / M39850 6171
蠟 J-X / M33786 5403
頸 J7074 / M43515 6638
馴 J466b / M44595 6729

Rad. 48 工

0 residual strokes

工 J3929 / M8714 1532

2 residual strokes

仝 J2138 / M378 114
功 J3879 / M2295 522
巧 J392a / M8721 1533

巨 J3570 / M8722 1534
左 J3a38 / M8720 1535
正 J4035 / M16255 2955

3 residual strokes

巧 J392a / M8721 1533
巨 J3570 / M8722 1534
式 J3c30 / M9663 1676
江 J393e / M17140 3045

4–5 residual strokes

佐 J3a34 / M506 155
攻 J3936 / M13120 2331
杢 J4c5d / M14487 2548
空 J3675 / M25415 4192

6 residual strokes

拭 J3f21 / M11989 2144
昂 J-X / M13885 2447
紅 J3948 / M27243 4441
虹 J467a / M32830 5279

7–8 residual strokes

差 J3a39 / M8732 1537
恐 J3632 / M10552 1853
控 J3935 / M12283 2202
紅 J3948 / M27243 4441
貢 J3957 / M36665 5772

9 residual strokes

尋 J3f52 / M7447 1385
惰 J4246 / M11055 1921
筑 J435e / M26002 4280
腔 J3950 / M29630 4826
項 J3960 / M43343 6617

10–17 residual strokes

嵯 J3a37 / M8363 1500
巖 J3460 / M8624ʼ 1521
楮 J424a / M15133 2780
橲 J5b6d / M15713 2897
濤 J5e34 / M18508 3361
瑳 J3a3c / M21170 3667
禱 J-X / M24852 4114
築 J435b / M26298 4343
鴻 J3963 / M46874 6963

Rad. 49 巳

0 residual strokes

巳 J4c26 / M8744 1538
己 J384a / M8742 1540

1–3 residual stroke

包 J4a71 / M2506ʼ 572
妃 J485e / M6061 1176
巴 J4743 / M8745 1541
色 J3f27 / M30602 4956

4 residual strokes

忌 J3477 / M10310 1786

把 J4744 / M11874 2083
改 J327e / M13114 2332
芭 J474e / M30730 4974
邑 J4d38 / M39269 6127

5 residual strokes

庖 J4a79 / M9266 1610
抱 J4a7a / M11917ʼ 2125
杷 J4747 / M14505 2575
泡 J4b22 / M17307 3093
肥 J486e / M29290 4774

6 residual strokes

巷 J392b / M-X 1543
卷 J342c / M8759ʼ 1545
紀 J352a / M27234 4439
胞 J4b26 / M29396ʼ 4788

7–8 residual strokes

倦 J3771 / M788 251
砲 J4b24 / M24120 3998
紀 J352a / M27234 4439
記 J352d / M35244 5563
起 J352f / M37048 5849
配 J475b / M39771 6163

9 residual strokes

圈 J3777 / M4815ʼ 960
巽 J4327 / M8765 1546
捲 J377e / M12208 2193
港 J3941 / M17783ʼ 3242

琶 J474a / M21081 3649
絕 J4064 / M-X 4490

10–11 residual strokes

巽 J4327 / M8765 1546
絕 J4064 / M-X 4490
遷 J412b / M39123ʼ 6113
選 J412a / M39127ʼ 6114
鞄 J3373 / M42781 6582
飽 J4b30 / M44109ʼ 6684

12–16 residual strokes

撰 J4071 / M12753 2277
艷 J3170 / M30632 4957
遷 J412b / M39123ʼ 6113
選 J412a / M39127ʼ 6114

Rad. 50 巾

0 residual strokes

巾 J3652 / M8771 1547

2 residual strokes

凧 J427c / M1749 434
匝 J4159 / M2599ʼ 586
布 J495b / M8778 1548
市 J3b54 / M8775 1549

3 residual strokes

匝 J4159/M2599 586
吊 J445f/M3291 710
帆 J4841/M8787 **1551**

4 residual strokes

希 J3475/M8813 **1553**

5 residual strokes

刷 J3a7e/M1964 479
刺 J3b49/M1969 480
制 J4029/M1961 481
姉 J3b50/M6165 1201
帖 J4421/M8849 **1558**
怖 J495d/M10450 1817

6 residual strokes

帥 J3f63/M8886 **1559**
帝 J446b/M8865 **1560**
柿 J3341/M14681 2624
肺 J4759/M29422′ 4791
逓 J447e/M38881′ 6055

7 residual strokes

席 J404a/M8926 **1561**
師 J3b55/M8916 **1562**
帯 J4253/M8929 **1563**
帰 J3522/M8930 **1564**
逓 J447e/M38881′ 6055

8 residual strokes

婦 J4958/M6432′ 1243
師 J3b55/M8916 **1562**
帳 J4422/M8939 **1568**
常 J3e6f/M8955 **1569**
掃 J415d/M12237′ 2207

9 residual strokes

帽 J4b39/M8971 **1573**
幅 J497d/M8995 **1574**
棉 J4c49/M14919 2741
滞 J425a/M18067′ 3280
稀 J3529/M25058 4145

10 residual strokes

幌 J4b5a/M9022 **1577**
幕 J4b6b/M9051 **1578**
滞 J425a/M18067′ 3280
獅 J3b62/M20609 3599
飾 J3e7e/M44111′ 6683

11–12 residual strokes

幡 J4828/M9086 **1584**
幣 J4a3e/M9088 **1585**
綿 J4c4a/M27592 4531
締 J4479/M27651 4549
飾 J3e7e/M44111′ 6683

13–14 residual strokes

綿 J4c4a/M27592 4531
締 J4479/M27651 4549
諦 J447c/M35716 5666
蹄 J447d/M37724 5893
錦 J3653/M40569 6301

Rad. 51 干

0 residual strokes

干 J3433/M9165 **1589**

1–4 residual stroke

刊 J3429/M1865 456
午 J3861/M2703 604
平 J4a3f/M9167 **1590**
年 J472f/M9168 **1593**
汗 J3440/M17130 3046
肝 J344e/M29273 4762

5 residual strokes

坪 J445a/M4976 998
岸 J345f/M8009 1459
幸 J392c/M9176 **1595**
杵 J354f/M14503 2581

6–8 residual strokes

南 J466e/M2750 619
執 J3c39/M5193 1039
梓 J3034/M14845 2688
秤 J4769/M24993 4134
竿 J3448/M25854 4250
軒 J382e/M38187 5944

9 residual strokes

報 J4a73/M5275 1059
揺 J4d49/M12445′ 2235
献 J3825/M20539 3596
評 J493e/M35383 5587

10–15 residual strokes

僻 J4a48/M1166 323
幹 J3434/M9183 **1596**
楠 J466f/M15152 2779
謡 J4d58/M35779′ 5666
辨 J5221/M38656 6003

Rad. 52 幺

1–7 residual stroke

幻 J3838/M9190 **1598**
幼 J4d44/M9193 **1599**
幽 J4d29/M9205 **1600**
弦 J3839/M9754 1688
後 J3865/M10098 1742
玄 J383c/M20814 3616
畜 J435c/M21814 3749
糸 J3b65/M27221 4431
胤 J307d/M29405 4786

8 residual strokes

牽 J3823/M20025 3544
絃 J383e/M27373 4468
舷 J383f/M30403 4938

9 residual strokes

幾 J3476/M9208 **1601**
滋 J3c22/M17919′ 3238

10 residual strokes

幾 J3476/M9208 **1601**
慈 J3b7c/M10980′ 1924
蓄 J435f/M31642 5161

11–20 residual strokes

幾 J3476/M9208 **1601**
機 J3521/M15561 2880
畿 J3526/M21925 3768
磁 J3c27/M24364 4029
磯 J306b/M24465 4049
聯 J4e7e/M29153 4737
響 J3641/M43318′ 6610
饗 J3642/M-X 6705
饗 J-X/M44431 6715

Rad. 53 广

2–3 residual strokes

庁 J4423/M9223 **1603**
広 J392d/M9224′ **1604**
庄 J3e31/M9234 **1605**

4 residual strokes

庇 J485f/M9239 **1606**
序 J3d78/M9253 **1607**

Rad.53: 4 residual strokes

床 J3e32 M9242 **1608**
応 J317e M10347 1789

---

5 residual strokes

庇 J485f M9239 **1606**
庚 J392e M9278 **1609**
炮 J4a79 M9266 **1610**
府 J495c M9283 **1611**
底 J446c M9262 **1612**
店 J4539 M9267 **1613**
拡 J3348 M11985 2118

6–7 residual strokes

唐 J4562 M3709 812
席 J404a M8926 1561
度 J4559 M9313 **1616**
庫 J384b M9330 **1617**
庭 J446d M9337 **1618**
座 J3a42 M9319 **1619**
砿 J395c M-X 3994

---

8 residual strokes

康 J392f M9376 **1621**
廊 J4f2d M-X **1622**
庵 J3043 M9369 **1623**
庸 J4d47 M9378 **1624**
庶 J3d6e M9373 **1625**
鹿 J3c2f M47586 7017
麻 J4b63 M47888 7040

---

9 residual strokes

廃 J4751 M9425 **1630**
渡 J454f M17765 3247
粧 J3e51 M26945 4400
鹿 J3c2f M47586 7017

---

10 residual strokes

備 J4d43 M1007 295
塘 J4564 M5340 1066
嫉 J3c3b M6611 1255
廓 J3347 M9461 **1633**
廉 J4e77 M9436 **1634**
遮 J3c57 M39086 6106
鉱 J395b M40340 6252

---

11 residual strokes

塵 J3f50 M5388 1087
滬 J3977 M18112 3300
腐 J4965 M29625 4835
遮 J3c57 M39086 6106

---

12 residual strokes

塵 J3f50 M5388 1087
廠 J3e33 M9490 **1643**
廟 J4940 M9489 **1645**
慶 J3744 M11145 1967
摩 J4b60 M12613 2264
滬 J3977 M18112 3300

---

13 residual strokes

磨 J4b61 M24449 4045
糖 J457c M27070 4420

鷹 J4126 M32143 5219

14–15 residual strokes

糠 J3947 M27105 4424
鍍 J4555 M40607 6312
麿 J4b7b M47909 7044

16–17 residual strokes

簾 J4e7c M26616 4365
麓 J4f3c M47658 7023
麗 J4e6f M47663 7026

18–33 residual strokes

纏 J453b M28043 4612
魔 J4b62 M45906 6843
鷹 J426b M47377 7007
麟 J4e5b M47690 7028

Rad. 54 廴

4–6 residual strokes

廷 J446e M9571 **1654**
延 J3164 M-X **1657**
廼 J4736 M9575 **1658**
廻 J3276 M9575 **1659**
建 J377a M9574 **1660**

7–9 residual strokes

健 J3772 M875 278
庭 J446d M9337 **1618**
挺 J4172 M12106 2164
虚 J3575 M32708 5269

10–14 residual strokes

艇 J447a M30440 4941
誕 J4342 M35692 5640
鍵 J3830 M40654 6317

Rad. 55 廾

1 residual stroke

升 J3e23 M2702 603
廿 J467b M9586 **1662**

2 residual strokes

弁 J4a5b M9588 **1663**
弁 J4a5b M9588 **1664**
弁 J4a5b M9588 **1665**
弁 J4a5b M9588 **1666**

3–7 residual strokes

共 J3626 M1458 373
奔 J4b5b M1148 1148
展 J4538 M7715 1425
巷 J392b M-X 1543
席 J404a M8926 1561
度 J4559 M9313 1616
弄 J4f2e M9596 **1668**
恭 J3633 M10596 1845

戒 J327c M11548 2027
昔 J404e M13816 2433
枡 J5b46 M14577 2587
洪 J393f M17402 3123

8 residual strokes

展 J4538 M7715 1425
庶 J3d6e M9373 1625
措 J413c M12286 2190
描 J4941 M12339 2196
曹 J4162 M14297 2477
械 J3323 M14882 2685
猫 J472d M20535 3586
異 J305b M21854 3757
黄 J322b M47926 7045

9 residual strokes

散 J3b36 M13265 2352
暁 J3647 M14031 2485
港 J3941 M17783 3242
渡 J454f M17765 3247
満 J4b7e M17921 3248
焼 J3e46 M19166 3438
葬 J4172 M31448 5128

10 residual strokes

嘆 J4332 M4138 872
弊 J4a40 M9644 **1670**
殿 J4542 M16651 3001
遮 J3c57 M39086 6106

11 residual strokes

暴 J4b3d M14137 2511
算 J3b3b M26146 4316
遮 J3c57 M39086 6106
鼻 J4921 M48498 7082

12 residual strokes

噴 J4a2e M4345 900
弊 J4a40 M9644 **1670**
憤 J4a30 M11239 1990
撲 J4071 M12753 2277
撒 J3b35 M12697 2279

13–20 residual strokes

曝 J4778 M14239 2524
爆 J477a M19540 3505
冀 J4a35 M27102 4425
翼 J4d63 M28801 4692
錯 J3a78 M40579 6299
鍍 J4555 M40607 6312

Rad. 56 弋
1–4 residual strokes

代 J4265 M386 125
弌 J4675 M-X **1675**
式 J3c30 M9663 **1676**

5–8 residual strokes

岱 J4252 M7997 1452

拭 J3f21 M11989 2144
武 J4970 M16273 2959
袋 J425e M34171 5443

9–16 residual strokes

斌 J494c M13468 2369
袋 J425e M34171 5443
試 J3b6e M35415 5611
貸 J425f M26709 5792
賦 J496a M36800 5811
鳶 J4650 M46674 6938
鴬 J4c39 M46963 6974
黛 J4263 M48075 7060

Rad. 57 弓
0 residual strokes

弓 J355d M9692 **1678**

1 residual stroke

弔 J4424 M9698 **1680**
引 J307a M9699 **1681**

2–4 residual strokes

夷 J3050 M5852 1143
弘 J3930 M9709 **1682**
弗 J4a26 M9708 **1683**
弛 J4350 M9724 **1684**
弟 J446f M9737 **1685**

5 residual strokes

弧 J384c M9757 **1687**
弦 J3839 M9754 **1688**
弥 J4c6f M9753 **1689**
沸 J4a28 M17251 3094

6 residual strokes

剃 J4466 M1989 489
矧 J476a M23938 3979
粥 J3421 M26938 4402

7 residual strokes

弦 J3839 M9754 **1688**
弱 J3c65 M9791 **1692**
張 J4425 M9812 **1694**
悌 J4470 M10642 1861

8 residual strokes

張 J4425 M9812 **1694**
強 J362f M9815 **1695**
梯 J4474 M14881 2706
第 J4268 M25943 4272

9 residual strokes

弼 J492b M9826 **1697**
弾 J4346 M9836 **1699**
濟 J4f51 M17920 3239
費 J4871 M36717 5786

10–26 residual strokes

疆 J3630 M9872 **1702**
溺 J452e M17990 3271
潑 J-X M18225 3325
窮 J3567 M25593 4212
醷 J4004l M46194 6194
鰯 J3073 M46413 6904
鵜 J312d M46952 6971

Rad. 58 彐
3–5 residual strokes

事 J3b76 M241 71
伊 J304b M432 134
君 J372f M3323 746
妻 J3a4a M6140 1200
庚 J392e M9278 1609
当 J4576 M9913 **1706**

6 residual strokes

侵 J3f2f M646 218
律 J4e27 M10097 1740
急 J355e M10475 1823
津 J4445 M17396 3122
浄 J3e74 M17451 3128
郡 J3734 M39436 6143

7 residual strokes

兼 J3773 M1483 381
凄 J4028 M1657 425
剥 J476d M48939 496
唐 J4562 M3709 812
帰 J3522 M8930 1564
書 J3d71 M14294 2463

浸 J3f3b M17505 3157
逮 J4261 M38931 6069

8 residual strokes

婦 J4958 M6432 1243
康 J392f M9376 1621
庸 J4d78 M9378 1624
捷 J3e39 M12216 2198
掃 J415d M12237 2207
逮 J4261 M38931 6069
雪 J3f5f M42216 6520

9 residual strokes

嫌 J3779 M6618 1257
尋 J3f52 M7447 1385
棲 J4033 M14980 2743
禄 J4f31 M24741 4096
筆 J492e M25987 4288
粛 J3d4d M29223 4747
葎 J4e2a M31397 5111

10 residual strokes

嫌 J3779 M6618 1257
寝 J3f32 M7278 1353
廉 J4e77 M9436 1634
群 J3732 M28498 4666
隠 J3123 M41836 6480

11–12 residual strokes

慧 J3745 M11116 1964

Rad.58: 12 residual strokes

緑 J4e50 M27541 4528
緑 J316f M27656 4553
静 J4045 M42574 6560

13 residual strokes

穏 J323a M25280 4175
糖 J457c M27070 4420
緑 J4e50 M27541 4528
録 J4f3f M40519 6298
鍵 J3830 M40654 6317

14 residual strokes

儘 J5056 M1234 327
瀞 J4654 M-X 3356
濯 J4275 M18532 3360
糠 J3947 M27105 4424
繊 J316f M27656 4553
繍 J3d2b M-X 4572
謙 J382c M35821 5686
鍵 J3830 M40654 6317

15-25 residual strokes

瀟 J-X M18659 3380
穰 J6354 M25381 4184
簾 J4e7c M26616 4365
繍 J3d2b M-X 4572
繡 J-X M27913 4600
鎌 J3379 M40693 6326
鱈 J432d M46470 6916

Rad. 59 彡

4-5 residual strokes

参 J3b32 M3090 666
形 J3741 M9969 1713
杉 J3f79 M14452 2562

6-7 residual strokes

修 J3d24 M721 260
彦 J4927 M9981 1714
珍 J4441 M20920 3631
疹 J3f3e M22097 3788

8 residual strokes

彪 J4937 M9993 1716
彬 J494b M9996 1717
彩 J3a4c M9992 1718
彫 J4426 M9995 1719
惨 J3b34 M10850 1896

9-12 residual strokes

彰 J3e34 M10015 1721
影 J3146 M10019 1722
診 J3f47 M35337 5586
須 J3f5c M43352 6618
髪 J4831 M45387 6804

13 residual strokes

穆 J4b54 M25251 4171
膨 J4b44 M29861 4874
謬 J3841 M-X 5659

髭 J4926 M45399 6812

15-26 residual strokes

謬 J4935 M35872 5695
顔 J3469 M43591 6648
鬖 J3033 M-X 6875
鬖 J724d M46442 6912

Rad. 60 彳

3-4 residual strokes

役 J4c72 M10057 1726
行 J3954 M34029 5419

5 residual strokes

径 J3742 M10080 1730
征 J402c M10077 1731
彼 J4860 M10066 1732
往 J317d M10073 1733

6 residual strokes

律 J4e27 M10097 1740
待 J4254 M10091 1741
後 J3865 M10098 1742

7 residual strokes

徐 J3d79 M10110 1744
従 J3d3e M10133 1745
徒 J454c M10121 1746
桁 J3765 M14754 2656

8 residual strokes

術 J3d51 M34046 1754
得 J4640 M10137 1755

9 residual strokes

循 J3d5b M10187 1758
街 J3339 M34051 1759
復 J497c M10183 1760
御 J3866 M10157 1761
葎 J4e2a M31397 5111

10-11 residual strokes

微 J4879 M10203 1765
徳 J4641 M10237 1767
徴 J4427 M10238 1768
跳 J4437 M37533 5877

12 residual strokes

履 J4d7a M7799 1434
徹 J4530 M10245 1771
衝 J3e57 M34069 1772
衛 J3152 M34073 1776

13 residual strokes

徽 J352b M-X 1773
衡 J3955 M34078 1775
衛 J3152 M34073 1776
縦 J3d44 M27804 4571

14 residual strokes

徽 J352b M-X 1773
徴 J-X M10267 1778
禦 J357a M24820 4111

15-21 residual strokes

徽 J-X M10267 1778
懲 J4428 M11399 2006
縦 J3d44 M27804 4571
覆 J4a24 M34789 5517

Rad. 61 心

0 residual strokes

心 J3f34 M10295 1780

1 residual stroke

必 J492c M10299 1781

3 residual strokes

忙 J4b3b M10334 1783
忘 J4b3a M10331 1784
志 J3b56 M10331 1785
忌 J3477 M10310 1786
忍 J4726 M10312 1787
応 J317e M10347 1789
芯 J3f44 M30732 4976

4 residual strokes

忽 J397a M10405 **1799**	恐 J3632 M10552 **1853**	**9 residual strokes**	慾 J4d5d M11163 **1951**	聴 J4430 M29173 **4740**
念 J4730 M10390 **1800**	秘 J486b M24977 **4140**		慮 J4e38 M11132 **1962**	臆 J3232 M29951 **4883**
忠 J4369 M10353 **1801**		愈 J4c7c M10904 **1909**	慧 J3745 M11116 **1964**	
快 J3277 M10369 **1802**		慌 J3932 M11057 **1917**	慶 J3744 M11145 **1967**	**14–18 residual strokes**
泌 J4867 M17279 **3092**	**7 residual strokes**	愉 J4c7b M10905 **1920**	慢 J4b7d M11110 **1968**	
		惰 J4246 M10855 **1921**	憎 J417e M11188 **1969**	懇 J3a29 M11326 **2002**
	偲 J3c45 M895 **266**	想 J415b M10858 **1922**	慣 J3437 M11111 **1970**	懐 J327b M11351 **2003**
5 residual strokes	密 J4c29 M7205 **1343**	愁 J3d25 M10885 **1923**	憂 J4d2b M11170 **1971**	懲 J4428 M11399 **2006**
	悌 J4470 M10642 **1861**	慈 J3b7c M10980 **1924**	慰 J3056 M11135 **1972**	擾 J3e71 M12920 **2314**
怡 J4e67 M10461 **1812**	悉 J3c3d M10635 **1864**	愚 J3672 M10946 **1925**	穂 J4a66 M25236 **4168**	癒 J4c7e M22545 **3847**
怯 J3631 M10491 **1816**	悩 J473a M10716 **1867**	意 J3055 M10921 **1926**	蕊 J3c49 M31939 **5188**	
怖 J495d M10450 **1817**	悦 J3159 M10629 **1868**	愛 J3026 M10947 **1927**		**Rad. 62 戈**
怠 J4255 M10469 **1818**	悟 J386 M10680 **1870**	感 J3436 M10953 **1928**		
怨 J3165 M10479 **1819**	患 J3435 M10691 **1871**	慨 J3334 M-X **1944**	**12 residual strokes**	**1–4 residual stroke**
怒 J455c M10439 **1820**	悠 J4d2a M10681 **1872**	稔 J4c2d M25107 **4149**		
怪 J3278 M10483 **1821**	悪 J302d M10483 **1873**	隠 J3123 M41836 **6480**	慶 J3744 M11145 **1967**	伐 J4832 M439 **132**
性 J402d M10478 **1822**	悼 J4657 M10759 **1887**		慣 J3437 M11111 **1970**	戊 J4a61 M11532 **2020**
急 J355e M10475 **1823**	捻 J4761 M12222 **2201**		憩 J3746 M11246 **1980**	戎 J3d3f M11539 **2024**
思 J3b57 M10462 **1824**	添 J453a M17698 **3201**	**10 residual strokes**	憧 J4634 M11242 **1982**	成 J402e M11542 **2025**
悌 J4470 M10642 **1861**	窓 J416b M25494 **4201**		憐 J4e79 M11206 **1987**	戒 J327c M11548 **2027**
		寧 J472b M7296 **1361**	憲 J377b M11269 **1988**	我 J3266 M11545 **2028**
		徳 J4641 M10237 **1767**	憤 J4a30 M11239 **1990**	或 J303f M11563 **2030**
6 residual strokes	**8 residual strokes**	慨 J3334 M-X **1944**	憾 J3438 M11312 **1999**	茂 J4c50 M30833 **4998**
		慎 J3f35 M11024 **1945**	憶 J3231 M11295 **2001**	
急 J4255 M10469 **1818**	惹 J3c66 M10866 **1886**	態 J4256 M11052 **1947**	穏 J323a M25280 **4175**	
恕 J3d7a M10560 **1834**	悼 J4657 M10759 **1887**	慕 J4a69 M11088 **1948**	総 J416d M27620 **4532**	**5 residual strokes**
恰 J3366 M10603 **1838**	惣 J415a M10829 **1889**	総 J416d M27620 **4532**		
恨 J3a28 M10588 **1842**	惟 J3054 M10820 **1890**	聡 J416f M29109 **4730**		俄 J3264 M665 **215**
恢 J327c M10577 **1843**	悼 J4569 M10738 **1891**	蜜 J4c2a M33143 **5343**	**13 residual strokes**	哉 J3a48 M3596 **779**
恭 J3633 M10585 **1845**	惑 J4f47 M10279 **1892**	誌 J3b6f M35501 **5620**		城 J3e6b M5086 **1011**
恥 J4351 M10585 **1846**	惣 J397b M10811 **1893**	認 J4727 M35502 **5623**	優 J4d25 M1261 **334**	威 J3052 M6239 **1219**
惠 J3743 M10618 **1847**	惜 J404b M10814 **1894**		慈 J3b7c M10980 **1924**	
悔 J3279 M10617 **1848**	悶 J4c65 M10729 **1895**		憐 J4e79 M11206 **1987**	
恒 J3931 M10617 **1849**	惨 J3b34 M10850 **1896**	**11 residual strokes**	憾 J3438 M11312 **1999**	**6 residual strokes**
息 J4229 M10601 **1850**	悲 J4861 M10720 **1897**		憶 J3231 M11295 **2001**	
恩 J3238 M10591 **1851**	情 J3e70 M10756 **1898**	億 J322f M1178 **321**	懇 J3a29 M11326 **2002**	峨 J3265 M8071 **1471**
恋 J4e78 M10537 **1852**	葱 J472c M31454 **5123**	態 J4256 M11052 **1947**	懐 J327b M11351 **2003**	栽 J3a4f M14750 **2654**

Rad.62: 6 residual strokes

栈 J3b37 M14796· 2658
残 J3b44 M16459 2976

---

7 residual strokes

域 J3068 M5158 1030
戚 J404c M11594 **2032**
械 J3323 M14882 2685
盛 J4039 M23001· 3895

8 residual strokes

幾 J3476 M9208 1601
惑 J4f47 M10789 1892
戟 J3761 M11606 **2035**
減 J383a M17759 3249
筬 J4835 M26000 4282
裁 J3a5b M34258 5454
越 J315b M37110 5851

9 residual strokes

感 J3436 M10953 1928
戦 J406f M11631 **2037**
歳 J3a50 M16326· 2962
滅 J4c47 M18008 3279
義 J3541 M28504 4668
蛾 J326b M33082 5325
誠 J403f M35497· 5606
賎 J4128 M-X 5796
賊 J4231 M36759 5801
越 J315b M37110 5851
践 J4129 M37547· 5873
載 J3a5c M38309 5960

---

10 residual strokes

摑 J-X M12572 2263
蔑 J4a4e M31781 5179
蔵 J4222 M31885· 5182
銭 J412c M40413 6264
閼 J4836 M41308 6398

---

11 residual strokes

儀 J3537 M1172 324
戯 J353a M11665 2041
畿 J3526 M21925 3768
蔵 J4222 M31885· 5182
賤 J6c4d M36826 5813
餓 J326e M44168· 6697

12 residual strokes

憾 J3438 M11312 1999
機 J3521 M15561 2880
餓 J326e M44168· 6697

13 residual strokes

戴 J4257 M11685 **2045**
犠 J353e M20190· 3550
磯 J306b M24465 4049
繊 J4121 M27874 4586

---

14 residual strokes

戴 J4257 M11685 **2045**
織 J3f25 M27892 4596
職 J3f26 M29183 4742

臓 J4221 M29995· 4886

15 residual strokes

繊 J4121 M27874 4586
臓 J4221 M29995· 4886
蟻 J3542 M33672 5397
識 J3c31 M35974 5704

16–17 residual strokes

機 J3521 M15561 2880
磯 J306b M24465 4049
織 J3f25 M27892 4596
議 J3544 M36027 5716

Rad. 63 戸

0 residual strokes

戸 J384d M11696 **2048**

3 residual strokes

戻 J4c61 M11707 **2051**
芦 J3032 M30716 4975

4–5 residual strokes

戻 J4c61 M11707 **2051**
房 J4b3c M11714 **2053**
所 J3d6a M11715 **2054**
炉 J4f27 M18902 3403
肩 J382a M29299 4776

6–7 residual strokes

偏 J4a50 M848 277
扇 J4070 M11743 **2056**
涙 J4e5e M17573 3154
遍 J4a57 M39001· 6086

8 residual strokes

扇 J4070 M11743 **2056**
扉 J4862 M11750 **2058**
遍 J4a57 M39001· 6086
雇 J385b M41976 6497

10–17 residual strokes

煽 J407a M19272 3469
篇 J4a53 M26257 4324
編 J4a54 M27665 4552
摩 J4825 M29228 4751
顧 J385c M43689· 6655

Rad. 64 手

0 residual strokes

才 J3a4d M11769 **2059**
手 J3c6a M11768 **2060**

1–3 residual strokes

払 J4a27 M11784 **2062**
打 J4247 M11781 **2063**
托 J4271 M11793 **2069**
扱 J3037 M-X **2070**

---

4 residual strokes

扱 J3037 M-X **2070**
扮 J4a31 M11830 **2080**
択 J4272 M11902 **2082**
把 J4744 M11874 **2083**
拒 J3571 M-X **2084**
批 J4863 M11845 **2086**
抄 J3e36 M11863 **2087**
承 J3e35 M11852 **2088**
扶 J495e M11840 **2089**
抑 J4d5e M11883 **2090**
抗 J3933 M11889 **2091**
技 J353b M11855 **2092**
抜 J4834 M11901· **2093**
折 J405e M11890 **2094**
投 J456a M11887 **2095**

---

5 residual strokes

拒 J3571 M-X **2084**
批 J4863 M11845 **2086**
抑 J4d5e M11883 **2090**
拐 J327d M11955 **2107**
抹 J4b75 M11926 **2112**
拠 J3572 M11985 **2113**
拍 J476f M11952 **2114**
拓 J4273 M11958 **2115**
披 J4864 M11909 **2116**
拡 J3348 M11985· **2118**
抽 J436a M11930 **2119**
抵 J4471 M11921 **2120**
担 J4334 M11941 **2121**
拙 J405b M11965 **2122**
拘 J3934 M11963 **2123**

招 J3e37 / M11968 2124
抱 J4a7a / M11917 2125
拝 J4752 / M11969 2126
押 J3221 / M11929 2128

6 residual strokes

峨 J3265 / M8071 1471
抵 J4471 / M11921 2120
拶 J3b22 / M12004 2134
拷 J3969 / M12006 2142
括 J3367 / M11988 2143
拭 J3f21 / M11989 2144
挑 J4429 / M12055 2145
挟 J3634 / M-X 2146
按 J3044 / M12038 2147
拳 J377d / M11996 2148
拾 J3d26 / M12014 2149
挙 J3573 / M12081 2150
持 J3b7d / M12019 2151
指 J3b58 / M12034 2152
捗 J-X / M12160 2161
挺 J4472 / M12106 2164
逝 J4042 / M38895 6051

7 residual strokes

哲 J452f / M3667 811
拷 J3969 / M12006 2142
捉 J422a / M12136 2159
挨 J3027 / M12082 2160
捗 J-X / M12160 2161
捌 J3b2b / M12141 2162
挫 J3a43 / M12087 2163
挺 J4472 / M12106 2164

挿 J415e / M12119 2167
捜 J415c / M12179 2168
挽 J-X / M12111 2169
捕 J4a61 / M12157 2170
振 J3f36 / M12093 2171
挽 J4854 / M-X 2172
逝 J4042 / M38895 6051

8 residual strokes

振 J3f36 / M12093 2171
挽 J4854 / M-X 2172
捗 J443d / M-X 2173
捫 J444f / M-X 2174
掻 J415f / M-X 2175
掠 J4668 / M12221 2189
措 J413c / M12286 2190
掠 J4e2b / M12273 2191
掩 J3166 / M12285 2192
捲 J377e / M12208 2193
掲 J3747 / M12311 2194
据 J3f78 / M12339 2195
描 J4941 / M12339 2196
掬 J3545 / M12290 2197
捷 J3e39 / M12216 2198
捧 J4a7b / M12189 2199
掌 J3e38 / M12248 2200
捻 J4731 / M12222 2201
控 J3935 / M12283 2202
掘 J3721 / M12264 2204
捨 J3c4e / M12191 2205
掃 J415d / M12237 2207
授 J3c78 / M12242 2208
採 J3a4e / M12259 2209
排 J4753 / M12256 2210

探 J4335 / M12211 2211
推 J3f64 / M12284 2212
接 J405c / M12280 2213
掛 J335d / M12267 2214

9 residual strokes

捲 J377e / M12208 2193
揖 J4d2c / M12351 2222
揃 J4237 / M12319 2226
搭 J456b / M12508 2228
揮 J3478 / M12394 2229
援 J3167 / M12407 2230
握 J302e / M12366 2232
換 J3439 / M12358 2233
揺 J4d49 / M12445 2235
揚 J4d48 / M12355 2236
提 J4473 / M12344 2237
義 J3541 / M28504 4668
蛾 J326b / M33082 5325

10 residual strokes

搬 J4842 / M12507 2249
摸 J4c4e / M12644 2250
搾 J3a71 / M12553 2251
摂 J405d / M12557 2252
携 J3748 / M12529 2253
損 J423b / M12459 2255
掻 J-X / M12477 2256

11 residual strokes

携 J3748 / M12529 2253
摺 J4022 / M12647 2262

摑 J-X / M12572 2263
摩 J4b60 / M12613 2264
撃 J3762 / M12674 2265
摘 J4526 / M12582 2266
誓 J4040 / M35514 5622
餓 J326e / M44168 6697

12 residual strokes

撹 J3349 / M-X 2267
播 J4745 / M12747 2273
撲 J4b50 / M12755 2274
撞 J4635 / M12717 2276
撰 J4071 / M12753 2277
撚 J4732 / M12713 2278
撒 J3b35 / M12697 2279
撤 J4531 / M12726 2280
撫 J496f / M12743 2281
撮 J3b23 / M12748 2282
餓 J326e / M44168 6697

13 residual strokes

擁 J4d4a / M12781 2294
操 J4160 / M12806 2296
犠 J353e / M20190 3550

14 residual strokes

擁 J4d4a / M12781 2294
擢 J4527 / M12852 2303
擦 J3b24 / M12862 2306
擬 J353c / M12870 2307

15–23 residual strokes

擾 J3e71 / M12920 2314
攬 J5978 / M13041 2322
蟻 J3542 / M33672 5397
議 J3544 / M36027 5716

Rad. 65 攴

0 residual strokes

支 J3b59 / M13061 2324

2–9 residual strokes

伎 J346c / M436 133
妓 J3538 / M6083 1185
技 J353b / M11855 2092
枝 J3b5e / M14557 2591
鼓 J385d / M48330 7076

Rad. 66 攴

1–3 residual strokes

勾 J4c68 / M2502 566
攷 J3b5a / M6951 1287
攻 J3936 / M13120 2331
改 J327e / M13114 2332

4–5 residual strokes

変 J4a51 / M5703 1119
放 J4a7c / M13133 2333
故 J384e / M13161 2334
政 J402f / M13135 2335

Rad.66: 5 residual strokes

枚 J4b67 M14554 2582
牧 J4b52 M19950 3537

---

6 residual strokes

俊 J3d53 M674 216
做 J4a6f M785 235
修 J3d42 M721 260
敏 J4952 M13202 2337
教 J3635 M13213 2345
致 J4357 M30149 4904

---

7 residual strokes

務 J4c33 M2394 546
啓 J373c M3820 828
悠 J4d2a M10681 1872
敏 J4952 M13202 2337
敗 J4754 M13227 2343
救 J355f M13221 2344
教 J3635 M13213 2345
敦 J4658 M13276 2349
赦 J3c4f M36999 5841

---

8 residual strokes

敦 J4658 M13276 2349
敢 J343a M13260 2350
敬 J3749 M13285 2351
散 J3b36 M13265 2352

---

9 residual strokes

微 J4879 M10203 1765
数 J3f74 M13319 2353

---

10 residual strokes

幣 J4a3e M9088 1585
弊 J4a40 M9644 1670
徴 J4427 M10238 1768
肇 J4825 M29228 4751
蔽 J4a43 M31888 5193

---

11 residual strokes

幣 J4a3e M9088 1585
廠 J3e33 M9490 1643
弊 J4a40 M9644 1670
徹 J4530 M10245 1771
撒 J3b35 M12697 2279
撤 J4531 M12720 2280
敷 J495f M13359 2357
敵 J4528 M13354 2359
蔽 J4a43 M31888 5193

---

12 residual strokes

整 J4030 M13394 2360
激 J3763 M18438 3350
斃 J4a4d M23672 3959
繁 J484b M27803 4570
薮 J4c79 M-X 5201

---

13 residual strokes

嚴 J3837 M3048 663
徽 J352b M-X 1773
斃 J4a4d M23672 3959
篠 J3c44 M-X 4352
繁 J484b M27803 4570

14–18 residual strokes

嚴 J3460 M8624 1521
懲 J4428 M11399 2006
繁 J484b M27803 4570
警 J3759 M35989 5705
轍 J4532 M38524 5988
霧 J4c38 M42418 6545
驚 J3643 M45013 6774

Rad. 67 文

0 residual strokes

文 J4a38 M13450 2364

2–6 residual strokes

対 J4250 M7419 1375
斉 J4046 M13454 2366
剤 J3a5e M2076 493
紋 J4c66 M27262 4451
蚊 J3263 M32849 5288

7–8 residual strokes

斎 J3a58 M13467 2368
斌 J494c M13468 2369
斐 J4865 M13469 2370
斑 J4843 M13470 2371
済 J3a51 M17749 3197
紋 J4c66 M27262 4451

Rad. 68 斗

0 residual strokes

斗 J454d M13489 2373

3–11 residual strokes

料 J4e41 M13501 2374
斜 J3c50 M13509 2376
幹 J3036 M13522 2378
科 J324a M24950 4130
魁 J3321 M45785 6834

Rad. 69 斤

0 residual strokes

斤 J3654 M13534 2379

1–2 residual strokes

丘 J3556 M33 19
匠 J3e22 M2605 588
斥 J404d M13535 2380
近 J3661 M38752 6021

---

3 residual strokes

兵 J4a3c M1462 374
匠 J3e22 M2605 588
折 J405e M11890 2094
芹 J365c M30742 4970
近 J3661 M38752 6021

---

4 residual strokes

岳 J3359 M8001 1457
所 J3d6a M11715 2054
斧 J4960 M13539 2382
析 J404f M14538 2574
欣 J3655 M16008 2930
祈 J3527 M24640 4071

5–9 residual strokes

哲 J452f M3667 811
啓 J373c M3820 828
斬 J3b42 M13555 2384
断 J4347 M13557 2385
斯 J3b5b M13563 2386
新 J3f37 M13572 2387
浜 J494d M17462 3152
訴 J4a1a M35325 5588
逝 J4042 M38895 6051
逝 J4042 M38895 6051

10–23 residual strokes

嘶 J4838 M4433 903
暫 J3b43 M12510 2510
漸 J4132 M18179 3305
薪 J3f45 M32149 5222
晢 J4040 M35514 5622
質 J3c41 M36833 5817
鋲 J4946 M40503 6277
駈 J366f M44636 6744

Rad. 70 方

0 residual strokes

方	J4a7d / M13620	**2389**

2–3 residual strokes

坊	J4b37 / M4924	986
妨	J4b38 / M6111	1187
芳	J4b27 / M30736'	4979
防	J4b49 / M41576	6429

4 residual strokes

房	J4b3c / M11714	2053
放	J4n7c / M13133	2333
於	J3177 / M13628	**2390**
肪	J4b43 / M29302	4766

5–6 residual strokes

做	J4a6f / M785	235
施	J3b5c / M13629	**2391**
旅	J4e39 / M-X	**2396**
紡	J4b42 / M27305	4450

7 residual strokes

族	J4232 / M13661	**2399**
旋	J407b / M13656	**2400**
訪	J4b2c / M35284	5571
遊	J4d37 / M38994'	6093

8 residual strokes

傍	J4b35 / M948	286
砺	J4557 / M-X	3993
紡	J4b42 / M27305	4450

蛎	J3342 / M-X	5291
遊	J4d37 / M38994	6093

10–12 residual strokes

敷	J495f / M13359'	2357
旗	J347a / M13687	**2402**
激	J3763 / M18438	3350

Rad. 71 无

5–10 residual strokes

厩	J3139 / M-X	654
慨	J3334 / M14283	1944
既	J347b / M13721	**2407**
概	J3335 / M15217'	2824

Rad. 72 日

0 residual strokes

日	J467c / M13733	**2410**

1 residual stroke

旦	J4336 / M13734	**2411**
旧	J356c / M13737	**2412**
由	J4d33 / M21724	3724
甲	J3943 / M21725	3725
申	J3f3d / M21726	3726
白	J4772 / M22678	3863

2 residual strokes

亘	J4f4b / M262	79

旨	J3b5d / M13738	**2414**
旬	J3d5c / M13746	**2415**
旭	J3030 / M13747	**2416**
曳	J3148 / M14282	**2417**
曲	J364a / M14280	**2418**
早	J4161 / M13742	**2419**
百	J4934 / M22679	3864

3 residual strokes

但	J4322 / M495	154
伯	J476c / M466	158
伸	J3f2d / M481	163
児	J3b79 / M1364	355
更	J3939 / M14283	**2422**
艮	J3a31 / M30596	4953
車	J3c56 / M38172	5939
迫	J4777 / M38797'	6031
里	J4e24 / M40131	6206

4 residual strokes

卓	J426e / M2741	616
厚	J387c / M2949	651
坤	J3a25 / M4969	996
坦	J4333 / M4971	997
奄	J3162 / M5881	1146
岬	J4c28 / M7992	1458
恵	J3743 / M10618'	1847
拍	J476f / M11952	2114
抽	J436a / M11930	2119
担	J4334 / M11941	2121
押	J3221 / M11929	2128
昂	J3937 / M13783	**2424**
旺	J3222 / M13774	**2427**

昌	J3b5d / M13803	**2428**
昆	J3a2b / M13806	**2430**
昏	J3a2a / M13806	**2431**
易	J3057 / M13814	**2432**
昔	J404e / M13816	**2433**
昇	J3e3a / M13794	**2434**
明	J4c40 / M13805	**2435**
果	J324c / M14556	2594
東	J456c / M14499	2596
沓	J3723 / M17206	3060
泊	J4771 / M17275	3099
狛	J397d / M20349	3566
的	J452a / M22692	3867
者	J3c54 / M28852	4698
艮	J3a31 / M30596	4953
良	J4e49 / M30597	4954
迫	J4777 / M38797'	6031

5 residual strokes

便	J4a58 / M659	219
単	J4331 / M2752	620
厚	J387c / M5060	651
垣	J3340 / M5060	1009
宣	J406b / M7132	1328
恒	J3931 / M10527	1849
指	J3b58 / M12034	2152
昂	J3937 / M13783	**2424**
昆	J3a2b / M13792	**2430**
昏	J3a2a / M13806	**2431**
昧	J4b66 / M13846	**2444**
昭	J3e3c / M13855	**2446**
昂	J-X / M13885	**2447**
映	J3147 / M13838	**2448**
昨	J3a72 / M13847	**2449**

昼	J436b / M13886	**2450**
是	J4027 / M13859	**2451**
星	J4031 / M13837	**2452**
春	J3d55 / M13844	**2453**
柏	J4770 / M14617	2623
沓	J3723 / M17206	3060
泉	J4074 / M17274	3095
洩	J314c / M17401	3118
皇	J3944 / M22701	3870
冒	J4b41 / M-X	3915
神	J3f40 / M24673'	4087
胆	J4340 / M29354	4790
良	J4e49 / M30597	4954
草	J3536 / M30945'	5032
軌	J3530 / M38176	5941
連	J4f22 / M38902	6062
陥	J3f58 / M41676	6446
陣	J3f58 / M41667	6448
音	J323b / M43265	6607
香	J3961 / M44518	6722

6 residual strokes

借	J3c5a / M781	259
冥	J4c3d / M1588	405
凍	J4560 / M1670	427
原	J3836 / M2973	652
宴	J3163 / M7166	1332
島	J4567 / M8108	1476
庫	J384b / M9330	1617
挿	J415e / M12119	2167
捜	J415c / M12179'	2168
晦	J3322 / M-X	**2454**
晋	J3f38 / M13899	**2455**
晃	J3938 / M13891	**2458**

晒	J3b2f	M13924	**2461**
時	J3b7e	M13890	**2462**
書	J3d71	M14294	**2463**
桓	J432c	M14774	2652
殉	J3d5e	M16448	2974
狸	J432c	M20427	3578
畠	J482b	M21827	3747
竜	J4e35	M25751	4232
脂	J3b69	M29463	4808
莫	J477c	M31078	5057
軒	J382e	M38187	5944
連	J422	M38902	6062
都	J4554	M39497	6148
陳	J4444	M41698	6457

7 residual strokes

亀	J3535	M210	62
乾	J3425	M204	63
動	J4630	M2390	549
喝	J3365	M-X	824
唱	J3e27	M3765	829
娟	J3e2b	M6376	1241
婚	J3a27	M6418	1242
宿	J3d49	M7195	1344
屠	J454b	M-X	1426
庵	J3043	M9369	1623
得	J4640	M10137	1755
悼	J4569	M10738	1891
惜	J404b	M10814	1894
措	J413c	M12286	2190
掩	J3166	M12285	2192
掲	J3747	M12311	2194
斬	J3b42	M13555	2384
曽	J413e	M-X	**2464**

曹	J4162	M14297	**2477**
晦	J-X	M13960	**2478**
梗	J393c	M14849	2698
渚	J3d6d	M-X	3164
渇	J3369	M17748	3195
混	J3a2e	M17694	3204
焔	J316b	M-X	3423
猪	J3a2f	M20511	3585
章	J3e4f	M25761	4235
粕	J4774	M26891	4391
紳	J27348		4467
習	J3d2c	M28672	4681
舶	J4775	M30402	4936
葛	J336b	M-X	5060
菖	J3e54	M31174	5085
萌	J4b28	M31265	5094
菓	J325b	M31168	5095
著	J4378	M31302	5098
軟	J4670	M38213	5947
転	J453e	M38234	5948
遇	J3678	M38991	6083
運	J313f	M38998	6092
隅	J3679	M41743	6467
陽	J4d5b	M41725	6470

8 residual strokes

募	J4a67	M2416	551
卿	J-X	M2880	643
喧	J3776	M3976	856
堵	J4548	M-X	1021
堵	J-X	M5279	1053
堤	J4469	M5259	1054
堰	J3161	M5274	1055
場	J3e6c	M5278	1058

寅	J3677	M7243	1348
帽	J4b39	M8971	1573
復	J497c	M10183	1760
戟	J3761	M11606	2035
揮	J3478	M12394	2229
揚	J4d48	M12355	2236
提	J4473	M12344	2237
晶	J413d	M14000	**2482**
曾	J413d	M14299	**2483**
暑	J3d6b	M14031	**2484**
暁	J3647	M14031	**2485**
替	J4258	M14300	**2486**
景	J375a	M13983	**2487**
晴	J4032	M13994	**2488**
普	J4961	M13982	**2489**
智	J4352	M14010	**2490**
晩	J4855	M14030	**2491**
最	J3a47	M14301	**2492**
相	J3f7a	M15063	2728
棉	J4c49	M14919	2741
棟	J456f	M14949	2747
棋	J4760	M15178	2754
混	J3a2e	M17694	3204
渚	J-X	M17758	3228
湿	J3c3e	M17920	3243
湯	J4572	M17874	3245
温	J3239	M17774	3246
煉	J4e7b	M-X	3428
煮	J3c51	M19165	3437
痩	J4169	M-X	3806
硬	J3945	M24230	4008
絢	J303c	M27427	4481
朝	J442b	M14374	4838
蓮	J4f21	M-X	5105
董	J4621	M31433	5118

萱	J337e	M31345	5121
葛	J-X		5126
軸	J3c34	M38269	5952
軽	J375a	M38281	5953
遇	J3678	M38991	6083
運	J313f	M38998	6092
間	J3456	M41249	6391
隙	J3764	M41792	6471

9 residual strokes

僧	J414e	M1076	300
傷	J3d7d	M1029	301
匙	J3a7c	M2590	582
墓	J4a68	M5431	1073
幌	J4b5a	M9022	1577
幕	J4b6b	M9051	1578
幹	J3434	M9183	1596
愚	J3672	M10946	1925
意	J3055	M10921	1926
戦	J406f	M11631	2037
摸	J4c4e	M12644	2250
暇	J324b	M14036	**2501**
暖	J4348	M14064	**2502**
暗	J3045	M14065	**2503**
暢	J442a	M14095	**2506**
榊	J3a67	M-X	2756
椿	J4458	M15090	2782
楊	J4c4c	M15112	2784
款	J343e	M16107	2938
漣	J4e7a	M-X	3210
漣	J-X	M18155	3259
漠	J4779	M18149	3268
滝	J426c	M18067	3273
源	J383b	M17926	3274

照	J3e48	M19226	3457
盟	J4c41	M23024	3899
碍	J3337	M24283	4016
禅	J4135	M24787	4104
紳	J3f42	M27348	4467
署	J3d70	M28311	4643
腫	J3c70	M29697	4848
腸	J4432	M29721	4849
腹	J4a22	M29722	4851
蓮	J4f21	M-X	5105
蒔	J3c2c	M31546	5153
蓮	J-X	M31722	5158
褐	J336c	M-X	5473
詣	J3758	M35412	5594
豊	J4b2d	M36263	5737
較	J3353	M38297	5959
農	J4740	M38688	6008
遭	J4178	M39082	6105
隙	J-X	M41813	6477
障	J3e63	M41821	6479
電	J4545	M42253	6526

10 residual strokes

僚	J4e3d	M1100	314
厭	J315e	M3025	662
嗜	J4139	M-X	873
嘗	J3e28	M4205	878
境	J362d	M5409	1085
増	J417d	M5448	1088
層	J4158	M-X	1432
彰	J3e34	M10015	1721
慕	J4a69	M11088	1948
憎	J3f41	M11188	1969
摺	J4022	M12647	2262

幹 J3036 M13522 2378	寮 J4e40 M7325 1366	
暢 J442a M14095 **2506**	履 J4d7a M7799 1434	
曆 J4e71 M14111‍ **2507**	廟 J4940 M9489 1645	
暮 J4a6b M14128 **2508**	影 J3146 M10019 1722	
榊 J-X M15352 2808	衝 J3e57 M34069 1772	
模 J4c4f M15453 2825	慢 J4b7d M11110 1968	
漣 J4e7a M-X 3210	撃 J3762 M12674‍ 2265	
漣 J3b23 M18155 3259	撮 J3b23 M12748 2282	
漸 J4132 M18179 3305	敷 J495f M13359‍ 2357	
漕 J4166 M18131 3306	暫 J3b43 M14120 **2510**	
漫 J4c21 M18166 3308	暴 J4b3d M14137 **2511**	
稲 J3070 M25187‍ 4158	槽 J4165 M15393 2844	
種 J3c6f M25174 4159	樟 J3e40 M15451 2851	
箸 J4824 M-X 4301	潤 J3442 M18277‍ 3329	
箔 J4773 M26142 4312	潮 J442c M18277‍ 3336	
絢 J303c M27427 4481	潜 J4078 M18241‍ 3337	
緒 J3d6f M27632 4521	稽 J374e M25218 4163	
練 J4e7d M27631‍ 4530	穂 J4a66 M25236‍ 4168	
綿 J4c4a M27592 4531	箪 J433d M-X 4321	
翰 J344d M28780 4690	範 J484f M26253‍ 4330	
膜 J4b6c M29808‍ 4854	縄 J466c M27729 4547	
蓮 J-X M31722 5158	線 J407e M27641‍ 4548	
蔓 J4c22 M31784 5180	瓢 J3465 M-X 4689	
複 J4a23 M34417 5484	蕩 J4622 M32002 5198	
貌 J4b46 M36556 5762	蝿 J4768 M-X 5344	
輔 J4a65 M38342 5964	諌 J3452 M35642 5630	
農 J4740 M38688 6008	諮 J315a M35690‍ 5637	
遭 J4178 M39082‍ 6105	諸 J3d74 M35691‍ 5648	
遼 J4e4b M39137 6111	賭 J4552 M-X 5807	
	賜 J3b72 M36809‍ 5812	

億 J322f M1178 321	踏 J4627 M37602 5889	
勲 J372e M2463 560	輦 J475a M38398 5971	
噌 J-X M4303 889	輪 J4e58 M38400 5973	
	遼 J4e4b M39137 6111	
	魯 J4f25 M46013 6848	

叡 J3143 M3214 683	
壇 J4a45 M5528 1101	
憶 J3231 M11295 2001	
曇 J465e M14172 **2518**	
濃 J473b M18442 3349	
激 J3763 M18438 3350	
甑 J3979 M-X 3706	
積 J302c M25281 4170	
穆 J4b54 M25251 4171	
穉 J-X M-X 4174	
篭 J4f36 M26371 4332	
緒 J3d6f M27632 4521	
練 J4e7d M27631‍ 4530	
綿 J4c4a M27592 4531	
縛 J477b M27771 4567	
薯 J3d72 M-X 5202	
薫 J3730 M32173 5223	
薬 J4c74 M32188‍ 5224	
輯 J3d34 M38420 5976	
輸 J4d22 M38438‍ 5978	
醍 J4269 M39924 6184	
醒 J4043 M39936 6185	
錫 J3c62 M40573 6292	
錯 J3a78 M40579 6299	
錬 J4f23 M40690‍ 6300	
韓 J345a M43159 6602	
鴨 J337b M46823 6955	

儲 J4c59 M-X 331	
曙 J3c6c M-X **2519**	
檜 J5b58 M15676 2894	

儲 J-X M1284 335	
曜 J4d4b M14227‍ **2522**	
曙 J-X M14220 **2523**	
篳 J-X M26509 4357	
簡 J344a M26520‍ 4358	
糧 J4e48 M27132 4426	
縛 J477b M27771 4567	
織 J3f25 M27892 4596	
職 J3f26 M29183 4742	
諸 J3d73 M-X 5237	
蝉 J-X M33616 5388	
覆 J4a24 M34789‍ 5517	
贈 J4223 M36920‍ 5827	
鞭 J4a2f M42937 6595	
題 J4a26 M43584 6645	
顕 J3832 M43609‍ 6646	

檀 J4349 M15632 2895	
濃 J473b M18442 3349	
療 J4e45 M22500 3842	
瞭 J4e46 M23697 3960	
竃 J3376 M-X 4216	
糟 J416c M27104 4423	
縄 J466c M27729 4547	
線 J407e M27641‍ 4548	
繋 J3752 M-X 4573	
縮 J3d4c M27815 4585	
膿 J3232 M29951 4883	
薯 J3c6f M32191 5230	
轄 J336d M38482‍ 5981	
鍾 J3661 M40672 6311	
闇 J3047 M41421 6414	
韓 J345a M43159 6602	

曝 J4778 M14239 **2524**	
檜 J4e59 M15798 2908	
濶 J4375 M-X 3377	
爆 J477a M19540 3505	
礎 J626a M24571‍ 4056	
簿 J4a6d M26623‍ 4364	
繋 J3752 M-X 4573	
縮 J3d4c M27815 4585	
諸 J-X M32391‍ 5247	
蘭 J4a66 M32477‍ 5255	
譜 J4968 M35990 5703	
識 J3c31 M35990 5704	
轍 J4532 M38524 5988	
鏡 J3640 M40812 6341	
響 J4e31 M43318‍ 6610	
韻 J3124 M43307 6611	
願 J346a M43623 6653	

欄 J4d73 M15880‍ 2914	
籍 J4052 M26676 4368	
織 J3f25 M27892 4596	
蠣 J695x M33799 5399	
鐘 J3e62 M40902 6352	
馨 J333e M44559 6724	

轟 J396c M38577 5991	
響 J3641 M43318‍ 6610	
饗 J-X M44431 6715	

Rad.72: 20 residual strokes

鰭 J4949 / M46400　6907

Rad. 73 日

0 residual strokes

日 J467c / M13733　2410

---

1 residual stroke

旦 J4336 / M13734　2411
旧 J356c / M13737　2412
由 J4d33 / M21724　3724
甲 J3943 / M21725　3725
申 J3f3d / M21726　3726
白 J4772 / M22678　3863

2 residual strokes

旨 J3b5d / M13738　2414
旬 J3d5c / M13746　2415
旭 J3030 / M13747　2416
曳 J3148 / M14282　2417
曲 J364a / M14280　2418
早 J4161 / M13742　2419

3 residual strokes

更 J3939 / M14283　2422
艮 J3a31 / M30596　4953
車 J3c56 / M38172　5939
迫 J4777 / M38797　6031
里 J4e24 / M40131　6206

4 residual strokes

卓 J426e / M2741　616
厚 J387c / M2949　651
坤 J3a25 / M4969　996
坦 J4333 / M4971　997
奄 J3162 / M5881　1146
岬 J4c28 / M7992　1458
惠 J3743 / M10618　1847
拍 J476f / M11952　2114
抽 J436a / M11930　2119
担 J4334 / M11941　2121
押 J3221 / M11929　2128
昂 J3937 / M13783　2424
旺 J3222 / M13774　2427
昌 J3e3b / M13803　2428
昆 J3a2b / M13792　2430
昏 J3a2a / M13806　2431
易 J3057 / M13814　2432
昔 J404e / M13816　2433
昇 J3e3a / M13794　2434
明 J4c40 / M13805　2435
果 J324c / M14556　2594
東 J4c56c / M14499　2596
沓 J3723 / M17206　3060
泊 J4771 / M17275　3099
狛 J397d / M20349　3566
的 J452a / M22692　3867
者 J3c54 / M28852　4698
艮 J3a31 / M30596　4953
良 J4e49 / M30597　4954
迫 J4777 / M38797　6031

5 residual strokes

便 J4a58 / M659　219
単 J4331 / M2752　620

厚 J387c / M2949　651
垣 J3340 / M5060　1009
宣 J406b / M7132　1328
恒 J3931 / M10527　1849
指 J3b58 / M12034　2152
昂 J3937 / M13783　2424
昆 J3a2b / M13792　2430
昏 J3a2a / M13806　2431
昧 J4b66　2444
昭 J3e3c / M13855　2446
昴 J-X / M13885　2447
映 J3147 / M13838　2448
昨 J3a72 / M13847　2449
昼 J436b / M13888　2450
是 J4027 / M13859　2451
星 J4031 / M13837　2452
春 J3d55 / M13844　2453
柏 J4770 / M14617　2623
沓 J3723 / M17206　3060
泉 J4c74 / M17274　3095
洩 J314c / M17401　3118
皇 J3944 / M13870... 3870
冒 J4b41 / M-X　3915
神 J3f40 / M24673　4087
胆 J4340 / M29354　4790
良 J4e49 / M30597　4954
草 J4170 / M30945　5032
軌 J3530 / M38176　5941
連 J4f22 / M38902　6062
陥 J3459 / M41676　6446
陣 J3f58 / M41667　6448
音 J323b / M43265　6607
香 J3961 / M44518　6722

6 residual strokes

借 J3c5a / M781　259
原 J3836 / M2973　652
宴 J3163 / M7166　1332
庫 J384b / M9330　1617
挿 J415c / M12119　2167
捜 J415c / M12179　2168
晦 J3322 / M-X　2454
晃 J3938 / M13891　2458
晒 J3b2f / M13924　2461
時 J3b7e / M13890　2462
書 J3d71 / M14294　2463
晦 J-X / M13960　2478
桓 J343c / M14774　2652
殉 J3d5e / M16448　2974
狸 J432c / M20427　3578
畠 J482b / M21827　3747
竜 J4e35 / M25751　4232
脂 J3b7e / M29463　4808
莫 J477c / M31078　5057
連 J4f22 / M38902　6062
陳 J4444 / M41698　6457

7 residual strokes

亀 J3535 / M210　62
乾 J3425 / M204　63
喝 J3365 / M-X　824
唱 J3e27 / M3765　829
娼 J3e2b / M6376　1241
婚 J4e22... / M6418　1242
宿 J3d49 / M7195　1344
屠 J454b / M... 1426
得 J4640 / M10137　1755

6 residual strokes

悼 J4569 / M10738　1891
惜 J404b / M10814　1894
措 J413c / M12286　2190
掩 J3166 / M12285　2192
揭 J3747 / M12311　2194
斬 J3b42 / M13555　2384
晦 J3322 / M-X　2454
曽 J413e / M14297... 2464
曹 J4162 / M14297　2477
晦 J-X / M13960　2478
梗 J393c / M14849　2698
渚 J3d6d / M-X　3164
渇 J3369 / M17748　3195
混 J3a2e / M17694　3204
焔 J316b / M-X　3423
猪 J4376 / M20511　3585
章 J3e4f / M25761　4235
紳 J3f42 / M27348　4467
習 J3d2c / M28672　4681
舶 J3d2c / M30402　4936
葛 J336b / M-X　5060
菖 J3e54 / M31174　5085
萌 J4b28 / M31265　5094
菓 J325b / M31168　5095
著 J4378 / M31302　5098
遇 J3678 / M38991　6083
隅 J3679 / M41743　6467
陽 J4d5b / M41725　6470

8 residual strokes

募 J4a67 / M2416　551
卿 J-X / M2880　643
喧 J3776 / M3976　856
堵 J4548 / M-X　1021

堤	J4469/M5259	1054	董	J4621/M31433	5118	碍	J3337/M24283	4016
堰	J3161/M5274	1055	萱	J337e/M31345	5121	禅	J4135/M24787	4104
場	J3e6c/M5278	1058	葛	J-X/M31420	5126	紳	J3f42/M27348	4467
寓	J3677/M7243	1348	遇	J3678/M38991	6083	署	J3d70/M28311	4643
帽	J4b39/M8971	1573	量	J4e4c/M40138	6209	腫	J3c70/M29697	4848
復	J497c/M10183	1760	間	J3456/M41249	6391	腸	J4432/M29721	4849
戟	J3761/M11606	2035	隙	J3764/M41792	6471	腹	J4o22/M29722	4851
揮	J3478/M12394	2229				蒔	J3c2c/M31546	5153

連 J-X/M18155 3259 樟 J3e40/M15451 2851

9 residual strokes / **10 residual strokes** ...

揚	J4d48/M12355	2236				蓮	J-X/M31722	5158
提	J4473/M12344	2237	**9 residual strokes**			褐	J336c/M-X	5473
晶	J3e3d/M14000	2482	僧	J414e/M1076	300	詣	J3758/M35412	5594
曾	J413d/M14299	2483	傷	J3d7d/M1029	301	豊	J4b2d/M36263	5737
暑	J3d6b/M14031	2484	匙	J-X/M2590	582	農	J4740/M38688	6008
暁	J3647/M14031	2485	墓	J4a68/M5431	1073	隈	J-X/M41813	6477
替	J4258/M14300	2486	幌	J4b5a/M9022	1577	障	J3e63/M41821	6479
景	J374a/M13983	2487	幕	J4b6b/M9051	1578	電	J4545/M42253	6526
晴	J4032/M13994	2488	幹	J3434/M9183	1596			
智	J4352/M14010	2490	愚	J3672/M10946	1925	**10 residual strokes**		
晩	J4855/M14030	2491	意	J3055/M10921	1926	僚	J4e3d/M1100	314
最	J3a47/M14301	2492	戦	J406f/M11631	2037	噌	J4139/M-X	873
椙	J3f7a/M15063	2728	摸	J4c4e/M12644	2250	嘗	J3e28/M4205	878
棉	J4c49/M14919	2741	暇	J324b/M14036	2501	境	J362d/M5409	1085
棟	J456f/M14949	2747	暖	J4348/M14064	2502	増	J417d/M5448	1088
楳	J4760/M15178	2754	暗	J3045/M14065	2503	層	J4158/M-X	1432
混	J3a2e/M17694	3204	暢	J442a/M14095	2506	彰	J3e34/M10015	1721
渚	J-X/M17758	3228	榊	J3d67/M-X	2756	慕	J4a69/M11088	1948
湿	J3c3e/M17920	3243	椿	J4458/M15090	2782	憎	J417e/M11188	1969
湯	J4572/M17874	3245	楊	J4d4c/M15112	2784	摺	J4022/M12647	2262
温	J3239/M17774	3246	漣	J4e7a/M-X	3210	斡	J3036/M13522	2378
煉	J4e7b/M-X	3428	漣	J-X/M18155	3259	暦	J4e71/M14111	2507
煮	J3c51/M19165	3437	漠	J4779/M18149	3268	暮	J4a6b/M14128	2508
痩	J4169/M-X	3806	滝	J426c/M18067	3273	榊	J-X/M15352	2808
硬	J3945/M24230	4008	源	J383b/M17926	3274	模	J4e57/M15453	2825
絢	J303c/M27427	4481	照	J3e48/M19226	3457	漣	J4e7a/M-X	3210
朝	J442b/M14374	4838	盟	J4c41/M23024	3899			

Column 4 & 5:

連	J-X/M18155	3259	樟	J3e40/M15451	2851
漸	J4132/M18179	3305	潤	J3442/M-X	3329
漕	J418f/M18131	3306	潮	J442c/M18277	3336
漫	J4c21/M18166	3308	潜	J4078/M18241	3337
稲	J3070/M25187	4158	稽	J374e/M25218	4163
種	J3c6f/M25236	4159	穂	J4a66/M25236	4168
箸	J4824/M-X	4301	筆	J433d/M-X	4321
箔	J4773/M26142	4312	箸	J-X/M26224	4328
絢	J303c/M27427	4481	範	J484f/M26253	4330
緒	J3d6f/M27632	4521	縄	J466c/M27729	4547
練	J4e7d/M27631	4530	線	J407e/M27641	4548
綿	J4c4a/M27592	4531	甌	J3465/M28766	4689
翰	J344d/M28780	4690	蕩	J4622/M32002	5198
膜	J4a23/M29808	4854	蝿	J4768/M-X	5344
蓮	J-X/M31722	5158	諌	J3452/M35642	5630
蔓	J4c22/M31784	5180	謁	J315a/M35690	5637
複	J4a23/M34417	5484	諸	J3d74/M35691	5648
貌	J4b46/M36556	5762	賭	J4552/M-X	5807
農	J4740/M38688	6008	賜	J3b72/M-X	5812
			踏	J4627/M37602	5889
11 residual strokes			輩	J475a/M38398	5971
億	J322f/M1178	321	魯	J4e3d/M46013	6848
勲	J372e/M2463	560			
寮	J4e40/M7325	1366	**12 residual strokes**		
履	J4d7a/M7799	1434	壇	J4345/M5528	1101
廟	J4940/M9489	1645	憶	J3231/M-X	2001
影	J3146/M10019	1722	曇	J465e/M14172	2518
衝	J3e57/M34069	1772	濃	J473b/M18442	3349
慢	J4b7d/M11110	1968	激	J3e57/M18438	3350
撃	J3762/M12674	2265	穐	J302c/M25281	4170
撮	J3b23/M12748	2282	穆	J4b54/M25251	4171
暫	J3b43/M14120	2510	稽	J-X/M-X	4174
暴	J4b3d/M14137	2511	篭	J4f36/M26371	4332
槽	J4165/M15393	2844	緒	J3d6f/M27632	4521

Rad.73: 12 residual strokes

練	J4e7d / M27631ˉ	4530
綿	J4c4a / M27592	4531
縛	J477b / M27771	4567
薯	J3d72 / M-X	5202
薫	J3730 / M32173	5223
薬	J4c74 / M32188ˉ	5224
醍	J4269 / M39924	6184
醒	J4043 / M39936	6185
錫	J3c62 / M40573	6292
錯	J3a78 / M40579	6299
錬	J4f23 / M40576	6300
韓	J345a / M43159	6602
鴨	J337b / M46823	6955

13 residual strokes

儲	J4c59 / M-X	331
曙	J3d6c / M-X	2519
檜	J5b58 / M15676	2894
檀	J4349 / M15632	2895
濃	J473b / M18442	3349
療	J4e45 / M22500	3842
瞭	J4e46 / M23697	3960
竃	J3376 / M-X	4216
糟	J416c / M27104	4423
縄	J466c / M27729	4547
線	J407e / M27641	4548
繋	J3752 / M-X	4573
縮	J3d4c / M27815	4585
膽	J3232 / M29951	4883
薯	J-X / M32191	5230
鍾	J3e61 / M40672	6311
闇	J3047 / M41421	6414
韓	J345a / M43159	6602

14 residual strokes

儲	J-X / M1284	335
曜	J4d4b / M14227ˉ	2522
曙	J-X / M14220	2523
甑	J3979 / M-X	3706
礪	J626a / M24571	4056
箪	J-X / M26509	4357
簡	J344a / M26520ˉ	4358
糧	J4e48 / M27132	4426
縛	J477b / M27892	4567
織	J3f25 / M27892	4596
職	J3f26 / M29183	4742
諸	J3d73 / M-X	5237
蝉	J-X / M33616	5388
覆	J4a24 / M34789ˉ	5517
贈	J4223 / M36920ˉ	5827
鞭	J4c5c / M42937	6595
題	J426a / M43584	6645
顕	J3832 / M43609ˉ	6646

15 residual strokes

曝	J4778 / M14239	2524
橙	J4f26 / M15798	2908
潴	J4829 / M-X	3377
爆	J477a / M19540	3505
礪	J626a / M24571	4056
簿	J4a6d / M26623ˉ	4364
繋	J3752 / M-X	4573
縮	J3d4c / M27815	4585
諸	J-X / M32391	5247
蘭	J4d76 / M32477ˉ	5255
譜	J4968 / M35990	5703
識	J3c31 / M35974	5704

鏡	J3640 / M40812	6341
響	J3641 / M43318ˉ	6610
韻	J3124 / M43307	6611
願	J346a / M43623	6653

16–17 residual strokes

欄	J4d73 / M15880ˉ	2914
籍	J4052 / M26676	4368
織	J3f25 / M27892	4596
蠣	J695a / M33799	5399
鐘	J3e62 / M40902	6352
響	J3641 / M43318ˉ	6610
馨	J333e / M44559	6724
鰭	J4949 / M46400	6907

Rad. 74 月

0 residual strokes

月	J376e / M14330	**2530**

2 residual strokes

肋	J4f3e / M29239	4754
肌	J4375 / M29242	4755
有	J4d2d / M14332	4756

3 residual strokes

肘	J492a / M29268	4761
肝	J344a / M29273	4762

4 residual strokes

明	J4c40 / M13805	2435
肪	J4b43 / M29302	4766
肴	J3a3a / M29322	4767
肢	J3b68 / M29285	4768
朋	J4c2e / M14340ˉ	4769
肱	J394f / M29315	4770
股	J3854 / M29284	4772
育	J3069 / M29318	4773
肥	J486e / M29290	4774
服	J497e / M14345ˉ	4775
肩	J382a / M29299	4776
胃	J305f / M29348	4793
青	J4044 / M42564ˉ	6557

5 residual strokes

削	J3a6f / M2000	488
前	J4130 / M2011	490
宥	J4d28 / M7137	1326
育	J3069 / M29318	4773
胤	J307d / M29405	4786
胞	J4b26 / M29396ˉ	4788
胎	J425b / M29369	4789
胆	J4340 / M29354	4790
肺	J4759 / M29422ˉ	4791
胡	J3855 / M29400	4792
背	J4758 / M29363	4794

6 residual strokes

宵	J3e2c / M7168	1334
屑	J367d / M7709	1424
消	J3e43 / M17529ˉ	3158
胤	J307d / M29405	4786
朕	J443f / M14361	4797

脆	J4048 / M29468	4800
朔	J3a73 / M14359	4801
朗	J4f2f / M14362ˉ	4802
脊	J4054 / M29472	4804
脈	J4c2e / M29470	4805
脇	J4f46 / M29467	4807
脂	J3b69 / M29458	4808
能	J473d / M29454	4809
胴	J4f3c / M29436	4810
胸	J363b / M29442	4811
随	J3f6f / M41764ˉ	6460
骨	J397c / M45098	6784

7 residual strokes

堕	J4244 / M-X	1033
崩	J4a78 / M8212	1491
情	J3e70 / M10756ˉ	1898
梢	J3e3f / M14866	2695
清	J4036 / M17695ˉ	3205
胤	J307d / M29405	4786
朗	J4f2f / M14362ˉ	4802
望	J4b3e / M14368ˉ	4819
脚	J3553 / M29502	4820
脳	J473e / M29567ˉ	4821
脱	J4326 / M29539ˉ	4822
膏	J3951 / M29800	4860
萌	J4b28 / M31265	5094
豚	J465a / M36352	5743
随	J3f6f / M41764ˉ	6460

8 residual strokes

勝	J3e21 / M2409	553
婿	J4c3b / M6470	1246

愉 J4c7b M10905 1920
惰 J4246 M10855 1921
揃 J4237 M12319 2226
散 J3b36 M13265 2352
晴 J4032 M13994 2488
棚 J432a M14941 2748
湖 J3850 M17836 3240
硝 J3e4b M24201 4007
筋 J365a M25994 4286
腔 J3950 M29630 4826
脹 J4431 M29570 4832
腎 J3f55 M29621 4834
期 J347c M14378 4836
腕 J4f53 M29631 4837
朝 J442b M14374 4838
腿 J425c M29747 4846

9 residual strokes

塑 J413a M5328 1068
愈 J4c7c M-X 1910
楮 J424a M15133 2780
溯 J5e6a M17975 3272
滑 J336a M18032 3282
煎 J4079 M19184 3453
瑚 J386a M21126 3662
盟 J4c41 M23024 3899
絹 J3828 M27470 4499
脹 J4431 M29570 4832
腎 J3f55 M29621 4834
腿 J425c M29747 4846
腺 J4123 M29746 4847
腫 J3c70 M29697 4848
腸 J4432 M29721 4849
腰 J3978 M29705 4850

腹 J4a22 M29722 4851
蛸 J427d M33072 5330
賄 J4f45 M36745 5800
靖 J4c77 M42570 6559

10 residual strokes

厭 J315e M3025 662
態 J4256 M11052 1947
熊 J3727 M19294 3468
精 J403a M26997 4411
腿 J425c M29747 4846
膜 J4b6c M29808 4854
膝 J4928 M29837 4868

11 residual strokes

廟 J4940 M9489 1645
徹 J4530 M10245 1771
態 J4256 M11052 1947
撒 J3b35 M12697 2279
撤 J4531 M12726 2280
潮 J442c M18277 3336
箭 J407d M26193 4325
糊 J3852 M27037 4415
絹 J3828 M27470 4499
罷 J486d M28650 4650
腿 J425c M29747 4846
膚 J4966 M29829 4867
膝 J4928 M29837 4868
請 J4041 M35640 5645

---

12 residual strokes

膳 J4137 M29891 4873

膨 J4b44 M29861 4874
謂 J3062 M35759 5656
諭 J4d21 M35727 5667
輸 J4d22 M38438 5978
醋 J386f M39930 6183
錆 J3b2c M40523 6296
鞘 J3e64 M42850 6587
骸 J333c M45164 6789
龍 J4e36 M48818 7103

13 residual strokes

瀞 J4654 M-X 3356
臀 J673d M29939 4880
臆 J3232 M29951 4883
膿 J473f M29938 4884
膾 J4625 M35780 5685
骸 J333c M45164 6789
鮪 J4b6e M46126 6858

14 residual strokes

癒 J4c7e M22545 3847
膿 J473f M29938 4884
臓 J4221 M29995 4886
藤 J4623 M32340 5241
髓 J3f71 M45240 6791

15–19 residual strokes

寵 J437e M7368 1370
瀧 J426d M18671 3376
聾 J4f38 M29212 4745
臓 J4221 M29995 4886

襲 J3d31 M34717 5510
覇 J4746 M34790 5519
轍 J4532 M38524 5988
騰 J462d M44915 6767
髓 J3f71 M45240 6791
鯖 J3b2a M46210 6883
鵬 J4b32 M47005 6979

Rad. 75 木

0 residual strokes

木 J4c5a M14415 2531

1 residual stroke

札 J3b25 M14422 2533
末 J4b76 M14420 2534
未 J4c24 M14419 2535
本 J4b5c M14421 2536
禾 J3253 M24906 4121

2 residual strokes

休 J3559 M440 142
机 J3479 M14435 2543
朴 J4b51 M14428 2544
杇 J3560 M14439 2545
朱 J3c6b M14424 2546
李 J4d7b M14459 2549
米 J4a46 M26832 1380

3 residual strokes

体 J424e M509 165
呆 J4a72 M3395 738

困 J3a24 M4717 946
宋 J4157 M7078 1313
床 J3e32 M9242 1608
杇 J3560 M14439 2545
杢 J4c5d M14487 2548
李 J4d7b M14459 2549
杏 J3049 M14461 2554
杖 J3e73 M14469 2555
杓 J3c5d M14466 2558
束 J422b M14480 2559
杜 J454e M14477 2560
材 J3a60 M14463 2561
杉 J3f59 M14452 2562
条 J3e72 M14486 2563
村 J423c M14464 2564
来 J4d68 M14489 2565

4 residual strokes

味 J4c23 M3456 766
妹 J4b65 M6138 1199
抹 J4b75 M11926 2112
析 J404f M14534 2574
杷 J4747 M14505 2575
枇 J487a M14528 2580
杵 J354f M14503 2581
枚 J4b67 M14552 2582
杭 J393a M14494 2583
枠 J4f48 M14576 2585
杯 J4748 M14497 2586
枡 J5b46 M14577 2587
枢 J3f75 M14577 2588
枕 J4b6d M14546 2589
林 J4e53 M14551 2590
枝 J3b5e M14557 2591

Rad.75: 4 residual strokes

松	J3e3e M14516 **2592**	栄	J3149 M14687 **2635**	殊	J3c6c M16451 2975	棄	J347e M14913 **2787**	榔	J4f31 M15226 **2766**
果	J324c M14556 **2594**	染	J4077 M14621 **2636**	殺	J3b26 M955 2994	淋	J4e54 M17626 3194	棄	J347e M14913 **2787**
板	J4844 M14518 **2595**	相	J416a M23151 3920	珠	J3c6e M20956 3637	深	J3f3c M17687 3206	湘	J3e45 M17842 3216
東	J456c M14499 **2596**	速	J422e M38897 6060	耗	J4c57 M28909 4709	渠	J3574 M17764 3230	渠	J3574 M17764 3230
某	J4b3f M14618 **2628**			耕	J394c M28907 4710	菓	J325b M31168 5095	煉	J4e7b M-X 3428
沫	J4b77 M17235 3085			速	J422e M38897 6060	菜	J3a5a M31184 5097	焚	J4a32 M19100 3434
采	J3a53 M40116 6201	**6 residual strokes**		陳	J4444 M41698 6457	葉	J4d55 M31387 5129	朕	J442d M19871 3529
		凍	J4560 M1670 427			集	J3d38 M41974 6500	琳	J4e56 M21077 3646
5 residual strokes		栂	J444e M14686 **2618**	**7 residual strokes**		麻	J4b63 M47888 7040	疎	J4142 M22002 3776
		柳	J4c78 M14662 **2629**					策	J3a76 M26009 4284
乗	J3e68 M153 54	栓	J4930 M-X **2637**	傑	J3766 M955 293			菓	J325b M31168 5095
保	J4a5d M702 222	柏	J337c M14714 **2638**	埜	J4738 M5154 1022	**8 residual strokes**		葉	J4d55 M31387 5129
勅	J443c M2354 540	栓	J4072 M14689 **2649**	彬	J494b M9996 1717			閑	J3457 M41247 6390
昧	J4b66 M13846 2444	栖	J4034 M14693 **2650**	彩	J3a4c M9992 1718	傑	J3766 M955 293	集	J3d38 M41974 6500
枇	J487a M14528 **2580**	柄	J4073 M14737 **2651**	術	J3d51 M34046 1754	喋	J437d M3917 850		
枢	J3f75 M14577 **2588**	桓	J343c M14774 **2652**	採	J3a4e M12274 2209	媒	J475e M6498 1247	**9 residual strokes**	
柁	J4248 M14599 **2597**	枯	J4335 M14777 **2653**	探	J4335 M12276 2211	屡	J3c48 M7770 1428		
枥	J464a M14687 **2613**	栽	J3a4f M14750 **2654**	核	J334b M14743 **2660**	巣	J4448 M8696 **2705**	想	J415b M10858 1922
柊	J4922 M14610 **2614**	桐	J364d M14770 **2655**	梅	J475f M14795 **2666**	槌	J4448 M-X **2709**	愁	J3d25 M10885 1923
栂	J444e M14686 **2618**	桁	J3765 M14754 **2656**	根	J3a2c M14745 **2670**	椋	J4c3a M15020 **2725**	新	J3f37 M13572 2387
柾	J4b6f M14675 **2619**	柴	J3c46 M14664 **2657**	梼	J456e M14911 **2672**	椙	J3f7a M15063 **2728**	槌	J4448 M-X **2709**
柵	J3a74 M14665 **2620**	桟	J3b37 M14796 **2658**	桝	J4b71 M-X **2673**	椀	J4033 M15001 **2732**	極	J364b M15181 **2753**
柑	J343b M14619 **2621**	桂	J374b M14755 **2659**	椛	J3371 M15065 **2683**	椅	J3058 M15009 **2737**	楳	J4760 M15178 **2754**
柚	J4d2e M14622 **2622**	核	J334b M14743 **2660**	械	J3323 M14882 **2685**	棉	J4c49 M15065 **2741**	榊	J3a67 M-X **2756**
柏	J4770 M14617 **2623**	桑	J372c M14772 **2661**	梓	J3034 M14845 **2688**	椎	J4447 M15024 **2742**	樋	J4875 M-X **2757**
柿	J3341 M14681 **2624**	栗	J3233 M14695 **2662**	桶	J3233 M14811 **2694**	楼	J4033 M14980 **2743**	榔	J4f31 M15226 **2766**
柘	J4453 M14626 **2626**	桃	J456d M14757 **2663**	梢	J3e3f M14866 **2695**	棋	J347d M14922 **2744**	槌	J-X M15318 **2767**
柄	J4a41 M14603 **2627**	桜	J3a79 M14796 **2664**	梱	J3a2d M14883 **2696**	棺	J343d M15065 **2746**	楮	J466a M15154 **2769**
某	J4b3f M14618 **2628**	株	J3374 M14723 **2665**	梨	J4d7c M14873 **2697**	棟	J456f M14949 **2747**	楚	J413f M15141 **2771**
柳	J4c78 M14662 **2629**	梅	J475f M14795 **2666**	梗	J393c M14849 **2698**	棚	J432a M14941 **2748**	椴	J464e M15075 **2772**
查	J3a3a M14643 2630	案	J3046 M14762 **2667**	梶	J3361 M14889 **2699**	森	J3f39 M14974 **2749**	楷	J3d5d M15173 **2776**
柱	J436c M14631 **2631**	格	J334a M14714 **2668**	梧	J3868 M14872 **2700**	棒	J4b40 M14889 **2750**	楓	J4976 M15126 **2777**
架	J324d M14586 **2632**	校	J393b M14713 **2669**	梁	J4e42 M14825 **2702**	植	J3f22 M15023 **2751**	楠	J466f M15152 **2779**
柔	J3d40 M14622 **2633**	根	J3a2c M14745 2670	巣	J4163 M8696 **2705**	検	J3821 M15065 **2752**	楢	J42da M15133 **2780**
枯	J384f M14579 **2634**	桝	J4b71 M-X **2673**	梯	J4474 M14881 **2706**	極	J364b M15181 **2753**	椿	J4458 M15090 **2782**
						楳	J4760 M15178 **2754**		

楊 J4d4c / M15112 **2784**
楼 J4f30 / M15212 **2785**
棗 J347e / M14913 **2787**
業 J3648 / M15170 **2789**
楽 J335a / M15213 **2790**
概 J3335 / M15217' **2824**
煤 J4761 / M19220 3452
煉 J-X / M19178 3455
腺 J442d / M19871 3529
禁 J3658 / M24743 4098
裸 J4d67 / M34371 5475
鉢 J482d / M40317 6249

10 residual strokes

厤 J4e71 / M14111' 2507
槌 J4448 / M-X **2709**
樋 J4875 / M-X **2757**
槌 J-X / M15318 **2767**
榊 J-X / M15352 **2808**
榎 J315d / M15219 **2810**
榛 J3f3a / M15240 **2811**
樋 J-X / M15415 **2816**
樺 J3372 / M15497 **2817**
槇 J7422 / M15310 **2818**
槙 J4b6a / M-X **2819**
様 J4d4d / M15352' **2821**
槍 J4164 / M15319 **2822**
構 J393d / M15317 **2823**
概 J3335 / M15217' **2824**
模 J4c4f / M15453 **2825**
歴 J4e72 / M16334' 2964
漆 J3c3f / M18108 3304
練 J4e7d / M27631' 4530
蝶 J4433 / M33333 5363

裸 J4d67 / M34371 5475
雑 J3b28 / M42022 6507

11 residual strokes

幡 J4828 / M9086 1584
摩 J4b60 / M12613' 2264
整 J4030 / M13394 2360
樋 J4875 / M-X **2757**
樋 J-X / M15415 **2816**
様 J4d4d / M15352 **2821**
概 J3335 / M15217 **2824**
楳 J4374 / M15438 **2841**
槽 J4165 / M15393 **2844**
槻 J4450 / M15390 **2845**
樫 J335f / M15485 **2849**
樟 J3e40 / M15451 **2851**
標 J4938 / M15442 **2852**
権 J3822 / M15484 **2853**
横 J3223 / M15484' **2854**
箱 J4822 / M26209 4331
蝶 J4433 / M33333 5363
襃 J4b2b / M34437 5483
諌 J3452 / M35642 5630
課 J325d / M35589 5644
謀 J4435 / M35697 5665
魅 J4c25 / M45811 6838

12 residual strokes

噺 J4838 / M4433 903
操 J4160 / M12801 2296
楳 J4374 / M15438 **2841**
樫 J335f / M15485 **2849**
橡 J464b / M15564 **2863**

橘 J354c / M15551 2868
樵 J3e41 / M15489 2871
樽 J432e / M15500 2875
樹 J3c79 / M15496 2878
橋 J3636 / M15526 2879
機 J3521 / M15561 2880
檎 J3869 / M15657 2888
磨 J4b61 / M24449' 4045
築 J435b / M26298 4343
練 J4e7d / M27631' 4530
薪 J3f45 / M32149 5222
薬 J4c74 / M32188' 5224
親 J3f46 / M34918 5534
課 J325d / M35589 5644
諫 J6b5d / M35724 5664
諜 J4435 / M35697 5665
謀 J4b45 / M35756 5671
錬 J4f23 / M40576 6300
頼 J4d6a / M43529' 6635

13 residual strokes

楳 J4374 / M15438 2841
櫛 J367b / M-X 2884
檎 J3869 / M15657 2888
橿 J3360 / M15629 2889
檜 J5b58 / M15676 2894
檀 J4349 / M15632 2895
燥 J4167 / M19467 3493
燦 J43c / M19468 3498
篠 J3c44 / M -- 4352
薫 J4f4e / M32222 5234
霜 J417a / M42363 6542

14 residual strokes

櫛 J367b / M-X **2884**
檮 J5b6d / M15713 **2897**
礎 J4143 / M24522 4054
襟 J365f / M34647 5504
麿 J4b7b / M47909' 7044

15 residual strokes

檮 J5b6d / M15713 **2897**
櫓 J4f26 / M15798 **2908**
瀬 J4025 / M18672' 3384
緑 J372b / M27953 4602
藻 J4174 / M32401 5254
蘭 J4d76 / M32477' 5255
麓 J4f23 / M47658 7023

16-22 residual strokes

機 J3521 / M15561 **2880**
櫨 J4827 / M15844 **2910**
欄 J4d73 / M15880' **2914**
欝 J3135 / M-X **2924**
欝 J-X / M15978 **2926**
籍 J4052 / M26676 4368
緑 J372b / M27953 4602
魔 J4b62 / M45906' 6843
麓 J4f3c / M47658 7023

Rad. 76 欠

0 residual strokes

欠 J3767 / M15991 **2928**

2-6 residual strokes

吹 J3f61 / M3373 747
姿 J3b51 / M6257 1216
次 J3c21 / M15992' **2929**
欣 J3655 / M16008 **2930**
欧 J3224 / M16024' **2931**
炊 J3f66 / M18904 3405
茨 J3071 / M30896 5017

7-9 residual strokes

欲 J4d5f / M16080 **2936**
款 J343e / M16107 **2938**
欺 J353d / M16097 **2939**
欽 J3656 / M16104 **2940**
羨 J4122 / M28503 4665
資 J3b71 / M36750 5803
軟 J372b / M38213 5947
飲 J307b / M44063' 6680

10-12 residual strokes

慾 J4d5d / M11163 1951
歌 J324e / M16167 **2945**
歎 J4337 / M16182 **2947**
歓 J343f / M16197 **2948**
盗 J4570 / M23000' 3894
蕨 J4f4f / M32001 5194
諧 J3b70 / M35728 5660

Rad. 77 止

0 residual strokes

止 J3b5f M16253 **2954**

1–2 residual stroke

企 J346b M422 135
凪 J4664 M1758 437
正 J4035 M16255 **2955**
此 J3a21 M16259 **2956**

---

4 residual strokes

些 J3a33 M268 84
征 J402c M10077 1731
步 J4a62 M16284 **2958**
武 J4970 M16273 **2959**
祉 J3b63 M24641 4069
肯 J394e M29311 4771

5–6 residual strokes

卸 J3237 M2861 641
捗 J-X M12160 2161
柾 J4b6f M14675 2619
柴 J3c46 M14664 2657
歪 J4f44 M16286 **2960**
症 J3e49 M22140 3795

---

7 residual strokes

帰 J3522 M8930 1564
捗 J443d M-X 2173
渉 J3e44 M17749 3190

渋 J3d42 M17750 3200
砦 J3a56 M24098 4002
距 J3577 M37481 5866

---

8 residual strokes

御 J3866 M10157 1761
斌 J494c M13468 2369
歯 J3b75 M16323 **2961**
疏 J4141 M22000 3775
疎 J4142 M22002 3776
紫 J3b67 M27337 4486
証 J3e5a M35341 5589
距 J3577 M37481 5866

---

9 residual strokes

歳 J3a50 M16326 **2962**
跨 J3859 M37504 5872
践 J4129 M37547 5873
跡 J4057 M37493 5875
路 J4f29 M37524 5876
跳 J4437 M37533 5877
鉦 J3e60 M40322 6246

---

10 residual strokes

歴 J4e72 M16334 **2964**
紫 J2733 M27337 4486
誕 J4342 M35692 5640
跨 J3859 M37504 5872
踊 J4d59 M37587 5882
雌 J3b73 M41998 6506

11–14 residual strokes

噛 J337a M-X 888
嚙 J-X M4516 921
整 J4030 M13394 2360
嚮 J357a M24820 4111
蹉 J4979 M31964 5203
誕 J4342 M35692 5640
賦 J496a M36800 5811
髭 J4926 M45399 6812
踏 J4627 M37602 5889
蹄 J4d77 M37724 5894
蹟 J4058 M37814 5905
頻 J4951 M-X 6641

15–20 residual strokes

瀕 J494e M18636 3381
蹴 J3d33 M37876 5913
躍 J4c76 M37955 5921
露 J4f2a M42463 6549
鷁 J4c39 M46963 6974
鷺 J3a6d M47362 7006
齢 J4e70 M48632 7093

Rad. 78 歹

2–5 residual strokes

例 J4e63 M587 193
列 J4e73 M1901 460
夙 J3d48 M5755 1126
死 J3b60 M16365 **2968**
殆 J4b58 M16430 **2972**

6–9 residual strokes

殉 J3d5e M16448 **2974**
殊 J3c6c M16451 **2975**
残 J3b44 M16459 **2976**
殖 J3f23 M16502 **2981**
烈 J4e75 M18987 3420
葬 J4172 M31448 5128
裂 J4e76 M34260 5453

Rad. 79 殳

3–6 residual strokes

役 J4c72 M10057 1726
投 J456a M11887 2095
殴 J3225 M16618 **2990**
段 J434a M16619 **2991**
殺 J3b26 M16629 **2994**
疫 J3156 M22069 3783
股 J3854 M29284 4772
般 J484c M30388 4931

7–10 residual strokes

搬 J4842 M12507 2249
槃 J464e M15075 2772
殻 J334c M-X **2996**
殿 J4542 M16651 **3001**
穀 J3972 M25188 4157
設 J405f M35293 5570

11–24 residual strokes

撃 J3762 M12674 2265

毅 J3523 M16673 **3003**
盤 J4857 M23036 3902
磐 J4858 M24401 4037
繋 J-X M-X 4573
臀 J673d M29939 4880
馨 J333e M44559 6724

Rad. 80 母

0 residual strokes

母 J4a6c M16723 **3005**

2–5 residual strokes

侮 J496e M629 187
悔 J3279 M10617 1848
梅 J444e M14686 2618
毎 J4b68 M16724 **3006**
毒 J4647 M16730 **3007**
海 J3324 M17450 3133

6–20 residual strokes

慣 J3437 M11111 1970
敏 J4952 M13202 2337
晦 J3322 M-X 2454
梅 J475f M14795 2666
繁 J484b M27803 4570
貫 J3453 M36681 5778

Rad. 81 比

0 residual strokes

比 J4866 M16743 **3010**

1–5 residual stroke

庇 J485f M9239 1606
批 J4863 M11845 2086
昆 J3a2b M13792 2430
枇 J487a M14528 2580
此 J3a21 M16259 2956
毘 J487b M16753 3011
皆 J3327 M22699 3869
陛 J4a45 M41654 6444

6–10 residual strokes

塵 J3f50 M5388 1087
混 J3a2e M17694 3204
漉 J3977 M18112 3300
琵 J487c M21080 3653
篦 J4a4f M26114 4310
階 J332c M41751 6469
雌 J3b73 M41998 6506
鹿 J3c2f M47586 7017

13–29 residual strokes

鍛 J4343 M40625 6318
麓 J4f3c M47658 7023
麗 J4e6f M47663 7026
麟 J4e5b M47690 7028

Rad. 82 毛

0 residual strokes

毛 J4c53 M16772 3013

3–7 residual strokes

尾 J4878 M7650 1411
梶 J3361 M14889 2699
耗 J4c30 M26881 4387
耗 J4c57 M28909 4709

Rad. 83 氏

0 residual strokes

氏 J3b61 M17026 3020

2–4 residual strokes

低 J4463 M504 166
底 J446c M9262 1612
抵 J4471 M11921 2120
昏 J3a2a M13806 2431
民 J4c31 M17028 3021
祇 J3540 M-X 4068

6 residual strokes

眠 J4c32 M23240 3925
砥 J4556 M24093 3997
紙 J3b66 M27293 4455
邸 J4521 M39347 6134

7–8 residual strokes

婚 J3a27 M6418 1242
眠 J4c32 M23240 3925
紙 J3b66 M27293 4455

Rad. 84 气

2–3 residual strokes

気 J3524 M17046 3025
汽 J3525 M17177 3068

Rad. 85 水

0 residual strokes

水 J3f65 M17083 3030

1 residual stroke

永 J314a M17088 3031
氷 J4939 M17087 3032

2 residual strokes

氾 J4845 M17101 3033
汀 J4475 M17103 3034
汁 J3d41 M17104 3035
求 J3561 M17105 3036

3 residual strokes

尿 J4722 M7651 1410
汝 J4672 M17138 3040
汐 J3c2e M17122 3041
池 J4353 M17141 3042
汎 J4846 M17120 3043
江 J393e M17140 3045
汗 J3440 M17130 3046
污 J3178 M17133 3047
沌 J4659 M17193 3054
汲 J3562 M17163 3064

4 residual strokes

承 J3e35 M11852 2088
污 J3178 M17133 3047
沌 J4659 M17193 3054
汰 J4241 M17160 3055
沓 J3723 M17206 3060
沃 J4d60 M17184 3061
沢 J4274 M17234 3062
沙 J3a3b M17212 3063
汲 J3562 M17163 3064
沖 J322d M17209 3065
没 J4b57 M17233 3066
汽 J3525 M17177 3068
沈 J4440 M17189 3069
決 J3768 M17174 3070

5 residual strokes

剥 J476d M48939 496
沫 J4b77 M17235 3085
況 J3637 M17264 3086
泳 J314b M17328 3090
沼 J3e42 M17257 3091
泌 J4867 M17279 3092
泡 J4b22 M17307 3093
沸 J4a28 M17251 3094
泉 J4074 M17274 3095
沿 J3168 M17260 3096
泰 J4259 M17325 3098
泊 J4771 M17275 3099
治 J3c23 M17256 3100
波 J4748 M17308 3101
河 J4245 M17245 3102
注 J436d M17316 3103

泣 J3563 M17309 3104
泥 J4525 M17311 3105
油 J4c7d M17253 3106
法 J4b21 M17290 3107

6 residual strokes

救 J355f M13221 2344
染 J4077 M14621 2636
洩 J314c M17401 3118
洛 J4d6c M17383 3119
洲 J3d27 M17413 3120
津 J4445 M17396 3122
洪 J393f M17402 3123
洞 J4636 M17363 3125
派 J4749 M17428 3126
浄 J3e74 M17451 3128
浅 J4075 M17452 3129
洋 J4d4e M17330 3130
洗 J4076 M17379 3131
活 J3368 M17423 3132
海 J3324 M17450 3133
浮 J4962 M17487 3159
球 J3565 M21011 3643
粛 J3d4d M29223 4747

7 residual strokes

康 J392f M9376 1621
救 J355f M13221 2344
海 J3324 M17450 3133
涜 J4642 M-X 3134
涛 J4573 M-X 3138
涅 J333d M17485 3142
浩 J3940 M17479 3147

Rad.85: 7 residual strokes

涌	J4d30 / M17534	3150
浜	J494d / M17462	3152
浴	J4d61 / M17496	3153
涙	J4e5e / M17573'	3154
浪	J4f32 / M17482	3155
浦	J313a / M17475	3156
浸	J3f3b / M17475'	3157
消	J3e43 / M17529'	3158
浮	J4962 / M17487	3159
流	J4e2e / M17572'	3160
淳	J3d5f / M17690	3189
禄	J4f3d / M24741'	4096
酒	J3c72 / M39776	6160
黍	J3550 / M47991	7048

8 residual strokes

婆	J474c / M6390	1240
梁	J4e42 / M14825	2702
浪	J4f32 / M17482	3155
渚	J3d6d / M-X	3164
涯	J3336 / M17582	3181
淀	J4d64 / M17610	3182
淘	J4571 / M17642	3187
淳	J3d5f / M17690	3189
渉	J3644 / M17749'	3190
淑	J3d4a / M17634	3191
淋	J4e54 / M17626	3194
渇	J3369 / M17748	3195
渓	J374c / M-X	3196
済	J3a51 / M17749	3197
涼	J4e43 / M17606	3198
液	J3155 / M17586	3199
渋	J3d42 / M17750'	3200
添	J453a / M17698	3201

淡	J4338 / M17660	3202
淫	J307c / M17678	3203
混	J3a2e / M17694	3204
清	J4036 / M17695'	3205
深	J3f3c / M17687	3206
渠	J3574 / M17764	3230
淵	J4a25 / M17692	3237
詠	J3153 / M35409	5584

9 residual strokes

様	J4d4d / M15352'	2821
混	J3a2e / M17694	3204
湧	J4d2f / M17862	3207
溌	J482e / M-X	3209
連	J4e7a / M-X	3210
湘	J3e45 / M17842	3216
渥	J302f / M17770	3224
湊	J4c2b / M17822	3226
渚	J-X / M17758	3228
渠	J3574 / M17764	3230
湛	J4339 / M17846	3234
淵	J4a25 / M17692	3237
滋	J3c22 / M17919'	3238
湾	J4f51 / M17920	3239
湖	J3850 / M17836	3240
渦	J3132 / M17771	3241
港	J3941 / M17783'	3242
湿	J3c3e / M17920'	3243
測	J422c / M17780	3244
湯	J4572 / M17874	3245
温	J3239 / M17774	3246
渡	J454f / M17765	3247
満	J4e7e / M17921'	3248
減	J383a / M17759	3249

滞	J425a / M18067'	3280
緑	J4e50 / M27541'	4528
腺	J4123 / M29746	4847
膝	J4928 / M29837	4868
落	J4d6e / M31362	5130
蒸	J3e78 / M31618'	5163

10 residual strokes

塗	J4549 / M5338'	1074
様	J4d4d / M15352'	2821
漣	J4e7a / M-X	3210
漣	J-X / M18155	3259
漠	J4779 / M18149	3268
溢	J306e / M17951	3270
溺	J452e / M17990	3271
溯	J5e6a / M17975	3272
滝	J426c / M18067	3273
源	J383b / M17926	3274
溝	J3942 / M17944	3275
溜	J4e2f / M17943	3276
溶	J4d4f / M17983	3277
準	J3d60 / M17934	3278
滅	J4c47 / M18008	3279
滞	J425a / M18067'	3280
漢	J3441 / M18068'	3281
滑	J336a / M18032	3282
羨	J4122 / M28503	4665
膝	J4928 / M29837	4868
蒲	J3377 / M31611	5156
袈	J3a40 / M34325	5457

11 residual strokes

暴	J4b3d / M14137	2511

連	J4e7a / M-X	3210
漣	J-X / M18155	3259
潅	J3443 / M18216	3287
滴	J4529 / M18084	3299
漉	J3977 / M18112	3300
潰	J4452 / M18167	3301
漂	J493a / M18102	3303
漆	J3c3f / M18108	3304
漸	J4132 / M18179	3305
漕	J4166 / M18131	3306
漏	J4f33 / M18120	3307
漫	J4c21 / M18166	3308
漁	J3579 / M18101	3309
演	J3169 / M18310	3310
窪	J3726 / M25580	4209
箔	J4773 / M26142	4312
緑	J4e50 / M27541'	4528
線	J407e / M27641	4548
裟	J3a40 / M34325	5457
踏	J4627 / M37602	5889
録	J4d519' / M40519'	6298
隷	J466c / M41928	6490

12 residual strokes

漉	J3977 / M18112	3300
潑	J-X / M18225	3325
潟	J3363 / M18247	3328
潤	J3442 / M-X	3329
潔	J3769 / M18231	3332
澄	J4021 / M18315	3333
潤	J3d61 / M18255	3334
潰	J4459 / M18281	3335
潮	J442c / M18277'	3336
潜	J4078 / M18241	3337

糠	J3947 / M27105	4424
蕩	J4622 / M32002	5198
隷	J4e6c / M41928	6490

13 residual strokes

滋	J3c22 / M17919'	3238
澱	J4543 / M18410	3347
濁	J4279 / M18440	3348
濃	J473b / M18442	3349
激	J3763 / M18438	3350
糠	J3947 / M27105	4424
線	J407e / M27641	4548
薄	J4776 / M32083'	5225
藤	J4623 / M32340'	5241

14 residual strokes

曝	J4778 / M14239'	2524
潔	J3769 / M18231	3332
濃	J473b / M18442	3349
瀞	J4654 / M-X	3356
濯	J4275 / M18532	3360
濤	J5e39 / M18508	3361
濠	J396a / M18502	3363
濡	J4728 / M18504	3365
濫	J4d74 / M18521	3366
爆	J477a / M19540	3505
鴻	J3963 / M46874	6963

15 residual strokes

濫	J4d74 / M18521	3366
瀆	J-X / M18591	3373
瀦	J4375 / M-X	3377

藩 J484d / M32346 5242

16–19 residual strokes

瀧 J426d / M18671 3376
濔 J4375 / M-X 3377
瀞 J-X / M18659 3380
瀬 J494e / M18636 3381
瀕 J4025 / M18672 3384
灌 J5e75 / M18759 3390
灘 J4667 / M18784 3391
薄 J4a6d / M26623 4364
藻 J4174 / M32401 5254

Rad. 86 火

0 residual strokes

火 J3250 / M18850 3394

2 residual strokes

灯 J4574 / M18855 3395
灰 J3325 / M18859 3396

3 residual strokes

灼 J3c5e / M18878 3398
灸 J3564 / M18872 3399
災 J3a52 / M18879 3400

4 residual strokes

炉 J4f27 / M18902 3403
炎 J316a / M18910 3404

炊 J3f66 / M18904 3405

5 residual strokes

恢 J327a / M10577 1843
為 J3059 / M18981 3411
点 J4540 / M18980 3412
炭 J433 / M18953 3413
畑 J482a / M21797 3741
秋 J3d29 / M24940 4131

6 residual strokes

烈 J4e75 / M18987 3420
烏 J3128 / M18998 3421
烹 J4b23 / M19049 3425
荻 J322e / M31005 5054
馬 J474f / M44572 6725

7 residual strokes

偽 J3536 / M927 276
庶 J3d6e / M9373 1625
淡 J4338 / M17660 3202
焔 J316b / M-X 3423
烹 J4b23 / M19049 3425
魚 J357b / M45956 6845
鳥 J443b / M46634 6931
黒 J3975 / M48040 7052

8 residual strokes

煉 J4e7b / M-X 3428
焚 J3975 / M19100 3434
然 J4133 / M19149 3435

焦 J3e47 / M19119 3436
煮 J3c51 / M19165 3437
焼 J3e46 / M19166 3438
無 J4c35 / M19113 3439
萩 J476b / M31333 5122
蒸 J3e78 / M31618 5163

9 residual strokes

営 J3144 / M4025 857
愁 J3d25 / M10885 1923
滅 J4c5b / M18008 3279
煤 J4761 / M19220 3452
煎 J4079 / M19184 3453
煩 J4851 / M19229 3454
焠 J316c / M19178 3455
煙 J316c / M19203 3456
照 J3e48 / M19129 3457
遮 J3c57 / M39086 6106

10 residual strokes

墨 J4b4f / M-X 1086
嶋 J4568 / M8434 1503
漁 J3579 / M18101 3309
熔 J4d50 / M19319 3458
熊 J3727 / M19294 3468
煽 J407a / M19272 3469
熟 J3975 / M19332 3472
遮 J3c57 / M39086 6106
鳶 J4650 / M46674 6938
鳴 J4c44 / M46672 6939

11 residual strokes

勲 J372e / M2463 560
撚 J4732 / M12713 2278
撫 J496f / M12743 2281
潟 J3363 / M18247 3328
熟 J3d4f / M19332 3472
熱 J472e / M19360 3473
窯 J4d52 / M25594 4210
蕉 J3e56 / M31937 5191
蕪 J4973 / M32004 5196
談 J434c / M35633 5643
駕 J326f / M44667 6743
黙 J4c5b / M48063 7055

12 residual strokes

儘 J5056 / M1234 327
樵 J3e41 / M15489 2871
燈 J4575 / M19402 3476
燕 J316d / M19429 3489
燃 J4733 / M19394 3490
燐 J4e55 / M19417 3499
薫 J3730 / M32173 5223
鴬 J3229 / M-X 6945
駕 J3175 / M46795 6953

13 residual strokes

燥 J4167 / M19467 3493
燭 J3f24 / M19480 3496
燦 J3b38 / M19468 3498
燐 J4e55 / M19417 3499
礁 J3e4c / M24502 4048
鍬 J372d / M40643 6314
黛 J4263 / M48075 7060

15–20 residual strokes

櫓 J4f26 / M15798 2908
爆 J477a / M19540 3505
繹 J6575 / M28058 4617
驚 J3643 / M45013 6774
鯵 J3033 / M-X 6875
鰍 J3362 / M46331 6895
鴬 J7274 / M47169 6994
鷲 J4f49 / M47345 7004
鷺 J3a6d / M47362 7006

Rad. 87 爪

0 residual strokes

爪 J445e / M19653 3509

2–4 residual strokes

争 J4168 / M236 69
受 J3c75 / M3159 678
妥 J4245 / M1188 1188
狐 J3851 / M20333 3568
瓜 J313b / M21371 3686
采 J3a53 / M40116 6201

5–6 residual strokes

孤 J3849 / M6966 1293
将 J3e2d / M7437 1379
浮 J4962 / M17487 3159

Rad.87: 7 residual strokes

7 residual strokes

彩 $\frac{J3a4c}{M9992}$ 1718

授 $\frac{J3c78}{M12242}$ 2208

採 $\frac{J3a4e}{M12274}$ 2209

渓 $\frac{J374c}{M-X}$ 3196

淫 $\frac{J307c}{M17678}$ 3203

菜 $\frac{J3a5a}{M31184}$ 5097

遙 $\frac{J4d5a}{M-X}$ 6075

8 residual strokes

媛 $\frac{J4932}{M6516}$ 1244

援 $\frac{J3167}{M12407}$ 2230

揺 $\frac{J4d49}{M12445}$ 2235

遥 $\frac{J4d5a}{M-X}$ 6075

9 residual strokes

奨 $\frac{J3e29}{M5990}$ 1167

媛 $\frac{J4932}{M6516}$ 1244

愛 $\frac{J3026}{M10947}$ 1927

暖 $\frac{J4348}{M14064}$ 2502

舜 $\frac{J3d58}{M30339}$ 4925

蒋 $\frac{J-X}{M-X}$ 5132

隠 $\frac{J3123}{M41836}$ 6480

10–12 residual strokes

墾 $\frac{J3a26}{M5509}$ 1097

稲 $\frac{J3070}{M25187}$ 4158

穏 $\frac{J323a}{M25280}$ 4175

綏 $\frac{J3c7a}{M27565}$ 4510

緩 $\frac{J344b}{M27669}$ 4551

謡 $\frac{J4d58}{M35779}$ 5666

13–15 residual strokes

瀞 $\frac{J-X}{M18659}$ 3380

爵 $\frac{J3c5f}{M19710}$ 3514

瞬 $\frac{J3d56}{M23694}$ 3969

緩 $\frac{J344b}{M27669}$ 4551

醤 $\frac{J3e5f}{M-X}$ 6186

鶏 $\frac{J375c}{M47074}$ 6980

Rad. 88 父

0 residual strokes

父 $\frac{J4963}{M19721}$ 3516

2–6 residual strokes

交 $\frac{J3872}{M291}$ 90

佼 $\frac{J3873}{M570}$ 175

効 $\frac{J387a}{M2334}$ 535

斈 $\frac{J4960}{M13539}$ 2382

校 $\frac{J393c}{M14713}$ 2669

郊 $\frac{J3959}{M39392}$ 6137

釜 $\frac{J3378}{M40164}$ 6215

7–10 residual strokes

爺 $\frac{J4c6c}{M19734}$ 3517

絞 $\frac{J394a}{M27421}$ 4485

較 $\frac{J3353}{M38297}$ 5959

鮫 $\frac{J3b2d}{M46127}$ 6863

Rad. 89 爻

5–10 residual strokes

爽 $\frac{J4156}{M19746}$ 3520

爾 $\frac{J3c24}{M19750}$ 3521

駁 $\frac{J477d}{M44619}$ 6733

12–22 residual strokes

攬 $\frac{J5978}{M13041}$ 2322

壐 $\frac{J3c25}{M21309}$ 3683

禰 $\frac{J-X}{M24851}$ 4115

襧 $\frac{J4729}{M-X}$ 4116

Rad. 90 爿

2–9 residual strokes

北 $\frac{J4b4c}{M2574}$ 581

壮 $\frac{J4154}{M5642}$ 974

将 $\frac{J3e2d}{M7437}$ 1379

状 $\frac{J3e75}{M20257}$ 3556

荘 $\frac{J4171}{M30890}$ 5031

装 $\frac{J4524}{M34283}$ 5455

鼎 $\frac{J4524}{M48315}$ 7074

10 residual strokes

奨 $\frac{J3e29}{M5990}$ 1167

寝 $\frac{J3f32}{M7278}$ 1353

蒋 $\frac{J3e55}{M-X}$ 5132

醤 $\frac{J3e5f}{M31820}$ 5177

装 $\frac{J4175}{M34283}$ 5455

Rad. 91 片

0 residual strokes

片 $\frac{J4a52}{M19813}$ 3525

4–17 residual strokes

版 $\frac{J4847}{M19817}$ 3526

牌 $\frac{J4757}{M19854}$ 3528

牒 $\frac{J442d}{M19871}$ 3529

繍 $\frac{J-X}{M27913}$ 4600

Rad. 92 牙

0 residual strokes

牙 $\frac{J3267}{M19909}$ 3531

2–11 residual strokes

穿 $\frac{J407c}{M25436}$ 4198

芽 $\frac{J326a}{M30860}$ 5002

邪 $\frac{J3c59}{M-X}$ 6135

雅 $\frac{J326d}{M41973}$ 6505

Rad. 93 牛

0 residual strokes

牛 $\frac{J356d}{M19922}$ 3532

2 residual strokes

件 $\frac{J376f}{M410}$ 130

牟 $\frac{J4c36}{M19928}$ 3533

牝 $\frac{J4c46}{M19925}$ 3534

3–5 residual strokes

牢 $\frac{J4f34}{M19934}$ 3535

牡 $\frac{J3234}{M19933}$ 3536

牧 $\frac{J4b52}{M19950}$ 3537

物 $\frac{J4a2a}{M19959}$ 3538

牲 $\frac{J4037}{M19986}$ 3539

6–16 residual strokes

惣 $\frac{J415a}{M10829}$ 1889

蟹 $\frac{J332a}{M33668}$ 5395

特 $\frac{J4643}{M20013}$ 3541

牽 $\frac{J3823}{M20025}$ 3544

犀 $\frac{J3a54}{M20045}$ 3546

犠 $\frac{J353e}{M20190}$ 3550

解 $\frac{J3272}{M35067}$ 5548

鉾 $\frac{J4b48}{M40353}$ 6255

Rad. 94 犬

0 residual strokes

犬 $\frac{J3824}{M20234}$ 3553

2–3 residual strokes

伏 $\frac{J497a}{M438}$ 139

吠 J4b4a M3331 739	犯 J4848 M20238 3554	状 J3e75 M20257 3556

4 residual strokes

戻 J4c61 M11707 2051
狂 J3638 M20287 3562

5 residual strokes

狗 J3669 M20345 3565
狛 J397d M20349 3566
狙 J4140 M20347 3567
狐 J3851 M20333 3568

6 residual strokes

狭 J3639 M20406 3572
狩 J3c6d M20390 3573
独 J4648 M20406 3574

7 residual strokes

狼 J4762 M20433 3576
狸 J432c M20427 3578
狼 J4f35 M20432 3579
猛 J4c54 M20498 3588
荻 J322e M31005 5054

8 residual strokes

然 J4133 M19149 3435
狼 J4f35 M20432 3579
猪 J4376 M20511 3585

猫 J472d M20535 3586
猟 J4e44 M20512 3587
猛 J4c54 M20498 3588

9–10 residual strokes

獄 J4d32 M20558 3590
猶 J4d31 M20557 3593
献 J3825 M20539 3596
獅 J3b62 M20609 3599
猿 J316e M20584 3600
獄 J3976 M20603 3602

11–13 residual strokes

撚 J4732 M12713 2278
燃 J4733 M19394 3490
獄 J3976 M20603 3602
獣 J3d43 M20714 3606
獲 J334d M20758 3609
黙 J4c5b M48063 7055

Rad. 95 玄

0 residual strokes

玄 J383c M20814 3616

3–10 residual strokes

弦 J3839 M9754 1688
牽 J3823 M20025 3544
率 J4e28 M20817 3618
畜 J435c M21814 3749
絃 J383e M27373 4468

舷 J383f M30403 4938
蓄 J435f M31642 5161

Rad. 96 王

0 residual strokes

壬 J3f51 M5639 968
王 J3226 M20823 3619
玉 J364c M20821 3620

1–2 residual strokes

主 J3c67 M100 38
任 J4724 M416 136
全 J4134 M1424 145
住 J3d3b M505 164
匡 J3629 M2606 587
玉 J364c M20821 3620

3 residual strokes

呈 J4468 M3401 734
国 J3971 M4752 950
妊 J4725 M6072 1189
宝 J4a75 M7122 1320
廷 J446e M9571 1654
弄 J4f2e M9596 1668
往 J317d M10073 1733
狂 J3638 M20287 3562
玖 J366a M20846 3621
麦 J477e M47718 7030

4 residual strokes

宝 J4a75 M7122 1320

廷 J446e M9571 1654
旺 J3222 M13774 2427
毒 J4647 M16730 3007
注 J436d M17316 3103
玩 J3461 M20872 3622
表 J493d M34105 5422
金 J3662 M40152 6211
青 J4044 M42564 6557

5 residual strokes

挺 J4472 M12106 2164
柱 J436c M14660 2631
毒 J4647 M16730 3007
珂 J3251 M20906 3625
玲 J4e68 M20888 3626
珊 J3b39 M20917 3630
珍 J4474 M20920 3631
皇 J3944 M22701 3870
茬 J3141 M30950 5022
表 J493d M34105 5422

6 residual strokes

害 J3332 M7165 1333
差 J3a39 M8732 1537
庭 J446d M9337 1618
挺 J4472 M12106 2164
捆 J444f M-X 2174
栓 J4072 M14889 2649
班 J4849 M20976 3636
珠 J3c6e M20956 3637
珪 J373e M20972 3638
素 J4147 M27300 4456

---

7 residual strokes

喫 J354a M3987 855
捆 J444f M-X 2174
淫 J307c M17678 3203
清 J4036 M17695 3205
琢 J4276 M-X 3640
琉 J4e30 M20978 3642
球 J3565 M21011 3643
理 J4d7d M21014 3644
現 J383d M21004 3645
望 J4b3e M14368 4819
責 J4055 M36682 5780

8 residual strokes

斑 J4843 M13470 2371
晴 J4032 M13994 2488
琳 J4e56 M21077 3646
瑛 J314d M21127 3647
琶 J474a M21081 3649
琢 J-X M21058 3650
琵 J487c M21080 3653
琴 J3657 M21079 3654
程 J4478 M25081 4144
素 J4147 M27300 4456
艇 J447a M30440 4941
註 J4540 M35340 5583
閏 J313c M41244 6389

9 residual strokes

僅 J-X M1048 292
嵯 J3a37 M8363 1500
琵 J487c M21080 3653

Rad.96: 9 residual strokes

瑚 $\frac{J386a}{M21126}$ **3662**	積 $\frac{J4051}{M25266}$ 4176	
瑞 $\frac{J3f70}{M21131}$ **3665**	錆 $\frac{J3b2c}{M40523}$ 6296	
聖 $\frac{J403b}{M29074}$ 4727	麪 $\frac{J4c4d}{M-X}$ 7038	
艇 $\frac{J447a}{M30440}$ 4941		
詮 $\frac{J4127}{M35435}$ 5604	**13 residual strokes**	
賃 $\frac{J4442}{M36743}$ 5802	潔 $\frac{J3769}{M18231}$ 3332	
鈷 $\frac{J385a}{M40270}$ 6236	瀞 $\frac{J4654}{M-X}$ 3356	
靖 $\frac{J4c77}{M42570}$ 6559	犧 $\frac{J353e}{M20190}$ 3550	

10 residual strokes

僅 $\frac{J-X}{M1048}$ 292	環 $\frac{J3444}{M21445}$ **3680**
徵 $\frac{J4427}{M10238}$ 1768	績 $\frac{J4053}{M27845}$ 4579
様 $\frac{J4d4d}{M15352}$ 2821	謹 $\frac{J3660}{M35850}$ 5688
潰 $\frac{J4452}{M18167}$ 3301	轄 $\frac{J336d}{M38482}$ 5981
瑳 $\frac{J3a3c}{M21170}$ **3667**	鎚 $\frac{J-X}{M40715}$ 6310
璃 $\frac{J4d7e}{M21196}$ **3669**	
瑠 $\frac{J4e5c}{M21143}$ **3673**	**14 residual strokes**
碧 $\frac{J4a4b}{M24334}$ 4027	叢 $\frac{J4151}{M3220}$ 684
精 $\frac{J403a}{M26997}$ 4411	懋 $\frac{J4428}{M11399}$ 2006
	璽 $\frac{J3c25}{M21309}$ **3683**

11 residual strokes

撲 $\frac{J4b50}{M12755}$ 2274	謹 $\frac{J3660}{M35850}$ 5688
様 $\frac{J4d4d}{M15352}$ 2821	蹟 $\frac{J4058}{M37814}$ 5905
潔 $\frac{J3769}{M18231}$ 3332	鎚 $\frac{J-X}{M40715}$ 6310
潤 $\frac{J3d61}{M18255}$ 3334	
璃 $\frac{J4d7e}{M21196}$ **3669**	**15–18 residual strokes**
請 $\frac{J4041}{M35640}$ 5645	績 $\frac{J4053}{M27845}$ 4579
駐 $\frac{J4373}{M44660}$ 6745	鑓 $\frac{J-X}{M40998}$ 6357
麹 $\frac{J396d}{M-X}$ 7036	鯖 $\frac{J3b2a}{M46210}$ 6883

12 residual strokes

Rad. 97 瓜

0 residual strokes

憲 $\frac{J377b}{M11269}$ 1988	瓜 $\frac{J313b}{M21371}$ **3686**

3–14 residual strokes

孤 $\frac{J3849}{M6966}$ 1293	
弧 $\frac{J384c}{M9757}$ 1687	
狐 $\frac{J3851}{M20333}$ 3568	
瓢 $\frac{J493b}{M21419}$ **3688**	
瓣 $\frac{J6122}{M21425}$ **3689**	
菰 $\frac{J3856}{M31217}$ 5079	

Rad. 98 瓦

0 residual strokes

瓦 $\frac{J3424}{M21438}$ **3690**	

6–11 residual strokes

瓶 $\frac{J4953}{M21486}$ **3699**	
甑 $\frac{J3979}{M-X}$ **3706**	

Rad. 99 甘

0 residual strokes

甘 $\frac{J3445}{M21643}$ **3710**	

2–6 residual strokes

勘 $\frac{J342a}{M2393}$ 548	
柑 $\frac{J343b}{M14619}$ 2621	
某 $\frac{J4b3f}{M14618}$ 2628	
甚 $\frac{J3f53}{M21648}$ **3711**	
甜 $\frac{J453c}{M21656}$ **3712**	
紺 $\frac{J3a30}{M27362}$ 4466	

7–12 residual strokes

媒 $\frac{J475e}{M6498}$ 1247	
惜 $\frac{J404b}{M10814}$ 1894	
棋 $\frac{J347d}{M14922}$ 2744	
椇 $\frac{J4760}{M15178}$ 2754	
煤 $\frac{J4761}{M19220}$ 3452	
紺 $\frac{J3a30}{M27362}$ 4466	
謀 $\frac{J4b45}{M35756}$ 5671	

6 residual strokes

庸 $\frac{J4d47}{M9378}$ 1624	
捕 $\frac{J4a61}{M12157}$ 2170	
桶 $\frac{J3233}{M14811}$ 2694	

7–8 residual strokes

備 $\frac{J4877}{M967}$ 284	
痛 $\frac{J444b}{M22195}$ 3814	
葡 $\frac{J4972}{M31430}$ 5127	
蒲 $\frac{J3377}{M31611}$ 5156	
補 $\frac{J4a64}{M34320}$ 5464	

9 residual strokes

傭 $\frac{J4d43}{M1007}$ 295	
樋 $\frac{J-X}{M15415}$ 2816	
蒲 $\frac{J3377}{M31611}$ 5156	
踊 $\frac{J4d59}{M37587}$ 5882	
輔 $\frac{J4a65}{M38342}$ 5964	

10–12 residual strokes

樋 $\frac{J4875}{M-X}$ 2757	
樋 $\frac{J-X}{M15415}$ 2816	
輔 $\frac{J4a65}{M38342}$ 5964	

圃 $\frac{J4a60}{M4774}$ 954		
捕 $\frac{J4a61}{M12157}$ 2170		
涌 $\frac{J4d30}{M17534}$ 3150		
浦 $\frac{J313a}{M17475}$ 3156		
甫 $\frac{J4a63}{M21706}$ **3722**		
通 $\frac{J444c}{M38892}$ 6063		

Rad. 100 生

0 residual strokes

生 $\frac{J4038}{M21670}$ **3715**	

2–5 residual strokes

姓 $\frac{J402b}{M6178}$ 1196	
性 $\frac{J402d}{M10478}$ 1822	
星 $\frac{J4031}{M13837}$ 2452	
牲 $\frac{J4037}{M19986}$ 3539	
隆 $\frac{J4e34}{M41720}$ 6455	

6–11 residual strokes

産 $\frac{J3b3a}{M21684}$ **3716**	
甥 $\frac{J3179}{M21689}$ **3719**	
薩 $\frac{J3b27}{M32189}$ 5217	
醒 $\frac{J4043}{M39936}$ 6185	

Rad. 101 用

0 residual strokes

用 $\frac{J4d51}{M21703}$ **3721**	

2–5 residual strokes

鋪 J4a5f M40491 6269

Rad. 102 田

0 residual strokes

由 J4d33 M21724 **3724**
甲 J3943 M21725 **3725**
申 J3f3d M21726 **3726**
田 J4544 M21723 **3727**

1 residual stroke

甲 J3943 M21725 **3725**

2 residual strokes

佃 J4451 M492 151
毎 J4b68 M16724 3006
申 J3f3d M21726 **3726**
町 J442e M21735 **3729**
男 J434b M21730 **3731**
里 J4e24 M40131 6206

3 residual strokes

岬 J4c28 M7992 1458
抽 J436a M11930 2119
押 J3221 M11929 2128
果 J324c M14556 2594
油 J4c7d M17253 3106
画 J3268 M21739 **3733**
苗 J4944 M30781 5004
里 M40131 6206

4 residual strokes

侮 J496e M629 187
勇 J4d26 M2360 541
卑 J485c M2751 618
厘 J4e52 M2946 650
届 J464f M7667 1413
思 J3b57 M10462 1824
柚 J4d2e M14629 2622
毘 J487b M16753 3011
油 J4c7d M17253 3106
画 J3268 M21739 **3733**
界 J3326 M21775 **3739**
畑 J482a M21797 **3741**
畏 J305a M21778 **3742**
胃 J305f M29348 4793
重 J3d45 M40132 6207

5 residual strokes

厘 J4e52 M2946 650
哩 J4b69 M3649 805
埋 J4b64 M5116 1020
恵 J3743 M10618 1847
捜 J415c M12179 2168
毘 J487b M16753 3011
涅 J333d M17485 3142
狸 J432c M20427 3578
畏 J305a M21778 **3742**
畔 J484a M21801 **3746**
畠 J482b M21827 **3747**
畝 J4026 M21815 **3748**
畜 J435c M21814 **3749**
留 J4e31 M21808 **3750**
畢 J492d M21829 **3754**

袖 J4235 M34192 5444
鬼 J3534 M45758 6833

6 residual strokes

偲 J3c45 M895 266
偶 J3676 M899 274
富 J495a M1592 406
副 J497b M2097 503
埋 J4b64 M5116 1020
婁 J4f2c M6383 1235
寅 J4652 M7204 1341
描 J4941 M12339 2196
曽 J413e M-X 2464
狸 J432c M20427 3578
猫 J472d M20535 3586
理 J4d7d M21014 3644
畢 J492d M21829 **3754**
略 J4e2c M21839 **3755**
異 J305b M21854 **3757**
笛 J452b M25917 4268
紬 J445d M27338 4462
累 J4e5f M27343 4469
細 J3a59 M27344 4472
逼 J492f M38973 6085
隈 J3728 M41748 6466
魚 J357b M45956 6845
黄 J322b M47926 7045
黒 J3975 M48040 7052

7 residual strokes

偶 J3676 M899 274
博 J476e M2761 621
堺 J3a66 M5289 1045

塁 J4e5d M5316 1056
寅 J4652 M7204 1341
寅 J3677 M7243 1348
富 J4959 M7230 1349
幅 J497d M8995 1574
巣 J4163 M8696 2705
湧 J4d2f M17862 3207
理 J4d7d M21014 3644
甥 J3179 M21689 **3719**
畜 J435c M21814 **3749**
番 J4856 M21858 **3762**
畳 J3e76 M21875 **3763**
童 J4638 M25775 4239
菓 J325b M31168 5095
軸 J3c34 M38269 5952
遇 J3678 M38991 6083
逼 J492f M38973 6085
野 J4c6e M40133 6208
量 J4e4c M40138 6209
隅 J3679 M41743 6467
黒 J3975 M48040 7052

8 residual strokes

僧 J414e M1076 300
博 J476e M2761 621
塊 J3274 M5319 1070
寅 J3677 M7243 1348
弾 J4346 M9836 1699
愚 J3272 M10946 1925
戦 J406f M11631 2037
暢 J442a M14095 2506
榊 J3a67 M-X 2756
溜 J4e2e M17943 3276
牌 J4757 M19854 3528

暖 J466d M21892 **3766**
禅 J4135 M24787 4104
福 J4a21 M24768 4105
童 J4638 M25775 4239
紬 J445d M27338 4462
累 J4e5f M27344 4469
細 J3a59 M27344 4472
菓 J325b M31168 5095
蒐 J4d2f M31539 5159
蓄 J435f M31642 5161
虜 J4e3a M32720 5273
裡 J4e23 M34295 5463
裸 J4d67 M34371 5475
遇 J3678 M38991 6083
量 J4e4c M40138 6209
雷 J4d6b M42245 6525

9 residual strokes

劃 J3344 M2193 513
噌 J4139 M-X 873
墨 J4b4f M-X 1086
増 J417d M-X 1088
審 J3f33 M7316 1367
層 J4158 M-X 1432
憎 J4e2e M11188 1969
戦 J406f M11631 2037
榊 J-X M15352 2808
漁 J3579 M18101 3309
演 J3169 M18130 3310
瑠 J4e5c M21143 3673
碑 J486a M24364 4028
禅 J4135 M24787 4104
稗 J4923 M-X 4156
裸 J4d67 M34371 5475

魁 J3321 M45785 6834
魂 J3a32 M45787 6835
鼻 J4921 M48498 7082

10 residual strokes

審 J3f33 M7316 1367
幡 J4828 M9086 1584
慮 J4e38 M11132 1962
憧 J4634 M11242 1982
播 J4745 M12747 2273
撞 J4635 M12717 2276
敷 J495f M13359 2357
横 J3223 M15484 2854
畿 J3526 M21925 **3768**
穂 J4a66 M25236 4168
箪 J433d M-X 4321
糊 J4138 M27057 4413
膚 J4966 M29829 4867
蓄 J435f M31642 5161
蕃 J4859 M31906 5199
蝉 J4066 M-X 5349
課 J325d M35589 5644
魅 J4c25 M45811 6838
魯 J4f25 M46013 6848

11 residual strokes

奮 J4a33 M6012 1172
彊 J3630 M9872 1702
衡 J3955 M34078 1775
憧 J4634 M11242 1982
撞 J4635 M12717 2276
敷 J495f M13359 2357
獣 J3d43 M20714 3606

顛 J3979 M-X 3706
穂 J4a66 M25236 4168
箪 J433d M-X 4321
糊 J4138 M27057 4413
薄 J4776 M32083 5225
蝉 J4066 M-X 5349
課 J325d M35589 5644
誹 J3062 M35759 5656
錨 J4945 M40598 6295
鮒 J4a2b M46075 6854
鮎 J303e M46070 6855
鳴 J3c32 M46831 6948
鴨 J337b M46823 6955
黙 J4c5b M48063 7055
黛 J4263 M48075 7060

12 residual strokes

彊 J3630 M9872 1702
戴 J4257 M11685 2045
橿 J3360 M15629 2889
畿 J3526 M21925 **3768**
瞳 J4637 M23707 3961
糞 J4a35 M27102 4425
翼 J4d63 M28801 4692
薄 J4776 M32083 5225
螺 J4d66 M33512 5382
醜 J3d39 M39969 6189
騨 J424d M-X 6762
鮪 J4b6e M46126 6858
鮭 J3a7a M46132 6859
鮫 J3b2d M46127 6863
鮮 J412f M46133 6864
黛 J4263 M48075 7060

13 residual strokes

彊 J3630 M9872 1702
瞳 J4637 M23707 3961
簞 J-X M26509 4357
薄 J4a6d M26623 4364
糧 J4e48 M27132 4426
翻 J4b5d M28814 4694
藩 J4a4d M32346 5242
贈 J4223 M36920 5827
鯉 J3871 M46182 6874

14 residual strokes

檜 J4f26 M15798 2908
簞 J-X M26509 4357
薄 J4a6d M26623 4364
糧 J4e48 M27132 4426
蘇 J4149 M32427 5252
螺 J4d66 M33512 5382
鯉 J3871 M46182 6874
鯵 J3033 M-X 6875
鯖 J3b2a M46210 6883
鯛 J4264 M46226 6884
鯨 J375f M46257 6886

15 residual strokes

櫨 J4827 M15844 2910
蠣 J695a M33799 5399
鐘 J3e62 M40902 6352
鰍 J3362 M46331 6895
鰐 J4f4c M46337 6901

16 residual strokes

鐘 J3e62 M40902 6352
魔 J4b62 M45906 6843
鰐 J4f4c M46337 6901
鰯 J3073 M46413 6904
鰭 J4949 M46400 6907

17 residual strokes

纏 J453b M28043 4612
鯵 J724d M46442 6912
鰻 J3137 M46443 6914
鰹 J336f M46437 6915
鱈 J432d M46470 6916

18 residual strokes

纓 J6575 M28058 4617
鰹 J336f M46437 6915
鱒 J4b70 M46492 6921
鱗 J4e5a M46502 6923

19–20 residual strokes

纏 J453b M28043 4612
纓 J6575 M28058 4617
鱗 J4e5a M46502 6923

Rad. 103 疋

0 residual strokes

疋 J4925 M21994 **3774**

3–5 residual strokes

定 J446a M7109 1323
従 J3d3e M10133 1745
徒 J454c M10121 1746
是 J4027 M13859 2451

6 residual strokes

匙 J3a7c M2590 582
旋 J407b M13656 2400
淀 J4d64 M17610 3182
蛋 J4341 M32977 5301

7 residual strokes

堤 J4469 M5259 1054
婿 J4c3b M6470 1246
御 J3866 M10157 1761
提 J4473 M12344 2237
疏 J4141 M22000 **3775**
疎 J4142 M22002 **3776**

8–10 residual strokes

楚 J413f M15141 2771
疑 J353f M22007 **3777**
碇 J4476 M24275 4019
綻 J433e M27587 4514

11 residual strokes

凝 J3645 M1720 431
綻 J433e M27587 4514
縦 J3d44 M27804 4571

醍 J4269 M39924 6184
錠 J3e7b M40559 6293

12–15 residual strokes

擬 J353c M12870 2307
礙 J4143 M24522 4054
縱 J3d44 M27804 4571
題 J426a M43584 6645

Rad. 104 疒

4 residual strokes

疫 J3156 M22069 3783

5 residual strokes

疹 J3f3e M22097 3788
症 J3e49 M22140 3795
疲 J4868 M22084 3796
疾 J3c40 M22112 3797
病 J4942 M22127 3798

6 residual strokes

痕 J3a2f M22171 3803
痔 J3c26 M22167 3804

7 residual strokes

痕 J3a2f M22171 3803
瘦 J4169 M-X 3806
痢 J4e21 M22213 3810
痘 J4577 M22185 3813

痛 J444b M22195 3814

8–14 residual strokes

嫉 J3c3b M6611 1255
痴 J4354 M22257 3823
癌 J3462 M22538 3840
療 J4e45 M22500 3842
癒 J4c7e M22545 3847
癖 J4a4a M22550 3848

Rad. 105 癶

4 residual strokes

発 J482f M22662 3860

7 residual strokes

廃 J4751 M9425 1630
溌 J482e M-X 3209
登 J4550 M22668 3862
葵 J302a M31458 5120

10–15 residual strokes

潑 J-X M18225 3325
澄 J4021 M18315 3333
燈 J4575 M19402 3476
醗 J4830 M-X 6182
醱 J-X M40041 6194
鐙 J462a M40904 6348

Rad. 106 白

0 residual strokes

白 J4772 M22678 3863

1 residual stroke

百 J4934 M22679 3864

2 residual strokes

伯 J476c M466 158
迫 J4777 M38797 6031

3 residual strokes

拍 J476f M11952 2114
泊 J4771 M17275 3099
狛 J397d M20349 3566
的 J452a M22692 3867
迫 J4777 M38797 6031

4 residual strokes

柏 J4770 M14617 2623
泉 J4074 M17274 3095
皆 J3327 M22699 3869
皇 J3944 M22701 3870

5 residual strokes

原 J3836 M2973 652
島 J4567 M8108 1476
栢 J337c M14714 2638
畠 J482b M21827 3747

皆 J3327 M22699 3869
貢 J3957 M36665 5772

6 residual strokes

兜 J3375 M1386 364
宿 J3d49 M7195 1344
皋 J3b29 M22727 3873
粕 J4774 M26891 4391
習 J3d2c M28672 4681
舶 J4775 M30402 4936
階 J332c M41755 6469

7 residual strokes

兜 J3375 M1386 364
卿 J-X M2880 643
堵 J4548 M-X 1021
弼 J492b M9826 1697
棉 J4c49 M14919 2741
階 J332c M41755 6469

8 residual strokes

兜 J3375 M1386 364
楽 J335a M15213 2790
源 J383b M17926 3274
腺 J4123 M29746 4847

9 residual strokes

寡 J3249 M7286 1363
弼 J492b M9826 1697
摺 J4022 M12647 2262
碧 J4a4b M24334 4027

箔 J4773 M26142 4312
綿 J4c4a M27592 4531
貌 J4b46 M36556 5762

---

10 residual strokes

潰 J4459 M18281 3335
線 J4c74 M27641 4548
甂 J3465 M28766 4689

11 residual strokes

弼 J492b M9826 1697
激 J3763 M18438 3350
綿 J4c4a M27592 4531
薬 J4c74 M32188 5224
錦 J3653 M40569 6301

12–17 residual strokes

優 J4d25 M1261 334
線 J407e M27641 4548
縮 J3d4c M27815 4585
饗 J-X M44431 6715

Rad. 107 皮

0 residual strokes

皮 J4869 M22823 3878

2–4 residual strokes

彼 J4860 M10066 1732
披 J4864 M11909 2116

波 J4748 M17308 3101

5–14 residual strokes

婆 J474c M6390 1240
疲 J4868 M22084 3796
破 J474b M24124 3999
簸 J4876 M26609 4363
被 J486f M34222 5445
頗 J3f7c M43415 6627

Rad. 108 皿

0 residual strokes

皿 J3b2e M22941 3885

1–4 residual strokes

孟 J4c52 M6960 1291
盃 J4756 M22955 3887
盈 J314e M22961 3888
盆 J4b5f M22959 3889
血 J376c M33964 5411

5–7 residual strokes

温 J3239 M17774 3246
猛 J4c54 M20498 3588
盈 J314e M22961 3888
益 J3157 M22972 3891
盗 J4570 M23000 3894
盛 J4039 M23001 3895

8 residual strokes

塩 J3176 M5382 1075
溢 J306e M17951 3270
盟 J4c41 M23024 3899
蓋 J3338 M31652 5155

9–13 residual strokes

盡 J5056 M1234 327
濫 J4d74 M18521 3366
監 J3446 M23032 3901
盤 J4857 M23036 3902
藍 J4d75 M32258 5233

15 residual strokes

櫨 J4827 M15844 2910
艦 J344f M30571 4950
鑑 J3455 M40988 6361

Rad. 109 目

0 residual strokes

且 J336e M29 17
目 J4c5c M23105 3906

1–2 residual strokes

自 J3c2b M30095 4900
見 J382b M34796 5522
貝 J332d M36656 5766
阻 J41b M41593 6434

3 residual strokes

具 J3671 M1473 376

姐 J3039 M6172 1195
宜 J3539 M7111 1317
岨 J413b M7984 1456
狙 J4c55 M20347 3567
盲 J443e M23132 3907
直 J443e M23136 3908

4 residual strokes

則 J4227 M1994 487
査 J3a3a M14643 2630
直 J443e M23136 3908
盾 J3d62 M23171 3912
冒 J4b41 M-X 3915
省 J3e4a M23179 3916
眉 J487d M23190 3917
県 J3829 M23210 3918
看 J3447 M23196 3919
相 J416a M23151 3920
祖 J4144 M24664 4083
臭 J3d2d M30103 4901
貞 J4467 M36658 5768
負 J4969 M-X 5769
頁 J4a47 M43333 6614
首 J3c73 M44489 6719

5 residual strokes

俱 J3666 M724 245
値 J434f M786 257
唄 J3134 M3694 802
員 J3077 M3633 808
夏 J3246 M5720 1120
息 J4229 M10601 1850
狼 J4762 M20433 3576

眠 J4c32 M23240 3925
真 J3f3f M23236 3926
租 J4145 M24988 4138
財 J3a62 M36664 5773

6 residual strokes

埴 J3e7d M5188 1031
基 J3453 M5197 1040
敗 J4754 M13227 2343
湛 J4339 M17846 3234
現 J383d M21004 3645
眺 J442f M23314 3933
眼 J3463 M23463 3935
粗 J4146 M26898 4394
組 J4148 M27374 4470
規 J34810 M34810 5524
視 J3b6b M34827 5525
販 J484e M36679 5779
責 J4055 M36682 5780
貨 J3f33 M36678 5781
貧 J494f M36677 5782
貫 J4c63 M36699 5789
逓 J465b M38982 6087
道 J463b M39010 6091
頃 J3a22 M43338 6615
頂 J443a M43335 6616

7 residual strokes

帽 J4b39 M8971 1573
循 J3d5b M10187 1758
植 J3f22 M15023 2751
殖 J3f23 M15023 2981
湘 J3e45 M17842 3216

測 J422c M17780 3244
畳 J3e76 M21875 3763
眼 J3463 M23318 3935
着 J4365 M23339 3938
督 J4647 M23457 3946

6 residual strokes

硯 J3827 M24233 4005
覗 J4741 M34839 5528
覚 J3350 M34846 5529
貫 J3453 M36681 5778
費 J4871 M36717 5786
貼 J453d M36718 5787
貿 J4b47 M36721 5788
賈 J4c63 M36699 5789
賀 J326c M36725 5790
貯 J4379 M36698 5791
貧 J425f M36709 5792
買 J4763 M36708 5793
貴 J352e M36704 5794
逓 J465b M38982 6087
道 J463b M39010 6091
項 J3960 M43343 6617
須 J3f5c M43352 6618
順 J3d67 M43349 6619
鼎 J4524 M48315 7074

8 residual strokes

傾 J3739 M1038 299
填 J4536 M-X 1072
寛 J3432 M7276 1352
想 J415b M10858 1922
慎 J3f35 M11024 1945
損 J423b M12459 2255
楷 J3d5d M15173 2776
煩 J4851 M19229 3454

Rad. 112 石

0 residual strokes

石 J4050/M24024 **3985**

3 residual strokes

姑 J454a/M6121 1197
宕 J4566/M7103 1316
岩 J3464/M7985 1461
拓 J4273/M11958 2115

4 residual strokes

垢 J3924/M5058 1008
柘 J4453/M14626 2626
砕 J3a55/M24080' **3990**
研 J3826/M24080 **3991**
砂 J3a3d/M24046 **3992**

5 residual strokes

砺 J4557/M-X **3993**
砧 J395c/M-X **3994**
砧 J354e/M24099 **3996**
砥 J4556/M24093 **3997**
砲 J4b24/M24120 **3998**
破 J47b/M24124 **3999**

6-7 residual strokes

砦 J3a56/M24098 **4002**
硲 J4823/M24243 **4004**
硯 J3872/M24233 **4005**
硫 J4e32/M24229 **4006**

硝 J3e4b/M24201' **4007**
硬 J3945/M24230 **4008**

8 residual strokes

碓 J3130/M24294 **4012**
碗 J4f52/M24306 **4014**
碕 J3a6c/M24296 **4015**
碍 J3337/M24283 **4016**
碇 J4476/M24275 **4019**
碁 J386b/M24261 **4020**

9 residual strokes

碩 J4059/M24338 **4026**
碧 J4a4b/M24334 **4027**
碑 J486a/M24080' **4028**
磁 J3c27/M24364 **4029**

10-15 residual strokes

磁 J3c27/M24364 **4029**
磐 J4858/M24401 **4037**
確 J334a/M24366 **4039**
磨 J4b61/M24449 **4045**
礁 J3e4c/M24502 **4048**
磯 J306b/M24465 **4049**
礎 J4143/M24522 **4054**
礦 J626a/M24571 **4056**

Rad. 113 示

0 residual strokes

示 J3c28/M24623 **4060**

1-3 residual strokes

奈 J4660/M5893 1147
宗 J3d21/M7106 1321
礼 J4e69/M24626' **4061**
祁 J3737/M24634 **4063**
社 J3c52/M24631' **4065**

4 residual strokes

祇 J3540/M-X **4068**
祖 J3b63/M24641' **4069**
祈 J3527/M24640' **4071**
途 J4553/M38882' 6057
除 J3d7c/M41669 6449

5 residual strokes

祇 J3540/M-X **4068**
祢 J472a/M-X **4074**
祐 J4d34/M24652' **4079**
祖 J4144/M24644' **4083**
祝 J3d4b/M24672' **4085**
神 J3f40/M24673' **4087**
途 J4553/M38882' 6057

6 residual strokes

尉 J3053/M7440 1383
崇 J3f72/M8152 1490
捺 J4668/M12221 2189
斎 J3a58/M13467 2368
票 J493c/M24694 **4089**
祥 J3e4d/M24689' **4090**
祭 J3a57/M24700 **4092**

7-8 residual strokes

款 J343e/M16107 2938
祷 J4578/M-X **4093**
禄 J4f3d/M24741' **4096**
禁 J3658/M24743 **4098**
蒜 J4947/M31562 5144
視 J3b6b/M34827' 5525
際 J3a5d/M41820 6478

9 residual strokes

察 J3b21/M7283 1360
榊 J3a67 2756
榊 J-X/M15352 2808
漂 J493a/M18102 3303
禎 J4477/M24767' **4099**
禍 J3252/M24766' **4102**
禅 J4135/M24787' **4104**
福 J4a21/M24768' **4105**
綜 J416e/M27535 4520
蔚 J3136/M31805 5181

10-11 residual strokes

慰 J3056/M11135 1972
標 J4938/M15442 2852
瓢 J493b/M21419 3688
穎 J3150/M24824 **4109**
綜 J416e/M27535 4520
隷 J4e6c/M41928 6490

12-14 residual strokes

擦 J3b24/M12862 2306
禦 J357a/M24820 **4111**
禧 J-X/M24852 **4114**
禰 J-X/M24851 **4115**
襧 J4729/M-X **4116**
標 J365f/M34647 5504

Rad. 114 内

4-7 residual strokes

偶 J3676/M899 274
寓 J3677/M7243 1348
遇 J3678/M38991' 6083
隅 J3679/M41743 6467

8-20 residual strokes

愚 J3672/M10946 1925
橋 J3869/M15657 2888
璃 J4d7e/M21196 3669
礦 J626a/M24571 4056
禽 J3659/M24893 **4120**
蠣 J695a/M33799 5399
離 J4e25/M42140 6517

Rad. 115 禾

0 residual strokes

禾 J3253/M24906 **4121**

2 residual strokes

利 $\frac{\text{J4d78}}{\text{M1932}}$ 466

季 $\frac{\text{J3528}}{\text{M6965}}$ 1292

禿 $\frac{\text{J4645}}{\text{M24910}}$ **4122**

秀 $\frac{\text{J3d28}}{\text{M24911}}$ **4123**

私 $\frac{\text{J3b64}}{\text{M24913}}$ **4124**

采 $\frac{\text{J4850}}{\text{M40115}}$ 6202

3 residual strokes

和 $\frac{\text{J4f42}}{\text{M3490}}$ 770

委 $\frac{\text{J3051}}{\text{M6181}}$ 1204

季 $\frac{\text{J3528}}{\text{M6965}}$ 1292

秀 $\frac{\text{J3d28}}{\text{M24911}}$ **4123**

4 residual strokes

秒 $\frac{\text{J4943}}{\text{M24952}}$ **4129**

科 $\frac{\text{J324a}}{\text{M24910}}$ **4130**

秋 $\frac{\text{J3d29}}{\text{M24910}}$ **4131**

透 $\frac{\text{J4629}}{\text{M38876}}$ 6059

香 $\frac{\text{J3961}}{\text{M44518}}$ 6722

5 residual strokes

倭 $\frac{\text{J4f41}}{\text{M796}}$ 242

秦 $\frac{\text{J3f41}}{\text{M24995}}$ **4133**

秤 $\frac{\text{J4769}}{\text{M24993}}$ **4134**

秩 $\frac{\text{J4361}}{\text{M24998}}$ **4135**

租 $\frac{\text{J4145}}{\text{M24988}}$ **4138**

称 $\frac{\text{J3e4e}}{\text{M25016}}$ **4139**

秘 $\frac{\text{J486b}}{\text{M24977}}$ **4140**

透 $\frac{\text{J4629}}{\text{M38876}}$ 6059

6 residual strokes

梨 $\frac{\text{J4d7c}}{\text{M14873}}$ 2697

移 $\frac{\text{J305c}}{\text{M25045}}$ **4141**

萎 $\frac{\text{J3060}}{\text{M31269}}$ 5087

菌 $\frac{\text{J365d}}{\text{M31156}}$ 5091

釈 $\frac{\text{J3c61}}{\text{M40120}}$ 6203

7 residual strokes

番 $\frac{\text{J4856}}{\text{M21858}}$ 3762

痢 $\frac{\text{J4e21}}{\text{M22213}}$ 3810

程 $\frac{\text{J4478}}{\text{M25081}}$ **4144**

稀 $\frac{\text{J3238}}{\text{M25058}}$ **4145**

税 $\frac{\text{J4047}}{\text{M25070}}$ **4146**

萩 $\frac{\text{J476b}}{\text{M31333}}$ 5122

黍 $\frac{\text{J3550}}{\text{M47991}}$ 7048

8 residual strokes

愁 $\frac{\text{J3d25}}{\text{M10005}}$ 1923

稔 $\frac{\text{J4c2d}}{\text{M25107}}$ **4149**

稜 $\frac{\text{J4e47}}{\text{M25123}}$ **4152**

稚 $\frac{\text{J4355}}{\text{M25120}}$ **4154**

9 residual strokes

榛 $\frac{\text{J3f3a}}{\text{M15240}}$ 2811

稗 $\frac{\text{J4923}}{\text{M-X}}$ **4156**

穀 $\frac{\text{J3972}}{\text{M25188}}$ **4157**

稲 $\frac{\text{J3070}}{\text{M25187}}$ **4158**

種 $\frac{\text{J3c6f}}{\text{M25174}}$ **4159**

誘 $\frac{\text{J4d36}}{\text{M35525}}$ 5625

10 residual strokes

稽 $\frac{\text{J374e}}{\text{M25218}}$ **4163**

稿 $\frac{\text{J3946}}{\text{M25220}}$ **4166**

穂 $\frac{\text{J4a66}}{\text{M25236}}$ **4168**

稼 $\frac{\text{J3254}}{\text{M25217}}$ **4169**

誘 $\frac{\text{J4d36}}{\text{M35525}}$ 5625

11 residual strokes

穐 $\frac{\text{J302c}}{\text{M25281}}$ **4170**

穆 $\frac{\text{J4b54}}{\text{M25251}}$ **4171**

穎 $\frac{\text{J314f}}{\text{M25267}}$ **4173**

稽 $\frac{\text{J-X}}{\text{M-X}}$ **4174**

穏 $\frac{\text{J3329}}{\text{M25280}}$ **4175**

積 $\frac{\text{J4051}}{\text{M25266}}$ **4176**

12–17 residual strokes

穣 $\frac{\text{J3e77}}{\text{M25335}}$ **4179**

穫 $\frac{\text{J334f}}{\text{M25334}}$ **4180**

穣 $\frac{\text{J6354}}{\text{M25381}}$ **4184**

蘇 $\frac{\text{J4149}}{\text{M32427}}$ 5252

鍬 $\frac{\text{J372d}}{\text{M40643}}$ 6314

馨 $\frac{\text{J333e}}{\text{M44559}}$ 6724

鰍 $\frac{\text{J3362}}{\text{M46331}}$ 6895

Rad. 116 穴

0 residual strokes

穴 $\frac{\text{J376a}}{\text{M25406}}$ **4187**

2–4 residual strokes

究 $\frac{\text{J3566}}{\text{M25409}}$ **4189**

突 $\frac{\text{J464d}}{\text{M25424}}$ **4191**

空 $\frac{\text{J3675}}{\text{M25415}}$ **4192**

窃 $\frac{\text{J4060}}{\text{M25453}}$ **4195**

穿 $\frac{\text{J407c}}{\text{M25436}}$ **4198**

5–7 residual strokes

控 $\frac{\text{J3935}}{\text{M12283}}$ 2202

窄 $\frac{\text{J3a75}}{\text{M25455}}$ **4197**

穿 $\frac{\text{J407c}}{\text{M25436}}$ **4198**

室 $\frac{\text{J4362}}{\text{M25493}}$ **4200**

窓 $\frac{\text{J416b}}{\text{M25494}}$ **4201**

腔 $\frac{\text{J3950}}{\text{M29630}}$ 4826

8–12 residual strokes

搾 $\frac{\text{J3a71}}{\text{M12553}}$ 2251

窟 $\frac{\text{J3722}}{\text{M25552}}$ **4206**

窪 $\frac{\text{J3726}}{\text{M25580}}$ **4209**

窯 $\frac{\text{J4d52}}{\text{M25593}}$ **4210**

窮 $\frac{\text{J3567}}{\text{M25593}}$ **4212**

窺 $\frac{\text{J312e}}{\text{M25633}}$ **4215**

竈 $\frac{\text{J3376}}{\text{M-X}}$ **4216**

Rad. 117 立

0 residual strokes

立 $\frac{\text{J4e29}}{\text{M25721}}$ **4223**

2–4 residual strokes

位 $\frac{\text{J304c}}{\text{M503}}$ 162

姜 $\frac{\text{J3e2a}}{\text{M6147}}$ 1198

彦 $\frac{\text{J4927}}{\text{M9981}}$ 1714

泣 $\frac{\text{J3563}}{\text{M17309}}$ 3104

音 $\frac{\text{J323b}}{\text{M43265}}$ 6607

---

5 residual strokes

倍 $\frac{\text{J475c}}{\text{M760}}$ 252

剖 $\frac{\text{J4b36}}{\text{M2034}}$ 492

竜 $\frac{\text{J4e35}}{\text{M25751}}$ **4232**

部 $\frac{\text{J4974}}{\text{M39460}}$ 6146

陪 $\frac{\text{J4766}}{\text{M41680}}$ 6458

6 residual strokes

培 $\frac{\text{J475d}}{\text{M5195}}$ 1032

接 $\frac{\text{J405c}}{\text{M12280}}$ 2213

梓 $\frac{\text{J3034}}{\text{M14845}}$ 2688

産 $\frac{\text{J3b3a}}{\text{M21684}}$ 3716

章 $\frac{\text{J3e4f}}{\text{M25761}}$ **4235**

笠 $\frac{\text{J335e}}{\text{M25924}}$ **4269**

粒 $\frac{\text{J4e33}}{\text{M26884}}$ **4392**

菩 $\frac{\text{J4a6a}}{\text{M31205}}$ 5093

7 residual strokes

傍 $\frac{\text{J4b35}}{\text{M948}}$ 286

竣 $\frac{\text{J3d57}}{\text{M25773}}$ **4238**

童 $\frac{\text{J4638}}{\text{M25775}}$ **4239**

8 residual strokes

意 $\frac{\text{J3055}}{\text{M10921}}$ 1926

新 $\frac{\text{J3f37}}{\text{M13572}}$ 2387

暗 $\frac{\text{J3045}}{\text{M14065}}$ 2503

滝 $\frac{\text{J426c}}{\text{M18067}}$ 3273

竪 $\frac{\text{J4328}}{\text{M25790}}$ **4240**

部 $\frac{\text{J3c43}}{\text{M31748}}$ 5138

障 $\frac{\text{J3e63}}{\text{M41821}}$ 6479

靖 J4c77 M42570 6559

9 residual strokes

境 J362d M5409 1085
嫡 J4364 M6656 1263
彰 J3e34 M10015 1721
竪 J4328 M25790 4240
端 J433c M25806 4243

10 residual strokes

億 J322f M1178 321
憧 J4634 M11242 1982
摘 J4526 M12582 2266
撞 J4635 M12717 2276
樟 J4850 M15451 2851
毅 J3523 M16673 3003
滴 J4529 M18084 3299
賠 J4765 M36818 5810

11 residual strokes

壁 J4a49 M5516 1103
憶 J3231 M11295 2001
敵 J4528 M13354 2359
篭 J4f36 M26371 4332
締 J4479 M27651 4549
薩 J3b27 M32189 5217
親 J3f46 M34918 5534
諺 J3841 M-X 5659
龍 J4e36 M48818 7103

12 residual strokes

瞳 J4637 M23707 3961
臆 J3232 M29951 4883
諦 J447c M35716 5663
蹄 J447d M37724 5894
闇 J3047 M41421 6414

13 residual strokes

締 J4479 M27651 4549
織 J3f25 M27892 4596
職 J3f26 M29183 4742
顔 J3469 M43591 6648

14 residual strokes

寵 J437e M7368 1370
瀧 J426d M18671 3376
識 J3c31 M35974 5704
鏡 J3640 M40812 6341
響 J3641 M43318 6610
韻 J3124 M43307 6611

15–18 residual strokes

競 J3625 M25831 4244
繊 J3f25 M27892 4596
聾 J4f38 M29212 4745
襲 J3d31 M34717 5510
鐘 J3e62 M40902 6352
響 J3641 M43318 6610

Rad. 118 竹

0 residual strokes

竹 J435d M25841 4246

2–4 residual strokes

竺 J3c33 M25842 4247
笈 J3568 M25869 4249
竿 J3448 M25854 4250
笑 J3e50 M25885 4256
笹 J3a7b M25968 4271

5 residual strokes

笥 J3f5a M25934 4265
笛 J452b M25917 4268
笠 J335e M25924 4269
符 J4964 M25935 4270
笹 J3a7b M25968 4271
第 J4268 M25943 4272

6 residual strokes

筈 J4826 M25990 4277
筑 J435e M26002 4280
筏 J4835 M26000 4282
筒 J457b M26004 4283
策 J3a76 M26009 4284
答 J457a M26006 4285
筋 J365a M25994 4286
等 J4579 M25992 4287
筆 J492e M25987 4288

7–8 residual strokes

節 J4061 M26102 4299
箸 J4824 M-X 4301

箕 J4c27 M26143 4307
箆 J4a4f M26114 4310
箔 J4773 M26142 4312
箇 J3255 M26116 4315
算 J3b3b M26146 4316
管 J3449 M26162 4317

9 residual strokes

箆 J4a4f M26114 4310
箪 J433d M-X 4321
篇 J4a53 M26257 4324
箭 J407d M26193 4325
箸 J-X M26224 4328
範 J484f M26253 4330
箱 J4822 M26209 4331

10–12 residual strokes

櫛 J367b M-X 2884
篭 J4f36 M26371 4332
篤 J4646 M26344 4342
築 J435b M26298 4343
篠 J3c44 M-X 4352
簞 J-X M-X 4357
簡 J344a M26520 4358

13–19 residual strokes

櫛 J-X M15817 2909
簸 J4876 M26609 4363
簿 J4a6d M26623 4364
簾 J4e7c M26616 4365

籍 J4052 M26676 4368
籠 J6446 M26752 4376
纂 J3b3c M28012 4608

Rad. 119 米

0 residual strokes

米 J4a46 M26832 4380

1–3 residual strokes

粂 J3729 M26860 4382
籽 J364e M26858 4383
籾 J4c62 M26857 4384
迷 J4c42 M38825 6037
釆 J4850 M40115 6202

4 residual strokes

料 J4e41 M13501 2374
耗 J4c30 M26881 4387
粋 J3f68 M26875 4389
粉 J4a34 M26872 4390
莱 J4d69 M-X 5039

5 residual strokes

悉 J3c3d M10635 1864
掬 J3545 M12290 2197
断 J4347 M13557 2385
粕 J4774 M26891 4391
粒 J4e33 M26884 4392
粘 J4734 M26901 4393
粗 J4146 M26894 4394
粛 J3d4d M29223 4747

菊 J3546 M31153 5096
積 J3c61 M40120 6203

6 residual strokes

奥 J317c M5981 1165
屡 J3c48 M7770 1428
断 J4347 M13557 2385
歯 J3b75 M16323 2961
番 J4856 M21858 3762
粗 J3e51 M26945 4400
粥 J3421 M26938 4402
粟 J3040 M26922 4403

7–8 residual strokes

数 J3f74 M13319 2353
楼 J4f30 M15212 2785
粥 J3421 M26938 4402
精 J403a M26997 4411
継 J3751 M27531 4501
隣 J4e59 M41847 6484

9 residual strokes

幡 J4828 M9086 1584
憐 J4e79 M11206 1987
糎 J4138 M27057 4413
糊 J3852 M27037 4415
継 J3751 M27531 4501
謎 J4666 M35800 5661
隣 J4e59 M41847 6484
麹 J396d M-X 7036

10 residual strokes

憐 J4e79 M11206 1987
燐 J4e55 M19417 3499
粥 J3421 M26938 4402
糟 J457c M27070 4420
薮 J4c79 M-X 5201
謎 J3569 M35800 5661

11 residual strokes

燦 J3b38 M19468 3498
燐 J4e55 M19417 3499
糟 J416c M27104 4423
糠 J3947 M27105 4424
糞 J4a35 M27102 4425
繍 J3d2b M-X 4572
襖 J3228 M-X 5498
鞠 J3547 M42892 6589

12–14 residual strokes

糧 J4e48 M27132 4426
繍 J3d2b M-X 4572
類 J4e60 M43608 6647
鱗 J4e5a M46502 6923
麟 J4e5b M47690 7028
麹 J-X M47818 7037
齢 J4e70 M48632 7093

Rad. 120 糸

0 residual strokes

糸 J3b65 M27221 4431

1 residual strokes

系 J374f M27223 4433

3 residual strokes

係 J3738 M663 217
級 J3569 M27258 4437
糾 J356a M-X 4438
紀 J352a M27234 4439
約 J4c73 M27242 4440
紅 J3948 M27243 4441

4 residual strokes

孫 J4239 M6987 1296
級 J3569 M27258 4437
紘 J3949 M27289 4445
紗 J3c53 M27287 4446
紐 J4933 M27268 4448
索 J3a77 M27306 4449
紡 J4b42 M27305 4450
紋 J4c66 M27262 4451
粉 J4a36 M27295 4452
納 J473c M27264 4453
純 J3d63 M27267 4454
紙 J3b66 M27293 4455
素 J4147 M27300 4456
紺 J3a30 M27362 4466

5 residual strokes

紙 J3b66 M27293 4455
紬 J445d M27338 4462
紹 J3e52 M27361 4465

紺 J3a30 M27362 4466
紳 J3f42 M27348 4467
絃 J383e M27373 4468
累 J4e5f M27343 4469
組 J4148 M27374 4470
終 J3d2a M27372 4471
細 J3a59 M27344 4472
経 J3750 M27392 4473

6 residual strokes

絢 J303c M27427 4481
絡 J4d6d M27426 4484
絞 J394a M27421 4485
紫 J3b67 M27337 4486
統 J457d M27447 4487
絵 J3328 M27464 4488
給 J356b M27432 4489
絶 J4064 M-X 4490
結 J376b M27398 4492
逓 J423d M39038 6098

7 residual strokes

絹 J3828 M27470 4499
続 J4233 M27533 4500
継 J3751 M27531 4501
逓 J423d M39038 6098

8 residual strokes

綏 J3c7a M27565 4510
綻 J433e M27587 4514
維 J305d M27568 4516
緋 J486c M27604 4517

綜 J416e M27535 4520
緒 J3d6f M27632 4521
綾 J303d M27591 4523
緊 J365b M27603 4524
綱 J394b M27576 4525
綴 J4456 M27579 4526
網 J4c56 M27577 4527
緑 J4e50 M27541 4528
練 J4e7d M27631 4530
綿 J4c4a M27592 4531
総 J416d M27620 4532

9 residual strokes

潔 J3769 M18231 3332
緊 J365b M27603 4524
緬 J4c4b M27674 4542
縄 J466c M27729 4547
線 J407e M27641 4548
締 J4479 M27651 4549
縫 J4b25 M27805 4550
緩 J344b M27669 4551
編 J4a54 M27665 4552
縁 J316f M27656 4553
緯 J305e M27682 4566

10 residual strokes

縫 J4b25 M27805 4550
緯 J305e M27682 4566
縛 J477b M27771 4567
縞 J3c4a M27777 4569
繁 J484b M27803 4570
縦 J3d44 M27804 4571

11 residual strokes

微 J352b / M-X 1773
徵 J-X / M10267 1778
縫 J4b25 / M27805 4550
繁 J484b / M27803 4570
繡 J3d2b / M-X 4572
繫 J3752 / M-X 4573
績 J4053 / M27845 4579
縮 J3d4c / M27815 4585
纖 J4121 / M27874 4586
螺 J4d66 / M33512 5382

12 residual strokes

縫 J4b25 / M27805 4550
繪 J4136 / M27893 4594
繭 J4b7a / M27944 4595
織 J3f25 / M27892 4596

13 residual strokes

繡 J3d2b / M-X 4572
繽 J-X / M27913 4600
繫 J-X / M27940 4601
線 J372b / M27953 4602
羅 J4d65 / M28397 4655

14–16 residual strokes

懸 J377c / M11462 2011
纂 J3b3c / M28012 4608
纏 J453b / M28043 4612
纓 J6575 / M28058 4617

彎 J3725 / M38587 5992

Rad. 121 缶

0–8 residual strokes

淘 J4571 / M17642 3187
缶 J344c / M28108 4624
匋 J463a / M31252 5075
遙 J7423 / M39035 6097
陶 J462b / M41705 6459

Rad. 122 网

7–8 residual strokes

夢 J4c34 / M5801 1131
罫 J3753 / M28295 4642
署 J3d70 / M28311 4643
罪 J3a61 / M28293 4644
置 J4356 / M28298 4645
買 J4763 / M36708 5793

9 residual strokes

寧 J472b / M7296 1361
德 J4641 / M10237 1767
漫 J4c21 / M18166 3308
罰 J4833 / M28315 4647
蔑 J4a4e / M31781 5179
蔓 J4c22 / M31784 5180

10 residual strokes

慢 J4b7d / M11110 1968
罵 J474d / M28333 4649
罷 J486d / M28336 4650

還 J3454 / M39174 6121

11 residual strokes

壞 J3275 / M5541 1102
憲 J377b / M11269 1988
懷 J327b / M11351 2003
濁 J / M18440 3348
還 J3454 / M39174 6121

12 residual strokes

懷 J327b / M11351 2003
曙 J3d6c / M-X 2519
燭 J3f24 / M19480 3496
爵 J3c5f / M19710 3514
環 J3444 / M-X 3680
聽 J4430 / M29173 4740

13–23 residual strokes

曜 J-X / M14220 2523
齵 J3135 / M-X 2924
爵 J3c5f / M19710 3514
羅 J4d65 / M28397 4655
鐸 J4278 / M40951 6356
鰻 J3137 / M46443 6914

Rad. 123 羊

0 residual strokes

羊 J4d53 / M28425 4658

3–5 residual strokes

差 J3a39 / M8732 1537
祥 J487e / M24689 4090
美 J4323 / M28435 4660
達 J4323 / M39011 6088
遲 J4359 / M38989 6089

6 residual strokes

善 J4131 / M3904 859
業 J3648 / M15170 2789
洋 J4d4e / M17363 3130
着 J4365 / M23339 3938
達 J4323 / M39011 6088
遲 J4359 / M38989 6089

7 residual strokes

嵯 J3a37 / M8363 1500
羨 J4122 / M28503 4665
群 J3732 / M28498 4666
義 J3541 / M28504 4668
詳 J3e5c / M35446 5607

8–9 residual strokes

儀 J3537 / M1172 324
樣 J4d4d / M15352 2821
瑳 J3a3c / M21170 3667
窯 J4d52 / M25594 4210
養 J4d5c / M44144 6691

10–14 residual strokes

叢 J4151 / M3220 684
撲 J4b50 / M12755 2274
犧 J353e / M20190 3550
繕 J4136 / M27893 4594
膳 J4137 / M29891 4873
蟻 J3542 / M36027 5397
議 J3544 / M36027 5716
養 J4d5c / M44144 6691
鮮 J412f / M46133 6864

Rad. 124 羽

0 residual strokes

羽 J3129 / M28614 4675

3–10 residual strokes

扇 J4070 / M11743 2056
摺 J4022 / M12647 2262
樛 J5c5c / M15445 2842
煽 J407a / M19272 3469
翁 J3227 / M28635 4677
翌 J4d62 / M28657 4679
習 J3d2c / M28672 4681
翠 J3f69 / M28732 4685
翫 J3465 / M28766 4689
翰 J344d / M28780 4690

11–12 residual strokes

擢 J4527 / M12852 2303

朋	J4a7e / M14340'	4769
胀	J394f / M29315	4770
肯	J394e / M29311	4771
股	J3854 / M29284	4772
育	J3069 / M29318	4773
肥	J486e / M29290	4774
服	J497e / M14345'	4775
肩	J382a / M29299	4776
郁	J306a / M39371	6136
青	J4044 / M42564'	6557

5 residual strokes

削	J3a6f / M2000	488
前	J4130 / M2011	490
宥	J4d28 / M7137	1326
育	J3069 / M29318	4773
胤	J307d / M29405	4786
胞	J4b26 / M29396'	4788
胎	J425b / M29369	4789
胆	J4340 / M29354	4790
肺	J4759 / M29422	4791
胡	J3855 / M29400	4792
胃	J305f / M29348	4793
背	J4758 / M29363	4794

6 residual strokes

哨	J3e25 / M3646	809
宵	J3e2c / M7168	1334
屑	J367d / M7709	1424
消	J3e43 / M17529'	3158
胤	J307d / M29405	4786
朕	J443f / M14361	4797
脆	J4048 / M29468	4800

朔	J3a73 / M14359	4801
朗	J4f2f / M14362'	4802
脅	J363c / M29466	4803
脊	J4054 / M29472	4804
脈	J4c2e / M29470	4805
脇	J4f46 / M29467	4807
脂	J3b69 / M29463	4808
能	J473d / M29454	4809
胴	J4639 / M24201'	4810
胸	J363b / M29442	4811
随	J3f6f / M41764'	6460
骨	J397c / M45098	6784

7 residual strokes

堕	J4244 / M-X	1033
崩	J4a78 / M8212	1491
庸	J4d47 / M9378	1624
情	J3e70 / M10756'	1898
梢	J4036 / M14866	2695
清	J3951 / M17695'	3205
胤	J307d / M29405	4786
朗	J4f2f / M14362'	4802
望	J4b3e / M14368'	4819
脚	J3553 / M29502	4820
脳	J473e / M29567'	4821
脱	J4326 / M29539'	4822
膏	J3951 / M29800	4860
萌	J4b28 / M31265	5094
豚	J465a / M36352	5743
随	J3f6f / M41764'	6460

8 residual strokes

勝	J3e21 / M2409	553

婿	J4c3b / M6470	1246
愉	J4c7b / M10905'	1920
惰	J4246 / M10855	1921
揃	J4237 / M12319	2226
散	J3b36 / M13265	2352
晴	J4032 / M13994'	2488
棚	J432a / M14941	2748
湖	J3850 / M17836	3240
硝	J3e4b / M24201'	4007
筋	J365a / M25994	4286
腔	J3950 / M29630	4826
腹	J4431 / M29570	4832
腎	J3f55 / M29621	4834
腐	J4965 / M29625	4835
期	J347c / M14378	4836
腕	J4f53 / M29631	4837
朝	J442b / M14374'	4838
腿	J425c / M29747	4846
遡	J414c / M39048	6094

9 residual strokes

塑	J413a / M5328	1068
愈	J4c7c / M-X	1910
楢	J424a / M15133	2780
溯	J5e6a / M17975	3272
滑	J336a / M18032	3282
瑚	J386a / M21126	3662
盟	J4c41 / M23024	3899
絹	J3828 / M27470	4499
腹	J4431 / M29570	4832
腎	J3f55 / M29621	4834
腿	J425c / M29747	4846
腺	J4123 / M29746	4847
腫	J3c70 / M29697	4848

腸	J4432 / M29721	4849
腰	J3978 / M29705	4850
腹	J4a22 / M29722	4851
蛸	J427d / M33072	5330
賄	J4f45 / M36745	5800
遡	J414c / M39048	6094
靖	J4c77 / M42570'	6559

10 residual strokes

厭	J315e / M3025	662
態	J4256 / M11052	1947
熊	J3727 / M11294	3468
精	J403a / M26997'	4411
腿	J425c / M29747	4846
膜	J4256 / M29808'	4854
膏	J3951 / M29800	4860
膝	J4928 / M29837	4868

11 residual strokes

廟	J4940 / M9489	1645
徹	J4530 / M10245	1771
態	J4256 / M11052	1947
撒	J3b35 / M12697	2279
撤	J4531 / M12780	2280
潮	J442c / M18277'	3336
箭	J407d / M26193	4325
糊	J3852 / M27037	4415
絹	J3828 / M27470	4499
罷	J486d / M28336	4650
腐	J4965 / M29625	4835
腿	J425c / M29747	4846
膚	J4966 / M29860	4867
膝	J4928 / M29837	4868

請	J4041 / M35640'	5645

12 residual strokes

膳	J4137 / M29891	4873
膨	J4b44 / M29861	4874
謂	J3062 / M35759	5656
諭	J4d21 / M35727'	5667
輸	J4d22 / M38438'	5978
醐	J386f / M39930	6183
錆	J3b2c / M40523	6296
鞘	J3664 / M42850	6587
骸	J333c / M45164	6789
龍	J4e36 / M48818	7103

13 residual strokes

濘	J4654 / M-X	3356
臀	J673d / M29939	4880
臆	J3232 / M29951	4883
膿	J473f / M29938	4884
膾	J4625 / M35780'	5685
骸	J333c / M45164	6789
鯖	J4b6e / M46126	6858

14 residual strokes

癒	J4c7e / M22545	3847
膿	J473f / M29938	4884
臓	J4221 / M29995'	4886
藤	J4623 / M32340'	5241
髄	J3f71 / M45240'	6791

15 residual strokes

寵	J437e M7368	1370
瀧	J426d M18671	3376
臟	J4221 M29995	**4886**
覇	J4746 M34790	5519
轍	J4532 M38524	5988
髓	J3f71 M45240	6791
鯖	J3b2a M46210	6883
鵬	J4b32 M47005	6979

16–19 residual strokes

聾	J4f38 M29212	4745
襲	J3d31 M34717	5510
騰	J462d M44915	6767

Rad. 131 臣

0 residual strokes

臣	J3f43 M30068	**4894**

2–9 residual strokes

堅	J3778 M5210	1038
姬	J4931 M6229	1217
樫	J335f M15485	2849
監	J3446 M23032	3901
堅	J4328 M25790	4240
緊	J365b M27603	4524
腎	J3f55 M29621	4834
臥	J3269 M30071	**4896**
蔵	J4222 M31885	5182
賢	J382d M36822	5816

10–17 residual strokes

濫	J4d74 M18521	3366
緊	J365b M27603	4524
臟	J4221 M29995	4886
臨	J4e57 M30087	**4899**
艦	J344f M30571	4950
藍	J4d75 M32258	5233
覧	J4d77 M34928	5533
鑑	J3455 M40988	6361
鱧	J336f M46437	6915

Rad. 132 自

0 residual strokes

自	J3c2b M30095	**4900**

3–4 residual strokes

息	J4229 M10601	1850
臭	J3d2d M30103	**4901**
頁	J4a47 M43333	6614
首	J3c73 M44489	6719

5 residual strokes

道	J463b M39010	6091
頃	J3a22 M43338	6615
頂	J443a M43335	6616

6 residual strokes

殖	J3f23 M16502	2981
道	J463b M39010	6091

項	J3960 M43343	6617
須	J3f5c M43352	6618
順	J3d67 M43349	6619

7 residual strokes

頌	J4852 M43378	6621
頓	J465c M43381	6623
頑	J3468 M43374	6624
預	J4d42 M43373	6625

8–9 residual strokes

導	J4633 M7463	1388
榎	J315d M15219	2810
碩	J4059 M24338	4026
頗	J3c2b M43415	6627
領	J4e4e M43423	6628
頬	J4b4b M-X	6629
頼	J4d6a M43529	6635
鼻	J4921 M48498	7082

10–11 residual strokes

嶺	J4e66 M8553	1517
憩	J3746 M11246	1980
穎	J314f M25267	4173
頴	J-X M43496	6637
頭	J462c M43490	6639
頻	J4951 M-X	6641

12 residual strokes

顎	J335c M43590	6643

額	J335b M43586	6644
題	J426a M43584	6645
顕	J3832 M43609	6646
類	J4e60 M43608	6647
顔	J3469 M43591	6648

13–16 residual strokes

攪	J3e71 M12920	2314
顎	J335c M43590	6643
顛	J453f M-X	6652
顧	J385c M43689	6655

Rad. 133 至

0 residual strokes

至	J3b6a M30142	**4903**

2–5 residual strokes

倒	J455d M767	256
到	J457e M1950	477
姪	J4c45 M6226	1209
室	J3c3c M7136	1327
屋	J3230 M7684	1421
窒	J4362 M25493	4200
致	J4357 M30149	**4904**

Rad. 134 臼

0 residual strokes

臼	J3131 M30173	**4907**

7–10 residual strokes

潟	J3363 M18247	3328
興	J363d M30226	**4913**
輿	J4d41 M38468	5983
鼠	J414d M48390	7078

Rad. 135 舌

0 residual strokes

舌	J4065 M30277	**4917**

1–10 residual strokes

乱	J4d70 M187	60
舎	J3c4b M30278	189
舗	J3a5e M30323	322
憩	J3746 M11246	1980
括	J3367 M11988	2143
活	J3368 M17423	3132
甜	J453c M21656	3712
筈	J4826 M25990	4277
舘	J345c M30326	**4923**
話	J4f43 M35441	5608
辞	J3c2d M38638	6000

Rad. 136 舛

0 residual strokes

舛	J4124 M30338	**4924**

4–9 residual strokes

傑	J3766 M955	293
憐	J4e79 M11206	1987

桝 J4b71/M-X 2673
舜 J3d58/M30339 **4925**
舞 J4971/M30342′ **4926**

Rad. 137 舟

0 residual strokes

舟 J3d2e/M30350 **4927**

3–5 residual strokes

般 J484c/M30388 **4931**
航 J3952/M30385 **4933**
舶 J4775/M30402 **4936**
舵 J4249/M30400 **4937**
舷 J383f/M30403 **4938**
船 J4125/M30407 **4939**

6–16 residual strokes

搬 J4842/M12507 2249
盤 J4857/M23036 3902
磐 J4858/M24401 4037
舷 J383f/M30403 **4938**
艇 J447a/M30440 **4941**
艦 J344f/M30571 **4950**

Rad. 138 艮

0 residual strokes

艮 J3a31/M30596 **4953**

1–2 residual strokes

即 J4228/M2855 633
良 J4e49/M30597 **4954**
退 J4260/M38839′ 6040
限 J3842/M41627 6439

3 residual strokes

恨 J3a28/M10588 1842
退 J4260/M38839′ 6040
郎 J4f3a/M39405′ 6138
食 J3f29/M44014 6674

4 residual strokes

娘 J4c3c/M6304 1230
既 J347b/M13721 2407
根 J3a2c/M14745 2670
浪 J4f32/M17482 3155
狼 J4f35/M20432 3579

5 residual strokes

卿 J362a/M2878 642
既 J347b/M13721 2407
痕 J3a2f/M22171 3803
眼 J3463/M23318 3935
朗 J4f2f/M14362′ 4802
郷 J363f/M39498′ 6145
飢 J3532/M44023′ 6675

6 residual strokes

厩 J3139/M-X 654
喰 J3674/M4015 849
廊 J4f2d/M-X 1622
既 J347b/M13721 2407
榔 J4f31/M15226 2766
腿 J425c/M29747 4846

7 residual strokes

厩 J3139/M-X 654
慨 J3334/M-X 1944
腿 J425c/M29747 4846
飯 J4853/M44064′ 6679
飲 J307b/M44063′ 6680

8 residual strokes

厩 J3139/M-X 654
慨 J3334/M-X 1944
概 J3335/M15217′ 2824
節 J4061/M26102 4299
腿 J425c/M29747 4846
銀 J3664/M40355 6268
飴 J303b/M44080′ 6682
飾 J3e7e/M44111′ 6683
飽 J4b30/M44109′ 6684
飼 J3b74/M44107′ 6685

9–20 residual strokes

墾 J3a26/M5509 1097
懇 J3a29/M11326 2002
概 J3335/M15217′ 2824
櫛 J367b/M-X 2884
鬱 J3135/M-X 2924
爵 J3c5f/M19710′ 3514
蝕 J3f2a/M-X 5333
響 J3641/M43318′ 6610
養 J4d5c/M44144 6691
餐 J3b41/M44160 6696
餓 J326e/M44168′ 6697
館 J345b/M44237′ 6701
饗 J3642/M-X 6705

Rad. 139 色

0 residual strokes

色 J3f27/M30602 **4956**

6–18 residual strokes

絶 J4064/M-X 4490
艶 J3170/M30632 **4957**

Rad. 140 艸

2–3 residual strokes

芝 J3c47/M30699′ **4961**
芋 J3072/M30670′ **4964**

4 residual strokes

芝 J3c47/M30699′ **4961**
芙 J4967/M30694 **4966**
苅 J3423/M30771 **4969**
芹 J365c/M30742 **4970**
芭 J474e/M30730 **4974**
芦 J3032/M30716 **4975**
芯 J3f44/M30732 **4976**
芥 J3329/M30715 **4977**
芸 J375d/M30741′ **4978**
芳 J4b27/M30736′ **4979**
花 J3256/M30734′ **4980**

5 residual strokes

供 J3621/M605 195
苓 J4e6a/M30777 **4981**
茎 J3754/M30861′ **4991**
茄 J3258/M30835 **4995**
苑 J3171/M30774 **4996**
茂 J4c50/M30833′ **4998**
苧 J4377/M30798 **5000**
苔 J425d/M30778 **5001**
芽 J326a/M30860′ **5002**
苫 J4651/M30802 **5003**
苗 J4944/M30781′ **5004**
茅 J337d/M30836 **5005**
苛 J3257/M30785 **5006**
若 J3c63/M30796′ **5007**
英 J3151/M30808′ **5008**
苦 J366c/M30797′ **5009**

6 residual strokes

茨 J3071/M30896 **5017**
茜 J302b/M30871 **5019**
荏 J3141/M30950 **5022**
茸 J427b/M30918 **5026**
荊 J3755/M-X **5027**
荘 J4171/M30890 **5031**
草 J4170/M30945′ **5032**
茶 J4363/M30915′ **5033**
荒 J3953/M30953′ **5034**
革 J3357/M42710 6570

7 residual strokes

匿 J463f/M2690 591

莱 J4d69/M-X **5039**	塔 J4563/M5332 1052	漠 J4779/M18149 3268	薦 J4126/M32143 **5219**
莞 J3450/M31063 **5052**	惹 J3c66/M10866 1886	漢 J3441/M18068 3281	薙 J4665/M32121 **5221**
狄 J322e/M31005 **5054**	慌 J3932/M11057 1917	蓬 J4b29/M-X **5099**	薪 J3f45/M32149 **5222**
莫 J477c/M31078 **5057**	搭 J456b/M12508 2228	蓮 J4f21/M-X **5105**	薫 J3730/M32173 **5223**
華 J325a/M31119 **5058**	敬 J3749/M13285 2351	蒋 J3e55/M-X **5132**	薬 J4c74/M32188 **5224**
荷 J3259/M31000 **5059**	瑛 J314d/M21127 3647	蓉 J4d56/M31648 **5135**	薄 J4776/M32185 **5225**
菰 J3856/M31217 **5079**	蓬 J4b29/M-X **5099**	蔀 J3c43/M31748 **5138**	錨 J4945/M40598 6295
	菟 J4551/M-X **5102**	蓑 J4c2c/M31661 **5143**	鞘 J3e64/M42850 6587

---

8 residual strokes

匩 J463f/M2690 591	蓮 J4f21/M-X **5105**	蒜 J4947/M31562 **5144**
椛 J3371/M15065 2683	葎 J4e2a/M31397 **5111**	蔭 J307e/M31840 **5151**
葛 J336b/M-X **5060**	董 J4621/M31433 **5118**	蒔 J3c2c/M31546 **5153**
蓞 J463a/M31252 **5075**	葵 J302a/M31458 **5120**	蒙 J4c58/M31555 **5154**
菀 J-X/M31189 **5077**	萱 J3338/M31345 **5121**	蓋 J3338/M31652 **5155**
菰 J3856/M31217 **5079**	萩 J476b/M31333 **5122**	蒲 J3377/M31611 **5156**
菖 J3e54/M31174 **5085**	葱 J472c/M31454 **5123**	蓬 J-X/M31720 **5157**
萎 J3060/M31269 **5087**	茸 J4978/M31465 **5125**	蓮 J-X/M31722 **5158**
菁 J3f7b/M31142 **5090**	葛 J-X/M31420 **5126**	蒐 J3d2f/M31539 **5159**
菌 J365d/M31156 **5091**	葡 J4972/M31430 **5127**	葦 J3031/M31437 **5160**
菱 J4929/M31219 **5092**	葬 J4172/M31440 **5128**	蓄 J435f/M31642 **5161**
菩 J4a6e/M31205 **5093**	葉 J4d55/M31387 **5129**	蒼 J4173/M31627 **5162**
萌 J4b28/M31265 **5094**	落 J4d6e/M31362 **5130**	蒸 J3e78/M31618 **5163**
菓 J325b/M31168 **5095**	蒸 J3e78/M31618 **5163**	靴 J3724/M42729 6576
菊 J3546/M31153 **5096**	靭 J3f59/M-X 6573	
菜 J3a5a/M31184 **5097**	韮 J4723/M43237 6605	
著 J4378/M31302 **5098**		
葉 J4d55/M31387 **5129**		

---

9 residual strokes

僅 J364f/M-X 279	**11 residual strokes**
備 J4877/M967 284	慕 J4a69/M11088 1948
募 J4a67/M2416 551	暮 J4a6b/M14128 2508
勤 J3650/M2415 552	樺 J3372/M15497 2817

10 residual strokes

僎 J364f/M-X 279	模 J4c4f/M15453 2825
僊 J-X/M1048 292	膜 J4b6c/M29808 4854
嘩 J325e/M-X 861	蓬 J4b29/M-X **5099**
墓 J4a68/M5431 1073	蓑 J4c2c/M31661 **5143**
夢 J4c34/M5801 1131	蓬 J-X/M31720 **5157**
寛 J3432/M7276 1352	蓮 J-X/M31722 **5158**
幕 J4b95/M9051 1578	醗 J-X/M31820 **5177**
摸 J4c4e/M12644 2250	

---

12 residual strokes

慶 J3744/M11145 1967
暴 J4b3d/M14137 2511
蕃 J435f/M31642 **5161**
蔵 J4222/M31885 **5182**
蕊 J3c49/M31939 **5188**
蕉 J3e56/M31937 **5191**
蔬 J6876/M31839 **5192**
蔽 J4a43/M31888 **5193**
蕨 J4f4f/M32001 **5194**
蕪 J4973/M32004 **5196**
蕎 J363e/M31946 **5197**
蕩 J4222/M32002 **5198**
蕃 J4859/M31906 **5199**
諾 J427a/M35687 5638
鞍 J3048/M42815 6586

13 residual strokes

燕 J316d/M19429 3489
獲 J334d/M20758 3609
薗 J3172/M32119 **5200**
薮 J4c79/M-X **5201**
薯 J3d72/M-X **5202**
蕗 J4979/M31964 **5203**
薩 J3b27/M32189 **5217**

---

14 residual strokes

薩 J3b27/M32189 **5217**
藍 J4d75/M32258 **5233**
藁 J4f4e/M32252 **5234**
謹 J3660/M35850 5688
鞠 J3547/M42892 6589

15 residual strokes

礦 J626a/M24571 4056
穫 J334f/M25334 4180
繭 J4b7a/M27944 4595
臓 J4221/M29995 4886
藍 J4d75/M32258 **5233**
藷 J3d73/M-X **5237**
藤 J4623/M32340 **5241**
潘 J484d/M32346 **5242**
難 J4671/M42128 6515
鞭 J4a5c/M42937 6595

16 residual strokes

礦 J626a/M24571 4056
臓 J4221/M29995 4886
藷 J-X/M32391 **5247**

Rad.140: 16 residual strokes

蘇 J4149/M32427 5252
藻 J4174/M32401 5254
蘭 J4d76/M32477 5255
警 J3759/M35989 5705

17–19 residual strokes

灌 J5e75/M18759 3390
灘 J4667/M18784 3391
蠶 J4b7a/M27944 4595
蠣 J695a/M33799 5399
護 J386e/M36038 5715
驚 J3643/M45013 6774

Rad. 141 虍

2–8 residual strokes

劇 J3760/M2218 517
噓 J3133/M-X 886
彪 J4937/M9993 1716
虎 J3857/M32675 5265
虐 J3554/M32678 5267
虛 J3575/M32708 5269
虞 J3673/M32723 5272
虜 J4e3a/M32720 5273

9–14 residual strokes

劇 J3760/M2218 517
噓 J-X/M4206 885
慮 J4e38/M11132 1962
櫨 J4827/M15844 2910
虜 J4966/M29829 4867

Rad. 142 虫

0 residual strokes

虫 J436e/M32804 5275

3 residual strokes

独 J4648/M20406 3574
虺 J303a/M32835 5277
虹 J467a/M32830 5279
風 J4977/M43756 6663

4 residual strokes

蚤 J4742/M32893 5287
蚊 J3263/M32849 5288
蚕 J3b3d/M32869 5290

5 residual strokes

強 J362f/M9815 1695
搔 J415f/M-X 2175
蛎 J3342/M-X 5291
蛋 J4341/M32977 5301
蛍 J3756/M32983 5302
蛇 J3c58/M32964 5303

6 residual strokes

属 J325c/M7754 1430
嵐 J4d72/M8289 1496
強 J362f/M9815 1695
蛭 J4948/M33048 5308
蛤 J483a/M33023 5312
蛙 J333f/M32997 5313

蛮 J485a/M33044 5314

7 residual strokes

強 J362f/M9815 1695
搔 J-X/M12477 2256
楓 J4976/M15126 2777
蛾 J326b/M33082 5325
蛸 J427d/M33072 5330
蜂 J4b2a/M33088 5331
触 J3f28/M35070 5547

8 residual strokes

蜥 J4f39/M-X 5332
蝕 J3f2a/M-X 5333
蜘 J4358/M33134 5342
蜜 J4c2a/M33143 5343
蝶 J4433/M33333 5363

9 residual strokes

嘱 J3e7c/M4249 894
蝕 J3f2a/M-X 5333
蠅 J4768/M-X 5344
蟬 J4066/M-X 5349
蝕 J-X/M33264 5358
蝶 J4433/M33333 5363
蝦 J325c/M33299 5364

10 residual strokes

濁 J4279/M18440 3348
融 J4d3b/M33384 5371

11–17 residual strokes

燭 J3f24/M19480 3496
繭 J4b7a/M27944 4595
螺 J4d66/M33512 5382
蟬 J-X/M33616 5388
蠅 J6a24/M33690 5394
蟹 J332a/M33668 5395
蟻 J3542/M33672 5397
蠣 J695a/M33799 5399
蠟 J-X/M33786 5403
騷 J417b/M44834 6760

Rad. 143 血

0 residual strokes

血 J376c/M33964 5411

7 residual strokes

衆 J3d30/M33981 5417

Rad. 144 行

0 residual strokes

行 J3954/M34029 5419

3–6 residual strokes

術 J3d51/M-X 1754
街 J3339/M34051 1759
桁 J3765/M14754 2656

9–18 residual strokes

衝 J3e57/M34069 1772
衡 J3955/M34078 1775
衛 J3152/M34073 1776

Rad. 145 衣

0 residual strokes

衣 J3061/M34091 5420

2 residual strokes

依 J304d/M607 191
初 J3d69/M1911 469

3 residual strokes

哀 J3025/M3580 791
表 J493d/M34105 5422
辰 J4324/M38682 6006

4 residual strokes

衷 J436f/M-X 31
娠 J3f31/M6322 1224
衿 J365e/M34149 5431
衰 J3f6a/M34127 5432

5 residual strokes

俵 J4936/M730 243
唇 J3f30/M3697 807
娠 J3f31/M6322 1224
袈 J3736/M34166 5442

袋 J425e M34171 **5443**				這 J4767 M38889 6058
袖 J4235 M34192 **5444**				
被 J486f M34222 **5445**				

9–10 residual strokes

4–6 residual strokes

6–8 residual strokes

3 residual strokes

---

6 residual strokes

- 喪 J4153 M3985 853
- 展 J4538 M7715 1425
- 袴 J3853 M34236 **5448**
- 袷 J3041 M34240 **5449**
- 裂 J4e76 M34260 **5453**
- 裁 J3a5b M34258 **5454**
- 裝 J4175 M34283 **5455**
- 辱 J3f2b M38686 6007

9–10 residual strokes

- 壊 J3e6d M-X 1098
- 壞 J3275 M5541 1102
- 孃 J3e6e M6807 1270
- 懐 J327b M11351 2003
- 褒 J4b2b M34437 **5483**
- 複 J4a23 M34417 **5484**
- 農 J4740 M38688 6008

4–6 residual strokes

- 晒 J3b2f M13924 2461
- 栖 J4034 M14693 2650
- 栗 J372a M14695 2662
- 票 J493c M24694 4089
- 粟 J3040 M26922 4403

6–8 residual strokes

- 寛 J3432 M7276 1352
- 攪 J3349 M-X 2267
- 槻 J4450 M15390 2845

3 residual strokes

- 訊 J3f56 M35224 **5559**
- 託 J4277 M35243 **5560**
- 討 J4624 M35231 **5561**
- 訓 J3731 M35238 **5562**
- 記 J352d M35244 **5563**
- 這 J4767 M38889 6058

7 residual strokes

- 喪 J4153 M3985 853
- 蓑 J4c2c M31661 5143
- 袴 J3853 M34236 **5448**
- 裟 J3d40 M34325 **5457**
- 裕 J4d35 M34305 **5461**
- 裏 J4e22 M34294 **5462**
- 裡 J4e23 M34295 **5463**
- 補 J4a64 M34320 **5464**

12–16 residual strokes

- 嚢 J-X M4633 933
- 穣 J3e77 M25335 4179
- 襖 J3228 M-X **5498**
- 嚢 J4739 M-X **5499**
- 襟 J365f M34647 **5504**
- 襲 J3d31 M34717 **5510**
- 讓 J3e79 M36037 5714
- 釀 J3e7a M40064 6197

7–13 residual strokes

- 標 J4938 M15442 2852
- 漂 J493a M18102 3303
- 煙 J316c M19203 3456
- 獣 J4d32 M20558 3590
- 瓢 J493b M21419 3688
- 腰 J3978 M29705 4850
- 覆 J4a24 M34789 **5517**
- 覇 J4746 M34790 **5519**
- 遷 J412b M39123 6113

9–16 residual strokes

- 攬 J5978 M13041 2322
- 窺 J312e M25633 4215
- 覧 J4d77 M34928 **5533**
- 親 J3f46 M34918 **5534**
- 観 J3451 M34955 **5538**

Rad. 148 角

0 residual strokes

- 角 J3351 M35003 **5543**

4 residual strokes

- 訟 J3e59 M35266 **5565**
- 訣 J376d M35267 **5567**
- 許 J3576 M35298 **5569**
- 設 J405f M35293 **5570**
- 訪 J4b2c M35284 **5571**
- 訳 J4c75 M35324 **5572**

8 residual strokes

- 裳 J3e58 M34357 **5472**
- 褐 J336c M-X **5473**
- 裾 J3f7e M34382 **5474**
- 裸 J4d67 M34371 **5475**
- 製 J403d M34380 **5476**

Rad. 146 西

0 residual strokes

- 西 J403e M34763 **5514**

2–3 residual strokes

- 価 J3241 M628 188
- 迺 J4736 M9576 1658
- 茜 J302b M30871 5019
- 要 J4d57 M34768 **5515**

Rad. 147 見

0 residual strokes

- 見 J382b M34796 **5522**

2–5 residual strokes

- 現 J383d M21004 3645
- 硯 J3827 M24233 4005
- 規 J352c M34810 **5524**
- 視 J3b6b M34825 **5525**
- 覘 J4741 M34839 **5528**
- 覚 J3350 M34846 **5529**

6–12 residual strokes

- 蟹 J332a M33668 5395
- 触 J3f28 M35070 **5547**
- 解 J3272 M35067 **5548**

Rad. 149 言

0 residual strokes

- 言 J3840 M35205 **5552**

2 residual strokes

- 信 J3f2e M707 221
- 訂 J447b M35211 **5553**
- 計 J3757 M35220 **5555**

5 residual strokes

- 詑 J4242 M35374 **5579**
- 詔 J3e5b M35379 **5581**
- 詞 J3b6c M35394 **5582**
- 註 J4370 M35340 **5583**
- 詠 J3153 M35409 **5584**
- 詐 J3a3e M35373 **5585**
- 診 J3f47 M35337 **5586**
- 評 J493e M35383 **5587**
- 訴 J414a M35388 **5588**
- 証 J3e5a M35341 **5589**

Rad. 149: 6 residual strokes

6 residual strokes

詣	J3758 M35412	5594
詫	J4f4d M35431	5598
該	J333a M35445	5601
譽	J4d40 M35498	5602
詮	J4127 M35435	5604
誇	J3858 M35474	5605
誠	J403f M35497	5606
詳	J3e5c M35446	5607
話	J4f43 M35441	5608
詰	J354d M35440	5609
詩	J3b6d M35427	5610
試	J3b6e M35415	5611

7 residual strokes

獄	J3976 M20603	3602
罰	J4833 M28315	4647
該	J333a M35445	5601
誇	J3858 M35474	5605
誌	J3b6f M35501	5620
誓	J4040 M35514	5622
認	J4727 M35502	5623
誘	J4d36 M35525	5625
誤	J386d M35546	5626
説	J4062 M35556	5627
語	J386c M35533	5628
誚	J4649 M35580	5629
誕	J4342 M35692	5640

8 residual strokes

誘	J4d36 M35525	5625
諫	J3452 M35642	5630

諷	J3f5b M35648	5632
誼	J3543 M35605	5634
調	J315a M35690	5637
諸	J427a M35687	5638
誹	J4870 M35601	5639
誕	J4342 M35692	5640
諒	J4e4a M35653	5641
誰	J432f M35586	5642
談	J434c M35633	5643
課	J325d M35589	5644
請	J4041 M35645	5645
論	J4f40 M35658	5646
調	J4434 M35609	5647
諸	J3d74 M35691	5648
謎	J4666 M35800	5661
諜	J4435 M35697	5665

9 residual strokes

謂	J3062 M35759	5656
諺	J3841 M-X	5659
諮	J3b70 M35728	5660
謎	J4666 M35800	5661
諦	J447c M35724	5663
諫	J6b5d M35724	5664
諜	J4435 M35697	5665
謡	J4d58 M35779	5666
諭	J4d21 M35727	5667
謀	J4b45 M35756	5671

10 residual strokes

儲	J4c59 M-X	331
謄	J4625 M35780	5685
謙	J382c M35821	5686

謝	J3c55 M35827	5687
謹	J3660 M35850	5688
講	J3956 M35824	5689

11 residual strokes

儲	J-X M1284	335
諸	J3d73 M-X	5237
謬	J4935 M35872	5695

12 residual strokes

諸	J-X M32391	5247
譜	J4968 M35990	5703
識	J3c31 M35974	5704
警	J3759 M35989	5705

13 residual strokes

讓	J3e79 M36037	5714
護	J386e M36038	5715
議	J3544 M36027	5716

14-20 residual strokes

讓	J3e79 M36037	5714
讚	J3b3e M36110	5720
讐	J3d32 M36125	5722
讚	J6c2d M36163	5729
辯	J6d67 M38677	6005

Rad. 150 谷

0 residual strokes

谷	J432b M36182	5730

2-5 residual strokes

俗	J422f M695	220
容	J4d46 M7172	1335
欲	J4d5f M16080	2936
浴	J4d61 M17496	3153
裕	J4d35 M34305	5461

6-12 residual strokes

慾	J4d5d M11163	1951
溶	J4d4f M17983	3277
熔	J4d50 M19319	3458
鎔	J6f30 M40704	6327

Rad. 151 豆

0 residual strokes

豆	J4626 M36245	5735

3-5 residual strokes

凱	J332e M1790	440
厨	J3f5f M3005	657
痘	J4577 M22185	3813
登	J4550 M22668	3862
短	J433b M23978	3982
逗	J3f60 M38887	6053

6-8 residual strokes

嘉	J3245 M4176	887
澄	J4021 M18315	3333

豐	J4b2d M36263	5737
鼓	J385d M48330	7076

9-13 residual strokes

樹	J3c79 M15496	2878
燈	J4575 M19402	3476
艷	J3170 M30632	4957
鎧	J333b M40735	6324
鐙	J462a M40904	6348
鬪	J462e M45649	6418
頭	J462c M43490	6639

Rad. 152 豕

2-3 residual strokes

家	J3248 M7169	1337
逐	J4360 M38877	6056

4 residual strokes

啄	J426f M-X	793
啄	J-X M3801	821
琢	J4276 M-X	3640
豚	J465a M36352	5743
遂	J3f6b M38985	6084
隊	J4262 M41750	6468

5 residual strokes

塚	J444d M-X	1048
琢	J-X M21058	3650
遂	J3f6b M38985	6084

6 residual strokes

嫁 J3247 / M6602 1256
蒙 J4c58 / M31555 5154
象 J3e5d / M36372 5744

7 residual strokes

墜 J4446 / M5451 1082
豪 J396b / M36406 5749

8 residual strokes

像 J417c / M1084 308
劇 J3760 / M2218 517
墜 J4446 / M5451 1082
毅 J3523 / M16673 3003
稼 J3254 / M25217 4169
緣 J316f / M27656 4553

10–11 residual strokes

壕 J3968 / M5559 1108
橡 J464b / M15564 2863
濠 J396a / M18502 3363
潴 J4375 / M-X 3377
緣 J316f / M27656 4553
緣 J-X / M27656 4554

Rad. 153 豸

3–10 residual strokes

懇 J3a29 / M11326 2002
豹 J493f / M36499 5753

貌 J4b46 / M36556 5762

Rad. 154 貝

0 residual strokes

貝 J332d / M36656 5766

2 residual strokes

則 J4227 / M1994 487
貞 J4467 / M36658 5768
負 J4969 / M-X 5769
頁 J4a47 / M43333 6614

3 residual strokes

唄 J3134 / M3694 802
員 J3077 / M3633 808
狽 J4762 / M20433 3576
貢 J3957 / M36665 5772
財 J3a62 / M36664 5773

4 residual strokes

偵 J4465 / M898 270
側 J4226 / M897 275
敗 J4754 / M13227 2343
貫 J3453 / M36681 5778
販 J484e / M36679 5779
責 J4055 / M36682 5780
貨 J325f / M36676 5781
貧 J494f / M36677 5782
貫 J4c63 / M36699 5789
頃 J3a22 / M43338 6615
頂 J443a / M43335 6616

5 residual strokes

測 J422c / M17780 3244
貫 J3453 / M36681 5778
費 J4871 / M36717 5786
貼 J453d / M36718 5787
貿 J4b47 / M36721 5788
賃 J4c63 / M36699 5789
賀 J326c / M36725 5790
貯 J4379 / M36698 5791
貸 J425f / M36709 5792
買 J4763 / M36708 5793
貴 J352e / M43343 5794
項 J3960 / M43343 6617
須 J3f5c / M43352 6618
順 J3d67 / M43349 6619

6 residual strokes

債 J3a44 / M1022 296
損 J423b / M12459 2255
煩 J4851 / M19229 3454
禎 J4477 / M24767 4099
賎 J4128 / M-X 5796
賂 J4f28 / M36738 5799
賄 J4f45 / M36759 5800
賊 J4231 / M36759 5801
賃 J4442 / M36743 5802
資 J3b71 / M36750 5803
頒 J4852 / M43378 6621
頓 J465c / M43381 6623
頑 J3468 / M43374 6624
預 J4d42 / M43373 6625

9 residual strokes

顋 J4655 / M4429 910

7 residual strokes

債 J3a44 / M1022 296
慣 J3437 / M11111 1970
潰 J4452 / M18167 3301
碩 J4059 / M24338 4026
賑 J4678 / M36785 5806
遺 J3064 / M39134 6115
頚 J375b / M43434 6626
頗 J3f7c / M43415 6627
領 J4e4e / M43423 6628

8 residual strokes

噴 J4a2e / M4345 900
墳 J4a2f / M5488 1095
實 J4950 / M-X 1365
慣 J3437 / M11111 1970
憤 J4a30 / M11239 1990
潰 J4459 / M18281 3335
賭 J4552 / M-X 5807
賠 J4765 / M36818 5810
賦 J496a / M36800 5811
賜 J3b72 / M36809 5812
賤 J6c4d / M36826 5813
賛 J3b3f / M36814 5814
賞 J3e5e / M36813 5815
賢 J382d / M36822 5816
質 J3c41 / M36833 5817
遺 J3064 / M39134 6115
頬 J4b4b / M-X 6629

12 residual strokes

瀬 J4025 / M18672 3384

潁 J3150 / M24824 4109
穎 J314f / M25267 4173
積 J4051 / M25266 4176
賢 J382d / M36822 5816
賭 J-X / M36847 5819
頼 J4d6a / M43529 6635
煩 J-X / M43496 6637
頸 J7074 / M43515 6638
頭 J462c / M43490 6639

10 residual strokes

償 J3d7e / M1245 333
嬰 J3145 / M6828 1273
嶺 J4e66 / M8553 1517
績 J4053 / M27845 4579
購 J3958 / M36885 5823
頻 J4951 / M-X 6641

11 residual strokes

潰 J-X / M18591 3373
贈 J4223 / M36920 5827
蹟 J4058 / M37814 5905
鎖 J3a3f / M40708 6325
顎 J335c / M43586 6643
額 J335b / M43586 6644
題 J426a / M43584 6645
顕 J3832 / M43609 6646
類 J4e60 / M43608 6647
顔 J3469 / M43591 6648

12 residual strokes

瀬 J4025 / M18672 3384

Rad.154: 12 residual strokes

績 J4053 M27845 **4579**
贋 J3466 M36943 **5830**
韻 J3124 M43307 6611
顎 J335c M43590 6643
顛 J453f M-X 6652
願 J346a M43623 6653

13–19 residual strokes

瀬 J494e M18636 3381
讃 J3b3e M36110 5720
讃 J6c2d M36163 5729
顧 J385c M43689 6655

Rad. 155 赤

0 residual strokes

赤 J4056 M36993 **5840**

4–7 residual strokes

赦 J3c4f M36999 **5841**
赫 J3352 M37010 **5843**

Rad. 156 走

0 residual strokes

走 J4176 M37034 **5845**

2–6 residual strokes

赴 J496b M37040 **5847**
起 J352f M37048 **5849**
越 J315b M37110 **5851**

超 J4436 M37096 **5852**

8–10 residual strokes

趣 J3c71 M37207 **5854**
趨 J3f76 M37258 **5855**

Rad. 157 足

0 residual strokes

足 J422d M37365 **5856**

2–5 residual strokes

促 J4225 M664 212
捉 J422a M12136 2159
距 J3577 M37481 **5866**

6 residual strokes

跨 J3859 M37504 **5872**
践 J4129 M37547 **5873**
跡 J4057 M37493 **5875**
路 J4f29 M37524 **5876**
跳 J4437 M37533 **5877**

7–9 residual strokes

蹄 J4979 M31964 5203
跨 J3859 M37504 **5872**
踊 J4d59 M37587 **5882**
踏 J4627 M37602 **5889**
蹄 J447d M37724 **5894**

11–21 residual strokes

蹟 J4058 M37814 **5905**
蹴 J3d33 M37876 **5913**
躍 J4c76 M37995 **5921**
露 J4f2a M42463 6549
鷺 J3a6d M47362 7006

Rad. 158 身

0 residual strokes

身 J3f48 M38034 **5928**

3–11 residual strokes

射 J3c4d M7434 1380
窮 J3567 M25593 4212
謝 J3c55 M35827 5687
躯 J366d M-X **5930**
軀 J-X M38137 **5935**

Rad. 159 車

0 residual strokes

車 J3c56 M38172 **5939**

2 residual strokes

軌 J3530 M38176 **5941**
軍 J3733 M38179 **5943**
連 J4f22 M38902 6062
陣 J3f58 M41667 6448

7 residual strokes

漣 J-X M18155 3259

---

3 residual strokes

庫 J384b M9330 1617
軒 J382e M38187 **5944**
連 J4f22 M38902 6062

4 residual strokes

動 J4630 M2390 549
斬 J3b42 M13555 2384
軟 J4670 M38213 **5947**
転 J453e M38234 **5948**
運 J313f M38998 6092

5 residual strokes

揮 J3478 M12394 2229
漣 J4e7a M-X 3210
蓮 J4f21 M-X 5105
軸 J3c34 M38269 **5952**
軽 J375a M38281 **5953**
運 J313f M38998 6092

6 residual strokes

漣 J4e7a M-X 3210
漣 J-X M18155 3259
蓮 J4f21 M-X 5105
蓮 J-X M31722 5158
較 J3353 M38297 **5959**
載 J3a5c M38309 **5960**

7 residual strokes

漣 J-X M18155 3259

漸 J4132 M18179 3305
蓮 J-X M31722 5158
輔 J4a65 M38342 **5964**

8 residual strokes

勲 J372e M2463 560
撃 J3762 M12674 2265
暫 J3b43 M14120 2510
範 J484f M26253 4330
輩 J475a M38398 **5971**
輝 J3531 M38372 **5972**
輪 J4e58 M38400 **5973**

9 residual strokes

輯 J3d34 M38420 **5976**
輸 J4d22 M38438 **5978**
輿 J4d41 M38468 **5983**

10 residual strokes

繋 J3752 M-X 4573
轄 J336d M38482 **5981**
輿 J4d41 M38468 **5983**

12–15 residual strokes

繋 J3752 M-X 4573
轍 J4532 M38524 **5988**
轟 J396c M38577 **5991**
轡 J3725 M38587 **5992**

Rad. 160 辛

0 residual strokes

辛 J3f49 M38630 **5996**

3–8 residual strokes

宰 J3a4b M7160 1330
新 J3f37 M13572 2387
辞 J3c2d M38638 **6000**
避 J4872 M39163 6120

9 residual strokes

壁 J4a49 M5516 1103
薪 J3f45 M32149 5222
辨 J517e M38657 **6002**
辦 J5221 M38656 **6003**
避 J4872 M39163 6120

11–14 residual strokes

瓣 J6122 M21425 3689
癖 J4a4a M22550 3848
辯 J6d67 M38677 **6005**

Rad. 161 辰

0 residual strokes

辰 J4324 M38682 **6006**

2–6 residual strokes

唇 J3f30 M3697 807

娠 J3f31 M6322 1224
振 J3f36 M12093 2171
辱 J3f2b M38686 **6007**
農 J4740 M38688 **6008**

7–10 residual strokes

濃 J473b M18442 3349
膿 J473f M29938 4884
賑 J4678 M36785 5806
農 J4740 M38688 **6008**
震 J3f4c M42300 6531

Rad. 162 辶

1–2 residual strokes

込 J397c M38712 **6010**
辺 J4a55 M38710 **6011**
辻 J4454 M38711 **6012**

3 residual strokes

巡 J3d64 M8680 1528
迄 J4b78 M38724 **6013**
迅 J3f57 M38727 **6014**
辿 J4329 M38718 **6015**
迂 J312a M38722 **6016**

4 residual strokes

迎 J375e M38748 **6019**
返 J4a56 M38758 **6020**
近 J3661 M38752 **6021**

---

5 residual strokes

迸 J4676 M38793 **6022**
迦 J3260 M38789 **6027**
迭 J4533 M38800 **6029**
述 J3d52 M38803 **6030**
迫 J4777 M38797 **6031**

6 residual strokes

迷 J4c42 M38825 **6037**
逃 J4628 M38845 **6038**
送 J4177 M38842 **6039**
退 J4260 M38839 **6040**
逆 J3555 M38849 **6041**
追 J4449 M38836 **6042**

7 residual strokes

逝 J4042 M38895 **6051**
逗 J3f60 M38887 **6053**
逢 J3029 M38901 **6054**
逼 J447e M38881 **6055**
逐 J4360 M38877 **6056**
途 J4553 M38882 **6057**
這 J4767 M38718 **6058**
透 J4629 M38876 **6059**
速 J422e M38897 **6060**
造 J4224 M38898 **6061**
連 J4f22 M38902 **6062**
通 J444c M38892 **6063**

8 residual strokes

逵 J4629 M38876 **6059**

逮 J4261 M38931 **6069**
週 J3d35 M38937 **6070**
逸 J306f M38951 **6071**
進 J3f4a M38943 **6073**
随 J3f6f M41764 6460

9 residual strokes

遥 J4d5a M-X **6075**
遇 J3678 M38991 **6083**
遂 J3f6b M38985 **6084**
逼 J492f M38973 **6085**
遍 J4a57 M39001 **6086**
遒 J465b M38982 **6087**
達 J4323 M39011 **6088**
遅 J4359 M38989 **6089**
過 J3261 M39002 **6090**
道 J463b M39091 **6091**
運 J313f M38998 **6092**
遊 J4d37 M38994 **6093**
違 J3063 M39067 6099

10 residual strokes

槌 J4448 M-X 2709
槌 J-X M15318 2767
溓 J4e7a M-X 3210
溓 J-X M18155 3259
腿 J425c M29747 4846
蓬 J4b29 M-X 5099
蓮 J4f21 M-X 5105
蓬 J-X M31720 5157
蓮 J-X M31722 5158
遇 J3678 M38991 **6083**
遡 J414c M39048 **6094**

遙 J7423 M39035 **6097**
遜 J423d M39038 **6098**
違 J3063 M39067 **6099**
遣 J382f M39052 **6100**
遠 J3173 M39047 **6101**

11 residual strokes

樋 J4875 M-X 2757
樋 J-X M15415 2816
腿 J425c M29747 4846
遭 J4178 M39082 **6105**
遮 J3c57 M39086 **6106**
適 J452c M39076 **6107**

12 residual strokes

導 J4633 M7463 1388
遼 J4a4b M39137 **6111**
遵 J3d65 M39118 **6112**
遷 J412b M39123 **6113**
選 J412a M39127 **6114**
遺 J3064 M39134 **6115**

13 residual strokes

縫 J4b25 M27805 4550
謎 J4666 M35800 5661
避 J4872 M39163 6120
還 J3454 M39174 **6121**

14–18 residual strokes

縫 J4b25 M27805 4550

種 $\frac{J3c6f}{M25174}$ 4159

糧 $\frac{J4138}{M27057}$ 4413

黙 $\frac{J4c5b}{M48063}$ 7055

9–18 residual strokes

瞳 $\frac{J4637}{M23707}$ 3961

糧 $\frac{J4e48}{M27132}$ 4426

纏 $\frac{J453b}{M28043}$ 4612

鐘 $\frac{J3e62}{M40902}$ 6352

鯉 $\frac{J3871}{M46182}$ 6874

Rad. 167 金

0 residual strokes

金 $\frac{J3662}{M40152}$ 6211

2 residual strokes

釜 $\frac{J3378}{M40164}$ 6215

釘 $\frac{J4523}{M40159}$ 6217

針 $\frac{J3f4b}{M40165}$ 6218

3 residual strokes

釧 $\frac{J367c}{M40176}$ 6222

釦 $\frac{J4b55}{M40175}$ 6223

釣 $\frac{J4460}{M40172}$ 6224

鈍 $\frac{J465f}{M40219}$ 6235

4 residual strokes

欽 $\frac{J3656}{M16104}$ 2940

鈎 $\frac{J3343}{M40220}$ 6226

鈍 $\frac{J465f}{M40219}$ 6235

5 residual strokes

鈷 $\frac{J385a}{M40270}$ 6236

鉦 $\frac{J3e60}{M40322}$ 6246

鈴 $\frac{J4e6b}{M40267}$ 6247

鉢 $\frac{J482d}{M40317}$ 6249

鉤 $\frac{J6e6c}{M40319}$ 6250

鉛 $\frac{J3174}{M40310}$ 6251

鉱 $\frac{J395b}{M40340}$ 6252

鉄 $\frac{J4534}{M40285}$ 6253

6 residual strokes

鉾 $\frac{J4b48}{M40353}$ 6255

銚 $\frac{J4438}{M40387}$ 6260

銑 $\frac{J412d}{M40376}$ 6263

銭 $\frac{J412c}{M40413}$ 6264

銘 $\frac{J4c43}{M40385}$ 6265

銅 $\frac{J463c}{M40361}$ 6266

銃 $\frac{J3d46}{M40359}$ 6267

銀 $\frac{J3664}{M40355}$ 6268

7 residual strokes

劉 $\frac{J4e2d}{M2224}$ 515

鋪 $\frac{J4a5f}{M40491}$ 6269

鋒 $\frac{J4b2f}{M40455}$ 6275

鋏 $\frac{J4946}{M40503}$ 6277

鋤 $\frac{J3d7b}{M40480}$ 6278

鋭 $\frac{J3154}{M40410}$ 6279

鋳 $\frac{J4372}{M40503}$ 6280

8 residual strokes

鎚 $\frac{J444a}{M-X}$ 6281

錘 $\frac{J3f6e}{M40547}$ 6291

錫 $\frac{J3c62}{M40573}$ 6292

錠 $\frac{J3e7b}{M40559}$ 6293

錐 $\frac{J3f6d}{M40536}$ 6294

錨 $\frac{J4945}{M40598}$ 6295

錆 $\frac{J3b2c}{M40523}$ 6296

鋸 $\frac{J3578}{M40505}$ 6297

録 $\frac{J4f3f}{M40519}$ 6298

錯 $\frac{J3a78}{M40579}$ 6299

錬 $\frac{J4f23}{M40600}$ 6300

錦 $\frac{J3653}{M40569}$ 6301

鋼 $\frac{J395d}{M40509}$ 6302

鍵 $\frac{J3830}{M40654}$ 6317

9 residual strokes

鎚 $\frac{J444a}{M-X}$ 6281

鎚 $\frac{J-X}{M40715}$ 6310

鍾 $\frac{J3e61}{M40672}$ 6311

鍍 $\frac{J4555}{M40607}$ 6312

鍔 $\frac{J4457}{M40617}$ 6313

鍬 $\frac{J372d}{M40643}$ 6314

鍋 $\frac{J4669}{M40603}$ 6315

鍵 $\frac{J3830}{M40654}$ 6317

鍛 $\frac{J4343}{M40625}$ 6318

10 residual strokes

鎚 $\frac{J444a}{M-X}$ 6281

鎚 $\frac{J-X}{M40715}$ 6310

鍔 $\frac{J4457}{M40617}$ 6313

鎗 $\frac{J4179}{M40709}$ 6320

鎧 $\frac{J333b}{M40735}$ 6324

鎖 $\frac{J3d7b}{M40708}$ 6325

鎌 $\frac{J3379}{M40693}$ 6326

鎔 $\frac{J6f30}{M40704}$ 6327

鎮 $\frac{J4443}{M40745}$ 6328

11–15 residual strokes

鏑 $\frac{J452d}{M40790}$ 6334

鏡 $\frac{J3640}{M40812}$ 6341

鏈 $\frac{J4c7a}{M-X}$ 6343

鐙 $\frac{J462a}{M40904}$ 6348

鐘 $\frac{J3e62}{M40902}$ 6352

鐸 $\frac{J4278}{M40951}$ 6356

鑓 $\frac{J-X}{M40998}$ 6357

鑑 $\frac{J3455}{M40988}$ 6361

Rad. 168 長

0 residual strokes

長 $\frac{J4439}{M41100}$ 6379

3 residual strokes

套 $\frac{J4565}{M5926}$ 1161

帳 $\frac{J4422}{M8939}$ 1568

張 $\frac{J4343}{M9812}$ 1694

4–11 residual strokes

張 $\frac{J4425}{M9812}$ 1694

脹 $\frac{J4431}{M29570}$ 4832

髪 $\frac{J4831}{M45387}$ 6804

髭 $\frac{J4926}{M45399}$ 6812

Rad. 169 門

0 residual strokes

門 $\frac{J4c67}{M41208}$ 6381

1–3 residual strokes

問 $\frac{J4c64}{M3814}$ 830

閃 $\frac{J412e}{M41214}$ 6383

閉 $\frac{J4a44}{M41222}$ 6385

4 residual strokes

悶 $\frac{J4c65}{M10729}$ 1895

閨 $\frac{J313c}{M41244}$ 6389

閑 $\frac{J3457}{M41247}$ 6390

間 $\frac{J3456}{M41249}$ 6391

開 $\frac{J332b}{M41233}$ 6393

6 residual strokes

聞 $\frac{J4a39}{M29104}$ 4732

閣 $\frac{J395e}{M41301}$ 6397

閥 $\frac{J4836}{M41308}$ 6398

閤 $\frac{J3355}{M41300}$ 6401

関 $\frac{J3458}{M41297}$ 6402

7–9 residual strokes

潤 $\frac{J3442}{M-X}$ 3329

潤 $\frac{J3d61}{M18255}$ 3334

閲 $\frac{J315c}{M41341}$ 6404

闇 $\frac{J3047}{M41421}$ 6414

10–12 residual strokes

欄 J4d73 / M15880 2914
簡 J344a / M26520 4358
蘭 J4d76 / M32477 5255
闘 J462e / M45649 6418

Rad. 170 阜

0 residual strokes

阜 J496c / M41534 6423

3–4 residual strokes

埠 J4956 / M5161 1029
阪 J3a65 / M41562 6428
防 J4b49 / M41576 6429

5–6 residual strokes

陀 J424b / M41600 6432
附 J496d / M41606 6433
阻 J414b / M41593 6434
阿 J3024 / M41599 6435
限 J3842 / M41627 6439

7 residual strokes

限 J3842 / M41627 6439
陛 J4a45 / M41654 6444
陥 J3459 / M41676 6446
院 J3121 / M41665 6447
陣 J3f58 / M41667 6448
除 J3d7c / M41669 6449

降 J395f / M41620 6450

8 residual strokes

陸 J4a45 / M41654 6444
陵 J4e4d / M41704 6454
隆 J4e34 / M41720 6455
険 J3831 / M41721 6456
陳 J4444 / M41698 6457
陪 J4766 / M41680 6458
陶 J462b / M41705 6459
随 J3f6f / M41764 6460
陸 J4e26 / M41708 6461
陰 J3122 / M41691 6462

9 residual strokes

堕 J4244 / M-X 1033
随 J3f6f / M41764 6460
隈 J3728 / M41748 6466
隅 J3679 / M41743 6467
隊 J4262 / M41750 6468
階 J332c / M41755 6469
陽 J4d5b / M41725 6470

10 residual strokes

階 J332c / M41755 6469
隙 J3764 / M41792 6471
隔 J3356 / M-X 6475

11 residual strokes

蔭 J307e / M31840 5151
隙 J-X / M41813 6477

際 J3a5d / M41820 6478
障 J3e63 / M41821 6479
隠 J3123 / M41836 6480

12–13 residual strokes

墜 J4446 / M5451 1082
隣 J4e59 / M41847 6484

Rad. 171 隶

2–4 residual strokes

康 J392f / M9376 1621
禄 J4f3d / M24741 4096
逮 J4261 / M38931 6069

6–9 residual strokes

糠 J3947 / M27105 4424
緑 J4e59 / M27541 4528
隷 J4e6c / M41928 6490

Rad. 172 隹

2 residual strokes

准 J3d5a / M1661 426
進 J3f4a / M38943 6073
隼 J483b / M41943 6493
隻 J4049 / M41941 6494
維 J305d / M27568 4516
雌 J3b73 / M41998 6506
雑 J3b28 / M22022 6507

3 residual strokes

唯 J4d23 / M3761 831
堆 J424f / M5211 1035

惟 J3054 / M10820 1890
推 J3f64 / M12284 2212
進 J3f4a / M38943 6073
雀 J3f7d / M41954 6496

4 residual strokes

椎 J4447 / M15024 2742
焦 J3e47 / M19119 3436
雀 J3f7d / M41954 6496
雇 J385b / M41976 6497
雁 J3e6f / M41960 6498
雄 J4d3a / M41972 6499
集 J3d38 / M41974 6500

5 residual strokes

催 J3a45 / M1005 298
勧 J342b / M2433 559
携 J3748 / M12529 2253
準 J3d60 / M17934 3278
碓 J3130 / M24294 4012
稚 J4355 / M25120 4154
雅 J326d / M41973 6505

6 residual strokes

奪 J4325 / M5994 1171
携 J3748 / M12529 2253
潅 J3443 / M18216 3287
維 J305d / M27568 4516
雌 J3b73 / M41998 6506
雑 J3b28 / M22022 6507

---

7 residual strokes

権 J3822 / M15484 2853
確 J334e / M24366 4039
蕉 J3e56 / M31937 5191
誰 J432f / M35586 5642

8 residual strokes

奮 J4a33 / M6012 1172
擁 J4d4a / M12781 2294
樵 J343f / M15489 2871
歓 J343f / M16197 2948
獲 J334d / M20758 3609
確 J334e / M24366 4039
維 J305d / M27568 4516
雍 J4665 / M32121 5221
錐 J3f6d / M40536 6294

9 residual strokes

擁 J4d4a / M12781 2294
擢 J4527 / M12852 2303
灌 J4275 / M18532 3360
礁 J3e4c / M24502 4048

10 residual strokes

曜 J4d4b / M14227 2522
穫 J334f / M25334 4180
観 J3451 / M34955 5538
雛 J3f77 / M42121 6514
難 J4671 / M42128 6515
離 J4e25 / M42140 6517

11 residual strokes

羅 J4d65 M28397 4655

贗 J3466 M36943 5830

離 J4e25 M42140 **6517**

12 residual strokes

灌 J5e75 M18759 3390

耀 J4d54 M28828 4695

護 J386e M36038 5715

13 residual strokes

灘 J4667 M18784 3391

羅 J4d65 M28397 4655

躍 J4c76 M37955 5921

顧 J385c M43689 6655

鶴 J4461 M47185 6995

14–16 residual strokes

讐 J3d32 M36125 5722

鶴 J4461 M47185 6995

鷹 J426b M47377 7007

Rad. 173 雨

0 residual strokes

雨 J312b M42210 **6518**

3–4 residual strokes

雫 J3c36 M42219 **6519**

雪 J4063 M42216 **6520**

雰 J4a37 M42231 **6521**

雲 J3140 M42235 **6522**

5 residual strokes

零 J4e6d M42242 **6524**

雷 J4d6b M42245 **6525**

電 J4545 M42253 **6526**

6 residual strokes

漏 J4f33 M18120 3307

需 J3c7b M42275 **6528**

7 residual strokes

橰 J4374 M15438 2841

震 J3f4c M42300 **6531**

靈 J4e6e M42309 **6532**

8 residual strokes

儒 J3c74 M1220 330

曇 J465e M14172 2518

橰 J4374 M15438 2841

9 residual strokes

嬬 J445c M6821 1271

橰 J4374 M15438 2841

濡 J4728 M18504 3365

霞 J3262 M42365 **6541**

霜 J417a M42363 **6542**

11–14 residual strokes

霧 J4c38 M42418 **6545**

露 J4f2a M42463 **6549**

鱈 J432d M46470 6916

Rad. 174 青

0 residual strokes

青 J4044 M42564 **6557**

2–6 residual strokes

情 J3e70 M10756 1898

晴 J4032 M13994 2488

清 J4036 M17695 3205

精 J403a M26997 4411

靖 J4c77 M42570 **6559**

静 J4045 M42574 **6560**

7–11 residual strokes

瀞 J4654 M-X 3356

瀞 J-X M18659 3380

請 J4041 M35640 5645

錆 J3b2c M40523 6296

鯖 J3b2a M46210 6883

Rad. 175 非

0 residual strokes

非 J4873 M42585 **6563**

2–5 residual strokes

靱 J3f59 M-X **6573**

2–4 residual strokes

俳 J4750 M726 254

匪 J485b M2629 592

悲 J4861 M10720 1897

扉 J4862 M11750 2058

排 J4753 M12256 2210

斐 J4865 M13469 2370

5–14 residual strokes

緋 J486c M27604 4517

罪 J3c61 M28293 4644

誹 J4870 M35601 5639

輩 J475a M38398 5971

Rad. 176 面

0 residual strokes

面 J4c4c M42618 **6566**

6–14 residual strokes

緬 J4c4b M27674 4542

麵 J4c4d M-X 7038

麺 J-X M47827 7039

Rad. 177 革

0 residual strokes

革 J3357 M42710 **6570**

2–5 residual strokes

靱 J3f59 M-X **6573**

靴 J3724 M42729 **6576**

鞄 J3373 M42781 **6582**

6–10 residual strokes

覇 J4746 M34790 5519

鞍 J3048 M42815 **6586**

鞘 J3e64 M42850 **6587**

鞠 J3547 M42892 **6589**

鞭 J4a5c M42937 **6595**

Rad. 178 韋

2–8 residual strokes

偉 J304e M837 285

衛 J3152 M34073 1776

韓 J3031 M31437 5160

韓 J345a M43159 **6602**

Rad. 179 韭

3 residual strokes

韮 J4723 M43237 **6605**

Rad. 180 音

0 residual strokes

音 J323b M43265 **6607**

2–8 residual strokes

意 J3055 M10921 1926

章 J3e4f M42561 4235

憶 J3231 M11295 2001

臆 J3232 M29951 4883

Rad. 180: 8 residual strokes

闇 J3047 M41421 6414 　領 J4e4e M43423 6628 　願 J346a M43623 6653

顧 J385c M43689ˊ 6655

9–14 residual strokes

織 J3f25 M27892 4596

響 J3641 M43318ˊ 6610

韻 J3124 M43307 6611

Rad. 181 頁

0 residual strokes

頁 J4a47 M43333 6614

2–3 residual strokes

頃 J3a22 M43338 6615

頂 J443a M43335 6616

項 J3960 M43343 6617

須 J3f5c M43352 6618

順 J3d67 M43349 6619

4 residual strokes

傾 J3739 M1038 299

煩 J4851 M19229 3454

頒 J4852 M43378 6621

頓 J465c M43381 6623

頑 J3468 M43374 6624

預 J4d42 M43373 6625

5 residual strokes

碩 J4059 M24338 4026

頚 J375b M43434 6626

頬 J3f7c M43415 6627

6 residual strokes

頬 J4b4b M-X 6629

7 residual strokes

頓 J4655 M4429 910

頴 J3150 M24824 4109

穎 J314f M25267 4173

頼 J4d6a M43529ˊ 6635

煩 J-X M43496 6637

頸 J7074 M43515 6638

頭 J462c M43490 6639

頻 J4951 M-X 6641

8–9 residual strokes

嶺 J4e66 M8553 1517

頻 J4951 M-X 6641

顎 J335c M43590 6643

額 J335b M43586 6644

題 J426a M43584 6645

顕 J3832 M43609ˊ 6646

類 J4e60 M43608ˊ 6647

顔 J3469 M43591ˊ 6648

10–12 residual strokes

瀬 J494e M18636 3381

瀕 J4025 M18672ˊ 3384

顎 J335c M43590 6643

顛 J453f M-X 6652

願 J346a M43623 6653

顧 J385c M43689ˊ 6655

Rad. 182 風

0 residual strokes

風 J4977 M43756 6663

4 residual strokes

楓 J4976 M15126 2777

Rad. 183 飛

飛 J4874 M44000 6672

Rad. 184 食

0 residual strokes

食 J3f29 M44014 6674

2–4 residual strokes

喰 J3674 M4015 849

飢 J3532 M44023ˊ 6675

飯 J4853 M44064ˊ 6679

飲 J307b M44063ˊ 6680

5 residual strokes

飴 J303b M44080ˊ 6682

飾 J3e7e M44111ˊ 6683

飽 J4b30 M44109ˊ 6684

飼 J3b74 M44107ˊ 6685

6 residual strokes

蝕 J3f2a M-X 5333

蝕 J-X M33264 5358

餅 J4c5f M44133 6689

餌 J3142 M44146 6690

養 J4d5c M44154 6691

7–12 residual strokes

餐 J3b41 M44160 6696

餓 J326e M44168ˊ 6697

館 J345b M44237ˊ 6701

饗 J3642 M-X 6705

Rad. 185 首

0 residual strokes

首 J3c73 M44489 6719

2–6 residual strokes

導 J4633 M7463ˊ 1388

道 J463b M39010ˊ 6091

Rad. 186 香

0–11 residual strokes

香 J3961 M44518 6722

馨 J333e M44559 6724

Rad. 187 馬

0 residual strokes

馬 J474f M44572 6725

3–4 residual strokes

馴 J466b M44595 6729

馳 J435a M44593 6730

駁 J477d M44619 6733

駄 J424c M44633 6734

駅 J3158 M44633ˊ 6735

駆 J366e M44634 6736

5 residual strokes

罵 J474d M28333 4649

駆 J366e M44634 6736

駒 J3670 M44663 6742

駕 J326f M44667 6743

駈 J3670 M44636 6744

駐 J4373 M44660 6745

6–12 residual strokes

篤 J4646 M26344 4342

駿 J3d59 M44775 6754

験 J3833 M44835 6758

騒 J417b M44834ˊ 6760

騎 J3533 M44817 6761

騨 J424d M-X 6762

騰 J462d M44915ˊ 6767

驚 J3643 M45013ˊ 6774

Rad. 188 骨

0 residual strokes

骨 J397c M45098 6784

3–9 residual strokes	鬼 J3534 M45758 **6833**	**8 residual strokes**	**2–3 residual strokes**

鬻 J4f49 M47345 **7004**

鬻 J3o6d M47362 **7006**

鷹 J426b M47377 **7007**

3–9 residual strokes

滑 J336a M18032 3282
骸 J333c M45164 **6789**
髓 J3f71 M45240 **6791**

3–4 residual strokes

塊 J3274 M5319 1070
蒐 J3d2f M31539 5159
魁 J3321 M45785 **6834**
魂 J3o32 M45787 **6835**

8 residual strokes

櫓 J4f26 M15798 2908
蘇 J4149 M32427 5252
鯵 J3033 M-X **6875**
鯖 J3b2o M46210 **6883**
鯛 J4264 M46226 **6884**
鯨 J375f M46257 **6886**

2–3 residual strokes

島 J4567 M8108 1476
嶋 J4568 M8434 1503
蔦 J4455 M31828 5178
鳩 J4837 M46648 **6936**
鳳 J4b31 M46671 **6937**
鳶 J4650 M46674 **6938**
鳴 J4c44 M46672 **6939**

Rad. 197 齒

齢 J3834 M-X **7013**
齬 J-X M47576 **7016**

Rad. 189 高

0 residual strokes

高 J3962 M45313 **6796**

5–11 residual strokes

醜 J3d39 M39969 6189
魅 J4c25 M45811 **6838**
魔 J4b62 M45906 **6843**

9–10 residual strokes

鰍 J3362 M46331 **6895**
鰐 J4f4c M46337 **6901**
鰯 J3073 M46413 **6904**
鰭 J4949 M46400 **6907**

4–6 residual strokes

鷗 J322a M-X **6941**
鴇 J463e M46730 **6943**
鴎 J322a M-X **6941**
鴬 J3229 M-X **6945**
鳴 J3c32 M46831 **6948**
鴛 J3175 M46795 **6953**
鴨 J337b M46823 **6955**
鴻 J3963 M46874 **6963**

Rad. 198 鹿

0 residual strokes

鹿 J3c2f M47586 **7017**

4–13 residual strokes

稿 J3946 M25220 4166
縞 J3c4a M27777 4569
膏 J3951 M29800 4860
藁 J4f4e M32222 5234

Rad. 195 魚

0 residual strokes

魚 J357b M45956 **6845**

11 residual strokes

鰺 J724d M46442 **6912**
鰻 J3137 M46443 **6914**
鰹 J336f M46437 **6915**
鱈 J432d M46470 **6916**

3–12 residual strokes

塵 J3f50 M5388 1087
慶 J3744 M11145 1967
濾 J3977 M18112 3300
麓 J4f3c M47658 **7023**
麗 J4e6f M47663 **7026**
麟 J4e5b M47690 **7028**

Rad. 190 髟

髪 J4831 M45387 **6804**
髭 J4926 M45399 **6812**

3–5 residual strokes

漁 J3579 M18101 3309
魯 J4f25 M46013 **6848**
魛 J4a2b M46075 **6854**
鮎 J303e M46070 **6855**

12–13 residual strokes

鰹 J336f M46437 **6915**
鱒 J4b70 M46492 **6921**
鱗 J4e6a M46502 **6923**

7–8 residual strokes

鵠 J3974 M46961 **6968**
鵜 J312d M46952 **6971**
鵡 J4c39 M46963 **6974**
鵬 J4b32 M47005 **6979**
鶏 J375c M47074 **6980**

Rad. 199 麥

0 residual strokes

麦 J477e M47718 **7030**

Rad. 191 鬥

Rad. 192 鬯

Rad. 193 鬲

融 J4d3b M33384 5371
隔 J3356 M-X 6475

6–7 residual strokes

鮪 J4b6e M46126 **6858**
鮭 J3a7a M46132 **6859**
鮫 J3b2d M46127 **6863**
鮮 J412f M46133 **6864**
鯉 J3871 M46182 **6874**

Rad. 196 鳥

0 residual strokes

烏 J3128 M18998 3421
鳥 J443b M46634 **6931**

10–14 residual strokes

鷲 J7274 M47169 **6994**
鶴 J4461 M47185 **6995**
鷗 J-X M47268 **6998**

Rad. 194 鬼

0 residual strokes

6–9 residual strokes

麹 J396d M-X **7036**
麺 J-X M47818 **7037**
麺 J4c4d M-X **7038**
麺 J-X M47827 **7039**

Rad. 200 麻

0 residual strokes

麻 J4b63 M47888 **7040**

4–10 residual strokes

摩 J4b60 M12613 2264
磨 J4b61 M24449 4045
魔 J4b62 M45906 6843
魘 J4b7b M47909 **7044**

Rad. 201 黄

0 residual strokes

黄 J322b M47926 **7045**

4 residual strokes

横 J3223 M15484 2854

Rad. 202 黍

黍 J3550 M47991 **7048**

Rad. 203 黒

0 residual strokes

黒 J3975 M48040 **7052**

3–11 residual strokes

勲 J372e M2463 560
墨 J4b4f M2076 1086
纆 J6575 M28058 4617

黙 J4c5b M48063 **7055**
黛 J4263 M48075 **7060**

Rad. 204 黹

Rad. 205 黽

竈 J635e M25703 4221
蠅 J6a24 M33690 5394

Rad. 206 鼎

鼎 J4524 M48315 **7074**

Rad. 207 鼓

鼓 J385d M48330 **7076**

Rad. 208 鼠

鼠 J414d M48390 **7078**

Rad. 209 鼻

鼻 J4921 M48498 **7082**

Rad. 210 齊

0 residual strokes

斉 J4046 M13454 2366

2–3 residual strokes

剤 J3a5e M2076 493
斎 J3a58 M13467 2368

済 J3a51 M17749 3197

Rad. 211 齒

0 residual strokes

歯 J3b75 M16323 2961

3–5 residual strokes

噛 J-X M4516 921
齢 J4e70 M48632 **7093**

Rad. 212 龍

0 residual strokes

竜 J4e35 M25751 4232
龍 J4e36 M48818 **7103**

3 residual strokes

籠 J437e M7368 1370
滝 J426c M18067 3273
瀧 J426d M18671 3376

6 residual strokes

篭 J4f36 M26371 4332
籠 J6446 M26752 4376
襲 J3d31 M34717 5510

Rad. 213 龜

0 residual strokes

亀 J3535 M210 62

5–10 residual strokes

龝 J302c M25281 4170
穐 J6354 M25381 4184

Rad. 214 龠

Rad. 301 ク

1 residual stroke

々 J2139 M97 45
久 J3557 M118 47
夕 J4d3c M5749 1123

4 residual strokes

争 J4168 M236 69
危 J346d M2849 629
色 J3f27 M30602 4956

5 residual strokes

免 J4c48 M-X 361
玖 J366a M20846 3621
角 J3351 M35003 5543

6–7 residual strokes

急 J355e M10475 1823
浄 J3e74 M17451 3128
粂 J3729 M26860 4382
負 J4969 M-X 5769
陥 J4641 M41676 6446

8 residual strokes

勉 J4a59 M2384 543
娩 J4a5a M6337 1233
挽 J4854 M-X 2172
脆 J4048 M29468 4800
逸 J306f M38951 6071

9 residual strokes

亀 J3535 M210 62
挽 J4854 M-X 2172
焔 J316b M-X 3423
菟 J-X M31189 5077
逸 J306f M38951 6071
魚 J357b M45956 6845

10 residual strokes

喚 J342d M3953 852
換 J3439 M12358 2233
晩 J4855 M14030 2491
絶 J4064 M-X 4490
菟 J4551 M-X 5102
象 J3e5d M36372 5744

11–13 residual strokes

像 J417c M1084 308
触 J3f28 M35070 5547
解 J3272 M35067 5548
漁 J3579 M18101 3309
箪 J433d M-X 4321
絶 J4064 M-X 4490

静 $\frac{J4045}{M42574}$ 6560

魯 $\frac{J4f25}{M46013}$ 6848

14 residual strokes

衡 $\frac{J3955}{M34078}$ 1775

橡 $\frac{J464b}{M15564}$ 2863

穋 $\frac{J302c}{M25281}$ 4170

鮒 $\frac{J4a2b}{M46075}$ 6854

鮎 $\frac{J303e}{M46070}$ 6855

15–16 residual strokes

瀞 $\frac{J4654}{M\text{-}X}$ 3356

鮪 $\frac{J4b6e}{M46126}$ 6858

鮭 $\frac{J3a7a}{M46132}$ 6859

鮫 $\frac{J3b2d}{M46127}$ 6863

鮮 $\frac{J412f}{M46133}$ 6864

鯉 $\frac{J3871}{M46182}$ 6874

17–18 residual strokes

櫓 $\frac{J4f26}{M15798}$ 2908

艶 $\frac{J3170}{M30632}$ 4957

蘇 $\frac{J4149}{M32427}$ 5252

蟹 $\frac{J332a}{M33668}$ 5395

鯖 $\frac{J3b2a}{M46210}$ 6883

鯛 $\frac{J4264}{M46220}$ 6884

鯨 $\frac{J375f}{M46257}$ 6886

鰍 $\frac{J3362}{M46331}$ 6895

鰐 $\frac{J4f4c}{M46337}$ 6901

19 residual strokes

穣 $\frac{J6354}{M25381}$ 4184

鰐 $\frac{J4f4c}{M46337}$ 6901

鰯 $\frac{J3073}{M46413}$ 6904

鰭 $\frac{J4949}{M46400}$ 6907

20 residual strokes

穰 $\frac{J6354}{M25381}$ 4184

鯵 $\frac{J724d}{M46442}$ 6912

鰻 $\frac{J3137}{M46443}$ 6914

鰹 $\frac{J336f}{M46437}$ 6915

鱈 $\frac{J432d}{M46470}$ 6916

21–22 residual strokes

鰹 $\frac{J336f}{M46437}$ 6915

鱒 $\frac{J4b70}{M46492}$ 6921

鱗 $\frac{J4e5a}{M46502}$ 6923

Rad. 302 マ

2–3 residual strokes

予 $\frac{J4d3d}{M231}$ 68

矛 $\frac{J4c37}{M23846}$ 3974

5–6 residual strokes

勇 $\frac{J4d26}{M2360}$ 541

序 $\frac{J3d78}{M9253}$ 1607

7 residual strokes

勇 $\frac{J4d26}{M2360}$ 541

柔 $\frac{J3d40}{M14622}$ 2633

茅 $\frac{J337d}{M30836}$ 5005

通 $\frac{J444c}{M38892}$ 6063

8–9 residual strokes

桶 $\frac{J3233}{M14811}$ 2694

涌 $\frac{J4d30}{M17534}$ 3150

通 $\frac{J444c}{M38892}$ 6063

野 $\frac{J4c6e}{M40133}$ 6208

10–11 residual strokes

樋 $\frac{J4875}{M\text{-}X}$ 2757

湧 $\frac{J4d2f}{M17862}$ 3207

痛 $\frac{J444b}{M22195}$ 3814

預 $\frac{J4d42}{M43373}$ 6625

12 residual strokes

樋 $\frac{J4875}{M\text{-}X}$ 2757

樋 $\frac{J\text{-}X}{M15415}$ 2816

疑 $\frac{J353f}{M22007}$ 3777

踊 $\frac{J4d59}{M37587}$ 5882

13–17 residual strokes

擬 $\frac{J353c}{M12870}$ 2307

樋 $\frac{J4875}{M\text{-}X}$ 2757

樋 $\frac{J\text{-}X}{M15415}$ 2816

橘 $\frac{J354c}{M15551}$ 2868

霧 $\frac{J4c38}{M42418}$ 6545

Rad. 303 ⺍

4–6 residual strokes

労 $\frac{J4f2b}{M2329}$ 531

単 $\frac{J4331}{M2752}$ 620

栄 $\frac{J3149}{M14687}$ 2635

7 residual strokes

悩 $\frac{J473a}{M10716}$ 1867

挙 $\frac{J3573}{M12081}$ 2150

桜 $\frac{J3a79}{M14796}$ 2664

8 residual strokes

巣 $\frac{J4163}{M8696}$ 2705

猟 $\frac{J4e44}{M20512}$ 3587

脳 $\frac{J473e}{M29567}$ 4821

蛍 $\frac{J3756}{M32983}$ 5302

9 residual strokes

営 $\frac{J3144}{M4025}$ 857

弾 $\frac{J4346}{M9836}$ 1699

覚 $\frac{J3350}{M34846}$ 5529

10–11 residual strokes

戦 $\frac{J406f}{M11631}$ 2037

禅 $\frac{J4135}{M24787}$ 4104

蝋 $\frac{J4f39}{M\text{-}X}$ 5332

誉 $\frac{J4d40}{M35498}$ 5602

12–17 residual strokes

厳 $\frac{J3837}{M3048}$ 663

厳 $\frac{J3460}{M8624}$ 1521

撹 $\frac{J3349}{M\text{-}X}$ 2267

獣 $\frac{J3d43}{M20714}$ 3606

蝉 $\frac{J4066}{M\text{-}X}$ 5349

騨 $\frac{J424d}{M\text{-}X}$ 6762

鴬 $\frac{J3229}{M\text{-}X}$ 6945

ANDREW NATHANIEL NELSON *was born in Great Falls, Montana, in 1893. He received his B.A. from Walla Walla College and his Ph.D. from the University of Washington. As a Seventh-day Adventist missionary in Asia between 1918 and 1961, Dr. Nelson played a prominent role in the fields of education and language training. Throughout his life, Dr. Nelson remained devoted to the study of the Japanese language and the fundamentals of Chinese.*

JOHN H. HAIG *is an associate professor of Japanese in the Department of East Asian Languages and Literatures at the University of Hawai'i at Mānoa, one of the largest departments of its kind in the United States.*

NOTE CONCERNING CHART INSIDE BACK COVER. These charts have been placed here as a handy reference for locating the more common radicals. The radicals are shown classified by the locations in which they most commonly appear (top, bottom, left, right, enclosure, lone). Not shown are the comparatively rare corner radicals or cases where the whole character is a radical.

See Appendices 3 and 4 for help in determining the radical of a character. The characters that are radicals by themselves are included in the charts of Appendix 5.

新版ネルソン漢英中辞典
The Compact Nelson
Japanese-English
Character Dictionary

1999年5月15日初版発行

編　者　ジョン・H・ヘイグ
　　　　ハワイ大学東アジア言語文学部

発行者　ステファン・フランツ
発行所　チャールズ・イー・タトル出版株式会社
　　　　神奈川県川崎市多摩区堰1-21-13
　　　　郵便番号214-0022
　　　　電話044-833-0228
発売所　株式会社タトル商会
　　　　神奈川県川崎市多摩区堰1-21-13
　　　　電話044-833-0225

© Periplus Editions (HK) Ltd., 1999
　Printed in Singapore

ISBN 4-8053-0574-6 (in Japan)

TOP
The Radicals Found at the Top

1	一 1	一 1	、 3	一 4	ノ	**2**	二 7	十 8	一 8	八 9	入 11
八 12	八 12	ソ 14	冖 14	刀 18	力 19	匕 21	十 24	十 25	ム 28	又 29	
3 口 30	土 32	士 32	夂 34	夕 36	大 37	女 38	子 39	宀 40	小 42	屮 42	
山 46	巛 47	工 48	己 49	彐 58	彐 58	彐 58	⺕ 58	艹 [140]	**4** 戈 62	父 66	
文 67	日 72	曰 72	木 75	止 77	比 80	民 81	水 85	火 86	灬 87	爪 87	
父 88	牛 93	王 [96]	⺾ [140]	**5** 玄 95	甘 99	田 102	癶 105	白 106	目 109	矛 110	
石 112	禾 115	穴 116	宀 116	穴 117	立 [122]	**6** 竹 118	米 119	羊 123	羽 110		
羽 124	老 125	而 126	耳 128	聿 129	自 132	臼 134	虫 142	血 143	衣 145	襾 146	襾 146
7 貝 154	車 159	辰 161	釆 165	**8** 隹 172	雨 173	非 175					
9 音 180	音 180	**10** 馬 187	高 190	彡 190	**11** 魚 195	鳥 196	鹿 198	麻 200			
麻 200	黑 [203]	**12** 黑 203		**13/16** 鼓 207	齊 210	龍 212					

LONE
The Common Characters Having But One Radical

メ 3	、	乃 1	ノ 4
久 4	ノ	了 1	亅 6

BOTTOM
The Radicals Found at the Bottom

1 一 1	、 3	**2** 二 7	儿 10	八 12	冫 15	几 16	刀 18	力 19
十 24	巳 26	ム 29	又 29	又	**3** 口 30	土 32	夂 34	夂 34	夕 36
大 37	女 38	子 39	寸 41	小 42	山 46	工 48	己 49	巾 50	干 51	廾 55	弓 57
彐 58	彡 59	**4** 心 61	小 61	手 64	斤 69	方 70	日 72	曰 72	木 75
止 77	毋 80	比 82	毛 85	水 86	火 86	灬 86	牛 93	犬 [96]	王 [96]	月 [130]
5 母 [80]	氷 [85]	玉 96	瓦 98	甘 99	用 101	疋 102	白 106	皿 108	目 109
5 矢 111	石 112	示 113	禾 115	**6** 米 119	糸 120	缶 121	羊 123	羽 124	羽 124
而 126	耳 128	聿 129	肉 130	至 133	臼 134	舌 135	舛 136	艮 138	虫 142	衣 145	豕 [152]
7 舛 [136]	見 147	角 148	言 149	豆 151	豕 152	貝 154	足 157	車 159	辛 160	辛 160
辰 161	酉 164	里 166	**8** 金 167	隹 172	非 175	**9** 面 176	革 177
韭 179	音 180	音 180	風 182	食 184	食 184	香 186	**10** 馬 187	髙 193	鬼 194
11 魚 195	鳥 196	鹿 198	**12** 黃 201	黑 203	**16** 龍 212

ENCLOSURE
The Radicals Found as Enclosures

1 ㄴ 5	**2** 冂 13	冂 13	凵 13	刂 13	几 16
八 16	囗 17	勹 20	匚 22	匸 22	厂 27	辶 [162]
3 囗 31	夂 34	尸 44	广 53	廴 54	弋 56	辶 [162]
4 戈 62	戶 63	戸 65	支 78	歹 82	毛 84	气 84
爪 87	**5** 瓦 98	疒 104	非	耳 128	虍 141	**7**
走 156	辰 161	辵 162	麥 [199]	**8** 門 169	**9** 風 182
10 鬥 191	鬼 194	**11** 鹿 198	麥 199	麻 200
13/14 鼠 208	齊 210			

LEFT
The Radicals Found at the Left

1	丨2	丨2	丿4	**2**	亻9	冫15	力19	十24	又29	ㄡ29	阝[170]
3	口30	土32	夕36	女38	子39	山46	川47	工48	己49	巾50	干51
幺52	弓57	彡59	彳60	忄[61]	扌[64]	氵[85]	丬[90]	犭[94]			
4	戸63	尸63	手64	文67	斤69	方70	日72	木75	止77	歹78	火86
爻89	爿90	片91	牙92	牛93	王[96]	礻[113]	月[130]	月[130]			
5	牙[92]	玄95	瓦98	甘99	生100	田102	疋103	白106	皮107	目109	矛110
矢111	石112	礻113	禾115	立117	具[138]	衤[145]	**6**	米119	糸120	缶121	羊123
羽124	羽124	而126	耒127	耒127	耳128	臣131	至133	舌135	角137	虫142	血143
7	臣[131]	角148	言149	谷150	豆151	豕152	豸153	貝154	赤157	足157	身158
車159	辛160	酉164	采165	里166	镸[168]	**8**	金167	隹172	青174	青174	食[184]
斉[210]	**9**	面176	革177	韋178	音180	音180	飠[184]	首185	香186		
10	韋[178]	馬187	骨188	鬲193	臾[195]	**11**	魚195	鳥196	歯197	鹿198	麥199
黄[201]	黒[203]	**12/17**	黄201	黍202	黑203	歯[211]	鼠208	鼻209	齊210	歯211	龍212

RIGHT
The Radicals Found at the Right

1	丨2	丨2	乚5	**2**	人9	几16	刀18	刂18	力19	匕21	十24
卜25	卩26	又29	阝[163]	**3**	口30	子39	寸41	彡59	**4**	戈62	支65
攴66	攵66	斗68	斤69	欠76	殳79	比81	毛82	犬94	月[130]	月[130]	
5	尢[71]	爪97	瓦98	甘99	皮107	目109	立117	**6**	羊123	羽124	羽124
耳128	聿129	艮138	色139	虫142	**7**	見147	角148	谷150	豸152	辛160	辛160
酉164	里166	**8**	隶171	隹172	青174	青174	**9**	韋178	頁181	風182	飛183
10	韋[178]	鬼194	**11**	鳥196